PROFESSOR McDONALD'S CONVEYANCING MANUAL

D1394412

For A J McDonald

PROFESSOR McDONALD'S CONVEYANCING MANUAL

Seventh Edition

David A Brand WS
*Solicitor, Senior Lecturer and Director of the Diploma in Legal Practice at
the University of Dundee*

Andrew J M Steven
Solicitor, Lecturer in Law at the University of Edinburgh

Scott Wortley
Solicitor, Lecturer in Law at the University of Strathclyde

Tottel
publishing

Published by

Tottel Publishing Ltd	Tottel Publishing Ltd
Maxwelton House	9-10 St Andrew Square
41-43 Boltro Road	Edinburgh
Haywards Heath	EH2 2AF
West Sussex	
RH16 1BJ	

ISBN 13: 978-1-84592-360-0
© Reed Elsevier (UK) 2004
First published 1982
Second edition 1983
Third edition 1986
Fourth edition 1989
Fifth edition 1993
Sixth edition 1997
Seventh edition 2004
Formerly published by LexisNexis Butterworths

This edition reprinted by Tottel Publishing Ltd 2006
Reprinted 2007

British Library Cataloguing-in-Publication Data.
A catalogue record for this book is available from the British Library.

Typeset by Phoenix Photosetting, Chatham, Kent
Printed and bound in Great Britain by
CPI Antony Rowe, Chippenham, Wiltshire

Preface

The first edition of Professor McDonald's *Conveyancing Manual* appeared in 1982. A J McDonald was for many years Professor of Conveyancing at the University of Dundee and is now Emeritus Professor of Conveyancing there. This, the seventh edition, has undoubtedly involved the most substantial changes in the history of the Manual, primarily due to the advent of devolution and human rights legislation. The main catalyst for this edition is the imminent abolition of the feudal system, which will take place on 28 November 2004. In previous editions, the Manual adopted a feudal structure and it was necessary for this to be removed. In addition to the Abolition of Feudal Tenure etc (Scotland) Act 2000 which prompted this change, the Scottish Parliament has passed recently a plethora of related legislation (such as the Title Conditions (Scotland) Act 2003) and unrelated legislation (such as the Building (Scotland) Act 2003), all of which affects conveyancers and requires treatment. As well as the 'defeudalisation', we have made a number of other changes, including the removal of the chapter on pre-1970 standard securities and the reduction of the material on pre-1995 authentication of deeds. We do, however, make various references to 'the sixth edition of this book', along with appropriate paragraph numbers, so the reader may pursue matters which have now become mainly of historical interest, if he or she so wishes.

In updating the Manual and in particular the digest of cases, we must acknowledge the specific help gained from reading the annual conveyancing updates of Professor Kenneth Reid and Professor George Gretton, which in recent years have been published, beginning with *Conveyancing 1999*. We were also assisted by the third edition of Professor McDonald's *Conveyancing Case Notes*, produced in electronic form by the University of Dundee.

Andrew Steven was primarily responsible for Part 2 and Chapters 21 to 23 and Scott Wortley for Part 3, except Chapter 20. With the exception of the specialist chapters detailed below, David Brand was primarily responsible for the remainder of the book.

A number of chapters, once again, have been updated by specialists. Chapter 5, which required to be rewritten to take account of the introduction of stamp duty land tax, is the work of Alan Barr, Director of the Legal Practice Unit in the University of Edinburgh and a partner in Brodies WS. Chapter 20, on public law restrictions on land use, involved substantial updating and was contributed by Professor Jeremy Rowan-Robinson, formerly of the University of Aberdeen. Chapter 25, on commercial leases, was revised by Stewart Brymer WS, a partner in Thorntons WS,

Honorary Professor of the University of Dundee and Convenor of the Conveyancing Committee of the Law Society of Scotland, who was chairman of the editorial board for the sixth edition of the Manual. Chapter 26, on agricultural leases, was again revised by Michael Blair WS, also a partner in Thorntons WS. This required a significant amount of work in the light of the new Agricultural Holdings (Scotland) Act 2003. The final chapter in the book, on transactions with companies, was updated by David Cabrelli, Lecturer in Law at the University of Dundee. We are grateful to them all.

We would also like to acknowledge the research assistance of Dot Reid, Lecturer in Law at the University of Strathclyde, in relation to the chapters on title conditions, as well as the help of many people including Professor Roderick Paisley of the University of Aberdeen; Alison Polson of Brodies WS; Professor Colin Reid of the University of Dundee; Colin Graham of Thorntons WS; Sandra Eden of the University of Edinburgh; Alan Eccles of Maclay, Murray and Spens and tutor at the University of Strathclyde; Kenneth McCaig of Dundee City Council; and Alistair Rennie, Deputy Keeper, and his colleagues Scott Bond, Alan Malone and Paul Singer, all of the Registers of Scotland. In addition, we acknowledge the assistance and considerable patience of the staff at LexisNexis. David Brand and Scott Wortley would particularly like to thank their wives, Helen and Heather, for their support during the preparation of this book.

Finally, we would like to pay tribute to the work of Professor McDonald. This is the first edition of the Manual in which he has had no direct involvement. However, his interest in the law and his powers of analysis remain undiminished, as anyone who has read his recent article on the Land Registration (Scotland) Act 1979 (published at (2001) 55 Greens PLB 6 and (2002) 56 Greens PLB 1) will realise. We have been pleased to refer to *Professor McDonald's Conveyancing Opinions*, published under the editorship of Dr Charlotte Waelde since the previous edition of the Manual. Our hope is that we have maintained his high standards.

We have attempted to state the law as at 31 July 2003, but it has been possible to take account of some later developments.

David A Brand
Andrew J M Steven
Scott Wortley

November 2003
Dundee

Contents

Bibliography

Note

This Bibliography provides details of material which is relevant to the whole Manual. For works of particular relevance to individual chapters, please see the Reading List.

References

Agnew of Lochnaw, Sir Crispin	*Agricultural Law in Scotland* (1996)
Agnew of Lochnaw, Sir Crispin	*Crofting Law* (2000)
Agnew of Lochnaw, Sir Crispin	*Variation and Discharge of Land Obligations* (1999)
Anton, A E	*Rights of Way: A Guide to the Law in Scotland* (revised edn by D J Cusine, 1996)
Barraclough, F R	*A Practical Guide to Rent Review of Agricultural Holdings in Scotland* (2002)
Bell, A M	*Lectures on Conveyancing* (1882)
Brand, D A (ed)	*Scottish Landlord and Tenant Legislation* (loose-leaf)
Brown, V	*Environmental Law and Property Transactions* (2003)
Burns, J	*Conveyancing Practice* (4th edn, 1957)
Burns, J	*Handbook of Conveyancing* (5th edn, 1938)
Butterworths	*Guide to Council Tax in Scotland*
Butterworths	*Scottish Local Government Handbook* (1990)
Butterworths	*The Laws of Scotland: Stair Memorial Encyclopaedia* ('*Stair Memorial Encyclopaedia*'), various volumes (1987–); in particular: Volume 6, paras 401–800, Conveyancing, including Registration of Title; Volume 13, Landlord and Tenant; Volume 18, Property; and Volume 20, Rights in Security
Cockburn, D W	*Commercial Leases* (2002)
Collar, N A	*Planning Law* (2nd edn, 1999)
Collar, N A	*Planning Law and Human Rights* (2001)
Rennie, D G and Agnew of Lochnaw, Sir Crispin (eds)	*The Agricultural Holdings (Scotland) Acts* (7th edn, 1996)
Coull, D	*The Law of Bankruptcy in Scotland* (1989)

Council of Mortgage Lenders	*Lenders' Handbook for Scotland* (2nd edn, 2003, available online only at www.cml.org.uk)
Craigie, J	*Elements of Conveyancing: Heritable Rights* (1908)
Craigie, J	*Scottish Law of Conveyancing: Heritable Rights* (1899)
Cusine, D J (ed)	*A Scots Conveyancing Miscellany: Essays in Honour of Professor J M Halliday* (1987)
Cusine, D J (ed)	*The Conveyancing Opinions of J M Halliday* (1992)
Cusine, D J and Paisley, R R M	*Servitudes and Rights of Way* (1998)
Cusine, D J and Rennie, R	*Missives* (2nd edn, 1999)
Cusine, D J and Rennie, R	*Standard Securities* (2nd edn, 2002)
Erskine, Sir J	*An Institute of the Law of Scotland* (2 Volumes, 1773)
Farran, C D	*The Principles of Scots and English Land Law* (1958)
Faulds, A and Hyslop, J	*Scottish Roads Law* (2000)
Flint, D	*Liquidation in Scotland* (1990)
Gamble, A J (ed)	*Obligations in Context: Essays in Honour of Professor D M Walker* (1990)
Garbutt, J	*Waste Management Law* (2nd edn, 1995)
Gill, The Hon Lord	*Law of Agricultural Holdings in Scotland* (3rd edn, 1997)
Gloag, W M	*Contract* (2nd edn, 1929)
Gloag, W M and Henderson, R C	*Introduction to the Law of Scotland* (11th edn, 2001)
Gordon, W M	*Scottish Land Law* (2nd edn, 1999)
Green, W	*Conveyancing Statutes* (current edn)
Green, W	*Encyclopaedia of the Laws of Scotland*, 16 Volumes (1926–35 with Supplements 1952) (*'Green's Encyclopaedia'*)
Green, W	*Property Law Bulletin* ('Greens PLB')
Greene, J H and Fletcher, I M	*The Law and Practice of Receivership in Scotland* (2nd edn, 1992)
Gregory	*Stamp Duties for Conveyancers* (1990) (an English text)
Gretton, G L	*Guide to Searches* (1991)
Gretton, G L	*The Law of Inhibition and Adjudication* (2nd edn, 1996)
Gretton, G L and Reid, K G C	*Conveyancing* (2nd edn, 1999)
Halliday, J M	*The Conveyancing and Feudal Reform (Scotland) Act 1970* (2nd edn, 1977)
Halliday, J M	*The Land Registration (Scotland) Act 1979* (1979)
Halliday, J M	*The Land Tenure Reform (Scotland) Act 1974* (1974)
Higgins, M	*Scottish Repossessions* (2002)
Himsworth, C	*Housing Law in Scotland* (4th edn, 1994)

Hiram, H	*The Scots Law of Succession* (2002)
Jauncey, The Hon Lord	*Fishing in Scotland: Law for the Angler* (2nd edn, 1984)
Johnston, D J	*Prescription and Limitation* (1999)
Kolbert, C F and Mackay, N A M (eds)	*History of Scots and English Land Law* (1977)
Logan, D J T	*Practical Debt Recovery* (2001)
McAllister, A	*Scottish Law of Leases* (3rd edn, 2002)
McAllister, A and Guthrie, T	*Scottish Property Law* (1992)
McBryde, W W	*Bankruptcy* (2nd edn, 1995)
McBryde, W W	*The Law of Contract in Scotland* (2nd edn, 2001)
MacCuish, D J and Flyn, D	*Crofting Law* (1990)
McDonald, A J	*Conveyancing Case Notes* (1980–81), Volumes 1 and 2
McDonald, A J	*Registration of Title Manual* (1986)
Macdonald, D R	*Succession* (3rd edn, 2001)
McKenzie Skene, D W	*Insolvency Law in Scotland* (1999)
MacQueen, H L and Thomson, J M	*Contract Law in Scotland* (2000)
Maher, G and Cusine, D J	*The Law and Practice of Diligence* (1990)
Menzies, A	*Lectures on Conveyancing* (Sturrock's edn, 1900)
Meston, M C	*The Succession (Scotland) Act 1964* (5th edn, 2002)
Mitchell, J J	*Eviction and Rent Arrears* (1995)
Mullen, T	*Scottish Housing Law Handbook* (1992)
Nichols, D I and Meston, M C	*The Matrimonial Homes (Family Protection) (Scotland) Act 1981* (2nd edn, 1986)
Ockrent, L	*Scottish Land Registration* (1942)
Paisley, R R M	*Land Law* (2000)
Paisley, R R M and Cusine, D J	*Unreported Property Cases from the Sheriff Courts* (2000)
Palmer, Sir F B	*Company Law* (25th edn) (looseleaf)
Paton, G C H and Cameron, J G S	*The Law of Landlord and Tenant in Scotland* (1967)
Rankine, J	*The Law of Landownership in Scotland* (4th edn, 1909)
Rankine, J	*The Law of Leases in Scotland* (3rd edn, 1916)
Registers of Scotland	*Registration of Title Practice Book* (2nd edn, 2000)
Reid, C T	*Green's Guide to Environmental Law* (1992)
Reid, K G C	*The Law of Property in Scotland* (1996)
Reid, K G C and Gretton, G L	*Conveyancing 1999* (2000)
Reid, K G C and Gretton, G L	*Conveyancing 2000* (2001)
Reid, K G C and Gretton, G L	*Conveyancing 2001* (2002)
Reid, K G C and Gretton, G L	*Conveyancing 2002* (2003)
Reid, K G C and Zimmermann, R (eds)	*A History of Private Law in Scotland*, Volume 1 (2000)
Rennie, R	*Minerals and the Law of Scotland* (2001)
Rennie, R	*Opinions on Professional Negligence in Conveyancing* (forthcoming)

Rennie, R — *Solicitors' Negligence* (1997)

Rennie, R and Cusine, D J — *The Requirements of Writing* (1995)

Robson, P and Halliday, S — *Residential Tenancies* (2nd edn, 1998)

Robson, P and McCowan, A — *Property Law* (2nd edn, 1999)

Rook, D — *Property Law and Human Rights* (2001)

Ross — *Leading Cases* (3 Volumes, 1849)

Ross, M J and McKichan, D J — *Drafting and Negotiating Commercial Leases in Scotland* (2nd edn, 1993)

Ross, W — *Lectures on the Law of Scotland* (1822)

Rowan-Robinson, J J — *Compulsory Purchase and Compensation* (2nd edn, 2003)

Rowan-Robinson, J J and McKenzie Skene, D W (eds) — *Countryside Law in Scotland* (2000)

Rowan-Robinson, J J and Young, E — *Planning by Agreement* (1989)

Rowan-Robinson, J J et al — *Scottish Planning Law and Procedure* (2001)

Scobbie, E (ed) — *Currie on Confirmation of Executors* (8th edn, 1996)

Scott Robinson, S — *The Law of Game Salmon and Freshwater Fishing in Scotland* (1990)

Scott Robinson, S — *The Law of Interdict* (2nd edn, 1994)

Sinclair, J H — *Handbook of Conveyancing Practice in Scotland* (4th edn, 2002)

Sinclair, J H — *Legal Drafting in Scotland* (2001)

Smith, Sir T B — *A Short Commentary on the Law of Scotland* (1962)

St Clair, J B and Drummond Young, J E — *The Law of Corporate Insolvency in Scotland* (2nd edn, 1992)

Stair, Viscount — *The Institutions of the Law of Scotland* (1681)

Stair Society — Volume 1, *Sources and Literature of Scots Law* (1936)

Volume 20, *Introduction to the History of Scots Law* (1959)

Talman, I J S (ed) — *Halliday's Conveyancing Law and Practice in Scotland* (2nd edn, 2 Volumes, 1996–97)

Tolley — *Stamp Duties and Stamp Duty Reserve Tax* (1990)

Waelde, C (ed) — *Professor McDonald's Conveyancing Opinions* (1998)

Walker, D M — *Civil Remedies* (1974)

Walker, D M — *Principles of Scottish Private Law* (4th edn, 1988)

Walker, D M — *The Law of Contracts and Related Obligations in Scotland* (3rd edn, 1995)

Walker, D M — *The Law of Prescription and Limitation of Actions in Scotland* (6th edn, 2002)

Ward, A — *Adult Incapacity* (2003)

Wilson, W A — *The Scottish Law of Debt* (2nd edn, 1991)

Wilson, W A and Duncan, A G M — *Trusts, Trustees and Executors* (2nd edn, 1995)

Wood — *Lectures on Conveyancing* (1903)

Young, E — *Scottish Planning Appeals* (1990)

Styles

Cusine, D J (ed)   *Green's Practice Styles* (looseleaf)
Gill, The Hon Lord and Fox, A   *Agricultural Holdings Styles* (1997)
Green, W   *Encyclopaedia of Scottish Legal Styles*, 10 Volumes (1935)

Appendix A to this Manual

Statutes

Royal Mines Act 1424
Leases Act 1449
Mines and Metals Act 1592
Registration Act 1617
Real Rights Act 1693
Registration of Sasines Act 1693
Infeftment Act 1845
Crown Charters Act 1847
Transference of Burgage Lands Act 1847
Transference of Lands Act 1847
Registration of Leases (Scotland) Act 1857
Titles to Lands Consolidation (Scotland) Act 1858
Titles to Land Consolidation (Scotland) Act 1860
Land Registers (Scotland) Act 1868
Registration of Writs (Scotland) Act 1868
Titles to Land Consolidation (Scotland) Act 1868
Titles to Land Consolidation (Scotland) Amendment Act 1869
Conveyancing (Scotland) Act 1874
Conveyancing Amendment (Scotland) Act 1887
Writs Execution (Scotland) Act 1887
Feudal Casualties (Scotland) Act 1914
Conveyancing (Scotland) Act 1924
Burgh Registers (Scotland) Act 1926
Conveyancing Amendment (Scotland) Act 1938
Public Registers and Records (Scotland) Acts 1948 and 1950
Tenancy of Shops (Scotland) Acts 1949 and 1964
Succession (Scotland) Act 1964
Conveyancing and Feudal Reform (Scotland) Act 1970
Redemption of Standard Securities (Scotland) Act 1971
Prescription and Limitation (Scotland) Acts 1973 and 1984
Land Tenure Reform (Scotland) Act 1974
Land Registration (Scotland) Act 1979
Law Reform (Miscellaneous Provisions) (Scotland) Act 1980
Matrimonial Homes (Family Protection) (Scotland) Act 1981
Law Reform (Miscellaneous Provisions) (Scotland) Act 1985
Prescription (Scotland) Act 1987
Register of Sasines (Scotland) Act 1987
Term and Quarter Days (Scotland) Act 1990

Property Misdescriptions Act 1991
Coal Industry Act 1994
Requirements of Writing (Scotland) Act 1995
Contract (Scotland) Act 1997
Abolition of Feudal Tenure etc (Scotland) Act 2000
Housing (Scotland) Act 2001
Leasehold Casualties (Scotland) Act 2001
Mortgage Rights (Scotland) Act 2001
Agricultural Holdings (Scotland) Act 2003
Buildings (Scotland) Act 2003
Land Reform (Scotland) Act 2003
Title Conditions (Scotland) Act 2003

Government reports and consultation papers

1963	*Registration of Title to Land* (Reid Committee Report) (Cmnd 2032)
1968	*Conveyancing Legislation and Practice* (Halliday Committee Report) (Cmnd 3118)
1969	*Registration of Title to Land* (Henry Committee Report) (Cmnd 4137)
1969	*Land Tenure in Scotland* (White Paper) (Cmnd 4009)
1972	*Land Tenure Reform in Scotland* (Green Paper)
2001	*Title Conditions (Scotland) Bill Consultation Paper* (Scottish Executive)
2002	*Enforcement of Civil Obligations in Scotland* (Scottish Executive)
2003	*Housing Improvement Task Force Report* (Scottish Executive)
2003	*Tenements (Scotland) Bill Consultation Paper* (Scottish Executive)

Scottish Law Commission consultative memoranda

No 1	*Probates or Letters of Administration as Links in Title to Heritable Property under the Succession (Scotland) Act 1964* (1966)
No 3	*Restrictions on the Creation of Liferents* (1967)
No 9	*Prescription and Limitation of Actions* (1969) (leading to Scot Law Com No 15)
No 10	*Examination of the Companies (Floating Charges) (Scotland) Act 1961* (1969) (leading to Scot Law Com No 14)
No 16	*Insolvency, Bankruptcy and Liquidation* (1971) (leading to Scot Law Com No 68)
No 33	*Law of Rights in Security - Company Law - Registration of Charges: Scotland* (1976)
No 43	*Defective Expression and its Correction* (1979) (leading to Scot Law Com No 79)
No 52	*Irritancies in Leases* (1980) (leading to Scot Law Com No 75)
No 59	*Recovery of Possession of Heritable Property* (1984) (leading to Scot Law Com No 118)
No 65	*Legal Capacity and Responsibility of Minors and Pupils* (1985) (leading to Scot Law Com No 110)
No 66	*Constitution and Proof of Voluntary Obligations and the Authentication of Writings* (1985)

(leading to Scot Law Com No 112)
No 69   *Intestate Succession and Legal Rights* (1986)
         (leading to Scot Law Com No 124)
No 70   *The Making and Revocation of Wills* (1986)
         (leading to Scot Law Com No 124)
No 71   *Some Miscellaneous Topics in the Law of Succession* (1986)
         (leading to Scot Law Com No 124)
No 72   *Floating Charges and Receivers* (1986)

Scottish Law Commission discussion papers

No 78   *Adjudication for Debt and Related Matters* (1987)
         (leading to Scot Law Com No 183)
No 81   *Passing of Risk in Contracts for the Sale of Land* (1989)
         (leading to Scot Law Com No 127)
No 91   *Law of the Tenement* (1990)
         (leading to Scot Law Com No 162)
No 93   *Property Law: Abolition of the Feudal System* (1991)
         (leading to Scot Law Com No 168)
No 97   *Contract Law: Extrinsic Evidence, Supersession and the Actio Quanti Minoris*
         (1994)   (leading to Scot Law Com No 152)
No 101   *Interpretation in Private Law* (1996)
         (leading to Scot Law Com No 160)
No 102   *Leasehold Casualties* (1997)
         (leading to Scot Law Com No 165)
No 106   *Real Burdens* (1998)
         (leading to Scot Law Com No 181)
No 107   *Diligence against Land* (1999)
         (leading to Scot Law Com No 183)
No 109   *Remedies for Breach of Contract* (1999)
         (leading to Scot Law Com No 174)
No 111   *Partnership Law* (2000)
         (a joint consultation paper with the English Law Commission)
No 112   *Conversion of Long Leases* (2001)
No 113   *Law of the Foreshore and Seabed* (2001)
         (leading to Scot Law Com No 190)
No 114   *Sharp v Thomson* (2001)
No 117   *Irritancy in Leases of Land* (2001)
         (leading to Scot Law Com No 191)
No 121   *Registration of Rights in Security by Companies* (2002)

Scottish Law Commission consultation papers

Mutual Boundary Walls (1992) (Scot Law Com No 163)

Scottish Law Commission reports

Scot Law Com No 14   *The Companies (Floating Charges) (Scotland) Act 1961*
                          (1970)

	(implemented by Companies (Floating Charges and Receivers) (Scotland) Act 1972)
Scot Law Com No 15	*Reform of the Law relating to Prescription and Limitation of Actions* (1970)
	(implemented by Prescription and Limitation (Scotland) Act 1973)
Scot Law Com No 68	*Report on Bankruptcy and Related Aspects of Insolvency and Liquidation* (1981)
	(implemented by Bankruptcy (Scotland) Act 1985)
Scot Law Com No 75	*Report on Irritancies in Leases* (1983)
	(implemented by Law Reform (Miscellaneous Provisions) (Scotland) Act 1985, ss 4–7)
Scot Law Com No 79	*Report on Rectification of Contractual and Other Documents* (1983)
	(implemented by Law Reform (Miscellaneous Provisions) (Scotland) Act 1985, ss 8 and 9)
Scot Law Com No 92	*Obligations – Report on Negligent Misrepresentation* (1985)
	(implemented by Law Reform (Miscellaneous Provisions) (Scotland) Act 1985, s 10)
Scot Law Com No 108	*Report on the Scottish Term and Quarter Days* (1987)
	(implemented by Term and Quarter Days (Scotland) Act 1990)
Scot Law Com No 110	*Report on the Legal Capacity and Responsibility of Minors and Pupils* (1987)
	(implemented by Age of Legal Capacity (Scotland) Act 1991)
Scot Law Com No 112	*Report on Requirements of Writing* (1988)
	(implemented by Requirements of Writing (Scotland) Act 1995)
Scot Law Com No 118	*Report on Recovery of Possession of Heritable Property* (1989)
Scot Law Com No 124	*Report on Succession* (1990)
Scot Law Com No 127	*Report on the Passing of Risk in Contracts for the Sale of Heritable Property* (1990)
Scot Law Com No 151	*Report on Incapable Adults* (1995)
	(implemented by Adults with Incapacity (Scotland) Act 2000)
Scot Law Com No 152	*Report on Three Bad Rules of Contract Law* (1996)
	(implemented by Contract (Scotland) Act 1997)
Scot Law Com No 160	*Report on Interpretation in Private Law* (1997)
Scot Law Com No 162	*Report on the Law of the Tenement* (1998)
Scot Law Com No 163	*Report on Boundary Walls* (1998)
Scot Law Com No 165	*Report on Leasehold Casualties* (1998)
	(implemented by Leasehold Casualties (Scotland) Act 2001)
Scot Law Com No 168	*Report on Abolition of the Feudal System* (1999)
	(implemented by Abolition of Feudal Tenure etc (Scotland) Act 2000)
Scot Law Com No 174	*Report on Remedies for Breach of Contract* (1999)
Scot Law Com No 181	*Report on Real Burdens* (2000)
	(implemented by Title Conditions (Scotland) Act 2003)
Scot Law Com No 183	*Report on Diligence* (2001)
Scot Law Com No 190	*Report on Law of the Foreshore and Seabed* (2003)

Scot Law Com No 191   *Report on Irritancy in Leases of Land* (2003)

Websites

Acts of the UK Parliament	www.hmso.gov.uk/acts.htm
The Coal Authority	www.coal.gov.uk
Coal Mining Reports	www.coalminingreports.co.uk
Companies House	www.companieshouse.gov.uk
The Council of Mortgage Lenders	www.cml.org.uk
The Inland Revenue	www.inlandrevenue.gov.uk
Stamp taxes section of the Inland Revenue	www.inlandrevenue.gov.uk/so
The Law Society of Scotland	www.lawscot.org.uk
The Law Society of Scotland, Conveyancing Essentials	www.lawscot.org.uk/members/conveyancing/index.html
LexisNexis	www.lexisnexis.co.uk
The National Archives of Scotland	www.nas.gov.uk
The Registers of Scotland	www.ros.gov.uk
The Scottish Courts	www.scotcourts.gov.uk
The Scottish Executive	www.scotland.gov.uk
The Scottish Law Agents' Society	www.slas.co.uk
The Scottish Law Commission	www.scotlawcom.gov.uk
Scottish legislation	www.scotland-legislation.hmso.gov.uk
The Scottish Parliament	www.scottish-parliament.uk

Reading List

Note
For material which is of relevance to the whole Manual, please see the Bibliography. The Bibliography also contains full details of most of the works which are referred to here.

PART I   PRELIMINARY MATTERS

Chapter 2   Authentication

References

Burns	*Conveyancing Practice* (4th edn, 1957), Chapter 1
Burns	*Handbook of Conveyancing* (5th edn, 1938), Chapters 2 and 3
Gloag	*Contract* (2nd edn, 1929), Chapters 10 and 11
Green's Encyclopaedia	Volume 2, paras 651–662, Blanks in Documents; Volume 5, paras 1071–1101, Execution of Deeds
Gretton and Reid	*Conveyancing* (2nd edn, 1999), Chapter 14
Menzies	*Lectures on Conveyancing* (Sturrock's edn, 1900), Part 1, Chapters 1–6
Reid	*The Requirements of Writing (Scotland) Act 1995* (1995)
Rennie and Cusine	*The Requirements of Writing* (1995)
Ross (ed)	*Walker and Walker: The Law of Evidence in Scotland* (2nd edn, 2000), Chapters 9–12, 16–19, 21, 22
Stair Memorial Encyclopaedia	Volume 6, paras 401–433
Talman (ed)	*Halliday's Conveyancing Law and Practice in Scotland* (2nd edn, 2 Volumes, 1996–97), Volume 1, Chapter 3
Waelde (ed)	*Professor McDonald's Conveyancing Opinions* (1998), pp 14–15

Styles

Encyclopaedia of Scottish Legal Styles	Volume 4, Execution of Deeds

Statutes

Subscription of Deeds Acts 1540, 1579 and 1584

Execution of Deeds Act 1593
Lyon King of Arms Act 1672
Subscription of Deeds Act 1681
Deeds Act 1696
Blank Bonds and Trusts Act 1696
Forms of Deeds (Scotland) Act 1856
Wills Act 1861
Titles to Land Consolidation (Scotland) Act 1868, ss 20, 139, 140, 144
Conveyancing (Scotland) Act 1874, ss 38, 39, 54
Partnership Act 1890, s 6
Conveyancing (Scotland) Act 1924, s 18 and Sch 1
Conveyancing and Feudal Reform (Scotland) Act 1970, s 44
Wills Act 1963
Local Government (Scotland) Act 1973, s 194
Companies Act 1985, s 36B
Law Reform (Miscellaneous Provisions) (Scotland) Act 1985, ss 8, 9
Requirements of Writing (Scotland) Act 1995

Scottish Law Commission Publications

1985 – *Constitution and Proof of Voluntary Obligations and Authentication of Writings* (Scot
    Law Com Memorandum No 66)
1988 – *Requirements of Writing* (Scot Law Com Report No 112)

Articles

1 *Conveyancing Review* 216	Adopted as holograph
1963 SLT (News) 161	The Wills Act 1963
1963 JLSS 99	The Wills Act 1963
1979 SLT (News) 173	Notarially Executed Wills
1980 JLSS 448	Testamentary Writings deemed to be Probative
1985 JLSS 308	What is a probative writ?
1986 SLT (News) 129	Execution or revocation?
1987 JLSS 148	Execution of deeds
1988 JLSS 228	Comments on Scottish Law Commission Report No 112
1989 JLSS 135	Execution of Deeds by Companies
1990 JLSS 358	Execution of Documents by Companies
1990 JLSS 498	Execution of Documents by Companies
1990 SLT (News) 241	Execution of Deeds by Companies: the New Law
1990 SLT (News) 369	Execution of Deeds by Companies: the Replacement Provisions
1991 SLT (News) 283	Bad Company: Companies' Executions
1991 SLT (News) 457	Good Company: Companies' Executions Once Again
1991 JLSS 73	Who signs for the Firm?
1993 JLSS 270	Execution of Deeds by a Mark
1994 JLSS 191	A note on the Foreign Companies (Execution of Deeds) Regulations 1994

1994 JLSS 450	Conveyancing – What's coming? An article on the proposed new statute on requirements of writing
1995 JLSS 221	A Commentary on the Requirements of Writing (Scotland) Act 1995
(1995) 15 Greens PLB 4	The Requirements of Writing (Scotland) Act 1995
(1995) 17 Greens PLB 7	The Requirements of Writing (Scotland) Act 1995 – Comment by the Keeper
1995 JLSS 405	The Requirements of Writing Act (Scotland) Act 1995 – Note by the Keeper
1996 SLT (News) 49	Constructing Ambiguities? Some problems of the Requirements of Writing (Scotland) Act 1995
(2000) 68 SLG 8	Bearing Witness to the Deed
(2001) SLPQ 197	Statutory Personal Bar: *Rei interventus* replaced

Chapter 3   Capacity

References

Burns	*Conveyancing Practice* (4th edn, 1957), pp 308–323
Gloag and Henderson	*Introduction to the Law of Scotland* (11th edn, 2001), Chapter 5
Gretton and Reid	*Conveyancing* (2nd edn, 1999), Chapters 25, 27, 28 and 29
McBryde	*Bankruptcy* (2nd edn, 1995)
Reid and Gretton	*Conveyancing 1999* (2000), pp 100–111
Stair Memorial Encyclopaedia	Volume 24, paras 1–300
Talman (ed)	*Halliday's Conveyancing Law and Practice in Scotland* (2nd edn, 2 Volumes, 1996–97), Chapter 2
Walker	*Judicial Factors* (1974)
Ward	*Adult Incapacity* (2003)
Wilson and Duncan	*Trusts, Trustees and Executors* (2nd edn, 1995)

Statutes

Judicial Factors (Scotland) Acts 1849, 1880 and 1889
Guardianship of Children Acts 1886, 1925 and 1973
Married Women's Property (Scotland) Act 1920
Conveyancing Amendment (Scotland) Act 1938, s 1
Succession (Scotland) Act 1964
Trusts (Scotland) Acts 1921 and 1961
Bankruptcy (Scotland) Act 1985
Family Law (Scotland) Act 1985, s 24
Companies Act 1985, s 35
Law Reform (Parent and Child) (Scotland) Act 1986
Recognition of Trusts Act 1987
Age of Legal Capacity (Scotland) Act 1991

Requirements of Writing (Scotland) Act 1995
Adults with Incapacity (Scotland) Act 2000
Limited Liability Partnerships Act 2000

Articles

Chapter 4   Delivery

References

Scottish Law Commission Publication

2001 – *Sharp v Thomson* (Scot Law Com Discussion Paper No 114)

Articles

1981 JLSS 132 and 181	Delivery of Deeds
1982 SLT (News) 149	Ownership on Delivery
1984 JLSS 400	Delivery of Deeds etc
1985 SLT (News) 165	Ownership on Delivery
1985 SLT (News) 280	Ownership on Registration
1986 SLT (News) 177	Constitution of Trust
1994 SLT (News) 183	Dead on Delivery – Comment on *Sharp v Thomson*
1994 SLT (News) 313	*Sharp* cases make good law
1994 JLSS 356, 371, 384, 444	Various Comments on *Sharp v Thomson*
1995 SLT (News) 75	*Sharp v Thomson* – A Civilian Perspective
1995 SLT (News) 79	*Sharp v Thomson*: identifying the mischief
1995 SLT (News) 91 and 101	Further Comments on *Sharp v Thomson*
1995 JLSS 256	*Sharp v Thomson*: What now?
1995 JLSS 323 Caveat	Delivery of Documents
1995 JLSS 311	A commentary on *Sharp v Thomson*
(1995) 1 SLPQ 53	*Sharp v Thomson*: property law preserved
1996 SLT (News) 365	The Perils of a Trusting Disposition
1996 SLT (News) 373	Intimation – The Equivalent Delivery of What?
1997 SLT (News) 79	Jam Today: *Sharp* in the House of Lords
(1997) 26 Greens PLB 5	*Sharp v Thomson* – The House of Lords strikes back
1997 JLSS 130	*Sharp v Thomson*: The Final Act
1997 SLT (News) 151 and 171	*Sharp v Thomson*: the impact on banking and insolvency law
(1997) 1 Edin LR 464	Equity triumphant: *Sharp v Thomson*
2001 SLT (News) 135	The Integrity of Property Law and the Property Registers
2001 SLT (News) 247	To *Sharp v Thomson*: an heir
2001 SLT (News) 305	Sharp pains for Scots property law
(2001) 5 Edin LR 72	Equitable Ownership in Scots Law?
(2002) 7 SLPQ 211	Mind the Gap: problems in the transfer of ownership
2002 SLT (News) 231	In Defence of the Trusting Conveyancer

Chapter 5   Stamp Duty Land Tax, Stamp Duty and VAT

References

BDO Stoy Hatward	*VAT and Property* (looseleaf)
Gammie and De Souza	*Land Taxation* (looseleaf)
Monroe and Nock	*Stamp Duties* (looseleaf)
Sergeant and Sims	*Stamp Duties* (looseleaf)
Soares	*VAT Planning for Property Transactions* (8th edn, 2002)
Tolley	*Stamp Duties and Stamp Duty Reserve Tax* (new edition, forthcoming, to include SDLT)

Tolley   *VAT on Construction, Land and Property* (loose-
                                          leaf))

Articles etc

Inland Revenue Statement of Practice   12 September 1991: Stamp Duty and VAT –
                                          Interaction (SP 11/91)
1992 PQLE   VAT on Property
(1993) 4 Greens PLB 4   Missives: VAT
(1993) 5 Greens PLB 2   Missives: VAT, Part 2
Update – November 1995   VAT on Property
1996 JLSS 398   VAT: Statement of Practice on Transfer of a
                                          Property – Letting Business as a Going Concern
1998 Tax 182   VAT: licence to occupy land
1999 EG 175   Going concerns and VAT
1999 Tax 109   Even more tax on tax
(2001) 50 Greens PLB 2   Something for nothing? (Rent-free periods and
                                          VAT)
HM Customs and Excise   Notice 742 March 2002, as amended – Land and
                                          Property HM Customs and Excise – Notice
                                          742/3 Jan 2002 – Scottish Land Law Terms
2003 Tax 430   The devil and the details
2003 JLSS Sep/28   Stamp Duty Land Tax
2003 Tax 256 and 284   Self-assessment Takes over Stamp Duty
(2003) 679 Tax J 15   VAT and Developing a Property Business
  and subsequent issues
(2003) 689 Tax J 5   Stamp Duty
  and subsequent issues
2003 NLJ 850   SDLT – A midsummer misnomer?
2003 NLJ 950   Stamping on Property Transactions
2003 SJ 558   Stamp Duty Update
2003 SJ 803   Land Tax: the basics

Statutes

Finance Acts, various, and especially the Finance Act 2003 for SDLT (together with regula-
        tions made thereunder)
Value Added Tax Act 1994 (as amended) and Regulations and Orders made thereunder.

PART 2   DISPOSITIONS

Chapter 6   Feudal Background

References

Burns   *Conveyancing Practice* (4th edn, 1957), Chapter 11

Burns	*Handbook of Conveyancing* (5th edn, 1938), Chapters 10 and 11
Gordon	*Scottish Land Law* (2nd edn, 1999), Chapters 2 and 3
Green's Encyclopaedia	Volume 2, paras 1066–1101, Burgage
	Volume 3, paras 236–296, Casualties
	Volume 3, paras 518–647, Charter – Feudal
	Volume 12, paras 758–863, Registration and Records
	Volume 14, paras 616–671, Superior and Vassal
Gretton and Reid	*Conveyancing* (2nd edn, 1999), Chapter 23
Paisley	*Land Law* (2000), paras 1.2–1.3
Reid	*The Abolition of Feudal Tenure in Scotland* (2003)
Reid and Gretton	*Conveyancing 2000* (2001), pp 123–143
Reid and Gretton	*Conveyancing 2002* (2003), p 42
Rennie	*Land Tenure Reform* (2003)
Robertson	'The Illusory Breve Testatum' in *The Scottish Tradition*, G W S Barrow (ed), (1974)
Stair Memorial Encyclopaedia	Volume 6, paras 401–411, History of Reform
	Volume 18, paras 41–113, Feudalism
	Volume 24, paras 301–329, Udal Law
Stair Society	Volume 20, Chapter 14
Talman (ed)	*Halliday's Conveyancing Law and Practice in Scotland* (2nd edn, 2 Volumes, 1996–97), Volume 2, Chapters 31 and 32
Waelde (ed)	*Professor McDonald's Conveyancing Opinions* (1998), pp 34–43 and 128–139

Styles

Encyclopaedia of Scottish Legal Styles   Volume 5, Feus

Statutes

Land Registers (Scotland) Act 1868
Titles to Land Consolidation (Scotland) Act 1868, ss 3, 5–10, 12–15, 17, 20, 21, 100, 138, 141–145, 147, 163
Conveyancing (Scotland) Act 1874, ss 4, 15, 16, 18, 20–23, 25–28, 32
Feudal Casualties (Scotland) Act 1914
Conveyancing (Scotland) Act 1924, ss 8–10, 12, 14, 48
Burgh Registers (Scotland) Act 1926
Conveyancing Amendment (Scotland) Act 1938, ss 8, 9
Conveyancing and Feudal Reform (Scotland) Act 1970, Part I
Land Tenure Reform (Scotland) Act 1974, ss 1–3
Land Registration (Scotland) Act 1979
Abolition of Feudal Tenure etc (Scotland) Act 2000

Government and Scottish Law Commission Publications

1969 – *Land Tenure in Scotland* (White Paper Cmnd 4009)
1972 – *Land Tenure Reform in Scotland* (Green Paper)

1991 – *Abolition of the Feudal System* (Scot Law Com Discussion Paper No 93)
1999 – *Abolition of the Feudal System* (Scot Law Com Report No 168)

Articles

1976 SLT (News) 257	Infeftment
(1988) 56 Leg Hist Rev 311	The Breve Testatum and Craig's *Jus Feudale*
1992 JLSS 306	Barony Title
1994 JR 283	The Theory and Ethics of Irritancy
1995 JR 321	The Feudal System – Going, Going, Gone?
1999 JLSS Feb/24	Abolition of the Feudal System
(2000) 47 Greens PLB 1	The Abolition of Feudal Tenure etc (Scotland) Act 2000 (part 1)
(2000) 48 Greens PLB 3	The Abolition of Feudal Tenure etc (Scotland) Act 2000 (part 2)
(2001) 69 SLG 46	Scottish Feudal Baronies in Reform
2001 SLT (News) 235	Leasehold Casualties
(2002) 60 Greens PLB 6	Preparing Superiors for Feudal Abolition (part 1)
(2002) 61 Greens PLB 7	Preparing Superiors for Feudal Abolition (part 2)
2002 JR 251	Udal Law and Coastal Land Ownership
2002 JBL 177	Scottish Land Law in a State of Reform
2003 SLT (News) 6	Court of the Lord Lyon: Baronial Titles
2003 JR 1	Tears of a Legal Historian: Scottish Feudalism and the *Ius Commune*

Chapter 7   The Disposition: General

References

Burns	*Conveyancing Practice* (4th edn, 1957), Chapter 16
Dobie	*Manual of the Law of Liferent and Fee* (1941)
Gordon	*Scottish Land Law* (2nd edn, 1999), Chapter 15: Co-ownership and common interest
Green's Encyclopaedia	Volume 1, paras 104–112, Accretion
	Volume 9, paras 502–557, Liferent and Fee
	Volume 14, paras 246–255, Singular Successor
Gretton and Reid	*Conveyancing* (2nd edn, 1999), Chapter 11
Paisley and Cusine	*Unreported Property Cases from the Sheriff Courts* (2000), Chapter 4
Reed, Lord (ed)	*A Practical Guide to Human Rights Law in Scotland* (2001), Chapter 7
Reid and Gretton	*Conveyancing 2002* (2003), pp 79–81
Stair Memorial Encyclopaedia	Volume 12, paras 1213–1262, Interpretation of Deeds
	Volume 13, paras 1601–1663, Liferents
	Volume 18, para 677, Accretion

Articles
Destinations

1984 JLSS 103	Heirs, Executors and Assignees
1985 SLT (News) 57	Common Property
1989 JLSS 299	Destinations
1990 JLSS 189	Survivorship Destinations in Scotland
2000 SLT (News) 203	Time for Special Destinations to Die
2003 JLSS May/32	A Matter of Opinion

Joint and common property and common interest

1 *Conveyancing Review* 17	Property Commonly Called Joint
1 *Conveyancing Review* 105	The Law of the Tenement
1 *Conveyancing Review* 143	Maintenance of Tenement Roofs
1 *Conveyancing Review* 239	The Law of the Tenement
1 *Conveyancing Review* 260	The Limitations of Common Interest
2 *Conveyancing Review* 102	The Law of the Tenement
1958 JLSS 217	Plans
1973 SLT (News) 68	Support of Buildings
1980 JLSS 141	Mutual Gable Walls
1983 JLSS 472	The Law of the Tenement
1985 SLT (News) 57	Common Property
1990 JLSS 368	Law of the Tenement
1993 SLT (News) 61	Joint or Common Property
1993 JLSS 465	Joint Property – Is this the best advice?
1993 JLSS 402	Maintenance of tenement roofs
1994 JLSS 423	A note from the Professional Practice Committee as to accounting on the sale of property held in common
1994 JLSS 398	Spousal Defences to division and sale
(1994) 11 Greens PLB 6	Law Reform: A comment on Scottish Law Commission Discussion Paper No 91 on the Law of the Tenement
1998 JLSS Apr/21	Reform of the Law of the Tenement
(2001) 52 Greens PLB 4	Reform of the Law of the Tenement (Part 1)
(2001) 53 Greens PLB 3	Reform of the Law of the Tenement (Part 2)

Chapter 8   Descriptions

References

Gilbert	*The Tenement Handbook: A Practical Guide to Living in a Tenement* (1992)
Gordon	*Scottish Land Law* (2nd edn, 1999)
	Chapter 4, Land and Boundaries
	Chapter 7, Water and Water Rights

Styles

Statutes and Statutory Instruments

Game (Scotland) Act 1772
Night Poaching Acts 1828 and 1844
Day Trespass Act 1832
Ground Game Act 1880
Trout (Scotland) Acts 1902 and 1933
Land Drainage (Scotland) Acts 1930 and 1958
Rivers (Prevention of Pollution) (Scotland) Acts 1951 and 1965
Salmon and Fresh Water Fisheries (Protection) (Scotland) Act 1951

Flood Prevention (Scotland) Act 1961
Control of Pollution Act 1974
Freshwater and Salmon Fisheries (Scotland) Act 1976
Water Act 1989
Environmental Protection Act 1990
Units of Measurement Regulations 1995, SI 1995/1804
Land Reform (Scotland) Act 2003
Salmon and Freshwater Fisheries (Consolidation) (Scotland) Act 2003
Agricultural Holdings (Scotland) Act 2003

Scottish Law Commission Publications

1990 – *Law of the Tenement* (Scot Law Com Discussion Paper No 91)
1992 – *Mutual Boundary Walls* (Scot Law Com Consultation Paper No 163)
1998 – *Law of the Tenement* (Scot Law Com Report No 162)
1998 – *Report on Mutual Boundary Walls* (Scot Law Com No 163)

Articles

Tenements

See Articles under Chapter 7   Joint and common property and common interest

General

1971 JLSS 62	Descriptions in Feu Dispositions
1973 JLSS 43, 78, 114, 141, 174	The Law of Pollution in Scotland
1984 SLT (News) 336	Regulation of salmon fishing
1985 SLT (News) 217	Salmon fishing in troubled waters
1985 JR 25	Tales from the river bank
1994 SLT (News) 75	Alluvio, avulsio and fluvial boundaries
1995 JLSS 41	Alluvio in the Land Register
1995 JLSS 402 Caveat	A reminder of the necessity of examining a title before committing the seller
1995 JLSS 481	Descriptions in standard securities – a note by the Keeper
1996 JLSS 209	Descriptions in standard securities, discussing *Beneficial Bank v McConnachie*
(1996) 19 Greens PLB 4	Metrication and Conveyancing Descriptions, discussing The Units of Measurement Regulations 1995
1994 JLSS 420 Caveat	The sale of older country properties with particular reference to boundaries and ownership
(1996) 20 Greens PLB 5	Boundaries and Roadside Verges
(1996) 22 Greens PLB 4	Drainage Systems and Rural Properties
(1996) 24 Greens PLB 11	Preparation of Conveyancing Deeds
(2000) 5 SLPQ 386	Parts and Pertinents in Conveyancing

2000 JR 39	The Ownership of Corporeal Property as a Separate Tenement
(2001) 6 SLPQ 137	Overcoming Practical Problems: The Law of Encroachment and the Function of Title Insurance
2001 SLT (News) 115	Boundary Disputes
2002 JR 251	Udal Law and Coastal Land Ownership
(2002) 6 Edin LR 67 and 199	Accession of Movables to Land

Other

Opinion of the Solicitor General in relation to shooting leases (1962), published as part of the Scottish Landowners Federation's evidence to the Justice 1 Committee in relation to the Title Conditions (Scotland) Bill. See http://www.scottish.parliament.uk/S1/official_report/cttee/just1-02/j1r02-09-vol02-03.htm#19.

Chapter 9   Reservations

References

Cusine (ed)	*The Conveyancing Opinions of J M Halliday* (1992), pp 437–439
Gordon	*Scottish Land Law* (2nd edn, 1999), Chapter 6: Horizontal Subdivision of Land, Minerals and Support
Green's Encyclopaedia	Volume 10, paras 1–54, Mines and Minerals
	Volume 14, paras 677–720, Support
	1949 Supplement Appendix, Coal Mines
Gretton and Reid	*Conveyancing* (2nd edn, 1999), para 4.05
Paisley	*Land Law* (2000), paras 1.13–1.15, 8.9, 10.18
Rankine	*The Law of Landownership in Scotland* (4th edn, 1909), Chapter 10
Registers of Scotland	*Registration of Title Practice Book* (2nd edn, 2000), paras 6.88–6.98
Rennie	*Minerals and the Law of Scotland* (2001)
Stair Memorial Encyclopaedia	Volume 18, paras 252–272, Minerals and support
Talman (ed)	*Halliday's Conveyancing Law and Practice in Scotland* (2nd edn, 2 Volumes, 1996–97), Volume 2, Chapter 34: Reservations etc
Waelde (ed)	*Professor McDonald's Conveyancing Opinions* (1998), pp 73–75

Statutes

Royal Mines Act 1424
Mines and Metals Act 1592
Coal Industry Nationalisation Act 1946
Mines (Working Facilities and Support) Act 1966

Coal Industry Act 1975
Coal Mining Subsidence Act 1991
Coal Industry Act 1994
Petroleum Act 1998

Styles

Encyclopaedia of Scottish Legal Styles   Volume 7, Mines and Minerals

Articles

Conveyancing Review 165	Mineral Reservations and the Unwilling Purchaser
1975 JLSS 205	Minerals
1988 PQLE	Minerals
(1994) 11 Greens PLB 2	Quarries etc
1995 JLSS 238, 259 and 326	Coal Mining Enquiries and Comments thereon
1996 JLSS 266	Minerals and the Land Register
2001 JLSS Aug/8	Coal Authority Online Mining Reports Service
(2002) 7 SLPQ 87	Mineral Rights

Websites

The Coal Authority	www.coal.gov.uk
Coal Mining Reports	www.coalminingreports.co.uk
Law Society Guidance Notes 1999	www.coalminingreports.co.uk/stLSGNFR.htm

Chapter 10   Other Clauses

References

Cusine (ed)	*A Scots Conveyancing Miscellany: Essays in Honour of Professor J M Halliday* (1987), p 152: Reid 'Warrandice etc'
Green's Encyclopaedia	Volume 15, paras 1107–1125, Warrandice
Gretton and Reid	*Conveyancing* (2nd edn, 1999), paras 18.04–18.13
Paisley	*Land Law* (2000), para 3.29
Reid and Gretton	*Conveyancing 2002* (2003), pp 8, 87–89 and 96
Stair Memorial Encyclopaedia	Volume 18, paras 701–714
Waelde (ed)	*Professor McDonald's Conveyancing Opinions* (1998), pp 101–105

Statute

Land Registration (Scotland) Act 1979, s 16

Articles

3 *Conveyancing Review* 144	Latent Defects in Heritable Property
1972 SLT (News) 41	An Aspect of Warrandice

1983 JR 1	The Scope of Warrandice in Conveyance of Land
1983 JLSS 228	Warrandice and Latent Defects in Heritage
1988 JLSS 162	Good and Marketable Title
(1993) 5 Greens PLB 6	Warrandice
1994 SLT (News) 183	Dead on Delivery
1996 SLT (News) 365	The Perils of a Trusting Disposition
1998 SLT (News) 283	Eviction Evicted? – Warrandice after the Contract (Scotland) Act 1997
2002 SLT (News) 231	In Defence of the Trusting Conveyancer

Chapter 11   Registration

References

Burns	*Conveyancing Practice* (4th edn, 1957), Chapter 12
Burns	*Handbook of Conveyancing (5th edn, 1938)*, Chapter 13
Green's Encyclopaedia	Volume 4, paras 387–390, 418–431, 449 and 457, Completion of Title
	Volume 12, paras 804–847, Registration and Records (part)
Gretton and Reid	*Conveyancing* (2nd edn, 1999), Chapter 16
Halliday	*The Land Tenure Reform (Scotland) Act 1974* (1974)
McDonald	*Registration of Title Manual* (1986)
Paisley	*Land Law* (2000), paras 3.14–3.15, 3.19–3.20
Registers of Scotland	*Registration of Title Practice Book* (2nd edn, 2000)
Registration of Title	(PQLE Papers: February 1991)
Reid and Gretton	*Conveyancing 1999* (2000), pp 12–16 and 66–72
Reid and Gretton	*Conveyancing 2000* (2001), pp 13–15 and 107–113
Reid and Gretton	*Conveyancing 2001* (2002), pp 14–15 and 108–115
Reid and Gretton	*Conveyancing 2002* (2003), p 11 and 83–87
Simpson	*Land Law and Registration* (1976)
Stair Memorial Encyclopaedia	Volume 6, paras 448–53, Sasine registration and paras 701–86, Registration of title
	Volume 19, paras 801–882, Public registers and records
Talman (ed)	*Halliday's Conveyancing Law and Practice in Scotland* (2nd edn, 2 Volumes, 1996–97), Volume 2, Chapter 39: Infeftment and Registration
Waelde (ed)	*Professor McDonald's Conveyancing Opinions* (1998), pp 106–116
Wood	*Lectures on Conveyancing* (1903), pp 44–60

Statutes and Statutory Instruments

Registration Act 1617
Subscription of Deeds Act 1681

Real Rights Act 1693
Register of Sasines Act 1693
Land Registers Act 1868
Titles to Land Consolidation (Scotland) Act 1868, ss 12, 15, 141–145
Conveyancing (Scotland) Act 1874, s 54
Conveyancing (Scotland) Act 1924, ss 10, 48
Burgh Registers (Scotland) Act 1926
Land Registration (Scotland) Act 1979
Land Registration (Scotland) Rules 1980, SI 1980/1413
Register of Sasines (Scotland) Act 1987
Land Registration (Scotland) Amendment Rules 1988, SI 1998/1143

Reports

1907 – *Royal Commission on Registration of Title* (Dunedin Committee Minutes of Evidence)
1963 – *Reid Committee Report* (Cmnd 2632)
Memorandum of Evidence to be Submitted by the Council of the Law Society of Scotland to the Reid Committee, pp 6–26
1969 – *Registration of Title to Land in Scotland* (Henry Report Cmnd 4137)

Articles

1957 JLSS 29	The Register of Sasines
1958 JLSS 217	The Register of Sasines
1963 SLT (News) 193	Registration of Title to Land in Scotland
1964 JLSS 285 and 320	The Torrens System in its Place of Origin: Registration of Title to Land in South Australia
1967 JLSS 17	The Origin of the Sasine Register
1 Conveyancing Review 13	Registration of Title in England
2 Conveyancing Review 83	Registration of Title in England
3 Conveyancing Review 108	Accretion
1969 JLSS 352	Registration of Title Pilot Scheme
1970 JLSS 8	Registration of Title
1976 SLT (News) 257	Infeftment
1979 JLSS 225	Registration of Title
1981 JLSS 219	Introduction of Registration of Title to Scotland
1982 JLSS 109	Titles to Land – The New System Considered
1984 JLSS 171, 212 and 260	Registration of Title – Comments on the 1979 Act
1988 JLSS 331	Note on the Land Registration Rules 1988
1988 JLSS 98	What is a Real Right?
1990 JLSS 200	*Brookfield Developments Ltd v The Keeper* – A commentary
1991 JR 70	*A Non Domino* Conveyances and the Land Register
1992 JLSS 120	Registration of Title – A comment on P16 reports
1993 SLT (News) 97	Registration or Rectification? (discussing *Short's Trustee*)
(1994) 12 Greens PLB 3	Comments by the Keeper on Recording of Deeds in the Sasine Register

1995 JLSS 283	A Comment by the Keeper on proposed changes in fees in the Registers of Scotland Executive Agency
1995 JLSS 482	A note by the Keeper on the introduction of pre-payment of fees in the Land Register and Sasine Register
(1995) 16 Greens PLB 8	A note on VAT in relation to registration fees
1996 JLSS 272	A note by the Keeper on Requisition Policy in the Land Register, and his discretion in accepting applications without all the necessary documentation
1999 SLT (News) 163	Problems in the Land Register
(2000) 46 Greens PLB 5	Land Registration Questions (but see clarifications at Issue 48 p 6)
2001 JLSS Feb/34	Substitute Land and Charge Certificates
2001 JLSS June/19	The Age of E-Conveyancing?
2001 JLSS Oct/28	Land Registry: Time to re-think conveyancing customs
2001 SLT (News) 58	Of Inoperative Deeds and Operational Areas
(2001) 55 Greens PLB 6	Rectification and Indemnity in the Land Register (part 1)
(2002) 56 Greens PLB 1	Rectification and Indemnity in the Land Register (part 2)
2002 JLSS Nov/25	Automated Registration of Title to Land
(2003) 8 SLPQ 95	The E-Conveyancing Matrix

Website

Registers of Scotland	www.ros.gov.uk

Chapter 12   The Effects of Possession: Prescription

References

Burns	*Conveyancing Practice* (4th edn, 1957), pp 200–206
Gordon	*Scottish Land Law* (2nd edn, 1999), paras 12-15–12-53 (prescription) paras 14-01–14-61 (possession)
Green's Encyclopaedia	Volume 12, paras 41–88, Prescription
Gretton and Reid	*Conveyancing* (2nd edn, 1999), paras 7.06–7.12
Johnston	*Prescription and Limitation* (1999), Chapters 14–16
Millar	*Prescription* (1893)
Napier	*Prescription* (2 Volumes, 1839)
Paisley	*Land Law* (2000), para 3.13
Rankine	*The Law of Landownership in Scotland* (4th edn, 1909), Chapters 1–4

Reid and Gretton	*Conveyancing 1999* (2000), p 25
Reid and Gretton	*Conveyancing 2000* (2001), pp 24–25
Reid and Gretton	*Conveyancing 2002* (2003), pp 26–27
Stair Memorial Encyclopaedia	Volume 18, paras 114–192, Possession
Waelde (ed)	*Professor McDonald's Conveyancing Opinions* (1998), pp 117–127
Walker	*Prescription and Limitation* (6th edn, 2002)

Statutes

Prescription Act 1469
Prescription Act 1474
Prescription Act 1617
Prescription and Limitation (Scotland) Act 1973
Land Registration (Scotland) Act 1979, s 10

Articles

1994 SLT (News) 261	Possession: nine-tenths of the law. A commentary on the decision in *Hamilton v McIntosh Donald Ltd*
(1997) 2 SLPQ 309	Prescriptive Possession in the Sasine and Land Registers
2001 SLT (News) 115	Boundary Disputes

PART 3   REGULATION OF LANDOWNERSHIP

Chapter 13   Land Regulation: Introduction

References

Gordon	*Scottish Land Law* (2nd edn, 1999), Chapter 26, Delicts affecting land
Stair Memorial Encyclopaedia	Volume 14, paras 2001–2158, Nuisance

Articles

(1982) 27 JLSS 497 and (1983) 28 JLSS 5	Reasonable Neighbourhood: The Province and Analysis of Private Nuisance in Scots law
1986 JR 107	Nuisance and Negligence
1994 SLT (News) 349	Liability as Occupier to User of a Right of Way
1995 JR 462	*Culpa* and the Law of Nuisance
(1995) 8 Env LB 4	Scots Law of Nuisance: *Kennedy v Glenbelle Ltd*
(1996) 7 Civ PB 2	Remedies in an Action for Nuisance
1997 SLT (News) 177	Damages for Nuisance
(1997) 2 SLPQ 214 and (1997) 2 SLPQ 274	Civil Liability for Injury and Damage Arising from Access to the Countryside: Time for Change?

1997 JR 162	The Basis of Liability in Nuisance
1997 JR 259	*Culpa* and the Law of Nuisance
(1998) 3 SLPQ 1	Nuisance in the Common Law of Scotland
1998 JR 281	Liability for *Opera Manufacta* (New Works) in Scots law
(1999) 4 SLPQ 303	Nuisance and Servitudes
(2000) 5 SLPQ 356	Strict Liability and the Rule in *Caledonian Railway Co v Greenock Corporation*
2000 SLT (News) 151	Financial Loss and Negligence Nuisance
2001 JR 223	Muddy Pavements and Murky Law: Intentional and Unintentional Nuisance and the Recovery of Pure Economic Loss
2002 SLG 150	Occupier's Liability and Natural Features giving rise to Danger
(2002) 6 Edin LR 117	*Effusia vel Deiecta* in Rome and Glasgow
(2003) 7 Edin LR 218	The Source of the *Plus Quam Tolerabile* Concept in Nuisance

Chapters 14, 15 and 17–19   Title Conditions

References

Agnew	*Variation and Discharge of Land Obligations* (1999)
Burns	*Conveyancing Practice* (4th edn, 1957), Chapters 11, 24
Craigie	*Scottish Law of Conveyancing: Heritable Rights* (1899), Volume I, Chapter 3
Cusine (ed)	*A Scots Conveyancing Miscellany: Essays in Honour of Professor J M Halliday* (1987), p 9: McDonald 'Third-party rights of enforcement of real burdens' and p 67: Gordon 'Variation and discharge of land obligations'
Cusine and Paisley	*Servitudes and Rights of Way* (1998)
Gloag	*Contract* (2nd edn, 1929), Chapters 13, 14, 34
Gordon	*Scottish Land Law* (2nd edn, 1999)
	Chapter 21, Introduction to restrictions on use of land
	Chapter 22, Feudal real burdens
	Chapter 23, Non-feudal real burdens
	Chapter 24, Servitudes and public rights of way
	Chapter 25, Variation and discharge by the Lands Tribunal
Green's Encyclopaedia	Volume 2, paras 876–987, Building restrictions
	Volume 3, paras 555–647, Charter, feudal
	Volume 8, paras 1361–1374, *Jus quaesitum tertio*
	Volume 9, paras 968–999, Irritancies

	Volume 13, paras 1215–1267, Servitudes
	Volume 14, paras 246–255, Singular successor
	paras 616–671, Superior and vassal
Gretton and Reid	*Conveyancing* (2nd edn, 1999)
	Chapter 13, Real burdens and servitudes
Johnston	*Prescription and Limitation* (1999)
	Chapter 3, Imprescriptible rights and obligations
	Chapter 7, Long negative prescription
	Chapter 17, Positive prescription for servitudes and public rights of way
Paisley	*Land Law* (2000)
	Chapter 8, Servitudes
	Chapter 9, Real Burdens and common interest
	Chapter 10, Public law rights affecting land
Rankine	*The Law of Landownership in Scotland* (4th edn, 1909), Chapters 5–11, 18, 19, 25–27
Reid	*The Abolition of Feudal Tenure in Scotland* (2003)
Stair Memorial Encyclopaedia	Volume 6, paras 401–641, Conveyancing in general
	Volume 12, paras 1213–1262, Interpretation of deeds
	Volume 18, paras 344–353, Real conditions
	paras 354–374 Common interest
	paras 375–438 Real burdens
	paras 439–493 Servitudes
	paras 494–513 Public rights of way
Talman (ed)	*Halliday's Conveyancing Law and Practice in Scotland* (2nd edn, 2 Volumes, 1996–97), Chapter 32: Feus, Chapter 34: Real burdens and Chapter 35: Servitudes

Styles

Encyclopaedia of Scottish Legal Styles   Volume 5, Feus
                                         Volume 8, Servitudes

Statutes

Abolition of Feudal Tenure etc (Scotland) Act 2000, Part 4
Title Conditions (Scotland) Act 2003

Government and other papers

1991 – *Abolition of the Feudal System* (Scot Law Com Discussion Paper No 93)
1998 – *Real Burdens* (Scot Law Com Discussion Paper No 106)
1999 – *Abolition of the Feudal System* (Scot Law Com Discussion Paper No 168)
2000 – *Report on Real Burdens* (Scot Law Com Discussion Paper No 181)
2001 – *Title Conditions (Scotland) Bill Consultation Paper* (Scottish Executive)

Chapters 15 and 17–19   Real Burdens (Including Feudal Real Burdens) and Variation and Discharge of Title Conditions

References

Cusine (ed)	*The Conveyancing Opinions of J M Halliday* (1992), pp 503–543 and 609–613

Opinion 118   Acquiescence
Opinion 119   Majority rule in deed of conditions
Opinion 120   Commercial restriction
Opinion 121   Which deed to create burdens?
Opinion 122   Can an uninfeft proprietor grant a deed of conditions?
Opinion 123   Implied third-party rights of enforcement
Opinion 124   Effect of consolidation on enforcement rights
Opinion 125   Common repairs
Opinion 126   Burdens in a tenement
Opinion 142   Negative servitude and real burden

Reid and Gretton	*Conveyancing 1999* (2000), pp 9–11, 57–61 and 74–79
Reid and Gretton	*Conveyancing 2000* (2001), pp 11, 12, 70–81 and 123–139 (the latter on the Abolition of Feudal Tenure etc (Scotland) Act 2000)
Reid and Gretton	*Conveyancing 2001* (2002), pp 9–11, 85–90 and 99–102
Reid and Gretton	*Conveyancing 2002* (2003), pp 7, 8 and 63–68
Waelde (ed)	*Professor McDonald's Conveyancing Opinions* (1998), pp 76–96, 117–122, 134–150 and 261–268

Opinion 19   Common charges and title to enforce
Opinion 20   Commercial burden and alternatives to express discharge
Opinion 21   Precision of burden (reference to statute) and irritancy
Opinion 22   Distinction between servitudes and burdens
Opinion 26   Extinction of feudal burdens by consolidation or prescription
Opinion 30   Pre-emption and prescription
Opinion 31   Implied third-party rights of enforcement and acquiescence
Opinion 32   Loss of interest to enforce and interpretation of burdens
Opinion 61   Right of pre-emption and the Conveyancing Amendment (Scotland) Act 1938

Opinion 62   Right of redemption: binding singular successors?

Articles etc

Chapter 16   Title Conditions: Servitudes

References

Reid and Gretton   *Conveyancing 2002* (2003), pp 4–7 and 72–78
Waelde (ed)   *Professor McDonald's Conveyancing Opinions* (1998), pp 22 and 23

         Opinion 22   Creation of valid servitude of drainage
         Opinion 23   Implied creation of servitude

See also general references for Chapters 14, 15 and 17–19

Articles

2 Conveyancing Review 97	Servitudes
1990 JLSS 57	Servitudes of Access, Rights of way and the Roads (Scotland) Act 1984
1993 JLSS 490 Caveat	A Problem of Access
(1993) 61 SLG 127	Servitudes of Access
(1993) 4 Greens PLB 6	New Buildings and Old Servitudes
1994 SLT (News) 349	Liability of an Occupier to a Person Using a Right of Way
1995 SLT (News) 228	The Extinction of Servitudes through Confusion
1995 JR 82	Discharge of Servitudes by Prescription
1997 JLSS 266	Keeper's Practice on Servitudes Constituted by Implication or Prescription
(1997) 2 SLPQ 90	Servitudes and Uninfeft Proprietors
(1998) 2 Edin LR 315	Common Interest Revisited
(1999) 4 SLPQ 64	Positive Servitudes and the Land Register
(1999) 4 SLPQ 176	Transmission of Servitudes and *Mortis Causa* Deeds
(1999) 4 SLPQ 303	Nuisance and Servitudes
(1999) 42 Greens PLB 5	Securing Access: On the Verges of the Law
(2000) 5 SLPQ 196 and 333	Perpetual Roads: A Never-Ending Story?
(2000) 5 SLPQ 435	Servitude Implied from Circumstances
2001 SLT (News) 25	The Land-Locked Proprietor's Right of Access
2001 JLSS March/48	Septic Tanks: Taking the Lid Off
(2001) 6 SLPQ 239	Access and Servitude
(2001) 6 SLPQ 261	The Modernisation of Real Burdens and Servitudes: Some Observations on the Title Conditions (Scotland) Bill Consultation Paper
(2001) 5 Edin LR 235	The Reform of Real Burdens
(2002) 6 Edin LR 101	Bower of Bliss?
(2003) 8 SLPQ 217	The Title Conditions (Scotland) Act 2003 and Servitudes
2003 JLSS May/32	A Matter of Opinion

Chapter 20   Public Law Restrictions on Land Use

References

Collar   *Planning* (2nd edn, 1999)
Collar   *Planning and Human Rights* (2001)

Faulds and Hyslop — *Scottish Roads Law* (2000)

Gill, Hon Lord (ed) — *Scottish Planning Encyclopaedia* (looseleaf)

Goodman (ed) — *Encyclopaedia of Health and Safety at Work: Law and Practice* (looseleaf)

Gordon — *Scottish Land Law* (2nd edn, 1999), Chapters 27–29

Himsworth — *Housing Law in Scotland* (2nd edn, 1994)

Himsworth — *Local Government Law in Scotland* (1995)

Laurence — *Waste Regulation Law* (1999)

McAllister and McMaster — *Scottish Planning Law* (2nd edn, 1999)

Reid — *Environmental Law in Scotland* (2nd edn, 1997)

Reid — *Nature Conservation Law* (2nd edn, 2002)

Rowan Robinson — *Compulsory Purchase and Compensation* (2nd edn, 2003)

Rowan Robinson and McKenzie-Skene (eds) — *Countryside Law in Scotland* (2000)

Rowan Robinson, Young, Purdue and Farquharson-Black — *Scottish Planning Law and Procedure* (2001)

Smith, Collar and Poustie — *Pollution Control: The Law in Scotland* (1997)

Stair Memorial Encyclopaedia — Volume 3, Building Controls

Volume 9, Environment

Volume 10, Fire Services

Tromans and Turrall-Clarke — *Contaminated Land* (2000)

Statutes

National Parks and Access to the Countryside Act 1949

Building (Scotland) Acts 1959 and 1970

Countryside (Scotland) Act 1967

Sewerage (Scotland) Act 1968

Fire Precautions Act 1971

Local Government (Scotland) Act 1973

Control of Pollution Act 1974

Health and Safety at Work etc Act 1974

Ancient Monuments and Archaeological Areas Act 1979

Water (Scotland) Act 1980

Wildlife and Countryside Act 1981

Roads (Scotland) Act 1984

Housing (Scotland) Act 1987

Housing (Scotland) Act 1988

Environmental Protection Act 1990

Natural Heritage (Scotland) Act 1991

Clean Air Act 1993

Local Government etc (Scotland) Act 1994

Disabilities Discrimination Act 1995

Environment Act 1995

Planning (Consequential Provisions) (Scotland) Act 1997

Planning (Listed Buildings and Conservation Areas) (Scotland) Act 1997

Planning (Hazardous Substances) (Scotland) Act 1997

Town and Country Planning (Scotland) Act 1997
Housing (Scotland) Act 2001
Land Reform (Scotland) Act 2003

Regulations

Fire Precautions (Hotels and Boarding Houses) (Scotland) Order 1972, SI 1972/382
Town and Country Planning (Tree Preservation Order and Trees in Conservation Areas) (Scotland) Regulations 1975, SI 1975/1204
Town and Country Planning (Control of Advertisements) (Scotland) Regulations 1984, SI 1984/467
Security for Private Road Works (Scotland) Order 1985, SI 1985/2080
Fire Precautions (Factories, Offices, Shops and Railway Premises) Order 1989, SI 1989/76
Building Standards (Scotland) Regulations 1990, SI 1990/2179
Town and Country Planning (Appeals) (Written Submissions Procedure) (Scotland) Regulations 1990, SI 1990/507
Environmental Protection (Prescribed Processes and Substances) Regulations 1991, SI 1991/472
Town and Country Planning (General Development Procedure) (Scotland) Order 1992, SI 1992/224
Town and Country Planning (General Permitted Development) (Scotland) Order 1992, SI 1992/223
Town and Country Planning (Hazardous Substances) (Scotland) Regulations 1993, SI 1993/323
Conservation (Natural Habitats etc) Regulations 1994, SI 1994/2716
Waste Management Licensing Regulations 1994, SI 1994/1056
Designation of Structure Plan Areas (Scotland) Order 1995, SI 1995/3002
Fire Precautions (Workplace) Regulations 1997, SI 1997/1840
Town and Country Planning Appeals (Determination by Appointed Persons) (Inquiries Procedure) (Scotland) Rules 1997, SI 1997/750
Town and Country Planning (Inquiries Procedure) (Scotland) Rules 1997, SI 1997/796
Town and Country Planning (Use Classes) (Scotland) Order 1997, SI 1997/3061
Environmental Impact Assessment (Scotland) Regulations 1999, SSI 1999/1
Management of Health and Safety at Work Regulations 1999, SI 1999/3242
Contaminated Land (Scotland) Regulations 2000, SSI 2000/178
Pollution Prevention and Control (Scotland) Regulations 2000, SSI 2000/323 (as amended)

Articles

(1995) 52 SPEL 102	The Environment Act 1995
(1996) 58 SPEL 110	Contaminated Land
(1999) 73 SPEL 60	Protection of Archaeological Sites: An Outline of the Law
(1999) 76 SPEL 127	Building Control
(2000) 77 SPEL 11	The Environmental Protection Act 1990 Part IIA
[2000] JPL 876	Environmental Impact Assessment
[2000] JPL 894	Statutory Nuisance: The Validity of Abatement Notices

[2000] JPL 1011	Statutory Nuisance Abatement Notices – A Response
[2000] JPL 1003	Waste Management Licensing: Benefit of Burden?
2000 SLT (News) 195	Human Rights and Planning
2000 JLSS Aug/45	Defining Contaminated Land
[2001] JPL 265	Managing Natura 2000: Priorities for Implementing European Wildlife Law
[2001] JPL 24	*Grampian and British Railways Board* Revisited – the use of negative pre-conditions in circumstances of uncertainty
(2002) 90 SPEL 36	Access to the Countryside: Reforming the Law
(2001) 91 SPEL 66	Validity of planning permission
(2002) 92 SPEL 83	Statutory nuisance
(2002) 94 SPEL 136	Waste: The Dirty Definition
[2002] JPL 1316	Environmental Impact Assessment: The Continuing Jurisprudence
(2002) 7 SLPQ 249	Tiptoeing around *Tesco*: the law on planning agreements
2003 JLSS Apr/30	Commonsense approach to contaminated land
2003 JLSS Apr/32	Contaminated Land Liabilities
(2003) 95 SPEL 3	Waste and Emissions Trading Bill
(2003) 66 Greens PLB 5	The Land Reform (Scotland) Act 2003

PART 4   SUBORDINATE RIGHTS: SECURITIES AND LEASES

Chapter 21   Securities: General

References

Cusine (ed)	*A Scots Conveyancing Miscellany: Essays in Honour of Professor J M Halliday* (1987), p 126: Gretton 'The Concept of Security'
Cusine and Rennie	*Standard Securities* (2nd edn, 2002), Chapter 1
Gloag and Irvine	*Rights in Security* (1897)
Gordon	*Scottish Land Law* (2nd edn, 1999), Chapter 20
Gretton and Reid	*Conveyancing* (2nd edn, 1999), Chapter 19
Higgins	*Scottish Repossessions* (2002), paras 5.3–5.12
Reid and Gretton	*Conveyancing 1999* (2000), pp 54–56
Reid and Gretton	*Conveyancing 2000* (2001), pp 86–91
Reid and Gretton	*Conveyancing 2001* (2002), pp 92–96
Reid and Gretton	*Conveyancing 2002* (2003), pp 59–63
Rennie	*Solicitors' Negligence* (1997), Chapters 1 and 5
Stair Memorial Encyclopaedia	Volume 8, paras 101–399

Statutes

Conveyancing and Feudal Reform (Scotland) Act 1970, Parts II and III
Mortgage Rights (Scotland) Act 2001

Articles

1993 JLSS 185	Mandates, Assignations and Arrestments
1994 JLSS 135	Negligence, Instructions and the Lender's Need to Know
1995 JLSS 58	Negligence, Securities and the Expanding Duty of Care
1997 JLSS 405	Negligence and the Duty to Disclose: A Turning of the Tide
1997 SLT (News) 195	Sexually Transmitted Debt
(1998) 2 Edin LR 90	The House of Lords applies *O'Brien* North of the Border
1998 SLT (News) 39	Good Faith in Contract, Spousal Guarantees and *Smith v Bank of Scotland*
1999 SLT (News) 53	Good News for Bankers, Bad News for Lawyers
1999 TSAR 419	Sexually Transmitted Debt
1999 JR 67	The dust settling: *Smith v Bank of Scotland*
1999 JR 382	*Watt v Bank of Scotland*: security advice for banks and solicitors: *Smith* reconsidered
(2001) 6 SLPQ 95	Solicitors' Negligence and the Judgment of Solomon
(2001) 6 SLPQ 304	Solicitors' Negligence: Third Parties Join the Queue
2002 SLT (News) 55	*Royal Bank of Scotland v Etridge (No 2)*: the end of a sorry tale
2002 SLT (News) 173	A break from the old routine: the doctrine in *Smith*
(2002) 7 SLPQ 87	Solicitors' Negligence: Rearguard Action?
(2003) 7 Edin LR 107	Cautionary Tales: The continued development of *Smith v Bank of Scotland*
2003 SLT (News) 215	Retroactivity and the Human Rights Act 1998

Chapter 22   Standard Securities

References

Cusine and Rennie	*Standard Securities* (2nd edn, 2002)
Gordon	*Scottish Land Law* (2nd edn, 1999), paras 20-119–20-204
Gretton and Reid	*Conveyancing* (2nd edn, 1999), Chapters 20 and 21
Higgins	*Scottish Repossessions* (2002)
Paisley	*Land Law* (2000), paras 11.3–11.24
Paisley and Cusine	*Unreported Property Cases from the Sheriff Courts* (2000), Chapter 11
Registers of Scotland	*Registration of Title Practice Book* (2nd edn, 2000), paras 6.65–6.76

Reid and Gretton	*Conveyancing 1999* (2000), pp 21–22 and 52–57
Reid and Gretton	*Conveyancing 2000* (2001), pp 20–22 and 81–92
Reid and Gretton	*Conveyancing 2001* (2002), pp 24–27, 75–85 and 90–99
Reid and Gretton	*Conveyancing 2002* (2003), pp 21–24, and 57–63
Talman (ed)	*Halliday's Conveyancing Law and Practice in Scotland* (2nd edn, 2 Volumes, 1996–97), Volume 2, Chapters 51–55 and 57
Waelde (ed)	*Professor McDonald's Conveyancing Opinions* (1998), pp 166–171

Statutes

Heritable Securities (Scotland) Act 1894
Conveyancing and Feudal Reform (Scotland) Act 1970, Part II and III
Consumer Credit Act 1974
Mortgage Rights (Scotland) Act 2001

Articles

1980 JLSS 275	Ranking of Heritable Creditors
1981 JLSS 26 and 280	Ranking of Heritable Creditors
(1983) 50 SLG 81	Securities over leases
1983 JR 177	Prescription and the foreclosure of adjudications
1983 SLT (News) 169 and 189	Real Conditions in Standard Securities
1985 JLSS 130 and 181	The Consumer Credit Act 1974
1985 JLSS 159	Bridging Loans and the Consumer Credit Regulations
1985 JLSS 222	The Consumer Credit Act 1974 – Loan Agreements and Standard Securities
1985 SLT (News) 125	Inhibitions and Standard Securities
1986 PQLE	The Consumer Credit Act and its implications for conveyancers
1988 PQLE	Lending and Financial Packages
1989 PQLE	Exercise of Power of Sale by Creditors Under Standard Securities
1989 SLT (News) 201	Creditor's Remedies under a Standard Security
1990 PQLE	Security Transactions and Related Matters
1990 JLSS 97 and 127	Descriptions in Standard Securities
1991 SLT (News) 195	Discharge of a Debtor and Securities
1991 JR 169	Power of Sale Under a Standard Security
1993 JLSS 158	A Note on Ranking Agreements
1993 JLSS 199 Caveat	Discharging Loans and Ranking Agreements
1994 JR 18	Expenses under a Standard Security
1994 JLSS 52	Inhibitions, Standard Securities and Further Advances
1994 SLT (News) 93	Controlling Creditors' Rights under Standard Securities

1994 JLSS 135	The Lender and the Solicitor's Duty of Care
(1994) 7 Greens PLB 5	Advertising Requirements in a Sale by a Heritable Creditor
1994 JLSS 257	The Duties of a Standard Security Holder
1994 SLT (News) 207	Assignation of All Sums Standard Securities
1994 JLSS 263	Note on *AIB Finance*
1995 JLSS 58	Negligence, Securities and the Expanding Duty of Care
1995 JLSS 245	Lending Institutions, Loan Instructions and Reports on Title
1995 JLSS 363 Caveat	Undisclosed Securities
1995 JLSS 357	Descriptions in Standard Securities
1995 JLSS 400	Enforcing Standard Securities
1995 JLSS 481	Descriptions in Standard Securities – (Note by the Keeper)
1995 Scolag 41	Mortgages Explained
1996 JLSS 209	Descriptions in Standard Securities – Where Now?
1996 JLSS 232 Caveat	Inadequate instructions from lenders
1996 JLSS 404	Certificates of Title
(2000) 5 SLPQ 72	Sale of Security Subjects: Applying the Free Proceeds
2001 SLT (News) 135	The Integrity of Property Law and the Property Registers
2001 SLT (News) 273	2001 – A Base (Rate) Odyssey
(2001) 53Greens PLB 1	Mortgage Rights (Scotland) Act 2001
(2001) 54 Greens PLB 5	Six Factors for Smoother Security Deals
(2002) 43 Greens CivPB 1	Circumventing the Mortgage Rights (Scotland) Act 2001
(2002) 45 Greens CivPB 3	Practical Aspects of Litigation arising out of the Mortgage Rights (Scotland) Act 2001
2002 JLSS May/22	Serving Notices under the Mortgage Rights Act
(2002) 70 SLG 5	Variable Mortgage Interest Rates
(2002) 70 SLG 32	Mortgage and Redemption Charges
(2002) 70 SLG 173	CML Handbook second edition
(2002) 70 SLG 180	The Regulation of Mortgage Advice

Website

Council of Mortgage Lenders	www.cml.org.uk

Chapter 23 Floating Charges

References

Cusine (ed)	*A Scots Conveyancing Miscellany: Essays in Honour of Professor J M Halliday* (1987), p 33: R B Jack 'The Coming of the Floating Charge'

Cusine (ed)	*The Conveyancing Opinions of J M Halliday* (1992), pp 437–439, pp 41–55
Gordon	*Scottish Land Law* (2nd edn, 1999), paras 20.205–20.226
Greene and Fletcher	*The Law and Practice of Receivership in Scotland* (2nd edn, 1992)
Gretton and Reid	*Conveyancing* (2nd edn, 1999), paras 28.06, 28.08–28.09, 29.06
Paisley	*Land Law* (2000), paras 11.25–11.31
Reid and Gretton	*Conveyancing 2000* (2001), pp 21–22
Reid and Gretton	*Conveyancing 2001* (2002), p 26
Reid and Gretton	*Conveyancing 2002* (2003), pp 22–24 and 89–92
St Clair and Drummond Young	*The Law of Corporate Insolvency in Scotland* (2nd edn, 1992)
Stair Memorial Encyclopaedia	Volume 4, paras 647–715
Talman (ed)	*Halliday's Conveyancing Law and Practice in Scotland* (2nd edn, 2 Volumes, 1996–97), Volume 2, Chapter 56
Waelde (ed)	*Professor McDonald's Conveyancing Opinions* (1998), pp 172–180

Statutes

Companies Act 1985, ss 410–424, 462 and 466
Insolvency Act 1986, ss 50–72
Companies Act 1989, ss 92–107 and 140
Enterprise Act 2002, ss 248–255

Scottish Law Commission Publications

2001 – *Sharp v Thomson* (Scot Law Com Discussion Paper No 114)
2002 – *Registration of Rights in Security by Companies* (Scot Law Com Discussion Paper No 121)

Articles

1981 JLSS 57 and 102	Diligence, Trusts and Floating Charges
1982 SLT (News) 177	The Registration of Charges
1983 SLT (News) 253	Floating Charges and Fraudulent Preferences
1984 SLT (News) 25	The Receiver and effectually executed diligence
1984 SLT (News) 105, 172, 177	The Nature of Receivership; Floating Charges; Receivers and Arresters
1985 JLSS 242	Future Assets and Double Attachments
1986 SLT (News) 325	Should Floating Charges and Receivership be Abolished?
1987 SLT (News) 113	Trusts and Floating Charges
1988 SLT (News) 194	Trusts and Liquidators – Further Thoughts
1988 JLSS 53	Using Trusts as Commercial Securities
1988 SLT (News) 81	Restitution and Property Law

1988 JLSS 357	Set–off and Receivership
1989 JLSS 50	Searches: (1) Companies
1989 SLT (News) 143	Trusts and Liquidators
1992 Update (April)	Heritable and Moveable Securities: Floating Charges, some problems of constitution and enforcement
1993 JLSS 199 Caveat	Discharging Loans and Ranking Agreements
(1993) 2 Greens PLB 5	Guidance on completion of forms for Register of Charges
1997 JLSS 181	Commercial law update: rights in security and insolvencies
(1998) 3 SLPQ 169	The Tragedy of the Floating Charge in Scots Law
(1999) 4 SLPQ 235	The Two Types of Floating Charge: The English and the Scots
2000 JR 325	Squaring the circle: revisiting the receiver and "effectually executed diligence"
(2001) 6 SLPQ 73	Floating charges and subsequent securities
2002) 6 Edin LR 146	Registration of Company Charges
2002 SLT (News) 289	The Registration of Rights in Security by Companies
2002 JLSS Dec/26	Reforming Registration of Company Charges
(2002) 7 SLPQ 18	Negative Pledges and Ranking Reconsidered

For articles on *Sharp v Thomson*, see the reading lists for Chapters 4 and 34.

Chapter 24   Leases: General

References

Burns	*Conveyancing Practice* (4th edn, 1957), Chapter 35
Burns	*Handbook of Conveyancing* (5th edn, 1938), Chapter 21
Cusine (ed)	*The Conveyancing Opinions of J M Halliday* (1992), pp 348–387
Gloag and Henderson	*Introduction to the Law of Scotland* (11th edn, 2001), Chapter 33
Gordon	*Scottish Land Law* (2nd edn, 1999), Chapter 19
Green's Encyclopaedia	Volume 9, paras 140–248, Leases
Himsworth	*Housing Law in Scotland* (4th edn, 1994)
McAllister	*Scottish Law of Leases* (3rd edn, 2002)
Megarry	*The Rent Acts* (11th edn, 1988)
Menzies	*Lectures on Conveyancing* (Sturrock's edn, 1900), Chapter 29
Paisley	*Land Law* (2000), Chapter 7
Paton and Cameron	*The Law of Landlord and Tenant in Scotland* (1967)
Rankine	*The Law of Leases in Scotland* (3rd edn, 1916)
Reid and Gretton	*Conveyancing 2000* (2001), pp 139–141
Robson	*Residential Tenancies* (2nd edn, 1998)

Stair Memorial Encyclopaedia	Volume 13, paras 101–548
Talman (ed)	*Halliday's Conveyancing Law and Practice in Scotland* (2nd edn, 2 Volumes, 1996–97), Volume 2, Chapters 40–44
Waelde (ed)	*Professor McDonald's Conveyancing Opinions* (1998), pp 189–204
Watchman	*The Housing (Scotland) Act 1987* (1991)

Statutes

Leases Act 1449
Registration of Leases (Scotland) Act 1857
Hypothec Abolition (Scotland) Act 1880
Removal Terms (Scotland) Act 1886
Heritable Securities (Scotland) Act 1894
Sheriff Courts (Scotland) Act 1907
Conveyancing (Scotland) Act 1924
Tenancy of Shops (Scotland) Act 1949 and 1964
Long Leases (Scotland) Act 1954
Succession (Scotland) Act 1964
Conveyancing and Feudal Reform (Scotland) Act 1970
Land Tenure Reform (Scotland) Act 1974
Crofting Reform (Scotland) Act 1976
Land Registration (Scotland) Act 1979
Tenants' Rights etc (Scotland) Act 1980
Law Reform (Miscellaneous Provisions) (Scotland) Act 1985
Term and Quarter Days (Scotland) Act 1990
Requirements of Writing (Scotland) Act 1995
Abolition of Feudal Tenure etc (Scotland) Act 2000
Leasehold Casualties (Scotland) Act 2001

Scottish Law Commission Publications

1997 – *Leasehold Casualties* (Scot Law Com Discussion Paper No 102)
1998 – *Leasehold Casualties* (Scot Law Com Report No 165)
2001 – *Conversion of Long Leases* (Scot Law Com Discussion Paper No 112)
2001 – *Irritancies in Leases of Land* (Scot Law Com Discussion Paper No 117)
2003 – *Irritancies in Leases of Land* (Scot Law Com Report No 191)

Articles

2 *Conveyancing Review* 47	The Tenancy of Shops Act 1949
1962 *Conveyancing Review* 39	*Rei interitus* in Leases
1972 JLSS 121	Crofting Law
1980 JLSS 319	The Tenants' Rights etc (Scotland) Bill
1980 SLT (News) 125	The Tenants' Rights etc (Scotland) Bill
1981 JLSS W 215, W 223, W 231	Calculating Fair Rents
1981 SLT (News) 101	The Tenants' Rights etc (Scotland) Act 1980 – Part IV

1981 JLSS 376 and 1982 JLSS 21	How irritating are Landlords actually?
1981 JLSS 383	The Tenants' Rights etc (Scotland) Act 1980 – Part II
1982 JLSS 161	The Tenants' Rights etc (Scotland) Act 1980 – Part I
(1983) 86 Scolag 169	Methods of Calculating Fair Rents
1983 2 CSW 534	Scots Law – Irritancies in Leases
1989 SLT (News) 431	Termination date in Notice to Quit
(1990) 160 Scolag	Security of Tenure
1990 SLT (News) 257	Term and Quarter Days defined
(1991) 173 Scolag 30, 174 Scolag 42	Resident Landlords and their Tenants
1992 Update (April)	Securities and Leases: Heritable and Moveable Securities
(1994) 9 Greens PLB 6	A Landlord's Common Law Obligations
(1995) 15 Greens PLB 8	Extraordinary Repairs
(1995) 16 Greens PLB 3	Tenancy of Shops (Scotland) Act 1949
(1995) 17 Greens PLB 5	To consent or not to consent: that is the question
(1995) 18 Greens PLB 3	Landlord's Hypothec
(1996) 20 Greens PLB 20	Schedules of Condition of Repair
(1996) 21 Greens PLB 4	Tenant's Repairing Obligation
(1996) 22 Greens PLB 7	Notices to Quit
(1996) 23 Greens PLB 11	Tenant Default: What are the Landlord's Options?
(1996) 24 Greens PLB 6	Tacit Relocation
(1996) 1 SLPQ 187	Requirements of Writing: Problems of Practice
(1998) 31 Greens PLB 6	Interposed Leases
(1998) 33 Greens PLB 1	Terrorism Insurance
1999 SLT (News) 1	To irritate or rescind: Two paths for the landlord?
(1999) 39 Greens PLB 1	Leasehold Irritancy: Is reform necessary?
2000 SLT (News) 143	Keeping the Goalposts in Sight
(2000) 44 Greens PLB 3	Length of Leases
(2000) 49 Greens PLB 4	Enforcing Commercial Lease Terms Against Successor Landlords (part 1)
(2000) 50 Greens PLB 4	Enforcing Commercial Lease Terms Against Successor Landlords (part 2)
2001 JR 201	Tacit relocation
2001 SLT (News) 235	Leasehold casualties
2002 SLT (News) 177	Goodbye to the landlord's hypothec?
(2002) 7 SLPQ 117	When is the refusal of consent by landlord or tenant unreasonable?
(2002) 7 SLPQ 141	Long Residential Leases – Some Unfinished Business
(2002) 57 Greens PLB 1	Reform of Irritancy in Leases of Land

Chapter 25   Commercial Leases

References

Aldridge	*Letting of Business Premises* (4th edn)
Bernstein and Reynolds	*Essentials of Rent Review* (1995)

Clarke and Adams	*Rent Reviews and Variable Rents* (1981)
Cockburn	*Commercial Leases* (2002)
Fleming	*Dilapidations* (2nd edn, 2002)
Lewison	*Drafting Business Leases* (1980)
McAllister	*The Scottish Law of Leases* (3rd edn, 2002)
Ross and McKichan	*Drafting and Negotiating Commercial Leases in Scotland* (2nd edn, 1993)
Stair Memorial Encyclopaedia	Volume 13, paras 555–589
Talman (ed)	*Halliday's Conveyancing Law and Practice in Scotland* (2nd edn, 2 Volumes, 1996–97), Volume 2: Leases, esp Chapter 29

Scottish Law Commission Publications

1981 – *Irritancies in Leases* (Scot Law Com Memorandum No 52)
1983 – *Irritancies in Leases* (Scot Law Com Report No 75)
2003 – *Irritancy in Leases of Land* (Scot Law Com Report No 191)

Articles

1976 JLSS 4	Irritancies in Leases
1976 JLSS 368	Irritability of the Rash Tenant
1977 JLSS 20	Rent Review: A Search for the True Purpose
1977 JLSS 309	Disaster in Leases: *Rei Interitus*
1979 JLSS (Workshop) 38	Policy Decisions: Analysis of Insurance Provisions in Leases
1979 JLSS (Workshop) (xxi)	Ground Leases: A consideration of pitfalls
1979 JLSS (Workshop) (xlv)	Ground Leases: Further consideration
1979 JLSS (Workshop) (v)	Assigning and subletting
1979 JLSS (Workshop) (lv)	Findings by Arbiters
1979 NLJ 839	The Lessons of *Ravenseft*
1980 JLSS (Workshop) 117	Styles Committee Lease
1980 JLSS (Workshop) 171	Comment on Style Lease
1981 JLSS 295	Less Irritating: Scottish Law Commission
1982 NLJ 993	Drafting Rent Review Clauses: A Cautionary Tale
1982 NLJ 677	Major Structural Repairs
1982 NLJ 786	Tenant's Right to Remove Fixtures
1983 JLSS (Workshop) April	Rent Review Clauses in Commercial Leases
1983 JLSS 519	The Scottish Commercial Lease: The Way Ahead
1985 JLSS 99	The Scottish Commercial Lease Grows Up
1985 JLSS 432	Enter the Fair and Reasonable Landlord
1988 PQLE	Commercial Conveyancing and Licensing Course
1989 PQLE	Commercial Leasing Course
1989 PQLE	Commercial Conveyancing Course
1989 PQLE	Landlord and Tenant Legislation Course
1990 PQLE	Commercial Leasing Course
1990 PQLE	Commercial Conveyancing Course

(2002) 59 Greens PLB 3	Commercial Leases: When is the refusal of Consent by a Landlord or Tenant unreasonable?
(2003) 62 Greens PLB 1	Construction Law
(2003) 63 Greens PLB 1	Collateral Warranty Agreements
(2002) 7 SLPQ 117	When is the refusal of consent by a Landlord or Tenant unreasonable? Further Guidance from the Courts
2002 SLT (News)177	Goodbye to the Landlord's Hypothec?
(2002) JLSS Jul/7	20 Things You Ought to Know about Leasing Commercial Property

Chapter 26   Agricultural Leases

References

Agnew of Lochnaw	*Agricultural Law in Scotland* (1996)
Barraclough	*A Practical Guide to Rent Review of Agricultural Holdings in Scotland* (2002)
Duncan	*The Agricultural Holdings (Scotland) Act 1991*
Gill	*The Law of Agricultural Holdings in Scotland* (3rd edn, 1997)
Law Society of Scotland	*Aspects of Agricultural Law*
Rennie, D G and Agnew of Lochnaw, Sir Crispin (eds)	*The Agricultural Holdings (Scotland) Acts* (7th edn, 1996)

Statutes

Hill Farming Act 1946
Agriculture (Scotland) Act 1948
Agricultural Holdings (Scotland) Act 1949
Agriculture Act 1958
Succession (Scotland) Act 1964
Agriculture (Miscellaneous Provisions) Act 1968
Agriculture (Miscellaneous Provisions) Act 1976
Agricultural Holdings (Amendment) (Scotland) Act 1983
Agricultural Holdings (Scotland) Act 1991
Scottish Land Court Act 1993
Agricultural Holdings (Scotland) Act 2003

Articles

1980 JLSS (Workshop) 135	Style Agricultural Lease
1988 SLT (News) 65	The Crofter and his Right to Buy
1989 SLT (News) 256	Special Destinations and Agricultural Leases
1990 JLSS 463	Land Tenure 40 years on
1990 JLSS 434	The value of an agricultural tenancy

1991 JLSS 465	The value of an agricultural tenancy – update
1992 SLT (News) 1	The Agricultural Holdings (Scotland) Act 1991
(1993) 2 Greens PLB 4	Procedure in the Scottish Land Court
(1998) 31 Greens PLB 7	Agricultural Lease: Notice to Quit
(1999) 67 SLG 61	What's happening in Agricultural Law?

Chapter 27   Residential Leases

References

Dailly	*Housing Law in Practice* (2003)
Himsworth	*Housing Law in Scotland* (4th edn, 1994)
McAllister	*Scottish Law of Leases* (3rd edn, 2002), Chapters 15 and 16
McKerrell	*The Rent Acts* (1985)
Mitchell	*Eviction and Rent Arrears* (1995)
Robson	*The Housing (Scotland) Act 1988* (1989)
Robson and Halliday	*Residential Tenancies* (2nd edn, 1998)

Statutes

Rent (Scotland) Act 1984
Housing (Scotland) Act 1987
Housing (Scotland) Act 1988
Leasehold Reform, Housing and Urban Development Act 1994
Housing (Scotland) Act 2001

Articles

1989 SLT (News) 245	The Housing (Scotland) Act 1988 and Private Sector Rented Accommodation
1990 SLT (News) 93	Assured and Short Assured Tenancies
1990 JLSS 425	The Rights of Secure Tenants
1992 SLT (News) 21	Assured Tenancies: Notices to Quit and Form AT6
(1992) Pilot Greens PLB 5	Residential Leases – Notices to Quit
(1993) 3 Greens PLB 8	Assured Tenancy Statutory Forms
(1995) 14 Greens PLB 2	Holiday Lettings
1994 JLSS 333	More Tenants' Rights
1995 JLSS 435	Ejection *brevi manu* and Hostel Dwellings
1999 SLT (News) 209	Antisocial Behaviour Orders and Neighbourhood Nuisance
(2001) 4 JHL 79	A Brief Commentary on the Housing (Scotland) Act 2001
2002 SLPQ 141	Long Residential Leases: Some Unfinished Business
(2002) 301 Scolag 201	Same Sex Couples in Scots Law

PART 5   TRANSMISSION

Chapter 28   Contracts of Sale and Purchase

References

Burns	*Conveyancing Practice* (4th edn, 1957), Chapters 9, 23
Burns	*Handbook of Conveyancing* (5th edn, 1938), Chapter 17
Cusine (ed)	*A Scots Conveyancing Miscellany: Essays in Honour of Professor J M Halliday* (1987), p 91: Cusine and Love 'Delays in Settlement of Conveyancing Transactions'
Cusine (ed)	*The Conveyancing Opinions of J M Halliday* (1992), pp 70–176
Cusine and Rennie	*Missives* (2nd edn, 1998)
Forte (ed)	*Good Faith in Contract and Property Law* (1999)
Gamble (ed)	*Obligations in Context: Essays in Honour of Professor D M Walker* (1990): Thomson 'Suspensive and Resolutive Conditions in the Scots Law of Contract'
Gloag	*Contract* (2nd edn, 1929), Chapters 10, 20, 23
Green's Encyclopaedia	Volume 6, paras 952–971, Excambion
	Volume 13, paras 317–451, Sale of Heritable Property (part)
Gretton and Reid	*Conveyancing* (2nd edn, 1999), Chapters 3–6
Hogg	*Obligations* (2003)
McBryde	*The Law of Contract in Scotland* (2nd edn, 2001), Chapters 14 and 20
MacQueen and Thomson	*Contract Law in Scotland* (2000)
Paisley and Cusine	*Unreported Property Cases from the Sheriff Courts* (2000), pp 139–144
Reid and Gretton	*Conveyancing 1999* (2000), pp 39–43
Reid and Gretton	*Conveyancing 2001* (2002), pp 61–64
Reid and Gretton	*Conveyancing 2002* (2003), pp 55–57
Rennie and Cusine	*The Requirements of Writing* (1995)
Sinclair	*Handbook of Conveyancing Practice in Scotland* (4th edn, 2002), Chapters 2 to 5
Stair Memorial Encyclopaedia	Volume 18, Property: Transfer of Ownership
Stair Society	Volume 20
Talman (ed)	*Halliday's Conveyancing Law and Practice in Scotland* (2nd edn, 2 Volumes, 1996–97), Volume 2, Chapter 30
Waelde (ed)	*Professor McDonald's Conveyancing Opinions* (1998), pp 216–243
Walker	*Damages* (1995), Chapter 12

Walker   *Principles of Scottish Private Law* (4th edn, 1988), Volume III, Chapter 5

Walker   *The Law of Contracts and Related Obligations in Scotland* (3rd edn, 1995)

Woolman   *Contract* (3rd edn, 2001)

Statutes

Titles to Land Consolidation (Scotland) Act 1868, ss 5, 8, 141–143
Conveyancing (Scotland) Act 1874, ss 4, 6, 32
Conveyancing (Scotland) Act 1924, ss 8–11, 48
Requirements of Writing (Scotland) Act 1995
Contract (Scotland) Act 1997

Scottish Law Commission Publications

1990 – *Passing of Risk in Contracts for the Sale of Land* (Scot Law Com Report No 127)
1994 – *Contract Law, Extrinsic Evidence, Supersession and the actio quanti minoris* (Scot Law Com Discussion Paper No 97)
1996 – *Three bad rules in contract law* (Scot Law Com Report No 152)
1999 – *Remedies for breach of contract* (Scot Law Com Discussion Paper No 109)
1999 – *Remedies for breach of contract* (Scot Law Com Report No 174)

Articles

1956 SLT (News) 137	Solicitor for Buyer and Seller
2 *Conveyancing Review* 165	Mineral Reservations and the Unwilling Purchaser
2 *Conveyancing Review* 193	Personal Rights
2 *Conveyancing Review* 189	Delays in Settlement
3 *Conveyancing Review* 13	Situation of Seller under Missives
3 *Conveyancing Review* 129	Remedies for Breach of Missives
1966 JLSS 124	The *Actio Quanti Minoris*
1966 JLSS 264	*Rei Interventus* Reconsidered
1967 SLT (News) 231	The Reserved Right to Bid
1968 JLSS 46	Sale by Instalments
1969 JLSS 138	Division of Large Industrial Units
1969 JLSS 70	Delayed Settlement
1970 JLSS 10	Sale of Heritage
1971 JLSS 179	The Purchase and Sale of Houses
1972 JLSS 315	Missives
1972 JLSS 316	Sale and Purchase of Heritage
1973 JLSS 29	Sale of Heritage: Fair Dealing
1976 JLSS 317	Notices of Change of Ownership
1976 JLSS 282	Conditions in Missives
1978 JLSS 277	Sale of Heritage – Interest
1979 JLSS 485	Housebuilders' Missives

(1996) 19 Greens PLB 11	Waiver of suspensive conditions. A note on *Manheath Ltd*
1996 JLSS 8	A comment in two letters on the foregoing regulations
1996 JLSS 191 Caveat	The problem of a purchaser's future plans for development etc not disclosed to the solicitors at the time of purchase, resulting in a claim for negligence for failing to provide for access etc
(1996) 20 Greens PLB 2 and 21 Greens PLB 2	The Construction (Design and Management) Regulations 1994
(1996) 23 Greens PLB 2	*Winston v Patrick* Revisited: The Two-Year Enforceability Clause
(1996) 24 Greens PLB 11	Preparing deeds for conveyancing
1996 SLT (News) 365	The Perils of a Trusting Disposition
(1997) 26 Greens PLB 1	The Seller's Remedies
1997 SLT (News) 225	Three Bad Rules of Contract Rectified
1997 SLT (News) 309	Endureth Forever?
1998 SLT (News) 282	Eviction Evicted? Warrandice after the Contract (Scotland) Act 1997
(1998) 3 SLPQ 24	The Passing of Risk in Contracts for the Sale and Purchase of Heritable Property
(1999) 38 Greens PLB 5	Buying Property at Auction
(1999) 37 Greens PLB 2	Title Insurance and Conveyancing in Scotland
2000 SLT (News) 65	The Modern Missive
(2000) 5 SLPQ 250	Charred or Chosen? Clauses dealing with Risk in Contacts for Sale of Heritable Property
(2000) 5 SLPQ 346	Conclusion of Missives in the Modern Age
(2002) 70 SLG 172	The End of Letters of Comfort
(2003) 60 Greens PLB 1	The Case for Standardisation of Builders' Missives
(2003) 21 SLG 33	Single Surveys and Purchasers Information Packs
2003 JLSS Aug/26	In My Considered Opinion (Comments by Professor Rennie on various matters including missives)

Chapter 29   Statutory Titles

References

Burns	*Conveyancing Practice* (4th edn, 1957), Chapter 15
Burns	*Handbook of Conveyancing* (5th edn, 1938), Chapter 19
Coull	*Bankruptcy* (2nd edn, 1995)
Cusine (ed)	*The Conveyancing Opinions of J M Halliday* (1992), pp 220–224, 405–415 and 423–433
Cusine and Paisley	*Servitudes and Rights of Way* (1998), para 17.42
Graham Stewart	*Diligence* (1898)

Green's Encyclopaedia	Volume 1, paras 298–372, Adjudication
	Volume 4, paras 564–567, Completion of Title
	Volume 4, paras 607–626 and 684–686, Compulsory Purchase
	1949 Supplement – Part 1: Acquisition of Land (Authorisation Procedure) (Scotland) Act 1947
	Volume 12, paras 736–752, Reduction
Gretton	*The Law of Inhibition and Adjudication* (2nd edn, 1996)
Gretton and Reid	*Conveyancing* (2nd edn, 1999), Chapter 17
Law Society of Scotland	*Compulsory Purchase in Scotland* (1983)
McBryde	*Bankruptcy* (2nd edn, 1995)
Maher and Cusine	*The Law and Practice of Diligence* (1990)
Murning	*Review of Compulsory Purchase and Land Compensation* (Scottish Executive Research Unit) (2001)
Rowan Robinson	*Compulsory Purchase and Compensation* (2nd edn, 2003)
Scott-Robinson	*The Law of Interdict* (2nd edn, 1994)
Scottish Office Development Department	*Compulsory Acquisition of Land: Land Compensation Rates of Interest* (1997)
Stair Memorial Encyclopaedia	Volume 5, para 24, Compulsory acquisition
	Volume 2, para 11, Bankruptcy
	Volume 8, para 34, Diligence etc
Talman (ed)	*Halliday's Conveyancing Law and Practice in Scotland* (2nd edn, 2 Volumes, 1996–97), Volume 1, Chapter 25
Waelde (ed)	*Professor McDonald's Conveyancing Opinions* (1998), pp 244–255

Scottish Law Commission Publications

1998 – *Diligence against Land* (Scot Law Com Discussion Paper No 107)
2001 – *Diligence against Land* (Scot Law Com Report No 183)

(I) JUDICIAL TITLES

Statutes

Titles to Land Consolidation (Scotland) Act 1868, ss 59, 62, 129
Conveyancing (Scotland) Act 1924, s 46

Articles

1979 JLSS 101	Ranking of Inhibitors
1982 JLSS 13 and 68	Inhibitions, Securities, Reductions and Multiple-poindings

1983 SLT (News) 145 and 177	Inhibitions and Company Insolvencies
1983 JR 177	Prescription and Foreclosure of Adjudications
1983 JLSS 495	Inhibitions and Securities for Future Advances
1984 JLSS 357	The Title of a Liquidator
1984 JLSS 400	Delivery of Deeds and the Race to the Register
1985 JLSS 20	Bankruptcy etc and the Race to the Register
1985 JLSS 109	Insolvency and Title: a Reply
1986 SLT (News) 125	Reduction of Heritable Titles
1990 JLSS 52	Property Transfer Orders under the Family Law (Scotland) Act 1985
1990 JLSS 236	Statutory Conveyances and Examination of Title
1990 JLSS 453 and 510	Positive and Negative Interdicts
1991 SLT (News) 258	Bankruptcy (Scotland) Act 1985
1991 SLT (News) 219	Development in Personal Insolvency Law
1992 JLSS 346	Aspects of Insolvency Conveyancing
1992 JLSS 326	A note on the Bankruptcy (Scotland) Bill
1992 SLT (News) 215	Error Revised
1993 JLSS 141	Gratuitous Alienations and Unfair Preferences in Insolvency
1993 JLSS 205	A cautionary note for conveyancers – the warrant to cite in the personal registers
1993 JLSS 261	Trust Deeds for Creditors
1994 JLSS 205	A cautionary note for conveyancers – sequestration
(1997) 65 SLG 132	Gratuitous Alienations
(1998) 33 Greens PLB 8	Power of Trustee in Sequestration to Sell Heritage
(2002) 55 Greens PLB 3	Rectification of the Register

(II) COMPULSORY PURCHASE

Statutes

Lands Clauses (Consolidation) (Scotland) Act 1845
Railways Clauses (Consolidation) (Scotland) Act 1845
Acquisition of Land (Authorisation Procedure) (Scotland) Act 1947
Land Compensation (Scotland) Acts 1963 and 1973
Housing (Scotland) Act 1987
Planning and Compensation Act 1991
Title Conditions (Scotland) 2003

Articles

1956 SLT (News) 103	Schedule Conveyances
1964 SLT (News) 205	Schedule Conveyances
1969 JLSS 321	Statutory Conveyances
1973 SLT (News) 47	Schedule Conveyances and the Lands Clauses (Consolidation) (Scotland) Act 1845
1980 JLSS Workshop 142	Statutory Conveyances

1985 SLT (News) 205	Compulsory Purchase and the Valuation Date
1990 JLSS 236 and	The effect of Schedule Conveyances under the Land
1992 JLSS 5, 68 and 182	Clauses (Consolidation) (Scotland) Act 1845, with particular reference to examination of title
(1996) 23 Greens PLB 7	Planning
(2001) 83 SPEL 13	Urban Redevelopment, Compulsory Purchase and Multiple Ownership
(2003) 95 SPEL 7	Compulsory Purchase and Compensation: Proposals for Change

Chapter 30   Transmission on Death

References

Burns	*Conveyancing Practice* (4th edn, 1957), Chapters 22, 38, 39, 45
Burns	*Handbook of Conveyancing* (5th edn, 1938), Chapters 24–27
Cusine (ed)	*The Conveyancing Opinions of J M Halliday* (1992), pp 625–710
Green's Encyclopaedia	Volume 3, paras 1236–1241, Commissary Court
	Volume 4, paras 463–499, 549–556, Completion of Title (part)
	Volume 4, paras 812–880, Confirmation of Executors
	Volume 6, paras 1116–1148, Executor
	Volume 15, paras 1083–1097, Vitious Intromission
Gretton and Reid	*Conveyancing* (2nd edn, 1999), Chapters 25 and 26
Meston	*The Succession (Scotland) Act 1964* (5th edn, 2002), Chapter 8
Meston	*Succession Opinions* (2000)
McDonald	*Succession* (3rd edn, 2001), Chapter 13
Scobbie (ed)	*Currie on Confirmation of Executors* (8th edn, 1996)
Talman (ed)	*Halliday's Conveyancing Law and Practice in Scotland* (2nd edn, 2 Volumes, 1996–97), Volume 1, Chapters 18–23
Waelde (ed)	*Professor McDonald's Conveyancing Opinions* (1998), pp 257–258
Walker	*Principles of Scottish Private Law* (4th edn, 1988), Volume III, Chapter 7, para 7.6

Statutes and Statutory Instruments

Confirmation of Executors (Scotland) Act 1823
Titles to Land Consolidation (Scotland) Act 1868, ss 19, 20, 27–50, 101–103, 125–128
Conveyancing (Scotland) Act 1874, ss 9, 10, 29, 31, 46
Executors (Scotland) Act 1900
Conveyancing (Scotland) Act 1924, s 5
Trusts (Scotland) Act 1961, s 2

Succession (Scotland) Act 1964, ss 14–22, 30, 36
Act of Sederunt (Confirmation of Executors Amendment) 1966, SI 1966/593
Act of Sederunt (Confirmation of Executors) 1967, SI 1967/789
Law Reform (Miscellaneous Provisions) (Scotland) Act 1968, s 19
Administration of Estates Act 1971

Scottish Law Commission Publication

1990 – *Succession* (Scot Law Com Report No 124)

Articles

1977 SLT (News) 197	Survivorship Destinations
1977 JLSS 16	What makes a Destination Special?
1979 SLT (News) 257	Deduction of Title – A Recurring Problem
1984 JLSS 103	Heirs, Executors and Assignees
1984 SLT (News) 133, 180 and 299	Special Destinations and Liability for Debt
1984 JLSS 154	Debts and Destinations
1984 SLT (News) 245	Notes on Petitions for Service of Heirs
1985 SLT (News) 57, 92 and 98	Common Property
1987 JLSS 111	Trust and Executry Conveyancing
1989 SLT (News) 256	Special Destinations and Agricultural Leases
1989 JLSS 299	Destinations
1990 JLSS 189	Special Destinations in Scotland
1991 SLT (News) 395	Age of Capacity under the 1991 Act. Can they or can't they?
1992 SLT (News) 77 and 91	Age of Capacity – Pitfalls
2000 SLT (News) 203	Time for Special Destinations to Die?

Chapter 31   Completion of Title

References

Burns	*Conveyancing Practice* (4th edn, 1957), Chapters 21, 33, 45 and 46
Cusine (ed)	*A Scots Conveyancing Miscellany: Essays in Honour of Professor J M Halliday* (1987), p 57: Meston 'Completion of Title'
Cusine (ed)	*The Conveyancing Opinions of J M Halliday* (1992), pp 56–69
Green's Encyclopaedia	Volume 4, paras 432–448 and 527–548, Completion of Title (parts)
	Volume 5, paras 1370–1378 and 1433–1440, Disposition (parts)
Gretton and Reid	*Conveyancing* (2nd edn, 1999), Chapter 24
Scobbie (ed)	*Currie on Confirmation of Executors* (8th edn, 1996)

Talman (ed)   *Halliday's Conveyancing Law and Practice in
                                       Scotland* (2nd edn, 2 Volumes, 1996–97),
                                       Volumes 1 and 2, Chapters 21 and 39

Styles

Encyclopaedia of Scottish Legal Styles   Volume 7, Notice of Title
                                            Volume 9, Trusts

Statutes

Titles to Land Consolidation (Scotland) Act 1868, ss 17, 19, 20, 22, 23, 25, 26, 125–128
Conveyancing (Scotland) Act 1874, ss 31, 45
Conveyancing (Scotland) Act 1924, ss 3–7
Conveyancing Amendment (Scotland) Act 1938, s 1
Conveyancing and Feudal Reform (Scotland) Act 1970, ss 12, 48

Scottish Law Commission Publication

1990 – *Succession* (Scot Law Com Report No 124)

Articles

1978 JLSS 438   Completion of Title
1980 SLT (News) 257   Deduction of Title – A Recurring Problem
1987 JLSS 111   Trust and Executry Conveyancing
1989 SLT (News) 256   Special Destinations in Agricultural Leases
1989 JLSS 299   Destinations
1990 JLSS 62   Appointing and Removing Executors
1990 JLSS 189   Special Destinations in Scotland
1993 JLSS 482   Continuity of Infeftment
1995 JLSS 30   Who is the Heir of Provision in Trust?
2000 SLT (News) 203   Time for Special Destinations to Die?

Chapter 32   Examination of Title

References

Burns   *Conveyancing Practice* (4th edn, 1957), Chapters
                                       10, 13, 15, 19, 24
Green's Encyclopaedia   Volume 8, paras 413–445, Inhibitions
                                     Volume 9, paras 719–722, Litigiosity
                                     Volume 13, paras 452–478, Sale of Heritable
                                       Property (part)
                                     Volume 13, paras 682–776, Searches
Gretton   *Guide to Searches* (1991)
Gretton   *The Law of Inhibition and Adjudication* (2nd edn,
                                       1996)

Gretton and Reid   *Conveyancing* (2nd edn, 1999), Chapters 7 and 8
Sinclair   *Handbook of Conveyancing Practice in Scotland*
                          (4th edn, 2002), Chapters 7 and 8
Talman (ed)   *Halliday's Conveyancing Law and Practice in*
                          Scotland (2nd edn, 2 Volumes, 1996–97),
                          Volume 2, Chapter 36

Statutes

Contract (Scotland) Act 1997
Abolition of Feudal Tenure etc (Scotland) Act 2000
Titles Conditions (Scotland) Act 2003
Land Reform (Scotland) Act 2003

Articles

1971 JLSS 104	Enquiries of Local Authorities
1972 SLT (News) 213	Period of Search
1975 JLSS 260	Letters of Obligation
1977 JLSS 212	Heritable Transactions by Companies
1978 JLSS 209 and 306	A Conveyancing Trap
1979 JLSS Workshop i	Heritable Transactions by Companies
1979 JLSS Workshop xxiv	Inhibition and Search
1982 JLSS 13 and 68	Inhibitions, Securities, Reductions and Multiplepoindings
1984 JLSS 75, 369 and 455	The Matrimonial Homes (Family Protection) (Scotland) Act 1981
1985 SLT (News) 125	Inhibitions and Standard Securities
1985 SLT (News) 177	The Law Reform (Miscellaneous Provisions) (Scotland) Act 1985
1985 JLSS 392	Inhibitions and Conveyancing Practice
1986 JLSS 486	Occupancy Rights in the Land Register
1987 JLSS 66	Further Thoughts on Inhibitions
1988 JLSS 162	Good and Marketable Title
1989 JLSS 50 and 85	Searches I and II
1989 JLSS 206	Planning and Building Control Warranties
1990 SLT (News) 104	Letters of Obligation
1991 JLSS 179, 349 and 450	Letters of Obligation
1991 JLSS 471	Inhibitions and Partnerships
1991 JLSS 444	Matrimonial Homes Deeds Furth of Scotland
1991 JLSS 23	Recording and Registration
1991 JLSS 450 Caveat	The cover provided by the Master Policy for letters of obligation
1992 JLSS 107 and 120	Recording and Registration
1992 JLSS 439	Conveyancing: The Profit Motive
1992 JLSS 448 Caveat	Unsigned deed presented for recording along with a standard security

1994 JLSS 205 — A Cautionary Note for Solicitors

1995 JLSS 155 Caveat — Grant of Security over Matrimonial Home by Joint Proprietors.

1995 JLSS 234 — Local Authority sales and pre-emption rights

(1995) 14 Greens PLB11 — The Register of Inhibitions and Adjudications: A Guide to Indexing Practice by the Manager of the Register at Meadowbank House

1995 JLSS 316 — Property Enquiry Certificates

1995 JLSS 323 Caveat — Delivery of Documents

1995 JLSS 323 Caveat — Letters of Obligation

1995 JLSS 58 — Negligence, Securities and the Duty of Care

1995 JLSS 363 Caveat — Undisclosed Securities

1995 JLSS 377 — Certificate of Title: Legal Context

1995 JLSS 482 — Pre-payment of fees in the Land Register and Sasines Register: the new provisions

1996 JLSS 150 — The Construction (Design and Management) Regulations 1994: implications for solicitors

1996 JLSS 232 Caveat — If in Doubt, Ask

1996 JLSS 255 — A Further Cautionary Note for Conveyancers (hazards of transactions with companies)

(1996) 20 Greens PLB 2 and (1996) 21 Greens PLB 2 — Construction (Design and Management) Regulations 1994

(1996) 24 Greens PLB 2 — Surveyors' Conditions of Engagement

(1996) 24 Greens PLB 3 — Contaminated Land

(1996) 1 SLPQ 76 — Letters of Obligation

1996 JLSS 298 — A Short History of Conveyancing Fees

1996 JLSS 341 — Conveyancing Fees: Are We Selling Ourselves Short?

1996 JLSS 379 — Conveyancing Fees: The Real Answer

1996 JLSS 436 — Conveyancing quality standards

(1997) 25 Greens PLB 2 — Landfill Tax

1997 JLSS 72 — The Sasine Register and Dispositions *a non domino*

1997 JLSS 266 — Occupancy rights and Powers of Attorney

1997 JLSS 508 — Servitudes: Affidavit Evidence

1998 JLSS 10 — A Cautionary Note on Searches

(1998) 66 SLG 178 — The Solicitor's Duty in Examining Title with Particular Reference to Roof Obligations

(1998) 36 Greens PLB 1 — Fraud, Forgery and Land Registration

(1999) 39 Greens PLB 4 — Title Insurance and Conveyancing

(2000) 45 Greens PLB 4 — Land Registration Questions

(2001) 6 SLPQ 137 — Overcoming Practical Problems: The Law of Encroachment and the Function of Title Insurance

2001 JLSS Oct/28 — Comparison of Scots Land Registration System with its English Equivalent

2001 JLSS Jun/19 — Electronic Conveyancing

(2002) 6 Edin LR 146 — Registration of Company Charges

(2002) 6 Edin LR 390 — The Progress of Article 1 Protocol 1 in Scotland

Chapter 33   A Typical Conveyancing Transaction

Articles

See also Articles listed under Chapters 28 and 32

Chapter 34   Transactions with Companies

References

Cusine and Rennie	*Standard Securities* (2nd edn, 2002), Chapter 11
Greene and Fletcher	*Law and Practice of Receivership in Scotland* (2nd edn, 1992), Chapters 1 to 4, 7, 8, 9 and 10
Gretton	*The Law of Inhibition and Adjudication* (2nd edn, 1996), Chapters 11 and 12
Gretton	*A Guide to Searches* (1991)
Gretton and Reid	*Conveyancing* (2nd edn, 1999), Chapters 20, 21, 28 and 29
Palmer	*Company Law* (25th edn, looseleaf), Chapters 8, 14 and 15
Palmer	*Insolvency Law* (1993)
Reid and Gretton	*Conveyancing 2002* (2003), pp 89–97
St Clair and Drummond Young	*The Law of Corporate Insolvency in Scotland* (2nd edn, 1992), Chapters 3–5 and 8
Stair Memorial Encyclopaedia	Volume 4, paras 221–744

Talman (ed)   *Halliday's Conveyancing Law and Practice in Scotland* (2nd edn, 2 Volumes, 1996–97), Volume 2, Chapters 48–57

Waelde (ed)   *Professor McDonald's Conveyancing Opinions* (1998), pp 270–271

Statutes

Bankruptcy (Scotland) Act 1985
Companies Act 1985
Insolvency Act 1986
Companies Act 1989
Law Reform (Miscellaneous Provisions) (Scotland) Act 1990
Requirements of Writing (Scotland) Act 1995
Enterprise Act 2002

Scottish Law Commission Publications

2001 – *Sharp v Thomson* (Scot Law Com Discussion Paper No 112)
2002 – *Registration of Rights in Security by Companies* (Scot Law Com Discussion Paper No 114)

Articles

1977 JLSS 212, 334 and 1978 JLSS 45	Heritable Transactions by Companies
1988 JLSS 357 and 392	Set-off and Receivership
1989 JLSS 50 and 85	Searches
1990 JLSS 358 and 498	Execution of Deeds by Companies
1991 SLT (News) 283 and 457	The Company Execution Provisions
1992 JLSS 346	Aspects of Insolvency Conveyancing
1992 JLSS 262	Set-off in receivership
1993 JLSS 199 Caveat	Discharging loans and Ranking Agreements
1994 JLSS 191	A note on the Foreign Companies (Execution of Documents) Regulations 1994
1994 JLSS 356	*Sharp v Thomson*
1994 JLSS 371	Notes on recent company cases
1994 JLSS 372	*Sharp v Thomson*
1994 JLSS 384	*Sharp v Thomson*
1994 JLSS 400	*Sharp v Thomson*
1994 JLSS 444	*Sharp v Thomson*
1994 SLT (News) 183	*Sharp v Thomson*
1994 SLT (News) 313	*Sharp v Thomson*
1994 JLSS 256	*Sharp v Thomson*: What Now?
(1994) 13 Greens PLB 2	Transactions with limited companies: *caveat emptor*?
1995 JLSS 438	Voluntary dissolution or liquidation? An ethical dilemma for practitioners
1995 SLT (News) 79	*Sharp v Thomson*: Identifying the Mischief

Digest of Cases

Notes

(1)   The cases in this digest are intented to illuminate the text. The list of cases included is by no means exhaustive.
(2)   The headings in the digest do not correspond exactly with the headings in the text. Where a case is referred to in the text under a different heading, this may be indicated at the end of the case note thus: '(Text 2.25)' etc.
(3)   An alphabetical table of cases appears later.

Chapter 1   General Introduction

1.3 The role of solicitors in heritable property transactions

Negligence

Watson v Swift & Co's Judicial Factor 1986 SC 55. Marketability of seller's title. Defect therein. Seller already committed to both sale and purchase. Both contracts were then rescinded. Held that the resulting loss was reasonably foreseeable and a claim against the solicitors was therefore relevant.

Ferguson v McIntyre 1993 SLT 1269. A solicitor failed to ensure that the title carried a share of common grazings. The purchaser claimed damages. Proof before answer allowed.

Paterson v Sturrock & Armstrong 1993 GWD 27-1706. The purchasers' solicitor knew that they intended to use property as a guest house but failed to advise them as to planning permission etc. Negligence was conceded. Quantum of damages discussed.

Moffat v Milne 1993 GWD 8-572. A solicitor failed to reserve a servitude of access to retained ground on a part sale. Proof before answer allowed.

Higginbotham v Paul Gebal & Co 1993 GWD 3-221. A solicitor who failed to advise the seller of a council house within the three-year period that there would be a clawback was held liable for negligence to the extent of the clawback amount.

MacQueen v J M Hodge & Son 1989 GWD 29-1365. Advice given by solicitors to a client affected a third party. Held that the solicitor was not liable to make reparation to a third party who might be injured by his negligent acts or omissions when acting for his own client.

Bolton v Jameson & Mackay 1987 SLT 291. Heritable property stood in name of a husband alone. With his wife's consent, he instructed solicitors to prepare an agreement to the effect that it was owned in common. The husband later sold the house and disappeared with the whole proceeds. Held that the wife had failed to establish that the solicitors had acted on her behalf as well as on behalf of her husband but that in disposing of all the free proceeds to the husband the solicitors may have acted improperly and proof before answer allowed.

Central Govan Housing Association Ltd v Maguire Cook & Co 1988 SC 137. Purchasers sued their solicitors for negligence at settlement of a transaction. Held that the only outstanding obligation at settlement was conditional and the solicitors were not at fault and could not have insisted either on retention or a letter of obligation.

Mason v A & R Robertson & Black 1993 SLT 773. The pursuers claimed damages against their solicitors for failing to advise on the merits and effect of a counterclaim. (Text 28.77)

Glasper v Rodger 1996 SLT 44. A claim against solicitors was restricted on the footing that it had prescribed. Held that the claimants had shown sufficient evidence to demonstrate that their ignorance of a potential claim might have been reasonable.

Clelland v Morton Fraser & Milligan 1997 SLT (Sh Ct) 57. On a previous sale of a house, the seller's solicitors made representations as to a building warrant which a subsequent purchaser allegedly relied on. The claim failed on the footing that there was no contract between the second purchaser and the original seller's solicitors.

The Mortgage Corporation v Mitchells Roberton 1997 SLT 1305. Solicitors for a lender passed a cheque to the borrowers' solicitors to be held as undelivered. The borrowers' solicitors cashed the cheque without authority. They could be held liable as acting in a constructive trust for the original lender. The case went to proof and is not further reported.

Tait v Brown & McRae 1997 SLT (Sh Ct) 63. The solicitors framed a lease for a three-year period. The owners intended to recover possession at the end of the lease but the lease gave security of tenure to the tenants and the solicitors were held liable in damages for negligence.

Cheltenham and Gloucester Building Society v Mackin 1997 GWD 32-1645. The solicitor for a building society failed to record the standard security within a reasonable time and in the interim two inhibitions were registered against the debtor which the building society required to clear before reselling on the debtor's default. The solicitors founded on *Sharp v Thomson* as establishing that the borrower did not have a real right and was therefore unaffected by the inhibitions. The case went to proof. The sheriff observed that while technically the inhibitions did not strike, it was the case that, as the law then stood, the building society did require to clear the inhibitions before they could sell and that constituted a sufficient basis for a claim for negligence.

Watson v Bogue 1998 SCLR 512, 1998 SCLR (Updates) 1132. This case involved the assignation of a standard security form B which contains no personal obligation. No assignation of the personal obligation was contained in the security and there was no separate assignation. The personal obligation did not transmit and damages were claimed against the solicitors who were held not liable.

Bristol and West Building Society v Rollo Steven & Bond 1998 SLT 9. Solicitors failed to advise a building society in the conveyancing transaction that the purchaser would not obtain vacant possession. The building society then sold subject to the sitting tenants, at a lesser price than with vacant possession and were awarded damages.

Jones v Kippen Campbell & Burt 1998 GWD 11-562. The claim for negligence in this case which involved the solicitor's duty in relation to a plan annexed to the missives failed on procedural grounds.

The Royal Bank of Scotland plc v Harper Macleod 1999 GWD 16-733. A bank claimed that it would not have lent over the subjects if the solicitors had advised that there was no title to the top floor and the subjects were listed. Proof allowed on the lower of the two sums the pursuers were claiming due to the way the pleadings were framed.

Smith v Lindsay & Kirk 2000 SLT 287. A claim for damages against solicitors who failed to take proceedings timeously to the prejudice of the client was initially held not to be barred by a supersession time limit in the missives. This was overturned on appeal.

Bristol and West Building Society v Aitken Nairn WS 2000 SLT 763. The building society agreed to advance on the security of a castle allegedly held on a barony title. The barony constituted a significant element in the valuation but this was not disclosed to their solicitors. The solicitors also acted for the borrower and adjusted the title in such a way that the barony was separated from the heritable subjects over which they then framed on the standard security. The debtor defaulted and the building society claimed damages on the footing that the owner's solicitors had acted to the prejudice of the building society in separating the barony from the security subjects. In the first instance it was held there was a lack of specific instructions by the building society but proof was allowed on appeal.

Lomond Assured Properties Ltd v McGrigor Donald 2000 SLT 797. Solicitors failed to obtain a deed of restriction relating to a prior security. The intervening delay in obtaining a clearance and related matters including vandalism caused expense to the pursuers. The solicitors were held partially liable and damages were awarded.

Cheltenham and Gloucester Building Society v Royal and Sun Alliance Insurance 2001 SLT 347. A lender sued a bankrupt solicitor's insurers who had suffered loss due to the solicitor's negligence. The claim was defended on the ground that the solicitor had acted in bad faith and the master policy of professional indemnity insurance only covers cases where a solicitor is acting in good faith. Proof was allowed.

Ross Harper & Murphy v Banks 2000 SLT 699. A former partner of a firm of solicitors had acted negligently while a partner resulting in a successful claim for damages against the firm. He was held personally liable to reimburse the firm.

Newcastle Building Society v Paterson Robertson & Graham 2001 SC 734. The building society claimed that solicitors had failed to report that all the conditions of their loan had not been complied with in their report on title and in particular that the borrowers were not owners of other property. Proof was allowed.

Leeds and Holbeck Building Society v Aitken Nairn WS 2001 SCLR 41. Solicitors failed to inform lenders that the borrowers were intending to convert the security subjects from a house to a hotel which was in breach of the terms of the security. It was held that the solicitors were under no duty to inform the lenders.

Smith v Gordon & Smyth 2001 GWD 26-1066. Solicitors were sued for failure to give proper tax advice when their client was selling property. Proof was allowed.

G W Tait & Sons v Taylor 2002 SLT 1285. This was an unsuccessful attempt by a firm of solicitors to recover a amount of a negligence claim they had settled with lenders on the basis of unjustified enrichment.

The Royal Bank of Scotland plc v Macbeth Currie 2002 SLT 128. The lender sued solicitors for alleged negligence for failure to obtain a standard security over the subjects over which they had lent. The solicitors argued that any defect in the borrowers title had been cured by positive prescription. Proof was allowed.

Adams v Thorntons 2002 SCLR 787. The solicitors were sued for negligence in a complicated property transaction and pled that the claim had prescribed. Proof was allowed.

The Guardian Investments Ltd v Iain Smith & Co 2002 GWD 8-264. In a claim by a company against two firms of solicitors, the sheriff required the pursuers to find caution for any expenses. The pursuers unsuccessfully appealed on the grounds that their case was a strong one and to find caution would be unjust and that a requirement to find caution contravened their human rights. The appeal was dismissed.

Cheltenham and Gloucester Building Society v Royal and Sun Alliance Insurance (No 2) 2002 GWD 18-605. In the proof of the above case it was held that the solicitor had not acted in good faith and the insurers under the master policy successfully denied liability.

Wylie v Jeffery Aitken 2002 GWD 40-1360. A problem relating to a sewage system occurred following a purchase. There were different recollections of the advice given at the time of the missives. The solicitors' recollection was preferred to their clients' recollection.

Measure of damages

Haberstitch v McCormick & Nicholson 1975 SLT 181. Solicitors acting for a purchaser accepted a title which was not marketable. The sheriff assessed damages on the basis of the difference between the value of the house with a good title and its value with a defective title, and was upheld on appeal.

Pollard v Speedie 1971 SLT (Sh Ct) 54. Solicitors bungled missives of sale and purchase but a settlement was subsequently agreed. There was no agreement as to expenses. Held that the parties' solicitors should each be personally liable for half of the whole expenses of the action.

Paterson v Sturrock & Armstrong 1993 GWD 27-1706. See under Negligence above.

Moffat v Milne 1993 GWD 8-572. See under Negligence above.

Higginbotham v Paul Gebal & Co 1993 GWD 3-221. See under Negligence above.

Stewart v Wright Johnston & MacKenzie 1994 GWD 22-1331. In an action for damages for negligence against a solicitor on the footing that he had failed to bid for property at an auction as instructed, proof before answer allowed with particular reference to quantum.

Di Ciacca v Archibald Sharp & Sons 1994 SLT 421, and, on appeal, 1995 SLT 380. Whether damages could include increased value of a comparable property to which the title was defective.

Smith v Lindsay & Kirk (No 2) 2002 SLT 335. Quantum of damages in the above case was set at £5,000 plus interest.

Prescription of claim: *terminus a quo*

Dunlop v McGowans 1980 SC (HL) 73. An action was raised in November 1976 against solicitors for failing to serve a timeous notice at Whitsunday 1971. Held that even if negligence were established, the claim had prescribed, and claim dismissed.

Duncan v Aitken, Malone & Mackay 1989 SCLR 1. Solicitors argued that a claim for damages had prescribed. The client argued that she had suffered no loss, and therefore had no actionable claim, until her husband's sequestration which caused her loss, and that the claim had not prescribed. Her argument was upheld.

Agency

Hopkinson v Williams 1993 SLT 907. Solicitors took instructions from the sister of the owner of heritable property and the seller later repudiated the bargain. Proof before answer allowed. (Text 28.4)

McCabe v Skipton Building Society 1994 SC 467. A solicitor fraudulently obtained a joint loan for himself and his wife and forged the wife's signature. Held that he was not acting as agent within the scope of his authority.

Bolton v Jameson & Mackay 1987 SLT 291. See under Negligence above.

Stewart v Wright Johnston & MacKenzie 1994 GWD 22-1331. See under Measure of damages above.

Brady v Neilsons 1999 GWD 4-209. In an action for damages against solicitors for professional negligence the solicitors argued that no solicitor/client relationship had been established. It was held that such a relationship could be inferred from the conduct of the parties even where there was no express agreement.

Chapter 2   Authentication

2.3 Faxes

Merrick Homes Ltd v Duff 1997 SLT 570. Missives for sale and purchase of heritage concluded by fax and by delivery of faxed letter. As faxed letter was delivered opinion was reserved on whether faxing sufficient. (Text 2.3)

Grovebury Management Ltd v McLelland 1997 SLT 1083. Following conclusion of probative missives and a breach by the purchaser, a faxed letter from the purchaser imtimating intention to proceed was an effective offer of performance.

McIntosh v Alam 1997 Hous LR 141; 1998 SLT (Sh Ct) 19. The last letter of missives for the sale and purchase of heritage was signed and faxed but not delivered. Held that the contract had been concluded. (Text 2.3)

Note
Many of the cases dealing with aspects of the rules prior to the Requirements of Writing (Scotland) Act 1995, such as rei interventus, *forged signatures etc, are still relevant under the rules in the 1995 Act. The cases in the sixth edition of this book are therefore included in this section of the Digest of Cases.*

2.16 Rei interventus, homologation and adoption

Henderson's Executors v Henderson 2003 SLT (Sh Ct) 34. Informal agreement relating to a proposed sale followed by actings and cicumstances insufficient to constitute homologation pre 1995.

2.16 Probativity

Stewart's Executors v Stewart 1993 SLT 440. Informal deed, proof by writ or oath. (Text 32.77).

Sereshky v Sereshky 1988 SLT 426. Forged signature.

McLeod v Cedar Holdings Ltd 1989 SLT 620. Forged signature.

Royal Bank of Scotland v Purvis 1990 SLT 262. Grantor bound by her signature of deed she had not read; uninduced unilateral error of grantor as to content irrelevant.

De Montfort Insurance Co v Dickson 1997 GWD 27-1348. Document not a cautionary obligation signed on first sheet only with clear link to second sheet sufficiently subscribed under pre-1995 rules.

Braithwaite v Bank of Scotland 1999 SLT 25. Where a witness deliberately gives a false designation this is curable under the Land Reform (Scotland) Act 1974, s 39.

McElveen v McQuillan's Executrix 1997 SLT (Sh Ct) 26. An agreement entered into before the Requirements of Writing (Scotland) Act 1995 must be probative and an action of implement raised after the passing of the Act was incompetent.

2.16 Form of deed

Simsons v Simsons (1893) 10 R 1247. Writing in pencil curable under s 39 of the Conveyancing (Scotland) Act 1874.

Munro v Butler Johnstone (1868) 7 M 250. Essential word interlined but not authenticated; whole deed invalidated.

Gollan v Gollan (1863) 1 M (HL) 65. Inessential words on erasure not authenticated; whole deed not invalidated.

Cattanach's Trustees v Jamieson (1884) 11 R 972. Inessential words on erasure not authenticated; deed not invalidated. (Text 8.22)

Pattison's Trustees v University of Edinburgh (1888) 16 R 73. Will altered in testator's own hand.

Syme's Executors v Cherrie 1986 SLT 161. Unauthenticated deletion and interlineation made to a will at the time of execution held unauthenticated.

Manson v Edinburgh Royal Institution 1948 SLT 196. Alterations by testator to copy will.

Thomson's Trustees v Bowhill Baptist Church 1956 SC 217. Alterations by testator to copy will duly authenticated; effective to revoke the will.

2.16 Execution by parties

Stuart v Crawford's Trustees (1885) 12 R 610. Signature illegible; touched up; stamp.

Donald v McGregor 1926 SLT 103. Partial signature and mark invalid.

Morton v French 1908 SC 171. Signature by mark on a testamentary nomination invalid.

American Express Europe Ltd v Royal Bank of Scotland plc 1989 SLT 266. Question whether an abbreviated signature complied with the Lyon King of Arms Act 1672.

American Express Europe Ltd v Royal Bank of Scotland plc (No 2) 1989 SLT 650. Signature by surname only valid execution. (Text 2.9)

Rhodes v Peterson 1971 SC 56. Signature 'Mum' on a testamentary letter held valid. (Text 2.9)

Draper v Thomason 1954 SC 136. Abbreviated signature competent in special circumstances; but see *American Express Europe Ltd (No 2)* above. (Text 2.9)

Brown v Duncan (1888) 15 R 511. Signature on erasure valid.

Gardner v Lucas (1878) 5 R (HL) 105. Signatures on last page, initials on preceding pages, invalid.

Lowrie's Judicial Factor v McMillan's Executrix 1972 SC 105. Signature by initials.

Elwick Bay Shipping Co Ltd v Royal Bank of Scotland plc 1982 SLT 62. Signature 'pro general manager' not equivalent to signature of general manager.

Moncrieff v Moneypenny (1710) Mor 15936. Signature must be spontaneous.

Crosbie v Picken (1749) M 16814. Signature must be spontaneous.

Noble v Noble (1875) 3 R 74. The hand must not be guided below the wrist.

Ker v Hotchkis (1837) 15 S 983. A blind person can validly subscribe.

Drummond v Farquhar 6 July 1809 FC. Status of bishops; but see *American Express Europe Ltd (No 2)* above.

Dunlop v Greenlee's Trustees (1863) 2 M 1. Married women may subscribe their maiden surname; but see *American Express Europe Ltd (No 2)*.

Bank of Scotland v Graham's Trustee 1992 SC 79. Application for rectification of standard security held relevant where grantor signed once as debtor, but failed to sign again as proprietor. (Text 29.17)

Subscription

McLay v Farrell 1950 SC 149. Holograph will subscribed; clause added below signature held unauthenticated.

Robbie v Carr 1959 SLT (Notes) 16. Holograph will; signature in margin; invalid.

Baird's Trustees v Baird 1955 SC 286. Signatures on reverse page; invalid.

McNeill v McNeill 1973 SLT (Sh Ct) 16. Signatures on reverse page; valid.

Ferguson, Petitioner 1959 SC 56. Writing on first page, signatures on third; valid. *Baird's Trustees v Baird*, above, distinguished.

2.16 Attestation

Allan and Crichton, Petitioners 1933 SLT (Sh Ct) 2. Witness signing 'Mrs Bernard' invalid.

Young v Paton 1910 SC 63. Allegation that witness did not see deed signed, nor hear acknowledgement; onus of proof.

Walker v Whitwell 1916 SC (HL) 75. Witness signing after death of grantor; invalid. (Text 2.4)

Murray, Petitioner (1904) 6 F 840. Witness signing ex intervallo; valid.

MacDougall v MacDougall's Executors 1993 SCLR 832; 1994 SLT 1178. Whether will validly attested. (Text 28.35, 30.17)

Grant v Keir (1694) Mor 16 913. Sufficiency of designation of witness.

Williamson v Williamson 1997 SLT 1044. A will was attested by two witnesses. One signed 'D.C.R. Williamson'. In the testing clause he was named D.C.R. Wilson. Held that the document failed to meet the requirements of probativity. (Text 2.4)

Lindsay v Milne 1995 SLT 487. A will was reduced as improperly attested, the second witness having not been present nor heard an acknowledgement of subscription.

Leggat v Lloyds Bank plc 1997 GWD 12-491. An action of reduction of a standard security on the grounds of forgery or alternatively improper execution failed.

McLure v McLure's Executrix 1997 SLT 127. A will was signed by witnesses when the testator was not present. The witnesses later went to see the testator who referred to the will and this was sufficientt acknowledgment of the signature by the testator.

Russo v Hardey 2000 GWD 27-1049. Probative writ relating to heritage reduced on grounds of force and fear.

Forsyth v Royal Bank of Scotland plc 2000 SLT 1295. Standard security granted by husband and wife in favour of bank to secure husband's business overdraft. Two witnesses did not see wife sign or acknowledge her signature. Held that wife had signed deed, knew it related to a security, the bank had relied on the security and *rei interventus* had taken place.

2.16 The testing clause

Blair v Assets Co Ltd (1896) 23 R (HL) 36. Operative words inserted in testing clause invalid.

Gibson's Trustees v Lamb 1931 SLT 22. Holograph provision in testing clause held valid in special circumstances.

McDougall v McDougall (1875) 2 R 814. Names in testing clause written on erasure did not invalidate.

Blair v Earl of Galloway (1827) 6 S 51. A 32-year interval in completing testing clause did not invalidate.

2.16 Notarial execution

Hynd's Trustee v Hynd's Executor 1955 SC (HL) 1. Statutory procedure not strictly observed; will invalidated.

Finlay v Finlay's Trustees 1948 SC 16. Interest of notary in will; power to charge; will invalidated.

Irving v Snow 1956 SC 257. Interest of notary in will; deed executed in England; will not invalidated.

McIldowie v Muller 1979 SC 271. Interest of notary in will; no power to charge; will not invalidated.

2.16 Informality of execution

Addison, Petitioner (1875) 2 R 457. Omitted testing clause may be added later; 1874 Act, s 39 petition probably unnecessary.

Elliot's Executors, Petitioners 1939 SLT 69. Witnesses' designations omitted; alterations not authenticated; deed curable under s 39 of the 1874 Act.

Grieve's Trustees v Japp's Trustees (1917) 1 SLT 70. Parties inaccurately designed; not sufficient to invalidate; s 39 petition not necessary.

Simsons v Simsons (1893) 10 R 1247. Writing in pencil curable under s 39 of the 1874 Act.

McLaren v Menzies (1876) 3 R 1151. Deed on several sheets signed on last page only; curable under s 39 of the 1874 Act.

McNeill v McNeill 1973 SLT (Sh Ct) 16. Signatures on reverse page; will held validly subscribed.

Baird's Trustees v Baird 1955 SC 286. Signatures on reverse page; document held not subscribed; compare McNeill above.

Walker v Whitwell 1916 SC (HL) 75. Defect in solemnities not curable under s 39. (Text 2.4)

Hynd's Trustee v Hynd's Executor 1955 SC (HL) 1. Defect in solemnities in notarial execution not curable under s 39 of the 1874 Act.

Thomson's Trustees v Easson (1878) 6 R 141. Failure to complete testing clause before registration or founding on not necessarily fatal.

Braithwaite v Bank of Scotland 1999 SLT 25. Where a witness deliberately gives a false designation this is curable under the 1874 Act, s 39.

2.16 The effect of ex facie probativity

Boyd v Shaw 1927 SC 414. Latent defect in probativity of onerous deed; personal bar.

2.16 Holograph writings

Harper v Green 1938 SC 198. Onus of proof lies on proponer, not challenger.

Harley v Harley's Executor 1957 SLT (Sh Ct) 17. Holograph will invalidly attested; valid notwithstanding.

Tucker v Canch's Trustee 1953 SC 270. Will partly printed, partly holograph; invalid.

Gillies v Glasgow Royal Infirmary 1960 SC 438. Will partly printed, partly holograph; valid.

Campbell, Petitioner 1963 SLT (Sh Ct) 10. Will partly printed, partly holograph; cases reviewed.

Merrick Homes Ltd v Duff 1997 SLT 570. Missives subscribed and adopted as holograph; validly executed. (Text 2.3)

Barker's Executors v Scottish Rights of Way Society 1996 SLT 1319. Whether documents partly printed and partly handwritten duly executed.

Adoption

Shiell v Shiell (1913) 1 SLT 62. Holograph docquet subscribed on backing ; invalid.

Campbell's Executors v Maudsley 1934 SLT 420. Holograph docquet subscribed on backing; valid.

Craik's Exx. v Samson 1929 SLT 592. Improbative will adopted by separate holograph codicil.

Stenhouse v Stenhouse 1922 SC 370. Improbative will in envelope bearing holograph signed docquet; invalid.

Chisholm v Chisholm 1949 SC 434. Typewritten document subscribed; 'Adopted as holograph' typed at foot but no statement *in gremio*; invalid.

2.16 Writings in re mercatoria

Caledonian Bank plc v St Aubyn 1994 GWD 30-1818. Question whether document solemnly executed or *in re mercatoria*.

Chapter 3   Capacity

3.5 Trustees

Darwin's Trustees, Petitioners 1924 SLT 778. Whether sale at variance with terms or purposes.

Campbell, Petitioner 1958 SC 275. Petition to court under *nobile officium* for power of sale. (Text 3.10)

Horne's Trustees, Petitioners 1952 SC 70. Petition by English trustees to court under *nobile officium* for power of sale; retrospective sanction of earlier sale not granted.

Fletcher's Trustees, Petitioners 1949 SC 330. Petition to court under Trusts Acts for power to purchase heritage.

Tod's Trustees, Petitioners 1999 SLT 308. Petition to court for power of sale where unclear whether trust was a public or private trust, charitable or otherwise.

Balgown Trustees, Petitioners 1999 SLT 817. Trustees of an old charitable trust which failed, acting *ex officio*, entitled to assume new trustees under the Trusts (Scotland) Act 1921.

3.11 Children

Cunningham's Tutrix, Petitioner 1949 SC 275. Tutor's power of sale. (Text 3.12)

3.14 Judicial Factors and Adults with Incapacity

Inland Revenue v McMillan's Curator Bonis 1956 SC 142. Nature of office of curator.

Bristow, Petitioner 1965 SLT 225, 1965 SLT (Notes) 42. Curator's power to purchase. (Text 3.9, 3.12)

Barclay, Petitioner 1962 SC 594. Curator may still require power from court to sell heritage, not for the purpose of giving title, but to exclude claims by beneficiaries.

Lothian's Curator Bonis, Petitioner 1927 SC 579. Whether sale at variance with terms or purposes.

Leslie's Judicial Factor, Petitioner 1925 SC 464. Power of JF to sell heritage; but see now Conveyancing Amendment (Scotland) Act 1938, s 1.

Cooper & Sons' Judicial Factor, Petitioner 1931 SLT 26. Power of JF to sell heritage.

Dunlop & Sons' Judicial Factor v Armstrong 1995 SLT 645. Court declined to interfere in dispute between judicial factor and heritable creditor.

Thurso Building Society's Judicial Factor v Robertson 2001 SLT 797. A judicial factor of a building society had a title to sue its former solicitor for negligence.

3.15 Corporations

James Finlay Corporation Ltd v R & R S Mearns 1988 SLT 302. Whether standard security to guarantee debts of another company *ultra vires*.

General Auction Co v Smith [1891] 3 Ch 432. A trading company has implied power to borrow.

Re Introductions Ltd, Introductions Ltd v National Provincial Bank Ltd [1969] 1 All ER 887. A creditor cannot rely on a power to borrow if the loan is patently for an *ultra vires* purpose.

Cockenzie Community Council v East Lothian District Council 1996 SCLR 209. Community council failed to prevent the sale by district council of part of common good under Local Government (Scotland) Act 1973, s 75(2).

West Dunbartonshire Council v Harvie 1997 SLT 979. Petition by council for authority to dispose of area of common ground, under 1973 Act, s 75, rejected on amenity grounds.

Stirling Council, Petitioners 2000 GWD 18-722. Permission granted for sale of a property which was part of the common good but was in a poor condition and could not be reasonably restored.

Wilson v Inverclyde Council 2003 GWD 8-237. An unsuccessful claim that a public trust had been set up in relation to a harbour which was separate from the common good.

3.19 Sequestration

Simpson's Trustee v Simpson 1993 SCLR 867. Division and sale of a matrimonial home; Bankruptcy (Scotland) Act 1985, s 40.

Clark's Trustee, Noter 1993 SLT 667. In exceptional circumstances, interim trustee in sequestration may be given power of sale under Bankruptcy (Scotland) Act 1985, s 18(3)(c).

3.23 Partnerships

Cameron v Lightheart 1995 SCLR 443. Title taken in name of A and B as trustees for their firm, but a special clause was added authorising either to sell and dispose without the consent of the other. B, acting alone, sold the subjects. A challenged the sale by an action of reduction but failed.

3. 25 Unincorporated associations

Lauder College, Petitioners 1996 GWD 12-719. Petition for judicial review of decision of a Commissioner regarding transfer of property and responsibility dismissed.

Piggins & Rix Ltd v Montrose Port Authority 1995 SLT 418. Held that in the particular circumstances it would be *ultra vires* for a port authority to sell surplus land. (Text 3.2, 3.15, 34.4)

Chapter 4   Delivery

4.1 The need for delivery

Life Association of Scotland v Black's Leisure Group plc 1989 SC 166. Discussion on effect of delivery of disposition as divesting disponer.

Life Association of Scotland v Douglas (1886) 13 R 910. Deed not delivered at grantor's death held undelivered.

Walker's Executor v Walker (1878) 5 R 965. Deed in favour of donor's wife undelivered; held donor not divested.

Connell's Trustees v Connell's Trustees 1955 SLT 125. Bond to trustees of wife of donor not exempt from need for delivery.

Clark's Executor v Clark 1943 SC 216. Delivery of testamentary writing does not prevent subsequent revocation. (Text 4.15)

McManus's Trustee v McManus 1981 SC 233. Deed to wife of donor in hands of his agent, but intimated to her, not sufficient to infer delivery.

Clark's Executor v Cameron 1982 SLT 68. Disposition improperly executed but delivered to grantor's agent did not, *per se*, constitute homologation.

Grant's Trustee v Grant 1986 SC 51. In bankruptcy, under Bankruptcy Act 1696 (now repealed), date of recording disposition, not the date of delivery, determining date for fraudulent preferences. (Text 29.12)

Gibson v Hunter Home Designs Ltd 1976 SC 23. Undelivered feu disposition held invalid although price paid and possession given. (Text 4.3, 32.44)

Russo's Trustee v Russo's Trustee 1996 GWD 21-1245. Alleged that shop premises in name of B were truly held in trust for A. Credibility of witnesses was suspect. Purported letters of trust rejected as evidence was dubious and insufficient to prove alleged trust. Accordingly, A's trustee in sequestration held entitled thereto

Sharp v Thomson 1995 SC 45 rev'd 1997 SC (HL) 66. A company executed and delivered a disposition of property to a *bona fide* purchaser for value. The company had already granted a floating charge which included that property. A receiver under the floating charge was appointed to the grantor of the disposition before the purchaser had recorded it. Held in the

Inner House that the property was attached by the floating charge. This was reversed on appeal to the House of Lords. (Text 4.4, 23.4, 29.8, 32.44, 34.7, 34.12, 34.15, 34.18)

Burnett's Trustee v Grainger 2002 SLT 699. Following a sale, the disposition in favour of the purchaser was delivered but not recorded. The seller was sequestrated and the trustee recorded a notice of title before the purchaser eventually recorded the disposition. The Inner House held that the decision in *Sharp v Thomson* only applied to floating charges in receiverships and not to sequestrations and the trustee had a good title to the subjects of sale. The case is under appeal to the House of Lords at the time of writing. (Text 4.5)

4.7 Presumptions arising from custody of the deed

McAslan v Glen (1859) 21 D 511. Deed held by donee not sufficient to infer delivery.

Mair v Thom's Trustees (1850) 12 D 748. Deed held by common agent not sufficient to infer delivery.

Lombardi's Trustee v Lombardi 1982 SLT 81. Delivery of disposition to common agent who intimated delivery to grantee. Deed held to be delivered.

4.11 Equivalents to delivery

Registration

(1) In the Register of Sasines

Linton v Inland Revenue 1928 SC 209. Registration in Sasines in names of donees held sufficient to imply delivery.

Cameron's Trustees v Cameron 1907 SC 407. Registration in Sasines in name of donor as trustee for donee did not create valid trust. (Text 4.12)

(2) In the Books of Council and Session

Tennent v Tennent's Trustees (1869) 7 M 936. Registration in Books of Council and Session is ordinarily equivalent to delivery. (Text 4.12)

(3) In the books of the company

Inland Revenue v Wilson 1928 SC (HL) 42. Registration in name of donee in books of company is a factor implying delivery.

4.13 Intimation to the debtor in an obligation

Smith v Place D'Or 1988 SLT (Sh Ct) 5. Assignation of lease held effective following intimation, despite the fact that the deed of assignation was not physically delivered.

4.14 Intimation to donee

Carmichael v Carmichael's Executors 1920 SC (HL) 195. Undelivered deed intimated to donee and held to create a *jus quaesitum tertio*. (Text 4.12)

Allan's Trustee v Lord Advocate 1971 SC (HL) 45. Intimation to donee equivalent to delivery. (Text 4.16)

Kerr's Trustees v Lord Advocate 1974 SC 115. Intimation to agent for donee equivalent to delivery.

Clark Taylor & Co Ltd v Quality Site Development (Edinburgh) Ltd 1981 SC 111. Contractual obligation, as 'continuing intimation' to obligee, is not equivalent to delivery.

4.16 Acceptance of delivery

Dowie & Co v Tennant (1891) 18 R 986. Need for acceptance of delivery. (Text 4.16)

Allans Trustees v Lord Advocate 1971 SC (HL) 45. Intimation to one donee, accepted, implies acceptance by all. (Text 4.16)

Chapter 5   Stamp Duty Land Tax, Stamp Duty and VAT

5.5 Rates of tax

Cohen v Attorney-General [1937] 1 KB 478. Definition of a series of transactions.

5.7 Exemptions and reliefs

Kildrummy (Jersey) Ltd v Inland Revenue Commissioners 1991 SC 1. A complex arrangement involving an allegedly voluntary disposition, a declaration of trust, a disposition and lease *in gremio* intended to avoid stamp duty failed in its purposes and duty held to be payable.

5.19 The election to waive exemption

Jaymarke Development Ltd v Elinacre Ltd 1992 SLT 1193. Construction of missives. Missives of sale and purchase were entered into between two companies. The purchase price was stipulated as a single sum stated to be deemed to be inclusive of VAT. The purchase price was duly paid at the date of entry as required by the missives. The sellers, however, did not elect to waive exemption from VAT. The purchaser then sought to recover from the sellers the VAT component in the purchase price. The court construed the missives as requiring payment by the purchasers of the full amount of the purchase price, whether the sellers paid VAT or not. The case also contains an excellent review of the operation of VAT on transfers of heritable property. (Text 5.19)

Hostgilt Ltd v Megahart Ltd [1999] STC 141. Term in a contract stating that 'sums payable … for the supply of goods and services are exclusive of VAT chargeable on the payment' meant that the price payable was the VAT exclusive price plus VAT at 17.5%, if VAT was chargeable on the transaction (Text 5.19)

5.21 The interaction between VAT and stamp duty land tax

Glenrothes Development Corporation v IRC 1994 SLT 1310. Obligation on purchasers of heritage to pay VAT is part of price for stamp duty purposes. (Text 5.21)

Chapter 7   The Disposition: General

7.3 Grantor

Swans v Western Bank (1866) 4 M 663. Accretion can operate even where grantor had no title to subjects at the time of grant.

7.9 Joint property

Magistrates of Banff v Ruthin Castle 1944 SC 36. Joint property or common property. (Text 30.10)

Munro v Munro 1972 SLT (Sh Ct) 6. Joint property or common property. (Text 30.10)

7.10 Common property : general

General rules

Cargill v Muir (1837) 15 S 408. Nature of common property; multiplication of superiors. (Text 7.9)

Deans v Woolfson 1922 SC 221. Common property; demolition and reconstruction.

Sutherland v Barbour (1887) 15 R 62. Common property or common interest; alterations to buildings.

Schaw v Black (1889) 16 R 336. Rights of individual *pro indiviso* proprietors; collecting rents.

Lade v Largs Banking Co (1863) 2 M 17. Right of *pro indiviso* proprietors to sue and defend.

Fearnan Partnership v Grindlay 1992 SC (HL) 38. Where property is owned in common, all proprietors must concur in granting servitude rights over the common property. (Text 16.5)

Grozier v Downie (1871) 9 M 826. Two out of three *pro indiviso* proprietors cannot remove a tenant without the participation of the third.

Price v Watson 1951 SC 359. Sale of *pro indiviso* share. Effect on other *pro indiviso* proprietors. Whether ejection of purchaser competent.

Bailey's Executors v Upper Crathes Fishing Ltd 1991 SC 30. Interdict is an appropriate remedy in dispute between co-proprietors of common property.

Wells v New House Purchasers Ltd 1964 SLT (Sh Ct) 2. Whether obligation to repair personal or real as between owners in common.

Carlton Place Properties v Richmond 1991 SCLR 151. Question whether single ownership of tenement property previously separately owned, with rights in common *inter se*, extinguishes those rights absolutely or whether they revive *sub silentio* on subsequent subdivision.

Midlothian District Council v McCulloch 1993 SCLR 152. Two properties were separated by a road serving both. One proprietor was held entitled to a right of access over the half of the road belonging to his neighbour.

Church of Scotland General Trustee v Phin 1987 SCLR 240. Liability for the cost of repairs to mutual fence and standard of repair required.

Rafique v Amin 1997 SLT 1385. Consent of all co-proprietors to alterations required, except those which are *de minimis*. Use of a common stair in a tenement is an ordinary use of the property.

Clydesdale Bank plc v Davidson 1998 SLT 522. Co-owners cannot lease to one of their number.

Michael v Carruthers 1998 SLT 1179. Disposition of whole subjects by a *pro indiviso* proprietor completely null. Compare *McLeod v Cedar Holdings Ltd* 1989 SLT 620.

Homecare Contracts (Scotland) Ltd v Scottish Midland Co-operative Society Ltd 1999 GWD 23-1111. Necessary repairs may be instructed by any co-proprietor.

McCafferty v McCafferty 2000 SCLR 256. Where disposition states that price paid by both co-proprietors, it is not competent to lead extrinsic evidence to the contrary.

Mackay v Gaylor 2001 GWD 1-59. Use of a common driveway by construction traffic instructed by one co-proprietor is an ordinary use, as is the laying of pipes, cables and drains underneath such a driveway.

7.11 Common property: division and sale

Milligan v Barnhill (1782) Mor 2486. Whether one co-proprietor may be made to transfer his share to another.

Grant v Heriot's Trust (1906) 8 F 647. Common property and common interest. Exclusion of right of division and sale.

D & S Miller v Crichton (1893) 1 SLT 262. On the division and sale of common property, one of the several proprietors who has been in possession may recover expenditure on maintenance but may be liable to pay rent.

Upper Crathes Fishings Ltd v Bailey's Executors 1991 SC 30. Absolute right to division or division and sale.

Morrison v Kirk 1912 SC 44. Division.

Scrimgeour v Scrimgeour 1988 SLT 590. Division and sale; purchase by co-proprietor.

Berry v Berry (No 2) 1989 SLT 292. Purchase by co-proprietor not allowed; sale to be on the open market; Scrimgeour, above, not followed.

The Miller Group Ltd v Tasker 1993 SLT 207. No fixed rule that judicial sale should be either by roup or by private bargain. Choice depends on which will achieve the highest price.

Williams v Cleveland and Highland Holdings Ltd 1993 SLT 398. Discussion of circumstances in which a *pro indiviso* owner can object to a report to the court on the respective merits of physical division and division and sale.

Hall v Hall 1987 SLT (Sh Ct) 15. Division and sale; matrimonial home.

Berry v Berry 1988 SLT 650. Division and sale; matrimonial home; divorce.

Milne v Milne 1994 SLT (Sh Ct) 57. Held that the court had discretion under the Matrimonial Homes (Family Protection) (Scotland) Act 1981. Application for division and sale refused on basis of balance of convenience.

Simpson's Trustee v Simpson 1993 SCLR 867. Action of division and sale of a matrimonial home, and the Bankruptcy (Scotland) Act 1985, s 40.

Burrows v Burrows 1996 GWD 25-1439. Held that, on divorce, one party had an absolute right to division and sale.

Grieve v Morrison 1993 SLT 852. Two parties purchased heritage jointly in contemplation of marriage which did not take place. The question was whether division and sale was appropriate or whether one party could purchase from the other.

Langstane (SP) Housing Association Ltd v Davie 1994 SCLR 158. A housing association, as *pro indiviso* proprietor, sought repossession of the other *pro indiviso* share from a defaulting owner/tenant and ran into procedural difficulties. Held that the action was incompetent in the circumstances.

Riddell v Morrisetti 1994 GWD 38-2238. A dispute involving two adjoining plots of land purchased for building, and question of access.

Gray v Kerner 1996 SCLR 331. Unmarried, cohabiting couple purchased a house in joint names. Held that the woman, who wished to remain in occupation, was entitled to purchase the *pro indiviso* share of the other cohabitee.

Ploetner v Ploetner 1997 SCLR 998. Where there are two co-owners and each wants to buy the share of the other, the court is likely to instruct division and sale.

Bush v Bush 2000 SLT (Sh Ct) 22. A co-owner may contract out of their absolute right to division and sale.

7.12 Common interest

Grant v Heriot's Trust (1906) 8 F 647. Common interest.

George Watson's Hospital v Cormack (1883) 11 R 320. Common interest in garden in square. Management.

Donald & Sons v Esslemont & Macintosh 1923 SC 122. Common interest in public street.

Calder v Merchant Co of Edinburgh (1886) 13 R 623. Common interest in tenement.

Taylor's Trustees v McGavigan (1896) 23 R 945. Prohibition against buildings.

Gray v MacLeod 1979 SLT (Sh Ct) 17. Common property or common interest, boundary wall.

Gill v Mitchell 1980 SLT 48. Common property or common interest, mutual wall.

Lyon v Findlay (April 1981, unreported), Aberdeen Sheriff Court, reported in Paisley and Cusine *Unreported Property Cases from the Sheriff Courts* (2000), pp 79–86. Right to light through glass panels in a tenement wall under common interest.

Thom v Hetherington 1988 SLT 724. Whether boundary wall mutual; consequences attaching to mutuality of wall.

Church of Scotland General Trustees v Phin 1987 SCLR 240. Liability for the cost of repairs to a mutual fence and standard of repair required.

Newton v Godfrey (19 June 2000, unreported), Stranraer Sheriff Court, reported in Paisley and Cusine *Unreported Property Cases from the Sheriff Courts*, pp 86–93. Proper liferenter can enforce common interest obligation.

7.13 Destinations

(See also para 30.9)

Hay's Trustee v Hay's Trustees 1951 SC 329. Criticism of use of special destinations. (Text 7.13, 30.9)

Redfern's Executors v Redfern 1996 SLT 900. Under a separation agreement, both parties relinquished any rights of succession in the estate of the other. Held that the agreement in its terms impliedly waived the normal prohibition against evacuation of a survivorship destination. (Text 30.13)

7.15 Liferents

Stronach's Executors v Robertson 2002 SLT 1044; 2002 SCLR 843. It is not competent for a fiar to obtain an order against the liferenter to get him to carry out repairs to the property. The appropriate remedy is to ask the court to make him find caution for any damages due at the expiry of the liferent in respect of failure to take reasonable care of the subjects. The caution is known as *cautio usufructuaria*.

Chapter 8   Descriptions

(See also Chapter 12.)

8.2 The extent of the grant

Hay v Aberdeen Corporation 1909 SC 554. 'Right and interest'. (Text 6.10)

Gordon v Grant (1851) 13 D 1. Parts and pertinents.

8.3 Separate tenements

McKendrick v Wilson 1970 SLT (Sh Ct) 39. Salmon fishings; need for conveyance. (Text 8.3, 28.23)

Munro Ferguson v Grant (1900) 8 SLT 326. Salmon fishings; illustration of express grant.

8.7 The common law of the tenement
Solum, front and rear ground

Johnston v White (1877) 4 R 721. An express conveyance of the right in common to the *solum*, on which a tenement is built, gives no right of ownership in the front area.

Barclay v McEwan (1880) 7 R 792. Same circumstances as in *Johnston*, above.

Boswell v Edinburgh Magistrates (1881) 8 R 986. Express conveyance of back ground; right to build.

Turner v Hamilton (1890) 17 R 494. Express conveyance of right to *solum*; proposed alterations thereon.

Arrol v Inches (1886) 14 R 394. Whether proprietor can build out over front area.

Bredero Aberdeen Centre Ltd v Aberdeen District Council. A small part of a building was constructed on the ground at ground-floor level. The remainder of that part of the building was supported by buildings on the ground floor in other ownerships. Held that the '*solum*' thereof extended to the whole area over which the upper floors were constructed.

City and County Investments (Scotland) Ltd v McIver 1997 GWD 6-248. Break-off disposition giving common right to *solum* 'on which the said whole subjects are erected', on the facts carried the land surrounding the tenement.

Main walls

Todd v Wilson (1894) 22 R 172. Alteration to main wall; no special provision in titles.

Rafique v Amin 1997 SLT 1385. Difficulties arising out of external walls being declared to be common property. (Text 8.9)

Floor and ceiling

Alexander v Butchart (1875) 3 R 156. Division line between upper and lower floors.

Roofs

Taylor v Dunlop (1872) 11 M 25. Where the roof of a tenement is not owned in common, the whole roof space and the roof itself belong exclusively to the top-floor proprietor.

Sanderson's Trustees v Yule (1897) 25 R 211. Ownership of roof; conversion of attics.

Watt v Burgess's Trustees (1891) 18 R 766. Ownership of roof; extension of attic upwards.

Duncan, Smith & MacLaren v Heatly 1952 JC 61. Maintenance; no provision in titles.

Duncan v Church of Scotland General Trustees 1941 SC 145. Maintenance; partial provision in titles.

Dunedin Property Management Services Ltd v Glamis Property Co Ltd 1993 GWD 31-2006. In a dispute as to the meaning of the term 'roof', the sheriff dismissed evidence based on leases as not forming part of the shop owner's title and was upheld on appeal.

Common passages and stairs

WVS Office Premises Ltd v Currie 1969 SC 170. Ownership of passage; no express provision in title.

Deans v Woolfson 1922 SC 221. Destruction of common stair; right to rebuild.

Common gables

Robertson v Scott (1886) 13 R 1127. Common gable; right to recompense; singular successor.

Houston v McLaren (1894) 21 R 923. Whether wall a common gable.

Lamont v Cumming (1875) 2 R 784. Adjoining proprietor is entitled to make vents in a mutual gable.

Baird v Alexander (1898) 25 R (HL) 35. Rights attaching to common gable at common law may be modified or excluded by contract.

Jack v Begg (1875) 3 R 35. One proprietor may not, without consent, remove a mutual boundary wall and erect a mutual gable in its place encroaching on a neighbouring property.

Wilson v Pottinger 1908 SC 580. Whether common gable encroaching on adjoining property.

Troup v Aberdeen Heritable Securities Co Ltd 1916 SC 918. Common gable resting on garden wall.

Trades House of Glasgow v Ferguson 1979 SLT 187. Liability for cost of demolition and reconstruction of exposed gable.

Demolition and reconstruction

Smith v Giuliani 1925 SC (HL) 45. Dangerous building; liability for cost of demolition.

Barr v Bass Ltd 1972 SLT (Lands Tr) 5. Partial demolition; resulting rights of several proprietors. (Text 16.13)

Deans v Woolfson 1922 SC 221. Common stair.

Liability for damage caused by alterations and reconstructions

Thomson v St Cuthbert's Co-operative Association Ltd 1958 SC 380. Nature and extent of obligation of support. (Text 8.7)

Kerr v McGreevy 1970 SLT (Sh Ct) 7. Nature and extent of obligation of support.

Doran v Smith 1971 SLT (Sh Ct) 46. Nature and extent of obligation of support.

Macnab v McDevitt 1971 SLT (Sh Ct) 41. Nature and extent of obligation of support. (Text 8.8)

Kennedy v Glenbelle Ltd 1996 SLT 1186. Contrary to professional advice, tenants in basement of tenement removed load-bearing wall with resulting damage to the upper floors. Pursuer claimed damages from occupiers and their consulting engineers, founding on nuisance and culpa. Proof allowed. (Text 8.8)

Powrie Castle Properties Ltd v Dundee City Council 2001 SCLR 146. Two tenements had a mutual gable. One was demolished. This cause damage by water penetration. The owners of the demolished tenement were liable for repairs necessitated by this.

Management and repairs

Wells v New House Purchasers Ltd 1964 SLT (Sh Ct) 2. Liability for repairs, personal or real.

Deans v Woolfson 1922 SC 221. Whether repairs necessary.

McNally & Miller v Mallinson 1977 SLT (Sh Ct) 33. Whether repairs necessary. 'Majority of proprietors'.

Schaw v Black (1889) 16 R 336. Discussion on right of one of several proprietors to collect rents.

Taylor v Irvine 1996 SCLR 937. Servitude right of access to part of tenement owned by another flat owner must be constituted by express provision or by implication.

Geary v Tellwright 1994 GWD 17-1077. Discussion on 'common repairs' between upper and lower proprietors.

McLay v Bennett 1998 GWD 16-810. Works carried out in relation to a lift were held on the facts to be improvements rather than repairs.

Richardson v Quercus Ltd 1999 SC 278, 1999 SLT 596. Proprietor of lower flat liable to proprietor of upper flats in damages for repairs necessitated by his actions.

Hamilton v Wahla 1999 GWD 25-1217. Tenant of shop liable to the proprietor of first floor flat in delict for damage caused by alterations.

Graham & Sibbald v Brash (21 March 2001, unreported), Dundee Sheriff Court. Defectively drawn deed of conditions in relation to payment of common charges for swimming pool serving the development. (Text 8.9)

8.12 Water rights
Surface water

Campbell v Bryson (1864) 3 M 254. Lower property not entitled to surface water from upper tenement as of right.

Anderson v Robertson 1958 SC 367. Lower property must accept natural flow of water from upper property.

Logan v Wang (UK) Ltd 1991 SLT 580. Upper proprietor entitled to collect water together and send it down in one body to lower property, provided the right is not 'overstretched'.

Crichton v Turnbull 1946 SC 52. Servitude of water; interference by drainage.

Noble's Trustees v Economic Forestry (Scotland) Ltd 1988 SLT 662. No liability, *ex dominio* and without *culpa*, for actings of a contractor causing damage by water; but interdict may be appropriate.

Scottish Highland Distillery v Reid (1887) 4 R 1118. Servitude of dam and aqueduct; interference therewith.

McLaren v British Railways Board 1971 SC 182. Circumstances where proprietor may have a duty to maintain his banks to prevent flooding his neighbour's land.

Rights in rivers and streams
Tidal and navigable waters

Bowie v Marquis of Ailsa (1887) 14 R 649. Fishings; express Crown grant.

Buchanan and Geils v Lord Advocate (1882) 9 R 1218. Right to foreshore of tidal river.

Lindsay v Robertson (1868) 7 M 239. Mussel fishing in tidal river; barony title and possession.

Smith v Lerwick Harbour Trustees (1903) 5 F 680; 10 SLT 742. Ownership of foreshore in udal law.

Mull Shellfish Ltd v Golden Sea Produce Ltd 1992 SLT 703. Mussel farming in the sea; reparation for damage to mussel larvae.

Walford v David 1989 SLT 876. Fish farm cages not a material interference with public right of navigation in the sea.

Shetland Salmon Farmers Association v Crown Estate Commissioners 1990 SCLR 484. The seabed within territorial waters belongs to the Crown by virtue of the prerogative, and may be alienated or leased by the Crown. This includes the sea around Shetland.

Lennox v Keith 1993 GWD 30-1913. The general public have no right to fish for trout in non-tidal waters, but may in tidal waters.

Non-tidal navigable rivers

Wills' Trustees v Cairngorm Canoeing and Sailing School Ltd 1976 SC (HL) 30. Right of public navigation in rivers.

Scammell v Scottish Sports Council 1983 SLT 462. Right of public navigation in rivers.

Campbell's Trustees v Sweeney 1911 SC 1319. Right of public to anchor and moor in rivers.

Orr Ewing v Colquhoun's Trustees (1877) 4 R (HL) 116. Private rights in *alveus*.

Grant v Henry (1894) 21 R 358. Fishings in navigable river.

Non-navigable rivers

Gibson v Bonnington Sugar Refining Co Ltd (1869) 7 M 394. 'Bounded by' a river implies ownership up to the *medium filum*. (Text 8.16)

Bicket v Morris (1866) 4 M (HL) 44. Opposite heritors; operations in *alveus*.

Menzies v Breadalbane (1901) 4 F 55. Opposite heritors; *medium filum*; main and subsidiary channel.

Cowan v Lord Kinnaird (1865) 4 M 236. Upper and lower heritor; operations in *alveus*.

Hood v Williamsons (1861) 23 D 496. Common interest in flow of water.

Young v Bankier Distillery Co (1893) 20 R (HL) 76. Pollution.

Macintyre Bros v McGavin (1893) 20 R (HL) 49. Pollution; prescriptive right.

Hardie v Walker 1948 SC 674. Operations in *alveus* interfering with passage of salmon.

Lochs

Macdonell v Caledonian Canal Commissioners (1830) 8 S 881. Loch surrounded by property of one proprietor.

Scott v Lord Napier (1869) 7 M (HL) 35. Competing titles of adjoining proprietors; joint or exclusive right.

Menzies v MacDonald (1856) 19 D (HL) 1. Joint right in loch; disposition 'with lakes and pertinents'.

Meacher v Blair-Oliphant 1913 SC 417. Competing titles; joint or exclusive right.

Mackenzie v Bankes (1878) 5 R 278. One loch or two.

Magistrates of Ardrossan v Dickie (1907) 14 SLT 349. Loch or stagnum.

Leith Buchanan v Hogg 1931 SC 204. Navigation on loch.

Menzies v Wentworth (1901) 3 F 941. Regulation of joint rights of fishing in lochs.

8.13 Fishings and game

Salmon fishings

Munro Ferguson v Grant (1900) 8 SLT 326. Express title.

McKendrick v Wilson 1970 SLT (Sh Ct) 39. Separate tenement; need for conveyance. (Text 8.3, 28.23)

Stuart v McBarnett (1868) 6 M (HL) 123. Crown grant with 'fishings'; construction.

Bowie v Marquis of Ailsa (1887) 14 R 649. Crown grant; tidal and navigable river; competing public rights.

Lord Advocate v Cathcart (1871) 9 M 744. Possession on barony title.

Farquharson v Lord Advocate 1932 SN 28. Competing titles.

Warrand's Trustees v Makintosh (1890) 17 R (HL) 13. Competing title.

Magistrates of Tain v Murray (1887) 15 R 83. Boundaries between fishings.

Lord Advocate v Balfour 1907 15 SLT 7. Udal law; salmon fishings not *inter regalia* in Orkney.

Gay v Malloch 1959 SC 110. River; regulation of rights of opposite heritors.

Fothringham v Passmore 1984 SC (HL) 96. River; *medium filum*; regulation of rights of opposite heritors.

Roxburghe v Waldie's Trustees (1879) 6 R 663. Method of exercising right.

Lord Advocate v Lovat (1880) 7 R (HL) 122. Express grant; possession; mode of exercise of right.

Lord Advocate v Sharp (1878) 6 R 108. Sea fishings exercisable from foreshore; right of access over adjoining land.

Middletweed Ltd v Murray 1989 SLT 11. Rights of access are those necessary for beneficial enjoyment of the fishings. Circumstances in which held that there was no right of vehicular access.

Trout fishings

Galloway v Duke of Bedford (1902) 4 F 851. Nature of right; lease of fishings.

Don District Board v Burnett 1918 SC 37. Nature of right.

Johnstone v Gilchrist 1934 SLT 271. Whether right of fishing and fowling real right or personal privilege.

Harper v Flaws 1940 SLT 150. Whether right of trout fishings a servitude or real burden.

Patrick v Napier (1867) 5 M 683. Whether right of angling right of property, burden or servitude.

Wemyss Water Trustees v Lawson 1924 SLT 162. Reservation of fishings; whether enforceable against a statutory successor.

Menzies v Wentworth (1901) 3 F 941. Regulation of joint rights of trout fishings in loch.

Meacher v Blair-Oliphant 1913 SC 417. Whether trout fishings in loch owned in common or exclusively.

Game

Welwood v Husband (1874) 1 R 507. Nature of right.

Johnstone v Gilchrist 1934 SLT 271. Nature of right.

Beckett v Bissett (1921) 2 SLT 33. Shooting rights as real burden.

Palmer's Trustees v Brown 1988 SCLR 499, 1989 SLT 128. Lease of shootings, if registered, transmits against singular successors of landlord. (Text 8.13, 24.8)

Adams v Scottish Ministers 2003 SLT 366. Protection of Wild Mammals (Scotland) Act 2002 does not contravene the Human Rights Act 1998. (Text 8.13)

8.15 Methods of description: general

Macdonald v Keeper of the General Register of Sasines 1914 SC 854. Description in general terms unacceptable for recording. (Text 8.14, 11.6)

Houldsworth v Gordon Cumming 1910 SC (HL) 49. General description.

Johnston's Trustees v Kinloch 1925 SLT 124. General description.

8.16 Methods of description: particular

Brown v North British Railway Co (1906) 8 F 534. Extrinsic evidence to identify boundary.

Oliver v Cameron 1994 GWD 8-505. Access road described as shown within red boundary lines on plan; ownership and servitude of access discussed.

Bennett v Beneficial Bank plc 1995 SLT 1105. Discussion on what constitutes a particular description for purposes of standard security.

Beneficial Bank plc v McConnachie 1996 SC 119, 1996 SLT 413. Held that description by postal address was not a particular description in standard security over a mid-terrace villa. (Text 8.16, 8.21, 8.23)

Beneficial Bank plc v Wardle 1996 GWD 30-1825. Rectification of defective description in standard security ordered.

Reid v McColl (1879) 7 R 84. 'Bounded by the lands of A.'

Strang v Steuart (1864) 2 M 1015. March fences.

Thom v Hetherington 1988 SLT 724. Mutual boundary wall; comments on nature of ownership of respective proprietors.

Gray v MacLeod 1979 SLT (Sh Ct) 17. Mutual wall.

Lord Advocate v Wemyss (1899) 2 F (HL) 1. 'Bounded by the sea.'

Gibson v Bonnington Sugar Co Ltd. (1869) 7 M 394. 'Bounded … along the Water of Leith'; boundary was *medium filum*. (Text 8.16)

Menzies v Breadalbane (1901) 4 F 55. River.

Magistrates of Hamilton v Bent Colliery 1929 SC 686. River.

Stirling v Bartlett 1992 SCLR 994. Effect on boundary of river changing course.

Magistrates of Ayr v Dobbie (1898) 25 R 1184. Public road.

Houstoun v Barr 1911 SC 134. Public road.

Louttit's Trustees v Highland Railway Co (1892) 19 R 791. Private road. (Text 28.32, 28.75)

Harris v Wishart 1996 SLT 12. Bounded by private road *prima facie* excludes whole road.

Butt v Galloway Motor Co Ltd 1996 SLT 1343. Held on appeal that word 'driveway' was bounding and excluded hedge and intervening verge. Boundary line lay along edge of tarmac of drive.

Suttie v Baird 1992 SLT 133. Written description ambiguous; shape of area possessed did not match plan; title not bounding. (Text 8.18, 12.7)

Mackenzie v Emms 1994 GWD 22-1363. Proof allowed in boundary dispute with strong recommendation to seek another form of resolution.

Boyd v Hamilton 1907 SC 912. Lane; conflicting titles; actings of parties.

Campbell v Paterson (1896) 4 SLT 79. Bounded by gable wall excludes the wall.

Hetherington v Galt (1905) 7 F 706. Line of trees.

Young v West 2000 GWD 7-262. Boundary feature (part of a railway bridge) no longer in existence.

8.18 Repugnancies and ambiguities

Currie v Campbell's Trustees (1888) 16 R 237. Boundaries and measurement inconsistent.

North British Railway Co v Moon's Trustees (1879) 6 R 640. Written description and plan inconsistent.

Royal and Sun Alliance Insurance v Wyman-Gordon Ltd 2001 SLT 1305; 2002 SCLR 34. Written description and plan inconsistent. Former prevailed as plan stated to be demonstrative. (Text 8.18)

8.19 Method of description: by reference

Murray's Trustees v Wood (1887) 14 R 856. Inept description by reference. (Text 8.22)

McLachlan v Bowie (1887) 25 SLR 734. Lost plan. (Text 8.16)

Matheson v Gemmell (1903) 5 F 448. Description by reference at common law. (Text 8.22)

Cattanach's Trustees v Jamieson (1884) 11 R 972. Error in date of recording deed held not to invalidate description by reference. (Text 8.22)

8.24 Methods of addenda: description

Gordon v Grant (1851) 13 D 1. Parts and pertinents.

Jamieson v Welsh (1900) 3 F 176. Fixtures and fittings.

Chapter 9   Reservations

9.1 The implication of reservations

Bain v Hamilton (1865) 3 M 821. Coal; constitution of title by reservation to superior.

Hamilton v Graham (1871) 9 M (HL) 98. Reservation of coal and limestone with right to sink pits.

Hamilton v Dunlop (1885) 12 R (HL) 65. Reservation of right to work.

Cadell v Allan (1905) 7 F 606. Minerals under foreshore; charter of novodamus; not reserving minerals, sufficient title to vassal.

Lord Advocate v Wemyss (1899) 2 F (HL) 1. Minerals under sea.

Millar v Marquess of Landsdowne 1910 SC 618. Competing titles; possession of surface.

Fleeming v Howden (1868) 6 M 782. Disposition of a bare superiority does not carry minerals previously reserved to, and owned by, disponing superior.

Craig v Jarvis (Scotland) Ltd 1997 GWD 20-979. Interpretation of terms of reservation in relation to extraction of minerals.

9.2 Definition of minerals

Caledonian Railway v Glenboig Union Fireclay Co Ltd 1910 SC 951. Fireclay a mineral in 1856.

Magistrates of Glasgow v Farie (1887) 15 R (HL) 94. Clay forming ordinary subsoil two or three feet below surface is not a mineral.

Linlithgow v North British Railway Co 1914 SC (HL) 38. Shale not a recognised mineral in 1818 but would be now.

North British Railway Co v Budhill Coal and Sandstone Co 1910 SC (HL) 1. Sandstone not a mineral in 1845.

Caledonian Railway v Symington 1912 SC (HL) 9. Whether freestone is a mineral is a question of fact; relevant factors discussed.

Borthwick-Norton v Gavin Paul & Sons 1947 SC 659. Whether sand a mineral.

9.4 Support

Buchanan v Andrew (1873) 11 M (HL) 13. Right of surface owner to prevent mineral working.

White v Dixon (1883) 10 R (HL) 45. Normal right of support may be excluded by express provision.

North British Railway Co v Turners Ltd (1904) 6 F 900. Nature of obligation to support.

Hamilton v Turner (1867) 5 M 1086. Support of buildings.

Bain v Hamilton (1867) 6 M 1. Support of buildings.

Dryburgh v Fife Coal Co Ltd (1905) 7 F 1083. Support of buildings.

Barr v Baird & Co (1904) 6 F 524. Support of existing buildings

Neill's Trustees v Wm Dixon Ltd (1880) 7 R 741. Support of building later erected.

British Coal Corporation v Netherlee Trust Trustees 1995 SLT 1038. Corporation was liable to carry out remedial action where damage was caused by the shifting of infill rather than true subsidence.

Osborne v British Coal Property 1996 SLT 736. The Lands Tribunal now has jurisdiction in compensation claims, but jurisdiction of Court of Session is not wholly excluded.

Brady v National Coal Board 1999 SC 621. Requirement to send timeous written notice under statutory subsidence compensation scheme.

Fitzpatrick v The Coal Authority 2001 GWD 7-282. Unsuccessful claim under statutory subsidence compensation scheme. In terms of Coal Mining (Subsidence) Act 1957, consent of both parties to refer matter to Lands Tribunal required. Compare Coal Mining Subsidence Act 1991, s 40.

Other reserved rights

Scottish Temperance Life Assurance Co Ltd v Law Union & Rock Insurance Co Ltd 1917 SC 175. Reservation of power to build on ground disponed held ineffective against singular successors.

Wemyss Water Trustees v Lawson 1924 SLT 162. Reservation of trout fishings. See also cases under 8.13.

Chapter 10   Other Clauses

10.5 Assignation of writs

Porteous v Henderson (1898) 25 R 563. Effect of assignation of writs.

10.6 Assignation of rents

Butter v Foster 1912 SC 1218. Interpretation of statutory clause.

10.7 Obligation of relief

Spottiswoode v Seymer (1853) 15 D 458. Special obligation of relief in disposition requires special assignation.

Duke of Montrose v Stewart (1863) 1 M (HL) 25. But not if undertaken by superior in feu charter.

North British Railway Co v Edinburgh Magistrates 1920 SC 409. Extent of obligation.

10.8 Warrandice

Cairns v Howden (1870) 9 M 284. Extent of claim.

Leith Heritages Co (Ltd) v Edinburgh and Leith Glass Co (1876) 3 R 789. Warrandice of 'all right, title and interest'.

Brownlie v Miller (1880) 7 R (HL) 66. Warrandice guarantees only against eviction and does not warrant the particular tenure. (Text 10.17)

Horsburgh's Trustees v Welch (1886) 14 R 67. Warrandice from fact and deed guarantees only against acts of grantor himself.

Duchess of Montrose v Stuart (1887) 15 R (HL) 19. Warrandice obligation strictly construed according to its terms. Express absolute warrandice in gratuitous deed so construed.

Welsh v Russell (1894) 21 R 769. Partial eviction. Nature of remedy. (Text 10.9, 28.32)

Lothian and Border Farmers Ltd v McCutcheon 1952 SLT 450. Existing lease not breach of warrandice. (Text 10.9, 28.30)

Christie v Cameron (1898) 25 R 824. Liability under warrandice persists and continues to bind original warrantor after grantee has sold subjects.

Young v McKellar Ltd 1909 SC 1340. Warrandice following articles of roup.

Fraser v Cox 1938 SC 506. Warrandice not reflecting prior agreement. (Text 16.8)

Watson v Swift & Co's Judicial Factor 1986 SC 55; 1986 SLT 217. Claim under warrandice is competent without actual ejection, if unquestionable burden on subjects can be proved which caused claimant to settle action with party who has better title. This may be regarded as equivalent to judicial eviction.

Cobham v Minter 1986 SLT 336. Claim by subsequent purchaser against earlier purchaser; transmission discussed. (Text 10.20)

Kildrummy (Jersey) Ltd v Inland Revenue Commissioners 1991 SC 1; 1992 SLT 787. Warrandice clause in disposition referred to lease. Lease void and held not to be capable of being validated by adoption by disposition. (Text 10.19, 12.7, 26.12)

Palmer v Beck 1993 SLT 485. No remedy in warrandice without judicial eviction. (Text 10.8, 28.72)

Clark v Lindale Homes Ltd 1994 SLT 1053. To establish eviction under warrandice, competing proprietor must actually have challenged the title.

Baird v Drumpelior & Mount Vernon Estates Ltd 2000 SC 103. Warrandice clause in disposition unqualified. Argued that this did not represent the intention of the parties. Claim for rectification failed.

Mutch v Mavisbank Properties Ltd 2002 SLT (Sh Ct) 91. In Land Register, rectification of Register not essential for there to be eviction, but there must be clear averments as to challenge to title.

Chapter 11 Registration

11.5 Registration

Ceres School Board v McFarlane (1895) 23 R 279. In a competition between recorded titles, priority of registration determines preference. (Text 31.1, 32.51)

11.6 Register of Sasines

Johnston v Fairfowl (1901) 8 SLT 480. Possession without title.

Cameron's Trustees v Cameron 1907 SC 407. Effect of recording. (Text 4.12)

Macdonald v Keeper of the General Register of Sasines 1914 SC 854. Need for adequate description. (Text 8.14)

Brown v North British Railway Co (1906) 8 F 534. Indefinite conveyance not mandate for infeftment.

Swans v Western Bank (1866) 4 M 663. Superior must be infeft; accretion. (Text 7.3)

11.26 Content of the title sheet

McCarthy & Stone (Developments) Ltd v Smith 1995 SLT (Lands Tr) 19. Owner of *dominium utile* acquired superiority and consolidated. His title was then registered in Land Register. Burdens section of title sheet disclosed burdens in *dominium utile* title as still subsisting. Held, in application to Tribunal for discharge thereof, that no *jus quaesitum* having been created, there were no longer enforceable burdens falling to be discharged, and application dismissed.

Marshall v Duffy 2002 GWD 10-318. Prior Sasine deeds may not be used to interpret the plan on a title sheet. (Text 11.28)

11.31 Rectification of the Register

Brookfield Developments Ltd v Keeper of the Registers of Scotland 1989 SLT (Lands Tr) 105. Keeper included burdens which were no longer subsisting; rectification allowed. (Text 18.54)

Short's Trustee v Keeper of the Registers of Scotland 1996 SLT 166. Decree of reduction not registrable under Land Registration (Scotland) Act 1979, s 2(4) and will not normally justify rectification of Register. (Text 11.35, 29.13, 32.65)

Scottish Enterprise v Ferguson 1996 GWD 26-1522. Disposition by registered proprietor immune from challenge based on an unregistered prohibition and Register would not be rectified.

Kaur v Singh 1998 SCLR 849. A heritable creditor is not a proprietor in possession in terms of 1979 Act, s 9(3). 'Proprietor' means the owner of property and 'possession' may include civil possession. (Text 11.33)

Short's Trustee v Chung (No 2) 1999 SLT 751. The Trustee was awarded an order in terms of the Bankruptcy (Scotland) Act 1985, s 34, for the proprietor in possession to convey the property to him. This seriously undermines the decision in *Short's Trustee v Keeper* (above). (Text 11.35)

Dougbar Properties Ltd v Keeper of the Registers of Scotland 1999 SC 513, 1999 SCLR 458. It is not careless for a party to rely on the Register where they know it to be inaccurate. (Text 11.34)

Wilson v Inverclyde Council 2000 SLT 267. Rectification not allowed because Register not shown to be inaccurate.

Keeper of the Registers of Scotland v MRS Hamilton Ltd 2000 SLT 352, reported as *MRS Hamilton Ltd v Keeper of the Registers of Scotland* 2000 SC 271. Rectification is not retrospective. Indemnity in terms of 1979 Act, s 12(1)(d), is only payable for discrepancies between the Title Sheet and the Land Certificate. (Text 11.37)

Kaur v Singh (No 2) 2000 SLT 1323; 2000 SCLR 944. Quantification of indemnity payable where rectification refused. (Text 11.37)

Stevenson-Hamilton's Executors v McStay (No 2) 2001 SLT 694. Rectification allowed due to fraud or carelessness on the part of the proprietors in possession. (Text 11.34)

Higgins v North Lanarkshire Council 2001 SLT (Lands Tr) 2. Register held to be inaccurate where disposition which induced the entry in it was voidable, but not yet actually reduced. (Text 11.32, 11.34)

Tesco Stores Ltd v Keeper of the Registers of Scotland 2001 SLT (Lands Tr) 23. Rectification allowed because proprietors were held not to be in possession. (Text 11.33)

Mutch v Mavisbank Properties Ltd 2002 SLT (Sh Ct) 91. Holder of a servitude may be a proprietor in possession. (Text 11.33)

Safeway Stores plc v Tesco Stores Ltd 2003 GWD 20-611. Decision of Lands Tribunal in *Tesco Stores* (above) upheld.

Chapter 12   The Effects of Possession: Prescription

12.5 *Positive prescription*

Scott v Bruce-Stewart (1779) 3 Ross LC 334. Purpose of positive prescription. (Text 12.6)

Lord Advocate v Graham (1844) 7 D 183. Working of positive prescription.

Edmonstone v Jeffray (1886) 13 R 1038. Possession without title cannot create proprietory rights by prescription.

Grant v Henry (1894) 21 R 358. Rights such as trout fishing cannot be acquired by prescriptive use.

Johnston v Fairfowl (1901) 8 SLT 480. Possession without title.

McLellan v Hunter 1987 GWD 21-803. Constitution of servitude right by possession for 20 years without title under Prescription and Limitation (Scotland) Act 1973, s 3.

12.6 The result of title and possession

Ex facie invalidity

Glen v Scales's Trustee (1881) 9 R 317. Title *a non domino*.

Hilson v Scott (1895) 23 R 241. Title *a non domino*.

Fraser v Lord Lovat (1898) 25 R 603. Possession on Crown grant disconform to enabling Act.

Ramsay v Spence 1909 SC 1441. Which register, county or burgh?

Meacher v Blair-Oliphant 1913 SC 417. Not competent to refer to earlier titles in order to qualify foundation writ.

Troup v Aberdeen Heritable Securities Co Ltd 1916 SC 918. Not competent to refer to earlier titles in order to make title bounding.

Cooper Scott v Gill Scott 1924 SC 309. Discussion on ex facie invalidity. (Text 12.7)

Lock v Taylor 1976 SLT 238. Was title express grant, or merely title habile to found prescription?

Love-Lee v Cameron of Lochiel 1991 SCLR 61. Even after granting a conveyance, grantor has, in original title, title which is habile for purposes of prescription. Hence if he retains possession for ten years after the grant, land reverts to his ownership.

Watson v Shields 1996 SCLR 81. If person in possession is challenged by alleged competitor, he cannot interdict that competitor to prevent challenge unless the competitor totally unable to demonstrate colourable title. (Text 12.2)

Ambiguity of description

Stuart v McBarnett (1868) 6 M (HL) 123. Crown grant of 'fishings'; possession of salmon fishings established title.

Fleeming v Howden (1868) 6 M 782. Title to 'superiority' not habile to acquisition of dominium utile.

Zetland v Glover Incorporation of Perth (1870) 8 M (HL) 144. Salmon fishings; consolidated title. (Text 12.7)

Agnew v Lord Advocate (1873) 11 M 309. No presumption that foreshore is a pertinent without express grant; prescriptive possession is necessary.

Zetland v Tennent's Trustees (1873) 11 M 469. Possession of salmon fishings beyond boundaries of associated land may create title thereto.

Stewart's Trustees v Robertson (1874) 1 R 334. Whether rights in lochs rights of property or servitude.

Auld v Hay (1880) 7 R 663. Ambiguity; title to *pro indiviso* shares; possession of whole.

Young v North British Railway Co (1887) 14 R (HL) 53. Possession of foreshore on title from subject superior sufficient.

Lord Advocate v Wemyss (1899) 2 F (HL) 1. Barony title, minerals under foreshore and sea.

Robertson's Trustees v Bruce (1905) 7 F 580. Right of property or right of servitude.

Millar v Marquess of Landsdowne 1910 SC 618. Minerals, competing titles, both claimants averring possession.

Meacher v Blair-Oliphant 1913 SC 417. Whether rights in lochs exclusive or common.

Farquharson v Lord Advocate 1932 SN 28. Possession of salmon fishings on base title may establish right.

Borthwick-Norton v Gavin Paul & Sons 1947 SC 659. Construction; minerals; sand.

Nisbet v Hogg 1950 SLT 289. 'All rights in any way competent to' disponers.

Luss Estates Co v British Petroleum Oil Grangemouth Refinery Ltd 1987 SLT 201. Foreshore – barony title with bounding description excludes acquisition by possession.

Suttie v Baird 1992 SLT 133. Ambiguous boundary sufficient title for prescription. (Text 8.18)

Michael v Carruthers 1998 SLT 1179. Disposition of flat referring to deed of conditions declaring basement of tenement to be common property not habile to include exclusive right to the basement.

Summers v Crichton 2000 GWD 40-1495. Erroneous judicial suggestion that earlier deeds may be considered when interpreting a description.

Parts and pertinents

Magistrates of Perth v Earl of Wemyss (1829) 8 S 82. Possession of island as a pertinent prevailed over express infeftment therein.

Gordon v Grant (1851) 13 D 1. Corporeal property cannot be acquired outwith bounding title.

McArly v French's Trustees (1883) 10 R 574. Right to retain signboard on a building established by prescriptive possession.

Cooper's Trustees v Stark's Trustees (1898) 25 R 1160. Saloon as pertinent of house.

Mead v Melville 1915 1 SLT 107. Title to basement flat habile to acquisition, by prescriptive possession, of cellar as a pertinent.

Bounding title

Gordon v Grant (1851) 13 D 1. Title bounding; statement of parish.

Zetland v Tennent's Trustees (1873) 11 M 469. Bounding title does not prevent acquisition of salmon fishings beyond boundaries.

North British Railway Co v Moon's Trustees (1879) 6 R 640. Title bounding; conflict between written description and plan.

Reid v McColl (1879) 7 R 84. Identification by reference to extrinsic evidence; adjoining title.

Watt v Burgess's Trustees (1891) 18 R 766. Title bounding; conveyance of attic storey.

North British Railway Co v Hutton (1896) 23 R 522. Particular description with exception; bounding so as to exclude exception.

Cooper's Trustees v Stark's Trustees (1898) 25 R 1160. Bounding title prevents acquisition of corporeal property outwith boundary.

Lord Advocate v Wemyss (1899) 2 F (HL) 1. Title bounding; statement of county.

Brown v North British Railway Co (1906) 8 F 534. Title bounding; identification by reference to extrinsic evidence; separate plan.

Houstoun v Barr 1911 SC 134. Title bounding; 'bounded by Quarrelton Street'. (Text 8.16)

Troup v Aberdeen Heritable Securities Co Ltd 1916 SC 918. Title not bounding; not competent to make it so by referring to earlier titles.

Nisbet v Hogg 1950 SLT 289. Title not bounding.

Anderson v Harrold 1991 SCLR 135. Title bounding; conflict between written description and plan.

12.8 The quality of title and nature of possession

Generally

Warrand's Trustees v McIntosh (1890) 17 R (HL) 13. Salmon fishings; possession relied on to construe express grant.

Robertson's Trustees v Bruce (1905) 7 F 580. Title must support possession.

Houstoun v Barr 1911 SC 134. Title must support possession; competent to refer to earlier titles to explain possession. (Text 8.16)

Argyll v Campbell 1912 SC 458. Title must support possession; competent to refer to earlier titles to explain possession.

Fothringham v Passmore 1984 SC (HL) 96. Salmon fishings; possession not referable to title.

Luss Estates Co v British Petroleum Oil Grangemouth Refinery Ltd 1987 SLT 201. Barony title; bounding title expressly excluding foreshore; possession did not create title.

McLellan v Hunter 1987 GWD 21-803. Constitution of a servitude right by possession for 20 years without title under the Prescription and Limitation (Scotland) Act 1973, s 3.

Landward Securities (Edinburgh) Ltd v Inhouse (Edinburgh) Ltd 1996 GWD 16-962.

Qualification 'so far as I have right thereto' no bar to prescription. (Text 8.24, 12.7)

Quality of possession

Young v North British Railway Co (1887) 14 R (HL) 53. Whether possession sufficient to create title; foreshore.

Warrand's Trustees v Mackintosh (1890) 17 R (HL) 13. Salmon fishing; barony title; possession by rod and line.

Maxwell v Lamont (1903) 6 F 245. Possession must be lawful and by legal methods; salmon fishings.

Millar v Marquess of Landsdowne 1910 SC 618. Possession must be exclusive.

Meacher v Blair-Oliphant 1913 SC 417. Whether possession sufficient to create title; salmon fishings.

Richardson v Cromarty Petroleum Co Ltd 1982 SLT 237. Quality of possession required to constitute public right of way.

Strathclyde (Hyndland) Housing Society Ltd v Cowie 1983 SLT (Sh Ct) 61. Quality of possession required to constitute public right of way.

Middletweed Ltd v Murray 1989 SLT 11. Quality of possession required to constitute servitude right of way.

Bain v Carrick 1983 SLT 675. Competing titles; use by one party; extent of use necessary.

Cumbernauld and Kilsyth District Council v Dollar Land Ltd 1993 SC (HL) 44. Quality of possession required to constitute public right of way. (Text 16.15)

Hamilton v McIntosh Donald Ltd 1994 SLT 793. Detailed analysis of requisites for prescriptive possession. (Text 12.11)

Patterson v Menzies 2001 SCLR 266. Where there is a title dispute, interdict appropriate to prevent one party altering the state of possession before dispute resolved.

Hoggan's Curator ad Litem v Cowan 2000 GWD 27-1050. Overlapping titles. Neither owner had the requisite ten years of possession.

Stevenson-Hamilton's Executors v McStay (No 2) 2001 SLT 694. Sporadic acts of possession over a ten year period, including clearing rubbish, trimming hedges and cutting grass held to be insufficient.

Royal Bank of Scotland plc v Macbeth Currie 2002 SLT (Sh Ct) 128. Possession may be civil.

Tantum praescriptum quantum possessum

Carstairs v Spence 1924 SC 380. Whether access for all, or limited, purposes.

Kerr v Brown 1939 SC 140. Limitation on right of drainage.

Interruption

Hogg v Campbell 1993 GWD 27-1712. Discussion on adverse actings and effect on continuity of peaceful possession.

Barratt Scotland Ltd v Keith 1993 SCLR 120. An obligation to deliver a disposition is an obligation in relation to land to which 20-year prescription is appropriate.

Lauder v MacColl 1993 SCLR 753. What acts of interruption are sufficient to break continuity of possession of a public right of way?

Renfrew District Council v Russell 1994 GWD 34-2032. What evidence of possession is necessary for declarator that there was a public right of way?

Royal Bank of Scotland plc v Macbeth Currie 2002 SLT (Sh Ct) 128. Where grantee in foundation write ejected by heritable creditor, this does not constitute interruption.

12.12 Interests in land under registration of title

MRS Hamilton Ltd v Baxter 1997 GWD 19-898. Raising an action of reduction in respect of disposition without conclusion for rectification of the Register sufficient to amount to judicial interruption.

12.15 The long negative prescription

Porteous's Executors v Ferguson 1995 SLT 649. Effect of negative prescription on personal unfeudalised rights. (Text 12.7, 31.42)

Chapter 13   Land Regulation: Introduction

13.5 Occupiers' liability

McGlone v British Railways Board 1966 SC (HL) 1. Nature of duty of care owed when injured party not invited onto premises.

Bermingham v Sher Brothers 1980 SC (HL) 67. Discussion of liability.

Titchener v British Railways Board 1984 SC (HL) 34. Discussion of s 2 of the Occupiers' Liability (Scotland) Act 1960.

Johnstone v Sweeney 1985 SLT (Sh Ct) 2. Liability to those using public right of way.

13.6 Nuisance

Inglis v Shotts Iron Co (1881) 8 R 1006. What amounts to nuisance.

Watt v Jamieson 1954 SC 56. Nuisance as damage to property.

Webster v Lord Advocate 1985 SLT 361. Nuisance and the Edinburgh military tattoo.

RHM Bakeries (Scotland) Ltd v Strathclyde Regional Council 1985 SC (HL) 66. Importance of fault.

Logan v Wang (UK) Ltd 1991 SLT 580. Interdict and fault.

Kennedy v Glenbelle Ltd 1996 SC 95. What amounts to fault.

Chapter 14   Title Conditions: General

14.3 Real burdens and servitudes

Tailors of Aberdeen v Coutts (1837) 2 Sh & Macl 609, (1840) 1 Robin 296. Real burdens, nature of content.

McLean v Marwhirn Developments Ltd 1976 SLT (Notes) 47. Distinction between servitude and real burden.

Chapter 15   Title Conditions: Real Burdens and their Creation

15.3 Praedial real burdens

Tailors of Aberdeen v Coutts (1837) 2 Sh & Macl 609, (1840) 1 Robin 296. Real burdens definition and rules of constitution.

15.6 Community burdens

Hislop v MacRitchie's Trustees (1881) 8 R (HL) 95. Situations when community burdens might arise.

15.7 Facility and service burdens

Tennant v Napier Smith's Trustees (1888) 15 R 671. Maintenance obligations regarding a canal, potentially facility burden in future.

Campbell's Trustees v Scottish Union & National Insurance Co (1893) 21 R 167. Obligation to maintain road, where road upgraded by local authority.

Wells v New House Purchasers Ltd 1964 SLT (Sh Ct) 2. Maintenance obligation in tenement, likely to be facility burdens in future.

15.9 Rights of pre-emption

Macdonald, Applicant 1973 SLT (Lands Tr) 26. Right of pre-emption is land obligation but Lands Tribunal has no jurisdiction to vary same if imposed by statute.

Spurway, Petitioner 1987 GWD 2-65. Title may contain right of pre-emption which overrides contract.

Banff and Buchan District Council v Earl of Seafield's Estate 1988 SLT (Lands Tr) 21. Lands Tribunal jurisdiction to vary right of pre-emption. Observations on effect of pre-emption.

Matheson v Tinney 1989 SLT 535. Right of pre-emption effect on singular successors to burdened property (application of rule penalising private knowledge of prior right).

Roebuck v Edmunds 1992 SLT 1055. Right of pre-emption effect on singular successors (application of private knowledge of prior right).

Waverley Housing Trust Ltd v Roxburgh District Council 1995 SLT (Lands Tr) 2. Local authority inserted pre-emption clause in two offers with no change of tenancy. Held condition unreasonable in terms of Housing (Scotland) Act 1988, s 58 and pre-emption clause conditions should be struck out from each offer.

Roberts v Tait & Peterson 1995 GWD 10-548. R bought a cottage. On later sale a pre-emption clause was discovered. Superior could not be traced and purchasers rescinded. R sued his agents. Proof before answer allowed.

Henderson v Glasgow District Council 1994 SLT 263. Prior titles contained right of pre-emption which was not brought to the attention of the Tribunal when they made their order effectively conferring title on the purchasing tenant. Tribunal satisfied that they were correct in issuing an offer to the tenant which took no account of the right of pre-emption, and were upheld.

Patience v Ross and Cromarty District Council 1997 SC (HL) 46. Right of pre-emption conflicts with statutory right to buy public sector housing.

Macdonald-Haig v Gerlings (3 December 2001, Inverness Sheriff Court). See text.

15.10 Rights of redemption

McElroy v Duke of Argyll (1902) 4 F 885. Feudal redemption entitling superior to buy back property on terms specified.

15.19 Manager burdens

Sheltered Housing Management Ltd v Aitken (1997, unreported), reported in Paisley and Cusine *Unreported Property Cases from the Sheriff Courts* (2000), p 225. Burden providing for appointment of manager.

Dumbarton District Council v McLaughlin 2000 Hous LR 16. Observations on validity of burden providing for appointment of manager

15.22 Affirmative and negative burdens
Affirmative burdens: some examples

See examples for para 15.7 and the following

Tailors of Aberdeen v Coutts (1840) 1 Robin 296. Obligation to maintain, obligation to pay maintenance costs, obligation to erect fences. Observations on invalidity of burdens where obligation to pay uncertain or indefinite amount.

Clark v City of Glasgow Life Assurance & Reversionary Co (1854) 1 Macq 668. Obligation to maintain mill and obligation to insure.

Stewart v Meikle (1874) 1 R 408. Obligation to pay construction costs of sewer is not real burden. Obligation to maintain is.

Welsh v Jack (1882) 10 R 113. Obligation to erect stables and coach-houses.

Magistrates of Glasgow v Hay (1883) 10 R 635. Obligation to erect houses.

Magistrates of Edinburgh v Begg (1883) 11 R 352. Maintenance burden effective (if for continuing obligations) but obligation to pay uncertain amount ineffective.

Tennant v Napier Smith's Trustees (1888) 15 R 671. Maintenance of canal.

Marshall's Trustee v Macneill & Co (1888) 15 R 762. Doubts about obligation to build being valid real burden.

Macrae v Mackenzie's Trustee (1891) 19 R 138. Obligation to build confirmed as valid real burden.

Charlton v Scott (1894) 22 R 109. Obligation to build road. Discussion of effects of failure to specify time limit for construction.

Marshall v Callander and Trossachs Hydropathic Co Ltd (1895) 22 R 954. Obligation to rebuild is an effective real burden.

Anderson v Valentine 1957 SLT 57. Obligation to build requires performance only once therefore doubts about validity as real burden

Secretary of State for Scotland v Portkill Estates 1957 SLT 209. Obligation to fence and enclose an area (with time limit).

Wells v New House Purchasers Ltd 1964 SLT (Sh Ct) 2. Obligation to maintain

Peter Walker & Son (Edinburgh) Ltd v Church of Scotland General Trustees 1967 SLT 297. Obligation to build does not imply obligation to maintain.

Gammell's Trustees v Land Commission 1970 SLT 254. Obligation to build with time limit effective burden, enforceable by singular successor.

David Watson Property Management v Woolwich Equitable Building Society 1992 SLT 430. Obligation to maintain, and obligation to pay. Enforceable against heritable creditor?

Negative burdens: some examples

Frame v Cameron (1864) 3 M 290. Prohibition on use of property for business purposes that might disturb neighbours, including erecting steam engines.

McNeill v Mackenzie (1870) 8 M 520. Prohibition on alterations to roof and chimneys not enforceable burden based on *de minimis* principle.

Ewing v Campbell (1877) 5 R 230. Prohibition on use of property other than dwellinghouse and prohibition on sale of alcohol.

Ewing v Hastie (1878) 5 R 439. Property to be used only as a dwellinghouse. Was use as girls' school a contravention?

Stewart v Bunten (1878) 5 R 1108. Prohibition on buildings above two storeys in height.

McEwan v Shaw Stewart (1880) 7 R 682. Prohibition on building above three storeys in height.

Earl of Zetland v Hislop (1882) 9 R (HL) 40. Prohibition on sale of alcohol or use as eating premises.

Calder v Merchant Co of Edinburgh (1886) 13 R 623. Prohibition on converting properties to shops and restrictions on height of building.

Walker & Dick v Park (1888) 15 R 477. Buildings to be used only as villas or cottages.

Hill v Millar (1900) 2 F 799. Prohibition on use of burdened property for shops; property only to be used for dwelling houses (not workmen's houses).

Graham v Shiels (1901) 8 SLT 368. Property to be used as a dwellinghouse and prohibition on conversion to shop or warehouse or trading place.

Thomson v Mackie (1903) 11 SLT 562. Buildings not to be used as shops, nor for any purpose that would be a nuisance.

J & F Forrest v Governors of George Watson's Hospital (1905) 8 F 341. Prohibition on building on vacant ground.

Braid Hills Hotel Co Ltd v Manuels 1909 SC 120. Prohibition on building other than ornamental greenhouse or summer-house on delineated area of ground.

Colquhoun's Curator Bonis v Glen's Trustees 1920 SC 737. Restriction on use to dwellinghouse. Was use of some rooms for nursery school a contravention?

Low v Scottish Amicable Building Society 1940 SLT 295. Restriction to use as a dwellinghouse. Was use of part of building as school contravention?

Fergusson v McCulloch 1953 SLT (Sh Ct) 113. Prohibition on use of ground for trade that might be deemed a nuisance. Covers sawmill?

Hunter v Fox 1963 SLT 314, 1964 SLT 201, HL. Prohibition on building, or planting trees or shrubs analysed as real burden by Court of Session and negative servitude by House of Lords.

Smith v Taylor 1972 SLT (Lands Tr) 34. Prohibition on sale of spirituous liquors.

Morris v Waverley 1973 SLT (Lands Tr) 6. Prohibition on use as shop, hotel, public house, or brothel.

Leney v Craig 1982 SLT (Lands Tr) 9. To use exclusively as dwellinghouse. Proposal to use as a hotel.

Mannofield Residents Property Co Ltd v Thomson 1983 SLT (Sh Ct) 71. Prohibition on activities that injure amenity of area or nuisance: does this prohibit chip shop?

Wimpey Homes Holdings Ltd v Macari (1985, unreported), reported in Paisley and Cusine *Unreported Property Cases from the Sheriff Courts* (2000), p 208. Prohibition on parking vehicles, on use of property for trade purposes: ice cream van parked, and produce (including cigarettes) stored on property.

Meriton Ltd v Winning 1995 SLT 76. Prohibition on running a business, or using property other than as private dwellinghouse. Would use as nursing home contravene burdens?

Anderson v Trotter 1999 SLT 442. Restriction to use as a private residence and no trade business or profession to be carried on. Use as children's nursery where planning permission granted. Contrary to burdens. Could Tribunal vary burden?

Burdens difficult to analyse

Co-operative Wholesale Society v Ushers Brewery 1975 SLT (Lands Tr) 9. Burdens requiring property to be used in a particular way, with related restrictions.

Lees v North East Fife District Council 1987 SLT 769. Part of property to be used for residential purposes, part to have swimming pool erected upon it. Would construction of car park contravene this? Burden relating to swimming pool seems to be affirmative, although analysis within case seems to suggest it is negative.

15.23 Change to pre-abolition law

Scott v Howard (1880) 8 R (HL) 59. Cannot create right of free admission to theatre as a real burden.

Glasgow School Board v Anderson Kirk Session 1901 1 SLT 59. Right of kirk session to use burdened property at time and for purposes that do not interfere with use as school.

Kirkintilloch Kirk Session v Kirkintilloch School Board 1911 SC 1127, 1911 2 SLT 146. Similar obligation to previous case.

B & C Group Management v Haren (4 December 1992, unreported). Obligation allowing use acceptable as burden.

15.25 Creation of real burdens

Tailors of Aberdeen v Coutts (1837) 2 Sh & Macl 609, (1840) 1 Robin 296. Sets out common law rules of constitution for real burdens generally restated in the paras on creation.

15.26 Praedial rule

Earl of Zetland v Hislop (1882) 9 R (HL) 40. Burden to be capable of benefiting property to be valid.

Aberdeen Varieties Ltd v James F Donald (Aberdeen Cinemas) Ltd 1939 SC 788. Distance between properties too far to be praedial.

Marsden v Craighelen Lawn Tennis and Squash Club 1999 GWD 37-1820. Restriction on use of tennis courts on Sunday. Is there praedial benefit?

15.31 Burdens cannot impose monopoly

Sheltered Housing Management Ltd v Aitken (1997, unreported), reported in Paisley and Cusine *Unreported Property Cases from the Sheriff Courts* (2000), p 225. Burden providing for appointment of manager in perpetuity.

15.32 Burdens in restraint of trade

Aberdeen Varieties Ltd v James F Donald (Aberdeen Cinemas) Ltd 1939 SC 788, 1940 SC (HL) 52. See text.

Co-operative Wholesale Society v Ushers Brewery 1975 SLT (Lands Tr) 9. See text.

Phillips v Lavery 1962 SLT (Sh Ct) 57. See text.

Giblin v Murdoch 1979 SLT (Sh Ct) 5. See text.

15.33 Burdens cannot be repugnant with ownership

Moir's Trustees v McEwan (1880) 7 R 1141. See text.

Grant v Heriot's Trust (1906) 8 F 647. See text.

15.37 Constitutive deed: pre-abolition law

Edinburgh Magistrates v Macfarlane (1857) 20 D 156. Feudal burdens created in charter of confirmation and not appearing on register.

Liddall v Duncan (1898) 25 R 1119. *Edinburgh Magistrates v Macfarlane* doubted. Burdens must be set out in full in register.

Jolly's Executrix v Viscount Stonehaven 1958 SC 635. Cannot create burdens in a conveyance of benefited property.

15.40 Voces signatae

Peter Walker & Son (Edinburgh) Ltd v Church of Scotland General Trustees 1967 SLT 297. Reference only to obligation binding named party means condition is not real.

15.42 Identification of burdened property

Anderson v Dickie 1914 SC 706. See text.

15.43 Setting out terms of burden in full

Liddall v Duncan (1898) 25 R 1119. Requirement to precisely set out terms of burden.

Anderson v Dickie 1914 SC 706. Where terms not precisely stated the burden is invalid.

Aberdeen Varieties Ltd v James F Donald (Aberdeen Cinemas) Ltd 1939 SC 788. See text.

Peter Walker & Son (Edinburgh) Ltd v Church of Scotland General Trustees 1967 SLT 297. Obligation to build does not include obligation to maintain.

David Watson Property Management v Woolwich Equitable Building Society 1992 SLT 430. Obligation to pay maintenance costs.

Heritage Fisheries Ltd v Duke of Roxburghe 2000 SLT 800. Reference to legislation in burden.

Sheltered Housing Management Ltd v Cairns 2002 Hous LR 126. See text.

15.45 Registration of constitutive deed

Liddall v Duncan (1898) 25 R 1119. Confirms requirement for registration of burden as essential precursor to validity.

15.53 Concurrent contractual liability

Kirkintilloch Kirk Session v Kirkintilloch School Board 1911 SC 1127, 1911 2 SLT 146. Obligation enforceable as contractual obligation if ineffective as burden.

Chapter 16   Title Conditions: Servitudes

16.1 Introduction

Patrick v Napier (1867) 5 M 683. Servitude a real right, not a personal right.

Cowan v Stewart (1872) 10 M 735. Whether obligation personal or real.

Allan v MacLachlan (1900) 2 F 699. Whether obligation to repair personal or real; no duty on servient owner to maintain.

Crichton v Turnbull 1946 SC 52. Servitude or right of property.

Taylor's Trustees v McGavigan (1896) 23 R 945. Prohibition on building to preserve light; servitude or burden.

16.2 Types of positive servitudes

Mendelssohn v The Wee Pub Co Ltd 1991 GWD 26-1518. Right to hang shop sign not one of known servitudes.

Neill v Scobbie 1993 GWD 13-887. Pipeline servitude.

Davidson v Wiseman 2001 GWD 9-317. Servitude of car parking?

Labinski Ltd v BP Oil Development Ltd 2002 GWD 1-46. Pipeline servitude.

16.3 Salient characteristics of servitudes

Hamilton v Elder 1968 SLT (Sh Ct) 53. Servitude cannot be created where same person owns both tenements.

Irvine Knitters v North Ayrshire Co-operative Society Ltd 1978 SC 109. Servitude is for benefit of dominant tenement only.

Hunter v Fox 1964 SC (HL) 95. Presumption for freedom.

Clark & Sons v Perth School Board (1898) 25 R 919. If ambiguous, least onerous construction is preferred.

Lanarkshire Water Board v Gilchrist 1973 SLT (Sh Ct) 58. Owner of dangerous bull may be interdicted from grazing it on land adjoining right of access.

Walker's Executrix v Carr 1973 SLT (Sh Ct) 77. Occasional access or regular daily use.

Fraser v Secretary of State for Scotland 1959 SLT (Notes) 36. Whether planting trees interference with right of pasturage.

Drury v McGarvie 1993 SC 95. Circumstances in which held that erection of unlocked gates by servient proprietor not interference with servitude of access.

Central Regional Council v Ferns 1979 SC 136. *Aquaeductus*; interference by overburdening by servient owner.

Baillie v Mackay 1994 GWD 25-1516. Road which had ceased to be public right of way held to be still subject to servitude rights of access.

MacKay v Lord Burton 1994 SLT (Lands Tr) 35. Servitude not a right capable of being held as separate interest by dominant proprietor who cannot therefore qualify as burdened proprietor.

Oliver v Cameron 1994 GWD 8-505. Only dominant owner has title to enforce servitude right.

16.5 Constitution of positive servitudes: express grant or express reservation

Cowan v Stewart (1872) 10 M 735. Agreement in missives.

North British Railway Co v Park Yard Co Ltd (1898) 25 R (HL) 47. Use of word 'servitude' unnecessary to expressly create servitude.

Campbell's Trustees v Glasgow Corporation (1902) 4 F 752. Unfeudalised grant not followed by possession.

Millar v McRobbie 1949 SC 1. Meaning and extent of express grant of access.

Stansfield v Findlay 1996 GWD 37-2170. Held that access route included verge. Access could be taken of route across verge at any one or more points.

Ross v Beck 1992 GWD 16-930. Original line of servitude constituted by express provision not affected by subsequent widening and other alterations to route.

Hermiston Securities Ltd v Kirkcaldy District Council 1994 GWD 39-2317. Agreement as to access by planning officer acting in that capacity did not bind council as owners.

Fearnan Partnership v Grindlay 1992 SC (HL) 38. See text.

Mackay v Burton 1994 SLT (Lands Tr) 35. Servitude not a right capable of being held as separate interest by dominant proprietor who cannot therefore qualify as burdened proprietor.

Brennan v Roberton's Executors 1997 GWD 1-32. There was nothing indefinite or uncertain in the undertaking as to servitude rights contracted for in missives, which were sufficient as a general obligation to render them enforceable. *Callander v Midlothian District Council* 1996 SCLR 955, involving a similar obligation, approved.

Callander v Midlothian District Council 1996 SCLR 955. In a contract for sale, purchasers of heritage were bound to permit owners and occupiers of adjoining land access over subjects of sale. Obligation in original missives was collateral and therefore not superseded, and language used was sufficient to determine intention.

Munro v Mclintock 1996 SLT (Sh Ct) 97. Dominant owner in servitude right of access sought interdict to prevent encroachment. Held that right having been precisely defined by express grant, it could not be altered, and decree in favour of the pursuer granted.

McEachen v Lister 1976 SLT (Sh Ct) 38. Express grant excludes alternative implied grant.

Balfour v Kinsey 1987 SLT 144. Possession is unnecessary if servitude enters titles of servient or dominant tenement.

Turner v Macmillan Douglas 1989 SLT 292. Question whether right of access stipulated for in missives was personal or servitude right.

Norcott v Sanderson 1990 SCLR 622. Right of access granted in favour of a named individual, and without reference to a dominant tenement, held not sufficient to constitute a servitude.

Robertson v Hossack 1995 SLT 291. Right of access granted in favour of named individual without reference to successors held not sufficient to constitute servitude.

Douglas v Crossflags (Motors) Ltd 1989 GWD 22-941. Servitude cannot be acquired by tenant in his own name.

Love-Lee v Cameron of Lochiel 1991 SCLR 61. Obligation on owner of land to maintain road giving access to that land cannot be read as conferring servitude right of access in respect of road.

Grant v Cameron 1991 GWD 6-328. Servitude of access 'for all purposes' held to include right to invite the public to use road.

Moss Bros Group plc v Scottish Mutual Assurance plc 2001 SC 779. Servitude does not require *voces signatae* for creation

16.6 Implied grant or implied reservation

Cochrane v Ewart (1860) 22 D 358. Implied grant of servitude of necessity for drainage.

Walton Brothers v Glasgow Magistrates (1876) 3 R 1130. Implied grant of servitude of necessity; access.

Fergusson v Campbell 1913 1 SLT 241. Implied reservation of servitude of necessity; aqueduct.

Shearer v Peddie (1899) 1 F 1201. Circumstances where right of access held not necessary for reasonable enjoyment.

Fraser v Cox 1938 SC 506. Circumstances where right of access held not to have been granted expressly or by implication.

Alexander v Butchart (1875) 3 R 156. No implied grant of servitude for shop sign.

Murray v Medley 1973 SLT (Sh Ct) 75. No implied reservation of servitude of necessity; water pipe.

Central Regional Council v Ferns 1979 SC 136. Grant of servitude of *aquaductus* created by statute, by implication.

Moffat v Milne 1993 GWD 8-572. On subdivision and sale of part, it does not necessarily follow that remainder is landlocked.

Midlothian District Council v McCulloch 1993 SCLR 152. Two properties separated by road. Owner of half the road held entitled to access over other half.

King v Brodt 1993 GWD 13-886. Circumstances where conveyance held to carry by implication right of access to disponee, formerly tenant.

Neill v Scobie 1993 GWD 13-887. For servitude by implication there must be presumption that granter intended it.

Harris v Wishart 1996 SLT 12. Question whether servitude right of access had been created.

Marshall v Duffy 2002 GWD 10-318. Servitude by implied grant.

16.7 Right of access to landlocked land

Bowers v Kennedy 2000 SC 555. See text.

Mackie v Donaldson (31 May 2000, unreported), Hamilton Sheriff Court. Landlocked plot with right of vehicular access implied if this in contemplation of parties at time of subdivision: see (2000) 5 SLPQ 432.

Inverness Seafield Co Ltd v Mackintosh 2001 SLT 118. Implied right of access to landlocked land contrasted with express right.

Hamilton v Mundell (20 November 2002, unreported), Dumfries Sheriff Court, discussed in Reid and Gretton *Conveyancing 2002* (2003), pp 6, 7 and 74. Discusses implications of *Bowers v Kennedy.*

16.9 Prescription

Scotland v Wallace 1964 SLT (Sh Ct) 9. Constitution of right of access by prescription.

Kerr v Brown 1939 SC 140. *Tantum praescriptum quantum possessum.*

Carstairs v Spence 1924 SC 380. *Tantum praescriptum quantum possessum.*

McLellan v Hunter 1987 GWD 21-803. Possession without title under Prescription and Limitation (Scotland) Act 1973, s 3.

Middletweed Ltd v Murray 1989 SLT 11. Discussion on constitution and extent of servitude right of access as accessory to right of salmon fishings.

Kennedy v MacDonald 1988 GWD 40-1653. Discussion on extent of right of access established by prescriptive possession; comments on incidental rights of parking, unloading etc.

Harris v Wishart 1996 SLT 12. See para 16.6 above.

Wilson v Ross 1993 GWD 31-2007. Claim to access by prescriptive use failed.

Lord Burton v Mackay 1995 SLT 507. See para 16.15 below.

Landward Securities (Edinburgh) Ltd v Inhouse (Edinburgh) Ltd 1996 GWD 16-962. Conveyance of heritable property 'but only so far as I have right thereto' held habile to acquisition by prescription.

Hogg v Campbell 1993 GWD 27-1712. Circumstances where servitude right of access held to have been abandoned.

Aberdeenshire County Council v Lord Glentanar 1999 SLT 1456. Servitude of vehicular access cannot be constituted by bicycling on an access route.

Davidson v Wiseman 2001 GWD 9-317. Insufficient possession to constitute servitude of car parking by prescription.

Hamilton v Mundell (20 November 2002, unreported), Dumfries Sheriff Court, discussed in Reid and Gretton *Conveyancing 2002* (2003), pp 6, 7 and 74. Discusses implications of *Bowers v Kennedy* 2000 SC 555.

16.10 Acquiescence

Macgregor v Balfour (1899) 2 F 345. Estate factor no implied authority to create servitude by express grant or acquiescence.

Robson v Chalmers Property Investment Co Ltd 1965 SLT 381. Laying of water pipes, known to servient owner.

More v Boyle 1967 SLT (Sh Ct) 38. Common water pipe.

16.11 Constitution of negative servitudes prior to 28 November 2004

Hunter v Fox 1964 SC (HL) 95. Constitution in disposition of servient tenement.

Cowan v Stewart (1872) 10 M 735. Constitution by agreement.

Inglis v Clark (1901) 4 F 288. Cannot be constituted by implication.

16.12 Enforcement or enjoyment of servitudes

Royal Exchange v Cotton 1912 SC 1151. Whether singular successor entitled to enforce.

Braid Hills Hotel Co Ltd v Manuels 1909 SC 120. Whether singular successor entitled to enforce.

Watson v Sinclair 1966 SLT (Sh Ct) 77. Communicating the right to tenant.

Keith v Texaco Ltd 1977 SLT (Lands Tr) 16. Communicating the right, increasing the burden.

Alba Homes Ltd v Duell 1993 SLT (Sh Ct) 49. Title to enforce after subdivision increasing the burden.

Oliver v Cameron 1994 GWD 8-505. Only benefited owner has title to enforce.

16.13 Interest to enforce

Royal Exchange Buildings, Glasgow, Proprietors v Cotton 1912 SC 1151. Presumption that benefited owner has interest to enforce.

16.14 Interpretation and exercise of servitudes

Hunter v Fox 1964 SC (HL) 95. Presumption for freedom.

Clark & Sons v Perth School Board (1898) 25 R 919. If ambiguous, least onerous construction is preferred.

Kerr v Brown 1939 SC 140. Increase in burden.

Smith v Saxton 1951 SLT 64. Does change of vehicles using servitude of access increase the burden?

McLean v Marwhirn Developments Ltd 1976 SLT (Notes) 47. Less severe principles of interpretation than for interpretation of real burdens.

Irvine Knitters Ltd v North Ayrshire Co-operative Society Ltd 1978 SC 109. See text.

Inverness Farmers' Dairy v Kinlochdamph Ltd 1989 GWD 25-1106. Right of access for purposes connected with boat house could be used for lorries carrying food to fish farm.

Alvis v Harrison 1991 SLT 64. Discussion of extent of use permitted and of right of dominant proprietor to repair servient tenement.

Alba Homes Ltd v Duell 1993 SLT (Sh Ct) 49. If dominant tenement subdivided, both parts can exercise servitude provided no increase in burden.

Stansfield v Findlay 1998 SLT 784. Does a servitude of access include access over the verges?

Wimpey Homes Holdings Ltd v Collins 1999 SLT (Sh Ct) 16. Servitude of access granted over route allows benefited owner to clear trees and hedges encroaching on the route (cf *Stansfield* above).

Axis West Developments Ltd v Chartwell 1999 SLT 1146. Interpretation of servitude and admissibility of extrinsic evidence in doing so.

Cloy v T M Adam & Sons 1999 GWD 19-908. Where exercise of a servitude would be dangerous the servitude ceases to be valid.

Aberdeenshire County Council v Lord Glentanar 1999 SLT 1456. A pedestrian right of way can be used by cyclists.

16.15 Public rights of way

Richardson v Cromarty Petroleum Co Ltd 1982 SLT 237. Quality of possession required to constitute public right of way.

Sutherland v Thomson (1876) 3 R 485. Erecting gate on public footpath.

Midlothian District Council v McKenzie 1985 SLT 36. Servient owner may not encroach unjustifiably on public right of way.

Love-Lee v Cameron of Lochiel 1991 SCLR 61. Sub-post office, part of a private house, held not to be public place in sense required for terminus of public right of way.

Cumbernauld & Kilsyth District Council v Dollar Land (Cumbernauld) Ltd 1993 SLT 1318. Cumbernauld Development Corporation constructed the new town with a public walkway through town centre. Defenders subsequently acquired new town and closed walkway to public at night. Held that nature of past use was not by mere tolerance but continuous and plain assertion of a public right of way.

Lauder v MacColl 1993 SCLR 753. Public right of way between two public places established by past use over long period.

Viewpoint Housing Association Ltd v Lothian Regional Council 1993 SLT 921. Road of a public character, used for less than prescriptive period, held not to have become public right of way.

Lord Burton v Mackay 1995 SLT 507. (Follow-up to *Mackay v Burton* 1994 SLT (Lands Tr) 35, noted above.) Mackay failed to establish ownership of *solum* of road. Lord Burton then sought to interdict him from taking access over that route. Held that, a public right of way having been established, proprietors along its route could continue to use it as access.

Renfrew District Council v Russell 1994 GWD 34-2032. Local authority obtained interdict against two persons who had attempted to deter public from exercising public right of way.

North East Fife District Council 2000 SCLR 413. Extent of possession required to constitute public right of way by prescription when use primarily 40–80 years before.

Chapter 17   Title Conditions: Enforcement

17.7 Constitutive deeds registered before 28 November 2004 creating express enforcement rights

Braid Hills Co Ltd v Manuels 1909 SC 120. Expressly created title to enforce.

Aberdeen Varieties Ltd v James F Donald (Aberdeen Cinemas) Ltd 1939 SC 788, 1940 SC (HL) 52. Expressly created title to enforce.

Macdonald v Douglas 1963 SLT 191. Expressly created third-party enforcement rights in feu.

Lawrence v Scott 1965 SC 403. Express creation of third-party enforcement rights where no such third-party rights would be implied.

Gorrie and Banks Ltd v Burgh of Musselburgh 1973 SC 33. Expressly created title to enforce.

Ness v Shannon 1978 SLT (Lands Tr) 13. Express creation of third-party enforcement rights.

17.10 Implied rights of enforcement of the disponer: law before 28 November 2004

J A Mactaggart & Co v Harrower (1906) 8 F 1101. Property retained by disponer implied to have title to enforce, and singular successors can therefore enforce.

Braid Hills Hotel Co Ltd v Manuels 1909 SC 120. No need to expressly assign title to enforce with conveyance of benefited property.

Botanic Gardens Picture House Ltd v Adamson 1924 SC 549. Where burdens are created as part of a common scheme then the property retained by the disponer does not have implied title to enforce.

Marsden v Craighelen Lawn Tennis and Squash Club 1999 GWD 37-1820. Decision wrongly doubts application of *Mactaggart v Harrower* where there is no express assignation of title to enforce in conveyance of benefited property.

17.15 Negative servitudes

Ogilvie v Donaldson (1678) Mor 14534. Servitude of light (*luminibus non officiendi*) does not create absolute prohibition on building.

Magistrates of Edinburgh v Brown (1833) 11 S 255. Servitude prohibiting building (*non aedificandi*) prohibits (in circumstances of case) construction of a shed.

Craig v Gould (1861) 24 D 20. Servitude prohibits building above a certain height.

Russell v Cowpar (1882) 9 R 660. Servitude of light does not encompass absolute prohibition on building.

17.23 Implied rights of enforcement for third parties (co-feuars or co-disponees) before 28 November 2004

Hislop v MacRitchie's Trustees (1881) 8 R (HL) 95. Circumstances in which co-feuars or co-disponees have implied rights of enforcement of real burdens. Generally relevant throughout following paragraphs.

Hislop type 1 cases (successive grants)

Botanic Gardens Picture House Ltd v Adamson 1924 SC 549. Similar burdens imposed on properties conveyed by successive grants.

Main v Doune 1972 SLT (Lands Tr) 14. Similar burdens and reference to common scheme imposed on properties conveyed by successive grants.

Hislop type 2 cases (single grant followed by subdivision of burdened property)

Low v Scottish Amicable Building Society 1940 SLT 295. Grant imposes burdens, then property subdivided.

Smith v Taylor 1972 SLT (Lands Tr) 34. Grant imposes burdens prior to subdivision of property.

Lees v North East Fife District Council 1987 SLT 769. Original imposition of burdens in disposition over area then subdivided.

17.26 Examination of the title of the burdened property

Notice of common scheme

McGibbin v Rankin (1871) 9 M 423. Notice given by developer of obligation to impose same burdens on other properties.

North British Railway Co v Moore (1891) 18 R 1021. While similar burdens on properties, lack of notice meant no third-party enforcement rights.

Johnston v The Walker Trustees (1897) 24 R 1061. See text.

Bannerman's Trustees v Howard & Wyndham (1902) 10 SLT 2. Observations on notice in title of burdened property and see text para 17.34.

Murray's Trustees v St Margaret's Convent Trustees (1906) 8 F 1109. A plan of larger area referred to for description of property not sufficient notice of common scheme of burdens.

Nicholson v Glasgow Blind Asylum 1911 SC 391. Notice of common scheme in title of burdened properties means implied enforcement rights regarding that property.

Wells v New House Purchasers Ltd 1964 SLT (Sh Ct) 2. Registration of deed of conditions over larger area deemed to give notice of common scheme.

Main v Lord Doune 1972 SLT (Lands Tr) 14. See text.

Nothing to negative common scheme

Thomson v Alley & Maclellan (1883) 10 R 433. Reserved right to vary burdens precludes possibility of implied third-party enforcement rights.

Walker & Dick v Park (1888) 15 R 477. Reserved right to superior to depart from common scheme precludes implied third-party enforcement rights.

Turner v Hamilton (1890) 17 R 494. Superior reserved power to vary terms in single grant envisaging subdivision of burdened property.

17.31 Same or similar burdens and common scheme

Botanic Gardens Picture House Ltd v Adamson 1924 SC 549. See text.

Lees v North East Fife District Council 1987 SLT 769. See text.

Other cases referred to in paras 17.24 and 17.26 above also discuss similarity of burdens.

17.33 The expression 'common scheme'

See references in para 17.31.

17.47 Which parties have title to enforce praedial real burdens?

Eagle Lodge Ltd v Keir & Cawder Estates Ltd 1964 SC 30. Only owner has title to enforce at common law, not non-owners such as tenants.

Smith v Taylor 1972 SLT (Lands Tr) 34. Heritable creditor has no title to enforce at common law.

17.51 Interest to enforce praedial real burdens

Magistrates of Edinburgh v Macfarlane (1857) 20 D 156. Where a burden is trivial there is no interest to enforce.

Maguire v Burges 1909 SC 1283. Nature of co-feuar's interest.

Scottish Co-operative Wholesale Society Ltd v Finnie 1937 SC 835. Where enforcement is between original contracting parties interest to enforce is presumed.

Aberdeen Varieties Ltd v James F Donald (Aberdeen Cinemas) Ltd 1939 SC 788. Distance between burdened and benefited properties relevant factor in determining interest to enforce.

Co-operative Wholesale Society v Ushers Brewery 1975 SLT (Lands Tr) 9. Proximity relevant factor in determining interest to enforce where burdens for commercial purposes.

See cases at para 15.32

17.56 Interpretation of burdens: the position prior to 28 November 2004

Frame v Cameron (1864) 3 M 290. See text.

Ewing v Campbells (1877) 5 R 230. See text.

Anderson v Dickie 1915 SC (HL) 79. Burden not expressly imposed.

Walker Trustees v Haldane (1902) 4 F 594. Restriction not expressly imposed.

Kemp v Largs Magistrates 1939 SC (HL) 6. Particular use not expressly prohibited.

Russell v Cowper (1882) 9 R 660. Building not expressly prohibited.

Cowan v Edinburgh Magistrates (1887) 14 R 682. Further buildings not expressly prohibited; vassal not restricted.

Carswell v Goldie 1967 SLT 339. Particular building not expressly prohibited.

Murray's Trustees v St Margaret's Convent Trustees 1907 SC (HL) 8. 'Unseemly building'.

Mannofield Residents Pty Co Ltd v Thomson 1983 SLT (Sh Ct) 71. Whether a prohibition against acts injurious to amenity too vague to be enforceable.

Lothian Regional Council v Rennie 1991 SC 212. Obligation to maintain the supply of water in a mill lade and to cleanse the remaining parts of the lade 'to the reasonable satisfaction' of the grantor held void from uncertainty.

Lawson v Hay 1989 GWD 24-1049. Requirement that dwellinghouse must be 'conventional' too vague for a real burden.

David Watson Property Management v Woolwich Equitable Building Society 1992 SLT 430. View expressed that an obligation of maintenance would not be enforceable if in the form of an obligation to pay an indefinite sum of money.

Dunedin Property Management Services Ltd v Glamis Property Ltd 1993 GWD 31-2006. Meaning of the term 'roof' in relation to a tenement comprising two single-storey shops and an adjacent tenement. Extrinsic evidence rejected.

Southwark Project Services Ltd v Granada Leisure Ltd 1993 GWD 2-126. The construction of a deed of conditions; effect of alleged omission of a comma.

Meriton Ltd v Winning 1995 SLT 76. Held that the word 'objectionable' was not so indefinite as to be incapable of enforcement.

Porter v Campbell's Trustees 1923 SC (HL) 94. Distinction between construction and use.

Mathieson v Allan's Trustees 1914 SC 464. Restrictions as to structure do not restrict subsequent change of use.

Hunter v Fox 1964 SC (HL) 95. Surplus words, if not ambiguous, treated as *pro non scripto*.

Arnold v Davidson Trust Ltd 1987 SCLR 213. Discussion on the powers of proprietors in applying the provisions of a deed of conditions.

Dumbarton District Council v McLaughlin 2000 Hous LR 16. See text.

Grampian Joint Police Board v Pearson 2001 SC 772. Benign approach to interpretation of burdens.

17.60 Identification of the burdened property

Anderson v Dickie 1915 SC (HL) 79. Failure to identify burdened property.

17.61 Subdivision of burdened property

See the cases on implied third-party rights of enforcement at para 17.24 above.

17.65 Liability of non-owners

Mathieson v Allan's Trustees 1914 SC 464. Interdict against landlord and tenant where negative burden contravened.

Colquhoun's Curator Bonis v Glen's Trustee 1920 SC 737. Interdict against landlord and tenant where negative burden contravened.

Eagle Lodge Ltd v Keir & Cawder Estates Ltd 1964 SC 30. See text.

Hampden Park Ltd v Dow 2002 SLT 95. Interdict for breach of burden at instance of superior against tenant in contravention of burden.

17.66 Liability in affirmative burdens

Hyslop v Shaw (1863) 1 M 535. Uninfeft proprietor liable for contravention of burden.

David Watson Property Management v Woolwich Equitable Building Society 1992 SC (HL) 21. Discussion of liability of heritable creditor in possession of burdened property where affirmative burden contravened.

17.68 Joint and several liability in affirmative burden

Marshall v Callander and Trossach Hydropathic Co Ltd (1895) 22 R 954. See text at para 17.69.

Rankine v Logie Den Land Co Ltd (1902) 4 F 1074. Follows *Marshall*.

Chapter 18   Title Conditions: Variation and Discharge

18.1 Introduction

McLennan v Warner & Co 1996 SLT 1349. Breach of obligation to give good and marketable title where title condition contravened without discharge.

18.4 Minutes of waiver

Campbell v Clydesdale Banking Co (1868) 6 M 943. Minute of waiver granted by co-feuar with third-party enforcement rights does not bind the superior.

Dalrymple v Herdman (1878) 5 R 847. Minute of waiver granted by superior does not bind feuars with third-party enforcement rights: see para 18.18.

Howard de Walden Estates Ltd v Bowmaker Ltd 1965 SC 163. See text.

McVey v Glasgow Corporation 1973 SLT (Lands Tr) 5. Benefited proprietor with interest to enforce can charge for minute of waiver.

Arnold v Davidson Trust Ltd 1987 SCLR 213. Minute of waiver granted by party with third-party enforcement rights does not bind other parties with third-party enforcement rights (see para 18.18).

18.9 Common law on minutes of waiver

McLennan v Warner & Co 1996 SLT 1349. Argued that minute of waiver can be granted by uninfeft proprietor.

18.30 Pre-sale undertakings regarding rights of pre-emption

Matheson v Tinney 1989 SLT 535. Where sale in contravention of right of pre-emption right can be exercised against purchaser.

Roebuck v Edmunds 1992 SLT 1055. Where sale in contravention of right of pre-emption the right of pre-emption can be exercised against the purchaser.

18.39 Implied consent: common law acquiescence

Muirhead v Glasgow Highland Society (1864) 2 M 420. Suggests singular successors bound by acquiescence of servitude, and that servitude extinguished only to extent of breach. See also text at para 18.39.

Campbell v Clydesdale Banking Co (1868) 6 M 943. Contravention throughout estate consented in by superior.

McGibbon v Rankin (1871) 9 R 423. Failure to object to application to dean of guild did not amount to acquiescence.

Stewart v Bunten (1878) 5 R 1108. Acquiescence only consents to the extent of the breach.

Ben Challum Ltd v Buchanan 1955 SC 348. Installation of petrol pumps in contravention of burdens was acquiesced in as a result of failure to object. Suggests singular successors bound by acquiescence of predecessor in title.

Gray v MacLeod 1979 SLT (Sh Ct) 17. Acquiescence and servitudes.

18.47 Loss of interest to enforce by material change of circumstances

Inglis v Boswall (1849) 6 Bell's App 427. Argued unsuccessfully that change of use of burdened property could prevent future challenge to a change of use where there was a negative servitude prohibiting building above a certain height.

Campbell v Clydesdale Banking Co (1868) 6 M 943. See text.

Gould v McCorquodale (1869) 8 M 165. Loss of interest to enforce and servitudes. The servitude survives but cannot be enforced.

Mactaggart & Co v Roemmele 1907 SC 1318. See text.

18.51 Non-use of a servitude

Campbell Douglas v Hozier (1878) 16 SLR 14. Case which suggests non-use for less than period of negative prescription could extinguish servitude, although decision on failure to constitute servitude.

Magistrates of Rutherglen v Bainbridge (1886) 13 R 745. Non-use for less than prescriptive period sufficient to extinguish servitude of access when accompanied with shutting up of route, and opening of new access route.

18.54 Registration of title and extinction of burdens

Brookfield Developments Ltd v Keeper of the Registers of Scotland 1989 SLT (Lands Tr) 105. Burdens on register that are not enforceable can be removed by rectification.

18.58 Negative prescription and servitudes

Brown v Carron & Co 1909 SC 452. Negative prescription and servitudes.

Walker's Executrix v Carr 1973 SLT (Sh Ct) 77. Non-use of servitude of access by vehicles for 20-year period can reduce servitude of access from vehicular to only pedestrian access.

18.62 Confusio and servitudes

Walton Bros v Magistrates of Glasgow (1876) 3 R 1130. Revival of servitude where burdened and benefited properties subdivided after previously coming into ownership of the same person.

18.64 Compulsory purchase

Wilson v Keeper of the Registers of Scotland (29 July 1998, unreported), Lands Tribunal. Effect of compulsory acquisition using schedule conveyance not compulsory purchase order on burdens.

18.66 Lands Tribunal

Conveyancing and Feudal Reform (Scotland) Act 1970: statutory jurisdiction of variation and discharge

George T Fraser v Aberdeen Harbour Board 1985 SC 127. Exclusion of assignees in lease not land obligation.

Macdonald, Applicant 1973 SLT (Lands Tr) 26. Right of pre-emption is land obligation but Lands Tribunal has no jurisdiction to vary same if imposed by statute. But see *Banff and Buchan District Council v Earl of Seafield's Estate* 1988 SLT (Lands Tr) 21, under s 1(3)(c) of the 1970 Act.

Ross and Cromarty District Council v Ullapool Property Co Ltd 1983 SLT (Lands Tr) 9. Tribunal may vary land obligation notwithstanding pending irritancy proceedings.

Fraser v Church of Scotland General Trustees 1986 SC 279. Discharge of real burdens by Lands Tribunal excluded possibility of subsequent irritancy by superior.

Watters v Motherwell District Council 1991 SLT (Lands Tr) 2. Date of creation of obligation is date of delivery of deed, not date of recording.

Mackay v Lord Burton 1994 SLT (Lands Tr) 35. Proprietor of dominant tenement in servitude is not burdened proprietor.

McCarthy & Stone (Developments) Ltd v Smith 1995 SLT (Lands Tr) 19. Where no implied third-party rights of enforcement created, adjacent proprietors are not benefited proprietors.

1970 Act: who may apply?

Walker v Strathclyde Regional Council 1990 SLT (Lands Tr) 17. Tribunal cannot vary landlord's title in application by secure tenant.

1970 Act, s 1(3)(a): circumstances justifying variation or discharge: 'by reason of' change in character of land

Bolton v Aberdeen Corporation 1972 SLT (Lands Tr) 26. Decline in trade is not.

Clarebrooke Holdings Ltd v Glentanar's Trustees 1975 SLT (Lands Tr) 8. Overgrown garden is not.

1970 Act, s 1(3)(a): change in character of neighbourhood

Manz v Butter's Trustees 1973 SLT (Lands Tr) 2. 'Neighbourhood'. Pitlochry, not merely its High Street.

Pickford v Young 1975 SLT (Lands Tr) 17. More restricted interpretation.

Stoddart v Glendinning 1993 SLT (Lands Tr) 12. Alterations to other properties in same street had not changed character of neighbourhood.

1970 Act, s 1(3)(a): other circumstances

Murrayfield Ice Rink Ltd v Scottish Rugby Union 1973 SC 21. Decline in skating as recreation etc.

James Miller & Partners Ltd v Hunt 1974 SLT (Lands Tr) 9. Drainage problems not amounting to.

Manz v Butter's Trustees 1973 SLT (Lands Tr) 2. Change in local habits in Pitlochry amounting to.

Owen v Mackenzie 1974 SLT (Lands Tr) 11. Change in social habits due to tourism etc amounting to.

Morris v Feuars of Waverley Park 1973 SLT (Lands Tr) 6. Disappearance of domestic staff amounting to.

Pickford v Young 1975 SLT (Lands Tr) 17. Change not sufficient to justify use of house as hotel.

Stoddart v Glendinning 1993 SLT (Lands Tr) 12. Alterations to other properties in same street had not changed character of neighbourhood.

1970 Act, s 1(3)(a): 'the obligation is or has become unreasonable or inappropriate'

Bolton v Aberdeen Corporation 1972 SLT (Lands Tr) 26. Reasonableness not related to profitability.

McArthur v Mahoney 1975 SLT (Lands Tr) 2. Tribunal's discretion to protect 'affected proprietor'.

United Auctions (Scotland) Ltd v British Railways Board 1991 SLT (Lands Tr) 71. Change of use from livestock auction mart to shopping development not unreasonable.

1970 Act, s 1(3)(b): 'the obligation is unduly burdensome'

Murrayfield Ice Rink Ltd v Scottish Rugby Union 1973 SC 21. Applies both to positive and negative obligations.

McQuiban v Eagle Star Insurance Co 1972 SLT (Lands Tr) 39. Circumstances in which restriction against assigning a lease, except as *unum quid*, unduly burdensome.

West Lothian Co-operative Society Ltd v Ashdale Land Property Co Ltd 1972 SLT (Lands Tr) 30. Circumstances in which obligation to maintain ruinous building, requiring pointless and expensive maintenance, unduly burdensome.

Nicolson v Campbell's Trustees 1981 SLT (Lands Tr) 10. Time-limit for reinstatement; application for extension of time under 1970 Act, s 1(3)(b) refused.

Miller Group Ltd v Gardner's Executors 1992 SLT (Lands Tr) 62. Inability to build flats not unduly burdensome compared with benefit of *status quo*.

Stoddart v Glendinning 1993 SLT (Lands Tr) 12. Alterations to other properties in same street had not changed character of neighbourhood.

Murray v Farquharson 1996 GWD 3-162. Application to make structural alterations granted; superior had previously given consent.

Cumbernauld Development Corporation v County Properties & Developments Ltd 1996 SLT 1106. Property purchased as ice rink, but that did not proceed; change to bingo hall permitted; compensation awarded.

1970 Act, s 1(3)(c): 'the obligation impedes some reasonable use'

Solway Cedar Ltd v Hendry 1972 SLT (Lands Tr) 42. Squeezing in one extra house in small development not reasonable use.

Main v Lord Doune 1972 SLT (Lands Tr) 14. Proposed use as nursery.

Devlin v Conn 1972 SLT (Lands Tr) 11. Circumstances justifying discharge of servitude of access.

Campbell v Edinburgh Corporation 1972 SLT (Lands Tr) 38. Subdivision into flats; application withdrawn after objection by superior.

Murrayfield Ice Rink Ltd v Scottish Rugby Union 1973 SC 21. Applicant must specify particular proposed use which land obligation impedes.

Gorrie & Banks Ltd v Musselburgh Town Council 1974 SLT (Lands Tr) 5. Planning permission not conclusive of reasonableness, but application granted.

Bachoo v George Wimpey & Co Ltd 1977 SLT (Lands Tr) 2. Grant of planning permission not conclusive of reasonableness; application refused.

Scott v Fulton 1982 SLT (Lands Tr) 18. Application for discharge of restriction on building in garden of subdivided house refused; refusal of planning permission indicating that proposed use is not reasonable.

Cameron v Stirling 1988 SLT (Lands Tr) 18. Observations on interrelationship between planning permission and Tribunal orders.

British Bakeries (Scotland) Ltd v Edinburgh District Council 1990 SLT (Lands Tr) 33. Grant of planning permission normally implies that proposed use is reasonable.

Tully v Armstrong 1990 SLT (Lands Tr) 42. Erection of house in garden ground not unreasonable.

Lees v North East Fife District Council 1989 SLT (Lands Tr) 30. Neighbouring proprietors held by Court of Session to have valid title to enforce land obligation very recently imposed on adjoining land, but Lands Tribunal nonetheless discharged it.

Macdonald v Stornoway Trust 1988 SC 299. Refusal to vary prohibition on sale of liquor in croft upheld as not impeding some reasonable use.

Banff and Buchan District Council v Earl of Seafield's Estate 1988 SLT (Lands Tr) 21. Observations on effect of right of pre-emption.

Spafford v Brydon 1991 SLT (Lands Tr) 49. Servitude right not discharged because still used.

British Steel plc v Kaye 1991 SLT (Lands Tr) 7. Antecedent breach ignored; courts to decide result if irritancy incurred following discharge by Tribunal.

Miller Group Ltd v Gardner's Executors 1992 SLT (Lands Tr) 62. See above.

Ramsay v Holmes 1992 SLT (Lands Tr) 53. Obligation to obtain consent can be waived or discharged; existence of obligation impeded proposed use; *British Bakeries*, above, not followed.

Murray v Farquharson 1996 GWD 3-162. See above.

Stoddart v Glendinning 1993 SLT (Lands Tr) 12. See above.

Harris v Douglass 1993 SLT (Lands Tr) 56. Alterations required superior's consent; superior sought compensation for giving consent; condition discharged; expenses against superior.

Irvine v John Dickie & Son Ltd 1996 GWD 3-163. Application for further access granted, subject to conditions.

1970 Act: variation or discharge

Crombie v George Heriot's Trust 1972 SLT (Lands Tr) 40. Restrictions on type of buildings and screening by trees.

Co-operative Wholesale Society v Ushers Brewery 1975 SLT (Lands Tr) 9. Limitation on use.

Brookfield Developments Ltd v Keeper of the Registers of Scotland 1989 SLT (Lands Tr) 105. Role of Keeper in registration of title.

1970 Act: procedure

Scott v Wilson 1993 SLT (Lands Tr) 52. Tribunal cannot consider only written submissions from objectors who did not appear at hearing.

Rowan Property Investments Ltd v Jack 1996 GWD 16-946. Tribunal decision to refuse application for a discharge of right of access upheld; observed that applicant might have been better to have raised ordinary court action because of uncertainty about title provisions.

18.78 Compensation

Conveyancing and Feudal Reform (Scotland) Act 1970: compensation

McVey v Glasgow Corporation 1973 SLT (Lands Tr) 15. Compensation claimed by superior refused under s 1(4)(i) of the 1970 Act.

Robertson v Church of Scotland General Trustees 1976 SLT (Lands Tr) 11. Compensation refused under s 1(4)(i).

Blythswood Friendly Society v Glasgow District Council 1979 SC (HL) 1. Compensation refused under s 1(4)(i).

Keith v Texaco Ltd 1977 SLT (Lands Tr) 16. Compensation refused under s 1(4)(i) and (ii) of the 1970 Act.

Sinclair v Gillon 1974 SLT (Lands Tr) 18. Application for change of use from dwellinghouse to coffee-house; compensation claimed by adjoining proprietor refused.

Co-operative Wholesale Society v Ushers Brewery 1975 SLT (Lands Tr) 9. Compensation granted under s 1(4)(i) of the 1970 Act for economic loss.

Smith v Taylor 1972 SC 258. Compensation granted under s 1(4)(i) for loss of amenity.

Gorrie & Banks Ltd v Musselburgh Town Council 1974 SLT (Lands Tr) 5. Compensation granted under s 1(4)(ii) of the 1970 Act.

Manz v Butter's Trustees 1973 SLT (Lands Tr) 2. 'Affected proprietor' has no claim.

Campbell v Edinburgh Corporation 1972 SLT (Lands Tr) 38. Expenses awarded against applicant on withdrawal of application.

McArthur v Mahoney 1975 SLT (Lands Tr) 2. Expenses awarded to successful objector.

Co-operative Wholesale Society v Ushers Brewery 1975 SLT (Lands Tr) 9. Compensation awarded but no expenses to either party.

Lees v North East Fife District Council 1989 SLT (Lands Tr) 30. Compensation refused.

United Auctions (Scotland) Ltd v British Railways Board 1991 SLT (Lands Tr) 71. Compensation refused.

Cumbernauld Development Corporation v County Properties & Developments Ltd 1996 SLT 1106. Appeal from decision of Lands Tribunal to award £206,000 refused.

Strathclyde Joint Police Board v The Elderslie Estates Ltd 2002 SLT (Lands Tr) 2. See text.

Chapter 19   Title Conditions: Feudal Real Burdens

19.3 Title to enforce

Nicholson v Glasgow Asylum for the Blind 1911 SC 391. See text.

19.4 Interest to enforce

Earl of Zetland v Hislop (1882) 9 R (HL) 40. Interest to enforce of superior is presumed.

Menzies v Caledonian Canal Commissioners (1900) 2 F 953. Is patrimonial interest enough?

Howard de Walden Estates Ltd v Bowmaker Ltd 1965 SC 163. Superior with bare superiority has interest to enforce.

19.13 Loss of interest to enforce

Campbell v Clydesdale Banking Co (1868) 6 M 943. See text.

19.14 Loss of interest to enforce as a result of bad faith

Eagle Lodge Ltd v Keir and Cawder Estates Ltd 1964 SC 30. Issue raised but undecided.

Howard de Walden Estates Ltd v Bowmaker Ltd 1965 SC 163. Proposal to charge for minute of waiver does not equal loss of interest to enforce through bad faith.

Harris v Douglas 1993 SLT (Lands Tr) 56. Superior bears cost of expenses of Lands Tribunal action to vary burden where only monetary interest in enforcement.

19.17 Consolidation extinguishing burdens

Calder v Merchant Co of Edinburgh (1886) 13 R 623. Decision suggesting consolidation extinguished third-party rights of enforcement of co-feuars.

Stevenson v Steel Co of Scotland Ltd (1899) 1 F (HL) 91. Consolidation does not extinguish third-party rights of enforcement of co-feuars.

Murray's Trustees v St Margaret's Convent Trustees (1906) 8 F 1109. Consolidation does not extinguish third-party rights of enforcement of co-feuars.

19.95 The cap on compensation

See cases on s 1(4)(ii) of the 1970 Act digested at para 18.78.

Chapter 20   Public Law Restrictions on Land Use

20.10 Development plans and development control

City of Edinburgh Council v Secretary of State for Scotland 1997 SCLR 1112. Status of the development plan in development control decisions.

20.12 Application for planning permission

Tesco Stores Ltd v Secretary of State for the Environment [1995] 1 WLR 759. Relationship between 'material considerations' and the subject matter of the planning application.

20.13 Determining an application

British Airports Authority v Secretary of State for Scotland 1979 SC 200. Scope of the power to impose conditions on a grant of planning permission.

20.14 Planning agreements

Good v Epping Forest District Council [1994] 1 WLR 376. The tests for planning agreements.

McIntosh v Aberdeenshire Council 1998 SCLR 435, 1999 SLT 93. Judicial review not generally available as regards planning agreements.

20.19 Human rights and planning

R (on the application of Holding & Barnes plc) v Secretary of State for the Environment, Transport and the Regions [2001] 2 WLR 1389. Compatibility of English planning procedures with Article 6 of the ECHR.

Country Properties Ltd v Scottish Ministers 2001 SLT 1125. Compatibility of Scottish planning procedures with Article 6 of the ECHR.

Chapter 21   Securities: General

21.4 The need for a principal obligation or debt

Albatown Ltd v Credential Group Ltd 2001 GWD 27-1102. Where principal obligation unenforceable, standard security becomes null. (Text 21.4)

Trotter v Trotter 2001 SLT (Sh Ct) 42. Standard security cannot be granted without a debt to secure. (Text 21.4)

21.8 Third-party security

Smith v Bank of Scotland 1997 SC (HL) 11. Lender has duty to act in good faith to wife acting as cautioner in connection with transaction being entered into by husband with her consent. She should be advised to obtain independent legal advice. (Text 21.8, 21.13 to 21.16)

21.11 The effect of the Consumer Credit Act 1974

Wilson v First County Trust (No 2) [2002] QB 74 rev'd [2003] 3 WLR 568. Whether s 127(3) of the Consumer Credit Act 1974 incompatible with the ECHR Article 1 protocol 1. (Text 21.11)

21.12 Creditors' duties to guarantors: introduction

Barclays Bank plc v O'Brien [1994] 1 AC 180. Creditor may be deemed to have notice that guarantor's consent is not free and informed where he knew that there was a close relationship between the debtor and guarantor but did not take steps to ensure that the consent was not vitiated. (Text 21.12)

21.13 Smith v Bank of Scotland

Hewit v Williamson 1998 SCLR 601. The rule in *Smith v Bank of Scotland* 1997 SC (HL) 11 only applies where a cautionary obligation genuinely exists, as opposed to where a third party has merely granted pure real security over their property.

21.14 The need for a vitiating factor

Braithwaite v Bank of Scotland 1999 SLT 25. There must be misrepresentation by the debtor to the cautioner or another vitiating factor for a cautioner to have a defence against a lender in terms of *Smith* (above). (Text 21.14)

Royal Bank of Scotland plc v Wilson 2001 SLT (Sh Ct) 2 aff'd 2003 SLT 910. Lender's duty to act in good faith to cautioners satisfied by them being given independent legal advice. (Text 21.14, 21.16)

Ahmed v Clydesdale Bank plc 2001 SLT 423. Lender's duty to act in good faith to cautioner satisfied by her being given independent legal advice. (Text 21.14)

Wright v Cotias Investments Inc 2001 SLT 353. (Text 21.14 to 21.15) Complex case, where guarantor a director and shareholder in the debtor company, but the company had been established at the instance of the guarantor's son.

21.16 What steps need to be taken?

Forsyth v Royal Bank of Scotland plc 2000 SLT 1295; 2000 SCLR 61. Lender's duty to act in good faith to a cautioner is satisfied where the same solicitors who are acting for the debtor give advice to the cautioner.

Broadway v Clydesdale Bank plc 2000 GWD 19-763. Lender under a duty to clarify whether cautioner has the benefit of independent legal advice.

Royal Bank of Scotland plc v Clark 2000 SLT (Sh Ct) 101; 2000 SCLR 193. Lender may assume that a cautioner who has been advised by a solicitor has given true and informed consent.

Broadway v Clydesdale Bank plc 2001 GWD 14-552. Proof before answer in the above mentioned case. Lender held to have reasonable grounds for believing that cautioner provided with independent legal advice.

Royal Bank of Scotland v Etridge (No 2) [2001] 4 All ER 449. Important English House of Lords case setting out the steps that a solicitor advising a cautioner must take where the cautioner could be unduly influenced by the debtor. (Text 21.16)

Clydesdale Bank plc v Black 2002 SLT 764; 2002 SCLR 857. The requirements placed upon solicitors by the House of Lords in *Etridge* (above) are not to be applied rigidly in Scotland. (Text 21.16)

21.17 Solicitors' duties to creditors

Bank of East Asia Ltd v Shepherd & Wedderburn WS 1995 SC 255. Solicitors may owe duty to lender to disclose information which could affect decision whether or not to lend. (Text 21.17)

The Mortgage Corporation v Mitchells Roberton 1997 SLT 1305. Claim made against two law firms for not following the lender's instructions. (Text 21.17)

Chapter 22   Standard Securities

22.1 Introduction

Pettit v Pettit [1970] AC 777. Comments from Lord Diplock on mortgages.

22.5 Style of deed

Bank of Scotland v Graham's Trustee 1992 SC 79. Debtors signed as debtors, but not as proprietors; rectification allowed. (Text 29.17)

Spowart v Wylie 1995 GWD 23-1257. Standard security in respect of sums set out in missives; held that obligation to pay was clear. (Text 22.5)

Bennett v Beneficial Bank plc 1995 SLT 1105. Description of whole tenement is not sufficient where security is over one flat.

Beneficial Bank plc v McConnachie 1996 SC 119. Postal address not a particular description. (Text 8.16, 8.21, 8.23)

Beneficial Bank plc v Wardle 1996 GWD 30-1825. Rectification of description in standard security which did not meet test as set out in *McConnachie*. (Text 8.16)

Royal Bank of Scotland v Marshall (5 June 1996, unreported), Glasgow Sheriff Court, reported in Paisley and Cusine *Unreported Property Cases from the Sheriff Courts* (2000), pp 445–477. Discussion of permitted level of deviation from statutory forms. (Text 22.5)

Hambros Bank Ltd v Lloyds Bank plc 1997 GWD 37-1915. Statement in standard security that 'all sums' are secured may be altered by unregistered document.

Norwich Union Life Insurance Society v Tanap Investments UK Ltd 1997 GWD 24-1183; 1997 GWD 32-1634. Action of declarator as to what loans were secured by a standard security.

Hambros Bank Ltd v Lloyds Bank plc (No 2) 1998 GWD 10-511. Proof in relation to the case reported at 1997 GWD 37-1915. Held, that prior correspondence did not alter the 'all sums' clause in the security.

Société General SA v Lloyds TSB Bank plc 1999 GWD 37-1822. Construction of standard security documentation as regards amount of debt.

Albatown Ltd v Credential Group Ltd 2001 GWD 27-1102. Whether standard security was Form A or B. (Text 21.4)

22.6 Statutory effect of security

Blackwood v The Other Creditors of Sir George Hamilton (1749) Mor 4898. Bad faith in relation to prior agreement to create another security not relevant. (Text 32.61)

Leslie v McIndoe's Trustees (1824) 3 S 48. Bad faith in relation to a prior agreement to create another security not relevant. (Text 32.61)

Trade Development Bank v Warriner & Mason 1980 SC 74. Creditor entitled to set aside unauthorised lease. Standard conditions; whether recording of standard security form B constituted notice of conditions in unrecorded minute of agreement; duty of enquiry. (Text 22.19, 24.21, 25.6, 32.55)

Trade Development Bank v David W Haig (Bellshill) Ltd; Trade Development Bank v Crittall Windows Ltd 1983 SLT 510. Standard conditions; heritable creditor not affected by personal obligations undertaken by debtor relating to security subjects. Effect of knowledge of prior personal right on subsequent real security. (Text 32.60)

David Watson Property Management v Woolwich Equitable Building Society 1992 SC (HL) 21. Heritable creditor in possession not liable for personal obligations entered into by debtor in relation to property. (Text 17.67, 22.50)

Bank of Scotland v T A Neilson & Co 1990 SC 284. Whether registration *de novo* validated standard security by company. (Text 22.6, 32.65)

Sanderson's Trustees v Ambion Scotland Ltd 1994 SLT 645. Assignation must follow statutory form, but need not be identical; assignation covers original and further advances, if these are covered by agreement.

Alliance and Leicester Building Society v Murray's Trustee 1994 SCLR 19. Warrant to cite purchaser granted prior to recording of disposition in his favour and standard security; held to be *acquirenda*. (Text 3.21)

Johnston v Robson 1995 SLT (Sh Ct) 26. House purchased in joint names of J and R; R contributed part of price in cash; balance obtained by loan in joint name; later, on division and sale, R sought to recover his cash contribution, based on recompense; proof before answer allowed.

Christie's Executor v Armstrong 1996 SLT 948. Endowment policy by H and W assigned in security; on death, proceeds paid to lender; executor sought to recover one half of proceeds from surviving W, based on recompense; proof before answer allowed.

Tamroui v Clydesdale Bank plc 1996 SCLR 732. T took lease from debtor under B's standard security, unaware of security; B obtained decree against debtor and sought to eject T; interim interdict granted.

MacNaught v MacNaught 1997 SLT (Sh Ct) 60, 1997 SCLR 151. Where a standard security provides that the property may not be transferred without the creditor's consent, a property transfer order in terms of the Family Law (Scotland) Act 1985, s 15(1), will require the creditor's consent.

Royal Bank of Scotland plc v Lamb's Trustee 1998 SCLR 923. Standard security granted by undischarged bankrupt held voidable at the instance of the trustee in sequestration who had not consented.

Cameron v Abbey National plc 1999 Hous LR 19. Whether heritable creditor can evict tenant with assured tenancy.

Watson v Bogue (No 1) 2000 SLT (Sh Ct) 125. In Form B security, express assignation of secured debt required. (Text 22.58)

22.8　Standard conditions

Clydesdale Bank plc v Mowbray 1998 GWD 34-1757. Action to recover expenses in terms of standard condition 12 competent in Court of Session.

22.10　Ranking of loans inter se

Sowman v Glasgow District Council 1984 SC 91. Ranking; statutory burden in favour of local authority.

Skipton Building Society v Wain 1986 SLT 96. Where there are two or more heritable securities on same property, creditor who first obtains decree under Conveyancing and Feudal Reform (Scotland) Act 1970, s 24, is entitled to retain possession to exclusion of other(s). (Text 22.50)

Alloa Brewery Co Ltd v Investors in Industry plc 1992 SLT 21. Meaning of 'charge' in ranking agreement. (Text 22.16, 34.37)

22.16　Ranking clauses

AIB Finance Ltd v Bank of Scotland 1993 SC 538. (Text 23.5, 34.7)

Scotlife Home Loans (No 2) v Muir 1994 SCLR 791. Debtor granted two securities, first was recorded second; held that intended first creditor had postponed ranking.

Griffith and Powdrill (Receivers of Lewis Holdings Ltd), Petitioners 1998 GWD 40-2037. Ranking of floating charges and standard security. (Text 34.9)

Bank of Ireland v Bass Brewers Ltd 2000 GWD 28-1077. Rectification action in relation to documents governing ranking of floating charges and standard security. (Text 34.7)

22.21 Calling-up notice

Bank of Scotland v Flett 1995 SCLR 591. Request by debtor for statement of amount due must comply with s 19(9); in any event, no prejudice to the debtor.

Clydesdale Bank plc v Davidson 1996 SLT 437. Calling-up notice served, but not obtempered; action of removal raised, but no notice requiring debtor to vacate; creditors not required to serve such a notice. (Text 25.9)

J Sykes & Sons (Fish Merchants) Ltd v Grieve 2002 SLT (Sh Ct) 15. Action for declarator of creditor's rights following service of calling-up notice. Defenders denied that any debt existed.

22.22 Form of notice

Clydesdale Bank plc v R Findlay & Co 1989 SLT (Sh Ct) 77. Calling up notice held not to be invalidated by statement in notice under s 19(9), to which debtor replied calling for amendment. (Text 22.22)

Royal Bank of Scotland plc v Shanks 1996 GWD 36-2124. No need for final determination of amount due when calling-up notice served.

Gallagher v Ferns 1998 SLT (Sh Ct) 79. Where property held by trustees, calling-up notice must refer expressly to this.

22.23 Service of the notice

Household Mortgage Corporation plc v Diggory (21 March 1997, unreported), Peterhead Sheriff Court, reported in Paisley and Cusine *Unreported Property Cases from the Sheriff Courts* (2000), pp 455–462. Notice sent by recorded delivery and accepted by neighbour is effectively served. (Text 22.23)

22.26 Default notice

Bank of Scotland v Fernand 1997 SLT (Sh Ct) 78; 1997 HousLR 65. Default notice procedure does of itself give right to enter into possession.

Bank of Scotland v Millward 1998 SCLR 577. Default notice procedure may be used as an alternative to the calling-up notice procedure where creditor wishes the entire debt repaid. (Text 22.26)

22.27 Objection by debtor

Wilson v Target Holdings 1995 GWD 31-1559. Calling-up notice may be challenged by action of reduction. (Text 22.27)

Gardiner v Jacques Vert plc 2001 GWD 38-1433 rev'd 2002 SLT 928. Petition for suspension of calling-up notice. (Text 22.27)

22.29 Application to the court

Halifax Building Society v Gupta 1994 SC 13. If sheriff is satisfied about creditor's entitlement to remedy, he has no discretion to refuse. (Text 22.32, 22.33)

22.30 Procedure: petition under Conveyancing and Feudal Reform (Scotland) Act 1970, s 24

Bradford and Bingley Building Society v Roddy 1987 SLT (Sh Ct) 109. Discussion on procedure on application by heritable creditor under Conveyancing and Feudal Reform (Scotland) Act 1970, s 24.

Hill Samuel & Co Ltd v Haas 1989 SLT (Sh Ct) 68. Discussion on procedure in petition under 1970 Act, s 24.

Clydesdale Bank plc v R Findlay & Co 1989 SLT (Sh Ct) 77. Discussion on correct procedure under 1970 Act, s 24, and interaction of ss 20–24 and standard condition 9. (Text 22.22)

Cedar Holdings Ltd v Iyyaz 1989 SLT (Sh Ct) 71. Discussion on procedure under 1970 Act, s24; not followed in *Clydesdale Bank plc* above.

Clydesdale Bank plc v Mowbray 1991 GWD 28-1686. Interdict of debtor trying to prevent sale.

Clydesdale Bank plc v Hyland 2002 GWD 37-1229. Where ejection is sought, ordinary action must be raised.

22.31 The creditor's powers on default

Commercial and General Acceptance Ltd v Nixon [1983] 152 CLR. Australian case on duty of creditor to obtain best price. (Text 22.43)

Armstrong, Petitioner 1988 SLT 255. Duty of creditor to exercise his power of sale and other powers *civiliter*. (Text 22.32)

Associated Displays v Turnbeam Ltd 1988 SCLR 220. Circumstances in which debtor held not entitled to prevent creditor exercising power of sale by interdict, on grounds that best price not being obtained. (Text 22.43)

Bank of Credit v Thompson 1987 GWD 10-341. Discussion on obtaining best price on exercise of power of sale. (Text 22.43)

UDT Ltd v Site Preparations Ltd (No 1) 1978 SLT (Sh Ct) 14. Default; application to court.

Dick v Clydesdale Bank plc 1991 SC 365. Duties of creditor in obtaining best price. (Text 22.43)

Dunlop & Son's Judicial Factor v Armstrong 1994 SLT 199. Creditor's right to sell and debtor's right to redeem can co-exist; if debtor tenders amount which is refused, that stops interest running on debt.

Halifax Building Society v Gupta 1994 SC 13. Creditor has discretion about which remedy to choose, but sheriff has no discretion to refuse. (Text 22.32, 22.33)

Gordaviran v Clydesdale Bank plc 1994 SCLR 248. Creditor not obliged to demonstrate to debtor that terms of Conveyancing and Feudal Reform (Scotland) Act 1970 complied with. (Text 22.43)

Thomson v Yorkshire Building Society 1994 SCLR 1014. Held incompetent for debtor to try to prevent creditor from exercising power of ejection. (Text 22.43)

Harris v Abbey National plc 1997 SCLR 359. Spuilzie action against creditor in respect of moveables in the property. Held, spuilzie not relevant as creditor in the position of a gratuitous depositary.

Gemmell v Bank of Scotland 1998 SCLR 144. Spuilzie action against creditor failed because bank had not dispossessed the debtor of the relevant moveables unlawfully.

Bissett v Standard Property Investment plc 1999 GWD 26-1253. Duty of creditor in obtaining best price, with particular comments on use of professional agents. (Text 22.43)

Grantly Developments v Clydesdale Bank plc 2000 GWD 6-213. Interim interdict sought against enforcement of security on ground of alleged breach of contract by the creditors. This was refused because no *prima facie* case had been made out.

Davidson v Clydesdale Bank plc 2002 SLT 1088. Duty of creditor in obtaining best price. (Text 22.43)

Clydesdale Bank plc v McCaw 2002 GWD 18-603. Enforcement of security in relation to debtor who had been sequestrated.

Newport Farm Ltd v Damesh Holdings Ltd [2003] UKPC 54. Privy Council appeal from New Zealand on creditor's duty to obtain the best price. (Text 22.43)

22.37 Mortgage Rights (Scotland) Act 2001: determination of the application

Halifax Building Society v Clark [1973] Ch 307. English case involving the counterpart legislation protecting debtors, which exposed a problem with the drafting of the relevant statute. (Text 22.37)

Abbey National v Briggs (20 June 2002, unreported), Glasgow Sheriff Court: see www.gov-anlc.com/abbeynational_v_briggs. Relevance of availability of other accommodation in relation to an application under the Mortgage Rights (Scotland) Act 2001. (Text 22.37)

22.41 Sale

Dunlop & Son's Judicial Factor v Armstrong 1995 SLT 645. Judicial factor is officer of court to which he has given undertaking protecting the interests of heritable creditor; so heritable creditor not entitled to interdict proposed sale by JF.

22.45 Clearing the record

Halifax Building Society v Smith 1985 SLT (Sh Ct) 25. Sale by heritable creditor; debtor inhibited; effect of inhibition on rights of unsecured creditors to surplus on sale. (Text 22.47)

Newcastle Building Society v White 1987 SLT (Sh Ct) 81. Inhibition registered against debtor after recording standard security does not prevent selling creditor, on default, from providing clear search. (Text 32.33)

Abbey National Building Society v Barclays Bank plc 1990 SCLR 639. Sale by heritable creditor; effect on free proceeds of inhibitions and arrestments. (Text 22.47)

Alliance and Leicester Building Society v Hecht 1991 SCLR 562. Inhibition is not a 'security' for the purposes of Conveyancing and Feudal Reform (Scotland) Act 1970, s 27(1). (Text 22.47)

22.46 Application of proceeds of sale

Bass Brewers Ltd v Humberclyde Finance Group Ltd 1996 GWD 19-1076. Challenge of various deductions made by prior-ranking creditor.

22.49 Entering into possession

Northern Rock Building Society v Wood 1990 SLT (Sh Ct) 109. Heritable creditor in possession not liable for community charge. (Text 22.50)

Skipton Building Society v Wain 1986 SLT 96. Creditor holding earlier of two competing decrees entitled to possession. (Text 22.50)

David Watson Property Management Ltd v Woolwich Equitable Building Society 1992 SC (HL) 21. Real conditions about repairs transmit against creditor in possession; but obligation to pay particular amount is personal to debtor and does not transmit against creditor. (Text 17.67, 22.50)

Clydesdale Bank plc v Davidson 1996 SLT 437: see 22.21.

Halifax Building Society v Gupta 1994 SC 13: see 22.29.

Bank of Scotland v Guardian Royal Exchange plc 1995 SLT 763. Where creditor's interest is endorsed on insurance policy, creditor has separate right thereunder.

Bass Brewers Ltd v Humberclyde Finance Group Ltd 1996 GWD 19-1076. Discussion of computing entitlements of creditors in ranking agreement.

Holt Leisure Parks Ltd v Scottish and Newcastle Breweries 1996 GWD 22-1284. Heritable creditor who has not entered into possession of lease has no liability thereunder.

Ascot Inns Ltd (In Receivership) v Braidwood Estates Ltd 1995 SCLR 390. If creditor does not enter into possession, no entitlement to rents.

UCB Bank plc v Hire Foulis Ltd 1999 SC 250; 1999 SLT 950; 1999 SCLR 35. Liquidator does not have to account to creditor for the rents until creditor enforces his right to enter into possession. (Text 22.49)

Abbey National plc v Arthur 2000 SLT 103. Unsuccessful attempt by sequestrated debtors to interdict the creditor from entering into possession.

22.54 Transmission

Sanderson's Trustees v Ambion Scotland Ltd 1994 SLT 645: see 22.6.

22.61 Discharge

Cameron v Williamson (1895) 22 R 293. Security may be extinguished by payment or discharge of debt. (Text 22.66)

Security Pacific Finance Ltd v Graham 1995 GWD 29-1545. Extrinsic evidence admissible to prove that discharge granted by mistake.

22.63 Redemption

Dunlop & Son's Judicial Factor v Armstrong 1995 SLT 645. Debtor has unfettered right to redeem, no matter whether creditor proceeding to sale; comments on calling up: see 22.41.

Chapter 23   Floating Charges

23.3 Effect of the charge

Forth and Clyde Construction Co Ltd v Trinity Timber and Plywood Co Ltd 1984 SC 1. Nature of fixed security on appointment of receiver.

Scottish and Newcastle Breweries v Liquidator of Rathburne Hotel Co Ltd 1970 SC 215. Extent of security; stated limit in back letter.

National Commercial Bank Ltd v Liquidators of Telford, Grier, Mackay & Co Ltd 1969 SC 181. Extent of security; interest due from date of liquidation.

Libertas-Kommerz v Johnson 1977 SC 191. Whether bond and floating charge assignable by creditor.

Hill Samuel & Co Ltd v Laing 1989 SC 301. Discussion on personal liability of receiver for debt incurred on behalf of company.

Shanks v Central Regional Council 1988 SC 14. Appointment of receiver does not necessarily exclude powers of directors of company to take action in certain circumstances.

23.4 Property affected

Sharp v Thomson 1995 SC 455, 1995 SLT 837, 1995 SCLR 683 rev'd 1997 SC(HL) 66, 1997 SLT 636, 1997 SCLR 328. Company which had granted a floating charge sold the property; before recording of disposition receiver was appointed; held in Inner House that property still subject to charge; reversed on appeal to House of Lords. See comment at 4.4 above. (Text 4.4, 10.23, 33.51, 34.7, 34.12, 34.15, 34.18)

23.5 Registration

Prior, Petitioner 1989 SLT 840. Petition to extend time for registration refused. (Text 23.9)

23.6 Ranking

Cumbernauld Development Corporation v Mustone Ltd 1983 SLT (Sh Ct) 55. Incorrect decision that floating charge prevails over landlord's hypothec.

AIB Finance Ltd v Bank of Scotland 1993 SC 538. A discussion of 'creation' in competition between floating charge and standard security: see also 22.16. (Text 34.7 and 34.9)

Ascot Inns Ltd (In Receivership) v Scottish and Newcastle Breweries plc 1994 SLT 1140. Certain subjects held to have been released from floating charge.

Grampian Regional Council v Drill Stem (Inspection Services) Ltd 1994 SCLR 36. Landlord's hypothec has priority over rights of receiver.

Griffith and Powdrill (Receivers of Lewis Lloyd Holdings) Ltd, Petitioners 1998 GWD 40-2037. Floating charge with negative pledge clause ranks above subsequent standard securities notwithstanding the consent of the charge holder to the grant of such securities.

Bank of Ireland v Bass Brewers Ltd 2000 GWD 28-1077. Ranking of floating charges and standard security. Letter of consent by floating charge holder to granting of standard security need not be registered in Charges Register to be effective. (Text 23.6, 34.7, 34.9)

23.9 Petition for rectification

Allan, Black & McCaskie, Petitioners 1987 GWD 19-709. Application by a company to extend 21-day period for registration of floating charge granted, subject to certain provisos.

Chapter 24   Leases: General

24.1 The creation of a lease

Millar v McRobbie 1949 SC 1. Possession by tenant in advance of date of entry does not bind a singular successor of landlord under Leases Act 1449. (Text 24.4)

Brador Properties Ltd v British Telecommunications plc 1992 SC 12. Description of a lease. (Text 25.83)

Goldston v Young (1868) 7 M 188. Lease perfected by *rei interventus*.

Ferryhill Property Investment Ltd v Technical Video Productions 1992 SCLR 282. Lease perfected by *rei interventus*.

Gray v Edinburgh University 1962 SC 157. The four cardinal elements in a lease are essential to bind singular successors under 1449 Act.

Kildrummy (Jersey) Ltd v Inland Revenue Commissioners 1991 SC 1. Lease by proprietor to company preceded by deed of trust by company which declared that it would hold subjects in trust for proprietor; lease a nullity. (Text 10.19, 12.7, 26.12)

Westend Business Centre Ltd v The Magregor Neil Partnership 1998 GWD 35-1818. Verbal agreement reached between tenant and sub-tenant for two-year lease. Sub-tenant took possession but left the tenancy two months later. Landlord sued for recovery of 10 months unpaid rent but court found in favour of the tenant and this was upheld on appeal.

Dougall v Lawrie 1999 SCLR 624. Agricultural lease terminated by notice following the sequestration of the tenant. Tenant argued that a new lease was created by his continued possession but decree of ejection was granted.

Ali v Khosla 2001 SCLR 1072. Existence of a lease. Verbal agreement to use certain land. Inconsistent occupation of land and payments made. Held no lease.

Gordon (A) Ritchie & Co v Ritchie 2001 GWD 36-1394. Constitution of lease. Dispute as to terms of verbal lease.

24.2 Lease as a real right

Formal requirements

Morrison Low v Paterson 1985 SC (HL) 49. Discussion on necessary requirements to establish a lease.

Buchanan v Harris & Sheldon (1900) 2 F 935. Effect of possession following on improbative missives of let.

Shetland Islands Council v British Petroleum Ltd 1989 SCLR 48. Whether possession by the tenant without specific agreement as to rent was sufficient to create a lease.

Trade Development Bank v David W Haig (Bellshill) Ltd; Trade Development Bank v Crittall Windows Ltd 1983 SLT 510. Effect of registration. (Text 32.60)

Andert Ltd v J & J Johnston 1987 SLT 268. Question whether, in the circumstances, the subjects of lease were sufficiently described.

Mann v Houston 1957 SLT 89. Lease must specify continuing rent to bind singular successors under 1449 Act.

Johnson v Cullen (1676) Mor 15231. Tenant must take possession to qualify for protection under Leases Act 1449.

British Petroleum Oil Ltd v Caledonian Heritable Estates Ltd 1990 SLT 114. Discussion on documentation required validly to vary formal lease.

Thomson v Thomas Muir (Waste Management) Ltd 1995 SLT 404. Implication of lease term.

Clydesdale Bank plc v Davidson 1998 SLT 522. A lease granted by *pro indiviso* proprietors in favour of one of their number is personally binding but will not transmit against nor bind singular successors as Landlords.

Richmond Securities Ltd v Weatherhead UK Ltd 1998 GWD 1-45. Proof allowed to determine whether notice to terminate the lease had been duly served by the tenants upon their landlord or not.

Taylor v Brunton 1998 SLT (Sh Ct) 72. A personal agreement, in this case creating occupancy rights, binds universal successors unless expressly excluded and accordingly in this case the heir succeeding to the property was held bound.

The need for consensus

Andert Ltd v J & J Johnston 1987 SLT 268. Necessity for *consensus in idem*.

Dickson Cameras (Glasgow) Ltd v Scotfilm Laboratories Ltd 1987 GWD 31-1152. Need for consensus.

McKenzie & Sons v Sutherland District Council 1987 GWD 16-611. Need for consensus – method of determining rent not precisely stated.

Smyth v Caledonian Racing (1984) Ltd 1987 GWD 16-612. Need for consensus – miscalculation in method of determining rent.

Pickard v Ritchie 1986 SLT 466. Need for consensus – whether lease constituted by *rei interventus*. Land originally leased to an individual but later farmed by partnership in succession. Rent accepted by landlord.

Dickson v MacGregor 1992 SLT (Land Ct) 83. Lease of farm to partnership, where landlord was the limited partner, held not to be illegal *per se*.

Pro indiviso proprietors

Bell's Executors v Inland Revenue Commissioners 1986 SC 252. Lease by several *pro indiviso* proprietors to one of their own number held to be competent and valid under 1449 Act in the circumstances; but with a caveat by the Lord President and Lord Grieve.

Pinkerton v Pinkerton 1986 SLT 672. Held, *inter alia*, that it was consistent with the definition of a lease that the landlord might also be one of a group of tenants in a joint tenancy. (Text 26.12)

Dickson v MacGregor 1992 SLT (Land Ct) 83. See above.

Clydesdale Bank plc v Davidson 1996 SLT 437. *Pro indiviso* proprietors granting lease of subjects to one of their number held to be a nullity. (Text 25.9, 26.12)

24.3 Assignability by tenant

Elliot v Duke of Buccleuch (1747) Mor 10329. Assignability of lease of exceptional duration.

Lousada & Co Ltd v J E Lesser (Properties) Ltd 1990 SC 178. Where lease requires landlord's consent to assignation, that consent must be clearly given. (Text 25.82)

Continvest Ltd v Dean Property Partnership 1993 GWD 40-2675. Reasonableness of landlord's refusal of consent. (Text 25.82)

Sears Properties Netherelands BV v Coal Pension Properties Ltd 2001 SLT 761. Whether landlord's consent required to assignation of previously approved sub-lease.

Scottish Ministers v Trustees of the Drummond Trust 2001 SLT 665. *Delectus personae*. Whether tenant's right under lease can be assigned.

24.4 Transmission

Donald Storrie (Estate Agency) Ltd, Petitioners 1987 GWD 20-774. Clause in assignation of lease restricting user by assignee held to be truly a provision in restraint of trade.

Bisset v Aberdeen Magistrates (1898) 1 F 87. Real and personal conditions; enforceability against singular successor of landlord. (Text 24.22)

Davidson v Zani 1992 SCLR 1001. Option to purchase; enforceable against singular successor of landlord; personal bar. (Text 24.22)

Waydale Ltd v DHL Holdings (UK) Ltd 1996 SCLR 391. Transmissibility of guarantee to the benefit of singular successor of landlord. (Text 25.18)

Kildrummy (Jersey) Ltd v Calder 1996 SCLR 727. Interposed lease granted after widow of agricultural tenant had agreed to vacate. Widow held not bound by agreement. (Text 26.5)

24.5 Rent

Wirral Borough Council v Currys Group plc 1997 SCLR 805 and 1998 SLT 463. Liquidate penalty clause in lease for late payment of rent. Held such clauses would only be upheld to the amount of the actual loss sustained by the landlord.

MacDonald's Trustees v Cunningham 1997 SCLR 986. A landlord sought to irritate a lease and the action was defended on the ground that the landlord had accepted rent from an associated company of the tenant after serving the notice of irritancy. This defence failed.

24.6 Possession

Jalota v Salvation Army Trustee Co 1994 GWD 12-770. Renewal of lease could cause hardship to landlord.

Dollar Land (Cumbernauld) Ltd v CIN Properties Ltd 1992 SLT 211 and 669 (HL). Highlights dangers which may rise from interposed leases. (Text 24.6, 24.20)

24.7 Registration

Roger v Crawfords (1867) 6 M 24. Registration not the only method of creating real right; but see now Land Registration (Scotland) Act 1979 for leases in operational areas. (Text 24.8)

Palmer's Trustees v Brown 1989 SLT 128. Lease of shootings, if registered under Registration of Leases (Scotland) Act 1857, binds singular successors. (Text 8.13, 24.8)

24.19 Interposed leases

Dollar Land (Cumbernauld) Ltd v CIN Properties Ltd 1992 SLT 211 and 669. Highlights dangers which may arise from interposed leases. (Text 24.6, 24.19)

Kildrummy (Jersey) Ltd v Calder 1994 SLT 888. See s 17 of Land Tenure Reform (Scotland) Act 1974 and para 24.1 above. Notwithstanding decision in *Kildrummy (Jersey) Ltd v Inland Revenue Commissioners* 1991 SC 1, Kildrummy Ltd ostensibly as landlords, served notice on a subtenant in possession of part of a farm, which was held invalid. (Text 26.5)

24.21 Examination of the landlord's title

Trade Development Bank Ltd v Warriner & Mason (Scotland) Ltd. Nature of obligation on tenant's agent to examine title of landlord. (Text 25.6, 32.55)

Cumming v Stewart 1928 SC 296. Need for obtaining consent of existing heritable creditor to granting of lease.

Armia Ltd v Daejan Developments Ltd 1979 SC (HL) 56. Examination of landlord's title. (Text 28.32, 28.57)

Hand v Hall (1877) 2 Ex D 355. Stamp duty on lease.

24.22 Real and personal conditions

McCall's Entertainments (Ayr) Ltd v South Ayrshire Council (No 1) 1998 SLT 1403. Tenants invoked an option to purchase. Following the exercise of the option, the landlord terminated the lease. The option was inoperable on termination of the lease. Held that the landlord's obligation to sell survived termination.

Seabreeze Properties Ltd v Bio-medical Systems Ltd 1998 SLT 319. Lease contained three options of which the tenant sought to exercise the first. Negotiations broke down and the lease continued on tacit relocation. Subsequently the tenant then removed which the landlord claimed to represent an exercise of the third option. The landlord's claim was rejected because (1) the earlier ineffectual exercise of the first option cancelled out the others and (2) in any event all the options were clearly exercisable only during the original term of the lease, not during the extension.

Richmond Securities Ltd v Weatherhead UK Ltd 1998 GWD 1-45. Proof before answer allowed to establish whether tenants had effectively notified their landlord that they were exercising their option to terminate.

Optical Express (Gyle) Ltd v Marks & Spencer plc 2000 SLT 644. Clause in a back letter granted by the landlord's predecessor in title was not deemed to be part of the lease and so could not bind the landlord. (Text 24.22, 32.55)

24.23 Notices to quit

Campbell's Trustees v O'Neill 1911 SC 18. Lease: removing by warrant for summary ejection through procedure laid down by Sheriff Courts (Scotland) Act 1907. (Text 24.24)

Urquhart v Hamilton 1996 GWD 37-2171. Notice to quit held invalid where the landlord had arbitrarily selected the termination date which was not prescribed precisely in the lease. Notice should have been given at the natural ish.

Capital Land Holdings Ltd v Secretary of State for the Environment 1996 SLT 1379. Lease ambiguous as to where notice should be served on landlord. Notice served at place of business but this was held to render the notice invalid as if the contract was read as a whole it was clear that the notice should have been served at the landlord's Registered Office.

Esson Properties Ltd v Dresser UK Ltd 1997 SLT 949. Clause in lease required a period of notice 'not less than nine months prior to the effective date' of the termination. Held that 'not less than' meant that the first and last day fell to be excluded when computing the period.

Chaplin v Caledonian Land Properties Ltd 1997 SLT 384. When the sending of notice to terminate a lease is proved, receipt thereof is presumed in the absence of evidence rebutting the presumption.

Signet Group plc v C & J Clark Retail Properties Ltd 1996 SLT 1325. Landlord argued that insufficient notice of termination given. Tenants argued that sufficient notice given and that the acting of the parties excluded the consensus required for tacit relocation. Held that tacit relocation had come into effect.

McGhie v Dunedin Property Investment Co 1998 GWD 39-2019. Tenants served notice to terminate their lease. The landlords argued the notice was invalid as it referred to the wrong clause of the lease and had been served on their property agents, not at their registered office.

Held that it was clear what the notice was and that it was possible to serve it on agents of the landlords.

James Howden & Co Ltd v Taylor Woodrow Property Co Ltd 1999 SLT 841. Dispute as to whether a right to resile a contract for the lease of heritage had been waived. Held that waiver of a right was permanent and postponement of the exercise of the right on the basis of an informal agreement did not constitute waiver.

Quarantelli v Forbes 2000 GWD 2-66. Decree of removing granted in landlord's favour where the tenants were in arrears with rent and an irritancy had been incurred by the sequestration of one of the partners in the tenant firm.

Keenan v Whitehead 2003 GWD 10-289. Lease continued by tacit relocation and variation of terms impossible.

Renunciation

B G Hamilton v Ready Mixed Concrete Ltd 1999 SLT 524. Registration of an *a non domino* disposition by a tenant in its own favour, later cancelled by rectification, did not constitute a renunciation of the lease, for which mutual consent was essential.

24.25 Periods of notice

Esson Properties Ltd v Dresser UK Ltd 1997 SLT 949. Timeous service of notice.

24.26 Service of notice

Capital Land Holdings Ltd v Secretary of State for the Environment 1996 SLT 1379. Lease stated means of service by which notice of termination was to be served: any other way was invalid.

Netherfield Visual Productions v Caledonian Land Properties Ltd 1996 GWD 19-1107. When serving a notice of termination there is a presumption in favour of delivery.

Chaplin v Caledonian Land Properties Ltd 1997 SLT 384. When the sending of notice to terminate a lease is proved, receipt thereof is presumed in the absence of evidence rebutting the presumption. (Text 24.26)

McGhie v Dunedin Property Investment Co 1998 GWD 39-2019. Tenants served notice to terminate their lease. The landlords argued the notice was invalid as it referred to the wrong clause of the lease and had been served on their property agents, not at their registered office. Held that it was clear what the notice was and that it was possible to serve it on agents of the landlords. (Text 24.26)

Miscellaneous

Life Association of Scotland Ltd v Black's Leisure Group plc 1989 SC 166. Whether singular successor has the benefit of notice of irritancy previously served by seller on tenant.

Walford v Crown Estate Commissioners 1988 SLT 377. Whether lease by Crown Commissioners of rights to fish farming interferes with inalienable right of public navigation.

Chevron Petroleum (UK) Ltd v Post Office 1987 SLT 588. Landlord not entitled to derogate from his lease by actings or otherwise.

The Hoy Trust v Thomson 2003 SLT 20. In general an action to remove a tenant must be by way of summary cause.

Chapter 25   Commercial Leases

25.4 Title

Trade Development Bank v Warriner & Mason (Scotland) Ltd 1980 SC 74. Consent of heritable creditor (Text 24.21, 25.6, 32.55)

25.8 Designations of parties to the lease

Clydesdale Bank plc v Davidson 1994 SCLR 828. Parties to a lease must be distinct from one another. (Text 26.10)

25.10 Guarantors

Waydale Ltd v DHL Holdings (UK) Ltd 1996 SCLR 391 and *Waydale Ltd v DHL Holdings (UK) Ltd (No 3)* 2000 GWD 38-1434.Transferability of guarantee. (Text 25.10)

25.11 Description of the leased subjects

Marfield Properties v Secretary of State for the Environment 1996 SC 362. What is a common part in a lease of part of multi-occupancy building? (Text 25.11)

Hand v Hall [1877] 2 Ex D 355. Calculation of stamp duty.

25.12 Duration

MacDougall v Guidi 1992 SCLR 167. Recovery of possession; tacit relocation; form of notice to quit. (Text 25.12)

25.14 Keep-open clauses

Whitelaw v Fulton (1871) 10 M 27. Obligation to keep premises plenished. (Text 25.16)

Grosvenor Developments (Scotland) plc v Argyll Stores Ltd 1987 SLT 738. Enforcement of keep-open obligation by interdict. (Text 25.17)

Postel Properties Ltd v Miller & Santhouse plc 1993 SLT 353. Enforcement of keep-open obligation. (Text 25.17)

Church Commissioners for England v Nationwide Anglia Building Society 1994 SLT 897. Keep-open obligation.

Church Commissioners for England v Abbey National plc 1994 SLT 959. Keep-open obligation. (Text 25.17)

Retail Parks Investments Ltd v Our Price Music Ltd 1995 SLT 1161. Interdict obtained by landlords to enforce keep-open clause recalled in part only.

Overgate Centre Ltd v Wm Low Supermarkets Ltd 1995 SLT 1181. Keep-open obligation.

Retail Parks Investments Ltd v The Royal Bank of Scotland plc (No 2) 1996 SLT 669. Keep-open obligation.

Co-operative Insurance Society Ltd v Argyll Stores (Holdings) Ltd [1997] 1 WLR 898. Keep-open obligation. (Text 25.17)

Co-operative Insurance Society Ltd v Halfords Ltd (No 2) 1999 SLT 685. (Text 25.17)

Highland & Universal Properties Ltd v Safeway Properties Ltd 2000 SLT 414. Keep-open obligation. Interim interdict granted. (Text 25.17)

25.19 Monetary obligations of tenant

Kleinwort Benson Ltd v Barbrak [1987] AC 597. Use of back letters. (Text 25.20)

Provincial Insurance plc v Valtos Ltd 1992 SCLR 203. Quarter days for payment. (Text 25.20)

25.29 Rent review

Montleigh Northern Developments Ltd v Ghai 1992 GWD 24-1381. Purchaser from landlord entitled to claim arrears of rent due to seller.

Pacitti v Manganiello 1995 SCLR 557. Withholding of rent.

Ravenseft Properties Ltd v Aberdeen District Council 1996 GWD 22-1285. Determination of fair market rent.

Visionhire Ltd v Britel Fund Trustees Ltd 1992 SCLR 236. Time of the essence. (Text 25.33, 28.15, 28.71)

Dunedin Property Investment Co Ltd v Wesleyan and General Assurance Society 1992 SCLR 159. Counter notice; time of the essence. (Text 25.33)

United Scientific Holdings Ltd v Burnley Borough Council [1978] AC 904. Time of the essence. (Text 25.33)

Prudential Assurance Co Ltd v Smiths Foods 1995 SLT 369. Notice by tenant whether validly served.

Banks v Mecca Bookmakers (Scotland) Ltd 1982 SLT 150. Waiver by landlord; time of the essence. (Text 25.33)

Waydale Ltd v MRM Engineering 1996 SLT (Sh Ct) 6. *Falkirk District Council v Falkirk Taverns Ltd* 1993 SLT 1097. Waiver by landlord-personal bar; waiver by landlord. (Text 25.33)

Scottish Development Agency v Morrisons Holdings Ltd 1986 SLT 59. Rent review procedure effective beyond review date.

Yates, Petitioner 1987 SLT 86. Landlord's notice of intention to review.

Leeds Permanent Pension Scheme Trustees Ltd v William Timpson Ltd 1987 SCLR 51. Time of the essence.

Legal and Commercial Properties Ltd v Lothian Regional Council 1988 SLT 463. Tenant's counter notice.

Crawford v Bruce 1992 SLT 524. Basis for review. (Text 25.36)

Beard v Beveridge, Herd & Sandilands 1990 SLT 609. Absence of basis for review. (Text 25.36)

Scottish Mutual Assurance Society v Secretary of State for the Environment 1992 SLT 617. Basis of review. (Text 25.36)

Unilodge v University of Dundee 2001 SCLR 1008. Basis of review. (Text 25.36)

Stylo Shoes Ltd v Manchester Royal Exchange Ltd [1967] 204 EG 803. Upwards-only review. (Text 25.37)

Plinth Property Investment Ltd v Mott, Hay & Anderson [1978] 249 EG 1167. Effect of restrictive user at rent reviews. (Text 25.41)

Campbell v Edwards [1976] 1 WLR 403. No appeal against decision of expert.

National Westminster Bank v Arthur Young McLelland Moores & Co [1985] 2 All ER 817. Disregard of future rent reviews. (Text 25.45)

Pugh v Smiths Industries Ltd [1982] 264 EG 823. Effect of provision for disregards. (Text 25.45)

British Gas Corporation v Universities Superannuation Scheme Ltd [1986] 1 All ER 978. Effect of exclusion of provisions as to rent. (Text 25.45)

F R Evans (Leeds) Ltd v English Electric Co Ltd (1977) 245 EG 657. Willing Landlord/Willing Tenant assumption. (Text 25.40)

Co-operative Wholesale Society Ltd v National Westminster Bank plc; Broadgate Square plc v Lehmann Brothers Ltd; Scottish Amicable Life Assurance Society v Middleton; Prudential Nominees Ltd v Greenham Trading Ltd [1995] 1 EGLR 97. Headline rents. (Text 25.36)

Church Commissioners for England and Sears Property Glasgow Ltd v Etam plc 1997 SLT 38. Headline rents v open market rents. (Text 25.36)

Colonial Mutual Group (UK Holdings) Ltd v National Industrial Fuel Efficiency Services Ltd 1994 GWD 29-1761. Basis of review. (Text 25.36)

Dennis & Robinson Ltd v Kiossis Establishment [1987] 1EGLR 133. Willing landlord/willing tenant. (Text 25.40)

99 Bishopsgate Ltd v Prudential Assurance Co Ltd [1985] 1 EGLR 72. Vacant possession assumption. (Text 25.44)

Ponsford v H M Aerosols Ltd [1979] AC 63. Effect of tenant's improvements. (Text 25.52)

Standard Life Assurance Co v Debenhams plc 1995 GWD 9-514. Tenant's improvements. (Text 25.52)

GREA Real Property Investments Ltd v Williams [1979] 250 EG 651. Disregards of tenant's improvements. (Text 25.52)

AGE Ltd v Kwik-Save Stores Ltd 2001 SLT 821. Arbiter or Expert. (Text 25.53)

Witan Properties Ltd v Lord Advocate 1993 GWD 29-1846. Disagreement with finding of arbiter.

EAE (RT) Ltd v EAE Property Ltd 1994 SLT 627. Fax transmission and delivery of copy to solicitors held to be sufficient service of notice of intention to review.

25.61 Tenant's repairing obligation

Turner's Trustees v Steel (1900) 2 F 363. Exclusion of common law. (Text 25.62)

Lowe v Quayle Munro Ltd 1997 GWD 10-438. Landlord's implied warranty. (Text 25.62)

Allan v Robertson's Trustees (1891) 18 R 932. Extent of repairing obligation. (Text 25.64)

Dickie v Amicable Property Investment Society 1911 SC 1079. Wind and watertight obligation. (Text 25.62)

Gunn v NCB 1982 SLT 526. Landlord's duty as to repair.

House of Clydesdale Ltd v Universities Superannuation Scheme Ltd 1992 GWD 23-1330. Landlord's duty as to repair.

Duff v Fleming (1870) 8 M 769. Damage to premises by *damnum fatale*.

Lurcott v Wakely & Wheeler [1911] 1 KB 905. Effect of obligation to repair. (Text 25.64)

Cantors Properties (Scotland) Ltd v Swears & Wells Ltd 1978 SC 310. *Rei interitus*. (Text 25.77)

Ravenseft Properties Ltd v Davstone (Holdings) Ltd [1980] 1 QB 12. Examination of concept of 'repair'.

Blackwell v Farmfoods (Aberdeen) Ltd 1991 GWD 4-219. Exclusion of common law. (Text 25.62)

House of Fraser plc v Prudential Assurance Co Ltd 1992 SCLR 884. Wording wide enough to cover ordinary and extraordinary repairs. (Text 25.64)

Taylor Woodrow Property Co Ltd v Strathclyde Regional Council 1996 GWD 7-397. Implication of reasonableness. (Text 25.64)

Mothercare UK Ltd v City Wall (Holdings) Ltd 1994 GWD 28-1712. Extent of premises for repairing obligation. (Text 25.67)

Lord Advocate v Shipbreaking Industries Ltd (No 2) 1993 SLT 995. Dispute re acceptance of site in good and tenantable condition.

25.68 Insurance

Carrick Furniture House Ltd v General Accident, Fire and Life Assurance Corporation Ltd 1977 SC 308. Underlying principle of insurance is indemnification for loss.

Muir v McIntyres (1887) 14 R 470. Rent abatement. (Text 25.75)

Allan v Markland (1881) 10 R 383. *Rei interitus*. (Text 25.77)

Fehilly v General Accident Fire and Life Assurance Corporation 1983 SC 163. Tenant's insurable interest in building.

Beacon Carpets Ltd v Kirby [1984] 2 All ER 726. Destruction to leased subjects; interest of tenant.

Mark Rowlands Ltd v Berni Inns Ltd [1985] QB 211. Insurer's right of subrogation.

Cantors Properties Ltd v Swears & Wells Ltd 1978 SC 310. *Rei interitus*. (Text 25.77)

Barras v Hamilton 1994 SLT 949. Where landlord agrees to insure whole and the tenant pays the premium for his part only, he remains liable for negligence if other parts are damaged. (Text 25.74)

25.79 Alienation

Skene v Greenhill (1825) 4 S 25. Termination of tenant's liability on assignation.

Burns v Martin (1887) 14 R (HL) 20. Joint and several liability of tenant.

Duke of Portland v Baird & Co (1865) 4 M 10. Landlord's power to refuse consent. (Text 25.82)

Walker v McKnights (1886) 13 R 599. Effect of exclusion of assignees and sub-tenants.

Renfrew District Council v AB Leisure (Renfrew) Ltd (In Liquidation) 1988 SLT 635. Landlord's consent not to be unreasonably withheld. (Text 25.82)

International Drilling Fluids Ltd v Louisville International Ltd [1986] 1 All ER 321. Refusal of consent by landlord. (Text 25.82)

Lousada & Co Ltd v J E Lesser (Properties) Ltd 1990 SLT 823. Landlord's consent subject to conditions. (Text 25.82)

John E Harrison Ltd v Sun Life Assurance Society plc (No 1) 1991 GWD 29-1761; and *John E Harrison Ltd v Sun Life Assurance Society plc (No 2)* 1992 GWD 38-226. Landlord's consent. (Text 25.82)

Brador Properties Ltd v British Telecommunications plc 1992 SLT 490. Constitution of sub-lease. (Text 24.1, 25.83)

Continvest Ltd v Dean Property Partnership 1993 GWD 40-2675. Assessment of financial strength of assignee. (Text 25.82)

Scotmore Developments Ltd v Anderton 1996 SLT 1304. Conditions on consent. (Text 25.82)

Legal and General Assurance Society Ltd v Tesco Stores Ltd 2001 GWD 18-707. Reasonableness of landlord's consent. (Text 25.82)

25.88 Irritancy

Dorchester Studios (Glasgow) Ltd v Stone 1975 SC (HL) 56. Effect of strict irritancy clause; but see now Law Reform (Miscellaneous Provisions) (Scotland) Act 1985. (Text 25.90)

HMV Fields Properties v Bracken Self-Selection Fabrics Ltd 1991 SLT 31. Acceptance of rent after notice of irritancy served. (Text 25.89)

Mountleigh Northern Developments Ltd v Ghai 1992 GWD 24-1381. Appeal against declarator of irritancy refused.

CIN Properties Ltd v Dollar Land (Cumbernauld) Ltd 1992 SC(HL) 104. Oppression. (Text 25.89)

Dollar Land (Cumbernauld) Ltd v CIN Properties Ltd 1998 SC(HL) 90. Claim for unjust enrichment. (Text 24.6, 24.19, 25.90)

Bellevue Cash and Carry Ltd v Singh 1996 GWD 4-220. Form of irritancy notice (Text 25.90)

Blythswood Investments (Scotland) Ltd v Clydesdale Electrical Stores Ltd (In Receivership) 1995 SLT 150. 'Fair and reasonable landlord'. (Text 25.90)

Auditglen Ltd v Scotec Industries Ltd 1996 SLT 493. Strict interpretation of irritancy clause.

Scottish Exhibition Centre v Mirestop Ltd 1996 SLT 8. Entitlement to irritate lease.

Holt Leisure Parks Ltd v Scottish and Newcastle plc 1996 GWD 22-1284. Liability of heritable creditor following upon irritancy.

Euro Properties Scotland Ltd v Alam & Mitchell 2000 GWD 23-896. Fair and reasonable landlord (Text 25.90)

25.92 Hypothec

Macpherson v Macpherson's Trustees 1905 8F 191. *Invecta et illata.* (Text 25.93)

Steuart v Stables (1878) 5 R 1025. Goods of sub-tenant. (Text 25.93)

Grampian Regional Council v Drill Stem (Inspection Services) Ltd 1994 SCLR 36. Procedure for hypothec.

Chapter 26   Agricultural Leases

Fothringham v Fotheringham 1987 SLT (Land Ct) 10. Proposed resumption of the majority of a hill farm by a landlord for planting was held to be in bad faith and not contemplated by the parties at time lease was entered into.

Baird's Executors v Inland Revenue Commissioners 1991 SLT (Lands Tr) 9. Tenant's interest in an agricultural tenancy can have a value for tax purposes. (Text 26.41)

Dickson v MacGregor 1992 SLT (Land Ct) 83. Letting to a limited partnership in which landlord is a partner is not *per se* illegal.

Kennedy v Johnstone 1956 SC 39. Discussion on whether exclusion of successors effectively brings tenancy to an end on death of tenant. (Text 26.13)

Kildrummy (Jersey) Ltd v Calder 1994 SLT 888. Contracting with a nominee is equivalent to contracting with oneself, and does not create a tenancy. (Text 26.32)

Morrison-Low v Paterson 1985 SLT 255. A tenancy can arise through the actings of the parties.

Edinburgh Corporation v Gray 1948 SC 538. Power of resumption under agricultural lease contested.

Turner v Wilson 1948 SC 296. Power of resumption under agricultural lease contested.

Glencruitten Trustees v Love 1966 SLT (Land Ct) 5. Power of resumption under agricultural lease contested.

Lady Auckland v Dowie 1964 SLT (Land Ct) 20. To avoid risk of claim for compensation for deer damage on arable land, it is necessary to allow tenant to kill and take deer. (Text 26.18)

Morrison's Executor v Rendall 1986 SLT 227. Informal undertakings to remove are invalid. (Text 26.32)

Johnston v Moreton [1980] AC 37. Public policy in regard to security of tenure reviewed.

Macfarlane v Falfield Investments Ltd 1996 SCLR 826. Position of a limited partnership as tenant. Intention of parties. (Text 26.10)

Pinkerton v Pinkerton 1986 SLT 376. Landlord can let to group of which he is a member. (Text 26.12)

Clydesdale Bank plc v Davidson 1998 SC (HL) 51. Several pro indiviso proprietors cannot let to one of their number. (Text 26.12)

Chapter 27 Residential Leases

27.2 Public sector tenancies

(Cases on the right to buy are dealt with generally in para 28.59)

Midlothian District Council v Tweedie 1993 GWD 16-1068. Circumstances in which decree for recovery of possession was upheld on appeal.

City of Edinburgh District Council v Lamb; City of Edinburgh District Council v Stirling 1993 SCLR 587. Sheriff principal, on appeal, reversed sheriff's dismissal of three actions for recovery of heritable property on grounds that he had moved too quickly in reaching his decision.

Glasgow District Council v Erhaiganoma 1993 SCLR 592. Inner House, on appeal, dismissed appeal against decision of sheriff granting possession to landlords on grounds of arrears of rent.

Midlothian District Council v Kerr 1995 GWD 30-1586. Local authority obtained decree for recovery of possession against troublesome tenant.

City of Edinburgh District Council v Lamb; City of Edinburgh District Council v Stirling 1993 SCLR 587. Recovery of possession sought by a council where the landlord could not deal with the question of reasonableness; Housing (Scotland) Act 1987, s 48.

Neilson v Scottish Homes 1998 GWD 6-286. Extent of obligations of landlord to provide subjects in habitable condition.

Glasgow City Council v Cavanagh 1999 Hous LR 7. Eviction refused following conviction for drug offences.

Perth and Kinross Council v Roy 1999 Hous LR 10. Secure tenant was removed following complaints as to condition of tenancy but tenancy was not terminated. Subsequent action for reinstatement but decree of eviction granted.

27.5 Protected tenancies

Margaret Blackwood Housing Association Ltd 1994 GWD 22-1368. Appeal against a decision of Rent Assessment Committee determining fair rent on grounds involving housing association service charge.

Milnbank Housing Association Ltd v Murdoch 1995 SLT (Sh Ct) 11. Held that secure tenancy which had purportedly been converted into an assured tenancy had not in fact been converted.

Quinn v Monklands District Council 1995 SCLR 393. Local authority tenant took occupation and house seemed to be in a satisfactory state of repair. Within two months black mould appeared caused by condensation; she claimed and was awarded damages.

Western Heritable Investment Co Ltd v Johnstone 1995 GWD 30-1584. Landlord appealed against decision of Rent Assessment Committee who assessed a fair rent for a substantial number of regulated tenancies. Landlord claimed that, since there was no substantial level of scarcity, comparable rents for regulated tenancies were no longer valid. Appeal refused.

Tamroui v Clydesdale Bank plc 1996 GWD 23-1340. Heritable creditor sought to eject short assured tenant. Landlord had granted lease without creditor's knowledge and should not have done so, given the standard conditions. Tenant argued that creditor would have to make application to court to dispense with requirement for notice of possible repossession under Housing (Scotland) Act 1988, s 18 and Schedule 5, ground (2), and was upheld in that argument.

Midlothian District Council v Kerr 1995 GWD 30-1586. See above at 27.2.

City of Edinburgh District Council v Lamb; City of Edinburgh District Council v Stirling 1993 SCLR 587. See above at 27.2.

McKay v Leask 1996 GWD 30-1828. Unlawful eviction of assured tenant while on holiday; damages awarded

Johnstone v Finneran 2003 GWD 17-541. A statutory assured tenancy was not brought to an end by entering into a short assured tenancy.

27.10 The Housing (Scotland) Act 1988

Govanhill Housing Association Ltd v Palmer 1998 SLT 887. Assured tenancy granted on basis of false information provided in application. Association sought reduction of tenancy agreement. Held that while the Association was entitled to their remedy, reduction of the agreement would create a statutory assured tenancy which could be terminated only in accordance with the conditions of the Housing (Scotland) Act 1988.

Key Housing Association Ltd v Cameron 1999 Hous LR 47. The requirements of notice to quit in an assured tenancy.

Royal Bank of Scotland plc v Boyle 1999 Hous LR 63. Assured tenancy where rent in arrears and no notice to quit served. Question whether notice to quit required where action for recovery based on irritancy. Held that grounds for recovery of possession must be set out in tenancy agreement provisions for termination.

Kinara Estate Trustees v Campbell 1999 Hous LR 55. A landlord in an assured tenancy sought to recover possession offering alternative accommodation but was refused.

Barns-Graham v Balance 2000 Hous LR 11. The 1988 Act grants assured tenancy rights only in houses occupied as the only or principal home; thus a tenant of a chalet for holiday use was not protected.

Knowes Housing Association v Millar 2001 SLT 1326. Transfer of landlord's interest from qualifying to non-qualifying landlord, whether tenancy remains secure.

Scott v Thomson 2003 SLT 99 Unlawful eviction by the son of the landlord. Held to be 'acting on [the landlord's] behalf.'

Queen's Cross Housing Association Ltd v McAllister 2003 GWD 17-541. A secure tenancy remains secure after transfer to property owned by the same landlord.

27.25 Gas Regulations

Mackenzie v Aberdeen City Council 2002 Hous LR 88. The regulations impose criminal liability and not civil liability. (See text 27.25)

Chapter 28   Contracts of Sale and Purchase

Note

With the passing of the Contract (Scotland) Act 1997, the problems caused by the rule excluding extrinsic evidence, the non-supersession rule and the rejection of the actio quanti minoris *ceased to have any significance in contracts concluded on or after 21 June 1997, but cases on these problems have been retained in the Digest for reference where appropriate.*

28.1 Constitution and essential content of the contract

Rockcliffe Estates plc v Co-operative Wholesale Society Ltd 1994 SLT 592. In a contract of sale and purchase for a portfolio of properties for a single global price, the purchasers were entitled to withdraw certain properties, and elected to do so, at prices fixed by them. The sellers declined to complete the sale on the footing that the purchasers had allocated artificially high prices on the withdrawn properties. Held that the purchasers must act reasonably and not capriciously. Proof allowed. (Text 28.17, 28.26)

Hopkinson v Williams 1993 SLT 907. Circumstances in which an agent was held to have ostensible authority to contract. (Text 28.4)

Cala Management Ltd v Corstorphine Piggeries Ltd 1996 GWD 34-2029. A contract included the option to purchase land which remained open either for 13 months or longer if awaiting Planning Committee approval. Application made to Planning Committee but by a different company. Application lapsed creating a deemed refusal of option.

Robertson v Secretary of State for Scotland 1999 GWD 26-1251. In a contract for sale of land the purchaser was entitled to rely on upon the 'current market value' rather than an earlier 1997 valuation due to the terms of the offer made.

Glasgow City Council v Peart 1999 GWD 29-1390. A deceased's solicitor signed a letter accepting the Council's offer to sell on the deceased's behalf. Held that it was essential that the deceased should have signed the acceptance himself and the letter of acceptance was reduced. (Text 28.4)

Miller Homes Ltd v Frame 2001 SLT 459. An agreement was reached for the sale of land with an option to purchase in the pursuer's favour. The defenders repudiated agreement arguing that it contained no enforceable agreement as to price. Held there was a concluded and enforceable bargain because the price was certain as it could be ascertained by machinery laid down in the agreement.

Bryant Homes (Scotland) Ltd v Secretary of State for Scotland 2001 GWD 19-738. Clause in missives stating that the purchaser would be entitled to recover from the purchase price paid any 'exceptional costs' incurred in the development of the heritable property bought. Arbiter's findings as to exceptional costs were approved.

28.2 Form and authentication

Davidson v Gregory 1988 GWD 25-1076. An alleged prior verbal agreement, referred to indirectly in a formal contract, is nonetheless extrinsic and cannot be considered in construing the formal document.

Caithness Flagstone v Sinclair (1880) 7 R 1117. Unsigned offer accepted in writing; no resulting contract.

McGinn v Shearer 1947 SC 334. Improbative acceptance; covering letter holograph.

Gavine's Trustee v Lee (1883) 10 R 448. 'Adopted as holograph' below signature effective to constitute binding offer.

Harvey v Smith (1904) 6 F 511. Circumstances where an individual, illiterate and without separate advice, held not bound by offer signed by him 'adopted as holograph'.

Maclaine v Murphy 1958 SLT (Sh Ct) 49. 'Adopted as holograph'; effect.

Whyte v Lee (1879) 6 R 699. Acceptance by agents, in proper form, binds the principal.

Findlater v Maan 1990 SC 150. When an offer for heritable property is met by qualified acceptance which rejects its terms, it is then too late subsequently to accept offer *de plano*. (Text 28.8, 28.18)

Scott v J B Livingstone & Nicol 1990 SLT 305. Where a firm makes an offer purportedly on behalf of named but non-existent principal, firm is delictually liable in damages for breach of warranty of its authority to contract.

Heron v Thomson 1989 GWD 11-469. Discussion on scope of agent's authority to conclude missives.

Inglis v Lowrie 1990 SLT (Sh Ct) 60. Formal, concluded missives of sale and purchase of heritage cannot be discharged or rescinded by oral agreement.

McMillan v Caldwell 1991 SLT 325. Formal written offer to purchase or sell heritage can be withdrawn verbally, provided withdrawal is intimated before acceptance. (Text 28.5)

Clyde Shopping Hall Ltd v Canning 1990 SLT (Sh Ct) 10. Agreement provided that either party must serve notice of termination in writing on other party to bring agreement to an end. Such a notice was posted by one party but not received by the other. Held that a proper construction of wording of the agreement required that the notice be actually received.

Edinburgh Property and Investment Co Ltd v Norfolk Capital Hotels Ltd 1988 GWD 27-1161. Proof allowed on averments of subsequent improbative variation of concluded missives. Question of personal bar considered but not decided.

Hamilton v Wakefield 1992 SCLR 740. Validity of contract made in England. (Text 28.5)

Stewart's Executors v Stewart 1993 SCLR 641. Held, that informal contract for sale and purchase of heritage cannot be proved simply by actings alone.

Abegg Ltd v Ladbrook Retail Parks Ltd 1993 GWD 14-947. Two separate contracts for sale and purchase of separate lots amended by subsequent missives. Held that terms of missives were not sufficient to overcome the presumption against novation and accordingly the two contracts remained separate and distinct.

Stewart Milne Group Ltd v Skateraw Development Co Ltd 1995 GWD 32-1650. Where a contract clearly assumed a knowledge of surrounding facts and circumstances not disclosed in the missives, it would be hazardous to attempt to interpret provisions therein without further evidence.

Littlejohn v Mackay 1974 SLT (Sh Ct) 82. A partner, not merely an assistant, must sign for a firm. But see now Requirements of Writing (Scotland) Act 1995, Schedule 2, para 2. (Text 2.14, 3.23)

Grovebury Management Ltd v McLaren 1997 SLT 1083. Missives provided that if price not paid 28 days after due date seller could rescind on giving written notice. After 28 days purchaser faxed that willing to settle. Sellers faxed back to rescind but held that not entitled to, as had not followed procedure by giving written notice. The fax by the purchaser was an an effective tender of performance. (Text 28.71)

Merrick Homes Ltd v Duff 1997 SLT 570. Missives for sale and purchase of heritage concluded by fax and by delivery of faxed letter. As faxed letter was also devilered, opinion was reserved on whether faxing sufficient. (Text 2.3, 28.4)

McIntosh v Alam 1998 SLT (Sh Ct) 19. Held that missives can be concluded by fax. (Text 2.3, 28.4)

Gawthorpe v Stewart 2000 GWD 39-1461. An informal verbal agreement to convey heritage is not binding. (Text 28.2)

28.4 Form and authentication – agents

Hopkinson v Williams 1993 SLT 907. Whether missives entered into were authorised. (Text 28.4)

28.7 Consensus in idem

Haldane v Watson 1972 SLT (Sh Ct) 8. Unilateral undertaking. (Text 28.2)

Dickson v Blair (1871) 10 M 41. No consensus; qualified acceptance. (Text 28.8)

Heiton v Waverley Hydropathic Co (1877) 4 R 830. No consensus; all conditions not agreed.

Stobo Ltd v Morrison's (Gowns) Ltd 1949 SC 184. No consensus; 'subject to contract'. (Text 28.9)

Westren v Millar (1879) 7 R 173. Consensus; purchaser taking possession and making alterations. (Text 28.9)

McCallum v Soudan 1989 SLT 522. Circumstances where, following general principle, uninduced error held not sufficient to avoid contract.

Angus v Bryden 1992 SLT 884. Disposition ostensibly implemented missives but disponer alleged error. Lord Cameron expressed opinion that unintentional essential error known to and taken advantage of by other party implied bad faith for which the law provided a remedy. *Steuart's Trustees v Hart* (1875) 3 R 192 applied and *Spook Erection (Northern) Ltd v Kaye* 1990 SLT 676 not followed. (Text 28.22)

McLeod's Executor v Barr's Trustees 1989 SC 72. Where price is not stated and no basis is given for fixing it in contract, there is no consensus and no contract. (Text 28.26)

Grant v Peter G Gauld & Co 1985 SC 251. Provision that 'the actual boundaries would be agreed between the parties' not sufficiently precise to create consensus. (Text 28.22)

Coomber v Ross 1987 SLT 266. Single contract for sale and purchase of two separate heritable properties held to be severable and individually enforceable.

Chapelcroft Ltd v Inverdon Egg Producers Ltd 1973 SLT (Notes) 37. Knowledge of agent imputed to principal.

Turner v Macmillan Douglas 1989 SLT 293. Subsequent writings can be taken into account in construing ambiguity in antecedent contract.

Barratt (Scotland) Ltd v Keith 1993 SC 142. Circumstances where lack of precision in defining subjects of offer in missives held not necessarily to exclude evidence of prior communings. But see *Angus v Bryden* above. (Text 32.44, 32.77)

Martone v Zani 1992 GWD 32-1903. Extrinsic evidence admitted to determine the extent of the property subject to an option to purchase. (Text 28.22, 28.76)

Aberdeen Rubber Ltd v Knowles & Sons (Fruiterers) Ltd 1995 SLT 870. A offered to purchase four areas of ground; disposition in implement conveyed five areas by mistake. Purchaser failed to satisfy court that the fifth area had been properly included in disposition, which was accordingly reduced. (Text 28.22)

McClymont v McCubbin 1995 SLT 1248. Held that where missives did not contain everything agreed, and which had to be agreed on, in order to constitute a contract, it was competent to prove that agreement had been reached by reference to prior communings taken together with missives themselves.

Tweedie v Ritchie 1992 GWD 34-2008. Held that there had been no consensus in relation to division and sale and alleged agreement as to unequal division of proceeds.

Colgan v Mooney 1992 GWD 34-2009. Seller and purchaser in dispute as to consensus on terms of contract, in particular provisions as to whether fire certificate required. (Text 28.74)

Callander v Midlothian District Council 1997 SLT 865. Clause in missives allowed adjoining proprietors access over the subject of sale but this was not referred to in subsequent disposition. Held that the obligation to allow access was a collateral obligation not superseded by the disposition. (However, this is no longer relevant due to the Contract (Scotland) Act 1997.)

Clelland v Morton Fraser & Milligan WS 1997 SLT (Sh Ct) 57. Contract concluded on the basis that evidence that alterations had been carried out in accordance with building warrants was presented. Later discovered that building warrants never existed. Purchaser raised action against selling solicitor which was unsuccessful as the solicitor, who was a third party, could not be held liable for damages.

Bogie (trading as Oakbank Services) v The Forestry Commission 2002 SCLR 278. The requirement of consensus as to the price and the subjects of sale applies equally to options as to an ordinary contract for sale and purchase.

28.8 The effect of a qualified acceptance

Rutterford Ltd v Allied Breweries Ltd 1990 SLT 249. Held, following *Wolf & Wolf v Forfar Potato Co* 1984 SLT 100, that latest qualified acceptance, in series of letters of offer and subsequent qualifications, represented a fresh counter-offer which supplanted and cancelled out previous counter-offer represented by original offer and earlier qualified acceptances which were therefore no longer open for *de plano* acceptance. (Text 28.8)

Findlater v Maan 1990 SC 150. When offer to purchase is met by a qualified acceptance, that is, in effect, a counter-offer. If purchaser accepted those qualifications but subject to a further qualification, that is, again, a new counter-offer. (Text 28.8, 28.18)

28.10 Personal Bar

Note

As the cases on rei interventus *remain relevant, this section of the Digest of Cases from the sixth edition of this book is included.*

Rei interventus and homologation

Colquhoun v Wilson's Trustees (1860) 22 D 1035. All conditions not explicitly agreed, but purchaser carrying out alterations to property.

Secretary of State for Scotland v Ravenstone Securities 1976 SC 171. Whether actings unequivocally referable to informal agreement.

Mitchell v Stornoway Trustees 1936 SC (HL) 56. Homologation of improbative agreement by actings.

East Kilbride Development Corporation v Pollock 1953 SC 370. Contract lacking essentials cannot be completed by *rei interventus*.

Errol v Walker 1966 SC 93. Proof of agreement to found *rei interventus*.

Mulhern v Mulhern 1987 SLT (Sh Ct) 62. Oral agreement to sell and purchase heritage can be proved only by writ or oath. *Errol v Walker* considered.

Law v Thomson 1978 SC 343. Circumstances insufficient to warrant *rei interventus* or homologation.

Clark's Executor v Cameron 1982 SLT 68. Delivery of improbative writ to grantor's agent does not normally constitute homologation; nor would the agent's actings constitute *rei interventus*.

Rutterford Ltd v Allied Breweries Ltd 1990 SLT 249. See para 28.8 above. Following exchange of missives, the sellers replied to the final but invalid acceptance in terms indicating that they were proceeding with the contract. This was held not sufficient to constitute homologation, there being no consensus. Fact that purchasers in turn embarked on examination of title and drafted a disposition and incidental documents held insufficient to constitute *rei interventus*.

Ferryhill Property Investments Ltd v Technical Video Productions 1992 SCLR 282. Circumstances in which actings of defenders held sufficient as evidence of consent to written lease, following *Errol v Walker*.

Shetland Islands Council v British Petroleum Ltd 1990 SLT 82. Discussion on actings sufficient to constitute *rei interventus*.

Stewart's Executors v Stewart 1994 SLT 466. In an *obligatio literis*, pursuer must prove informal agreement by writ or oath before he can attempt to prove homologation.

Ferryhill Property Investments Ltd v Technical Video Productions 1992 SCLR 282. Held that actings of the defender following on a written offer of lease were sufficient evidence of consent for *rei interventus* and proof before answer allowed.

Tomorrow's World v Burgess 1993 GWD 29-1845. In the case of a draft lease followed by actings, court admitted evidence *habili modo* on footing that the tenant claimed entitlement by *rei interventus*.

Barratt (Scotland) Ltd v Keith 1994 SLT 1343. See para 28.7 above.

Nelson v Gerrard 1994 SCLR 1052. Binding contract (here, lease) could be constituted by actings following prior informal communings.

Hamilton v Wakefield 1992 SCLR 740. See para 28.2 above. (Text 2.15)

Henderson's Executors v Henderson 2003 SLT (Sh Ct) 34. Informal agreement followed by actings which were held insufficient to hold a contract existed.

Statutory personal bar

Bryce v Marwick (29 March 1999, unreported), Aberdeen Sheriff Court. (Text 28.10)

Super (Tom) Printing and Supplies Ltd v South Lanarkshire Council 1999 GWD 31-1496 and 38-1854. Negotiations took place but no formal contract between parties. Certain subsequent actings insufficient to hold that a contract existed. (Text 28.10)

28.11 Factors which affect the normal content of missives

Note

After the Contract (Scotland) Act 1997 the cases in the Digest on Winston v Patrick *and the* actio quanti minoris *are of little relevance but are included for the sake of completeness.*

Winston v Patrick

Meek v Bell 1993 GWD 20-1238. Question as to how far missives were superseded by delivery of lease.

Aberdeen Rubber Ltd v Knowles & Sons (Fruiterers) Ltd 1995 SLT 870. Delivery of disposition totally supersedes antecedent missives but only on matters which it is intended to implement. (Text 28.22)

McClymont v McCubbin 1995 SLT 1248. See 28.7 above. (Text 28.7)

The *actio quanti minoris* and collateral obligations

King v Gebbie 1993 SLT 512. Under missives, a house was still uncompleted at date of entry.

After settlement, defects were discovered in structure. Obligations to perform building work held collateral, following *McKillop v Mutual Securities Ltd* 1945 SC 166; and the missives were not superseded.

Hardwick v Gebbie 1991 SLT 258. Circumstances where obligation to build house held to be intended as continuing obligation, notwithstanding delivery of disposition but only *quoad* matters not reasonably discoverable on inspection. Remedy was damages for breach of contract, not *actio quanti minoris*.

Black v Gibson 1992 SLT 1076. Obligation to build house held to be a single complete collateral obligation. Building partly completed before missives concluded; but held not appropriate to apportion collateral obligation with reference to that part of building already completed, and the remaining part not completed until after conclusion of missives.

Fortune v Fraser 1996 SLT 878. Purchasers contracted to acquire a business. Sellers warranted, *inter alia*, correctness of accounts, which were materially inaccurate. Full discussion in Inner House on *actio quanti minoris* and effect of misrepresentation.

Tomorrow's World v Burgess 1993 GWD 29-1845. See para 28.10 above.

Colgan v Mooney 1994 GWD 1-43. M sold a guest house with certain assurances as to fire certificate. M qualified a condition as to fire certificate 'to the extent that the subjects are too small to require a full fire certificate' and disclosed fire officer's letter confirming that safety standards were met. Held on appeal that M not liable under *actio quanti minoris* clause. Lord Clyde doubted whether, in any event, claim properly fell within scope of that clause. (Text 28.74)

Adams v Whatlings plc 1995 SCLR 185. Whether implied term that house to be erected to reasonable workmanlike standards. See para 28.16 below.

28.13 Survey reports

Martin v Bell-Ingram 1986 SLT 575. Discussion on duty owed by surveyor when inspecting a property for building society in anticipation of purchase.

Crouches v Murray & Muir 1987 GWD 12-428. Discussion on measure of damages in claim against surveyor.

UCB Bank plc v Dundas & Wilson 1990 SC 377. Liability of solicitors and surveyors for depreciation in land value due to subsidence.

Robbie v Graham & Sibbald 1989 SLT 870. Liability for negligent survey.

Melrose v Davidson & Robertson 1993 SLT 611. Validity of disclaimer of liability on survey report discussed.

Hunter v J & E Shepherd 1991 GWD 17-1043. Discussion on the basis of assessment of damages arising out of negligent survey.

Peach v Iain G Chalmers 1992 SCLR 423. Discussion on basis of assessment of damages arising out of negligent survey.

Smith v Carter 1994 SCLR 539. Discussion on duty of care owed by a surveyor to undisclosed co-purchaser.

Alliance and Leicester Building Society v J & E Shepherd 1995 GWD 11-608. Firm of surveyors stated that they had not seen any evidence of flood damage and that property had no unusual hazard. In following year and in two subsequent years property was seriously flooded and the owner abandoned property to building society, who sold it for half the amount of their loan. They sued surveyors in contract and delict for failing to take reasonable care. On evidence produced by surveyors, they were exonerated.

Mortgage Express Ltd v Dunsmore Reid & Smith 1996 GWD 10-590. Claim for negligence in two mortgage valuations, and dispute as to persons liable in negligence claim, given that surveyors operated in Scotland and in England and there was a question whether one of surveyor group was to be treated as partner.

Fraser v D M Hall & Son 1997 SLT 808. In a case of negligent survey it was held that it was not possible to state that averments of distress were inevitably irrelevant.

Lawson v McHugh 1998 GWD 31-1618. In an action for damages against surveyor for loss from negligent valuation it was held that the proper measure of damages was the difference between the price paid and the actual market price which the subjects would have fetched at the date of sale. A further modest sum might be allowed for *solatium*.

28.16 The need for express provision

Fortune v Fraser 1996 SLT 878. See para 28.11 above. Standing this decision, it may not be sufficient simply to include warranty in missives without declaration that clause is material and breach thereof will entitle purchaser to certain remedies by express provision.

Rockcliffe Estates plc v Co-operative Wholesale Society Ltd 1994 SLT 592. See 28.1. Parties presumed by implication to act reasonably, not capriciously, in relation to contract conditions. (Text 28.17, 28.26)

Adams v Whatlings plc 1995 SCLR 185. Contract to purchase land incorporated obligation to erect a house thereon. After completion, defects developed and purchaser claimed damages for defective workmanship. Seller was held liable on footing that condition as to good workmanship, though not express, was necessarily implied and not extinguished by delivery of the disposition.

Scottish Youth Theatre (Property) Ltd v Anderson 2002 SCLR 945. A contract contained express provision that the parties would act in good faith. In a dispute as to the conduct of one of the parties it was held that while the conduct was disappointing to the other party it did not amount to repudiation of the contract.

28.17 Effect of conditions in contracts

Burnside v James Harrison (Developers) Ltd 1989 GWD 11-468. Provision in contract that either party may resile if completion certificate not obtained by specified date binding and enforceable even if certificate later obtained. Specific provisions in missives as to notice superseded and excluded normal ultimatum rule. (Text 28.19, 28.73)

Park v Morrison Developments Ltd 1993 GWD 8-571. Missives included suspensive conditions to be implemented by successive stated dates. Purchaser was held entitled to resile, when first fixed date had passed, without implement of that condition. Both sides having been legally advised on complicated missives, *contra proferentem* rule inapplicable.

Manheath Ltd v H J Banks & Co Ltd 1996 SLT 1006. Purchaser was to apply for planning permission on which the contract was conditional and, unless purchaser intimated within five years that permission had been granted, missives would fall. Planning permission not granted. Purchaser intimated that suspensive condition as to planning permission had been purified although permission had not been granted. Held that condition was not conceived solely in favour of purchaser and therefore not capable of unilateral waiver. (Text 28.19)

Khazaka v Drysdale 1995 GWD 23-1258. Contract conditional upon the purchaser obtaining planning permission. Time-limit for lodging application specified. Seller qualified missives to effect that purchaser would have four weeks in which to make application. Seller purportedly resiled when the purchaser's application was lodged six days late, on the footing that suspensive condition required strict adherence to time limit specified. Held that time-limit fixed for lodging application was not of same character; and ultimatum procedure was appropriate. (Text 28.40)

28.18 Effect of conditions inserted for the benefit of one party

Dewar & Finlay Ltd v Blackwood 1968 SLT 196. Condition as to planning permission.

Ellis & Sons Ltd v Pringle 1974 SC 200. Condition as to planning permission. (Text 28.18)

Imry Property Holdings Ltd v Glasgow YMCA 1979 SLT 262. Whether seller entitled to waive condition.

Gilchrist v Payton 1979 SC 380, 1979 SLT 135. Whether purchaser entitled to waive condition. (Text 28.17)

Zebmoon Ltd v Akinbrook Investment Development Ltd 1988 SLT 146. Condition in missives may be waived by one party unilaterally if it satisfies two tests: (i) that it is in the interests of that party only; (ii) that it is not inextricably connected with other parts of contract.

Manheath Ltd v H J Banks & Co Ltd 1996 SLT 1006. See 28.17 above.

28.21 Identification of the subjects sold

Macdonald v Newall (1898) 1 F 68. 'Property known as the Royal Hotel.' (Text 28.22, 32.43)

Houldsworth v Gordon Cumming 1910 SC (HL) 49. 'The Estate of Dallas.' Prior negotiations. (Text 28.22)

McKendrick v Wilson 1970 SLT (Sh Ct) 39. Whether salmon fishing included in sale. (Text 8.3, 28.23)

Davidson v Gregory 1988 GWD 25-1076. Alleged prior verbal agreement, referred to indirectly in formal contract, is nonetheless extrinsic and cannot be considered in construing formal document.

Grant v Peter G Gauld & Co 1985 SC 251. Provision to the effect that 'the actual boundaries would be agreed between the parties' not sufficiently precise to create consensus. (Text 28.7, 28.22)

Anderson v Lambie 1954 SC (HL) 43. Farm and other subjects; prior communings. (Text 28.77)

Murray v Cherry 1980 SLT (Sh Ct) 131. Not legitimate to refer to prior negotiations to contradict terms of missives, unless ambiguous. (Text 28.22)

Turner v Macmillan Douglas 1989 SLT 293. Subsequent writings can be taken into account in construing ambiguity in antecedent contract.

Russell's Executor v Russell's Executors 1983 SLT 385. Discussion of rule in *Anderson v Lambie* above.

Martone v Zani 1992 GWD 32-1903. Extrinsic evidence admitted to determine extent of property subject to option to purchase. (Text 28.22, 28.76)

Angus v Bryden 1992 SLT 884. Discussion on proper construction of contract of sale or purchase where parties took different views as to what was included. (Text 28.22)

Merrick Homes v Duff 1997 SLT 570. Adequacy of the description of the subjects in a contract for sale and purchase discussed. (Text 2.3, 28.4)

Shoprite Group Ltd v Kwik Save Stores Ltd 1999 GWD 5-233. Contract for the sale and purchase of heritable and leasehold properties used for a business containing complex and conflicting provisions especially as regards the definition of the subjects and the completion dates.

N J & J Macfarlane (Developments) Ltd v MacSween's Trustees 1999 SLT 619. Sellers challenged a contract for the sale and purchase of ground with workshops and attached land on the basis that it lacked sufficient specification on the extent and identity of the subjects, price, possession and entry. No valid contract as there was uncertainty as to the identify of the subjects and the how the price was to be fixed. (Text 28.22, 28.26)

28.24 Fixtures and fittings

Nisbet v Mitchell-Innes (1880) 7 R 575. Vegetables, grapes etc.

Cochrane v Stevenson (1891) 18 R 1208. Picture in panel.

Christie v Smith's Executrix 1949 SC 572. Summerhouse.

Assessor for Fife v Hodgson 1966 SC 30. Storage heaters.

Assessor for Lothian Region v Blue Circle Industries plc 1986 SLT 537. Discussion on whether semi-mobile plant heritable or moveable.

Scottish Discount Co Ltd v Blin 1985 SC 216. Whether plant, on hire purchase and affixed to hirer's yard, heritable or moveable.

Jamieson v Welsh (1900) 3 F 176. Passing of moveables.

Glasgow City Council v Cannell 1999 SCLR 385. The Council obtained an interdict to prevent the owner selling eight stained glass panels in a listed building on the footing that the panels were fixtures.

28.25 Price

Stirling v Honyman (1824) 2 S 765. No binding contract if price not fixed.

McLeod's Executor v Barr's Trustees 1989 SC 72. Price must be stated or precise method prescribed for ascertaining it. (Text 28.7, 28.26)

Zemhunt (Holdings) Ltd v Control Securities Ltd 1992 SLT 151. Where deposit paid in terms of a contract of sale and purchase of heritage, the term will normally be construed as meaning that purchaser guarantees he will complete, and that deposit will be forfeited if he is in breach. (Text 28.27)

Inverkip Building Co Ltd v City Ploy Ltd 1992 GWD 8-433. Purchaser can insist on recovering deposit if he is not in default, in cases where contract cannot be implemented. (Text 28.27)

Singh v Cross Entertainments Ltd 1990 SLT 77. Purchaser may be entitled to recover deposit if justified, on principle *causa data causa non secuta*. (Text 28.27)

Scottish Wholefoods Collective Warehouse Ltd v Raye Investments 1994 SCLR 60. Clause in a lease giving option to purchase to tenant at 'the current open market price pertaining at the time ... as between a willing buyer or a willing seller ... and as the said price shall be mutually agreed between the parties ...' held to be sufficiently precise and therefore enforceable according to its terms, on footing that, if parties failed to agree, court would determine price. (Text 28.26)

Rockcliffe Estates plc v Co-operative Wholesale Society Ltd 1994 SLT 592. In contract of sale and purchase for a portfolio of properties for a single global price, purchasers were to intimate individual prices for dispositions, with right to withdraw properties at their discretion. Purchasers elected to withdraw certain properties and sellers declined to complete sale, on footing that purchasers had allocated artificially high prices on withdrawn properties. Held that there could be no implication that the purchasers would allocate prices on reasonable basis, having regard to market values because contract otherwise provided, but that it was implied that purchasers would act reasonably and not capriciously and proof before answer allowed with certain limitations. (Text 28.17, 28.26)

Stewart Milne Group Ltd v Skateraw Development Co Ltd 1995 GWD 32-1650. Purchasers of land sued sellers for cost of constructing part of road. Whether sellers were liable depended on meaning of obscure provision in contract. Court declined to interpret provision without further information as to background to purchase, since it would be 'hazardous' to do so.

Sutherland v The Royal Bank of Scotland plc 1997 SLT 329. Contains a complex technical argument as to the method of payment and the validity of the methods proposed in terms of the Bills of Exchange Act 1882.

Rapide Enterprises v Midgley 1998 SLT 504. Builders' missives stated that the builders were entitled to treat contract as void and resell property if the purchaser failed to pay the price. Purchasers failed to pay and builder resold. Builder sought damages representing the loss on resale and for a sum representing the interest which would have been earned on the original purchase price if duly paid. The second claim was excluded from the proof. (Text 28.28)

Hamilton v Rodwell 1998 SCLR 418. Missives which were to continue in force for two-year period contained clause requiring seller to meet cost of repairs. Money placed on deposit receipt to meet such costs. The two-year period expired before work was completed. Held that the seller was under no obligation to meet the cost of the repairs and therefore the money on deposit receipt became part of the purchase price payable to the seller. (Text 28.43)

N J & J Macfarlane (Developments) Ltd v MacSween's Trustees 1999 SLT 619. Sellers challenged a contract for the sale and purchase of ground with workshops and attached land on the basis that it lacked sufficient specification on the extent and identity of the subjects, price, possession and entry. No valid contract as there was uncertainty as to the identity of the subjects and the how the price was to be fixed. (Text 28.22, 28.26)

Robertson v Secretary of State for Scotland 1999 GWD 26-1251 (Sh Ct). Obligation to sell heritage on 'current market value' basis. Offer made on 'best price' basis which was held not an appropriate valuation.

Morston Assets Ltd v City of Edinburgh Council 2001 SLT 613. Petition for judicial review by potential purchasers who had submitted highest offer after closing date which was not accepted. Unsuccessfully argued that council under statutory duty to obtain best price.

City of Glasgow Council v Castrop Ltd 2003 SLT 526. Missives provided for additional payment if planning permission for extra houses obtained. Permission was so obtained by a wholly owned subsidiary of purchasers and additional payment was due.

28.28 Interest on the price

Zani v Martone 1997 SLT 1269. A tenant wished to exercise option to purchase subjects of lease and landlord/seller delayed implement. The tenant/purchaser was obliged to pay deposit receipt rate interest up to the date of granting of the disposition and thereafter interest at the judicial rate until the date of payment. (Text 28.28)

Keenan v Aberdeen Slating Co 2000 SC 81. Where a seller has been in breach and then offers performance the purchaser must pay the full price and cannot deduct any interest paid on the price. Any loss suffered by the purchaser due to the seller's breach can only be recovered by a claim for damages. (Text 28.28)

28.30 Entry

Sloan's Dairies Ltd v Glasgow Corporation 1977 SC 223. Agreed date of entry not essential. (Text 28.30, 28.42)

Law v Thomson 1978 SC 343. Date of entry essential.

Secretary of State for Scotland v Ravenstone Securities 1976 SC 171. Question whether date of entry would always be implied.

Gordon District Council v Wimpey Homes Holdings Ltd 1988 SLT 481. Entry 'not earlier than …' sufficient to create valid contract; exact date of entry not necessary. (Text 28.30)

Speevak v Robson 1949 SLT (Notes) 39. 'Entry' and 'settlement' contemporaneous.

Heys v Kimball & Morton (1890) 17 R 381. 'Immediate entry' means such early possession as is possible and practicable. (Text 28.30, 28.69)

Bosal Scotland Ltd v Anderson 1988 GWD 30-1275. Seller of property may have implied duty to take reasonable care to maintain property until entry, notwithstanding that risk may pass to purchaser. (Text 28.42)

28.31 Title

Christie v Cameron (1898) 25 R 824. Seller bound to clear title.

McConnell v Chassels (1903) 10 SLT 790. Long lease not a marketable title. (Text 28.32)

Bruce v Stewart (1900) 2 F 948. Decree of irritancy in absence.

Dryburgh v Gordon (1896) 24 R 1. Undischarged inhibitions. (Text 32.33)

Hamilton v Western Bank of Scotland (1861) 23 D 1033. Title defective; buildings erected in part on adjoining feu.

Baird v Drumpellier & Mount Vernon Estates Ltd 1999 GWD 39-1896 and 2000 GWD 12-427. Court affirmed the general rule that missives of sale and purchase contain an implied term that the seller warrants that he owns the property and will confer ownership on the purchaser.

28.32 Good and marketable title

Title to whole and identical property

Whyte v Lee (1879) 6 R 699. Purchaser entitled to resile.

Campbell v McCutcheon 1963 SC 505. Purchaser entitled to resile. (Text 28.32, 28.51, 28.76)

Macdonald v Newall (1898) 1 F 68. Purchaser's knowledge; personal bar. (Text 28.22, 32.43)

Mossend Theatre Co v Livingstone 1930 SC 90. Whether knowledge to be imputed to purchaser. (Text 28.35)

Burdens and conditions

Corbett v Robertson (1872) 10 M 329. Personal, not real, condition.

Smith v Soeder (1895) 23 R 60. Undisclosed burden. (Text 28.32)

Welsh v Russell (1894) 21 R 769. Undisclosed servitude. (Text 10.9, 28.32)

Cameron v Williamson (1895) 22 R 293. Undischarged security. (Text 22.66)

Bremner v Dick 1911 SC 887. Unallocated feuduty renders title unmarketable.

Armia v Daejan Developments Ltd 1979 SC (HL) 56. Purchaser not bound to accept undisclosed burdens. (Text 28.32, 28.59)

Umar v Murtaza 1983 SLT (Sh Ct) 79. Seller bound to disclose all restrictions on title. (Text 28.32)

Morris v Ritchie 1992 GWD 33-1950. In contract of sale and purchase, seller bound to disclose all burdens, existing or proposed, if material. (Text 28.32)

28.33 Variation of the obligation as to marketable title

Morton v Smith (1877) 5 R 83. Observations on effect of this clause.

Young v McKellar Ltd 1909 SC 1340. No title to 25 sq yds out of 383 sq yds. Purchaser bound to accept title.

Wood v Magistrates of Edinburgh (1886) 13 R 1006. Purchaser must accept real conditions in title.

Davidson v Dalziel (1881) 8 R 990. Purchaser must accept real undischarged burdens.

Carter v Lornie (1890) 18 R 353. Purchaser not bound to accept incurable defects.

Leith Heritages Co v Edinburgh and Leith Glass Co (1876) 3 R 789. Effect of obligation 'to put purchaser in the sellers' place'.

Mackenzie v Clark (1895) 3 SLT 128. Provision that purchaser not entitled to search does not deprive him of right to marketable title.

Morris v Ritchie 1992 GWD 33-1950. Held that purchaser entitled to resile on account of burden restricting parking places substantially below total originally contracted for. (Text 28.32)

MacDougall v MacDougall's Executors 1994 SLT 1178. Sellers' title unmarketable, but they pleaded, *inter alia*, that as *bona fide* purchasers for value without notice, recorded disposition in their favour was exempt from challenge by way of reduction. Held, on this point, that, when purchasing subjects, sellers had been put on notice by narrative in earlier writ and had failed to make due enquiry as to facts. (Text 28.35, 30.17)

Watson v Gillespie MacAndrew 1995 GWD 13-750. Purchaser sought damages from his solicitors for failing to disclose existence over part of estate which he had purchased of servitude right of access and wayleave agreement for electricity pylons. (Text 28.38)

28.35 Personal bar

Ceres School Board v McFarlane (1895) 23 R 279. Unrecorded charter granted by seller. (Text 11.5, 32.51)

Davidson v Dalziel (1881) 8 R 990. Burden in a will not made real.

Stodart v Dalzell (1876) 4 R 236. Purchaser barred by knowledge from objecting to right of occupancy. (Text 32.53)

Campbell's Trustees v Glasgow Corporation (1902) 4 F 752. Personal contract not binding on singular successor.

Rodger (Builders) Ltd v Fawdry 1950 SC 483. Second purchaser having notice of prior sale. (Text 28.73, 28.76, 28.77, 32.52, 32.56, 32.59)

Trade Development Bank v David W Haig (Bellshill) Ltd; Trade Development Bank v Crittal Windows Ltd 1983 SLT 510. Creditor taking real security with knowledge of prior personal obligation; whether affected thereby. (Text 32.60)

28.40 Planning and other statutory matters

See also paras 28.18 and 28.60.

Murray v Hillhouse Estates Ltd 1960 SLT (Notes) 48. Meaning and effect of condition as to 'unqualified planning permission'.

Bradley v Scott 1966 SLT (Sh Ct) 25. Closing order an 'outstanding notice'.

Kelly v A & J Clark Ltd 1968 SLT 141. 'Notices etc under Town and Country Planning Acts.'

McFadden v Wells (15 November 1994, unreported), Banff Sheriff Court, reported in Paisley and Cusine *Unreported Property Cases from the Sheriff Courts* (2000), p 139. Requirement to act reasonably. Purchaser cannot rescind because subjects located in Outstanding Conservation Area. (Text 28.17)

Hood v Clarkson 1995 SLT 98. Offer contained standard clause to effect that there were no existing applications, orders, notices etc and seller had no knowledge that any such were intended. Qualified acceptance modified that provision, stating that, with regard thereto, the usual local authority letter would be exhibited and, if letter disclosed any materially prejudicial matter, purchaser could resile. After settlement, disponee discovered that seller had negotiated with local authority for sale of the land for roadworks, which did not show up in local authority letter. Purchaser maintained that seller had misrepresented position and claimed damages. There was a non-supersession clause. Claim rejected, court holding that seller obliged to provide local authority letter and nothing more. He had not made any misrepresentations as to his knowledge at date of sale.

Khazaka v Drysdale 1995 SLT 1108. See para 28.17 above. (Text 28.17)

Smith v Renfrew District Council 1997 SCLR 354. Flat subject to a statutory repair notice which owners failed to implement. Local authority carried out repairs and sought costs from subsequent purchaser. Held purchaser had no notice that works carried out and the charging order should be quashed. (Serious doubts exist about competency of this decision.)

Clelland v Morton Fraser & Milligan WS 1997 SLT (Sh Ct) 57. Purchaser sued selling solicitors following a revelation that the property did not have adequate building warrants despite representations to the contrary. Action unsuccessful as selling solicitors were not a contracting party.

Donald v Hutchinson 2000 GWD 21-834. Condition in missives that no matters requiring repair were known to sellers. Following purchase the Council passed resolution declaring area housing action area for improvement. Claim for damages on basis of breach of missives in light of seller's knowledge of possibility of resolution was unsuccessful.

28.42 Structure and passing of the risk

Structure

See also para 28.13.

Martin v Bell-Ingram 1986 SLT 575. Discussion on duty owed by surveyor when inspecting property for building society in anticipation of purchase. (Text 28.13)

Crouches v Murray & Muir 1987 GWD 12-428. Discussion on measure of damages in claim against surveyor.

UCB Bank plc v Dundas & Wilson 1990 SC 377. Liability of solicitors and surveyors for depreciation in land value due to subsidence.

McKay v Leigh Estates (Scotland) Ltd 1987 GWD 16-609. Missives contained condition that purchaser should receive a satisfactory report on suitability of ground for development. Purchaser did not adequately investigate ground and then purportedly resiled. Purchaser was ordained to lead proof to establish that decision to resile reasonable. (Text 28.17, 28.60)

Passing of the risk

Sloan's Dairies Ltd v Glasgow Corporation 1977 SC 223. Risk of damage to subjects of purchase passes from seller to purchaser at date of completion of contract. (Text 28.30, 28.42)

Bosal Scotland Ltd v Anderson 1988 GWD 30-1275. Notwithstanding rule as to risk, seller may have duty to take reasonable care to maintain property until entry.

Hall v McWilliam 1993 GWD 23-1457. Missives included standard clause that subjects would be in substantially same condition at date of entry. After conclusion of missives and before entry, house flooded. Seller undertook remedial work, which was completed by date of entry, and purchaser held bound to proceed.

Homecare Contracts (Scotland) Ltd v Scottish Midland Co-operative Society Ltd 1999 GWD 23-1111. Missives specifically outlined provision for passing of risk which was different from the common law position. (Text 28.42)

28.43 Contract to remain in full force and effect

See also cases under para 28.73.

Lee v Alexander (1883) 10 R (HL) 91. General principles.

Orr v Mitchell (1893) 20 R (HL) 27. General principles.

Butter v Foster 1912 SC 1218. General principles.

Winston v Patrick 1980 SC 246. General principles. (Text 28.11, 28.43)

Hayes v Robinson 1984 SLT 300. General rule excluded by specific clause in missives to that effect.

Pena v Ray 1987 SLT 609. Non-supersession clause in missives competent and will keep contract open, notwithstanding delivery of a disposition in implement which does not refer to it.

Ferguson v McIntyre 1993 SLT 1269. Time-limit in non-supersession clause not invalidated by Prescription and Limitation (Scotland) Act 1973, s 13.

Sinclair-MacDonald v Haitt 1987 GWD 7-232. Agreement in missives, supported by non-supersession clause, that seller would remain in occupation beyond date of entry held not to be superseded by delivery of disposition as being personal right affecting the parties within exception (3) in *Winston v Patrick*.

Jamieson v Stewart 1989 SLT (Sh Ct) 13. Non-supersession clause need not be included in disposition to be effective after delivery thereof, under exception (3) to rule in *Winston v Patrick*.

Finlayson v McRobb 1987 SLT (Sh Ct) 150. Non-supersession clause not effective unless incorporated in disposition. Observed that *actio quanti minoris* incompetent in sale and purchase of heritage.

Jones v Stewart 1988 SLT (Sh Ct) 13. Obligation in missives as to condition of swimming pool held to be collateral. Several earlier cases reviewed and discussed in the context of *Winston v Patrick*.

Wood v Edwards 1988 SLT (Sh Ct) 17. Condition as to planning permission etc held not to be collateral; but condition as to state of repair of central heating system at date of entry might be so.

Fetherston v McDonald (No 1) 1988 SLT (Sh Ct) 16. Where non-supersession clause effective and contains time-limit, it is sufficient to raise action within time-limit, even though action not disposed of until later. See also *Pena v Ray* above.

Fetherston v McDonald (No 2) 1988 SLT (Sh Ct) 39. Provision in missives as to condition of central heating system at date of entry held collateral and so not superseded by disposition.

Hardwick v Gebbie 1991 SLT 258. Circumstances where obligation to build house held to be intended as continuing obligation, notwithstanding delivery of disposition, but only *quoad* matters not reasonably discoverable on inspection. Remedy was damages for breach of contract, not *actio quanti minoris*.

Black v Gibson 1992 SLT 1076. Obligation to build house held to be single complete collateral obligation. Building partly completed before missives were concluded; but, on this basis, held not appropriate to apportion collateral obligation with reference to part already implemented prior to missives and part not implemented until after conclusion of missives.

King v Gebbie 1993 SLT 512. Under missives, house to be completed before date of entry. After settlement, defects discovered in structure. Held that missives not superseded. Obligations to perform building work held collateral, following *McKillop v Mutual Securities Ltd* 1945 SC 166.

Porch v MacLeod 1992 SLT 661. Contract of sale and purchase of heritage contained warranty that all consents and warrants had been obtained for work carried out or for change of use; and undertaking to exhibit evidence thereof. There was also a non-supersession clause, limited to two years. Held that undertaking to exhibit evidence was a personal obligation collateral to the warranty; but it fell on delivery of disposition because it did not come within one or other of three express exceptions in *Winston v Patrick* 1980 SC 246 which are exhaustive.

Parker v O'Brien 1992 SLT (Sh Ct) 31. Contract of sale and purchase of heritage contained phrase 'the seller will warrant' condition of fitments and appliances. Held that wording implied a future promise or warranty and thus did not fall within collateral obligation exception in *Winston v Patrick* 1980 SC 246.

Taylor v McLeod 1990 SLT 194. Undertaking in missives by seller of heritage to put machinery thereon in working order held to be both collateral obligation and personal obligation covered by a non-supersession clause included in missives but not in disposition. On both grounds, undertaking survived delivery of disposition. Authorities discussed.

Bourton v Claydon 1990 SLT (Sh Ct) 7. Undertaking by seller to bear cost of repairs to any defect in central heating system held to survive delivery of disposition on footing that it was a collateral obligation which had nothing to do with conveyance. *Wood v Edwards* 1988 SLT (Sh Ct) 17 and *Finlayson v McRobb* 1987 SLT (Sh Ct) 150 not followed. No non-supersession clause in contract and the sheriff proceeded on footing that, since this was a collateral obligation, it automatically survived delivery of disposition.

Robson v Inglis 1990 GWD 2-92. In special circumstances, involving obligations clearly intended to remain enforceable beyond a contractual time-limit, time-limit held inapplicable and Pena v Ray 1987 SLT 607 distinguished.

University of Strathclyde (Properties) Ltd v Fleeting Organisation Ltd 1992 GWD 14-822. Parties free to contract for time-limit different from statutory period laid down in Prescription and Limitation (Scotland) Act 1973 or elsewhere.

Meek v Bell 1993 GWD 20-1238. Missives for sale of business included benefit of a lease. In addition, missives provided that purchaser should have option to purchase. Purchaser exercised right, which seller disputed, basing his argument on fact that contract had been implemented by delivery, in this case, of lease which superseded whole missives. Held that delivery of lease had superseded only that clause in missives which provided that lease should be entered into. All other provisions in missives collateral and therefore survived *proprio vigore*.

Rae v Middleton 1995 SLT (Sh Ct) 60. Offer for sale provided that, where subjects had been altered, consents and certificates should wherever applicable be exhibited prior to settlement and delivered with titles. Purchaser maintained that this was collateral obligation which survived delivery of disposition. Held that clause was operative only up to the date of settlement and not beyond and was not saved by non-supersession clause. *Greaves v Abercromby* 1989 SCLR 11 and *Porch v MacLeod* 1992 SLT 661 followed.

Spowart v Wylie 1995 GWD 23-1257. Purchaser maintained that he had no liability under a clause in the missives in terms of which, if planning permission were obtained, he would pay additional sum. He granted a standard security covering the additional sum. Missives also contained a two-year non-supersession clause which had expired. Held that standard security contained obligation to pay the additional sum in clear terms and was in substance self-contained. Purpose of standard security was to protect seller's position; and in terms of the missives it was clear that parties intended liability to survive beyond two-year period.

Glazick v Iyer 1996 SCLR 270. Missives contained usual clause as to planning permission, building warrants etc and non-supersession clause with two-year time-limit. Transaction settled and disposition delivered. It then turned out that building alterations had previously been carried out without building warrant which was clearly in breach of consents clause. Held that, since disposition in its terms incorporated antecedent contract by specific reference, it then formed part of the conveyance and as such became 'sole measure of the rights and liabilities'.

Callander v Midlothian District Council 1996 SCLR 955. Missives of sale and purchase provided, *inter alia*, for right of access. Seller argued that missives provision as to access, not repeated in disposition, was superseded thereby. Held that access provision remained enforceable and was not too unspecific to be implemented. Not superseded by disposition, being collateral; and it was not an obligation personal to the parties but in the nature of a servitude. (Text 17.56)

Aberdeen Rubber Ltd v Knowles & Sons (Fruiterers) Ltd 1995 SLT 870. Held, in House of Lords on the non-supersession point, that additional area of land was conveyed patently by mistake and formed no part of antecedent contract. Accordingly, non-supersession not in point.

Smith v Lindsay & Kirk 1998 SLT 1096 and 2000 SLT 287. Non-supersession clause with two year time limit. Purchaser instructed solicitor to sue but solicitor failed to raise action within two-year period. Held that a provision requiring enforcement within two years could not cut off the right to sue for damages for breach but this was overruled on appeal.

Hamilton v Rodwell 1998 SCLR 418. Missives which were to continue in force for two-year period contained clause requiring seller to meet cost of repairs. Money placed on deposit receipt to meet such costs. The two-year period expired before work was completed. Held that the seller was under no obligation to meet the cost of the repairs and therefore the money on deposit receipt became part of the purchase price payable to the seller. (Text 28.43)

Albatown Ltd v Credential Group Ltd 2001 GWD 27-1102. A property was sold and the disposition narrated that the full price had been paid. In fact only part of the price was paid and the purchasers granted a standard security to the sellers over the property in respect of the obligations in terms of the missives. There was a two-year supersession clause in the missives. After two years the balance of the price was still unpaid and it was held that this was no longer payable and no longer secured by the standard security. (Text 21.4, 28.43)

Lonergan v W & P Food Services Ltd 2002 SLT 908. A clause in the missives provided that the missives would remain in effect ' notwithstatnding payment of the price and delivery of the disposition but that for a period of two years.' It was held this clause was void from uncertainty as no starting date was specified. (Text 28.43)

Spence v W & R Murray (Alford) Ltd 2002 SLT 918. Condition that missives would cease to be enforceable two years after date of entry. Settlement was delayed for more than two years and the contract was held to be unenforceable. (Text 28.43)

28.44 Matrimonial Homes (Family Protection) (Scotland) Act 1981

Verity v Fenner 1993 SCLR 223. In the case of cohabiting couples under s 18 of Matrimonial Homes (Family Protection) (Scotland) Act 1981, primary condition to establish is that cohabitation existed at date when court considered the case.

Armour v Anderson 1994 SLT 1127. Discussion on 1981 Act, s 18(3), as it applies to cohabiting couples. By the time action raised parties no longer cohabiting and held by the sheriff principal to be outwith provisions of 1981 Act. On appeal, decision of sheriff principal reversed, holding that, since parties were co-habiting when relevant events occurred, application was competent.

Stevenson v Roy 2002 SLT 445. Discusses a non-entitled spouse's rights to occupy and be protected against the transfer of heritable property under s 6(3)(f) of the 1981 Act. Loss of rights due to lapse of time and relevance of unsuccessful attempt to reoccupy. (Text 28.44)

28.47 Time of the essence

Toynar Ltd v R & A Properties (Fife) Ltd 1989 GWD 2-92. Discussion on effect of making time of essence of contract, and then giving time to pay. (Text 28.73)

Ford Sellar Morris Properties plc v E W Hutchison Ltd 1990 SC 34. Where time-limit is specified for implement of contractual condition, whether suspensive or resolutive, and is made of essence of contract, time-limit must be adhered to, failing which either party may resile. (Text 28.73)

Ahmed v Akhtar 1997 SLT 218. Contract for sale of business included provision for assignation of lease of premises from which business conducted. 'Material condition' that landlords gave consent to assignation. When landlords had failed to give consent by date of entry, purchaser withdrew from bargain. Seller argued that withdrawal unlawful. Action dismissed. Rule that time is not of essence is a rule of sale of heritable property. This was sale of business conducted from leased premises, and rule did not apply. Thus it was not necessary for contract to provide in terms that obtaining of consent by date of entry was of essence. Words of contract supported view that time ought to be of essence. Hence purchaser justified in rescinding.

The following section is included for the sake of completeness.

The actio quanti minoris clause

Hayes v Robinson 1984 SLT 300. Purchaser, after completion, sought to retain subjects and claim damages for breach of collateral obligation. Held premature to consider whether claim *quanti minoris.*

Neilson v Barratt 1987 GWD 13-467. Discussion as to whether claim for damages in circumstances amounted to *actio quanti minoris*.

McKillop v Mutual Securities Ltd 1945 SC 166. Combined sale and building contract; distinguished in *Winston v Patrick*.

Fallis v Brown 1987 GWD 13-466. Discussion on claim arising out of damage between completion of contract and date of settlement, where missives contained clause requiring seller to maintain non-supersession clause. (Text 28.42)

Fortune v Fraser 1996 SLT 878. See para 28.16 above.

Colgan v Mooney 1994 GWD 1-43. See para 28.11 above.

28.48 Time-limit for acceptance

Effold Properties Ltd v Sprot 1979 SLT (Notes) 84. Condition as to time-limit in qualified acceptance did not prevent withdrawal of acceptance within the time-limit.

28.50 Let property – vacant possession

Lothian and Border Farmers v McCutcheon 1952 SLT 450. Tenant in occupation under lease. (Text 10.8, 28.30)

Stuart v Lort-Phillips 1977 SC 244. Provision for 'actual occupation' entitles purchaser to insist on vacant possession of whole subjects. (Text 28.30, 28.69)

28.52 New Houses

Cormack v NHBC 1997 GWD 24-1218. Discusses what defects are covered by the NHBC policy.

28.58 Intended development

See also paras 28.18 and 28.40 above.

Gordon District Council v Wimpey Homes Holdings Ltd 1989 SLT 141. Where contract contains suspensive conditions as to planning permission etc, it is normally implied that parties will act reasonably in determining whether or not condition has been implemented. (Text 28.60)

John H Wyllie v Ryan Industrial Fuels Ltd 1989 SLT 302. In the ordinary case each party to contract entitled to assume that the other will act reasonably with particular reference to suspensive conditions. (Text 28.60)

McKay v Leigh Estates (Scotland) Ltd 1987 GWD 16-609. Missives contained condition that purchaser should receive satisfactory report on suitability of ground for development. Purchaser did not adequately investigate ground and then purportedly resiled. Purchaser ordained to lead proof to establish that decision to resile was reasonable. (Text 28.17, 28.60)

Burnside v James Harrison (Developers) Ltd 1989 GWD 11-468. Provision in contract that either party may resile if completion certificate not obtained by specified date binding and enforceable even if certificate later obtained. (Text 28.19, 28.73)

Elwood v Ravenseft Properties Ltd 1991 SLT 44. Sellers in contract undertook to use all reasonable endeavours to obtain consent. Held competent for purchaser to seek order from court ordaining sellers to raise action against landlord seeking to procure consent.

28.61 Purchase of public sector houses and the right to buy

Dundee District Council v Anderson 1994 SLT 46. Tenants' rights to purchase a dwellinghouse provided with facilities specially designed or adapted for persons of pensionable age or disabled persons; call/alarm system installed but not connected. Held that correct approach to the Housing (Scotland) Act 1987, s 61, was to consider whether, at the material date, house satisfied statutory conditions.

McLoughlin's Curator Bonis v Motherwell District Council 1994 SLT (Lands Tr) 31. Purchase of dwellinghouse; tenant incapax and permanently hospitalised. Held that tenancy not abandoned, curator could competently make application.

Jack's Executrix v Falkirk District Council 1992 SLT 5. Sheriff of opinion that ss 72 and 73 of 1987 Act in effect incorporated into missives. Held further that executrix of deceased tenant who had contracted to buy but died before delivery of disposition entitled to implement of bargain. Discussion of concept of ownership arising under missives as opposed to mere jus crediti.

Glasgow District Council v Doyle 1993 SLT 604. Held on appeal that legislation envisaged the tenants becoming proprietors of the same subjects which they held on lease as tenants and that local authority had no discretion to vary extent of the ground in tenancy except in unusual cases where local authority might find themselves incapable of making offer to sell the whole.

Drummond v Dundee District Council 1993 GWD 26-1637. Discussion on level of discount where continuous occupation had been interrupted.

Lamont v Glenrothes Development Corporation 1993 SLT (Lands Tr) 2. Onus lies on tenant to show that she has secure tenancy to entitle her to right to buy.

McLuskey v Scottish Homes 1993 SLT (Lands Tr) 17. Tenant maintained that potential liability, under existing deeds of conditions, to contribute towards maintenance of common parts unreasonable. Held that, in circumstances, conditions reasonable and tenant's contention rejected. Tribunal made observations on disapplying Land Registration (Scotland) Act 1979, s 17, in case of houses built for letting, some of which were being sold.

Henderson v Glasgow District Council 1994 SLT 263. Under earlier procedure, Lands Tribunal had found that tenant had right to purchase and ordered local authority to issue appropriate papers. Offer duly made subject to right of pre-emption but no bargain concluded. Thereafter, Lands Tribunal served on tenant offer to sell under s 63(2) of Housing (Scotland) Act 1987 without reference to pre-emption. Offer accepted. On appeal, Inner House held Tribunal correct in issuing offer without reference to right of pre-emption.

Ross and Cromarty District Council v Patience 1995 SLT 1292. Held by Lord Marnoch that superior entitled to right of pre-emption on right-to-buy offer. Decision reversed in House of Lords – see 1997 SLT 463.

Clydebank District Council v Keeper of the Registers of Scotland 1994 SLT (Lands Tr) 2. Held that sale of dwellinghouse purchased under right-to-buy legislation by executors of deceased purchaser discharged obligations of deceased to repay discount. (Text 28.67)

Cumbernauld and Kilsyth District Council, Reference by 1993 SLT (Lands Tr) 51. Dispute arose between adjoining proprietors as to how much should be included in the offer to sell.

Fernie v Strathclyde Regional Council 1994 SLT (Lands Tr) 11. Held that in application under s 68(4). Tribunal not restricted to deciding whether ground of refusal valid, but could competently consider other reasons why tenant had no right to purchase.

Dundee District Council v Kelly 1994 SLT 1268. Discussion on meaning of the term 'succession' under Housing (Scotland) Act 1987, s 61(5). Held that 'succession' not limited to succession on death. But occupation by child of tenant during tenancy which ended before 1980 did not count for continuous occupation.

Beggs v Kilmarnock and Loudoun District Council 1996 SLT 461. Local authority tenant opted to purchase his house but Lands Tribunal refused his application to find that he had been a secure tenant since 1990. Immediately prior to his application in 1992, tenant given six years' imprisonment. His furniture and personal effects, however, remained in house, and he continued to pay rent. He received housing benefit. His aunt occupied the house in 1992 and removed at the request of council. On release from prison tenant returned to house and argued that he had been only temporarily absent and was technically 'in occupation'. Lands Tribunal refused tenant's application on the basis that occupation for this purpose required physical presence in house. Tenant appealed to Court of Session, arguing that, in all the circumstances, he was 'in possession' and intended to return as soon as released, which meant he was in possession. Court of Session upheld appeal and referred case back to Lands Tribunal.

Waverley Housing Trust Ltd v Roxburgh District Council 1995 SLT (Lands Tr) 2. Trust applied to purchase two houses owned by the district council with no change of tenancy. Council offered to sell on condition that, subject to statutory rights of occupying tenants, houses were not to be sold with vacant possession until they had first been offered to council at equivalent value of tenanted property. Held that, in absence of evidence that pre-emption clause depressed value placed on the two houses, Lands Tribunal could not assume that this was so and condition did not prevent giving good and marketable title, but right of pre-emption in this form would contravene Housing (Scotland) Act 1988, s 63, and so should be struck out.

McKay v Dundee District Council 1996 SLT (Lands Tr) 9. Tenant of local authority, being undoubtedly a secure tenant, sought to purchase her house. Landlords failed to issue offer to sell or a refusal in good time. Accordingly, the tenant referred to Lands Tribunal. While case was before Tribunal, local authority obtained order for ejection and then argued that tenant was no longer entitled to purchase, not being secure tenant any more. Held that exercise of right to buy occurred when tenant accepted offer to sell. To exercise that right, tenant had to remain secure until such offer was received and accepted. That was not the position here and accordingly tenant was disqualified.

McLean v Cunninghame District Council 1996 SLT (Lands Tr) 2. Husband and wife, joint secure tenants, applied to purchase. Wife had longer period of occupation as wife of former husband during his tenancy of a public sector house. Held that her period of occupancy, being longer, counted in calculating discount.

Hamilton v Glasgow District Council 1996 SLT (Lands Tr) 14. Wife succeeded husband as tenant of public sector house. Later, son became joint tenant along with her. She died and son became sole tenant. He applied to purchase. Local authority offered discount of sum calculated from date when he became joint tenant. Son appealed. Held that son not entitled to discount in respect of occupation during the tenancy of his father.

Kennedy v Hamilton District Council 1995 SCLR 980. Lands Tribunal rejected application to purchase council house on grounds that, at date of application, house formed one of a group of houses with special facilities. Tenant appealed but was refused.

Houston v East Kilbride Development Corporation 1995 SLT (Lands Tr) 12. Lands Tribunal allowed application by tenant to purchase her house. Decided that house had not been provided with facilities specified in s 61(4)(a) of Housing (Scotland) Act 1987.

Hamilton v City of Glasgow District Council 1997 SLT 243. A discussion as to what constitutes qualifying occupation.

Tennant v East Kilbride District Council 1997 SLT (Lands Tr) 14. Discussion on calculation of the discount from price with particular reference to previous discount allowed.

Livingstone v East of Scotland Water Authority 1999 SLT 869. Dispute as to right to buy procedure in which it was held that there is a duty on the landlord to ascertain whether the tenancy was secure.

Ross v City of Dundee Council 2000 GWD 18-719. Discussion on rights of the executors of a deceased qualifying tenant under the right to buy scheme.

McDonald's Trustee v Aberdeen City Council 2000 GWD 1-24. Registration of a trust deed in Books of Council and Session represented a disposal for the purposes of the right to buy legislation and the discount was recoverable by the council from the trustee under the deed.

Lock v City of Edinburgh Council 2000 GWD 31-1237. Discussion of what constitutes qualifying occupation for the purposes of the right to buy scheme and the effect of interruption to occupation.

Smith v Dundee City Council 2001 GWD 20-778. Purchase by a tenant janitor of house which was within school grounds. Discussion on the right to buy scheme in relation to such houses and whether employee required to occupy for better performance of duties. .

Nicol v Shetland Islands Council 2001 GWD 7-274. Timeous issue of notice to sell or notice of refusal to sell in response to tenant's application under right to buy scheme. Delay due to concerns as to whether the local authority held a valid title to the property.

Davidson v Dundee City Council 2002 Hous LR 104. Exclusion from right to buy scheme due to adaptation of dwelling for elderly persons.

Forsyth v South Ayrshire Council 2002 Hous LR 101. Exclusion from right to buy scheme where house equipped with facilities to assist elderly or disabled persons.

Queens Cross Housing Association Ltd v McAllister 2003 GWD 17-541. A secure tenancy remains secure after transfer to property owned by the same landlord.

28.68 Resulting obligations of seller and purchaser

Inglis v Lowrie 1990 SLT (Sh Ct) 60. Concluded formal missives for sale and purchase of heritage cannot be discharged by oral agreement.

Rockcliffe Estates plc v Co-operative Wholesale Society Ltd 1994 SLT 592. Reminder that parties are presumed by implication to act reasonably, and not capriciously, in relation to contract conditions. Compare *Hutton v Barrett* 1994 GWD 37-2188, para 28.75 below.

28.69 Seller's obligations – to deliver a valid disposition

For title, possession, and searches etc, see above.

Leith Heritages Co (Ltd) v Edinburgh and Leith Glass Co (1876) 3 R 789. General principles.

Anderson v Lambie 1954 SC (HL) 43. Reduction of disposition as erroneous; effect on prior contract. (Text 28.77)

Russell's Executor v Russell's Executors 1983 SLT 385. If formal contract does not properly reflect intentions of both parties, and that can be proved, court will correct error.

Johnston's Trustees v Kinloch 1925 SLT 124. Terms of description to be inserted in disposition.

Equitable Loan Co v Storie 1972 SLT (Notes) 20. Disposition not conveying whole subjects sold.

Hay v Aberdeen Corporation 1909 SC 554. Sale of 'right and interest'; seller bound to dispone land.

Cowan v Stewart (1872) 10 M 735. Servitude to be inserted in disposition.

Mackenzie v Neill 37 SLR 666. Seller must grant absolute warrandice.

Young v McKellar Ltd 1909 SC 1340. Warrandice following articles of roup.

Fraser v Cox 1938 SC 506. Warrandice not reflecting terms of antecedent contract. (Text 16.6)

Porteous v Henderson (1898) 25 R 563. Writs.

28.70 Purchaser's obligations

Payment of the price

Rodger (Builders) Ltd v Fawdry 1950 SC 483. Date of payment. (Text 28.73, 28.76, 28.77, 32.52, 32.56, 32.59)

Prestwick Cinema Co v Gardiner 1951 SC 98. Interest on unpaid price. (Text 28.28)

Bowie v Semple's Executors 1978 SLT (Sh Ct) 9. Purchaser not in possession; interest. (Text 28.28, 28.69)

Chapman's Trustees v Anglo-Scottish Group Services Ltd 1980 SLT (Sh Ct) 27. Delay in payment of price; whether sellers entitled to claim damages or merely interest.

Tiffney v Bachurzewski 1985 SLT 165. Seller not entitled to interest unless purchaser actually in possession; interest not due *ex mora*. (Text 28.28, 28.47)

Davidson v Tilburg Ltd 1991 GWD 2-115; 1991 GWD 18-1109. Purchaser cannot be required to settle contract of sale and purchase of heritage except in exchange for delivery of disposition. Sellers not entitled to resile on account of purchaser's refusal to settle on this ground unless sellers themselves in position to settle, notwithstanding apparently contradictory provision in missives. (Text 28.69)

28.72 Default by the purchaser – seller's remedies

Carter v Lornie (1890) 18 R 353. Action for implement.

British Railways Board v Birrell 1971 SLT (Notes) 17. Action for payment.

Muir & Black v Nee 1981 SLT (Sh Ct) 68. Action for payment – whether purchaser's obligations extinguished by the short negative prescription.

Inveresk Paper Co Ltd v Pembury Machinery Co Ltd 1972 SLT (Notes) 63. Rescission. (Text 28.71)

Rodger (Builders) Ltd v Fawdry 1950 SC 483. Circumstances not justifying rescission. Disposition to second purchaser reduced. (Text 28.73, 28.76, 28.77, 32.52, 32.56, 32.59)

Grant v Ullah 1987 SLT 639. Discussion on quantum of damages on breach by purchaser. (Text 28.74)

Johnstone v Harris 1977 SC 365. Rescission; seller's duty to mitigate damages.

Commercial Bank v Beal (1890) 18 R 80. Forfeiture of deposit. (Text 28.27)

Reid v Campbell 1958 SLT (Sh Ct) 45. Forfeiture of instalments paid to account of price. (Text 28.29)

Geo Packman & Sons v Dunbar's Trustees 1977 SLT 140. Impossibility, delay; seller entitled to rescind without notice. (Text 28.73)

Robson v Inglis 1990 GWD 2-92. Time-limit in non-supersession clause held not to apply to recovery of damages by seller following on breach by purchaser.

Atlas Assurance Co Ltd v Dollar Land Holdings plc 1993 SLT 892. Actings of parties, in particular delay in enforcing contract, may imply that right to resile has been waived. (Text 28.73)

University of Strathclyde (Properties) Ltd v Fleeting Organisations Ltd 1992 GWD 14-822. Claim for damages founded on clause in missives but not in disposition; non-supersession clause limited to 18 months after settlement. Held that action raised outwith that period was out of time.

Mills v Findlay 1994 SCLR 397. Purchaser defaulted and sellers rescinded and resold, then raised action of damages against defaulting purchaser for, *inter alia, solatium,* and each awarded £1,100. On appeal to sheriff principal, *solatium* reduced to £500 for each pursuer. (Text 28.74)

Hall v McWilliam 1993 GWD 23-1457. See para 28.42 above. (Text 28.42)

Cumming v Brown 1993 SCLR 707. Held that, while the seller could have resiled in interval between date of entry and date of tender by purchaser, he had not done so and was therefore bound to proceed with bargain. Decree of specific implement granted. (Text 28.73)

Charisma Properties Ltd v Grayling 1997 SLT 449. Missives of sale and purchase provided that it was a material condition that price was paid by certain date and time. If price was not paid within 21 days, seller could treat purchaser as in material breach and rescind on giving prior notice to that effect. On stipulated date, no payment had been made. Seller's solicitors sent letter purportedly giving notice that the missives were rescinded with immediate effect. Purchaser's solicitors responded by refusing to accept that intimation on footing that seller not entitled immediately to resile, and prior notice required. Held that contract itself declared breach material and no further indulgence beyond stipulated 21-day period was necessary. (Text 28.73)

Owen v Fotheringham 1997 SLT (Sh Ct) 28. Contract for sale of land and erection of house. Purchasers sought to rescind on the basis that the house was not built in a good and workman-like manner. Proof allowed.

Grovebury Management Ltd v McLaren 1997 SLT 1083. Missives provided that if price remained unpaid 28 days after entry the sellers could rescind on giving written notice. Such notice was given after fax received from purchasers offering to settle. Held contract could not be rescinded until written notice given and the fax was an effective tender of performance. (Text 28.73)

James Howden & Co Ltd v Taylor Woodrow Property Co Ltd 1998 SCLR 903. When a single right emerges on the occurrence of a specified event, postponement of the exercise of the right for a limited period does not constitute waiver.

Palmer v Forsyth 1999 SLT (Sh Ct) 93. Missives provided that the purchasers could resile if the title deeds were not entirely satisfactory to them of which they were to be the sole judges. The purchasers considered the tiles unsatisfactory and resiled .The sellers argued that they had to give reasons for resiling and that there was an implied term to act reasonably. Held that no reason need be given and although the purchasers did have to act reasonably the sellers had failed to show that they had not acted reasonably.

28.74 Default by the purchaser: measure of damages

Lloyds Bank plc v Bamberger 1993 SCLR 727. Missives contained standard clause for payment of interest if not paid on date of entry. Purchasers defaulted and sellers resiled. Sellers claimed that purchasers were liable for interest at rate specified in interest clause over period from due date of payment to date of resiling. Sellers held not entitled to interest. There was a total failure to pay the price, following on which sellers had rescinded and resulting entitlement was damages, not contractually stipulated rate. (Text 28.28)

Palmer v Beck 1993 SLT 485. Held that (1) if there is no actual eviction, there is no claim under warrandice; (2) if claim is for fraudulent misrepresentation, *solatium* is element in damages; (3) not so if claim is under warrandice. (Text 10.8, 28.74)

Colgan v Mooney 1994 GWD 1-43. See para 28.11 above. (Text 28.74)

King v Moore 1993 SLT 1117. Award of damages for purchasers' failure to implement contract based on difference between (1) the contract price of two years ago and (2) present value of subjects about £100,000 less plus interest.

Rapide Enterprises v Midgley 1998 SLT 504. Held that where parties make specific provision for the quantum calculation on breach, an additional claim for interest is assumed not to have been contemplated. (Text 28.28)

28.75 Default by the seller

Time for implement

Gilfillan v Cadell & Grant (1893) 21 R 269. Valid title tendered too late.

Kelman v Barr's Trustee (1878) 5 R 816. Valid title tendered too late.

Campbell v McCutcheon 1963 SC 505. Where defect fundamental, purchaser not obliged to give time. (Text 28.32, 28.51, 28.76)

Carter v Lornie (1890) 18 R 353. Circumstances in which purchaser bound to take title tendered late.

Kinnear v Young 1936 SLT 574. Defect incurable; purchaser having taken possession and given time still entitled to resile.

Rodger (Builders) Ltd v Fawdry 1950 SC 483. Price not tendered at date of entry. (Text 28.73, 28.76, 28.77, 32.52, 32.56, 32.59)

Burns v Garscadden (1901) 8 SLT 321. Circumstances in which seller held not to have given sufficient notice to defaulting purchaser of intention to rescind and resell.

Macdonald v Newall (1898) 1 F 68. Purchaser's objection to title made too late. (Text 28.22, 32.43)

Crofts v Stewart's Trustees 1927 SC (HL) 65. Instalment purchase; no objection to title until after instalment paid.

Morrison v Gray 1932 SC 712. Purchaser held not barred from objecting until disposition delivered.

Speevak v Robson 1949 SLT (Notes) 39. Seller contractually bound to effect alterations to subjects by date of entry; alterations not completed. Seller held to be in breach and liable in damages; but purchaser not entitled to resile.

Boland & Co Ltd v Dundas Trustees 1975 SLT (Notes) 80. Suspensive condition not within power of contracting party to purify. (Text 28.73)

Macdonald v Scott 1981 SC 75. Obligation to deliver conveyance of heritable property not imprescriptible.

Burnside v James Harrison (Developers) Ltd 1989 GWD 11-468. Provision in contract that either party may resile if completion certificate not obtained by specified date is binding and enforceable even if certificate later obtained. (Text 28.19, 28.73)

Ford Sellar Morris Properties plc v E W Hutchison Ltd 1990 SC 34. Where date is fixed in contract for purification of condition, that date must be strictly adhered to. *Boland & Co Ltd*, above, followed. (Text 28.73)

Stewart's Executors v Stewart 1993 SLT 440. Opinion that mere contractual obligation to grant disposition not imprescriptible under Prescription and Limitation (Scotland) Act 1973, Schedule 3(h). Schedule 3(h) applies to personal titles which are imprescriptible. (Text 32.77)

Barratt Scotland Ltd v Keith 1994 SLT 1343. Obligations of seller under missives are obligations relating to land, as such are subject to 20-year prescription, not 5-year prescription. (Text 32.77)

Wright v Frame 1992 GWD 8-447. Obligation relating to land, for the purposes of Prescription and Limitation (Scotland) Act 1973, falls under the long negative prescription, not five-year prescription, following *Barratt* above. (Text 32.44, 32.77)

Clancy v Caird (No 2) 2000 GWD 18-716. Claim for damages by purchaser of a residential home on basis of misrepresentation on number of residents dismissed as no misrepresentation proved and purchaser had relied on other matters in making the purchase.

Evans v Argus Healthcare (Glenesk) Ltd 2001 GWD 2-96. Missives for sale of nursing home. Seller in breach in relation to provision for servitude. Proof before answer allowed on whether right to rescind waived by actings.

Adams v Young 2001 GWD 3-127. House purchased which had formerly been a shop and was converted by the seller. Three years after the purchase a secret room was discovered which contained builders' waste and was alleged to have caused some dry rot in the house. Purchaser sued for damages on the ground of fraudulent misrepresentation. Proof before answer was allowed on whether the house was worth less than the price paid due to the existence of this secret room.

Barry v Sutherland 2001 GWD 38-1431. Proof before answer allowed where purchasers averred that they had been induced to pay a certain price for the commercial premises due to fraudulent trading accounts.

Argus Care Ltd v Balmoral Nursing Homes Ltd 2001 GWD 29-1155. Purchasers of a nursing home failed in an action for damages due to negligent misrepresentation regarding compliance with health board regulations.

Purchaser's remedies

Smith v Soeder (1895) 23 R 60. Title not marketable; rescission. (Text 28.32)

Campbell v McCutcheon 1963 SC 505. Undisclosed mineral reservation; rescission. (Text 28.32, 28.51, 28.76)

Louttit's Trustees v Highland Railway Co (1892) 19 R 791. Remedies of purchaser after settlement. (Text 28.32, 28.77)

Welsh v Russell (1894) 21 R 769. Remedies of purchaser after settlement. (Text 10.9, 28.32)

Fielding v Newell 1987 SLT 530. Discussion on quantum of damages on breach by seller.

McKillop v Mutual Securities Ltd 1945 SC 166. Retention and damages.

Bradley v Scott 1966 SLT (Sh Ct) 25. Retention and damages.

Hayes v Robinson 1984 SLT 300. Retention and damages; whether *quanti minoris*.

Neilson v Barratt 1987 GWD 13-467. Discussion as to whether a claim for damages amounted to *actio quanti minoris*.

Steuart's Trustees v Hart (1875) 3 R 192. Circumstances justifying restitutio after settlement.

Angus v Bryden 1992 SLT 884. Disposition ostensibly implemented missives but disponer alleged error. Lord Cameron expressed opinion that unintentional essential error known to and taken advantage of by other party implied bad faith for which law provided remedy. *Steuart's*

Trustees, above, applied; *Spook Erection (Northern) Ltd v Kaye* 1990 SLT 676 not followed. (Text 28.22)

Hamilton v Western Bank of Scotland (1861) 23 D 1033. Circumstances justifying *restitutio* after settlement.

Stewart v Kennedy (1890) 17 R (HL) 1. Specific implement; general observations.

McKellar v Dallors Ltd 1928 SC 503. Specific implement.

Mackay v Campbell 1967 SC (HL) 53. Specific implement.

Hoey v Butler 1975 SC 87. Specific implement and damages.

Speevak v Robson 1949 SLT (Notes) 39. Purchaser held not entitled to resile on breach by seller but awarded damages.

Plato v Newman 1950 SLT (Notes) 30. Specific implement, seller claiming implement impossible.

Boag, Petitioner 1967 SC 322. Seller disappeared; clerk of court empowered to execute disposition. (Text 28.76)

Mowbray v Mathieson 1989 GWD 6-267. Purchaser had been in possession for over two years and had already sued for implement; no longer open to him to rescind. (Text 28.77)

Tainsh v McLaughlin 1990 SLT (Sh Ct) 102. Discussion on measure of damages. (Text 28.72)

Caledonian Property Group Ltd v Queensferry Property Group Ltd 1992 SLT 738. Discussion on quantum of damages (anticipated capital loss and interest) on default by the seller after settlement. (Text 28.77)

Martone v Zani 1992 GWD 32-1903. Decree in an action of implement; clerk of court authorised to sign disposition. (Text, 28.22, 28.76)

Parker v O'Brien 1992 SLT (Sh Ct) 31. Held that (1) condition in missives fell to be construed as future promise to grant warranty and was not a collateral obligation; and (2) mere warranty is nothing more than that, whether present or future, and in particular does not oblige warrantor to do anything. In the result, any claim for damages based on such warranty is illegitimate attempt to use *actio quanti minoris* in circumstances which do not support it.

Hutton v Barrett 1994 GWD 37-2188. Following on concluded missives, which provided for preliminary variation of seller's title, seller then produced title duly varied, but purchaser demurred at new burdens imposed, on footing that they materially diminished value and prevented parking, which in turn rendered planning permission valueless. Held that purchaser entitled to resile without proof and that question of his acting reasonably did not arise since seller clearly could not perform his obligation.

MacDougall v MacDougall's Executors 1994 SLT 1178. See para 28.35 above. (Text 28.35)

McLennan v Warner & Co 1996 GWD 22-1281. In terms of titles, right of access provided for limited purposes by path to be made, six feet wide, stretching from back of building. Owner of upper flat subsequently built garage over access without consent. Held that seller in breach; that purchaser could not be required to implement bargain and take entry pending resolution of title problem; and, when title problem later resolved, seller not entitled unilaterally to seek to revive contract already earlier validly terminated on this ground. (Text 28.76)

28.78 Collateral obligations

(See also cases under 28.75)

Taylor v McLeod 1990 SLT 194. Obligation to repair defects in lift held collateral.

Bourton v Claydon 1990 SLT (Sh Ct) 7. Obligation on seller to bear cost of repairs to central heating held collateral.

Hardwick v Gebbie 1991 SLT 258. Circumstances where obligation to build house held to be intended as continuing obligation, notwithstanding delivery of disposition but only *quoad* matters not reasonably discoverable on inspection. Remedy was damages for breach of contract, not *actio quanti minoris*.

Porch v MacLeod 1992 SLT 661. Missives provided that all necessary consents etc had been obtained for any work on subjects, 'and satisfactory evidence to substantiate this will be exhibited ... and delivered at ... entry'. Missives also contained non-supersession clause, not repeated in subsequent disposition. Held that the warranty clause contained warranty as to condition at date of missives and 'a personal and collateral obligation on the sellers' to produce satisfactory evidence, but that warranty and obligation ancillary thereto (ie the obligation to produce evidence) had both terminated on delivery of disposition in implement.

University of Strathclyde (Properties) Ltd v Fleeting Organisations Ltd 1992 GWD 14-822. Where claim for damages founded on clause in missives but not in disposition and non-supersession clause was limited to 18 months after settlement, held that action raised outwith that period was out of time.

Meek v Bell 1993 GWD 20-1238. Following on concluded missives for sale and purchase of business, which involved *inter alia* lease and option to purchase, held that delivery of lease superseded missives only to extent that missives provided for lease being entered into in terms of agreed draft. Also held that all other provisions in missives were collateral and so excluded from rule in *Winston v Patrick*.

King v Gebbie 1993 SLT 512. Composite contract for sale and purchase of ground including an obligation on the seller to construct a dwellinghouse according to certain specifications. Held that obligation imposed in missives to give entry to house according to certain specifications etc covered works carried out before and after conclusion of missives; that obligation to build etc was collateral; and that missives could not be so construed as to prevent purchaser claiming damages for reasonably discoverable defects. Observed that condition in missives obliging seller to produce planning permission, building warrants and completion certificates not collateral and would be superseded by delivery of disposition.

Rae v Middleton 1995 SLT (Sh Ct) 60. Offer for sale provided that, where subjects had been altered, consents and certificates should wherever applicable be exhibited prior to settlement and delivered with titles. Purchaser maintained that this was a collateral obligation which survived delivery of disposition. Held that clause operative only up to date of settlement, not beyond, and not saved by non-supersession clause. *Greaves v Abercromby* 1989 SCLR 11 and *Porch v MacLeod* followed.

Adams v Whatlings plc 1995 SCLR 185. On purchase of building plot from builder who undertook to build dwellinghouse thereon, builder, by implication, was held to have warranted quality of building.

28.79 Both parties in breach

Mason v A & R Robertson & Black 1993 SLT 773. Complex case involving breach or alleged breach on both sides and professional negligence. Held: that letter of obligation was contract collateral to missives, to be read in context thereof; that pursuer by taking decree had not irrevocably elected because, as a matter of law, missives were not automatically terminated by decree; and accordingly pursuer's averment that letter of obligation became ineffective was irrelevant. Subsequently, decree of dismissal granted. See 1.3 above (Text 28.79)

Chapter 29   Statutory Titles

29.2 Adjudication in implement

Boag, Petitioner 1967 SC 322. Seller disappeared. Clerk of court authorised to sign disposition. (Text 28.76)

Martone v Zani 1992 GWD 32-1903. Decree in action of implement. Clerk of court authorised to sign disposition. (Text 28.22, 28.76)

29.5 Adjudication for debt

Watson v Swift & Co's Judicial Factor 1986 SC 55. Effect on title of decree of redeemable adjudication within the ten-year period of the legal.

29.8 Bankruptcy and sequestration

Boyle's Trustee v Boyle 1988 SLT 581. Discussion on gratuitous alienations as between husband and wife in a sequestration. (Text 29.12)

Bank of Scotland, Petitioners 1988 SLT 690. A creditor is entitled, at common law, to challenge actings of a debtor company in making a gratuitous alienation and that right not excluded by Insolvency Act 1986, s 242.

Matheson's Trustee v Matheson 1992 SLT 685. A husband conveyed a dwellinghouse to his wife and claimed he was solvent, notwithstanding his subsequent sequestration. This was held to be a suitable question for proof.

Clark's Trustee, Noter 1993 SLT 667. In special circumstances power of sale may be conferred on interim trustee.

Rankin v McMahon 1997 SCLR 439. Matrimonial home owned in common by spouses. After parties separated wife made all payments for mortgage and endowment policy. Husband sequestrated. Trustee in sequestration raised action against wife for division and sale. Wife relied on s 40 of the Bankruptcy (Scotland) Act 1985 which requires trustee to obtain consent from court before selling. Proof before answer allowed on wife's entitlement to share of proceeds of sale.

Royal Bank of Scotland plc v Lamb's Trustee 1998 SCLR 923. The bank granted a security to enable the purchase of heritage by an undischarged bankrupt. The trustee in sequestration claimed the property as acquirenda and claimed that the security was void. Held that the trustee had a right to aquire the property but subject to the standard security.

Sutherland v Inland Revenue Commissioners 1999 SC 104. Held that a sequestration could not be reduced merely due to a procedural defect in its registration.

Thoar's Judicial Factor v Ramlort Ltd 1999 SLT 1153. Gratuitous alienation. Held that the creation of an English trust was not struck at by s 34 of the Bankruptcy (Scotland) Act 1985 because that section did not confer jurisdiction.

Rankin's Trustee v Somerville and Russell 1999 SLT 65. Vesting of the debtor's acquirenda in the Trustee in sequestration.

Anderson v White 2000 SLT 37. Owners of a farm sued their neighbour on the basis of nuisance. Nuisance was established and the Trustee in sequestration was found personally liable as he had continued to run the business as a going concern.

Fleming's Trustee v Fleming 2000 SLT 406. A title was in name of a husband and wife and survivor. The husband was sequestrated and subsequently died. It was held that the wife took the husband's one half share subject to his debts. *Barclays Bank Ltd v McGreish* 1983 SLT 344 was overruled. (Text 30.13)

Halifax plc v Gorman's Trustee 2000 GWD 8-312. Debtor not informed about sequestration due to late execution of petition. In meantime debtor granted a standard security in favour of the Halifax. The Keeper then refused to register the standard security anfd the trustee registered a notice of title. Held that the Halifax were entitled to be treated as preferred creditors. (Text 3.21)

Rush's Trustees v Rush 2002 GWD 1-16. Petition by trustee in sequestration to uplift consigned funds comprising compensation for compulsory purchase. Bankrupt challenged acquisition procedure. Trustee's petition granted.

29.10 Completion of title by trustee

Alliance and Leicester Building Society v Murray's Trustees 1995 SLT (Sh Ct) 77. Bankrupt acquired heritable property after the date of sequestration. The bankrupt granted a standard security in favour of the building society, and both deeds were recorded in the Register of Sasines. The court held that the property vested in the trustee in sequestration notwithstanding that the conveyance in favour of the bankrupt was granted after the date of sequestration. If the property had formed part of the bankrupt's estate at the date of sequestration it would have vested automatically in the trustee at that date. The bankrupt could not therefore grant a valid standard security. (Text 3.21)

29.12 Gratuitous alienation and unfair preferences

Bank of Scotland v T A Neilson & Co 1990 SC 284. Common law rule against gratuitous alienation applies to companies. (Text 32.65)

Short's Trustee v Chung 1991 SLT 472. Sale at undervalue is gratuitous alienation for purposes of Bankruptcy (Scotland) Act 1985, s 34; and reduction of the offending disposition is the appropriate remedy.

Latif's Trustee v Latif 1992 GWD 14-784. Disposition granted gratuitously by husband to his wife reduced on subsequent sequestration.

McLuckie Brothers Ltd v Newhouse Contracts Ltd 1993 SLT 641. Price paid for a property prior to sequestration inadequate and reduction granted.

Stuart Eves Ltd (In Liquidation) v Smiths Gore 1993 SLT 1274. In the circumstances liquidator sufficiently averred gratuitous alienation at common law.

MacFadyen's Trustee v MacFadyen 1994 SLT 1245. The owner of a dwellinghouse conveyed half to his mother. He was then sequestrated within the relevant period. The trustee in sequestration sought to have the disposition of the one half share reduced, not having been made for adequate consideration. The mother argued that there had been consideration – she had paid the purchase price, the running costs, and the title was in joint names of herself and her son because the bank had insisted. The arguments were rejected on the grounds that consideration, in the Bankruptcy (Scotland) Act 1985, implied something which had patrimonial worth at the time at which it was given. The disposition was reduced.

Ashraf's Trustee v Ashraf 1994 GWD 24-1440. Argument that property had been purchased and held in trust rejected.

Thomson v M B Trustees Ltd 1994 GWD 32-1894. Liquidator raised action against trustees of a pension fund and a bank seeking reduction of a disposition granted by the company in favour of the pension fund. The company acquired the property by disposition dated August 1988 and recorded in March 1989. The company conveyed the subjects to the pension fund in August 1988, recorded October 1988. The liquidator averred that the company was insolvent, or the granting of the disposition rendered it insolvent, and persons associated with the company benefited as a result. The pension fund trustees argued they paid full consideration. Proof before answer was allowed. The onus of establishing consideration was with the pension fund trustees.

Rankin v Meek 1995 SLT 526. On the winding up of a company, if a claim against a company has been discharged by an alienation made by the company within two years prior to the winding up, the alienation can be challenged and can only be upheld if made for adequate consideration.

Short's Trustee v Keeper of the Registers of Scotland 1996 SLT 166. Decree of reduction not registrable under Land Registration (Scotland) Act 1979, s 2(4), and will not normally justify rectification of Register. (Text 11.35, 29.13, 32.65)

Short's Trustee v Chung (No 2) 1999 SC 471. Reduction of original gratuitous alienation to Chung by bankrupt could not be registered in the land register. The trustee in sequestration achieved the desired result, however, by obtaining decree of restoration against Chung which was upheld on appeal. (Text 11.35)

Nottay's Trustees v Nottay 2001 SLT 769. Transfer of heritable property by debtor to spouse for 'love, favour, and affection'. Subsequent bankruptcy. Proof before answer allowed on relevancy of spouse's averments that the statement was made in error and adequate consideration paid.

29.13 Reduction

Mulhearn v Dunlop 1929 SLT 59. Extent of protection of s 46 of Conveyancing (Scotland) Act 1924. (Text 29.15, 32.50)

Grant's Trustee v Grant 1986 SC 51. Disposition granted in 1978 but not recorded in Sasines until March 1980. In August 1980, the disponer went bankrupt. Held that relevant date was date of recording, not delivery; and disposition was accordingly reduced. (Text 29.12)

McLeod v Cedar Holdings Ltd 1989 SLT 620. When a husband forged his wife's signature on a standard security over a dwellinghouse held in joint names, partial reduction of the security was held appropriate in order to maintain the obligation against the grantor but to release his wife therefrom. (Text 29.14)

Sereshky v Sereshky 1988 SLT 426. Where a signature on a power of attorney was alleged to have been forged, the onus lay on the challenger; but expert evidence was admitted to disprove authenticity and, on the basis of that and other evidence, the power of attorney was reduced as a forgery. (Text 29.13)

Hughes v McCluskie 1991 GWD 3-177. In an action for reduction of a disposition, the principal deed must be produced.

Leslie v Leslie 1987 SLT 232. Illustration of reduction of disposition under the Divorce (Scotland) Act 1976 (now the Family Law (Scotland) Act 1985).

Stockton Park (Leisure) Ltd v Border Oats Ltd 1991 SLT 333. In special circumstances and in the exercise of its equitable jurisdiction, the court may refuse to reduce a disposition although ex facie reducible, but compensation is payable.

Broadley v Wilson 1991 SLT 69. In appropriate circumstances, partial reduction only of a disposition held to be appropriate remedy. (Text 29.14)

Matheson's Trustee v Matheson 1992 SLT 685. A husband conveyed a dwellinghouse to his wife and claimed he was solvent notwithstanding his subsequent sequestration. This was held to be a suitable question for proof.

Angus v Bryden 1992 SLT 884. Missives included sea fishings in subjects of sale, but Lord Cameron held that as a matter of construction, it was intended that the river fishings only be included. (Text 28.22)

Aberdeen Rubber Ltd v Knowles & Sons (Fruiterers) Ltd 1995 SLT 870. An offer was made to purchase four areas of ground. Subsequently informal letters passed between the agents, one referring to the fact that it was intended that a fifth area be included. The offer was met by a qualified acceptance which was accepted *de plano* disposition conveyed all five areas. Sellers sought reduction on ground that the fifth area not mentioned in missives. House of Lords found no element of common error had been established. (Text 28.22)

Stirling v Bartlett 1992 SC 523. Partial reduction of a disposition which exceeded the extent of the subjects sold was appropriate.

Dougherty v MacLeod 1993 GWD 39-2599. Disposition in favour of mother and daughter contained a special disposition in favour of the survivor. Another daughter sought to have disposition reduced on ground that the mother had not intended there to be a survivorship destination. The action failed.

MacDougall v MacDougall's Executors 1994 SLT 1178. This case involved a challenge to the validity of a will; the granting of a Charter of Novodamus in favour of the alleged heir-at-law; and completion of title. Could the disponee from the wrong heir defend this title against an action of reduction brought by the true heir within the prescriptive period? The court held that completion of title by someone not the true heir is worthless in defence of a challenge by the true heir, however the mistake arose. This applies against the wrong heir as against *bona fide* third parties. The Charter of Novodamus fell to be reduced together with a disposition in favour of a purchaser for value. (Text 28.35, 30.17)

Bain v Bain 1994 GWD 7-410. A proprietor who had personal right, but no title to heritable property sold it to a purchaser but died before making up title and conveying it to the purchaser. A heritable creditor sought to make up title and obtained a disposition from two members of the family which he recorded. At the time of recording the disposition, the disponee was aware of the previous sale by the beneficial owner and the subsequent proceedings by which the purchaser sought to implement the missives. Held that in these circumstances the recorded disposition fell to be reduced under the offside goal rule in *Rodger (Builders) Ltd v Fawdry* 1950 SC 483.

Gordaviran Ltd v Clydesdale Bank plc 1994 SCLR 248. A debtor challenged the sufficiency of the advertisement by the creditor on the exercise of a power of sale. Held that s 25 of the Conveyancing and Feudal Reform (Scotland) Act 1970 confers no right on the debtor to require the creditor to demonstrate that he has fulfilled his duties, and so interim interdict of the proposed sale was refused. (Text 22.43)

Dunlop & Son's Judicial Factor v Armstrong 1995 SLT 645. The judicial factor appointed to the sequestrated estate of a firm sought to sell its heritable property which was subject to a standard security. Members of the family manipulated the standard security by clearing an assignation immediately prior to the appointment. They then sought to block the sale. Held that the judicial factor, as an officer of the court, had given an undertaking which fully secured the interests of the holder of the standard security, and on a balance of convenience he should be entitled to sell.

Johnstone & Clark (Engineers) Ltd v Graham 1994 SCLR 1100. Discharge of a standard security wrongly granted on a misunderstanding on the part of the solicitors. There was a subsequent sequestration and the discharge was challenged by the trustees. Proof before answer was allowed on the basis that, in a reduction, proof of error could be led by parole, and in this case the error was essential.

McCabe v Skipton Building Society 1994 SC 467. A standard security was granted by a husband and wife. The husband acted fraudulently in obtaining a further advance. The wife's action for reduction was dismissed.

Mumford v Bank of Scotland; Smith v Bank of Scotland 1996 SLT 392. Two partners in the same firm fraudulently obtained loans on security from the bank. In one case the property was in joint names and the wife signed at the request of the husband. In the other case the wife signed a consent under the Matrimonial Homes (Family Protection) (Scotland) Act 1981. Both wives argued they had been induced to sign by their husbands on fraudulent misrepresentations. Neither wife had been separately advised. Held, except in the case of agency, the law of Scotland did not confer constructive notice simply because of surrounding circumstances; and so, in the absence of actual knowledge on the part of the bank, the bank had no implied duty to explain to each wife the nature of the transaction or the consequences. Reversed on appeal to the House of Lords.

Sanderson's Trustees v Ambion Scotland Ltd 1994 SLT 645. Where a standard security is assigned the form of assignation must conform as nearly as may be to the statutory form but not necessarily verbatim, and the standard security so assigned may secure both original and further advances by the assignee if that is covered by the agreement.

Cameron v Lightheart 1996 SLT 1038. An application for reduction of a disposition granted 10 years previously by L in favour of C's husband, H, and subsequent disposition from H to X. The first title was a disposition in favour of C and L as trustees for a firm in which C and L were the partners. C argued that this disposition had been granted without her consent. The disposition contained the proviso that L and C and their successors in office were entitled to sell the subjects without limitation of anything contained in it, or otherwise dispose of the subjects in whole or in part by themselves or herself alone as if they or she were absolute beneficial owners and without consent of the other partners. The court refused to reduce the disposition. (Text 3.23)

Short's Trustee v Keeper of the Registers of Scotland 1996 SLT (HL) 166. A trustee in sequestration obtained a decree of reduction of a disposition as a gratuitous alienation. The subjects had, however, been registered as being in an operational area, and the gratuitous disponee had registered title. That title, in Sasines, would have been open to reduction under the Bankruptcy (Scotland) Act 1985 and the decree of reduction could have been recorded under the Conveyancing (Scotland) Act 1924. However, the Court of Session (upheld by the House of Lords in this reference) held that a decree of reduction was not registrable in the Land Register. For more details see 13.16 above. (Text 11.35, 29.13, 32.65)

Frost v Unity Trust Bank plc 1996 GWD 14-813. This case, involving allegations of misrepresentation, concerned an attempted reduction of a standard security. The pursuer failed to sustain relevant averments and the action was dismissed.

Russo v Hardey 1997 GWD 6-246. Decree of reduction of disposition granted on the grounds of force and fear.

City and County Investments (Scotland) Ltd v McIver 1998 SLT 541. Decree of reduction granted in case of an *a non domino* disposition.

Boyle v Boyle's Executor 1999 SC 479. Will reduced either (1) on grounds of incapacity or (2) on grounds of facility.

Young v Archibald 1999 GWD 4-205. Pursuer failed to have disposition reduced on the basis that the signature was allegedly forged as neither party was found to be a credible witness.

29.17 Rectification

Shaw v Wm Grant (Minerals) Ltd 1989 SLT 121. Requirements of rectification provisions in s 8 of Law Reform (Miscellaneous Provisions) (Scotland) Act 1985 discussed.

MAC Electrical & Heating Engineers Ltd v Calscot Electrical Distributors Ltd 1989 SCLR 498. Discussion on relevancy of averments in petition for rectification.

Oliver v Gaughan 1990 GWD 22-1247. Circumstances in which an order granted rectifying disposition as disconform to missives.

Bank of Scotland v Graham's Trustee 1993 SLT 252. A standard security, imperfectly completed, can nonetheless be rectified under the 1985 Act, s 8, even although the defects were *in substantialibus*.

Rehman v Ahmad 1993 SLT 741. A dispute between two partners. Lord Penrose, in a lengthy judgment, held that there had to be proof of agreement and of consensus independent of and prior to the document intended to give effect to it; and there had to be proof that the document failed to express accurately the common intention.

George Thompson Services Ltd v Moore 1993 SLT 634. Following the conclusion of missives, a disposition was delivered which the purchaser later maintained to be incorrect. He sued for rectification. The action was dismissed on the basis that, to rectify a disposition, a prior agreement had to be founded on disclosing the common intention which it was alleged the disposition did not reflect.

Angus v Bryden 1992 SLT 884. Held that missives of sale and purchase of salmon fishings were intended to be, as a matter of construction, restricted to river fishings only and not to include sea fishings, although these were included in the express terms of the missives. Reduction and rectification under the 1985 Act were discussed. (Text 28.22)

Aberdeen Rubber Ltd v Knowles & Sons (Fruiterers) Ltd 1995 SLT 870 (HL). A offered to purchase four areas of ground. Informal letters passed between the agents. One mentioned that the offer had been intended to cover a fifth area of ground not mentioned. The offer was met by a qualified acceptance and the purchasers concluded the bargain *de plano*. The disposition conveyed all five areas. The seller sought reduction on the basis that a fifth area was conveyed which was not referred to in the missives. The court held that the disposition was the ruling document, and on the face of it there was no apparent error. Accordingly the onus on the sellers to show that it did not accurately implement the missives. The purchasers were not obliged to establish the terms of the prior agreement, but were entitled to lead evidence to support their claim that the fifth area was intended to be included and that reflected the common intention. Furthermore, the provision for non-supersession did not prevent or render invalid the conveyance of the fifth area if that was the common intention, and proof allowed. (Text 28.22)

McClymont v McCubbin 1995 SLT 1248. In a boundary dispute, a petition for rectification was dismissed. On appeal, proof before answer allowed. (Text 28.7)

Huewind Ltd v Clydesdale Bank plc 1996 SLT 369. A question of the construction of a guarantee. The points involved patent and latent defects and ambiguity as to interest. On appeal the petition relating to rectification refused and proof before answer allowed on the question of interest only.

Bank of Scotland v Brunswick Developments (1987) Ltd 1995 SLT 689. On a petition for rectification of instructions to a bank in relation to a transfer of funds, it was held that the letter of instruction was in fact an assignation and therefore within the Law Reform (Miscellaneous Provisions) (Scotland) Act 1985, s 8(1)(b). Rectification competent even where mistake related to identity of grantor.

Belhaven Brewery Co Ltd v Swift 1996 SLT (Sh Ct) 127. Rectification refused where it became apparent that the pursuers were asking the court to rewrite the contract on a material matter. Discussion on the appropriateness of granting decree of rectification in absence.

Bovis Construction (Scotland) Ltd v Glantre Engineering Ltd 1997 GWD 32-1609. Rectification of building contract refused as the principal contractor could not prove that the sub-contractors had agreed to accelerate works.

Bank of Scotland v Brunswick Developments (1987) Ltd 1998 SLT 439. Director and Secretary of principal company signed documents to secure a loan which on the face of it appeared to be made on behalf of another borrowing company. The bank petitioned the court for rectification stating that the signatories had intended to sign on behalf of principal company rather than the borrowing company. Rectification granted but reversed on appeal to the House of Lords 1999 SLT 716.

Royal Bank of Scotland plc v Shanks 1998 SLT 355. Wife's action for rectification of a standard security and personal bond in respect of the debts of her husband's business was dismissed even although she alleged misrepresentation by her husband.

Norwich Union Life Insurance Society v Tanap Investments (No 2) 1999 SLT 204. Continuation of case reported at para 22.5 above. Norwich Union dropped the request for declarator and sought rectification. The court allowed a proof. Appeal and cross appeal were both refused: see 2000 SLT 819.

Baird v Drumpellier & Mount Vernon Estates Ltd 2000 GWD 12-427. Seller sought rectification of warrandice clause but this was refused on basis that missives of sale and purchase contain an implied term that the seller warranted that he owned the property and would confer ownership on the purchaser.

Delikes Ltd v Scottish and Newcastle plc 2000 SLT (Sh Ct) 67. Debtors under a standard security which had been varied to include a loan to a third part sought rectification of the variation. Held that s 8(1)(b) of the 1985 Act applied only where the parties to the document to be rectified were the same as the parties to the antecedent agreement: and further, the variation in this case was a collateral agreement not covered by the terms of that section.

Bank of Ireland v Bass Brewers Ltd 2000 GWD 20-786. Bank sought rectification of a Letter of Consent by Bass to a Standard Security granted by another company in favour of the bank. Proof before answer allowed. Established that s 8(1)(b) of the 1985 Act could apply when the language of the document repeated exactly the language that the grantor intended to use but which failed to achieve the intended result. (Text 29.17)

Sheltered Housing Management Ltd v Cairns 2003 SLT 578. Builders executed a deed of conditions relating to a sheltered housing complex built by them on land owned by them at that time. The deed mistakenly omitted a clause which related to a management scheme for the complex with the result that there was no provision for payment of a service charge. A petition for rectification was granted. (Text 29.17)

29.19 Compulsory purchase

Argyll v LMS Railway Co 1931 SC 309. Statutory and common law title compared; authorities reviewed.

Magistrates of Elgin v Highland Railway Co (1884) 11 R 950. Effect of statutory title.

Campbell's Trustees v London and North-Eastern Railway Co 1930 SC 182. Effect of statutory title.

Barr v Glasgow Corporation 1972 SLT (Sh Ct) 63. Statutory title; effect on superior's right to feuduty.

Heriot's Trust v Caledonian Railway Co 1915 SC (HL) 52. Discussion on nature and effect of statutory conveyance.

Rush v Fife Regional Council 1994 SCLR 231. Notices to treat: some observations on the implications of a notice to treat with substantial citation of authority. (Text 29.22)

JDP Investments Ltd v Strathclyde Regional Council 1996 SCLR 243. Sale of surplus land which had previously been acquired by a local authority. Subjects had not been compulsorily acquired. Held that Crichel Down rules inapplicable. (Text 29.22)

Standard Commercial Property Securities Ltd v City of Glasgow Council 2001 SC 177. Circumstances where compulsory purchase order made *ultra vires*.

Reside v North Ayrshire Council 2001 SLT 6. Validity of purchase notice. Effect of failure to respond to notice. Held Council deemed to have served a notice to treat.

South Lanarkshire Council v Lord Advocate 2002 SC 88. Whether planning authority entitled to grant certificate of appropriate alternative development.

Prestige Assets Ltd v Renfrewshire Council 2003 SLT 679. Derelict listed building. Judicial review. Reduction of repairs notice. Competency where no compulsory purchase order made.

Chapter 30   Transmission on Death

30.2 Position before the Succession (Scotland) Act 1964

Intestacy

MacRae v MacDonald 1980 SC 337. Special service; effect of decree.

Stobie v Smith 1921 SC 894. Special service. Wrong heir served; effect of decree.

Mackay's Executrix v Schonbach 1933 SC 747. General service; validity and effect of decree.

Sibbald's Heirs v Harris 1947 SC 601. General service. (Text 30.17, 32.49)

McAdam v McAdam (1879) 6 R 1256. Conveyancing (Scotland) Act 1874, s 9. Vesting in the heir.

Robertson, Petitioner 1978 SLT (Sh Ct) 30. 1874 Act, s 10. Petition for authority to complete title may be presented by an executor.

Fraser, Petitioner 1978 SLT (Sh Ct) 5. 1874 Act, s 10. Petition for authority to complete title may be presented by a surviving spouse entitled to prior rights.

McKenzie, Applicant 1979 SLT (Sh Ct) 68. 1874 Act, s 10. Petition for authority to complete title not competent where the property was last vested in an ex facie absolute disponee.

Robertson, Petitioner 1980 SLT (Sh Ct) 73. The heir of a deceased heir at law cannot serve as heir in trust under the 1874 Act, s 43.

MacMillan, Petitioner 1987 SLT (Sh Ct) 50. In determining the identity of an heir of provision in trust where the deceased in question died after 10 September 1964, the new statutory code of succession must be applied and not the old rule operating prior to that date.

MacDougall v MacDougall's Executors 1994 SLT 1178. The validity of a will was questioned. The heir-at-law obtained a Charter of Novodamus which was used as a link in title by apparently bona fide purchasers for value. Held that completion of title by service or otherwise by one who is not the heir is valueless if challenged by the true proprietor. (Text 28.35, 30.17)

Testate succession

Smith v Wallace (1869) 8 M 204. Effect of general disposition at common law.

Thoms v Thoms (1864) 6 M 174. Effect of general disposition *mortis causa* at common law.

Studd v Cook (1883) 10 R (HL) 53. Effect of general disposition under Titles to Land Consolidation (Scotland) Act 1868, s 20.

Grant v Morren (1893) 20 R 404. Effect of general disposition under 1868 Act, s 20.

Lawson's Executor v Lawson 1958 SLT (Notes) 38. Estate carried by the will. 'Money'.

Crozier's Trustee v Underwood 1963 SLT 69. Estate carried by the will. 'All my other affect'.

Taylor v Brunton 1998 SLT (Sh Ct) 72. Held that where a person entered into a personal agreement with another party, that agreement would bind the heirs and successors of the grantor in the absence of contrary express provision.

30.6 Special destinations

(See also cases under para 7.13 above.)

Haddow's Executors v Haddow 1943 SC 44. A destination to A and B in conjunct fee and liferent, for A's liferent and for B in fee, is not a special destination.

Cormack v McIldowie's Executors 1975 SC 161. Definition of special destination.

Hay's Trustee v Hay's Trustees 1951 SC 329. Whether destination revocable. (Text 7.13, 30.9)

Gordon-Rogers v Thomson's Trustees 1988 SC 145. Extrinsic evidence not admissible to contradict plain terms of the narrative clause in a disposition; and, in the instant case, there was sufficient in the deed to infer that the destination was contractual and therefore irrevocable. (Text 30.9)

Shand's Trustees v Shand's Trustees 1966 SC 178. Whether destination revocable; price jointly contributed. (Text 30.9)

Brown's Trustee v Brown 1943 SC 488. Whether destination revocable; condition of gift. (Text 30.9)

Munro v Munro 1972 SLT (Sh Ct) 6. Whether destination revocable; joint or common property. (Text 30.10)

Perrett's Trustees v Perrett 1909 SC 522. Revocation; destination created by testator.

Campbell v Campbell (1880) 7 R (HL) 100. Revocation; destination created by another.

Stirling's Trustees v Stirling 1977 SC 139. Revocation; Succession (Scotland) Act 1964, s 30. (Text 30.11)

Steele v Caldwell 1979 SLT 228. Effect of survivorship destination on inter vivos deed.

Smith v Mackintosh 1988 SC 453. A special destination in the title, even if contractual, cannot prevent inter vivos disposal; nor is it legitimate to look behind the disposition to determine whether or not the destination is contractual. (Text 30.9)

Marshall v Marshall's Executor 1987 SLT 49. A contractual special destination is irrevocable by mortis causa deed; and, in any event, even if revocable, the revocation must comply with 1964 Act, s 30. If a special destination is claimed to be contractual, that must appear ex facie of the deed. (Text 30.11)

Barclays Bank Ltd v McGreish 1983 SLT 344. Property passing on a special destination is not subject to personal debts of deceased institute.

Gardner's Executors v Raeburn 1996 SLT 745. Title to matrimonial home taken in name of husband and wife and survivor. The parties then divorced. The wife conveyed to her husband her one half pro indiviso share. The husband then died. Held that the disposition was restricted in its terms to the wife's one half pro indiviso share only. As a result the wife was entitled to succeed to the husband's original share. (Text 30.13)

Redfern's Executors v Redfern 1996 SLT 900. Following a separation, the parties entered into an agreement regulating *inter alia* sale of the matrimonial home. The title stood in joint names of both parties and the survivor. Under the agreement, both relinquished any rights of succession in the estate of the other. Held that the agreement in its terms impliedly waived normal prohibition against evacuation. (Text 30.13)

Fleming's Trustee v Fleming 2000 SLT 406. A title was in name of a husband and wife and survivor. The husband was sequestrated and subsequently died. It was held that the wife took the husband's one half share subject to his debts. *Barclay's Bank v McGreish* 1983 SLT 344 was overruled. (Text 30.13)

Chapter 31 Completion of Title

31.8 Lapsed trusts

Browning, Petitioner 1976 SLT (Sh Ct) 87. Service as heir in trust.

MacMillan, Petitioner 1987 SLT (Sh Ct) 50. Service as heir in trust and the Law Reform (Miscellaneous Provisions) (Scotland) Act 1980, s 6.

31.24 Notarial instrument

Kerr's Trustee v Yeaman's Trustee (1888) 15 R 520. Effect of notice of title. (Text 31.24)

Sutherland v Garrity 1941 SC 146. Effect of notice of title. (Text 31.24)

Cowie v Muirden (1893) 20 R (HL) 81. Real burden in favour of third party can be duly constituted by recording notice of title, if general disposition on which it proceeds so warrants. (Text 31.34)

MacKenzie v Clark (1903) 11 SLT 428. *Cowie v Muirden*, above, not followed because burden not set out in the notice.

Chapter 32 Examination of Title

32.2 Conditions in the contract

Hood v Clarkson 1995 SLT 98. Standard clause that there are no existing applications, orders, notices etc modified to effect that the usual local authority letter would be exhibited. After settlement, the disponee discovered that the seller had previously received notice of proposed roadworks. Purchaser's claim rejected. (Text 28.40)

Hawke v W B Mathers 1995 SCLR 1004. Sellers, prior to settlement, offered purchasers a letter of comfort instead of a completion certificate. Purchasers held entitled to resile. (Text 28.40)

32.3 Proprietary title

Prescriptive progress of titles

Scott v Bruce-Stewart (1779) Mor 13519. General principle of positive prescription.

Lord Advocate v Graham (1844) 7 D 183. General principle of positive prescription.

Wallace v St Andrews University (1904) 6 F 1093. Title.

Fraser v Lord Lovat (1898) 25 R 603. Title.

Meacher v Blair-Oliphant 1913 SC 417. Ex facie validity.

Cooper Scott v Gill Scott 1924 SC 309. Ex facie validity. (Text 32.4)

Troup v Aberdeen Heritable Securities Co Ltd 1916 SC 918. Ex facie validity.

Hilson v Scott (1895) 23 R 241. Ex facie validity.

Glen v Scales's Trustee (1881) 9 R 317. Ex facie validity.

Ramsay v Spence 1909 SC 1441. Recording in 'appropriate register' – BRS or GRS? (See now Land Registration (Scotland) Act 1979, s 15(1) – 'Recording' means recording in GRS).

Auld v Hay (1880) 7 R 663. Title need not be unambiguous.

Troup v Aberdeen Heritable Securities Co Ltd 1916 SC 918. Title need not be unambiguous.

Hay v Aberdeen Corporation 1909 SC 554. Title must be definite.

Brown v North British Railway Co (1906) 8 F 534. Title must be definite.

MacDougall v MacDougall's Executors 1994 SLT 1178. See 31.3 above. (Text 28.35, 30.17)

Stewart v J M Hodge & Son 1995 GWD 12-691, OH. Partnership bought property in 1974. In 1990 it was found that part of the property lay outwith the title boundary.

32.8 Burdens

Campbell v McCutcheon 1963 SC 505. Where the contract made no mention of minerals, which were reserved, purchaser was entitled to resile. (Text 28.32, 28.51, 28.76)

Bremner v Dick 1911 SC 887. Unallocated feuduty entitles purchaser to resile.

Armia v Daejan Developments Ltd 1979 SC (HL) 56. Material undisclosed burdens entitle purchaser to resile. (Text 28.32, 28.59)

Umar v Murtaza 1983 SLT (Sh Ct) 79. Unless seller discloses all restrictions on title, purchaser may resile. (Text 28.32)

Spurway, Petitioner 1987 GWD 2-65. Title may contain right of pre-emption which overrides contract. (Text 32.10, 32.11)

Welsh v Russell (1894) 21 R 769. Undisclosed servitude, if material, may entitle purchaser to resile. (Text 28.32)

Cameron v Williamson (1895) 22 R 293. Purchaser not obliged to take a title subject to outstanding heritable securities; but something less than a formal discharge may suffice. (Text 22.66)

Watson v Gillespie MacAndrew 1995 GWD 13-750. Solicitors for purchaser of landed estate failed to advise purchaser of existence of servitude right of access. Solicitors held negligent. (Text 28.38)

32.11 Other real burdens

Matheson v Tinney 1989 SLT 535. Right of pre-emption in feudal writ not struck at as a prohibition against alienation under Tenures Abolition Act 1746.

Spurway, Petitioner 1987 GWD 2-65. Where title contains right of pre-emption, seller must make formal offer to creditor in the pre-emption. (Text 32.9, 32.11)

Roebuck v Edmonds 1992 SLT 1055. Disposition granted in contravention of clause of pre-emption may be reduced; but the clause is strictly construed and reduction will not necessarily entitle the creditor to take up the right.

Ross and Cromarty District Council v Patience 1997 SLT 463. Effect of right of pre-emption.

Waverley Housing Trust Ltd v Roxburgh District Council 1995 SLT (Lands Tr) 2. Local authority inserted pre-emption clause in two offers with no change of tenancy. Held condition unreasonable in terms of Housing (Scotland) Act 1988, s 58 and pre-emption clause conditions should be struck out from each offer.

Henderson v Glasgow District Council 1994 SLT 263. Prior titles contained right of pre-emption which were not brought to the attention of the Tribunal when they made their order effectively conferring title on the purchasing tenant. Tribunal satisfied that they were correct in issuing an offer to the tenant which took no account of the right of pre-emption, upheld.

Roberts v Tait & Peterson 1995 GWD 10-548. R bought a cottage. On later sale a pre-emption clause was discovered. Superior could not be traced and purchasers rescinded. R sued his agents. Proof before answer allowed.

Hamilton v Grampian Regional Council 1996 GWD 5-277. Purchaser of large landed estate successfully sought declarator that ground conveyed in 1858 to trustees under the School Sites Act 1841 belonged to him on ceasing to be so used.

Grampian Joint Police Board v Pearson 2000 SLT 90, aff'd 2001 SC 772, 2001 SLT 734. Uncertainty of pre-emption clause as to price meant that the burden was unenforceable as a real burden.

Macdonald-Haig v Gerlings (3 December 2001, unreported), Inverness Sheriff Court; see Reid and Gretton *Conveyancing 2002* (2003), pp 63–65. Pre-emption not contrary to ECHR.

32.14 Possession in support of the title

(See also generally Chapter 12.)

Robertson's Trustees v Bruce (1905) 7 F 580. The title must support the possession.

Meacher v Blair-Oliphant 1913 SC 417. Discussion on quality of possession required to support title.

Houstoun v Barr 1911 SC 134. Possession must be directly referable to title it allegedly supports.

32.17 The Property Register (now Form 10 and Form 11 reports)

Cameron v Williamson (1895) 22 R 293. Purchaser entitled to clear search in Property Register. (Text 22.66)

Rodger (Builders) Ltd v Fawdry 1950 SC 483. Purchaser may be personally barred from relying on title as disclosed by search. (Text 28.69, 28.72, 28.73, 32.52, 32.54, 35.10)

Robson v Chalmers Property Investment Co Ltd 1965 SLT 381. Purchaser, as singular successor, may be affected by actings or acquiescence on the part of a predecessor in title although nothing is disclosed on Record. (Compare overriding interests in Registration of Title.)

32.20 The Register of Inhibitions
General effect

Menzies v Murdoch (1841) 4 D 257. Preference created by inhibition over other creditors.

Murphy's Trustees v Aitken 1983 SLT 78. Effect of inhibition in English bankruptcy.

Dryburgh v Gordon (1896) 24 R 1. Inhibition effective even where no feudal title. (Text 32.33)

Leeds Permanent Building Society v Aitken, Malone and Mackay 1986 SLT 338. Right of purchaser under missives not heritable and so not caught by inhibition until a disposition in implement thereof has been delivered in his favour.

Scottish Wagon Co Ltd v James Hamilton's Trustee (1906) 13 SLT 779. Inhibition is negative in nature.

McInally v Kildonan Homes Ltd 1979 SLT (Notes) 89. Partial recall of inhibition competent.

Customs and Excise Commissioners, Applicants 1992 SLT 11. Inhibition in security (a rare bird) competent only to cover future or contingent debts.

Murray v Long 1992 SLT 292. Pursuer claimed that inhibition on the dependence was effectually executed diligence in a question with a receiver but the point was not decided. Opinion that interdict may be a competent remedy to support an inhibition but only on cause shown.

Rhodes v Boswell 1994 SLT 371. Circumstances in which recall of inhibition granted.

M T Group v Howden Group plc 1993 SLT 345. Danish company, seeking performance of obligations undertaken by a Scottish company had obtained inhibition on the dependence which the inhibited debtor moved to recall. They argued, *inter alia, forum non conveniens*. Motion for recall refused.

Hogg v Prentice 1994 SCLR 426. Held that service and registration of letters of inhibition on the dependence of an action constituted a relevant claim for purposes of Limitation and Prescription (Scotland) Act 1973, s 6(1) and so interrupted running of prescription. Prescription starts running again from that date.

Modern Housing Ltd v Love 1998 SLT 1188. Trivial defect in inhibition as to company's place of business did not effect the validity of the inhibition.

Karl Construction Ltd v Palisade Properties plc 2002 SC 270, 2002 SLT 312. Inhibition on the dependence contrary to ECHR, Article 1, Protocol 1 where no judicial involvement. (Text 32.24)

Advocate General for Scotland v Taylor 2003 SLT 1340. Judicial involvement in inhibition on the dependence does not require an actual hearing.

Effect on heritable creditors

McGowan v A Middlemass and Sons Ltd 1977 SLT (Sh Ct) 41. Inhibition does not prevent sale by bondholder but creates no preference for inhibitor.

Newcastle Building Society v White 1987 SLT (Sh Ct) 81. In view of provisions of the Conveyancing and Feudal Reform (Scotland) Act 1970, s 26, it was clear ex facie of the Record that the property was disencumbered and the search was therefore clear for purposes of marketable title as provided for in the missives. (Text 22.45, 32.33)

Bank of Scotland v Lord Advocate 1977 SLT 24. Inhibition does not prevent sale by holder of standard security, but creates a preference for inhibitor on any surplus as against other creditors.

Abbey National Building Society v Sheik Aziz 1981 SLT (Sh Ct) 29. Inhibition creates preference for inhibiting creditor on free proceeds of sale over posterior arresting creditors.

Ferguson & Forster v Dalbeattie Finance Co 1981 SLT (Sh Ct) 53. Subjects sold by secured creditors. Inhibiting creditor not to be preferred to free proceeds over unsecured creditors. Cf. *Abbey National Building Society v Sheik Aziz*, above, and *Halifax Building Society v Smith* below.

Halifax Building Society v Smith 1985 SLT (Sh Ct) 25. Nature of preference created by inhibition. (Text 22.47)

Mackintosh's Trustees v Davidson and Garden (1898) 25 R 554. Inhibition does not prevent debtor discharging heritable security.

Henderson v Dawson (1895) 22 R 895. A creditor, who had inhibited, agreed to a discharge on receiving an assurance as to payment; and was held entitled to enforce that assurance.

Atlas Appointments Ltd v Tinsley 1998 SLT 395. Accurate information needed when instructing inhibitions. (Text 32.23)

Allied Irish Bank plc v GPT Sales & Service Ltd 1995 SLT 163. Owner of a hotel subjected to an inhibition by a company GS, formerly known as GR. GR and GS exchanged names. There was a confusion of dates. Heritable creditors successfully petitioned for the recall of inhibition.

32.26 Sequestration

Alliance and Leicester Building Society v Murray's Trustees 1995 SLT (Sh Ct) 77. Heritable property acquired by bankrupt, by disposition in his favour granted after date of sequestration. The bankrupt then immediately granted a standard security in favour of the building society and both deeds were recorded in Sasines. Held that the property vested in the trustee notwithstanding the conveyance in favour of the bankrupt. Since the bankrupt had no right to the subjects, he could not have granted a valid standard security. (Text 3.21)

Sharp v Thomson 1995 SC 45, 1997 SC (HL) 66. A company executed and delivered a disposition of property to a bona fide purchaser for value. The company had already granted a floating charge which included that property. A receiver under the floating charge was appointed to the granter of the disposition before the purchaser had recorded it. Held in the Inner House that the property was attached by the floating charge. This was reversed on appeal to the House of Lords: see 1997 SLT 636. (Text 4.4–4.6, 11.5, 23.4, 29.8, 32.44, 34.7, 34.12, 34.15, 34.18)

Halifax v Gorman's Trustee 2000 SLT 1409 Security granted by an undischarged bankrupt held to be effective. (Text 3.21, 32.26)

Burnett's Trustee v Grainger 2002 SLT 699. Following a sale, the disposition in favour of the purchaser was delivered but not recorded. The seller was sequestrated and the trustee recorded a notice of title before the purchaser eventually recorded the disposition. The Inner House held that the decision in *Sharp v Thomson* only applied to floating charges in receiverships and not to sequestrations and the trustee had a good title to the subjects of sale. The case is under appeal to the House of Lords at the time of writing. (Text 4.5, 32.44)

32.37 Settlement obligations

Johnston v Little 1960 SLT 129. Letter of obligation is personally binding on the solicitor who grants it. (Text 32.35)

Gibson v Hunter Home Designs Ltd 1976 SC 23. Effect of payment of price in exchange for letter of obligation only but no title. (Text 4.3, 32.44)

Richardson v MacGeoch's Trustees (1898) 1 F 145. Obligation by agent to deliver discharge of a loan does not bind principal creditor if the agent embezzles the money.

McGillivary v Davidson 1993 SLT 693. Seller's solicitors gave a letter of obligation undertaking to deliver planning permission, building warrant and completion certificates. After settlement, the purchasers discovered that the local authority had served an enforcement notice. Held that the seller and his solicitors were jointly and severally liable. Purchaser entitled to sue both the solicitors granting a letter of obligation at settlement and their client jointly, if obligation not implemented. (Text 32.35)

Emslie v James Thomson & Sons (1991, unreported): see 1991 JLSS 349. Where solicitors have granted a letter of obligation which is not implemented, the purchaser can sue them in his own name although the obligation was granted to his own agents.

Mason v A & R Robertson & Black 1993 SLT 773. Seller's solicitors granted a letter of obligation giving certain undertakings which they were not able to implement. The solicitors were exonerated but the case underlines the danger of giving such letters. (Text 28.79)

Warners v Beveridge & Kellas 1994 SLT (Sh Ct) 29. Solicitors granted an obligation to deliver within a specified time-limit a search brought down in terms of an agreed memorandum showing clear records 'which search will disclose your client's title, provided your client's title is recorded within 21 days from this date'. The purchaser's solicitors failed to record within the 21-day time-limit. The selling solicitors, having granted an obligation in these terms, argued that they escaped liability because of the failure of the purchaser's solicitors. Held that, since the primary obligation was to give a clear search and this did not depend on recording within 21 days, there was no reason why an alternative construction should not be adopted limiting the proviso to the phrase immediately preceding it. The decision underlines the need for care in drafting letters of obligation. (Text 32.39)

Digby Brown & Co v Lyall 1995 SLT 932. Solicitors granted letter of obligation 'on behalf of their clients' which was signed by them without any reference to their agency. Lord Cullen held the letter of obligation was not personally binding on the firm who granted it.

Carlin v Trainor Alston 1998 GWD 39-2020. Seller's solicitor gave personal obligations to the purchaser on the basis of information available to him from the seller. Information was incorrect and proof before answer allowed to ascertain whether the solicitor was entitled to rely on the information without any further investigation.

32.49 Latent defects

Taylor v Brunton 1998 SLT (Sh Ct) 72. Where a person entered into a personal agreement with another party, that agreement would bind the successors of the granter in the absence of contrary express provision.

32.65 Gratuitous alienations

Leslie v Leslie 1987 SLT 232. Reduction of a disposition under Divorce (Scotland) Act 1976, s 6 does not necessarily imply that a standard security over the property will also fall, looking to the proviso to s 6(2). (See now the Family Law (Scotland) Act 1985, s 18 for equivalent provisions now in force.)

Bank of Scotland, Petitioners 1988 SLT 690. Common law rule against gratuitous alienation applies to companies.

32.67 Occupancy rights of non-entitled spouses

Murphy v Murphy 1992 SCLR (Sh Ct) 62. A dwellinghouse was purchased in joint names of A and B. B then married C who moved into the house and it became their matrimonial home. The marriage broke up and B moved out leaving C in occupation. Held that, since A had never occupied the house and allowed B to occupy it with his wife C, A had waived her rights of occupation in favour of B under s 1(2) of the Matrimonial Homes (Family Protection) (Scotland) Act 1981. (Text 32.69)

Stevenson v Roy 2002 SLT 445 Discusses a non-entitled spouse's rights to occupy and be protected against the transfer of heritable property under s 6(3)(f) of the 1981 Act. Loss of rights due to lapse of time and relevance of unsuccessful attempt to reoccupy. (Text 28.44, 32.67)

32.77 Negative prescription

Barratt (Scotland) Ltd v Keith 1993 SC 1420. Seller's obligation to grant a disposition is an obligation relating to land, not imprescriptible but subject to the 20-year prescription. (Text 32.44, 32.77)

Wright v Frame 1992 GWD 8-447. Discussion on interaction of Prescription and Limitation (Scotland) Act 1973, Sch 1, para 1(g) – obligations arising from contract; and para 2(e) – obligations relating to land. (Text 32.44, 32.77)

Stewart's Executors v Stewart 1993 SLT 440. Obligation to grant a disposition not imprescriptible. Exclusion in Prescription and Limitation (Scotland) Act 1973, Sch 3, para (h) applies only where a disponee holds an unrecorded disposition. Sch 3(h) allows completion of title thereon indefinitely. (Text 32.77)

Hogg v Prentice 1994 SCLR 426. See 33.22 above.

Porteous's Executors v Ferguson 1995 SLT 649. The defender granted a disposition in his own favour *a non domino* recorded 17 January 1992. Executors took out Confirmation as representing the reputed owner of the same ground and then recorded a Notice of Title on 5 August 1992. Executors then sought to reduce the *a non domino* disposition but failed on the footing that the personal right of the deceased who died in 1952 had been extinguished by the long negative prescription before 25 July 1976 when the 1973 Act came into force, since no action and no infeftment was taken following her death. (Text 31.42)

MRS Hamilton Ltd v Arlott 1995 GWD 25-1355. Short negative prescription of five years did not apply to arrears of leasehold casualties which were not, in terms of the Prescription and Limitation (Scotland) Act 1973, periodical payments.

Beveridge & Kellas WS v Abercromby 1997 SLT 1086. Discussion on the requirement that the *terminus a quo* is the date when an obligation would have become enforceable unless the creditor was not aware and could not with diligence have been made aware that loss had been incurred.

Lowland Glazing Co Ltd v G A Group 1997 SLT 257. The date of termination of a contract, duly terminated on breach, is the *terminus a quo* for prescription nothwithstanding an arbitration clause which barred proceedings thereunder until a later date.

Strathclyde Regional Council v W A Fairhurst & Partners 1997 SLT 658. The onus of proof in negative prescription normally lies on the party seeking to maintain that prescription had extinguished the obligation.

Hamilton v Baxter 1998 SLT 1075. Any form of claim which competently puts the validity of possession or title in issue is 'judicial interruption'.

Chapter 33   A Typical Conveyancing Transaction

There is no digest of cases for this chapter, although the digest of cases for other chapters should be referred to, especially Chapters 28 and 32.

Chapter 34   Transactions with Companies

34.1 General

Weir v Rees 1991 SLT 345. Circumstances where it was held appropriate to appoint an interim judicial factor to a company without directors.

34.3 Company name

Penrose v Martyr (1858) 120 ER 595. English decision. Omission of word 'Limited' fatal to validity of document.

Hendon v Adelman (1973) 117 SJ 631. English court found that in the case of a company called 'L & R Agencies Ltd', a document in which the '&' was omitted did not reproduce the company name correctly.

Banque de l'Indochine etc v Euroseas Group Finance Co Ltd [1981] 3 All ER 198. Held, by an English court, that the abbreviation of the word 'Company' to 'Co' does not invalidate the document at common law.

Jenice v Dan [1994] BCC 43 at 48F–G. Held, by an English court, that the misspelling of a word will generally be insufficient to render a deed void.

Modern Housing Ltd v Love 1998 SLT 1191. Court stated that an error as to company name must plainly be regarded as of first importance.

Orkney Islands Council v S & J D Robertson & Co Ltd 2003 SLT 775. Inaccurate narration of a company's name in a court summons. Motion granted to amend a court summons which narrated the name of the company as 'S & J D Robertson & Co Ltd' instead of its true name 'S & J D Robertson Oils Ltd'

34.4 Capacity

James Finlay Corporation Ltd v R & R S Mearns 1988 SLT 302. Discussion on *ultra vires* actings.

Re Introductions Ltd, Introductions Ltd v National Provincial Bank Ltd [1969] 1 All ER 887. Discussion on actings.

Piggins & Rix Ltd v Montrose Port Authority 1995 SLT 418. Montrose Port Authority wished to sell some land that was surplus to its requirements. A special case was presented to the court to ascertain whether it had the capacity to do so. The court concluded that it did not, and to do so would be *ultra vires*. The court did however consider, obiter dictum, that the Port Authority may have power to enter into long leases. (Text 3.2, 3.15)

34.5 Execution of deeds

Liquidator of Style and Mantle Ltd v Prices Tailors Ltd 1934 SC 548. Discussion on form of disposition granted by a company in liquidation.

34.7 Floating charges

Forth and Clyde Construction Co Ltd v Trinity Timber and Plywood Co Ltd 1984 SC 1. Nature of fixed security on appointment of receiver.

Lord Advocate v Aero Technologies Ltd 1991 SLT 134. No reason in principle why a company and its receivers should not be regarded as joint occupiers for various statutory and other purposes.

Iona Hotels Ltd (In Receivership) v Craig 1990 SC 330. Held, distinguishing *Lord Advocate v Royal Bank of Scotland Ltd* 1977 SC 155, that if a security is prior in date to registration of a charge, it takes priority.

National Commercial Bank Ltd v Liquidators of Telford, Grier, Mackay & Co Ltd 1969 SC 181. Extent of security; interest due from date of liquidation.

Libertas-Kommerz v Johnson 1977 SC 191. Bond and floating charge is assignable by creditor.

Hill Samuel & Co Ltd v Laing 1989 SC 301. Discussion on personal liability of receiver for debt incurred on behalf of the company.

Shanks v Central RC 1988 SC 14. Appointment of receiver does not necessarily exclude powers of directors of company to take action in certain circumstances.

Taymech Ltd v Rush and Tompkins Ltd 1990 SLT 681. Conceded by counsel that an inhibition, registered after creation of the charge, was ineffective in a question with a receiver subsequently appointed.

Myles J Callaghan Ltd v City of Glasgow District Council 1987 SC 171. Discussion on nature of crystallisation of a charge on appointment of a receiver.

Bank of Scotland, Petitioners 1988 SLT 690. Held, notwithstanding provisions of Insolvency Act 1986, creditors still retained the right to challenge transactions as gratuitous alienations at common law.

Bank of Scotland v T A Neilson & Co 1990 SC 284. Standard security by a company, recorded in Sasines, was not registered in the Register of Charges. Second security recorded simultaneously was duly registered. There was a ranking agreement in terms of which the unregistered security was intended to have prior ranking. Held that the ranking agreement could not alter the effect of the statutory ranking provisions then in force. (Text 22.6)

Prior, Petitioner 1989 SLT 840. Application for extension of time to register a floating charge, with or without conditions attached, was refused. (Text 23.5, 23.9)

Scottish and Newcastle plc v Ascot Inns Ltd 1994 SLT 1140. Informal letter from creditor in a floating charge to solicitors for the company amounted to a release of the properties specified in the letter. The letter did not require to be registered to be valid. (Text 34.12, 34.18)

AIB Finance Ltd v Bank of Scotland 1993 SC 538. Dispute as to ranking between heritable creditor holding a fixed security and creditor holding a floating charge. The court held that the existence of a 'negative pledge' in a floating charge is sufficient to displace the statutory order of ranking set out in subss (2) and (4) of s 464 Companies Act 1985. It was also held that the word 'create' in the negative pledge and s 410(5) and s 464 meant (1), in relation to a fixed security, the date of the real right coming into existence and accordingly, the date of recording of the fixed security in the Register of Sasines or registration in the Land Register and (2) in relation to a floating charge, the date of execution of the floating charge instrument.

Sharp v Thomson 1995 SC 45 rev'd 1997 SC (HL) 66. A company as a going concern executed and delivered a disposition of property to a bona fide purchaser for value. The company had already granted a floating charge which included that property. On the day after settlement, a receiver was appointed to the disponer before the purchaser had recorded the disposition. Held, the property was caught by the floating charge. This decision was reversed in the House of Lords. (Text 4.4–4.6, 11.5, 23.4, 29.8, 32.44, 34.7, 34.12, 34.15 and 34.18)

Bass Brewers Ltd v Humberclyde Finance Group Ltd 1996 GWD 1076. Bass objected to certain payments made to Humberclyde, prior security holders. Humberclyde's security was ranked and preferred to that of Bass. Discussion on the payments permitted on construction of the ranking agreement.

Bank of Ireland v Bass Brewers Ltd 2000 GWD 28-1077. In this case, it was held that a negative pledge in a floating charge had to be read as part of a single scheme of regulation so that the absolute prohibition on the grant of securities having priority to, or ranking *pari passu* with the floating charge containing the negative pledge was qualified by the exception of securities granted with that floating charge holder's consent. Accordingly, there is no universal rule to the effect that the existence of a negative pledge in a floating charge will, as a matter of course, elevate such a floating charge to a prior ranking security, notwithstanding the terms of the Companies Act 1985, s 464(1A). Each negative pledge will be interpreted and applied strictly according to its particular terms.

Burnett's Trustee v Grainger 2002 SLT 699 (under appeal to the House of Lords). Delivery of a disposition of property by a person who was subsequently sequestrated thereafter, but before the disposition was recorded in favour of the *bona fide* purchaser for value. Trustee in sequestration preferred. (Text 4.5, 32.44)

34.18 Alternative methods of protecting the purchaser

Bank of Scotland, Petitioner 1988 SLT 690. Common law rule against gratuitous alienations applies to companies.

34.19 Purchase of heritage from an administrator

Scottish Exhibition Centre Ltd v Mirestop Ltd 1996 SLT 8. Landlord can serve an irritancy notice on a tenant in administration notwithstanding Insolvency Act 1986, s 11.

34.24 Purchase of heritage from a receiver

Norfolk House plc v Repsol Petroleum Ltd (In Receivership) 1992 SLT 235. Section 72 of the Insolvency Act 1986 is designed to operate as a bridge from creation of floating charge to the receiver's appointment, in order to ensure that a receiver can exercise his powers under Schedule 1 to the 1986 Act in relation to Scottish property untrammelled by Scottish conveyancing and property law. (Text 34.7, 34.12)

Independent Pension Trustee Ltd v LAW Construction Co 1996 GWD 33-1956. On the attachment of a floating charge, the directors of the company are implicitly divested of their powers.

34.28 Title

Iona Hotels Ltd (In Receivership) v Craig 1990 SC 330. Arrestment, not followed by forthcoming, nonetheless constituted effectually executed diligence in a question with a receiver.

Taymech Ltd v Rush & Tompkins Ltd 1990 SLT 681. Inhibition against a company, not followed by adjudication, is of no effect in a question with a receiver subsequently appointed and has nuisance value only, which justifies recall of the inhibition; but cf *Iona Hotels Ltd* above.

Murray v Long 1992 SLT 292. Question raised, but not resolved as to whether or not an inhibition registered before receivership was effective against the receiver.

Alloa Brewery Co Ltd v Investors in Industry plc 1992 SLT 121. Discussion on the meaning of 'charge'. (Text 22.16, 34.36)

Grampian RC v Drill Stem (Inspection Services) Ltd 1994 SCLR 36. In a competition between landlord and tenant in receivership, landlord's hypothec takes precedence. (Text 23.6)

Scottish and Newcastle Breweries plc v Ascot Inns Ltd 1994 SLT 1140. Informal letter from creditor in a floating charge to solicitors for the company amounted to release of the properties specified in the letter. Letter did not require to be registered to be valid. (Text 34.12, 34.18)

34.30 Consent of creditor or application to the court

Murray v Long 1992 SLT 292. Discussion on effect of inhibition on powers of receiver to sell heritable property.

34.33 Liquidation

McLuckie Brothers Ltd v Newhouse Contracts Ltd 1993 SLT 641. Gratuitous alienation by a company reduced. Onus on the disponee seeking to uphold the transaction to prove that it was not either gratuitous or a sale at under value.

Stuart Eves Ltd (In Liquidation) v Smiths Gore 1993 SLT 1274. In the circumstances of the case, the liquidator had sufficiently averred a gratuitous alienation at common law.

John E. Rae (Electrical Services) Linlithgow Ltd v Lord Advocate 1994 SLT 788. Bond granted to Inland Revenue was an alienation for adequate consideration.

Thomson v MB Trustees Ltd 1994 GWD 32-1894. Liquidator raised action against trustees of a pension fund and a bank seeking reduction of a disposition granted by the company in favour of the pension fund. The company acquired the property by disposition dated August 1988 and recorded in March 1989. The company conveyed the subjects to the pension fund in August 1988, recorded October 1988. The liquidator averred that the company was insolvent, or the granting of the disposition rendered it insolvent, and persons associated with the company benefited as a result. The pension fund trustees argued they paid full consideration. Proof before answer was allowed. Onus of establishing consideration was with the pension fund trustees.

Rankin v Meek 1995 SLT 526. Gratuitous alienation by a company in liquidation, and a question as to whether valuable consideration had been given in exchange for a grant by the company.

34.37 Second securities by companies

Armour and Mycroft, Petitioners 1983 SLT 453. Affirmation of general rule that, where there is competition between creditors with equal security rights, preference is given according to the dates of the securities.

Table of Statutes

Table of Orders, Rules and Regulations

Table of European Legislation

Table of Cases

Note
Cases for which there are paragraph numbers in bold are referred to in the text. All other paragraph numbers refer to the Digest of Cases.

PART I

PRELIMINARY MATTERS

Chapter 1

General Introduction

1.1 General

This Manual is intended primarily for students following the degree and diploma classes of conveyancing, although it is hoped that it will also be of assistance to practitioners. It deals only with conveyancing in the narrow sense, and those seeking information on the wider aspects of the law of heritable property, ie land law, are directed to works such as Professor Paisley's *Land Law* (2000), Professor Gordon's *Scottish Land Law* (2nd edn, 1999) and the *Stair Memorial Encyclopaedia*, Volume 18: Property, paras 1–718. (The principal author of Volume 18 was Professor Reid. The work was subsequently published separately as *The Law of Property in Scotland* (1996). In general, reference here will be made to Volume 18 as, by implication, it includes the ongoing updates to the *Stair Memorial Encyclopaedia*.)

An extensive Bibliography and Reading List is included at the front of the book. Further and more detailed information on the Reading List is contained later in this chapter.

1.2 Content and scope

As a general indication of the content and scope of this subject, for the degree and diploma student, one can do no better than quote directly from the Law Society's submission to the Royal Commission on Legal Services in Scotland, Volume 1, published in 1977.

'Conveyancing has been defined as "the art which deals with the transfer of property in writing" (Wood's Lectures). The essence of the definition is some form of writing or deed. Wood uses the word "property" in its widest sense as meaning everything which can be possessed. The expression "transfer" includes every kind of right relating to such property which can be created, conveyed or extinguished in writing. Such a transfer may be an absolute one of ownership as from seller to purchaser or donor to donee, it may be redeemable ie subject to extinction at a future date such as a security or a lease. It includes the preparation of those documents which are preliminary to the actual deed of transfer, such as missives of sale. Conveyancing therefore embraces the preparation of contracts, writs and deeds of every kind, and is not confined to the transfer of heritable property or rights therein. Settlements, trusts, wills, contracts for the purchase or sale of businesses or shares, debentures and loan agreements, leases, leasing or hire purchase agreements, building contracts, contracts of employment, partnership, patent, licence and "know-how" agreements and indeed every contract or writing of any kind which is preliminary to or in itself creates, transfers, modifies or extinguishes a right or obligation, falls within the work of a conveyancer.

It is of course true that the greater part of the conveyancer's work is concerned with heritable property. This work covers not only the buying and selling of such properties and the preparation of conveyances and securities, but also the preparation of tenancy agreements and leases, deeds granting limited rights such as servitudes or wayleaves, and deeds extinguishing or varying rights or obligations. Further, the conveyancer's duty is not limited to the mere preparation of the deed giving effect to the transaction in question. He must be able to advise his client on the effect of the transaction generally, as to the ways of achieving the desired result, the financing of the transaction and its effect on his client's affairs, for example, in relation to taxation, insurances, succession, etc. When acting for a seller of property or the grantor of a right, discharge or waiver, he must ensure that his client can give a good title and does not contract to do something which he cannot fulfil or, if the consents of other persons are required, that these can be obtained. When acting for a purchaser or for the person in whose favour the right, discharge or waiver is being granted he must ensure that any preliminary contract is correctly and sufficiently drawn and, by examination of the grantor's title, that the grantor can grant and that his client will obtain a valid and enforceable title good against all parties and free from any burdens or restrictions prejudicial to his client's interests. He must also ensure that all necessary permissions for the transactions have been obtained from any third party who may have rights in the matter such as the feudal superior [as will be discussed in Chapter 6, feudal superiors will have their rights extinguished on 28 November 2004], heritable creditor, landlord or over-landlord, or in respect of any statutory requirements or regulations such as planning permission, building regulations, fire certificates, or licensing requirements. Where there are title restrictions the conveyancer may also be involved in an application to the Land Tribunal.'

1.3   The role of solicitors in heritable property transactions

The Law Society's submission to the Royal Commission continued as follows.

'In relation to heritable property transactions, the work of the solicitor in Scotland is not confined to carrying out the conveyancing, as the solicitor in

Scotland, unlike his English counterpart, is also engaged in the negotiations leading up to the purchase and sale which in England are, with few exceptions, handled by the estate agent. Indeed, the majority of properties in Scotland are bought and sold by solicitors. This fact is undoubtedly to the advantage of the public for, of all the advisers who may or should be involved at one stage or another in the sale of the house such as a surveyor, estate agent, insurance broker, banker, building society or accountant, only the solicitor has the overall knowledge and training to co-ordinate all the various steps and carry through the transaction from the point when the seller first decides to put his property on the market to the point where the purchaser completes the purchase by settling the price, taking possession of the property and recording his title in the Sasine Register. Furthermore, it has already been shown that the solicitor's duty does not stop at the transaction in question. He is also expected to advise his client on the effect which it may have on that client's other affairs and it is only the legal profession which is trained to look at and appreciate the overall picture. This is not to say that the profession is blind to the considerable specialist expertise which other advisers can offer and in many cases the solicitor will advise his client to make use of these services. For example, when selling commercial or industrial property, the client may well be advised to put the sale in the hands of a firm of estate agents specialising in the sale of this kind of property. If this is to be done, the solicitor will consider the client's title and the other aspects of the transaction before instructing the estate agents. On the other hand, the profession is only too well aware of the dangers to the client who instructs someone who has only a limited sphere of activity and is unable to take a broad view of the subject, for example, the client who is persuaded to take out a large endowment policy on the explanation that he will not obtain a building society loan unless he does, or where the policy is not suitable for his needs or he cannot really afford the premiums or where the client incurs heavy and unnecessary advertising costs because he has been advised to advertise on four successive days each week, every fourth advertisement being free.

Heritable property ranges from the small tenement flat on the one hand to the large housing development, on the other, from the small shop to the large shopping development, from the single factory to the industrial estate and from the country cottage or smallholding to the large landed estate. The work can, and does, vary enormously from one type of property to another but the difference can be said to be one of degree, for the steps which the solicitor has to take and the considerations which he has to have in mind are normally much the same.'

The monopoly previously enjoyed by solicitors in the provision of conveyancing services for money was ended by Part II of the Law Reform (Miscellaneous Provisions) (Scotland) Act 1990. The 1990 Act established the Conveyancing and Executry Services Board which was charged with the regulation of a new profession of non-solicitor conveyancers, known as qualified conveyancers. The reference in the final paragraph of the foregoing quotation should therefore now be to the conveyancer, rather than the solicitor. The Conveyancing and Executry Services Board has now been abolished and its functions transferred to the Law Society of Scotland in terms of the Public Appointments and Public Bodies etc (Scotland) Act 2003, ss 11–13.

As an illustration of the great variety of situations where a solicitor may be held liable for negligence, see the Digest of Cases for para 1.3. The test of whether a solicitor is professionally negligent follows the principles set out in the leading professional negligence case, *Hunter v Hanley* 1955 SC 200, a medical negligence case, under which it must be shown that a professional person of ordinary skill would not have followed the course of action taken. See further Professor Rennie *Solicitors' Negligence* (1997) and *Opinions on Professional Negligence in Conveyancing* (forthcoming). It will be seen from the Digest of Cases that the number of such cases continues to rise.

1.4   Heritable and moveable

As the foregoing summary indicates, heritable property includes primarily land and everything affixed to or growing on land such as buildings and trees. It also includes rights directly connected with land such as servitudes.

In contrast, moveable property, which includes both corporeal and incorporeal assets, has no direct connection with land. See further *Stair Memorial Encyclopaedia*, Volume 18, paras 11–16.

This Manual is confined almost exclusively to heritable property, heritable rights and heritable titles.

1.5   Heritable property

There are two main aspects to the law of heritable property:

(1) the substantive law, which is dealt with in some textbooks under such headings as 'Landownership', 'Rights in Security', 'Leases' etc. The substantive law regulates the rights and liabilities of the owner or occupant, on the assumption that his right as such has been properly constituted by the appropriate title;

(2) conveyancing, which is primarily concerned with the constitution and transmission of the right of property (or occupancy) in the form appropriate to the type of property being dealt with. The conveyance is the traditional document of title by which a right of property in land is transferred from one person to another – hence the term.

As indicated above, rights to land in Scotland generally require a written title to constitute and to transmit the right. In many cases, rights and liabilities of the proprietor of land are implied at common law but these rights may be varied to a greater or lesser extent by the terms of his particular title; that is, by 'conventional provision'. Therefore, although the substantive law of landownership is concerned with rights and liabilities of owners and occupiers generally, it is also necessary in each individual case to examine the individual title to the property concerned and consider the particular terms of that title and the extent to which, if any, the title modifies what the common law would otherwise imply. This, in turn, involves the application of conveyancing principles in construing the terms of the documents constituting the title.

So, under the common law of the tenement, as applied to tenement property generally, the proprietor of the top flat is by implication responsible for the whole cost of maintaining the roof. In many cases, however, this common law liability is modified by the terms of the titles to the individual flats in that tenement. See para 8.7.

Similarly, the owner of a vacant piece of land has, at common law, an unqualified right to build on or use that land as he pleases. In his particular title, however, he may be prevented from building altogether; or at least limited in his freedom to use land for building or other purposes. See Part 3.

1.6 Devolution and human rights

Two significant events have taken place recently with devolution of government to Scotland under the Scotland Act 1998 and the passing of the Human Rights Act 1998.

Under the Scotland Act 1998, property law and conveyancing are devolved matters and the new Scottish Parliament has been very active in passing legislation which is rapidly updating and reforming Scottish property law and substantially altering conveyancing practice as a result. A glance at the Reading List discloses the fact that eight major Acts were passed in the first four years of the Scottish Parliament, indicating the rapid pace of reform compared with the previous position under Westminster government.

The Human Rights Act 1998 gives effect to the European Convention on Human Rights, including the First Protocol, which makes provision on Property. The general intention is to protect property rights of individuals from abuse by the State as opposed to by other individuals. The main protection of property rights is in Article 1 of the First Protocol, but Article 6, which provides procedural guarantees in the determination of rights and Article 8, which protects private and family life, are also relevant. The effect will be wide reaching but it is too early in the development of human rights law in relation to property to predict how conveyancing practice may be affected. The first major human rights challenge impinging on property law was in relation to planning procedure in *County Properties Ltd v The Scottish Ministers* 2001 SLT 1125. In the small number of cases dealing with property matters to date, Scottish property law generally seems robust enough to comply with the Convention.

See, for example, *Strathclyde Joint Police Board v The Elderslie Estates Ltd* 2002 SLT (Lands Tr) 2. Where human rights are an issue, this is mentioned in the text.

1.7   Reading and references

This is a big subject and there is a good deal of material in statutes, decisions, institutional writers and textbooks. A detailed Bibliography and Reading List will be found at the beginning of the book, divided up to correspond to the different chapters. The Bibliography sets out the principal texts and statutory provisions which deal with conveyancing and related areas of law. Note that some of the abbreviations used there are used hereafter in the text. The Reading List for each subsequent chapter relates only to the content of that chapter and is divided into separate sections for books, statutes and for articles. No individual cases are listed in the Reading List but a Digest of Cases is also included at the beginning of this work, divided once again according to chapters.

Many of the matters dealt with in this Manual are treated much more fully, and with ample citation of authority in I J S Talman (ed) *Halliday's Conveyancing Law and Practice in Scotland* (2nd edn, 2 Volumes, 1996–97), to which reference should be made on points of difficulty.

1.8   Recording and registration

Since the first edition of this Manual was published, registration of title has been introduced and the whole of Scotland is now operational for land registration – see Chapter 11.

To avoid unnecessary repetition, the reader should assume that, whenever the expression 'Sasines' or 'Register of Sasines' or 'GRS' or the term 'recording' is used, this includes registration of the appropriate writ in the Land Register unless the context otherwise requires.

Chapter 2

Authentication

2.1 The significance of written documents

Conveyancing involves the preparation of written evidence in competent form to constitute rights or obligations. Is writing essential for this purpose?

The general principle is that, in a court action to establish or enforce a right or obligation, every kind of evidence is admissible to prove the facts and circumstances out of which the action arose. Apart from special cases, the intention of the parties, in any transaction, can be proved without recourse to writing as evidence. But that general principle is subject to a considerable number of exceptions and qualifications.

Obviously, written documents form an important category of evidence; and, in this context, may be classed as public or private.

(1) *Public writings.* These are documents and records specially prepared by duly authorised officials for the express purpose of preserving evidence in matters of public interest, such as Acts of Parliament, rules of court, court records, public registers, such as the Registers of Births, Deaths and Marriages, and so on. See M L Ross (ed) *Walker and Walker: The Law of Evidence in Scotland* (2nd edn, 2000), Chapter 18.

(2) *Private writings.* These are documents prepared by individuals either:
   (a) because writing is an essential to the constitution of the right or obligation; or
   (b) because the parties simply wish to preserve evidence of the terms of a transaction, although a written document may not be an essential to the constitution of the right.

The foregoing general principles still apply but, in the case of private writings executed on or after 1 August 1995, the whole of the previous law governing the authentication of documents of various kinds, both at common law and under a number of earlier statutory provisions, was replaced by a new statutory code introduced under the Requirements of Writing (Scotland) Act 1995.

The 1995 Act does not, however, have any effect whatever on the law of authentication as it applied prior to 1 August 1995 in the case of any document executed before that date. In the result, for several decades, it will remain essential for the practitioner to be familiar with the rules of authentication as they applied prior to this Act. This is particularly so in the following instances.

(1) *Heritable titles* where, inevitably, as will later emerge, Register of Sasines titles normally have to be examined for at least ten years prior to the current transaction and, in many cases, deeds of a very much earlier date also have to be examined for various purposes. One important point which has to be considered when examining such titles is whether or not they were duly executed, that is according to the law as it applied prior to the 1995 Act.

(2) In the case of *testamentary writings*, again, notwithstanding that the death occurred after the 1995 Act came into operation, if the testamentary writings were executed prior to 1 August 1995, the validity of the document so far as authentication is concerned will be tested according to the rules in force prior to the 1995 Act.

(3) In a great variety of *other writs*, the old rules will be applied to determine whether or not a deed was validly executed according to the rules in force before the 1995 Act.

This chapter deals with the rules on authentication for documents executed on or after 1 August 1995. For details of the old rules for documents executed before 1 August 1995 see the sixth edition of this book, Chapter 2. A brief summary of those rules is given at para 2.14 below.

2.2   **When is a written document obligatory?**

The general provision under the Requirements of Writing (Scotland) Act 1995, s 1(1) is that, with certain exceptions, a written document is not required for the constitution of any contract, unilateral obligation or trust.

The principal qualification to that rule is then set out in s 1(2) in terms of which a formal written document, properly subscribed, is required for any writ relating to the constitution of a contract or unilateral obligation for the creation, transfer, variation or extinction of an interest in land; for any gratuitous unilateral obligation except in the course of business; to establish any trust by which the truster declares himself to be the sole trustee of his own property including *acquirenda*; and for any testamentary writing in any form.

Section 1(3) to (6) of the 1995 Act then provide a qualification to the new rule requiring formal writing for the various transactions referred to in s 1(2)(a) where there has been what, under the old rules, would have amounted to *rei interventus* or possibly homologation. So, under these sections, lacking the necessary formal written document, if a creditor in an obligation which was intended to be constituted thereby or a beneficiary under such a trust as is referred to above has acted in reliance thereon to the knowledge and with the acquiescence of the other party, that other party, notwithstanding the lack of the required formal writing, is personally barred from withdrawing from the contractual obligation or trust which, as a result, is not to be treated as invalid if the conditions of s 1(4) are satisfied. Under that subsection, the requirement is that the aggrieved party, by so acting or refraining from so acting, has been, and would be, materially and adversely affected if the transaction was not implemented. By express provision in s 1(5) these rules replace *rei interventus* and homologation under the old rules.

The same principles are then applied with the like effect under s 1(6) to a variation of any such transaction where the variation itself lacks the necessary formal documentation.

An interest in land is defined under s 1(7) as any estate, interest or right in or over land including any right to occupy or use land or to restrict the occupation or use of land. Under this subsection a tenancy, a right to occupy or use land or a right to restrict the occupation or use of land where the tenancy or right is granted for not more than a year is excluded. Growing crops and moveable buildings or other structures are also specifically excluded under s 1(8).

It should be noted that after feudal abolition on 28 November 2004, 'interest in land' will be replaced by 'land or real right in land'.

2.3 Faxes

Faxes are a common feature of modern conveyancing and the question arises whether a fax is sufficient to satisfy the rules on requirements of writing. In *Merrick Homes Ltd v Duff* 1997 SLT 570 missives for the sale and purchase of heritage were concluded both by fax and by delivery of the faxed letter. Although it was unnecessary to decide the point, in the Outer House Lord Gill expressed the view that missives could be concluded by fax. No view was expressed in the Inner House. In *McIntosh v Alam* 1997 Hous LR 141 missives were concluded by exchange of letters, the last of which was faxed but never posted. It was admitted that the letter had been signed. The sheriff held that the fax was sufficient communication to the other party and the contract was validly concluded.

The decision in *McIntosh v Alam* raises the question of whether other electronic means of communication, such as email, will be regarded as sufficient communication. At present, it is unlikely that an email is sufficient, as it is not signed. In the not too distant future, however, electronic signatures may be introduced and it is the policy of the Law Society of Scotland to progress the use by the Scottish legal profession of electronic signatures: see (2002) 47 JLSS Feb/44. Under the Electronic Communications Act 2000, s 8, Scottish Ministers are empowered to alter legislation by statutory instrument to facilitate the use of electronic communications. This power could be used to amend the 1995 Act. Developments in this area are inevitable and are awaited with interest.

2.4 Formal validity and presumption of subscription

Under the Requirements of Writing (Scotland) Act 1995, s 2(1), formality of execution as required by s 1(2) means subscription on the last page by the grantor of the relevant document or by each grantor where there is more than one. Nothing other than such subscription is required to validate the document. Under s 2(2), two or more contractual documents taken together satisfy these requirements if each is so subscribed. Section 2(3) permits the use of an informal document as evidence in cases where a formal document is strictly required.

Subject to detailed and elaborate provisions in s 3(2) to (7) of the 1995 Act, noted below, s 3(1) provides that, where a document bears to be subscribed by the grantor, bears to have been signed by a witness, bears to state therein or in the testing clause the name and address of the witness; and where there is no contra-indication in the document, then that document is presumed to have been subscribed by that grantor. It should be noted particularly that only one witness is required.

A document which is thus on the face of it presumed to have been so subscribed is self-proving in the sense that the authenticity of the grantor's subscription and of the content of the deed requires no further corroborative evidence to establish its terms and the formality of its execution. To put it another way, it is probative. Note particularly that attestation, although necessary for this purpose, is no longer a necessary element in the solemnity of execution. Under the old rules, attestation by two witnesses was a requirement for formal validity.

Two cases neatly illustrate this fundamental difference between the old rules and the rules under the 1995 Act. In *Walker v Whitwell* 1926 SC (HL) 75, a will was signed in front of two witnesses. One witness signed as witness but the other did not, under the mistaken belief that he could not as he was a beneficiary under the will. After the testator died, this witness did add his signature but the will was held to be invalid. After 1 August 1995, in the same circumstances the will would be formally valid but not self-proving. Similarly, in a much more recent case, *Williamson v Williamson* 1997 SLT 1044, a will was executed in 1988 by a Mrs Williamson. One of the witnesses to her signature, a solicitor, D C R Wilson, for some extraordinary reason signed 'D. C. R. Williamson'. This defect in the attestation by this witness rendered the will void. Again, if the will had been signed after 1 August 1995 it would have been formally valid.

There are a number of qualifications to the rule for the presumption of validity under s 3(1).

(1) Under s 3(2), testamentary writings must be subscribed on every sheet.
(2) Under s 3(3), the name and address of the witness may be added at any time before the document is founded on or registered, and need not be written by the witness himself.
(3) Under s 3(4), if a question arises as to formality of subscription and if it is proved that the signature of the witness is false, or is the signature of another party to the deed, or if the witness did not know the grantor, was under 16 years of age, or *incapax*, or if the witness failed properly to attest, *unico contextu*, or if the name and address of the witness were added after the time limit in s 3(3) above, then there is no presumption that the document was subscribed by the grantor. The same result follows in the case of a testamentary writing on more

than one sheet if a signature on any of the sheets is proved not to be the signature of the testator.

(4) Under s 3(5), knowing the grantor merely means having credible information as to his identity.

(5) Under s 3(6), where there is more than one party to a deed and the same witness attests two or more signatures, the fact that an interval occurs between the signature of the parties and the subscription by the witness does not disqualify the attestation as failing to satisfy the *unico contextu* rule.

(6) Under s 3(7), the witness must see the grantor subscribe or the grantor must acknowledge his subscription to the witness.

(7) Under s 3(8), if the document is so authenticated and bears to state, *in gremio* thereof or in a testing clause, the date or place of subscription, that statement is presumed to be correct in the absence of any contra-indication, except in the case of a testamentary writing, under s 3(9). But, under s 3(10), an equivalent rule applies to testamentary writings, even if not self-proving. This avoids problems of the relative dates of several codicils which may be valid but not self-proving.

2.5 PRESUMPTIONS IN COURT PROCEEDINGS

The provisions in the Requirements of Writing (Scotland) Act 1995, s 4, arise out of the alteration in the rules by virtue of which a subscribed document is formally valid although, if not attested, it is not self-proving. Normally, that is not important. But it can be where the writ is to be registered or used to obtain confirmation. In such cases, if not self-proving as to signature, date or place, application can be made to the court for certification of all or any of these facts. Procedure is regulated by the Act of Sederunt (Requirements of Writing) 1996, SI 1996/1534.

2.6 ALTERATIONS TO DOCUMENTS

The general effect of the Requirements of Writing (Scotland) Act 1995, s 5, is to validate any alteration to a document:

(1) if made before the document is subscribed by the first or the only grantor, in which case the alteration forms part of the document; or

(2) if made after subscription and if the alteration is then signed by the grantor, or by all grantors when there is more than one.

Otherwise, alterations are not valid, unless so declared on application to the court. The facts may be established by any evidence, for which detailed provision is made in Schedule 1 to the 1995 Act.

An alteration to a document subscribed by the grantor or all the grantors is presumed to have been made before subscription and therefore to form part of the document:

(1) where the document is self-proving, the alteration is declared, and there is no contra-indication in the document; or

(2) if (1) is not applicable, the same result is achieved if application is made to the court, if the facts are established and if the document is suitably endorsed.

The provisions of s 4 apply generally to any such application.

Where the alteration is made after subscription, certain presumptions apply as set out in Schedule 1 to the 1995 Act.

2.7   ALTERATIONS AFTER SUBSCRIPTION

Schedule 1 to the Requirements of Writing (Scotland) Act 1995 deals with alterations made to a document after it has been subscribed. There are two main paragraphs. The first deals with the presumption in such circumstances as to the signature of the grantor or date or place of signing.

Contemporaneous alterations to documents have been dealt with above. The provisions of Schedule 1 apparently envisage later additions or alterations to a document previously executed. The provisions are lengthy and cumbersome.

Broadly speaking, Schedule 1, para 1 deals with a subsequent alteration to a self-proving deed previously executed as such and involves substantially the same formalities as apply in the case of the execution of the self-proving deed itself.

Paragraph 2 deals with alterations to a document not in form self-proving for which an application to the court is required. No doubt it will be useful to have these provisions in place as a fall back in unusual and unexpected circumstances but normally they will not be used.

Alterations to testamentary writings using these provisions are particularly undesirable.

2.8   REGISTRATION

Under the pre-1995 Act statutory rules covering registration in the Books of Council and Session or Sheriff Court Books, a deed would normally only be accepted for such registration if it was probative. Where executed under the 1995 Act, the position is now regulated by s 6 of the 1995 Act. Generally speaking, to be registrable, the document must be self-proving except in the case of a testamentary document or a deed executed abroad. No consent to registration is required.

2.9   SUBSCRIPTION AND SIGNING

Under s 7(1) of the Requirements of Writing (Scotland) Act 1995, subscription means signing the document at the end of the last page.

(1) Signing as grantor means:
    (a) signing with the full name as stated in the document; or
    (b) with the surname preceded by at least one forename or initial or abbreviation; or
    (c) in the case of subscribed but not self-proving documents, other modes of signature are permitted. These include initials or mark; but in all such cases it must be established that this was the usual mode of executing that type of writing and was intended as a signature. This will cover situations in such cases before the 1995 Act where deeds were held valid when signed with family names, as with holograph letters signed 'Connie' in *Draper v Thomason* 1954 SC 136 and ' lots of love, Mum' in *Rhodes v Peterson* 1972 SLT 98.
(2) Where there is more than one grantor, signing at the end of the last page is achieved if at least one grantor so signs; but the others must also sign on that page or on an additional page or pages.
(3) One signature covers all capacities in which a party signs.
(4) An attesting witness must sign with the full name as in the document, or testing clause or at least with the surname preceded by one forename or an initial or abbreviation. A witness need not sign more than once when attesting several signatures.

There are rules which permit members of the Royal family, peers and other privileged persons to sign in a special manner, as was the position prior to the 1995 Act. See *American Express Europe Ltd v Royal Bank of Scotland plc (No 2)* 1989 SLT 650.

The foregoing rules apply to subscription and signing by individual natural persons. Schedule 2 to the 1995 Act contains a number of provisions for execution of documents by various non-natural persons, for which see below.

2.10 ANNEXATIONS

These have always caused problems. Under the rules in s 8 of the Requirements of Writing (Scotland) Act 1995, any annexation is regarded as incorporated in a document if the document refers to it and if the annexation is on the face of it identified as being the annexation so referred to. The identification should be in particular, not merely general, terms. If these conditions are observed, no signature or subscription is required. The annexation, unsigned, is regarded as incorporated in the document.

Under s 8(2), however, there is a special provision, applicable only to a document relating to land, which incorporates an annexation and only where that annexation describes or shows all or part of the land to which the document relates. In that case, but in that case only, the annexation is regarded as incorporated in the document if, in addition to the above requirements, it is signed on the last page or, where the annexation takes the form of a plan, drawing, photograph or other representation, on every page thereof. The Keeper takes the view that this should normally include a reference to the parties to the deed and to the date. See 1995 JLSS 405.

The Keeper also takes the view that some schedules, such as a schedule of condition or dilapidations annexed to a lease, must be signed on every page, being annexed to a document relating to land and containing a plan, drawing, photograph or 'other representation'. This is the Keeper's position where the schedule in question consists entirely of plans, drawings, photographs or other representations. Where the schedule consists of both pages of text in addition to plans etc, the Keeper's position is that only the last page and any pages of plans etc must be signed.

Under s 8(3) of the 1995 Act, if an annexation requires a signature and bears to have been signed by the grantor, it is presumed to have been signed by the person who subscribed the deed as that grantor. Accordingly, if so signed, the annexation is self-proving. The provisions of s 7(2) apply to the signing of any annexation and, under s 8(6), if any one of several grantors signs on the last page of an annexation, the other grantor or grantors must also all sign, but may competently do so on an additional page. It is not clear how this applies (if at all) where an annexation must be signed on every page under s 8(2)(c)(i).

Section 8(5) alters the old *unico contextu* rule to the extent that an annexation to a self-proving document need not be signed at the same time as the document itself. It must, however, be signed before the document itself is founded on, registered for preservation, or recorded or registered in the General Register of Sasines or Land Register. No doubt this is a convenient relaxation but it may produce unexpected problems.

2.11 VICARIOUS SUBSCRIPTION

Where a grantor is blind or unable to write there are rules for execution on behalf of that person. These were previously known as notarial execution. The rules introduced to replace notarial execution under the Requirements of Writing (Scotland) Act 1995 are similar but are in a simplified form under s 9 and Schedule 3. The requirements under these rules are:

(1) The grantor must declare to 'a relevant person' that he is blind or cannot write. Notwithstanding this provision, blind persons may themselves still competently sign a document as before.

(2) A relevant person means a solicitor with a practising certificate, an advocate, a Justice of the Peace or a Sheriff Clerk. Where the document is executed outwith Scotland, it also includes a Notary Public or anyone else who, in the place of execution, has official authority so to execute documents.

(3) In the presence of a witness, the relevant person must read the document to the grantor unless the grantor otherwise declares this to be unnecessary. If then authorised by the grantor, he may then subscribe the document on the grantor's behalf. In the case of testamentary writings only, the relevant person must subscribe each sheet as in s 3(2) of the 1995 Act. In all cases, the signature must be in the presence of the grantor.

(4) The witness then signs.

(5) A testing clause is added and must contain, or if there is no testing clause, the document must contain, a statement that the document was read or not read and the grantor gave the relevant person authority to sign.

The same provisions apply, generally, to vicarious execution of annexations and alterations as apply in the case of personal subscription by the grantor but with the special qualification that the reference above to reading the document to the grantor includes, where appropriate, describing a plan, photograph or other representation, however best that can be achieved.

Section 9(4) of the 1995 Act now provides that, under the new rules, a document vicariously subscribed which confers a benefit on the subscriber or his or her spouse, son or daughter is invalidated only to the extent that it confers such a benefit. This is a welcome improvement on the position under the old rules, where any interest of the notary invalidated the whole deed.

As mentioned above, a blind person does not require to adopt vicarious execution but may himself validly subscribe. However, this is not to be recommended in practice. The document may either be read over to the grantor or the grantor may dispense of that requirement. In practice, while that may be convenient, it is almost certainly not advisable to encourage dispensation but instead it is better, if practicable, to read the document over to the grantor.

If there is any likelihood that vicarious execution may have to be resorted to in individual cases, the alternative of a power of attorney should always be seriously considered.

2.12 TESTING CLAUSES

A testing clause is a convenient way to set out the designations of the witnesses and the date and place of execution. Under s 10 of the Requirements of Writing (Scotland) Act 1995, the information required for the rules for creating a self-proving document can be incorporated in the deed itself, but a testing clause is commonly used, in practice.

Scottish Ministers (formerly the Secretary of State) are empowered to prescribe a form of testing clause under s 10 but this power has not been exercised yet. Accordingly, conventional forms of testing clause incorporating the necessary information can be and are used.

2.13 PROOF BY WRIT OR OATH

Under the Requirements of Writing (Scotland) Act 1995, s 14(3), nothing in the 1995 Act applies to any document executed under the old rules nor affects the operation of any procedure for establishing the authenticity of any such document, for example under the Conveyancing (Scotland) Act 1874, s 39. That is, however, subject to an exception in the case of proof by writ or oath which is abolished under s 11 of the 1995 Act. In that special case, unless proceedings have been commenced before the commencement of the 1995 Act, proof by writ or oath is no longer applicable. Instead, any evidence, including parole evidence will be competent from and after 1 August 1995 to establish transactions or obligations already entered into or undertaken prior to 1 August 1995 which, under the old rules, could only have been proved by writ or oath.

2.14 SPECIAL PERSONS

Schedule 2 to the Requirements of Writing (Scotland) Act 1995 sets out in detail special provisions which apply where the deed is subscribed or signed by or on behalf of various special categories of persons other than individuals.

(1) *Partnerships*
Under the pre-1995 Act rules, there was no statutory provision for execution of deeds by partnerships and this occasionally caused problems. See *Littlejohn v Mackay* 1974 SLT (Sh Ct) 82. Provision is now made in Schedule 2.

Where the grantor of a document is a partnership, it is duly executed if signed on its behalf by a partner or by a duly authorised person. The person signing signs in his own name, or in the partnership name. Where the firm name is used, there seems to be no need for the signatory to declare his personal identity or authority.

Alterations are similarly dealt with.

No special provision is made for the self-proving quality of a deed so signed but since, in every case, the signature required is the signature of an individual, it is assumed that, if attested, a document so signed on behalf of a partnership will have self-proving status, as signed by the firm.

This does not, however, in addition imply that a partner or an authorised person was, or is presumed to be, duly authorised to sign; nor does the self-proving quality carry with it a guarantee that the signatory was in fact a partner. Some investigation may therefore be required, even in the case of *ex facie* self-proving documents.

Execution of documents by limited liability partnerships, a new type of partnership – see para 3.24 – is set out in the Limited Liability Partnerships (Scotland) Regulations 2001, SSI 2001/128 under which a new paragraph 3A is added to Schedule 2 to the 1995 Act. The provisions are similar to those for companies. The partnership name is not used. In general, the document is signed by a member of the limited liability partnership. To enable the presumption under s 1(3) of the 1995 Act to apply, the document must be signed by either two members or one member and a witness with the name and address of the witness included. There is no presumption that the person signing is a member of the limited liability partnership.

(2) *Companies*
Between 1985 and 1995, the rules for the execution of deeds by companies were confused. For a helpful table, see G L Gretton and K G C Reid *Conveyancing* (2nd edn, 1999), para 14.16.

Under the 1995 Act rules, the position is as follows:

(a) Self-proving status:

(i) *Attested documents.* Where a document appears to have been subscribed on behalf of a company by a director, or the secretary, or a duly authorised person and, in addition, it bears to be signed by a witness whose name and address are given, then, in the absence of any contrary indication on the face of the document, a document so subscribed is formally valid and is self-proving.

(ii) *Unattested documents.* If the document is not attested but is subscribed on behalf of the company by two directors, or by a director and the secretary, or by two duly authorised persons but is otherwise unattested, and in the absence of any contrary indication on the face of the document, then, in this alternative form, the document is formally valid and is self-proving.

(b) Formal validity

If self-proving status is not required, a document is validly executed on behalf of a company if signed by one director, or the secretary, or one duly authorised person.

A company no longer requires to have a common seal and so, in any of the foregoing alternatives, the seal is unnecessary.

Note that, as in the case of partnerships, the foregoing provisions as to execution are restricted to authentication only and in no circumstances imply that any person so signing is in fact a director, or the secretary, or an authorised person.

Equivalent provision is then made for subsequent alterations of any writings so executed on behalf of a company.

(3) *Local authorities*

Again, there have been changes over the years in the mode of execution of documents by local authorities. Under the old rules, the latest of these was in the Local Government (Scotland) Act 1973, s 194.

Until 1 April 1996, 'local authority' meant a Regional or District Council. As from that date, it means a new Unitary Council established under the Local Government etc (Scotland) Act 1994. There is no equivalent provision for execution of deeds in that Act and instead execution is dealt with under the 1995 Act rules. They apply to the new Unitary Councils.

The requirements in Schedule 2 to the Requirements of Writing (Scotland) Act 1995 for execution by a local authority are as follows.

Where the grantor of the document is a local authority, it is signed by the authority if signed on its behalf by the proper officer of the authority. That, by itself, creates formal validity. No additional signatures of members of the authority or witnesses and no corporate seal are required.

For the purpose above stated, however, a person purporting to sign on behalf of a local authority as the proper officer of the authority is presumed to be the proper officer. Note the difference between other juristic persons and local authorities. Here, there is a presumption that the signatory is authorised to sign. Accordingly, no further enquiry is necessary in such cases.

Consistent with the other provisions in the 1995 Act, such a signature creates formal validity. If the document is to be self-proving, then either the signature must be witnessed by one witness and the attestation details must be incorporated in the deed or, if not witnessed, the deed must also carry the common seal.

Again, there is the usual provision that there is no contra-indication on the face of the deed.

Provisions similar to those noted above apply to contemporaneous and subsequent alterations.

(4) *Bodies corporate*

There is an infinite number of bodies corporate, whether under statute or Royal Charter, each of which has its own special provision for authentication of documents. This is clearly troublesome and the provision in Schedule 2 to the 1995 Act for bodies corporate generally is welcome. The provision applies to any body corporate except a company or local authority, both of which have been dealt with above.

Where the grantor of a document is a body corporate, it is to be signed by either:

(a) a member of the governing board or a member of the body if there is no board; or

(b) the secretary of the body by whatever name he is called; or

(c) a duly authorised person.

Such signature confers formal validity.

For self-proving status, consistent with the other provisions in the 1995 Act, attestation of the signature by one witness is required, with the inclusion of the name and address of the witness; or, in the absence of attestation, the document must carry the common seal.

Again, there is the standard provision that there is no contra-indication in the document itself.

When so executed, the document is self-proving.

As with companies, so with bodies corporate, the presumptions referred to above relate only to authentication. There is no additional presumption that the subscriber satisfies the statutory requirement.

(5) *Ministers of the Crown and office holders*

Where the grantor of a document is a Minister or office holder, it is signed by him if signed:

(a) personally; or

(b) if authorised by statute, by an officer of the Minister or some other authorised person; or

(c) in the case of an office holder who is duly authorised to delegate, it may be signed by the authorised person; or

(d) in any case, by any other person who is duly authorised to sign.

Such signature satisfies the formality validity rule. If in addition the document is to have self-proving status, there must be attestation and the document must disclose the name and address of the witness.

There is the usual provision that the deed contains no contra-indication.

2.15 **Writs executed abroad**

The general rule of private international law, applied in Scotland, is that any deed executed abroad will receive effect here if executed in accordance with the required formalities in the place of execution.

The rule is most commonly applied in the case of wills, and powers of attorney.

In the case of wills, the common law rule has been reinforced with modifications under the Wills Act 1963 which continues to apply under the new rules.

Some authors treat this exception for writs executed abroad as falling under the general heading of privileged writings and they are so treated here. See J Burns *Conveyancing Practice* (4th edn, 1957), p 14 and also R Rennie and D J Cusine *The Requirements of Writing* (1995), p 40. For a recent illustration of the application of the rule in practice, see *Hamilton v Wakefield* 1992 SCLR 740 where it was held in the Scottish Courts that a contract for the sale and purchase of a superiority, being heritable property, had been validly created under the English rule which provides that, where a person bids at an auction, he incurs a binding legal obligation, even where the subject matter is heritable.

The only mention in the Requirements of Writing (Scotland) Act 1995 of documents executed abroad is in s 6 (3)(c)(iii), which authorises registration in the Books of Council and Session or Sheriff Court Books if the Keeper or Sheriff Clerk is satisfied that the document is formally valid according to the law governing its validity.

The 1995 Act abolishes holograph writings and writs *in re mercatoria* as privileged writings. Except for the speciality of registration, however, writs executed abroad are not otherwise referred to in the Act. It is presumed that the privilege accorded to a deed executed abroad under the old rules will continue to apply, but no express provision seems to be made in the 1995 Act.

Prior to the 1995 Act, titles to heritable property in Scotland form an exception; they must conform to the Scottish requirements of authentication, regardless of other factors. It is assumed that this continues to apply.

2.16 **The old rules prior to 1 August 1995**

Full details of the old rules can be found in Chapter 2 of the sixth edition of this book. A brief summary is as follows:

Prior to 1 August 1995, in many transactions the law required some formal written deed in order to create certain rights or obligations, which were known as *obligationes literis*. Deeds were formally valid if subscribed by the grantor and witnessed by two witnesses. Detailed rules set out the various requirements in relation to the subscription and the witnesses. Such formally valid deeds were also probative. If a deed was not properly subscribed and witnessed it was not valid. Where such an invalid deed was a contract it could become binding by the subsequent actions of the parties which amounted to *rei interventus* or homologation.

Certain deeds, known as privileged writings, were valid without the need for witnesses. The main type was holograph writings which were in the handwriting of the grantor or had the words 'adopted as holograph' in the grantor's handwriting above the grantor's signature. Although valid, such deeds were not probative.

Where the grantor was blind or unable to write, there was a procedure known as 'notarial execution' whereby the deed could be signed on behalf of the grantor: see para 2.11.

Chapter 3
Capacity

3.1 Capacity

On the general question of capacity, and its effect on the ability of a person to contract, see W M Gloag and R C Henderson *Introduction to the Law of Scotland* (11th edn, 2001), Chapter 4.

Broadly speaking, the same general principles apply to the ownership of, title to and disposal of, heritable property.

3.2 Power

In addition to capacity, the party must also have power to make contracts. In the case of individuals acting for their own beneficial interest, if such an individual has capacity, he also has, by necessary implication, power to deal with his proprietary rights in any way. If, however, a person acts in a representative capacity, such as a trustee, or as an agent, the trustee or agent may have capacity but may lack power. If so, any deed granted by him may be voidable or even void. For example, in *Piggins & Rix Ltd v Montrose Port Authority* 1995 SLT 418, a port authority acquired heritable property under statutory powers which also conferred on the authority a number of other powers but not power of sale. In a special case presented to the Court of Session to determine whether or not power of sale could be implied, the court held that the reasonable inference to be drawn from the omission of this power in the relevant statutory provisions was that Parliament did not intend that the authority should have power of sale, and that power was not considered to be reasonably incidental to the main purposes of the corporation.

3.3 Domicile

In relation to capacity, the question of domicile may be significant. The general rule, which applies to Scottish heritage, is that the *lex situs*, ie the law of the place where the land is situated, determines whether or not a person has capacity to deal with his heritable property in Scotland. See A E Anton *Private International Law* (2nd edn,

1990), p 604. But that general principle is hedged about with certain limitations and qualifications. So, in the case of children, there is some support for the view that the *lex domicilii*, ie the law of the place of domicile, may determine the capacity of a foreign child to deal with Scottish heritage.

Clearly, in such cases, the ideal rule is to ascertain the position under both systems of law, *lex situs* and *lex domicilii*; and only to act in reliance on a deed by a person domiciled abroad if that deed is valid under both systems.

Further, where a person acts in a representative capacity in reliance on statutory powers, for example, trustees, corporations etc, their powers are necessarily limited by the relevant statutory authority in their own jurisdiction. Scottish Acts, in particular the Trusts (Scotland) Acts, have no application in such cases.

3.4   Title

The question of title is distinct and separate from the question of capacity and power. The case of trustees is typical. The constituent deed, ie the deed of trust, must itself be valid before the trustees can act. But, in addition, the trustees must themselves be capable of acting, which does not depend on the terms of the deed, but on personal factors; and they must also have power to act with reference to the trust assets which, again, involves different considerations. The technicalities of title will be dealt with later.

3.5   Trustees

The case of Scottish trustees is taken first because some of the rules applicable to trustees apply also in other comparable cases, for example guardians and children etc.

3.6   CAPACITY

The individual trustee is generally subject to the same rules as to capacity as is any individual. So, a person who is insane cannot effectively deal with his own property; and although he may validly be appointed as a trustee, he cannot effectively deal with trust assets.

3.7   TITLE

Normally, there is a deed of trust (or its equivalent, for example confirmation-dative) which constitutes the trustees' title. That deed must, of course, be intrinsically valid in itself. It may take various forms and, in relation to *mortis causa* trusts, there are special rules, supplementing the common law position, under the Succession (Scotland) Act 1964. In *inter vivos* trusts, assets of various kinds may pass to the trustee under the constituent deed or by separate conveyance or transfer; *mortis causa*, assets pass to the trustees either directly under the constituent deed, or, since 1964, indirectly by virtue of confirmation. In certain circumstances, with both *inter vivos* and *mortis causa* trusts, the trustees may later acquire assets during the course of administration of the trust. In all cases, they may also come to dispose of trust assets. In addition, during the course of administration, there may be supplementary trust titles in the form of deeds of assumption and conveyance and minutes of resignation of trustees, and decrees of appointment of new trustees by the court etc. In any given trust, there may therefore be a whole series of formal deeds which, together, make up the title of the trustees for the time being to a particular asset in the estate.

3.8   SALE OF HERITAGE

At common law, trustees had no implied power to dispose of heritage conveyed to them by the truster. Instead, the necessary implication was that any such heritable estate was to be retained by the trustees for the ultimate benefit of the beneficiaries. Thus, if A died leaving a will conveying his whole estate to trustees, including heritage, the trustees had a title to that heritage and capacity to deal with it; but they had no power to sell or dispose of it, except in terms of the will. This rule could, and can, be displaced in the following ways:

(1) *Express power of sale*. The truster might competently confer on his trustees an express power of sale; and this express power is still regularly met with in practice in deeds of trust. For a typical illustration, see J Burns *Conveyancing Practice* (4th edn, 1957), p 802, and A H Elder *Forms of Wills in Accordance with the Law of Scotland* (1947), p 165.

> 'My trustees ... shall have power ... to sell or otherwise realise the trust estate or any part or parts thereof, heritable and moveable.'

(2) *Implied power*. The Trusts (Scotland) Act 1921, s 4 provides that, in all trusts, the trustees have power to do certain acts, provided that the act is not at variance with the terms or the purposes of the trust; and any such act, when done, is as effectual as if the trust deed had contained an express power to that effect. These powers in s 4 include:
  (a) to sell the trust estate or any part thereof, heritable as well as moveable;
  (b) to grant feus of heritage (which will be no longer possible after feudal abolition);
  (c) to grant leases;
  (d) to borrow money on security;
  (e) to excamb (or exchange) land;
  (f) to grant all deeds necessary for carrying into effect the powers vested in the trustees.

Section 6 prescribes the method of sale, which may be by public roup or private bargain.

Prior to the Trusts (Scotland) Act 1961, in all cases when dealing with trustees, a purchaser had to examine not only the trustees' title to satisfy himself as to its intrinsic validity, but, in addition, he had to consider the purposes of the deed, and the powers of the trustees thereunder, to see whether or not they had power of sale. Otherwise, he might find himself with an invalid title.

The 1961 Act, s 2 has improved the position of the purchaser, although it does not in any way alter the strict rules as to trustees' power of sale. The sole purpose of the section is to protect the purchaser and to spare him the necessity of enquiring into trustees' powers. Note the following features of this section:

(i) It applies to any of the powers in the 1921 Act, s 4, not merely sale of heritage.

(ii) If, after 27 August 1961, the trustees exercise one of the implied powers in s 4, for example sale, the validity of the sale, and of the purchaser's title, cannot be challenged by any person merely on the grounds that the sale is at variance with the terms or purposes of the trust. Good faith on the part of the purchaser is not required. See *Brodie v Secretary of State for Scotland* 2002 GWD 20-698.

(iii) If trustees are acting under the supervision of the accountant of court, s 2 only applies if the accountant of court consents. This applies only in special cases, such as where a guardian is selling heritage for a person who lacks capacity.

(iv) The section does not in any way affect the relationship between trustees and beneficiaries. Thus, trustees who sell *ultra vires* may now confer a valid title and the purchaser is no longer concerned with their powers; but, in so doing, they lay themselves open to an action for breach of trust at the instance of an aggrieved beneficiary.

(3) *Power granted by the court.* If the deed of trust contains no express power, and if no effective power is implied under s 4, trustees may not sell unless specially authorised by the court under the 1921 Act, s 5. Prior to the 1961 Act, such petitions to the court were commonplace, and are still competent and not unusual. Undoubtedly, however, petitions under s 5 are less frequent than they were before 1961, when purchasers were scrutinising trustees' titles, and challenging their powers. Note that the petition in this case is not concerned with matters of title, but only with power of sale. Provided the trustees have power (express, implied or from the court), the purchaser is not further concerned to consider whether or not the power is being properly exercised. An improper exercise of the power would not in any way invalidate the purchaser's title.

3.9   PURCHASE OR ACQUISITION OF ASSETS

The same problem does not here arise, in that a person selling any asset, heritable or moveable, to trustees has no duty whatever to consider, or enquire into, the powers of the purchasing trustees. If, having sold to trustees, it turns out that the trustees do not have power to purchase, the trustees cannot rescind the contract nor retract in a question with the seller. Contrast the position of a purchaser from trustees without power of sale, prior to 1961; his title was open to reduction and, if reduced, he lost the property. If trustees do make an unauthorised purchase, they have implied power to resell: see A MacKenzie Stuart *The Law of Trusts* (1932), p 237.

On the other hand, as between trustees and a beneficiary, the trustees cannot properly purchase any asset, heritable or moveable, unless they are duly authorised by:

(1) express powers of purchase, or investment, in the deed of trust, which often are expressly conferred;

(2) implied powers under the Trusts (Scotland) Act 1921, now substantially supplemented by the Trustee Investments Act 1961;

(3) the Trusts (Scotland) Act 1961, s 4 which empowers trustees to acquire an interest in residential accommodation in Scotland or elsewhere, if it is reasonably required as a residence for a beneficiary. This power to purchase under the 1961 Act is added as one of the implied powers in the 1921 Act, s 4, now s 4(1)(ee). It is, therefore, still competent to petition the court, under the 1921 Act, s 5, for authority to purchase heritage in cases not within the new s 4(1)(ee) – see *Bristow, Petitioner* 1965 SLT 225 where, in special circumstances, a *curator bonis* applied for special powers to purchase under this section. The petition was dismissed as unnecessary on the basis that the curator did have implied power; but, as in other similar cases, Lord Cameron stated 'It may well be that curators will decide to err on the side of caution in determining whether to seek the Court's authority for the exercise of such a power as is sought here, or to act at their own hands'. On *curators bonis*, see further para 3.14.

3.10 Foreign trusts

The foreign trust most commonly encountered in practice is an English trust. Trust law in England differs radically from trust law in Scotland. In particular, the Trusts (Scotland) Acts 1921 and 1961 have no application whatsoever in an English trust. But, on the basis of international comity, the Court of Session in Scotland will exercise its *nobile officium* to make an order in a foreign trust, if required. Therefore, English trustees may petition the Scottish court under the *nobile officium*, but not under the 1921 Act, s 5, for, *inter alia*, power of sale. The Scottish court must then consider how English law views the powers of trustees in relation to the sale of immoveable property.

For a typical case see *Campbell, Petitioner* 1958 SC 275, where the court granted power of sale to English trustees, but declined to include in the order an English provision regulating the exercise of the power. Lord President Clyde said: 'It is clear that, as this is an English trust, the Trusts (Scotland) Act 1921 does not apply ... and it is equally clear that, as the English Court does not operate in Scotland, an application to this Court is necessary to enable the trustees to give the purchaser of Scottish subjects a good marketable title.'

It can be argued that this is no longer necessary after the passing of the Recognition of Trusts Act 1987, which permitted ratification of the Hague Trusts Convention and which was ratified by the United Kingdom in 1989. This argument is that trustees have such powers as may be implied in their own system and if the matter came before a Scottish court, the court should attempt to give effect to the objects of an English trust which might include the power of sale. However, the position is not clear. See further A E Anton *Private International Law* (2nd edn, 1990), Chapter 25, especially at p 643.

Note, particularly, that the 1961 Act, s 2 applies only to Scottish trusts. It does not protect a purchaser from, for example, English trustees; and so a purchaser must still satisfy himself that English (or other foreign) trustees do have the requisite power to deal with Scottish heritage under the proper law of jurisdiction of the trust.

The same considerations apply where English trustees purchase Scottish heritage, but again, with this difference, that, in such cases, the seller is not concerned with the powers of a purchasing trustee after the transaction has settled. In all such cases, it is as well to take advice from a lawyer practising in the country having jurisdiction over the trust.

3.11 Children

The common law rules relating to capacity of children were substantially recast by the Age of Legal Capacity (Scotland) Act 1991, which came into force on 25 September 1991.

The common law distinguished between pupil children and minor children. A pupil was a girl under 12 or a boy under 14, while a minor was a child above these ages but who had not yet attained the age of 18. Pupils had no legal capacity and their property was administered by a tutor or tutors, in practice usually a parent. Minors had full legal capacity subject to the need to obtain the consent of a curator if there was one, which there usually was.

Under the 1991 Act, which replaces the common law rules, a dividing line is set at the age of 16. Children under that age have no active legal capacity except in certain limited circumstances which do not usually affect rights to heritage. Children aged 16 or over have full legal capacity and there is no equivalent, in the new law, to the minor's curator at common law.

3.12 CHILDREN UNDER 16

Subject to a small number of exceptions, a child under the age of 16 has no legal capacity to enter into any transaction. Thus a child cannot buy or sell a house, or burden it with a standard security. But a child aged 12 or over has testamentary capacity and may bequeath heritable property by will.

Juristic acts are performed on behalf of a child by the child's guardian or guardians. The appointment of guardians is regulated by the Law Reform (Parent and Child) (Scotland) Act 1986, ss 2–4 (as amended). In the normal case the guardian is the mother of the child and, provided that he was married to the mother at the time of conception or subsequently, the father also. Where there are two guardians, each may exercise guardianship rights without the consent of the other.

Guardians are trustees within the meaning of the Trusts (Scotland) Acts 1921 and 1961. Thus purchasers are protected by s 2 of the 1961 Act (see above) and may take title from a guardian without inquiry into his powers. But a guardian who sells beyond his powers is liable in damages in a question with his ward. The question of power of sale was considered in *Cunningham's Tutrix, Petitioner* 1949 SC 275, where a distinction was made between heritage held as an investment and heritage in the nature of a family estate or residence. It was suggested that a guardian was empowered to sell the former but not the latter.

The position of a guardian differs from that of a trustee, in that the property of the child is held, and title is taken, in the name of the child. The guardian merely acts as an administrator and will make up title in name of the child and not in his own name as guardian. In practice, purchase of heritage by a guardian is unusual, although it is authorised under s 4 of the 1961 Act where its purpose is to provide a residence for the child – see *Bristow, Petitioner* 1965 SLT 225. Further, a child may, for example, inherit heritage by will.

As pointed out in para 3.8 above, the 1961 Act, s 2 only operates to protect parties transacting onerously with trustees. It does not prevent a beneficiary from suing for breach of trust.

3.13 CHILDREN AGED 16–18

A child aged 16 or over has full legal capacity and may buy and sell heritable property in his own name. However, it is provided by the Age of Legal Capacity (Scotland) Act 1991, s 3 that a child between the ages of 16 and 18 who enters into a prejudicial transaction may apply to the court at any time before attaining the age of 21 to have the transaction set aside.

A transaction is prejudicial within the 1991 Act if (a) an adult, exercising reasonable prudence, would not have entered into it, and (b) it has caused, or is likely to cause, substantial prejudice to the child. Obviously, sales and purchases of heritable property will not ordinarily be prejudicial within this definition. Nonetheless a seller to or a purchaser from a child between 16 and 18 will need to be cautious. There are various ways in which his position might be protected. First, s 3(3) of the 1991 Act lists a number of transactions which cannot be set aside. These include transactions in the course of the child's trade and transactions induced by fraudulent misrepresentation on the part of the child. Secondly, a projected transaction can be ratified by the court in advance under s 4 of the 1991 Act. Thereafter it cannot be set aside. Thirdly, the child can himself ratify a transaction if he is over the age of 18. Finally, care can be taken to ensure that the transaction is not in fact prejudicial. Thus in the case of a sale by a child there should be sufficient advertising of the property and, preferably, an independent valuation. See I J S Talman (ed) *Halliday's Conveyancing Law and Practice in Scotland* (2nd edn, 2 Volumes, 1996–97), paras 2–04 to 2–40.

The position of children under the age of 18 has been affected further by the Children (Scotland) Act 1995. This Act is primarily concerned with family relationships and parental responsibilities, and also deals at considerable length with promotion of the welfare of children by local authorities. In large measure, therefore, the Children (Scotland) Act 1995 is outwith the scope of this Manual. There are, however, two provisions to which attention should be given in this context. First, in the 1995 Act, ss 1 and 2, certain parental responsibilities are imposed on a parent which include, *inter alia*, power to act as the child's legal representative and, under s 2, a variety of parental rights which are less relevant in this context are conferred on a parent. For the purposes of these two sections, 'child' means a person under 16 years of age. Further elaborate provisions deal with these responsibilities and rights and with the appointment of guardians.

Sections 9 and 10 of the Children (Scotland) Act 1995 deal with the safeguarding of the property of a child and with its administration by the legal representatives.

Section 9 imposes quite onerous provisions on persons who hold property to which a child (again under 16 years of age) has an absolute indefeasible and vested right and would therefore be entitled to call for immediate payment and delivery, were the child not under 16 years of age. Section 9 applies *inter alia* both to trustees and to executors holding such property for a child under the age. A trustee or executor in that position comes under certain obligations as to how to deal with the property of the child, which in turn depends on the value of the property.

Section 10 is perhaps the most important section in the context of this chapter. In terms of that section, a person acting as a child's legal representative in relation to administration of assets comes under a statutory duty to act reasonably and prudently but, with that qualification, is generally entitled to do anything which the child could do in relation to the child's property if that child were of full age. The 'child', in this provision, apparently means a child under 18 years of age, although the ability so to act ceases at age 16.

These provisions are supplementary to the provisions in the Age of Legal Capacity (Scotland) Act 1991 referred to above which continues to apply as summarised under this sub-head.

The foregoing provisions came into force on 1 November 1996.

3.14 Judicial factors and adults with incapacity

A judicial factor may be appointed by the court in various circumstances to safeguard and administer an estate, both heritable and moveable.

The decree or act and warrant appointing the judicial factor operates as his title to the estate coming under his control. A judicial factor is a trustee for the purposes of the Trusts Acts; and the Trusts (Scotland) Act 1961, s 2 applies to protect a purchaser in dealings with a judicial factor. See para 3.8.

A common type of judicial factor prior to the introduction of the provisions of the Adults with Incapacity (Scotland) Act 2000 was a *curator bonis* to an adult who lacked capacity. See the sixth edition of this book. Under the 2000 Act it is no longer competent to appoint a *curator bonis* and new statutory provisions are introduced in Part 6, with effect from 1 April 2002. There are two new types of appointees whom a court can empower to act on behalf of an adult who lacks capacity. Authorised persons or interveners can be given power, on application to a sheriff, to act in relation to a specific matter and guardians, similar to *curators bonis*, can be appointed by a sheriff and given wide-ranging powers to act in relation to all or most matters on behalf of the adult. Both authorised persons and guardians are supervised by the Public Guardian, a new post. For further details, see A Ward *Adult Incapacity* (2003).

Once a sheriff grants an interlocutor which gives an authorised person or guardian power to deal with heritable property, an application to the Keeper must be made forthwith under the 2000 Act, s 56 or s 61 respectively, to record the interlocutor in the Register of Sasines or register it in the Land Register. This applies to any order which gives the power 'to deal, convey or manage any interest in land' which is registered or capable of being registered in the Register of Sasines or Land Register. This ensures that any search of the Registers for conveyancing purposes will reveal the intervention order.

The interlocutor must specify the property adequately to make it identifiable in either the Register of Sasines or Land Register. It is not possible to deduce title through an interlocutor using it as a midcouple. Third-party purchasers for good faith from an authorised person or guardian are protected against any irregularity in the making of an order or exceeding of authority under s 53(13) and s 79(a) and against termination of authority prior to the transfer of title to the third party under s 77(4) of the 2000 Act. See further Steven and Barr in Reid and Gretton *Conveyancing 2002* (2003) at pp 100–111.

3.15 Corporations

A corporation is a separate legal person and may hold property in its own name. Of necessity, however, all contracts and deeds relating to the corporation's assets must be entered into and granted by the directors or other officer. The mode of execution of a deed by a corporation is discussed in Chapter 2.

Every statutory and chartered corporation enjoys powers conferred on it by the relevant statute or charter, and these should be consulted in all cases. *Piggins & Rix Ltd v Montrose Port Authority* 1995 SLT 418, referred to above, at para 3.2, serves as a warning.

The commonest corporation met with in practice is the company incorporated under the Companies Acts 1985 and 1989. Every such company must have a memorandum and articles of association. In the objects clause of the memorandum, the company's powers and the limits of those powers are defined; and the articles prescribe the mode in which those powers may be exercised. Thus, the memorandum of every incorporated company will, in practice, include a power to the company to acquire and to dispose of property of all kinds, and to borrow on the security thereof.

Typical objects clauses in a memorandum of association of a company, taken from K W Mackinnon and R Buchanan-Dunlop (eds) *Palmer's Company Precedents* (17th edn, 1956), Part 1: General Forms, pp 303 and 310, read:

'To purchase, take on lease or in exchange, hire or otherwise acquire, any real and personal property and any rights or privileges which the company may think necessary or convenient for the purposes of its business'.

'To sell, lease, mortgage or otherwise dispose of the property, assets, or undertaking of the company or any part thereof for such consideration as the company may think fit.'

For the exercise of these powers, a typical clause in articles of association, taken from *Palmer's Company Precedents*, p 543, might read:

'The business of the company shall be managed by the directors who ... may exercise all such powers of the company as are not, by the Act or by these regulations, required to be exercised by the company in general meeting ...'

The power to borrow is often limited by the articles to a stated maximum. Often there is no power in the memorandum to guarantee borrowing by some other person and to grant security therefor. In recent years, this created problems in the case of groups of companies where the parent company borrows for the benefit of the whole group on the footing that the subsidiary companies will guarantee the parent company's borrowing.

At common law a transaction was void if it was beyond the powers of the company as set out in its memorandum, but this *ultra vires* rule has been displaced by statute. The current provision is in the Companies Act 1985, s 35 (inserted by the Companies Act 1989, s 108 with effect from 4 February 1991). This provides that the validity of an act done by a company shall not be called into question on the ground of lack of capacity by reason of anything in the company's memorandum. Thus, where A purchases property from a company, the company is able to confer a good title even although there is no express power of sale in its memorandum. Unlike the original version of s 35, which was in force until 4 February 1991, there is now no requirement that the purchaser is unaware that the company had no power to make the transaction. Section 35A provides that a third party dealing with the Board of a company is protected if in good faith, even though the Board acted beyond its powers. The third party is not to be regarded as in bad faith by reason only of knowing that the transaction was beyond the Board's powers. Section 35 does not alter the rule that directors are liable to the members of the company in respect of any breach of the memorandum or articles, but a party transacting with the company is unaffected.

3.16 LIQUIDATION

A company may be wound up voluntarily, either in a members' or in a creditors' liquidation; or it may be wound up compulsorily by the court. In all cases, a liquidator, or joint liquidators, is or are appointed. In contrast to the sequestration of an individual (see below), liquidation does not divest the company of its assets; but an order or resolution for the winding-up of the company has the effect of suspending the powers of the directors and, by statute, the liquidator is invested with comparable powers. In particular, the liquidator may, without the sanction of the court, sell both heritable and moveable property belonging to the company by public roup or private bargain. A deed granted by a company in liquidation runs in name of the company, but the fact of liquidation is referred to; and the deed is executed by the liquidator in place of the directors.

3.17 RECEIVERSHIP

A holder of any floating charge over a company's assets created before 15 September 2003 may appoint or petition the court to appoint a receiver to take over the management of the property which is subject to the floating charge under the Insolvency Act 1986, Part II. Often this will be the whole property of the company and the object of receivership is to make the best use of the property to enable the floating charge holder to be repaid. A receiver has the powers contained in the instrument creating the floating charge and statutory powers under the 1986 Act, Schedule 2. These include power to take possession of the property and to sell both heritable and moveable property by public roup or private bargain. A deed granted by a receiver is executed by the receiver in the company name. Although there are no express statutory provisions on how the receivership affects the powers of the directors, when a receiver takes possession of the company property this effectively suspends the directors' powers. For floating charges created since 15 September 2003, the Enterprise Act 2002 has significantly limited the availability of receivership: see para 23.4.

3.18 ADMINISTRATORS

Under the Insolvency Act 1986, Part II, the court has power, in specified circumstances, to make an order appointing an administrator as an alternative procedure to liquidation in the case of a potentially or actually insolvent company which, it is thought, may be rescued by competent administration.

In terms of the 1986 Act, s 11, during the period of administration, the company cannot be wound up; no creditor can take steps to enforce any security; and no other proceedings, and no diligence, are competent against the company or its assets except with the leave of the court.

Further, on the making of the order, any petition for the winding-up of the company is automatically dismissed.

Under s 15(7), the administrator is required, within 14 days of his appointment, to notify the Registrar of Companies.

Wide powers are conferred on the administrator under ss 14 and 15 of the 1986 Act. In particular, under s 15, the administrator is empowered to deal with and dispose of any asset of the company which is subject to any form of security or diligence; but the preference of the secured creditor is preserved in the net proceeds of such disposal. In terms of s 14(6), a person dealing with an administrator in good faith and for value is not under any obligation to enquire whether he is acting within his powers.

In terms of s 16(1) of the 1986 Act, when the administrator disposes of an asset in Scotland, the recording, intimation or registration of the document of transfer (as appropriate) has the effect of disencumbering the property from the security thereon.

During the period of administration, the assets of the company remain vested in the company; and deeds relating thereto will run in name of, and be granted by, the company. For this purpose, the administrator is given power to use the company's seal and to do all acts and execute in name and on behalf of the company any deed, receipt or other document.

As with the case of the liquidator, so with the administrator it is safest to assume that, in executing deeds intended to be self-proving, the signature of the administrator should be attested.

The execution of documents on behalf of a company by a liquidator or administrator is dealt with in the Insolvency Act 1986: see now the Requirements of Writing (Scotland) Act 1995, Schedule 2, para 3(2).

3.19 Sequestration

Where an individual becomes apparently insolvent and is sequestrated, a trustee in sequestration is appointed by the court. His position is analogous to that of a judicial factor, but he is appointed under special procedure, and with special powers, under the Bankruptcy (Scotland) Act 1985.

No attempt is made here to deal in detail with the provisions of the Bankruptcy (Scotland) Act 1985 but attention is drawn to certain sections which apply with particular reference to title to heritable property. See further W W McBryde *Bankruptcy* (2nd edn, 1995).

3.20 PROCEDURE

Firstly, in a sequestration, various steps in procedure are laid down in the Bankruptcy (Scotland) Act 1985 leading to the election and confirmation by the court of a permanent trustee. The primary responsibility of the trustee is to ingather and safeguard the estate of the sequestrated debtor for the benefit generally of his creditors. The decree confirming the appointment of the permanent trustee in office is termed the act and warrant.

3.21 VESTING

Sections 31–33 of the Bankruptcy (Scotland) Act 1985 deal with the vesting of the estate of the debtor in the permanent trustee as at the date of sequestration. Under s 31 of the 1985 Act, the whole estate of the debtor vests at the date of sequestration in the permanent trustee for the benefit of the creditors by virtue of the act and warrant. The act and warrant has the same effect on the heritable estate of the debtor by statute as if a decree of adjudication in implement of a sale as well as a decree of adjudication for payment and in security of a debt, subject to no legal reversion, had been pronounced in favour of the permanent trustee. For adjudication and its effect, see Chapter 29. For a discussion of s 31, see *Burnett's Trustee v Grainger* 2002 SLT 699.

Under s 31(2), the exercise by the permanent trustee of any power conferred on him by the 1985 Act in respect of any heritable estate vesting in him under the act and warrant is not subject to challenge on the ground of any prior inhibition.

In cases where the debtor has an incomplete title to heritable estate in Scotland, the permanent trustee is empowered under s 31(3) to complete title to that estate either in his own name or in the name of the debtor but completion of title in the name of the debtor is not permitted, under the 1985 Act, to validate by accretion any unperfected right in favour of any person other than the permanent trustee. For the effect of accretion in ordinary cases, see Chapter 7.

By s 33(1), property held in trust by the debtor for any other person is expressly excluded from the sequestration and does not vest in the permanent trustee. Further, the vesting of the heritable estate in the permanent trustee is without prejudice to the rights of any secured creditor preferable to the right of the permanent trustee.

Under s 32(6), assets subsequently acquired by the debtor after the date of sequestration also vest in the permanent trustee who is entitled, by virtue of that provision, to require a conveyance of that estate from any person holding the same. So if, after sequestration, the debtor succeeds to a heritable estate under the will of his father, the executors of the father would be obliged to convey that heritable estate to the permanent trustee for the benefit of the general body of creditors.

For a discussion on the position of the bankrupt after sequestration, see *Alliance & Leicester Building Society v Murray's Trustees* 1995 SLT (Sh Ct) 77. In that case, a debtor, although sequestrated, succeeded in acquiring title to a heritable property by way of a feu disposition in his favour and he then granted a standard security in favour of the building society. Both documents post-dated the registration of the sequestration order. The argument for the debtor, that both deeds were interlinked and together constituted *acquirenda*, was rejected by the Sheriff who held, instead, that the subjects conveyed by the feu disposition vested in the trustee as *acquirenda*, not in the debtor; and accordingly that the standard security granted in favour of the building society was a separate transaction, struck at by the deemed inhibition on the debtor created by the sequestration.

The argument of the bankrupt and the significance of *acquirenda* derive from the Titles to Land Consolidation (Scotland) Act 1868, s 157, in terms of which no inhibition is effective against any heritable property acquired by the inhibited debtor after the date when the inhibition was laid on. The flaw in the argument in this case was that, under the Bankruptcy Act 1985, s 32(6), the subjects conveyed to the debtor by the feu disposition vested immediately and directly in the trustee in sequestration, not in the debtor, and accordingly the 1868 Act, s 157 had no application.

Further cases have not resolved the position of securities granted by an undischarged bankrupt where the property in question has been acquired after the sequestration. See *Royal Bank of Scotland plc v Lamb's Trustee* 1998 SCLR 923, *Halifax plc v Gorman's Trustee* 2000 SLT 1409 and Reid and Gretton *Conveyancing 2000* (2001), pp 98–101.

3.22   SEQUESTRATION AND LIQUIDATION CONTRASTED

Note the significant difference between sequestration and liquidation. As already mentioned, in liquidation, the title to heritable property remains vested in the company although the directors are stripped of their powers. In contrast, in sequestration, all the assets of the debtor, both heritable and moveable, are transferred as if by conveyance from the debtor to the trustee who thereby acquires a title to these assets in his own person as trustee and thereafter deals with them as such. The act and warrant is the link in title.

The equivalent vesting provisions under the Bankruptcy (Scotland) Act 1913 created certain problems as between the trustee in sequestration and third parties in certain situations. The vesting provisions in the Bankruptcy (Scotland) Act 1985 do not seem to have resolved all of these problems, some of which, and some related problems in liquidations, are discussed in the articles in the Reading List, to which reference is made.

3.23 **Partnerships**

In Scotland, a firm has a distinct legal *persona*, in contrast to an English firm which is simply a number of individuals trading together. But the legal status of a Scottish firm is not equivalent to a corporation. A Scottish firm may own, hold and deal with moveable property *socio nomine*. It may also be the beneficial owner of heritage, but it is not feudally possible to take the title to land in name of a firm. Instead, title must be taken in name of trustees acting on behalf of the firm. The partners normally (but not necessarily) act as trustees. Prior to the Trusts (Scotland) Act 1961, this could cause problems in partnership titles; but, by s 2 of that Act, a purchaser has no concern with beneficial ownership and can safely take a title from the trustees for a firm. Nonetheless, problems can still arise. In particular, if heritage was purchased many years ago by a firm and the title taken in name of the then partners as trustees, all the original partners may now be dead, with a resulting lapsed trust, which produces a technical difficulty in the title.

Under the Abolition of Feudal Tenure etc (Scotland) Act 2000, s 70, from the appointed day it will be possible for a partnership to own heritage in its own name. It is unlikely that this provision will be widely used as partnerships can be dissolved quickly and sometimes unexpectedly and holding heritage in the partnership name may not be the most sensible option. It is more likely that title to partnership heritage will normally continue to be held by partners as trustees for the firm.

Cameron v Lightheart 1996 SLT 1038 is a most unusual case. Heritable property was acquired by a partnership and, following the rule stated above, the title was taken, as is standard practice, in name of the two partners as trustees for the firm. Trustees are empowered to act by majority and quorum and of course this cannot apply where there are only two trustees. Presumably with that in view, the conveyance to the partners as trustees contained an additional clause in which, by express provision, each partner as such trustee had power to sell the subjects without the consent of her co-trustee or any other present or future partner. The intervening transactions are not relevant here. Ultimately, however, purportedly exercising the express power so conferred, one partner then conveyed the subjects to a disponee who in turn sold them to *bona fide* purchasers for value. The other partner, some years later, having disappeared in the interim, then raised an action of reduction to set aside the disposition by her former partner. Her argument, however, was rejected on appeal on the footing that, in the circumstances, reduction of that disposition would achieve no useful purpose. On the merits of the clause itself, Lord McCluskey took the view that any such unusual power would have to be created in words which were absolutely unambiguous; but, subject to that proviso, he seemed clearly of the view that such a provision was in principle competent. In his opinion, however, the clause in this case did not meet the strict test which he applied and so in terms of that clause alone, a valid title could only be granted by both trustees conjoined together.

However, for other reasons indicated above, the court considered that no useful purpose could be achieved by reducing the disposition in question and so the title remained valid. It would therefore clearly be inadvisable in such circumstances to attempt to achieve the desired result by the insertion of such a clause. Other means should always be used.

Under the Requirements of Writing (Scotland) Act 1995, Schedule 2, special provision is now made for the execution of documents by a partnership. These are discussed in Chapter 2, para 2.14. While this removes some uncertainties illustrated in *Littlejohn* referred to in that paragraph, the provisions in the 1995 Act as to execution will not normally be relevant in the context of title to heritage, because such titles are invariably taken in name of trust.

3.24 **Limited liability partnerships**

Under the Limited Liability Partnerships Act 2000, a new form of organisation is created, known as a limited liability partnership. This is a body corporate with a separate legal personality and is largely regulated by the provisions of company and corporate insolvency law rather than partnership law. All contracts including those relating to property are made by the limited liability partnership although under s 6(1) every member of the limited liability partnership is the agent of the partnership. See further D A Bennett 'Limited Liability Partnerships: the conveyancing aspects' (2001) 54 Greens PLB 1.

3.25 **Unincorporated associations**

Any association which is not incorporated may beneficially own heritable property but cannot take the title in its own name. It must always act through the medium of trustees. Since 1961, this does not normally present any significant problem not already mentioned; but, again, lapsed trusts are not unusual.

In appropriate cases, the Titles to Land (Consolidation) (Scotland) Act 1868, s 26 and, less commonly, the Conveyancing (Scotland) Act 1874, s 45 may be used when taking a title in name of trustees for the association to ensure continuity of registration.

3.26 **Bodies corporate**

The Requirements of Writing (Scotland) Act 1995, Schedule 2 also makes elaborate provision for the execution of documents by any body corporate other than a company or local authority which are separately dealt with in the same Schedule. This has been referred to in more detail in Chapter 2, para 2.14.

Chapter 4

Delivery

4.1 The need for delivery

In a number of important transactions, the law requires a formal written document to effect that transaction. But the mere fact that a party has executed a formal written document does not automatically bind the party in terms of that deed. In most cases, something more is required to make the writing obligatory on the grantor; and that further requirement is delivery of the deed into the hands of the grantee, or its equivalent. So, with limited exceptions dealt with below, the standard rule is that any deed, whether onerous or gratuitous, becomes effective, irrevocable and binding on the grantor only if it is delivered; and, similarly, that the grantee thereunder cannot enforce that writ against the grantor unless and until he has taken delivery thereof.

It follows that, particularly in the case of gifts and other gratuitous transactions, delivery is a vital element in completing the rights and obligations of the parties. Perhaps rather surprisingly, no formal legal act or procedure is required to effect delivery. In all cases, delivery is a question of fact and intention.

In practice, difficulties do not often arise. A deed is normally delivered simply by handing it over physically to the grantee or his agent, either gratuitously or, in the case of onerous deeds, in exchange for the consideration thereunder. The fact of physical handing over, coupled with intention to make the deed operative, is of itself sufficient delivery. Similarly, a deed is not delivered by physical handing over of a deed if accompanied by a covering letter, which says: 'You are to hold the accompanying deed as undelivered'. This is quite a commonplace qualification when physically parting with a deed.

4.2 Heritable titles: *Heritable Reversionary Company Ltd v Millar*

In the context of heritable titles, delivery of the appropriate deed to a disponee or heritable creditor is an essential first step towards establishing the real right by registration. The requirements for registration are dealt with in greater detail in Chapter 11. This proposition was always generally accepted in the past but some difficulties could arise. In a competition between two parties claiming the same property, whether as proprietors or heritable creditors, each having taken a delivered deed from the same grantor, priority of registration determined the real right. In a question between a disponee or creditor on the one hand and a trustee in sequestration or the equivalent on the liquidation of a company on the other, doubts had been expressed as to the effect of delivery. These doubts at least in part date back to the decision in *Heritable Reversionary Company Ltd v Millar* (1892) 19 R (HL) 43. In that case, a bankrupt was registered as owner of certain heritable property *ex facie* absolutely, but truly in trust for a beneficiary. No indication of the existence of the trust was disclosed on the record. Accordingly, on the face of it, since he was the registered owner and had the real right in his own person, then, applying the strict rule, the trust property so held by him but truly as trustee should have passed to the trustee in sequestration of the bankrupt to the exclusion of the person beneficially entitled thereto under the undisclosed trust. This, of course, was manifestly inequitable and was so held in the House of Lords, reversing the judgment of the First Division and holding that a heritable property to which the bankrupt had an unqualified feudal title but which did not belong to him was not his property in the sense of the Bankruptcy Act then in force and so did not vest in his trustee.

Extrapolating on that argument, it was possible then to argue that in other comparable situations, but where there was no established trust, the strict rule should not be applied and, in comparable cases, property should not pass to a trustee in sequestration, or the equivalent when a company went into liquidation. This in turn involved an argument as to the proper construction of the language used in the insolvency legislation, with reference to both individuals and companies, to determine what was the property of the bankrupt, or of the company, which was affected by insolvency in the context of that legislation. In the Bankruptcy (Scotland) Act 1913, s 97, which was the vesting section in that Act, it was provided that, at the date of sequestration, the act and warrant should *ipso jure* transfer to and vest in the trustee in sequestration 'the whole property of the debtor'. Notwithstanding the earlier decision in *Heritable Reversionary Company*, however, no special exception was made in the 1913 Act to exclude trust property from the sequestration but the rule already established in that case continued to be applied nonetheless. That apparent omission has now been corrected by statute in the Bankruptcy (Scotland) Act 1985, s 33(1)(b) which expressly provides that property held on trust by the debtor shall not vest in the permanent trustee.

In the case of companies, a comparable question of construction arose particularly in relation to the floating charge. Under the Companies Act 1985, s 462 and earlier legislation which originally introduced the floating charge into Scotland in 1961, it is competent for a company in Scotland to create a floating charge in favour of a creditor over all or any part of 'the property which may from time to time be comprised in the property and undertaking of the company'. Again, there is no special exclusion of property held in trust.

Thus there was failure to make specific provision to exclude trust property in the situations envisaged above and instead to rely on the common law rule in *Heritable Reversionary Company*. This left the way open for an argument that if, at common

law, trust property was not the property of the debtor vesting in his trustee in sequestration, then there might be other situations where, on an application of the *tantum et
tale* rule or of the rule in *Heritable Reversionary Company*, property in which the
debtor was still registered at the date of sequestration but truly had no beneficial interest should be excluded from vesting in the trustee in sequestration on the same argument as succeeded in *Heritable Reversionary Company*. A typical situation where this
argument could be most persuasively applied is the case where a disposition of heritable property has been delivered to a *bona fide* purchaser for value by the registered
owner who, in exchange, has received the price, but where, for whatever reason, on
insolvency or on the appointment of a receiver, a real right has been created for the
benefit of the trustee in sequestration or the receiver before the disponee has recorded
his title. Applying the strict rule referred to above in that situation, where the property has been ostensibly transferred to the purchaser on a delivered but unrecorded
disposition, it nonetheless still remained vulnerable to the acts and deeds of the
disponer until he was feudally divested, and the disponee was invested in the real right
by the recording of his disposition. See *Mitchells v Ferguson* (1781) Mor 10296.

4.3   *Gibson v Hunter Homes Design Ltd*

The decision in *Gibson v Hunter Home Designs Ltd* 1976 SC 23 apparently added
some support for the foregoing argument. In that case, there was a binding contract
for sale and purchase of heritable property. On the strength of that contract, but without taking delivery of a disposition, the purchaser took possession and paid the price,
assuming he would then get a delivered title which he could record to perfect his real
right. Unfortunately, before the relevant title was delivered and recorded, the company which sold the subjects went into liquidation and a debate then arose as to
whether, in these circumstances, the property had already passed to the purchaser by
virtue of the missives, the taking of possession and payment of the price, or whether
it fell under the liquidation. Given that, at the date of liquidation, no title had been
delivered, and the purchaser's right rested simply on missives and nothing more, his
position was fairly hopeless and the argument that he had acquired a right preferable
to that of the liquidator was scarcely tenable. However, in the course of his judgment,
the Lord President, admittedly in an *obiter dictum*, stated:

> '[I]n the law of Scotland, no right of property vests in a purchaser until there
> has been delivered to him the relevant disposition. On delivery of the disposi-
> tion the purchaser becomes vested in a personal right to the subjects in
> question and his acquisition of a real right to the subjects is dependent upon the
> recording of the disposition in the appropriate Register of Sasines. Putting the
> matter in another way, the seller of subjects under the missives is not, in a ques-
> tion with the purchaser, divested of any part of his right of property in the
> subjects until, in implement of his contractual obligation to do so, he delivers
> to the purchaser the appropriate disposition'.

He then observed that the purchaser in this position has no more than a *jus crediti* until delivery of the disposition. It is really quite clear from the language used by the Lord President that, when he refers to the vesting of the personal right in the purchaser and the divesting of the seller by delivery of a disposition, he was looking at the resulting position merely as between seller and purchaser. However, in the way in which the judgment was phrased, it did add force to the argument that a delivered disposition might be said to have divested the disponer at least to the extent of taking the subjects out of the property of the insolvent or out of the property and undertaking of the company for the purposes of the insolvency legislation referred to above.

In the result, as the Reading List discloses, this question was debated in a number of articles in the journals between 1981 and 1986. The matter rested there until the case of *Sharp v Thomson* 1997 SC (HL) 66.

4.4   *Sharp v Thomson*

No recent conveyancing case has been so controversial or resulted in so much comment as *Sharp*. The Reading List details the articles it has inspired and the potential problems as a result of the decision are discussed in a Scottish Law Commission Discussion Paper: *Sharp v Thomson* (No 114, 2001). The extent of the application of this decision is not yet certain as a subsequent case, *Burnett's Trustee v Grainger* is under appeal to the House of Lords at the time of writing.

In *Sharp*, a company had granted a floating charge in the statutory terms. Several years later it then sold a heritable property to a *bona fide* purchaser for value who, very unusually, more than a year later, took delivery of a disposition of the subjects in proper form in exchange for the purchase price. On the day after the disposition was delivered, a receiver was appointed to the selling company, so creating an immediate real right in security. The disposition in favour of the purchaser was subsequently recorded. The essential question therefore was whether, at the date of delivery of the disposition to the purchaser, the subjects conveyed by that disposition had ceased to be part of the property and undertaking of the company or whether the subjects remained part of that property and as such were subject to a real right created for the benefit of the creditor under the floating charge on the date when the receiver was appointed. In the Outer House, Lord Penrose found in favour of the receiver and, on appeal, reported in 1995 SC 455, following on exhaustive argument by both sides with an extensive citation of authorities, his decision was unanimously upheld. The Lord President delivered a lengthy, learned and detailed judgment in which the competing arguments are closely examined in the context of property law and the law of contract. At the same time, he considered and rejected arguments founded on the wording of the relevant insolvency legislation, and he dismissed the idea of a resulting constructive trust. He was supported in his views by Lord Sutherland and Lord Coulsfield, each of whom delivered equally conclusive opinions. All four judgments, in the Outer House and in the Inner House, merit careful study.

The decision was, however, appealed to the House of Lords by the Woolwich Building Society who financed the purchase, and the appeal was allowed. The reasons for allowing the appeal are not entirely clear. Lord Clyde and Lord Jauncey delivered speeches which differed in their approach. Lord Clyde appeared to take the view that the decision was based on the interpretation of the legislation on floating charges. The subjects did not form part of the 'property and undertaking' of the company under the Companies Act 1985, s 462(1) and therefore were not caught by the floating charge. The purchasers had an unencumbered right to the subjects. Lord Jauncey's approach was more controversial. He took the view that at the time when the floating charge crystallised by the appointment of the receiver, the disponer still held the recorded title to the subjects and therefore the real right but, by delivery of the disposition, the disponer had divested himself of all beneficial interest in the property. Accordingly, although the real right still remained vested in the disponer at that date, that residual ownership did not amount to a right of property in this context, and any deed granted by that registered proprietor in these circumstances would necessarily be a deed granted in fraud of the delivered disposition. The effect of the Insolvency Act 1986, s 53(7) is to make available as security to the holder of the floating charge all property in which the company had a beneficial interest at the date of crystallisation. By delivery of the disposition, the company in this case had no remaining beneficial interest in the property and accordingly the charge did not attach thereto. This concept of beneficial interest passing on delivery without registration was the subject of much subsequent debate, most of which was critical, because the concept had not previously been found outwith the law of trusts.

4.5 *Burnett's Trustee v Grainger*

Sharp v Thomson 1997 SC (HL) 66 was concerned with a floating charge and a receiver and the facts were unusual as there had been a long delay between settlement and delivery and registration of the disposition in favour of the purchasers. The question arose whether the decision was limited to receiverships only or whether it applied to insolvency procedures and would therefore affect sequestrations and liquidations. This was the subject of litigation in *Burnett's Trustee v Grainger* 2002 SLT 699. In that case a heritable property was sold to purchasers. The transaction settled when the price was paid and the disposition was delivered. The disposition was not recorded straight away. This was a similar failing as in *Sharp*. The seller was sequestrated and the trustee in sequestration recorded a notice of title before the disposition was eventually recorded. The purchaser argued that the decision in *Sharp* included sequestrations, whereas the trustee argued that the decision was confined to receiverships. The Sheriff Principal held that *Sharp* also applied to sequestrations but an Extra Division of the Inner House reversed this on appeal.

The Inner House considered that no clear *ratio* could be taken from *Sharp* on the extent of its application as Lord Clyde appeared to limit his view to floating charges whereas Lord Jauncey appeared to extend his to all insolvency procedures. The Inner

House decided that *Sharp* was confined to floating charges only and that in the present case delivery to the purchasers did not give them a beneficial right which would be preferred to the trustee's right achieved by registering first. Lord Coulsfield repeated his view expressed in *Sharp* that the recognition of some kind of property right intermediate between a real and a personal right is repugnant to the underlying principles of Scots law.

This decision has been welcomed by commentators (see the Reading List), but the case has been appealed to the House of Lords and the appeal hearing is pending at the time of writing. It remains to be seen whether the House of Lords will uphold the Inner House and confine *Sharp* to floating charges only.

4.6   Dealing with the gap period

Both *Sharp v Thomson* 1997 SC (HL) 66 and *Burnett's Trustee v Grainger* 2002 SLT 699 were cases where the insolvency occurred after delivery but before registration. This gap is normally very short and the delay of over a year in both cases between payment of the price and eventual registration is not normal conveyancing practice. A gap, however short, does remain. In the Discussion Paper on *Sharp v Thomson*, which was published before the Court of Session appeal in *Burnett's Trustee,* the Scottish Law Commission propose, firstly, that *Sharp* is overturned by statute and, secondly, that the gap problem is remedied by preventing a trustee in sequestration from completing title during a period of 21 days after public notification of appointment in the Register of Inhibitions and Adjudications. This will remove the gap problem in sequestrations. There is no similar proposal in relation to liquidations since there will be no gap if normal practice is followed: see Chapter 34. The gap problem in relation to floating charges in receiverships is presently covered by the decision in *Sharp* and receiverships are not possible for most floating charges created since 15 September 2003: see Chapter 23.

After *Sharp*, it was a suggested that a way round the problem was to insert a trust clause in a disposition. This is not without its own difficulties: see para 10.23.

For a general discussion on the gap period and means of protecting the purchaser, see Scott Wortley and Dot Reid 'Mind the Gap: problems in the transfer of ownership' (2001) 7 SLPQ 211.

4.7   Presumptions arising from the custody of the deed

Occasionally, a doubt arises as to whether or not a deed is to be treated as delivered in particular circumstances. In these cases, there are certain presumptions, arising out of the surrounding circumstances, but in all cases these are rebuttable. The presumptions may be summarised as set out in the following three paragraphs.

4.8 DEED HELD BY GRANTEE

Where a deed, gratuitous or onerous, is held by the disponee or grantee thereunder, this raises a strong presumption that the deed was delivered and is, therefore, operative. But mere possession of the deed alone does not *per se* imply delivery; in doubtful cases, it is necessary to establish *animus* or intention.

4.9 DEED IN THE HANDS OF AN AGENT

Frequently, in practice, deeds are delivered and accepted, and held, by solicitors or other agents. The rule is that the agent is equivalent to the party whom he represents.

4.10 DEED IN HANDS OF COMMON AGENT

If, as often happens, a common agent acts for grantor and grantee (for example, the family solicitor acting for father and son as donor and donee) the fact that the common agent holds a deed, which apparently effects donation, raises no presumption one way or the other. In such cases, therefore, it is very important to establish delivery by other means; for example, a separate letter confirming the fact of delivery and a signed acknowledgement thereof.

4.11 Equivalents to delivery

Certain acts by the grantor may imply delivery.

4.12 REGISTRATION

There are two main types of registration which may or may not raise presumptions, according to circumstances. These are:

(1) *Registration for publication in the Register of Sasines or the Land Register.* Registration of a deed in the Register of Sasines or the Land Register is the final step in perfecting the real right of a disponee of heritage. It follows that if A, as owner of a heritable property, dispones that property to B, and thereafter the disposition is recorded in the Register of Sasines or the Land Register on behalf of B, the disponee, this necessarily raises an almost irrebuttable presumption that the deed has been delivered. See *Carmichael v Carmichael's Executors* 1920 SC (HL) 195 for the ordinary case. But compare *Cameron's Trustees v Cameron* 1907 SC 407 for a speciality, where title was taken in name of A as trustee for his daughter B, and was recorded on A's behalf; recording was not sufficient to establish delivery as between A and B.

(2) *Registration for preservation in the Books of Council and Session.* In this case, registration does not create rights. The only purpose is to avoid the loss of the principal deed. As a result, registration for preservation is less significant than registration for publication. See *Tennent v Tennent's Trustees* (1869) 7 M 936.

4.13 INTIMATION TO THE DEBTOR IN AN OBLIGATION

When an incorporeal moveable right is assigned, the assignee completes his title by intimating the assignation to the debtor in the obligation. Intimation here is equivalent to registration in the Register of Sasines or the Land Register in the case of heritage. In exactly the same way as with heritage, intimation will normally infer delivery.

4.14 INTIMATION TO DONEE

This too may imply delivery. This question has been considered in a number of modern cases, which are listed in the Digest of Cases.

4.15 Deeds not requiring delivery

Contrary to the general rule, certain deeds do not require to be delivered in order to become effective. The principal cases are:

(1) *testamentary writings.* Delivery is never necessary; and, even if a testamentary deed is delivered to the beneficiary, that does not make it irrevocable nor confer any enforceable rights on the beneficiary *inter vivos*: see *Clark's Executor v Clark* 1943 SC 216; and
(2) *bilateral contracts.* A contract becomes immediately binding, once executed by all parties. This is an important point to consider when dealing with leases.

4.16 Acceptance of delivery

The grantee is not normally obliged to accept delivery; he or she has the option to accept or reject it. But apparently, a deed may be delivered so as to bind the grantor even although the grantee may be unaware of its existence. Therefore, although delivery is conditional upon acceptance by the grantee, that condition is resolutive and not suspensive. See *Dowie & Co v Tennant* (1891) 18 R 986 and *Allan's Trustee v Lord Advocate* 1971 SC (HL) 45.

Chapter 5

Stamp Duty Land Tax, Stamp Duty and VAT

5.1 Introduction to stamp duty land tax and stamp duty

Stamp duty land tax (SDLT) was introduced in the Finance Act 2003 as a virtually total replacement for stamp duties. This followed what was (for tax matters) a relatively long and detailed period of consultation, during which the replacement tax appeared under the rather more accurate name of 'land transaction tax'. It was made clear that the part of the intention behind the new legislation was to counter what was perceived as substantial avoidance of stamp duty.

SDLT affects transactions which settle on or after 1 December 2003, including those for which there was a contract concluded after the date on which the Finance Act received Royal Assent, 10 July 2003. Transactions settled before 1 December 2003, or those settled on or after that date in pursuance of contracts concluded before 11 July 2003, continue to be governed by the rules on stamp duty.

In these circumstances, it is appropriate first to outline the rules on SDLT in more detail than those on stamp duty. However, as stamp duty will remain relevant when looking at titles for some years to come, the treatment of SDLT is followed by some brief details on its predecessor.

5.2 Legislative background to stamp duty land tax

The basic legislative framework for SDLT is found in Part 4 of the Finance Act 2003 (ss 42 to 124), backed by Schedules 3 to 19. More detail is supplied by regulations made under various of the primary provisions, which were not published until shortly before the new tax came into force. The regulation-making power is extremely wide and it is possible that even quite fundamental rules about the tax will be altered by regulation.

5.3   SCOPE OF THE TAX

Unlike stamp duty, SDLT is a tax on land transactions. It applies whether or not there exists any instrument to effect the transaction; whether or not any instrument is executed in the UK; and whether or not any party to the transaction is present or resident in the UK: see Finance Act 2003, s 42(2).

A land transaction means any acquisition of a chargeable interest: Finance Act 2003, s 43(1). A chargeable interest is defined extremely widely: Finance Act 2003, s 48. It means an estate, interest, right or power in or over land in the United Kingdom, or the benefit of an obligation, restriction or condition affecting the value of any such interest, right or power. Certain interests are designated as exempt. The ones relevant in Scotland are any security interest; and any licence to use or occupy land. There are other exemptions, however (see below).

It is also made clear that the creation, renunciation or variation of a chargeable interest are all to be treated as acquisitions of chargeable interests; and that in all those cases the person benefiting from the transaction is to be treated as the purchaser under a land transaction. The tenant under a lease will thus be treated as a 'purchaser' for the purposes of SDLT.

Special provision is made under the Finance Act 2003, s 44, for situations where a land transaction involves both a contract and a conveyance, as will most sales of land in Scotland, with missives to be followed by a disposition. In general, the contract will not be treated as a separate land transaction – there will be a single land transaction for which the effective date will be the date of settlement.

However, if the contract is substantially performed before it actually settles or completes, then that substantial performance becomes the effective date of the transaction. 'Substantial performance' takes place where the purchaser (as widely defined, above) takes possession of the whole, or substantially the whole of the subject matter of the contract or a substantial amount of the consideration is paid.

If such a contract is later completed, that completion will also be a notifiable transaction, but any tax paid on the earlier substantial performance can be set off against that due on completion. If the contract is later annulled, tax can be repaid.

In effect, these new rules mean that there may be a tax point much earlier than that which applied under stamp duty, which could not arise until the appropriate conveyance had been executed.

It is also made clear that the creation of options and rights of pre-emption are themselves land transactions, distinct from the exercise of the option or right of pre-emption. This appears to mean that the creation of a right of pre-emption for the seller in a sale transaction would involve two land transactions: the obvious one, in which the acquirer is the purchaser; and the creation of the pre-emption, in which the purchaser (of that right) would be the seller of the land.

Excambions (or exchanges) are very clearly to be treated as two distinct land transactions.

5.4 CONSIDERATION

Extensive provision is made to establish the consideration which is to be subject to SDLT. It certainly includes 'any consideration in money or money's worth given for the subject matter of the transaction, directly or indirectly, by the purchaser or a person connected with him': Finance Act 2003, Schedule 4, para 1(1).

Value added tax will be included if it is chargeable in respect of the transaction – but not if it can only be charged by virtue on an election to waive exemption after the effective date of a transaction (see below). This is a slight relaxation from the rule under stamp duty.

If payment of the consideration is to be postponed, there will generally be no discount for that postponement.

It may be necessary to make apportionments in relation to consideration, where part of that consideration relates to a chargeable land transaction and part does not. This apportionment has to be made on a just and reasonable basis. The most obvious example of this is on the sale of a house along with some moveable contents. It is even clearer under SDLT than under stamp duty that the attribution of part of the overall purchase price to moveable items (on which SDLT will not be payable) will have to be on a reasonable and justifiable basis – and, if necessary, that attribution will require to be justified.

Clearly, there can be consideration other than money. In general, non-monetary consideration will be valued at its open market value. Special provision is made for such relatively unusual consideration as debt, foreign currency, the carrying out of works, the provision of services, the payment of an annuity and the creation of obligations under a lease.

If consideration is contingent, it has to be assumed that the contingency leading to the payment of the consideration will occur; if chargeable consideration is uncertain or unascertained, a reasonable estimate requires to be made: Finance Act 2003, s 51. There are provisions for adjustments to be made when the position becomes more certain, which could lead to the payment of additional tax or a repayment by the Inland Revenue: see Finance Act 2003, s 80.

5.5 RATES OF TAX

The amount of SDLT payable is a percentage of the chargeable consideration, now rounded down to the nearest whole pound of tax. In the case of consideration other than rent under a lease, the size of this percentage depends on the total amount of consideration, either in relation to the transaction in question on its own, or in relation to that transaction along with any linked transactions (see below).

The percentage is 0% where the consideration falls below a set threshold. There is now a differentiation between that threshold as it applies to residential property as compared to where it applies to non-residential or mixed property. In the former case, as at 1 December 2003, the 0% threshold was set at £60,000; whereas for non-residential or mixed property it was set at £150,000.

It is thus necessary to have a definition of 'residential property'. This is found now in the Finance Act 2003, s 116. The general definition revolves round the concept of a building being used or suitable for use as a dwelling. Certain buildings are then specifically defined as being used as dwellings, such as residential accommodation for school pupils; and others are specifically defined as not being used as dwellings, such as children's homes, hospitals, hospices, prisons and 'a hotel or inn or similar establishment'. It can be seen that there are some grey areas in such definitions, doubtless to be resolved in due course. There is also an extension of the non-residential category to include transactions involving six or more dwellings.

Beyond the 0% threshold, the percentage rates of tax are set at the same levels for residential and non-residential property. From 1 December 2003, for consideration between the 0% threshold and £250,000, the rate is 1%; for consideration between £250,000 and £500,000, the rate is 3%; and for consideration in excess of £500,000, the rate is 4%.

In this context, it is necessary to look at the consideration for all 'linked transactions'. This is a new concept for SDLT, but it extends a rule which was in place for stamp duty. Transactions are 'linked' if they form part of a single scheme, arrangement or series of transactions between the same vendor and purchaser or persons connected with them, with 'connection' being very widely defined in keeping with other tax provisions: see the Income and Corporation Taxes Act 1988, s 839.

For instance, under stamp duty, if there was a single sale of one piece of land for £100,000 between two individuals, it is not permissible to split this into two transactions between the same two parties, each for £50,000 and apparently below the 0% threshold. However, the position may have been different where there were actually two transactions, perhaps involving related but separate parties (such as husband and wife) on one or both sides of the transaction. The intention of the new concept is apparently that these transactions would be treated as linked and charged to tax at the rate appropriate to the total consideration. Under stamp duty law, there was the same restriction on a 'series of transactions' being treated as separate and this has been subsumed into the new concept of linked transactions: on this aspect, see *Cohen v Attorney General* [1937] 1 KB 478. The exact scope of the new concept will doubtless become clearer in due course.

5.6   LEASES

Leases were treated differently under stamp duty and also receive separate consideration under SDLT. However, these rules in particular changed before their introduction on 1 December 2003.

Premiums and other capital payments in relation to leases are simply treated in the same way as consideration for other land transactions, with an exception where the annual rent exceeds £600 a year. (In that case, the 0% thresholds for consideration do not apply and consideration within these thresholds will instead be taxed at 1%.)

Rent is treated differently. It is taxed at 1% of the amount by which the 'net present value' of the rent exceeds specified thresholds, these being £60,000 for residential leases and £150,000 otherwise. No tax is charged on the present value within these thresholds. The calculation of the net present value is quite complex – it requires taking the total rent payable over the term of the lease, but applying an annual discount for the rents to be paid in and beyond the first year. An online calculator will be available from the Inland Revenue.

Provision is made to exclude the effect of rent reviews and other charges more than five years after the commencement of the lease; and there is a range of anti-avoidance provisions.

In Scotland, special provision is made to define the 'completion' of a lease, as being when it is signed by the parties (presumably by the last of them, if different dates are involved), or constituted by any means (which would cover oral leases and missives of let without a formal lease). The date of completion is important is determining when SDLT becomes due.

5.7   EXEMPTIONS AND RELIEFS

A number of exemptions and reliefs are provided from SDLT, quite apart from transactions excluded from its scope altogether, such as those involving securities and licences. Among the most important are:

(1)   exemption for transactions where there is no chargeable consideration. Thus gifts are generally exempt from SDLT, but gifts subject to accepting liability for a debt will be chargeable;
(2)   exemption for transactions in connection with divorce;
(3)   exemption for transactions deriving from the variation of testamentary dispositions within two years of death;
(4)   exemption for purchases by charities and certain bodies established for national purposes (although there are anti-avoidance provisions attached);
(5)   relief for transactions involving land in so-called 'disadvantaged areas'. This provides complete exemption where the property is all non-residential. Where residential property is involved, the consideration must not exceed £150,000, whether in the form of price or the net present value of the rent.

Disadvantaged areas are defined in Scotland by postcode. The Inland Revenue maintains a website which is of assistance (but which is not conclusive) in establishing whether this relief is available. This is www.inlandrevenue.gov.ukso/pcode_search.htm.

(6) exemption for transactions between companies within the same group. This relief is subject to a range of complex definitional provisions; and to clawback in a number of circumstances, notably where the recipient company ceases to be a member of the same group as the transferor within three years of he effective date of the transaction;

(7) exemption where a reconstruction of a company is involved; and reduction of the rate of duty to 0.5% where the acquisition of an undertaking of a company is involved. Both of these are subject to a range of conditions and possible clawback;

(8) exemption for the grant of certain leases by registered social landlords, in Scotland under s 57 of the Housing (Scotland) Act 2001;

(9) relief for exchanges involving house-building companies;

(10) exemption for certain purchases by employers or relocation companies where this results from the relocation of an employee and various other conditions are met;

(11) exemption for compulsory purchases facilitating development;

(12) exemption for purchases by public authorities where these arise to comply with a planning obligation;

(13) exemption for certain transfers following the incorporation of a limited liability partnership;

(14) exemption for various reorganisations of public bodies under statute; and

(15) relief where the crofting community right to buy (under Part 3 of the Land Reform (Scotland) Act 2003) is exercised, allowing the total consideration to be divided by the number of crofts being bought when establishing the rate of SDLT to be charged.

5.8   ADMINISTRATIVE PROVISIONS

The purchaser is required to deliver to the Inland Revenue a land transaction return in respect of every notifiable transaction within 30 days after the effective date of a transaction (generally the date of settlement). As with other tax matters, this return must include a self-assessment of the SDLT that is chargeable.

Most transactions are notifiable. These include all acquisitions of major interests in land (that is, ownership or the right of a tenant), but with the exception of some leases for a term of less than seven years. Also excepted are exempt transactions in categories (1), (2), (3) and (7) above.

Transactions other than the acquisition of a major interest are only notifiable if there is tax chargeable at a rate of 1% or higher.

The return is a six-page form (SDLT 1), with pay-slip attached. Further details are required on supplementary forms in certain cases, notably where a new lease or a purchase by a company is involved. The form requires to be signed by the purchaser himself (with an agent's signature being insufficient unless under Power of

Attorney), which is a very different requirement than existed for stamp duty, although there is some provision in connection with those who lack capacity.

Where there is more than one purchaser involved in a single transaction, only one return is required.

After completion, the form requires to be sent to a central Inland Revenue address. Provisions are to be introduced for electronic submission and payment.

Payment is made an explicit liability of the purchaser, with joint and several liability applying to purchasers in common.

There can be an application for deferment of payment where the consideration is contingent or uncertain.

When the form has been completed correctly, submitted and payment has been made, the Revenue will issue a certificate confirming compliance with SDLT requirements. In cases where a return is not required, a certificate is required to be completed by the purchaser to this effect (appropriate wording has been issued in Regulations, along with further details about the returns and certification).

It is only on production of this certificate that the Keeper will accept any document for registration in any register maintained by him including the Books of Council and Session. This is a very important encouragement to compliance with SDLT.

Special arrangements are being made to allow personal presentation in certain cases, to prevent the delay and risk which would ensue from awaiting return of the certificate through the post or other delivery method.

The legislation contains a vast amount of regulatory provisions on the administration of the tax, mostly imported directly from other tax regimes. There are rules on the duty to keep and preserve records; on the power of the Revenue to make enquiries and to make determinations where no return is delivered; on the power of the Revenue to make assessments; and in relation to appeals against Revenue decisions on the tax.

The various regulatory requirements are supported by provisions for interest and penalties for failure to pay the tax or to comply more generally – for instance, by supplying incorrect information. There are also extensive and detailed provisions allowing the Revenue to obtain information in relation to tax compliance. These are of particular importance in relation to solicitors involved in the completion and submission of returns, given their professional obligation of confidentiality of their clients.

5.9 The continued application of stamp duty

On or after 1 December 2003, stamp duty will continue to apply to instruments relating to stock or marketable securities: see the Finance Act 2003, s 125.

Rather more surprisingly, stamp duty in its unamended form continues to apply to the transfer by partners or prospective partners of land into and out of partnerships; and to the acquisition of partnership interests. Such transactions are excluded from stamp duty land tax. On this aspect, see the Finance Act 2003, Schedule 15, and Part 3 of the Act.

5.10   STAMP DUTY: HISTORIC NOTE

In conveyancing terms, it may of course still be important to be aware of whether a document was properly stamped. There follows a brief discussion of the rules on stamp duty. Further details can be found in previous editions of this book.

Stamp duty is simply one form of taxation. All the older taxing provisions were consolidated and re-enacted in two principal Acts: the Stamp Act of 1891, which imposed the duties, and the Stamp Duties Management Act 1891, which dealt with administration. Much of the former Act was replaced by new provisions in the Finance Act 1999, although intervening Finance Acts had already substantially altered the 1891 provisions.

Stamp duty was (and remains) a tax on documents; no document, no duty. This leads to a further point. Stamp duty was only payable when expressly imposed in terms of the relevant Act. Sometimes it was possible, by framing a document in one way, to avoid paying stamp duty which would be chargeable on that document were it framed in another way. Provided that the writ as framed achieved its purpose, and that there was no concealment or distortion of the facts, it was perfectly legitimate so to frame it that stamp duty was altogether avoided or perhaps was payable at a lesser rate. Care was required because the Inland Revenue has the power to request sight of all antecedent relevant documents. This type of possibility is now much restricted under stamp duty land tax, where the tax is due in respect of the transaction itself rather than being dependent on the mere forms of document used in the transaction.

The duty was paid by way of impressed stamps, which involved the lodging of the document with the Revenue for stamping, together with the duty itself. As a precaution against evasion, every document (if liable) required to have the stamp duty impressed thereon within 30 days after execution. In practice, where there were several parties to a deed, the time limit ran from the date on which the last party signed.

5.11   STAMP DUTY: SANCTIONS

To ensure that in every case the duty was paid when due, two separate sanctions were imposed:

(1) that a document which was not duly stamped was not admissible as evidence in any civil action (this rule no longer exists under SDLT); and
(2) that any document not timeously stamped incurred a penalty over and above the duty due, when eventually presented. The penalty could be up to £10, plus the amount of the duty, plus interest. But this potentially large amount was normally remitted in whole or in part.

These two provisions were essentially complementary. The effect, with certain limited exceptions, was not to render an unstamped document invalid, because (with few exceptions) any document might be presented out of time for stamping. But if so, then the second proviso operated, and a penalty was payable in addition to the duty. The result was that, if you ever have to found on an unstamped document in any action, the court would not reject it out of hand, but would insist that it be properly stamped, before considering its terms; and that of course means payment of duty, plus penalty.

Fines were also imposed in limited circumstances. It followed that a writ which was insufficiently stamped would not be accepted for registration, nor as a link in title by any agent. Nor would the Revenue, for income tax and other purposes, accept a writ as effective unless it were stamped. This, in practice, was sufficient to ensure, in a great number of cases, that stamping was timeously effected.

5.12   STAMP DUTY: BASIS OF ASSESSMENT

Two methods were used to arrive at the actual duty payable on any particular document. These were either a fixed duty of a stated amount for the particular document regardless of the value of the property to which it relates; or *ad valorem* duty, calculated as a percentage on the amount involved. A disposition (a conveyance) might carry either fixed duty of (most recently £5, raised from 50p from 1 October 1999), or *ad valorem* duty calculated by reference to the price paid for, or the value of, the property conveyed; it would depend on circumstances which mode of fixing the duty applied.

After various reforms, fixed duties were removed from a very large number of documents, especially when they could be certified under the Stamp Duty (Exempt Instruments) Regulations 1987, SI 1987/516, as being within one of the various categories specified. *Ad valorem* duties were (as a general rule) fixed, not according to the type of document, but according to the nature of the transaction. The most important was conveyance on sale duty, which was imposed on every instrument and every decree of court whereby any property was, on sale, transferred to a purchaser. This extended to every form of property, not merely land.' Sale' necessarily involves some element of consideration, and it was the value of the consideration on which (as a rule) the amount of duty was based.

The deed on which the duty was charged was normally the conventional document whereby the actual transfer was effected, for example, on sale of land, the disposition; on sale of stock, the transfer. But, in many cases, other documents were found liable under this head because they in fact effected a conveyance on sale, though not in conventional form. The emphasis was on the nature of the transaction, not on the nature of the deed.

The rate of duty in the original Stamp Act 1891 for all conveyances on sale was 10 shillings per £100 of consideration. There have been frequent alterations to the basic rate in subsequent Finance Acts and on the virtual abolition of stamp duty in 2003, the rate on sale was the same as the first imposed rate of stamp duty land tax (see above). Although of no significance now from the point of view of stamping a deed, it may be important to know the various rates of duty from time to time in force in the past when examining a heritable title, because one of the things you have to check is that each writ in the title is properly stamped.

Since reduced rates were introduced (including a zero rate for consideration below a stated threshold), it has been required to qualify for the exemption or for the reduced rates from time to time in force that the deed contained a certificate of value. If the clause was not included, the full rate was exigible, no matter how small the consideration. The clause certified that 'the transaction hereby effected does not form part of a larger transaction or of a series of transactions in respect of which the amount or value or the aggregate amount or value of the consideration exceeds [a stated limit]'. This was designed to prevent evasion of duty by breaking down a single large transaction into a number or series of smaller transactions.

There were special rules, which changed over the years, to deal with excambions (exchanges) of property. These have been tightened up under stamp duty land tax.

There were a number of special rules and exemptions on (for instance) transfers to charities, voluntary dispositions and testamentary documents, most of which are carried forward to stamp duty land tax.

5.13   STAMP DUTY: SOME ADMINISTRATIVE MATTERS

The Revenue, if required, would adjudicate the stamp duty on any document, and in certain cases adjudication was obligatory. If adjudicated and duly stamped, the document was impressed with a further stamp, in addition to the duty, called an adjudication stamp. That was then conclusive evidence that the proper duty had been paid.

There was a general obligation under the Stamp Act 1891, s 5, to set out all material facts relevant to stamping in the body of the deed and, where this was done, adjudication was normally unnecessary. But if the case was complicated, then adjudication was appropriate.

Denoting stamps were a method of marking a document to the effect that the correct stamp duty had been paid, usually on another document linked to the one on which the denoting stamp was placed.

5.14   **VAT: general**

The rules relating to VAT in the UK are complex. It is not the intention here to give detailed information as to the applicability of VAT, but rather to provide a general outline of some of the more common areas when a professional adviser acting for a commercial client will require to consider VAT implications.

VAT was introduced into the UK in 1973 as a result of joining the European Community. It has its origins in Article 99 of the 1957 Treaty establishing the European Economic Community which requires a 'harmonized system of indirect taxes' to prevail throughout the Community.

The VAT rules applicable to land and property transactions were changed in the Finance Act 1989, as a result of a judgment of the European Court handed down on 21 June 1988, which decided that the UK had not implemented its obligations under an EEC directive with regard to VAT provisions. Introduction of these rules has led to numerous anomalies, which consequently make it difficult for advisers to extract general principles.

VAT will not be applicable on the normal domestic conveyancing transaction. However, when considering the sale or purchase of land and/or property by a commercial client, or a leasehold transaction, VAT will be an element that will require to be considered.

If a commercial client buys, sells, leases, licenses, rents or hires out land or buildings or parts of a building on a regular basis, then he will be seen as acting in the course or furtherance of a business, and the VAT liability of the supply will require to be considered. Property development or redevelopment on a 'one off' basis is also seen as carrying on a business for the purpose of VAT.

5.15   TYPES OF SUPPLY

Supplies are categorised for VAT purposes into taxable and exempt supplies. Taxable supplies fall into three categories:

(1) zero-rated supplies;
(2) standard-rated supplies, which are those on which VAT is paid at the current rate of 17.5%; and
(3) reduced-rate supplies, which are those on which VAT is paid at the reduced rate of 5%. (In the present context the reduced rate is only relevant to supplies of certain energy-saving materials.)

However, supplies made in the course of the transfer of a business as a going concern are outside the scope of VAT entirely: see the Value Added Tax (Special Provisions) Order 1995, SI 1995/1268. The concept of 'business' can include a let investment property.

The difference between taxable and exempt supplies is that input VAT (VAT on expenses for the business) related to taxable supplies may be recovered whereas input VAT related to exempt supplies is in principle not recoverable.

Prior to 1 April 1989 the supply of an interest in land and buildings (sale or lease) was exempt with certain exceptions. The supply of a major interest in a building by the person constructing the same was zero-rated. 'Major interest' meant an outright transfer of ownership or lease for more than 21 years. The provision of construction services for the construction of a new building was also zero-rated. After 1 April 1989 the position changed substantially.

5.16   Zero-rated supplies

Zero-rating is now restricted to prescribed instances in which a supply has as its subject a 'qualifying' building. 'Qualifying' buildings include a dwelling or group of dwellings, but excludes those which cannot be occupied throughout the year by the person to whom the grant is made, such as timeshare accommodation. The sale of timeshare accommodation is standard rated where the property involved was completed less than three years before the sale, and is otherwise exempt. 'Qualifying' buildings also include a building or part of a building to be used for charitable purposes; and a residential building or residential part of a building which will be used as *inter alia* a children's home or a home for old or disabled persons. The person constructing such a qualifying building can zero rate the supply of such a building provided that the undernoted conditions are met.

(1) The building must 'qualify' as explained above.
(2) A certificate of proposed use must be obtained from the purchaser or grantee where the intended use is for relevant residential or relevant charitable purposes.
(3) A major interest in all or part of the building must be granted.
(4) The supplier must qualify as the person constructing the building and, with effect from 1 March 1995, the supply must be the first grant of a major interest.
(5) The building formerly required to be new but, since 1 March 1995, a non-residential building converted for a residential or other qualifying purpose would also generally attract zero-rating.

A major interest includes a grant of the *dominium utile* or a long lease – one which is capable of exceeding 20 (now reduced from 21 years to ensure consistency with the normal definition of a long lease).

Any supply of a qualifying building which does not meet these criteria will be exempt.

Note that if, within ten years of its completion, a zero-rated qualifying building (other than a dwelling) is used for non-qualifying purposes, the then owner or tenant must account for VAT.

5.17   Standard-rated supplies

Any sale of a new 'non-qualifying' building will be standard rated for VAT. 'New' is defined as up to three years old from the date of first occupation or the date of practical completion (whichever is the earlier).

5.18   Exempt supplies

All supplies of buildings or land which do not meet the criteria to be zero-rated, as discussed above, and which do not fall to be standard rated will be exempt with the option to tax (see below).

5.19 THE ELECTION TO WAIVE EXEMPTION

The election to waive exemption (or option to tax) for a supply which is otherwise exempt, is now to be found in paras 2 to 4 of Schedule 10 to the Value Added Tax Act 1994. Subject to the rules, the option to tax means that if it is exercised by the supplier, supplies which would otherwise be exempt will become taxable at the standard rate. Thus a landlord of non-residential property, any supply of which is exempt, can waive this exemption and opt to tax the rental income received by him, whereupon VAT will become payable on rents. Similarly the seller of used non-residential property which does not 'qualify' for zero-rating and is not mandatorily standard rated can opt to tax the property whereupon VAT will become payable on the sale price. However, the Finance Act 1997 contains provisions restricting the option. Its effects are removed where the developer of property which falls within the Capital Goods Scheme makes a grant in relation to the property, with the intention or expectation that the property would be occupied other than mainly for taxable business purposes by the grantor, or a person funding the development, or a person connected with either of them. This complicated anti-avoidance provision has been extended further by later Finance Acts.

This option is virtually irrevocable, although provisions were introduced in 1995 allowing an option to be revoked in certain circumstances within less than three months, or after more than 20 years, of its exercise. Subject to this, once the option has been exercised for a given building or area of land, the choice is binding for all future supplies by the person exercising the option; after a change of ownership the new owner has the right to exercise the option or not as he chooses. Therefore while a property remains in the ownership of the person who has exercised the option the rents cannot be taxed without taxing any subsequent sale. Furthermore, if the option is exercised, it must be exercised for a building as a whole. Customs and Excise treats buildings linked internally or by a covered walkway as single buildings for the purposes of the option to tax. Certain buildings, including private dwellings, and all other 'qualifying' buildings cannot be the subjects of an option to tax. Further, supplies of land to D.I.Y. homebuilders or to housing associations for the construction of dwellings cannot be subject to the option.

The option takes effect from the beginning of the day on which it is exercised, or at a later date if specified. The option can be exercised without prior consultation with tenants or a purchaser, no matter what the stage of the transaction. If negotiations have proceeded on the basis that the building is exempt, then the purchasers must obtain a binding undertaking from the seller not to exercise the option. If a seller exercises the option, VAT becomes payable on the purchase price. If an agreement has been entered into which is silent on VAT, the VAT payable as a result of the exercise of the option will be payable in addition to the agreed price. Given that the option can be exercised at any time, these issues should be resolved prior to conclusion of missives: on this aspect, see *Jaymarke Developments Ltd v Elinacre Ltd* 1992 SLT 1193 and *Hostgilt Ltd v Megahart Ltd* [1999] STC 141.

5.20   THE ADVANTAGES AND DISADVANTAGES OF OPTING TO TAX

If an option to tax is exercised, input tax relating to the supply, such as VAT on land purchases and construction costs, can be recovered. However, disadvantages include the indirect effect on the residual value of the property, together with the irrevocable nature of the option. Furthermore, opting to tax when dealing with a building that will subsequently be leased will mean that subsequent rents will be subject to VAT. Potential tenants may include those not subject to the VAT regime who would thus be unable to reclaim their input VAT.

5.21   INTERACTION BETWEEN VAT AND STAMP DUTY LAND TAX

The Inland Revenue issued a Statement of Practice on 12 September 1991 highlighting the interaction between stamp duty and VAT. A number of points arise from this Statement of Practice which should be borne in mind and are still likely to be applicable in relation to stamp duty land tax.

(1) For stamp duty land tax purposes, on sale of a new non-domestic building, the amount or value of the consideration is the gross amount inclusive of VAT. Therefore, where VAT is payable on the sale of new, non-residential property, stamp duty is calculated on the VAT inclusive consideration. This point was confirmed in *Glenrothes Development Corporation v Inland Revenue Commissioners* 1994 SLT 1310.

(2) As discussed above, certain transactions with non-residential property other than the sales of new buildings are exempt from VAT. However, where the seller or landlord opts to tax, then:

   (a) where the election has already been exercised at the time of the transaction, stamp duty land tax is chargeable on the purchase price, premium or rent (depending on the transaction) including VAT;

   (b) where the election has not been exercised at the time of the transaction, for stamp duty purposes VAT had to be included in any payments to which an election could still apply. This used to mean that there was a VAT element in the stamp duty charge in cases where an election to waive the exemption has not been exercised but it was still possible to exercise it. However, with effect from the introduction of stamp duty land tax, SDLT will not be chargeable unless the election is actually made before the effective date of the transaction;

   (c) where VAT is charged on the rent under a lease, subject to certain considerations, stamp duty land tax will be charged on the VAT inclusive figure for the net present value. The rate of VAT in force at the effective date of the lease will be used in the calculation;

(d) where there is a formal Deed of Variation varying the terms of a lease so as to provide payment of VAT by way of additional rent, further stamp duty land tax will be payable.

PART 2

DISPOSITIONS

Chapter 6

Feudal Background

6.1 Historical overview

In common with other European countries in the medieval period, land in Scotland came to be held on feudal tenure, although feudalism was probably not a significant force until the twelfth century, which is late by comparison with other countries. Feudalism became and remained the dominant form of land tenure throughout Western Europe from the late medieval period until the early modern period. The feudal system was abolished in France with the Revolution of 1789, and in most other countries in the 50 years which followed. England had effectively dismantled its feudal system a century earlier. By about 1850 Scotland was the only country in Europe to retain a feudal system of land tenure. On 28 November 2004, the Scottish feudal system will finally be abolished by virtue of the Abolition of Feudal Tenure etc (Scotland) Act 2000, one of the first pieces of legislation to be passed by the new Scottish Parliament. For valuable accounts of the feudal system, see Professor Gretton in *Stair Memorial Encyclopaedia*, Volume 18, paras 41–113 and Professor Reid *The Abolition of Feudal Tenure in Scotland* (2003), Chapter 1.

6.2 Characteristics of feudal land tenure

Feudal land tenure is difficult to characterise succinctly. Partly this is because of the vast historical time span which it has occupied. Partly it is because feudalism seems to have been in a state of almost constant evolution, a process which has accelerated in modern times. Partly also it is because legal theory, perhaps necessarily, pays little regard to the evidence as uncovered by historians, so that feudal theory in the form in which it is usually expressed by lawyers is profoundly unhistorical.

Feudal theory holds that all land in Scotland belonged, and indeed, in a sense which is explained below, belongs still, to the Crown. Much of that land was then feued out to the Crown's supporters in return for a periodic rendering of services or, in the later period, of money, known as *reddendo*. A number of different feudal tenures existed, and the nature of the *reddendo* depended on the type of tenure. The person to whom the land was feued was known as the vassal or feuar, and the Crown was referred to as his feudal superior. The vassal was entitled to the use of the land but only in exchange for payment of the *reddendo*. If he failed to pay the *reddendo* he could lose the feu by the process known as irritancy. In effect therefore, a feu is much like a perpetual lease, and indeed in analysing feudalism the institutional writers drew parallels with the *emphyteusis* of Roman law.

6.3   The feudal tenures

Land could be held on a number of different tenures. Apart from mortification, which was granted to religious houses and which did not survive the Reformation, the available tenures were the following:

(1) *Wardholding.* This was the paradigm feudal tenure. In exchange for his land the vassal was subject to the *reddendo* of hunting and hosting, which was the rendering of military services to the superior by the provision of men and equipment.

(2) *Feu-farm.* 'Farm' means rent, and in feu-farm tenure the *reddendo* was the payment of feuduty, whether in coin or in kind. A variant of feu-farm was, and is, the tenure of the kindly tenants of Lochmaben, which is found in four villages in the parish of Lochmaben. 'Kindly' in this context means hereditary, and in origin kindly tenancies appear to have been perpetual leases. The *reddendo* is rent rather than feuduty and is payable to the hereditary Keeper, who is the Earl of Mansfield.

(3) *Blench.* In blench tenure the *reddendo* was purely nominal, so that the vassal took the land for nothing. A typical blench *reddendo* was one penny Scots a year, if asked only.

(4) *Burgage.* Burgage was the only tenure permissible within the royal burghs. No *reddendo* was payable other than watching and warding, which meant assisting in the keeping of the peace within the burgh. Subinfeudation was prohibited and it seems likely that the vassals held directly from the Crown, although the precise position is obscure.

Of these four traditional tenures, effectively only two now survive. Wardholding was converted to blench tenure by the Tenures Abolition Act 1746, following the 1745 Rebellion, and burgage tenure was equated to feu-farm by the Conveyancing (Scotland) Act 1874, s 25. Today almost all land is held on feu-farm tenure, although blench holdings are found occasionally. The Land Tenure Reform (Scotland) Act 1974, ss 4–6, contains provisions for the redemption of feuduty by a single payment to the superior of its capitalised value, and many feuduties have now disappeared. No new feuduty may be imposed after 1974. Where feuduty remains payable today, it is payable in coin and not in kind.

6.4   Casualties

Unlike *reddendo*, which was a regular payment due periodically, a casualty was a single payment which was due on the occurrence of a certain event. Casualties often involved substantial liability and were of considerable importance, but they were abolished by the Feudal Casualties (Scotland) Act 1914 and are now of historical interest only. The casualties payable depended on the tenure on which the land was held and no casualties at all were due in burgage tenure. Typical were the casualties of composition and relief, payable when a new vassal entered with the superior, respectively by *inter vivos* transfer and by inheritance.

6.5 Baronies

As part of a feu of land the Crown could confer upon favoured vassals the right of heritable jurisdiction. The technical means by which this was done was by a grant of barony, the grantee being known as a baron. A baron was entitled to hold baron's courts. Jurisdiction was determined by the terms of the grant and usually included both civil and criminal jurisdiction. For all practical purposes, baron courts were abolished by the Heritable Jurisdictions (Scotland) Act 1746, but barony grants remain in existence, giving rise to certain conveyancing peculiarities and conferring on the holder the right to use the title of baron. For further detail, see *Report on the Abolition of the Feudal System* (Scot Law Com No 181, 1999), paras 2.31–2.45. In recent years there has been a growing market for barony titles. Time will tell whether this remains the case following feudal abolition and its impact upon such titles (see para 6.27).

6.6 Allodial land

Not absolutely all land in Scotland is held on feudal tenure. There is also a small amount of allodial land, that is to say, land which is owned outright and without reference to a feudal superior. The main example of allodial land is udal land in Orkney and Shetland, which is Scandinavian in origin. In udal land the owner (or 'udaller') holds the land absolutely, subject to the payment of a land tax known as skat. But over the centuries a considerable quantity of udal land has become feudalised and is now indistinguishable from ordinary feudal land.

Other examples of allodial land are land which has not been feued by the Crown, and certain churchyards in the ownership of the Church of Scotland. It is sometimes said that land which has been acquired by compulsory purchase is allodial, but the case law is inconclusive.

6.7 Substitution and subinfeudation

In the modern law a vassal is free to transfer his interest in the land, either by substitution or by subinfeudation. This was not always so, and in earlier times transfer could be restricted or prevented altogether by the terms of the original feudal grant or by the refusal of the superior to give entry to the new vassal. Restrictions of this kind cannot now receive effect: see the Tenures Abolition Act 1746, s 20; the Conveyancing (Scotland) Act 1874, s 22 and the Conveyancing Amendment (Scotland) Act 1938, s 8.

The distinction between substitution and subinfeudation is simple, but of fundamental importance to an understanding of feudal law. In substitution the vassal transfers his entire interest in the land to someone else. In subinfeudation he replicates the original act of the Crown by feuing the land to another party, who then holds of him and, until 1974, when new feuduties ceased to be possible, was bound to pay him *reddendo*. An example illustrates the difference. Suppose that A holds land directly from the Crown. If A then transfers to B by substitution, the effect is that B takes A's place as vassal of the Crown, with the same rights and liabilities as were formerly held by A. A then has no further interest in the land. By contrast, if A subfeus to B, B becomes the vassal of A (and not of the Crown), and A remains as the vassal of the Crown. In principle, B must pay *reddendo* to A, and A must pay to the Crown. Only B is entitled to possession of the land, and historically the main value to A of subfeuing was where the *reddendo* paid to him exceeded the *reddendo* which he required to pay to his superior. There is no direct relationship between B and the Crown, but the Crown is said to be the over-superior of B, and B the subvassal of the Crown.

6.8   Divided *dominium*

There is no restriction on the number of times the same piece of land may be subfeued. Thus A, who holds of the Crown, may subfeu to B, who subfeus to C, who subfeus in turn to D. The result is five different parties holding simultaneous interests in the same property. How are these interests to be classified? The answer to this question puzzled Continental jurists in the early modern period. Roman law taught that there could only be one right of ownership in respect of any one thing at any one time. But in the case of feudal land it was difficult to identify which one of the various parties was the owner. The solution ultimately adopted was to say that each had *dominium* (ownership), but *dominium* of a different kind. Thus the ultimate vassal (D in our example) had *dominium utile*, the intermediate or 'subject' superiors (A, B and C) had *dominium directum* and the Crown had *dominium eminens*. There was no single owner of the land. Each party had ownership of a different and distinctive type; and the totality of these different kinds of ownership was full ownership of the land.

In Scotland this idea of divided ownership was adopted, first by Craig, in his *Jus Feudale*, and then later by Stair. It remains the accepted view in the modern law. But it is necessary to emphasise that legal theory is here utterly remote from economic reality. Thus Mr Smith buys a house and moves into it. He believes that he owns it, and so he does, at least in the sense that he has *dominium utile*. But Mr Smith would be surprised to learn that he is not the only owner of the house, and that *dominium* is held also by his superior, by his over-superior, by the Crown, and possibly by other subject superiors as well. Of course the economic reality is otherwise. Mr Smith is entitled to live in the house and no one else is. Probably no feuduty is now payable. In practice the interest of the superiors is likely to be almost valueless. Nonetheless the full feudal hierarchy remains in place. As this example shows, in modern times feudalism is often complex without actually being useful. This was one of the most powerful arguments in favour of its abolition, which led to the Abolition of Feudal Tenure etc (Scotland) Act 2000.

In our example the sequence of subfeus occurred in rapid succession. In practice the timescale is much more likely to involve several centuries. So the Crown might have feued to A in 1600 whereupon for the next hundred years the feu might have been transferred only by substitution. Then in 1700 A(5), a successor (by substitution) of A and, like A, holding directly from the Crown, might have subfeued to B. Another 100 years might have passed before B(5), B's successor by substitution, subfeued to C. And so on. Once a new interest in land is created, by subinfeudation, that interest remains in existence unless or until it is extinguished either by irritancy or by consolidation. Consolidation is relatively rare. For an account, see the sixth edition of this book, paras 29.43–29.45. Irritancy has been incompetent since 9 June 2000 in terms of the 2000 Act, s 53. See para 6.28. A superiority interest (*dominium directum*) is perpetual in precisely the same manner as the *dominium utile* and may likewise be transferred by substitution.

6.9 Subinfeudation before the nineteenth-century reforms

As might be expected, the precise method by which subinfeudation was carried out was not constant through time. In recent years legal historians have done much to revise and to clarify our view of early conveyancing practice, for example by casting doubt on the existence of the *breve testatum*, which was once thought to be a precursor of the modern feu charter. This is not, however, the place to trace the evolution of the different feudal forms. On the matter of the *breve testatum*, see further J J Robertson 'The Illusory *Breve Testatum*' in G W S Barrow (ed) *The Scottish Tradition* (1974) and J W Cairns 'The *Breve Testatum* and Craig's *Jus Feudale*' (1988) 56 Leg Hist Rev 311. For present purposes it is sufficient to examine feuing practice as it existed in the years between the establishment of the Register of Sasines in 1617 and the sequence of major statutory reforms which began in 1845.

If, between 1617 and 1845, A wished to subfeu his land to B, the following steps were required to be taken:

(1) A executed and delivered to B a charter granting the lands in feu. The charter described the land, stipulated the tenure and fixed the *reddendo*.

(2)   An agent of A ('bailie') and an agent of B ('procurator') proceeded to the land itself. A's agent derived his authority to act from a precept of sasine contained in the charter. At the land A's agent 'gave sasine' (ie possession) to B's agent by delivery of the appropriate symbol for the land. The choice of symbol was regulated by feudal law, and in the case of land with a building on was earth and stone. This symbolical delivery took place in the presence of a notary public and two witnesses.

(3)   Subsequently, the notary public drew up an instrument of sasine which summarised the terms of the charter and narrated the ceremony of giving of sasine. The witnesses signed.

(4)   Finally, the instrument of sasine was recorded on B's behalf in the Register of Sasines. This had to be done within 60 days of its date. Only the instrument could be recorded, which explains the name of the Register. On registration, the instrument of sasine was minuted, engrossed in the Register, and returned to the presenter duly certified as registered.

All four steps were mandatory, and only on completion of registration, the fourth and final step, was B infeft, that is to say, entered with A as his vassal. Until infeftment B did not have *dominium* and his right was personal and not real.

6.10   Subinfeudation after 1845

Between 1845 and 1858, an initial series of conveyancing statutes simplified and modernised the system of land tenure. These were consolidated in 1868. Further reforms were introduced in 1874 and 1924 but, by and large, the fundamental feudal principles of tenure remained unimpaired. The new simplified procedures and writs 'merely introduced shorthand means of expressing what was formerly stated at length, but made no difference in the import of the clauses or the true principles on which our feudal system is based'. See *Hay v Aberdeen Corporation* 1909 SC 554 at 558, per Lord President Dunedin.

Since 1964, however, there has been a gradual movement away from the original common law forms and procedures, thus:

(1)   The Succession (Scotland) Act 1964 completely altered transmission of heritage on death.

(2)   The Halliday Committee *Report on Conveyancing Legislation and Practice* (Cmnd 3118) (1968) recommended a large number of reforms. The report has been substantially implemented by the Conveyancing and Feudal Reform (Scotland) Act 1970, which completely altered the law of heritable securities and made other major changes to the law of land tenure; and by the Land Tenure Reform (Scotland) Act 1974, mainly relating to feuduty but introducing certain further reforms.

(3)   In a White Paper produced by the Labour Government in 1969, 'Land Tenure in Scotland – a Plan for Reform' (Cmnd 4099), and in a Green Paper produced by

the Conservative Government in 1972, 'Land Tenure Reform in Scotland', further major reforms are discussed; and these were in part implemented by the Land Tenure Reform (Scotland) Act 1974, altering the law on subinfeudation and on feuduty.

In addition, the Land Registration (Scotland) Act 1979 introduced registration of title to Scotland. This has meant that the final step in the process of subinfeudation increasingly has become registration in the Land Register rather than in the General Register of Sasines. Registration of title is discussed in detail in Chapter 11.

6.11 The Conveyancing Acts

The main purpose of the series of Conveyancing Acts, commencing with the Infeftment Act 1845, was simplification, in part by providing short clauses with a long statutory interpretation which would serve for practically all situations; and in part by eliminating unnecessary steps in the procedure. But all this was achieved within the framework of the feudal system and hitherto the fundamental principles of tenure have remained unaltered.

6.12 THE CONVEYANCING ACTS: HISTORY

The Conveyancing Acts fall conveniently into two parts:

(1) The initial series. Between 1845 and 1868 there were a number of statutes, each making further amendments to the system. All of these are now consolidated and re-enacted in an Act of 1868 called the Titles to Land Consolidation (Scotland) Act 1868. Such consolidation, while convenient for the practitioner, is confusing for the student because it blurs the process of gradual statutory development.

(2) Since 1868, the 1868 Act itself has been radically amended by a number of subsequent statutes, principally the Conveyancing (Scotland) Act 1874; the Conveyancing (Scotland) Act 1924; the Conveyancing Amendment (Scotland) Act 1938; the Succession (Scotland) Act 1964; the Conveyancing and Feudal Reform (Scotland) Act 1970; the Land Tenure Reform (Scotland) Act 1974; and the Land Registration (Scotland) Act 1979. But there has been no subsequent consolidating statute.

The main simplifications to subinfeudation effected by the Acts 1845 to 1868 were:

(a) Abolition of symbolic delivery on the ground; and
(b) Direct recording of charters and other conveyances in the Register of Sasines in place of the recording of the instrument of sasine, which, as a result, disappeared.

6.13 THE CONVEYANCING ACTS: CONSOLIDATION

The Titles to Land Consolidation (Scotland) Act 1868 ('the 1868 Act') consolidates the foregoing provisions and a number of other earlier ones as well. Originally, it formed a comprehensive statutory conveyancing code but was fairly quickly amended and has now been largely superseded by later legislation.

It suffices to mention at this stage ss 141 to 143 of the 1868 Act, which deal with the direct recording of conveyances which are endorsed with a warrant of registration. Section 15 provides that a conveyance endorsed with a warrant, when recorded, has the same legal effect as if a conveyance in the old form had been followed by the recording of an instrument of sasine. This is termed 'the system of equivalents', often adopted in this and other conveyancing statutes. The general effect is that a new or shorthand method or formula introduced in a later Act is equated to the position under the earlier rules.

6.14 **Specific reforms**

The later Conveyancing Acts made various changes on particular matters affecting subinfeudation, dealt with under the following subject headings. These matters include:

(1) burgage;
(2) subinfeudation;
(3) casualties; and
(4) *reddendo*.

6.15 BURGAGE

Burgage is a distinct and separate tenure within the feudal system applicable to lands within the Royal Burghs, and was always separately treated in the Conveyancing Acts. Thus, Burgh Registers were introduced separately for burgage under an Act of 1681 (c 11); and the Titles to Land Consolidation (Scotland) Act 1868 makes separate provision for burgage and non-burgage property. However, reforms were made by:

(1) the Conveyancing (Scotland) Act 1874, s 25 which provides for the right to subinfeudate in burgage tenure; and
(2) the Burgh Registers (Scotland) Act 1926, under which, by a gradual process, Burgh Registers were all absorbed into the Register of Sasines. The last such separate register closed in 1963.

6.16 SUBINFEUDATION

Subinfeudation was often expressly prohibited in a feu charter and any such prohibition was binding on the vassal. Such prohibitions were made unenforceable by the Conveyancing Amendment (Scotland) Act 1938, s 8.

6.17   CASUALTIES

Casualties were due *ex lege* (as a matter of law), the actual casualties exigible depending on the nature of the tenure. But the nature of the casualty might be (and often was) varied by the express terms of a feu charter. This was known as taxing the casualty. The point of taxing casualties was to substitute casualties definite in amount, or in point of time (or both), in place of the indefinite casualties due *ex lege*.

All casualties, *ex lege* and taxed, have ceased to be exigible as a result of:

(1) the Conveyancing (Scotland) Act 1874, ss 4, 15, 16, 18 and 23; and
(2) the Feudal Casualties (Scotland) Act 1914.

From a practical point of view, the result is that in examining a title, the question of casualties can be ignored altogether, except in so far as the parties have agreed to commute the casualty by payment of additional feuduty, in which case there had to be an agreement setting out the amount of the additional feuduty payable, recorded in the General Register of Sasines under the Acts above cited. Leasehold casualties have also now been abolished by the Leasehold Casualties (Scotland) Act 2001: see para 24.18 below and Professor Rennie 'Leasehold Casualties' 2001 SLT (News) 235.

6.18   *REDDENDO*

Historically the *reddendo* to be rendered by a vassal to his superior might take various forms, including military services, watching and warding, hunting and hosting, agricultural non-military services, known as carriages and services, and feuduty which might be payable in cash or in kind. All services have disappeared and all feuduties are now expressed in money sterling under:

(1) the Conveyancing (Scotland) Act 1874, ss 20 and 21;
(2) the Feudal Casualties (Scotland) Act 1914, s 18;
(3) the Conveyancing (Scotland) Act 1924, s 12.

Until 1974, it was still competent to provide for a permanent increase or permanent reduction in the amount of feuduty payable, such increase or reduction to take effect on a definite date or on the happening of a definite event. Any such provision in a pre-1974 deed is still effective.

It became incompetent to impose feuduty by virtue of the Land Tenure Reform (Scotland) Act 1974, s 1(1) which applies to all deeds executed after 1 September 1974. An attempt to impose feuduty after that date does not render the deed invalid, but the feuduty clause itself is null: 1974 Act, s 1(2). Similar rules are applied to other perpetual outgoings, such as ground annual and skat: 1974 Act, s 2. It is not competent to contract out of these provisions: 1974 Act, s 21.

6.19 Allocation and redemption of feuduty

Where feuduty has been imposed on an area of ground which is subsequently subdivided, the land as a whole remains liable. For example, if a field is divided into ten plots for housing, the owner of each plot is jointly and severally liable for the entire feuduty, which is known technically as the *cumulo* feuduty. Thus, if the *cumulo* feuduty is £100, the superior can proceed against any of the plot owners for this. In practice, developers informally apportioned the *cumulo* between the plot owners. The superior, however, is not bound by this apportionment. The only way to bind the superior is to have the portion of the *cumulo* formally allocated. Prior to the passing of the Conveyancing and Feudal Reform (Scotland) Act 1970, allocation required the consent of the superior. Now, in terms of ss 3–7 of that Act the vassal has a right to have the feuduty allocated by serving an appropriate notice on the superior. For a detailed account of the relevant procedure, see paras 16.10–16.16 of the sixth edition of this book.

At common law, a vassal can redeem his or her feuduty, but only by agreement with the superior. In other words, it can be agreed that feuduty will no longer be paid, normally in return for compensation. The Land Tenure Reform (Scotland) Act 1974, s 4 gives the vassal the right to redeem the feuduty allocated upon his or her land by serving a notice upon the superior and paying compensation. The level of compensation is calculated by reference to the market price of 2.5% Consolidated Stock. The calculation is not without difficulty and solicitors were helped in this regard for many years by a feuduty factor being published in the Journal of the Law Society of Scotland. Multiplying the annual feuduty by the feuduty factor gives the compensation payable. Unfortunately, the factor is no longer published in the Journal: see 1998 JLSS June/12. It is, however, available in the financial pages of *The Scotsman* newspaper.

The s 4 procedure is voluntary at the instance of the vassal. Far more important is compulsory redemption, in terms of s 5 of the 1974 Act. In summary, the feuduty must be redeemed the first time the land is sold after 31 August 1974. The same level of compensation is payable as under s 4. The normal date of redemption is the date of entry specified in the conveyance which gives effect to the sale. Only allocated feuduty is subject to the compulsory redemption procedure. For more detail, see paras 16.17–16.29 of the sixth edition of this book. Given that s 5 has been in force for almost 30 years, the majority of feuduties have now been redeemed.

6.20 Summary of subinfeudation process immediately prior to feudal abolition

What we have so far done is to consider the historical origins and common law development, and later the statutory development, in the process of subinfeudation. The position immediately prior to the final abolition of the feudal system by the Abolition of Feudal Tenure etc (Scotland) Act 2000, resulting from the developments above referred to, is:

(1) Agreement by the parties which is incorporated in the formal vesting document, namely, the feu charter. The content and terms of the feu charter are dealt with in Chapter 7 of the sixth edition of this book.

(2) The charter is (a) duly executed, and (b) delivered to the vassal. Stamp duty land tax is paid where applicable.

(3) The charter is then presented to the Keeper of the Registers with the appropriate Land Registration Application Form for registration of the title in the Land Register. All counties are now operational for the Land Register and therefore a feu charter must be registered there: Land Registration (Scotland) Act 1979, s 2(1)(a)(i).

Registration of the charter in name of the vassal is essential to complete the infeftment of the vassal and perfect his real right of ownership (*dominium*). As a result, infeftment and sasine have lost their old meaning. An infeft proprietor has come to mean a proprietor who has perfected his real right in the subjects by the registering in the Land Register of an appropriate written title. Nonetheless, by his charter, the vassal obtains his grant of land and establishes his right of tenure to which the basic feudal rules still apply. He is the vassal holding of and under the grantor, his superior, subject to the real burdens imposed in his charter.

6.21 The road to feudal abolition

The feudal system in Scotland has suffered a slow death. Piecemeal abolition has been effected over the centuries: for a summary see Professor Gretton in *Stair Memorial Encyclopaedia*, Volume 18, para 113. The Land Tenure Reform (Scotland) Act 1974 has had a pronounced effect, in prohibiting new feuduties and providing for the compulsory redemption of existing ones. The final chapter in the story began with the publication of *Property Law: Abolition of the Feudal System* (Scot Law Com Disc Paper No 93, 1991). After a consultation period, this was eventually followed by the Commission issuing its *Report on the Abolition of the Feudal System* (Scot Law Com No 181, 1999). The Report contained a draft Abolition of Feudal Tenure etc (Scotland) Bill. The issue which has held up feudal abolition for so long is the fate of feudal real burdens. The right to enforce real burdens has become the last valuable right held by superiors, particularly following the 1974 Act and its provisions on feuduty. The Commission's proposals were largely accepted by the Scottish Executive and its draft Bill formed the basis of the Abolition of Feudal Tenure etc (Scotland) Act 2000, which received Royal Assent on 9 June 2000.

6.22   Abolition of Feudal Tenure etc (Scotland) Act 2000

The Abolition of Feudal Tenure etc (Scotland) Act 2000 has a three-stage implementation process. The first stage was Royal Assent, when a small number of provisions came into force. These are discussed in para 6.28. The second stage began on 1 November 2003, when much of Part 4 of the 2000 Act was brought into force: see the Abolition of Feudal Tenure etc (Scotland) Act 2000 (Commencement No 1) Order 2003, SSI 2003/455. This is the part which contains the provisions allowing superiors to preserve certain feudal real burdens. It is discussed in detail in Chapter 19. The third stage is when the remainder of the 2000 Act comes into force. That will happen on the 'appointed day' for feudal abolition. This has now been fixed as 28 November 2004: see the Abolition of Feudal Tenure etc (Scotland) Act 2000 (Commencement No 2) (Appointed Day) Order 2003, SSI 2003/456. In terms of s 71 of the 2000 Act, the appointed day had to be fixed as either Whitsunday (28 May) or Martinmas (28 November) to simplify the compensation payment for loss of the right to feuduty (see para 6.25), feuduty being traditionally payable at these dates.

The date of the appointed day was first announced by the Justice Minister in the Scottish Parliament on 21 November 2002. The date could realistically not be any sooner than 28 November 2004 for two reasons. First, at the time of the announcement, the Title Conditions (Scotland) Act 2003 had not completed its legislative passage. The reform of real burdens carried out that by Act and feudal abolition are part of the same property law reform programme. Secondly, there needs to be a reasonable period of time between Part 4 being brought into force and the appointed day, to give superiors a fair opportunity to preserve the burdens which the 2000 Act allows them to preserve.

6.23   What will happen on the appointed day?

'The feudal system of land tenure, that is to say the entire system whereby land is held by a vassal on perpetual tenure from a superior is, on the appointed day, abolished.' So states s 1, the grand opening provision of the Abolition of Feudal Tenure etc (Scotland) Act 2000. The spirit is similar to s 1 of the Scotland Act 1998: 'There shall be a Scottish Parliament'. The overarching principle of s 1 of the 2000 Act is given specific effect by the following provision, s 2. Section 2(1) provides that the feudal estate of *dominium utile* will be converted into absolute ownership on the appointed day. That ownership, however, will remain burdened by the subordinate real rights and other encumbrances which burdened the *dominium utile*. So, for example, a standard security or a servitude over the *dominium utile* will subsist over the land. In terms of s 2(2), all other feudal estates will be extinguished upon the appointed day. This includes the paramount superiority of the Crown. Finally, s 2(3) provides that subinfeudation will no longer be competent.

6.24 **Transfer of ownership**

Currently, as para 6.20 notes, registration is required to make the vassal infeft, in other words to let him hold the land from his superior under feudal tenure. As there will no longer be any feudal structure, the effect of registration requires to be statutorily recast by the Abolition of Feudal Tenure etc (Scotland) Act 2000. This is done by s 4, which simply provides that the effect of registration is to transfer ownership. Rather than becoming infeft, the transferee becomes absolute owner.

6.25 **Feuduty**

Part 3 of the Abolition of Feudal Tenure etc (Scotland) Act 2000 deals with feuduty. Section 7 provides that all remaining feuduties are extinguished on the appointed day. Superiors, however, are to be given the right to claim compensation for any feuduty still then exigible. The relevant provisions apply equally to other periodical payments such as ground annual and skat: 2000 Act, s 56. As noted earlier, most feuduties have already been redeemed under the Land Tenure Reform (Scotland) Act 1974. Feuduties still in existence tend to be in respect of unallocated *cumulos*.

Following the appointed day, the erstwhile superior has two years in which to make a compensation claim: 2000 Act, s 8(1). In other words, he must do so before 28 November 2006. If no claim is made, no compensation is due. A contrast can be made with the 1974 Act where compensation is always payable. The value of compensation is the same as under that earlier Act: 2000 Act, s 9(1). To claim, the appropriate notice must be served on the former vassal.

Where there is a *cumulo* feuduty the notice must be in the form set out in Schedule 1 to the 2000 Act. This requires the compensation to be allocated amongst the former vassals. In terms of s 9(3) of the 2000 Act, the allocation must be carried out reasonably. Where the *cumulo* has already been apportioned, the allocation will be presumed to be reasonable if it adheres to that apportionment: 2000 Act, s 9(4). In the more straightforward case of allocated feuduty, the form of compensation notice is set out in Schedule 2 to the 2000 Act.

If the compensation payable is £50 or more, the former vassal can choose to pay in instalments. In this case, the Schedule 1 or 2 notice must be accompanied by an instalment document in terms of Schedule 3 to the 2000 Act. This must be returned to the former superior within eight weeks, together with an additional sum amounting to 10% of the compensation, in lieu of interest: 2000 Act, s 10(2). Section 10(4) sets out how the instalments are to be paid at Whitsunday (28 May) and Martinmas (28 November) as follows:

Amount of compensatory payment	Number of instalments
£500 or less (but £50 minimum)	5
More than £500, but not more than £1,000	10
More than £1,000, but not more than £1,500	15
More than £1,500	20

In a case where the compensation was greater than £1,500, the final payment could be made as late as 2016 (if the superior did not make a claim until 2006). But note s 10(3) of the 2000 Act, which provides that where the property is sold, the compensation remaining due is payable immediately. Often, however, the compensation due will be too small to justify the expense of claiming it at all.

In contrast to the 1974 Act, the compensation is not secured on the land in the event of non-payment. Effectively, this removes feuduty as a matter to be considered when purchasing land following feudal abolition. Only the individual who was the vassal immediately prior to the appointed day, ie on 27 November 2004, is liable for the compensation and any arrears of feuduty: see 2000 Act, s 13(2), (3). The former superior's claim is merely a personal right against that individual. For further commentary, see K G C Reid and G L Gretton *Conveyancing 2000* (2001), pp 125–127, and S Brymer and S Wortley 'Preparing Superiors for Feudal Abolition, Part 2' (2002) 61 Greens PLB 7.

6.26   Real burdens

The right of superiors to enforce real burdens is abolished on the appointed day: Abolition of Feudal Tenure etc (Scotland) Act 2000, s 17(1). This, however, is subject to the provisions in Part 4 of the 2000 Act, which as noted above, allow superiors to preserve enforcement rights in certain cases. See further Chapter 19.

6.27   Other provisions which will come into force on the appointed day

The Abolition of Feudal Tenure etc (Scotland) Act 2000 makes some other changes which will affect conveyancing. Section 5(1) abolishes the need for warrants of registration. With most transactions now involving the Land Register, the use of warrants is becoming more occasional. The warrant will soon only be of historical interest. Section 70 of the 2000 Act allows partnerships to hold land in their own name. Under the current law, it is generally accepted that land must be held by the partners as trustees for the firm, despite the firm having legal personality in terms of the Partnership Act 1890, s 4(2). It may be expected that practice will not be quick to change here. Section 63 of the 2000 Act will sever the link between barony titles and land. The actual titles and any associated heraldic privilege will persist. The Lord Lyon King of Arms has issued a practice note in relation to this provision. See 'Court of the Lord Lyon: Baronial Titles' 2003 SLT (News) 6. Less important changes are the abolition of entails or tailzies (2000 Act, ss 50–52), thirlage (s 55) and kindly tenancies (which are converted into ownership by s 64). Finally, Schedules 12 and 13 contain a considerable number of amendments and repeals, which are necessary to wipe feudal terminology from the statute book.

6.28 Provisions in the 2000 Act which came into force on Royal Assent

Three key provisions came into force on 9 June 2000. The first of these relaxes the rules for descriptions in standard securities and has no real connection with feudal abolition. It is discussed at para 8.14.

The second, s 53 of the Abolition of Feudal Tenure etc (Scotland) Act 2000, abolishes the right of the superior to irritate the feu. The effect of irritancy was to extinguish the feudal grant and the remedy was a draconian one: see R Rennie 'The Theory and Ethics of Irritancy' 1994 JR 283. The feu could be irritated for non-payment of feuduty for five years (irritancy *ob non solutum canonem*). The same remedy was available for breach of a real burden, but only where the feu charter expressly authorised it. For further detail, which is now only of historical value, see the sixth edition of this book at paras 16.3–16.6.

Thirdly, s 67 restricts the lengths of leases to 175 years. This is an anti-avoidance provision, which was introduced to stop the feudal system being re-created by landowners granting extraodinarily long leases in place of feu charters. See Scottish Law Commission *Report on the Abolition of the Feudal System* (Scot Law Com No 168, 1999), paras 2.9 and 9.40–9.42. See para 24.1 below.

6.29 The future without the feudal system

The extrication of feudalism from Scottish land law will ultimately result in a far simpler and more coherent body of rules. In the short term, life for the conveyancer will, if anything, become more complicated as he or she has to grasp the new law and also use the transitional provisions in the Abolition of Feudal Tenure etc (Scotland) Act 2000 to help superiors, where it is viable to preserve rights. The Title Conditions

(Scotland) Act 2003 and the forthcoming legislation on the law of the tenement will also require careful study. It will also take some time for new case law to develop. But the end result, undoubtedly, will be Scotland with a system of land law fit for the twenty-first century.

Chapter 7

The Disposition: General

7.1 General form

A disposition, in its standard form, is unilateral. A typical example will be found in the Appendix of Styles. The disposition runs in the name of and is executed by the grantor (disponer) alone. It contains, in essence, the identification of the parties; the consideration; the identification of the subjects; certain other clauses, in particular, the entry clause which states when the disponee can enter into possession and the warrandice clause, which warrants the title. The disposition may be sub-divided into:

(1) the narrative, or inductive, clause or clauses;
(2) the operative clauses, which may again be sub-divided into the dispositive clause, which rules, and other clauses, conferring rights ancillary to the main or dispositive clause; and
(3) the testing clause (see Chapter 2).

7.2 Narrative clause

The standard content of the narrative clause is set out in the following paragraphs.

7.3 GRANTOR

The name and designation of the grantor will be given followed by a description of his or her status, normally 'heritable proprietor of the subjects and others hereinafter disponed' which implies that the grantor is the registered owner. There are a number of variants to meet special cases.

If the disposition is to be effective as a title to the disponee, then the grantor must have title and capacity to grant it.

(1) *Title.* It is not necessary that the land falls within the private patrimony (personal estate) of the grantor. He may, for example, hold the property as trustee or in some other representative capacity. If so, it may be relevant to consider his powers (for example, if he is a trustee). But, to enable him effectively to convey he must either be the registered proprietor or have the right to complete title. In the latter case,

a deduction of title clause will be required where the subjects are currently registered in the Register of Sasines. Where they are in the Land Register, the relevant link(s) in title will need to be produced to the Keeper. See the Land Registration (Scotland) Act 1979, s 15(3), and the *Registration of Title Practice Book*, para 5.28.

Absence of title at the time of making a grant is cured if the grantor comes subsequently to own the property. This is by virtue of the doctrine of accretion. Accretion applies to all conveyancing deeds provided that they contain either a grant of absolute warrandice or a conveyance by the grantor of his whole right, title and interest, present and future, in the property. Dispositions in practice usually contain both. Accretion is not restricted to the case of grantors without registered title but applies even where there was no shadow of a title at the time of making the grant. See *Swans v Western Bank* (1866) 4 M 663. Initially a grant by a non-owner is ineffective, because no one can convey that which he does not have. This is a fundamental rule of the law of property, often expressed in terms of the Latin maxims *nemo dat quod non habet* or *nemo plus juris ad alienum transferre potest, quam ipse haberet*. But if, after registration of the ineffective grant, the grantor comes to own the property, the title of the grantee is immediately and automatically perfected by accretion. If there are competing grantees, priority is determined by applying the fiction that accretion is retrospective, so that the grantee who registered first prevails. Note that accretion operates in practice differently in the Land Register, but the principle is the same. See further *Stair Memorial Encyclopaedia*, Volume 18, para 677.

(2) *Capacity.* Mere title is not enough, standing alone. The grantor of the disposition must also have legal capacity. See Chapter 3.

7.4   CONSENTORS

In addition, for various reasons, it may be appropriate for a party or parties to consent to the disposition in which case they are also named and designed in the narrative clause and the reason for their consent is there stated. Probably the most common type of consent is by a non-entitled spouse in terms of the Matrimonial Homes (Family Protection) (Scotland) Act 1981.

7.5   CONSIDERATION

It is usual but not essential for a conveyance to set out explicitly the consideration. Normally the consideration is a monetary one, because the land has been sold. Here it is usual practice to state the price paid both in words and in figures. If any moveables are included, the consideration paid for these should not be included. Where no price has been paid, the practice is to state that the disposition is either granted 'for love, favour and affection' (for example, for a gift to a relative) or 'for certain good and onerous causes' (for example, for a transfer between corporate bodies).

7.6 Operative clauses

The dispositive clause is the main or ruling clause in the disposition. The remaining operative clauses are subordinate to it. Its essential elements are:

(1) *Words of conveyance.* To be effective, every disposition must contain clear words expressing an immediate present transfer (or conveyance) of the right to the disponee. Thus, a mere agreement to convey was not (and is not) a conveyance. It merely creates a personal obligation on one contracting party to convey property to the other contracting party. The word 'dispone' has ceased to be a *verbum solemne* (essential) (Conveyancing (Scotland) Act 1874, s 27) although it is invariably used in practice.

(2) *Identity of the grantee and the destination.*

7.7 CAPACITY OF DISPONEE

Subject in certain cases to the consent of some other person (for example, parents for children under 16), there is now no legal bar arising out of nationality, domicile, residence, age, sex or capacity to prevent or disable anyone from owning heritage in Scotland. This includes both natural and legal persons. Partnerships, however, are currently unable to hold title in their own name, so hold through the medium of trustees. As of the appointed day for feudal abolition, they will be able to take title in their own name: see para 6.27.

Unincorporated associations do not have legal personality and therefore can only hold title through their members or through trustees. On capacity generally, see Chapter 3.

7.8 PLURAL DISPONEES

In Scotland, heritage may competently be conveyed to, and held by, several persons. There is no legal limit on the total number. If there are two or more co-proprietors, then they hold either as joint proprietors or as proprietors in common.

7.9 Joint property

Joint property vests as a single undivided unit in two (or more) persons, no one of whom has any absolute beneficial or exclusive right to an aliquot or severable share of the subjects. Instead, each has a joint right in the whole subjects along with all his co-proprietors 'not merely *pro indiviso* in respect of possession, but altogether *pro indiviso* in respect of the right': Lord Moncreiff in *Cargill v Muir* (1837) 15 S 408. Joint property arises automatically wherever title to land is taken by trustees. This includes property taken by trustees for behoof of a partnership. It is thought that joint property can also arise where land is held by the members of an unincorporated association or club, but direct authority is lacking. In practice, such bodies hold land through trustees. Outwith the sphere of trusts and unincorporated associations, it is not possible to create joint property, even by the use of express words. See para 30.10 and *Stair Memorial Encyclopaedia*, Volume 18, para 34.

One of several joint proprietors cannot separately dispose of his joint interest in the property to a third party; and, on his death or resignation as trustee or member, his right and interest in the joint property automatically accresce to the survivor(s). No deed or other procedure is required to vest the joint property exclusively in the survivor(s).

7.10   Common property: general

This is the usual form of co-proprietorship. A right of common property may arise simply because several separate persons come to be interested in the same undivided property, whether by joint purchase, succession or otherwise. It also often arises in special cases, such as tenements where certain parts of the building are owned in common.

In common property, each of the several proprietors has an absolute, unrestricted right to a fractional or aliquot share of the whole property so long as it remains undivided. The relative size of his share (ie the amount of the fraction) may be stated expressly in terms of the titles. The shares of owners in common are not necessarily equal; but, failing any express statement in the title, the implication is that all co-proprietors own equal *pro indiviso* shares.

A fundamental rule of common property is that each co-proprietor is entitled to possess the entire property. Consequently, it is not possible for one co-proprietor to obtain an order for ejection against another: see *Price v Watson* 1951 SC 359. The point is also made by *Langstone (SP) Housing Association Ltd v Davie* 1994 SCLR 158. The pursuers were a housing association whose policy was to encourage shared ownership of individual houses in the association's complex. In this case, the individual occupier owned one half and was 'tenant' of the association in the other half. But of course this was a half *pro indiviso*, not a physical one half of a divisible property. Accordingly, the owner/tenant occupied the whole house on the foregoing basis. He then defaulted on his loan arrangements and the creditor, who had a standard security over the defaulter's one half *pro indiviso* share, sought to recover possession. The association also sought to take possession and raised an action for that purpose. The action was undefended. In giving judgment, the sheriff underlined the difficulties which such a socially desirable arrangement might produce in law, but concluded that, in the circumstances, an action of eviction or for recovery of possession was not competent. In the result, the crave by the housing association for eviction was dismissed. In so doing, the sheriff emphasised that the only competent legal remedy was division and sale: see para 7.11.

Each co-proprietor is entitled to make ordinary use of the property as a whole, but extraordinary use will require the consent of all fellow co-owners. Similarly, alterations and repairs need the permission of all co-proprietors, except where they can be regarded as 'necessary' or *de minimis*.

One of several co-proprietors, owning a *pro indiviso* share, may dispose of that *pro indiviso* share without consulting his co-owners or may burden it with debt; and on his death, the *pro indiviso* share passes to his representatives and does not accresce by implication to the remaining co-proprietors.

See further *Stair Memorial Encyclopaedia*, Volume 18, paras 22–26, W M Gordon *Scottish Land Law* (2nd edn, 1999), para 15.13–15.21, and R R M Paisley *Land Law* (2000), paras 5.5–5.8.

7.11 Common property: division and sale

In general, there is an absolute right to have the property divided at any time or, where physical division is impractical, as it usually is, to have the property sold and the proceeds divided: see *Upper Crathes Fishings Ltd v Bailey's Executors* 1991 SLT 747. The appropriate court action is one of division or of division and sale. The method of sale is the one which is considered will produce the best price: *Miller Group Ltd v Tasker* 1993 SLT 207. In practice this is usually sale by private bargain nowadays. There are limited circumstances in which an order for division and sale will not be granted. The most important is arguably property which, in the words of Bell, is 'of common and indispensable use, as a stair case or vestibule': Bell, *Principles*, s 1082. Other cases are where an owner in common is contractually or personally barred from seeking the remedy: see *Stair Memorial Encyclopaedia*, Volume 18, para 32.

The court also has a discretion whether to grant decree in matrimonial cases: Matrimonial Homes (Family Protection) (Scotland) Act 1981, s 19. Several illustrations are given in the Digest of Cases for para 7.11.

Rather than seeking division and sale, there is nothing to prevent the parties simply agreeing between themselves on a sale by one to the other at an agreed price. A somewhat unresolved issue, however, is whether a co-proprietor can obtain a court order compelling a fellow co-proprietor to sell to him. The early case of *Milligan v Barnhill* (1782) Mor 2486 appears to support such a rule. But there have been a number of recent cases which are not easy to reconcile. In *Scrimgeour v Scrimgeour* 1988 SLT 590, a wife obtained decree in the Court of Session to purchase her husband's share of their house at market value. However, the action was undefended. *Scrimgeour* was not followed in *Berry v Berry (No 2)* 1989 SLT 292. There, Lord Cowie considered it to be in the best interests of the parties that the subjects be placed on the open market, as this would raise the highest price. In *Gray v Kerner* 1996 SCLR 331, a sheriff court case, the property was the family home of a couple and their four children. The mother wished to buy the father's share for market value. The father wanted sale on the open market. The mother obtained decree: it was held that there was no finding in fact to justify the property being sold on the open market. Such a sale would not necessarily guarantee a higher price being achieved. Finally, in *Ploetner v Ploetner* 1997 SCLR 998 the two co-proprietors of a farm each wished to buy the other out. The sheriff said that this created an impasse. He also expressed the view that where one party wanted to buy the other's share, then the remedy could be refused if the other party persuasively argued that sale on the open market would achieve a better price. Further, it was of course open to the party wishing to buy to put in an offer if the whole property was put on the market. The sheriff ultimately sent the matter to a proof. It is tentatively suggested that the decision in *Ploetner* is sound, but further Court of Session authority is awaited.

It has been suggested that the remedy of division and sale will be affected by the incorporation of the European Convention on Human Rights into Scots law: see K Springham 'Property Law' in Lord Reed (ed) *A Practical Guide to Human Rights Law in Scotland* (2001), p 235, at pp 264–267. The view taken here is that it is unlikely that Article 1 of Protocol 1 of the Convention (the right to property) will have any impact, because the defender in an action of division and sale will always be compensated for loss of their share in the property, by being entitled to the sale proceeds. Moreover, the right to division and sale has long been justified in terms of public policy: see Bankton *Institute*, I, 8, 36. Co-proprietors should not be compelled to stay together. On the other hand, it is felt that Article 8 (the right to respect for one's home and family life) might assist a spouse who continues to live in the family home following marital breakdown to insist that that the other spouses's share in the property be sold directly to him or her, rather than face bidding for it on the open market. It should be remembered, however, that the courts already have a discretion in such circumstances in terms of s 19 of the Matrimonial Homes (Family Protection) (Scotland) Act 1981 (see above).

7.12   Common interest

In certain special situations, separate proprietors owning separate properties are united by a common interest which entitles each of them to object to certain acts by any other proprietor which may interfere with the comfortable enjoyment of his property.

This body of rules is known generally as 'the law of common interest'. The significant difference between the restrictions arising out of property owned in common, and arising out of common interest, is that, in the first case, the individual has, at most, a right to a share only, and not the whole, of a particular property; whereas, with common interest, each individual owns the full and exclusive right of property in his own land, subject only to special restrictions for the benefit of his neighbours. These restrictions need not appear in his title, but arise by operation of law. In effect, common interest is like an implied title condition. However, it is not a title condition within the meaning of the Title Conditions (Scotland) Act 2003, as it is not subject to variation or discharge by the Lands Tribunal. Section 118 of the 2003 Act also makes it clear that it is not possible to create common interest expressly. Currently there is some doubt on this matter: see *Stair Memorial Encyclopaedia*, Volume 18, para 358.

7.13 DESTINATIONS

There are two forms:

(1) *A general destination.* In this case, the property is conveyed to the named disponee 'to his executors [or successors, formerly heirs] and assignees whomsoever'. A general destination adds nothing, and, if omitted, would have no adverse effect. Thus the statutory form of standard security contains no destination; and under the Conveyancing and Feudal Reform (Scotland) Act 1970, s 11(1), a standard security operates to vest the interest in the grantee. There is no reference to executors or successors, since that is inevitably implied.

(2) *The special destination.* This was a device, of ancient origin, frequently adopted to circumvent feudal limitations on the free power of *mortis causa* disposal. Typically, and in its simplest form, the subjects were disponed on a special destination 'to A (designed) whom failing' (or 'on his death') 'to B (designed)'; or, commonly, 'to A and B (both designed) and to the survivor of them and to the heirs and assignees whomsoever of the survivor'. In considering the rights of the parties to a destination (for example, in the illustrations A and/or B) a number of technical and complex rules may have to be taken into account. For some problems which the special destination creates, see para 30.13.

All valid reasons for resorting to the special destination in a conveyance of land disappeared under the Titles to Land Consolidation (Scotland) Act 1868, s 20; but the device still continues to be used as one method of controlling the devolution of a heritable property on the death of the proprietor for the time being. A much more common method (and a preferable one) is to arrange for the devolution of the property through a will or other general *mortis causa* deed; and the use of the special destination is now generally discouraged. See Lord President Cooper in *Hay's Trustee v Hay's Trustees* 1951 SC 329. Notwithstanding the foregoing comments and criticisms, the special destination continues to be used regularly, particularly in the title to matrimonial homes, and difficulties continue to arise: see D A Brand 'Time for Special Destinations to Die?' 2000 SLT (News) 203. The valuable advice given by Professors Gretton and Reid in *Conveyancing* (2nd edn, 1999), para 26.05, is that a special destination should only be used where its consequences have been carefully discussed with the client and he has given clear instructions to proceed, confirmed in writing.

7.14 NATURE OF CONVEYANCE

Finally, the subjects are disponed 'heritably and irredeemably', which establishes:

(1) that the disponee's right is inheritable (ie transmissible *mortis causa*, that is to say on death) as of right in perpetuity. But this has always been so in Scotland; and

(2) that the disponee's right is an absolute and irredeemable one. This can be compared with heritable securities in the old forms used before the Conveyancing

and Feudal Reform (Scotland) Act 1970, where the debtor as proprietor, having pledged his land in security by conveyance to the creditor, may nonetheless redeem his land on payment of the secured debt. See the sixth edition of this book, Chapter 21.

Both elements are implied, if not express, and the phrase, though invariably included in any disposition, is strictly redundant.

7.15   Liferents

Land can be disponed to A in liferent and B in fee. This gives rise to what is known as a proper liferent. It may be contrasted with improper liferent. There, the liferent is created through the medium of a trust, whereby the liferented property is conveyed to trustees and held by them for the liferenter's use and enjoyment. With a proper liferent, the liferenter (A) receives a subordinate real right in the land, whereas the fiar (B) receives ownership. A is entitled to the beneficial enjoyment of the property during his lifetime, to the total exclusion of B. The liferent burdens B's ownership. A is entitled to occupy the property free of rent, but has certain obligations as to outlays and repairs. Proper liferents are relatively rare and not without their problems, as the recent case of *Stronach's Executors v Robertson* 2002 SLT 1044 demonstrates. See further W J Dobie *Manual of the Law of Liferent and Fee* (1941); *Stair Memorial Encyclopaedia*, Volume 13, paras 1601–1663; and K G C Reid and G L Gretton *Conveyancing 2002* (2003), pp 79–81.

7.16   Specimen style

There follows an example of a typical narrative clause in a disposition:
'I AB (design) heritable proprietor of the subjects and others hereinafter disponed in consideration of the sum of £   paid to me by CD (design) HAVE SOLD and DO HEREBY DISPONE to and in favour of the said CD and his successors and assignees whomsoever heritably and irredeemably ALL and WHOLE . . .'

There then follows the description (see Chapter 8), the reservations (if any) (see Chapter 9), real burdens (see Chapter 15) and other clauses (see Chapter 10).

Chapter 8

Descriptions

8.1 Identification of subjects

A conveyance of land, to be valid, must properly and distinctively identify the subjects conveyed. Complete lack of identification completely invalidates the conveyance; this occasionally occurs, for technical reasons, in a blundered description by reference.

The part of the dispositive clause which so identifies the subjects conveyed is termed the description. There are two aspects to descriptions:

(1) Given that a heritable property is to be conveyed, how do you set about identifying it in the disposition?
(2) Assuming that land has been conveyed in a disposition containing a description, what is carried to the disponee under that description?

The vast majority of titles in Scotland deal primarily with land as the subject of the conveyance, other rights being carried to the grantee as incidental thereto. But this is not necessarily so in every case, since a variety of incorporeal heritable rights are capable of separate transfer. Such rights include, generally, all the *regalia minora* and certain other rights. See *Stair Memorial Encyclopaedia*, Volume 18, paras 207–213. By contrast, certain rights associated with heritable property can never be severed from land and can never be held separately on a separate title. Contrast salmon fishings which can be separately held on a separate title, and trout fishings which cannot be so held, except under the special circumstances set out in the Abolition of Feudal Tenure etc (Scotland) Act 2000: see paras 8.13 and 19.98.

Further, land or buildings may be divided both in the vertical and in the horizontal planes. Therefore, any given surface area of land can be sub-divided into any number of smaller separate surface areas, each held on a separate title; and in the horizontal plane, land can be divided into layers or strata, each layer or stratum being held on a separate title by separate registration. The same applies to buildings, both vertical and horizontal division being permitted within a building. But there are practical limits. So, the Keeper using his common law discretion refused to record souvenir plot titles, on the footing, *inter alia*, that each plot was not 'separately identifiable by description or plan' (Keeper's Report 1969); and, for registration of title, this rule is now statutory by the Land Registration (Scotland) Act 1979, s 4(2)(b).

Whatever the nature of the property (or right) to be conveyed, the general rule in all cases is that, in a conveyance, any words which are sufficient to identify the subject matter of the conveyance are in themselves an adequate description. There are no *verba solemnia* (special words), there are no statutory formulae for an identifying description and no hard and fast rules at common law. But that general principle falls to be applied in accordance with the following general rules.

8.2   THE EXTENT OF THE GRANT

Land is described in a conveyance in terms of two dimensions only, ie in the horizontal plane, by reference to surface features only; it is nonetheless normally implied that this carries to the disponee everything *a coelo usque ad centrum*, ie all subjacent minerals and sub-strata to the centre of the earth and everything above the surface, including air space indefinitely upwards.

8.3   SEPARATE TENEMENTS

As explained, land and buildings can be divided vertically and horizontally, the resulting divisions each being capable of separate registration and known as separate tenements. Some, but not all, heritable rights are also capable of separate registration as separate tenements, such as salmon fishings. The rule is that each separate tenement must be separately and specifically described (or properly referred to) in a conveyance. Otherwise, it will not pass to a disponee. Thus, a conveyance of land, described as such, will not carry automatically to the disponee the right of salmon fishings: see *McKendrick v Wilson* 1970 SLT (Sh Ct) 39. A farm was conveyed 'with parts and pertinents', but no reference was made to salmon fishings to which the disponee laid claim. It was held that, as the title did not expressly include salmon fishings, the action by the disponee must be dismissed.

As a result of this rule, a separate lease of salmon fishings has always been regarded as competent and as binding a singular successor of the landlord. On the other hand, a lease of trout fishings has always been regarded as purely a personal contract, not running with the land. This rule was altered by the Freshwater and Salmon Fisheries (Scotland) Act 1976, s 4, in terms of which a lease of freshwater fish (ie trout) in inland waters for more than one year will bind a singular successor of the landlord and thus, for this limited purpose, is created a *quasi* separate tenement. This provision will be repealed and replaced by the Salmon and Freshwater Fisheries (Consolidation) (Scotland) Act 2003, s 67 which is to similar effect. At the time of writing it has not yet been brought into force.

Discontiguous areas of ground are also separate tenements. Suppose A owns a plot of ground with a house on it. He also owns an allotment, 50 yards away on the other side of the public road. A conveyance which describes the house and garden would not normally carry the allotment as well; special reference to the allotment is required. Similarly, a conveyance of land will automatically carry to the disponee all subjacent minerals, unless and until the minerals are severed from the surface and held on a separate title. Thereafter, the minerals having become a separate tenement, they must be separately conveyed.

8.4 FIXTURES

Corporeal things are heritable or moveable according to their physical state. The general rule is that, when moveable things are affixed to land, they lose their moveable character and become heritable by accession. This is summed up in the Latin brocard, *inaedificatum aut plantatum solo, solo cedit.* When moveables have become heritable in this way by physical annexation, then on a conveyance of land, described as such, fixtures pass to the disponee without express reference thereto. Thus a conveyance of land automatically carries to the disponee all buildings thereon, all fixtures within the buildings, growing timber and the like. In practice this is an area, both on contracts and on subsequent conveyances, where disputes frequently arise; and the question of fixtures should always be carefully considered. See further *Stair Memorial Encyclopaedia*, Volume 18, paras 570–587.

8.5 IMPLIED OR INHERENT RIGHTS

A conveyance of land, described as such, automatically carries to the disponee certain natural and ancillary rights. It is, therefore, unnecessary in any description of land expressly to define, describe or refer to rights in this category. The implied rights, which are carried automatically to the disponee with a conveyance of land, are summarised here for convenience in the context of the description in the disposition. Strictly, they are a matter for the law of landownership and the reader is referred to the further reading suggested. They include the rights to:

(1) *Exclusive possession.* This entitles the disponee to prevent trespass or encroachment within his boundaries. See W M Gordon *Scottish Land Law* (2nd edn, 1999), paras 13.07–13.15; R R M Paisley *Land Law* (2000), paras 4.28–4.30; *Stair Memorial Encyclopaedia*, Volume 18, paras 174–190.

(2) *Unrestricted user.* In practice, the theoretical unrestricted right of user is now severely limited by a variety of statutory provisions of general application, and by conventional provisions in particular cases. See Gordon, paras 13.16–13.17; Paisley *Land Law*, paras 4.7–4.17; *Stair Memorial Encyclopaedia*, Volume 18, para 195.

(3) *Support.* The disponee is entitled to require his neighbours, laterally and vertically, to support his land, unless that right is expressly varied in the titles. See Chapter 9.

Certain of these rights may be varied or negatived by the express terms of the conveyance. But, in the absence of any express provision, they pass automatically on a conveyance of the land.

8.6 Special cases: tenements

The ownership of heritable property in Scotland, including buildings, may be split laterally in strata and vertically within a single building. This longstanding rule has tended to encourage, in Scotland, the development of flatted tenements particularly in large towns and cities in which several flats on several floors are owned outright (not merely held on lease) by several independent heritable proprietors. Clearly, this is a situation in which each owner is peculiarly vulnerable to prejudice from the actings of his neighbour.

Very often (but not by any means universally, especially in older titles), the rights and obligations of the owners of individual flats in a tenement are regulated, *inter se*, in great detail in their respective titles. But, where no provision is so made (or where the provision so made is not exhaustive), then (or to that extent at any rate) the law in Scotland implies certain rights and obligations based on common interest and in this context known as the law of the tenement. It should be noted at the outset that the law here will soon be codified by virtue of the Tenements (Scotland) Bill: see paras 8.10–8.11. However, the Bill essentially builds on the common law. Hence, there is value in setting it out.

8.7 THE COMMON LAW OF THE TENEMENT

Very briefly, and in outline, the rules are:

(1) Each flat-owner has an exclusive right of property in the air space within his flat; and may use it as he pleases, subject to the common interest of other owners in the tenement.

(2) The owner of a flat on the lowest floor of the building has an exclusive right of property in the *solum* of the tenement below his flat and in the front area and the back ground *ex adverso* thereof; but subject to the common interest of other proprietors which allows any one of them to prevent the use of the *solum* or front and back ground in a manner injurious to the amenity of the objector's property, such as building thereon in such a way as to exclude light.

(3) In each individual flat, each proprietor owns the enclosing walls, except where these separate him from an adjoining property in which case they are mutual. In other words, they are owned to the centre line (*ad medium filum*). This applies both to gables and to internal division walls. But each such proprietor must uphold his main walls in order to afford support to proprietors above him. Note particularly the positive obligation to maintain. In the case of common gables, there are cross rights of common interest between the whole proprietors of all houses in each tenement on either side of the gable, to prevent interference with the gable so as to render the building unstable.

(4) As between upper and lower flat, the floor/ceiling are notionally divided along an imaginary line drawn along the centre of the joists. But again, neither party may interfere with or weaken the joists to the detriment of the other.

(5) The roof and the space between the ceiling and the roof beams belong to the top-floor proprietor (or severally to two or more top-floor proprietors); but again, they are bound to maintain the roof (so far as it covers their individual houses) in order to afford protection to the floors below them. This places a heavy financial burden on the top-floor proprietors, therefore the title deeds normally vary this.

(6) The common passage and stair in the tenement, the *solum* of such passage etc and the enclosing walls thereof (to the centre line), are common property vested in the whole proprietors of the several flats in the tenement served by that passage and stair (but no others) as *pro indiviso* owners.

(7) The cost of repairs to common parts and the cost of demolition of the whole tenement will be divided equally amongst all proprietors.

(8) It is said that one proprietor may insist that the others conjoin with him in rebuilding a destroyed or demolished tenement. In such rebuilding, the rights originally enjoyed must be preserved, but there seems to be no reported case in which this rule has been applied; and according to Professor Reid in 'The Law of the Tenement' 1983 JLSS 472 at 477, it can no longer be relied on, following *Thomson v St Cuthbert's Co-operative Association Ltd* 1958 SC 380, unless there is a specific provision in the title. See also *Stair Memorial Encyclopaedia*, Volume 18, para 250.

8.8 DISTINCTION BETWEEN COMMON PROPERTY AND COMMON INTEREST

There is a very important difference in effect to be noted between a right of common property in, for example, a main wall where no operation can be carried out without the consent of all proprietors; and a main wall owned by a particular flat owner, and not owned in common, where any operations may be carried out on that main wall (for example, converting it into a shop front) provided other proprietors are not endangered by these operations. The law of the tenement does not impose absolute liability. Proof of negligence, in commission or omission, is required.

In the Digest of Cases for para 8.6, a number of cases are listed under the heading 'Liability for damage caused by alterations and reconstruction' which confirm the foregoing rule that no liability arises *ex dominio*, in other words, merely from ownership. Therefore, no claim for damages is available to the proprietor of any flat in a tenement arising out of operations in some other flat, or from the failure in the structure in some other flat, unless it can be shown that an operation was carried out negligently, or negligence can otherwise be proved, as the direct cause of the damage.

In *Macnab v McDevitt* 1971 SLT (Sh Ct) 41, a successful attempt was made to escape from the rule of liability requiring evidence of *culpa* (fault) by relying instead on the law of nuisance as the basis of the claim for damages. This case, however, pre-dates the important decision of the House of Lords in *RHM Bakeries (Scotland) Ltd v Strathclyde Regional Council* 1985 SC (HL) 17. There, bakery premises were flooded as the result of the collapse of a sewer maintained by the local authority. The bakery company sued for damages on the grounds of nuisance at common law. On that point, the House of Lords held that the case as so pleaded was irrelevant because there was no averment of fault on the part of the defenders. According to Professor Reid in the *Stair Memorial Encyclopaedia*, Volume 18, para 233, note 8, this decision closed the door which appeared to be opened by the decision in *Macnab*. However, in *Kennedy v Glenbelle Ltd* 1996 SLT 1186 the point was raised again in comparable circumstances. The tenants of the basement in that case, against the advice of the consulting engineers, removed a wall which was known to be load bearing, and the removal caused cracking and settlement. The owner of the basement was advised by the consulting engineers that this was a probable outcome but nonetheless proceeded with the work. On appeal, the Inner House held that a case of nuisance was appropriate in these circumstances where the consulting engineers knew that the work constituted a positive interference with support and that the proposed works would probably result in damage to the upper floor proprietors, but observed that averments of fault were irrelevant in a claim for damages without supporting averments of negligence. Thus, liability for damages arising out of both common interest and nuisance is not strict. Fault requires to be shown: for a fuller analysis, see E Reid 'The Basis of Liability in Nuisance' 1997 JR 162. See also the articles referred to in the Reading List for Chapter 13.

8.9 VARIATION OF THE COMMON LAW

In practice, in modern titles, the law of the tenement is substantially excluded by express provision in the title to each separate flat, as follows.

The conveyance to the disponee often includes a right of common ownership with the other proprietors to the solum on which the tenement is erected, the front ground and back green, the roof, rhones, and down pipes, and all pipes, drains and cables serving the whole tenement. It is normal nowadays to list the common parts in a deed of conditions, but the relevant part of that deed must then be expressly incorporated by reference into each break-off disposition: see I J S Talman (ed) *Halliday's Conveyancing Law and Practice in Scotland* (2nd edn, 2 volumes, 1996–97), para 33.57. When deciding which parts are to be held in common caution should be exercised. The temptation to over-use common property should be resisted. The case of *Rafique v Amin* 1997 SLT 1385 makes the point well. There, the proprietors of one of the flats in a tenement wished to carry out alterations. In particular, they intended to insert steel beams into a gable wall bounding their flat. The title deeds, however, provided that the outside walls and gables were the common property of both flats in the building. The proprietor of the other flat successfully obtained interdict against the proposed work on the ground that alterations to common property generally require the consent of all co-proprietors: see para 7.10. This caused Lord Justice-Clerk Ross at p 1387F to comment on the practical difficulties caused by over-use of common property: 'It is somewhat ironical that if, instead of making these elaborate provisions regarding common property, the granter had allowed the more usual law of the tenement to prevail, many of these difficulties would not have arisen.'

Real burdens will also be imposed in the conveyance to regulate maintenance and repair to key parts of the tenement, in particular the roof and the common stair. It is usual practice nowadays to make all the flat proprietors equally liable for repairs. Previously, it was common to apportion liability by reference to the feuduty or rateable value in respect of the individual flat set against that for the building as a whole, although the validity of such burdens was often doubted: see para 15.43. The demise of both feuduty and domestic rates has ended this practice. Usually, modern tenements will be governed by deeds of conditions. These deeds normally provide that a majority of the proprietors can decide to carry out repairs. There are often complex provisions regulating the appointment of factors and the establishment of residents' associations. Great care needs to be exercised in the drafting of such deeds. For a salutary tale, see *Graham & Sibbald v Brash* (21 March 2001, unreported), Dundee Sheriff Court, discussed in K G C Reid and G L Gretton *Conveyancing 2001* (2002), pp 85–88. Many of the issues relating to the drafting of a deed of conditions are not tenement specific, but relate to all modern developments. For further discussion, see Chapter 15.

A final possible feature of tenement title deeds is an express right of access in favour of the proprietors into other proprietors' flats, for the purpose of carrying out repairs to the building.

See further *Halliday's Conveyancing Law and Practice*, para 33.22 and *Stair Memorial Encyclopaedia*, Volume 18, paras 240–241.

8.10   THE TENEMENTS (SCOTLAND) BILL: BACKGROUND

The Scottish Law Commission began work on reform of the law of the tenement in the 1980s and published *Law of the Tenement* in 1990 (Scot Law Com Disc Paper No 91, 1990). A consultation period followed and the *Report on the Law of the Tenement* was eventually published in 1998 (Scot Law Com No 162, 1998), together with a draft Bill. The decision was taken by the Scottish Executive that the Bill should not be introduced to the Scottish Parliament until the legislation on feudal abolition and title conditions was passed. Changes effected by this legislation would mean that some redrafting of the Commission's original Bill was required. In March 2003, shortly after the Title Conditions (Scotland) Act 2003 was passed and in fact before it received Royal Assent, the Executive duly published a consultation paper, containing a lightly revised version of the Bill. It is available at http://www.scotland.gov.uk/consultations/housing/tsbc-00.asp. The paper takes account of recommendations of the Housing Improvement Task Force in relation to tenements in its report, also published in March 2003: see Annex B. The consultation period ended on 13 June 2003 and at the time of writing, introduction of the Bill into Parliament is awaited. The Executive has announced that this will be in early 2004.

Why is the law of the tenement to be reformed? The Commission points to a number of reasons in paras 2.13–2.22 of its Report. These include:

(1) *Uncertainty.* The common law is based on a small number of mainly nineteenth-century cases. This means that there is no authority on the ownership of entryphones or satellite dishes. Other areas are also unclear, for example the question of who owns pipes running down an outside wall.

(2) *Unfairness.* Some aspects of the common law are inequitable. The prime example is that in the absence of express stipulation in the title deeds, only the proprietors of the top-floor flats are liable for the maintenance of the roof, even though this benefits the whole tenement.

(3) *Insolvent or absconding owners.* The common law does not satisfactorily address the question of who must meet the share of repair costs due by a defaulting flat proprietor.

(4) *No management system.* The absence of a specific management scheme in the common law means that recourse often has to be made to the general rules of common property. This means that unanimity is required, so that one awkward flat proprietor can block repairs. For a cautionary tale, see 'Editional' (1997) 1 Edin LR 280.

8.11 TENEMENTS (SCOTLAND) BILL: SPECIFIC FEATURES

A comprehensive account will not be given, as the Bill may be amended when it passes through Parliament. (In this regard, the section numbers referred to below are obviously subject to change.) That said, it is not anticipated that substantial changes will be made. The Bill builds on the existing law, effectively codifying the law of the tenement, but at the same time removing the uncertainties which currently exist. Like the common law, the new statutory law will be subject to the terms of the title deeds. In other words, it will be a 'default' law. It will apply to both existing and new tenements. The Schedule to the Bill contains a management scheme which will regulate all tenements, subject to the title deeds. This is known as the 'Tenement Management Scheme' and practitioners can expect to become very familiar with it. The original version of the Bill also contained a more sophisticated scheme which developers or proprietors could choose to adopt. Such a scheme, known as the 'Development Management Scheme', now exists by virtue of Part 6 of the Title Conditions (Scotland) Act 2003 (see para 15.55) for developments in general and no longer requires to be included.

(1) *Definitions.* Section 26 of the Bill contains two key definitions. 'Tenement' is defined to mean a building, comprising of two or more flats, at least two of which are (or are designed to be) in separate ownership and which are divided from each other horizontally. It includes the *solum* and land pertaining to the building. The words '(or are designed to be)' did not appear in the definition in the Scottish Law Commission's Bill, nor indeed do they appear in the definition

on p 7 of the Executive's Consultation Paper. It would seem that they come from the definition of 'tenement' in s 122(1) of the Title Conditions (Scotland) Act 2003. Their inclusion appears to be a mistake, since the aim of the Bill is to regulate tenements where more than one party owns the units therein. 'Flat' itself is defined to mean a dwelling-house, or any business or other premises. So the Bill applies to an office block of independently owned offices.

(2) *Ownership*. Sections 1 to 3 of the Bill regulate boundaries and pertinents within a tenement. Their effect is to codify the common law. For example, the top flat will continue to include the roof above it (subject, as always, to the titles). Human rights law makes it practically impossible to redistribute ownership. In addition, as the case of *Rafique v Amin* 1997 SLT 1385 shows, making more parts of the tenement common property leads to its own problems. As for parts where ownership is currently uncertain, the Bill provides that these shall be a pertinent of the flat(s) which they benefit: s 3(4). Where more than one flat benefits, the pertinent will be held in common. The provision will apply, for example, to cables, fire escapes, rhones and pipes.

(3) *Management*. Sections 4 and 5 provide for the Tenement Management Scheme which, as mentioned above, is set out in the Schedule. This scheme will apply to all tenements, except those governed by the Development Management Scheme. The Commission's original proposal was that a developer or the flat proprietors could also disapply the Tenement Management Scheme by providing for his or their own scheme. The Executive, however, believes that it would be simpler, if all tenements are governed by either one of the two statutory schemes, subject to the terms of the title deeds. The Bill is duly amended to this affect. See Consultation Paper, p 15.

In general, the Tenement Management Scheme provides that a majority of the proprietors can make 'scheme decisions' in relation to 'scheme property'. The number of 'scheme decisions' is limited: see rule 2.2. Included are decisions to carry out maintenance, appoint a factor and arrange a common insurance policy. 'Scheme property' effectively means the parts of the tenement which all the proprietors have an interest in maintaining and includes the roof, the foundations, external and load-bearing walls and any parts of the tenement owned in common. A proprietor who objects to a scheme decision can apply to the sheriff to have it annulled, but must do so within 21 days: see s 5. The sheriff must be satisfied that the decision is not in the best interests of all the proprietors or unfairly prejudicial to one or more of them.

(4) *Liability for costs*. Rule 5 governs liability for 'scheme costs', which effectively means costs arising from scheme decisions. Where provision for payment of the full cost is made in real burdens in the title deeds, these will prevail. If this is not the case, but the relevant part of the tenement is owned in common, the proprietors will be liable in proportion to their shares. If the part is not owned in common, and there are no real burdens covering the full cost, the proprietors will be liable equally, save that if the larger or largest flat has a floor space one and half times greater than that of the smaller or smallest flat, then the cost is

apportioned in accordance with floor space. The most notable effect of this is that where the title deeds are silent as to maintenance and ownership of the roof, the top floor proprietors will no longer be solely liable.

(5) *Other matters.* Sections 7 to 10 of the Bill codify the common interest obligations of proprietors, in particular the duties to provide support and shelter. However, these obligations will not be enforceable where this is unreasonable in the circumstances involved, in particular considering the age and condition of the tenement and the likely maintenance costs which would be incurred. Thus common interest obligations may cease in dilapidated tenements. Section 15 introduces a compulsory obligation on proprietors to insure their flats and any pertinents attaching thereto. Unlike motor car insurance, there is no criminal sanction for non-compliance, but other proprietors are given the right to demand sight of the policy and evidence that the premium is paid. It is questionable the extent to which this right will be enforced. The Housing Improvement Task Force has recommended that common insurance policies should be mandatory for new developments, but at the time of writing the Executive had yet to accept this proposal.

Section 16 of the Bill gives a right, subject to building and planning laws, to install television aerials on the roof or a chimney stack. Similarly, s 17 authorises the leading of pipes and other conduits through the building for the provision of gas and other services to be prescribed by statutory instrument. Sections 18 to 22 deal with demolition and abandonment of a tenement. Subject to the title deeds, where a tenement has been demolished, any proprietor is entitled to have the site sold and the proceeds divided (s 20). The same right applies where a tenement has been entirely unoccupied for six months because it is in a poor condition (s 22). Finally, s 6 gives the sheriff power to resolve disputes in relation to both the new statutory law of the tenement and the management scheme governing the tenement in question.

For further discussion, see K G C Reid 'Reform of the Law of the Tenement' 1998 JLSS Apr/21 and A J M Steven 'Reform of the Law of the Tenement' (2001) 52 Greens PLB 4 and (2001) 53 Greens PLB 3, but note that these discuss the original version of the Bill.

8.12   Special cases: water rights

(1) *Surface water.* Surface water, and water percolating underground, which, in each case, is not confined in a definite bed or channel, may be appropriated by the owner of the land. This rule operates even if, by such appropriation, the owner interferes with the legitimate enjoyment of his neighbours, so there is no common interest in this case. Further, each neighbouring proprietor is bound to accept the natural flow of water from an adjoining property in its natural state; and the neighbour cannot complain if the natural flow is artificially interrupted by some other proprietor on whose land the water falls or flows.

A case in point is *RHM Bakeries v Strathclyde Regional Council* 1985 SC (HL) 17, referred to in para 8.8. It was cited in *G A Estates Ltd v Caviapen Trustees Ltd (No 1)* 1993 SLT 1037. In that case, in the construction of a new development, a stream which flowed across the site was diverted through a culvert. Subsequently, after completion of the works, the development flooded as a result of heavy rainfall which the culvert was inadequate to cope with. In the course of his judgment, Lord Coulsfield referred to a *dictum* of Lord Jauncey in the earlier case of *Noble's Trustees v Economic Forestry (Scotland) Ltd* 1988 SLT 662 at 664, where Lord Jauncey states that, if the owner knows that an operation on his land will or will probably cause damage, however much care is exercised, that amounts to *culpa*. This is also the case where the owner knows that certain steps are necessary to prevent damage to a neighbour and, notwithstanding, proceeds with his operations without taking those precautions. This still, however, necessitates proof of *culpa*, although possibly in a special form.

(2) *Rights in rivers, streams and the foreshore.* The ownership of waters depends upon whether they are tidal or non-tidal. The *alveus* (bed) of the sea and other tidal waters belongs to the Crown. Non-tidal streams, rivers and lochs are in private ownership and are presumed the property of the owner or owners of the banks. Thus, if land being conveyed extends across both banks, so that the river (or as the case may be) runs through the land, the *alveus* of the river is carried by the conveyance. Conversely, if the river forms a boundary, there is a presumption that the *alveus* is carried *ad medium filum* (to the mid-point). Similarly, possession *ad medium filum* is presumed: see *Tesco Stores Ltd v Keeper of the Registers of Scotland* 2001 SLT (Lands Tr) 23, affirmed at 2003 GWD 20-610. If the river permanently alters its course because of extraordinary flooding or other natural cause, then the boundary line may shift to coincide with the new *medium filum*. See *Stirling v Bartlett* 1993 SLT 763, discussed in D L Carey Miller 'Alluvio, avulsio and fluvial boundaries' 1994 SLT (News) 75.

Unless it is very short, a non-tidal river or stream is likely to be owned in sections by a number of different people. In such a case all proprietors of land through (or along) which the stream flows, from its source to its mouth, are united together in a common interest, to preserve their individual rights in the flow of water in its usual channel, undiminished in quantity and without any deterioration in its quality. Any one riparian proprietor may object if any of these rights is imperilled through the operation of any other riparian proprietor; but he must show actual or probable interference with his rights, arising from some such operation. If his rights are not interfered with in any way, then he has no cause to object. Subject to that common interest, each individual riparian proprietor is entitled as of right, and without express provision in his title, to appropriate the water in the stream (a) for primary purposes, ie for domestic use and for animals; and (b) for secondary uses, but only if he does not interfere with the enjoyment of others.

There is no presumption as to the ownership of the foreshore. Sometimes it is owned privately. If, however, it has never been never feued or acquired by positive prescription, it is owned by the Crown. In Orkney and Shetland, where there is udal tenure, the foreshore is normally held by the proprietor of the land bounding it: *Smith v Lerwick Harbour Trustees* (1903) 5 F 680.

A number of public rights exist in respect of waters and the foreshore. These are quite extensive in the case of tidal waters and the foreshore, and include a right of navigation and a right of fishing (other than for salmon). There is also a public right of navigation in non-tidal waters, but only where the waters are 'navigable' in the sense of having been used for navigation for a period of at least 40 years. See *Wills' Trustees v Cairngorm Canoeing and Sailing School Ltd* 1976 SC (HL) 30.

In March 2003, the Scottish Law Commission published its *Report on the Law of the Foreshore and the Seabed* (Scot Law Com No 190), which has a draft Sea, Shore and Inland Waters (Scotland) Bill annexed to it. The Bill effectively codifies the common law. The public rights over the foreshore are expressly defined and these include sunbathing and making sandcastles.

8.13 Special cases: fishing and game

At common law, every riparian proprietor enjoys an absolute right to fish, as a natural incident of ownership, for any fish except salmon. Salmon fishings are a separate heritable right and require a separate conveyance. But the methods of fishing are controlled by statute. The relevant legislation has recently been consolidated by the Salmon and Freshwater Fisheries (Consolidation) (Scotland) Act 2003, which is expected to come into force shortly.

Except for the purposes of s 65A of the Abolition of Feudal Tenure etc (Scotland) Act 2000, the right to fish for trout etc ('white fish') cannot vest as a separate and independent heritable right, in someone who is not the owner of land adjacent to the stream (or loch). Section 65A, which was added to the 2000 Act by the Title Conditions (Scotland) Act 2003, allows superiors to preserve so called 'sporting rights', ie rights of fishing and game as a separate tenement. The provision is a very odd one because, unlike all other separate tenements, this type gives a non-exclusive right to property. See further para 19.98.

The Salmon and Freshwater Fisheries (Consolidation) (Scotland) Act 2003, like its predecessor legislation, faciliates the preservation of freshwater and salmon fisheries in Scotland. In particular, it regulates close times and allows the Scottish Ministers to make protection orders in respect of freshwater fish if they are satisfied that this will increase the availability of fishing in inland waters. Provision is also made for policing by wardens etc, with fines for contravention. The legislation also permits the leasing of freshwater fishing rights: see para 8.3.

Game, like fish, are *ferae naturae* and, therefore, *res nullius*. The term 'game' includes a variety of animals, variously defined in various statutes. Nonetheless, mere ownership of land carries with it by implication the right to take or kill all kinds of game on that land as a natural incident of the right of property. A recent important development, however, has been the Scottish Parliament passing legislation to prohibit the hunting of wild animals with dogs: see the Protection of Wild Mammals (Scotland) Act 2002. This Act was unsuccessfully challenged on human rights grounds: see *Adams v Scottish Ministers* 2003 SLT 366.

The right to game is personal to the landowner, as landowner, and not inherent in or necessarily associated with the use or occupancy of land. Therefore, where land is let to an agricultural tenant or for other purposes, there is no implication that the tenant has the right to take or kill game. Under the Ground Game (Scotland) Act 1880, an agricultural tenant does have the right to kill rabbits and hares on the subjects of lease; and there is no contracting out of the provisions of this Act. The same applies to vermin unless protected by statute as an endangered species.

The right to take game may be the subject matter of a valid contract of lease; and, possibly, particularly where the lease is a lease of land with right to shoot thereover, it may come within the provisions of the Leases Act 1449 and so transmit against a singular successor. Until recently, it was not considered possible legally to constitute a lease of shooting over land as a separate and independent heritable right transmissible against, and binding on, singular successors of the landlord. See Paton and Cameron *Leases*, p 106, and the authorities there cited.

In *Palmer's Trustees v Brown* 1989 SLT 128, however, the court held that an ordinary game lease, if otherwise in appropriate terms, is registrable under the Registration of Leases (Scotland) Act 1857 and, if so registered, transmits against and is binding on singular successors. It was unnecessary in that case to decide whether or not such a lease, without registration, would transmit against singular successors under the Leases Act 1449; and that question is therefore not yet finally decided, but the indications in this decision are that a game lease is protected by the 1449 Act. The justification for this decision lies in the wording of the 1857 Act, s 2. A lease which is binding on the grantor and which is registered is effectual against any singular successor. The decision may be questioned on the ground that game is not a separate tenement in Scots law (except for the limited purposes of Abolition of Feudal Tenure etc (Scotland) Act 2000, discussed above) and therefore it is difficult to understand how a real right can be granted in respect of it. But see C Waelde (ed) *Professor McDonald's Conveyancing Opinions* (1998), pp 192–197, as well as the recently published 1962 opinion of the then Solicitor General referred to in the Reading List.

8.14 Conveyancing descriptions: general

In order to be registrable, dispositions and other conveyances require a description 'recognised in Scots conveyancing, for example, general or particular description or a description in statutory form'. See *Macdonald v Keeper of the Register of Sasines* 1914 SC 854. But want of such a description does not render a conveyance invalid, provided the subjects are identifiable, for example, by description in general terms.

Such a conveyance cannot, however, be recorded of itself; a notice of title is needed to supply the want of description if the grantee is to become heritable proprietor. Typically, before the Succession (Scotland) Act 1964, heritable property passed to trustees under a will which described the property in general terms, thus, 'the whole means and estate, heritable and moveable, real and personal which shall belong to me at my death'. A will in this form was a valid general disposition and, as such, operated of itself as a title to the trustees but it was not recordable in the General Register of Sasines. Since 1964, heritage vests in executors by confirmation thereto; and confirmation is also for practical purposes a general disposition, not recordable itself.

Very much stricter rules were formerly applied in the case of standard securities. In its original form, note 1 to Schedule 2 to the Conveyancing and Feudal Reform (Scotland) Act 1970 required that a particular description be used. For the meaning of a particular description, see para 8.16. The problems with this requirement became apparent in the series of *Beneficial Bank* cases: *Bennett v Beneficial Bank plc* 1995 SLT 1105; *Beneficial Bank v McConnachie* 1996 SC 119, 1996 SLT 413; and *Beneficial Bank plc v Wardle* 1996 GWD 30–1825. These are noted in the Digest of Cases and discussed at length in para 8.11 of the sixth edition of this book. The situation was remedied by the Abolition of Feudal Tenure etc (Scotland) Act 2000, Schedule 12, para 30(23)(a) which replaces the original version of Note 1 as follows: 'The security subjects shall be described sufficiently to identify them; but this note is without prejudice to any additional requirement imposed as respects any register'. The change is retrospective: 2000 Act, s 77(3). Consequently, the requirements for descriptions in standard securities are now the same as for those in other deeds. See further Reid and Gretton *Conveyancing 2000* (2001), pp 141–143.

8.15   Methods of description: general

This is not to be confused with a general disposition (on which, see para 31.2). Under this method, the subjects are identified simply by name, and no attempt is made to define the property by reference to physical features on the ground. Such descriptions are common in older titles, but are not now normally employed in a conveyance of new except in conjunction with a particular description. The identification of the property so conveyed, and its limits, are determined by possession following on the title, and by the operation of the positive prescription. But, clearly, it may often be extremely difficult to identify precisely on the ground the extent of the subjects conveyed under this form of description, and this is often a major problem when examining older titles. In practice, these difficulties are in most cases resolved by reliance on the Prescription and Limitation (Scotland) Act 1973, s 1, taken together with occupation of the subjects within defined physical boundaries on the ground for the prescriptive period. This is dealt with at greater length in Chapter 12. In the Land Register it is not possible to register a deed which only has a vague general description, unless the Keeper is separately advised of the precise location of the subjects, because he must be able to identify the subjects on the Ordnance Survey Map: see para 8.27.

8.16 Methods of description: particular

Under this method, the subjects conveyed are identified by actual physical features on the ground, whether these features be natural or artificial. This is the method now normally used in practice where land is first conveyed as a separate tenement. Obviously, the variety of possible circumstances is almost infinite and there are no hard and fast rules. There is still, however, some difference of opinion as to what amount of detail is required to constitute a particular description. I J S Talman (ed) *Halliday's Conveyancing Law and Practice in Scotland* (2nd edn, 2 Volumes, 1996–97), appears to equate a particular description with a bounding title. The court would appear to adopt that view in *Beneficial Bank plc v McConnachie* 1996 SC 119 at 126B, where the Lord President says that a particular description is one which makes it unnecessary to refer to any extraneous material to define the extent of the subjects, such as the state of possession. That seems to be an unnecessarily stringent requirement. A particular description can, it is thought, quite easily be achieved with sufficient precision without creating a bounding title and without incorporating every individual boundary in the description itself. However, given the *dictum* of the Lord President in *Beneficial Bank plc v McConnachie*, the matter is unsettled, but of far less practical importance following the recent statutory relaxation of the description rules for standard securities (see para 8.14).

Subject to these comments, any particular description will, or may, contain the following elements:

(1) The name or postal address of the property, with a reference to the parish and county; but none of this is necessary, provided the location of the property is clear.

(2) Identification of the boundary line or boundary feature on each side of the property; but very often only some of the boundaries are so described. For this purpose, natural or artificial features are used where appropriate, for example, walls, streams, roads etc and the length of each such boundary is normally given. This may raise difficulties as to the actual extent of the property conveyed in relation to that boundary feature. Thus, where property is described as bounded, on one side, by a wall, it is assumed that the whole wall is excluded altogether on that particular wording. In contrast, where the words used are 'enclosed by a wall', the presumption is that the whole wall is included. Where the boundary is a public road, the presumption is *medium filum*, ie to the centre line; but 'bounded by a road' has been held to exclude the whole road, at least if supported by plan and/or measurements: see *Houston v Barr* 1911 SC 134 and J Burns *Conveyancing Practice* (4th edn, 1957), p 328. But compare *Magistrates of Hamilton v Bent Colliery* 1929 SC 686 at 694, where 'bounded by a public road' was stated to include it to *medium filum*.

In relation to a non-tidal stream, 'Bounded by the Water of Leith', was held to included the stream to the *medium filum*, even in the face of measurements, which were ruled not to be taxative. See *Gibson v Bonnington Sugar Refining Co Ltd* (1869) 7 M 394.

For the presumptions which apply for various other features on the ground, see J Burns *Conveyancing Practice* (4th edn, 1957), pp 327–329; W M Gordon *Scottish Land Law* (2nd edn, 1999), paras 4.24–4.51; and *Halliday's Conveyancing Law and Practice*, para 33.11. Any such presumption can be altered by express provision in the deed, for example, bounded, on the north, 'by the southern face of a wall' or 'by the northern edge of the road', or 'by the mid-line'.

More recent examples of individual boundary features are given in the Digest of Cases for para 8.16.

(3) Often the length of the boundaries is given, and there may also be a statement of the superficial area. Until 30 September 1995 measurements could be given either in imperial or in metric measure, but new descriptions after that date require to use metric measure. This requirement derives from the Units of Measurement Regulations 1995, SI 1995/1804 implementing EEC/Directive 80/181. The requirements of these regulations are discussed in detail in the *Registration of Title Practice Book*, paras 4.44–4.51 and Chapter 4, Appendix 1.

Briefly, for conveyancing and registration purposes, the rule is that in any description, every measurement of length, depth, height or area must be in metric and not Imperial measure. There is one exception in that it remains permissible to use the acre as an indicator of area, although the use of the hectare in lieu is common-place and recommended. The regulations have no effect on descriptions in existing documents prior to 1 September 1995.

The more important conversions can be summarised as follows:

- one yard equals 0.9144 metres
- one foot equals 0.3048 metres
- one square foot equals 0.0929 square metres
- one inch equals 0.0254 metres
- one acre equals 0.4047 hectares.

Reversing the measurements:

- one metre equals 3.2808 feet
- one hectare equals 10,000 square metres or 2.471 acres
- one square metre equals 10.764 square feet.

If an acre is used as an indicator of area, the old sub-divisions of the acre cannot also be used, ie roods, poles etc. Instead any sub-division of an acre must be in decimal terms. So 'one acre, one rood' or 'one acre, 40 poles' will each become '1.25 acres'.

The use of Imperial measure in addition to metric units of measurement is permitted, provided the metric unit is given first, which seems unnecessarily pedantic.

Scales on plans are similarly affected. A plan can no longer be described as to the scale of one inch to eight feet and instead must be represented by the ratio equivalent, for example, 1:500.

The effect of failure to observe the new requirements is not entirely clear. The Keeper indicates that he would almost certainly refuse to accept for recording or registration any description, written or by plan, which fails to conform to the new requirements. That is not to say, however, that a conveyance which uses old measurements of length or area is in itself invalid. It may not itself be capable of registration, but may operate effectively as a link in title. The Keeper's bar on accepting deeds for registration would appear to apply only to the Register of Sasines and Land Register. So, such a deed could be recorded for preservation in the Books of Council and Session or Sheriff Court Books. Thus, any such link in title can be effectively preserved. The safest course of action, however, is to ensure that the deed complies with the regulations and therefore can be registered.

(4) A plan is not essential to supplement a written particular description; but, even in the simplest case, it is always desirable. Normally, the plan is not embodied in the deed but is appended as a schedule, being referred to and adopted as part of the deed by a reference in the description; and as such it is signed and referred to in the testing clause.

It is perfectly competent, and increasingly common, to describe properties simply by reference to a plan, without incorporating any written description in the deed. Formerly, there were disadavantages in this practice, as discussed in para 8.13 of the sixth edition of this book. In particular, until 1934 no record of plans appended to deeds was kept by the Keeper at Register House. This meant that where a description depended solely on a plan and the principal deed was lost, the title might well be rendered invalid: see *McLachlan v Bowie* (1887) 25 SLR 734. Nowadays, particularly with the advent of registration of title, which is plan based (see para 8.26), it is common practice to give a particular description by reference to a plan only. See further G L Gretton and K G C Reid *Conveyancing* (2nd edn, 1999), paras 12.11–12.12.

8.17 PART AND PORTION CLAUSE

Any piece of ground which, on a sub-division, is conveyed for the first time as a separate heritable unit, and particularly described as such, necessarily forms part of a larger area of ground already held on its own title in name of the disponer. It is customary, although not essential, to link up the new particular description with the previous titles by a 'part and portion' clause. This simply repeats, in the most convenient form (normally a description by reference) the description of the larger property of which the subjects (now described for the first time as a separate unit) form part.

8.18   REPUGNANCIES AND AMBIGUITIES

Information in a particular description may be duplicated, for example, written boundaries and plan, or measurement, which carries with it the possibility of some conflict or discrepancy. Thus, property may be described as 'bounded on the north by an existing stone wall along which it extends for one hundred metres or thereby'; but it turns out on inspection that the wall is only eighty metres long. Or again, property may be described in a written description by reference to physical features 'all as delineated and coloured pink on the plan annexed'; but, when the written description is related to physical features on the ground, it may turn out that the area delineated and coloured pink on the plan is not the same area. In the ordinary way, discrepancies of this type will not invalidate the deed. Instead, rules have been developed in the reported cases for reconciling such discrepancies. These are discussed in J Rankine *The Law of Landownership in Scotland* (4th edn, 1909), Chapter 6; *Halliday's Conveyancing Law and Practice*, para 33.13; and Gordon *Scottish Land Law*, para 4.08.

Everything depends on the particular title and particular circumstances but some general rules emerge from the cases:

(1)   If, in the deed, there are written boundaries with stated measurements, and these conflict with a plan annexed, the plan will normally be treated as demonstrative and the written boundaries rule.

(2)   If, in the deed, there are written boundaries without measurements, and these conflict with a plan containing measurements, the plan will normally be preferred. But the deed may declare expressly that the plan is 'demonstrative only and not taxative', in which case the written boundaries normally prevail. See, for example, *Royal and Sun Alliance Insurance v Wyman-Gordon Ltd* 2001 SLT 1305.

(3)   The deed may contain written boundaries with stated measurements which cannot be reconciled on the ground, for example, 'bounded by a wall along which it extends 25m' and, on checking the wall, it is found to be 20m only. If the written description of the boundary feature is clear and specific, the measurement will be rejected, and the written description is taxative. For a case involving an ambiguous written description and a plan annexed, see *Suttie v Baird* 1992 SLT 133.

(4)   In the converse case where the written boundary is clearly stated and is greater than the stated measurement, the written boundary again will rule, and the smaller measurement will not be held to limit the grant, for example, 'bounded by a wall running from the road to the southeast corner of the tenement at 5 King Street a distance of 100m' which turns out to be 200m on the ground.

8.19   Methods of description: by reference

In this method of description, there is no specific identification of the property conveyed. Instead, to identify the subjects, a previous recorded deed containing either a general or a particular description is referred to. Therefore, with limited exceptions, this form of description is only suitable for a conveyance which transmits to the disponee an entire separate tenement which is already held on a separate title and is already separately described as such in a prior title. The principal types of description by reference (though not always so referred to in the textbooks) are (a) description by reference at common law and (b) statutory description by reference.

8.20 DESCRIPTION BY REFERENCE AT COMMON LAW

In older conveyances, it was normal to find the description of the property repeated in each successive conveyance of that property. But it is now accepted that, at common law, it never was necessary to repeat, word for word, the previous description of the property conveyed. Instead, the property could be identified (or described) in a conveyance simply by reference to some prior writ which itself contained an identifying description. For a description by reference at common law (as opposed to a statutory description by reference, see below), there are no settled rules except the over-riding principle that the words used must be sufficient to identify the property. This means that the writ referred to for description must be identifiable. In practice, however, this method of description is seldom relied on and, instead, the next method should always be employed.

8.21 STATUTORY DESCRIPTION BY REFERENCE

The relevant statutory provisions are the Conveyancing (Scotland) Act 1874, s 61; the Conveyancing (Scotland) Act 1924, s 8; and the 1924 Act, Schedule D. Under these sections and Schedule, the requirements for a valid statutory description by reference can be summarised thus:

(1) The deed referred to may be a deed of any type, provided it contains a particular description and has been recorded in the Register of Sasines. Note the requirement that the deed referred to in a statutory description by reference must itself contain a particular description. In the *Beneficial Bank* cases (see para 8.14), the requirements for a particular description are discussed and are, it is thought, a great deal more stringent than had previously been imagined. Apart from the case of an upper tenement flat, in *Beneficial Bank plc v McConnachie* 1996 SC 119 the court appear to lay down that a particular description must be complete and self-contained and in itself constitute a bounding title. Admittedly, that case was concerned with a particular description as required for a standard security. But the term 'particular description' has been used for more than a century in other contexts, especially in the context of the notarial instrument and notice of title, and there seems to be no reason to suppose that the requirement that a statutory description by reference should refer to a deed which itself contains a particular description would be any less rigorously construed.

There are almost certainly a considerable number of what were thought to be statutory descriptions by reference which refer back to a deed containing a fairly specific description but not one which satisfies the stringent rules which now apparently have to be applied in determining whether a description, in whatever form of deed, constitutes a particular description or not. Given, however, the very lenient rules applied to determine whether or not a description meets the requirements for a description by reference at common law, this will probably not create any serious problems in practice, at least where the prescriptive period has run on such a description.

(2) The description by reference must:

(a) state the County (for land originally held on burgage tenure, the burgh and county) in which the property is situated: Conveyancing (Scotland) Act 1874, s 61. This has not been altered by the introduction of regions and districts; nor by the further replacement of regional and district councils by the unitary councils under the Local Government etc (Scotland) Act 1994.

(b) specify the prior deed referred to for description in terms of the Conveyancing (Scotland) Act 1924, Schedule D. The basic requirements of such specification are not itemised in the Acts or Schedule; but normally a description by reference should specify:

- the type of deed referred to, for example, disposition.
- the parties, without designations.
- the date of the deed – but is this necessary?
- the Division of the General Register of Sasines.
- the date of recording.
- the Book and Folio, or, for recent deeds which are held on microfiche, the fiche and frame number – but only if otherwise there would be ambiguity. This is rare.

See the 1924 Act, s 8(3), and see especially notes 1 and 4 to Schedule D for further detail.

Nothing more is required; but it is normal to preface the statutory description by reference with a short identifying description, effectively a general description. This is usually the postal address. See the 1924 Act, Schedule D, note 2.

By the 1874 Act, s 61, such specification and reference to the prior recorded deed in any conveyance etc are equivalent to the full insertion in that conveyance of the particular description contained in the prior deed to which reference has been made.

8.22   Statutory description by reference: examination of title

These are the rules for a statutory description by reference and in practice they should always be strictly followed, when framing new descriptions. But when examining a title it will sometimes be found, that a description by reference in one of the existing deeds does not comply in some respect with the statutory rules. The question then is whether the deed is valid or not, and in deciding this question there are three main considerations to keep in view:

(1) The strict statutory essentials are a particular description in the prior deed, specification of the county, the Register, the date of recording and a reference to the prior deed in such terms as shall be sufficient to identify it on record. Omission of county, which is common, or of Register Division is probably fatal. But an error in the date of recording, for example, wrong day of month, may not be, if the deed can be clearly identified notwithstanding. The same applies to minor errors, for example, in the names of parties. An error in or omission of the date(s) of the deed (not the date of recording) is never fatal, except in very exceptional cases (for example, two deeds, same parties, same recording date, no Book and Folio number, and different dates).

(2) Even if the error is sufficiently serious to disqualify the description under statute, it may nevertheless be a valid description by reference at common law; such a description has always been competent, and in the past was not infrequently employed for 'eking out a generalised or incomplete description'. The statutory facilities do not exclude it, or render it invalid in any way; they merely provide a convenient alternative with statutory sanction. As stated above, the exact requirements for a valid common law description by reference are not defined. See *Murray's Trustees v Wood* (1887) 14 R 856, *Matheson v Gemmell* (1903) 5 F 448, and *Cattanach's Trustees v Jamieson* (1884) 11 R 972.

(3) Even if the description by reference has been so hopelessly bungled that it is invalid as such both under statute and at common law, it may still contain sufficient in itself to constitute a general description, in terms sufficient to identify the subjects. Here, very little will suffice. The normal short introductory words will certainly serve in most cases, for example, 'All and Whole that dwellinghouse and pertinents No. 10 Glebe Road, Dundee' standing alone are an adequate general description of a detached dwellinghouse. Again, if a deed contains only a bare reference, without identifying words, to a deed itself containing a description by reference, that is not a valid statutory description. But if the deed referred to contains anything which could amount to an identifying description, that will be valid at common law.

8.23 Methods of description: illustrative style

In practice, with a modern description, there is often a combination of two or even all three of the foregoing methods of description, for example:

'ALL and WHOLE the farm and lands of Nether Mains in the Parish of Strathmartine and County of Angus' (a general description) 'being the subjects delineated and enclosed within the red line on the plan annexed and signed as relative hereto' (a particular description) 'which subjects hereinbefore disponed form part and portion of all and whole the subjects in said Parish and County particularly described in and disponed by Disposition by John Smith in my favour dated seventh and recorded in the Division of the General Register of Sasines for the County of Angus twelfth both days of August, Nineteen hundred and Fifty-nine'.

If the prior deed so referred to itself contains a particular description which meets the requirements laid down in *Beneficial Bank plc v McConnachie* 1996 SC 119 (see para 8.16), that is a statutory description by reference. If not, it is still a description by reference at common law.

8.24   Methods of description: addenda

In any heritable conveyance, in practice, it is normal to find (appended at the end of the description of the property) certain additional incidentals, varying in number and nature according to the nature of the property conveyed. Sometimes, such addenda do materially add to the main description, for example, in the case of separate tenements in the form of incorporeal rights such as salmon fishings where, following on a description of a landed estate, you may find some such right as:

'Together with the salmon fishings in the River Isla, bounding the said subjects hereinbefore disponed on the north and west sides, but only up to the *medium filum* thereof *ex adverso* of the said subjects hereinbefore disponed'.

For reasons already examined (see para 8.3) if salmon fishings are to pass with a conveyance of land, they must be expressly described; accordingly, this addendum to the description forms a material addition to the subjects conveyed. So also new servitude rights and privileges, typically free ish and entry, or access, drainage and other like rights materially add to the description of the land. In other cases, standard and typical addenda in fact add little or nothing to the description of the subjects. Thus, in practice, you will often find in a conveyance three typical addenda, which are:

(1) 'The whole parts, privileges and pertinents of and effeiring to the said subjects hereinbefore disponed.' The exact implication of the term 'parts, privileges and pertinents' is nowhere clearly defined. The general principle has already been mentioned above, namely: that all implied rights inherent in the ownership of the land pass automatically on a conveyance of the same. In contrast, separate tenements must be separately identified and conveyed. It is, therefore, unnecessary, and adds nothing, to itemise or list implied rights in a charter or disposition. The term 'parts, privileges and pertinents' is a general phrase wide enough to embrace all the normal implied rights. Any right not ordinarily implied must be distinctly specified; otherwise, the disponee could not lay claim to it. Therefore,

the parts and pertinents clause normally adds nothing but is nonetheless normally included as an addendum. In rare cases, some weight may be placed on the presence of a 'parts and pertinents' clause; for this, see Chapter 12: Prescription.

(2) 'The whole fittings and fixtures in and upon the said subjects hereinbefore disponed.' Again it is doubtful whether this can ever add anything. If the fittings etc are heritable in law they pass *sub silentio*; if moveable, they pass under the Sale of Goods Act 1979 and not by virtue of the conveyance. As Lord Kinnear stated in *Jamieson v Welsh* (1900) 3 F 176 at 182, 'a sound conveyancer in framing a disposition . . . will not think it necessary to insert a futile conveyance of the moveables which would carry nothing'.

(3) 'My whole right, title and interest, present and future, in the subjects disponed.' This is probably implied, at least in onerous conveyances. But the express clause has the advantage of enabling the operation of accretion, should that prove necessary. See para 7.3. Occasionally, where the title of the grantor is in doubt and it is uncertain whether or not he owns the whole or certain parts of the subjects conveyed, this last addendum may be modified to the effect that the subjects, or a specified part thereof, are conveyed but only in so far as the disponer has right thereto. It seems settled that this does allow the grantee to found on that conveyance as a title habile to the running of the positive prescription. In addition, it will of course be necessary to protect the disponer by excepting the title or that part thereof which is in doubt, at least from absolute warrandice and possibly to restrict it to simple warrandice only *quoad* the parts in doubt. For a recent illustration of a comparable case, see *Landward Securities (Edinburgh) Ltd v Inhouse (Edinburgh) Ltd* 1996 GWD 16-962.

8.25 Methods of description: by exception

As a general rule, in practice, the most convenient method of describing any particular subjects is always used. Suppose that a person acquires a hectare of ground, area X, by disposition containing a detailed particular description; later she dispones one-half hectare, area Y, by disposition containing a particular description. She is left with the remaining half hectare, X–Y. The whole area X is already particularly described, and so is the lesser area Y, the remaining area X–Y is nowhere particularly described as such. Supposing she sells it; there are two alternatives:

(1) to describe the area X–Y using a particular description incorporating boundaries, measurements etc and plan; or

(2) much more simply by describing it as the whole area X by reference under exception of subjects Y, also by reference. The form is suggested in the Conveyancing (Scotland) Act 1924, Schedule D, note 3. This is one example of ground first conveyed as a separate entity where a new particular description is not necessary.

8.26   Descriptions in registration of title

Registration of title is map based. With limited exceptions, every title sheet (and therefore every land certificate) will include a plan which is an excerpt from the Ordnance Survey Map of an appropriate scale coloured to indicate the registered property. Therefore, every description, at the date of first registration, whatever its form has been in the past progress of titles, must at that point be translated onto the Ordnance Survey Map. Obviously this will to some extent affect conveyancing practice both before and after registration of each individual title.

For more detail on the use of Ordnance Survey plans in registration of title, see the *Registration of Title Practice Book*, paras 4.22–4.26.

8.27   PRE-REGISTRATION PRACTICE

The deed inducing first registration in the Land Register (normally the disposition implementing the first sale of the property after the relevant County became operational) need not itself contain a particular description, need not constitute a bounding title, and need not contain a plan. Further, if the deed does contain a plan, it need not be exact and to scale nor on the Ordnance Survey, nor on one of the Ordnance Survey recognised scales of 1:1,250, 1:2,500, 1:10,000. Nonetheless, at the time of application for registration, the applicant must provide the Keeper with sufficient information on the property to be registered to allow him to translate that information on to an Ordnance Survey Map. But the information required for this purpose can be given separately from the title deed itself.

8.28   Boundaries

Registration of title produces a new problem in that, on the 1:1,250 scale (the largest scale normally used), boundary features such as walls are represented by a single black line, and it is impossible to represent such features diagrammatically on the Ordnance Survey so as to show whether the boundary lies on one or other side thereof or on the mid-line. To get over this difficulty, the Land Certificate provides for the use of arrows to indicate where the boundary line lies in relation to particular boundary features. An arrow across the boundary line indicates the mid-line thereof. An arrow pointing at one or other face of the boundary feature indicates that the boundary line is on that side of the feature. See the note on the Land Certificate and also, the *Registration of Title Practice Book*, para 4.30. In practice, however, the Keeper seems to prefer in most cases to indicate the exact position of the boundary in the written description in the property section of the title sheet rather than to resort to arrows.

One standard exception to the rule that registration of title is map based is the tenement flat or part of a building separately conveyed. In this case, the postal address and a verbal description of the location of the flat in the tenement will suffice, provided that reference is made to a fixed compass point, for example, the southmost first-floor flat at Two High Street, Banff. See ROTPB, paras 5.63 and 6.67. In addition, where appropriate, the Keeper will plot the *solum* of the tenement and the front and back ground, if any, on an Ordnance Survey Map incorporated in the title sheet and Land Certificate.

If no visible feature exists on a particular boundary, the Keeper indicates this by a dotted line on the plan; and the plan will carry a legend, thus:

'The boundary shown by dotted lines has been plotted from the Deeds. Physical boundaries will be indicated after their delineation on the Ordnance Map'.

At a later date, when the boundary features, such as fences, have been constructed on the ground, and then plotted on the Ordnance Survey Map, they will then find their way on to the title sheet.

8.29   REGISTERED LAND

Here the title has already been registered in the Land Register. Therefore:

(1) the property will already appear on the Master Index Map in the Land Register and will have an individual title plan in its title sheet, all on the appropriate Ordnance Survey scale; and

(2) a title number will have been allocated to that property on the title sheet. Therefore, any subsequent transfer of the whole of the property can be simply and precisely effected by reference to the title number. The position is regulated by the Land Registration (Scotland) Act 1979, s 15(1) and the Land Registration (Scotland) Rules 1980, SI 1980/1413, Schedule B. An example which complies with the statutory guidelines is 'ALL and WHOLE the dwellinghouse known as One Graham Road, Dundee, being the subjects registered under Title Number ANG 1697'.

Nothing more is required. In particular, note:

(1) No reference is required to any prior recorded deed: 1979 Act, s 15(1).

(2) No addenda are necessary – they are all set out in the title sheet. See the 1979 Act, s 3(1)(a).

(3) No part and portion clause is necessary – the part and portion element is all dealt with by reference to the Index Map.

(4) There is no need to refer to burdens, as these are already set out at full length in the burdens section of the title sheet. See the 1979 Act, s 15(2).

See, in general, the *Registration of Title Practice Book*, para 8.47.

If, alternatively, part only of One Graham Road was to be disponed, a particular description would be required in the disposition in implement of that part sale, in order to identify separately the part of the property being given off for the first time as a separate heritable unit. The disposition may proceed substantially as at present, with a written description of the boundaries and a reference to a plan. But, bearing in mind that there will already be in existence in the title sheet an accurate Ordnance Survey plan, the particular description may be much more simply and effectively accomplished than at present, by reference to that Ordnance Survey Map.

In any event, whatever method is adopted to identify the separate part, it will have to be followed with a reference as follows:

'being part of the subjects registered under Title No. ANG 1697'.

See the Land Registration (Scotland) Rules 1980, SI 1980/1413, rule 25 and Schedule B.

Chapter 9

Reservations

9.1 General

Where a conveyance contains a reservation, this implies that a right which, under the description, would ordinarily be conveyed to the disponee, is by express reservation excluded from the conveyance, and retained by the disponer.

This is always competent, subject to the proviso that a right can only be thus reserved to the disponer if it is capable of separate registration as a separate heritable right on a separate heritable title, ie as a separate tenement.

A clause of reservation is, therefore, strictly speaking, part of the description since it defines some thing or right which is to be excluded from the major or larger thing conveyed. In practice, however, reservations tend to be treated in the same category as burdens, because by far the commonest reservation in a conveyance in practice is a reservation of minerals which usually contains elaborate burdens clauses regulating the working of the minerals for the protection of the surface owner.

As a matter of standard practice, reservations of minerals to the disponer, which in the past were very common in feu charters, define the thing reserved by reference to its physical substance; and do not attempt to describe the reserved minerals in the same way in which land is described. Accordingly, a typical clause of reservation of minerals qualifying a conveyance of land reads (J Burns *Conveyancing Practice* (4th edn, 1957), p 243):

> 'Reserving always to the superiors all stone, iron stone, shale, and all metals, mineral substances and things in or under the subjects hereby feued with full power by themselves or through lessees or others to work and carry away the same ...'

Compare I J S Talman (ed) *Halliday's Conveyancing Law and Practice in Scotland* (2nd edn, 2 Volumes, 1996–97), para 32.83.

Where a conveyance contains a clause of this kind, it qualifies the implied rule that a conveyance of land carries to the disponee everything *a coelo usque ad centrum* and excludes from the conveyance everything falling within the categories of things defined in the reservation; in this case, that would include stone, iron stone, shale and 'minerals'. In other typical clauses, the thing reserved is 'minerals' alone, without any specific narration of particular types of minerals; or again other types of mineral may be separately specified and identified by name.

Note that, while minerals are often severed from the surface by way of reservation in a charter or disposition, it is equally competent for the owner of surface and sub-strata to convey the minerals as a separate heritable right, or 'separate tenement'.

Once minerals have been severed from the surface, they will not pass in any future conveyance of the surface. But because ownership is deemed to be *a coelo usque ad centrum*, the granter must exclude the minerals from the dispositive clause if he is not to be liable to the grantee in warrandice. In practice this is usually done by making reference to the deed in which the minerals were reserved or conveyed.

9.2   Definition of minerals

Clearly, since the accepted method of defining minerals in a reservation or con-veyance thereof, is by reference to their physical substance and by using such terms as 'minerals' (or 'mines and minerals'; or 'quarries, mines and minerals' etc) rather than describing their geographical location, it becomes necessary to consider (for the purpose of defining the thing conveyed or reserved) what the terms mean.

Note, first, three specialities:

(1) Mines of gold and silver are *regalia minora*, and a conveyance of land does not by implication carry such minerals. By the Royal Mines Act 1424, they remain vested in the Crown; but the Crown is bound to make a grant of such minerals to the owner for the time being of the surface, on payment of 1/10th royalties in terms of the Mines and Metals Act 1592. See *Stair Memorial Encyclopaedia*, Volume 18, para 210.

(2) Coal and associated minerals. Under the Coal Industry Nationalisation Act 1946, all coal and certain associated minerals, wherever situated, and whether being worked or not, vested in and were managed by the National Coal Board. Under the Coal Industry Act 1987 the name was changed to the British Coal Corporation. Under the Coal Industry Act 1994, a new regulatory body was established known as the Coal Authority. The 1994 Act creates a new structure for the ownership and control of the industry, provides for the transfer from the Corporation of its assets and liabilities and for the dissolution of the Corporation, and sets out the regime for the licensing of coal-mining operations. More generally, it amends the law relating to coal-mining operations (including the legislation relating to liability for subsidence damage) mainly to take account of restructuring and makes clear that the ownership of coal-bed methane existing in its natural condition in strata is vested in the Crown.

A search can be obtained from the Coal Authority on any given area to determine whether or not, and if so to what extent, the area is or may have been affected by coal mining and therefore may be liable to subsidence. Details are contained in the Law Society of Scotland Guidance Notes 1999 reprinted in R Rennie *Minerals and the Law of Scotland* (2001), Appendix 2. These notes currently require updating and the secretary of the Law Society's Conveyancing Committee advises that the Coal

Authority's website (www.coal.gov.uk) should be consulted. See L J Lewin 'Coal Mining Guidance Notes 1999' 2003 JLSS May/70. Coal mining reports may be ordered online at www.coalminingreports.co.uk. When the search facility, which had operated successfully in England and Wales for a number of years, was first introduced to Scotland in 1995, controversy raged over the circumstances in which a report must be obtained. See 'Forum' 1995 JLSS 259 and 'Coal Mining Searches' 1995 JLSS 326. Professor Rennie, in his comprehensive work on minerals *Minerals and the Law of Scotland*, at para 8.3, takes the view 'that whether a coal mining search or report should be obtained will always be a matter of judgement having regard to the terms of any survey report and mineral reservation clause'. The difficulty, however, for practitioners is that the Law Society's Guidance Notes must be read in conjunction with a directory which lists 'Places where a coal mining search *is* required' and 'Places where a coal mining search *is not* required' (emphasis added). Although Professor Rennie may well be correct when he states that the wording is to protect the Coal Authority, the safest approach (albeit one which will involve additional cost to the client) is to obtain in a report where the directory states that it is required.

(3) Petroleum and natural gas are vested in the Crown under the Petroleum Act 1998. Provision is made in the 1998 Act for the issuing of licences to work onshore and offshore.

It follows that the term 'minerals' or 'mines and minerals' reserved in a conveyance cannot include the above substances. As to what else the terms include depends, to some extent, on surrounding circumstances. As Rankine states, the word 'mineral' 'is of flexible meaning, to be construed very generally if there be nothing in the deed or in the surrounding circumstances to control this construction': *The Law of Landownership in Scotland* (4th edn, 1909), p 171. See also Rennie, Chapter 2.

9.3 Rights of parties

Normally (but not necessarily) the rights and obligations of the surface owner and of the mineral owner or lessee who is to work the subjacent minerals under reservation, are set out in detail in the relevant title. These clauses normally cover three main points, namely:

(1) *The nature of the reserved right.* There are two possibilities, namely that the right reserved is:
   (a) an express right of property in the minerals, which carries with it by implication the right to work them and carry them away; or
   (b) a privilege or servitude of working the minerals.
   It is recommended that in every case a right of property should be reserved rather than a mere servitude or privilege of working, since under the latter right the person working the minerals may not enjoy the right to use the resulting shaft or gallery as a pipe-line for transporting minerals extracted from adjoining properties.

(2) *The right to work.* The method of working is normally laid down in the title.
(3) *The right of support.* A landowner is inherently entitled to support, both lateral and vertical, from adjoining proprietors of land abutting his boundaries and from the owner of subjacent minerals. The mere fact that minerals have passed into the ownership of another person does not of itself in any way limit or derogate from the surface owner's right. So far as mineral reservations are concerned, the right of support extends to and includes land in its natural state and (subject to possible qualifications) buildings erected on the land.

9.4 Support

The right of support of land is often expressed as being a natural right consequent on ownership. In English law the natural right ceases if land is built upon, support thereafter depending on whether or not a servitude (easement) right can be established. The rule in Scotland is sometimes said to be the same, but the balance of authority favours the view that the natural right of support continues even in respect of buildings. See *Stair Memorial Encyclopaedia*, Volume 18, para 260.

The term 'right of support' is, perhaps, misleading. There is no positive obligation on the mineral owner to provide support. Rather he is bound to avoid acts which interfere with the existing support, however adequate or inadequate that support might be. Further, the mineral owner is not under any duty to refrain from excavations altogether, leaving the whole sub-strata in the original state; if this were so, then severance of minerals from the surface would be of no practical importance. Instead, his duty is to refrain from carrying on his mineral operations in such a way that the surface is (or will probably be) damaged thereby. Admittedly, this may result in an absolute bar on mineral working in certain circumstances, for example where the top and sub-soil is of such a kind and the mineral operations are of such a kind, that, taken together, the surface is bound to come down. But this will be a question of facts and circumstances to be considered in each individual case. As a result, if the surface owner has reason to believe that the operations of the mineral owner will inevitably bring down the surface, he has the right, by interdict, to prevent the mineral owner from carrying out any such operations. In any other case, his remedy is damages for injury caused, each recurrent subsidence creating a fresh ground of action.

This is only a very brief summary of some of the complex rules which control the relationship between surface and mineral owners. For a detailed account, see R Rennie *Minerals and the Law of Scotland*, Chapter 4. All or any of these general rules may be expressly varied in terms of the respective titles and in practically all cases there is some degree of variation. For typical clauses, see J Burns *Conveyancing Practice*, pp 243–244 and *Halliday's Conveyancing Law and Practice*, para 32.83. Further, in certain special cases, the ordinary rules have been varied by statute, for example in terms of the Coal Mining Subsidence Act 1991, s 2, as modified by the Coal Industry Act 1994, s 43, the 'responsible person' must execute remedial works (or pay for the cost thereof) in respect of any damage caused to land or buildings due to the lawful working of coal. The 'responsible person' will either be the holder of a licence from the Coal Authority to work the coal, or, if no licence has been granted, the Authority itself.

In *British Coal Corporation v Netherlee Trust Trustees* 1995 SLT 1038 a question arose as to the meaning of subsidence. In the ordinary way, subsidence implies that a vacant space left behind in the empty gallery or shaft from which coal has been extracted simply implodes on itself and so brings down the surface. In this case, however, the empty shaft had been filled in and the argument was that the Corporation (as it then was) was not liable for damage caused by a shifting of the material used for in-filling. The argument was rejected and the Corporation was held liable to carry out remedial works.

In cases where the right is not available at common law or under the titles, a mineral owner may apply to the Court for power to bring down the surface under the Mines (Working Facilities and Support) Act 1966, but subject in all such cases to payment of compensation. The Coal Authority likewise enjoys comparable powers under the Coal Industry Act 1994, and that also applies to any licensed operator under s 38 of that Act.

Chapter 10

Other Clauses

10.1 General

In a disposition, the narrative clause and the dispositive clause, including the description and any reservations, are followed by a number of other clauses. These are the burdens clause, the subordinate clauses, the certificate for stamp duty or stamp duty land tax, and the testing clause.

10.2 Burdens clause

The burdens clause sets forth the real burdens affecting the property. Existing burdens are incorporated by referring to the deed in which they were created. New burdens must be set out in full. If, as is the case occasionally, the property is not subject to burdens then the clause can be omitted. Further, once the subjects have been registered in the Land Register, the burdens need not be listed: see the Land Registration (Scotland) Act 1979, s 15(2). The reference to the Title Sheet number suffices. Burdens are dealt with at length in Chapters 15, 17 and 18.

10.3 Subordinate clauses

In the original form of disposition all these clauses were set out at great length, but now they are considerably abbreviated. The abbreviated forms are statutory, first introduced by the Lands Transference Act 1847 and re-enacted in the Titles to Land Consolidation (Scotland) Act 1868, ss 5, 8 and Schedule B1. Each short clause authorised in s 5 receives a lengthy and detailed interpretation in s 8.

10.4 ENTRY

Schedule B1 to the Titles to Land Consolidation (Scotland) Act 1868 sets out the form of the entry clause. A typical modern example based on this is 'With entry on 28 November 2003'. This clause determines the date at which the grantee is entitled to possession (which may either be civil possession or, more usually, natural posses-sion). See the Conveyancing (Scotland) Act 1874, s 28 for implied dates, if this clause is omitted. If the grantee himself intends to occupy the subjects it is essential to stipulate in the missives for 'entry and actual occupation (or vacant possession)'. This is because the existence of a lease may not give rise to a claim in warrandice (see below), and, if not, the grantee would be left without a remedy against the grantor.

10.5   ASSIGNATION OF WRITS

Under the Sasine system, recording of the appropriate writ is the final, mandatory step in the acquisition of the real right of ownership. By recording the appropriate title, the disponee thereunder establishes his real right if, but only if, the recorded title is itself valid and proceeds upon a valid prior progress of titles. The mere fact that A holds land on a recorded title is not, *per se*, conclusive evidence of his right; some enquiry into (a) the antecedents of that recorded title and/or (b) possession for the prescriptive period, is always necessary. Therefore, every disponee, whether under a feu charter or under a disposition, normally has an interest in the prior titles in order to maintain his own right. If these titles are not delivered to him (as they may not be), then he should have the right to call for production or exhibition of the prior titles when required; but, since 1970, this right has become of less importance because, under the Conveyancing and Feudal Reform (Scotland) Act 1970, s 45, an extract of a deed from the Register of Sasines must be accepted for all purposes as sufficient evidence of the contents of the original. In other words, a Sasine extract is now equivalent to the principal writ; and so the want of missing principal deeds can be made good by producing Sasine extracts.

Schedule B1 to the Titles to Land Consolidation (Scotland) Act 1868 states: 'And I assign the writs and have delivered the same according to Inventory'.

For deeds executed after 4 April 1979 – the date of the passing of the Land Registration (Scotland) Act 1979 – the assignation of writs clause need no longer be included in a disposition and, if omitted, as invariably it is, the disposition implies:

(1) an assignation to the disponee of all prior title deeds and searches, to the effect of maintaining and defending him in the subjects; and
(2) that the disponer is obliged for that purpose to lend to the disponee any title deeds and searches relating in part to the subjects disponed and which he still holds on all necessary occasions at the disponee's expense. See the 1979 Act, s 16(1)(a).

Where the subjects are registered in the Land Register, the assignation of the writs applies only to the Land Certificate and Charge Certificate (if there is one), unless indemnity has been excluded by the Keeper. See the 1979 Act, s 3(5).

10.6 ASSIGNATION OF RENTS

Schedule B1 to the Titles to Land Consolidation (Scotland) Act 1868 reads: 'And I assign the rents'. The disponee may himself enter into natural possession of the subjects conveyed to him and usually does so. Alternatively, having acquired the right of property under the disposition, he may part with natural possession of the property for a term of years to a tenant under a temporary arrangement known as a lease, in virtue of which, *inter alia*, the proprietor becomes entitled to an annual rent from the tenant. If the lease is to be valid, the proprietor as landlord must himself be registered as owner. If the subjects are sold and disponed to a disponee, that does not automatically bring the lease to an end; but the disponee becomes entitled to the rents in place of the disponer. It is the person registered for the time being as owner who is entitled to rent; and rents follow registration. Accordingly, the assignation of rents clause in a conveyance is not necessary to confer a title on the disponee to collect rents; but it does serve to determine the basis of apportionment of the rent payable by the tenant, as between disponer and disponee with reference to the date of entry.

In deeds executed after 4 April 1979, the assignation of rents clause need no longer be included and, if omitted, the disposition itself implies an assignation to the disponee of the rent payable in respect of the subjects, if any. See the Land Registration (Scotland) Act 1979, s 16(3)(a).

10.7 OBLIGATION OF RELIEF

Schedule B1 to the Titles to Land Consolidation (Scotland) Act 1868 in its post feudal form reads: 'And I bind myself to free and relieve the said disponee and his foresaids of all public burdens'. By s 8 of the 1868 Act, this imports an obligation to relieve of all public, parochial and local burdens due from or on account of the lands conveyed, prior to the date of entry. In other words, as between grantor and grantee all outgoings are apportioned at entry.

In deeds executed after 4 April 1979, the clause of obligation of relief is implied in dispositions by virtue of the Land Registration (Scotland) Act 1979, s 16(3)(b).

10.8 WARRANDICE

In any transaction for sale and purchase of heritage, there are three stages; first, completion of the contract; second, delivery of the conveyance to the purchaser against payment of the price when the purchaser takes actual possession; and third, registration of the conveyance. The rights and obligations of the parties differ at stages one and two. On completion of the contract, the seller's obligations are briefly to give a good title, possession, and a clear search. If at that stage the purchaser finds that the seller cannot fulfil any of these obligations, his remedy is rescission of the contract and an action of damages for breach thereof. But once the conveyance has been delivered and the transaction completed, the seller's obligation under that conveyance, in the absence of special provisions in the missives, is warrandice against eviction; it is then normally too late for rescission. If, after completion, the purchaser then discovers some defect in the title or some impingement on his possession, he cannot normally then reduce the contract, and return the property to the seller. His only action is for damages *quanti minoris*, and it is on the seller's warrandice that this action is based. This is dealt with again in more detail in Chapter 28.

In its absolute form, the warrandice obligation represents a personal guarantee by the disponer that he will indemnify the disponee against any loss or damage which the disponee may suffer owing to a diminution in the value of his real right arising out of:

(1) complete eviction of the disponee from the whole subjects, or partial eviction from part, owing to a defect in the title; or

(2) a real burden, or other adverse real right, affecting the subjects, actually made effective against the disponee, which he was unaware of at date of delivery of the disposition. This is often referred to as 'partial eviction'. In practice, however, the purchaser's solicitor will have examined the title deeds prior to delivery and have noted the relevant burdens.

It is important to be clear on the fairly narrow scope of the warrandice obligation in case (1), ie where the title is defective. Eviction normally means that the title has been successfully challenged by a third party in court, in other words judicial eviction. So in *Palmer v Beck* 1993 SLT 485 a purchaser, having taken delivery of a disposition with the usual warrandice clause, then sought to claim damages from the seller on the grounds of alleged misrepresentation, basing her claim on the warrandice obligation in the disposition in her favour. The claim was rejected on the grounds that there had been no actual eviction or even a threat thereof although there may have been an undeniable absence of title. Lord Kirkwood took the view that, if there had been a claim under warrandice, damages would have been limited to indemnity only and not *solatium* as well. See further Professor Rennie 'Warrandice: A Guarantee with Small Print' at (1993) 5 Greens PLB 6.

Similarly, in *Clark v Lindale Homes Ltd* 1994 SLT 1053, the pursuer purchased a flat and occupied it for two years. She then resold it. The purchaser declined to take the title. The defect was eventually cured, but only after long delay. Consistent with previous authority, the court held that indemnity under absolute warrandice extended only to eviction or threatened eviction and that nothing less than a challenge from a competing title holder would be deemed to be eviction for this purpose. Her claim therefore failed.

In the Land Register, the requirement for eviction will be satisfied by rectification of the Register by the Keeper: see *Stair Memorial Encyclopaedia*, Volume 18, para 707. But, in the view of Sheriff Principal Bowen in *Mutch v Mavisbank Properties Ltd* 2002 SLT (Sh Ct) 91 at 94, rectification is not necessarily required if there are 'clear averments' setting out the challenge to the title.

10.9 Nature of obligation

Warrandice is necessarily and, of its nature, a personal guarantee only; and of course, as with any personal obligation, the value of the indemnity to the purchaser depends entirely on the financial stability of the seller and his ability to pay. Thus warrandice by a disponer who later has become bankrupt, although it infers an obligation to indemnify the purchaser to the extent of his loss, may well in fact be worthless. That, however, is a risk which the purchaser must take. He cannot ask for more than the seller's warrandice, and he cannot insist that the obligation be fortified either by security or by a third party's guarantee, except by express provision in the contract of sale and purchase, which is rare.

The warrandice obligation does not indemnify against loss or damage which the grantee may suffer from any cause, other than actual or constructive eviction by an adverse real right.

Servitudes will found a claim, if patrimonial loss can be demonstrated. Leases, on the other hand, may not found a claim. See the questionable decision of *Lothian and Border Farmers Ltd v McCutcheon* 1952 SLT 450, and compare I J S Talman (ed) *Halliday's Conveyancing Law and Practice* (2nd edn, 2 volumes, 1996–97), para 30.82 and Professor Reid 'Good and Marketable Title' 1988 JLSS 162 at 164.

In every case, the disponer's obligation is to indemnify. He is not obliged to take any steps to put the title right, nor can the disponee claim *restitutio in integrum*. This is most strongly emphasised in *Welsh v Russell* (1894) 21 R 769. In that case, after completion of the purchase of a house and garden, a right of way was later established across the garden by an adjoining owner. Founding on warrandice, the disponee sued for the present value of the whole subjects, offering to reconvey them as they stood to the seller; in other words, he sought restitution, not indemnity. It was held that the purchaser's right under warrandice was limited to indemnification for the loss sustained.

10.10 Extent of claim

Warrandice is indemnity and the quantum of any claim must therefore be calculated on the basis of the actual pecuniary loss suffered by the purchaser. In cases of total eviction, it is settled that, if the value at the time of eviction is greater than the price paid, then warrandice covers the excess and is not limited to the original price. Thus, if A buys land for £10,000 and builds to the value of £100,000 on it, A can (if evicted) claim £110,000, not merely the original £10,000. The converse case, where the value at eviction is less than the original price, is not settled; but presumably, only that value could be recovered. In cases of partial eviction, the quantum of the claim is the amount in money terms by which the adverse right diminishes the value of the property. If the adverse right is, for example, a standard security for an exact amount, no question arises; the sum in the standard security is the amount claimed. In other circumstances, it is a question of valuation.

10.11   Degrees of warrandice

The extent or degree of warrandice to be undertaken by the grantor of a deed varies according to circumstances. In every heritable conveyance, warrandice is almost invariably expressed. But, if no warrandice is expressed, then in every case some degree of warrandice will be implied. To omit the clause of warrandice altogether does not therefore mean that the grantor gives no warrandice; in the result, a higher degree of warrandice may be implied against him than that which he would have undertaken or been obliged to undertake had the clause been expressed in the deed. The nature of the transaction and the capacity of the grantor will normally determine what degree of warrandice is appropriate in any particular case. But, of course, it is always open to the parties to agree to specialties to meet special circumstances. This must then be given effect to accurately in the disposition, otherwise the only way of correcting matters may be a rectification action (on which, see para 29.17) and such an action may not succeed: see *Baird v Drumpellier & Mount Vernon Estates Ltd* 2000 SC 103.

10.12   *Absolute warrandice*

This is the highest degree of warrandice and indemnifies against loss arising from any defect in the title or any adverse right, not attributable to the act or neglect of the grantee. Absolute warrandice is implied in onerous transactions, for example, sale for adequate price.

10.13   *Warrandice from fact and deed*

Here the grantor is bound to indemnify the grantee against loss arising from any act or deed, past, present or future of the grantor himself. He is not liable for any defects not personally attributable to him. This degree is implied where the consideration is not a full one; and probably also where the grantor acts in a representative capacity only. Certainly, in the last case, this is the degree of warrandice always expressed by trustees, thus – 'I as trustee foresaid grant warrandice from my own facts and deeds only'. It would be unfair if a trustee were personally liable to indemnify for all defects, because he has no patrimonial or beneficial interest in the price; but, in onerous transactions, the trust estate is also taken bound in absolute warrandice.

10.14   *Simple warrandice*

Here the grantor is liable only for future voluntary deeds adverse to the grantee's right. It carries no indemnity against past acts of the grantor, nor against future acts in implement of a prior binding obligation. It is implied in all gratuitous transactions; if expressed, the term used is 'I grant simple warrandice' or 'I grant warrandice, but only against all voluntary acts and deeds hereinafter to be executed or done by me', and this, or fact and deed warrandice, is normally expressed in any gratuitous deed.

10.15 Combined degrees

It is quite common for two separate degrees of warrandice to be combined expressly in a deed. The normal clause in an onerous deed by a trustee exemplifies: 'And I as trustee foresaid grant warrandice from my own facts and deeds only and I bind the trust estate under my charge in absolute warrandice'.

10.16 Consenters

Pure consent alone will not normally imply warrandice in any degree against the consenter; but, where the consenter is conjoined in the operative clause, some warrandice will probably be inferred, at least simple warrandice, possibly more according to the nature of the consent; consenter's warrandice should always be express. Usually fact and deed will serve, sometimes absolute is required. It depends on the circumstances in which consent is required.

10.17 The statutory clause

This is governed by the Titles to Land Consolidation (Scotland) Act 1868, s 5 and Schedule B1. The clause in the Schedule reads 'I grant warrandice'. The interpretation of that clause in s 8 implies '... unless especially qualified ... absolute warrandice as regards the lands and writs and evidents, and warrandice from fact and deed as regards the rents ...'. This means:

(1) absolute warrandice as to title, discussed above;

(2) the same for the title deeds. In other words, the grantor warrants that the whole progress of titles is good and sufficient to maintain the grantee in possession in terms of the dispositive clause of his conveyance. It is not necessarily an absolute warranty that each individual writ is wholly valid according to its terms. This distinction is drawn in *Brownlie v Miller* (1880) 7 R (HL) 66 (and see (1880) 5 R 1076);

(3) the rents are warranted from fact and deed only. The rents are assigned, as noted above. In any assignation of a debt the degree of warrandice implied is fact and deed only and *debitum subesse* – that the debt subsists and is owing. There is no guarantee that the debtor is solvent or that he will pay; if that were inferred, the grantor would be in the position of guarantor to all the tenants. In practice, it means that the leases are valid and are effectually assigned, for what they are worth. *Debitum subesse* is implied, see A Menzies *Lectures on Conveyancing* (Sturrock's edition, 1900), p 179. See also *Stair Memorial Encyclopaedia*, Volume 18, para 717.

10.18 Implied warrandice

If no warrandice is expressed, it will be implied in one degree or another, according to the nature of the transaction and capacity. The converse also holds, namely: that where warrandice is express, it will entirely supersede whatever obligation would otherwise have been implied by law. Further, any express warrandice is strictly interpreted according to its terms. This may have unfortunate results. Thus, the use of the statutory clause 'I grant warrandice' is not appropriate in a gratuitous conveyance; fact and deed is the most that should be given, more often simple warrandice only; but if 'I grant warrandice' is so used, it will receive full effect. On the other hand, where fact and deed warrandice only is given in an onerous disposition, that is all that the grantee can later found on, although, had no warrandice been expressed, then absolute warrandice would have been implied.

10.19   Qualifications of warrandice

In an onerous conveyance, the statutory clause is almost always used but it may require qualification. One example – trustees – has already been given; a similar qualification is appropriate in any conveyance granted by someone who is not the true owner.

Where there are adverse rights subsisting at the date of conveyance of which the purchaser is aware and which he is to accept (for example, servitudes, leases, securities etc), all such rights must be excepted from warrandice to prevent any possibility of future claims against the grantor.

As already noted, where property is sold subject to a lease, it is usual and possibly necessary, in order to protect the seller, to except leases from warrandice, so limiting the seller's liability by excluding any possible claim on that ground. But that is the only effect of such a qualification. In *Kildrummy (Jersey) Ltd v Inland Revenue Commissioners* 1992 SLT 787, as part of a tax-minimisation exercise, title to a heritable property was taken in name of a Jersey company, subject to a lease. For technical reasons, the lease was held to be void. In the disposition in favour of the company, however, the lease was excepted from warrandice under a general exclusion of all current leases. The company then argued that, having accepted a disposition with that exclusion, it had effectively adopted the lease and thus had validated it. The argument was rejected on the footing that, since the lease was a nullity *ab initio*, it could not be so validated; and in any event the warrandice clause in the disposition was, according to its own terms, merely an obligation of relief and nothing more.

10.20   Transmission

It is settled that the assignation of writs clause in a conveyance passes on the benefit of existing warrandice obligations to the grantee under a conveyance. Probably, this passed by implication on a disposition alone without assignation of writs before the Land Registration (Scotland) Act 1979; but this is now implied by the 1979 Act, s 16(1).

This in turn, however, creates a trap for the unwary. Suppose that A dispones heritable property to B with absolute warrandice. B then dispones the same property to

C with absolute warrandice. Having taken delivery of the disposition B to C, suppose that C is then physically evicted and claims damages against B under the warrandice obligation in the disposition by B to C. The claim would almost certainly succeed. That same defect in title, however, was warranted by A in the warrandice obligation in the disposition A to B. On the face of it, B has in turn a claim for damages against A under that warrandice obligation. In theory, this is undoubtedly correct. But the disposition by B to C impliedly assigned to C the benefit of the warrandice obligation in the disposition by A to B. B was therefore divested of the benefit of that obligation by A in his favour. Accordingly, if B is to claim effectively against A, he requires a retrocession or a reassignation in his own favour by C of the transmitted warrandice obligation in the disposition A to B. In *Cobham v Minter* 1986 SLT 336 a situation along these lines occurred. Using the same scenario, C, the ultimate disponee, after recording his disposition, was evicted. He claimed damages against B under the warrandice obligation in the disposition B to C and recovered damages from B. B in turn sought to recover damages from A, the original disponer under the warrandice obligation in the disposition A to B. However, that warrandice obligation had passed to C under the implied assignation of writs clause in the disposition B to C and B had not obtained a retrocession or reassignation before A was conjoined as a third party when B sought relief against A in the claim by C against B. C's claim was settled. B pursued his claim against the third party, A, but, because B had not obtained a reassignation before A was conjoined as a third party, his claim was rejected and he recovered nothing from A. No doubt on strictly technical grounds that decision was correct. However, Lord Kincraig stated his view that, since B himself had not actually been evicted, he had no grounds of claim against A. It was conceded that there was no authority on this point. If that view is correct, however, it produces a very inequitable result. Professor Reid, in his article on warrandice in D J Cusine (ed) *A Scots Conveyancing Miscellany: Essays in Honour of Professor J M Halliday* (1987), p 152 at pp 169–170, rightly considers this dictum by Lord Kincraig to be unsound. 'It is manifestly unjust that B should be unable to recover from A'. See also *Stair Memorial Encyclopaedia,* Volume 18, para 712.

10.21   CERTIFICATE OF STAMP DUTY OR STAMP DUTY LAND TAX

See Chapter 5.

10.22   CONSENT TO REGISTRATION FOR EXECUTION

A deed may be registered for publication, for preservation, or for execution; and the same deed may be registered for all three purposes. Registration for publication means registration in the Register of Sasines. Registration for preservation or for execution means registration in the court books, either the Books of Council and Session in Edinburgh or the books of the local sheriff court.

Each type of registration has a different purpose. Registration for publication is the means of obtaining a real right in land. A copy of the deed (now a microcopy) is held by the Register of Sasines and the original is returned.

By contrast, no rights are conferred on the grantee by registration for preservation, the sole purpose of which is the physical preservation of the deed, which is retained in the court books. Registration for preservation is routinely used for deeds such as wills and powers of attorney; but it is not normally used for deeds which have already been registered in the Register of Sasines because, even if Sasine deeds are lost, an extract copy from the Register is as good as the original: see the Conveyancing and Feudal Reform (Scotland) Act 1970, s 45.

Finally, registration for execution enables the creditor in a deed to use the expedited procedure of summary diligence against the debtor. The debtor's consent is required for registration for execution, and, if forthcoming, a short clause of consent is included in the deed, normally at the end. A clause of consent is appropriate only for deeds which impose a pecuniary obligation on one of the parties, and in normal conveyancing practice they are found mainly in standard securities and in leases.

10.23   TRUST CLAUSES

Following the Outer House decision in *Sharp v Thomson* 1994 SLT 1068, Professor Rennie recommended, in an article entitled 'Dead on Delivery' 1994 SLT (News) 183, that solicitors should insert a trust clause in dispositions, to protect the purchaser in the event of the seller becoming insolvent in the gap period prior to registration. Subsequently, Dr Steven and Mr Wortley in 'The Perils of a Trusting Disposition' 1996 SLT (News) 365 suggested that there could be some technical difficulties with the operation of such a clause and that careful consideration should be exercised before adopting Professor Rennie's suggestion. In a more recent article, 'In Defence of the Trusting Conveyancer' 2002 SLT (News) 231, Mr Chalmers disagrees with the analysis of Dr Steven and Mr Wortley, but very fairly concedes that the efficacy of the trust clause cannot be guaranteed. It is not intended to rehearse the various arguments here, but it should perhaps be noted that the trust clause would not offer any protection against insolvency before delivery. Given that the House of Lords decision in *Sharp* (see para 4.4) means that a purchaser cannot be affected by a receiver appointed after delivery and that the risk from other insolvency processes is remote, as Professors Reid and Gretton state in *Conveyancing 2002* (2003), p 96, the use of the trust clause does not seem justified.

10.24   TESTING CLAUSE

See Chapter 2.

Chapter 11

Registration

11.1 The requirements for registration

The mere fact that a disposition is prepared containing all the requisite clauses does not, of itself, operate to confer any right on the disponee and imposes no obligations on the grantor thereof. Before the disponee can perfect his real right and become owner, a number of further steps are necessary. The further elements involve:

(1) authentication;
(2) delivery;
(3) stamp duty land tax and VAT; and
(4) registration.

11.2 AUTHENTICATION

The disposition must be properly executed. See Chapter 2 and relevant Reading List references.

11.3 DELIVERY

The disposition must be delivered. The mere execution of the deed by the grantor does not, of itself, immediately create binding rights and obligations. So long as the deed remains in the possession of the grantor or under his control, it is inoperative; to make it operative, it must be delivered to the disponee who must accept delivery. See Chapter 4 and relevant Reading List references.

11.4 STAMP DUTY LAND TAX AND VAT

Where appropriate, stamp duty land tax must be paid on the disposition. See Chapter 5 and relevant Reading List references.

11.5 REGISTRATION

The disposition must be registered. This is the focus of this chapter. Mere delivery of a disposition, although essential to the disponee's right, does not of itself operate to divest the disponer nor to perfect the disponee's real right in the subjects. Instead, delivery of the disposition merely confers upon the disponee a personal right to complete title, which is of itself a mandate for registration and assignable as such by disposition (and pre-1970 also by special assignation). To convert his personal right into a real right, good against the world, the disponee must register the disposition. See *Ceres School Board v McFarlane* (1895) 23 R 279, for an illustration of the general principle 'that a singular successor takes the lands free from the personal obligations of his predecessor and unaffected by burdens not appearing on the Records', and the cases of *Sharp v Thomson* 1997 SC (HL) 66 and *Burnett's Trustee v Grainger* 2002 SLT 699 discussed in Chapter 4.

Two separate registers for land are currently in operation: the Register of Sasines and the Land Register. As will be seen, the latter is slowly superseding the former. They are dealt with in turn.

11.6   **The Register of Sasines**

When the Register of Sasines was first set up, in 1617, feu charters and dispositions could not be directly recorded. A special deed, known as an instrument of sasine, which summarised the content of the charter or disposition, had to be drawn up and recorded, rather than the charter or disposition itself. But direct recording has been possible since 1858, and instruments of sasine are no longer used. Before a writ can be recorded, it must satisfy certain requirements: see *Macdonald v Keeper of the General Register of Sasines* 1914 SC 854. Briefly, these are:

(1) that the writ is self-proving (see Chapter 2);
(2) that stamp duty land tax has been paid upon it, if appropiate (see Chapter 5);
(3) that it is appropriate to the Register of Sasines, ie that it deals with a real right in land;
(4) that it contains an identifying description. See generally *Macdonald*, above;
(5) that it carries the statutory warrant of registration;
(6) that the deed is presented along with the relevant application form CPB2, and the recording dues, for recording in the Sasine Register.

On grounds of public policy the Keeper of the Register also feels constrained to refuse to record deeds of a frivolous or vexatious nature. Thus conveyances of souvenir plots are not accepted for recording; and in recent years a number of dispositions *a non domino* presented for registration in competition with the true owners have been refused registration. The Keeper's stance against recording souvenir plots in Sasines is similar to the statutory position in s 4(2)(c) of the Land Registration (Scotland) Act 1979 in relation to the Land Register. See the *Registration of Title Practice Book*, para 6.4.

Refusal to record or register an *a non domino* disposition is certainly consistent with the Keeper's discretion referred to in *Macdonald* above. In that case, the pursuer, who sought to record a deed which did not contain a sufficient description, argued that the Keeper had no duty, and therefore no right, to question the sufficiency of the description and that he had no discretionary power in the matter but was bound, without question, to record the deed as presented to him. Exactly the same argument can be put forward in the case of the *a non domino* disposition. However, that view was roundly rejected by the court. The Lord President stated in unqualified terms that the court were wholly unable to accede to that view. The Keeper was a highly placed official in charge of the Register, and was bound, in the faithful discharge of his statutory duty, to exercise due care and control over the Register in order to secure its efficiency for the purpose for which it was created.

11.7 WARRANTS OF REGISTRATION

The Titles to Land (Scotland) Act 1858, when abolishing the instrument of sasine, also introduced as a new requirement that the conveyance when presented for registration should carry a warrant of registration endorsed thereon, authorising the Keeper to record the writ. In terms of the 1858 Act, the warrant must identify the person becoming owner and must be signed by him or his authorised agent.

When, in 1868, all land registers were centralised in Edinburgh, a further statutory requirement was added to the warrant of registration, in that from 1868 onwards the warrant must also direct the division of the Register in which the writ is to be recorded. Here is a typical form of warrant:

'Register on behalf of the within-named Andrew Baillie in the Register of the County of Dumfries.
Edwards and Fraser
W.S., Edinburgh,
Agents'.

The detailed statutory requirements are set out in paras 13.7–13.9 of the sixth edition of this book, and in an article by Gretton and Wortley 'Warrants of Registration: Who Signs?' at 1997 JLSS 110. As of 28 November 2004, it will no longer be necessary for a deed to have a warrant of registration before it can be recorded: see the Abolition of Feudal Tenure etc (Scotland) Act 2000, s 5(1).

11.8 PRESENTATION FOR REGISTRATION

Following on delivery of the disposition and payment, where appropriate, of stamp duty land tax, and the signing of the warrant of registration, the deed is ready to be presented for registration. The deed is delivered, by hand or by post, to the Register of Sasines at Meadowbank House in Edinburgh. It must be accompanied by the appropriate fee. Prepayment of recording and registration dues in the Register of Sasines or Land Register, effective from 1 April 1996, was introduced by the Land Register (Scotland) Act 1995: see 'Prepayment of Fees in the Land Register and Sasine Register' 1995 JLSS 482.

On presentation, brief details of the deed are entered in the Presentment Book, and the date of this entry there is the date of registration. The Presentment Book has been computerised since 1 April 1992, and all applications for registration must now be accompanied by a special application form (form CPB2) which is machine-readable.

A number of further registration processes then follow. First, the deed is minuted, ie a short summary of its terms is prepared for the Minute Book. A copy of the minute is entered on the search sheet for the property in question. Next, a microcopy is made of the deed. (Previously this was a photocopy, and earlier still a copy written out by hand.) Finally, the deed is stamped with the Keeper's certificate showing that it has been recorded in the Register of Sasines and is then returned to the ingiver. The whole registration process takes several weeks.

The certificate of registration endorsed by the Keeper on the deed merely certifies that the deed has been recorded on a given date, but goes no further than that. In particular, the certificate does not guarantee the validity or sufficiency of the deed. At the date of recording, the disponee may or may not be in possession, and he may or may not be the person properly entitled to the land, in that the deed may or may not be valid; but, unless the deed is grossly inept, the Keeper will accept and record it, although he may raise matters of substance or of detail with the ingiver, as a matter of Register House practice. As noted, the Keeper does have discretion to refuse to accept a writ in special circumstances: see para 11.6 above.

11.9   Disadvantages of the Register of Sasines

The Register of Sasines has proved remarkably efficient and effective over a period of more than 300 years. In modern times, however, it was seen as suffering from a number of disadvantages, which, viewed cumulatively, were deemed sufficient to justify the introduction of registration of title.

The perceived disadvantages of the Register of Sasines were, and are, the following.

11.10   IDENTIFICATION

Until, perhaps, 100 years ago, it was commonplace to describe properties, particularly rural properties, simply by their name alone, without any attempt to define area or boundaries on a plan. Detailed particular descriptions, usually supported by plans, are now the accepted norm for 'new' properties, but modernisation or redrafting of an inadequate description in an existing title is relatively unusual. Even the modern particular description is very often inadequate and does not precisely define and delimit the subject matter of the grant. Further, deed plans are not always accurate;

and Register House has never been in a position to correlate plans of adjoining properties in order to make sure that boundaries coincide.

One remedy would be to improve the standard of conveyancing and, in particular, to make it obligatory, in any description of old or new properties, to refer to a plan prepared by a person properly qualified. Normally, a simple two-dimensional plan on one sheet would suffice. For more complex subjects, plans on several sheets, possibly in three dimensions, or showing different elevations, might be required, for example for mineral strata, parts of buildings etc.

Accurate mapping of individual properties on Ordnance Survey maps, and correlation of individual properties and their boundaries *inter se* on index or master plans, is one of the cardinal features of any system of registration of title; and the introduction of registration of title will cure this weakness in the existing system.

The same criticism applies to the identification of ancillary rights, for example servitudes, fishings, the right to enforce burdens etc. Here, precision, in the nature of things, is much more difficult to attain, and registration of title is not such a certain solution.

11.11 TITLE CONDITIONS

Another criticism of the existing system is that the burdens and conditions affecting the title (and to some extent reservations, although this is perhaps a criticism of the identification system) are difficult to discover and may be uncertain. But at least with our system of registration for publication, any title conditions, to be effective, must be recorded in the Register of Sasines; and to this standard rule there are only very limited exceptions, for example in the case of servitudes and leases, where there are other means of discovering the adverse right.

Apart from these limited exceptions, all title conditions are ascertainable by searching in the Register of Sasines. Again, registration of title is not the only and necessary cure for this weakness in the system and other solutions are possible. But registration of title will improve the position here, in that burdens and conditions will be readily ascertainable from the one title sheet.

11.12 HERITABLE SECURITIES

The same principles apply to heritable securities as apply to title conditions, although, in practice, it is usually easier to ascertain whether or not securities are outstanding than to ascertain the position as to old burdens. Again, registration of title will improve the position.

11.13 PROOF OF OWNERSHIP

Finally, and most importantly, the mere recording of a title in the Register of Sasines is never in any circumstances a guarantee of the validity of that title nor of the right of the party on whose behalf the title was recorded. The grantee has an indefeasible real right if, but only if, his deed derives from a grantor whose own title is in turn valid and unchallengeable. But a defect in the title of the grantor is not cured by the recording of the grantee's deed and the deed may later be reduced, notwithstanding that it has been recorded, if it turns out that the grantor's title was invalid.

The consequence is that in practice proof of title depends upon the operation of positive prescription (for which see Chapter 12). Therefore, in every title, some examination of the titles for at least 10 years back is always necessary. Often, such examination is time-consuming, repetitive and uncertain. The reduction in 1970 of the period of positive prescription from 20 years to 10 years (with certain exceptions) cut down the necessary period over which the title must be examined but did not eliminate examination, nor did it eliminate the risks inherent in the Register of Sasines system.

The only true cure for this defect is a system of registration of title. Under registration of title, the state assumes responsibility for registering the ownership of every individual heritable property throughout the country or in defined areas; and, on such registration, issues a certificate to reputed owners which, when issued, becomes conclusive evidence of title and, therefore, in principle bars all questions as to, and investigation of, antecedent titles. In the process, this eliminates all earlier invalidities or doubtful points and defects in the earlier titles on which the right depends. Registration, thus, can be described as having a 'curative' effect. See K G C Reid '*A Non Domino* Conveyances and the Land Register' 1991 JR 79.

11.14   Registration of title and the Land Register

After protracted delays, registration of title was introduced to Scotland by the Land Registration (Scotland) Act 1979. The new Scottish registration system follows, fairly closely, the system of registration of title which has been operating in England on a compulsory basis for nearly 80 years. It was introduced by the Land Registration Act 1925, which has recently been replaced by the Land Registration Act 2002, most of which was brought into force in October 2003. But there are significant differences between the English and Scottish systems, in part reflecting differences in the land tenure north and south of the border; and in part reflecting ideas which emerged in the preparation of the Reid and Henry Committee Reports. In the result, the Scottish statutory scheme is simpler than the English one. But, nonetheless, it has been problematic.

In contrast to the Register of Sasines, in registration of title, the role of the registrar is an active one, in that the Keeper, as registrar, must scrutinise the individual title, must satisfy himself that the reputed owner has a valid title, and must satisfy himself as to identity and burdens affecting the property which he is registering. He must then positively certify that the individual proprietor is indeed the proprietor of that particular property. By so certifying, he makes correct as a matter of law what was possibly an invalid or vulnerable title.

Note also, in contrast to certain other forms of registration, that the state here intervenes, in the public interest, to certify ownership. Compare, in particular, motor vehicle registration where, for fiscal purposes, and also for the purpose of control and law enforcement in traffic offences, every vehicle operating on the public roads in Britain must be registered. But the certificate issued under statutory authority has no effect whatsoever *quoad* title.

11.15   The Register and the Keeper

Obviously, a new register of title was required. But, in Scotland, this was a relatively simple problem. A comprehensive system of registration already exists, with a central Register House in Edinburgh fully and efficiently staffed with sophisticated techniques for the existing system of registration. The Register of Sasines contains, in readily accessible form, a great deal of information which will be translated onto the title sheet on registration of title. Logically, under the Land Registration (Scotland) Act 1979, the new Land Register is placed under the control of the Keeper of the Registers. It is housed partly in the same premises (Meadowbank House in Edinburgh) and partly in Glasgow, and the two registers work in parallel and are closely co-ordinated. But, in registration of title, the role of the Keeper alters from a mere passive role in the controlling of intake of deeds for publication to the much more important and active role of examining and adjudicating upon titles presented for registration. In the new system of registration of title, he is given a great deal of discretion as to what he registers and more importantly as to what he guarantees.

11.16   Registration

For practical reasons, the process of registration of title could only be introduced gradually. It would have been quite impossible to introduce it instantaneously for every title throughout the whole of the country.

The original intention was to introduce the new system, area by area throughout Scotland, on a nine-year programme starting in April 1981 with the County of Renfrew. For some years previously, the Keeper had been operating a pilot scheme for this county and a good deal of practical experience had thus been gained. However, the original programme fell badly behind. It was only on 1 April 2003 that all counties finally became operational. Here is a table of the commencement dates:

County	Commencement date
Renfrew	6 April 1981
Dumbarton	4 October 1982
Lanark	3 January 1984
Glasgow	30 September 1985
Clackmannan	1 October 1992
Stirling	1 April 1993
West Lothian	1 October 1993
Fife	1 April 1995
Aberdeen, Kincardine	1 April 1996
Ayr, Dumfries,	1 April 1997
Kirkcudbright, Wigtown	
Angus, Kinross, Perth	1 April 1999
Berwick, East Lothian,	
Peebles, Roxburgh, Selkirk	1 October 1999
Argyll, Bute	1 April 2000
Midlothian	1 April 2001
Inverness, Nairn	1 April 2002
Banff, Caithness, Moray,	1 April 2003
Orkney and Zetland, Ross	
and Cromarty, Sutherland	

Once an area has been declared a compulsory registration area in terms of s 30 of the Land Registration (Scotland) Act 1979 ('an operational area'), then broadly speaking (for details see later) on any sale of heritage within that area after that date, the title of the purchaser must be registered in the new Land Register.

In urban areas, properties change hands about once every seven or eight years on average, and much less frequently in rural areas. On that average, it will therefore be at least a further ten years from the date when the area is declared operational until a majority of the titles in that area have been registered.

At at March 2003, approximately one third of Scottish titles have been registered in the Land Register (source: Registers of Scotland). In Renfrew, the first county to become operational, the figure is 62.9%, whereas in Midlothian, which has only been operational since April 2001, it is unsurprisingly only 12.4%. However, the fact that approximately one eighth of titles in Midlothian have transferred in two years, shows how active the Edinburgh housing market is. In Glasgow, as of May 2003, 79.5% of titles were held in the Land Register. This figure rose from one of 53% earlier in the year, due to a large scale voluntary transfer of council houses. Registration of title is therefore a very gradual remedy for the imperfections which it eventually will cure. A matter of further interest is that as of January 2003, only 4.93% of Scotland's land mass was registered in the Land Register. This statistic can be explained to a certain extent by the fact that the large northern counties were not yet operational at that date. The principal reason, however, is that landed estates which remain owned by the same family, passing from one generation to the next, stay in the Register of Sasines, because a transfer on death does not induce first registration.

11.17 Certificate of title

On receiving an application for registration of a title to a particular property the Keeper examines the whole progress of titles, satisfies himself as to its validity, and then certifies that the applicant is the owner of the property, which he identifies on an official certificate known as a land certificate. The extent and particulars of the property are similarly certified, subject to the burdens and conditions specified in the certificate; and subject also to certain inherent qualifications which apply to every certificate.

Therefore, the system of registration embodies machinery for the identification of:

(1) the property and its ancillary rights, with plan;
(2) the burdens affecting the title which include:
    (a) the conditions of tenure;
    (b) heritable securities;
(3) the owner of the property, with a specification of the nature of his right therein.

All this is contained in the land certificate issued to the owner; and the certificate exactly reproduces the entries in the title sheet maintained in the Register itself.

Again, in the Register of Sasines, this machinery exists in embryo in the search sheets maintained in Register House; but, of course, a new format is required and substantial additional information appears on the certificate of title. But, in Scotland, we are a good deal further ahead than, say, in England, where registration of title is superimposed on unregistered titles.

The land certificate almost wholly replaces and supersedes the title deeds; but a reference back to the earlier titles may still be necessary in limited and unusual cases. Therefore, the owner may still have an interest to retain his title deeds.

11.18 Overriding interests

Some interests are too ill-defined or indeterminate to register on individual certificates; and certain interests are too insignificant to register. In any system of registration of title, this is inevitable. In the result, the legislature has the choice either:

(1) of eliminating all such interests in land, so that the certificate of title can be a complete and exhaustive record of every single minute item in or affecting that title; or

(2) of permitting these minor and indeterminate adverse rights to co-exist along with the registered title and to affect the registered land, although they may not appear in the certificate of title.

In Scotland, as in England, we have adopted the second alternative, and these adverse interests are termed 'overriding interests'. We are already familiar with the general principle of 'overriding interests' north of the border in the sense that certain rights prevail against the proprietor holding on a recorded title without these rights themselves entering the Register of Sasines. Thus, servitudes, although normally constituted by recorded deed, do not require to enter the Register of Sasines; and the same applies to public rights of way. Nonetheless, these rights prevail against singular successors in perpetuity. So also leases, under the Leases Act 1449, bind singular successors although not disclosed on the Record.

11.19 **Rectification and indemnification**

The Register of Sasines is negative in this sense that, unless a title is recorded, no real right is obtained. But it does not necessarily follow that recording automatically creates a real right; a recorded title is not beyond challenge. Suppose that A, improperly and without having right or title to do so, dispones land to B who in good faith and for value accepts the disposition and records it. Suppose the property really belongs to C who has an unchallengeable right and title thereto. The fact that B, in good faith, has recorded a putative title does not prevent C from attacking that title by an action of reduction. If he successfully attacks B's title and if that title is reduced, then B's only remedy is an action of damages against A. If A cannot pay, B is the loser. C, the true owner, emerges virtually unscathed.

In contrast, in a system of registration of title, if B has become the proprietor on a fully indemnified registered title, and has taken possession, his registered title in principle is beyond challenge. Even although C may be able to demonstrate beyond doubt that he had a valid right and title to the property registered in B's name, C cannot, as of right, reduce B's title. On the other hand, in certain circumstances a discretion is vested in the Keeper to amend or rectify the Register where it appears to him that a mistake has been made. But in any such case, whether the Register is rectified or not, if anyone can show that, as a result of registration or rectification, he has suffered loss, then he may be able to claim compensation from the state. The provision of state indemnification is discussed more fully below. Thus in the A–B–C case above, in a system of registration of title, where A wrongly and without any power to do so transfers his registered title to B (if that were possible), C cannot challenge B's title as of right, unless of course B's title is subject to a relevant exclusion of indemnity. He may, however, make representations to the Keeper; and the Keeper in certain circumstances may at his own hand rectify the Register by removing B from the Register and putting C in his place. If he does so, then he may have to compensate B for his loss; if he does not rectify the Register in this way but if C can satisfy him as to the rights which he has lost, then the Keeper would normally be bound to indemnify C.

Further, as will be seen, under the Land Registration (Scotland) Act 1979, the Keeper is not allowed to rectify the Register to the disadvantage of the proprietor in possession; and the court cannot so require the Keeper, except in certain specified situations.

11.20 The Land Registration (Scotland) Act 1979

Section 1 is the formal section under which the new Register was created, known as 'The Land Register of Scotland'. The Register is public, and is placed under the management of the Keeper of the Registers.

Throughout the 1979 Act, the words 'register', 'registered' etc mean the new Land Register and registration of title therein.

11.21 COMMENCEMENT

Section 1 of the Land Registration (Scotland) Act 1979, setting up the Register, came into operation on 4 April 1979 under s 30. The remaining sections in Parts I and II of the Act, dealing with the mechanics of registration, have been introduced for particular defined areas of Scotland on the phased programme referred to above. This was achieved by Statutory Instrument; and different days were appointed under s 30 for different areas, as indicated in the timetable outlined above. 'The commencement of the Act' in ss 2–14 therefore means, in relation to each operational area only, the date on which it became operational.

11.22 COMPULSORY REGISTRATION

Within each operational area, and from and after the operational date as fixed in the Statutory Instrument, broadly speaking, every title must be registered in the Land Register when the property is sold or leased on a long lease. See the *Registration of Title Practice Book*, paras 2.3–2.5. The Keeper, however, has been prepared nevertheless still to record dispositions in the Register of Sasines if the relevant transaction settled on a date before the county became operational: see ROTPB, para 2.6. This practice, however, does not seem to be justified by the Land Registration (Scotland) Act 1979 and a call has been made for remedial legislation to homologate it: see S Wortley 'Of Inoperative Deeds and Operational Areas' 2001 SLT (News) 79.

In limited circumstances, the Keeper may be willing to accept a title on a voluntary registration, but this facility will be sparingly used in Scotland, although more common in England. See ROTPB, paras 2.8–2.10.

Once a title to a property has been so registered under this section, thereafter (but only thereafter) every subsequent transaction relating to that property also becomes registrable, for example the transfer of the registered interest, a heritable security over the registered interest, a liferent of the registered interest, and generally any other transaction which affects the registered title. Further, under s 2(5) of the 1979 Act (as amended), the Scottish Ministers may, at some future date, require certain interests in land, not then registered, to be brought onto the Register, so as to complete registration in a particular area. It is thought that this power will not be used for a long time to come.

11.23   THE EFFECT OF REGISTRATION

Registration is defined in s 3 of the Land Registration (Scotland) Act 1979 as having the following effects.

(1) Under s 3(1)(a) it vests in the registered proprietor a real right in the registered interest as also in any right, pertinent or servitude, express or implied, forming part of that registered interest. The right so vests subject only to:
  (a) any adverse entries in the title sheet itself, for example heritable securities, title conditions, notices of improvement grants etc actually entered in the title sheet and land certificate; and
  (b) any overriding interest, whether entered in the title sheet or not.
(2) Under s 3(1)(b), on registration, all rights and obligations entered in the title sheet are similarly made real.
(3) Under s 3(1)(c) registration also 'affects' any registered real right or obligation relating to the registered interest in land.

These three subsections, however, are qualified by a proviso to the effect that registration only has these effects insofar as the right or obligation in question is capable, under existing law, of being made real.

Further, under s 3(3), from the date when a particular area becomes an operational area, certain transactions have to be registered in the Land Register which, at the moment, do not require to be recorded in the Register of Sasines. In these cases, registration is obligatory in the sense of being the only means of making the right or obligation real. These cases, where registration is obligatory, are:

• the right of the lessee under a long lease;
• the right of the udal proprietor; and
• the right of a kindly tenant of Lochmaben.

It should be noted that rights of kindly tenants will be converted into ownership of the property upon feudal abolition: see the Abolition of Feudal Tenure etc (Scotland) Act 2000, s 64.

In contrast, in any other case, rights can be made real by any other means which are effective at present. Thus under the existing law a short lease is made real, under the Leases Act of 1449, by the granting of a lease in certain terms, followed by possession by the tenant. In the case of long leases (ie leases for more than 20 years) granted before a county became operational, recording was an alternative to possession. But once an area has been declared operational, then, on the granting of such a lease possession ceases to be available as a method of making the right real. The long lease must be registered, whether or not the landlord's title has been registered. In contrast, under a short lease, possession still makes the right of the tenant real, and indeed registration is incompetent.

11.24 MECHANICS OF REGISTRATION

The mechanics of registration are controlled by ss 4–6 of the Land Registration (Scotland) Act 1979 and are considered more fully in Chapter 32. They differ in some important respects from the procedure applicable to the Register or Sasines. Thus:

(1) A formal deed in normal form is still required to vest the right in the disponee, although the Keeper may be prepared to allow some shortcuts in the completion of the required formalities.

(2) No warrant of registration is required. Instead, under s 4(1), the vesting deed is sent to the Keeper along with an application for registration of the title. If it is a first registration, ie if the interest in land is held on a Register of Sasines title and is being presented to the Land Register for the first time, the applicant sends all relevant Register of Sasines deeds with the application. The Keeper examines the title, just as a purchaser would examine it, for validity, burdens etc; and may require the applicant to furnish further information, for example as to identification of the property, boundaries, servitudes, possession etc.

(3) The Keeper must reject the application if:
   (a) the property is not sufficiently described to allow him to identify it on the Ordnance Survey map;
   (b) it relates to a souvenir plot;
   (c) it is frivolous or vexatious; or
   (d) the title is already registered, and the deed omits to mention the title number.
   In addition, the Keeper has discretion to reject an application which is not accompanied by such documents and other evidence as he may require. On this principle the Keeper could, if he wished, reject a conveyance which was granted *a non domino*. The Keeper's policy here, which has become stricter in recent years, is to reject such deeds if he deems them to be 'speculative'. In other words, the applicant must demonstrate good reason why registration should be allowed. See the *Registration of Title Practice Book*, para 6.4.

(4) On receipt of that application for registration, the Keeper notes the date of receipt thereof which is deemed to be the date of registration unless the application is rejected by the Keeper or is withdrawn.

11.25 THE TITLE SHEET

Under s 5 of the Land Registration (Scotland) Act 1979, the process of first registration of a title involves, in the case of proprietary rights, ie resulting from a disposition etc, the preparation, by the Keeper, of a title sheet to the property (or rather, to the interest being registered). The title sheet is a summary of all the salient features in the title to that interest and is dealt with in detail in s 6. The essential content of the title sheet comprises:

(1) a description of the property by reference to an Ordnance Survey plan;
(2) the name of the proprietor;
(3) any adverse entries in the Personal Register;
(4) any heritable securities;
(5) any enforceable real right or subsisting real burden;
(6) any exclusion of indemnity;
(7) such other information as the Keeper may think fit to enter.

Further, in terms of s 6(2) of the 1979 Act, the Keeper is empowered either to repeat verbatim rights or burdens, or to summarise these, or to refer to them in the title sheet by reference to a previous recorded deed, a copy of which is put up with the title sheet for completeness. The Keeper tends to narrate burdens verbatim in practice.

Under s 5(4), overriding interests will also be noted by the Keeper in most cases, if drawn to his notice.

11.26 CONTENT OF TITLE SHEET

The content of the title sheet is set out in detail in Part II of the Land Registration (Scotland) Rules 1980, SI 1980/1413. The title sheet contains four parts, namely:

(1) the property section – the description of the property;
(2) the proprietorship section – the identity of the owner;
(3) the charges section – heritable securities etc;
(4) the burdens section – title conditions etc.

Every title sheet will be given a distinguishing number (the 'title number'); and, in any future transaction relating to that title, the number must be quoted. The title number is a combination of three letters denoting the relevant county, for example GLA for Glasgow, and numerals.

The title sheet is part of the Land Register and is retained permanently by the Keeper. It will be updated from time to time whenever information reaches the Keeper relating to any individual property in the Register.

11.27 LAND AND CHARGE CERTIFICATES

For each individual owner, a formal copy of the title sheet, containing all the same information, will be issued on registration, and it will be updated from time to time as required. In the case of proprietary interests, the copy of the title sheet issued to the owner takes the form of a land certificate which certifies that he is the owner of the land described in the property section.

Lesser interests, such as heritable securities, liferents etc, are also registrable; but only after the title to the property itself has been registered. Thus, if the proprietor of heritable property in Renfrew holding on a Register of Sasines title sells and dispones it to a purchaser, the purchaser must apply for the registration of his title as purchaser: Land Registration (Scotland) Act 1979, s 2(1)(a)(ii).

If that same owner of property in Renfrew, instead of selling it, grants a standard security in favour of a creditor, the standard security will be recorded in the Register of Sasines. Registration in the Land Register is not required, and indeed not competent, merely on the granting of securities etc.

If, however, the property in Renfrew has been sold and the purchaser has registered his title as purchaser, a title sheet will have been prepared in the Land Register and a land certificate will have been issued to him. If he then grants a standard security, the creditor must register that standard security in the Land Register and it is then entered on the title sheet of that proprietor: 1979 Act, s 2(3)(i). In other words, once the title of the proprietor has been registered, every subsequent transaction is registrable in the Land Register; and nothing can subsequently be recorded in the Register of Sasines to affect that title.

As will be later explained, the land certificate issued to the registered proprietor, and any other writ issued or updated by the Keeper of the Registers, is guaranteed by the Keeper, with certain exceptions.

Because the Keeper normally guarantees a registered title, and every subsequent transaction relating thereto, he has to examine the title on first registration, as indicated above, in exactly the same way as the purchaser's solicitor examines the title at the present time in the Register of Sasines system, in order to satisfy himself as to the validity of the proprietary title and the burdens and heritable securities thereon.

If he is not satisfied with the validity of the title, then he may still register it, but will exclude indemnity either generally or on certain aspects of that title. If there is any exclusion of indemnity, this must be explicitly expressed on the title sheet and on the land certificate. See para 11.39.

11.28 THE LAND CERTIFICATE

The form of land certificate, which mirrors the title sheet, is prescribed in Schedule A, Form 6 of the Land Registration (Scotland) Rules 1980, SI 1980/1413. An example is given in the Appendix of Styles. The land certificate consists of at least eight separate pages and, in addition, there may be incorporated in, or annexed to it,

schedules of burdens, or copies of whole writs. Minor amendments have been made
to the form of land certificate and certain other forms by the Land Registration
(Scotland) Amendment Rules 1988, SI 1988/1143, with effect from 1 October 1988.
Further minor amendments to the form of land certificate and significant changes to
the layout and content of some other forms were introduced by the Land Registration
(Scotland) Amendment Rules 1995, SI 1995/248, with effect from 1 April 1995. The
salient features of the land certificate are as follows.

Page 1 contains:

(1) the title number;
(2) the postal address;
(3) standard information about the indemnity.

Page 2 contains a series of boxes for inserting the date to which the land certificate
has been updated. As indicated above, the land certificate is a document issued to the
individual registered proprietor. With limited exceptions, the land certificate will
have to be produced to the Keeper by the registered proprietor on any subsequent
transaction affecting the registered interest. The land certificate is then made to correspond with the title sheet by adding whatever additional information is required.
The successive dates to which the land certificate is thus updated will be shown in the
boxes on page 2.

Page 3 reproduces the plan of the individual property, an essential feature of the
system of registration of title. It is simply a copy of the relevant section of the
Ordnance Survey map and the property in question is outlined with a heavy red line
or tinted or otherwise delineated. The title number appears again at the top right-hand
corner. Three scales of Ordnance Survey plan are used:

- 1:1,250 which will be used for all normal urban property. In exceptional cases,
  however, the Keeper may produce a special plan on a larger scale, for example
  1:500, if that is necessary to show details.
- 1:2,500 which is the scale to be used for rural properties, farms etc
- 1:10,000 – a much smaller scale for use in hill and moorland properties.

One weakness of the plan system is that, because of limitations of scale, it is
impossible in many cases exactly to define the boundary line in relation to the
boundary feature, for example the centre line of a wall etc; but the Keeper overcomes
this difficulty either by verbal description or by a system of arrows, mentioned
below. Differing colours will be used in appropriate cases to distinguish different
areas or rights. See generally the *Registration of Title Practice Book*, paras
4.22–4.30. It is not competent to interpret the plan by reference to the preceding
Register of Sasines deeds upon which the title is based: *Marshall v Duffy* 2002 GWD
10-318. But it would be possible to found on such deeds in an application to rectify
a plan which was alleged to be incorrect.

The next pages of the land certificate reproduce the four sections referred to in
para 11.26 above, with the individual information for each of these four sections in
the standard form.

(1) *The property section.* The property section gives the title number, the county, the nature of the interest, and a description of the property, primarily by reference to the plan. The verbal description is cut to the minimum. Strictly speaking, the plan forms part of the property section. Ancillary rights, for example servitudes of access for the benefit of the property will be added to the description, as additional proprietorial rights. The requirement for dual registration of real burdens under the Title Conditions (Scotland) Act 2003 (see Chapters 15 and 19) means that the right to enforce burdens will also have to be stated in land certificates. It is anticipated that the statement will be in the property section, but confirmation is awaited from the Keeper.

(2) *The proprietorship section* gives the name and address of the proprietor, the date of his registration as such, and a note of the price paid.

(3) *The charges section* lists the outstanding heritable securities on the property. Sections B and C may be updated by deletion of spent items and the addition of new entries, without reframing the entire land certificate afresh on each registration.

(4) *The burdens section.* This is the final section of the land certificate and will normally be the longest one. For this reason, it is put as the last section of the land certificate to allow for additional pages and for the annexing of copy deeds etc.

In general there are three ways in which title conditions etc will be introduced into the title sheet, thus:

(1) Feu charter by ... etc 'Note: Copy in certificate'. This means that a full and complete copy of the feu charter referred to in this entry will be attached to the land certificate.

(2) Feu charter etc ... 'Contains the following burdens'. In this case, the terms of the burdens are reproduced verbatim, so that the full original text thereof is copied in the land certificate.

(3) Minute of waiver etc. The import of the minute of waiver is then summarised by the Keeper in the entry itself, but is not reproduced at full length. The Keeper guarantees the accuracy of this summary.

In the amended form of land certificate introduced by the Land Registration (Scotland) Amendment Rules 1988, SI 1988/1143, general information appears on the last page and covers the following matters:

(a) Overriding interests. The full definition of overriding interests is contained in the interpretation section, s 28(1), of the Land Registration (Scotland) Act 1979. The land certificate details overriding interests, thus:

 (i) short leases (ie leases not exceeding 20 years);

 (ii) long leases where the lessee acquired the real right (by recording in the Register of Sasines or by possession) prior to the area becoming operational;

 (iii) the right of crofters or cottars under statute;

(iv)   the right of the benefited proprietor in a servitude – although in many cases servitudes will in fact be disclosed on the land certificate;

(v)   public interests generally, except those which, in the Sasines system, require the recording of a deed in the Register of Sasines. This includes, for example, matters affecting property under the Planning Acts, Housing Acts, Health and Safety at Work Acts, Fire Precaution Acts etc. But a notice of improvement grant which, under the present housing legislation, requires to be recorded in the Register of Sasines will, under the new system, have to be registered in the Land Register as a burden on the title sheet of the property concerned and these will not override;

(vi)   rights created by the Telecommunications Act 1984;

(vii)   certain rights of licence holders under the Electricity Act 1989;

(viii)   an interest vesting in the Coal Authority by virtue of s 7(3) of the Coal Industry Act 1994;

(ix)   floating charges (whether or not they have attached);

(x)   public rights of way;

(xi)   the rights of the non-entitled spouse under the Matrimonial Homes (Family Protection) (Scotland) Act 1981;

(xii)   real rights which have become real otherwise than by recording of a deed in the Register of Sasines;

(xiii)   rights relating to common interest and common property generally, excluding such rights as have been constituted by recorded or registered deed. Therefore, only the common law rights override under this head.

See further the *Registration of Title Practice Book*, paras 5.67–5.73.

(b)   The use of arrows on title plans. This has already been referred to above. The intention is to indicate the actual boundary line as defined in the title with reference to a boundary feature by the use of arrows. As already mentioned, because of limitations of scaling, the plan itself cannot accurately show whether the boundary line is, say, to the east or west of an existing wall or along the middle of the line of it. This may be important. To get over the limitations of scaling, the Keeper may indicate by the use of arrows (or, in the case of some irregular areas, a combination of arrows and letters) whether, according to the titles, the boundary line lies on one side or other of the physical features on the ground, or along the mid line thereof, as indicated in this note, but the information so given is not guaranteed. Alternatively, this information may be incorporated in the property section as a verbal addendum to the written description.

(c)   Measurements. All measurements on title plans are subject to the qualification 'or thereby'; and indemnity is excluded in respect of such measurements.

(d)   The land certificate must be produced on any application to the Keeper.

(e)   Finally, there is a warning that no unauthorised alteration should be made to the land certificate.

11.29 CHARGE CERTIFICATE

The charge certificate is the equivalent document issued to the creditor in a heritable security and contains similar entries to those in the land certificate. The security document itself is attached to it. An example is given in the Appendix of Styles.

11.30 RANKING

Section 7 of the Land Registration (Scotland) Act 1979 preserves the general principle which applies to recording in the Register of Sasines, namely, that, subject to the terms of any ranking agreement, titles to land rank according to the date of registration. Thus if A grants a standard security to B and a second standard security to C, priority of ranking is determined by the order in which the securities are registered and not by the order in which they were granted. See the *Registration of Title Practice Book*, para 2.16.

As between the two Registers, the Register of Sasines and Land Registers, again, priority of registration determines priority of right (s 7(3) of the 1979 Act), but with qualifications. Thus, A, the registered proprietor, grants a standard security to B which B records in the Register of Sasines under the present rule; and, at the same time, A dispones the property to C who applies for registration of the title. If B records the heritable security before C applies for registration, B is preferred. If not, B acquires no real right by his security but has a personal right of action against A under warrandice.

If, however, in the same situation, A sells land to B and, simultaneously, sells the same land to C; and B and C are both *bona fide* purchasers for value without notice of each other's claim, the two dispositions to B and C will each be registrable in the Land Register. The first to apply for registration will obtain a fully indemnified title. The Keeper's original practice, as discussed in K G C Reid *The Law of Property in Scotland* (1996), para 685, was also to give the latecomer a registered title but under exclusion of indemnity in the respect of the prior title of the first party. The practice was an odd one, because ownership rights cannot rank like security rights. One must exclude the other. But, as discussed above, the Keeper's policy on *a non domino* dispositions has recently become stricter (see ROTPB, para 6.4) and it is now unlikely that he would register the second disposition, unless satisfied of special circumstances from the presenting agent. In the event that both applications for registration are lodged on the same day, the Keeper will either exclude indemnity from both titles or simply refuse the applications for registration until the parties sort out amongst themselves who has the better right to become owner.

Under s 3(2) and s 8(4) of the 1979 Act, the Keeper should refuse to record either of these two dispositions if presented for recording in the Register of Sasines in the traditional way. Suppose, however, that, by oversight, the disposition A to B entered the Register of Sasines and, later, C applied for registration of his title and had his application accepted by the Keeper. In this case, even although B has the first recorded title, the title has been wrongly recorded; and C would prevail over B.

11.31 RECTIFICATION OF THE REGISTER: GENERAL

In contrast to the present system, under registration of title the document of title issued to the registered proprietor is the land certificate which in turn exactly reflects the content of the title sheet when granted. The title sheet is the creation of the Keeper and determines the rights and obligations of the individual proprietor to the exclusion of the contents of the earlier titles. That being so, there must clearly be, and under s 9 of the Land Registration (Scotland) Act 1979 there is, provision for correcting errors or mistakes in the title sheet and land certificate in relation to individual properties.

Thus, under s 9(1) of the 1979 Act, the Keeper in certain circumstances may, and if so required by the court or the Lands Tribunal shall, rectify any inaccuracy in a title sheet which is brought to his notice. But this power to rectify the register is very severely restricted by s 9(3). Under that section, the Keeper may not rectify the Register to the prejudice of the proprietor in possession of the registered interest except in very limited circumstances; and so, with these limited exceptions, the proprietor in possession on a registered title is now in principle immune from the challenge of that title on any grounds whatever. But see para 11.35.

11.32 Rectification: what is an 'inaccuracy'?

The Land Registration (Scotland) Act 1979 is short on definition. 'Inaccuracy' is not defined. The generally accepted meaning is that an entry in the Register is inaccurate if it is (one) not justified or (two) is no longer justified by the deed which induced it, in terms of Register of Sasines rules. An example of the former would be a deed granted by an adult with incapacity. An example of the latter would be a deed which was reduced as a gratuitous alienation. See G L Gretton and K G C Reid *Conveyancing* (2nd edn, 1999) para 8.07. A rather wider meaning, however, was given by the Lands Tribunal in *Higgins v North Lanarkshire Council* 2001 SLT (Lands Tr) 2. There, the disposition which induced the entry was voidable but had not actually been reduced by court order. The Tribunal took the view that the Register was inaccurate. But this is surely wrong. A voidable disposition is good until such time that it is reduced. See Reid and Gretton *Conveyancing 2000* (2001), pp 110–111.

11.33 Rectification: what is a 'proprietor in possession'?

This term is also not defined in the Land Registration (Scotland) Act 1979. Over recent years, however, there has been some judicial interpretation. In *Kaur v Singh* 1997 SCLR 1075, reversed 1999 SC 180, 1998 SCLR 849, the Inner House held that 'proprietor' was to be given its ordinary meaning. Accordingly, an owner of land is a 'proprietor', but a heritable creditor is not. Whilst the decision did not make the position clear, it is generally thought that the tenant under a registered long lease should also be regarded as a 'proprietor', because he, like an owner, has his own title sheet.

In *Mutch v Mavisbank Properties Ltd* 2002 SLT (Sh Ct) 91, the sheriff principal in *obiter* remarks expressed the view that the holder of a servitude was also a 'proprietor', on the basis that a servitude is a pertinent of the land which he owns. Thus to remove such a servitude from his title sheet must be to his prejudice as 'proprietor'. As Professors Reid and Gretton point out in *Conveyancing 2002* (2003), pp 85–86, definitive authority is awaited on the matter and a different view might be reached where the servitude does not appear on the holder's title sheet.

On 'possession', the Inner House in *Kaur* stated that this meant natural possession and could mean possession 'in other ways' such as where parents had purchased a flat which was then possessed civilly through their student daughter. 'But there is no need in this case to go further and attempt to map the boundaries of possession for these purposes' (1999 SC 180 at 191; 1998 SCLR 849 at 860). This is not very helpful. Thus for example we are left with no clear authority as to whether a landlord possessing through a commercial tenant is a 'proprietor in possession'. The view expressed here is that he is, but judicial confirmation would be welcome.

It may be questioned whether the exalted place given to 'possession' in the 1979 Act is wise. In *Kaur*, the state of possession was altered more than once by the use of a locksmith whilst the opposing party in the action was out of the property. In *Tesco Stores Ltd v Keeper of the Registers of Scotland* 2001 SLT (Lands Tr) 23, affirmed 2003 GWD 20-610, ownership of part of a river was in dispute. The disputing parties used various tactics involving bollards and divers to establish possession as against the other, before court action eventually commenced. These activities were described by counsel for one of the parties as a 'tennis match'. A system of land registration should not encourage tussles such as this and the issue is something which the Scottish Law Commission will no doubt consider in its review of the 1979 Act. See para 11.40.

11.34 Rectification against a proprietor in possession

The Keeper can only rectify the title sheet and land certificate to the prejudice of the proprietor in possession in the following circumstances set out in s 9(3) of the Land Registration (Scotland) Act 1979:

(1) to note an overriding interest; but the overriding interest would, of course, override in any event, whether noted or not. This, therefore, does not truly prejudice the registered proprietor. This provision appears otiose.

(2) where everyone concerned has consented. This provision too is of little importance.

(3) where the error was caused by the fraud or carelessness of the proprietor in possession – and therefore he has only himself to blame. 'Fraud' or 'carelessness' are not defined in the 1979 Act, but it was stated in *Dougbar Properties Ltd v Keeper of the Registers of Scotland* 1999 SC 513 at 532 by Lord Macfadyen, that carelessness involves reasonable foresight of the inaccuracy by the proprietor and failure on her part, where possible, to take steps to obviate the inaccuracy. He held, however, that mere knowledge that the Register is inaccurate is insuffi-

cient to amount to carelessness. The result is that rectification may not be possible against a proprietor who knows that there is a mistake in the Register, or, alternatively, indemnity may be payable to such a party following rectification. In policy terms, this seems wrong. There would also appear to be difficulties here with the so-called 'offside goals' doctrine: see paras 32.51–32.62. Say A concludes missives with B. Say A then dispones to C who knows about B. C then registers. Is it possible for B to obtain rectification against C (following reduction of the disposition in his favour) on the ground of 'carelessness' if mere knowledge is not 'carelessness'? The decision of the Lands Tribunal in *Higgins v North Lanarkshire Council* 2001 SLT (Lands Tr) 2 is authority that rectification would indeed be available here. Whilst agreeable on grounds of policy, the decision does not sit well with that in *Dougbar* and higher authority is awaited. In order to establish fraud or carelessness, the Keeper will make reference to the application forms submitted in relation to the application for registration. Thus in *Stevenson-Hamilton's Executors v McStay (No 2)* 2001 SLT 694, giving factually incorrect answers to the questions on the relevant form, in particular not declaring that there was another party who had adverse possession of the subjects, was held to be, at the least, careless. Solicitors therefore need to be very careful when completing these forms or the answers may come back to haunt them in the future.

(4) where rectification relates to something against which the Keeper has previously declined to indemnify the proprietor in possession, by an express exclusion of indemnity on the title sheet and land certificate. The Keeper will exclude indemnity if he is doubtful about the validity of the proprietor's right to the subjects. This allows the Register to be rectified even where the proprietor is in possession.

Similarly, on the application of an interested party to the Lands Tribunal or to the court, rectification may be ordered; but the Lands Tribunal and court are similarly restricted in ordering rectification to the prejudice of a proprietor in possession.

11.35   Rectification: circumvention of the rule protecting the proprietor in possession

In principle, under registration of title, if a *bona fide* grantee registers a title and enters into possession of the registered land, then, assuming that indemnity has not been excluded, his title is immediately put beyond challenge and he does not require to possess on that title for ten years in order to validate it. This is in theory a very considerable improvement on the present law of positive prescription, so far as the owner in possession is concerned. This fundamental principle of registration of title has, however, been undermined by *Short's Trustee v Keeper of the Registers of Scotland* 1996 SC (HL) 14.

In 1986, Mr Short conveyed two properties by separate dispositions, both at undervalue, to a purchaser who in turn, in May 1987, by two separate dispositions conveyed them gratuitously to his wife. All four dispositions were duly registered in the Land Register. When Mr Short was subsequently sequestrated, his permanent trustee successfully applied for a decree of reduction of all four dispositions, on the footing that the two original dispositions at under-value were gratuitous alienations struck at by the Bankruptcy (Scotland) Act 1985, s 34(4): see *Short's Trustee v Chung* 1991 SLT 472. Having reduced the dispositions, the trustee applied to the court for an order requiring the Keeper to register the decrees of reduction under the Land Registration (Scotland) Act 1979, s 2(4)(c) as a transaction or event which is capable, under any enactment or rule of law, of affecting the title to a registered interest in land. There was clearly some force in the permanent trustee's argument in that a decree of reduction, in a Register of Sasines title, is recordable by express statutory provision in the Conveyancing (Scotland) Act 1924, s 46 and, if so recorded, subject to the qualifications in that section, has the effect of restoring the title to the state it would have been in if the reduced deed(s) had never been granted. In other words, in this particular case, the properties would have reverted to the debtor's estate for the benefit of his general creditors.

Notwithstanding a vigorous argument along these lines by the permanent trustee, however, both the Outer House (1993 SLT 1291) and the Inner House (1994 SLT 65) rejected the application as being incompatible with the provisions of the 1979 Act and the clear underlying purpose and principles of registration of title.

The trustee appealed to the House of Lords unsuccessfully: see 1996 SC (HL) 14, 1996 SLT 166; 1996 SCLR 571. His arguments were again rejected, but on somewhat different grounds. The court considered that Parliament could not have intended that reduction should be an event capable of affecting a registered interest. Accordingly, the decree could not be registered; instead, the trustee was entitled to claim compensation under 1979 Act, s 12(1)(b). However, this is difficult to understand because s 12(3)(b) of the 1979 Act provides that no indemnity is payable in respect of titles reduced under the Bankruptcy (Scotland) Act 1985.

The litigation, however, did not end there. The trustee sought an order under s 34 of the 1985 Act requiring Mrs Chung to reconvey the property to him. The point about a reconveyance was that it could simply enter the Register by s 2 of the 1979 Act, as an ordinary disposition: prejudice to a proprietor in possession would be irrelevant. The trustee was successful in both the Outer and Inner House. The case is reported as *Short's Trustee v Chung (No 2)* 1998 SC 105, 1998 SLT 200, affirmed 1999 SLT 751. There was no appeal to the House of Lords. The decision is a problematic one. If the rule that there should be no prejudice to a proprietor in possession can be avoided by registration the Register becomes unreliable. Moreover, indemnity is not available in this situation. So, conveyancers may have to consider looking at the previous Sasine deeds. The operation of the 1979 Act in this context badly requires reappraisal. For further discussion, see Steven 'Problems in the Land Register' 1999 SLT (News) 163 and Reid and Gretton *Conveyancing 1999* (2000), pp 70–71.

11.36 INDEMNITY: GENERAL

Closely linked with the question of rectification is the matter of indemnity. Not only does the Keeper usually guarantee the validity of every title which is registered, subject only to those cases where he excludes indemnity. In addition, where the registered proprietor or a third party can demonstrate that, because of entries made in the Register by the Keeper, he has suffered loss, then he normally has a claim for compensation against the Keeper. This right to indemnity is expressly conferred by s 12(1) of the Land Registration (Scotland) Act 1979 in terms of which any person who suffers loss as a result of any of the following is entitled to be indemnified by the Keeper:

(1) a rectification of the Register;
(2) the refusal of the Keeper to rectify the Register;
(3) the loss or destruction of any document whilst lodged with the Keeper;
(4) any error or omission in a land or charge certificate or in other information given by the Keeper in writing, for example in a search.

The value of indemnity paid out each year has varied. For example, in 1992/93, according to Registers of Scotland statistics, there were 18 payments totalling £62,779.96. In 1999/2000, there were 44 payments, totalling £73,347.47.

11.37   Indemnity: where rectification refused

It has been held that the value of the indemnity payable under heading (b) above is measured as at the date of refusal to rectify, rather than at the date at which the inaccuracy which triggered the rectification arose: see *MRS Hamilton Ltd v Keeper of the Registers of Scotland* 2000 SC 271. As Professor McDonald has shown in 'Rectification and Indemnity in the Land Register' (2001) 55 Greens PLB 6 and (2002) 56 Greens PLB 1, this leads to some very unsatisfactory results. A variant of one of the examples given by Professor McDonald provides a good illustration. Say A holds a registered title to a field. The field is worth £10,000. B forges A's signature and sells the field to C for £10,000. The Keeper, unaware of the forgery, accepts the disposition for registration and enters C in the Register as proprietor. C takes possession of the field and after obtaining planning permission builds a factory on it. The field is now worth £100,000. A, who has been abroad, comes back and discovers what has happened. He applies for rectification of the Register, but this is refused because C is in possession. A therefore applies for indemnity in terms of s 12(1)(b) of the Land Registration (Scotland) Act 1979. To what sum is he entitled? If the Register had been rectified, he would now have an asset worth £100,000. Therefore as a result of the refusal to rectify, he has lost £100,000. *MRS Hamilton* makes it clear that the date for quantifying the loss is the date the Keeper refuses to rectify.

It is possible to argue that A should only receive £10,000 because if the Register had been rectified, although A would have received title to land worth £100,000, C would have had a £90,000 unjustified enrichment claim against him for the improvements made to the land. Such an enrichment claim would be valid: see, for example *Magistrates of Selkirk v Clapperton* (1830) 9 S 9 and *McDowel v McDowel* (1906) 14 SLT 125. For such an argument to succeed, however, it would involve reading words into s 12(1)(b) and reading words into the 1979 Act is something which the courts appear unwilling to do. Rather, they prefer a literal interpretation of the legislation.

This approach is exemplified by *Kaur v Singh (No 2)* 2000 SLT 1323. The facts were that Mr Kaur had fraudulently sold the flat which he co-owned with Mrs Kaur to Mr Singh. He forged his wife's signature on the disposition and the Keeper, who naturally was unaware of this, duly gave effect to the disposition by entering Mr Singh in the Register as proprietor. Mrs Kaur initially sought rectification, leading to the case discussed in para 11.33 above. But she later decided not to pursue the case, choosing instead to make a claim for indemnity against the Keeper under s 12(1)(b) of the 1979 Act. Both Mrs Kaur and the Keeper agreed that her loss was to be valued as at 8 March 1996. This was the date at which the Keeper registered the disposition in favour of Mr Singh, in other words the date that the inaccuracy entered the Register. Interestingly, this contrasts with the earlier ruling in *MRS Hamilton Ltd v Keeper of the Registers of Scotland* 2000 SC 271 that the loss should be measured as at the date of the refusal to rectify. The court did not require to explore the matter as the parties were agreed. What the parties disagreed on was the level of the indemnity.

On 8 March 1996 the flat was worth £51,000. Mrs Kaur therefore argued that her loss was half of that ie £25,500. The Keeper pointed out, however, that until 7 March the flat had been burdened by a standard security for £41,000 which Mr Kaur redeemed as part of the sale to Mr Singh. The Keeper therefore argued that the true value of Mrs Kaur's loss was one half of (£51,000–£41,000) = £5,000. Both the Outer House and the Inner House found for Mrs Kaur. Their reasoning was simple. If the Register had been rectified in favour of Mrs Kaur on the agreed date, then she would have received a half share in a flat worth £51,000 which was not burdened by a standard security. Her loss was therefore £25,500.

On the wording of s 12(1)(b) of the 1979 Act as it presently stands it is difficult to come to any other conclusion. Of course it may be the case that a claim could be made by Mr Kaur against Mrs Kaur in respect of half the cost of redeeming the standard security prior to the sale to Mr Singh. But such a claim might not be made or indeed might not succeed. The result in *Kaur* therefore is an inequitable one. In the article referred to at the start of this paragraph, Professor McDonald sensibly calls for legislation to amend s 12(1)(b). One possibility would be to follow the example of England, where indemnity is payable as a result of a loss arising from 'a mistake whose correction would involve rectification of the register': see the Land Registration Act 2002, Schedule 8, para 1(1)(b). This means that the loss is quantified at the date of the mistake and not of the date of refusal to rectify. Such a change would address most of Professor McDonald's concerns. However, it would not have changed the result in *Kaur* where the parties had agreed themselves that the date of the inaccuracy was the date upon indemnity should be valued. What caused the problem there was the forgery. It surely must be questioned whether the state should be liable financially in such circumstances.

11.38   Indemnity: errors or omissions in land or charge certificates

There are two possible interpretations of s 12(1)(d) of the Land Registration (Scotland) Act 1979. The wide interpretation is that indemnity is available where the Land/Charge Certificate contains an error or omission which is on the actual Title Sheet. In other words, the Land/Charge Certificate simply copies that error or omission. The narrow interpretation is that indemnity is only available if the Land/Charge Certificate is an incorrect copy of the Title Sheet. If the wide view is correct, then there would seem to be no need for s 12(1)(a) and (b) as any loss under these sub-sections would be covered by s 12(1)(d). Rather than claiming because of a loss suffered because of rectification or because of the Keeper's refusal to rectify, one could simply claim because of a loss arising out of the error or omission in the Land/Charge Certificate. Both Lord Hamilton in the Outer House decision of *MRS Hamilton Ltd v Keeper of the Registers of Scotland (No 1)* 1999 SLT 829 and the Lands Tribunal in *MRS Hamilton Ltd v Keeper of the Registers of Scotland* (19 May 1998, unreported) took the wide interpretation. The latter case was appealed to the Inner House: see *M R S Hamilton Ltd v Keeper of the Registers of Scotland* 2000 SC 271. The court ruled that the narrow view was correct. The Lord President stated (at p 281): 'I find that the wording of the provision leaves no room for doubt as to the correct interpretation.' Section 12(1)(d) only covers errors or omissions in the Land/Charge Certificate rather than the Title Sheet.

11.39   Indemnity: where not payable

Clearly, there will be quite a number of cases where, because of known or suspected defects, the title is not marketable; and in these cases it clearly would be impracticable for the Keeper to guarantee the title absolutely. In exactly the same way, where a seller under the present system knows that there is a defect in his title, he is at risk if he grants absolute warrandice. In any such case, the Keeper is empowered by s 12(2) of the Land Registration (Scotland) Act 1979, on registration, to exclude the right of the registered proprietor to indemnity in respect of anything appearing in, or omitted from, the title sheet of that interest, by an express exclusion of indemnity endorsed on and appearing in the title sheet and land certificate.

Thus, A is the reputed owner of 100 hectares. He has an *ex facie* valid title to 95 hectares, supported by possession, but not to the remaining 5 hectares. He sells and dispones the whole property to B. B applies for registration of the title. The Keeper may, depending on the case made by the presenting agent, register the title to the whole 100 hectares; but would exclude indemnity in respect of the 5 doubtful hectares. The title to those 5 hectares will be cured in the end of the day by the operation of the normal rules of positive prescription, ie possession following on a recorded or registered title for the relevant period; and, on application, the exclusion of indemnity is then deleted. For prescription, see Chapter 12.

Additionally, even where indemnity has not been expressly excluded by the Keeper, there is a long list of circumstances where it is not payable in terms of s 12(3) of the 1979 Act. In particular, fraud or carelessness on the part of the claimant will debar the claim. See the *Registration of Title Practice Book*, paras 7.18–7.32.

11.40   The future for registration of title

In the case of *Short's Trustee v Chung* 1996 SC (HL) 14 at 26, Lord Jauncey commented: 'Nobody could accuse the Act of being well drafted'. That comment is supported in the note by Professor Gretton, reporting on the House of Lords' decision in 1996 SCLR 571 at 585. The drafting of the Act has been criticised in several other sources, many of which are listed as articles under this chapter heading in the Reading List at the beginning of this volume. The criticisms seem well justified, even on the basis of the relatively small number of cases which have come to the courts since 1979. On the other hand, while that is so, critics of the drafting must perhaps keep in mind that the Land Registration (Scotland) Act 1979 was drafted hurriedly and under considerable pressure. It only just clawed its way on to the statute book in the very last days of the Labour government in 1979. If it had not then received royal assent, registration of title would certainly have been delayed, possibly for a considerable time, and that would undoubtedly have been unfortunate. Nonetheless, the drafting has presented problems and, as we have seen, the operation of the 1979 Act in general has not been without difficulty.

The Scottish Law Commission, accordingly, is reviewing registration of title as part of its Sixth Programme of Law Reform. The suggestion that such a review should take place was in fact made by the Keeper with the support of the Civil Law Division of the Scottish Executive Justice Department. The Commission discusses its plans at paras 2.13–2.17 of its *Sixth Programme of Law Reform* (Scot Law Com No 176, 2000). It refers to the lack of conceptual framework in the 1979 Act and to some of the difficulties identified by the case law, including:

(1)   the relationship between rectification and registration;
(2)   the meaning of key terms in the 1979 Act, such as 'proprietor in possession' and 'carelessness';
(3)   the circumstances in which indemnity is payable; and
(4)   the amount of indemnity due.

A Discussion Paper is anticipated in 2004, with a subsequent Report and draft Bill.

11.41   AUTOMATED REGISTRATION OF TITLE TO LAND

In recent years, the Registers of Scotland have piloted a system of automated registration of title to land (ARTL). The idea is that titles will be transferred electronically and that there will no longer be any need for paper deeds. This will involve solicitors completing registration forms online, with little direct involvement from the Keeper's staff. It will also be possible for stamp duty land tax and registration dues to be paid electronically. At least initially, ARTL will be restricted to dealings with the whole of an interest already registered in the Land Register. More details may be found by referring to 'ARTL' 2001 JLSS June/20; L J Lewin 'Automated Registration of Title to Land' 2002 JLSS Nov/25 and www.ros.gov.uk/solicitor/artl.html. A pilot model has been developed by the Registers of Scotland over recent years and fine tuned in the light of comments from the profession and other interested parties, such as the Council of Mortgage Lenders.

An ARTL Stakeholders' Meeting was held in Edinburgh in late July 2003, where the implementation strategy was discussed. It is intended that the technical specification will be carried out during 2004 and 2005, with a live six-month trial of the system from March to August 2006 in one or two of the counties which have been operational for a long time, such as Glasgow. It is envisaged that ARTL will be introduced across the country in 2007.

Clearly legal issues arise out of this development and an opinion was obtained in 2003 from Professors Brymer, Gretton, Paisley and Rennie on what legislation will be needed to implement such a system. At the time of writing it has not fully been made public as it is still being considered by the Keeper and his staff. Obviously, the Requirements of Writing (Scotland) Act 1995 will require amendment. The professors were asked to advise whether primary legislation would be needed or whether an order under s 8 of the Electronic Communications Act 2000 would suffice. If primary legislation is required, then this will probably form part of the draft Bill to be produced by the Scottish Law Commission mentioned above.

Chapter 12

The Effects of Possession: Prescription

12.1 Sasine and possession

'Sasine' in its original sense involved physical symbolic delivery on the ground. The last traces of sasine in this sense disappeared in 1858; and, since then, the real right of ownership of land has come to depend solely on title. Delivery (other than delivery of the appropriate title, which is not the same thing) and subsequent possession of heritage are no longer pre-requisites for obtaining ownership. Thus, A, owner of the lands of X on a valid progress of titles, has delivered by post to B, then resident in Hong Kong, a disposition by A to B of the lands of X, in usual form. Delivery of the disposition confers a valid personal right on B to become owner. By posting the disposition from Hong Kong to the General Register of Sasines in Edinburgh, B is able to convert his personal right into a real right; and, at the moment of recording, his real right is perfected, notwithstanding that B still remains in Hong Kong and that the property remains unoccupied for the next 30 years. At the end of that period, B still has the real right unimpaired, subject only to one possible qualification explained below.

But possession of heritage may be significant in three ways.

12.2 POSSESSORY REMEDIES

A person in possession of land has the right not to be dispossessed against his will except by judicial order. This right arises from possession alone and no title is required. Wrongful dispossession founds an action of ejection, allowing recovery of the land. But if the possessor does not have a title to the land, he is vulnerable to subsequent dispossession by judicial process.

Further rights arise where possession has subsisted for a period of seven years, and where the possession was based on a *prima facie* title to the land, such as a recorded disposition. In this case the possessor is entitled to remain in possession of the land unless or until his *prima facie* title is reduced; and to protect his possession against an action of ejection or trespass. This rule was of considerable importance when the period of positive prescription was 40 years, but today it is of historical interest only and the seven-year possessory judgment is unknown in modern practice. Thus the reduction in the period of the positive prescription to ten years has rendered these remedies largely academic. See *Stair Memorial Encyclopaedia*, Volume 18, paras 145–146.

A recent case where two parties claimed ownership on competing titles is *Watson v Shields* 1996 SCLR 81. The outcome was that the person in actual possession of heritable property was held not to be entitled to obtain interdict against anyone challenging his possession unless the challenger in turn is unable to show any right whatsoever to support his claim. On the other hand, if the possessor has *prima facie* evidence of title, that title must first be reduced before the challenger can succeed.

12.3   *BONA FIDE* POSSESSION

Where a person possesses land in the reasonable but mistaken belief that he is the owner, or is otherwise entitled to possession, he is said to be a *bona fide* possessor. As such he has certain privileges in the event of ultimate dispossession by the true owner. In particular, a *bona fide* possessor is not required to account to the owner for the fruits of his period of possession. See *Stair Memorial Encyclopaedia*, Volume 18, paras 131–137 and 171.

12.4   PRESCRIPTION

The general principle is that mere lapse of time, of itself, may operate to create, modify or extinguish rights or obligations in land. Two applications of the rule apply to heritable titles, namely, positive prescription which applies only in the case of heritage, and long negative prescription (formerly the negative prescription) which applies generally to all rights, including rights relating to heritable property.

The positive and long negative prescriptions now rest wholly on statutory provision, as interpreted by judicial decision.

All earlier statutory provisions were repealed by the Prescription and Limitation (Scotland) Act 1973, with effect from 25 July 1976. The 1973 Act therefore now provides a complete and self-contained statutory code for both the positive and the long negative prescriptions. However, the old law is to a large extent re-enacted in the 1973 Act, albeit with some significant modifications; and, in the result, the basic underlying principles of earlier legislation on both prescriptions are substantially preserved. Therefore, many of the cases decided under previous statutory provisions still remain relevant to the new code.

Under the 1973 Act, the period of the positive prescription in most cases is now ten years, but remains at 20 years in certain special cases dealt with below. The period of long negative prescription is 20 years in all cases although recent amendment provides that short negative prescription applies to real burdens as of 28 November 2004. See the Title Conditions (Scotland) Act 2003, s 18.

12.5 Positive prescription

Positive prescription operates actively to create, enlarge, or fortify rights in land which did not previously exist or which, previously, were at least open to challenge.

In feudal theory, all land belongs to the Crown. Therefore, at common law, in order to establish a good title to land, it is essential to trace back the title to an original Crown grant and to produce all the links in title intervening between the original Crown grant and the present proprietor. These links must, in themselves, be valid and sufficient to transmit the right. In almost every case, this would involve enormous labour; and the result might well be inconclusive. The original object of the Prescription Act 1617 was to secure a proprietor in possession against spurious challenge; but the emphasis has shifted and the main object of the modern legislation on the positive prescription is to limit the period of research and enquiry, in any particular case, to the title, in the progress, last recorded more than ten years ago; and to declare that such title, so recorded, is absolute in the person of the possessor, no matter what other competing titles may be produced against him. The implications of this for examination of title are considered at para 32.15. Note the two separate elements. There must be, firstly, a title; and, following thereon, possession for a period. In the result, the rule stated above that title alone, without possession, confers real rights, suffers a qualification to this extent that, in a competition, where two competing parties can both produce titles and registration in the same subjects, the one who can prove possession, in addition, for the ten-year period will be preferred.

Certain specialities arise in the case of land registered in the Land Register, and these are discussed later in the chapter.

Since the sixth edition of this book was written, Professor Johnston in his *Prescription and Limitation* (1999), Chapter 14, has argued that the effect of positive prescription is not acquisitive, in other words it does not vest a new title in the party in whose favour prescription has run. Rather, he writes, at para 14.14: 'The title simply becomes exempt from challenge, and all inquiry into the title prior to the prescriptive period is excluded.' Professor Reid takes the opposite view, namely, that positive prescription is acquisitive: see *Stair Memorial Encyclopaedia*, Volume 18, para 674. So too does Professor Paisley in his *Land Law* (2000), para 3.13. Whilst it is accepted that the Prescription and Limitation (Scotland) Act 1973 could be more clearly drafted, the view expressed here, in accordance with the first sentence of this paragraph, which has appeared in previous editions of this work, is that this is acquisitive prescription.

12.6 The result of title and possession

If title and possession for the prescriptive period do coincide, all enquiry into the *initium possessionis*, and into the validity of prior titles, is altogether barred. It does not matter that the basic title originated from someone who had no right to grant it ie *a non domino*, or *a non habente potestatem*. It does not matter that the original title was granted in bad faith. Indeed, the basic title may have been granted *a non domino*, with the sole purpose of possessing thereon for the prescriptive period in order to create a real right in the subjects to which, prior to the granting of the disposition, the possessor had no colourable right or title.

One of the leading early cases on prescription contains the frequently quoted statement: 'It is the great purpose of prescription to support bad titles. Good titles stand in no need of prescription' *Scott v Bruce-Stewart* (1779) 3 Ross LC 334. This proposition is perfectly correct, so far as it goes. But, since a bad title can be validated by prescription, a bad title may prevail in a question with a title originally good on which possession has not followed. Accordingly, a good title may require possession following thereon to maintain it if, or to the extent to which, it conflicts with another competing title.

12.7   **Practical consequences**

The positive prescription has two important practical consequences.

(1)   Ex facie *invalidity*. Prescription cannot cure a title which is itself *ex facie* invalid or which is forged. With these two exceptions, a recorded title initially defective from whatever other cause is validated and put completely beyond challenge by possession for the necessary period. So, if A occupies land without any right or title thereto, he can get a friend to grant a disposition of that land in favour of himself and record it in the Register of Sasines. If he continues to occupy that land for ten years thereafter, then, on the expiry of the ten-year period, the disposition, which was granted in his favour and which was originally totally invalid, becomes valid and unchallengeable; and the true owner of the land, whoever he may be, is no longer able to reduce the disposition, as he could have done initially, and so loses his right of property altogether.

The meaning of *ex facie* invalidity has caused some difficulty and has been discussed in a number of reported cases. It appears that a deed is *ex facie* invalid if, and only if, its invalidity is clearly apparent on its face and without recourse to extrinsic evidence. So a deed which is neither clearly valid nor clearly invalid is not considered to be *ex facie* invalid in the sense meant by the law of prescription and is capable of founding a prescriptive title.

The case of *Watson v Shields* 1996 SCLR 81 is referred to in para 12.2, in the context of mere possession and the possessory remedies. In relation to prescription and the question of *ex facie* invalidity, the same case raises two further points.

Firstly, in an attempt to create a title for themselves, the parties in actual possession granted a disposition in their own favour *a non domino* since they had no prior colourable disposition. Presumably, the intention was to continue in possession on that title and in the fullness of time to validate it by prescription. However, at the date of the raising of the action, the prescriptive period had not run. The Prescription and

Limitation (Scotland) Act 1973, s 1(1)(b) requires that possession should follow on the recording of a deed sufficient in its terms to constitute a title. Further, under s 1(1A) that does not apply if the deed is invalid *ex facie*. This echoes the earlier provision in the Conveyancing (Scotland) Act 1924, s 16 which required possession following on an *ex facie* valid irredeemable title to an estate in land duly recorded. Given the similarity of the wording, it was not thought in the sixth edition of the Manual that this represented any change in the law; and the preceding paragraph dealing with invalidity was written on that assumption.

In his decision in *Watson*, however, the sheriff seems to have taken the view that, because the narrative of the *a non domino* disposition expressly stated that it was granted *a non domino*, that constituted an *ex facie* invalidity. Professors Reid and Gretton, in 'Conveyancing: What Changed in 1994' and 'Conveyancing: What Changed in 1995' (unpublished University of Edinburgh seminar papers), positively expressed the view that to state in the narrative that the disponers had no title was an elementary blunder and automatically rendered the deed *ex facie* invalid. The sixth edition of this book (at para 14.7) disagreed with this view on the basis that whether the disponers had title or not was an extrinsic matter which cannot be determined from the deed itself. It is submitted here, however, that a statement denying title does render the deed 'self destructive' within the meaning of the leading case of *Cooper Scott v Gill Scott* 1924 SC 309 and therefore it cannot be a good foundation writ.

Professors Reid and Gretton suggest in the papers above referred to that where the grantor of an *a non domino* disposition conveys the subjects to himself, as in *Watson*, that deed is a nullity. See also Gretton and Reid *Conveyancing* (2nd edn, 1999), para 7.13. There is certainly some force in this argument, looking to the case which they cite, *Kildrummy (Jersey) Ltd v Inland Revenue Commissioners* 1992 SLT 787. The facts are simply stated. With a view to minimising stamp duty, the owners of a landed estate first set up a company. They then entered into an agreement with the company which took the form of a declaration by the company, delivered to and accepted by the estate owners, that the company would enter into a lease with the estate owners and would hold the lease in trust and as nominees for the estate owners. Having entered into that arrangement, the estate owners then granted a lease to the company. A month later, the estate owners conveyed the estate a Jersey company which they had established. A further month elapsed and the tenant company then assigned their rights as tenants under the lease to the true proprietors, ie the estate owners. The court held that the lease was a nullity because it was a contract entered into between the estate owners as the proprietors of the dominium utile and their own nominees, under the earlier deed of trust. They held the tenants' interest under the lease for the benefit of the true proprietors. In the view of the court, in so doing, the true proprietors were in effect contracting with themselves and so the lease was null. Note, however, that there is no suggestion in any of the judgments in this case that the disposition by the estate owners as true proprietors in favour of their own nominees was void on the footing that they were contracting with themselves, which would seem to destroy the argument that a disposition by A in his own favour is intrinsically null.

That point apart, however, there is ample precedent for the view that a disposition by the true proprietor *a non domino* in his own favour is perfectly valid. Indeed, this device with modifications was regularly used, in the nineteenth century and before, in the setting up of entails. In any number of such cases a disposition by the proprietor in fee simple in favour of himself as institute and his heirs male, or whatever, as substitutes was treated, without question, as a perfectly valid disposition. Likewise, in the context of tenure in the feudal system, A could grant a feu charter in favour of B. There was nothing to prevent A, later, from acquiring the *dominium utile* of the feu by disposition in his own favour. That does not automatically produce consolidation or *confusio* for which some further action on the part of the superior as owner of the two estates, *dominium directum* and *dominium utile,* is required. This may take a variety of forms; but whatever form it takes it inevitably involves a grant by conveyance or resignation by the same person as the proprietor of the dominium utile in favour of himself as his own superior which, subject to certain procedure, then produces consolidation. This is a familiar feature of the feudal system and is illustrated in *Zetland v Glover Incorporation of Perth* (1870) 8 M (HL) 144. Lord Westbury, at 154, deals with the point. There is no suggestion by him or any of the other judges in the House of Lords that a resignation *ad remanentiam* by the proprietor of the dominium utile as vassal in favour of himself as superior was in any way objectionable on these grounds. But any such grant is in essence a conveyance by A to A.

A further example is *Porteous's Executors v Ferguson* 1995 SLT 649. This was a case of competing claimants, one of whom, within the prescriptive period, recorded a disposition *a non domino* in favour of himself. Since prescription had not run on that disposition for the benefit of the disponee thereunder and since that was his only title, it was challenged by the pursuers on the basis that the disponer and disponee had no personal right or title to the property. The case was dismissed on other grounds, dealt with in Chapter 31, but, so far as the report discloses, there was no attempt on the part of counsel for the pursuers to challenge the validity of a disposition *a non domino* by the disponer in favour of himself as disponee, although it was attacked on other grounds.

Finally, it may be noted that Professors Gretton and Reid correctly advise that where A and B hold land under a title with a survivorship destination and B wishes to convey his half to A, the way to do this so that the destination is evacuated is for A and B to convey the whole property to A. See Gretton and Reid *Conveyancing,* para 26.14. Whilst the facts here are not precisely the same, this advice does not sit very easily with their view that the same party cannot be both granter and grantee in the one disposition.

(2) *Ambiguity of description.* In many cases, the description in a title is indefinite or ambiguous, in that the description is not precisely bounding on all sides. In such cases, the extent of the land contained in that title is defined by possession for the necessary period. In order for prescription to operate, the land as possessed must be capable of being reconciled with the land as described; but in the application of this rule

an ambiguous description need not be given its most natural interpretation provided that it is given a possible interpretation, and prescriptive possession may produce a result which might not be anticipated from a first reading of the deed. For a recent and instructive example, see *Suttie v Baird* 1992 SLT 133, discussed by Professor Rennie in 'Prescriptive Possession in the Sasine and Land Registers' (1997) 2 SLPQ 309.

If, however, a description is precise and bounding, possession of land beyond those precise boundaries cannot be founded on or referred to that title, in that the possession on the face of it contradicts the title. Hence the importance of the distinction between bounding titles and titles which are not bounding.

A bounding title in this context is one where the description so precisely defines all the boundaries of the land that the exact extent of it can be ascertained from the title itself.

Where the title is so bounding, corporeal property, such as land and buildings etc, cannot be acquired by prescriptive possession beyond those boundaries; but incorporeal rights, for example a servitude right of access, or a right of fishings, may be acquired beyond the boundaries. The rule is the same even where the property sought to be acquired is being claimed as a part and pertinent. See also C Waelde (ed) *Professor McDonald's Conveyancing Opinions* (1998), pp 122–124.

Not infrequently, there may be some doubt as to the extent of the subjects conveyed or as to the nature of the title in relation to, for example, a particular pertinent. In such cases, to limit the liability of the disponer, but to allow for prescription to operate for the benefit of the disponee, it is common practice for the subjects or the pertinents conveyed to be qualified by some such terms as 'but only insofar as I have right thereto'. This then raises a doubt as to whether or not that is a title sufficient in its terms for the positive prescription to run thereon in terms of the Prescription and Limitation (Scotland) Act 1973, s 1.

It is generally accepted that a title so qualified will operate as a valid foundation title for the running of prescription, and that view is confirmed in the recent decision in *Landward Securities (Edinburgh) Ltd v Inhouse (Edinburgh) Ltd* 1996 GWD 16-962, where a title in these terms was held habile to the running of prescription. The words 'but only insofar as I have right thereto' did not detract from or qualify the description which preceded them.

12.8 The quality of title and nature of possession: earlier provisions

Until 1976, the basic Act was the Prescription Act 1617 which provided, in outline, that possession of land, following on a recorded title, for 40 years, continually and together, peaceably and without lawful interruption, secured the right and title of such possessor beyond challenge, whatever the nature of any competing title may be, unless the title on which he possessed was a forgery. For further detail, see the sixth edition of this book, at para 14.8.

12.9   The quality of title and nature of possession: the 1973 Act

Three distinct but parallel provisions are made in the Prescription and Limitation (Scotland) Act 1973 for three separate cases dealt with in ss 1, 2 and 3.

(1)   *Section 1.* This applies to interests in land generally, and covers, *inter alia*, ownership of land and recorded leases, but not servitudes.
(2)   *Section 2.* This deals with unusual special cases where, for technical reasons, the title has not been recorded, for example allodial land, unrecorded leases etc as in s 2(2)(b) and (a) respectively.
(3)   *Section 3.* This deals exclusively with servitudes and public rights of way.

The general principle of each of the three sections is the same, namely, if in any given case the owner (and his predecessors in title, if any) have possessed a heritable property or exercised a heritable right for the appropriate period following on the appropriate title, then on the expiry of the period, the validity of the title or right is put beyond challenge. But the detail differs in each of the three sections to take account of the different nature of the title, and of the property or interest in each case.

12.10   SECTION 1. INTERESTS IN LAND: GENERAL

So far as Register of Sasines titles are concerned, the provision takes the following form under the Prescription and Limitation (Scotland) Act 1973.

(1)   *Section 1(1).* If:
   (a)   an interest in land has been possessed by the reputed owner (and his predecessors in title, if any), for a continuous period of ten years, openly and peaceably; and
   (b)   that possession was founded on, and followed, the recording in the General Register of Sasines of a deed sufficient in its terms to constitute a title to that interest;
   then, on the expiry of that ten-year period, the validity of that title so far as relating to that interest is exempt from challenge except on the grounds that the deed is *ex facie* invalid; or was forged.
(2)   *Section 1(2).* The section applies to any interest in land, the title to which can competently be recorded. Obviously, this covers ownership and recorded leases as stated above; but, by virtue of the definition in s 15 of the 1973 Act, interest in land here specifically excludes servitudes, which are specially dealt with in s 3.

Upon feudal abolition, on 28 November 2004, the expression 'interest in land' will be replaced by 'land or real right in land': see the Abolition of Feudal Tenure etc (Scotland) Act 2000, s 76 and Schedule 12, para 33.

12.11 Possession

In terms of s 1(1)(a) of the Prescription and Limitation (Scotland) Act 1973 there must have been possession for a continuous period of ten years which has been held: 'openly, peaceably and without any judicial interruption.'

In one special case, under s 1(4) of the 1973 Act, possession must be for 20 years, not 10 years. This is where the right claimed by possession is a right to the foreshore or to salmon fishings as against the Crown, as owner of the *regalia*. This only applies as between the proprietor claiming the right and the Crown. Thus, if the Crown has granted salmon fishings on a Crown charter to a Crown vassal who in turn sub-feus on a charter which refers to fishings but not 'salmon fishings', and if the sub-vassal possesses the salmon fishings on that title for ten years, he has a good claim to the salmon fishings as against his superior. The superior's right as against the Crown is established by the plain terms of the title and requires no possession to validate it.

This requirement as to possession is then further amplified by s 4 of the 1973 Act dealing with interruption, by s 14 dealing with the computation of the period, and by the definitions in s 15.

The possession may be natural, by actual physical occupation on the part of the proprietor claiming the right; or it may be civil, by actual occupation on behalf of the owner by his tenants or some other person: see the 1973 Act, s 15(1). See also D E L Johnston *Prescription and Limitation* (1999), paras 16.13–16.14.

In either case, 'possession' implies *animus*, ie it must be either in the belief that the occupant is in possession as of right, or with the intention of establishing a right. Possession *in mala fide* counts. But none of this is statutory. See Johnston, para 16.05.

The possession must be in support of and consistent with, the title, not 'in the teeth of the title'. See above, with particular reference to bounding titles.

The possession must be exclusive, and sufficient in extent to support the right claimed by it. The extent and nature of possession vary according to circumstances. Where the possessor has an alternative right to possess, eg as a tenant, possession arising out of this right is insufficient for prescriptive purposes. See C Waelde (ed) *Professor McDonald's Conveyancing Opinions* (1998), pp 124–127.

Under s 1(1)(a) of the 1973 Act, the possession must be for a continuous period of 10 years (or, under s 1(4), 20 years) 'openly, peaceably and without any judicial interruption'. As to continuity, the term 'continuous' is interpreted in relation to the subjects in question. Thus, it is not necessary, in order to establish a right to salmon fishing by prescription, to show that the claimant has fished continuously, 24 hours a day throughout the 10-year period (or 20-year period in a question with the Crown); nor, in the case of a right of way, that someone has walked continuously over it throughout the 20-year period. On the other hand, mere occasional acts of apparent possession will not serve. There must be regular and continuing acts throughout the period.

Further, the possession must be open and peaceable, not clandestine or in the face of opposition.

The leading modern case on the nature, extent and quality of possession required to establish a prescriptive title is *Hamilton v McIntosh Donald* 1994 SLT 793. The pursuer had an unchallengeable title to the subjects, but had never had possession; the defenders had a title recorded in 1950 but *a non domino* which was habile to acquisition by prescriptive possession. A number of acts of possession were alleged by the defenders and the critical question was whether, in the circumstances and looking to the nature of the subjects, these acts of possession, some of which were proved, were sufficient to establish possession of the whole subjects for a ten-year period openly, peaceably and without any judicial interruption. There had been no judicial interruption and the question therefore was whether there had been open and peaceable possession sufficient to constitute a valid title.

The Lord Justice-Clerk, in his judgment commencing at p 796, lays down nine requirements which the alleged possessor must satisfy in order to establish title. These can be summarised briefly.

(1) There must be a habile title. In this case, although *a non domino*, the title was otherwise habile and was not significantly challenged.

(2) Possession must be continuous, open and peaceable without judicial interruption.

(3) It may be natural or civil which was important here because most of the acts of possession were acts arguably in the latter category.

(4) The required acts of possession depend on the nature of the subjects. Again, that was important here because the subjects were of an unusual nature, being largely a marsh or peat bog which, arguably, was largely unusable for any reasonable purpose.

(5) Possession must be directly referable to the title. That did not cause any problem in this case.

(6) It must be continuous. This did cause problems in this case, because the continuity was arguably insufficient to justify the defender's claims.

(7) *Tantum prescriptum quantum possessum* (the measure of prescription is the amount of possession). Again, that was important here in that, arguably, such possession as could be established might be said to have been localised to very small areas, and might not justify treating that limited possession as possession of the whole. A distinction falls to be made between the cases where prescription is relied on to constitute a new right and cases where it is relied on for the purpose of establishing the extent of the right. That distinction has been criticised.

(8) In appropriate cases, circumstantial evidence is acceptable, with the proviso that the claimant must nonetheless establish whether there has in fact been requisite possession.

(9) The onus of establishing possession lies on the party claiming to have acquired by prescriptive possession.

This is undoubtedly a useful and exhaustive survey of the law of possession. It was particularly important in the case in question and the decision was very evenly balanced. One of the judges in the Inner House dissented, and in a subsequent article

'Possession: Nine Tenths of the Law' published at 1994 SLT (News) 261, Professor Rennie concludes that the defenders had not in fact made out a sufficient case. See also D E L Johnston *Prescription and Limitation* (1999), para 16.14. If the possession is physically interrupted either because, for a definite period, the possessor excludes himself from possession or is excluded by another, that will interrupt the prescription and the period would have to start to run again entire from the date when possession was resumed. The same effect follows on judicial interruption, ie where a competing claimant has raised an action to exclude the possessor from his possession.

For a discussion of acts of interruption and whether or not they can be treated as excluding a claim to continuous peaceable possession, see *Hogg v Campbell* 1993 GWD 27-1712.

12.12 SECTION 1. INTERESTS IN LAND UNDER REGISTRATION OF TITLE

For titles registered in the Land Register, certain modifications are made to s 1 of the Prescription and Limitation (Scotland) Act 1973 by s 10 of the Land Registration (Scotland) Act 1979. This is in recognition of the fact that, on registration in the Land Register without exclusion of indemnity, an immediate and, in principle, unchallengeable title is conferred on the non-fraudulent or careless applicant, provided that he enters into and continues in possession. Hence in the normal case there is no need for positive prescription.

However, where an applicant for registration of title presents to the Keeper a title which is clearly defective, the Keeper may exclude indemnity, in which case, under the rectification rules, if the invalidity is later established by appropriate action by a competing proprietor, this is one of the cases where the Keeper can rectify the Register to the disadvantage of the proprietor in possession. Therefore, if a title is registered with exclusion of indemnity, it still requires the ten-year prescription to cure that defect. On the expiry of the ten-year period, the proprietor with a registered title excluding indemnity simply applies to the Keeper for the removal of that exclusion, whereupon his title immediately becomes virtually unchallengeable.

The detailed rules for positive prescription are set out in s 1 of the 1973 Act (as amended), and follow closely the equivalent rules for Sasines titles. There are three requirements. First, the interest in land in question must be registered in the Land Register in the name of the person founding on prescription. Secondly, indemnity must be excluded by the Keeper. Where it is not excluded, positive prescription cannot fortify the title, even where the proprietor was fraudulent or careless. This contrasts with the Register of Sasines. Thirdly, the land must be possessed in precisely the same way and for precisely the same period as for Sasines land (for which see above). Prescription is excluded if the registration proceeded on a forged deed and the applicant was aware of the forgery at the time of registration.

Contrary to what might at first sight appear, a title recorded in the Register of Sasines can still effectively compete with a registered title.

Suppose that A is already in possession of one hectare of ground on a title recorded in the Register of Sasines, which either expressly includes, or is habile to include, that hectare; but the title to that hectare is defective.

Under the present rule, possession on that title for ten years will cure the defect, and give A an absolute right thereto.

Suppose that B acquires an adjoining estate by disposition which expressly includes A's one hectare. B registers the title in the Land Register, and so becomes the registered proprietor of A's hectare. If, in that situation, A continues in possession for the ten-year period and so validates his right by prescription, A could then apply to the Keeper for a rectification of the Register so as to exclude A's hectare from B's registered title. This is not one of the cases where B could object to rectification because, since A is in possession, B, the registered proprietor, is not the proprietor in possession. On rectification, B might have a claim against the Keeper, but he could not insist on retaining his title to the one hectare because, lacking possession, the Register will be rectified against B, to exclude that one hectare from B's earlier registration.

In the converse situation, where B registers a title to 100 hectares in the Land Register and where, after the date of that registration, A then records a title habile to include the one hectare in the Register of Sasines, A can never prevail against B on a title recorded in the Register of Sasines because, the 100-hectare title having first been registered, it is no longer competent to record a title in the Register of Sasines which includes any part of that 100 hectares under s 8(4) of the 1979 Act. If A is to compete with B, whose title is already registered, A himself must apply for registration of a title to the one hectare. Depending on the circumstances presented to him, the Keeper may be prepared to accept that application and register A as proprietor to the one hectare only, even although B is already shown as the proprietor of that hectare and 99 more; but, when registering A's title, the Keeper will exclude indemnity.

If A then possesses the one hectare on that registered title, excluding indemnity, for the period of positive prescription, he can then prevail against B, and require rectification of the Register in his favour in respect of that one hectare because B is not in possession. See, generally, the *Registration of Title Practice Book*, paras 6.5–6.11.

12.13   SECTION 2. INTERESTS IN LAND: SPECIAL CASES

Almost identical provision is made in this section for special and very unusual cases where, for technical reasons, the title is not recorded or is not recordable: see para 12.9.

In contrast to s 1 of the Prescription and Limitation (Scotland) Act 1973, under s 2 possession is founded on and follows the execution of a deed (whether recorded or not) which is sufficient to constitute a title to that interest. Note particularly that the initial title need not be recorded. But, in all these cases, the necessary period of possession is, under s 2(1)(a), 20 years, not 10 years as in s 1.

12.14 SECTION 3. POSITIVE SERVITUDES AND PUBLIC RIGHTS OF WAY

Under this section, alternative provisions are made for the establishing of servitude rights and public right of way by prescription, taking account of the special nature of a servitude right. This is discussed at para 16.9.

12.15 The long negative prescription

This is dealt with in the context of Examination of Title at paras 32.77 and 32.78.

12.16 Evidence of possession

In all the foregoing situations, the critical question frequently turns on possession over a period of years. In practice, possession is normally taken for granted unless there is something in the title to create a reasonable doubt. If so, it may be necessary to obtain a declarator of ownership.

In certain situations, to avoid expense and unnecessary delay, the parties may be content to rely on affidavit evidence by two or more parties as to possession or lack of possession over the relevant period; and it may be useful to obtain this coupled with indemnity to protect the interests of one party or the other. It is unlikely, however, that affidavit evidence alone would be accepted by the court (or the Keeper).

Similar situations arise in other contexts, for example under the Matrimonial Homes (Family Protection) (Scotland) Act 1981 where the affidavits provided at the time of the original transfer have been lost. Again, facts reinforced by affidavit evidence with a statement of indemnity may serve the purpose. There is no situation, however, in the absence of any positive provision in the missives, in which a purchaser could be compelled to accept a title where there is any genuine possibility that the position is not in fact as it seems to be.

PART 3

REGULATION OF LANDOWNERSHIP

Chapter 13

Land Regulation: Introduction

13.1 The nature of ownership

It is often stated that ownership is 'absolute': see, for example, Bell *Principles*, s 939. Inherent in this is the idea that ownership is unititular. There can be only one real right of ownership of one piece of property at any one time, and the owner has the right of exclusive use of the land, and the freedom to use the land as he or she wishes. However, the absolute nature of ownership is qualified in various ways. There are various restrictions imposed as a consequence of owners living in proximity to other owners, and as part of a greater society.

Generally, regulation arises in one of two ways: by public law or by private law.

13.2 REGULATION BY PUBLIC LAW

Regulation by public law is referred to by Professor Gordon as 'social control of land use': W M Gordon *Scottish Land Law* (2nd edn, 1999), Chapter 27. Public law regulation allows the interests of society and the public to be taken account of in determining how an individual may use the land. These interests can conflict with the interests of the individual landowner. Chapter 20 of this Manual gives an overview of such public law regulation.

13.3 REGULATION BY PRIVATE LAW

Regulation by private law can be either by the law of delict or through the use of the law of property.

Property law deals with rights and obligations that affect individual parcels of property in perpetuity. Consequently, these affect the owners and occupiers of the land at any given instant. As a result, property law will be used prospectively. It will attempt to regulate the way land is used in future through allowing individuals to impose restrictions and other obligations on the way land is used in perpetuity. It attempts to anticipate what people would wish to do with their land, and to regulate that. The obligations imposed through using property law are referred to as title conditions. These form the basis of much of the rest of this Part of this Manual.

13.4   Delicts

The law of delict deals with relationships between individuals. It creates personal rights and obligations, generally providing by involuntary application of law based on the fault of an individual that the wrongdoer must desist from acting in a certain way that affects or causes damage to (or that will affect or cause damage to) another party, or by providing that where the wrongdoer has acted in a certain way causing damage or loss to an innocent party the wrongdoer must compensate the party affected by that action. In imposing obligations that generally arise from events that have happened, the law of delict typically applies retrospectively. The development of case law in delict, however, allows an owner to anticipate how a court will react to certain activities on his or her property, and will therefore also serve to act as a means of regulating how an owner will use his or her property. There are a number of delicts that relate to the use of land. In this chapter the two principal delicts affecting land use are examined: liability under the Occupiers' Liability (Scotland) Act 1960; and the law of nuisance. Other delicts are beyond the scope of this Manual, but the interested reader is referred to Gordon *Scottish Land Law*, Chapter 26, for a valuable study of delicts affecting land.

13.5   OCCUPIERS' LIABILITY

Certain acts, or omissions, by a proprietor of land are regarded by the law as innocuous in themselves; but if the landowner (or occupier) in the doing of such an act or in such an omission is negligent or reckless and, as a result, injury or damage is caused to some other person or property, then he may be liable in damages. The law of delict is concerned with compensating a person who has suffered loss as a result of the wrongful actions of another. To succeed in a claim it is necessary to establish that the defender owed the pursuer a duty of care and that there was a breach of that duty giving rise to the injury or damage complained of. Liability in such cases is based on *culpa*.

Potential liability will be a consideration for any proprietor of land or buildings to which the public has access. The reform of the law relating to public access to the countryside by the Land Reform (Scotland) Act 2003 (discussed in Chapter 20) has focused particular attention on the potential liability of a heritable proprietor for injury sustained by a member of the public taking access to his land. Quite apart from the duty of care that arises at common law, persons occupying or having control of land or other premises owe a duty of care to all persons entering thereon, including trespassers, by virtue of the Occupiers' Liability (Scotland) Act 1960. Section 2(1) of the 1960 Act provides that the occupier must show to persons entering the premises 'such care as in all the circumstances of the case is reasonable' to ensure that they do not suffer injury or damage as a result of dangers due to the state of the premises or anything done or omitted to be done on them. What is reasonable is very much a matter of fact and degree. The extent to which a person may be expected to be on the premises, the characteristics of the claimant (young, infirm, etc) and the nature of the dangers will all be relevant in determining what is reasonable in the circumstances. Whilst s 5(2) of the Land Reform (Scotland) Act 2003 provides that in principle an occupier's duty of care is unaffected by the new legislation, it may be the case that if more individuals are encouraged to take access to land as a result, then in practice the risk of a claim against him or her is more likely.

There will be no liability in respect of risks which the claimant has voluntarily accepted: s 2(3) of the 1960 Act. This may be helpful in the context of access to the countryside because people engage in open-air recreation very much at their own risk. They do not, however, accept the risk of injury from land management operations carried on by the defender; nor do they accept the risk of injury resulting from latent defects in the state of the premises (for example, an underwater hazard in a popular bathing area). They would, however, be expected to take suitable precautions against patent hazards such as steep ground.

13.6 NUISANCE

In certain circumstances, the law regards particular acts by the heritable proprietor as unacceptable in that they occasion 'serious disturbance or substantial inconvenience to his neighbour or material damage to his neighbour's property': *Watt v Jamieson* 1954 SC 56. Such conduct is referred to as a 'nuisance'. The law of nuisance operates as some constraint on an owner's freedom to enjoy his land in the manner of his choice.

A nuisance occurs when a person so uses his property as to cause unreasonable interference in the comfortable enjoyment by a neighbour of his property. The onus of proof in a nuisance action lies on the pursuer: *Webster v Lord Advocate* 1984 SLT 13. While nuisance is judged from the standpoint of the victim, it is necessary to show that the activity complained of is *plus quam tolerabile*: *Watt v Jamieson*. In other words, the harm must be material. In an action for nuisance based on disturbance to the comfortable enjoyment of property, as opposed to material damage, it will also be necessary to show that the activity complained of was out of place in the locality: *Inglis v Shotts Iron Co* (1881) 8 R 1006. As the editors of *Gloag and Henderson* observe, in *Introduction to the Law of Scotland* (11th edn, 2001), para 31.10, 'what is a nuisance in a residential neighbourhood would not necessarily be one in an industrial district'.

Nuisance, at least in the context of disturbance to the comfortable enjoyment of property, generally involves conduct which is continuing rather than one-off so that interdict will be the principal remedy sought. It has been established that it is not necessary to prove *culpa* where the only remedy sought is interdict: *Logan v Wang (UK) Ltd* 1991 SLT 580. However, a claim for damages for nuisance, for example for material damage to property, is classified as a delictual claim so that *culpa* would have to be shown: *RHM Bakeries (Scotland) Ltd v Strathclyde Regional Council* 1985 SC (HL) 17.

Chapter 14

Title Conditions: General

14.1 Introduction

Property law regulates land use through the imposition of title conditions. These are obligations encumbering land (or a right in land) imposed voluntarily by the landowner (or holder of the right in land). Unlike obligations undertaken by contract, the utility of title conditions as a means of regulation is that, once validly imposed, the obligation 'runs with' the land (or the right), rather than merely being enforceable only against the person that undertook the obligation. An example illustrates how this operates.

Angela owns a house and grants a title condition in favour of Brian: that obligation encumbers the house, not Angela as an individual, and is enforced against Angela as the owner of the house, not in her personal capacity. Thus, if Angela sells the house to Christopher, it is not Angela that the condition can be enforced against but Christopher in his capacity as owner of the house encumbered by the title condition.

14.2 'Title conditions'

The term 'title condition' is a new one and is used in the Title Conditions (Scotland) Act 2003. It defines the obligations that can be varied or discharged by the Lands Tribunal for Scotland. The statutory definition is in s 122(1) of the 2003 Act. It provides:

"'title condition" means—
(a) a real burden;
(b) a servitude;
(c) an affirmative obligation imposed, in a servitude, on the person who is in right of the servitude;
(d) a condition in a registrable lease if it is a condition which relates to the land (but not a condition which imposes either an obligation to pay rent or an obligation of relief relating to the payment of rent);
(e) a condition or stipulation –
    (i) imposed under subsection (2) of s 3 of the Registration of Leases

(Scotland) Act 1857 (assignation of recorded leases) in an assignation which has been duly registered; or

(ii) contained in a deed registered under subsection (2A) or (5) of that section;

(f) a condition in an agreement entered into under s 7 of the National Trust for Scotland Order Confirmation Act 1938; or

(g) such other condition relating to land as the Scottish Ministers may, for the purposes of this paragraph, prescribe by order'.

This definition replaces and expands the definition of 'land obligation' used in the Conveyancing and Feudal Reform (Scotland) Act 1970 to determine the obligations that could be varied or discharged by the Lands Tribunal.

Many of the title conditions listed in s 122(1) of the 2003 Act are not considered in detail in this Part of this book. Instead, attention is focused on the two most important types: real burdens and servitudes.

14.3   Real burdens and servitudes

Real burdens and servitudes are members of the same genus: K G C Reid *The Law of Property in Scotland* (1996), Chapter 7, and K G C Reid 'Defining Real Conditions' 1989 JR 69. Both are title conditions affecting land or buildings (rather than affecting a subordinate real right in land). In addition, in both title to enforce the condition is generally annexed to other land in the neighbourhood of the affected land, rather than an individual. However, personal real burdens – introduced by the Title Conditions (Scotland) Act 2003 – are an exception to this.

Thus, in the example given above, if Angela had created a servitude or real burden over her house in favour of Brian, this would have been required to have been created in favour of Brian in his capacity as owner of neighbouring land. As with other title conditions, the obligation would affect the property, meaning that successors in title to Angela as owner of this property would be liable to perform the condition. The property encumbered in the obligation is referred to as 'the burdened property'. However, where the condition is a servitude or real burden it would be enforced by Brian in his capacity as owner of the neighbouring land. If Brian were to sell this land to Diane, Brian would no longer be able to enforce the condition. Instead, Diane could enforce the condition in her capacity as owner of the neighbouring land. The land that has title to enforce the condition is referred to as 'the benefited property'.

14.4   Purpose of real burdens and servitudes

As members of the same genus, servitudes and real burdens perform slightly different functions.

Real burdens can regulate the burdened property by imposing obligations requiring the burdened owner to do something (such as to maintain or rebuild property); or not to do something (such as a prohibition of running a business from the burdened property, or building on the burdened property).

Servitudes can regulate the burdened property by imposing an obligation allowing the benefited owner to make some use of it, such as allowing the benefited owner to traverse the property, or to make use of a water supply there.

14.5 BEFORE FEUDAL ABOLITION

Prior to feudal abolition there was some overlap between servitudes and real burdens. Servitudes could impose obligations allowing the benefited owner to use the burdened property ('positive servitudes') or prohibiting certain building operations on the burdened property ('negative servitudes'). As well as imposing obligations to do, or obligations not to do something, a real burden could impose an obligation allowing the benefited owner to use the burdened property (for example, to use part of it as a car parking space).

The Title Conditions (Scotland) Act 2003 rationalises the overlap. Negative servitudes are converted into real burdens: s 80 of the 2003 Act, discussed at paras 17.16 to 17.21; and real burdens allowing use are converted into positive servitudes: s 81 of the 2003 Act, discussed at paras 16.1 and 16.2.

14.6 Title Conditions (Scotland) Act 2003

The Title Conditions (Scotland) Act 2003 codifies and amends the law of real burdens; and makes certain amendments (wide-ranging in effect) to the law of servitudes. Chapters 15 to 18 generally cover the 2003 Act, and the surviving common law principles regarding real burdens and servitudes: Chapter 15 deals with the new taxonomy and creation of real burdens; Chapter 16 with general principles applicable to and creation of servitudes; Chapter 17 with the enforcement of real burdens; and Chapter 18 with the variation and discharge of real burdens and servitudes, and the Lands Tribunal jurisdiction to vary or discharge title conditions.

Chapter 15

Title Conditions: Real Burdens and their Creation

15.1 Introduction

The Title Conditions (Scotland) Act 2003 contains a statutory statement of virtually the whole of the law of real burdens. Part 1 is a restatement of the common law (with improvements) and provides detailed rules of content, creation, enforcement, interpretation, and variation and discharge. Variation and discharge is dealt with in Chapter 18 of this book. Enforcement of real burdens (including interpretation) is dealt with in Chapter 17. In this chapter the law and practice on creation is examined. The model development management scheme introduced by the 2003 Act is also briefly considered.

As well as restating the current law, the 2003 Act introduces a number of new types of real burden and provides a more rational framework for some innovations introduced by the Abolition of Feudal Tenure etc (Scotland) Act 2000.

This chapter will not consider feudal real burdens. These are the real burdens created by feudal superiors over the *dominium utile* of land. Feudal real burdens are to be abolished from the appointed day (28 November 2004). The current law relating to feudal real burdens, and the rules for preservation and conversion of certain feudal real burdens are found in Chapter 19. Prior to the appointed day new feudal real burdens should not be created if the burdens can be readily created using the mechanisms to be described in this chapter. Nor should feudal real burdens be created prior to the appointed day if they cannot be readily preserved under Part 4 of the 2000 Act (as discussed in Chapter 19). For the creation of feudal burdens – a matter now primarily of historical interest – see paras 10.8 to 10.20 of the sixth edition of this book.

15.2 The types of real burdens: taxonomy and definitions

The Title Conditions (Scotland) Act 2003 refers to a number of different types of real burden. These can be analysed based on: where enforcement rights rest; content; or the nature of the obligation. If analysis is based on enforcement there are two principal types of real burden: praedial real burdens – where enforcement rights lie with the owner (or other occupier) of land in the neighbourhood of the property encumbered; and personal real burdens – where enforcement lies with an individual. However, one type – the manager burden – while stated to be a personal real burden in s 1(3) of the 2003 Act, shares characteristics with praedial real burdens in that the existence of the burden is dependent on the person appointing the manager owning property in the neighbourhood of the burdened property (and in the view of Professor Reid can be a praedial burden: see K G C Reid *The Abolition of Feudal Tenure in Scotland* (2003), para 4.27, n 1). If analysis is based on content there are a number of discrete types of burden, including: maritime burdens; facility burdens; conservation burdens; and economic development burdens. These types are considered later in this chapter. If analysis is based on the type of obligation there are only two permissible types of real burden: affirmative burdens; and negative burdens. These are examined at para 15.22.

15.3   Praedial real burdens

The term 'praedial real burden' is not used in the Title Conditions (Scotland) Act 2003, but it is useful nonetheless. It is 'an encumbrance on land constituted in favour of the owner of other land in that person's capacity as owner of that other land': s 1(1) of the 2003 Act. In relation to burdens created before the appointed day it includes all non-feudal burdens (including those where title to enforce is implied in common schemes: see paras 17.32–17.45) where there are two pieces of land. In nature a praedial real burden is like a servitude. One parcel of land is encumbered; the other parcel of land benefits from that encumbrance and can enforce it. The land encumbered is the 'burdened property', although previous legislation referred to 'the servient tenement': see the Abolition of Feudal Tenure etc (Scotland) Act 2000. The land that benefits from the encumbrance is referred to as the 'benefited property', although it is referred to as 'the dominant tenement' in the 2000 Act. Typically, these two properties will be in close proximity. It is the property that is burdened and benefited, not the individual owners (or tenants or other occupiers such as non-entitled spouses). A praedial real burden 'runs with' the land, meaning that the owner at any particular point in time of the parcel of land that forms the benefited or burdened property can enforce or is restricted by the burden. However, when that owner sells the parcel of land on to a third party his or her right to enforce, or obligation imposed by the restriction, will cease.

For example, if Ann owns a property that benefits from a burden, and Brian owns the property encumbered by the burden, Ann can enforce the burden against Brian. If Ann sells her property on to Carol, now Carol can enforce against Brian. Ann has no residual right to enforce against Brian. If Brian then sells his property on to Donna, it is Donna that must comply with the burden. Brian generally has no residual liability. For praedial real burdens, enforcement and liability are dependent on ownership (or occupation) of the land.

15.4 Personal real burdens

Personal real burdens are defined in s 1(3) of the Title Conditions (Scotland) Act 2003: they are 'burdens constituted in favour of a person other than by reference to the person's capacity as owner of any land'. Personal real burdens are also encumbrances on land. As with praedial real burdens, the property encumbered by a personal real burden is known as the 'burdened property': the encumbrance running with the land binding whomsoever the owner (or in certain cases the occupier) is at any particular point in time. It is in enforcement that personal real burdens differ. The right to enforce a personal real burden lies with a person, juristic or natural; that person need not own any property in the vicinity of the burdened property.

15.5 Types of praedial real burdens

In addition to a set of general rules applicable to all burdens, there are special rules applicable to what are referred to as 'community burdens'. Those praedial real burdens that are not community burdens are sometimes referred to as 'neighbour burdens': see, for example, K G C Reid *The Abolition of Feudal Tenure in Scotland* (2003), para 2.8. This was the terminology in the Scottish Law Commission *Report on Real Burdens* (Scot Law Com No 181, 2000), para 1.9. Neighbour burdens are burdens where the benefited property has the right to enforce against the burdened property, but the burdened property has no reciprocal right of enforcement. Community burdens involve reciprocal enforcement rights. While as descriptive terms these provided a useful distinction for real burdens pre-abolition, it is questionable how useful the distinction is after the appointed day. The statutory definition of community burdens precludes the inclusion of some burdens where there are reciprocal rights of enforcement; and may not apply to some burdens where there are no reciprocal rights of enforcement within a common scheme: Title Conditions (Scotland) Act 2003, s 52. See para 17.34. In the latter case the existence of the common scheme means that description of the burdens as 'neighbour burdens' is misleading.

15.6 COMMUNITY BURDENS

The term 'Community burdens' is defined in s 25 of the Title Conditions (Scotland) Act 2003. This provides that:

'where –
(a) real burdens are imposed under a common scheme on four or more units; and
(b) each of those units is, in relation to some or all of those burdens, both a benefited property and a burdened property,
the burdens shall, in relation to the units, be known as "community burdens"'.

There must be a common scheme, an expression not defined in the legislation. This is unfortunate as the term is the central concept for a number of sections in the 2003 Act (including ss 52 and 53, as well as the community burdens scheme). The explanatory notes on community burdens offer indirect assistance. In para 127 it is provided that 'A community is a group of four or more properties all subject to the same or similar burdens and which can be mutually enforced'. The requirement that a minimum of four properties are affected means that burdens such as those regulating the small commercial development comprising a convenience store, a public house and a bookmakers described in *Co-operative Wholesale Society v Ushers Brewery* 1975 SLT (Lands Tr) 9 will not be community burdens.

Community burdens apply to properties subject to the same or similar burdens. This will arise where an area is developed and subject to burdens imposed in a common deed covering the whole of the area (such as a deed of conditions, or a conveyance of the area); or may arise if the same or similar burdens have been imposed in successive sales or conveyances of individual plots within the area. These two instances mirror the examples given by Lord Watson, in determining whether there are implied rights of enforcement, in *Hislop v MacRitchie's Trustees* (1881) 8 R (HL) 95 at 103.

Such instances can arise after the appointed day (where community burdens will generally be expressly created), or will apply to burdens created before the appointed day, either through the express creation of enforcement rights or through the implication of title to enforce within common schemes under ss 52 to 54 of the 2003 Act (discussed at paras 17.33 to 17.45).

Community burdens have special provisions for enforcement, and variation and discharge, dealt with in Chapters 17 and 18 respectively.

15.7   FACILITY AND SERVICE BURDENS

Facility and service burdens are types of praedial burdens. They were introduced by s 23 of the Abolition of Feudal Tenure etc (Scotland) Act 2000. However, this provision was repealed by the Title Conditions (Scotland) Act 2003 and the operative provision for the burdens is now s 56 of the 2003 Act. This provides that, where there are facility or service burdens, every property benefiting from the facility or service shall have title to enforce the burdens.

'Facility burden' is defined in s 122 of the 2003 Act, which provides that it is 'a real burden which regulates the maintenance, management, reinstatement or use of heritable property which constitutes, and is intended to constitute, a facility of benefit to other land'. Subsection (3) then gives illustrative examples of types of property that may be facilities of benefit to other land. They include: common parts of a tenement; common recreation areas; boundary walls; and private roads. Examples of facility burdens would be burdens to maintain a tenement roof, or burdens to maintain a private water supply. In many housing developments it will be provided that the owners are to maintain roads or water supplies. However, when the local (or other public) authority takes over the maintenance, the burden cannot be a facility burden. This is a matter that can be checked in the property enquiry certificate: see para 33.4.

Service burdens are more unusual. They are real burdens which relate 'to the provision of services to land other than the burdened property': s 122(1) of the 2003 Act. This could involve an obligation on a burdened owner to provide a water supply or electricity supply.

Often facility burdens will also be community burdens in that the properties burdened will typically also be the properties that are given title to enforce. For example, in a tenement, often every flat would be encumbered by the obligation to maintain the roof evidencing a common scheme in the tenement. Each flat benefits from the maintenance of the roof. Accordingly, there are reciprocal enforcement rights. However, facility (and service) burdens do not require to be part of a common scheme. The rules on variation and discharge for facility and service burdens therefore depend on attributes other than merely being a facility or service burden.

15.8 RIGHTS OF PRE-EMPTION AND OPTIONS TO ACQUIRE

Prior to the implementation of the Title Conditions (Scotland) Act 2003 it was possible to create a number of options to acquire property as real burdens. An option to acquire property is an undertaking by the owner of land that on the occurrence of a specific event a third party will have the opportunity to acquire the property. Such options are generally constituted contractually. However, some are constituted as real burdens. The most common form of option to acquire created as a real burden is a right of pre-emption: see para 15.9. Although, prior to the 2003 Act, it was possible to create rights of redemption (see para 15.10) as real burdens, and rights of reversion could also be created (see para 15.11), it will no longer be possible to create rights of redemption or rights of reversion as real burdens (praedial or personal) after the appointed day: s 3(5) of the 2003 Act. However, it will still be possible to create a right of pre-emption as a real burden.

15.9 Rights of pre-emption

A right of pre-emption is a right of first refusal common in many areas of property law. In conveyancing practice it will typically be constituted as a real burden on the sale of land. For example, Zoe owns a farm and sells part of the farmland to Yann. She provides in the sale that, if Yann wishes to sell the land on to a third party, Zoe can acquire the property at the price that a third party may offer. Zoe's option to acquire is protected by the imposition of a right of pre-emption as a real burden in the sale. Yann's property is encumbered by the right of pre-emption which is constituted in favour of Zoe's farmland. The right of pre-emption cannot be exercised by Zoe until the owner of the burdened property (Yann, or his successors) decides to sell the property on.

Rights of pre-emption tended to be created as feudal real burdens prior to the appointed day, but were sometimes created as praedial real burdens. If created as a feudal real burden, the right of pre-emption can be preserved as a praedial real burden under s 18(7)(b)(ii) of the Abolition of Feudal Tenure etc (Scotland) Act 2000, or as a personal real burden under s 18A of the 2000 Act. For details, see para 19.78.

There has been a special regime for the exercise and extinction of all rights of pre-emption since 1938. Special rules continue to apply under the Title Conditions (Scotland) Act 2003: see the discussion at paras 18.30 and 18.52.

Rights of pre-emption can still be constituted as praedial real burdens subsequent to the appointed day: s 3(5) of the 2003 Act.

In a sheriff court decision in 2001, *Macdonald-Haig v Gerlings* (3 December 2001, unreported), Inverness Sheriff Court, a right of pre-emption was challenged as being contrary to Article 1 of the first Protocol to the European Convention on Human Rights. For a discussion of the case, see K G C Reid and G L Gretton *Conveyancing 2002* (2003), pp 63–65. The challenge was unsuccessful. The sheriff noted that:

'I am not persuaded that the terms of the Article can properly be applied to a situation such as the present where, in effect, the Defender seeks to avoid the consequences of a contract, the terms of which were known to him before he possessed the property, freely entered into between two private individuals, albeit two individuals other than the Defender himself'.

15.10   Rights of redemption

A right of redemption differs from a right of pre-emption. It is a right of repurchase granted to the benefited owner: when the right can be exercised depends on the terms of its creation. Some examples are given by the Scottish Law Commission in its *Report on Real Burdens* (Scot Law Com No 181, 2000) at para 10.3. It can be exercised at the instance of the holder, exercised on occurrence of a trigger event, or after the expiry of a pre-determined period of time.

Since 1 September 1974 it has not been possible to create a right of redemption with a duration of more than 20 years: see the Land Tenure Reform (Scotland) Act 1974, s 12. From the appointed day it will not be possible to create a right of redemption as a real burden running with land.

Those rights of redemption created as praedial real burdens before 1 September 1974 remain effective in perpetuity, subject to the general rules on extinction of real burdens. If created after that date they are subject to the 20-year duration.

If a right of redemption was created as a feudal real burden it can be preserved under s 18(7)(b)(ii) of the Abolition of Feudal Tenure etc (Scotland) Act 2000 as a praedial real burden, or as a personal redemption burden under s 18A of the 2000 Act. For details, see para 19.78.

15.11   Rights of reversion

Related to rights of redemption are rights of reversion: these provided that the holder of the right could automatically reacquire the burdened property on the satisfaction of certain conditions. Rights of reversion tended to be used in pre-1970 *ex facie* conveyances in security to allow the debtor to reacquire the property on repayment of his or her loan. However, it appears that their use was not limited to securities, although reversions were created not as praedial but as personal encumbrances running with the land provided they were registered: see the Reversion Act 1469 and the Registration Act 1617. It is not clear how many rights of reversion are on the registers created outwith the context of securities. Ordinary clauses of irritancy that have appeared in feudal charters and dispositions to buttress real burdens may be framed in such a way that they suggest the property will automatically revert to the benefited owner. However, these are not thought to be rights of reversion but irritancy clauses. As such, they ceased to have effect for feudal obligations under s 53 of the Abolition of Feudal Tenure etc (Scotland) Act 2000 (in force from 9 June 2000), and for non-feudal burdens under s 67 of the Title Conditions (Scotland) Act 2003 (in force since 4 April 2003).

From the appointed day it is not possible to create a right of reversion as a real burden running with land and the Reversion Act 1469 is repealed: s 89 of the 2003 Act. Rights of reversion created since 1 September 1974 have been limited in duration to 20 years: Land Tenure Reform (Scotland) Act 1974, s 12. If still in existence at the appointed day they will continue to encumber the burdened property until expiry of this period or exercise. If a right of reversion was created prior to 1 September 1974 it will continue in existence in perpetuity (although will be extinguished when exercised).

15.12   Types of personal real burden

Personal real burdens did not exist prior to the Abolition of Feudal Tenure etc (Scotland) Act 2000, as originally enacted. Under the 2000 Act it was provided that certain burdens could be preserved by an individual conservation body or were automatically preserved in favour of the Crown. The types of personal burden proliferated after the Title Conditions (Scotland) Act 2003, when many more were introduced. Although there are a number of different types of personal real burden, they will be relatively uncommon as the rules for each personal real burden restrict either the content of burdens or the individuals that can hold such burdens.

There are eight types of personal real burden: conservation burdens; economic development burdens; health care burdens; maritime burdens; personal pre-emption burdens; personal redemption burdens; rural housing burdens; and manager burdens. Each is considered in turn.

15.13   CONSERVATION BURDENS

Conservation burdens were introduced by the Abolition of Feudal Tenure etc (Scotland) Act 2000, which provides a preservation mechanism for existing feudal burdens that serve the function of conservation burdens: for details, see paras 19.75–19.77. The Title Conditions (Scotland) Act 2003 provides that such burdens can also be created after the appointed day.

The term 'conservation burden' is defined in s 38 of the 2003 Act. It is a real burden created in favour of a conservation body or the Scottish Ministers:

'for the purpose of preserving, or protecting, for the benefit of the public – (a) the architectural or historical characteristics of any land; or (b) any other special characteristics of any land (including, without prejudice to the generality of this paragraph, a special characteristic derived from the flora, fauna or general appearance of the land)'.

There are two restrictive strands to the definition: one based on the purpose of the burden (rather than on its content); the other based on the body that can hold title to enforce.

(1) *Restrictions based on purpose of the burden.* The burdens are to have the purpose of protecting or preserving buildings and the natural environment. Conservation burdens are permitted only in so far as they protect or preserve these special elements. So, if there were burdens restricting the building materials that could be used in an historic village or restricting the extent to which alterations could be made to buildings constructed 200 years ago, these could be conservation burdens under s 38(1)(a). If there were burdens restricting development in land that was home to a rare amphibian, these could be conservation burdens under s 38(1)(b) of the 2003 Act.

(2) *Restrictions based on the persons that can hold the burden.* Whilst any person can create conservation burdens (see para 15.39), only certain bodies are permitted to have title to enforce conservation burdens. These include the Scottish Ministers and certain prescribed conservation bodies. The conservation bodies that can hold conservation burdens are to be prescribed by the Scottish Ministers under s 38(4) of the 2003 Act (and bodies can be removed from the prescribed list too: s 38(7) of the 2003 Act). In order to be prescribed, the body must have as an object or function the preservation or protection 'for the benefit of the public such characteristics of any land as are mentioned in paragraph (a) or (b) of subsection (1)'. A Parliamentary written answer of 25 June 2003 (S2W-1100) invited applications from those interested in becoming conservation bodies, requesting interested parties to contact Iain Hockenhull, Civil Law Division, 2 West Rear, St Andrew's House, Edinburgh, EH1 3DG. The initial list of conservation bodies was prescribed by the Title Conditions (Scotland) Act 2003 (Conservation Bodies) Order 2003, SSI 2003/453, which came into force on 1 November 2003. It prescribes various bodies, including all local authorities in Scotland, the National Trust, Scottish Natural Heritage, the John Muir Trust, the

Royal Society for the Protection of Birds, the Woodland Trust and various local interest preservation trusts. The list will be kept under review, and names can be added or removed. Those bodies not on the list who wish to be so should make representations to Iain Hockenhull. If the prescribed conservation body is a conservation trust then the trustees will be the holders of the burdens.

15.14 ECONOMIC DEVELOPMENT BURDENS

Economic development burdens were introduced by the Title Conditions (Scotland) Act 2003. The term is defined in s 45 of the 2003 Act. It is a real burden 'in favour of a local authority, or of the Scottish Ministers, for the purpose of promoting economic development'. The expression 'promoting economic development' is not defined in the legislation, nor is the expression glossed in the explanatory notes to the 2003 Act. The background to the provision is based on representations by local authorities during the parliamentary progress of the 2003 Act. When the provision was introduced at Stage 2 of the parliamentary consideration of the Act, the Justice Minister, Jim Wallace MSP noted:

'Local authorities will be able to create economic development burdens in circumstances in which they wish to sell land with a view to encouraging economic development within their area. They might wish to impose a burden that includes a clawback condition if there is likely to be a windfall increase in the value of land as a result of a change in use. Authorities will be able to use the new burdens for that purpose'. (Justice 1 Committee, Official Report, 10 December 2002, meeting no 42, 2002, col 4355)

It appears that this provision is designed to allow local authorities or the Scottish Ministers to sell properties at undervalue to encourage investment in an area. It may be suggested that the imposition of restrictions on the way that property can be used (as would be inherent in a burden encumbering land) does not necessarily promote economic development and this, coupled with the uncertainty as to definition, means that it is not clear to what extent such burdens will be used after the appointed day.

There are two restrictions inherent in economic development burdens: one based on the parties that can hold economic development burdens; the second based on the purpose of the burden.

(1) *Restriction based on person that can hold the burden.* Economic development burdens can only be held by local authorities or the Scottish Ministers.

(2) *Restriction based on purpose of the burden.* An economic development burden must promote economic development. It is not clear how this can be ascertained objectively by the Keeper or purchasers. While for preservation of economic development burdens under the 2000 Act it is necessary to provide evidence to support an assertion that the burden was imposed to promote economic devel-

opment, there is no equivalent requirement for economic development burdens created after the appointed day.

Economic development burdens can be created after the appointed day in favour of local authorities or the Scottish Ministers. Feudal burdens which serve the same function can be preserved under s 18B of the 2000 Act (added by the 2003 Act). This is discussed at para 19.79.

Unlike other real burdens (aside from health care burdens), economic development burdens specifically allow for the payment of a sum of money, and can reserve clawback arrangements. This is considered at para 15.44.

15.15 HEALTH CARE BURDENS

Like economic development burdens, health care burdens were introduced by the Title Conditions (Scotland) Act 2003. The term is defined by s 46 of the 2003 Act. It is a 'real burden in favour of a National Health Service Trust, or of the Scottish Ministers, for the purpose of promoting the provision of facilities for health care'. The expression 'facilities for health care' is defined to include ancillary facilities, such as the provision of accommodation: s 46(6). Health care burdens were introduced at Stage 3 of the parliamentary consideration of the Act (see Stage 3 debate, Scottish Parliament Official Report, 26 February 2003, col 18694). A useful example of when health care burdens may arise is given in the explanatory notes to the 2003 Act, at para 208:

> 'Health care burdens can be created where land is being sold but it is intended that it should continue to be used for health care purposes. This could, for example, occur where land is being sold to a developer to build accommodation for hospital staff and nurses. A health care burden could allow the health body to ensure that the land is developed for that purpose, and to secure compensation if another type of development occurs'.

As for other personal real burdens, there are two restrictions inherent in health care burdens: a restriction based on the person that can hold the burden; and one based on the purpose of the burden.

(1) *Restriction based on person holding the burden.* Only NHS trusts and the Scottish Ministers can hold the benefit of health care burdens. NHS trusts are established by s 12A of the National Health Service (Scotland) Act 1978.

(2) *Restrictions based on purpose of the burden.* The burden has to be imposed with the purpose of promoting the provision of facilities for health care. This can be demonstrated by making express reference to the relevant facilities (such as hospitals, health centres, general practitioner surgeries or accommodation for hospital employees) in the deed creating the burdens, and should be determinable by examination of the register.

Health care burdens can be created after the appointed day in favour of NHS Trusts or the Scottish Ministers. Feudal burdens which serve the same function can be preserved under s 18C of the 2000 Act (added by the 2003 Act). This is discussed at para 19.80.

As is the case for economic development burdens, but not for other burdens, it is possible to use a health care burden to require the burdened owner to make payment. The burden can be used to reserve clawback. This aspect is discussed at para 15.44.

15.16 MARITIME BURDENS

Maritime burdens were initially introduced by the Abolition of Feudal Tenure etc (Scotland) Act 2000, where in s 60 a mechanism was provided for the conversion of certain feudal burdens enforceable by the Crown: see para 19.29. The Title Conditions (Scotland) Act 2003 makes provision for the creation of maritime burdens in future, the relevant provision being s 44: a maritime burden is a real burden 'over the sea bed or foreshore in favour of the Crown for the benefit of the public'. 'Sea bed' is defined to cover the bed of the territorial waters (including tidal waters) around Scotland.

As with the other personal real burdens, there are restrictions inherent in the definition, based on the holder of the burden; and the purpose of the burden.

(1) *Restriction based on person holding the burden.* Only the Crown can hold a maritime burden, and the Crown's right cannot be assigned to a third party.

(2) *Restriction based on purpose of the burden.* A maritime burden can be an affirmative or negative burden imposed for the benefit of the public over the foreshore or sea bed.

The extent of the foreshore is 'that part of the shore which is wholly covered by the sea at high tide and wholly uncovered at low tide': see K G C Reid *The Law of Property in Scotland* (1996), para 313.

15.17 PERSONAL PRE-EMPTION AND REDEMPTION BURDENS

Personal pre-emption and redemption burdens are introduced by the Title Conditions (Scotland) Act 2003, by adding new s 18A into the Abolition of Feudal Tenure etc (Scotland) Act 2000. It is not possible to create these burdens after the appointed day.

A personal pre-emption burden is a feudal right of pre-emption preserved by a superior, not for the benefit of a parcel of land owned in the vicinity of the burdened property, but instead for the benefit of a superior as an individual. A personal redemption burden makes similar provision for a right of redemption created in a feu. The requirements for preservation of personal pre-emption and redemption burdens are detailed at para 19.78. If the holder of the personal pre-emption burden is a rural housing body (see para 15.18), the personal pre-emption burden is a rural housing burden: s 122 of the 2003 Act.

Personal pre-emption burdens are subject to the general rules on personal real burdens and to the general rules on rights of pre-emption. The rules in s 18 and Part 8 of the 2003 Act for the extinction of rights of pre-emption are equally applicable to personal pre-emption burdens.

Personal redemption burdens are subject to the restrictions on rights of redemption detailed above at para 15.10.

These personal real burdens have transitional effect.

15.18   RURAL HOUSING BURDENS

Rural housing burdens were introduced by the Title Conditions (Scotland) Act 2003 in response to an issue raised by Maureen Macmillan MSP, a list MSP from the Highlands. The rural housing burden is defined in s 43 as 'a right of pre-emption in favour of a rural housing body other than by reference to the body's capacity as owner of any land'. Rural housing burdens are restricted in two ways: by the body that can hold the burden; and by content.

(1) *Restriction based on content.* Rural housing burdens can only be rights of pre-emption.
(2) *Restriction based on person holding the burden.* Whilst any person can create rural housing burdens (see para 15.39), only prescribed rural housing bodies are permitted to have title to enforce them. The rural housing bodies that can hold rural housing burdens are to be prescribed by Scottish Ministers under s 43(5) of the 2003 Act (and bodies can be removed from the prescribed list too: s 43(8) of the 2003 Act). If the prescribed rural housing body is a trust, the holders of the burden are the trustees. In order to be prescribed as such the body must have as an object or function the provision of housing on rural land or rural land for housing: s 43(6). Rural land is defined in s 43(9) to tie the definition to that used in the Land Reform (Scotland) Act 2003, s 33. At the time of writing the list has not been prescribed. However, during the Stage 3 debate, the Justice Minister, Jim Wallace, indicated that a draft list would be published before the appointed day and bodies could make applications to appear on the list. This list will be compiled in consultation with the Scottish Federation of Housing Associations, and the Highlands Small Communities Housing Trust (Scottish Parliament, Official Report, 26 February 2003, col 18693). However, there is no statutory obligation to consult these bodies.

Rural housing burdens also include personal pre-emption burdens that have as their holder a rural housing body: s 122(1) of the Title Conditions (Scotland) Act 2003; and are subject to the general rules on rights of pre-emption, subject to various amendments. A rural housing burden will not be extinguished by non-exercise as a result of negative prescription under s 18(2) and (6) of the 2003 Act. Where the holder of a rural housing burden gives an undertaking as to non-exercise under s 83 of the 2003 Act (on which see para 18.30), this will not extinguish the burden; and where the burdened owner makes an offer to a rural housing body holding a rural housing burden under s 84 of the 2003 Act (see para 18.52), the body has 42 days, not 21, to accept; and, if the right is not exercised, the rural housing burden (unlike other rights of pre-emption) will not be extinguished by s 84 of the 2003 Act.

15.19 MANAGER BURDENS

Manager burdens are burdens which allow a developer to manage a development personally, or to appoint a manager to the development, while the development is being constructed. For the purpose of the Title Conditions (Scotland) Act 2003, manager burdens are defined as personal real burdens. However, as noted previously, they have praedial elements. In some ways, then, it is better to characterise manager burdens as a hybrid form of burden.

Manager burdens were introduced by the 2003 Act and the relevant provisions have been in force since 4 April 2003. The purpose underlying their introduction is to protect developers during the construction of housing or commercial developments. Under the law prior to the appointed day developers may have feued the property and retained control over the property as feudal superior during the construction of the development. Thus, if a purchaser in the development proposed to contravene a burden in such a way that this would affect the developer's investment and subsequent sales of properties in the development, the developer could enforce the feudal burden and prevent the contravention. After feudal abolition such control would not be possible without a special mechanism. The manager burden solves this problem by adapting existing practice.

In modern housing developments real burdens are typically accompanied by a burden appointing a manager for the development. This is done in various ways. The developer can attempt to retain a right to appoint the manager in perpetuity (an invalid attempt to create a monopoly: see para 15.31). The developer can attempt to retain a right to appoint the manager only during the early years of the development, while the developer still retains ownership of certain plots. Alternatively, the residents of the development may be given the right to appoint the manager.

Prior to the 2003 Act there was doubt as to the validity of burdens appointing managers, as it was not clear that such burdens complied with the praedial rule (see para 15.26): see Professor Rennie 'The Reality of Real Burdens' 1998 SLT (News) 149. However, a validly appointed manager would allow the developer to keep control of the development during its construction. To achieve this, manager burdens were introduced by s 63 of the 2003 Act. To further the effect of this provision, s 65 provides that if a person is appointed as a manager by virtue of a real burden (or purported real burden) created before 4 April 2003 then the appointment is retrospectively validated.

The manager burden provisions apply to burdens created both before and after the appointed day, under feudal or non-feudal burdens: s 63(9) of the 2003 Act. They will have effect to affirm the appointment of managers prior to 28 November 2004 and allow a developer constructing a development during the period when feudalism is abolished to retain control of the development.

15.20   Related properties

In general terms it is provided in s 63 of the Title Conditions (Scotland) Act 2003 that burdens can validly make provision for the developer to have power to appoint (or dismiss) a manager of 'related properties' for a temporary period, provided it retains ownership of one of the related properties. 'Related properties' is defined in s 66; whether or not properties are related properties is to be 'inferred from all the circumstances'. However, illustrative examples are given, including: where properties share common features or common maintenance obligations; where the properties are a group subject to the same common scheme (which includes community burdens imposed expressly or by implication: see para 15.6); and where there are properties with shared ownership.

Section 63(2) provides that in various situations properties will not be related properties for the purposes of the manager burden provisions. These include properties used as a warden's flat in a retirement or sheltered housing development; or facilities that benefit two or more properties (such as private roads or common recreational areas). Subsection (2) also provides that properties covered by the development management scheme (see paras 15.55 to 15.57) can not be covered by manager burdens.

15.21   Duration of manager burdens

Manager burdens are temporary burdens. The developer can retain a right to appoint the manager only during a limited period. The deed creating the burdens may specify when the developer's right to appoint a manager will terminate. This will prevail unless the default grounds set out in s 63(4) of the Title Conditions (Scotland) Act 2003 would mean that the manager burden terminated at an earlier date. The earlier date will be the earliest of the expiry of a continuous 90-day period during which time the developer has ceased to own one of the related properties (s 63(4)(c)) or a fixed (or other) time period dependent on the nature of the development. There are three relevant types of development:

(1) where a manager burden is imposed on a retirement or sheltered housing development;

(2) where a manager burden is imposed on an estate subject to the 'right to buy' legislation: s 61 of the Housing (Scotland) Act 1987; and

(3) any other development (including commercial developments as well as residential developments).

(1) *Retirement or sheltered housing.* The fixed period is three years from the day on which the deed creating the burdens affecting the development is registered. The effect of the definition of related properties in s 66 of the 2003 Act, coupled with s 63, is that in a retirement or sheltered housing development the developer can retain the power to appoint the manager while it retains ownership of at least one of the units in the development (excluding any flat retained by the developer for use by a

resident warden or such like) for a period of three years from the date of registration of the deed of conditions covering the development, or the date of the registration of the first conveyance imposing burdens in the development if there is no deed of conditions.

During the period that the manager burden is enforceable the owner-occupiers of the development are not permitted to dismiss the manager under s 28(1)(d) of the 2003 Act (where the owners subject to community burdens can dismiss a manager by simple majority if the terms of the burden do not provide otherwise) or s 64 (where the owners of related properties ordinarily have an absolute right to dismiss the manager by a two thirds majority vote irrespective of the wording of the burden).

(2) *Mixed tenure estates.* Mixed tenure estates arise where a local authority (or other provider of public sector housing) owns and lets some of the properties in an estate while other properties have been acquired under the 'right to buy' legislation – discussed at paras 28.61 to 28.66. Here, over a period of years, the housing authority will have sold off a number of properties and imposed burdens, while retaining ownership of others. Often the housing authority will have retained a right to appoint a property manager during that period (in order to ensure consistency of treatment between the tenanted and owner-occupied properties). However, unlike ordinary developments the developer authority will retain ownership of some properties in the development for a prolonged period. Accordingly, the time period during which the authority can retain the power to appoint a manager (provided it retains ownership of at least one of the related properties) is 30 years, although this period runs from the date in which burdens allowing the manager to be appointed were first registered in the estate (either generally over the estate or over a specific property). As many estates have been subject to the right to buy since the early 1980s, the 30-year period has in those estates less than ten years to run.

Further, unlike the position in relation to manager burdens in other estates or developments, it is expressly provided in s 63(8) of the 2003 Act that, as long as the manager burden is enforceable by the housing authority (ie as long as it retains ownership of at least one related property), a two-thirds majority of owners of the related properties within the estate can dismiss the manager appointed by the housing authority, irrespective of the wording of the burden. It is not competent during the currency of the manager burden, though, for a simple majority of owners to dismiss the manager under s 28(1)(d) of the 2003 Act: see s 63(8).

(3) *Other estates.* In other developments the developer retains the power to appoint the manager for five years, as long as it retains ownership of at least one property in the development. This period begins with the original imposition of burdens in the development.

As is the case for manager burdens in sheltered housing developments, the owners cannot dismiss the manager under s 28(1)(d) or s 64 while the developer can enforce the manager burden.

15.22   AFFIRMATIVE AND NEGATIVE BURDENS

As well as a division between praedial and personal real burdens, it is possible to divide burdens based on the type of obligation imposed. Burdens can be affirmative burdens or negative burdens.

(1) *Affirmative burdens.* Affirmative burdens are obligations on the burdened owner to do something, or to defray or contribute towards a cost: see s 2(1)(a) of the Title Conditions (Scotland) Act 2003. They can include obligations to maintain or to pay the cost of maintenance, or to rebuild. (They do not generally cover obligations to make payment.)

(2) *Negative burdens.* Negative burdens are restrictions on use of the burdened property: 'an obligation to refrain from doing something' – see s 2(1)(b) of the 2003 Act. They can include prohibitions on building or running a business, restrictions on the number of families that may occupy a property, or restrictions on the sale of alcohol or keeping of pets.

The distinction between affirmative and negative burdens applies whether the burden is praedial or personal. It is important in determining enforcement of the burden because, generally, affirmative burdens are enforceable only against the burdened owners; negative burdens are enforceable against any occupier of the burdened property (see paras 17.64 to 17.69).

While ordinarily it will be straightforward to determine whether a burden is affirmative or negative, there will be times when that is not the case. It is useful to consider some examples. A burden providing that the burdened property shall be used for no purpose other than residential purposes is framed as a negative burden. However, it may be argued that its effect is to require the burdened owner to use the property for residential purposes and is therefore an affirmative burden. It is suggested that such an argument would be unsuccessful as the burden would not impose an obligation to use the property at all. However, this demonstrates the potential difficulties that may arise. In such cases, s 2(5) of the 2003 Act provides that, in determining whether a burden is affirmative or negative, regard is paid to the function of the burden rather than its form.

In some cases, determining the nature of the burden may be very difficult: *Co-operative Wholesale Society v Ushers Brewery* 1975 SLT (Lands Tr) 9 provides an illustration. There, a burden provided that 'the buildings erected or to be erected on the [property] shall be used as a retail shop (but not as a betting shop) and for no other purposes ... and neither the [property] nor the buildings thereon shall at any time be used in whole or in part for ... the sale or manufacture of excisable liquors'. This is framed as an affirmative obligation – 'the [property] shall be used' – although it also contains a restriction – 'neither the [property] nor the buildings shall ... be used'. It appears that the effect of the 2003 Act is that the differing strands of the burden are treated differently.

15.23 CHANGE TO PRE-ABOLITION LAW

Prior to the appointed day it was possible to create burdens that imposed obligations to do; obligations not to do; or obligations allowing use. The last were accepted in only one case: Lord Cullen's Outer House decision in *B & C Group Management v Haren* (4 December 1992, unreported). Burdens allowing use created before the appointed day are converted into positive servitudes: s 81 of the Title Conditions (Scotland) Act 2003, discussed in paras 16.1 and 16.2. It is not possible to create an obligation allowing use as a real burden after the appointed day, other than as an ancillary burden.

15.24 ANCILLARY BURDENS

Sometimes burdens are imposed for the better enforcement of affirmative or negative burdens. For example, a maintenance obligation may be coupled with an obligation allowing the benefited owner to enter the burdened property if the burdened owner fails to perform the obligation; or a burden providing for a management scheme or for the appointment of a property factor is not an affirmative or negative burden, but is an obligation enabling the better enforcement of the negative and affirmative burdens. Burdens such as this are referred to in s 2(3) of the Title Conditions (Scotland) Act 2003 as 'ancillary burdens'.

15.25 **Creation of burdens**

Sections 3 to 5 of the Title Conditions (Scotland) Act 2003 provide the general rules for creation of real burdens. These rules are, for the most part, a restatement of the common law rules for creation of burdens set out in *Tailors of Aberdeen v Coutts* (1837) 2 Sh & Macl 609, (1840) 1 Robin 296. The common law rules were set out in detail at paras 10.8–10.14 of the sixth edition of this book. They are broadly restated in the 2003 Act. The common law rules are applicable if the burdens were created before 28 November 2004, subject to the retrospective changes of s 5 of the 2003 Act. For burdens created on or after 28 November 2004, the rules in ss 3 to 5 apply.

The rules on creation include rules relating to content and rules relating to form. Each is considered in the following paragraphs. The general position for praedial real burdens is stated, with qualifications applicable to personal real burdens or community burdens noted where appropriate.

15.26 RULES ON CONTENT: PRAEDIAL RULE

Real burdens must be praedial. They have to impose an obligation affecting the land, and have to be (for praedial real burdens) for the benefit of other land.

The praedial rule is relatively flexible but, prior to the Title Conditions (Scotland) Act 2003, was subject to little case law. Its principal role was and is to act as a check on the types of obligation permitted as real burdens and to prevent merely personal obligations from running with the land. Thus, while it is permissible to require a burdened proprietor to maintain a garage building erected on his property, it is not permissible to require the burdened owner to use that garage regularly to maintain and repair the benefited owner's car. The former maintenance obligation is praedial in that it relates to land; the latter is personal in that it does not.

One recent case turned on the praedial rule: *Marsden v Craighelen Lawn Tennis and Squash Club* 1999 GWD 37-1820 involved a burden prohibiting the playing of tennis on a Sunday. It was held that the burden imposed only a personal benefit (given the restriction to Sundays) and not a benefit to the benefited property. This decision was doubted by the Scottish Law Commission *Report on Real Burdens* (Scot Law Com No 181, 2000), para 2.13, but it can be persuasively argued that the decision is correct in this regard.

The praedial requirement for the burdened property is set out in s 3(1) and (2) of the 2003 Act. Section 3(1) provides that 'a real burden must relate in some way to the burdened property'; and s 3(2) provides that 'the relationship may be direct or indirect but shall not merely be that the obligated person is the owner of the burdened property'.

These subsections are glossed by the Scottish Law Commission *Report on Real Burdens*, para 2.12. Negative burdens will typically have a direct relationship to the burdened property. For example, a prohibition on using the property for business purposes, or a prohibition on tallow chandling in the property will clearly relate to the property. Affirmative burdens may directly or indirectly relate to the burdened property. Indirect relationship arises where the burdened property is removed from the subject of the obligation. For example, in a tenement a typical burden imposed on every owner will require the upkeep of the tenement roof. The owner of the top flat has a direct relationship with the top flat. However, the owner of the ground- floor flat (if he or she is not a co-owner of the roof) does not. The burden would be an obligation to upkeep someone else's property, but this indirect relationship would be sufficient to be valid.

The praedial requirement for the benefited property is set out in s 3(3) and (4) of the 2003 Act. Section 3(3) provides that 'a real burden must, unless it is a community burden, be for the benefit of that [benefited] property'. This is normally easily satisfied as the putative burdened and benefited properties will be physically proximate. However, case law prior to the 2003 Act suggested that, where the benefited and burdened properties were too far apart, the praedial rule may not be satisfied. An illustration is *Aberdeen Varieties Ltd v James F Donald (Aberdeen Cinemas) Ltd* 1939 SC 788, which held that a distance of half a mile between benefited and burdened theatres was too far for there to be praedial benefit. However, in a rural context such a distance may be acceptable.

15.27 Variant on general rule for community burdens

It is provided under s 3(4) of the Title Conditions (Scotland) Act 2003 that where the burden is a community burden the praedial rule is satisfied if the burden is 'for the benefit of the community to which it relates or of some part of that community'. This means that burdens imposed for the general benefit of the community may be acceptable. Thus, under the law prior to the 2003 Act, Professor Rennie, in 'The Reality of Real Burdens' 1998 SLT (News) 149 at 149–151, suggested that some burdens encountered commonly in practice would not be valid. He argued under the common law praedial rule that a burden in a sheltered housing development restricting occupation to residents over a certain age would not be praedial because it could not be shown to benefit each benefited property. He also argued that burdens requiring the appointment of a property manager would not be valid because this is not really for the benefit of the benefited property, but for the better administration of the development.

By permitting burdens for 'the benefit of the community', s 3(4) of the 2003 Act addresses these concerns by allowing burdens to benefit an entire development, rather than each individual property within that development. So, an age restriction imposed in a sheltered housing development will maintain the amenity of the development as a whole; or a provision allowing the appointment of a property manager is for the better administration of the development.

15.28 Variant on general rule for personal real burdens

Where the burden is a personal real burden there is obviously no requirement that the burden be for the benefit of property. However, the praedial rule continues to affect the obligation imposed by the burden. A personal real burden must relate (directly or indirectly) to the burdened property.

15.29 RULES ON CONTENT: POLICY-BASED GROUNDS OF INVALIDITY

Since Lord Corehouse's judgment in *Tailors of Aberdeen v Coutts* (1840) 1 Robin 296, it has been accepted that burdens cannot be illegal, *contra bones mores*, or contrary to public policy. This has been restated in s 3(6) and (7) of the Title Conditions (Scotland) Act 2003 for burdens created after 28 November 2004, with a new policy-based ground set out in s 3(8). The following provisions apply equally to praedial and personal real burdens.

15.30 Burdens cannot be illegal

A real burden cannot be illegal: s 3(6) of the Title Conditions (Scotland) Act 2003. Thus, it is not possible to restrict occupancy based on grounds of sex or race: Sex Discrimination Act 1975, ss 30 and 77; Race Relations Act 1976, ss 21 and 72.

15.31   Burdens cannot impose a monopoly: general

Apart from the transitory manager burden, a real burden cannot impose a monopoly: s 3(7) of the Title Conditions (Scotland) Act 2003. The provision makes clear that this applies to the appointment of managers or other providers of services. It is therefore not competent for a developer to reserve the right to appoint a manager of property in perpetuity, or for the benefited owner to require the burdened owner to use the benefited owner's solicitor when dealing with the property (abolished by the Conveyancing (Scotland) Act 1874, s 22), or for a commercial developer to require the use of a specified private security firm on an industrial estate.

15.32   Burdens cannot impose a monopoly: unreasonable restraints of trade

Although in *Tailors of Aberdeen v Coutts* (1840) 1 Robin 296, Lord Corehouse suggested (at 307 and 317–319) that burdens cannot impede commerce, this has never been applied strictly in all cases. Burdens can impose obligations restricting commercial use of property. In a residential area it is possible to expressly prohibit the use of property for business purposes. However, where the benefited property is other commercial property different considerations apply. This will continue to be the case with the statutory restatement in s 3(6) of the Title Conditions (Scotland) Act 2003, which provides that a burden cannot be an unreasonable restraint of trade.

Prior to the 2003 Act there has been little case law in this area. In *Co-operative Wholesale Society v Ushers Brewery* 1975 SLT (Lands Tr) 9 it was held that the burdens were unobjectionable where the burdens protected a small commercial development comprising a bookmakers, a grocers and a public house. Each property was prohibited from carrying out any activity carried on by the other stores (thus, the grocers could not sell alcohol). The burdens were treated as being valid as they were intended to support the economic viability of the area as a whole.

However, in other cases the burden has been struck down, although seldom solely on the basis that it is an unreasonable restraint of trade. For example, in *Aberdeen Varieties v James F Donald (Aberdeen Cinemas) Ltd* 1939 SC 788, 1940 SC (HL) 52, the owner of two theatres sold one, imposing a burden preventing the use of the building as a theatre for the performance of stage plays of a certain kind. The burden was ineffective. However, the decision was based on the pursuer's lack of interest to enforce or failure to comply with the praedial rule, rather than the burden being struck down simply because it was an unreasonable restraint of trade.

Other cases in this area include *Giblin v Murdoch* 1979 SLT (Sh Ct) 5, where a putative burden was imposed prohibiting use of the burdened property as a hairdressers – where the seller retained a competing business as benefited property. See also *Phillips v Lavery* 1962 SLT (Sh Ct) 57, where the putative burden prohibited use of the burdened property as a butchers and grocers when the benefited property retained a competing business. In both cases the pursuer and defender were the original contracting parties and the decision was based on the general principles regulating restraints of trade imposed in contracts.

Given the terms of Sheriff Gordon's decision in *Giblin*, it seems that similar considerations to those applicable in considering contractual clauses in restraint of trade would apply in determining the validity of burdens. Factors to take into account include: the purpose of the restriction; the geographical area; and the duration of the proposed restriction. There is a full discussion of the Scottish case law on contractual restraints of trade in W W McBryde *The Law of Contract in Scotland* (2nd edn, 2001), at paras 19-86 to 19-146. Professor McBryde's treatment includes guidance on relevant factors to be considered when attempting to draft clauses in this area.

15.33   Burdens cannot be repugnant with ownership

Section 3(6) of the Title Conditions (Scotland) Act 2003 restates the common law rule that burdens cannot be repugnant with ownership. The broad principle is that 'you cannot make a man proprietor and yet prohibit him from exercising his ownership': *Moir's Trustees v McEwan* (1880) 7 R 1141 at 1145, per Lord Young. Lord Young would have taken a view that would have seen many acceptable burdens struck down. While the principle remains, his interpretation of it does not. He believed that general restrictions on the sale of alcohol were repugnant with a man's ownership of property: see *Earl of Zetland v Hislop* (1881) 8 R 675 at 681–82, reversed (1882) 9 R (HL) 40. However, the House of Lords indicated that negative obligations would generally be acceptable, because a restriction on one activity does not preclude the property being used for many other activities. However, affirmative obligations that greatly restricted the use that could be made of property may be more problematic. If a burden required an owner to sell alcohol then this may be unduly restrictive of his ownership.

This principle also prevents burdens from imposing restrictions on juristic acts affecting the property. It is not possible to impose burdens absolutely prohibiting sales or leases; and, where property is co-owned, it is not possible to use a real burden to prevent the co-owner's absolute entitlement to raise an action of division and sale: *Grant v Heriot's Trust* (1906) 8 F 647.

15.34   Burdens cannot give title to vary or waive compliance to a third party

Section 3(8) of the Title Conditions (Scotland) Act 2003 provides that burdens cannot provide that a party other than the holder (or party with title to enforce) can discharge or vary the burden. This means that in future, when creating burdens, developers cannot provide that the burden can be waived only with the assent of the developer – where the developer does not own benefited property or hold the personal real burden. Read strictly, subsection (8) provides that, where there are multiple benefited owners in relation to a burdened property, it is not competent to provide that only some of them have to be consulted in relation to variation or discharge of the burdens. It will no longer be possible, therefore, to provide that a burden can be complied with simply with the consent of one benefited owner (as is the case under the current law, where the superior's consent can effectively waive a burden enforceable by many parties). However, subsection (9) makes clear that subsection (8) does not apply where the burdened property is part of a community covered by a community burden where express provisions for waiver or discharge are made in the deeds creating the community burdens.

Section 3(8) applies to burdens created after the appointed day. An equivalent provision is made for burdens created prior to the appointed day, in s 73(2A) of the 2000 Act: see para 19.108. However, s 73(2A) does not include a reference to the variation and discharge of community burdens under the 2003 Act. It is not clear if community burdens created before the appointed day (expressly or by implication) can effectively provide for variation or discharge by designated owners (or a percentage of designated owners) rather than by every benefited owner. If this is the effect of s 73(2A) it is particularly unfortunate because a number of developments in recent years include provisions for variation and discharge by, for example, the consent of only those immediately adjacent owners to the burdened property.

15.35   RULES ON FORM AND DRAFTING

Section 4 of the Title Conditions (Scotland) Act 2003 sets out the rules for creation of burdens after the appointed day. They broadly restate the rules set out by Lord Corehouse in *Tailors of Aberdeen v Coutts* (1840) 1 Robin 296. However, there are some important changes. The following paragraphs consider the new rules and detail changes to the law applicable immediately before abolition.

15.36   Constitutive deed

The constitutive deed is defined in s 122 when read with s 4(2) of the Title Conditions (Scotland) Act 2003: it is a deed which sets out the terms of real burdens. The nature of the deed is not specified. Accordingly, unlike the law prior to feudal abolition, there is no restriction on the types of deed that can validly create real burdens. Burdens can be created: in a disposition of the burdened (or benefited) property; in a deed of conditions; or by imposing new burdens in a minute of waiver. As the deed is to be registered in the property register, it requires to be signed and witnessed in accordance with the Requirements of Writing (Scotland) Act 1995.

A disposition of the burdened property will provide, as a qualification to the dispositive clause, details of the burdens that encumber the property disponed. This is similar to creation of a servitude by reservation.

A disposition of the benefited property will grant, as a pertinent to the benefited owner, the right to enforce certain burdens encumbering land retained by the seller. This is similar to creation of a servitude by grant.

Deeds of conditions were introduced by s 32 of the Conveyancing (Scotland) Act 1874, which was amended by s 17 of the Land Registration (Scotland) Act 1979. Both sections are repealed by the 2003 Act, but the style of deed continues to be used. It is a deed covering an area which imposes burdens (or other title conditions) on that area; and is often used by developers in new developments.

Minutes of waiver are discussed at paras 18.4 to 18.25.

Where the burdens are personal real burdens, it is possible that they will be created not in a conveyance of the burdened property but, instead, in a grant by the burdened owner of the property. The deed in this case will in form be rather like a deed of servitude. In such cases the burdened owner may need the consent of the prospective holder of the personal real burden: see para 15.39.

15.37 Change to pre-abolition law

Before 28 November 2004 real burdens could be created only in a conveyance of the burdened property or in a deed of conditions. It was not possible to create a real burden in a conveyance of the benefited property; and, where a deed of conditions was used, reference had to be made to s 32 of the Conveyancing (Scotland) Act 1874. This provided that such a deed could be granted by an owner where 'he is to feu or otherwise deal with or affect his lands'. It was suggested by the Scottish Law Commission that a deed of conditions could not be used 'if the granter does not have a conveyance in contemplation': *Report on Real Burdens* (Scot Law Com No 181, 2000), para 3.13. If this was the case then deeds of conditions could not be used as self-standing deeds. However, such deeds are sometimes used, and the position is unclear. The possible restriction on use of deeds of conditions is not replicated by the Title Conditions (Scotland) Act 2003.

15.38 Who grants the constitutive deed?

The deed creating burdens is to be granted by the owner of the land which is to be burdened: s 4(2)(b) of the Title Conditions (Scotland) Act 2003. In the ordinary case of a burden being created in a disposition, the disponer will (at the time he or she sets out the burden) be the owner of the burdened property (be it the land conveyed or retained land); or, when a deed of conditions is granted it will typically be granted, by a developer owning the large development site.

'Owner' is defined in s 123 of the 2003 Act and includes the registered owner, and any unregistered owner – that is to say, the holder of an unregistered conveyance derived from the owner, formerly referred to as the 'uninfeft proprietor': see, generally, Chapter 31. It is expressly provided in s 123(1)(a) that, for the purpose of s 4(2)(b), any one of the unregistered proprietors can create burdens. Thus, if Alfred owns land and conveys to Bertram, who does not register prior to conveying to Carol, who dies before registering, and whose executor is Dora, then Alfred, Bertram and Dora are all owners for the purposes of s 123 and each could validly grant burdens.

Thus far, the statutory provisions generally mirror the common law. However, there are two extensions. Firstly, in s 123 of the 2003 Act, the definition of owner also includes a heritable creditor in possession. Secondly, s 60 provides that any constitutive deed granted by someone who is not on the register will require a deduction of title clause if it applies to a property that is not yet on the Land Register. No deduction of title clause is required if the property is on the Land Register, due to the effect of s 15(3) of the Land Registration (Scotland) Act 1979. Prior to 28 November 2004, it was not possible for an unregistered owner to grant a deed of conditions.

15.39 Special rules for personal real burdens

It is generally the burdened owner that grants the constitutive deed. If the granter of the deed creating personal burdens is the relevant body that can hold the personal real burden (be it a local authority, the Scottish Ministers, a rural housing body, or NHS trust), selling the burdened property on and creating the personal real burden in the conveyance, then the holder of the personal real burden is its granter.

However, an altruistic landowner may wish to create a personal real burden by setting aside part of his or her land and providing that it shall be used for health care purposes or for conservation purposes. In such a case the creation of the personal real burden is not by the holder. However, for some personal real burdens the burden cannot be created without the consent of the proposed holder of the burden: s 38(2) of the Title Conditions (Scotland) Act 2003 for conservation burdens; s 43(2) for rural housing burdens; s 45(2) for economic development burdens; and s 46(2) for health care burdens.

15.40 Voces signatae (special words)

The Title Conditions (Scotland) Act 2003 requires the deed creating burdens to use the expression 'real burden' or (if a specific type of real burden is being created such as community burdens or economic development burdens) to refer to a specific type of real burden: s 4(2)(a) and (3). This can be done by a clause providing that 'the following obligations are declared to be real burdens'. If there is no express reference, then no real burdens are created.

If the deed states that the burden is a community burden, the effect is that subsequent registration of the constitutive deed means that each unit within the community is both a burdened and a benefited property: s 27 of the 2003 Act.

This is a change from the law prior to abolition, where no special form of words was required in order validly to create burdens, although it was necessary to draft the burdens in such a way that it was clear that they ran with the land. See K G C Reid *The Law of Property in Scotland* (1996), para 390.

15.41 The constitutive deed must identify the burdened property and the benefited property

Section 4(2)(c) of the Title Conditions (Scotland) Act 2003 requires the granter to identify the property to be burdened and, if it is a praedial burden, the land which is to be benefited property, or, if it is a personal real burden, the person in whose favour the burden is created. If the burdens to be imposed are community burdens, the constitutive deed must identify the community to be affected: s 4(4).

There is no specific requirement as to how the relevant properties should be identified; but, as the constitutive deed requires to be registered in order validly to create the burdens, the identification of the relevant properties must be in such a way that it complies with s 4(2)(a) of the Land Registration (Scotland) Act 1979. When deeds are registered in the Land Register, the Keeper is under a statutory obligation to reject deeds in which land is 'not sufficiently described to enable him to identify it by reference to the Ordnance Map'. The identification of the burdened and benefited properties (or of the community) is therefore to be by reference to a plan, or (if the property is already registered in the Land Register) by reference to the title number of the relevant property.

15.42   *Change to pre-abolition law.*

For burdens created before the appointed day there is a requirement to describe precisely the burdened property: *Anderson v Dickie* 1914 SC 706, affirmed 1915 SC (HL) 79. Here, the description of the burdened property as comprising 'the ground occupied as the lawn' was held to be insufficient to identify the burdened property. There was no such requirement to describe the benefited property and it is therefore common to have title to enforce implied in burdens created prior to 28 November 2004.

15.43   **The terms of the burden must be set out in full within the constitutive deed**

Section 4(2)(a) of the Title Conditions (Scotland) Act 2003 requires the terms of the burden to be set out in full within the constitutive deed. This mirrors the common law rule that the terms of the burden must appear within 'the four corners of the deed'. The common law application of this can be seen at its most extreme in *Aberdeen Varieties Ltd v James F Donald (Aberdeen Cinemas) Ltd* 1939 SC 788: the burden there provided that the burdened property should not be used for the performance of 'any stage play which requires to be submitted to the Lord Chamberlain under the Act for regulating Theatres Sixth and Seventh Victoria Chapter Sixty Eight'. It was held that, as the relevant terms of that Act were not set out, the full extent of the burden was not specified within the four corners of the deed, and the burden was accordingly invalid. Compare *Heritage Fisheries Ltd v Duke of Roxburghe* 2000 SLT 800, discussed in K G C Reid and G L Gretton *Conveyancing 1999* (2000), at pp 57–59. Many burdens created prior to 28 November 2004 are framed by making reference to matters outwith the four corners of the deed, such as legislation, or local valuation rolls. While the general rule will apply to all burdens, it is qualified by s 5 of the 2003 Act.

Section 5 of the 2003 Act provides that, where the burden relates to payment of a cost incurred, and either (1) the amount payable or (2) the proportion payable by the burdened owner is not specified within the four corners of the deed, this is not in itself an objection to the validity of a burden. If the burden provides that a proportion of the cost is to be paid, the burden will be valid provided there is a mechanism within the deed for calculating the relevant proportion. The proportion can be determined by reference to extrinsic material, provided that that material is found in a 'public document' (which is defined in s 5(2) to be 'an enactment or a public register or some record or roll to which the public readily has access'). Section 5 applies to burdens whenever they were created and will serve to validate retrospectively some burdens that were previously thought to be invalid. Some examples can illustrate how ss 4 and 5 will operate.

Example 1 If there is a maintenance burden in a tenement providing that the burdened owner shall pay the costs of maintenance of the roof, this burden is validated by s 5(1)(a) of the 2003 Act.

Prior to the passage of the 2003 Act opinion was divided as to whether such burdens were valid. Professor Rennie argued that they were not enforceable because the extent of the obligation (ie how much was to be paid) was not set out within the four corners of the deed: 'The Reality of Real Burdens' 1998 SLT (News) 149 at 151–152. Professor Reid took the opposite view: *The Law of Property in Scotland* (1996), para 418. A recent decision suggests that such burdens were enforceable, although there remains no case directly in point: *Sheltered Housing Management Ltd v Cairns* 2002 Hous LR 126 at para 22, per Lord Nimmo Smith.

Example 2 If there is a maintenance burden in a tenement apportioning liability for common repairs by reference to rateable value (meaning that the owner must examine the valuation roll), or by reference to feuduty, this will be validated by s 5(1)(b) and (2) of the 2003 Act. However, the retrospective validation is dependent on the document referred to (ie the valuation roll, or the deeds which imposed feuduty) being something to which the public readily has access. It is arguable that, as the valuation roll for residential properties was closed some years ago prior to the introduction of the community charge, which itself predates council tax, references requiring examination of the valuation roll may not be sufficient to comply with s 5(2). Despite this doubt, para 53 of the explanatory notes to the 2003 Act expressly refers to the valuation roll as an example of the operation of s 5(2).

Example 3 In *Sheltered Housing Management Ltd v Cairns* 2002 Hous LR 126 it was provided in the constitutive deed (a deed of conditions) that 'A Management Scheme comprising regulations shall be drawn up by the Superiors and these shall be enforceable against the feuars. These Management Regulations shall contain rules governing the management and administration of the complex and the payment of Charges by feuars for such management and administration'. The Management Regulations were not included within the deed of conditions. Professors Reid and

Gretton argue that the Regulations would not be effective to encumber the property as burdens because they were not set out in full in the constitutive deed: Reid and Gretton *Conveyancing 2002* (2003), p 67. If such a provision was inserted in a burden after the appointed day, the regulations would similarly be invalid.

15.44 *Clawback arrangements*

The rule that the terms of a burden must be set out in full when coupled with the praedial rule has particular impact in relation to clawback arrangements. In a clawback arrangement, land is disponed and the disponer has an expectation when the land is sold the value of the land may be enhanced in some way by the actions of the purchaser. For example, land may be sold that for agricultural purposes but if planning permission was granted for residential development then the value of the property would be increased.

Clawback arrangements can take various forms. Often they are accompanied by a standard security in favour of the disponer providing that if a certain event happens (such as the grant of planning permission) the seller will receive further payment from the purchaser. This enables the disponer to claw back some of the enhanced value that would otherwise accrue to the purchaser disponee.

Alternatively, the clawback arrangement (prior to the appointed day) could be imposed using a feudal real burden restricting the use of the property sold on. The transferor remains as superior but otherwise retains no land neighbouring the burdened property. As superior, the transferor could take legal action if the burden was breached, despite no longer having any patrimonial interest in the property other than his or her financial interest. Such burdens will be abolished with feudal abolition and, unless they can be converted under Part 4 of the Abolition of Feudal Tenure etc (Scotland) Act 2000, will not affect property in future.

The third means by which clawback can be attempted to be arranged is that a real burden is imposed and provides a mechanism for a payment to be made to the disponer in the event of certain events happening. Prior to 28 November 2004, if such an arrangement imposed a burden for payment of an uncertain sum of money, the burden would not be valid and the mechanism would fail. It is also arguable that such arrangements would not be praedial – the burden is a personal benefit to the holder of the burden, not for the benefit of land. As a personal benefit, such arrangements will not be effective praedial real burdens; that continues to be the case for clawback arrangements that a transferor seeks to impose after 28 November 2004.

However, could a clawback mechanism be used in a personal real burden? In such cases there is no requirement that there be a benefit to land, but instead it is a person who is to benefit. However, is a clawback mechanism praedial: is it an obligation encumbering the property? This may depend on the wording of the condition, but it is perhaps difficult to see how an obligation to pay an uplift relates to the burdened property. Further, the rules on content provide that affirmative burdens are permitted to cover only obligations to defray or contribute to some cost, not general obligations to make payment to the holder of the burden: s 2(1)(a) of the Title Conditions

(Scotland) Act 2003. There is the further difficulty that a clawback mechanism may not provide for a fixed sum to be paid and, as a burden for payment of an uncertain amount, the full terms of the burden are not set out within the four corners of the constitutive deed. It is suggested that s 5 of the 2003 Act will not save such a mechanism because it relates to burdens where a cost has been incurred (which will cover maintenance payments or service charges), which runs contrary to the purpose of the legislation. See paras 162 to 165 of the policy memorandum for the Act (SP Bill 54-PM). This makes clear that the Executive felt that burdens were not an effective means of protecting clawback arrangements. However, it is difficult to know how a court will deal with matters if faced with such a mechanism.

There are, however, two cases where clawback mechanisms are permitted. The rules on economic development burdens and health care burdens expressly provide that these personal real burdens can comprise an obligation to pay money, provided the mechanism for calculating the payment is set out in the deed.

15.45   Registration of the constitutive deed

In order validly to create the real burdens the constitutive deed must be registered. Section 4(5) of the Title Conditions (Scotland) Act 2003 provides that registration is to be against both the burdened and the benefited properties (ie dual registration). The burden is not effective as a burden until it is so registered.

The law pre-abolition provided that registration of a disposition or deed of conditions was required in order to ensure that the burdens appeared in the title of the burdened property; there was no requirement to register against the benefited property. If a deed purporting to create burdens did not appear in the title of the burdened property any obligations contained therein did not encumber the burdened property.

15.46   When do the burdens become effective?

Section 4(1) of the Title Conditions (Scotland) Act 2003 details when the burdens become effective to encumber the burdened property. There are three possibilities.

(1) The default position. If the constitutive deed is silent as to when burdens become effective then they become so from the date the constitutive deed is registered against both burdened and benefited properties.

(2) The constitutive deed specifies a fixed date. The constitutive deed may expressly provide that the burdens are to come into effect on a specified day: s 4(1)(a). In using this provision it is necessary to provide a fixed date, not a reference to a specified event or other occurrence.

(3) The constitutive deed specifies a date of registration of another deed. The constitutive deed may specify that the burdens become effective when another deed is registered and will therefore come into effect on registration of that deed: s 4(1)(b). For example, a deed of conditions may cover a development and be imposed prior to building work being carried out. However, in order to retain flexibility while building, the developer may provide that the burdens do not

come into effect immediately. The developer may wish to vary the burdens to take account of building conditions within the development. In order to postpone the burdens coming into effect, the developer may provide that the burdens are not effective until the first conveyance of a unit of the development is registered, or may specify that burdens do not affect individual units until the conveyance for each individual unit is registered.

15.47   Change in the pre-abolition law

Where a burden was created before the appointed day, the date on which the burdens became effective was determined by the deed in which the burdens were created. If the burdens were created in a disposition (or other conveyance), they were effective from the date the disposition was registered against the burdened property.

If the burdens were created in a deed of conditions, registration did not necessarily mean the burden was effective: it depended on the date of the deed of conditions.

(1) Where the deed of conditions was executed before 4 April 1979, s 32 of the Conveyancing (Scotland) Act 1874 governed creation. This provided that the burden was not created until the deed of conditions was incorporated into a conveyance of the burdened property. It was only on registration of that conveyance that the burden was created as against the specific burdened property.

(2) Where the deed of conditions was executed on or after 4 April 1979, s 32 of the 1874 Act required to be read alongside s 17 of the Land Registration (Scotland) 1979. This provided that, unless s 17 of the 1979 Act was expressly disapplied, the burdens were effective on registration of the deed of conditions. If s 17 of the 1979 Act was disapplied, then s 32 of the 1874 Act alone governed creation and the rule stated in the preceding paragraph applied. In some cases, s 17 could mean that the deed of conditions was not effective to create real burdens immediately, or – in some cases – at all. Praedial real burdens require both benefited and burdened properties. Accordingly, until there was a conveyance of at least one plot in the area covered by the deed of conditions, the burdens could not encumber the property because there were no benefited properties. However, if the deed contained a clause reserving to the developer the right to waive or vary the burdens (thereby excluding implied third party rights of enforcement under *Hislop v MacRitchie's Trustees* (1881) 8 R (HL) 95: see paras 17.26 and 17.27), no express rights of enforcement were granted in the deed of conditions and the conveyance was a disposition, then no benefited property existed and any obligations detailed in the deed of conditions could not be valid. These results are altered by the effect of Part 4 of the Title Conditions (Scotland) Act 2003, discussed in Chapter 17.

15.48   Transitional rules of creation

Where a deed of conditions is registered before the appointed day and s 17 of the Land Registration (Scotland) Act 1979 has been disapplied, the obligations imposed in the deed of conditions are not effective real burdens until incorporated into a conveyance of the burdened property (or other constitutive deed). Where the conveyance of the burdened property is to be registered after the appointed day, the prospective burdens in the deed of conditions registered before 28 November 2004 can be 'imported' into the conveyance. This is done in the form set out in Schedule 1 to the Title Conditions (Scotland) Act 2003.

15.49   How long do burdens last?

Unless a real burden expressly provides that it is restricted in duration, it will last in perpetuity (at least until varied or discharged): s 7 of the Title Conditions (Scotland) Act 2003. However, manager burdens have a transitory duration: see para 15.21.

15.50   Co-owned property

It is not possible to create burdens over or have burdens benefiting an individual co-owner's share of property: ss 4(6) and 6(3) of the Title Conditions (Scotland) Act 2003. This prevents the use of real burdens to regulate co-owned property as between the co-owners and means that real burdens cannot be used as the principal form of regulation of timeshare developments.

15.51   REPETITION OF REAL BURDENS IN SUBSEQUENT CONVEYANCES

Some constitutive deeds provide that the terms of burdens require to be repeated in each subsequent conveyance of the burdened property, and that failure to do so will extinguish the burdens. Any such provision is, as a result of s 68 of the Title Conditions (Scotland) Act 2003, of no effect in future. However, in practice, where there is a conveyance of the burdened property to be registered in the General Register of Sasines, or a first registration in the Land Register, the burdens will typically be referred to in the dispositive clause in order to avoid the possibility of a claim in warrandice against the transferor.

15.52   Change in pre-abolition law

The position prior to 28 November 2004 was that, while such clauses were commonplace, their efficacy was uncertain and their effect could be avoided by using the corrective mechanisms provided in s 9(3) and (4) of the Conveyancing (Scotland) Act 1924. In respect of an omission in a current title of the burdened property, s 9(4) provided that the burdened owner could register a deed of acknowledgement of omitted conditions in accordance with Schedule E to the 1924 Act. In respect of omissions in previous conveyances of the property, s 9(3) provided that the omission was cured if burdens were listed in the current conveyance. These provisions are repealed by the Title Conditions (Scotland) Act 2003.

15.53 CONCURRENT CONTRACTUAL LIABILITY

Prior to feudal abolition, where burdens were imposed in a conveyance the conveyance was treated as a contract between disponer and disponee and the disponee was liable in contract to the disponer, as well as the property transferred being encumbered by a real burden (if validly constituted). Section 61 of the Title Conditions (Scotland) Act 2003 provides that, where a burden is created, there is now no concurrent contractual liability.

15.54 FACTORS TO TAKE INTO ACCOUNT WHEN CREATING BURDENS

As well as complying with the general requirements of content and creation, it is necessary to consider various other issues when drafting burdens.

Firstly, although the rules of interpretation of burdens have been liberalised (see s 14 of the Title Conditions (Scotland) Act 2003, discussed at paras 17.55 to 17.57), certain general presumptions of interpretation continue to apply. These include:

(1) the presumption that real burdens will be interpreted *contra proferentem* (against the interests of the party relying on the burden, ie against the interests of the benefited owner);
(2) the related presumption that land is free from encumbrances; and
(3) that the terms of burdens affecting land are to be interpreted objectively and not to be based on the subjective intention of the benefited (or burdened) owner.

Burdens need to be precisely drafted and, when drafting burdens, the conveyancer must remember the rules of interpretation. However, while precisely drafting burdens it is necessary to remember that, if framed too narrowly, burdens may not cover matters they are intended to cover. For example, listing matters that are prohibited may mean that other matters not listed, or not of the same type as the matters that are listed, are not included. Nevertheless, this factor needs to be set against the following factor.

Secondly, there has been a tendency in recent years for burdens to proliferate, and to be unthinkingly imposed. When styles are held on a computer, it is very tempting for the burdens contained in the general styles to be incorporated into the relevant deed of conditions or conveyance. As the Scottish Law Commission noted in its *Report on Real Burdens* (Scot Law Com No 181, 2000), paras 1.34–1.35:

'Some deeds seek to regulate matters of the utmost triviality. Others impose broad general restrictions, not unreasonable in themselves, but which hit a much wider target than is really intended. For example, a prohibition on building is probably aimed at extensions and new double garages rather than at

Wendy houses and fences. Yet, unless the burden attempts some discrimination, all are equally prohibited. In practice the affected owner will probably build the Wendy house anyway, either in ignorance of the burden or on the view that it would not be enforced. In most cases this judgment would be sound. Nonetheless it is unsatisfactory that owners should be put in the position of having to act in deliberate disregard of the provisions of their titles. Law reform can help in a small way by making burdens easier to discharge. But even a simplified system of discharge involves trouble and, often, money. It is irksome to have to discharge a burden which should not have been there in the first place. In the development of a modern system of real burdens, changes in conveyancing practice will be as important as changes in the law'.

It is necessary to consider carefully what burdens are appropriate in the specific development or against the specific burdened properties. A style deed of conditions used for a residential estate comprising tenement properties is not applicable in relation to a residential estate comprising bungalows or detached properties. The drafting of burdens must be tailored to the specific development and should not simply be lifted from a bank of styles with the assumption that the burdens will be appropriate.

Thirdly, in many cases the 2003 Act is providing a set of default rules that can be trumped by express provision within the constitutive deed creating the burdens. For example, the default rules on variation and discharge of community burdens (see paras 18.19 to 18.25) will in many cases be unworkable in practice. If drafting burdens against a background that would require 100 owners to agree to the variation of a burden prohibiting building, the view could be reasonably taken that an alternative mechanism be put in place in the constitutive deed. It would be possible for the constitutive deed to provide that for certain burdens only those immediately adjacent to the burdened property would require to consent to proposed variations, while retaining the default rules for other burdens; or the constitutive deed could provide that certain burdens could be varied for the whole community if 30 per cent of owners in the community agree. By providing specific mechanisms for discharge or variation within the constitutive deed, the drafter can distinguish between burdens fundamental to a development and those intended to provide for the better amenity of individuals. If such mechanisms are not put in place, in future developments there will be particular problems in operating the default rules for express variation and discharge.

Fourthly, s 92 of the 2003 Act provides that a constitutive deed can provide that no Lands Tribunal application for variation or discharge is permissible before a date specified within the constitutive deed (within five years of the date of creation). Consideration requires to be given as to whether such a clause should be included.

15.55 Development management scheme

The Title Conditions (Scotland) Act 2003 provides that detailed rules to manage a community can be applied to it through the application of a development management scheme. This is a scheme of management rules that will be set out in an order to be made by the Westminster Parliament. At the time of writing the rules have not been promulgated. The intent is that the scheme will be a model set of management rules indicating good practice in the area and establishing an owners' association as a body corporate. It is likely that the statutory instrument will provide detailed rules regulating objections to management decisions taken, rules on variation and discharge of the scheme provisions, and rules regulating liability, as well as the model scheme itself. It is likely that these rules will be based on the scheme and rules recommended by the Scottish Law Commission in Part 8 of its *Report on Real Burdens* (Scot Law Com No 181, 2000).

The 2003 Act sets out a structure for the development management scheme, providing when the scheme applies and when it will cease to apply.

15.56 APPLICATION

The development management scheme cannot apply to a community unless a deed of application is registered in the property register against the properties comprising the community. The deed of application is a declaration that the scheme is to apply to specified land, made under s 71 of the Title Conditions (Scotland) Act 2003. The deed is to be granted by the owners of the community, which means that the scheme is unlikely to be used for existing communities where there will be difficulty in obtaining the written agreement of every owner. However, in new developments a developer may grant and register the deed of application. If a development management scheme is set up, the developer cannot impose manager burdens: s 66(2)(b) of the 2003 Act.

In granting the deed of application the developer can vary the terms of the model development management scheme to be specified.

The deed of application must specify the extent of the development; property which is to be referred to as 'scheme property' (those parts of the development to be maintained under the scheme); what is to be meant by a 'unit' within the development (be it houses, flats or such like); the name of the Owners' Association; and the name and address of the first manager.

The deed of application takes effect on registration or such later date as the deed may specify. The rules set out in s 71(1) mirror the rules on when burdens created under s 4 of the 2003 Act are to be effective: see para 15.46.

When the development management scheme applies to regulate a community, the provisions of the 2003 Act specified in s 72 will be adapted to apply to it. Those adapted include rules on the content of obligations, acquiescence, negative prescription, and Lands Tribunal applications.

15.57 DISAPPLICATION

A development management scheme will be disapplied by registering a deed of disapplication granted in conformity with s 73 of the Title Conditions (Scotland) Act

2003. Disapplication will completely remove the scheme from the community. The deed of disapplication is to be granted by the owners' association created under the scheme, and may be granted on the basis set out in the scheme. The deed of disapplication need not leave the community unregulated in that it is competent to create real burdens in a deed of disapplication, and the general rules in s 4 of the 2003 Act are applied by s 73(2).

Where there is a proposal to register a deed of disapplication, the owners' association require to intimate the proposal to register such a deed to the owners within the community. Intimation is made under s 74, and every owner is given eight weeks to apply to the Lands Tribunal to argue that the scheme should be preserved. The deed cannot be registered unless the Tribunal has certified the deed, confirming that no application was received.

Chapter 16

Title Conditions: Servitudes

16.1 Introduction

A servitude is a title condition running with land. It is created for the benefit of a proprietor of land – traditionally referred to as 'the dominant tenement', although referred to as 'the benefited property' in the Title Conditions (Scotland) Act 2003 – and entitles the benefited owner to exercise certain rights on or over an adjoining piece of land – traditionally 'the servient tenement', but referred to as 'the burdened property' in the 2003 Act. The terminology of the 2003 Act is used in this chapter.

Servitudes are subordinate real rights (meaning a real right held by a person in land owned by another), which (as real rights) once effectively created attach to the burdened property, and are enforceable against anyone on that property.

Prior to the 2003 Act, servitudes could impose obligations restricting use of the burdened property (typically by prohibiting building) as well as imposing obligations allowing the benefited owner to make some use of or to enter the burdened property. The latter are referred to as 'positive servitudes', and are, from 28 November 2004, the sole species of servitudes. These are the principal focus of this chapter. The former are referred to as 'negative servitudes' and, on 28 November 2004, are converted into real burdens preserved, in the case of those not constituted in the title of the burdened property, through registration of a notice of converted servitude: s 80 of the 2003 Act. See the discussion at paras 17.15 to 17.19. No new negative servitudes can be created from 28 November 2004: s 79 of the 2003 Act. Consequently, this chapter will not generally consider negative servitudes, other than to note the previous rules of creation which are relevant in determining whether negative servitudes require to be preserved through use of a notice of converted servitude. The distinction was important because the mode of constitution differed for each. Since positive servitudes allow the benefited owner to enter or use the burdened property, they may be actively possessed or enjoyed; while negative servitudes could not.

As explained at para 14.5, the overlap between real burdens and servitudes was not simply negative servitudes and negative burdens. At common law it appeared that a real burden could impose an obligation allowing the benefited owner to make some use of the burdened property: see para 15.23. On the appointed day (28 November 2004) such burdens (including those feudal burdens that are preserved under s 18 of the Abolition of Feudal Tenure etc (Scotland) Act 2000, having satisfied subs (7)(b) of that section) are converted into positive servitudes: s 81 of the 2003 Act.

From the point of view of the owner of the burdened property there is little difference in practical effect between a real burden in the title, and a servitude. Both
derogate from the absolute quality of his ownership; both entitle some other party to
exercise a right or enforce a restriction affecting the landowner as such. But in law,
there are certain important distinctions concerning: their function (see para 14.4);
their nature; constitution of the respective rights; their enforcement; and their variation and discharge (the latter being dealt with along with consideration of variation
and discharge of real burdens in Chapter 18).

Since the sixth edition of this book, Sheriff Douglas Cusine and Professor
Roderick Paisley have published *Servitudes and Rights of Way* (1998). This is a mag-
isterial volume and is the primary point of reference for any questions on law or
practice in this area. Appropriate reference to the relevant sections of Cusine and
Paisley is given in the text.

16.2   Types of positive servitudes

Prior to the Title Conditions (Scotland) Act 2003, the general position was that servitudes required to conform to certain recognised types known to law, or at least analogous to known servitudes. It was sometimes said that there was 'in effect, a fixed list
of servitudes in Scotland': see, for example, *Report on Real Burdens* (Scot Law Com
No 181, 2000), para 12.22. The various types of servitude right on this list are of long
standing (often traceable back to Roman law), well defined and well established, and
are natural incidents to the proper enjoyment of heritable property. The same, or counterpart, rights exist in other systems: see, for example, English 'easements' and 'profits à prendre'. But, nonetheless, in a system of conveyancing heavily dependent on
registration the servitudes on the fixed list are, in some ways, an anomaly in that, in
some cases, written title is not necessary for their constitution. Nothing need enter the
Land Register (servitudes being an 'overriding interest' under s 28 of the Land
Registration (Scotland) Act 1979), although s 75 of the 2003 Act, discussed below,
provides a new rule of constitution. This common law position can be contrasted with
the law for real burdens, where validity is dependent on registration in the title of the
burdened (and from 28 November 2004, also the benefited) property.

Writers have attempted to detail the list: see W M Gordon *Scottish Land Law* (2nd
edn, 1999), paras 24-20 to 24-26; and D J Cusine and R R M Paisley *Servitudes and
Rights of Way* (1998), Chapter 3. Common examples of these servitudes found in
practice, often in rural areas, include:

(1) the right of access or passage (the right to traverse the burdened property on
    foot, or by vehicle, or to drive animals through the burdened property);
(2) the rights of *aquaehaustus* and aqueduct (the rights to draw water from and to
    lead it through the burdened property);
(3) the servitude of sinks or drainage (the right to drain water into a property, typi-
    cally through draining into a septic tank); and

(4) the right of pasturage (the right to pasture animals on the burdened property).

The 2003 Act amends the law in two primary ways. Firstly, it clears up uncertainty in the pre-feudal abolition law as to the efficacy of pipeline servitudes. Secondly, it ends the fixed list of positive servitudes.

Pipeline servitudes are dealt with by s 77: it provides that a right to lead a cable, pipe or wire is deemed always to have been competently created as a servitude. The effect is to add pipeline servitudes to the fixed list. This accords with general conveyancing practice, and reverses the unfortunate decision in *Neill v Scobbie* 1993 GWD 13-887, where it was held that it was not competent to grant a servitude for the transmission of an electricity cable. Contrast that decision with *Labinski Ltd v BP Oil Development Ltd* 2002 GWD 1-46.

In relation to the fixed list, there are two provisions that have effect to bring it to an end: firstly, in relation to new obligations allowing use created from 28 November 2004; and, secondly, those obligations allowing use created prior to 28 November 2004.

For those obligations to be created from 28 November 2004, it is provided that where there is a servitude created in writing and registered in accordance with s 75 of the 2003 Act (discussed at para 16.5), which is of the general character of servitudes (discussed at para 16.3), then 'any rule of law that requires that a positive servitude be of a type known to the law shall not apply'. See s 76(1) of the 2003 Act, discussed in *Report on Real Burdens* (Scot Law Com No 181, 2000), at paras 12.22–12.25. This would allow the creation of general obligations allowing use, such as the right to use the burdened property to have a bonfire. One other instance where there may be clarification regards an obligation allowing car parking. There is some doubt as to the best analysis in the current law. Cusine and Paisley think it is a servitude: *Servitudes and Rights of Way*, paras 3.45–3.52. This view was also held in *Davidson v Wiseman* 2001 GWD 9-317, discussed in K G C Reid and G L Gretton *Conveyancing 2001* (2002) at pp 72–73. The position, though, is not free from doubt. If the right of car parking is not a servitude, it could be constituted as a servitude under ss 75 and 76 of the 2003 Act.

For those obligations allowing use created before 28 November 2004, the obligation could only be validly constituted to run with the land if created as a real burden. Section 81 of the 2003 Act provides that such burdens are converted into positive servitudes on the appointed day.

16.3 Salient characteristics of servitudes

(1) There must be two separate properties – the benefited and the burdened – in separate ownership. However, this may not be possible where servitudes are created in a deed of conditions over a development, prior to the sale of the initial plots. In this situation the deed creating the servitude is registered when there is only

one owner of benefited and burdened properties. Section 75(2) of the Title Conditions (Scotland) Act 2003 provides that the validity of the servitude cannot be questioned if so created, although the servitude will not come into existence until there are two properties.

(2) Servitudes are praedial. They are created for the benefit of the benefited property, not the individual that happens to own the benefited property; and they must encumber the burdened property, not the individual burdened owner. This means that the servitude cannot be held in isolation: *MacKay v Lord Burton* 1994 SLT (Lands Tr) 35. Title to enforce attaches to the benefited property, and 'runs with the land' in the same manner as praedial real burdens: see the example in para 15.3, which illustrates how this operates. The praedial requirement means that the burdened and benefited properties must be in the same neighbourhood, although not necessarily contiguous.

(3) The burdened owner must suffer or permit a restriction on his freedom of use of his or her property at the instance of the benefited owner. But there can be no positive obligation on him or her to do or execute any act or thing. The burdened owner's role is purely passive: in other words, the obligation must be *in patiendo*.

(4) Although a servitude necessarily infringes on, and derogates from, the absolute freedom of the burdened owner, it must nonetheless be consistent with his or her right of ownership; in other words, it cannot be so extensive or so burdensome that the burdened owner is entirely precluded from using his land. This rule is restated for those servitudes not on the fixed list: s 76(2) of the 2003 Act.

For general discussion of the characteristics of servitudes, see Cusine and Paisley *Servitudes and Rights of Way*, Chapter 2.

16.4   Constitution of positive servitudes

Positive servitudes may be constituted in three or, possibly, four ways:

(1) express grant or express reservation;
(2) implied grant or implied reservation;
(3) prescription; and
(4) acquiescence.

16.5   EXPRESS GRANT OR EXPRESS RESERVATION

Such express provision may occur in a conveyance of the benefited or burdened property respectively; in a deed of conditions; or there may be a separate minute of agreement or deed of servitude. A deed creating a servitude must be granted only by the registered owner of the burdened property (at the time of grant). It is not possible for a servitude to be effectively created by an unregistered proprietor of the burdened property unless the deed creating the servitude is a disposition: see the discussion in D J Cusine and R R M Paisley *Servitudes and Rights of Way* (1998), para 4.08. In the case of a co-owned burdened property, all proprietors must concur to create a servitude right. See *Fearnan Partnership v Grindlay* 1992 SC (HL) 38.

In a disposition, the disponer may expressly confer on the disponee a right of access over other land retained by the disponer (creation by grant); or the disponer may reserve a right of access to him or herself, or to a third party, over the disponee's property (creation by reservation). Alternatively, positive servitudes may be constituted by mere written agreement between the burdened owner and benefited owner; or by a unilateral deed of servitude granted by the burdened owner. For guidance on drafting, see Cusine and Paisley *Servitudes and Rights of Way*, Chapter 5 and 6. The deed creating a servitude must identify the burdened and benefited property. Given the requirements for land registration (see s 4 of the Land Registration (Scotland) Act 1979), it is necessary to describe the properties in such a way that they can be identified on the Ordnance Map. Prior to 28 November 2004, the precision with which the properties are identified is dependent on the deed used. Conveyances required conveyancing descriptions, other deeds did not: Cusine and Paisley *Servitudes and Rights of Way*, paras 2.25–2.39.

Any deed creating a servitude and executed prior to 1 August 1995 must be in formal writing (probative, holograph or adopted as holograph); or, if in informal writing, be followed by *rei interventus*. Any such deed, executed on or after 1 August 1995, must be a formal document in terms of the Requirements of Writing (Scotland) Act 1995, s 2 and, for practical purposes, should always be self-proving, as it must be if the deed is to be registered. Section 75(1) of the Title Conditions (Scotland) Act 2003 provides that, from 28 November 2004, 'A deed is not effective to create a positive servitude by express provision unless it is registered against both the benefited property and the burdened property.' The servitude is then not constituted as a real right until dual registration takes place. Section 75 applies to servitudes that appear on the fixed list if they are created in writing after the appointed day, as well as to new positive servitudes (not on the fixed list): s 76 of the 2003 Act.

However, if a servitude was created before 28 November 2004, the vesting of the real right could arise in one of two ways. Where the deed containing the servitude was registered in the title of either the benefited or the burdened property, nothing further is required. The benefited owner (and his or her successors) may exercise the right, or not, as he or she pleases in perpetuity, subject only to the servitude being discharged: see Chapter 18. But, where the servitude is not registered then the benefited owner must enter into possession of the servitude right (ie to commence, and continue, to exercise the right) in order to make it effective against singular successors in the burdened property. The relevant authorities are gathered by Cusine and Paisley *Servitudes and Rights of Way*, at para 6.31.

As the creation of real rights generally requires an element of publicity in order to advertise the right to the world, it is said that possession is required as an alternative to publication by registration to ensure that, by possession and public enjoyment, the existence of the servitude is made known openly, and can be ascertained from inspection of the property. In this way, a purchaser of the burdened property is protected. However, possession is, in practice, a haphazard and uncertain method of discovering encumbrances, which may be very onerous and can altogether frustrate the intentions of a purchaser.

An express grant or reservation of servitude, as with reservations and burdens in titles generally, will be strictly construed in favour of the burdened property. The terms of the grant must be clear and there must be a definite intention to create a servitude running with the lands; but there are no statutory forms or any necessary words of style. Use of the word 'servitude' is not necessary for creation: *North British Railway v Park Yard Co Ltd* (1898) 25 R (HL) 47 and *Moss Bros Group plc v Scottish Mutual Assurance plc* 2001 SC 779. See Cusine and Paisley *Servitudes and Rights of Way*, paras 2.54 ff and Chapter 15. The discussion in paras 2.54 ff gives indications of factors that will be considered in determining whether the deed can be treated as creating a servitude. It is necessary to show that there was intention to create a permanent servitude.

16.6   IMPLIED GRANT OR IMPLIED RESERVATION

An implied servitude can be created only when the two properties, benefited and burdened, have previously been owned by the same proprietor, who has disposed of one (or both) of them, and in so doing has omitted to express such servitude rights as are either absolutely necessary or, in certain circumstances, reasonably necessary for the proper enjoyment of the subjects disponed. As with express grants and reservations, where an implied grant or reservation is claimed, the benefited owner must be able to demonstrate a deemed intention to create the right. The law does not generally imply servitudes as there is a general presumption that property is free from encumbrances: see W M Gordon *Scottish Land Law* (2nd edn, 1999), para 24-34. The following paragraphs examine when servitudes may be created by implied grant or reservation, and touch on a related matter which involves landlocked land, where, in certain cases, a right of access will be implied under the rule in *Bowers v Kennedy* 2000 SC 555.

16.7   Rights absolutely necessary to the use or enjoyment of the dominant tenement: the right of access to landlocked land

Suppose, for example, A sells to B land completely surrounded by other land of A, but gives B no express right of access; a right of access over A's land will be implied. Likewise, if A disponed the other land to B, retaining the landlocked subjects without reserving to himself access in B's disposition, a right of access is implied for A's benefit. Such access can be implied only where claimed over property from which the landlocked plot has been sub-divided, and will not be implied at all if an alternative access route is available. The right of access to landlocked land arises as of necessity.

In the sixth edition of this book, at para 11.7, in accordance with the analysis of the time, this right of access was analysed as a servitude of necessity: see the discussion in D J Cusine and R R M Paisley *Servitudes and Rights of Way* (1998), paras 11.18–11.26. However, since then the doctrinal basis of the right has been clarified by the Inner House decision in *Bowers v Kennedy* 2000 SC 555. This case is discussed in Reid and Gretton *Conveyancing 2000* (2001) at pp 52–55; Cabrelli 'The Landlocked Proprietor's Right of Access' 2001 SLT (News) 25; and Paisley 'Bower of Bliss?' (2002) 6 Edin LR 101.

In *Bowers*, land was divided into two plots: plot A was landlocked by plot B. Plot B was sold first; a servitude of access was expressly reserved over plot B. Plot A ceased to be used and the servitude of access was not used for a period of time. It was held that, even though non-use of the servitude for 20 years would have seen it extinguished by long negative prescription (see para 18.58), the owner of plot A would still have an implied right of access over plot B. This access would be a right inherent in the ownership of plot A, and as such could not be extinguished by long negative prescription being a right *res merae facultatis*: see the Prescription and Limitation (Scotland) Act 1973, Schedule 3, para (c). The full implications of *Bowers* remain uncertain.

16.8 Rights necessary for the proper, comfortable enjoyment of the dominant tenement.

The extent and limits within which servitudes may be constituted in these circumstances are less certain. There is a general discussion in D J Cusine and R R M Paisley *Servitudes and Rights of Way* (1998) at Chapter 8. Professor Gordon, in *Scottish Land Law* (2nd edn, 1999), at para 24-35, aside from stating that it is possible to create positive servitudes only by implication, identifies the following conditions for creation by implied grant:

'… the [benefited] and [burdened] properties must originally have been possessed together and subsequently severed;

… the "servitude" claimed must be absolutely necessary, or at least reasonably necessary, for the comfortable enjoyment of the [property] first disponed by the common author;

… the 'servitude' must be in existence at the date of severance, or more exactly, must have been used before the severance or have become necessary by reason of the severance; and

… the servitude must be over land of the grantor and not the granted, as a general rule [ie generally implied grant, rather than implied reservation]'.

The general principle seems firmly established in *Cochrane v Ewart* (1861) 23 D (HL) 3. This case involved the continued use, following sub-division of a property, of a pre-existing drain serving the benefited and passing through the burdened property. As Lord Campbell, LC, put it at p 4:

'Where two properties are possessed by the same owner, and there has been a severance, anything which was used and which was necessary for the comfortable enjoyment of that part of the property which is granted [ie the part sold and disponed] shall be considered to follow from the grant'.

In contrast, in *Murray v Medley* 1973 SLT (Sh Ct) 75, the owner of a group of buildings sold one of them, together with a small area of ground. Unknown to the purchaser, a water pipe ran under the subjects of sale, supplying mains water to the remaining buildings retained by the seller. In the disposition in favour of the purchaser, there was no reserved right to continue using this pipe. The sheriff rejected an argument that an existing mains water supply was necessary for the reasonable enjoyment of a dwellinghouse. He held that plenty of dwellinghouses in Scotland have no mains water, and that the property in question was capable of being used as a house without a mains supply. A servitude right for this mains supply pipe would clearly derogate from the grant in favour of the purchaser and so requires an express reservation, except in cases of necessity. Since there was no 'necessity' in this instance, there could be no implied reservation of the necessary servitude right. In the result, by failing to reserve an express servitude right, the seller was deprived of his existing mains water supply. It is questionable if a similar decision would be reached today. For a comparable case, where the omission to make express provision for an electricity supply was held to be deliberate and did not justify an implied grant, see *Neill v Scobbie* 1993 GWD 13-887, discussed at para 16.2.

These cases confirm the general suggestion of Professor Gordon that a servitude under this head (necessary for comfortable enjoyment) will generally be created only by implied grant for the benefit of the disponee; and rarely be created by implied reservation for the benefit of the disponer. Indeed, it appears that a servitude can be implied, by reservation, only if absolutely necessary for the property to be used at all: see Gordon *Scottish Land Law*, para 24-40.

If, in *Murray*, the facts had been reversed, and if the water mains serving the sold property had passed through the retained property, it might have been possible to establish a servitude by implication for the benefit of the disponee.

In *McEachen v Lister* 1976 SLT (Sh Ct) 38, A owned and occupied a dwellinghouse with land attached. He sold and disponed the dwellinghouse and part of his land to B. In the disposition, A conveyed to B the benefit of all rights of way etc in general terms. He specifically conferred on B a servitude right of access to the house by a road leading thereto from the public road across the remainder of A's land, the route being coloured blue on the attached plan. It later transpired that, when A himself had occupied the house, he had also taken access thereto by a second route over the retained land, but in the disposition no right was conferred on B to use this second route. Following on the sale, A closed the second route, leaving the first route open. B objected, claiming access to the dwellinghouse by both routes. It was held that, since a right of access had been specifically conferred in the purchaser's title by the first route, this by itself automatically excluded the possibility of any implied right of access by the second route.

There is a discussion in this case on the requisites for a servitude of access necessary for convenient and comfortable enjoyment. The sheriff principal reviewed the authorities at p 41 and concluded:

'I find it difficult to presume an intention to create by implication a right of way in a case where the proprietor took pains to provide for access to the property disponed by making an express grant of a right of way'.

He then distinguished *Cochrane v Ewart* (1861) 23 D (HL) 3 on the grounds that, in that case, the title was silent as to the mode of access; and followed *Fraser v Cox* 1938 SC 506.

The wording in *McEachen* also discloses a common trap for the draftsman, which frequently passes unnoticed and on which the sheriff principal made comment in his decision in this case. The subjects conveyed were part of a larger estate. As stated in para 16.3 above, for the existence of a servitude there must be two separate tenements in separate ownership. Accordingly, on a sub-division, if the intention is to create servitude rights as between the sub-divided parts, it must be borne in mind that there are at that date no existing 'servitudes' serving the disponed part over the retained part or vice versa. This is a contradiction in terms: no such servitude can exist until there has been actual sub-division. However, *Cochrane* and *Shearer v Peddie* (1899) 1 F 1201 make clear that for a servitude to be created by implied grant it is necessary to show that it existed, or that the right of use claimed existed, prior to the sub-division. In *Shearer* a building company was formed to construct terraced houses as per a building plan. Each member of the company was to purchase one dwellinghouse and each of them saw the building plan; the plan showed a lane to the rear. The houses were duly completed and conveyances granted to the individual members of the company as purchasers, in which no reference was made to the plan. Each conveyance included a portion of the lane adjoining each individual house but no servitude rights of access were created over the remainder of the land. Some owners raised an action seeking the implication of a servitude in the conveyances in their favour. This was rejected because the lane had not been used prior to sub-division (and could not be used, because the lane had not been constructed).

16.9 PRESCRIPTION

Servitudes can be created by positive prescription. Until 1976, the period of possession required for this was 40 years, with added years for non-age and disability. By virtue of s 3(1) and (2) of the Prescription and Limitation (Scotland) Act 1973, which came into force on 25 July 1976, the period is now 20 years in all cases. Possession before the commencement of the 1973 Act was counted towards the 20 years, provided that it continued at least for a time, however short, after the Act came into force: see 1973 Act, s 14(1)(a).

Section 3 of the 1973 Act must now be read alongside ss 75 and 76 of the Title Conditions (Scotland) Act 2003.

Under s 3(1) of the 1973 Act, possession of the servitude for 20 years following on the execution of a deed will establish the right beyond challenge, subject to the same exceptions as are provided in s 1 of the 1973 Act. The deed must be sufficient in its term to constitute the servitude either by express provision therein or by necessary implication. For servitudes created expressly on or after 28 November 2004, the deed will require to be registered under s 75 of the 2003 Act.

Alternatively, under s 3(2) of the 1973 Act, if a positive servitude has been possessed for 20 years, without reference to any written deed, the existence of the servitude as so possessed is exempt from challenge. Both before and after the appointed day of 28 November 2004, this will only apply to positive servitudes appearing on the fixed list. It cannot apply to positive servitudes to be created under s 76 of the 2003 Act.

Section 3 of the 1973 Act simply re-enacts, in a modified form, the former rule that positive servitudes can be created either by deed followed by possession or by mere possession. It underlines the peculiar feature of servitudes, with particular reference to prescription, that a written title is not necessary and nothing need appear on the register. This will apply only to servitudes appearing on the fixed list from 28 November 2004.

The person claiming the right must be the proprietor (registered or, probably, unregistered) of the benefited property; and he must show possession of the right, as of right, throughout the full period by him or herself, the previous owners, and/or representatives (including tenants, and family members): 1973 Act, s 3(4). Possession is not only proof that the right exists but also proof of the measure and extent of the right; it defines the dominant tenement, and probably the servient tenement affected by the right, and the degree, and way, in which the right may be exercised. This is what is meant by the maxim *tantum praescriptum quantum possessum*.

The most important case on servitudes created by prescription is *Carstairs v Spence* 1924 SC 380. Here, the owner of the burdened property attempted to interdict the benefited owner from using an access route constituted by prescription to transport building materials to the benefited property to construct a residential development. The servitude had been constituted while the benefited property was used for agricultural purposes and the burdened owner claimed that this use limited the extent of the servitude. The First Division held that the servitude could be used for the transporting of building materials. Once it is clear into what category the servitude falls (in this case, a servitude of vehicular access), the purpose for which it was acquired does not determine its extent. However, this is subject to the general principle that the servitude should not be exercised in such a way as to increase the burden on the burdened owner.

The creation of servitudes by positive prescription is considered in detail by D J Cusine and R R M Paisley *Servitudes and Rights of Way* (1998), Chapter 10. The acquisition of heritable rights by prescription generally is dealt with in Chapter 12.

16.10 ACQUIESCENCE

'It does appear that, in certain circumstances, a servitude or some similar right (*sic*) may be created by acquiescence': Bell's *Principles*, s 947. In addition, there is authority for the view that, in some cases, singular successors in lands will be bound by the acquiescence of their predecessors: *Macgregor v Balfour* (1899) 2 F 345. This has been stated to occur when the thing acquiesced in is visible and obvious, especially where it is of such a character or cost as to be inconsistent with its having been allowed merely during pleasure. See, for detailed consideration of relevant authorities in the area, Cusine and Paisley *Servitudes and Rights of Way*, paras 11.37–11.46.

16.11 Constitution of negative servitudes prior to 28 November 2004

As negative servitudes will be converted into real burdens by s 80 of the Title Conditions (Scotland) Act 2003, it is necessary to know the rules of constitution of negative servitudes that applied prior to 28 November 2004. They could be constituted by express grant or reservation in a conveyance or by agreement in writing. As a negative servitude did not involve the benefited owner having an active right over the burdened property, constitution by prescription was not possible, nor was constitution by implied grant or reservation. However, see the view of Cusine and Paisley *Servitudes and Rights of Way*, Chapter 9.

When constituted in writing, the writing had to be probative or, if executed on or after 1 August 1995, formal and, if registered, self-proving. However, as for positive servitudes, the writing did not need to be registered. This places the burdened owner (and singular successors of the burdened owner) in a difficult position: if the negative servitude did not appear in the title of the burdened property then the burdened owner could not know of the obligation; and nothing may show, on the register or from inspection of the property, that a negative servitude exists. Further, there cannot be any active exercise or enjoyment of the right until the burdened owner actually contravenes the servitude obligation.

16.12 Enforcement and enjoyment of servitudes

The person entitled to exercise the servitude is so entitled, not personally as an individual, but as owner of the benefited property. Only the benefited owner has a title to enforce: *Oliver v Cameron* 1994 GWD 8-505. However, the servitude can be enjoyed by non-owners, as the benefited owner can communicate the right to enjoy to those with an interest in the benefited property, such as family members and, occasionally, tenants. See Cusine and Paisley *Servitudes and Rights of Way*, paras 1.55–1.61, where the contrary approach suggested in para 11.12 in the sixth edition of this book is criticised. It is inherent in the nature of a servitude that, once properly constituted in any of the ways indicated above, it runs with the lands so far as the burdened property is concerned and will continue to affect it no matter into whose ownership it may pass. A servitude is, therefore, effective not only against the original owner of the burdened property but against singular successors whether they have prior notice of the right or not, and whether they acquire the whole, or part only, of the burdened property. For example, a burdened property subject to a right of way is later sold in 50 lots as a building estate; all 50 lots remain encumbered if the right of way is through each lot.

So far as the benefited owner is concerned, the right subsists for the benefit of the benefited property. Two results follow:

(1)   singular successors, as owners of the benefited property, require no express assignation of the servitude; mere title to the benefited property entitles them to exercise or enforce it; and

(2)   since the servitude is praedial, it generally cannot be divorced from the benefited property so as to benefit someone other than a party with a 'nexus' in the benefited property. So the benefited owner cannot assign the right to a third party. However, sub-division of the benefited property is permissible, and each subdivided part will be entitled to exercise the servitude subject to the general principle that the burden on the burdened property cannot be increased. The qualification is crucial. Clearly, to communicate a servitude of taking peat (the servitude of fuel, feal and divot) to several purchasers on the break-up of a benefited property materially increases the burden and would be objectionable. There would be less of a problem in the case of access or way, and no problem at all in, for example, communicating a stillicide from a tenement roof, when flats are sold individually, with a common right or interest in the roof. See *Watson v Sinclair* 1966 SLT (Sh Ct) 77; *Keith v Texaco Ltd* 1977 SLT (Lands Tr) 16; and *Alba Homes Ltd v Duell* 1993 SLT (Sh Ct) 49.

16.13   INTEREST TO ENFORCE

As with other title conditions, the benefited owner must have an interest to enforce. However, the rule now seems to be that interest to enforce is presumed and it is up to the burdened owner to show that the benefited owner has no interest to enforce: *Royal Exchange Buildings, Glasgow, Proprietors v Cotton* 1912 SC 1151. See also Cusine and Paisley *Servitudes and Rights of Way*, para 12.50.

16.14   INTERPRETATION AND EXERCISE OF SERVITUDES

The presumption for freedom operates here, as with real burdens (see paras 17.55 to 17.58). But the strict rules applied in construing real burdens do not apply so rigorously when the right created is a servitude of a well-known kind. See *McLean v*

Marwhirn Developments Ltd 1976 SLT (Notes) 47 and Cusine and Paisley *Servitudes and Rights of Way*, Chapter 12 (which details the rights and obligations implied in the exercise of servitudes) and Chapter 16 (on construction of servitudes).

The principles for the construction and the exercise of servitudes are that:

(1) in cases of ambiguity, the least onerous result is preferred, applying the general principle of interpretation *contra proferentem*;

(2) the benefited owner must exercise the right *civiliter*, that is to say in the least burdensome manner. In *Alba Homes Ltd v Duell* 1993 SLT (Sh Ct) 49, a servitude right of access was created for the benefit of a plot of land and of a neighbouring plot. The owner of the first plot built a dwellinghouse thereon and intended to build a second dwellinghouse, to which the owner of the neighbouring plot objected on a curious argument that the purchaser of part only, but not the whole, of the benefited property was not entitled to the benefit of the right. The argument was rejected: 'The dominant tenement in favour of which the servitude is constituted is the whole of the land conveyed to the defenders by the disposition in their favour and not any particular part of that land'. This is the standard rule in such cases. The decision in this case would, of course, be subject to the standard proviso that there must be no overburdening of the right; but there was no element of overburdening in this case.

See also *Irvine Knitters Ltd v North Ayrshire Co-operative Society Ltd* 1978 SC 109. In that case the pursuers had granted a servitude right of access over a lane to the defenders' predecessors in title at 84–90 High Street, Irvine. The defenders also acquired 78–82 and 92–106 High Street, Irvine and used the whole property, 78–106 High Street, as a supermarket. Deliveries to the supermarket made use of the servitude right of access and were delivered at what had been 84–90 High Street, but were then taken through that property to the rest of the store. It was held that the servitude could not be used in this way. The benefited property in the servitude could not be used as a 'bridge' by the benefited owner truly to benefit other properties;

(3) the burdened owner is limited in his freedom of use only to the extent necessary to allow the proper exercise of the servitude. So, with a servitude of way, the burdened owner may use it himself, may erect unlocked gates, or, in rural areas, if the exact line is not defined precisely, may alter the line to another route equally convenient. A servitude of access constituted by express grant along a defined line cannot be altered unilaterally by the benefited owner; nor may the burdened owner encroach thereon;

(4) the benefited owner cannot increase the burden on the burdened property (either through excessive multiplication of those enforcing the servitude, or through increasing the use of the servitude). An example of the former would be where benefited property in a servitude of access is developed. The benefited property may originally be farmland, but that land is sold for residential development. The increase from one benefited owner to 50 or 100 benefited owners would be an unwarranted increase in the burden. Advising in this area is dependent on the

individual facts of each case but useful guidance is given in K G C Reid 'New Buildings and Old Servitudes' (1993) 4 Greens PLB 6 and Cusine and Paisley *Servitudes and Rights of Way*, para 12.193. There is more case law on the latter, where the benefited owner's use of the burdened property changes and increases the burden on the servitude. *Smith v Saxton* 1951 SLT 64, where a servitude of carriage could be used by motor vehicles, can be contrasted with *Kerr v Brown* 1939 SC 140, which considered whether there was an increase in burden where a servitude for drainage of waste water was used for the discharge of 'closet sewage'.

16.15   Public rights of way

A servitude exists for the benefit of an adjoining benefited property. A public right of way exists for the benefit of the public, between and connecting two public places. It may be of the same degree as the servitude right of way, ie footpath, horse road, drove road or carriage road. It may be constituted by express grant, but in the great majority of cases public rights of way exist by virtue of prescriptive possession for the full prescriptive period of 20 years in terms of s 3(3) of the Prescription and Limitation (Scotland) Act 1973. A public right of way may be lost by disuse for the full prescriptive period; or by disuse coupled with actings by the servient proprietor which are inconsistent with the existence of the right and which are unchallenged over a period of time of lesser duration than the prescriptive period.

Public rights of way may be vindicated by the general public, or by public bodies such as local authorities and Rights of Way societies. Two recent cases illustrate the distinctive features of this right.

In *Cumbernauld and Kilsyth District Council v Dollar Land (Cumbernauld) Ltd* 1993 SC (HL) 44 it was held in the House of Lords, affirming earlier decisions in the lower courts, that a public right of way had been constituted by a continuous and plain assertion of a public right. The Development Corporation originally constructed the new town of Cumbernauld, which incorporated a public walkway through the town centre. The defenders purchased the whole development in 1987 and, shortly after completion, locked the doors on this walkway at night to prevent vandalism.

They argued principally that, even although there had apparently been prescriptive possession, there was no evidence that the public use was an assertion of a public right; it could equally be ascribed to tolerance on the part of the then proprietors. But that argument was rejected in the First Division: see *Cumbernauld and Kilsyth District Council v Dollar Land (Cumbernauld) Ltd* 1992 SC 357. Lord President Hope stated at 366 that:

> 'where the use is of such amount and in such manner as would reasonably be regarded as being the assertion of a public right, the owner cannot stand by and ask that his inaction be ascribed to his good nature, or to tolerance'.

In *Burton v Mackay* 1995 SLT 507 the pursuer sought to interdict a neighbouring proprietor from using an old road as a means of access to his property. The road had ceased to qualify as a public right of way. The court held that, given that a public right of way had been established, it necessarily followed that proprietors along that route remained entitled to use it for access to their individual properties, even although the road itself had ceased to be public because it no longer led from one public place to another. Accordingly, the higher right of public right of way would seem to carry with it, by implication, the lesser right of private servitude of access.

It is, of course, obviously difficult to disentangle and distinguish between use by the public in the assertion of a public right of way concurrently with private use by individual proprietors of the public right of way as a means of access to their own individual properties. But, as Lord Coulsfield observed, although the point was without authority, it would be extraordinary if an established right of use along a public right of way enjoyed by intermediate proprietors was to be lost when the road ceased to be public. He stated that the defenders must at least continue to enjoy a private right of access to their own property, and for that purpose he considered that there was sufficient evidence of material use as of right without interruption to sustain a servitude right of access to the property in question. Notwithstanding this decision, however, there clearly could be cases where the distinction between the use of a public right of way and an assertion of a public right would not, of itself, be sufficient to satisfy the requirements for the creation of a private servitude right of access although, on the evidence in this case, Lord Coulsfield did not consider that point significant. See in this regard *Hamilton v Mundell; Hamilton v J & J Currie Ltd* (20 November 2002, unreported), Dumfries Sheriff Court, discussed in K G C Reid and G L Gretton *Conveyancing 2002* (2003), pp 74–76.

The Land Reform (Scotland) Act 2003 gives a general right of recreational access and is discussed in Chapter 20. This, in general, does not affect the law on public rights of way.

Chapter 17

Title Conditions: Enforcement of Real Burdens

17.1 Introduction

Real burdens are enforced when the burdened owner or, in some cases, another person occupying the burdened property either contravenes a real burden or proposes to do so.

Examination of enforcement involves consideration of the issue of title to enforce burdens (both expressly granted and arising by implication); interest to enforce; the liability of the burdened owner and others in the obligation; the interpretation of burdens; and remedies available for their breach. In considering title to enforce praedial real burdens the rules on subdivision of benefited properties will be examined. In considering liability of the burdened property, rules on subdivision of burdened properties will be considered. Some of the powers held by and enforceable by a community and inherent in community burdens are also outlined.

The rules on title and interest to enforce burdens are required in relation to variation and discharge of burdens – in order to determine who must be approached for express consent to a proposed contravention of a burden. The rules on interpretation are also useful to remember when there is a proposed action that may contravene a burden as they may indicate that this does not actually do so and therefore there is no requirement for variation or discharge.

17.2 General position

Section 8(1) of the Title Conditions (Scotland) Act 2003 provides: 'a real burden is enforceable by any person who has both title and interest to enforce it'. In the following paragraphs we examine title and interest to enforce.

17.3 Title to enforce burdens

The rules here differ depending on whether the burden is a praedial real burden or a personal real burden.

Title to enforce praedial real burdens is considered at paras 17.4–17.48. The rules on title to enforce personal real burdens are considered at para 17.49.

17.4   Title to enforce praedial real burdens

The following will be considered: identification of the benefited property or properties; and detailing the people with an interest in the benefited property that have title to enforce.

17.5   IDENTIFYING BENEFITED PROPERTIES

There are three possible situations:

(1) where the benefited property is expressly identified in a constitutive deed registered after the appointed day;
(2) where the benefited property is expressly identified in a constitutive deed registered before the appointed day; and
(3) where benefited properties are implied.

When benefited properties are expressly identified there is no requirement that the owners of the properties identified have any relation to the granter of the constitutive deed. Equally, the properties identified need not have been previously owned by him or her (although in many cases they will have been).

17.6   Expressly granted rights of enforcement: all constitutive deeds registered after 28 November 2004

As detailed at para 15.41, when burdens are created after the appointed day the constitutive deed must expressly identify the benefited property: s 4(2)(c)(ii) of the Title Conditions (Scotland) Act 2003. In the ordinary case where the property is in (or is to be registered in) the Land Register this will require the benefited property to be described in such a way that it can be identified on the Ordnance Map or by reference to a title number. See s 4(2)(a) of the Land Registration (Scotland) Act 1979. Where constitutive deeds are registered after 28 November 2004, the deed has to be registered against both the benefited and burdened properties: s 4(5) of the 2003 Act.

Where the constitutive deed expressly creates community burdens the community must be identified: s 4(4) of the 2003 Act. Identification of the burdens as community burdens provides that every property in the community is both burdened and benefited: s 27 of the 2003 Act.

Thus, the benefited owner can look at his or her title and confirm that the property has title to enforce the burden. Additionally, the burdened owner can look at his or her title and see which property holds title to enforce the burdens against him or her.

17.7 Constitutive deeds registered before 28 November 2004 creating express enforcement rights

Prior to 28 November 2004 it was not necessary for a constitutive deed to expressly identify the benefited property, and – unless the constitutive deed was a deed of conditions – the constitutive deed in practice could not be registered against the benefited property. While express identification of the benefited property was not required it was not uncommon. A deed of conditions can provide that each transferee from the developer will have reciprocal enforcement rights. Or if burdens are created in a conveyance the developer may have expressly identified property as having title to enforce the burden. This can be by giving a verbal description of the properties with title to enforce; by identifying properties on a map; or by simply referring to land retained by the developer/transferor or owned by named individuals.

As the deed need not be registered against the benefited property, the benefited owner may not know from examination of his or her title that the property has title to enforce the burden (although this should be apparent in the case of community burdens created in a deed of conditions or other constitutive deed covering the entire community). Prior to 28 November 2004 the constitutive deed did have to be registered against the burdened property, and examination of the title to the burdened property would reveal the expressly granted enforcement rights. However, even though expressly granted enforcement rights are apparent from examination of the burdened title where there is no conveyancing description of the benefited properties it will not be clear where the benefited properties are. Examination of other titles may be necessary.

Where express enforcement rights are granted this does not preclude the possibility that there are concurrent implied enforcement rights also applicable, which may serve to expand the number of properties with title to enforce.

17.8 IMPLIED ENFORCEMENT RIGHTS

The law on implied enforcement rights prior to the Title Conditions (Scotland) Act 2003 was complicated, and difficult to operate in practice. The rules were subject to criticism in *Report on Real Burdens* (Scot Law Com No 181, 2000), paras 11.20–11.27. The principal problems were that the rules meant that it was difficult to determine which properties held title to enforce and overgenerous in extending title to enforce to too many properties.

Different rules applied to the implied rights of enforcement held by a disponer of property and those held by co-feuars or co-disponees. Given the constraints of the European Convention on Human Rights Article 1 of Protocol 1 (see para 1.6) it was not possible in the 2003 Act to extinguish all implied rights of enforcement without some form of preservation or replacement. The 2003 Act resolves some problems in the pre-abolition law. But, some of the provisions are themselves somewhat complicated and may create new difficulties.

17.9   Implied rights of enforcement: general provision

Where implied rights of enforcement were created before the appointed day of 28 November 2004, s 49 of the Title Conditions (Scotland) Act 2003 provides that the implied rights of enforcement are abolished. This is subject to ss 50 and 80 of the 2003 Act. These provide that the benefited owner can preserve certain implied rights of enforcement (based on the implied title to enforce given to land retained by a disponer when the burdened property was disponed and where negative servitudes are converted) during a ten-year period after the appointed day. This general provision means that where ss 52 to 57 of the 2003 Act provide rules on implied rights of enforcement, those rules replace the pre-abolition law. However, some of these provisions replicate the pre-abolition law.

The provisions in ss 50, 52 to 57 and 80 of the 2003 Act are transitional, in that they generally apply to burdens created prior to the appointed day. However, as burdens have been imposed since the late eighteenth and early nineteenth centuries there will be many burdens that are affected by these provisions, and will remain affected by these provisions in years to come.

In the following paragraphs the rules on implied rights of enforcement are considered as follows:

(1) those rights held by disponers;
(2) converted servitudes;
(3) implied rights of enforcement held by co-feuars or co-disponees (based on *Hislop v MacRitchie's Trustees* (1881) 8 R (HL) 95);
(4) implied rights of enforcement for common schemes over related properties;
(5) implied rights of enforcement for sheltered housing;
(6) the creation of new burdens and rights under s 57 of the 2003 Act; and
(7) implied rights of enforcement for facility and service burdens.

In considering each it is necessary to briefly detail the law applicable prior to 28 November 2004.

17.10   Implied rights of the disponer: law before 28 November 2004

The leading case here is *J A Mactaggart & Co v Harrower* (1906) 8 F 1101. If an owner sub-divides his land and transfers one plot (plot B) by disposition while retaining another plot (plot A), it is implied that the real burdens imposed on plot B in the disposition are for the benefit of plot A, the retained plot. Once the implied rights of enforcement attach to plot A this is the benefited property. The burdens can then be enforced by the owner of plot A at the time of contravention, without any requirement that the right to enforce be assigned in subsequent conveyances of the benefited property: *Braid Hills Hotel Co Ltd v Manuels* 1909 SC 120. This is doubted incorrectly in *Marsden v Craighelen Lawn Tennis and Squash Club* 1999 GWD 37-1820: see Reid and Gretton *Conveyancing 1999* (2000), pp 59–61.

17.11 Implied rights of the disponer: treatment after 28 November 2004

Where a benefited property is implied as a result of the rule in *J A Mactaggart & Co v Harrower* (1906) 8 F 1101, title to enforce will be extinguished ten years after the appointed day, ie from 28 November 2014: s 49(2) of the Title Conditions (Scotland) Act 2003. During this ten-year period, the owner of the benefited property can register a notice of preservation under s 50 of the 2003 Act.

The notice is to be in the form provided in Schedule 7 to the 2003 Act. It is similar in form to the notices prescribed under the Abolition of Feudal Tenure etc (Scotland) Act 2000 for the preservation of feudal burdens and the general observations made in the context of those notices are equally applicable here: see paras 19.32 to 19.37. Most importantly, registration of a notice of preservation under s 50 of the 2003 Act will not validate an invalid burden. The notice must:

(1) identify the burdened property;
(2) identify the benefited property;
(3) set out the terms of the burdens to be preserved;
(4) detail – if required – any mid-couples linking the benefited owner applying to register the notice to the last registered owner of the property; and
(5) set out the legal and factual reasons why the property nominated in the notice as the benefited property is the benefited property.

17.12 *Notice of preservation: contents*

Let us look at the notice of preservation in more detail.

(1) *Who can complete and register a notice?* The notice must be completed by an owner of the land that is the benefited property. 'Owner' is defined in s 123 of the Title Conditions (Scotland) Act 2003 and for the purposes of s 50 is the person that has most recently acquired right: s 123(1)(b). This means that the person entitled to register the notice may not be the person who is last registered owner. Instead if the last registered owner had conveyed to a third party that had not yet registered, it is the third party that is the person that 'has most recently acquired right' and is therefore entitled to register the notice. Where the person registering the notice is not the last registered owner he or she is required to set out the mid-couples linking his or her title to the last registered title.

If the benefited property is owned by co-owners there is no requirement that all agree to the preservation of title to enforce. One of the co-owners is permitted to register the notice of preservation.

(2) *Description of the benefited and burdened properties.* Unlike the position for notices under the Abolition of Feudal Tenure etc (Scotland) Act 2000, there is no requirement that the properties be described in such a way that they can be identified on the Ordnance Map (although this would be best practice). If the relevant property is already in the Land Register, reference should be made to the title number. If the relevant property is not yet registered in the Land Register, reference should be made to the deed containing the particular description recorded in the General Register of Sasines. It is thought that following the usual principles of description by reference will suffice: see para 8.19.

If subsequent to creation of the burdens the properties have been subdivided the notice can apply to all (or some) benefited or all (or some) burdened properties provided each is identified. Thus, if the burdened property had been sub-divided into four plots the benefited owner could detail each of these in the notice of preservation: s 115 (4) of the 2003 Act.

(3) *Identifying the burdens.* It is not necessary (although it is permissible) to set out the terms of the burdens in full. Instead, reference can be made to the constitutive deed and the relevant burdens therein.

(4) *Setting out the grounds for preservation.* The notice for preservation must detail the factual and legal grounds justifying registration. In the ordinary case reference will be required to the rule in *J A Mactaggart & Co v Harrower* (1906) 8 F 1101, implying benefited properties where the disponer retains land, and the form will require information as to the land retained at the time the burden was originally imposed.

17.13   *Notice of preservation: procedure*

Once the notice is prepared the benefited owner requires to send it to the burdened owner, intimating that it is to be registered. The notice is to be sent, together with the explanatory notes set out in Schedule 7 to the Title Conditions (Scotland) Act 2003. Sending of the notice is to be in accordance with s 124 of the 2003 Act and is to be to the burdened owner or his or her agents (and can therefore be sent to solicitors on behalf of the burdened owner). If the benefited owner does not know the name of the burdened owner the notice can be sent to 'the owner'. Service can be by post, delivery, or in electronic form. Once sent the benefited owner requires to state in the notice that intimation has been made (or narrate that service was not reasonably practicable if that was the case). An appropriate form of wording for this statement is set out in note 5 to Schedule 9 to the 2003 Act.

Once the notice is complete and intimation has been given to the burdened owner, the benefited owner requires to swear or to affirm that the contents of the notice are true: s 50 (4) of the 2003 Act. The observations relevant to the similar provision in notices under the Abolition of Feudal Tenure etc (Scotland) Act 2000 (see para 19.37) are equally applicable here. The benefited owner is swearing or affirming that information that cannot be readily ascertained by a third party (such as the Keeper) is true.

The notice is then registered against the burdened and benefited properties: s 50(3) of the 2003 Act. Registration means that on expiry of the ten-year transitional period set out in s 49(2) of the 2003 Act, the property identified as the benefited property will retain title to enforce and the burden (if valid) will continue to be enforceable.

17.14   Notice of preservation: where it cannot be used

The Schedule 7 notice cannot be used in every case in which *J A Mactaggart & Co v Harrower* (1906) 8 F 1101 may have applied prior to 28 November 2004. Subsection (6) precludes the application of s 50 where the burdens encumbering the burdened property have been imposed as part of a 'common scheme'. This is because common schemes are covered by ss 52 to 54 of the Title Conditions (Scotland) Act 2003. Unfortunately the term is not defined in the legislation. There is, though, guidance in the explanatory notes. It is suggested at para 235 of these notes that a common scheme is where properties are 'subject to the same of similar burdens'. See also para 221.

It appears that the subsection is targeting the following situation. Under the law prior to abolition there was some overlap between the rules in *Hislop v MacRitchie's Trustees* (1881) 8 R (HL) 95 (see paras 17.23 to 17.31) and the rule in *Mactaggart*. It is possible that a benefited property may be implied under both rules. For example, where Alfred owns land and subdivides it into three plots, X, Y, and Z. When Alfred sells plot X to Brian he imposes burdens. Under the rule in *Mactaggart* plots Y and Z would (as retained properties) be implied benefited properties. However, if Brian then sells plot Y to Carol, imposing the same burdens, if the rules in *Hislop* are satisfied, plot Y may be a benefited property as against plot X under these rules as well as the rules in *Mactaggart*. Prior to 28 November 2004 it was not clear whether the rules could co-exist, or (as was implied from the decision in *Botanic Gardens Picture House Ltd v Adamson* 1924 SC 549) that the rule in *Mactaggart* did not apply where the rules in *Hislop* might. It appears that s 50(6) of the 2003 Act adopts the approach in *Botanic Gardens*.

17.15   Conversion of negative servitudes

The Title Conditions (Scotland) Act 2003 rationalises the law of title conditions by providing that obligations allowing a benefited owner to make use of the burdened property are servitudes; and obligations restricting use of the burdened property requiring the burdened owner to do something are real burdens. Prior to 28 November 2004, though, there was some overlap between real burdens and servitudes. Servitudes could be obligations allowing the benefited owner to make some use of the burdened property (positive servitudes) or prohibiting the burdened owner from building (negative servitudes). Real burdens could be obligations allowing use, restrictions on use (negative burdens), or impose positive obligations to do (affirmative burdens). There was overlap between positive servitudes and real burdens allowing use. This is rationalised by providing that real burdens cannot be created as obligations allowing use after the appointed day (other than ancillary burdens): s 2 of the 2003 Act; and existing real burdens allowing use become positive servitudes: s 81 of the 2003 Act. There was also overlap between negative servitudes and negative burdens. On negative servitudes see paras 16.1 and 16.11. This is rationalised by providing that no new negative servitudes can be created: s 79; and that existing negative servitudes are converted into negative burdens: s 80 of the 2003 Act.

17.16   Rules of conversion

Section 80 of Title Conditions (Scotland) Act 2003 provides different rules for conversion dependent on how the negative servitude had been created. If it is created in a deed registered against the burdened property, or appears in the title sheet of the burdened property, then it is automatically converted into a real burden on the appointed day (under s 80(1)) and is not extinguished on expiry of a ten-year transitional period: s 80(3). However, if that deed (or entry) does not expressly identify a benefited property for the former negative servitude then while a notice of converted servitude is not required it is arguable that it will be caught by s 49 of the 2003 Act and a notice of preservation under s 50 is required. This appears to be the combined effect of s 80(1) which on the appointed day converts a negative servitude into a real burden, s 80(3) and ss 49(2) and 50(1) of the 2003 Act. There is no guidance in the background policy papers on this issue.

17.17   Notice of converted servitude

If the negative servitude is not registered against the burdened property, it will be extinguished automatically on expiry of a ten-year transitional period commencing on the appointed day of 28 November 2004, unless the benefited owner registers a notice of converted servitude in the form required by Schedule 9 to the Title Conditions (Scotland) Act 2003 Act: s 80(2) and (4). Prior to the appointed day it was possible for negative servitudes to be created in various ways: either by implication (which was very uncommon); or by a deed registered only against the benefited property (where the negative servitude was created by grant); or by an unregistered deed. In all of these cases a notice of converted servitude must be registered. The notice is very similar to the Schedule 7 notice of preservation registered under s 50 of the 2003 Act. A number of the observations made in consideration of that notice (in paras 17.11–17.14) are equally relevant here.

   The notice is to be completed by the owner of the benefited property, covering the following matters:

(1) it must identify the burdened property;
(2) it must identify the benefited property;
(3) if the benefited owner is not the registered owner, the mid-couples linking the registered owner to the benefited owner must be specified;
(4) it must set out the terms of the converted servitude (that is, the negative servitude that was converted into a negative burden on the appointed day under s 80(1) of the 2003 Act); and

(5) if the benefited property is not identified in the deed creating the negative servitude (for example, because the constitutive deed had not been registered), the legal and factual reasons why the benefited property is identified as such must be stated.

The notice must have annexed to it a copy of the constitutive deed (unless the servitude had been created by implication).

17.18 *Notice of converted servitude: contents*

Let us look at the notice of converted servitude in more detail.

(1) *Who can complete and register a notice?* As with s 50 of the Title Conditions (Scotland) Act 2003, the notice is to be completed by an owner of the land that is the benefited property. 'Owner' is defined in s 123 of the 2003 Act and as for s 50 will be the person that has most recently acquired right: s 123(1)(b). Again, as for s 50, if the benefited property is owned by co-owners only one of the co-owners need complete and register the notice of preservation.

(2) *Description of the benefited and burdened properties.* The provisions on describing properties are as for s 50 of the 2003 Act and as discussed at para 17.11. As for s 50, if there are multiple benefited properties or burdened properties (as a result of subdivision of burdened or benefited property after creation of the servitude) the same notice can be used for each: s 115(4) of the 2003 Act.

(3) *Identifying the converted servitude.* The converted servitude to be preserved is to be set out in full or by reference to the constitutive deed. However, if the negative servitude is created by implication (which is virtually unknown in practice) the benefited owner must set out the factual and legal circumstances in which the servitude was created.

(4) *Setting out why the benefited property is the benefited property.* If the benefited property is not identified in the constitutive deed the notice of converted servitude must detail the factual and legal grounds justifying why the property identified is the benefited property.

(5) *Annexation of the constitutive deed.* When the constitutive deed or a copy of it (where appropriate) is annexed it should have an unsigned endorsement on it providing that 'This is the constitutive deed referred to in the notice of converted servitude by [the granter] dated [date]'.

17.19 *Notice of converted servitude: procedure*

The notice of converted servitude, the constitutive deed, and the explanatory note in Schedule 9 to the Title Conditions (Scotland) Act 2003 are to be intimated to the burdened owner or owners in accordance with s 124 (discussed at para 17.13). When this is done a statement as to service must be completed. A form of words is set out in note 5 in Schedule 9 to the 2003 Act.

When the form is complete the benefited owner must swear an oath or affirm as to the accuracy of the contents of the notice: s 80(7) of the 2003 Act applies s 50(4) to notices of converted servitude. Again, as for s 50, the observations relevant to the similar provision in notices under the Abolition of Feudal Tenure etc (Scotland) Act 2000 (see para 19.37) are equally applicable here. The benefited owner is swearing or affirming that information that cannot be readily ascertained by a third party (such as the Keeper) is true.

When complete, the notice of converted servitude is to be registered against both the burdened and benefited properties. Registration does not convert the negative servitude into a negative burden. Conversion is by s 80(1) of the 2003 Act. Instead, registration has the effect that, on expiry of the transitional ten-year period on 28 November 2014, the converted servitude is not extinguished under s 49 of the 2003 Act.

17.20   Keeper refuses to register notice of converted servitude or notice of preservation

The Keeper will have a discretion to refuse to register notices if they do not provide the relevant information or have the relevant signatures. He is not to check the statements of fact, but may reject the notice due to omission of a signature or if it is otherwise incomplete. Where the Keeper has rejected the notice under s 4 of the Land Registration (Scotland) Act 1979, this may be challenged by application to the Lands Tribunal. If the Tribunal (or court) does not reach a decision before expiry of the ten-year transitional period then the burden or converted servitude need not be extinguished. Section 115(6) of the Title Conditions (Scotland) Act 2003 provides that if the application to the Tribunal or court has been made within a prescribed time (s 115(7)), and the Tribunal or court found that the notice was registrable, then the notice can be registered within two months of the decision and shall be treated as if it had been registered within the ten-year transitional period.

17.21   Challenges to notice of converted servitude or notice of preservation

Where there is a dispute about a notice of converted servitude or notice of preservation (for example, as to the legal or factual basis purportedly justifying execution and registration of the notice, or as to the validity of a burden preserved) this matter may be referred to the Lands Tribunal under s 102 of the Title Conditions (Scotland) Act 2003. The tribunal can make such order as it thinks fit. The order is to be registered, and is ineffective against third parties until registration: s 102(3).

17.22   Implied rights of enforcement in common schemes

Sections 52 to 54 of the Title Conditions (Scotland) Act 2003 provide new rules establishing implied rights of enforcement within 'common schemes'. These rules restate and replace the implied rights arising from *Hislop v MacRitchie's Trustees* (1881) 8 R (HL) 95. There is a useful discussion of the common law and new regime in A Steven 'Implied Enforcement Rights in Relation to Real Burdens in terms of the Title Conditions (Scotland) Act 2003' (2003) 71 SLG 146.

17.23 **Implied rights of enforcement for third parties (co-feuars and co-disponees) before 28 November 2004**

The following paragraphs briefly detail the law on implied rights of enforcement for co-feuars and co-disponees under *Hislop v MacRitchie's Trustees* (1881) 8 R (HL) 95. The leading treatment of this area is Professor McDonald's article 'The Enforcement of Title Conditions by Neighbouring Proprietors' in D J Cusine (ed) *A Scots Conveyancing Miscellany: Essays in Honour of Professor J M Halliday* (1987), pp 9–32.

17.24 **Hislop v MacRitchie's Trustees: 2 examples**

Lord Watson in *Hislop v MacRitchie's Trustees* (1881) 8 R (HL) 95 at 102 identifies two situations in which such implied rights of enforcement may arise.

'(1) where the superior feus out his land in separate lots for the erection of houses, in streets or squares, upon a uniform plan; or (2) where the superior feus out a considerable area with a view to its being subdivided and built upon, without prescribing any definite plan, but imposing certain general restrictions which the feuar is taken bound to insert in all sub-feus or dispositions granted by him'.

The first example involves successive sales (or other conveyances, be they feus or ordinary dispositions) of the properties, where in each the developer has imposed the same or similar burdens; this is referred to here as '*Hislop* type 1'. The second example involves the imposition of burdens over a large area (either through an initial sale of the area imposing burdens, or the imposition of a deed of conditions over the area) followed by subdivision of that area. This is referred to as '*Hislop* type 2'.

17.25 **Case law since Hislop**

While Lord Watson's two examples describe when implied rights of enforcement for co-feuars and co-disponees arise, he does not prescribe when such rights arise. From the case law subsequent to *Hislop v MacRitchie's Trustees* (1881) 8 R (HL) 95 collected in Professor McDonald's article and the Digest of Cases, the rules can be summarised as follows:

(1) the burdened property and the property seeking implied title to enforce as a benefited property must share the same or similar burdens;
(2) these burdens must have been imposed by a common author;
(3) the prospective benefited property seeking title to enforce will only have title if the title deeds or title sheet of the burdened property contains notice that there is a common scheme of burdens; and
(4) there is nothing in the title of the burdened property that negatives the existence of implied third-party rights of enforcement.

These common law rules are complicated. It is perhaps useful to consider the rules as involving two facets in practice: one from examination of the title of the burdened property; the other from examination of the title of other properties.

17.26 Examination of the title of the burdened property: the positive requirement

The application of rules (3) and (4) involves examination of the title of the burdened property.

The requirement that the burdened title contains notice of a common scheme of burdens covering properties including the burdened property is a positive require-ment. It is not enough that the burdened and neighbouring properties are encumbered by the same or similar burdens: see, for example, *North British Railway Co v Moore* (1891) 18 R 1021. There has to be an indication in the title of the burdened property that third-party enforcement rights may arise because the burdened property is part of a larger area encumbered (or to be encumbered) by the same or similar burdens. If there is no notice in the constitutive deed there are no implied third-party enforce-ment rights under *Hislop v MacRitchie's Trustees* (1881) 8 R (HL) 95.

For *Hislop* type 2 cases the notice requirement is generally easily satisfied. Examination of the title of the burdened property will indicate that the constitutive deed covers a larger area than just the burdened property.

For *Hislop* type 1 cases the notice requirement is generally satisfied by one of two means: the grantor of the constitutive deed imposes an obligation on him or herself to create similar burdens in subsequent sales on the development; or he makes express reference to a common scheme (or in the parlance of the older cases, a com-mon feuing plan). This indicates that the plot conveyed is part of a larger development and can be achieved by express reference to a written plan indicating there are common conditions in every conveyance: *Main v Lord Doune* 1972 SLT (Lands Tr) 14. But it has been held in some cases that less is sufficient: see *Johnston v The Walker Trustees* (1897) 24 R 1061. Here, a clause in the conveyance indicated that 'the tenement built on the … area has been erected in strict conformity to the plan and elevation adopted for [Coates Crescent and Manor Place]', although other factors were relevant in confirming that implied third-party enforcement rights arose there. See K G C Reid *The Law of Property in Scotland* (1996), para 400, n 20.

17.27 Examination of the title of the burdened property: the negative requirement

Requirement (4) is a negative requirement. There is to be nothing in the title of the bur-dened property that would exclude implied enforcement rights. If there is a clause or form of wording that suggests there is no common scheme then there can be no implied third-party enforcement rights under *Hislop v MacRitchie's Trustees* (1881) 8 R (HL) 95.

The most common means of preventing implied third-party enforcement rights arising was for the granter of the constitutive deed in either *Hislop* type 1 or type 2 cases to reserve the unilateral right to vary or waive the burdens. Such clauses are found as a matter of course in a number of constitutive deeds. Many conveyancers insert the clause in order to prevent possible third-party enforcement rights, but others do so to protect the developer's interest during the erection of the development by allowing them to change the burdens to respond to conditions on the ground. A typical example of such a clause is the following

'It is expressly provided and declared that there shall be reserved to the [developers] full power to make or allow whatever alterations or deviations they may consider proper upon any feuing plans of the feuing area or any part thereof or to the layout thereof or of the roads, footpaths, sewers, and other services within or outwith the same or even to depart entirely therefrom and the [developers] expressly reserve to themselves the right and power to alter and modify in whole or in part the foregoing burdens, obligations, conditions and other clauses with respect to any particular feu or feus and in the event of their doing so the feuars shall have no right or title to object thereto and shall have no claim in respect thereof' (quoted in Scottish Law Commission, *Report on Real Burdens* (Scot Law Com no 181) (2000) para 11.15).

In *Hislop* type 2 cases implied third-party rights of enforcement can also be prevented by a clause prohibiting sub-division of the larger area covered by the constitutive deed: *Girls School Company Ltd v Buchanan* 1958 SLT (Notes) 2. This continues to prevent the imposition of implied third-party enforcement rights even if that clause is later discharged: *Williamson v Hubbard* 1970 SLT 346.

17.28 Examination of the title of the burdened property: summary

If examination of the title of the burdened property reveals that there is notice of the common scheme in the constitutive deed, and nothing in the constitutive deed to prevent the implication of implied third-party enforcement rights this does not in itself indicate that there are implied third-party enforcement rights. These will arise only if requirements (1) and (2) – that the same or similar burdens have been imposed by a common author on the burdened property and the property seeking title to enforce – are satisfied. To determine this it is then necessary to look at the titles of the properties neighbouring the burdened property.

The extent of the research required beyond the title of the burdened property is dependent on whether research is carried out by an owner wishing to enforce a burden against the burdened property, or by the burdened owner attempting to ascertain the properties that have title to enforce that must be approached for express consent to a proposed contravention.

In both cases it is necessary to demonstrate that the burdened and prospective benefited properties are subject to the same or similar burdens imposed by the same granter.

17.29 Examination of titles beyond the burdened property: Hislop type 2 cases

For *Hislop* type 2 cases confirming whether burdened and prospective benefited properties share the same burden is generally straightforward. A property will be an implied benefited property if it is covered by the same constitutive deed. The burdens affecting both properties will necessarily have been imposed by the same granter and the burdens will be sufficiently similar. *Lees v North East Fife District Council* 1987 SLT 769 is a relatively recent illustration of this. There, burdens on one part of the area provided for the erection of a swimming pool, burdens on the rest of the area provided for use of the property for residential purposes. However, because the burdens were imposed in the same constitutive deed they were part of a larger scheme and were deemed to be sufficiently similar to justify the implication of title to enforce on the residential properties as against the owner of the area that was to be used as a pool.

17.30   Examination of titles beyond the burdened property: Hislop type 1 cases

Difficulties arise when considering *Hislop* type 1 cases. If the research is carried out by a neighbour that wishes to enforce a burden once he or she has examined the title of the burdened property he or she then requires to examine his or her own title to determine if the property is subject to the same or similar burdens imposed by the same person. Determining whether burdens are the same or similar is considered in the next paragraph.

If the research is carried out by a burdened owner determining which properties have title to enforce in order to approach them for consent to a proposed contravention of the burden the same requirements must be shown. Properties with title to enforce will have the same or similar burdens imposed by a common author. Finding the properties transferred by a common author can be determined by carrying out a search of the registers. Identifying which of those properties have the same or similar burdens requires examination of the individual titles. However, examining some titles and discovering that some properties do not have the same or similar burdens will not preclude the possibility that there are others further away that have the same or similar burdens imposed by the same common author. The process of determining which properties have the same burdens can seem never ending (although application of the rules on interest to enforce provides a limitation of sorts). The practical operation of the rules in *Hislop v MacRitchie's Trustees* (1881) 8 R (HL) 95 is very difficult and can lead to multiple benefited properties, making variation and discharge of burdens difficult: as discussed in Chapter 18.

17.31   The same or similar burdens

Implied third-party enforcement rights arise where properties are subject to the same or similar burdens. In *Hislop v MacRitchie's Trustees* (1881) 8 R (HL) 95 itself the burdens were not deemed to be sufficiently similar. There the burdens affecting the putative benefited property and burdened property were both restrictions on building. However, the specific building restrictions were not worded in an identical way and had been tailored to each individual plot in the small development. The most helpful observations in this area are those of Lord President Clyde in *Botanic Gardens Picture House Ltd* 1924 SC 549 at 563. He stated:

'I am not prepared to hold that restrictions must be absolutely identical in order to make them mutually enforceable. It may well be that conformity to a general plan (not necessarily a plan drawn out on paper) for streets and buildings, by which the character of corner tenements may vary from those forming the general line, and so on, may be made mutually enforceable as between the feuars or disponees of corner tenements and of front-line tenements ... Indeed I see no reason, as at present advised, why a vassal or disponee should not be asked, and (if he agrees) should not be bound, to subject his lands to a restriction upon condition that other vassals or disponees subject their lands to a different restriction enforceable by him'.

The burdens covered by such a scheme may not be that similar: see *Lees v North East Fife District Council* 1987 SLT 769 (discussed at para 17.29). Case law gives guidance as to when burdens will be sufficiently similar. An important factor is that the burdens encumbering benefited and burdened properties have a degree of equivalence: see, for example, *Co-operative Wholesale Society v Ushers Brewery* 1975 SLT (Lands Tr) 9. Here, burdens restricted the use of three commercial properties to use as a public house, a grocers and convenience store, and a bookmakers. Despite the burdens differing, there was sufficient equivalence between the burdens to warrant the implication of third-party enforcement rights to the other properties.

17.32 What happens to implied title to enforce arising under Hislop after abolition?

Under s 49 of the Title Conditions (Scotland) Act 2003, on 28 November 2004 the implied title to enforce arising from application of the rules in *Hislop v MacRitchie's Trustees* (1881) 8 R (HL) 95 will be extinguished. It will be replaced with new statutory rules under ss 52–54 of the 2003 Act. However, these three sections are very different in effect and expand the grant of implied title to enforce burdens beyond the parameters established in *Hislop*.

The provisions granting new implied title to enforce may overlap, and properties may be treated as being benefited properties under more than one of the schemes.

17.33 The expression 'common scheme'

Central to the application of each is the idea of a 'common scheme'. As noted previously, this expression is not defined in the Title Conditions (Scotland) Act 2003. During its consideration of the 2003 Act, the Justice 1 Committee of the Scottish Parliament sought clarification on the meaning of the expression. The sole guidance on meaning that can be discerned is by implication from the interaction of ss 52–54 of the 2003 Act, from the explanatory notes to the 2003 Act, and from the *Report on Real Burdens* (Scot Law Com No 181, 2000).

For most conveyancers prior to the appointed day 'common scheme' would be equated to the expression 'common feuing plan' and be determined as being whether or not implied title to enforce arose under the rules in *Hislop v MacRitchie's Trustees* (1881) 8 R (HL) 95. However, the scheme of s 52 precludes this interpretation, because the fourth requirement of the rules in *Hislop* (there is to be nothing to negative the possibility of implied third-party rights of enforcement) is in subsection (2) expressly stated and qualifies the requirement that there be a common scheme: s 52(1)). As properties contained in a 'common scheme' does not have the same meaning as the properties that would be covered by the rules in *Hislop* it is necessary to seek further guidance.

Para 234 of the explanatory notes to the 2003 Act states: 'Common schemes exist where there are several burdened properties all subject to the same or similar burdens.' This then seems to be the first requirement of *Hislop*, that the properties share the same or similar burdens. It is therefore suggested, pending the first cases on the expression after 28 November 2004, that such case law as there is on this topic under *Hislop* will probably be helpful in interpreting the provision in the 2003 Act. Relevant cases are cited in para 17.31 above, and the Digest of Cases.

It is suggested in the explanatory notes at para 238 that 'it will no longer be necessary for title to have been obtained from a common granter'. While this may be the intention, and there is no explicit requirement for this in the legislation the lack of definition of 'common scheme' may mean that it is subsequently interpreted to include only those properties where the same or similar burdens have been imposed by a common author.

17.34 *Section 52 of the 2003 Act: a statutory restatement of* Hislop

Under s 52 of the Title Conditions (Scotland) Act 2003 new implied rights of enforcement are created which substantially replicate the law on third-party implied enforcement rights prior to feudal abolition. The position as detailed at paras 17.25 to 17.31 remains relevant for consideration of the application of this section after the appointed day. There is though potentially one variation, given the suggestion in the explanatory notes that the expression 'common scheme' does not require the burdens to be imposed by a common author. If this approach is adopted this will expand the number of properties with implied title to enforce, but not to any great extent.

Where implied title to enforce is granted under s 52 it is possible that the burdens will be community burdens and subject to Part 2 of the 2003 Act. However, it will be difficult to determine if properties are community burdens as a result of the application of s 52. While it is easy to determine if there are four or more properties encumbered by the burdens, community burdens require reciprocal enforcement between the affected properties. However, the rules in *Hislop v MacRitchie's Trustees* (1881) 8 R (HL) 95, being dependent on notice in the title of the burdened property, and there being nothing in that title to negative the existence of a common scheme, do not necessarily lead to reciprocal enforcement rights. For example, where plot A and plot B are both subject to the same burdens, plot A will not be subject to implied enforcement rights under s 52 if there is no notice in the title of plot A that the same burdens are imposed on other properties. The owner of plot A may enforce against plot B, but no owner can enforce against plot A in that case: see *Bannerman's Trustees v Howard & Wyndham* (1902) 10 SLT 2.

Any implied title to enforce granted under s 52 will not include title to enforce a right of pre-emption, redemption, or reversion: s 52(3). In addition, it cannot include title to enforce a maintenance burden where the obligation to maintain has been taken over by a local authority: s 52(4), applying s 122(2)(ii) of the 2003 Act.

17.35 Section 53 of the 2003 Act: common schemes affecting related properties

Section 53 of the Title Conditions (Scotland) Act 2003 potentially greatly expands the number of properties with implied title to enforce in relation to any burdens. Subsection (1) provides that

'Where real burdens are imposed under a common scheme, the deed by which they are imposed on any unit comprised within a group of related properties being a deed registered before the appointed day, then all units comprised within that group and subject to the common scheme (whether or not by virtue of a deed registered before the appointed day) shall be benefited properties in relation to the real burdens'.

'Common scheme' is undefined but the earlier observations on its meaning are equally applicable here: see para 17.33. This provision differs from s 52 of the 2003 Act and the old common law rules in *Hislop v MacRitchie's Trustees* (1881) 8 R (HL) 95 in two principal ways. Firstly, there is no requirement that there be notice of a common scheme in the title of the burdened property. Secondly, there is no restriction on the existence of implied title to enforce where the constitutive deed contains factors that would – for the purposes of *Hislop* – negate the existence of a common scheme. Its effect is that clauses in the constitutive deed reserving the right to unilaterally vary or waive the burdens are irrelevant in determining whether or not there are implied third-party rights of enforcement. As both requirements relate to examination of the title of the burdened property the effect of s 53 is that it is no longer possible to tell if there are such implied rights merely by looking at the title of the burdened property.

17.36 'Related properties': definition

Section 53 of the Title Conditions (Scotland) Act 2003 provides that where a common scheme is imposed on a group of 'related properties' all of the units within that group will have implied title to enforce.

'Related properties' is defined in s 53(2). It does not have the same meaning as 'related properties' in the context of manager burdens: s 66 of the 2003 Act (discussed at para 15.20). The definition in s 53(2) provides that 'Whether properties are related properties for the purposes of subsection (1) above is to be inferred from all the circumstances'. The legislation gives various examples of situations where the inference would arise. These include situations where the properties:

(1) share common features (such as a common recreational area in a modern housing estate, or a shared car park in a modern tenemental development);
(2) are all subject to the same deed of conditions (registered before 28 November 2004); and
(3) are all flats in the same tenement.

In an urban context the number of properties covered by the expression 'related properties' is potentially substantial. When a precursor of s 53 was introduced during parliamentary consideration of the 2003 Act, the Minister for Justice, Jim Wallace MSP, identified the purpose of the provision as: 'to ensure that amenity burdens in all housing estates or tenements should be mutually enforceable by the owners of houses in the estate or flats in the tenement.' (Scottish Parliament *Official Report Justice 1 Committee*, 10 December 2002, col 4371). This is confirmed in the explanatory notes at para 246, where it states: 'properties on a residential housing estate or in a sheltered or retirement housing development would normally be related properties.'

Properties will be 'related' if they are physically proximate and may be related if they share certain common characteristics (such as building style). Many modern housing estates comprising tens (and sometimes hundreds) of properties are covered by one deed of conditions and the effect of s 53 will be, in many cases, to make the variation and discharge of burdens more difficult.

17.37   'Related properties': complications

Often the parameters of the properties that will have implied title to enforce are readily determinable (for example, where the burdens affect a tenement all of the properties within that tenement will have title to enforce; or if the burdens are imposed by a deed of conditions that deed will set out the boundaries of the property affected). In other cases, though, it will be more difficult. For example, it is difficult to determine the boundaries of enforcement where there is a development comprising various types of property – tenement flats, terraced, detached, and semi-detached houses – sharing a central common car parking area (that serves some but not all of these properties), and common bin stores for some of the properties. It may be necessary to examine the titles of all properties to determine if the burdens are the same or sufficiently similar. This issue will be a particular problem in relation to variation and discharge of burdens where it may be necessary to seek consent from a majority of benefited owners to waive the burden: s 33 of the Title Conditions (Scotland) Act 2003. The result may be that if the parties that have to be approached for consents or waivers cannot be readily determined it is safer to apply to the Lands Tribunal to vary the burden, or burdens may simply be breached without obtaining consent.

17.38 *Expansion of implied title to enforce burdens*

The effect of s 53 of the Title Conditions (Scotland) Act 2003 is that even though the developer may not have intended to grant implied title to enforce to every property in the development (for example, by expressly reserving the right to vary or waive burdens or not giving notice of the scheme), this will nevertheless be the case. Section 53 then serves to create title to enforce burdens where such title did not exist prior to feudal abolition. In doing so, s 53 serves as a substantial automatic exception to the extinction of burdens under Part 4 of the Abolition of Feudal Tenure etc (Scotland) Act 2000 (discussed in Chapter 19).

If a superior has imposed burdens on an area (subsequently sub-divided) while reserving the right to vary or waive the burdens prior to feudal abolition the superior will have title to enforce and there will be no implied third-party enforcement rights. However, after the appointed day the superior will lose his title to enforce and all the proprietors within that large area will not have title to enforce. The effect may be that where previously only one person had title to enforce (and had to be approached for consent to proposed contraventions) after the appointed day there may be tens or hundreds of benefited proprietors. The effect of s 53 of the 2003 Act is therefore very different in its consequences to that of Part 4 of the 2000 Act where typically title to enforce was transferred from the superior to one proprietor – thereby not penalising the vassal in any way.

17.39 *New implied rights arising after the appointed day*

Section 53(1) of the Title Conditions (Scotland) Act 2003 provides that as long as one deed imposing the burdens as part of the common scheme was registered before the appointed day then all units forming part of that common scheme shall have title to enforce, whenever the burdens affecting their own properties were registered. This is intended to deal with two situations: a development partially constructed and sold before the appointed day; and mixed tenure estates where there have been 'right to buy' sales before the appointed day.

In the former case a development may comprise a number of properties and be partially sold prior to the appointed day without express provision for enforcement rights. This may be because a deed of conditions over the area (whether or not s 17 of the Land Registration (Scotland) Act 1979 has been disapplied: see para 15.47) or the individual conveyances over the area (imposing the burdens, possibly by reference to a deed of conditions disapplying s 17 of the 1979 Act) do not make provision for title to enforce the burdens. The developer will continue to sell properties in the same manner and subject to the same burdens after the appointed day. The deeds registered after the appointed day will require to make express provision for title to enforce. However, because the properties conveyed form part of a common scheme which began before the appointed day, s 53 of the 2003 Act provides that all properties within that common scheme have reciprocal implied enforcement rights (and specifically those conveyed after the appointed day will have implied title to enforce against those conveyed before).

This provision has similar effect for estates where properties are held subject to the statutory right to buy under the Housing (Scotland) Act 1987. While in some estates a local authority will have imposed a deed of conditions over the whole area which is then incorporated into each property sold, in many other instances no deed of conditions was used. Instead the local authority (or housing authority) will have sold some properties subject to burdens. These sales may have been by ordinary dispositions or by feus. However, typically each sale will be subject to the same or equivalent burdens, and (as is common) no express provision for title to enforce will be made. On the appointed day the local (or housing) authority is likely to hold properties in a mixed tenure estate. A number of properties are owner-occupied and subject to burdens imposed by the authority. The remaining properties are owned by the local (or housing authority) but are tenanted and are subject to the statutory right to buy. Prior to the appointed day the local authority can register a deed of conditions covering the retained properties and imposing the same burdens. This will make clear that the properties previously sold and those retained are part of a common scheme and properties sold after the appointed day will remain part of that common scheme and be subject to reciprocal enforcement rights within the scheme. This will allow local authorities to continue to enforce the burdens against properties sold prior to the appointed day (in their capacity as owner of an implied benefited property under s 53 of the 2003 Act).

The above option is envisaged by the Executive as the appropriate approach for local authorities with mixed tenure estates: see *Title Conditions (Scotland) Bill Policy Memorandum* (SP Bill 54-PM) at para 140). Professor Reid in *The Abolition of Feudal Tenure in Scotland* (2003) suggests a further possible approach that would not retain the local authority's title to enforce. At para 5.10 he writes that the common scheme can expand by 'the gradual sale of the remaining houses. As a house is sold, subject to the same burdens, so it joins, and swells, the existing community. The owner of the new house can enforce the burdens against houses previously sold; and in exchange the owners of the latter can enforce against the owner of the former'.

17.40   Miscellaneous effects of section 53

Like s 52, s 53 of the Title Conditions (Scotland) Act 2003 does not create implied enforcement rights for rights of pre-emption, redemption, or reversion (s 53(3)) or for maintenance burdens where the maintenance obligation has been taken over by the local authority: s 53(4), applying s 122(2)(ii) of the 2003 Act.

As section 53 gives reciprocal enforcement rights to every property within the common scheme, if there are four or more properties, section 53 has effect to create – by implication – community burdens. This means that the general principle of majority rule inherent in community burdens will apply (see later at para 17.72) and ss 32 to 36 of the 2003 Act will govern variation and discharge (discussed at paras 18.19 to 18.25).

It is possible that implied title to enforce will arise under s 53 as well as under s 52, s 54, or s 56 of the 2003 Act. The sections are not mutually exclusive.

17.41 *Implied rights of enforcement in sheltered housing developments*

Section 54 of the Title Conditions (Scotland) Act 2003 provides detailed rules regulating title to enforce in sheltered and retirement housing developments created before the appointed day. These are developments where there are a group of owner-occupied houses which, as s 54(3) puts it:

'having regard to their design, size and other features, are particularly suitable for occupation by elderly people (or by people who are disabled or infirm or in some other way vulnerable) and which, for the purposes of such occupation, are provided with facilities substantially different from those of ordinary dwelling houses'.

Where there is a sheltered or retirement housing development every property within the development (except any unit used in a special way – such as a flat retained by the developer for occupation by a resident warden) will have title to enforce in relation to the burdens: s 54(1). This makes the burdens community burdens and subject to the general principle of majority rule inherent in community burdens (see para 17.72) and that ss 32 to 36 of the 2003 Act will govern variation and discharge (discussed generally at paras 18.19 to 18.25).

However, while majority rule is the default position where burdens in the development regulate management or maintenance of facilities or services they are core burdens and are subject to special rules for variation and discharge requiring a two-thirds majority: s 54(5)(b) of the 2003 Act. If burdens regulate the age of occupiers within the development they cannot be varied unless with the assent of all owners in the development: s 54(5)(c) of the 2003 Act.

As with ss 52 and 53, s 54 does not confer implied title to enforce in relation to rights of pre-emption, redemption, or reversion.

17.42 *Facility and service burdens*

Facility and service burdens are defined at para 15.7. Where there are facility or service burdens any property which benefits from the facility or service (or the facility itself) will be implied as a benefited property: s 56 of the 2003 Act. Thus, where the facility burden is a maintenance obligation in a tenement requiring the owners to upkeep the roof, the roof is the facility and all of the flats within the tenement have title to enforce the maintenance burdens because each flat benefits from the roof.

17.43 *Breaches before the appointed day when implied title to enforce is granted under ss 53 to 56 of the 2003 Act*

The structure of Part 4 of the Title Conditions (Scotland) Act 2003 is to extinguish all implied rights of enforcement that applied as at the appointed day by s 49 (subject to implied rights under *J A Mactaggart & Co v Harrower* (1906) 8 F 1101 being saved for ten years). Sections 52 to 56 then establish new implied rights of enforcement which may replicate the pre-abolition law, but in many cases will expand it. Section 57(1) provides that where a right of enforcement had been waived or lost (for example through acquiescence or lack of interest to enforce) prior to the appointed day it is not revived by the new common scheme provisions. And s 57(3) provides that where there has been a contravention of a burden before the appointed day ss 53 to 56 (which create new rights of enforcement) do not give title to enforce in relation to those breaches.

However, s 52 of the 2003 Act, which restates *Hislop v MacRitchie's Trustees* (1881) 8 R (HL) 95, can found title for breaches before the appointed day. In certain circumstances this may mean that parties that had no title before the appointed day have title to enforce subsequent to it. This will arise where benefited properties implied under s 52 did not have the burdens imposed by a common author (assuming that 'common scheme' does not require the burdens to be imposed by a common author – see para 17.33).

17.44   New burdens created

Most startling of the provisions in Part 4 of the Title Conditions (Scotland) Act 2003 is s 57(2). This provides that:

'Where there is a common scheme, and a deed, had it nominated and identified a benefited property, would have imposed under that scheme the real burdens whose terms the deed sets out, the deed shall, for the purposes of sections 25 [the general provision defining community burdens] and 53 to 56 of this Act, be deemed so to have imposed them'.

In certain cases it is possible that burdens have not been validly imposed. A deed of conditions may have been registered prior to the appointed day and s 17 of the Land Registration (Scotland) Act 1979 not disapplied. If no express enforcement rights are granted, and the developer reserves the right to vary or waive burdens (thereby excluding implied rights of enforcement) then burdens may not be validly imposed. This is discussed at para 15.47.

The effect of s 57(2) is to treat the burdens as if they had been validly imposed, creating new obligations affecting properties, and in consequence implying multiple benefited properties in accordance with ss 53, 54 or 56 of the 2003 Act. This provision only applies where the reason the burdens are not valid is that there is no benefited property nominated, and no benefited property has arisen by implication.

The imposition of new obligations on properties where none existed previously seems potentially at risk from challenge under Article 1 of Protocol 1 to the European Convention on Human Rights as the imposition of new negative and affirmative obligations will be a control of use of the property. If this is the case the provision will be *ultra vires* the Scottish Parliament. While there is no European case law directly in point, a number of decisions suggest that the point is arguable. See *Denev v Sweden* (1989) 59 DR 127, where there was an imposition of a positive obligation on the landowner, and *Banér v Sweden* (App No 11763/85), where the loss of an exclusive right of use of property was a control of use. See also *Pine Valley Developments Ltd v Ireland* (1991) 14 EHRR 319.

17.45 Summary on implied title to enforce

The rules set out in Part 4 of the Title Conditions (Scotland) Act 2003 are potentially complex in their operation. Despite being intended to act as transitional rules to deal with title to enforce for burdens created before the appointed day in some cases (detailed at para 17.39), the rules will see new implied title to enforce created after the appointed day in some cases. The provisions lead – especially in urban areas as a result of s 53 of the 2003 Act – to a multiplicity of benefited properties and may cause difficulties in variation and discharge of burdens.

17.46 SUB-DIVISION OF BENEFITED PROPERTIES

As has been seen benefited properties may be expressly identified, and generally have to be so identified if the burdens are created after 28 November 2004, or may arise by implication. In certain cases the benefited property may be sub-divided. Under the law prior to abolition it was thought that sub-division of a benefited property meant that every subdivided plot had title to enforce the burden (although the rules on interest to enforce may mean that the burdens cannot be enforced by all parts of the sub-divided plot). Thus, if a landowner owns an estate and sells off a cottage the retained land is the benefited property. If the landowner then sells another cottage this second cottage will probably also be a benefited property in relation to the first – no matter how far away it is from the burdened property. This is the case unless the deed sub-dividing the benefited property provided otherwise. This is very uncommon.

Section 12 of the Title Conditions (Scotland) Act 2003 makes new provision for sub-division of benefited properties after the appointed day. However, it does not apply to:

(1) community burdens (where burdens benefit the community);
(2) those properties where title to enforce is implied as a result of the application of the rules in ss 52 to 56 of the 2003 Act; or
(3) properties covered by a deed of conditions registered either before or after the appointed day where sub-division of the property would be anticipated during the course of development.

The provision then generally applies to – what are sometimes referred to as – neighbour burdens, where there is no reciprocity of enforcement rights. It is provided that where a benefited property is sub-divided the part retained will retain title to enforce the burden, unless there is contrary provision in the conveyance: s 12(1) of the 2003 Act.

If it is decided in the transfer that the break-off plot be granted title to enforce a clause to that effect must be inserted in the conveyance: s 12(1)(a) of the 2003 Act. This clause must make reference to the constitutive deed (giving registration details), identifying the burdens: s 12(3). This may be appropriate in some cases, such as in the example above. If the second cottage neighboured the first cottage it may be more appropriate for title to enforce to lie with that second cottage rather than the retained land.

Alternatively, it may be expressly provided that title to enforce is to be granted to the break-off plot as well as being retained by the retained plot. Again the clause so providing must refer to the constitutive deed (with registration details) and identify the burdens affected, although this cannot apply to rights of pre-emption, redemption, or reversion where only one party can appropriately hold title to enforce: s 12(3).

17.47   WHICH PARTIES HAVE TITLE TO ENFORCE PRAEDIAL REAL BURDENS?

Section 8(2) of the Title Conditions (Scotland) Act 2003 details the parties that have title to enforce praedial real burdens. They are:

(1) the owner of the benefited property – including, if it is co-owned, any one of the co-owners. 'Owner' is defined in s 123 of the 2003 Act. It need not be the registered owner of the property but may be the unregistered owner (holder of an unregistered conveyance of the property) that has most recently acquired right to the property if the benefited property is the subject of an unregistered conveyance. The definition in s 123 also includes a heritable creditor in possession of the benefited property;

(2) a tenant of the benefited property. The tenant can hold a short or long lease. Any one of co-tenants will be able to enforce the burden;

(3) a proper liferenter of the benefited property. A liferenter holding as beneficiary under a trust does not have title to enforce the burden;

(4) a non-entitled spouse of the owner holding occupancy rights under the Matrimonial Homes (Family Protection) (Scotland) Act 1981; and

(5) where the burden is an affirmative burden requiring the burdened owner to defray or contribute towards a cost incurred by an owner, tenant, proper liferenter, or non-entitled spouse with occupancy rights, that individual at the time the cost was incurred.

The multiplication of individuals with title to enforce does not have an impact on title to grant discharges or variations of burdens. It is only the owner that can grant variations and discharges of burdens. See para 18.6.

Title to enforce rights of pre-emption, redemption, or reversion rests only with the owner of the benefited property and cannot be exercised by those with lesser interests in the property.

17.48 Variant of rule for community burdens

Within a community every property has title to enforce against every other property. However, a community may decide to delegate its power to enforce to a third party, or a manager burden may govern the community in its early days.

Under s 28(1) of the Title Conditions (Scotland) Act 2003 a community by simple majority vote (unless the community burdens make express provision in which case that provision must be followed) may appoint a person to be manager of the community, conferring on the manager the right to revoke, vary or exercise such powers as may be specified. These powers can include the power to enforce community burdens: s 28(2)(b) of the 2003 Act.

If a manager burden applies to the community the manager may also be delegated power to enforce the community burdens: s 28(4) of the 2003 Act.

In both cases the manager can enforce the community burdens.

17.49 Title to enforce personal real burdens

The holder of a personal real burden has title to enforce the burden. The rule is set out in s 40 of the Title Conditions (Scotland) Act 2003 for conservation burdens and this section is applied to rural housing burdens by s 43(10), to economic development burdens by s 45(5), and to health care burdens by s 46(5) of the 2003 Act. For these personal real burdens holder includes an unregistered holder that has not yet completed title to the personal real burden.

Maritime burdens are enforceable by the Crown: s 44 of the 2003 Act.

Personal pre-emption and personal redemption burdens are enforceable by the former superior: s 18A(5) of the Abolition of Feudal Tenure etc (Scotland) Act 2000. The right to enforce personal pre-emption and redemption burdens can be assigned to third parties although the assignation is not effective until registration: s 18A(7) of the 2000 Act, implying that title to enforce for personal pre-emption and redemption burdens is dependent on registration.

17.50 Interest to enforce

It is not enough to have merely title to enforce a burden. It is also necessary to have interest to enforce. Interest is dependent on the nature of the burden enforced, the nature of the enforcer, and the nature of the contravention. The rules for praedial and personal real burdens differ in approach.

17.51 Interest to enforce praedial real burdens

Prior to the appointed day there was little authority on interest to enforce, and a tendency to conflate the issue with the praedial rule. Cases include *Aberdeen Varieties*

Ltd v James F Donald (Cinemas) Ltd 1939 SC 788, where a distance of half a mile between burdened and benefited property was a relevant factor in determining that the putative benefited owner could not enforce the burden. However, other aspects of this case suggest the decision is not actually based on interest to enforce but is instead based on consideration of the praedial rule. It is necessary to stress the distinction between the praedial rule and interest to enforce. The praedial rule looks in the abstract at whether a burden is for the benefit of an identified property and at the nature of the obligation. The rule on interest to enforce relates to whether an individual with ownership of a specific property can enforce in relation to a specific contravention of a specific burden. As the Scottish Law Commission notes, 'the specificity makes all the difference': *Report on Real Burdens* (Scot Law Com No 181, 2000), para 4.16.

The general rule on interest to enforce is set out in s 8(3)(a) of the Title Conditions (Scotland) Act 2003. It provides that interest to enforce will exist if 'in the circumstances of any case, failure to comply with the real burden is resulting in, or will result in, material detriment to the value or enjoyment of the person's ownership of, or right in, the benefited property'.

In determining whether or not there is interest to enforce it is necessary to consider various factors, including the nature of the contravention of the burden; the nature of the enforcer's interest in the benefited property, and the nature of the benefited property.

An example can demonstrate this. If plot A is subject to a negative burden prohibiting building this could be enforced by two benefited properties plot B which adjoins plot A, and plot C which is 50 metres away. If the burdened owner wishes to erect a small Wendy house for her child in the garden of plot A, this would technically contravene the burden. However, it is unlikely that the owner of plot B or of plot C could show that this was to the material detriment of their properties. Although both would have title, it is likely that neither would have interest to enforce. However, if the owner of plot A wished to erect a conservatory, this would also contravene the burden. The erection of the conservatory is unlikely to be to the material detriment of plot C, 50 metres away, but will probably be to the material detriment of plot B next door if it impinges on plot B's visual amenity. The owner of plot C will have title, but no interest to enforce. The owner of plot B will have both title and interest. If finally the owner of plot A wished to erect a house in the garden this will probably be to the material detriment of plot B and plot C meaning both proprietors would have title and interest to enforce. As can be seen interest to enforce is dependent on the severity of the breach, and in ascertaining its impact on the benefited property holding title to enforce the distance between burdened and benefited properties is relevant.

17.52   INTEREST TO ENFORCE: QUALIFICATION

The previous paragraph noted that the nature of the enforcer's interest in the benefited property is a relevant factor in determining whether or not he or she has interest (as well as title) to enforce. This is the effect of the words 'material detriment to the value or enjoyment of the person's ... right in, the benefited property'. This is a crucial qualification given the extension of title to enforce as implicit in it is the duration of the right.

For example, if in the example given in the previous paragraph plot B was tenanted, the tenant will have title to enforce the contraventions by the owner of plot A. However, if the tenant had only weeks left on her lease, she would probably not be able to show that the contravention of the burden by erection of a conservatory would be to the material detriment of her lease. However, if the tenant had 20 years left on the lease, she would be more likely to do so.

17.53 INTEREST TO ENFORCE: RECOVERING COSTS INCURRED

In para 17.47 it was noted that where an owner (or other person with a lesser interest in the benefited property) had incurred costs under an affirmative burden requiring payment (such as an obligation to pay for maintenance), the party that incurs payment will have a right of relief against those owners that do not pay. If the party that incurred payment moves on – and is no longer resident in the benefited property – he or she will have both title and interest to enforce to recover their expenditure.

17.54 Interest to enforce personal real burdens

It is provided in s 47 of the Title Conditions (Scotland) Act 2003 that in personal real burdens the holder will be presumed to have interest to enforce. This mirrors the position for feudal superiors discussed at paras 19.4 to 19.5.

17.55 Interpretation of burdens

We shall consider the interpretation of burdens under two headings: the position prior to 28 November 2004 and the position under the Title Conditions (Scotland) Act 2003.

17.56 THE POSITION PRIOR TO 28 NOVEMBER 2004

At common law burdens were interpreted in a hostile way. The general position could be summarised in the following statement of Lord Curriehill in *Frame v Cameron* (1864) 3 M 290 at 292:

'restrictions upon the use of property in onerous contracts are not to be implied; and ... if the sentence imposing restrictions admits fairly of two readings you are to take the reading that is in favour of freedom'.

By 'freedom' is meant that the burdened property is free from the burden. Lord Curriehill was proposing a principle of interpretation in cases of ambiguity Effectively, he was proposing the principle of *contra proferentem*, that ambiguities are interpreted against the interest of the party relying on the burden (ie against the interest of the benefited owner). This principle is applicable in the interpretation of other deeds and contractual provisions. Lord President Inglis held that in interpreting burdens while courts should not interpret burdens so as to give a 'loose or wide interpretation against the proprietor', nor should there be a 'malignant interpretation' against the interests of the benefited owner: *Ewing v Campbells* (1877) 5 R 230 at 233. However, at times the courts took such a malignant interpretation. The burden was not merely given a *contra proferentem* interpretation, but was interpreted in such a way that it was held to be invalid through being insufficiently precise in setting out the extent of the obligation. When contravention of a burden risked irritancy, and the burdened owner losing the property, and the modes of extinction of burdens were solely dependent on the actions of the benefited owner or owners such an approach was understandable. However, after the introduction of judicial variation of burdens by the Lands Tribunal under the Conveyancing and Feudal Reform (Scotland) Act 1970, such an approach was harder to justify. Despite this there continued to be cases where burdens were interpreted in a strict way.

Sometimes this seemed justified, as in *Dumbarton District Council v McLaughlin* 2000 Hous LR 16 which provided that the benefited owner (the Council) was entitled to claim 'normal factorage and expenses' in respect of 'normal functions' of property managers. This was held to be insufficiently precise and the burden was extinguished given that normality in property management is difficult to determine.

However, sometimes the approach is harder to justify. In *Lothian Regional Council v Rennie* 1991 SC 212 the burden contained an obligation to maintain a water supply to provide 'an adequate flow to the reasonable satisfaction' of the benefited owner. It was held by a majority that 'the reasonable satisfaction' of the benefited owner was a subjectively determined test that was insufficiently precise to be enforceable. Lord McCluskey dissented, and it must be noted that such clauses are commonly enforced in ordinary contracts (including leases encumbering land): *Callander v Midlothian District Council* 1996 SCLR 955 and *Brennan v Robertson* 1997 SC 36.

In the years immediately prior to the passage of the Title Conditions (Scotland) Act 2003, a more benign approach to interpretation was being adopted in some cases: see *Grampian Joint Police Board v Pearson* 2001 SC 772, discussed in Reid and Gretton *Conveyancing 2001* (2002) at pp 88–89.

Much of the case law on burdens prior to the passage of the 2003 Act involves issues relating to interpretation. These cases can give valuable guidance on the drafting of burdens. Some of them are referred to in the Digest of Cases. In addition, see the cases gathered thematically by Professor Gordon in *Scottish Land Law* (2nd edn, 1999), paras 22-44 to 22-50, and Professor Reid in *The Law of Property in Scotland* (1996), paras 416 to 422.

17.57 THE POSITION UNDER THE 2003 ACT

The Title Conditions (Scotland) Act 2003 provides that the construction of burdens is to be 'in the same manner as other provisions of deeds which relate to land and are intended for registration'. The intention behind this provision is that burdens are interpreted in much the same way as servitudes, and that the hostile approach to interpretation ceases.

Given the burden relates to land and will encumber singular successors of the burdened owner the general approach to interpretation will be objective: looking at what is expressed, not what the party that imposed the burdens thinks the burden means. If the burden is ambiguous it will still be interpreted in accordance with a presumption in favour of freedom, and ambiguities will be interpreted *contra proferentem*. However, Professor Reid suggests that this approach will not be appropriate for community burdens where benefited and burdened owners are all subject to the same burdens: *The Law of Property in Scotland* (1996), para 415.

Given the recent decision in *Grampian Joint Police Board v Pearson* 2001 SC 772 it may be the case that the reform will not make much difference in practice.

17.58 FUTURE REFORM?

The Scottish Law Commission has proposed a restatement of the principles of interpretation in private law in its *Report on Interpretation in Private Law* (Scot Law Com No 160, 1997), which has a draft Private Law (Interpretation) (Scotland) Bill annexed. This draft Bill contains a new general principle of interpretation. Rule 1 in the Schedule to the draft Bill provides:

'(1) Any expression which forms part of a juridical act shall have the meaning which would reasonably be given to it in its context; and in determining that meaning regard may be had to –
    (a) the surrounding circumstances; and
    (b) in so far as they can be objectively ascertained, the nature and purpose of the juridical act.
(2) For the purposes of this rule the surrounding circumstances do not include:
    (a) statements of intention;
    (b) instructions, communings or negotiations forming part of the process of preparation of the juridical act;
    (c) conduct subsequent to the juridical act'.

17.59   Liability in burdens

Having considered title and interest to enforce it is now necessary to examine enforcement from the perspective of the burdened property. The following paragraphs examine: the identification of the burdened property; liability for negative burdens; liability for affirmative burdens; and sub-division of the burdened property.

17.60   IDENTIFICATION OF THE BURDENED PROPERTY

It has always been necessary to expressly identify the property encumbered by the burdens. Failure to do so means that the burden is not validly created: *Anderson v Dickie* 1915 SC (HL) 79. Prior to the Title Conditions (Scotland) Act 2003, if the burdens were created in a conveyance the burdened property is generally the property transferred, while if the burdens were created in a deed of conditions then ordinarily the area affected is typically described sufficiently for conveyancing purposes within the deed of conditions. Under the 2003 Act express identification of burdened and benefited property is an essential aspect of creation of the burden: see para 15.41.

17.61   SUB-DIVISION OF THE BURDENED PROPERTY

Where burdened property is subdivided each sub-divided part of the burdened property remains liable in the burden. If Angela owns a burdened property comprising house and garden, then selling the garden to Brian will not affect liability in relation to the plot. Both the part retained by Angela and the part conveyed to Brian will be burdened properties in future: s 13 of the Title Conditions (Scotland) Act 2003.

However, this is not the case if the burden cannot relate to either the plot conveyed or plot retained. For example, a burden regarding a water supply could not apply to the plot that did not contain the water supply.

Where the burden is an affirmative burden, s 11 of the 2003 Act applies. Both retained and conveyed plot remain burdened properties. However, as there is an obligation to carry out an action (such as rebuilding, or paying maintenance costs) it is provided that the owners of the retained and conveyed burdened properties are jointly and severally liable. Liability *inter se* (between the respective burdened owners) is based on the proportion the area of the burdened plot bears to the original burdened area, although special rules are provided for tenement flats: s 11(1)(b) and (3) of the 2003 Act.

17.62   Change in pre-abolition law

Section 11 of the Title Conditions (Scotland) Act 2003 restates the common law position in determining the burdened property. However, in *Hislop* type 2 cases (see para

17.24), where a burdened property was subdivided this created third-party implied enforcement rights within the original burdened property unless there was an indication in the constitutive deed that there was no intention to create implied third-party enforcement rights. This rule is not enforceable after the appointed day.

17.63 WHO IS LIABLE?

Section 9 of the Title Conditions (Scotland) Act 2003 details against whom burdens are enforceable. Negative and affirmative burdens are treated differently.

17.64 LIABILITY IN NEGATIVE BURDENS

Negative burdens (and ancillary burdens) are enforceable against any person having use of the burdened property: s 9 (2) of the Title Conditions (Scotland) Act 2003. The effect of this is to make negative burdens subordinate real rights in land. This means that burdens can be enforced against tenants or other occupiers of the burdened property.

17.65 Change in pre-abolition law

At common law real burdens were not real rights. They were enforceable only against the owner of the burdened property. However, owners included not just registered owners but also uninfeft proprietors: *Hyslop v Shaw* (1863) 1 M 535.

There were cases in which burdens were enforced (or proceedings were raised) against tenants including *Colquhoun's Curator Bonis v Glen's Trustee* 1920 SC 737, and *Mathieson v Allan's Trustees* 1914 SC 464. However, in these cases the action was raised against landlord as well as the tenant. And in the later case of *Eagle Lodge Ltd v Keir & Cawder Estates Ltd* 1964 SC 30 at 45, it was suggested by Lord Sorn that while the tenant of the burdened property may be a co-defender primary liability rested with the landlord. There was no case law providing that burdens could be enforced against other parties occupying or using the burdened property.

Where negative servitudes have been converted to real burdens, s 9(2) of the Title Conditions (Scotland) Act 2003 means that liability remains unaltered. Negative servitudes were real rights.

17.66 LIABILITY IN AFFIRMATIVE BURDENS

An affirmative burden imposes a positive obligation to do something. There has to be one party with primary responsibility for performance. Affirmative burdens are enforceable only against the owner of the burdened property: s 9(1) of the Title Conditions (Scotland) Act 2003. 'Owner' is defined in s 123 and for the purposes of s 9 means either the registered owner, or if the property has been conveyed subsequent to the last registration and no conveyance has been registered by the most recent unregistered owner. Where there is a heritable creditor in possession of the burdened property it will be liable as 'owner': s 123(2).

If the burdened property is co-owned the co-owners are jointly and severally liable: s 11(5)(a); liability *inter se* being based on the proportion in which the co-owners own the property: s 11(5)(b) of the 2003 Act.

Thus, if there is a burden providing for payment of the cost of maintenance the burdened owner requires to meet this obligation. If the burdened property is co-owned by Mr and Mrs Smith, the benefited owner may raise enforcement proceedings against either Mr or Mrs Smith (or both).

17.67   Change in pre-abolition law

This does not change the pre-abolition law. Uninfeft proprietors were liable in burdens: *Hyslop v Shaw* (1863) 1 M 535. And a heritable creditor in lawful possession of the burdened property was liable for the performance of maintenance burdens under s 20(5)(b) of the Conveyancing and Feudal Reform (Scotland) Act 1970. However, the House of Lords decision in *David Watson Property Management v Woolwich Equitable Building Society* 1992 SC (HL) 21 has been viewed as throwing some doubt on this.

17.68   Joint and several liability in affirmative burdens

When an action to enforce an affirmative burden is raised by a benefited owner he or she will typically raise the action against the party that is the current owner of the property (or the party that is identified as the registered owner). However, the current burdened owner may not be the party that breached the burden. For example, if there is a burden containing an obligation to rebuild property breached by Alpha Ltd as owners of the burdened property, should a transferee, Beta Ltd, be liable to bear the substantial cost of rebuilding? However, to require the benefited owner to sue a party that owned the property some time ago is unfair to him or her. There may also be difficulty in identifying the current owner particularly if there is an unregistered conveyance.

This is addressed in two ways: s 70 of the Title Conditions (Scotland) Act 2003 deals with identifying the parties; and s 10 deals with liability.

Section 70 provides that a former burdened owner can be contacted by the benefited owner and required to disclose the name and address of the current owner, or information to enable the current owner to be discovered. Secondly, s 10 deals with liability.

The approach in s 10 of the 2003 Act is to strike a balance. It provides that the current owner on acquiring ownership incurs joint and several liability with the previous owner of the property (the party that breached the burden): s 10(2). The wrongdoer does not escape liability by transferring the property: s 10(1). This means that from the perspective of the benefited owner an action can be raised against the current owner of the benefited property, whether or not he or she breached the burden.

However, if the current owner incurs expenditure in performing the obligation he or she has a right of relief as against the wrongdoer enabling the recovery of this expenditure: s 10(3).

It is necessary to determine the identity of the wrongdoer. A mechanism is put in place to determine the instant at which liability is incurred: s 10(4). Generally, it is when the obligation becomes due although there are special rules for some community burdens involving expenditure.

17.69 Change in pre-abolition law

The pre-abolition law was based on *Marshall v Callander and Trossach Hydropathic Co Ltd* (1895) 22 R 954, where a burdened owner attempted to escape liability to rebuild a property destroyed by fire by transferring the burdened property to a shell company holding no assets. It was held that new and previous owners were jointly and severally liable, although liability *inter se* was not clear. The legislation restates and clarifies the case law.

17.70 Remedies

When burdens have been contravened (or there is a risk of contravention), the appropriate remedies are:

(1) specific implement – to require a burdened owner to perform his obligations;
(2) an interdict – to prevent a burdened owner from breaching the burden;
(3) an action of damages – to compensate the benefited owner for the loss suffered as a result of the breach of the burden;
(4) a requirement to the burdened owner to remove buildings – if the burden breached is a building restriction.

For negative burdens the primary remedies are interdict and damages. Interdicts will be of little value where the burden has been contravened.

In actions for damages quantification may be difficult. For example, if a burden prohibits building and the burdened owner erects a conservatory, the loss to the benefited owner is the diminution in value of the benefited property as a result of the burdened owner's construction. For discussion see W M Gordon *Scottish Land Law* (2nd edn, 1999), para 23-16, and K G C Reid *The Law of Property in Scotland* (1996), para 423.

Irritancy in relation to praedial real burdens is abolished by s 67 of the Title Conditions (Scotland) Act 2003. See para 6.28 for discussion of irritancy.

17.71 CHANGE IN PRE-ABOLITION LAW

Although irritancy is abolished by s 67 of the Title Conditions (Scotland) Act 2003, it was probably ineffective as a remedy for non-feudal praedial real burdens prior to feudal abolition. See K G C Reid *The Law of Property in Scotland* (1996), para 424.

There had been debate as to whether real remedies such as adjudication or poinding of the ground were applicable to praedial real burdens prior to feudal abolition. The sixth edition of this book details the debate at paras 10.4 to 10.7. Reference must also be made to Professor Gordon's consideration of the topic at para 23-16 of *Scottish Land Law* (2nd edn, 1999) and *Report on Real Burdens* (Scot Law Com No 181, 2000), paras 4.68–4.70. Given the statutory clarification that real burdens run with the land without requiring assignation or some other special element, the policy reasons in support of the approach argued for in the sixth edition of this book no longer seem persuasive. Real remedies will not have a role in future enforcement of real burdens.

17.72   Miscellaneous enforcement issues in community burdens

The provisions on community burdens allow for majority rule in various cases. The decision of the majority in these matters binds the owners within the community and their successors in title: s 30 of the Title Conditions (Scotland) Act 2003. The two principal issues on which majority rule applies (aside from on variation and discharge) relate to:

(1) the power to appoint, or dismiss, a manager to administer the community and to delegate powers to the manager (which powers can include power to carry out maintenance, and to enforce or vary burdens): s 28 of the 2003 Act; and

(2) the power to instruct maintenance where community burdens provide for maintenance of the whole or the part of the community: s 29 of the 2003 Act. The latter provision contains a detailed scheme for instruction and authorisation of, and payment for the work.

Chapter 18

Title Conditions: Variation and Discharge

18.1 Introduction

Title conditions are perpetual in nature, unless expressly provided to be of limited duration. And although title conditions serve a useful function in regulating areas to a higher standard than the planning system, their perpetual nature can have detrimental effects. Conditions that are relevant when a property was constructed may restrict development. For example, burdens restricting the carrying on of a business in a residential area imposed in the nineteenth century may prevent an owner working from home, using on-line connections, today. It is necessary to allow the conditions to be discharged or varied.

Conveyancers encounter the rules on discharge and variation of title conditions in two main contexts. The first is where the conveyancer is approached by a client who wishes to carry out work or some other activity that would contravene (or has contravened) a title condition.

The second is during a sale or purchase of property when it is discovered that the seller has contravened a title condition (whether knowingly or not). While a homeowner will be aware of many public law obligations affecting his or her property (such as the need for planning permission), research suggests that there is a lack of awareness of title conditions. See Andra Laird and Emma Peden *Survey of Owner Occupiers' Understanding of Title Conditions* (Scottish Executive Central Research Unit, 2000), Chapter 2. Unknowing breach is therefore very common. However, the motivation in breaching is of no interest to the purchaser. As liability in a title condition rests with the current owner (subject to such rights of relief as he or she may have against his or her predecessors in title) a purchaser will wish to ensure that the title condition cannot be enforced against him or her in future. This will involve ensuring that the title condition is varied or discharged (or otherwise extinguished). Failure to do so may render a title not good and marketable: *McLennan v Warner & Co* 1996 SLT 1349. This can cause particular problems where the burdened owner has not obtained express consent or negative prescription has not applied. Where there are disputes as to facts in relation to matters of implied extinction a purchaser may refuse to accept the position (as was the case in *McLennan v Warner*). This is a particular problem where the rules on implied extinction appear to involve matters of judgment, or issues that are subjective.

From 28 November 2004, the Title Conditions (Scotland) Act 2003 will regulate the matter. It provides that title conditions can be varied or discharged by:

(1) express consent;
(2) the 'sunset rule';
(3) implied consent;
(4) other forms of implied extinction;
(5) negative prescription;
(6) *confusio*;
(7) compulsory purchase; and
(8) the Lands Tribunal for Scotland.

In this chapter the primary focus will be on the rules for variation and extinction to be introduced from 28 November 2004. Where this amends the law, reference will be made to the pre-abolition position through reference to either the sixth edition of this book or a brief summary of the current law. Special rules for feudal title conditions are considered at paras 19.7 to 19.19.

18.2   Total or partial discharge?

Title conditions can be discharged in whole or in part. An example of the former would be a servitude of access over land where the benefited proprietor simply agrees to renounce the servitude in full. Or if there was a burden prohibiting building, total discharge would mean the agreement of the benefited proprietor to any form of building in future, be that the construction of a rabbit hutch, a garden shed, a garage or a factory.

Partial discharge is sometimes referred to as variation of the title condition. The condition remains in force but its terms are restricted in some way. For example, if there is a servitude of vehicular access the benefited proprietor may agree to the servitude being restricted to only pedestrian access. Or if there is a burden prohibiting building, the benefited proprietor may agree to the construction of a garage. This partial discharge of the original burden will not permit the burdened proprietor to construct a factory. Partial discharge then extinguishes the title condition only to the extent specified.

Throughout this chapter reference is made to 'variation' of title conditions. By this is meant partial discharge, not the imposition of new title conditions which requires the consent of the burdened proprietor – and is subject to the rules on creation of title conditions set out at paras 15.25 to 15.50.

In this part 'discharge' will be used to refer to 'total discharge', and 'variation' will generally be used to refer to 'partial discharge'.

18.3   Express consent

There is one form of express consent that is applicable to all title conditions: the minute of waiver (or deed of renunciation), which is discussed in general terms at paras 18.4 to 18.16. Special rules apply where the title condition is a praedial burden (see para 18.18) or a community burden (see paras 18.19 to 18.25). Where the title condition is a real burden it is possible that an informal letter of consent may be used, discussed at paras 18.27 to 18.29. There are special rules for the consensual discharge of rights of pre-emption and these are discussed at paras 18.30 to 18.31.

18.4 MINUTE OF WAIVER: GENERAL RULES

The minute of waiver is the most common method of variation or discharge. In a study of feuing conditions (feudal real burdens) carried out by Cusine and Egan in 1995 it was found that a minute of waiver was used in almost two thirds of cases where consent to the proposed contravention of a burden was sought. See Cusine and Egan *Feuing Conditions in Scotland* (Scottish Office Central Research Unit, 1995), Chapter 4.

Normally the benefited owner is approached by the burdened owner and asked to agree that the burden should be varied or extinguished. Typically, the benefited proprietor will agree to do so only if the burdened proprietor is prepared to pay a consideration. Prior to the introduction of the jurisdiction of the Lands Tribunal for Scotland in 1970, the consideration requested could be excessive. See, for example, *Howard de Walden Estates Ltd v Bowmaker Ltd* 1965 SC 163, where £1,250 was sought for waiver of a burden that had been contravened (with or without consent) by 19 of the burdened owner's 60 neighbours. However, since 1970 it is thought that the cost of minutes of waiver is not excessive.

As an example of its use consider the situation where there is a burden prohibiting alterations to the external features of the property. The burdened owner wishes to install new windows. The new windows would comprise an alteration. The burdened owner would therefore approach the benefited owner for consent. The benefited owner will agree to consent if the burdened owner pays a *grassum* (one-off payment) of, say, £100, plus a payment covering the benefited owner's legal fees. This will be the case even if the burdened owner has obtained planning permission to carry out the work, and the benefited owner is the local authority that granted planning permission. Provided the benefited owner has interest to enforce the burden he or she is at liberty to charge for the provision of a minute of waiver and 'the amount of this money payment would be limited only by what the burdened proprietor might be prepared to pay': *McVey v Glasgow Corporation* 1973 SLT (Lands Tr) 15 at 20.

Unlike real burdens, servitudes need not be created in writing (being created through positive prescription or – in some cases – by implication, on which see Chapter 16) but it is competent to grant a minute of waiver in relation to an unwritten servitude.

18.5 The five provisions

Under the Title Conditions (Scotland) Act 2003 there are five separate provisions dealing with minutes of waiver (or as they are referred to in the statute, deeds of

variation or discharge). Section 15 regulates the use of a minute of waiver for praedial real burdens. Sections 33 and 35 provide special rules for minutes of waiver for
community burdens. Section 48 regulates the use of minutes of waiver for personal
real burdens. Section 76 regulates the use of minutes of waiver for certain positive
servitudes. These provisions share some common features, which we shall look at
now.

18.6　Who can grant the minute of waiver?

The minute of waiver has to be granted by or on behalf of the benefited owner or
holder of the burden. Thus, while title to enforce has been extended to include non-
owners such as tenants (see para 17.47), it is only the owner of the property (or
holder of the personal burden) who can agree to the variation or discharge of the burden. If the right to enforce the burden is held by co-owners, all must assent. There are
exceptions to this general principle, applicable where ss 33 or 35 of the Title
Conditions (Scotland) Act 2003 are used. These provisions (discussed at paras 18.20
to 18.23) provide that all benefited owners do not need to consent to vary a community burden. Additionally, where there is a manager of the community who has been
given authority to grant discharges, then the manager can consent. This, though, can
be viewed as the manager granting the waiver on behalf of the owners as the manager
is their agent.

Ordinarily the benefited owner or holder will be the registered proprietor although
there are variants for minutes of waiver relating to real burdens.

The benefited owner to be approached should be a party with interest to enforce.
However, it is often difficult to determine if an individual has interest to enforce or
not. As discussed at paras 17.50 to 17.52, interest to enforce is considered in the context of a specific breach, or in this regard in the context of a specific proposed
contravention of the burden. If the minute of waiver is granted by all parties with
interest to enforce then, if no party has interest to enforce, s 17 of the 2003 Act will
apply (discussed at para 18.48).

18.7　*Special rules for praedial real burdens*

Where the minute of waiver relates to a praedial real burden (be it a neighbour burden or community burden: see paras 15.5 to 15.6) 'owner' is given a statutory
meaning in s 123 of the Title Conditions (Scotland) Act 2003. It includes transferees
of the benefited property who have not completed title, formerly referred to as 'uninfeft proprietors' (that is where a person has a general or special conveyance to the
property but has not registered, such as the holder of a delivered but unregistered disposition). Any person falling into this category will be able to grant the minute of
waiver in addition to the registered owner: s 123(1) of the 2003 Act. Thus, assume
Alfred conveyed a house to Brenda. Brenda did not register the conveyance before
she died. Carol confirms as executor to Brenda. Brenda's will provides that David is
to inherit the house. Carol executes a docket transfer in favour of David. Alfred, as

registered owner, and Carol, and David (as transferees who have not completed title) will all be able to grant a minute of waiver if the house is a benefited property.

Section 123(1) also provides that where a heritable creditor is in lawful possession of the benefited property, then they too may grant a minute of waiver.

Where a minute of waiver is to be granted by a transferee who has not completed title (or, it appears, a heritable creditor in lawful possession) then one of two rules will apply:

(1) if the granter's property is not yet registered in the Land Register a deduction of title clause is required: s 60(1) of the 2003 Act (for deduction of title see para 31.41); or

(2) if the granter's property is registered in the Land Register then no deduction of title clause is necessary although the application for registration must provide evidence linking the grantor to the last registered owner: s 15(3) of the Land Registration (Scotland) Act 1979.

18.8 Special rules for personal real burdens

Where the minute of waiver relates to a personal real burden it will be granted by the registered holder of the burden typically. However, s 41(b)(ii) of the Title Conditions (Scotland) Act 2003 provides that if the burdened property is not registered in the Land Register the holder will have to deduce title linking to the last registered holder of the personal real burden. For deduction of title, see para 31.41. However, if the property is registered in the Land Register then no deduction of title clause is required provided that evidence linking the grantor to the last registered holder is submitted with the application for registration: s 15(3) of the Land Registration (Scotland) Act 1979.

This provision is applied to all personal real burdens excepting maritime burdens and personal pre-emption and personal redemption burdens. For maritime burdens the Crown is the only party that can ever have title to enforce and so the provision is unnecessary. For personal pre-emption and personal redemption burdens, the terms of s 41(b)(ii) of the 2003 Act are repeated in s 18A(8)(b)(ii) of the Abolition of Feudal Tenure etc (Scotland) Act 2000.

18.9 Change to pre-feudal abolition law

Under the law prior to 28 November 2004 it is thought that it is not possible for an uninfeft proprietor to grant a minute of waiver as this is not a deed listed in the statutory provisions on deduction of title: primarily s 3 of the Conveyancing (Scotland) Act 1924. It was suggested in *McLennan v Warner & Co* 1996 SLT 1349 that an uninfeft proprietor can grant a minute of waiver of a servitude although this assertion has been persuasively criticised. See further G L Gretton 'Servitudes and Uninfeft Proprietors' (1997) 2 SLPQ 90 and D J Cusine and R R M Paisley *Servitudes and Rights of Way* (1998), para 17.05.

18.10   The minute of waiver may be a variation or a discharge

A minute of waiver can competently be granted to discharge fully a title condition or to waive it only to a limited extent. It is therefore permissible to provide that a title condition is varied only to permit a specified potential contravention.

18.11   The minute of waiver must be in writing and capable of being registered

The minute of waiver is a deed which affects a real right in land and therefore requires to be formally valid in accordance with s 2 of the Requirements of Writing (Scotland) Act 1995. As it requires to be registered it should also comply with s 3 of the 1995 Act. See Chapter 2 for details.

18.12   The minute of waiver must be registered against burdened property

It is always necessary to register the minute of waiver against the burdened property in order that it be effective. However, prior to that an enforcement action by the benefited owner or holder would fail on the basis of personal bar.

Registration is to be by the burdened owner: s 69(2) of the Title Conditions (Scotland) Act 2003. Although this provision does not apply to servitudes, it represents the common law.

18.13   *Special rules for praedial burdens*

Where the minute of waiver relates to a praedial burden that has been registered against both burdened and benefited property (for example, through the new rules for creation – see para 15.45 – or conversion of the burden under Part 4 of the Abolition of Feudal Tenure etc (Scotland) Act 2000), registration against only the burdened property may mislead a purchaser of the benefited property. The Keeper is therefore given discretion (although is under no obligation) to alter the title to the benefited property to take account of the minute of waiver: s 105(1) of the Title Conditions (Scotland) Act 2003.

If the minute of waiver relates to community burdens being granted under ss 33 or 35 of the 2003 Act, registration can be made by a grantor (including a manager): s 69(3). After grant of the deed (with no challenge to the Tribunal from a dissatisfied owner in the minority) this provision therefore prevents unsatisfied owners in the community from preventing the registration of the burden.

18.14   *Special rules for servitudes*

The requirement for registration of the minute of waiver only applies to positive servitudes that have been registered against, or noted in the title sheet of, the burdened property: s 78 of the Title Conditions (Scotland) Act 2003. Accordingly, the common law position applies to servitudes created by positive prescription or created prior to 28 November 2004 and registered against only the benefited property. Although there is no requirement that minutes of waiver relating to these other servitudes be registered, it is permissible to do so, despite the repeal of s 18 of the Land Registration (Scotland) Act 1979: see para 18.15.

It is argued by Sheriff Cusine and Professor Paisley that unregistered minutes of waiver of servitudes are effective to bind singular successors of the benefited proprietor: *Servitudes and Rights of Way* (1998), para 17.04. It is suggested that this approach would continue to apply to minutes of waiver for unregistered servitudes.

18.15   *Changes to pre-feudal abolition law*

Prior to the Title Conditions (Scotland) Act 2003 the relevant statutory provision was s 18 of the Land Registration (Scotland) Act 1979. This provided that a registered minute of waiver of a 'land obligation' (which term included servitudes and real burdens) would bind singular successors of both benefited and burdened owners. An unregistered minute of waiver of real burdens is merely a personal agreement between benefited and burdened proprietor and not binding on singular successors of either (and arguably this applied also to registered minutes of waiver at common law: see para 17.17 of the sixth edition of this book).

18.16   **The minute of waiver does not require a grantee**

When a minute of waiver of a real burden (praedial or personal) is drafted it does not require a grantee to be identified: s 69(1) of the Title Conditions (Scotland) Act 2003. It will often be framed as a unilateral deed running in the name of the grantor for the benefit of the burdened owner. However, the importance of this provision is that the minute of waiver can now be sought by a non-owner possessing the burdened property (such as a tenant or a liferenter). The non-owner could pay the appropriate *grassum*.

While the provisions do not apply to servitudes, it is thought they represent the common law.

18.17   MINUTE OF WAIVER: VARIANTS ON THE GENERAL RULES

In the following paragraphs the detailed schemes for minutes of waiver are considered in so far as they depart from the general principles detailed above.

18.18   **Praedial real burdens**

Section 15 of the Title Conditions (Scotland) Act 2003 applies to all praedial real burdens (neighbour and community burdens). It specifies that the minute of waiver discharges (in whole or in part) 'as respects a benefited property'. This confirms the common law position that a minute of waiver only relates to the property owned by the grantor. For example, where there are multiple benefited proprietors, Alfred, Brian, and Carol, if only Carol grants the minute of waiver this will have no effect on the enforcement rights of Alfred and Brian as owners of the other benefited properties. See *Dalrymple v Herdman* (1878) 5 R 847 and *Arnold v Davidson Trust Ltd* 1987 SCLR 213. If a burdened owner wishes to contravene (or has contravened) a burden it is therefore essential to obtain the approval of all benefited proprietors (subject to the caveat that only the consent of those with interest to enforce is required – see para 18.6). However, there are special rules that can be used for community burdens, meaning that the assent of all benefited proprietors is not required (see paras 18.19 to 18.25); and those who do not expressly consent may be bound by rules on implied consent (see paras 18.38 to 18.44).

18.19　Community burdens

The expansion of implied rights of enforcement (see paras 17.32 to 17.45) means that many properties will be subject to community burdens. The general position under s 15 of the Title Conditions (Scotland) Act 2003 (as at common law) could require all proprietors in a community to agree to the variation or discharge of burdens. This position is mitigated by ss 32 to 37 of the 2003 Act. Unlike s 15, a minute of waiver granted under ss 33 or 35 may bind benefited owners who do not assent expressly to its terms. Sections 33 and 35 provide two distinct schemes for variation and are considered in the following paragraphs. Given that one of the reasons for their introduction was the difficulty of obtaining consent of all proprietors, it is unfortunate that both schemes will be impractical for many estates regulated by community burdens and force burdened owners instead to rely on rules of implied consent, negative prescription or judicial variation.

18.20　*Majority rule*

Section 33 of the Title Conditions (Scotland) Act 2003 allows community burdens to be varied or discharged by majority. In this case, and importantly, variation can include the imposition of new burdens. The provision can be used in relation to only one property or in relation to the broader community. For example, if eight properties are in the community and subject to a burden prohibiting the carrying on of a business and the owner of one plot wishes to start a business contravening the burden, s 33 can be used. Or similarly, if the owners get together and decide that the burden is no longer relevant to their community, s 33 can be used.

If the deed creating the community burdens makes special provision for variation and discharge then this may be complied with: s 33(1)(a). However, where community burdens arise from constitutive deeds registered before the appointed day s 73(2A) of the 2003 Act means that some special provisions may not be effective. (This issue is discussed at para 15.34.) Given the impracticality of obtaining waiver or discharge in many communities the developer should, when drafting burdens, carefully frame the deed to include provisions for discharge and variation. Doing so means that the complex intimation provisions in s 34 do not apply and therefore makes discharge or variation easier.

However, many communities will have no special provision. In these cases the default position is that a deed of variation (the statutory name for a minute of waiver of community burdens) can be granted either: (1) by, or on behalf of, the owners of a majority of the units in the community; or (2) by the manager of the community if authorised so to do: s 33(2) of the 2003 Act. The majority can include properties that are burdened where the owners are seeking the variation or discharge of the community burden (such properties are referred to as 'affected units' in these sections).

Although it is possible for the owners of the majority of units to vary or discharge the burden, if only one proprietor owns the majority of properties the assent of a further owner is necessary.

Where the majority has signed the deed, it is not possible to register it immediately. The minority may be unaware of the proposed variation and could therefore be subject to the imposition of new burdens on their property or removal of the right to enforce burdens against their neighbours. Section 34 of the 2003 Act therefore provides that those in the community who have not agreed to the deed of variation must receive intimation of this. The notice of intimation is sent to the owner or his or her agent by either posting, personal delivery or sending in electronic format: s 124 of the 2003 Act. It is to be in the form provided in Schedule 4 to the 2003 Act identifying the properties which will be affected by the deed of variation and detail its nature (ie discharge, variation or imposition of burdens). The notice will also notify the recipients of a date not less than eight weeks after intimation. If the recipient wishes to preserve the burden (or right to enforce the burden) in relation to his or her property and any unit whose owners have not granted the deed then he or she can apply to the Lands Tribunal.

18.21 Registration

Registration of the deed of variation requires the Tribunal clerk to sign a certificate on the deed: s 37(2) of the Title Conditions (Scotland) Act 2003. This confirms that:

(1) no objections were received; or
(2) objections were received but withdrawn; or
(3) objections were received in relation only to the proposed variation or discharge of specified burdens (in which case those variations and discharges not objected to would be effective).

In applying for such certification the applicant must use form TC37 and the Tribunal requires evidence of intimation under s 34 of the 2003 Act. See the Lands Tribunal for Scotland Rules 2003, SSI 2003/452, r 5.

Once the Tribunal has certified the position, the party proposing to register the deed of variation must swear or affirm that s 33(1) and (2) have been complied with and that the date by which applications to the Tribunal had to be made has expired.

The provision regarding swearing or affirming is similar to that in relation to preservation of feudal burdens and is considered at para 19.37.

After the Tribunal certificate is endorsed and the oath is taken, the deed can be registered. Registration will then vary or discharge the burden (but not in so far as it relates to the objections).

Objections are considered by the Tribunal (see para 18.83) and its disposal of the case will determine whether the community burden will be preserved or varied.

18.22 An example

The effect of ss 33 and 34 of the Title Conditions (Scotland) Act 2003 can be seen from the following example. If there is an eight-property development where building is prohibited and one owner, Alfred, wishes to build a garage, the consent of the owners of four other properties in the development would satisfy s 33. If this was in relation to a development where one person (such as the developer) owned a majority (say, six) of the other properties, but Zoe owned the other, the consent of the developer would not in itself be enough, despite the developer owning a majority of units. Alfred would also have to sign (and can do so: s 33(3) of the 2003 Act). In the former case once Alfred obtained the consent of four owners he would intimate to the other owners his intention to register the deed of variation. They would then have eight weeks to apply to the Tribunal to preserve the burden. In the latter case intimation must be sent to Zoe.

While the scheme may be practical for small developments where a majority comprises only a few people, in housing estates where there are tens or hundreds of properties it is not. If Alfred lived in a community of 100 properties he would require the assent of the owners of a further 50 properties. Paying for the legal costs of signature for each signatory means that in such estates use of the procedure would be prohibitively expensive. Further, even where the scheme is practical the eight-week time period during which the notice cannot be registered means that the procedure cannot be used when minutes of waiver are most frequently sought: during the sale and purchase of property. Accordingly, the scheme is unlikely to be much used.

18.23 *Variation or discharge by neighbours*

Given the impracticality of the general rule in s 15 and the provisions on majority rule in s 33, the Title Conditions (Scotland) Act 2003 also provides an alternative default scheme for variation and discharge of community burdens. Section 35 provides that where an individual in a community wishes to vary or discharge a burden, he or she can do so by obtaining a minute of waiver that is signed by the owners of all properties that are within four metres of the burdened property (referred to in the Act as 'adjacent units': s 32). In calculating the four metres no account is to be taken of public roads (if less than 20 metres wide). Further, the four metres is calculated along the horizontal plane: s 125 of the 2003 Act. This latter requirement means that where properties are built on top of each other they will all lie within the same distance of the burdened property. Thus, if the community burden is enforceable by tenement properties the owners of each tenement flat will have to be consulted. Or if the burdened owner lives in a housing estate the adjacent units may comprise the properties on either side of the burdened property, and the properties directly opposite the burdened property. In large housing estates this will mean that in place of requiring the consent of a simple majority of tens or hundreds of proprietors, a maximum of eight will typically require to assent to the deed of variation or discharge.

Section 35 does not apply to facility and service burdens (see para 15.7).

Nor will s 35 apply if expressly disapplied in the deed creating the burdens. Express disapplication of s 35 should only be considered if an alternative mode of discharge is provided in the constitutive deed. Removing the s 35 procedure may make variation or discharge of community burdens wholly impractical and consequently increase the number of applications to the Lands Tribunal. As it stands the s 35 procedure has practical difficulties that will affect its operation in practice. These difficulties arise from the notification procedure.

Section 36 of the 2003 Act regulates intimation of a proposal to register a deed of variation or discharge granted under s 35. Failure to provide for intimation would mean that benefited proprietors would lose their right to enforce without an opportunity to preserve their right. However, while laudable in principle the scheme of intimation in s 36 is somewhat complicated in practice. Once the burdened owner has obtained the signatures of every proprietor within four metres of the burdened property the burdened owner must intimate his or her intention to register the deed of variation or discharge to the other proprietors in the community. Notification is through: (1) sending notice in the form set out in Schedule 5; (2) the 'lamp post rule' using the form set out in Schedule 6; or (3) newspaper advertisement providing the information set out in s 36(3), where a Schedule 6 notice is not possible.

The Schedule 5 notice is to be sent to the benefited owners (or their agents) either by post or by hand delivery, or through electronic mail. When Schedule 5 is used the notice must detail the burdened property, the burdens to be varied or discharged, and whether the burdened owner is seeking to register a variation or a discharge. The benefited owners are also to be advised that they have power to preserve the burdens through a Lands Tribunal application and (as with s 34) given at least eight weeks so to do.

Similar information is required on a Schedule 6 notice. This notice requires to be 'conspicuous' and to be affixed to lamp posts within 100 metres of the burdened property: s 36(2)(b). Care must be taken to ensure that no lamp post is damaged during the affixing, nor can the notice be attached to the lamp post for too long after the expiry of the date to apply to the Tribunal. This is because detailed rules protecting the integrity of lamp posts are provided, although the sanction for failure to comply with these rules is not specified: s 36(5), applying s 21(6) of the 2003 Act. Burdened owners will be relieved to know that affixing the notice to the lamp post will not require planning permission: s 36(5), applying s 21(7). Where a community is free from lamp posts the burdened owner is permitted to place a local newspaper advertisement giving the information set out in s 36(3). The Schedule 6 procedure will be of most use in large estates or where benefited proprietors are determined by the application of rules on implied rights.

Where a benefited owner wishes to preserve his or her right to enforce the community burden they may apply to the Lands Tribunal under s 37.

Registration of the deed of variation or discharge requires an endorsement from the clerk of the Tribunal that no objections have been received. The position set out at para 18.21 applies here also with two amendments: the oath or affirmation relates to compliance with s 36; and the application to the Tribunal for certification requires evidence of intimation under s 36.

18.24   Another example

The effect of ss 35 and 36 of the Title Conditions (Scotland) Act 2003 can be seen from a variant of the example given at para 18.22. Where Alfred lives in the estate of 100 properties, rather than obtaining the consent of the majority of proprietors in the community he would only require the assent of his immediate neighbours (likely to be a maximum of eight people) for his proposal to contravene the burden. This is clearly more practical than s 33 of the 2003 Act in large estates, although obtaining the assent of eight people may still prove problematic where personal matters (or disputes) between neighbours may be influential. However, even where the signatures were obtained Alfred would have to notify the other proprietors in the community of his plans and would be unable to register the deed of variation for the eight-week period. Again, this would cause severe problems where Alfred was under time pressure to obtain the minute of waiver.

18.25   Complexity

The schemes for variation and discharge of community burdens involve such complexity in the intimation and registration procedures that it is suggested that they will be little used in practice. Given that burdens can quickly become outdated and obstruct reasonable development of an area it is necessary to make discharge and variation reasonably straightforward. Indeed, para 9 of the explanatory notes to the Title Conditions (Scotland) Act 2003 states that the Act 'reduces the number of outdated burdens by making it easier to discharge or vary them'. While the provisions for variation and discharge of community burdens make things easier than the current law, coupled with the expansion of implied rights of enforcement they may ironically serve to make obtaining express consent more difficult in future. It will probably be necessary, then, in dealing with properties in a community to rely on the rules on implied consent, or negative prescription, or to apply to the Lands Tribunal.

18.26   Servitudes

As with praedial real burdens, a minute of waiver of a servitude granted by a benefited proprietor will not bind other benefited proprietors (for example, where the benefited property has been sub-divided). See D J Cusine and R R M Paisley *Servitudes and Rights of Way* (1998), para 17.06. Care must be taken to ensure that the minute of waiver is granted by all benefited proprietors.

18.27 INFORMAL LETTERS OF CONSENT

Informal letters of consent are used in two ways: where there is express provision in the burden; or as an informal method of express consent.

18.28 The 'without the consent of' provision in burdens

Burdens may be drafted to provide that the burdened owner may not use the property in a certain way or may not carry out certain work on it 'without the consent of [the benefited owner]'. In such cases the signature of an informal letter of consent by the benefited owner will be sufficient for the burdened owner to carry out the work. Before feudal abolition it would often be provided that work could be carried out with the sole consent of the feudal superior whether or not neighbours of the burdened owner had title to enforce the burden. As the letter of consent was not registered it was in such cases a cheap alternative to obtaining a full minute of waiver. Such burdens are affected in two ways by abolition. Firstly, s 73(2) of the Abolition of Feudal Tenure etc (Scotland) 2000 provides that where a burden expressly refers to the superior, it is to be interpreted post-abolition as covering all benefited proprietors where the final burden has been converted into a non-feudal burden under Part 4 of the 2000 Act or s 56 of the Title Conditions (Scotland) Act 2003. However, it does not include neighbours granted rights of enforcement under the new rule on implied rights of enforcement discussed at paras 17.32 to 17.45. Secondly, where a burden (whether created in a feudal deed or otherwise before the appointed day) provides that persons other than all of the benefited owners may consent, s 73(2A) of the 2000 Act provides that the clause so providing is disregarded. Accordingly, the informal means of consent is ineffective. See para 15.34, which also discusses the mirror provision: s 3(8) of the Title Conditions (Scotland) Act 2003. The effect of these provisions (discussed at para 19.108) will particularly in the second case be to increase the numbers that must be approached for consent, making even the informal method of express consent more expensive.

18.29 Inexpensive form of express consent

A letter of consent is frequently used in practice as an inexpensive form of discharge. The benefited owner is approached for consent to a proposed contravention of a burden. A letter is provided in exchange for a small payment. The letter does not contain a conveyancing description of the burdened (or benefited) property and is not attested. The letter of consent cannot be registered. For these reasons it is cheaper than a minute of waiver. However, the letter of consent is simply a personal agreement between the benefited owner and burdened owner. This will not bind singular successors of either. A letter of consent used in this way cannot expressly vary or discharge a burden but may be relevant when looking at the provisions on acquiescence: see para 18.43.

18.30   PRE-SALE UNDERTAKINGS REGARDING RIGHTS OF PRE-EMPTION

Section 83 of the Title Conditions (Scotland) Act 2003 introduces a new provision allowing the benefited proprietor in a right of pre-emption (on which see para 15.9) to consent expressly to its extinction prior to a sale.

It applies to rights of pre-emption created in feudal conveyances or to rights of pre-emption created in other deeds signed after 1 September 1974. This will therefore include those rights of pre-emption preserved under s 18(7) of the Abolition of Feudal Tenure etc (Scotland) Act 2000 (see para 19.55), personal pre-emption burdens and rural housing burdens. Most rights of pre-emption were created in feudal conveyances. Those that were created in ordinary conveyances executed before 1 September 1974 remain effective in perpetuity (subject to the general rules on variation and discharge of praedial burdens).

Section 83 of the 2003 Act provides that where the benefited proprietor (or holder of the right of pre-emption) is contacted by the burdened owner in advance of a proposed sale (typically when the burdened owner is intending to market the property), the benefited proprietor may give a statutory undertaking (in accordance with Schedule 10 to the 2003 Act) that he or she will not exercise the right of pre-emption during a specified time period provided certain conditions are satisfied. The benefited proprietor can determine both the conditions and the time period. For example, the benefited proprietor may provide that he will not exercise his right of pre-emption if the sale price of the property reaches a certain threshold ('if the consideration is £100,000 or more'). In relation to the time period the benefited proprietor may require the sale of the property to be completed within three months of the undertaking.

If the burdened property is then sold and the conveyance registered within the specified time period then, provided the conditions set out by the benefited proprietor are satisfied, the right of pre-emption is extinguished. As registration of the conveyance is the key date for extinction of the right of pre-emption this is a further incentive to the purchaser to register promptly. For, failure to register the conveyance timeously or to satisfy the conditions means that the right of pre-emption will continue to encumber the burdened property, putting any purchaser at risk of an action based on the 'offside goals rule': *Matheson v Tinney* 1989 SLT 535. If it becomes apparent during the sale of the property that there is a risk that the sale may extend beyond the time period, or the offers received do not satisfy the conditions prescribed by the benefited owner, the burdened owner can seek a new Schedule 10 undertaking. Alternatively, he or she can instead rely on the s 84 procedure whereby an offer is made to the benefited owner. This is discussed at para 18.52 with the rules on implied extinction.

Where neither of the s 83 or s 84 procedures is complied with the right can be extinguished by negative prescription where the benefited owner does not enforce the right of pre-emption within five years: s 18(2) of the 2003 Act. See further para 18.57.

If the right of pre-emption is a rural housing burden s 83 will not extinguish the burden – although compliance with s 83 will be sufficient to satisfy the terms of the burden.

18.31   Registration

The Schedule 10 undertaking is a personal agreement between benefited owner and burdened owner. However, if the undertaking is registered then it will bind singular successors of both parties. Registration is therefore encouraged as a matter of course.

Where the right of pre-emption appears in the Land Register the Schedule 10 undertaking will be submitted with the application for registration to support an application to remove the right of pre-emption from the title sheet.

18.32   The 'sunset rule': notices of termination

In the policy papers from the Scottish Law Commission and the Scottish Executive before the passage of the Title Conditions (Scotland) Act 2003, one problem was regularly identified: that of obsolete and anachronistic burdens. Given that burdens have existed in Scots law for nearly 200 years, many that were initially valuable have outlived their usefulness due to changing social circumstances. Prohibitions on running piggeries, tanneries and tallow chandlers remain in city centre titles, despite modern planning law making inconceivable the likelihood of such developments. Such burdens, though, are harmless. Or prohibitions on running businesses from residential properties seem outdated where technological developments allow individuals to work on-line from their homes. Such burdens are more harmful. In some countries the problem of anachronistic burdens has led to the introduction of strict rules extinguishing burdens when the burden reaches a certain age (often referred to as a 'sunset rule'). However, simply because burdens are old does not mean that they do not serve a valuable purpose. Taking account of this, the 2003 Act provides a more targeted approach than a general sunset rule.

Sections 20 to 24 provide a procedure for a burdened owner to initiate the termination of burdens where the burden is more than 100 years old. A person against whom the burden is enforceable can seek variation or discharge of the burden through execution and registration of a notice of termination. Prior to registration this notice must be intimated to all benefited owners. They are then given a limited time period during which they can object and apply to the Lands Tribunal to preserve the burden.

18.33   SCOPE OF THE SUNSET RULE

The termination procedure does not apply to conservation burdens; facility or service burdens; maritime burdens; or burdens excluded from the jurisdiction of the Lands Tribunal: s 20(3) of the Title Conditions (Scotland) Act 2003. This means the procedure primarily applies to amenity burdens.

18.34   INTIMATION

The procedure is initiated by the burdened owner, or other person against whom the burden is enforceable, such as a tenant. This person is referred to in the legislation as 'the terminator'. He or she has to complete a Schedule 2 notice. This notice:

(1) identifies the terminator and his or her relationship to the burdened property;
(2) describes the burdened property;
(3) identifies the burdens the application relates to (which can be multiple burdens from the same constitutive deed);
(4) confirms whether discharge of variation is sought; and
(5) provides a date by which the benefited owners are to apply to the Lands Tribunal if they wish to preserve the burdens (the date being a minimum of eight weeks after intimation is last given): the 'renewal date'.

The notice is then to be intimated to the owners of the benefited properties (or holders of the personal real burden) and the owner of the burdened property (if he or she is not the terminator). Intimation is to be given by sending a copy of the notice of termination; placing notices on lamp posts; or (in unusual cases) by newspaper advertisement.

For praedial real burdens the notice is to be sent to those benefited owners who own properties within four metres of the burdened property (discounting public roads). Sending is to be by personal delivery, post, or in electronic form: s 124 of the Title Conditions (Scotland) Act 2003. As evidence of intimation will be required for any Tribunal application or application to register the notice, it is suggested that recorded delivery should be used. When sending the notice, the explanatory note in Schedule 2 must be sent as well. This note advises the benefited owner that he or she can object to the notice and apply to the Tribunal to preserve the burden. A similar rule applies for intimation to the holder where the notice is used for personal real burdens.

Intimation to those benefited properties more than four metres from the burdened property is by affixing a notice to a lamp post in the form prescribed in Schedule 3 to the 2003 Act. This notice must be conspicuous and will detail the burdened property, the burdens that the terminator proposes to vary or discharge, the proposed extent of variation or discharge, and the renewal date before which a benefited owner wishing to preserve the burden must make objection to the Tribunal. The process is similar to that used for intimation to benefited owners under s 35 of the 2003 Act (see para 18.23). The notice must be affixed to lamp posts within 100 metres of the burdened property (and no planning permission is required) and the lamp post must not be damaged: s 21 of the 2003 Act.

If there is no lamp post within 100 metres of the burdened property, or if the burdened property comprises minerals or salmon fishings, then intimation to the benefited owners more than four metres from the burdened property requires the terminator to place an advertisement in a local newspaper detailing his or her contact details, the burdened property, the burdens that he or she proposes to vary or discharge, and the renewal date.

18.35 OBJECTIONS

If a benefited owner or the holder of the burden wishes to preserve it he or she can object to the notice of termination. Objection is made to the Lands Tribunal before the renewal date through an application for renewal of the burden. The general rules on Tribunal applications will then apply, determining whether the burdens should be preserved, varied or discharged. Any order by the Tribunal will then be registered. These are discussed at para 18.81.

Where an application for renewal of the burden has been made this may encourage the terminator to negotiate with the objector. If the objector withdraws the application for whatever reason (including the terminator making a payment in exchange for such withdrawal) the notice can be registered in relation to that objector's benefited property. Further, if objections are not received from every benefited owner the notice can be registered in relation to those benefited properties that did not object. See para 18.36.

18.36 REGISTRATION IF NO OUTSTANDING APPLICATIONS FOR RENEWAL

In so far as a benefited owner does not object to the proposed notice of termination, the notice can then be registered. Prior to registration the notice requires the terminator to swear an oath or make affirmation confirming that the notice was appropriately intimated under s 21: s 22 of the Title Conditions (Scotland) Act 2003. As is the case for the notices regarding variation or discharge of community burdens, the provision regarding swearing or affirming is similar to that in relation to preservation of feudal burdens, and is considered at para 19.37.

Prior to registration, the notice of termination requires to be certified by the clerk to the Tribunal: s 23 of the 2003 Act. In any application the applicant must use form TC23, and the Tribunal requires evidence of intimation to benefited owners. See the Lands Tribunal for Scotland Rules 2003, SSI 2003/452, r 5. No certification will be provided if the terminator indicates to the Tribunal that the proposal to register a notice of termination is withdrawn. The certification will provide that: there are no outstanding applications for renewal (either because no applications for renewal were received; or because there were applications received but subsequently withdrawn); or there are outstanding applications relating to some but not all of the burdens specified in the notice; or there are outstanding applications from one or more, but not all, benefited proprietors. The content of the certification determines the effect of the notice.

Where the certificate provides that there are no outstanding objections the notice can then be registered against the burdened property. On registration the notice takes effect to vary or discharge the burden: s 24(1) of the 2003 Act.

Where the certificate is qualified by reference to outstanding applications registration of the notice against the burdened property will not have effect in relation to those outstanding applications: s 24(2) of the 2003 Act. Thus, if there is an outstanding application from one benefited proprietor in relation to specific burdens, registration of the notice will vary or discharge the burdens specified in the notice as against all other benefited properties. Registration of the notice will also vary or discharge the burdens not specified in the application against the benefited property owned by the applicant.

It is possible for an application to be withdrawn after a notice of termination has been registered. In such cases the terminator can request a new certificate from the Tribunal. Registration of the notice following a second certificate will take effect only as provided in that second certificate.

18.37　POSSIBLE OPERATION IN PRACTICE?

It is not clear how the termination procedure will operate in practice. It may be that purchasers – to open negotiations – generally insert in their offers a requirement that sellers should serve a notice of termination regarding burdens more than 100 years old. However, it seems more likely that the procedure will be used by burdened owners proposing to carry out an act that would contravene the burden. Intimation of the proposal would then lead to objections, identifying those benefited proprietors that were concerned about the loss of the right to enforce the burden. The objectors may be approached and offered the payment of a *grassum* to drop their objections or to agree to enter a formal minute of waiver. Used in this way the termination procedure, when used with the general rules on minutes of waiver, may serve to make these general rules workable in practice. If no agreement can be reached it requires the benefited owner to meet the initial expenses and initiate a Tribunal action to consider preservation of the burden.

18.38　Implied consent: acquiescence

Acquiescence is an aspect of personal bar. Where a title condition is breached with the knowledge or consent of the benefited owner (or other holder of enforcement rights), and the title condition is not enforced, then the benefited owner may lose the right to enforce the title condition through acquiescence. There are two possible situations in which acquiescence will arise: (1) where there has been material expenditure in relation to a burden triggering s 16 of the Title Conditions (Scotland) Act 2003; and (2) where it is not covered by s 16 of the 2003 Act (the position at common law).

The increasing importance of community burdens (created expressly or through the new implied enforcement rights created under the 2003 Act) means that express consent will be more difficult to obtain, particularly if required in short time (such as during a sale and purchase) due to an existing breach. Therefore increasing reliance on acquiescence will be necessary after the appointed day. However, this will require a change in practice. Currently, solicitors often require written evidence that can be registered (such as minutes of waiver) or transmitted with the titles (such as letters of consent). This is, in part, because the common law rules on acquiescence are unsatisfactory (see paras 18.39 to 18.42). Without a judicial declarator it may be difficult to satisfy a purchaser that the conditions have been satisfied. However, the statutory rules on acquiescence introduce a time limit of 12 weeks for objections to be made to prevent the application of acquiescence. This will be of particular utility in practice – if bolstered by certain warranties in the missives. See paras 18.43 to 18.44.

18.39 COMMON LAW ACQUIESCENCE

There are three requirements: (1) the benefited owner knows of the contravention; (2) the benefited owner (or other holder of enforcement rights) does not enforce the title condition; and (3) the burdened owner relies on the benefited owner's non-enforcement to his or her prejudice. Together these elements imply that the benefited owner consents to the contravention of the title condition. While the rules for acquiescence in relation to real burdens are restated by statute the common law position will be relevant to servitudes and may have a residual role for real burdens where the breach of the burden did not involve the burdened owner in making material expenditure.

(1) *Knowledge of contravention.* Where the burdened owner contravenes the title condition acquiescence will apply where the benefited owner knows of the contravention. This is generally satisfied where the contravention of the burden is patent for the benefited owner to see, such as building works.

However, even notification of proposed works may not be sufficient to trigger acquiescence. In *McGibbon v Rankin* (1871) 9 R 423 a negative servitude provided that buildings could not be constructed above a certain height. Notification of proposed works on the burdened property did not specify the proposed height and the benefited owner made no objection. However, when it became apparent that the buildings were to exceed the maximum height, the benefited owner raised interdict proceedings. Failure to object initially had not founded acquiescence because the benefited proprietor did not know that the proposed work would contravene the burdens.

Knowledge can probably be actual or constructive. There is academic and judicial approval: see *Ben Challum Ltd v Buchanan* 1955 SC 348 at 355 to 356, per Lord President Clyde; W M Gloag *Contract* (2nd edn, 1929), p 253; and D J Cusine and R R M Paisley *Servitudes and Rights of Way* (1998), para 17.18. However, there is no direct authority on constructive knowledge. An example would be where a non-resident landlord of the benefited property can object but does not know about work carried out by the burdened owner contravening a burden. It is not clear if the landlord's failure to enforce the condition is sufficient to found acquiescence. If it is, the obviousness of the work contravening the burden will clearly be a relevant factor. Is the work patent for the world to see? This means that if the contravention is not obvious (for example, where there is a prohibition on use, and such a use is made within the burdened property) there will be difficulties of proof.

(2) *Failure to object.* Acquiescence only arises where a benefited owner fails to object. While failure to raise court proceedings to enforce the condition is sufficient for acquiescence, it is not clear if that is necessarily required for the doctrine to apply. The Scottish Law Commission discusses the situation where a benefited owner receives notification under planning law of proposed work that would contravene the burden and suggest that objection under the planning

system would not be sufficient to prevent the operation of acquiescence. See *Report on Real Burdens* (Scot Law Com No 181, 2000), para 5.62. The statutory change in s 16 of the Title Conditions (Scotland) Act 2003 (see para 18.43) will impact on the common law treatment of this in relation to real burdens.

(3) *The burdened owner relies on the benefited owner's failure to object to the contravention.* The burdened owner's contravention of the burden must rely to some degree on the benefited owner's knowledge and inaction. Thus, where the burdened owner erects a garage in contravention of a prohibition on building, by the time the garage is completed the work will have relied to a degree on the benefited owner's failure to object.

It is sometimes suggested that acquiescence will only apply where there has been material expenditure by the burdened owner: see, for example, *Muirhead v Glasgow Highland Society* (1864) 2 M 420; *Report on Real Burdens* (Scot Law Com No 181, 2000), para 5.60. However, this does not appear to be a necessary requirement, provided that there is reliance by the burdened owner on the benefited owner's failure and the burdened owner has acted to his prejudice. See Cusine and Paisley *Servitudes and Rights of Way*, para 17.16, and W M Gordon *Scottish Land Law* (2nd edn, 1999), para 22-75. Thus, erection of a fence over a servitude access route would be sufficient for the doctrine to apply but need not involve substantial expenditure.

18.40   Proving acquiescence

It is difficult to prove the necessary elements of acquiescence. However, one means by which it can be evidenced in relation to a specific benefited owner is through obtaining a letter of consent. That indicates that the benefited owner knew about the breach, and agreed to it, and the burdened owner will rely on this letter.

18.41   Where acquiescence applies

Where acquiescence applies at common law its effect is not wholly clear. Personal bar is usually personal between the party who fails to enforce, and the party against whom the obligation was not enforced. However, it is not clear if singular successors of the benefited owner are bound by the actions of their predecessor in title. The issue was discussed in a valuable article by Professor Halliday in 'Acquiescence, Singular Successors and the Baby Linnet' 1977 JR 89. Although there is no direct authority, the consensus of opinion is that singular successors are bound where the contravention is patent and the burdened owner has incurred substantial expenditure. See K G C Reid *The Law of Property in Scotland* (1996), para 427; W M Gordon *Scottish Land Law* (2nd edn, 1999), paras 22-76 and 24-89; D J Cusine and R R M Paisley *Servitudes and Rights of Way* (1998), para 17.20. See also *Muirhead v Glasgow Highland Society* (1864) 2 M 420 and *Ben Challum Ltd v Buchanan* 1955 SC 348. However, it may be a difficult question of fact to determine when the contravention is sufficiently patent for acquiescence to affect singular successors. This problem arises even where the elements of acquiescence can be proved through provision of an informal letter of consent between burdened and benefited owners.

Acquiescence does not necessarily discharge the condition. It is extinguished only to the extent of the breach: *Stewart v Bunten* (1878) 5 R 1108. For servitudes it is necessary to determine if the breach renders the servitude wholly inoperable. If it does the servitude will be extinguished. If not, the servitude will subsist. The issue is discussed in Cusine and Paisley *Servitudes and Rights of Way*, para 17.19.

18.42 Uncertainties

At common law a purchaser of the burdened property is unlikely to rely on acquiescence to vary or discharge the condition. There are too many uncertainties. There are difficulties of both fact and law. Can a purchaser be sure that the benefited owner knows of the breach? That there was no objection raised? That the burdened owner relied on the failure to object? That singular successors are bound? Statutory acquiescence under s 16 of the Title Conditions (Scotland) Act 2003 is designed to remedy some of these problems and to encourage the use of acquiescence to address the difficulties of obtaining express consent.

18.43 STATUTORY ACQUIESCENCE OF BREACHES OF REAL BURDENS

The rules in s 16 of the Title Conditions (Scotland) Act 2003 apply only to real burdens (both praedial and personal). They are largely based on the common law with minor amendments and clarifications. There are three prerequisites:

(1) the burden is breached by the burdened owner (or occupier of the burdened property) in such a way that material expenditure is incurred;
(2) the party breaching the burden would lose the benefit of his or her expenditure if the burden was enforced; and
(3) the benefited owner (or other party with title to enforce) has consented to the breach either actively or by implication.

The first two elements refine the requirements for reliance and prejudice under common law acquiescence discussed above. The latter element deals with the issue of consent and restates (and amends) the common law provisions regarding knowledge and failure to object.

The section distinguishes between active consent and implied consent. In both cases consent is not to the breach of a burden, but to the carrying out of a certain activity.

Active consent does not require any special form. Best practice would involve the burdened owner obtaining an informal letter of consent, although verbal consent, such as 'a casual word exchanged over the garden fence', is acceptable: see para 93 of the explanatory notes to the 2003 Act. It is not necessary to obtain active consent from any party with title and interest to enforce. However, for evidential reasons a burdened owner may wish to obtain consents from immediate neighbours.

Passive consent is consent not to the breach, but to the activity that constitutes the breach. It is given where a party with title and interest to enforce knows about the activity and does not object. In determining the knowledge of those with title to enforce it is not necessary that they know that a burden has been contravened; only to know that certain works have been carried out. Thus, the provision will apply to patent contraventions (primarily external building works). It is not necessary for actual knowledge to be shown. If the burdened owner can show that those with title to enforce ought to have known of the work (such as the erection of a two-storey extension or garage) then this will suffice. There is, though, a long stop provision whereby a person with title to enforce is presumed to know of the work on expiry of 12 weeks from substantial completion of the activity. No objection within the 12-week period will mean that passive consent is presumed (although evidence to the contrary can be led). Objection in this context does not require the party with title to enforce to raise a court action to enforce the burden as it is the activity that constitutes the contravention that must be objected to. Mere objection (including objection made under planning law) would therefore suffice to prevent the operation of acquiescence.

All parties with title and interest to enforce the burden must consent (either actively or passively). However, this does not require the burdened owner to obtain letters of consent from every benefited owner, or every tenant, non-entitled spouse, or heritable creditor in possession of benefited property. A mixture of passive and active consent is acceptable. However, if any person entitled to enforce objects acquiescence cannot apply.

If there are no objections then the burden is varied: extinguished to the extent of the breach. This will bind singular successors of burdened and benefited owners (and others with title).

Where the requirements for statutory acquiescence are not satisfied the common law will apply to a limited extent. As it appears arguable that it did not require the burdened owner's breach to involve material expenditure, where there was no such expenditure the common law applies.

18.44 STATUTORY ACQUIESCENCE AND PRACTICE

For a purchaser (and seller) of the burdened property, s 16 of the Title Conditions (Scotland) Act 2003 provides special problems. If a seller cannot demonstrate that a burden has been extinguished by express consent or negative prescription, he or she will attempt to argue that there has been acquiescence. This will often be the case in communities in relation to community burdens where express consent is very difficult to obtain. Provided the work is patent (a matter on which a purchaser will have to take a view), then if at least 12 weeks have expired since completion of the work and there were no objections from any benefited owner (or other party with title to enforce), the breach is not enforceable against the purchaser.

However, the efficacy of the provision is dependent on two elements: the work must involve material expenditure and be clear for all to see (meaning that it will be of little or no value in relation to breaches carried out within the burdened property, such as changes of use); and the seller has to satisfy the purchaser that no objections were received. The seller is then left with having to prove a negative. A purchaser may require the burdened owner selling to warrant that no objections were received.

Aside from these difficulties there is the general problem for implied variation and discharge that the matters are not clear from the register. Will a purchaser rely on implication with no documentation? In this regard the 12-week provision will be of assistance to burdened owners selling on property. Further, given the complexity of the rules on express consent, if purchasers do not apply s 16 and take a commercial view then there will be difficulties in dealing with properties at all without either requiring the burdened owner to apply to the Lands Tribunal for judicial pronouncement or through requiring the burdened owner to obtain some form of guarantee as to unenforceability of the burdens (such as some form of private title insurance).

It is difficult to foresee how practice will develop in this regard but it is suggested that conveyancing practicalities mean that a pragmatic approach should be adopted.

18.45 Other circumstances where title conditions are extinguished by implication

There are other modes of extinction of title conditions that arise by implication. These include:

(1) the benefited owner or holder losing interest to enforce the title condition;
(2) the benefited property being destroyed or otherwise changed;
(3) the benefited owner giving up a servitude through renunciation;
(4) the benefited owner giving up use of a servitude;
(5) a right of pre-emption being extinguished under s 84 of the Title Conditions (Scotland) Act 2003;
(6) where a real burden does not appear on the Land Register; and
(7) lapse of time or fulfilment of purpose.

For the first four examples it will be difficult for a seller of burdened property to demonstrate extinction to the satisfaction of a purchaser's agents as the justification for extinction may not be apparent from the face of the register. It will be necessary to determine if a commercial view should be taken. In order to fully protect his or her position, the purchaser may insist on a declarator being obtained or a Lands Tribunal order for variation or discharge. This will not be feasible in the short time span of a conveyancing transaction. However, in some cases a pragmatic view can be effectively adopted. For example, generally a party will not have interest to enforce a breach of a burden prohibiting building where the benefited property is some distance from the burdened property.

In the latter two modes of extinction, however, the position can be confirmed from examination of the register.

18.46   LOSS OF INTEREST TO ENFORCE

To enforce title conditions the benefited owner or holder must have both title and interest to enforce. For personal real burdens, interest to enforce is presumed. However, for praedial title conditions, interest must be proved. Where there is no interest to enforce then in certain cases the title condition will be extinguished. This arises in two principal situations: where there is a material change in circumstances; or where s 17 of the Title Conditions (Scotland) Act 2003 applies. Both cases, though, may be difficult to prove and may mean that a purchaser of the burdened property (or the Keeper) is unlikely to be satisfied that the burden has been extinguished or varied. However, in certain instances where used in conjunction with other modes of variation and discharge, a pragmatic view can be taken.

18.47   Material change of circumstances

This arises where the burdened or benefited property changes to such an extent that the title condition can no longer be enforceable. The main example is where the property has been destroyed: see para 18.49. However, it is also possible that a consistent practice of multiple burdened owners breaching burdens may lead the benefited owner to lose interest to enforce the burden, therefore extinguishing (or varying) the burden in relation to all burdened properties. As will be discussed at para 19.13, this primarily arose where the feudal superior had enforcement rights in relation to an estate. However, it may equally arise where one benefited owner has title to enforce against multiple burdened properties (such as would have arisen for the original disponer in *Lees v North East Fife District Council* 1987 SLT 769) or where there are community burdens (created expressly or through implied rights of enforcement).

Where there is a community and burdens are contravened in some parts this is not in itself an indication that the burden ceases to apply in relation to the whole community. For example, if there are fifty properties in an estate burdened with a prohibition on constructing conservatories the ten owners at the north of the estate may all have built conservatories without any objection from the owners at the south of the estate. However, when Alice, an owner at the south of the estate, proposes to build a conservatory she is faced with interdict proceedings raised by an immediate neighbour. It would not be enough for Alice to argue that the burden has been breached elsewhere in the estate. As Lord McLaren noted in *Mactaggart & Co v Roemmele* 1907 SC 1318 at 1325:

'... it would be a very inconvenient, not to say inequitable, rule that a feuar who becomes aware of some infraction of building conditions by a feuar from the same superior, but at such a distance from himself that the infraction causes no inconvenience to him, must either apply for an interdict or be taken to have waived his right to enforce the condition in a question with conterminous feuars or disponees'.

However, where the burden has been breached throughout the estate, this may result in the benefited owners losing their interest to enforce and the burden being extinguished. An example would be in George Street in Glasgow, where burdens provided that properties should not exceed two storeys high. It is now the case that there are few, if any, properties there less than three storeys high. See *Campbell v Clydesdale Banking Co* (1868) 6 M 943, discussed at para 19.13. It is not clear to what extent the burden must have been contravened (or waived) throughout the community. As Professor Reid notes in *The Law of Property in Scotland* (1996), para 429:

'no simple arithmetical formula exists to determine the answer, and it appears the position will depend at least to some extent on the size of the estate, [and] on the location of the properties in respect of which discharges have been given in relation to the property'.

Such uncertainty means that this principle is unlikely to be relied on by a purchaser of the burdened property without declarator confirming its operation.

18.48 Extinction of real burdens where no person has interest to enforce

Section 17 of the Title Conditions (Scotland) Act 2003 provides that where a burden is breached and no person with title (be they owner, tenant, or other holder of a possessory real right in the benefited property) has interest to enforce then the burden is extinguished to the extent of the breach (that is, varied in the language used in this chapter). This provision was introduced at Stage 3 of the parliamentary consideration of the 2003 Act. No examples of the operation of this provision were given in the explanatory notes on the Act. However, the Justice Minister, Jim Wallace, when moving the amendment inserting the provision noted that it

'will ... clarify that only those who would actually be able to enforce the burden are required to give their consent. That means, for example, that consent is not needed from owners of a distant property who, in spite of having a title to enforce, would not have any interest in doing so because the particular breach would not be to the detriment of their property. In this case, a burden could be extinguished, but only to the extent of the actual breach, without the consent of that distant owner'.

See the Scottish Parliament Official Report, 26 February 2003, col 18701.

This suggests that where a burden is breached then if a holder of title to enforce does not have interest to enforce that burden he or she (or his or her successors) cannot subsequently object to the contravention as the burden is varied to the extent of the breach. It appears from the wording of the section that the section only applies if there is no party (on any benefited property) with interest to enforce, although this is only implicit in the legislation through the omission of the words 'as respects a benefited property' that appear in relation to express consent in s 15(1) of the 2003 Act.

The provision then requires to be used in conjunction with other rules on variation and discharge. For example, if Alan owns a burdened property where there are multiple benefited properties, and obtains express consent under s 15 (through a minute of waiver) from immediate neighbours with interest to enforce and benefited owners not approached have no interest to enforce, then once the minute of waiver is registered, s 17 can apply if no non-signatory to the minute of waiver has interest to enforce.

It will be interesting to see how this provision will be used in practice. Interest to enforce a burden is dependent on the nature of the breach. This is a matter that is determined subjectively and, apart from some clear cut cases (such as where burdened and benefited properties are a substantial distance apart), without judicial determination, opinions could reasonably differ. For example, a burdened owner may not seek minutes of waiver from benefited proprietors because he takes the view that the benefited owners have no interest to enforce, although a purchaser from the burdened owner may not be satisfied that there was no interest to enforce. The efficacy of the provision is then dependent on the extent to which purchasers are prepared to rely on judgment rather than documentation that can be registered.

18.49   DESTRUCTION OF THE PROPERTY

If the benefited property (or burdened property) is destroyed, this will, in certain circumstances, extinguish the title condition. See W M Gordon *Scottish Land Law* (2nd edn, 1999), paras 22-78 and 24-92; and Cusine and Paisley *Servitudes and Rights of Way* (1998), para 17.21. Destruction of heritable property is very unusual but this principle may apply where a title condition is for the benefit of a specific part of benefited property, implying that the condition has a restricted purpose.

18.50   RENUNCIATION OF A SERVITUDE

While real burdens require registration to be validly constituted, servitudes do not. A servitude in writing may be made a real right prior to the Title Conditions (Scotland) Act 2003 by the benefited owner taking possession. Accordingly, a servitude can be renounced before it is formally constituted if no possession is taken.

18.51 NON-USE OF A SERVITUDE

It is possible for a positive servitude to be extinguished by non-use coupled with an intention on the part of the benefited owner to give up the servitude. This is discussed by Sheriff Cusine and Professor Paisley in *Servitudes and Rights of Way* at para 17.15; and Professor Gordon in *Scottish Land Law* at paras 24-84 to 24-87, with reference to the relevant case law. This is not the same as negative prescription, where non-use can extinguish a servitude without intention on the part of the benefited owner. See para 18.58.

18.52 EXTINCTION OF RIGHTS OF PRE-EMPTION AFTER OFFERS TO SELL

Section 84 of the Title Conditions (Scotland) Act 2003 is an improved restatement of s 9 of the Conveyancing Amendment (Scotland) Act 1938. It applies to rights of pre-emption created in feudal conveyances or to rights of pre-emption created in other deeds signed after 1 September 1974, including those preserved under s 18(7) of the Abolition of Feudal Tenure etc (Scotland) Act 2000 (see para 19.55), personal pre-emption burdens, and rural housing burdens. Most rights of pre-emption were created in feudal conveyances. Those that were created in ordinary conveyances executed before 1 September 1974 remain effective in perpetuity (subject to the general rules on variation and discharge of praedial burdens).

Section 84 of the 2003 Act provides that a right of pre-emption is extinguished if on sale (or such other trigger event as is specified in the pre-emption) the burdened owner offers to sell the property to the party with title to enforce the pre-emption. The offer is to be formally valid and to be made on such terms as provided in the pre-emption. If no terms are so provided the offer is to be 'on such terms ... as are reasonable in the circumstances': s 84(4). Typically the right of pre-emption will provide that the property is to be offered to the benefited owner at the same price and on the same conditions as the seller was prepared to accept from offers received on marketing of the property. However, as offers are typically framed for the primary benefit of the purchaser there are clauses that a seller would wish to add to protect their position (for example, by providing contractual remedies for a delay in settlement). The intention of s 84(4) is to allow the seller to 'include only such terms as are reasonable in the circumstances, by which is meant terms which a reasonable purchaser, properly advised, would be inclined to accept. In appropriate cases he could add terms of his own': *Report on Real Burdens* (Scot Law Com No 181, 2000), para 10.39.

The benefited owner (or holder) is to be given 21 days (or such lesser period as is specified in the pre-emption) to accept the offer. If the benefited owner (or holder) is not persuaded that the offer is reasonable he or she can intimate such to the burdened owner. If the offer is not reasonable then the right of pre-emption will continue. If the benefited owner does not intimate that the offer is unreasonable within the time period, the offer will be deemed to be reasonable: s 84(5) of the 2003 Act.

If the offer is accepted the right of pre-emption is extinguished, but the benefited owner (or holder of the pre-emption) will acquire ownership of the property and can in any subsequent sale impose a new right of pre-emption. If the offer to the benefited owner is not accepted, the right of pre-emption is extinguished.

The s 84 procedure being dependent for its operation on the seller marketing the property, setting a closing date, and receiving offers, can introduce a delay into the proceedings. The seller (burdened owner) cannot accept any offers he or she receives pending a decision from the benefited owner (or holder). Given the possible delays in the s 84 procedure, burdened owners should use the s 83 procedure if possible (see para 18.30).

18.53   Changes to pre-abolition law

Section 84 of the Title Conditions (Scotland) Act 2003 broadly re-enacts s 9 of the Conveyancing Amendment (Scotland) Act 1938. It provided that the right of pre-emption was extinguished where the burdened owner offered the property back to the benefited owner and the offer was not accepted. For discussion, see para 33.13 of the sixth edition of this book.

18.54   LAND REGISTER

In land registration a burdened owner owns the property subject only to those real burdens that appear in the title sheet: s 3(1)(a) of the Land Registration (Scotland) Act 1979. Thus, if a real burden does not appear in the title sheet it does not encumber the property (subject to the possibility of rectification: see paras 11.31 to 11.35). However, appearance in the title sheet is not a guarantee as to the validity and effectiveness of the burden: s 12(3)(g) of the 1979 Act. In the Register of Sasines the Keeper is not required to take a view on whether real burdens are subsisting or enforceable. The position differs for land registration. Section 6(1)(e) of the 1979 Act provides that the Keeper is only to enter 'subsisting real burdens' in the title sheet. This means that the Keeper is obliged to take a view on whether the burden is subsisting. If he does not do so, the burdened owner can apply to the Tribunal to have the position clarified: *Brookfield Developments Ltd v Keeper of the Registers of Scotland* 1989 SLT (Lands Tr) 105.

18.55   LAPSE OF TIME OR FULFILMENT OF PURPOSE

Although ordinarily servitudes and real burdens are intended to be perpetual, it is possible to provide that the condition is effective only for a limited period. See Cusine and Paisley *Servitudes and Rights of Way* (1998), paras 2.89 to 2.98 and 17.32 for the position regarding servitudes, and s 7 of the Title Conditions (Scotland) Act 2003 for the position regarding real burdens. Where the title condition is intended to have a temporary duration it will come to an end on expiry of that period or fulfilment of the relevant purpose. The restriction on duration requires to be clearly stated in the deed creating the title condition, and will, therefore, generally be apparent from examination of the register.

18.56 Negative prescription

After the appointed day there are separate regimes for negative prescription applicable to real burdens and servitudes.

18.57 REAL BURDENS

The rules for real burdens are found in s 18 of the Title Conditions (Scotland) Act 2003. This provides that where a burden has been breached after the appointed day and there has for five years been no relevant claim in court proceedings by a party with title to enforce and no relevant acknowledgement by the burdened owner (or party against whom the burden can be enforced) that the burden is still effective, the burden will be extinguished to the extent of the breach. Thus, if there is a prohibition on building and the burdened owner constructs a garage then if there is no enforcement action within five years there can be no enforcement action in respect of that breach. However, if the burdened owner wished to construct a further building (such as a conservatory) this could be prevented by the benefited owner.

The period runs from the date on which the burden is breached, and takes no account of the incapacity of benefited owners to enforce the burden.

The short negative prescription is equally applicable to rights of pre-emption or other options to purchase, although in this case non-enforcement of the right of pre-emption will extinguish the right of pre-emption. Thus, if the burdened owner does not offer the property to the benefited owner then on expiry of the five-year period without enforcement the right of pre-emption is extinguished.

18.58 SERVITUDES

The position for servitudes differs. As real rights, servitudes are rights without correlative obligations. As servitudes are not imprescriptible under Schedule 3 to the Prescription and Limitation (Scotland) Act 1973, s 8 of the 1973 Act applies, despite the wording of s 3 of the 1973 Act. See D E L Johnston *Prescription and Limitation* (1999), para 7-14 and Cusine and Paisley *Servitudes and Rights of Way*, paras 17.33 and 17.34. Where a servitude is not exercised, long negative prescription (20 years) applies. If the 20-year period expires without exercise of the servitude or a relevant claim by the benefited owner (as defined in s 9 of the 1973 Act), the servitude is extinguished. This is the case even if the benefited owner lacks capacity to enforce the servitude. For positive servitudes the period runs from the last active exercise of the right by the benefited owner.

However, if a servitude is not wholly exercised for a 20-year period, it is not clear if the servitude is extinguished to the extent of the failure to use, or if the servitude remains wholly effective. For example, if there is a servitude of vehicular access and the benefited owner only exercises pedestrian access for 20 years, can the benefited owner then use the access route for vehicular access? The sheriff court decision in *Walker's Executrix v Carr* 1973 SLT (Sh Ct) 77 suggests that the benefited owner could not use the servitude in this way. However, Sheriff Cusine and Professor Paisley suggest that where the servitude is for specified purposes and it is only used in a limited way for 20 years, the servitude will not be restricted to that limited purpose: *Servitudes and Rights of Way*, para 17.33.

18.59   CHANGE FROM PRE-ABOLITION LAW

Prior to the coming into force of the Title Conditions (Scotland) Act 2003, real burdens are covered by long negative prescription of 20 years under s 7 of the Prescription and Limitation (Scotland) Act 1973 (because there is a correlative obligation: Johnston *Prescription and Limitation*, para 7.14). Accordingly, if there were a burden prohibiting the carrying on of a business on the burdened property, if a car business were to operate for 20 years from the premises, negative prescription would apply. It was not clear under the pre-abolition law if the burden is extinguished only to the extent of the breach (in the example, only car repairs will be permitted in future); or if the burden is wholly extinguished (in the example, the burdened owner can now operate a road haulage firm and coffee shop from the burdened property). It is probable that the burden is extinguished only to the extent of the breach. As argued by David Johnston: 'to conclude that the burden is wholly extinguished would be odd': *Prescription and Limitation*, para 2.11.

Section 18(5) of the 2003 Act provides a transitional rule for real burdens where there is a breach before the appointed day. The prescriptive period will be the shorter of 20 years from the date of breach, or five years from the appointed day. This means that breaches before 28 November 1989 will prescribe on expiry of 20 years from the date of the breach. Breaches after 28 November 1989 will prescribe five years after the appointed day on 27 November 2009. This provision will also apply to those negative servitudes converted into real burdens by s 80 of the 2003 Act. Prior to the appointed day, negative servitudes were subject to long negative prescription running from the date of the first act inconsistent with the servitude.

18.60   *Confusio*

Confusio arises where both burdened and benefited properties (or, for personal real burdens, ownership of the burdened property and the right to enforce the burden) come into the ownership of the same person holding in the same capacity. In such cases the title condition cannot be enforced by that owner against him or herself. However, the effect of *confusio* differs for servitudes and real burdens.

18.61 REAL BURDENS

Under s 19 of the Title Conditions (Scotland) Act 2003 real burdens are not extinguished by reason only of *confusio*. Where there are no subordinate real rights in, or occupiers other than the owners of, either benefited or burdened property the burden remains on the register and if either property is (or both are) sold on, the burden will be enforceable between benefited and burdened owners. Where there are subordinate real rights or occupiers, the burdens can be enforced by those holding possessory real rights (such as tenants) in the benefited property against the owner, as owner of the burdened property: s 8 of the 2003 Act. Or – where the burden is a negative burden – it can be enforced by the owner of the benefited property (or holder of a personal burden) against tenants or other occupiers of the burdened property: s 9 of the 2003 Act.

18.62 SERVITUDES

For servitudes, title to enforce arises solely from ownership of the benefited property. Where both benefited and burdened property come into ownership of the same person in the same capacity, the servitude is extinguished. However, if the properties then come into separate ownership the servitude is probably revived: see the discussion by Sheriff Cusine and Professor Paisley *Servitudes and Rights of Way* (1998), at paras 17.22 to 17.25; and Professor Gordon *Scottish Land Law* (2nd edn, 1999) paras 24-96 to 24-98 for full details.

Mr O'Brien suggested that *confusio* would not operate to extinguish a servitude where the burdened property was tenanted: 'The Extinction of Servitudes through *Confusio*' 1995 SLT (News) 228. However, the better view is that the servitude is extinguished and any residual entitlement held by the tenant to 'enforce' the servitude arises as a pertinent of the lease. See further Cusine and Paisley *Servitudes and Rights of Way*, para 17.30, and Gordon *Scottish Land Law*, para 24-98.

18.63 CHANGES TO PRE-FEUDAL ABOLITION POSITION

Prior to 28 November 2004 the effect of *confusio* on real burdens is not clear. Professor Gordon suggests that the burden is suspended, not extinguished: *Scottish Land Law*, para 23-18. This is probably the case and finds some support in *Botanic Gardens Picture House Ltd v Adamson* 1924 SC 549 at 564, per Lord President Clyde.

18.64   Compulsory purchase

The procedure on compulsory acquisition is briefly outlined at paras 29.16 to 29.20. Prior to the passage of the Title Conditions (Scotland) Act 2003, the effect of compulsory purchase on title conditions was unclear. The issue had never been subject to judicial decision, although there is a comprehensive discussion in an unreported decision of Mr Robin Edwards WS in the Lands Tribunal decision in *Wilson v Keeper of the Registers of Scotland* (29 July 1998, unreported). The position was debated in articles by I J Ghosh 'Statutory Conveyances: Examination of Title' (1990) 35 JLSS 236 at 238; and Professor McDonald 'Schedule Conveyances under the Lands Clauses Consolidation (Scotland) Act 1845' (1992) 37 JLSS 68. It was not clear if title conditions were extinguished, or their efficacy suspended pending a subsequent sale of the property. It was also uncertain if the effect was the same if the acquiring authority made use of a compulsory purchase order or an agreement had been entered into under threat of the use of a compulsory purchase order.

18.65   THE EFFECT OF COMPULSORY PURCHASE

The effect of compulsory purchase on title conditions is clarified by ss 106, 107, 109 and 110 of the Title Conditions (Scotland) Act 2003. These provisions came into force on 1 November 2003: the Title Conditions (Scotland) Act 2003 (Commencement No 1) Order 2003, SSI 2003/454.

Section 109 of the 2003 Act introduces new notification procedures into the Acquisition of Land (Authorisation Procedure) (Scotland) Act 1947 where an acquiring authority proposes to make a compulsory purchase order in relation to a burdened property. The detailed regulations on notification, incorporating the new procedures, are found in the Compulsory Purchase of Land (Scotland) Regulations 2003, SSI 2003/446. Similar amendment is made by s 110 to the equivalent provisions in the Forestry Act 1967. The acquiring authority is required to notify the benefited owners in title conditions and the holders of personal real burdens through delivery of notice, advertisement, or intimation through notice on a lamp post. The benefited owners or holders are then entitled to object to the proposed order and have a right to be heard.

Section 106 of the 2003 Act applies where a compulsory purchase order is made under the Acquisition of Land (Authorisation Procedure) (Scotland) Act 1947 or under the Forestry Act 1967. On registration of a conveyance (be it a general vesting declaration, a Schedule A conveyance under the Lands Clauses Consolidation (Scotland) Act 1845, a notice of title, or an ordinary disposition) following the order then all title conditions affecting the property will be extinguished. Failure to refer to s 106 in a notice of title or disposition will mean the title conditions survive. No such reference is required in general vesting declarations or Schedule A conveyances. The conveyance or compulsory purchase order can limit the full application of s 106, for example by only extinguishing some conditions, or only applying to part of the burdened property. See SSI 2003/446, Schedule, Form 6.

Section 107 of the 2003 Act applies where the burdened property is acquired by agreement where compulsory purchase powers could have been used. In such cases the disponee authority has to give notice to benefited owners of title conditions, or holders of personal real burdens by sending to those with right to enforce, advertising, or affixing notices to lamp posts. In giving notice the authority intimates that title conditions may be extinguished and the person with right to enforce can apply to the Lands Tribunal to preserve the title conditions by a specified date (which is at least 21 days after intimation). The Tribunal is to certify that no objections have been received (or have been received but withdrawn) before the notice can be registered. The provisions are similar to those applicable to Tribunal certification in relation to the 'sunset rule': see para 18.36. On registration the title conditions are extinguished (except in so far as otherwise specified in the conveyance or certificate).

18.66 The jurisdiction of the Lands Tribunal for Scotland

The Lands Tribunal for Scotland was established under the Lands Tribunal Act 1949. It has had jurisdiction to vary and discharge title conditions (originally referred to as 'land obligations') since the Conveyancing and Feudal Reform (Scotland) Act 1970. This jurisdiction is retained and expanded by Part 9 of the Title Conditions (Scotland) Act 2003. In the following paragraphs the provisions of the 1970 Act are not considered in detail, other than to note some substantial changes enacted by the 2003 Act, and to highlight some areas where case law pre-abolition will remain relevant after 28 November 2003. The restatement and expansion of the Lands Tribunal jurisdiction means that cases decided before 28 November 2004 may not be relevant in future applications. The restatement and expansion of the Lands Tribunal jurisdiction has led to the promulgation of new rules dealing with Tribunal applications. These are found in the Lands Tribunal for Scotland Rules 2003, SSI 2003/452. The Rules prescribe that applications under the 2003 Act require to be made in the appropriate form. Details are given below during the consideration of each application.

The provisions of the 1970 Act are considered in the sixth edition of this book at paras 17.18 to 17.35 and in fuller detail by Sir Crispin Agnew of Lochnaw in *Variation and Discharge of Land Obligations* (1999).

18.67 JURISDICTION OF THE LANDS TRIBUNAL

As was seen earlier in this chapter, the Lands Tribunal has various jurisdictions under the Title Conditions (Scotland) Act 2003 as well as the power to judicially vary or discharge burdens. The following list details the powers and where time limits and other elements are discussed elsewhere in the text reference is given. The Tribunal can:

(1) deal with applications to vary or discharge title conditions (or purported title conditions) in relation to a specific burdened property raised by anyone against whom the title condition is enforceable: s 90(1)(a)(i) of the 2003 Act;

(2) deal with applications to vary or discharge community burdens in relation to an entire community (or part of that community) if the application is made by owners of at least one quarter of the units in the community: s 91;

(3) determine the validity, enforceability and interpretation of real burdens (or purported real burdens) or rules of a development management scheme: s 90(1)(a)(ii);

(4) preserve (or vary) burdens which would be extinguished by registration of a notice of termination (under s 21: see paras 18.32 to 18.37) on application by an owner of the benefited property or holder of the personal real burden: s 90(1)(b)(i) and (2);

(5) preserve (or vary) burdens or a development management scheme which would be extinguished by registration of a conveyance of the burdened property where compulsory purchase powers could be used (under s 107: see para 18.65) on application by an owner of the benefited property or holder of the personal real burden: s 90(1)(b)(ii) and (2) or in the case of the development management scheme by the owners' association of the development: s 90(1)(e) of the 2003 Act;

(6) preserve a community burden that would be extinguished by registration of a deed of variation and discharge under ss 33 or 35 of the 2003 Act (see paras 18.20 to 18.25) on application of an owner within the community: s 90(1)(c); and

(7) preserve a development management scheme which would be extinguished by registration of a deed of disapplication under s 74 (see para 15.57 on application of an owner within the development): s 90(1)(d).

Aside from the power to vary and discharge title conditions, all other jurisdictions are new. Even in considering the power to vary and discharge title conditions, the Tribunal is now empowered to consider purported title conditions, and is therefore not prohibited from making a decision on a title condition that would be invalid (as it would have been under the 1970 Act).

18.68   APPLICATIONS FOR VARIATION AND DISCHARGE OF TITLE CONDITIONS

The following points briefly detail the procedure for applications under the Title Conditions (Scotland) Act 2003 to vary or discharge burdens. These also act as the general rules for the other powers. Variations for these will be noted below. Applications must be made using Form TC90(1)(a). See Lands Tribunal for Scotland Rules 2003, SSI 2003/452.

18.69   Who can apply?

An application for variation and discharge of a title condition (or purported title condition) can be made by any party against whom the condition can be enforced (or purportedly enforced). Thus for negative burdens or servitudes the application can be by a tenant or unregistered owner who uses the burdened property, as well as by the owner of the burdened property: s 90(1) of the Title Conditions (Scotland) Act 2003.

If the application relates to variation or discharge of a community burden (in relation to the whole community or a sizeable part of the community) then owners of at least one quarter of the units within the community must apply: s 91 of the 2003 Act.

18.70 When can the application be made?

If the title condition contains an express provision that no application is permitted within a period up to five years from creation of the condition, this provision will be effective: s 92 of the Title Conditions (Scotland) Act 2003. Otherwise the application to vary or discharge the burden can be made at any time.

18.71 What title conditions can be the subject of an application?

The jurisdiction of the Tribunal generally covers title conditions. The term is defined in s 122(1) of the Title Conditions (Scotland) Act 2003 and includes: real burdens; servitudes; affirmative conditions in servitudes; conditions in long leases (other than those relating to rent); conditions imposed in assignations of leases; conditions contained in conservation agreements entered into under s 7 of the National Trust for Scotland Order Confirmation Act 1938; and other conditions prescribed by the ministers. See para 14.2.

It excludes title conditions which impose obligations of the type specified in Schedule 11 to the 2003 Act: s 90(3). These include title conditions relating to the right to work minerals; title conditions enforceable by the Crown for defence purposes or by the Crown or public authorities for civil aviation purposes, or relating to land used as an aerodrome; or certain obligations created in leases of agricultural land or crofts. It is noteworthy that planning agreements entered into under s 75 of the Town and Country Planning (Scotland) Act 1997 are not subject to the Tribunal jurisdiction.

18.72 Intimation of the application

When the Tribunal receives the application it must notify the application to burdened owners (necessary if the applicant is a burdened co-owner, or holder of a lesser right in the burdened property), benefited owners, the holders of personal burdens, or other holders of title conditions: s 93 of the Title Conditions (Scotland) Act 2003. Other parties (such as others with title to enforce such as tenants or non-entitled spouses) may receive intimation of the application: s 93(3). Intimation is by sending the notice to the relevant parties by post, or electronic transmission (ss 93 and 124) unless there are difficulties in identifying or otherwise tracing the relevant parties, or parties would not have title to enforce. In such cases notice can be by advertisement or such other means as the Tribunal thinks fit (such as notification made on lamp posts in the area): s 93(2). This also applies where the Tribunal is concerned that the numbers of people requiring notification mean that the boundaries of the properties with title to enforce cannot readily be identified. This would be the case where there is a multiplicity of benefited properties, or implied rights of enforcement under ss 52 or 53 of the 2003 Act.

Such intimation is to summarise the application, to give the party receiving notification at least 21 days to make representations, and to indicate the fee to be charged for making representations. If the application relates to real burdens the intimation must indicate that an unopposed application can be granted automatically.

18.73   Who can make representations?

Representations can be made by benefited owners, holders of title conditions, or anyone against whom the condition is enforceable (including non-owners such as tenants or non-entitled spouses): s 95 of the Title Conditions (Scotland) Act 2003.

Representations are to be made initially in writing indicating the facts and contentions upon which the objector wishes to rely, and must be accompanied by payment of a fee: s 96 of the 2003 Act. The representations must generally be made within the time period specified in the notice of intimation, but the Tribunal can accept later representations.

18.74   Unopposed applications

If the application for variation and discharge relates to real burdens, s 97 of the Title Conditions (Scotland) Act 2003 applies. This provides that the application will be automatically granted if unopposed unless the application relates to facility or service burdens: s 97(1) and (2). Where the application is made to vary or discharge a community burden by owners of at least one quarter of properties in the community, under s 91 the application will not automatically be granted if it relates to retirement or sheltered housing: s 97(2)(c).

Applications are treated as being unopposed where no representations are received from either a benefited owner, or the holder of a personal real burden (or where representations have been received and withdrawn). Objections from those with mere possessory interests or subordinate real rights in the benefited property do not mean that the application is opposed: s 97(3).

An order by the Tribunal in an unopposed application cannot order payment of compensation, or require the imposition of a new title condition.

18.75   Opposed applications or applications where the Tribunal has to consider the merits

If representations are received from a benefited owner or the holder of a personal real burden, or if the application relates to facility or service burdens, or is in relation to an application to vary or discharge a community burden under s 91 of the Title Conditions (Scotland) Act 2003, the Tribunal will hold a hearing. The Tribunal can only grant the application for variation or discharge if it is satisfied having regard to certain factors that 'it is reasonable to grant the application': s 98 of the 2003 Act.

18.76   The factors the Tribunal is to consider

The factors to be considered in determining whether it is reasonable to grant the application are detailed in s 100 of the Title Conditions (Scotland) Act 2003. They are:

'(a) any change in circumstances since the title condition was created (including, without prejudice to that generality, any change in the character of the benefited property, of the burdened property or of the neighbourhood of the properties);
(b) the extent to which the condition–
 (i) confers benefit on the benefited property; or
 (ii) where there is no benefited property, confers benefit on the public;
(c) the extent to which the condition impedes enjoyment of the burdened property;
(d) if the condition is an obligation to do something, how
 (i)   practicable; or
 (ii) costly,
it is to comply with the condition;
(e) the time that has elapsed since the condition was created;
(f) the purpose of the title condition;
(g) whether in relation to the burdened property there is the consent, or deemed consent, of a planning authority, or the consent of some other regulatory authority, for a use which the condition prevents;
(h) whether the owner of the burdened property is willing to pay compensation;
(i) if the application is under section 90(1)(b)(ii) of this Act, the purpose for which the land is being acquired by the person proposing to register the conveyance; and
(j) any other factor which the Lands Tribunal consider to be material.'

The factors are discussed in detail in *Report on Real Burdens* (Scot Law Com No 181, 2000, paras 6.70 to 6.84. The Tribunal is to balance consideration of the factors in reaching the decision whether variation or discharge is reasonable.

The first factor, change of circumstances, is intended to mirror s 1(3)(a) of the Conveyancing and Feudal Reform (Scotland) Act 1970. There was a sizeable case law on this provision, which is discussed in W M Gordon *Scottish Land Law* (2nd edn, 1999), paras 25-14 to 25-21, and Sir Crispin Agnew of Lochnaw *Variation and*

Discharge of Land Obligations (1999), paras 6-02 to 6-11. The Tribunal can look to see if the burden operates in the manner in which it was originally intended, and determine if the change of circumstances has rendered it obsolete, or it is serving no useful purpose. A typical case under this head would be a restriction limiting the use of a building in a town centre to a dwellinghouse only, where, with the passage of time, surrounding properties generally have been converted to commercial uses as offices and shops.

The second factor, extent of benefit to the benefited property or (if a personal real burden) the benefit to the public, is intended to deal with title conditions where it is not a change of circumstances that has rendered it unnecessary, but where the condition has been an unnecessary clog on title since creation.

The third factor, impeding enjoyment of the burdened property, is intended to mirror s 1(3)(c) of the 1970 Act and to act as a balance to consideration of benefit in the second factor. Through mirroring s 1(3)(c), some of the previous case law gathered in Gordon *Scottish Land Law*, paras 25-23 to 25-26 and Agnew *Variation and Discharge of Land Obligations*, paras 6-18 to 6-28 will be of interest. However, the provision differs from s 1(3)(c) of the 1970 Act, in that the burdened owner (or applicant) will no longer need to show that the burden impedes a reasonable use of the burdened property. While the use proposed by the burdened owner will remain relevant it is not necessary that the applicant requires to show that the use proposed is reasonable. The *Report on Real Burdens* (Scot Law Com No 181, 2000), para 6.76, notes that:

> 'The central issue is the reasonableness of the condition rather than of the use. Whether a proposed use is reasonable or unreasonable seems unimportant. In general, an owner can use his property as he wishes, provided that no harm is done to anyone else. If he chooses to act selfishly, or foolishly, it is perhaps not for the Lands Tribunal to stop him.'

The fourth factor, the cost and practicability of compliance of affirmative burdens or other positive obligations, is intended to deal with cases where affirmative burdens become inappropriate. If a burdened property is derelict, or has been destroyed, the cost of compliance may be disproportionate.

The fifth factor, the age of the condition, suggests that older conditions will be treated less favourably than conditions more recently imposed. This accords with current practice under the 1970 Act: Sir Crispin Agnew of Lochnaw *Variation and Discharge of Land Obligations*, paras 5-11 to 5-13.

The sixth factor, the purpose of the condition, was not recommended by the Scottish Law Commission. It is not explained in the explanatory notes to the 2003 Act why the provision was introduced.

The seventh factor allows the Tribunal to consider whether planning permission has been granted or is deemed to be granted under the Town and Country Planning (General Permitted Development) (Scotland) Order 1992, SI 1992/223 (as amended). Under the 1970 Act the Tribunal considers whether planning permission has been granted in reaching its decisions and this can be influential (see, for example, *Cameron v Stirling* 1988 SLT (Lands Tr) 18) but not decisive: *Bachoo v George Wimpey & Co* 1977 SLT (Lands Tr) 2.

The eighth factor, whether the burdened owner is willing to pay compensation, was not recommended by the Scottish Law Commission (see *Report on Real Burdens* (Scot Law Com No 181, 2000), para 6.90), but is relevant to the remedies that can be granted by the Tribunal. On compensation, see para 18.78.

18.77   Decision of the Tribunal

If satisfied that the application is reasonable the Tribunal can order the variation or discharge of the burden. The Tribunal can also make ancillary orders including (1) requiring the burdened owner to pay the benefited owner compensation: s 90(6) and (7); and (2) the imposition of a new burden on the burdened property.

If not satisfied that the application is reasonable the Tribunal will not so order.

18.78   Compensation

The grant of compensation will be unusual. However, if the Tribunal decides that compensation is to be awarded to the benefited owner, this can be done on the basis of one of the two heads set out in s 90(7) of the Title Conditions (Scotland) Act 2003, provided that the burdened owner consents: s 90(9) of the 2003 Act. If the burdened owner does not agree, the Tribunal may decide not to grant the discharge.

The grounds set out in s 90(7) repeat those in s 1(4) of the Conveyancing and Feudal Reform (Scotland) Act 1970.

Head (1) provides that compensation can be paid to compensate the benefited owner, or holder of a personal real burden, for any substantial loss or disadvantage suffered as a result of discharge of the title condition. The loss must be substantial. The Tribunal does not grant compensation for the loss of possible payments for minutes of waiver (*Harris v Douglass, Erskine v Douglass* 1993 SLT (Lands Tr) 56) or for loss of the right to control a development (*United Auctions (Scotland) Ltd v British Railways Board* 1991 SLT (Lands Tr) 71). The case law is discussed in Gordon *Scottish Land Law*, paras 25-32 to 25-35, and Agnew *Variation and Discharge of Land Obligations*, paras 7-06 to 7-21.

Head (2) provides that compensation can be paid to compensate 'for any effect which the title condition produced, at the time when it was created, in reducing the consideration then paid or made payable for the burdened property': s 90(7)(ii) of the 2003 Act. The precursor of this provision formed the basis of the compensation provisions for development value burdens under the Abolition of Feudal Tenure etc (Scotland) Act 2000, and the case law in relation to this head is discussed at para 19.95.

It should be noted that despite a human rights based challenge to the compensation provisions, it has been held that the provisions are compliant with the European Convention on Human Rights. See *Strathclyde Joint Police Board v The Elderslie Estates Ltd* 2002 SLT (Lands Tr) 2, discussed in K G C Reid and G L Gretton

Conveyancing 2001 (2002), pp 35 to 36, and A Steven 'The Progress of Article 1, Protocol 1 in Scotland' (2002) 6 Edin LR 396.

18.79   Imposition of a new condition to replace the discharged provision

Section 90(8) of the Title Conditions (Scotland) Act 2003 provides that an order varying or discharging a title condition can impose a new condition to replace the discharged provision. However, this is only possible with the consent of the burdened owner: s 90(11) of the 2003 Act. This provision replicates that in s 1(5) of the Conveyancing and Feudal Reform (Scotland) Act 1970. The case law on that provision is discussed in Gordon *Scottish Land Law*, paras 25-27 to 25-29, and Agnew *Variation and Discharge of Land Obligations*, paras 8-04 to 8-06.

18.80   Registration of the Tribunal order

The order of the Tribunal can be registered: s 104 of the Title Conditions (Scotland) Act 2003. Registration will typically take place only if the title condition is to be varied or discharged, and it is only on registration that the condition will be varied or discharged.

18.81   APPLICATIONS TO PRESERVE REAL BURDENS SUBJECT TO A PROPOSED NOTICE OF TERMINATION

For applications in connection with paras 18.81 to 18.84, see the Lands Tribunal for Scotland Rules 2003, SSI 2003/452. The position is as generally stated in paras 18.69 to 18.80 subject to the following variations.

(1) *Who can apply?* Applications to preserve the burden can only be made by the owner of a benefited property. Owners include unregistered owners: s 90(1)(b)(i) and s 123 of the Title Conditions (Scotland) Act 2003.

(2) *When can the application be made?* Applications have to be made before the renewal date specified in the notice of termination (see s 20(4)(d) of the 2003 Act and paras 18.34 and 18.35), although late applications are permitted with the consent of the terminator: s 90(4) of the 2003 Act.

(3) *Intimation of the application.* Intimation must be made to the terminator and burdened owners: s 93(1)(b) of the 2003 Act.

(4) *Unopposed applications.* Unopposed applications for renewal of the burden will be granted automatically: s 97(1)(b) of the 2003 Act, other than for applications regarding facility or service burdens. An application is unopposed if there are no representations from the terminator. The Tribunal may order the terminator to pay the expenses of the party opposing the application: s 97(4).

(5) *Decision of the Tribunal.* If the Tribunal refuses the application to renew the burden this will mean that the notice of termination can be registered. The Tribunal may decide to refuse the application subject to an ancillary order requiring the

terminator to compensate the benefited owner, or to impose a new burden in substitution for the burden to be extinguished by the notice of termination.

18.82 APPLICATIONS TO RENEW BURDENS THAT WOULD BE EXTINGUISHED WITH REGISTRATION OF A CONVEYANCE GRANTED UNDER S 107 OF THE 2003 ACT

The position is as generally stated in paras 18.69 to 18.80 subject to the following variations.

(1) *Who can apply?* Application is to be made by an owner of the benefited property.
(2) *When can the application be made?* The application is to be made before the specified date under s 107(6)(d)(ii) of the Title Conditions (Scotland) Act 2003.
(3) *Intimation of the application.* Intimation is to be given to the burdened owners, and the person proposing to register the conveyance under s 107: s 93(1)(b) of the 2003 Act.
(4) *Who can make representations?* Representations can be made by the burdened owners, other persons against whom the burdens are enforceable, and the person proposing to register the conveyance under s 107: s 95 of the 2003 Act.
(5) *Unopposed applications.* Where an application is unopposed the application (other than applications relating to facility and service burdens) will be granted automatically, and the burden renewed: s 97(1) of the 2003 Act. Applications are unopposed where no representations are received from the person proposing to register the conveyance: s 97(3)(b) of the 2003 Act. The Tribunal may order the person proposing to register the conveyance to pay the expenses of the applicant: s 97(4).
(6) *Decision of the Tribunal.* If the Tribunal refuses the application the conveyance under s 107 can be registered. The Tribunal may decide to refuse the application subject to an ancillary order requiring the person proposing to register the conveyance to compensate the benefited owner, or to impose a new burden in substitution for the burden to be extinguished by registration of the conveyance under s 107.

18.83 APPLICATIONS TO PRESERVE COMMUNITY BURDENS SUBJECT TO A PROPOSED VARIATION OR DISCHARGE UNDER SS 33 OR 35 OF THE 2003 ACT

Again, the position is as generally stated in paras 18.69 to 18.80, subject to the following variations.

(1) *Who can apply?* In the case of a deed of variation or discharge granted by the majority of owners in a community under s 33 of the Title Conditions (Scotland)

Act 2003 the application may be made by any owner who has not granted the deed: s 34(3) of the 2003 Act. For deeds of variation or discharge granted by those owners within four metres of the burdened property under s 35 of the 2003 Act, the application may be made by any owner in the community who has not granted the deed: s 37(1) of the 2003 Act.

(2) *When can the application be made?* The application is to be made within eight weeks of the non-signatories receiving intimation of the proposal to register the deed of variation and discharge: ss 34 (3) and 37(1) of the 2003 Act.

(3) *Intimation of the application.* The application must be notified to the person proposing to register the deed of variation and discharge: s 93(1)(c) of the 2003 Act.

(4) *Unopposed applications.* Where there is an unopposed application to preserve a community burden, other than a facility or service burden, it will be granted automatically. The application is unopposed when no representations are made by the person proposing to register the deed of variation or discharge: s 97(3)(c) of the 2003 Act. In making the order the Tribunal can make an order requiring the person to proposing to register the deed of variation or discharge to pay expenses: s 97(4) of the 2003 Act.

(5) *Opposed applications or applications where the Tribunal has to consider the merits.* In considering an application to preserve the community burden the Tribunal is to determine whether it is in the best interests of the owners of all units in the community to grant the application, or if the applicant (or another benefited owner) would be unfairly prejudiced by the variation or discharge: s 98(b) of the 2003 Act. In considering this the Tribunal is to consider the factors detailed in s 100 of the 2003 Act.

(6) *Decision of the Tribunal.* If the Tribunal refuses the application to preserve the community burden the deed of variation or discharge granted under ss 33 or 35 of the 2003 Act can be registered. Again, the Tribunal may decide to refuse the application subject to an ancillary order requiring the person proposing to register the conveyance to compensate the benefited owner, or to impose a new burden in substitution for the burden to be varied or discharged: s 90(6) of the 2003 Act.

18.84   APPLICATIONS TO PRESERVE A DEVELOPMENT MANAGEMENT SCHEME

Again, the position is as generally stated in paras 18.69 to 18.80 subject to the following variations.

(1) *Who can apply and when?* In the case of applications to preserve a development management scheme where there is a proposal to register a deed of disapplication any owner within the community who has not agreed to the disapplication may apply within eight weeks of intimation of the intention to register the deed of disapplication: s 74(3) of the Title Conditions (Scotland) Act 2003.

In the case of applications to preserve a development management scheme that would be extinguished by registration of a conveyance under s 107 of the 2003 Act, the owners' association may apply to preserve the scheme: s 107(5).

(2) *Intimation of the application.* The application to preserve a development management scheme where there is a proposal to register a deed of disapplication must be intimated to the owners' association: s 93(1)(d) of the 2003 Act. In the case of an application in relation to a conveyance granted under s 107 of the 2003 Act, notice must be given to the person proposing to register the conveyance: s 93(1)(e) of the 2003 Act.

(3) *Unopposed applications.* As the development management scheme creates rules administering a community (on which see paras 15.55 to 15.57) not real burdens, s 97 of the 2003 Act does not apply to allow automatic preservation of the scheme. Instead, s 99(1) provides that an unopposed application for preservation will be granted automatically. An application is unopposed where the party who receives intimation (be it the owners' association or the proposer) has not made representations: s 99(2) of the 2003 Act, although the Tribunal may provide that the owners' association has to pay expenses to the applicant: s 99(3).

(4) *Applications where the Tribunal has to consider the merits and factors to be considered.* In considering an application to preserve the scheme where there is a proposal to register a deed of disapplication the Tribunal is to determine whether it is in the best interests of the owners of all units in the development to grant the application, or if the applicant (or another owner in the development) would be unfairly prejudiced by the variation or discharge: s 99(4)(a) of the 2003 Act. This provision does not make reference to the factors set out in s 100 of the 2003 Act, and accordingly they do not apply. It is not clear what factors will be considered by the Tribunal.

In considering an application to preserve the scheme where there is a proposal to register a conveyance under s 107 of the 2003 Act the Tribunal will grant the application only if it is reasonable to do so having regard 'to the purpose for which the land is being acquired': s 99(4)(b) of the 2003 Act. Again the s 100 factors do not apply, and it is not clear what factors will be considered by the Tribunal.

(5) *Decision of the Tribunal.* If the Tribunal refuses the application to preserve the scheme the scheme will be disapplied on registration of the deed of disapplication or conveyance: s 90(1) of the 2003 Act.

Chapter 19

Title Conditions: Feudal Real Burdens

19.1 Introduction

Real burdens became an established part of conveyancing practice following *Tailors of Aberdeen v Coutts* (1840) 1 Robin 296. Although that case itself involved burdens created in an ordinary disposition, many have assumed that real burdens are feudal in nature. This is a misconception. Since *Tailors of Aberdeen*, burdens have been created in conveyances of property. Such conveyances can involve the transferor either feuing the land to the transferee using a feu charter (a process known as subinfeudation: see para 15.1 of the sixth edition of this book) or disponing the land using a disposition (a process known as substitution – discussed in para 29.1 of the sixth edition of this book). If the burdens are created using a feu charter they may be referred to as feudal real burdens. If created using a disposition they may be referred to as non-feudal real burdens. In previous chapters non-feudal real burdens have been considered. The general position stated there is equally applicable to feudal real burdens. However, there are some variations considered in this chapter. For more detail the reader is referred to Chapter 17 of the sixth edition of this book. The mechanisms whereby the feudal superior can preserve his or her right to enforce a feudal real burden after the appointed day for feudal abolition are then considered.

19.2 Enforcement of feudal real burdens prior to 28 November 2004

The feudal system of land tenure is abolished on 28 November 2004 when the Abolition of Feudal Tenure etc (Scotland) Act 2000 comes fully into force (see Chapter 6). Prior to that date the feudal superior as benefited owner can enforce feudal real burdens against the vassal. In order to do so as is the case with any benefited owner the superior must demonstrate (1) title; and (2) interest, to enforce the burden.

19.3   TITLE TO ENFORCE

As between superior and vassal, title to enforce causes no problem. The superior's title to enforce feudal real burdens (and other feuing conditions) forms part of the *dominium directum*. As stated by Lord Dunedin in *Nicholson v Glasgow Asylum for the Blind* 1911 SC 391 at 399:

'The title of the superior to enforce a restriction contained in a vassal's title is always to be found in that title, because it begins as a contract between the original superior and the vassal and continues as between succeeding superiors and succeeding vassals by virtue of the tenure which, in the case of each succeeding vassal, binds him by the contract'.

Again, as between superior and vassal, the general rule is that:

(1) conditions in a feu charter are a private matter between the superior and the vassal for the time being. No one can compel the superior to insist on feuing conditions in a question with his own vassal, if the superior himself does not so choose; and

(2) no one other than the superior can so enforce feuing conditions.

19.4   INTEREST TO ENFORCE

As explained in Chapter 17, title to enforce real burdens is an essential pre-requisite; but this alone is not enough. In addition, the benefited owner must have an interest to enforce the real burden. Here, there is a significant difference between the position of the superior and other benefited owners.

The superior's interest to enforce is presumed; and the onus lies on the burdened owner to prove (if he or she can) that the legitimate interest (which presumably the superior originally had to enforce the charter conditions) now no longer exists. See *Earl of Zetland v Hislop* (1882) 9 R (HL) 40.

19.5   Nature of superior's interest

The nature of the superior's interest is not defined; but some cases suggest that his interest need not be patrimonial, involving financial loss. For example, in *Menzies v Caledonian Canal Commissioners* (1900) 2 F 953 the superiors sought to enforce a burden prohibiting the sale of alcohol. Their motivation was said to arise on public safety grounds. They wished to restrict the sale of alcohol to workmen constructing a nearby canal, owned by a third party. Reliance on the public safety argument to support the superiors' interest to enforce meant that interest was not patrimonial (in the sense of affecting property owned by the superior), but was justified on other grounds.

In the sixth edition of this book it was argued that the interest need not be patrimonial, but may be merely financial (see para 17.7). This view is disputed by some other writers. Professor Reid, in *The Law of Property in Scotland* (1996), para 408, supports the view of the Lord Ordinary (Kincairney) in *Menzies* and argues that:

'a superior will always have a personal interest to enforce at least in the sense that the vassal may be willing to pay for a minute of waiver, and consequently a rule admitting personal interest collapses into a rule that interest to enforce is always and under all circumstances conclusively present'.

19.6 Bare superiority

While interest to enforce is presumed it is not clear if the vassal can challenge it if the superior has only a bare superiority and does not own the *dominium utile* of heritable property in the vicinity of the burdened property. The Scottish Law Commission suggests that the superior may not: see *Report on Abolition of the Feudal System* (Scot Law Com No 168, 1999), para 4.26. The judgments of the Lord Chancellor in *Earl of Zetland v Hislop* (1882) 9 R (HL) 40 and the Lord Ordinary in *Menzies v Caledonian Canal Commissioners* (1900) 2 F 953 tend to support this view. However, there is no direct authority, and in *Howard de Walden Estates Ltd v Bowmaker Ltd* 1965 SC 163 the holder of a bare superiority was held to have interest to enforce feudal burdens.

In the period before feudal abolition conveyancers cannot safely assume that a superior will not have both title and interest to enforce a feudal burden if the superior does not hold other property in the neighbourhood of the burdened property.

This will also have implications after feudal abolition because burdens to be preserved under the preservation schemes (see paras 19.30 to 19.87) are only preserved if on the day immediately preceding the appointed day the burden was enforceable. If the superior owning a bare superiority does not have interest to enforce then it may not be possible for such superiors to preserve the burdens or rights to claim compensation.

19.7 The law of variation and discharge of feudal real burdens prior to 28 November 2004

Feudal burdens can be discharged or varied by:

(1) the express consent of the benefited proprietor;
(2) implied consent or otherwise by implication;
(3) negative prescription;
(4) consolidation of the feu; or
(5) judicial intervention.

The general principles stated in Chapter 18 are equally applicable to feudal superiors, with some variations.

19.8   EXPRESS CONSENT

There are three possible forms of express consent by a feudal superior. The superior may grant (1) a charter of *novodamus*; (2) a minute of waiver; or (3) an informal letter of consent. However, the express consent of the superior using any mechanism will have no effect on the independent right of enforcement held by any co-feuars with third-party enforcement rights.

19.9   Charter of *novodamus*

Where the superior agrees to the vassal's request for an alteration in the real burdens, or to an alteration in the feuduty, the appropriate feudal process is for the vassal to surrender his feu into the hands of the superior. The *dominium utile* having then merged with the *dominium directum*, all existing feuing conditions are extinguished. Technically, as a preliminary to the granting of a *novodamus*, the superior should be reinvested; but by statute this is made unnecessary: Conveyancing Amendment (Scotland) Act 1887, s 3. The superior is then in a position to make a new grant of the original feu to the vassal, on new conditions. This new grant differs from an original feu charter in that it represents the renewal of an existing investiture. The writ is therefore called a charter of *novodamus*.

Charters of *novodamus* are relatively uncommon at the time of writing. They are typically used where superior and vassal have agreed that new feudal real burdens are to be imposed when the burdens are waived or varied as this is the only competent method of imposing new feudal real burdens.

As a feudal deed, the charter of *novodamus* will cease to be effective with feudal abolition from 28 November 2004 and may not be used to vary or discharge burdens after that date.

19.10   Minute of waiver

The charter of *novodamus*, although the correct and recommended method for varying feudal real burdens, is elaborate and expensive. In practice, where no new or varied condition is to be imposed but where the parties have simply agreed that the superior will not insist on a particular feudal burden, it is common to incorporate such a variation in a minute of waiver. This is shorter and cheaper than a charter of *novodamus*, but cannot be used to impose new feudal real burdens. Minutes of waiver granted by feudal superiors are similar to those granted by other benefited owners and are discussed in paras 18.4 to 18.18.

19.11 Informal letter of consent

Sometimes, rather than pay the cost of a minute of waiver, a vassal may seek a less formal option. The vassal seeks an informal letter of consent from the superior, assenting to a proposed contravention of the burden, or waiving the burden. The superior will typically require payment, but as no formal deed for registration is prepared the cost to the burdened owner is reduced. Informal letters of consent arise in two main situations.

(1) Occasionally burdens will be framed in such a way that an activity is prohibited unless with 'the consent of the superior'. In these cases an informal letter from the superior may be granted in order to comply with the terms of the burden.

(2) However, even if a feudal real burden is not framed in this way but a superior has title to enforce, a burdened owner wishing to contravene the terms of the burden may still approach the superior for informal consent. Rather than pay the cost of a minute of waiver, the vassal obtains a 'letter of comfort' from the superior which purports to waive the condition.

In neither case will the letter be registered. And as the letter is a personal correspondence from superior to vassal the letter, while binding on the superior who grants it, may not be enforceable against his or her singular successors.

Informal consents of both types are relevant when considering acquiescence and are discussed in this regard in paras 18.38 to 18.40 and 18.43.

19.12 VARIATION OR DISCHARGE BY IMPLICATION

As discussed in paras 18.38 to 18.42, a real burden may be varied or discharged (to the extent that it is contravened) by acquiescence. This is the implied consent of the benefited proprietor to a breach of a burden and can be evidenced by the failure of the benefited proprietor to object to an obvious contravention of the burden. Acquiescence and the problems that led to the introduction of s 16 of the 2003 Act apply equally to feudal real burdens.

However, feudal real burdens may be extinguished by implication in two other primary ways: (1) where there are multiple burdened properties and a change of circumstances in the neighbourhood means the burden ceases to be enforceable; or (2) where the superior would be in bad faith in enforcing the burden. In both cases the superior loses his interest to enforce the burden.

19.13 Loss of interest to enforce by change of circumstances

The superior will be unable to enforce the burden where, owing to change of circumstances in the neighbourhood, it can be shown that feudal real burdens have ceased to have any content or meaning. It is not enough that there have been one or two unchallenged contraventions (either through failure to enforce or by express consent of the superior). Instead the superior will lose all interest to enforce a feudal burden which is useless to him or to anyone else. This may occur where there has been a general abandonment of the whole plan of development owing to supervening circumstances. Where, for example, 'the superior had permitted a continuous and systematic departure from the conditions of feu' as in *Campbell v Clydesdale Banking Co* (1868) 6 M 943. Here, the feu contracts of plots on the north side of George Street, Glasgow, dating from 1825, provided for erection of houses not exceeding two full storeys. In 1866 Clydesdale Banking Company had bought the feu and were proceeding to erect a three-storey building for use as a bank. The superior sought to interdict them. The majority of the other feus on the street had either had another storey erected or the original buildings had been demolished and replaced with higher ones. It was held that the superior had lost interest to enforce. Lord Cowan noted at p 948 that:

'[H]ere the restriction has been departed from by most of the feuars in the compartment in which the defenders' building stands, so that by the tolerated acts of these feuars the condition is inapplicable to the present condition of the street. It is not the street which it was at the date of these feu contracts. It now contains many buildings much higher than the feu contracts permitted . . . [T]he superior has no personal or private interest in enforcing the condition . . .'.

However, the loss of interest to enforce on the part of the superior does not necessarily mean that where there are co-feuars' third-party rights of enforcement the co-feuars similarly lose their interest to enforce on account of the general change of circumstances in the neighbourhood. This is illustrated by *Mactaggart & Co v Roemmele* 1907 SC 1318, and is discussed at paras 18.46 and 18.47.

19.14   Loss of interest to enforce as a result of the superior's bad faith

A superior is presumed to have interest to enforce feudal burdens. However, it is sometimes suggested that if in withholding consent to a variation or discharge of a condition of tenure, it can be shown that the superior is acting *in mala fide* or oppressively, or capriciously, then the superior is treated as having lost interest to enforce and the burden will be extinguished. However, there has been no reported case where a burdened owner has successfully argued that a feudal superior has lost interest to enforce leading to extinction of the burden.

It has been argued that where the superior requests a substantial monetary consideration for expressly consenting to the variation of a feudal burden then the superior has demonstrated loss of interest to enforce. In *Eagle Lodge Ltd v Keir and Cawder Estates Ltd* 1964 SC 30 the superior withheld his consent to a variation in feudal burdens, except upon payment of £1,000. The vassal argued that, by suggesting a monetary consideration for a waiver, he had either demonstrated his lack of interest or put himself *in mala fide*; but the point was not decided. Similarly, in *Howard de*

Walden Estates Ltd v Bowmaker Ltd 1965 SC 163 the superior asked for a payment of £1,250 as consideration for his consent; the defender did not press the argument that in so doing he was *in mala fide*. In any event, Lord Guthrie noted: 'The fact that the superior demanded a sum of £1,250 in consideration of their consent ... does not indicate a change of circumstances showing a loss of interest'.

19.15 Grassum

The superior may propose to charge a *grassum* (ie a fixed sum) for a minute of waiver. Although this is unlikely to have an impact on the superior's interest to enforce the burden it may – if the burdened proprietor was to apply to the Lands Tribunal for Scotland to have the burden varied – be a factor in determining who should bear the expenses of the action. For example, in *Harris v Douglas* 1993 SLT (Lands Tr) 56 the superiors who lived in England proposed a *grassum* of at least £500 to waive a feudal burden. After the superiors raised an action of irritancy, the burdened vassal applied to the Tribunal to vary the burden. The Tribunal awarded expenses against the superiors, because their action 'was both vexatious and unreasonable being wholly designed to extract money payments'.

19.16 DISCHARGE OR VARIATION BY NEGATIVE PRESCRIPTION

The general position on negative prescription is dealt with in paras 18.57 and 18.59. Under the current law the relevant statutory provision is s 7 of the Prescription and Limitation (Scotland) Act 1973. Section 7 applies to feudal real burdens because a feudal real burden is enforceable *in personam* by the superior against only the vassal.

The consensus of modern academic opinion is that negative prescription does apply to feudal real burdens. This view is supported by Professor Reid *The Law of Property in Scotland* (1996), para 431; Professor Paisley *Land Law* (2000), para 9.24; and David Johnston *Prescription and Limitation* (1999), para 7.14. However, at para 22-82 of *Scottish Land Law* (2nd edn, 1999), Professor Gordon argues that 'in general, real conditions in a feudal grant are not subject to prescription'. He argues that a feudal real burden may be an obligation *res merae facultatis* or an attribute of the *dominium directum* and as such would be imprescriptible under Schedule 3 to the 1973 Act. The subject of *res merae facultatis* is not without uncertainty. However, David Johnston, in *Prescription and Limitation*, paras 3.07 to 3.17, illustrates that *res merae facultatis* applies where there is 'no right, no action and no defence but simply the free choice of the person who exercises it' (para 3.12). To put it another way, it is a power without a correlative duty. Given that there is a clearly constituted obligation on the vassal, the view expressed here is that the right to enforce feudal burdens is not a right *res merae facultatis* and that accordingly long negative prescription applies.

19.17   DISCHARGE OR VARIATION BY CONSOLIDATION

Where the *dominium utile* and *dominium directum* come into the ownership of the same person in the same capacity it is possible for the owner to take the formal step of consolidation of the feu. This has effect to extinguish the *dominium utile* through merger with the superiority title. The mechanics are discussed in detail at paras 29.42 to 29.48 of the sixth edition of this book. Any feudal real burdens created in the original feu charter will be extinguished as between superior and vassal. However, if third-party enforcement rights were created in favour of co-feuars under the original feu charter through application of the rules in *Hislop v MacRitchie's Trustees* (1881) 8 R (HL) 95 then the consolidation of the feu will not effect these. Consolidation will therefore extinguish the feudal real burden but will leave the non-feudal aspect of the burden untouched. See *Stevenson v Steel Co of Scotland Ltd* (1899) 1 F (HL) 91 at 93, per Lord Watson, and *Murray's Trustees v St Margaret's Convent Trustees* (1906) 8 F 1109 at 1117, per Lord Kinnear. A contrary approach is wrongly adopted in *Calder v Merchant Co of Edinburgh* (1886) 13 R 623. See further Professor McDonald 'The Enforcement of Title Conditions by Neighbouring Proprietors' in D J Cusine (ed) *A Scots Conveyancing Miscellany: Essays in Honour of J M Halliday* (1987), p 9 at p 21.

19.18   EXTINCTION BY IRRITANCY

Prior to 9 June 2000 it was permissible for a feudal superior to raise an action of irritancy if a feudal real burden was breached. The effect of irritancy was to extinguish the *dominium utile* through merger with the *dominium directum*. The remedy is discussed at para 6.27 and in the sixth edition of this book at paras 16.3 to 16.6. As with consolidation, irritancy of the feu extinguished feudal real burdens as between superior and vassal. It was not clear whether irritancy of the feu would extinguish co-feuars' third-party enforcement rights, although in principle it would seem that the approach in *Stevenson v Steel Co of Scotland Ltd* (1899) 1 F (HL) 91 should be adopted for irritancy as it is for consolidation. This is the view of Professor Reid in *The Law of Property in Scotland* (1996), para 432. Despite the abolition of irritancy by s 53 of the Abolition of Feudal Tenure etc (Scotland) Act 2000, consideration of the effect of irritancy on co-feuars' enforcement rights may still arise in practice in determining which individuals should be approached for consents or waivers of burdens.

19.19   VARIATION OR DISCHARGE BY JUDICIAL INTERVENTION

The jurisdiction of the Lands Tribunal for Scotland to vary or discharge 'land obligations' under s 1 of the Conveyancing and Feudal Reform (Scotland) Act 1970 applies to feudal as well as non-feudal real burdens. The current law is discussed in detail at paras 17.18 to 17.34 of the sixth edition of this book. If a burdened owner applies for variation of a feudal burden, superiors should note *Harris v Douglas* 1993 SLT (Lands Tr) 56, discussed at para 19.13. This indicates that superiors may have expenses of the Tribunal action awarded against them where they propose to charge an unreasonable amount for a minute of waiver.

The existing jurisdiction will be replaced by the scheme in Part 9 of the Title Conditions (Scotland) Act 2003. This is discussed in Chapter 18 at paras 18.66 to 18.84.

19.20 The Abolition of Feudal Tenure etc (Scotland) Act 2000

The remainder of this chapter considers the effect of the Abolition of Feudal Tenure etc (Scotland) Act 2000 on feudal real burdens, under the following headings:

(1) background to feudal real burdens (see paras 19.21 ff);
(2) the preservation of praedial real burdens (see paras 19.41 ff);
(3) the preservation of personal real burdens (see paras 19.74 ff);
(4) the preservation of the right to claim compensation: development value burdens (see paras 19.81 ff);
(5) the preservation of sporting rights (see para 19.98); and
(6) general observations on the preservation of burdens (see paras 19.99 ff).

19.21 Background to feudal real burdens

As discussed in Chapter 6, on 28 November 2004 the Abolition of Feudal Tenure etc (Scotland) Act 2000 will abolish the feudal system of land tenure. The removal of the feudal superstructure would – without special provision – extinguish all feudal burdens and indeed this is the effect of s 17 of the 2000 Act. This could lead to the loss of valuable rights of enforcement without compensation. This would cause problems under the European Convention on Human Rights, Protocol 1, Article 1. Additionally, some feudal real burdens serve a wider function and can be said to protect aspects of the public interest. Further, the effect of feudal abolition may be retrospectively to penalise superiors for conveyancing advice that turns out, as a result of the legislation, to be misguided.

For example, if a client wished to sub-divide a plot of ground, retaining part, the client may seek to preserve his amenity by imposing burdens restricting use of the property. Before feudal abolition this could be done by conveying the property by an ordinary disposition, imposing burdens therein; or alternatively the seller could convey the property by feu charter, imposing feudal burdens. An adviser for the seller could suggest either mechanism and may have preferred to recommend the latter given that a superior has presumed interest to enforce the feudal burdens. Without a mechanism to preserve the feudal burdens, though, abolition of the feudal system would extinguish the feudal burdens, leaving the seller unprotected, whereas if the seller had disponed the property the burdens would remain in place.

Given the potential inequities that might arise, it was decided to allow feudal superiors to preserve their rights to enforce some feudal burdens through converting the burdens to non-feudal burdens or rights to claim compensation.

The scheme for preservation has been considered by Professors Kenneth Reid and George Gretton in *Conveyancing 2000* (2001), pp 129 to 136, and by Stewart Brymer and Scott Wortley in 'Preparing Superiors for Feudal Abolition' at (2002) 60 Greens PLB 6 and (2002) 61 Greens PLB 1.

Conversion of burdens is also possible under ss 52 to 54 of the Title Conditions (Scotland) Act 2003 which provides for implied rights of enforcement to arise automatically in certain scenarios where burdens were created before the appointed day. The purpose of these sections is found in para 244 of the explanatory notes to the 2003 Act in that 'in many cases it will represent a transfer of rights of enforcement from the feudal superior to the owners of the related properties'. These sections are considered in more detail at paras 17.34 to 17.45.

19.22   THREE KEY DATES

The implementation of the Abolition of Feudal Tenure etc (Scotland) Act 2000 is based on three key dates: the date of royal assent; the 'preservation day' (an expression used by Brymer and Wortley, but not found in the 2000 Act); and the appointed day.

19.23   Royal assent

Royal assent was given on 9 June 2000. The immediate effects are discussed at para 6.27. In relation to feudal real burdens the primary effect was that s 53 of the Abolition of Feudal Tenure etc (Scotland) Act 2000 ended the remedy of irritancy for superiors.

19.24   The appointed day: 28 November 2004

The appointed day was fixed by Scottish Ministers by the Abolition of Feudal Tenure etc (Scotland) Act 2000 (Commencement No 2) (Appointed Day) Order 2003, SSI 2003/456 as 28 November 2004: see para 6.23. For superiors the primary effect is that with the loss of their superiority they will generally lose the right to enforce real burdens: s 17 of the 2000 Act. However, this is subject to the remainder of Part 4 of the 2000 Act (as amended by the Title Conditions (Scotland) Act 2003). This Part permits the preservation of certain feudal real burdens through their conversion to non-feudal real burdens, or by preserving a right to claim compensation. Where preservation requires some action of the superior in order to be effective, that action must take place in a period between the preservation day and the appointed day.

19.25 The preservation day: 1 November 2003

Some feudal real burdens are converted automatically on the appointed day into non-feudal burdens. But, generally the preservation and conversion of feudal real burdens will require some action by the superior through the registration of a notice prior to the appointed day, identifying the burdens to be preserved. This notice requires to be registered between the 'preservation day' of 1 November 2003 and the appointed day of 28 November 2004. The preservation day was the date on which the majority of Part 4 of the Abolition of Feudal Tenure etc (Scotland) Act 2000 came into force and was fixed by the Abolition of Feudal Tenure etc (Scotland) Act 2000 (Commencement No 1) Order 2003, SSI 2003/455.

19.26 THE APPROACHES TO PRESERVATION AND CONVERSION

Under Part 4 of the Abolition of Feudal Tenure etc (Scotland) Act 2000, read in conjunction with the Title Conditions (Scotland) Act 2003, there are two broad approaches to preservation of feudal burdens. Some feudal burdens will be preserved and converted automatically; others require the superior to take some action to preserve and convert the burden into either a non-feudal burden or a right to claim compensation.

19.27 AUTOMATIC PRESERVATION

Some burdens will be converted automatically on the appointed day. These include the feudal burdens preserved and converted by the granting of implied rights of enforcement to neighbours under ss 52 to 54 of the Title Conditions (Scotland) Act 2003: maritime burdens; and facility and service burdens. Preservation does not validate invalid burdens. The former provisions are considered at paras 17.34 to 17.45.

19.28 Facility and service burdens

Under s 56 of the Title Conditions (Scotland) Act 2003 it is provided that where facility or service burdens are created before the appointed day then those properties that benefit from the facility or service shall be benefited properties. This applies irrespective of whether the burdens were created originally in feus or dispositions of the burdened property. The effect of the provisions for feudal burdens can be illustrated by the following example.

There is a block of tenement flats feued by the superior subject to burdens providing that all flat owners are to maintain the roof, but with the superior reserving the right to vary the burdens, therefore precluding a common scheme under *Hislop v MacRitchie's Trustees* (1881) 8 R (HL) 95. As the roof is a facility that benefits the entire tenement, any burdens regulating its maintenance are caught by the facility burden provisions. Section 56 of the 2003 Act has the effect that when the feudal system is abolished the superior's right to enforce is effectively transferred to all of those who benefit from the facility, ie every flat owner.

Facility and service burdens are discussed more fully at para 15.7.

19.29   Maritime burdens

Maritime burdens are personal real burdens in favour of the Crown. They were created where the Crown feued the foreshore or seabed (defined to include the territorial sea adjacent to Scotland) imposing burdens. The burdens were imposed for the benefit of the public. On the appointed day the Crown's paramount superiority will be extinguished. However, under s 60 of the Abolition of Feudal Tenure etc (Scotland) Act 2000, the Crown will retain the right to enforce the burdens as a person. Like other personal real burdens, the Crown will be presumed to have interest to enforce in future. Maritime burdens cannot be assigned.

19.30   PRESERVATION BY ACTION OF THE SUPERIOR

The feudal burdens capable of reallotment will be preserved through the registration of a notice. On the appointed day the preserved feudal burden will be converted into a praedial real burden; a personal real burden; or a right to claim compensation. It is also necessary to consider certain anomalous rights that are sometimes analysed as burdens that can be preserved.

19.31   General observations

There is a separate statutory form for each preservation notice, but the forms for both personal and praedial real burdens share certain characteristics and requirements that must be satisfied in each case.

19.32   Notices for preservation: general

The statutory notices under Schedules 5 to 9 to the Abolition of Feudal Tenure etc (Scotland) Act 2000 share certain common features. In each notice:

(1) the burdened property must be identified;
(2) the real burdens and any counter-obligations require to be set out;

(3) the superior must set out his or her title to the superiority; and

(4) details as to service of the notice on the vassal must be provided.

In addition, some notices require the superior to swear or affirm before a notary public confirming the accuracy of the information contained within the notice.

19.33 *Identification of the burdened property*

The burdened property must be described. It is provided that the description has to be sufficient to identify the property on the Ordnance map (taking account of the fact that the Land Register now covers the whole of Scotland: the requirements for descriptions in the Land Register are discussed at para 8.26 ff). The notes for completion of the statutory forms provide that if the burdened property is in the Land Register then the burdened property should be identified by its title number. If the burdened property is not yet on the Land Register it should normally be identified by reference to a deed recorded in the General Register of Sasines. Although the notes do not indicate the appropriate form of wording, it would appear that following the usual principles for description by reference (see para 8.19 ff) would be sufficient.

The statutory rule that description must be sufficient to identify the property on the Ordnance map may not be satisfied by reference to a deed recorded in the Register of Sasines. As is discussed at para 8.15, for older titles the property may have been described using a general description. While the notes for completion of the form indicate reference to a recorded deed may be sufficient, these notes do not have statutory effect. In order to satisfy the statutory rule it may be necessary in such cases to obtain a plan of the burdened property, identifying it on the Ordnance map.

There is, though, one exception to the general statutory rule for notice. The Schedule 6 notice which deals with preservation of feudal burdens by agreement of vassal and superior under s 19 of the Abolition of Feudal Tenure etc (Scotland) Act 2000 does not require identification by reference to the Ordnance Map. Unlike the Schedule 5 to 5C and Schedule 7 to 9 notices, the Schedule 6 notice does not require to be registered in the property register to confirm its effectiveness.

19.34 *Setting out real burdens and counter-obligations*

When preparing the notice it is necessary to identify the burdens that are to be preserved. Some feudal burdens, though, were imposed subject to an obligation on the superior. An example is given by the Scottish Law Commission in its *Report on Abolition of the Feudal System* (Scot Law Com no 168, 1999) at para 4.92. '[T]he superior might undertake to maintain some facility in exchange for an obligation on the grantee to pay the cost'. Where the superior preserves a burden if there is an obligation that is its direct counterpart then that counter-obligation shall be preserved too.

In setting out the burdens and counter-obligations to be preserved it is necessary to identify the deeds in which the burdens are imposed, the burdens being identified by reference to the deed in which they were constituted, or by being set out in full.

19.35   Title to the superiority

The person attempting to register the notice must show that they are entitled to the superiority. This is done by referring to the title number if the superiority is in the Land Register. If, though, the person seeking to register the notice is not the registered proprietor of the superiority then he or she must list the mid-couples linking him or her to the last registered superior.

If the superiority is not registered in the Land Register but remains recorded in the General Register of Sasines then the superior will show his or her title by referring to the deed constituting his or her title. If the person seeking to register the notice is not infeft in the superiority then he or she must list the mid-couples linking him or her to the last recorded title to the superiority.

In certain cases the superior's title may not be on the property registers at all. For example, if the superior is a body corporate and has held the property since before the institution of the General Register of Sasines in 1617 then the superior's title may have been properly constituted by an unrecorded charter that remains effective today. This would be the case for some University titles in Scotland. If this is the case then the superior must give details of their title to the superiority.

19.36   Service of the notice

Although the effect of the notices is to preserve existing burdens, the Scottish Law Commission took the view that each notice required to be served on the burdened owner: *Report on the Abolition of Feudal Tenure* (Scot Law Com No 168, 1999), para 4.66. This view was accepted on passage of the Abolition of Feudal Tenure etc (Scotland) Act 2000. Section 41 regulates service. It provides that the superior shall post a copy of the notice (and relevant explanatory note) to the vassal. The letter to the vassal shall be addressed to 'The Proprietor' and posted to the burdened property if the name of the vassal is unknown. It is not provided that postage of the notice must be by recorded or registered delivery, and ordinary post is therefore effective. Indeed, it was identified as being sufficient by the Commission in its report, at para 4.66. The use of ordinary post will have particular utility if the vassal lives overseas. While not strictly necessary it is suggested that recorded or registered delivery should be used if the vassal lives within the UK. This will allow the superior to retain proof of posting.

Service is a prerequisite for registration. Every notice requires a statement by the superior on service. This statement either notes that the notice was posted (and will specify if posted by recorded delivery, registered delivery, or ordinary post); or will state that posting was not reasonably practicable, and will give reasons for this. For example, there may be cases where it is difficult to identify the owner of the burdened property, or the vassal may have owned the property for some time, letting the property, and the contact address for the vassal may not be readily accessible.

Although service is a prerequisite for registration under s 43 of the 2000 Act, the Keeper is under no obligation to determine whether or not the notice has been served and is only required to consider that the notice is on its face valid. Despite this, the Keeper is given discretion to refuse to register deeds under s 4(1) of the Land Registration (Scotland) Act 1979. A more restricted discretion is also applicable for deeds recorded in the Register of Sasines: *Macdonald v Keeper of the General Register of Sasines* 1914 SC 854 (see Chapter 11). On the basis it would be possible for the Keeper to reject a notice if dissatisfied as to the statement on service in the notice.

The sanction for failure to serve the notice as required then will not necessarily be that registration cannot take place. However, under s 44 of the 2000 Act a dispute regarding a notice may be referred to the Lands Tribunal at any time before or after the appointed day. This is discussed at para 19.103 below.

19.37 *Swearing or affirming*

Not every notice requires the superior to swear an oath or make an affirmation before a notary public. The notices under s 18 of and Schedule 5 to the Abolition of Feudal Tenure etc (Scotland) Act 2000 for reallotment of burdens, s 18A and Schedule 5A for reallotment of personal pre-emption and personal redemption burdens, and s 33 and Schedule 9 for development value real burdens all require the superior to swear or to affirm. However, the notices which involve a public interest element do not require the superior to swear or to affirm as to the validity of the contents of the notice: see s 18B and Schedule 5B for economic development burdens; s 18C and Schedule 5C for health care burdens; s 27 and Schedule 8 for conservation burdens; and s 27A and Schedule 8A for nominating a conservation body. It is not clear why those burdens preserved for 'the public interest' are treated more leniently in this regard. No rationale is given for this different treatment in the explanatory notes to the 2000 Act. The Scottish Law Commission did not consider the introduction of economic development or health care burdens but noted that for conservation burdens the information was easily verifiable (Scot Law Com No 168, 1999, para 4.65) and did not require the added solemnity of an oath or affirmation. While this is the case for conservation burdens it is difficult to see how the same rationale applies to economic development burdens particularly where the notice requires evidence that the burden was to promote economic development.

The content of what must be affirmed is discussed in the context of each individual notice. Here, though, the general elements are considered. The superior is to swear or affirm before a notary public that the information contained within the notice is to the best of the superior's knowledge and belief is true. This assertion covers the various special elements of the notice including statements that cannot be readily verified by an external party simply examining the title of the burdened property.

If the superior is *incapax* through non-age or mental incapacity it is provided that a representative of the superior (for example, a guardian under the Adults with Incapacity (Scotland) Act 2000) can swear or affirm on the superior's behalf.

Where the superior is a juristic person such as a British company or other body corporate then clearly it is not possible for the superior to swear in person. In such circumstances any party authorised to sign documents on behalf of the juristic person (either by express authorisation – such as a designated authorised signatory – or by implication – such as a company director or company secretary) may sign on its behalf.

While the identity of notaries public is clear if the oath is administered within Scotland there may be problems if the superior is situated outwith Scotland. The statutory definition of notary public for Part IV of the 2000 Act (in s 49) makes provision for the swearing or affirming of the oath if administered furth of Scotland. The oath can be administered by a person duly authorised so to administer oaths in the relevant country. Thus, if the superior is situated in England, the oath can probably be administered by any solicitor (given that the Solicitors Act 1974, s 81, provides that solicitors are Commissioners for Oaths in England). However, the problem identified by Scott Styles in 'The Taking of Matrimonial Homes Deeds Furth of Scotland' at 1991 JLSS 444 in the context of matrimonial homes conveyancing may be equally applicable here.

If there are inaccuracies in the notice known to the party swearing or affirming he or she will be committing a criminal offence. The sanctions of the False Oaths (Scotland) Act 1933 are applicable.

19.38   Summary

Other general features regarding the notices and challenges to notices are considered at paras 19.99 to 19.104.

19.39   Notices for preservation: registration

The preparation of a notice requires the superior to identify the burdens that he or she wishes to preserve. However, in order to be preserved the burdens must be valid and enforceable. Occasionally, the burdens that are set out within the notice may not be valid. For example, a burden may fail to satisfy the rules of constitution set out in *Tailors of Aberdeen v Coutts* (1840) 1 Rob 296. It may impose an invalid monopoly (for example, requiring the vassal to use a property manager appointed by the superior), or be illegal (for example, a burden discriminating on sexual grounds – such as prohibiting the property from being occupied by men). Or alternatively, the burden may not be enforceable. It may have been extinguished by acquiescence or negative prescription prior to the appointed day. If the superior attempts to preserve a burden that is not valid and enforceable the burden will not be validated by registration of the notice in the Sasine or Land Register. The Keeper is under no obligation to determine the enforceability of burdens contained within the notices: s 43(3)(a) of the Abolition of Feudal Tenure etc (Scotland) Act 2000.

This is a particular issue in relation to development value burdens where many burdens intended to reserve to the superior an uplift in value if the property is used for alternative purposes in future are invalid and consequently incapable of conversion under the scheme.

19.40 Notices for preservation: mechanisms

Feudal real burdens may be preserved by conversion of the burden into either a praedial or a personal real burden. Conversion into personal real burdens is considered later in this chapter. The process of conversion into praedial real burdens is known as reallotment, and is considered now.

19.41 The preservation of praedial real burdens

The reallotment of feudal burdens involves the superior nominating property in the neighbourhood of the burdened property as the new benefited property. If successful, reallotment will effectively transfer the right of enforcement from the superiority to the nominated property on the appointed day, thereby converting the feudal burden into a non-feudal praedial burden. Reallotment can take one of three forms:

(1) unilateral reallotment (under s 18 of the Abolition of Feudal Tenure etc (Scotland) Act 2000);
(2) bilateral reallotment (under s 19 of the 2000 Act); or
(3) judicial reallotment (under s 20 of the 2000 Act).

These are considered in detail by Scott Wortley in 'Preserving Feudal Real Burdens as Praedial Real Burdens' in (2003) 71 *Scottish Law Gazette* 73. The following paragraphs draw on the analysis in that article.

19.42 UNILATERAL REALLOTMENT

This is governed by s 18 of the Abolition of Feudal Tenure etc (Scotland) Act 2000. It provides that the superior can unilaterally nominate property within the vicinity of the burdened property to become benefited property for the preserved burdens. Nomination is through the completion of a Schedule 5 notice. Aside from general information required for notices (details above at paras 19.32 to 19.37) it is also necessary for the superior to provide further information.

(1) The land nominated to be the benefited property must be described sufficiently to enable identification on the Ordnance map (the observations applicable to the description of the burdened property are equally applicable to the benefited property: see para 19.33).

(2) The superior must state which of the conditions specified in s 18(7) (and discussed below at paras 19.46 to 19.56) is applicable.

In swearing or affirming as to the accuracy of the contents of the notice the superior is confirming that the information regarding the satisfaction of the s 18(7) conditions is accurate.

19.43   Registration

After the notice is served on the vassal, and the superior has sworn or affirmed, it is registered. In accordance with the new general principle for registration of burdens the notice is to be registered against both the burdened property and the nominated benefited property: s 18(3) of the Abolition of Feudal Tenure etc (Scotland) Act 2000.

19.44   Restrictions: general

The superior cannot use unilateral reallotment to preserve every feudal burden. There are various restrictions imposed under s 18 of the Abolition of Feudal Tenure etc (Scotland) Act 2000. The validity and effectiveness of the notice is dependent on satisfaction of these conditions.

19.45   Restrictions: the nominated land must be owned by the superior

Under s 18(1) of the Abolition of Feudal Tenure etc (Scotland) Act 2000, whatever condition in s 18(7) is satisfied, it is necessary for the feudal superior to own the property nominated as the prospective benefited property. Mere ownership of both superiority and nominated property is not sufficient. Firstly, the superior is to own the nominated property in the same capacity as he or she owns the superiority. Secondly, the superior is to be the sole owner of the nominated property.

Thus, if A is the superior, then if the other s 18 conditions discussed below are satisfied A can nominate land he owns in the neighbourhood of the burdened property as the prospective benefited property. But, if A co-owns the neighbouring land with B then the neighbouring land cannot be nominated. Or if A owns the superiority as trustee for X, but owns the neighbouring land in his own name, then the neighbouring land cannot be nominated. Or if A co-owns the superiority but owns the neighbouring land in his own name, again the neighbouring land cannot be nominated.

19.46   Restrictions: the s 18(7) conditions

If the superior owns land in the neighbourhood of the burdened property, that in itself is not sufficient to allow the superior to register a notice. In addition the superior must comply with one of the three conditions set down in s 18(7) of the Abolition of Feudal Tenure etc (Scotland) Act 2000. These conditions are:

(1) the hundred-metre rule (discussed at paras 19.47 to 19.54);
(2) that the burden is of a designated type (ie a right of pre-emption or redemption or a burden allowing the superior to use the burdened property); or
(3) that the property nominated comprises a right to minerals or salmon fishings.

19.47 The hundred-metre rule

This applies to burdens that regulate the appearance and amenity of a property. It does not apply to those burdens for which there is a special public interest in their preservation (which can generally be preserved under the provisions preserving personal real burdens). It does not apply to those feudal burdens that are of their nature not amenity burdens (such as burdens allowing use or facility burdens) that are preserved under an alternative mechanism in the Abolition of Feudal Tenure etc (Scotland) Act 2000 or the Title Conditions (Scotland) Act 2003. Where a superior seeks to preserve feudal burdens it is this condition that will in most cases require to be satisfied.

19.48 Purpose

The condition is designed to preserve burdens that are truly for the benefit of neighbouring property rather than simply to preserve an income stream for the superior from minutes of waiver. There was some debate within the Scottish Parliament during the passage of the Abolition of Feudal Tenure etc (Scotland) Act 2000 and the Title Conditions (Scotland) Act 2003 as to whether the distance limitation should apply to every property, both rural and urban. In the end, it was decided that in the interests of certainty a general rule should apply across Scotland. However, those burdens that could not be preserved under s 18 of the 2000 Act may be capable of preservation under the schemes for bilateral reallotment under s 19 or judicial reallotment under s 20. The details of the parliamentary debates can be found in (2003) 71 *Scottish Law Gazette* 72 at 76, nn 26 and 28 and text.

19.49 Definition

The hundred-metre rule is found in s 18(7)(a) of the Abolition of Feudal Tenure etc (Scotland) Act 2000, which provides:

> 'that the land which ... would become the dominant tenement has on it a permanent building which is in use wholly or mainly as a place of human
> (i) habitation; or
> (ii) resort
> and that building is, at some point, within one hundred metres (measuring along a horizontal plane) of the land which would be the servient tenement'.

Within the 2000 Act the terms 'dominant' and 'servient tenement' are used where in the Title Conditions (Scotland) Act 2003 the terms 'benefited' and 'burdened property' are used.

The rule has four elements:

(1) that the prospective benefited property has on it a building;
(2) that the building is used wholly or mainly as a place of human habitation or resort;
(3) that the building is permanent; and
(4) that the building is within one hundred metres of the burdened property.

As the rule is not based on the nature of the burden, nor on the nature of the benefited property, to these four elements can be added a fifth: when is the hundred-metre rule to be satisfied?

The elements are considered in the following paragraphs.

19.50   There must be a building on the nominated benefited property

In order to avoid the perpetuation of the feudal system particularly in rural areas through a mere distance limitation the Scottish Law Commission in its *Report on Abolition of the Feudal System* (Scot Law Com No 168, 1999) at para 4.34 argued that some refinement was required. Given that burdens were to preserve amenity, the Commission took the view that open fields did not justify special treatment for protection. This view was endorsed by the Scottish Executive and Parliament. Accordingly, it is necessary that the nominated benefited property has erected upon it a building. But, not every building that will satisfy the condition.

19.51   The building must be for human habitation or resort

The only buildings that benefit from the condition are those that are for human habitation or resort. Therefore, buildings intended only for the use of animals such as barns, or used only for storage, such as grain stores, do not benefit. The expression is undefined, although generally it will be clear. It will apply to those places where people live or go to for recreational purposes. This approach is confirmed by the explanatory notes to the Abolition of Feudal Tenure etc (Scotland) Act 2000, para 79.

Accordingly, the superior will be able to nominate a benefited property upon which is situated a house or a hotel, a restaurant or pub, or a factory or leisure centre. The position is more uncertain where the building is less substantial, such as a conservatory or summerhouse. The Commission report appears to suggest that the size of the building does not matter provided the building is for human use. However, the further elements of the hundred-metre rule impose their own restrictions.

19.52   The building must be permanent

The building must be a permanent structure. Thus, a temporary construction, such as a marquee or circus tent, is insufficient. However, it is not clear what degree of permanence is required for structures. It is argued at (2003) 71 *Scottish Law Gazette* 73 at 77 that:

'it may be helpful to consider the test of permanence in the law of accession for buildings. If a construction on land is not of sufficient permanence to become a fixture under the law of accession it would seem ... to be unlikely the construction be sufficiently permanent under s 18(7)(a)'.

While the test under s 18 may be more liberal than the common law of accession, this would seem to be a useful guide.

It is also not clear what the position would be if a building was only partially built. No guidance can be found in the Commission report or the explanatory notes on this point. It may be difficult to argue that a burden is for the protection of the amenity of a partially constructed building, particularly when there has been a substantial lead in from the passage of the Abolition of Feudal Tenure etc (Scotland) Act 2000 in June 2000 to its final implementation on 28 November 2004.

19.53 The building must be within one hundred metres of the burdened property

It is not enough that the prospective benefited property is within one hundred metres of the burdened property. It is the building that has to be within one hundred metres of the burdened property, the distance being calculated by measuring along the horizontal plane. Therefore distance is measured as it would appear on a map rather than the physical distance between properties measured along the ground, taking account of gradients.

The one hundred-metre distance can run from any point of the building. Therefore a rural superior may have a large house extending for many metres, but as long as the house is at one point within one hundred metres of the burdened property then the condition is satisfied.

19.54 When is the condition to be satisfied?

The hundred-metre rule is transitional in some ways. It is not necessary that it be satisfied throughout the (potentially perpetual) existence of the burden.

It is not necessary for compliance as at the appointed day itself as the operative provision for conversion does not require it: s 18(6) of the Abolition of Feudal Tenure etc (Scotland) Act 2000. Thus, if the nominated benefited property has erected upon it at the time of registration of the notice a building for human habitation or resort and that building is subsequently destroyed prior to the appointed day, the validity of the notice will be unaffected. Section 18(6) will continue to apply.

There may be a lag between execution of the notice and registration and it is necessary to consider whether the condition should be satisfied at both times. The condition must be satisfied at the date of execution of the deed given that the superior must swear or affirm as to the accuracy of its contents. It has been stated by Professors Reid and Gretton that the condition must also be satisfied at the date of registration of the notice: see *Conveyancing 2000* (2001), p 131. This view is supported by the analysis of s 18(1) of the 2000 Act in (2003) 71 *Scottish Law Gazette* 73 at 78, and it appears that the hundred-metre rule must be satisfied at the date of both execution and registration.

19.55   The real burden is of a specified type allowing nomination of property within any distance of the burdened property

Section 18(7)(b) of the Abolition of Feudal Tenure etc (Scotland) Act 2000 provides a condition based on the type of burden. Burdens allowing use (other than sporting rights) or burdens creating rights of pre-emption or rights of redemption are capable of preservation without distance limitation between the nominated and burdened properties.

Where the burden to be preserved is a right of pre-emption then if effectively preserved from the appointed day it will be subject to the provisions of Part 8 of the Title Conditions (Scotland) Act 2003. As such, if the burden is preserved, then the owner of the nominated benefited property will have only one opportunity to exercise the pre-emption. The rules on this are discussed at paras 18.30 and 18.52 to 18.53.

Where the burden to be preserved is a burden allowing the benefited owner to use the burdened property (such as a burden allowing the superior to park his car on the burdened property) then, if effectively preserved from the appointed day, it will be subject to s 81 of the 2003 Act. This provides that burdens allowing use shall become positive servitudes on the appointed day.

The position for burdens allowing use can be contrasted with the position for positive servitudes created in a feu. When this occurs the servitude is not for the benefit of the superiority, but for the *dominium utile* of any retained land held by the superior: *Stewart v Steuart* (1877) 4 R 981. Thus, it is unnecessary to use the preservation notice for such servitudes. It is incompetent to create a servitude in favour of the superiority: see *Report on Abolition of the Feudal System* (Scot Law Com No 168, 1999), paras 6.18 to 6.21.

19.56   The type of property nominated as benefited property has a special characteristic

Section 18(7)(c) of the Abolition of Feudal Tenure etc (Scotland) Act 2000 deals with the situation where the feudal burden truly benefits the separate tenement of minerals or salmon fishings the *dominium utile* of which is held by the superior. For example, a superior may hold the right to the salmon fishings or own a *stratum* of minerals. In such cases the superior is entitled to nominate the separate tenement as the new benefited property.

19.57   The effect of unilateral reallotment

Where a Schedule 5 notice is registered against both nominated property and burdened property, s 18(6) of the Abolition of Feudal Tenure etc (Scotland) Act 2000 determines that provided the burden was still enforceable by the superior on the day preceding the appointed day, thereafter the nominated property becomes the benefited property, and the burdened property remains encumbered. The feudal burden is therefore converted into a non-feudal praedial burden, and as such burden is subject to the general principles applicable to real burdens under the Title Conditions (Scotland) Act 2003.

19.58   Failure or inability to use the s 18 reallotment procedure

Often the burden cannot be preserved through registering a Schedule 5 notice under s 18 of the Abolition of Feudal Tenure etc (Scotland) Act 2000. For example, there may be no building on the property the superior wishes to nominate, or the superior may not own property in the vicinity of the burdened property in the same capacity as he or she owns the superiority. In such cases the superior can attempt to negotiate with the vassal for preservation of the burden and attempt bilateral reallotment of the burden under s 19 of the 2000 Act. If negotiation fails the superior can then apply to the Lands Tribunal under s 20 of the 2000 Act to seek judicial reallotment of the burden.

19.59   BILATERAL REALLOTMENT

Section 19 of the Abolition of Feudal Tenure etc (Scotland) Act 2000 was not found in the original Scottish Law Commission draft Bill. It is a provision inserted into the 2000 Act by the Scottish Executive. It provides that before the appointed day the superior can serve a Schedule 6 notice on the vassal seeking to enter an agreement to preserve feudal burdens for the benefit of property owned by the superior in the vicinity of the burdened property. If the vassal is amenable for whatever reason (for example, a *grassum* is paid), such an agreement can be entered into and registered. If the burdens were enforceable immediately prior to the appointed day they will then be preserved.

The s 19 procedure was subject to criticism in (2003) 71 *Scottish Law Gazette* 73 at 78 to 80. It is there argued that the provision 'seems … to be of no utility', given that it allows the parties to enter an agreement which would broadly replicate in effect a free-standing deed of conditions (under s 32 of the Conveyancing (Scotland) Act 1874 when read with s 17 of the Land Registration (Scotland) Act 1979). However, whether such deeds are competent is a moot point: see para 15.37. It is further argued there that an attempt to enter a deed of conditions would occasionally offer more flexibility to the superior and is arguably sufficient to comply with the threshold requirements for a Tribunal application under s 20 of the 2000 Act.

The one important use for the s 19 procedure would be to permit the superior to continue to enforce burdens breached before the appointed day. This is due to the effect of s 17 of the 2000 Act, which permits the superior to continue to enforce burdens breached before the appointed day if the burden has been preserved under the

Part 4 procedures (including bilateral reallotment). This provision is discussed at para 19.106. However, it is difficult to see why a vassal would agree to the preservation of a burden that he or she has breached using the s 19 procedure.

19.60   Schedule 6 notice

The process of bilateral reallotment is initiated by the superior serving a Schedule 6 notice on the vassal accompanied by the relevant explanatory note. Unlike other notices, this does not require to be registered and it appears that there is no sanction for failure to serve on the vassal. However, evidence of its service will be of use when applying to the Lands Tribunal for judicial reallotment under s 20 of the Abolition of Feudal Tenure etc (Scotland) Act 2000: see para 19.63. This notice contains the same general information as the other notices, but like the Schedule 5 notice it identifies a prospective benefited property that must be owned by the superior in the same capacity in which he or she owns the superiority. The observations in para 19.45 are equally applicable here.

The Schedule 6 notice differs from others in that it does not does not require nominated or benefited properties to be identified in a manner sufficient to identify them on the Ordnance Map, although given that an agreement will follow the notice, best practice would be to do so.

The explanatory note accompanying the notice explains that if no agreement is reached then the superior may apply to the Lands Tribunal to preserve the feudal burden.

19.61   The s 19 agreement

If vassal and superior agree to the preservation of feudal burdens for the benefit of the nominated benefited property then they can enter an agreement broadly equivalent to a deed of conditions. The agreement must:

(1) identify the burdened and nominated benefited property. It is not stated that it is necessary to identify the property sufficiently to permit identification on the Ordnance Map, but s 4(2)(a) of the Land Registration (Scotland) Act 1979 will require such identification if the property is registered in the Land Register;

(2) set out the burdens and any counter-obligations (subject to any modifications agreed between the parties) in the manner required generally for notices: see para 19.34;

(3) set out the title of the superior to the superiority and the nominated property (detailing if the superior is uninfeft in relation to either property mid-couples linking him or her to the last registered owner); and

(4) state expressly that it is being entered into under s 19 of the Abolition of Feudal Tenure etc (Scotland) Act 2000.

It appears that a deed similar to a deed of conditions with appropriate amendment to contain the relevant statutory statements will suffice to comply with this provision.

The deed will be granted by the owner of the burdened property (the vassal) and the owner of the property nominated to be the benefited property (who is also the superior). Since it will be registered, the deed must be executed and witnessed in accordance with ss 2 and 3 of the Requirements of Writing (Scotland) Act 1995.

If either burdened or prospective benefited owner is uninfeft then – unlike the position for an ordinary deed of conditions – the agreement may contain a deduction of title clause linking the uninfeft owner to the last registered owner.

The agreement then requires to be registered against both the burdened property and the benefited property in accordance with the new principle of dual registration.

19.62   Effect of s 19 agreement

As with unilateral reallotment under s 18 of the Abolition of Feudal Tenure etc (Scotland) Act 2000, where a s 19 agreement is registered and the burden remains enforceable immediately before the appointed day, the nominated property becomes the benefited property, and the burdened property remains encumbered by the burden. The feudal burden is again converted into a non-feudal praedial burden, and as such is subject to the general principles applicable to real burdens under the Title Conditions (Scotland) Act 2003.

19.63   JUDICIAL REALLOTMENT

If the superior has been unable to reallot under s 18 of the Abolition of Feudal Tenure etc (Scotland) Act 2000, and has attempted – but failed – to have the burden reallotted by agreement under s 19, he or she can seek to have the feudal burden preserved through judicial reallotment. Under s 20 of the 2000 Act the superior can apply to the Lands Tribunal prior to the appointed day seeking an order to reallot the right to enforce the burden to an identified nominated benefited property.

In the application the superior is to detail his or her attempts to reach an agreement under s 19 of the 2000 Act. A copy of a Schedule 6 notice could be used to prove this.

The property nominated as the benefited property is – as for ss 18 and 19 – to be property owned by the superior in the same capacity in which he or she owns the superiority: see para 19.45 for comment.

The Tribunal, on receipt of the s 20 application, is, under s 21 of the 2000 Act, to give notice of the application to the owner of the burdened property or to such other persons as the Tribunal thinks fit (examples could be secured creditors or tenants with an interest in the burdened property). Such notice can be given through advertisement or in the manner prescribed by the Lands Tribunal for Scotland Rules 2003, SSI 2003/452, r 4.

19.64   Schedule 7 notice

When the superior applies to the Tribunal, he or she may within 42 days of applying (or such longer period as the Tribunal may permit) execute, serve and register a

Schedule 7 notice. While the words of the statute are permissive, the explanatory notes state (at para 95) that the superior is required so to do. It is suggested that the mandatory reading should apply here for two reasons.

Firstly, the purpose of the notice is to provide public notice to all interested parties (such as prospective purchasers or heritable creditors or tenants). Without registration of the notice someone may purchase property prior to the Tribunal decision and subsequently discover that burdens that appeared to be extinguished under the Abolition of Feudal Tenure etc (Scotland) Act 2000 had in fact survived. This would be an odd result.

Secondly, the order that may be made by the Tribunal under s 20(7) of the 2000 Act (if the decision is reached after the appointed day) may confirm that the position during the transitional period becomes permanent. The transitional position arises only on the registration of a Schedule 7 notice, suggesting that registration is a mandatory rather than discretionary element of the s 20 procedure.

The notice contains the usual general information (see paras 19.33 to 19.36) and must be served on the vassal. The vassal will therefore receive notification of the application from the Tribunal under s 21 of the 2000 Act and the superior through service of the Schedule 7 notice. The Schedule 7 notice will protect the superior's interest through disapplying the general rule for extinction of the feudal burden: see para 19.65. If the effect of the provision is permissive rather than mandatory this consequence acts as an incentive for registration.

The notice is to detail the superior's attempts to enter the agreement under s 19 of the 2000 Act. Like the Schedule 5 notice, the Schedule 7 notice is to include details of the property the superior nominates as the benefited property, and prior to registration of the notice the superior is to swear or affirm as to the accuracy of its contents. The oath or affirmation is primarily of importance in relation to the superior's statement of the attempt to enter the agreement. Details of the principles applicable to taking the oath or affirming are found at para 19.37.

19.65   Registration of the Schedule 7 notice

The notice is to be registered against both the burdened property and the property nominated as the benefited property within 42 days of the application to the Tribunal (or such longer period as the Tribunal may allow).

Under s 43(2)(d) and (3)(a) of the Abolition of Feudal Tenure etc (Scotland) Act 2000, the Keeper is under no obligation to determine:

(1) that the notice has been registered timeously;
(2) that the information provided in the notice regarding the superior's attempt under s 19 to reach an agreement with the vassal is correct; or
(3) whether the burden is enforceable on the day preceding the appointed day.

On registration, provided that the burden is enforceable, the notice takes effect to preserve and convert the feudal burden on a temporary basis. Section 20(5) of the 2000 Act provides that from the appointed day the nominated benefited property shall become the benefited property and the burdened property remain the burdened property for a transitional period.

The transitional period is defined in s 20(6) of the 2000 Act and runs from the appointed day until the Tribunal has reached a decision on the application for judicial reallotment and the order of the Tribunal has been registered. However, if the application has commenced but no order of the Tribunal has been registered (for example, because the Tribunal did not reach a decision on the merits of the case) then the transitional period runs until a prescribed date (referred to in the statute as the 'specified day').

19.66 Timing of registration

Although s 20(6) of the Abolition of Feudal Tenure etc (Scotland) Act 2000 provides for the temporary reallotment of the feudal burden from the appointed day, the legislation (as amended) appears to create a *lacuna*. An application to the Tribunal is to be made before the appointed day. Originally, a time period was to be prescribed for applications, but the qualification was repealed by Schedule 13, para 4(a) to the Title Conditions (Scotland) Act 2003. Thus, an application at any time before the appointed day will be effective. Under s 20(3) of the 2000 Act, which provides for registration of the Schedule 7 notice, registration must take place within 42 days of the application, or

'such longer period of days (being a period which ends before the appointed day) as the Lands Tribunal may allow if it is satisfied that there is good cause for so allowing'.

The parenthetical qualification does not appear as a qualification to the 42-day period but only the latter period, meaning that on a strict reading of s 20(3) of the 2000 Act the following scenario could arise.

A superior applies to the Tribunal for judicial reallotment on 26 November 2004. The superior registers the Schedule 7 notice on 5 January 2005. The notice is registered within the 42-day period and therefore satisfies s 20(3) and (5) of the 2000 Act.

The effect of this would be that the feudal burden would be extinguished on 28 November 2004 but then be revived by s 20(5) of the 2000 Act on registration. The effect of s 20(5) would be retrospectively to validate the feudal burden from the appointed day to the specified day. Thus a purchaser of the burdened property during the blind period may not be aware that an application for judicial reallotment has been made. Even a probing provision in the missives requiring the burdened owner to advise of any applications for judicial reallotment may not be wholly sufficient as the superior is only obliged to serve the Schedule 7 notice at some point prior to registration of the notice. There is some utility in such a provision in the missives because the burdened owner will have received notification of the application from the Tribunal under s 21 of the 2000 Act – although there may be a slight time lag between application and notification.

While this consequence would be the natural reading of the provision, to invalidate and then validate the burden would be a peculiar consequence and there is – it is suggested – a strong possibility that such a result would not be reached.

In order to avoid problems in the application of this provision it is suggested that Schedule 7 notices should be registered prior to the appointed day in order to give appropriate publicity, thereby protecting prospective purchasers and other interested third parties.

19.67   Determination by the Tribunal: who may be heard?

In determining any application for judicial reallotment the Tribunal can consider representations made by the (former) superior, the burdened owner, and others who would be affected by reallotment of the burden (even if they have not received notice): s 21(2) of the Abolition of Feudal Tenure etc (Scotland) Act 2000. Thus, a tenant of property who would be liable to comply with a converted feudal burden under s 9 of the Title Conditions (Scotland) Act 2003 (which comes into force on the same date) may seek to object to a burden that if preserved by the s 20 procedure would lead to the tenant being directly liable. Those who object to the application for judicial reallotment will ordinarily not be liable for the expenses of the application: s 20(13) of the 2000 Act. However, they may incur liability for the expenses of the action if their objections are frivolous or vexatious.

19.68   Determination by the Tribunal: consideration of the merits

The Tribunal will initially confirm that the s 20 application is appropriate by examining the evidence regarding the superior's attempt to reach an agreement under s 19 of the Abolition of Feudal Tenure etc (Scotland) Act 2000.

The Tribunal will then consider the merits of the application to determine whether, if the feudal burden that the superior is attempting to preserve was extinguished under s 17 of the 2000 Act, this would lead to 'material detriment to the value or enjoyment of the applicant's ownership ... of the dominant tenement': s 20(7)(a) (as amended)). The form of wording was substituted by the Title Conditions (Scotland) Act 2003 and is based on the test for interest to enforce in s 8 of the 2003 Act.

In considering 'material detriment', argument will require to focus on specific examples to demonstrate the utility of the burden. Suppose, for example, the superior is attempting to preserve a burden prohibiting building and he or she nominates as benefited property land more than one hundred metres from the burdened property. Consideration of 'material detriment', to the nominated benefited property will be illustrated by considering possible contraventions of the burden (such as the building of a housing estate or factory or industrial estate) and their potential impact on the value or amenity of the nominated property.

19.69 The order of the Tribunal

If the Tribunal is satisfied that the extinction of the burden would be to the 'material detriment' of the nominated benefited property, it can make an order that will reallot the burden subject to such modification of the burden or counter-obligations that the Tribunal thinks fit: s 20(7) and (9) of the Abolition of Feudal Tenure etc (Scotland) Act 2000.

Section 20(10) of the 2000 Act and s 11 of the Tribunals and Inquiries Act 1992 provide that the decision of the Tribunal is final and cannot be appealed. However, this is subject to the usual principles of judicial review regarding jurisdictional error applicable to preclusive clauses in legislation: see, for example, *Campbell v Brown* (1829) 3 W & S 441 and *Anisminic Ltd v Foreign Compensation Commission* [1969] 2 AC 147.

19.70 *When the decision is made*

The order of the Tribunal preserving and converting the burden may be made either (1) before the appointed day; or (2) on or after the appointed day.

(1) If the decision is made before the appointed day (and it is possible to register the order before the appointed day) then the order will provide that the right to enforce is transferred from superiority to the nominated benefited property.
(2) If the decision is made on or after the appointed day then the order will provide that the position during the transitional period (where the nominated benefited property has title to enforce the burden and the burdened property remains encumbered) will become permanent.

19.71 *When an order is not made*

If the Tribunal is not satisfied that the nominated benefited property will suffer 'material detriment', the Tribunal can make an order refusing the application under s 20(7)(b) of the Abolition of Feudal Tenure etc (Scotland) Act 2000 (inserted by the Title Conditions (Scotland) Act 2003 (Consequential Provisions) Order 2003, SSI 2003/503, Schedule 1, para 4(b)). The amendment addresses a concern identified by Professor Reid where the previous wording allowed the burden to remain, encumbering the burdened property until the end of the transitional period. See K G C Reid *The Abolition of Feudal Tenure in Scotland* (2003), para 3.33, n 4.

19.72 Registration of the order

The order will be registered by the Tribunal, not the parties. As usual, registration must be against both burdened and nominated benefited property: s 20(11) of the Abolition of Feudal Tenure etc (Scotland) Act 2000.

When the order is registered the effect is permanently to reallot the burden and therefore convert the burden into a non-feudal praedial real burden subject to the general provisions of the Title Conditions (Scotland) Act 2003.

(1) Where the order under s 20(7) of the 2000 Act is registered before the appointed day, the application of s 20(8)(a)(i) is that the right to enforce the burden is effectively transferred from the superiority to the nominated benefited property, provided that the burden was enforceable by the superior immediately before the appointed day.

(2) Where the order under s 20(7) is registered on or after the appointed day, the application of s 20(8)(a)(ii) is that the nominated property that has during the transitional period temporarily been the benefited property will remain the benefited property. Registration confirms that the burdened property remains encumbered by the former feudal burden.

19.73   GENERAL EFFECT OF REALLOTMENT.

As has been explained, reallotment under ss 18, 19 or 20 of the Abolition of Feudal Tenure etc (Scotland) Act 2000 converts the feudal burden on the appointed day into a non-feudal praedial real burden. As a praedial real burden, the converted burden is subject to the general provisions of the Title Conditions (Scotland) Act 2003 on enforcement, variation and discharge.

The preservation and conversion of burdens under ss 18, 19 and 20 of the 2000 Act has implications for court actions in relation to breaches of feudal burdens arising before the appointed day. This is discussed in relation to all preserved burdens at para 19.106.

19.74   The preservation of personal real burdens

There are mechanisms in the Abolition of Feudal Tenure etc (Scotland) Act 2000 to preserve the following personal real burdens: conservation burdens; personal preemption burdens; personal redemption burdens; economic development burdens; or health care burdens. These will be relatively uncommon.

19.75   CONSERVATION BURDENS

Under s 27 of the Abolition of Feudal Tenure etc (Scotland) Act 2000, a feudal burden can be preserved if it has been imposed for the purpose of:

'preserving, or protecting, (a) the architectural or historical characteristics of the land; or (b) any other special characteristics of the land (including, without prejudice to the foregoing generality of this paragraph, a special characteristic derived from the flora, fauna or general appearance of the land)'.

This burden is a conservation burden, and the definition quoted is virtually identical to that in s 38(1) of the Title Conditions (Scotland) Act 2003: see the discussion at para 15.13.

There are two possible mechanisms whereby a feudal superior can preserve conservation burdens:

(1) through using s 27 of and Schedule 8 to the 2000 Act, where the feudal superior is a conservation body itself; or
(2) through using s 27A and Schedule 8A, where the feudal superior is not itself a conservation body but nominates a conservation body to benefit from the burdens.

19.76 Preservation by conservation body

Under s 27 of the Abolition of Feudal Tenure etc (Scotland) Act 2000, if the superior is a conservation body or the Scottish ministers, the superior can register a Schedule 8 notice to preserve conservation burdens. The notice requires the usual information (see paras 19.32 to 19.36), together with a statement by the superior detailing the statutory instrument under which the body was prescribed as a conservation body.

If the notice is registered against the burdened property and the burden is enforceable before the appointed day, under s 28 of the 2000 Act, from the appointed day the feudal burden is converted into a conservation burden. As a personal real burden, it is therefore subject to Part 3 of the Title Conditions (Scotland) Act 2003. On conversion the former superior becomes the holder of the conservation burden and therefore has title to enforce the burden against the burdened property and like a superior is presumed to have interest to enforce the burden.

19.77 Nomination of body to enforce preserved conservation burdens

Under s 27A of the Abolition of Feudal Tenure etc (Scotland) Act 2000 (added by s 114(3) of the Title Conditions (Scotland) Act 2003), where a feu contains burdens that fall within the definition of conservation burdens, the superior can transfer the right to enforce the burdens to a conservation body. This could have been achieved through transfer of the superiority to a conservation body. However, this would not have enabled the superior to otherwise preserve feudal burdens. Section 27A then allows the superior to execute and register a Schedule 8A notice. The superior nominates a conservation body (or the Scottish Ministers) to enforce the conservation burdens and if the conservation body (or Ministers) consents prior to the service of the notice then the superior can register the Schedule 8A notice.

The notice again requires the usual information (see paras 19.32 to 19.36) together with (1) a statement giving details of the statutory instrument prescribing the nominated conservation body as a conservation body; and (2) signature on behalf of the nominee body indicating their assent to the nomination.

If the Schedule 8A notice is executed and registered against the burdened property before the appointed day and immediately preceding the appointed day the burdens are enforceable by the superior, then from the appointed day the burden is preserved and converted into a conservation burden enforceable by the nominee conservation body. As a conservation burden the burden is subject to Part 3 of the 2003 Act: the holder having title to enforce the burden and again being presumed to have interest to enforce.

19.78   PERSONAL PRE-EMPTION AND PERSONAL REDEMPTION BURDENS

Under s 18 of the Abolition of Feudal Tenure etc (Scotland) Act 2000, a superior can preserve a right of pre-emption (a right of first refusal held by the superior) or redemption (a right of repurchase held by the superior and exercised either at the instance of the superior or at a determined time) as a praedial real burden through nominating benefited property and registering a Schedule 5 notice. However, the efficacy of the s 18 procedure is dependent on the superior having property in the neighbourhood. The Executive took the view that a feudal right of pre-emption should be capable of preservation even if the superior did not own property in the vicinity of the burdened property, and inserted s 18A and Schedule 5A into the 2000 Act (by s 114(2) of the Title Conditions (Scotland) Act 2003). These provisions will allow superiors to preserve rights of pre-emption or redemption as personal real burdens.

The superior can execute and register a Schedule 5A notice. The notice is to contain the usual information: see paras 19.32 to 19.36. Further, the superior is to swear or affirm as to the accuracy of its contents (although it is difficult to see why this notice requires this and others relating to personal real burdens do not, given that all relevant information will appear on the property register).

If the notice is registered against the burdened property before the appointed day then if the right of pre-emption or redemption was enforceable on the day immediately preceding the appointed day, thereafter the right is preserved and is converted into a personal pre-emption burden or personal redemption burden. The burdened property remains encumbered by the burden. The former superior becomes the holder of the burden. As holder he or she has title to enforce the burden and is presumed to have interest to enforce it. It is also open to the holder to assign the right to a third party.

As the burden preserved is a right of pre-emption or redemption the personal real burden will be subject to s 82 of the 2003 Act. This provision broadly re-enacts s 9 of the Conveyancing Amendment (Scotland) Act 1938 and in general terms allows the holder of the burden one opportunity to enforce the burden before it is extinguished.

19.79 ECONOMIC DEVELOPMENT BURDENS

Under s 18B of the Abolition of Feudal Tenure etc (Scotland) Act 2000, where a feudal burden was imposed for the purpose of promoting economic development (an expression undefined), provided that the superior is a local authority or the Scottish Ministers, the burden can be preserved by the superior by executing and registering a Schedule 5B notice.

The Schedule 5B notice is to contain the usual information (see paras 19.32 to 19.36) together with a statement that the burden was imposed for the promotion of economic development together with evidence to support this statement. There is no requirement that the superior swear or affirm as to the accuracy of this statement. It is not apparent why this is the case when other notices require the superior to swear or affirm as to the accuracy of statements that can not easily be externally verified. The notice is then registered against the burdened property. The Keeper is under no obligation to check the accuracy of the statement: s 43(2)(bb) of the 2000 Act.

If the notice is registered before the appointed day then if the feudal burden is enforceable by the local authority or Scottish Ministers as superior immediately before the appointed day, from the appointed day the burden will be preserved and converted into an economic development burden. This is a personal real burden subject to Part 3 of the Title Conditions (Scotland) Act 2003. It is enforceable by the local authority or Ministers and they are presumed to have interest to enforce.

19.80 HEALTH CARE BURDENS

Under s 18C of the Abolition of Feudal Tenure etc (Scotland) Act 2000, where a feudal burden has been imposed for 'the purpose of promoting the provision of facilities for health care' and is enforceable by a National Health Service trust or the Scottish Ministers as superiors, then the burden can be preserved by the superiors by executing and registering a Schedule 5C notice.

The notice again contains the usual information (see paras 19.32 to 19.36) together with a statement that the burden was imposed for the purpose of promoting the provision of facilities for health care, together with evidence to support this statement. Like the Schedule 5B notice, there is no requirement for the superior to swear or affirm as to the accuracy of the contents of this notice. The notice is registered against the burdened property. As for the Schedule 5B notice, the Keeper is under no obligation to check the accuracy of the statement: s 43(2)(bb) of the 2000 Act.

If the notice is registered before the appointed day then if the feudal burden is enforceable by an NHS trust or the Scottish Ministers as superior immediately before the appointed day, from the appointed day the burden will be preserved and converted into a health care burden. This is a personal real burden subject to Part 3 of the 2003 Act. It is enforceable by the NHS trust or ministers and they are presumed to have interest to enforce.

19.81   The preservation of the right to claim compensation: development value burdens

Feudal burdens are not always imposed to provide for maintenance or to regulate the amenity of a property. Sometimes burdens are imposed to protect development value. For example, a benevolent landowner may gift land to a local community to use as a community centre with playing field. If the site was sold for development then the landowner could expect to make a substantial profit. If the community then sold on the property for this substantial sum the landowner would be understandably aggrieved. In order to protect his or her benevolence the landowner may impose a feudal burden to restrict the use of the property to use as a community centre and playing field and prohibiting other buildings. If the community then sells on the property for development, breaching the burden, the landowner will be able to recoup his lost development value through charging for the minute of waiver, or through detailed provision of a mechanism for compensation within the deed creating the burden. If the burden had been created by the landowner in a feu of the property then the vassal would obtain a windfall benefit from feudal abolition if the superior was unable to preserve the burden. Preservation in this case, though, does not convert the feudal burden into a perpetual personal or praedial real burden. Instead, preservation gives the former superior a temporary right to claim compensation in certain limited circumstances.

Preservation of the right to claim compensation under s 33 of the Abolition of Feudal Tenure etc (Scotland) Act 2000 is through registration of the Schedule 9 notice against the burdened property which is registered against the burdened property.

The Schedule 9 procedure cannot be used to preserve the right to claim compensation in relation to every burden that cannot otherwise be preserved by the superior. Two principal criteria are applicable before the scheme can be used: (1) the burdens converted by the notice must have been imposed to reserve to the superior 'development value'; and (2) the property was conveyed to the vassal at undervalue or gifted to the vassal as a result of the imposition of the burden reserving development value.

19.82   DEVELOPMENT VALUE

The notice is to be used to preserve a right to claim compensation in relation to those burdens that reserved 'development value'. This expression is defined in s 33(5) of the Abolition of Feudal Tenure etc (Scotland) Act 2000. It provides that '"development value" ... means any significant increase in the value of the land arising as a result of the land becoming free to be used, or dealt with, in some way not permitted under the grant in feu'. An illustration would be a variant of the example given in para 19.81. For example, if there were a feudal burden restricting use to only agricultural purposes, the extinction of the burden would free the land to be used for commercial or residential purposes. Freedom from the burden will therefore significantly increase the value of the property.

Development value is not the final value of the property taking account of any buildings that are subsequently erected upon it, but is instead the increase in value as a result of removing the burden from the property. For example, where there is a feudal burden restricting use to only agricultural uses, when this is removed development value will not take account of the ultimate purchase of the property by a supermarket and construction of a large supermarket building. This is, in the words of the Scottish Law Commission, 'added value': *Report on Abolition of the Feudal System* (Scot Law Com No 168, 1999), para 5.21. Instead, 'it is the increase in value due to the fact that land which could formerly only have been used as a sports field can now be used for the construction of a supermarket that constitutes the development value'.

19.83 BURDEN RESERVED FOR THE BENEFIT OF THE SUPERIOR

The superior must show that the burden 'reserved for the superior the benefit ... of any development value': s 33(1)(a) of the Abolition of Feudal Tenure etc (Scotland) Act 2000. While the notion of 'development value' itself is readily understandable, the requirement that the superior 'reserved' the benefit of development value is more problematic. The purpose of this provision is to ensure that burdens which were imposed merely for the preservation of amenity will not be covered by the scheme. Examples include the imposition of burdens in a community allowing properties to be used only for residential purposes, or prohibiting the erection of buildings in a residential area. The *Report on Abolition of the Feudal System* (Scot Law Com No 168, 1999), para 5.21, states that the provision is intended to cover:

'a burden which was designed to ensure that any significant increase in the value of the land due to its being freed for development for a purpose other than those permitted under the feudal grant will accrue to the superior'.

If this is used to aid interpretation of the provision, it appears that the requirement is that the burden 'was designed' to secure development value. Although the wording of the subsection indicates an objective approach should be taken, the background material suggests a subjective element: the intention of the creator of the burden. The superior imposed the burden with a view to recovering the development value in the event of breach of the burden.

In some cases it may be possible to determine this through examination of the property register – for example, where the burden contains a mechanism to deal with development value, as in *Cumbernauld Development Corporation v County Properties and Developments Ltd* 1996 SLT 1106. There, the superior feued property as an ice rink. If the property were to be used for other purposes, the sale price would have been substantially higher. While restricting use to that of an ice rink, the feu provided in a further condition that if the initial development proved unviable then an alternative (viable) use of the property should be adopted and a compensatory sum paid to the superior. Such a mechanism would clearly indicate the superior's intention to reserve development value.

Generally, though, the intent for which the burden was imposed is something that cannot be readily determined through examination of the property register. It may therefore be difficult to determine whether or not a burden was truly an amenity burden (which should not be capable of preservation through the scheme) or a burden reserving development value. To this end, when the Schedule 9 notice is prepared the superior is required to make a statement that the burden reserved development value and to provide supporting information. The superior then requires to swear or affirm as to the accuracy of the contents of the notice: see para 19.37.

19.84   CONVEYANCE AT UNDERVALUE

The notice can only be used to preserve a right to claim compensation if the property was feued at undervalue. This can mean either that the superior feued the property for no consideration at all (such as a gift to a community) or that the superior reduced the sale price as a result of the imposition of the relevant burden. An example of this is, as mentioned above, the sale of property with a burden restricting the use to that of an ice rink, leading to a substantially lower sale price than if the property could be used for other purposes.

In completing the Schedule 9 notice the superior must narrate – to the best of his or her knowledge or belief – the amount by which the consideration was reduced as a result of the imposition of the burden or burdens. In many cases this will be educated guesswork based on an awareness of the market value at the time of the grant of the original feu. However, in some instances there may be more accurate information – based on survey valuations carried out on the assumption that property was available for commercial purposes. In order to avoid contentious disputes at a later date, some superiors may seek to instruct surveys to assess historic valuations based on the assumption that property was free for commercial use.

As with the other contents of the notice, the accuracy of the information regarding the reduction in value is verified by the superior swearing or affirming as to its accuracy: see para 19.37.

The amount by which the consideration was reduced is of crucial importance in the compensation scheme. Under s 37(2) of the Abolition of Feudal Tenure etc (Scotland) Act 2000, the maximum amount of compensation will typically be the reduction in consideration at the time the burden was imposed: see paras 19.92 to 19.96. This means that in relation to older feudal burdens the reduction in consideration is – in modern terms – a trivial amount. Accordingly, it will often not be worth preserving a right to claim compensation using the scheme.

19.85 MULTIPLE DEVELOPMENT VALUE BURDENS

The final point to be noted in relation to development value is that the burden which is converted into the right to claim compensation must be ascertainable as a burden that reserved development value and led to a consequent reduction of the sale price. It is not enough to look at a multi-page feu charter and note that the cumulative effect of the imposition of the burdens was to see the sale price reduced from what it might otherwise have been. Instead, a distinct reduction in the price attributable to individually ascertained burdens must be identified. This has consequences for the completion of the Schedule 9 notice. Where the superior attempts to convert multiple burdens into compensation claims the reduction in consideration must be apportioned and attributed to each burden. Again, the accuracy of this attribution is supported by the superior swearing or affirming as to its accuracy: see para 19.37.

19.86 SCHEDULE 9 NOTICE

The Schedule 9 notice is to contain the usual information (see paras 19.32 to 19.36). In addition the superior is to narrate:

(1) that the burden was imposed for the reservation of development value and provide information to support that;
(2) the amount by which consideration was reduced as a result of the imposition of the burden (an amount being attributed to each burden), to the best of the superior's knowledge and belief; and
(3) that the superior is reserving the right to claim compensation.

The notice is to be served on the vassal in the normal way, and the superior is to swear or affirm as to the accuracy of the contents of the notice: see para 19.37.

The notice is then registered against the burdened property. Such registration must take place before the appointed day. On registration the Keeper is under no obligation to verify the accuracy of the statements within the Schedule 9 notice, nor is he obliged to verify whether the burden was truly imposed to reserve development value, or that the imposition of the burden had led to a reduction in consideration: s 43(2)(c) of the Abolition of Feudal Tenure etc (Scotland) Act 2000.

19.87 THE EFFECT OF REGISTRATION OF THE SCHEDULE 9 NOTICE

If the Schedule 9 notice is executed and registered before the appointed day this does not preserve the burden. The burden is extinguished under s 17 of the Abolition of Feudal Tenure etc (Scotland) Act 2000. However, registration has effect to reserve to the superior a personal right to claim compensation in the event of certain conditions being satisfied: s 35 of the 2000 Act. As will be seen in para 19.89, the effect of this is to give the former feudal burden a temporary afterlife. As Professors Reid and Gretton note, the burden will 'live on in a shadow form': *Conveyancing 2000* (2001), p 135. The former burden will continue to appear on the register, but breach will have only financial consequences for the owner of the property.

That an unenforceable burden cannot be preserved is fundamental to Part 4 of the 2000 Act. It is a particular issue in relation to the compensation scheme. If a feudal burden intended to reserve development value to the superior contains a mechanism for payment to be made to the superior, the burden may be invalid. For example, where the burden contains an obligation on the vassal to pay money, if the amount is uncertain the burden may potentially be struck down. In *Tailors of Aberdeen v Coutts* (1840) 1 Robin 296 at 340, Lord Brougham stated: 'an obligation to bear an unascertained expense, that is, an unascertained sum of money, which it is on all hands agreed cannot be imposed'. Or if the burden contains an obligation to pay an amount certain or uncertain, the burden may not be sufficiently praedial to be valid. An obligation to make payment may simply be a personal obligation on the vassal – based on contract – and not relate to the land itself. In cases where the burden itself is invalid the scheme cannot be used to preserve an effective right to claim compensation.

There is one other element that may be relevant in considering enforceability. In its *Report on Abolition of the Feudal System* (Scot Law Com No 168, 1999), para 5.22, the Scottish Law Commission discusses the question of interest to enforce. The current law is stated at paras 19.4 to 19.6 above. While interest to enforce is presumed, it is possible for the vassal to challenge that presumption. As stated at para 19.6, it has been suggested that the superior will not have interest to enforce a feudal burden if he or she does not own property in the vicinity of the burdened property. If this is the case then a feudal superior who owned a bare superiority with no property in the neighbourhood would not be able to convert that burden into a right to claim compensation, as the burden would not have been enforceable on the day immediately preceding the appointed day. However, conflicting authorities in this area mean that the issue will be open for argument during judicial consideration of the development value burdens scheme.

19.88 TRANSMISSION OF THE RIGHT TO CLAIM COMPENSATION

The right to claim compensation is an unusual personal right. It can be exercised by the superior against the current owner of the property and is not simply enforceable against the owner of the property at the time the feudal system was abolished. The transmission of the obligation may initially seem unfair, but the right is publicised to prospective purchasers through the property register.

Like other personal rights, the right to claim compensation is capable of transfer to third parties, either voluntarily through *inter vivos* assignation or involuntarily through insolvency or in succession: s 34 of the Abolition of Feudal Tenure etc (Scotland) Act 2000. Assignation can be of the whole right or part of it.

A statutory application of the maxim *assignatus utitur jure auctoris* (the transferee's rights can be no greater than those of the transferor) applies in assignation of the right to claim compensation. Under s 37(3)(b) of the 2000 Act, if the assignee seeks to enforce a claim for compensation under s 35(3) of the 2000 Act, the assignee's claim can be no greater than that claimable by the former superior. Thus, the former superior cannot use the compensation scheme if he or she was precluded from claiming compensation as a result of the application of s 37(3)(a), ie if the superior is able to recover development value in another way (such as under the original contract between superior and vassal).

A statutory model for assignation is provided in Schedule 11 to the 2000 Act. Execution of the assignation in accordance with s 3 of the Requirements of Writing (Scotland) Act 1995, followed by registration of the assignation, is required to transfer the right to the assignee effectively.

19.89 THE CONDITIONS FOR CLAIMING COMPENSATION

The conditions for claiming compensation are:

(1) If the burden was breached prior to the appointed day then the superior may not have had an opportunity to enforce the burden prior to its extinction. Extinction of the burden would without some special preservation see the vassal gain a windfall benefit from abolition. The statute provides a transitional rule to deal with this case. If the burden is breached in the five years before the appointed day the former superior will be entitled to claim compensation if the Schedule 9 notice has been registered effectively: s 35(2)(c)(i) of the the Abolition of Feudal Tenure etc (Scotland) Act 2000.

(2) When the burden has been extinguished by s 17 of the 2000 Act, the scheme differs. Here, the right to claim compensation relates to the afterlife of the former feudal burden. If in the 20 years after the appointed day the owner of the property acts in a way that would have contravened the burden if the burden had been preserved, then the shadow burden would be 'breached'. 'Breach' of this 'shadow burden' triggers the right to claim compensation: s 35(2)(c)(ii) of the 2000 Act.

For example, say there is a feudal burden providing that property shall be used only for agricultural purposes and a right to claim compensation is preserved in relation to that burden in accordance with the 2000 Act. The burden itself is extinguished on the appointed day. However, if a supermarket is then constructed on the property this would have contravened the burden if the burden had been preserved. This 'breach' of the 'shadow burden' would entitle the former superior to claim compensation.

19.90   SUMMARY OF THE CONDITIONS TRIGGERING A COMPENSATION CLAIM

The conditions for claiming compensation in relation to the development value burden are as follows:

(1) the superior has duly completed and registered a Schedule 9 notice before the appointed day (see paras 19.85 to 19.86);
(2) the burden was enforceable on the day immediately preceding the appointed day (see para 19.87);
(3) the superior's right to enforce the burden was extinguished on the appointed day under s 17 of the Abolition of Feudal Tenure etc (Scotland) Act 2000;
(4) the burden was breached in the five years before the appointed day or the 'shadow burden' is 'breached' during the 20 years after the appointed day.

19.91   THE MECHANICS OF CLAIMING COMPENSATION

If the holder of the right to claim compensation (the former superior or any assignee) is able to claim compensation as a result of the breach (or 'breach') of the development value burden (or shadow burden), then one of two things must happen.

(1) The holder must serve a notice on the owner of the property in accordance with s 36 of the Abolition of Feudal Tenure etc (Scotland) Act 2000. Service requires the holder to either: (a) personally deliver the notice to the owner – in which case service is proved through the owner's signed acknowledgment in conformity with Form A of Schedule 10 to the 2000 Act; or (b) send the notice to the owner by recorded or registered delivery – in which case service is proved either by a Form A notice or by a certificate in conformity with Form B of Schedule 10 to the 2000 Act accompanied by a receipt of posting. Form B of Schedule 10 is framed in a peculiar way requiring the signature of the 'owner'. As the owner is the burdened person, not the party claiming compensation, this appears to have been made in error as the owner will not necessarily be aware of the posting of the notice.

For the purposes of these provisions 'owner' means the registered owner, or – if there are unregistered proprietors – the most recent unregistered proprietor: s 39 of the 2000 Act. For example, assume that the registered owner of the burdened property is Alan, but Alan has died and his executor Ben, having confirmed to Alan's estate, transferred the burdened property to Carol. Ben and Carol are both unregistered proprietors but it is Carol who would be potentially liable to pay compensation, being the person who has most recently acquired title to the property.

It may be difficult for the holder of the right to claim compensation to determine who the most recent 'owner' is. For example, the former superior may be aware that Alan died and that Ben confirmed to his estate but may have no idea that Alan's executor transferred the right to Carol. In this case s 38 of the 2000 Act provides that where notice is served on a party who was entitled to the property prior to the breach taking place, this person shall pass on contact details of their successor unregistered proprietor. Alternatively, he or she must provide information to enable the holder to trace the most recent unregistered proprietor.

The s 35(3) notice claiming compensation is to specify the amount of compensation claimed in accordance with s 37. This is discussed at paras 19.92 to 19.96.

(2) The holder must make the claim within three years of (a) the appointed day if the claim relates to a breach of the development value burden where that breach took place before the appointed day; or (b) the 'breach' if the claim relates to 'breach' of a development value burden taking place after the appointed day: s 35(4) of the 2000 Act.

The starting point for this three-year period is the date that the breach commences if the breach is ongoing: s 35(6). For example, if the burden provided that property shall not be used other than for agricultural purposes and the property is used as a supermarket, every day that it operates as a supermarket is a contravention of the burden. However, the claim for compensation must be raised within three years of the time that the property was first not used for agricultural purposes.

19.92 THE AMOUNT OF COMPENSATION

When claiming compensation under s 35(3) of the Abolition of Feudal Tenure etc (Scotland) Act 2000, the holder of the right to claim compensation must assert the compensation claimed. In paras 5.41 to 5.46 of its *Report on Abolition of the Feudal System* (Scot Law Com No 168, 1999), the Scottish Law Commission explained its thinking on *quantum* in detail. Compensation is to be the lower sum of (1) the loss to the superior as the result of the loss of his or her right to enforce the development value burden; or (2) the benefit to the owner of the burdened property of contravention of the shadow burden.

This scheme is implemented through s 37 of the 2000 Act where quantification of compensation has two elements:

(1) the calculation of the benefit to the owner;
(2) capped by calculation of the loss to the superior.

19.93 The benefit to the owner

Calculation of the benefit to the owner is in accordance with s 37(1) of the Abolition of Feudal Tenure etc (Scotland) Act 2000. This provides that compensation is:

> 'such sum, as represents, at the time of the breach or occurrence in question, any development value which would have accrued to the owner had the burden been modified to the extent necessary to permit the land to be used, or dealt

with, in the way that constituted the breach or, as the case may be, occurrence on which the claim is based'.

Thus, the benefit to the owner is the increase in development value (ie the increase in value of the property) arising as a result of the specific breach. In some cases the breach may not relate to the whole of the burdened property. For example, if there is a burden restricting the use of one hectare to agricultural purposes and a small bungalow is constructed on one part of the property, the site has not realised the full development value that would have arisen if it had been developed as a supermarket. The benefit to the owner is the land being freed for the construction of a bungalow and the compensation to be paid should reflect that rather than the potential maximum. Compensation then will reflect the difference in value between a valuation made on the assumption that no bungalow could be constructed and a valuation made on the assumption that a bungalow could be constructed.

19.94   No double claims

Although the former superior (or his or her successor) can claim compensation for the benefit arising in a claim under s 35(3) of the Abolition of Feudal Tenure etc (Scotland) Act 2000, no compensation will be payable if the development value can be claimed in another way. The holder of the right is not to be entitled to double compensation: s 37(3)(a) of the 2000 Act. For example, if the holder of the right to claim compensation and the owner of the burdened property were the original contracting parties, liability for breach of the development value burden would be incurred under the contract. This is because contractual provisions between the original parties are not affected by feudal abolition under s 75(1) of the 2000 Act. This would preclude the possibility of compensation under s 35(3) of the 2000 Act.

The principle that double claims are precluded will also affect assignees of the holder of the development value burden. If the holder of the right to claim compensation is an original contracting party then if he or she assigns the right to a third party the assignee cannot claim any more than the former superior: s 37(3)(b) of the 2000 Act. This is discussed at para 19.88.

19.95   The cap on compensation

The compensation scheme provides that the superior can claim (in total) no more than he or she lost. The loss is not calculated as the windfall benefit to the owner – made sometimes years after the superior sold on the property. Instead, it 'shall not exceed such sum as will make up for any effect which the burden produced, at the time when it was imposed, in reducing the consideration then paid or made payable for the feu': s 37(2) of the Abolition of Feudal Tenure etc (Scotland) Act 2000. This is not unfamiliar, and is derived from the compensation scheme for variation or discharge of burdens in the Lands Tribunal jurisdiction under s 1(4)(ii) of the

Conveyancing and Feudal Reform (Scotland) Act 1970. There have been a number of cases on this provision in the 1970 Act. They are discussed at para 17.31 of the sixth edition of this book and more fully in Agnew *Variation and Discharge of Land Obligations* (1999) at paras 7-22 to 7-27 (although note that a number of the cases therein cited relate to the English legislation). There is also a useful discussion of the background to the provision in W M Gordon 'Variation and Discharge of Land Obligations' in D J Cusine (ed) *A Scots Conveyancing Miscellany: Essays in Honour of Professor J M Halliday* (1987), p 67 at pp 82 to 84.

The following factors seem to be relevant in calculating the maximum amount of compensation.

(1) The holder of the right to claim compensation must be able to lead evidence to demonstrate the reduction in consideration attributable to the burden. This is implied in completion of the Schedule 9 notice (and is discussed at para 19.84), and has been relevant in various cases under the equivalent provision in the 1970 Act. See, for example, *Manz v Butter's Trustees* 1973 SLT (Lands Tr) 2, where the superior could not demonstrate that the sale price of a temperance hotel in the 1920s was substantially less than it would have been without the imposition of the burden prohibiting the sale of alcohol.

(2) Calculation of the reduction in consideration will probably not make an allowance for inflation. This is the assumption upon which the legislation was framed: see *Report on Abolition of the Feudal System* (Scot Law Com No 168, 1999), para 5.46. See also the explanatory notes to the 2000 Act, para 144, where it is stated that, 'In relation to [s 1(4)(ii) of the 1970 Act], the practice of the Lands Tribunal for Scotland has been to make no allowance for inflation in the calculation of compensation'. This assumption seems to be based on the approach in two cases: *Manz v Butter's Trustees* 1973 SLT (Lands Tr) 2 and *Gorrie & Banks Ltd v Musselburgh Town Council* 1974 SLT (Lands Tr) 5.

In *Manz* the observations of the Tribunal were *obiter* comments, but useful nonetheless. In that case the Tribunal rejected the claim for compensation under s 1(4)(ii) of the Conveyancing and Feudal Reform (Scotland) Act 1970, because the superior could not show that a reduction in consideration resulted from the imposition of the burden. The superior had argued that compensation should be based on the amount that would have been paid for a minute of waiver at the time of creation of the burden. The superior then proposed doubling the figure to take account of the passage of time from imposition of the burden to the Tribunal application. The Tribunal rejected this view given that the superior had had the benefit of the burden for a substantial period of time. The Tribunal also noted that there would be various problems in the application of this approach to nineteenth-century burdens. Instead, the Tribunal suggested an approach based on the differential of capitalisation of feuduties – *Manz v Butter's Trustees* 1973 SLT (Lands Tr) 2 at 5:

'Let us assume for the sake of illustration that a fair consideration for an unrestricted feu of McKay's Hotel in 1924 was £50, 10 s and not £10, 10 s. Then the superiors in the intervening years would have been paid and even now would have as their asset the annual feuduty of £50, 10 s. At the date of the Tribunal's order that feuduty would have a capital value relative to the appropriate year's purchase. In fact at present the superiors are entitled to a feuduty of only £10, 10 s, which again has a capital value relative to the appropriate year's purchase. A possible approach to assessing compensation would then be to take the difference between these two capital values as representing a fair sum to make up for the effect which the obligation produced at the time when it was imposed in reducing the consideration made payable for the interest in land affected by it'.

This approach was adopted by the Tribunal in *Gorrie & Banks Ltd v Musselburgh Town Council* 1974 SLT (Lands Tr) 5. A burden agreed in 1913 but not registered until 1920 restricted the building of residential properties on an area. The area had originally been feued in 1888 for a feuduty of £19, 12 s. This feuduty was reduced to £9, 12 s in 1920 with the imposition of the burden. When the burden was varied by the Tribunal in 1973 it was held that the appropriate method of calculating compensation was the capitalisation at the time of variation (1973) of the extra feuduty that would have been charged if no burden was imposed. The extra feuduty could be shown to be £10. The capitalisation was based on a multiplier of 15 years' purchase. This was agreed between the parties and the Tribunal endorsed the approach without reasons. The focus on the reduction of feuduty (and by implication reduction in the purchase price) suggests that inflation will not be considered in the calculation of compensation. However, there is no case law directly in point where there was a reduction in the *grassum* (sale price) rather than reduction in feuduty.

If the assumption lying behind the legislation is correct then unless the burden was imposed recently there will be little reason to preserve the burden using the development value burden scheme. If property was sold for £15 in 1899 subject to a burden restricting use only as a sports field, instead of the price of £30 that would have been paid if the property had been sold free from the burden, the development of the property in 2005 as a million-pound supermarket development would trigger a claim for compensation of only £15 – the reduction in consideration in 1899. However, if property was feued subject to a burden restricting use to a sports field in 1999 for no consideration when a property free from the burden would have sold for £250,000 then a multi-million pound supermarket development in 2005 would trigger a compensation claim of £250,000 – the reduction in consideration in 1999.

(3) Is the claimant the original grantor of the feu? Under s 1(4)(ii) of the Conveyancing and Feudal Reform (Scotland) Act 1970, there is a suggestion in some cases that the superior will only be able to claim compensation if he or she was the original grantor who imposed the burden: *Devlin v Conn* 1972 SLT (Lands Tr) 11 at 14. Sir Crispin Agnew suggests that there is case law where a subsequent purchaser has benefited from the provision: *Variation and Discharge of Land Obligations* (1999), para 7-24. He cites *Gorrie & Banks Ltd v Musselburgh Town Council* 1974 SLT (Lands Tr) 5 as authority for this. However, in that case Musselburgh Town Council successfully claimed com-

pensation, and was the original superior. There has been no reported case where a successor in title has successfully claimed compensation under s 1(4)(ii) of the 1970 Act. This is a reasonable result. Any purchaser of the superiority will have acquired it at market value and will not have suffered the loss of development value inherent in the original conveyance of the burdened property. If this principle is applied in relation to s 37(2) of the 2000 Act, then, coupled with s 37(3), it may limit the circumstances in which compensation could be successfully claimed. As s 37(3) would appear to exclude liability where both owner and claimant were the original contracting parties to the feudal grant imposing the development value burden, if *Devlin* was applied the circumstances in which compensation could be claimed would be restricted to claims by the original superior (or assignee) against singular successors of the original vassal. It is not clear that this is the intention of the legislation, and this possibility is not canvassed in the Scottish Law Commission report or Executive explanatory notes.

(4) The Tribunal will take account of any mechanism to calculate development value. Aside from *Gorrie & Banks Ltd*, the only case in which compensation has been paid under s 1(4)(ii) of the 1970 Act is *Cumbernauld Development Corporation v County Properties and Developments Ltd* 1996 SLT 1106. The facts of that case are summarised at para 19.83. The burden restricting use to that of an ice rink was accompanied by a condition providing a mechanism for compensation if the ice rink was not financially viable and the superior agreed to the conversion of use to use for retail purposes. It was provided that £650,000 compensation would be payable. However, when the Tribunal varied the burden to allow the property to be used as a bingo hall, it held that under s 1(4)(ii), compensation should be assessed at £206,000. This took account of the specific wording of the mechanism which referred to a £650,000 payment for change of use from that of an ice rink to retail use. As a bingo hall was a leisure use, and as only leisure uses would probably be permitted in future, compensation would be assessed at a figure substantially less than that specified in the deed.

19.96 QUANTIFICATION OF THE COMPENSATION: CONCLUSION

Assessment of compensation is the lower of the benefit to the owner, and the loss to the claimant (the former superior). The mode of determining the loss to the claimant will typically act as a cap on the amount of compensation that can be claimed. The case law of the Tribunal in relation to s 1(4)(ii) of the Conveyancing and Feudal Reform (Scotland) Act 1970 suggests that this maximum figure for compensation will often be insignificant. This has clear implications for practice in preserving the right to claim compensation.

If there is a dispute about the amount of compensation the matter may be referred to the Lands Tribunal: s 44(2) of the Abolition of Feudal Tenure etc (Scotland) Act 2000 using form AFT 44 in the Lands Tribunal for Scotland Rules 2003, SSI 2003/452. It has discretion to make such order as it thinks fit. This discretion includes a power to determine the amount of compensation to be paid. In a case before the Tribunal the claimant bears the onus of proof on disputes as to fact. Accordingly, the claimant has to prove that the burden did reserve development value, that the original feu was at undervalue, what was the reduction of consideration, and whether there was a 'breach' (or 'breach') of the burden (or 'shadow burden'). Any order of the Tribunal may be registered.

19.97   DISCHARGE OF DEVELOPMENT VALUE BURDENS

In certain cases the owner may wish to cleanse the register. If the superior has received compensation under s 35(3) of the Abolition of Feudal Tenure etc (Scotland) Act 2000 for a 'breach', the owner would wish to notify third parties that no further claim can be made, or that the maximum sum claimable has been reduced as a result of an earlier claim. Alternatively, the owner may negotiate with the holder of the right to claim compensation and through payment of a *grassum* in anticipation of work that would constitute a breach seek to prevent a compensation claim being raised. In these cases the owner would seek an executed deed from the holder discharging their claim. Such a deed would be broadly equivalent to a minute of waiver and is competent under s 40 of the 2000 Act. The deed of discharge, or restriction, is to be executed in accordance with s 3 of the Requirements of Writing (Scotland) Act 1995 and should be registered.

19.98   **The preservation of sporting rights**

Scots law recognises certain separate tenements in relation to sport: see Chapter 8. The right to fish for salmon is a legal separate tenement that can be owned separately from the ownership of the riverbanks or river bed (*alveus*). The treatment of other sporting rights is less clear, for example where the superior feued land reserving the right to use the *dominium utile* for sporting purposes (such as the right to fish for trout or hunt game). Under the current law these rights are difficult to classify: see *Report on Abolition of the Feudal System* (Scot Law Com No 168, 1999), paras 6.22 to 6.35. The original approach in the Abolition of Feudal Tenure etc (Scotland) Act 2000 was that the right was viewed as a real burden allowing use, and was preserved by the reallotment procedures. This would then have been converted into a servitude under s 81 of the 2003 Act. However, this approach was criticised by Dr Andrew Steven in a series of articles: A J M Steven 'The Reform of Real Burdens' (2001) 5 Edin LR 235; and S Wortley and A J M Steven 'The Modernisation of Real Burdens and Servitudes: some observations on the Title Conditions (Scotland) Bill Consultation Paper' (2001) 6 SLPQ 261 at 281f. Dr Steven argued that the case law on feudal sporting rights suggested that the right could not be a servitude: see, for example, *Patrick v Napier* (1867) 5 M 683. See also D J Cusine and R R M Paisley *Servitudes and Rights of Way* (1998), paras 3.08 and 3.63.

The 2000 Act was amended by s 114 of the Title Conditions (Scotland) Act 2003, which added s 65A to the 2000 Act. This provides that the superior is entitled to preserve sporting rights through execution and registration of a Schedule 11A notice. This notice is to contain the usual information (see paras 19.32 to 19.36) with one amendment. Rather than stating the burden to be preserved, the superior is to describe the rights to be preserved (and any counter-obligations). When the Schedule 11A notice is preserved the superior is to swear or affirm as to the accuracy of the contents of the notice (see para 19.37). The notice is to be registered against the property subject to the sporting rights. Again, s 43 of the 2000 Act (as read with s 65A) provides that the Keeper is not to verify the accuracy of the contents of the notice.

If the notice is executed and registered before the appointed day, and the sporting rights have been validly constituted before the appointed day, then, under s 65A(5) of the 2000 Act, from the appointed day the sporting rights will be converted into a separate tenement in land. However, unlike other separate tenements that are not derived directly from the *regalia* of the Crown, the separate tenement of converted sporting rights is expressly provided to be non-exclusive: s 65A(6) of the 2000 Act. Accordingly, the right to hunt or fish (for fish other than salmon) may be shared with the owner of the riverbank or riverbed: see W M Gordon *Scottish Land Law* (2nd edn, 1999), para 8-131.

In land registration other separate tenements, such as the right to salmon fishings, have their own title sheet. The 2003 Act amends the Land Registration (Scotland) Act 1979 to provide that sporting rights preserved under s 65A of the 2000 Act are not 'incorporeal heritable rights' leading to similar treatment. Thus, s 2(1) of the 1979 Act will apply to transfers of sporting rights. In order to be effective the transfer of sporting rights must be registered. Section 5(1)(a) of the 1979 Act provides that where there is an interest in land that is not an incorporeal heritable right (such as s 65A sporting rights) registration of that interest will lead to the creation of a new title sheet for the interest.

19.99 General observations on the preservation of burdens

It is necessary to consider the further general rules applicable to each preservation scheme.

19.100 CAN MORE THAN ONE SCHEME BE USED?

Section 42(1) of the Abolition of Feudal Tenure etc (Scotland) Act 2000 provides that any one burden can only be preserved under one scheme. This is subject to the exception that an unsuccessful attempt to reach an agreement for bilateral reallotment under s 19 of the 2000 Act will not preclude another scheme being used. Typically, the feudal superior will not have any choice. For example, a feudal superior who wishes to preserve general amenity burdens while owning land in the vicinity of the burdened property will not use the development value burden scheme, will typically not be able to fit the burdens within the definition of conservation, health care, or economic development burdens, but will seek reallotment of the burden to neighbouring property.

Sometimes, though, the superior will have a choice. For example, a health service trust may own property in the vicinity of property where use is restricted by a burden to a nurses' home. The trust will typically seek to preserve the burden as a health care burden. This will allow the trust to preserve control of the home for itself rather than attaching title to enforce to a neighbouring property it may wish to sell off in a few years. In some circumstances the choice may be more difficult.

For example, a property may be encumbered by a feudal burden restricting use of burdened property only to agricultural purposes. The superior may own property one hundred and fifty metres from the burdened property. The superior may therefore have the option of using the procedure to reserve a right to claim using the Schedule 9 notice or may seek to preserve the burden through judicial reallotment using the Schedule 7 procedure (therefore initially seeking bilateral reallotment). Registering a Schedule 7 notice and applying to the Tribunal in the hope that the burden will be preserved in perpetuity will preclude the registration of a Schedule 9 notice. If the Tribunal was to reject the attempt to reallot then it is too late to use an alternative procedure.

The only circumstances in which the superior can attempt to preserve a burden under more than one procedure is where the notice has been discharged either through an order of the Lands Tribunal after challenge to a notice (under s 44(1) of the 2000 Act) or if the superior has executed and registered a deed discharging the notice: s 41(1)(i) of the 2000 Act. Registration of the discharge and subsequent registration of the other notice would both have to take place before the appointed day.

19.101   PRESERVATION OF MULTIPLE BURDENS AGAINST ONE *DOMINIUM UTILE*

Where a superior wishes to preserve more than one burden using one scheme then the superior can preserve these burdens in one notice: s 42(4) of the Abolition of Feudal Tenure etc (Scotland) Act 2000. Thus, if the superior owned property within one hundred metres of the burdened property, and the feu charter contained ten burdens, each burden could be preserved using the same Schedule 5 notice.

19.102   PRESERVATION WHERE MORE THAN ONE *DOMINIUM UTILE* IS SUBJECT TO THE SAME BURDEN

Often a superior will have the *dominium directum* for multiple burdened properties. The original single *dominium utile* may have been sub-divided many times.

This will typically be the case in housing estates. The same feudal burdens imposed in the same feu charter will encumber each *dominium utile*. If the superior wishes to preserve these feudal burdens, he or she must register a separate notice against each *dominium utile*: s 42(3) of the Abolition of Feudal Tenure etc (Scotland) Act 2000.

19.103 DISPUTES REGARDING NOTICES

It is possible for many disputes to arise in relation to notices. A vassal (or former vassal) may argue that the burdens preserved by a notice were not enforceable (either because the superior did not have interest to enforce or the burden was invalid). Alternatively, he or she may argue that the person registering the notice did not have title, or that in completing the Schedule 5 notice the superior did not own the benefited property. Or he or she may argue that the nominated benefited property did not have constructed upon it a building within one hundred metres of the burdened property; or, in relation to a Schedule 9 notice, that the property had not been conveyed at undervalue, or that the reduction in consideration was inaccurate.

If registered in the Land Register the notice may be rectified in certain cases: s 9 of the Land Registration (Scotland) Act 1979, discussed in K G C Reid *The Abolition of Feudal Tenure in Scotland* (2003), para 11.18.

Any dispute in relation to a registered notice may be referred to the Lands Tribunal: s 44 of the Abolition of Feudal Tenure etc (Scotland) Act 2000 using form AFT 44 in the Lands Tribunal for Scotland Rules 2003, SSI 2003/452. There is no time limit. Accordingly, a notice could be registered in 2004 but no issue arise in relation to the notice until the former superior attempted to enforce the burden or to claim compensation in 2014. At this stage the former vassal (or his or her successor in title) could challenge the validity of the notice on the basis that the burden was not valid. An unchallenged registered notice will not validate a burden that is otherwise invalid or unenforceable.

In a referral under s 44(1) of the 2000 Act, the onus of proof in relation to disputed questions of fact lies with the person relying on the notice. The Tribunal has a wide discretion in reaching its decision and is empowered to make 'such order as it thinks fit discharging or, to such extent as may be specified in the order, restricting the notice in question'. Unlike the position in the Conveyancing and Feudal Reform (Scotland) Act 1970, the power of the Tribunal under s 44(1) of the 2000 Act includes the power to determine the validity of the burden.

Any order made by the Tribunal is capable of registration and when registered will take effect as regards third parties: s 44(4) of the 2000 Act.

19.104 Disputes arising in relation to unregistered notices

When an application is made to register a notice the Keeper may reject the application. In the Register of Sasines such rejection may be based on the common law principles of *Macdonald v Keeper of the Registers of Scotland* 1914 SC 854. In the Land Register the Keeper has a broad discretion to reject applications under s 4 of the Land Registration (Scotland) Act 1979. If an application for registration has been rejected the applicant may challenge the rejection in court (for decisions relating to the Sasine register) or in the Lands Tribunal (for decisions relating to the Land Register: s 25(1) of the 1979 Act). Under s 45(2) of the Abolition of Feudal Tenure etc (Scotland) Act 2000, a time period during which such challenges must be made will be prescribed by Ministers. No time period has been prescribed at the time of writing.

If the court or Tribunal reaches a decision prior to the appointed day the notice may be appropriately registered: s 45(2) of the 2000 Act. However, if the notice has not been registered before the appointed day or if the decision of the court or Tribunal takes place after the appointed day, the notice may be registered in a limited period. In this case the burden will have been extinguished under s 17 of the 2000 Act as no notice was registered before the appointed day. However, registration within two months of the decision and before such time period as the Ministers prescribe will be retrospectively treated as being effectively registered prior to the appointed day: s 45(1)(b) of the 2000 Act.

19.105   EXTINCTION OF FEUDAL BURDENS ON ABOLITION

Under s 17 of the Abolition of Feudal Tenure etc (Scotland) Act 2000, unless a feudal burden is preserved or converted using one of the procedures detailed above, on the appointed day it will be extinguished. It is the superior's right to enforce that vanishes. Any manager burdens (as defined in s 63 of the Title Conditions (Scotland) Act 2003, discussed at paras 15.19 to 15.21), or rights of enforcement arising through the creation of new implied rights of enforcement under ss 52 to 56 of the 2003 Act (discussed at paras 17.34 to 17.45) are unaffected. This means that any rights of enforcement held by the superior in his or her capacity as owner of neighbouring land (either through preservation of the burden under Part 4 of the 2000 Act or under the implied rights provisions in the 2003 Act) are unaffected.

This is not to say, though, that where the superior feued land while retaining ownership of property in the vicinity of the burdened property, the superior can benefit from the rule in *J & A Mactaggart v Harrower* (1906) 8 F 1101 which would imply the retained land as benefited property (see para 17.10). This possibility is expressly precluded under s 48 of the 2000 Act. The superior cannot therefore rely on this rule to circumvent the rules on preservation.

19.106   Breaches of feudal burdens before the appointed day

The extinction of feudal burdens under s 17 of the Abolition of Feudal Tenure etc (Scotland) Act 2000 has implications in relation to breaches that took place before the appointed day. Under s 17(2) of the 2000 Act it will not be competent to raise actions for enforcement after the appointed day (other than for damages or the payment of money); and any proceedings that were commenced before the appointed day will be deemed to be abandoned.

If a decree had been granted before the appointed day, such as an interdict in relation to a proposed contravention of a burden restricting the use of the burdened property, that decree will (unless it related to the payment of damages or other payment) be deemed to be reduced or recalled on the appointed day. In the case of the burdened proprietor extinction of the feudal burden restricting use would see the recall of the interdict and the burdened proprietor permitted to carry out the action in contravention of the burden (provided that no implied third-party enforcement rights existed).

If the burden had been preserved and converted under the procedures in Part 4 of the 2000 Act (excepting the development value burden provisions) then any court proceedings raised, or court decrees pronounced, before the appointed day would not fall. The action for breach of the burden could proceed – despite the change in nature of the burden.

The position for development value burdens differs slightly because under s 35(2) of the 2000 Act it is only possible to claim compensation in respect of breaches taking place in the five years immediately preceding the appointed day. Court proceedings raised, or court decrees pronounced, before the appointed day in relation to breach of a burden subsequently preserved as a development value burden will fall with feudal abolition, although this does not preclude a subsequent claim for compensation.

19.107 MISCELLANEOUS ITEMS

Feudal abolition has implications on other aspects of burdens aside from their extinction or preservation. Two are of particular importance. Firstly, where feudal burdens are preserved under Part 4 of the Abolition of Feudal Tenure etc (Scotland) Act 2000, or where new implied enforcement rights are granted in relation to former feudal burdens under ss 52 to 56 of the Title Condition (Scotland) Act 2003, it is necessary to convert feudal terminology into appropriate post-feudal language. Secondly, the theory that feudal superior and vassal are bound together in a perpetual contract must be considered to determine if there will be continuing contractual relations between the former vassal and superior.

19.108 Interpretation of burdens containing feudal terminology in the future

Section 73 of the Abolition of Feudal Tenure etc (Scotland) Act 2000 provides detailed conversion provisions for any feudal terminology found in deeds or in a title sheet in the Land Register (or any land certificate). Subsection (1) provides that where a deed contains a reference to:

'(i) the dominium utile of the land, that reference shall be construed either as a
      reference to the land or as a reference to the ownership of that land;
(ii) an estate in land, that reference shall be construed as a reference to a right
      in land, and as including ownership of land;
(iii) a vassal in relation to land that reference shall be construed as a reference
      to the owner of the land;
(iv) feuing, that reference shall be construed as a reference to disponing;
(v) a feu disposition, that reference shall be construed as a reference to a dis-
      position;
(vi) taking infeftment, that reference shall be construed as a reference to com-
      pleting title'.

Subsection (2) provides that where there is a reference to the superior in relation
to a former feudal burden then that shall become a reference to the party that obtains
title to enforce as a result of the conversion procedure. Thus, if a Schedule 5 notice
was registered, preserving a burden as a praedial real burden, any reference in the
burden to the superior must be interpreted as a reference to the owner of the nominated property. Or if a Schedule 8 notice was registered, preserving a conservation
burden, any reference in the burden to the superior must be interpreted as a reference
to the holder of the conservation burden. Subsection (2), however, does not provide
that superior means the holders of implied title to enforce where such title is given to
properties neighbouring the burdened property under ss 52 to 54 of the Title
Conditions (Scotland) Act 2003.

A new subsection (2A) was introduced by para 13 (c) of Schedule 13 to the Title
Conditions (Scotland) Act 2003. This provides that 'any provision ... to the effect
that a person other than the person entitled to enforce the burden may waive compliance with or mitigate or otherwise vary a condition of, the burden shall be
disregarded'. This provision is wide-ranging in effect and applies to rights enforceable on and after the appointed day. It is not limited to feudal abolition and would
appear to apply to burdens created both before and after the appointed day. It is
intended to mirror s 3(8) of the 2003 Act (discussed at para 15.34). It appears to have
various effects.

It has implications if a burden provides that parties other than the benefited owners can vary or discharge the burden. The use of the definite article in subsection (2A)
suggests that the subsection covers burdens which do not provide for consent of *all*
parties entitled to enforce the burden. The provision is intended to prevent developers retaining control over developments (and a stream of income for variations and
discharges) when their interest in the development has ceased. However, the effect is
broader than intended. A burden may provide that title to vary burdens differs from
title to enforce. For example, it may be provided in a feudal development that burdens can be varied or discharged by the superior or failing that by immediate
neighbours of the burdened property. This, though, is not permitted if title to enforce
extends beyond these immediate neighbours. In a modern housing estate with such a
burden where under the pre-abolition law a vassal could approach the superior for

consent, post-abolition the owner will require to approach every proprietor with title to enforce (or rely on the provisions for variation of community burdens under ss 32 to 37 of the 2003 Act, discussed at paras 18.19 to 18.25). This will generally not be practical and lead to increased reliance on implied variation and discharge and applications to the Tribunal for variation: see Chapter 18.

19.109 Contractual effect of feu

Where at the time of feudal abolition the original contracting parties remain vassal and superior s 75(1) of the Abolition of Feudal Tenure etc (Scotland) Act 2000 provides that in so far as the contract remains effective it will be unaffected. This will be of importance in relation to compensation mechanisms established in relation to development value burdens. Such mechanisms will often not be valid real burdens and therefore could not be converted into a right to claim compensation under the development value burden procedure.

It is sometimes suggested that the enforcement of feudal burdens can be attributed, to some degree, to an ongoing contractual relationship between superior and vassal, based on the requirement in feudal law for the vassal to take entry with the superior. This approach was often asserted as the juridical basis for the enforceability of burdens: see for example, W M Gloag *Contract* (2nd edn, 1929), pp 228 to 229. The approach is difficult to reconcile with the facts of *Tailors of Aberdeen v Coutts* (1837) 2 Sh & Macl 609 and (1840) 1 Robin 296 and is criticised by K G C Reid in *The Law of Property in Scotland* (1996), paras 382 and 393. Any doubts regarding this have been dealt with by s 75(2) of the 2000 Act (added by para 14 of Schedule 13 to the Title Conditions (Scotland) Act 2003). It provides that in considering the contractual relationship between the parties any perpetual feudal contract based on renewal of investiture is disregarded.

Chapter 20

Public Law Restrictions on the Use of Land

20.1 Introduction

The limitations imposed on individual owners by the common law have been dealt with already in Chapter 13 and restrictions in individual titles in Chapters 14 to 19. But landowners are also subject to a large number of public law restraints. The principal ones are examined briefly in this chapter. For a fuller treatment, reference should be made to the texts cited in the Reading List for this chapter.

A purchaser will need to be alert to public law controls because they may impose constraints, sometimes serious, on what may be done on or with the land with a consequent effect on land value or they may require the carrying out of works with consequent costs. The rule of *caveat emptor* will apply, unless suitable provision has been made in the antecedent contract. This underlines the need either for prior inquiry before a contract is concluded; or for the making of suitable provisions as to statutory controls in the contract of sale and purchase (see Chapter 28).

The subjects which will be discussed here are:

(1) town and country planning;
(2) compulsory purchase;
(3) building control;
(4) the countryside;
(5) ancient monuments;
(6) fire precautions;
(7) housing;
(8) roads;
(9) health and safety at work;
(10) disability discrimination; and
(11) environmental controls.

20.2 Town and country planning: general

The most comprehensive of the controls over what may be done on or with land is to be found in the planning legislation. What follows is an outline of some of the more important points in relation to town and country planning which may affect a purchaser of heritable property. No attempt is made here to deal in detail with the law of town and country planning.

20.3   LEGAL FRAMEWORK

The main statutes at present governing town and country planning in Scotland are the Town and Country Planning (Scotland) Act 1997 (henceforth 'the principal statute' or 'the 1997 Act'), the Planning (Listed Buildings and Conservation Areas) (Scotland) Act 1997 ('the Listed Buildings Act 1997'), the Planning (Hazardous Substances) (Scotland) Act 1997, and the Planning (Consequential Provisions) (Scotland) Act 1997, all of which consolidated the law as at 27 May 1997.

Planning law is, however, in a continuous state of change. Legislation covering related areas, such as housing and roads, may also be relevant in dealing with planning matters. But the above statutes, together with regulations made thereunder, form the legislative framework of planning in Scotland.

Most procedural matters are dealt with by regulation. The principal regulations include the Town and Country Planning (General Permitted Development) (Scotland) Order 1992, SI 1992/223 (as amended), referred to as 'the Permitted Development Order'; the Town and Country Planning (General Development Procedure) (Scotland) Order 1992, SI 1992/224 (as amended), referred to as 'the Procedure Order' (both 1992 orders came into effect on 13 March 1992); and the Town and Country Planning (Use Classes) (Scotland) Order 1997, SI 1997/3061, referred to as 'the Use Classes Order', which came into effect on 2 February 1998. There are numerous other regulations and orders covering in detail specific aspects of planning procedure.

Planning law is required to be compatible with European Community law and certain rights created by the European Convention on Human Rights. The Scottish Executive, in the form of the First Minister and Scottish Ministers, have executive responsibility for the Scottish planning system. This responsibility includes initiating new legislation and drawing up national planning policies and issuing guidelines on policy in the form of SPPs (Scottish Planning Policies); PANs (Planning Advice Notes); and Circulars which provide guidance on policy as a result of legislative or procedural change.

20.4   HISTORY

Town and country planning in Scotland goes back to 1909; but, for practical purposes, the origin of the modern system was the Town and Country Planning (Scotland) Act 1947. The provisions of that Act have now been wholly superseded and it is only rarely that it will have any continuing relevance in conveyancing.

The Local Government (Scotland) Act 1973 provided for a two-tier planning system in the six 'urban' regions of Scotland reflecting the distribution of local government functions between regional and district councils. This was thought to fit well with the two-tier development plan system of structure and local plans which had been introduced by the Town and Country Planning (Scotland) Act 1969 and consolidated in the Town and Country Planning (Scotland) Act 1972. In the three rural regions and the three islands areas, regional and islands councils exercised all planning functions.

This arrangement continued until 1996 when the two-tier system of regional and district councils was abolished by the provisions of the Local Government etc (Scotland) Act 1994. The 1994 Act established in its place a single-tier system of local authorities. The two-tier development plan system remained and is reflected in the Town and Country Planning (Scotland) Act 1997, the principal planning Act today.

However, s 33 of the 1994 Act provides that the Scottish Ministers may by order provide for structure plan areas overlapping local authority boundaries and that where a structure plan area extends to the district of more than one planning authority, the planning authorities concerned shall jointly carry out certain structure planning functions under the principal statute. The precise arrangements for carrying out these functions jointly are to be such as the authorities concerned may agree. Such an order, namely the Designation of Structure Plan Areas (Scotland) Order 1995, SI 1995/3002, came into effect on 1 April 1996 and, for example, the former structure plan area of Tayside was divided into two structure plan areas: (1) Perth and Kinross; and (2) Dundee and Angus.

As explained below, the Scottish Executive is presently undertaking a review of the Scottish planning system with a view to streamlining development plans.

Development planning is only one of the two main roles of planning authorities. The other is development control, which provides for the comprehensive regulation of land development. Although the detail of the development control system has changed considerably over the years, its essentials remain much as they were under the 1947 Act. The law relating to development control is now to be found in the 1997 Act and in the related regulations.

20.5   OVERALL RESPONSIBILITY FOR PLANNING

Following devolution, the Scottish Ministers have overall responsibility for town and country planning in Scotland, exercised principally through the Scottish Executive Development Department, while the actual day-to-day administration of the planning system is carried out by the planning authorities as defined in the principal statute.

20.6   DEVELOPMENT PLANS: 1947–1996

Because of the importance of the development plan in the planning system (see below) and because of the way in which the plan has changed over the years, it is appropriate to take a moment to map out these changes before moving on to outline the development control process.

Under the Town and Country Planning (Scotland) Act 1947 every planning authority (which, by and large, meant every large burgh and county authority in Scotland) was charged with the duty of preparing a development plan for its planning area. The plan was map based and, once prepared, it had to be reviewed every five years. These 'old style' single-tier development plans have little continuing relevance and a new two-tier regime was introduced by the Town and Country Planning (Scotland) Act 1969. The two tiers are considered in turn.

(1) *Structure plans*. The intention of the system introduced by the 1969 Act was to separate strategic planning from the detailed land use planning of an area. The old-style development plans had attempted unsuccessfully to combine both. The regional and islands planning authorities set up under the Local Government (Scotland) Act 1973 considered the policy implications for their whole area and then prepared a structure plan. The structure plan comprised a written statement supplemented by diagrams setting out strategic policies for development and land use. Considerable preparatory study and discussion were required before the structure plan could be prepared; and the approval of the Secretary of State was then required. Thereafter the plans were to be kept under review.

(2) *Local plans*. Detailed land use planning was contained in the local plans, which were the responsibility of the district planning authorities, except in the three rural regions and the three islands areas. They consisted of a written statement and a map or maps. They either covered a specified, and usually a fairly restricted, area (such as a town) or they could take the form of a subject plan (such as mineral development). They could not be adopted unless they conformed to the approved structure plan. Once adopted by the planning authority (the approval of the Secretary of State was not normally required) local plans offered detailed guidance to developers and purchasers.

The development plan for an area therefore comprised the structure plan and one or more local plans.

20.7   POST-1996 DEVELOPMENT PLANNING

(1) *Structure plans*. The preparation of a structure plan for a structure plan area follows very closely the procedure described above for regional planning authorities. Schedule 4 to the Local Government etc (Scotland) Act 1994 makes further and transitional provisions, particularly where the new structure plan area differs from the previous one. Since new structure plans are in the majority of cases now prepared by several authorities acting together, the Schedule provides for dealing with disagreements through each authority setting out its own reasoned alternative proposals and powers to the Scottish Ministers to issue directions. Also, with the new structure plan

areas being generally smaller than the previous ones, consultation is required with any other planning authority which is likely to be affected, before submission of a structure plan to the Scottish Ministers or before its alteration.

(2) *Local plans.* Under the 1994 Act the provisions relating to local plans are virtually identical to those already described, but every planning authority is now required to pre-pare local plans for all parts of its area and it is now competent for two or more plan-ning authorities to make a joint local plan extending to parts of each of their districts.

Section 24 of the Town and Country Planning (Scotland) Act 1997 states that struc-ture and local plans made prior to 1 April 1996 remain in force until replaced by new plans.

(3) *Advisory plans.* These do not have statutory effect and may consist of a statement of policy (perhaps to be found in the planning authority's minutes) or a more formal document (such as a proposed local plan which has not yet entered the consultation process). Such advisory plans do, however, carry weight in practice and should be given consideration.

20.8   THE REVIEW OF STRATEGIC PLANNING (2001)

The two-tier development plan system has not worked well. Planning authorities have struggled, often unsuccessfully, to keep them up to date and local plans have been held up by delays with structure plans. By law, the local plan must conform to the structure plan. *The Review of Strategic Planning* (SEDD, 2001) has accordingly proposed the abolition of structure plans for all but the four largest cities. The four city regions would continue with a two-tier development plan with the top tier com-prising a strategic development plan and the bottom tier a local development plan. Outside the four city areas, the two-tier development plan would be replaced by a one-tier local development plan to be prepared by each planning authority. Legislation is awaited.

Legislation is also awaited to implement EC Council Directive 2001/42 on strate-gic environmental assessment. The Directive must be implemented by 21 July 2004 and will require environmental assessment to be a part of the preparation of devel-opment plans.

20.9   DEVELOPMENT PLANS AND THE PURCHASER

The concern in describing the arrangements for development plans is with their rele-vance to a purchaser. A purchaser will normally make his offer conditional upon there being no adverse planning implications in the development plan (which may require definition).

20.10   DEVELOPMENT PLANS AND DEVELOPMENT CONTROL

It should not be assumed that an individual application for planning permission will receive automatic approval simply because the application appears to fall within the guidelines set out in a development plan. Nor should it be assumed that an application which departs from the plan will be refused. Each application requires to be considered on its own merits. However, s 25 of the Town and Country Planning (Scotland) Act 1997 provides that where, in making any determination under the Act, regard is to be had to the development plan, the determination shall be made in accordance with the plan unless material considerations indicate otherwise. Section 25 does not make the plan binding; development control remains a discretionary exercise. It does, however, give the plan primacy in the decision-making process.

20.11   'DEVELOPMENT'

(1)   *Definition.* The principal statute operates by imposing a statutory control on all development of land. 'Development' is comprehensively defined in the Town and Country Planning (Scotland) Act 1997, s 26(1) as:

   (i)   '... the carrying out of building, engineering, mining, or other operations in, on, over or under land, or

   (ii) '... the making of any material change in the use of any buildings or other land'.

Certain of these expressions are defined in the 1997 Act. Section 28(1) provides that planning permission is required for the development of land (a term which includes buildings or structures and land covered by water). Unless and until planning permission is obtained, it is unlawful to carry out any proposed development on land and enforcement action may be initiated against a breach of control.

As a result of conflicting court cases, demolition is now specifically included in the list of building operations in s 26 of the 1997 Act which amount to development which requires planning permission. However, many forms of demolition outwith residential areas do not in fact require permission as a result of the Town and Country Planning (Demolition which is not Development) (Scotland) Direction 1995 and Class 70 of the Permitted Development Order (see below).

For the avoidance of doubt, certain activities (to use a neutral term) are specifically declared not to involve development (s 26(2) of the 1997 Act). These include:

(1) the maintenance, improvement or other alteration of a building, affecting only the interior or not materially affecting the external appearance (this does not however avoid the need for listed building consent where applicable, nor building warrant);

(2) the use of any building or land within the 'curtilage' of a dwellinghouse for any purpose incidental to the enjoyment of that dwellinghouse as such;

(3) the use of land, or buildings thereon, for agriculture or forestry;
(4) a change of use of land or building which is authorised by or falls within any of the use classes specified by the Use Classes Order.

(2) *The Use Classes Order.* The current Use Classes Order at the time of writing is the Town and Country Planning (Use Classes) (Scotland) Order 1997, SI 1997/3061. This came into operation on 2 February 1998. There are 11 separate classes of use. A change from one activity to another within the same class of the Order does not constitute development. The classes include:

Class 1 – Use as a shop where the sale, display or service is principally to visiting members of the public. Use as a shop for the sale of motor vehicles is excluded by article 3(5)(d) of the Order and motor fuel by article (3)(5)(c).

Class 2 – Use for the provision of financial services, professional services or any other service including use as a betting office where such provision is appropriate in a shopping area and the services are provided principally to visiting members of the public.

Class 3 – Use for the sale of food or drink for consumption on the premises. Public houses are expressly excluded by article 3(5)(h) of the Order. The sale of cold food (but not hot food) for consumption off the premises is permitted by Class 1.

Class 4 – Use (a) as an office other than a use within Class 2, (b) for research and development of products or processes, or (c) for any industrial process, being a use which can be carried on in any residential area without detriment to the amenity of the area.

Class 5 – Use for an industrial process other than one falling within Class 4.

The Use Classes Order is not a comprehensive listing of all possible uses of land but merely catalogues certain types of use. Some uses are expressly excluded, such as use as an amusement arcade and always require planning permission as they are considered to be *sui generis* uses, ie non-classified uses.

While a change from a use within one class to a use in another class will generally constitute development, a general planning permission is granted by the Town and Country Planning (General Permitted Development) (Scotland) Order 1992, SI 1992/223 for certain changes between classes (see below). These are cases where in effect the proposed use is less detrimental than the previous use, for example, a café can be changed to a shop, but not vice versa: see Part 3 of Schedule 1 to the Permitted Development Order.

The Use Classes Order retains effective control over changes of use which, because of environmental consequences or relationship with other uses, need to be the subject of a specific planning permission but the scope of each class is wide enough to take in changes of use which generally do not need to be subject to specific planning control.

(3) *The Permitted Development Order*. Article 3 of the Town and Country Planning (General Permitted Development) (Scotland) Order 1992, SI 1992/223, as amended, grants a general planning permission for the 72 classes of development set out in Schedule 1 to the Order. Many of these are generally of little relevance to the individual purchaser or developer, but Part 1, Classes 1 to 6, Part 2, Classes 7 to 9 and Part 3, Classes 10 to 13, could be important. Thus, under the Permitted Development Order:

- Part 1, Classes 1–6, development within the curtilage of a dwellinghouse (not including a flat) is permitted within certain tolerances without an application for planning permission being required (but see Part 1, Class 6, and Part 21, Classes 6–8 as to satellite dishes).
- Part 2, Classes 7–9, permit sundry minor operations, such as erecting fences within certain prescribed dimensions.
- Part 3, Classes 10–13, permit a change from a use within one class of the Use Classes Order to a use within another class of the Use Classes Order. As we have already seen, although a change within the same class of the Use Classes Order is not development, a change between classes is likely to be. For example, change of use from a hairdresser's to a sweet shop would not require planning permission as they are both uses within Class 1. However, changing from a hairdresser's to a restaurant would require permission because the Class 1 use is changing to a Class 3 use. As mentioned above, this part of the PDO permits change of use from café (Class 3) to shop (Class 1) but not vice versa.

(4) *Simplified planning zones*. In terms of the Town and Country Planning (Scotland) Act 1997, ss 49 to 54 and Schedule 5, planning authorities have a duty to consider whether it would be desirable to establish simplified planning zones in their area. The effect of a simplified planning zone scheme, if adopted, is to grant planning permission for the types of development specified therein. Few such areas have been established.

20.12   APPLICATION FOR PLANNING PERMISSION.

An application for planning permission can be made by anyone, but if the applicant is not the owner, notification of the application must be given to the owner and the appropriate certificate must accompany the application: Town and Country Planning (Scotland) Act 1997, s 35. The application is made to the planning authority on a form obtained from that authority. An environmental statement must be lodged with an application for certain types of development and may be requested in others: Environmental Impact Assessment (Scotland) Regulations 1999, SSI 1999/1. The authority may seek additional information from the applicant about the proposed development. A fee is payable at the time of submission of the application. Public notice must be given of certain applications, including those regarded as 'bad neighbour' developments (listed in Schedule 2 to the Permitted Development Order).

If an applicant intends to build a house on a particular plot of land, he lodges an application for full planning permission and, with it, detailed plans showing the layout of the house and details of the building itself. Permission may be granted with or without modification. If the applicant intends to develop a housing estate with, say, 200 houses, it would obviously be a very laborious and expensive job to lodge detailed layout and building plans for each plot when, at the end of the day, the planning authority may be opposed in principle to the development. It is, therefore, competent, for an applicant to apply for 'outline planning permission' (often referred to as planning permission in principle) indicating the general intention without specifying all the detail of the proposals for which planning permission is, ultimately, required. A grant of outline planning permission means that the developer has approval in principle for his proposals but must submit thereafter one or more applications for approval of the 'reserved matters', ie the details which were not included in the outline application.

Intimation of every application (with very limited exceptions) must be given either to neighbouring proprietors or to the public in general. Every application must be notified to 'persons having a notifiable interest in neighbouring land': article 9 of the Town and Country Planning (General Development Procedure) (Scotland) Order 1992, SI 1992/224. Due to the fact that domestic property is no longer entered in the valuation roll, article 9 of the Procedure Order requires notices to 'the owner' and 'the occupier' in respect of each address of premises comprising neighbouring land.

Planning authorities may also give public notice of certain other applications (for example, in conservation areas or of public interest) and must take any representations into account when dealing with the application. It should be noted, however, that, while a planning authority must 'take into account' representations made to it, neither these, nor an objector's strongly held views, can derogate from the right and duty of the planning authority to take whatever decision it feels correct in all the circumstances.

Under s 36 of the Town and Country Planning (Scotland) Act 1997, every planning authority is obliged to maintain a register of applications for, and grants of, planning permission. The register is open to the public and may be consulted at any time during working hours.

20.13 DETERMINING AN APPLICATION

Planning authorities will, by the nature of the size of their area or their organisation, adopt different procedures for dealing with planning applications. Section 56(1) of the Local Government (Scotland) Act 1973 provides for powers to be delegated by the authority to a committee, a sub-committee or an official and the majority of straightforward planning applications will be dealt with under delegated powers. Certain authorities may hear representations in respect of particular applications; certain may only be prepared to consider written representations.

A planning authority must issue its decision on a planning application within two months of submission of the application (four months for an application accompanied by an environmental impact assessment (EIA)). It may, however, if necessary consultations are numerous or if the application is of more than ordinary importance, seek the applicant's consent for an extension of this period. If no timeous decision is issued, the applicant may appeal to the Scottish Ministers against a 'deemed refusal'. A determination must be issued in respect of each application.

The planning authority may refuse an application, or may grant it – unconditionally, or subject to stated conditions which must be observed in carrying out the development. Depending on the application, a grant of permission may be for outline permission, ie a decision in principle, leaving the reserved matters as defined in article 2 of the Town and Country Planning (General Development Procedure) (Scotland) Order 1992, SI 1992/224 for later approval. Alternatively, it may be for full permission, allowing the development to be commenced without further planning approval being required; this is sometimes colloquially referred to as 'detailed permission'.

Under s 44 of the Town and Country Planning (Scotland) Act 1997, any planning permission which is granted attaches to the land irrespective of who is the owner for the time being.

Sections 58 and 59 of the 1997 Act require any development normally to commence within five years from the date of the granting of permission. Where outline permission has been granted, application for approval of reserved matters must be made within three years of the outline permission; and the development must normally commence within a further two years of final approval of the reserved matters.

20.14   PLANNING AGREEMENTS

A planning authority may enter into agreement with any person having an interest in land, such as would allow him to bind the land for the purpose of restricting or regulating development or use of that land: Town and Country Planning (Scotland) Act 1997, s 75. Section 75 agreements are widely employed in the development control process to give the planning authority stronger or more extensive control over the development for which planning permission has been applied or for securing the provision of the necessary supporting infrastructure and other community benefits. The agreement is normally registered in the Register of Sasines or in the Land Register, as appropriate, and can then be enforced by the planning authority against the owner for the time being. The Lands Tribunal for Scotland has no jurisdiction to review such agreements and they can only be varied by agreement with the planning authority. In negotiating a planning agreement it is crucial to ensure that provision is made within it for discharge and variation. A purchaser will need to check carefully for the existence of such an agreement relating to the land and for compliance with its terms. Purchasers of properties subject to planning agreements should check for discharge and variation provisions.

A search will disclose a registered planning agreement and any discharge or variation. If an agreement is not registered it does not bind the land in perpetuity but is a contract nonetheless. The courts have held that, as contracts, the terms of section 75 agreements cannot easily be the subject of judicial review.

Some local authorities are prepared to enter into personal agreements under the Local Government (Scotland) Act 1973, s 69, usually in relation to minor or temporary matters, but such an agreement is not registered and the obligations in such an agreement do not attach to the land.

20.15 APPEAL

If no timeous decision is issued, if the application is refused, or if the application is granted subject to conditions which the applicant considers to be unacceptable, the applicant has a right of appeal to the Scottish Ministers. The right of appeal must be exercised within six months of the decision or, in the absence of a decision, within six months of the date by which a decision should have been given. The applicant has the right to have his appeal heard, usually by way of a public local inquiry or alternatively by way of a hearing. The extent of public interest and the complexities of the law and policy at issue influence the choice of forum. Public inquiries are more usual. However the vast majority of appeals are not 'heard' but dealt with on the basis of the written submission procedure. This procedure allows each side to present a written statement of their position and avoids the delay and expense inherent in the public local inquiry. Following the 'closing of the record' in the written submissions procedure, or the completion of the report following upon the public local inquiry, the decision on the appeal is then taken, in the vast majority of cases by a reporter (a Scottish Executive official) who has the necessary power delegated to him. The principal parties (usually the appellant and the planning authority) must agree to adopt the written submissions procedure, otherwise a public local inquiry will be held. In the case of a major application, or one which has generated considerable local concern, a public local inquiry is likely to be held.

Normally, all relevant and non-repetitive evidence will be heard at a public inquiry. There is, however, nothing to prevent written representations being made by any interested party.

20.16 ENFORCEMENT OF PLANNING CONTROL

There is no point in having a detailed system of development control unless it is backed up with sanctions for a breach of control. These sanctions are provided in Part VI of the Town and Country Planning (Scotland) Act 1997.

Where a proprietor or occupier of the land either:

(1) carries out development without permission; or
(2) fails to comply with the conditions subject to which planning permission was granted,

a breach of planning control has occurred.

The planning authority's powers to take enforcement action against a breach of control are subject to time limits in terms of s 124 of the 1997 Act. Thus, where there has been a breach of planning control consisting of the carrying out without planning permission of operational development, enforcement action must be taken within four years of the date on which the operations were substantially completed. The four-year period also extends to the situation where the use of a building has been changed to that of a single dwellinghouse without planning permission. For any other breach of planning control (like change of use or breach of planning condition), there is a limitation period of ten years for enforcement action to be taken.

This immunity from enforcement is important because s 150(2) of the 1997 Act provides that uses and operations are 'lawful' if no enforcement action may be taken against them because the time for taking enforcement action has expired. A purchaser should always confirm carefully that the current use of the property is the authorised use or, alternatively, if it is unauthorised, that it is immune from enforcement action. The lawful use of any property is clearly critical to a purchaser. In many cases, no problem arises and there will be no need to make special inquiry, for example for a dwellinghouse clearly used as such for 60 years. For more recent development it is sensible to request a copy of the planning permission. For unauthorised but immune uses, it may be wise, in the absence of a letter of comfort from the planning authority (which, since a planning authority cannot bind itself by letter, may well be insufficient), to ask that a certificate of lawful use or development be obtained (see below).

Where a breach of control has occurred and the development is not immune from enforcement action, the planning authority is not obliged to take enforcement action. It has a discretion which will be exercised having regard to the development plan and all other material considerations. The authority cannot, however, be compelled to commence enforcement action by, for example, an affected neighbour.

The first step, where enforcement action is to be taken, may be the service of a planning contravention notice. This will be employed where the planning authority requires information about activities on the land, or the nature of the recipient's interest in the land (s 125 of the 1997 Act). A planning contravention notice does not constitute taking enforcement action (as defined in s 123 of the 1997 Act). Recipients of a notice are required to provide such information as the notice specifies regarding any operations being carried out on the land, any use of the land, and any conditions which apply to any planning permission that has been granted in respect of the land. Failure to comply with a notice within 21 days of it being served is an offence.

A planning authority has at its disposal a number of enforcement mechanisms. Of these, the most used is the enforcement notice. This may be served where it appears to the authority that there has been a breach of control. The provisions are to be found in ss 127–139 of the 1997 Act (see too SEDD Circular 4/1999). An enforcement notice must state the matters which constitute the breach of planning control and specify the steps required to remedy this. There is no prescribed form of notice. A right of appeal lies within 28 days to the Scottish Ministers and the grounds of appeal are specified in the 1997 Act, s 130. An appeal has the effect of suspending the notice until it is determined. Once an enforcement notice takes effect, a time is allowed for compliance. Failure to comply with a notice is an offence and the authority has power to take direct action and to recover the cost.

Where the planning authority serves an enforcement notice but considers that the consequences of the breach of control are such that the activity, or some of it, should cease immediately, it may also serve a stop notice (s 140 of the 1997 Act). A stop notice takes effect immediately on service but cannot be used to prohibit the use of any building as a dwellinghouse. Failure to comply with a stop notice is an offence. There is no right of appeal against such a notice. The notice remains in effect until the related enforcement notice is quashed or withdrawn or the time for compliance with it has passed.

Where the breach of control comprises a failure to comply with a condition, a planning authority may decide to serve a breach of condition notice (s 145 of the 1997 Act). A breach of condition notice can be served on any person carrying out a development on the ground or on the person having control of the ground. The notice must specify the steps which the planning authority considers should be taken, or the activities which the authority considers should cease, to secure compliance with the condition(s) specified in the notice. The recipient of the notice has 28 days from service of the notice to comply and failure to do so constitutes an offence. There is no right of appeal.

Offences may be prosecuted at the hands of the procurator fiscal by way of summary cause or solemn procedure. Fines can be substantial and are unlimited in solemn procedure.

As well as, or as an alternative to, taking any of the steps described above, a planning authority may seek an interdict to restrain any actual or apprehended breach of planning control (s 146 of the 1997 Act). The application to either the Court of Session or the sheriff court for interdict is not dependent on the exercise of any other powers under the 1997 Act. Whether an interdict should be used as opposed to other powers may depend on the seriousness of the breach of control and the particular circumstances of the persons against whom proceedings are initiated.

20.17   CERTIFICATE OF LAWFUL USE OR DEVELOPMENT

If a person wishes to ascertain whether a use or operation is lawful, or whether the carrying on of development without complying with a condition on the consent is lawful, he may apply for a certificate of lawful use or development. A use or operation is being carried on lawfully if it is not development, if it is covered by a general or specific grant of planning permission, if it is not being carried on in contravention of a consent or if it is immune from enforcement action. If a planning authority refuses to grant the certificate applied for, the refusal may be appealed to the Scottish Ministers.

20.18   SPECIAL CONTROLS

In addition to mainstream planning control outlined above, planning authorities are also responsible for a number of other controls which operate either alongside or instead of mainstream planning control.

(1) *Listed buildings and conservation areas.* The most important of the special controls are those relating to listed buildings. The Planning (Listed Buildings and Conservation Areas) (Scotland) Act 1997 ('the Listed Buildings Act 1997') requires the Scottish Ministers to compile a list of buildings of special architectural or historic interest – listed buildings – throughout Scotland. A listing applies not just to the building but also to an object or structure fixed to the building, whether internal or external and also to certain objects or structures within the curtilage of the building. The list may be amended from time to time. There is no right of appeal against a decision to list a building. A copy of the list is maintained by the planning authority and is available for public inspection.

The effect of listing is that the building in question cannot be demolished, nor can it be altered or extended in such a way as to affect its character as a listed building, without first obtaining listed building consent from the planning authority. There is a right of appeal on statutory grounds (including the ground that the building is not worthy of listing) to the Scottish Ministers against an adverse decision on a listed building application. A breach of listed building control is an offence and may be the subject also of a listed building enforcement notice. Listed building control is a separate procedure which runs in parallel with mainstream planning control. Unlike breach of planning control, breach of listed building control can never become lawful by passage of time. A separate planning permission will be required for any 'development' of the building and in exercising development control functions a planning authority must have special regard to the desirability of preserving the building or its setting or any features of special interest which it possesses: Listed Buildings Act 1997, s 59. A purchaser should check to see whether a building is listed because a listing could well affect any future plans for development.

A separate but parallel regime of control applies to 'conservation areas'. A planning authority is under a duty to designate as conservation areas those parts of its district of special architectural or historic interest, the character or appearance of which it is considered desirable to preserve or enhance. A conservation area may well include one or more listed buildings to which listed building control will apply.

A conservation area is first and foremost a development control designation. In exercising planning powers, a planning authority must pay special regard to the desirability of preserving or enhancing the character of appearance of the area: Listed Buildings Act 1997, s 64. However, the designation also confers control over the demolition of unlisted buildings and gives some protection to trees. A purchaser should check whether a property is in a conservation area, although the designation has less significance for an owner than listing.

(2) *Trees.* The felling or lopping of a tree does not constitute 'development' for the purposes of the Town and Country Planning (Scotland) Act 1997 and does not therefore require planning permission. There are, however, two ways in which planning authorities can exercise control over what happens to trees. First of all, when granting planning permission for development, the authority may impose conditions

safeguarding existing trees and requiring the planting of new trees. Secondly, an authority may make a tree preservation order (TPO) to protect existing trees in the interests of amenity. A purchaser of land with development in mind will need to watch for both of these.

TPO procedure is set out in the Town and Country Planning (Tree Preservation Order and Trees in Conservation Areas) (Scotland) Regulations 1975, SI 1975/1204, as amended. A TPO may be made to protect a single tree, a group of trees or wood-lands. The effect of the order will be to prohibit, without the prior approval of the authority, the cutting down, topping, lopping uprooting or the wilful damage or destruction of a protected tree(s). While there is a right to make representations to the authority against a TPO, it can be, and often is, drafted so as to have immediate effect. The authority will make the final decision on the order after taking account of any representations. Contravention of a TPO is an offence and the owner of the land must replace any tree removed with another of an appropriate size and species. The TPO will apply to any replacement tree. There is a right of appeal to the Scottish Ministers against an adverse decision on an application for consent under an order. Any consent to remove a tree may be subject to a replanting obligation. A TPO will be registered in the Register of Sasines or Land Register, as appropriate.

(3) *Advertisements*. Although the display of an advertisement may amount to 'devel-opment', no planning permission is required provided the advertisement is displayed in accordance with the Town and Country Planning (Control of Advertisements) (Scotland) Regulations 1984, SI 1984/467. The regulations provide a self-contained code dealing with the control of the display of advertisements. 'Advertisement' is given a wide definition in the Town and Country Planning (Scotland) Act 1997, s 277(1). Advertisement control may be exercised only in the interests of amenity and public safety: s 182(2) of the 1997 Act.

(4) *Waste land*. If it appears to a planning authority that the amenity of its district is adversely affected by the condition of any land in its district, it may serve a notice on those with an interest in the land under s 179 of the 1997 Act, requiring the proper maintenance of the land. The power would seem to be available to deal with both 'built' and 'unbuilt' land and provides planning authorities with a tool for tackling problems caused by passive neglect, although it is not confined to that. There is a right of appeal against such a notice to the Scottish Ministers on prescribed grounds. Failure to comply with such a notice may lead to direct action by the authority and recovery of costs.

(5) *Hazardous substances*. The Planning (Hazardous Substances) (Scotland) Act 1997 requires hazardous substances consent to be obtained from a planning author-ity for the presence of a hazardous substance on land at or above its controlled quantity. The hazardous substances and their controlled quantity are set out in the Town and Country Planning (Hazardous Substances) (Scotland) Regulations 1993, SI 1993/323, as amended.

20.19   HUMAN RIGHTS AND PLANNING

Whilst there are no specific rights in the European Convention on Human Rights in respect of planning, the fact that Convention rights are broadly expressed means they have a potential to apply to many areas of activity like trade or planning.

The framework of the Town and Country Planning (Scotland) Act 1997 tends to involve duties or obligations rather than rights, for example, the obligation to obtain planning permission. Convention rights do not fit easily with the planning system. The interpretation of Convention rights and planning law is a balancing exercise.

For example, the right to peaceful enjoyment of possessions (Article 1, Protocol 1 of the Convention) does not prevent the state from having the right to control the use of the property. Convention rights like this tend to indicate their own restrictions. So Article 1, Protocol 1 states that a person may be deprived of his possessions in the public interest subject to legal conditions and the general principles of international law. Therefore, for example, compulsory purchase of land by a public authority can be competently done.

Similarly, a developer and an objector could rely on the same Convention rights to support their opposing cases. For example, the developer extending his house could rely on Article 8 (right to respect for private and family life) and Article 1, Protocol 1 to argue that planning permission should be granted for his house extension. His neighbours could rely on the same Convention rights to argue permission should be refused.

The Human Rights Act 1998 makes it unlawful for a public authority to act in a way that is incompatible with Convention rights. All parties involved in the planning system, other than the public authorities, have Convention rights. The planning authority, as the public authority in this case, has to balance the competing Convention rights when making its decisions. The actual decisions reached by planning authorities may in the main be effectively the same as they would have been before the 1998 Act, albeit that the considerations may have increased.

In addition to Article 8 and Article 1, Protocol 1 referred to above, there are procedural rights secured by Article 6(1) (right to a fair trial). It should be noted that there is much overlap between the provisions of Article 6(1) and the common law requirements for procedural fairness and the rules of natural justice.

Given the broad terms of the House of Lords decision in *R (on the application of Holding & Barnes plc) v Secretary of State for the Environment, Transport and the Regions* [2001] 2 WLR 1389 (known generally as 'the *Alconbury* case') and the Inner House of the Court of Session decision in *County Properties Ltd v Scottish Ministers* 2001 SLT 1125, it seems unlikely that Article 6 will found a successful planning challenge unless the European Court of Human Rights changes its view on the adequacy of the British system of planning appeal and judicial review. In these cases, any lack of independence and impartiality on the part of the decision maker is held cured by the availability of recourse to the courts. In Scotland most planning procedures carry a statutory right of appeal to the Court of Session or there is potential for non-statutory judicial review. These cases indicate that such recourse satisfies the requirements of Article 6(1).

20.20 **Compulsory purchase**

Part VIII of the Town and Country Planning (Scotland) Act 1997 makes provision for the acquisition of land by agreement or compulsorily for various planning purposes to be carried out by the authority or by others. Compulsory acquisition is subject to confirmation by the Scottish Ministers and to the payment of compensation to the expropriated proprietor. Power is given elsewhere also to various authorities and utilities to acquire land compulsorily for the purposes of their functions. This is discussed below at paras 29.19 to 29.33.

20.21 **Building control**

The Building (Scotland) Acts 1959 and 1970, and regulations made thereunder, deal with the setting of building standards, the conduct of building operations and the treatment of dangerous buildings. Virtually all building operations and most changes of use anywhere in Scotland come under the supervision and control of the local authority and require a building warrant. It is an offence under s 6 of the 1959 Act to carry out building operations unless a warrant has been obtained and, where this happens, local authorities have power to require works to be undertaken to ensure that the building conforms to standards. Local authorities have delegated powers to grant building warrant relaxations in appropriate cases. A warrant will be granted only if the local authority is satisfied that the works will be carried out in accordance with the requirements of the building standards and the building operations regulations. A self-certification procedure is available. Class warrants may be issued by the Scottish Ministers for a particular design of building.

Warrants are conditional and satisfactory completion of building operations in accordance with conditions and in accordance with the building standards is signalled by the issuing by the local authority of a completion certificate. Except in 'exceptional circumstances', it is an offence wilfully to occupy a building before a completion certificate has been granted. Purchasers of buildings can avoid difficulties with local authorities by checking warrants and certificates, not only for new buildings, but for alterations or extensions to existing buildings. Local authorities also have power to deal with dangerous buildings, including power to require the demolition of such a building.

While the legislation is concerned mainly with the construction of new buildings or with changes of use, local authorities have power, having regard to the health, safety and convenience of those who will inhabit or frequent the building, to require existing buildings to conform to standards where it is reasonably practicable to require this. This provision is not often invoked in practice.

The 1959 and 1970 Acts are to be repealed and replaced by the Building (Scotland) Act 2003. The 2003 Act is to be brought into effect by commencement order. The new Act will set out the framework for a new building standards system, as opposed to a building control system. This reflects in part the harmonisation of construction standards throughout the European Community as a result of EC Council Directive 89/106. However, the general framework of control, involving an application for a warrant in advance of undertaking the works and the granting of a completion certificate on satisfactory conclusion is continued. The 2003 Act aims to simplify the process and also opens the door for building standards work being undertaken not just by local authorities but also by other 'verifiers'. Letters of comfort will be replaced with 'building standard assessments', although there may be difficulties with this: see A D Anderson 'The End of Letters of Comfort' (2002) 70 SLG 172.

20.22   The countryside

There are two main aspects to the countryside that we shall consider here: access and habitat.

20.23   ACCESS

Subject to what is said below about Part 1 of the Land Reform (Scotland) Act 2003, a landowner in Scotland has the right to the exclusive use of the land. The corollary of this right to the exclusive use of land is that anyone who enters the land without right or permission commits a trespass.

  One such right of access which may have consequences for what can be done with land is a public right of way. Public rights of way in Scotland are created by prescriptive use. Certain conditions must be fulfilled for a route to constitute a public right of way: it must lead from one public place to another, it must follow a more or less defined route and it must have been used by the public as of right openly, peaceably and without judicial interruption for a continuous period of at least 20 years (see para 16.15). Unlike England and Wales, there is no definitive map of such routes in Scotland so that the status of a 'claimed' public right of way is in fact often uncertain. As a result, it seems that a considerable part of Scotland's heritage of routes has been lost through land development, intensive agriculture, afforestation, the construction of by-passes, the electrification of railways and the construction of hydro-electric schemes.

  Because of shortcomings in the network of access routes in Scotland, the Countryside (Scotland) Act 1967, as amended, made provision for planning authorities to promote public path creation agreements and public path creation orders thereby conferring a statutory right of access on the public. Such agreements and orders must be registered in the Register of Sasines or the Land Register, as appropriate, and are enforceable at the instance of the planning authority against successors in title. Further provision is made in the 1967 Act for creating access rights on an area rather than a linear basis through access agreements and orders. Such agreements and orders must also be registered and are enforceable against successors in title. A person interested in land comprised in an access agreement or order is not to carry out work on the land which would have the effect of reducing public access to the land. In fact, relatively little use has been made of statutory agreements and orders, except in connection with long distance routes. They have proved to be difficult to promote, landowners have been reluctant to lose control and planning authorities have not been keen to take on the commitment.

Partly because of continuing problems in promoting secure access to the country-side in Scotland, particularly in lowland areas and on the urban fringe, partly because of widespread uncertainty about the legal basis on which people can enjoy access to the countryside, partly because of the lack of effective support for land managers facing problems with access and partly because of a commitment in the Labour Party manifesto for the 1997 election to improve access arrangements, Part 1 of the Land Reform (Scotland) Act 2003 will radically change the position from the date on which it takes effect. The landowner's right to the exclusive use of land will be qualified by a general right of public access to all land (subject to exceptions) and inland water for recreation and passage: 2003 Act, s 1. The right is a right of non-motorised access. The exercise of access rights should not impede land management operations and there are safeguards for privacy. Excluded from access rights are, amongst others, buildings and, in non-residential cases, their curtilage, land required to secure for a dwelling a reasonable measure of privacy, land on which crops have been sown or are growing, and land to which the public have been and are admitted only on payment of a charge: 2003 Act, s 6. Local authorities will have power to exempt other land at the request of a landowner by order: 2003 Act, s 11. Access rights are to be exercised responsibly and Scottish Natural Heritage (SNH) is required to prepare and publish a Scottish Outdoor Access Code. Questions about the extent of access rights and about responsible behaviour may be determined by way of summary application to the sheriff: 2003 Act, s 28. See further A J M Steven and A Barr 'The Land Reform (Scotland) Act 2003' (2003) 66 Greens PLB 5.

20.24 HABITAT PROTECTION

There has been a long history of legislative intervention to protect species; but it was not until the middle of the twentieth century that Parliament took steps to safeguard the habitats of species and habitats of nature conservation interest. More recently, the European Union has intervened to strengthen this protection. Purchasers of land in rural areas need to be aware of the implications of the regime for habitat protection as it can have important implications for the use and management of the land. It has been estimated that some 11% of Scotland's land surface is subject to some form of nature conservation protection. There are three levels of protection: nature reserves, Sites of Special Scientific Interest and European sites. These are considered in turn.

(1) *Nature reserves.* The National Parks and Access to the Countryside Act 1949 makes provision for nature reserves. Nature reserves are areas of land managed primarily for the study and conservation of nature (s 15). National nature reserves may

be 'declared' (in effect designated) by SNH on land held or leased by SNH, or by a body recognised by it for the management of such reserves, or on land subject to what is in effect a management agreement entered into by SNH under s 16 of the 1949 Act with an owner or occupier. An agreement will include provision for compensation where a landowner forgoes some alternative more profitable use of the land. Although powers of compulsory acquisition exist they have never been employed and Scotland's portfolio of national nature reserves therefore relies on the continued willingness of landowners to sell or lease land or to enter into an agreement which gives effect to the primacy of nature. It is essentially a voluntary approach to habitat protection.

Local authorities also have power under s 21 of the 1949 Act to establish local nature reserves in much the same way.

(2) *Sites of Special Scientific Interest (SSSIs).* The most commonly employed means of safeguarding habitats is through the designation by SNH of an SSSI. The legislative provisions are to be found in Part II of the Wildlife and Countryside Act 1981. They revolve around a system of reciprocal notification. SNH has a duty to notify owners and occupiers and the local authority of a site which in its opinion is of special scientific interest. There is an opportunity to make representations although the notification takes effect immediately. The effect of the notification is to trigger two different forms of control. Accompanying the notification will be a list of potentially damaging operations. If such an operation constitutes 'development' within the meaning of the Town and Country Planning (Scotland) Act 1997, then it will be subject to development control (above). SNH will be a statutory consultee under the planning procedure. If, on the other hand, the activity does not constitute development, then the owner or occupier wishing to carry out such an operation must first notify SNH (the reciprocal notification). Failure to notify is an offence. SNH has four months in which to consider the likely impact of the operation. It may consent to the operation or seek to negotiate a management agreement modifying or preventing the operation. There is no obligation on an owner or occupier to fall in with SNH's wishes. Part II of the 1981 Act operates on a voluntary basis. At the conclusion of the period of four months the owner or occupier may proceed with the operation as planned. However, there could be an incentive to enter into an agreement because SNH may pay compensation for profit forgone in not carrying on the operation or not carrying it on in the way proposed. In practice, with most agreements compensation tends to be paid now for undertaking positive management in the interests of nature conservation rather than for not undertaking a damaging operation. It should also be noted that SNH can seek a nature conservation order from the Scottish Ministers if negotiations break down. There is a right of objection. Such orders are used to safeguard the more important SSSIs. The effect of such an order will be to extend the period of restraint so that agreement can be reached. Whether land has been designated as an SSSI can be checked through SNH or via the local plan.

Purchasers of land in rural areas should note that the Nature Conservation Bill, published by the Scottish Executive for consultation in April 2003, proposes to move away from a system of compensation for not damaging a site of nature conservation interest. Instead, SNH will be able to refuse a notice of intention to carry out an operation and there will be a right of appeal against the refusal to the Scottish Land Court. No compensation will be payable if an operation is prevented from going ahead. In other words, the intention is to move away from the present voluntary system for safeguarding SSSIs towards a conventional system of regulation.

(3) *European Sites*. The government is under an obligation under the Birds Directive (EC Council Directive 79/409) to classify special protection areas for birds (SPAs), and under the Habitats Directive (EC Council Directive 92/43) to propose to the European Union sites for designation as special areas of conservation (SACs). The object is to establish a coherent ecological network of sites across Europe. SPAs and SACs are together known as 'European sites'.

The protection of European sites relies up to a point on the provisions of Part II of the Wildlife and Countryside Act 1981 outlined above. Government policy has been to designate nearly all European sites as SSSIs. However, purchasers of land should be aware that European sites do not depend on a voluntary system for protection. The Conservation (Natural Habitats etc) Regulations 1994, SI 1994/2716 provide that where a notified operation is likely, in SNH's view, to have a significant effect on a European site, SNH must make an assessment of the implications for the site and consent to the operation can only be given if SNH concludes that it will not adversely affect the integrity of the site. Exceptionally, such an operation could be allowed to proceed if there are imperative reasons of overriding public interest. If the owner or occupier, nonetheless, indicates an intention to proceed with the operation otherwise than in these exceptional circumstances, SNH will seek a special nature conservation order from the Scottish Ministers. Such an order will delay the operation indefinitely. It is worth stressing that the rules on European sites apply to all operations that may have an effect on the site, not just those taking place within its designated boundaries, so landowners outwith the area are also subject to them.

20.25 Ancient monuments

The protection of ancient monuments is governed by the Ancient Monuments and Archaeological Areas Act 1979. Under the 1979 Act, the Scottish Ministers are required to compile and maintain a 'Schedule' of important monuments. The Schedule may be added to from time to time. Owners and occupiers must be notified of scheduling. It is an offence to carry out work affecting a scheduled monument without first obtaining authorisation. An application for 'scheduled monument consent' is made to the Scottish Ministers. Any such consent may be conditional and one such condition which is commonly imposed permits the carrying out of an archaeological investigation before the works are undertaken. A consent lasts for five years. A refusal of consent, and in some cases a conditional grant, can give rise to compensation for resulting expenditure, loss or damage: s 7 of the 1979 Act. There is provision for the Scottish Ministers or a local authority to enter into an agreement with the occupier of land dealing with the maintenance and preservation of the monument, the restriction of use of the land, public access and other matters. An agreement may provide for payment to be made in respect of obligations undertaken. Such an agreement may be registered in the Register of Sasines or the Land Register, as appropriate, and, in that event, can bind successors in title.

Part II of the 1979 Act also makes provision for the designation by the Scottish Ministers or by a local authority of areas of archaeological importance. Any person wishing to carry out an operation in such an area which may disturb the ground or which involve flooding or tipping operations must first notify the local authority. Failure to do so is an offence. The prior notice procedure will allow an investigation to be made of the site before the operation proceeds with a view to recording any matters of archaeological or historic interest.

20.26   **Fire precautions**

While a number of legislative codes, particularly those dealing with building control and with health and safety at work, make provision with regard to fire precautions, a purchaser should pay special attention in this regard to the requirements of the Fire Precautions Act 1971. The 1971 Act requires a fire certificate to be obtained from the fire authority for all designated premises. The requirement for a fire certificate turns on the use of the premises. It is an offence to put premises to a designated use in the absence of a current fire certificate.

Fire certificates are required for a number of uses designated by secondary legislation. In particular, a certificate is required for use as a hotel, boarding house, factory, office, shop, sporting and leisure complex and place of public entertainment. For details, see the Fire Precautions (Hotels and Boarding Houses) Order 1972, SI 1972/238; the Fire Precautions (Factories, Offices, Shops and Railway Premises) Order 1989, SI 1989/76; and the Fire Precautions (Workplace) Regulations 1997, SI 1997/1840. The requirement for a fire certificate is generally triggered by a threshold in terms of numbers of persons likely to use the premises and numbers likely to be present above ground-floor level.

An applicant for a fire certificate may be faced with a requirement to put in place onerous fire precautions. The certificate will specify the use for which the premises is certified and will deal with such matters as fire alarm, means of escape in the case of fire and fire fighting provision. The local authority has wide powers of inspection to determine whether a fire certificate is required and whether the terms of a certificate are being observed and may require remedial action to be taken where appropriate. Failure to comply with any remedial requirement may result in a fire certificate being cancelled and the use of the premises being prohibited or restricted.

20.27 **Housing**

Local authorities have a wide range of powers and duties relating to housing in their area. These include the provision of new housing, the management of their own housing stock, tackling sub-standard housing, making provision for the homeless and dealing with houses which are overcrowded or in multiple-occupation. Attention is focused in this section of this chapter only on the powers and duties under the housing legislation with regard to the standard of the housing stock, public and private, in the area. Depending on the standard of the property, a purchaser of a house may need to be alert to the exercise of these powers and duties.

Local authorities have a duty to ensure that sub-standard housing in their area is brought up to the necessary standard within a reasonable time. Central to this duty is the term 'tolerable standard'. Section 85 of the Housing (Scotland) Act 1987 provides that every local authority is under a duty to secure that all houses in its area which do not meet the tolerable standard are closed, demolished or brought up to that standard within a reasonable period. Section 86(1), as amended by the Housing (Scotland) Act 2001, provides that a house meets the 'tolerable standard' if it:

- is structurally stable;
- is substantially free from rising or penetrating damp;
- has satisfactory provision for natural and artificial lighting, for ventilation and for heating;
- has an adequate piped supply of wholesome water available within the house;
- has a sink provided with a satisfactory supply of both hot and cold water within the house;
- has a water closet available for the exclusive use of the occupants of the house and suitably located within the house;
- has a fixed bath or shower and a wash-hand basin, each provided with a satisfactory supply of both hot and cold water and suitably located within the house;
- has an effective system for the drainage and disposal of foul and surface water;
- has satisfactory facilities for the cooking of food within the house;
- has satisfactory access to all external doors and outbuildings.

Sub-standard housing may be tackled in one of two ways. First of all, local authorities have powers to tackle individual sub-standard houses. Secondly, local authorities may tackle sub-standard housing on an area basis. These are considered in turn.

20.28 INDIVIDUAL SUB-STANDARD HOUSING

Local authorities may tackle individual sub-standard houses through closing orders, demolition orders, improvement orders and repairs notices. These are considered briefly in turn.

(1) *Closing and demolition orders*. If the local authority is satisfied that a house does not meet the tolerable standard and ought to be demolished, but it forms part only of a building, it may make a closing order prohibiting human habitation: Housing (Scotland) Act 1987, s 114. Where a single house or single houses do not meet the tolerable standard and ought to be demolished, it may make a demolition order requiring the vacation of the building and its subsequent demolition: 1987 Act, s 115. There is a right of appeal against either order to the sheriff.

The owner of a house served with such an order has the option either of carrying out repairs necessary to bring the house up to the tolerable standard in which case the closing order or demolition order can then be removed; or of leaving the property as it is in the case of a closing order or demolishing in the case of a demolition order. In many of these cases, the local authority takes over the tenement from the owner at a nominal figure and carry out the work themselves; but the local authority has no obligation so to do.

Under the 1987 Act, s 123, if a demolition order is not complied with, the local authority may itself demolish and recover the cost from the owner. Under s 131, it may then make a charging order on the property to secure payment of the cost of any works.

If property is purchased subject to a closing order or a demolition order, the effect transmits against a purchaser.

(2) *Improvement orders*. A local authority may require a sub-tolerable house to be brought up to the tolerable standard and put into a good state of repair by an improvement order: Housing (Scotland) Act 1987, s 88. Where the house will have a future life of not less than ten years, the authority may also require the house to be provided with all standard amenities (as listed in Schedule 18). Such an order requires the owner to carry out works within 180 days to bring the house up to standard. The owner has a right of appeal against the order to the sheriff. The house may be acquired by the authority by agreement or, if necessary, by compulsion to secure enforcement.

(3) *Repairs notices*. A local authority may serve a repairs notice in respect of a house which is in a serious state of disrepair: Housing (Scotland) Act 1987, s 108. The repairs notice procedure is concerned with restoring a house to its former condition; the improvement order procedure is concerned with improving on that condition. The house does not necessarily have to be below the tolerable standard. The notice is served on the person having control of that house, requiring him, within a reasonable time, to execute works specified in the notice in order to bring the house up to a standard of reasonable repair. If a property is purchased subject to such a notice, the onus lies on the purchaser to carry out the work. The local authority may itself carry out the necessary work, if the owner fails or refuses, and recover the cost from the owners. The authority may make a charging order burdening the property with the cost.

Under the repairs notice procedure each person having control of premises (including non-residential premises) in a building should receive a notice referring to defects for which that owner would have some responsibility, even if this is only a partial responsibility. Failing collective action by the recipients, if that is necessary for example to secure common repairs, the local authority may itself undertake the necessary repairs after the expiry of the specified period which must not be less than 21 days. The expenses incurred by the local authority may be apportioned amongst the persons having control of premises in the building concerned, and retrieved (by charging order if appropriate) from such persons following service of a demand for payment.

There is no requirement, under the provisions referred to above relating to repairs, closing, demolition or improvement orders, which makes it obligatory to register the order in the Register of Sasines or the Land Register, as appropriate, as a necessary prerequisite of liability. So, a purchaser will not be put on his guard by a search over the title of the property. He has to make inquiry of the local authority direct to see whether or not any such order has been issued or is pending.

(4) *Grants*. Dealing with sub-standard housing is not just a matter of submitting to orders and notices. Implementation relies also on a system of repairs and improvement grants, some of which are mandatory and some discretionary. The grant arrangements are to be found in Part XIII of the Housing (Scotland) Act 1987, as amended by the Housing (Scotland) Act 1988 and subsequently by the Housing (Scotland) Act 2001 which provided for means testing. They are complex and are beyond the scope of this chapter.

20.29   SUB-STANDARD AREAS OF HOUSING

Local authorities have power to tackle sub-standard housing in a more comprehensive way where the situation requires such an approach. Authorities may designate a housing action area for demolition, for improvement or for both.

(1) *Housing action area for demolition*. Where an authority is satisfied that the houses, or the greater part of them, in an area do not meet the tolerable standard and that the most effective way of dealing with the area is to secure the demolition of the houses, it may declare the area to be a housing action area for demolition (HAAD): Housing (Scotland) Act 1987, s 89. An HAAD may not include the site of a building unless at least part of the building consists of a house which does not meet the tolerable standard and there may be excluded from demolition any part of a building which is used for commercial purposes. The resolution declaring the HAAD will identify the houses for demolition. A resolution is made first in draft form and is submitted to the Scottish Ministers who may direct that it be rescinded. Notice of the resolution must be served on those with an interest in the affected property and publication of the resolution in a local newspaper is also required. Representations in respect of the resolution may be submitted to the authority. Thereafter the authority must consider whether to make the resolution final. The authority has power to

acquire land by agreement or compulsorily to implement the resolution; but grants and loans are available for those willing to implement the works themselves.

(2) *Housing action area for improvement.* Where an authority is satisfied that the houses, or the greater part of them, in an area lack one or more of the standard amenities or do not meet the tolerable standard and that the most effective way of dealing with the area is to secure the improvement of the houses, it may declare the area to be a housing action area for improvement (HAAI): Housing (Scotland) Act 1987, s 90. The resolution declaring such an area will define the standard which the houses must attain on completion of the necessary works. They must meet the tolerable standard and be in a good state of repair. Where the houses will have a life of at least ten years, the resolution may also require the provision of all standard amenities An HAAI must not include the site of a building unless at least part of the building consists of a house which lacks one or more of the standard amenities or is not in a good state of repair. The procedure for an HAAI is as for an HAAD. As with an HAAD, an authority may acquire land by agreement or compulsorily to implement the resolution; but the hope is that in an HAAI the necessary work may be undertaken by or on behalf of those with an interest in the properties. To encourage this, improvement and repairs grants are available at special rates in such areas. Loans may also be available.

(3) *Housing action area for demolition and improvement.* Where the conditions for an HAAI exist but the authority considers that the best approach lies in a combination of demolition and improvement, it may designate a housing action area for demolition and improvement (HAADI): Housing (Scotland) Act 1987, s 91. The procedure for an HAADI is as for an HAAD. Implementation may be undertaken by those with an interest in the properties with the support of grants and loans or by the local authority through acquisition of the land.

Lastly, reference may be made to the final report of the Housing Improvement Task Force *Stewardship and Responsibility: A Policy Framework for Private Housing in Scotland* (March 2003), available at www.scotland.gov.uk/library5/housing/pfph.pdf. This addresses a number of areas, in particular updating the repairing standard for private landlords and improving mechanisms for common repairs.

20.30 Roads

Roads may be public or private, in the sense that they are either open to the public or under private control. Roads may, however, also be public or private in relation to the liability to maintain, in that a road which is open to the public as a public thoroughfare may nonetheless be maintainable by private individuals, normally the frontagers on that road. A road does not pass automatically to the council upon construction unless and until, following an application by an interested party such as a developer, the council has agreed to take over the road. It will probably do so if and when the owner or frontagers make up the road to the required standard at their own expense. Thereafter, the council will assume liability for maintenance. The council is obliged to maintain a list of roads maintainable at the public expense and this is available for public inspection.

The same applies, generally speaking, to foot pavements adjacent to public streets. The liability to make up and maintain rests with the individual frontagers according to the length of their frontage unless this liability has been assumed by the council. This is, therefore, a relevant point of inquiry when examining title to see whether there is any liability on the purchaser for making up or maintenance.

Under the Roads (Scotland) Act 1984, the council has power to require frontagers to make up a road, failing which the council will itself make it up and charge the frontagers with the due proportion of the cost.

In dealing with the acquisition of a house in a new housing development, it should be established with the local authority whether the developer has deposited with the local authority, or secured to the authority's satisfaction, a sum of money sufficient to meet the cost of constructing the road in accordance with the road construction consent and to the standard required by the authority under s 17 of the Roads (Scotland) Act 1984 and the Security for Private Road Works (Scotland) Regulations 1985, SI 1995/2080, as amended by the Security for Private Road Works (Scotland) Amendment Regulations 1998, SI 1998/3220. Development cannot commence until road construction consent has been obtained and the security has been lodged. Failure by the builder to lodge such security is a criminal offence. If, for any reason, work has commenced without a security having been lodged, a purchaser's agent should consider the desirability of retaining an appropriate part of the price until either a security is lodged, or the road has actually been constructed to an appropriate standard.

The Water Environment and Water Services (Scotland) Act 2003 makes provision for the construction and adoption of water and drainage services in new developments along broadly similar lines as roads. These are not yet in force, as detailed regulations made under the 2003 Act are awaited.

20.31 Health and Safety at Work etc Act 1974

The Health and Safety at Work etc Act 1974 imposes a duty on every employer to ensure, so far as it is reasonably practicable, the health, safety and welfare at work of all employees: s 2. Employers, and all self-employed persons, are similarly under a duty to conduct their undertaking in such a way as to ensure that persons not in their employment, who may be affected thereby, are not exposed to risks to their health or safety: s 3. The 1974 Act is very much general principle legislation and it is for employers and self-employed persons to determine what is required to achieve the goals of the legislation in their own particular circumstances. The legislation is supported by a host of regulations directed at specific aspects of work and by codes of practice.

Of particular relevance are the Management of Health and Safety at Work Regulations 1999, SI 1999/3242 which require employers and self-employed persons to carry out a suitable and sufficient assessment of risks to employees and visitors arising out of or in connection with the undertaking and to identify measures to be taken to comply with their obligations under health and safety legislation. The assessment is to be kept under review. The regulations go on to provide that employers are to implement any preventative or protection measures in accordance with the general principles of prevention set out in Schedule 1. The extent of the employer's obligation under the legislation is to do all that is reasonably practicable in the circumstances.

Responsibility for enforcement rests with the Health and Safety Executive and a failure to discharge his obligations under the legislation could lay an employer open to prosecution for an offence under s 33 of the 1974 Act and the Health and Safety Executive may invoke administrative notice procedure in the form of an improvement notice or a prohibition notice to secure compliance.

As with the fire precautions legislation, compliance with health and safety requirements can be expensive and a purchaser of a work place should consider what may be required.

20.32 Disability discrimination

In terms of the acquisition of property for the purpose of providing goods, facilities and services, it should be noted that Part III of the Disability Discrimination Act 1995 provides that it is unlawful for a service provider to discriminate against a disabled person (s 19). A person is a 'provider of services' if he is concerned with the provision of services to the public or to a section of the public, whether or not for payment. The White Paper *Ending Discrimination Against Disabled People* (Cmnd 2729, 1995) stated that the right of access to goods, facilities and services granted by the legislation will not only prohibit discriminatory behaviour but also require positive action which is reasonably and readily achievable to overcome physical and communication barriers which impede disabled people's access. A service provider discriminates against a disabled person if he treats that person less favourably than others because of the disability or if he fails to make reasonable adjustments. Discrimination may be justified in certain circumstances as for example where it is necessary so as not to endanger health and safety.

The duty on service providers to make adjustments is set out in the Disability Discrimination Act 1995, s 21. This includes a duty to take reasonable steps to remove or alter any physical feature which makes it impossible or unreasonably difficult for disabled people to make use of a service which he provides to other members of the public. This might extend to widening a door, providing ramps or installing a lift or, possibly, arranging for the service to be brought to the disabled person. The intention is to provide low-cost accessibility solutions, but 'low-cost' is a relative term.

The requirement to make adjustments could raise issues as between a landlord and a tenant if a lease prohibits alterations. It could present particular difficulties with buildings on the list of buildings of architectural or historic interest. And such adjustments may require approval under other systems of regulation such as planning and building control.

Section 22 of the 1995 Act makes it unlawful for a person with the power to dispose of premises to discriminate against a disabled person in the sale or letting of the premises. This might take the form of refusing to dispose of the premises to a disabled person or by offering it on less favourable terms than to others. Section 22 does not apply to small dwellings (as defined in s 23).

A claim of unlawful discrimination is brought by way of civil proceedings before the sheriff court. The remedies available are those available in the Court of Session and may include damages including compensation for injury to feelings.

20.33 Environmental controls

Probably the fastest developing area of statutory regulation of the use and management of land relates to environmental protection. Environmental controls can have far reaching effects on the activities that may be carried out on land and on the way in which the activities may be carried out. Purchasers of industrial sites, in particular, will need to check carefully what activities have been carried out on the site, whether they were authorised and whether there has been compliance with the necessary regimes. Some of the regimes of control are complex and sophisticated. It is only possible in this chapter to touch briefly on the more important of these.

20.34 CONTAMINATED LAND

A new regime for dealing with contaminated land came into force in Scotland in 2000. It is designed to deal with contaminated land which poses an immediate and potentially serious threat to human health or the environment. Its focus is on historic contamination – typically contamination arising from past industrial activity and inadequate waste disposal arrangements. Purchasers of existing or former industrial sites will need to consider whether the land is 'contaminated' within the meaning of the regime.

The regime replaces the statutory nuisance provisions so far as contaminated land is concerned, although it operates in much the same way. It was introduced by the

Environment Act 1995 as Part IIA of the Environmental Protection Act 1990. Reference should also be made to SERAD Circular 1/2000, which contains very extensive guidance – some of which is mandatory – and the Contaminated Land (Scotland) Regulations 2000, SSI 2000/178.

The regime is structured around two key duties:

(1) Local authorities must inspect their areas with a view to identifying and designating contaminated land. To assist this process, authorities should have published a strategy for identifying contaminated land in their area. This should enable authorities to identify from historic records and other sources, in a rational, ordered and efficient manner, land which merits detailed inspection.

(2) Failing agreement on how the contamination is to be dealt with, the authority, or in some cases SEPA, must then serve a remediation notice requiring the liable person to clean up the land.

The definition of 'contaminated land' is therefore central to the regime. It is defined as land which appears to the authority to be in such a condition, because of substances in, on or under it, that:

(a) significant harm is being caused or is likely; or

(b) the pollution of controlled waters is being, or is likely to be caused.

As regards the first part of the definition, the authority must satisfy itself as regards the land that there is:

- a contaminant (there may be more than one);
- a receptor at risk from the contaminant. Risk is defined in terms of 'harm to the health of living organisms or other interference with ecological systems of which they form part and, in case of man, includes harm to property'; and
- a pathway by means of which the contaminant is causing, or likely to cause, significant harm to the receptor.

The second part of the definition of 'contaminated land' relates to water pollution. This part of the definition is likely to be more easily satisfied. There is no threshold of 'significance', although it seems likely that such a threshold will be introduced before long. On the face of it, small quantities of contaminant might satisfy the definition and invoke the duty to designate the land as contaminated. However, it is a requirement that any remediation must be reasonable having regard to the cost involved and the seriousness of the pollution.

Where any land has been identified as contaminated, the enforcing authority has a duty to require appropriate remediation. Notice of the designation of a site as contaminated will be given to the owners and occupiers and to any other person who appears to the authority to be an 'appropriate person' (ie a person who caused or permitted the substance causing the contamination to be on the land).

Unless urgent remediation is required, there is then a three-month consultation period before any further formal action can be initiated. The hope is that the process of consultation will lead to agreement on the remedial action required. Where, however, agreement cannot be reached or such agreement is not implemented, the authority has a duty to serve a remediation notice. Care will need to be taken in the drafting of a lease to anticipate the distribution of liability between landlord and tenant in the event of the service of such a notice.

The objective of the remediation notice will be to secure the remediation of the land to the appropriate standard. The appropriate standard is 'suitable for use' (ie the land should be brought into such a condition that, in its current use, it is no longer 'contaminated land'). The steps required by such a notice must be reasonable having regard to the cost involved and the seriousness of the harm or of the pollution of controlled water.

There is a right of appeal to the sheriff (Scottish Ministers if the notice is served by SEPA) on one or more of the statutory grounds against a remediation notice. There are 24 such grounds.

Details of land identified as contaminated must be logged in a public register maintained by the local authority. The register will also contain details of any remediation statement which has been agreed or remediation notice which has been served. This register should be a useful source of information in property transactions.

Where a remediation notice is to be served, the authority will have to determine who is liable for clean up. The most complex provisions of the regime and the accompanying guidance are those relating to the determination of liability.

The Environmental Protection Act 1990 recognises two categories of liable persons, referred to as 'appropriate persons'. These are referred to as 'Class A' and 'Class B' persons.

Those who caused or knowingly permitted the circumstances to arise by virtue of which the land is contaminated are known as 'Class A' persons. Such persons are responsible for remediating the pollution they have caused. Of course, such persons can only be made liable if they still exist and can be found.

The words 'causing or knowingly permitting' deserve attention. 'Causing' requires that the person concerned was involved in some active operation or operations to which the presence of the contaminating substance is attributable or, conceivably, was involved in a failure to act which gave rise to the presence of the contaminant. The phrase 'knowingly permitting' is wider and includes persons, such as the present owner or occupier, who know of the presence of the pollutant, who had the ability to take steps to prevent or remove the pollutant and who had a reasonable opportunity to do so but did not.

Where, after reasonable inquiry by the authority, no Class A person can be found, then the owner or occupier, if they are not a Class A person, will be liable. It should be noted, however, that a Class B person can never be liable for the remediation of land which is designated as contaminated because of the pollution of controlled waters.

It is thought that in most cases, the process of identifying the appropriate person should be straightforward. However, more complex situations will arise where there is one contaminant with significant pollution linkages to more than one person or where there are several contaminants linked to several persons. The Environmental Protection Act 1990 and the guidance provide assistance in determining liability where there are multiple appropriate persons.

20.35   INTEGRATED POLLUTION CONTROL, AIR POLLUTION CONTROL AND INTEGRATED POLLUTION PREVENTION AND CONTROL

Part I of the Environmental Protection Act 1990 regulates pollution from industrial processes carried out on land. The Integrated Pollution Control (IPC) regime takes an holistic approach to pollution control from the larger industrial processes, of which there are some 200 in Scotland. It is concerned with preventing or minimising pollution from emissions to the air, water or land; in other words, it brings under one control regime discharges to all environmental media and seeks to minimise pollution by achieving the best practicable environmental option. The Air Pollution Control (APC) regime, also contained in Part I of the 1990 Act, is concerned with preventing or minimising air pollution from smaller, less polluting industrial processes. Many of the rules in Part I apply to both regimes. The Scottish Environment Protection Agency (SEPA) is the regulator in both cases.

In both cases, the Environmental Protection Act 1990, s 6, makes it an offence to carry on a prescribed process in the absence of an authorisation granted under Part I. The processes are prescribed in the Environmental Protection (Prescribed Processes and Substances) Regulations 1991, SI 1991/472, as amended. The regulations designate processes as either Part A processes subject to IPC or Part B processes subject to APC.

An application for an authorisation must be accompanied by full information and by the appropriate fee. Applications are lodged in a register and are the subject of public notice. Authorisations will be conditional. In particular, nearly all authorisations will be subject to a condition that the process(es) will be carried on using the best available techniques not entailing excessive cost (BATNEEC) to prevent or minimise the release of prescribed substances.

Authorisations may be varied by way of notice at the request of the operator or on the initiative of SEPA. In particular, provision is made for the review and upgrading of authorisations at the expense of the operator by way of a variation notice in the light of advances in technology and the advent of more rigorous standards. To assist this process, an annual fee is paid by the operator to cover the cost of monitoring by SEPA of the activities being carried on.

There is a right of appeal to the Scottish Ministers against the refusal of an authorisation or against conditions imposed on a grant.

The industrial processes regulated by IPC and some of those regulated by APC and by the waste management licensing regime (see below) are to be subject to a new control regime known as Integrated Pollution Prevention and Control (IPPC). This is the result of the Pollution Prevention and Control Act 1999 passed to implement the requirements of EC Council Directive 96/61 on integrated pollution prevention and control. The details of the new pollution control system are to be found in the Pollution Prevention and Control (Scotland) Regulations 2000, SSI 2000/323. The regulations will control installations and mobile plants carrying on prescribed activities listed in Part I of Schedule I to the Regulations. The new regime, which already applies to new installations, is to be phased in for existing installations over an eight-year period. Operators will be required as a pre-requisite to an application for an IPPC permit, to undertake a baseline environmental investigation to provide a detailed picture of the condition of the site and a similar report will be required if and when the permit is eventually surrendered. The new regime will eventually replace the IPC regime but the APC and waste management licensing regime will continue for installations not caught by IPPC. As with IPC and APC, SEPA is to be the regulator.

Installations caught by the regulations, whether new or existing, will have to apply for an IPPC permit from SEPA. The procedure is modelled on that for IPC but is focused on installations rather than processes and is concerned not only with the consequences of processes in terms of emissions but also on what goes in to the process. It extends the scope of control to embrace matters such as energy efficiency, the use of raw materials, noise, waste minimisation and safety.

20.36 WASTE MANAGEMENT

Part II of the Environmental Protection Act 1990 introduced a new regime for the control of the production, management and disposal of waste. Details of the regime were provided in the Waste Management Licensing Regulations 1994, SI 1994/1056 (as amended). The regime is administered by the Scottish Environment Protection Agency (SEPA) having regard to the objectives of the national waste strategy.

'Waste' is defined as 'any substance or object in the categories set out in Schedule 2B to this Act which the holder discards or intends or is required to discard' (s 75, as amended). The list in Schedule 2B is wide ranging.

Under s 33 of the 1990 Act it is an offence to deposit controlled waste or to keep, treat or dispose of controlled waste in the absence of a waste management licence from SEPA. Certain waste management activities may be the subject of an IPC or IPPC authorisation (above) in which case a waste management licence will not be required. 'Controlled waste' means household, commercial or industrial waste. The 1994 Regulations contain an extensive list of exemptions from the requirement to obtain a waste management licence. The exemptions apply, for the most part, to wastes which are unlikely to give rise to environmental problems.

A licence can only be granted for a site if the activity being carried on on the land is the subject of an extant planning permission. A waste management licence may be refused if the applicant is not a 'fit and proper person' or if the proposals for the handling of waste are such as to be likely to give rise to environmental risk. A licence will be subject to conditions.

Part II of the 1990 Act provides that SEPA may only accept the surrender of a licence if it satisfied that the condition of the land arising from the handling of waste is unlikely to give rise to pollution or harm to human health.

In addition to the licensing regime, Part II of the 1990 Act provides that everyone in the waste chain is subject to a duty of care: s 34. This requires everyone to take such steps as are reasonable to prevent others committing an offence under Part II, to prevent the escape of waste under their control and to ensure that waste is properly packaged for carriage, is transferred to an authorised person and is accompanied by an adequate written description of the waste.

20.37   TRADE EFFLUENT

The discharge of trade effluent into a sewer requires the consent of Scottish Water under the Sewerage (Scotland) Act 1968, s 26. Consent may be secured by serving a trade effluent notice on the authority, stating the nature, quantity and rate of the proposed discharge. An application may be approved unconditionally or subject to conditions or it may be refused. An unconditional consent is unlikely. Conditions may deal with such matters as the nature, quantity, timing and rate of discharge, the installation of monitoring equipment and the payment to be made for receiving the discharge in the sewer. There is a right of appeal against an adverse decision to the Scottish Ministers.

Alternatively, consent to discharge may be secured by way of an agreement entered between the owner or occupier of the premises and Scottish Water in terms of s 37 of the 1968 Act. This offers a more flexible alternative to the notice procedure, particularly where the discharge will require new sewerage infrastructure provision. The agreement will stipulate the terms governing the discharge and will deal with any financial arrangements between the parties.

20.38   WATER POLLUTION

The discharge of noxious, poisonous or polluting matter or any solid matter into controlled waters, in the absence of a discharge consent, is an offence under s 30F of the Control of Pollution Act 1974 (inserted by the Environment Act 1995). 'Controlled waters' are defined in s 30A and include coastal, inland and ground water. Discharges governed by the IPC or IPPC regimes (above) are exempt from the provisions of the 1974 Act.

An application for a discharge consent is made to SEPA. An application may be granted unconditionally or subject to conditions or it may be refused. An unconditional discharge consent is unlikely. Conditions may deal with such matters as the place of discharge, the nature, quantity and rate of discharge, and the installation of monitoring equipment. An appeal lies to the Scottish Ministers against a refusal or against the imposition of onerous conditions.

20.39   STATUTORY NUISANCE

Part III of the Environmental Protection Act 1990 dealing with statutory nuisance was applied to Scotland by s 107 of and Schedule 17 to the Environment Act 1995.

The relevant provisions of the Public Health (Scotland) Act 1897 dealing with statutory nuisance were repealed.

The following matters are stated in s 79 of the 1990 Act to constitute 'statutory nuisances':

- any premises in such a state as to be prejudicial to health or a nuisance;
- smoke emitted from premises so as to be prejudicial to health or a nuisance;
- fumes or gases emitted from premises so as to be prejudicial to health of a nuisance;
- any dust, steam, smell or other effluvia arising on industrial, trade or business premises and being prejudicial to health or a nuisance;
- any accumulation or deposit which is prejudicial to health or a nuisance;
- any animal kept in such a place or manner as to be prejudicial to health or a nuisance;
- noise emitted from premises so as to be prejudicial to health or a nuisance;
- noise that is prejudicial to health or a nuisance and is emitted from or caused by a vehicle, machinery or equipment in a road;
- any other matter declared by any enactment to be a statutory nuisance.

It is the duty of every local authority to cause its area to be inspected from time to time to detect any statutory nuisances (s 79) and the authority must investigate any complaint made to them about such a nuisance.

Where land is contaminated within the meaning of Part IIA of the 1990 Act and the new contaminated land regime (see above), it may not be dealt with under the statutory nuisance regime. And if proceedings might be commenced against the nuisance under the provisions of Part I of the 1990 Act or under the Pollution Prevention and Control Act 1999 (IPC/ APC/ IPPC), the consent of the Scottish Ministers is required to commence proceedings under Part III of the 1990 Act.

Where a local authority is satisfied that a statutory nuisance exists or is likely to occur or recur, it must serve an abatement notice requiring the abatement of the nuisance or prohibiting or restricting its occurrence or recurrence or requiring the execution of such works and the taking of such other steps as may be necessary for any of those purposes and stipulating a time for compliance: Environmental Protection Act 1990, s 80. The local authority has no discretion with regard to the service of a notice. An appeal may be made against such a notice to the sheriff court. Failure to comply with the notice without reasonable excuse is an offence and the authority may also take direct action to abate the nuisance and recover the cost. In certain circumstances, it will be a defence to a prosecution for failure to comply with a notice to show that the best practicable means were used to prevent, or to counteract the effects of, the nuisance.

An abatement notice is to be served on the person responsible for the notice or, where that person cannot be found, on the owner or occupier of the premises: 1990 Act, s 80(2).

Quite apart from action by the local authority, it should be noted that any person aggrieved by the existence of a statutory nuisance may make a summary application to the sheriff for a remedy: 1990 Act, s 82.

20.40 CLEAN AIR

Under the Clean Air Act 1993, it is an offence to emit 'dark smoke' (as defined) from premises. The regulator in this case is the local authority. Where the premises are subject to regulation under the IPC/APC or IPPC regimes, the provisions of the 1993 Act do not apply. Local authorities are also given control over the installation of new furnaces and may prescribe limits for the emission of grit and dust from furnaces. In addition, furnace chimney heights are subject to local authority approval.

Local authorities may designate areas within their districts to be 'smoke control areas' in which, subject to certain exemptions and limitations, the emission of smoke, or of smoke of certain qualities, from chimneys is an offence. Such smoke control orders require the consent of the Scottish Ministers.

PART 4

SUBORDINATE RIGHTS: SECURITIES AND LEASES

Chapter 21

Securities: General

21.1 The concept of security

The normal rule in Scotland is that a debtor's whole estate, both heritable and moveable, is liable for payment of his whole debts. If, therefore, A lends £1,000 to B, the debtor, without security, A can enforce repayment of his loan by the appropriate diligence out of any of the assets, heritable or moveable, belonging to B at the time of enforcement. But, when A calls for repayment, B may have no assets; and so, in the result, A gets nothing. Or B's assets may prove insufficient to repay the debts of A and others in full; and in insolvency no one ordinary creditor has any preference over another. A creditor may however acquire a preference by taking security under which, as a matter of contractual arrangement, the creditor obtains a nexus in respect of a specified asset or assets of the debtor, in advance, at the date when the debt is contracted, and retains his nexus until such time as the debt has been paid.

The nexus which the creditor receives is usually a real right (but compare floating charges where the creditor's right only becomes real when the charge attaches: see para 23.4). As a real right, it will prevail against the debtor's singular successors. Thus the security will remain good, if the debtor transfers the property. Equally, it will prevail against the debtor's other creditors, thus giving the security holder priority if the debtor becomes insolvent. It is little wonder therefore that creditors often insist on taking security.

For a general discussion on the theory and practice of securities, both over heritage and moveables, see Gloag and Irvine *Rights in Security*, Chapter 1 and Gretton 'The Concept of Security' in D J Cusine (ed) *A Scots Conveyancing Miscellany: Essays in Honour of Professor J M Halliday* (1987).

21.2 Express, tacit and judicial securities

Securities can be divided into three categories. First, a security can be granted voluntarily by the creditor, in other words the security can be express. This is by far the most important type of security in practice and both the standard security and the floating charge are examples. Secondly, a security may arise by operation of law, in other words be tacit. Such securities are more common in relation to moveable property, for example the landlord's hypothec (see paras 25.92 to 25.96). The tacit security of lien, which normally gives the right to retain property until a debt incurred in relation to it is satisfied has typically been viewed as confined to moveable property. But there is no reason in principle, why such a security should not be exercised in respect of land: see H L MacQueen and J M Thomson *Contract Law in Scotland* (2000), para 5.16, and R R M Paisley *Land Law* (2000), para 11.2. The third type of security, judicial security, which includes some forms of diligence, will not be discussed further in this chapter. But, on adjudication, see paras 29.5 to 29.7. See also G L Gretton *The Law of Inhibition and Adjudication* (2nd edn, 1996), and the *Stair Memorial Encyclopaedia,* Volume 8, paras 101–399.

One type of security which is difficult to place within the tripartite classification is the charging order. It exists under statute. Local authorities and certain other public bodies are given the right to 'charge' land for debts owed by its owner. A typical example is where a local authority has exercised its statutory power to repair a dangerous building. It may register a charging order in the Register of Sasines or Land Register in respect of the cost. The owner will need to meet the debt, before the order will be discharged. See para 20.28 and Paisley *Land Law,* para 11.32.

21.3   True and functional securities

In a true security, the creditor receives a subordinate real right (*jus in re aliena*) in the relevant property. The debtor retains ownership (*dominium*). Consequently, two real rights exist in the property at the same time. The position is similar to that of lease, where the landlord remains owner, but the tenant has a subordinate real right. The standard security over land is a true right in security. Sometimes, however, other legal devices are used to act as a security. Thus, in the old form of heritable security known as the *ex facie* absolute disposition (see para 22.3), ownership was actually transferred to the creditor. He or she would contractually agree to reconvey the land when the debt was discharged. If the debtor became insolvent without having paid, the creditor was duly protected. The trust is another example of a functional security. On the use of trust clauses in dispositions, see para 10.23.

21.4   The need for a principal obligation or debt

As its name suggests, a right in security requires to secure something. This may be either a monetary debt or an obligation *ad factum praestandum*. Normally, it is a debt which is secured, although as discussed in the next paragraph, securities are often granted in respect of all sums owed by the debtor to the creditor rather than a fixed amount. An example of a secured obligation *ad factum praestandum* would be if A granted B an option to purchase a field and that option was then secured by a standard security over the field in B's favour. This would protect B if A breached the option by conveying the land to another party or if he became insolvent. The security would secure the damages claim available to B because the option was not fulfilled. See G L Gretton and K G C Reid *Conveyancing* (2nd edn, 1999), para 20.05.

The need for an underlying debt or obligation was confirmed recently in *Albatown Ltd v Credential Group Ltd* 2001 GWD 27-1102, where a standard security was granted in order to secure obligations under missives entered into by the parties. However, as is typical practice (see para 28.43), the missives were held to be unenforceable two years after the transaction settled. It was held that the security could not be enforced after that date, because there was no longer a valid principal obligation. For another example, see *Trotter v Trotter* 2001 SLT (Sh Ct) 42.

21.5 Special and general security

A right in security may be special or restricted, in that it secures the payment of a fixed sum. Thus a charging order could secure the sum of, say, £15,000 owed to the local authority following the repair to a building. The order would not be enforceable in respect of other sums owed by the property owner to the authority, for example arrears of Council Tax. Only the repair bill would be secured. It is usual practice, however, for standard securities and floating charges to be general or unrestricted. When signing the relevant document, the debtor will agree that the security will cover 'all sums due and which may become due' to the bank or other creditor. This means that it can be enforced in relation to the original loan, subsequent advances and indeed any debts owed to the creditor whatsoever. Of course, it might prove to be the case that the value of the property is insufficient upon sale to meet the entirety of the debt, in which case the creditor will be unsecured in relation to the shortfall.

21.6 The right to redeem

It is an implied condition of a security that it may be redeemed by the debtor upon payment of the sum secured. For example, an individual may have granted a standard security to a bank in respect of a sum of £100,000 to be repaid over 25 years. If, after two years, he received an unexpected legacy from a long lost aunt, which allowed him to repay the whole loan there and then, he could exercise his right of redemption: see para 22.63. A common example of debtors exercising their right of redemption is where they are remortgaging, in other words changing their lender. However, many lenders charge a financial penalty for this.

21.7 The property secured

The nature of the property determines the method by which an effective voluntary security can be created. So far as heritage is concerned, the standard security is the only security which all landowners may grant nowadays. It is discussed in detail in the next chapter. In addition, certain corporate debtors, most notably companies, can grant a floating charge. But, as will be seen in Chapter 23, this form of security is normally created over the debtor's entire estate, rather than land alone.

21.8   Third-party security

Normally, the debtor and the owner of the property are one and the same person. Nevertheless, it is competent for one party to grant a security over his or her property in respect of the debt of another. A good example is where a wife is prepared to grant a standard security over her share of the matrimonial home in order to secure her husband's business debts. This situation has given rise to a stream of case law following the decision of the House of Lords in *Smith v Bank of Scotland* 1997 SC (HL) 111 (see para 21.13), with a number of wives seeking to have the security reduced because they did not receive independent legal advice. Third-party security is also recognised by the Mortgage Rights (Scotland) Act 2001, s 1 which separately provides that owners and debtors may invoke this legislation, assuming that they satisfy the relevant criteria. See para 22.35.

21.9   Enforcement

A security will be typically enforced by the creditor selling the property and using the proceeds to pay off the debt. The sale procedure varies depending on the security and judicial permission may need to be sought. There are, however, two particularly important principles. The first is that any surplus following the sale must be returned to the debtor. The creditor is only entitled to a sum equal to the value of the debt. The second and related principle is that the creditor is under a duty to sell the property at the best price which may be reasonably obtainable in the circumstances. See, for example, the Conveyancing and Feudal Reform (Scotland) Act 1970, s 25. This protects the debtor, because the creditor only needs to achieve a sum which will pay the debt. Consequently, if a house was worth £200,000, but the secured debt plus expenses amounted only to £120,000, the creditor would not be unduly bothered if he only sold it for £120,000. But there would then be nothing to return to the debtor, which would be inequitable, given the true value of the property.

21.10   Ranking

More than one security may be granted over the same asset. For example, a debtor could grant a standard security to Bank A and then a second standard security to Bank

B. In such a situation, the usual rule is that the securities rank in order of creation, or to be more precise, by the dates upon which they became real rights. This means that earlier creditors take priority over later creditors. It is possible for the parties to vary that rule contractually by means of a ranking agreement. Ranking in the case of standard securities and floating charges is subject to specific statutory rules and these are discussed in the next two chapters.

21.11   The effect of the Consumer Credit Act 1974

Under the Consumer Credit Act 1974, loans below the statutory limit may be 'regulated agreements' which have to comply with certain statutory requirements. The limit is currently £25,000: see the Consumer Credit (Increase of Monetary Limits) Order 1983, SI 1983/1878, as amended by the Consumer Credit (Increase of Monetary Limits) (Amendment) Order 1998, SI 1998/996. However, the 1974 Act does not apply where the lender is an exempt institution such as recognised banks, building societies and local authorities. This means that most standard securities are unaffected by this legislation. Where it does apply, failure to comply with the statutory requirements may result in the agreement being unenforceable. But, one of the relevant provisions in the 1974 Act was recently held by the Court of Appeal in England to be incompatible with the European Convention on Human Rights: see *Wilson v First County Trust (No 2)* [2002] QB 74. This decision was overturned by the House of Lords, but on the narrow ground that the Convention had not been directly incorporated into English law at the time of the events which gave rise to the case. See [2003] 3 WLR 568 and P W Ferguson 'Retroactivity and the Human Rights Act 1998' 2003 SLT (News) 215. For further discussion of the 1974 Act, see J M Halliday *Conveyancing Law and Practice* (2nd edn, 2 volumes, 1996–97, edited by I J S Talman), paras 52.69–52.73 and M Higgins *Scottish Repossessions* (2002), para 2.5.

21.12   Creditors' duties to guarantors: introduction

As noted in para 21.8, it is common for an individual to provide security for the business debts of her spouse. Typically, but not necessarily, it tends to be a wife who acts as a guarantor. This is why Professors Reid and Gretton in their annual updates, *Conveyancing 2001* (2002), *Conveyancing 2002* (2003) etc (see Reading List), have come to refer to this area of law under the heading 'cautionary wives'. Here the word 'guarantor' is used, to reflect the fact that what is being granted by the (typically said)

wife is either (a) a true guarantee, ie caution or (b) third-party security, ie real security over the property owned by the guarantor, for example, their *pro indiviso* share
in the matrimonial home. Historically, creditors did not owe a wife, or indeed any
other party who had a close personal relationship with the debtor, any duty to ensure
that her consent was freely given. She could therefore normally not have had the
security reduced on the ground that the debtor had misled her as to the meaning of
the document which she had signed. See G L Gretton 'Sexually Transmitted Debt'
1997 SLT (News) 195.

   The position has, however, changed, the catalyst being the landmark English decision of *Barclays Bank plc v O'Brien* [1994] 1 AC 180. There, the House of Lords
held that where a creditor has knowledge that the debtor is in a close relationship
with the would-be guarantor, then he or she is put on notice that the would-be guarantor's consent could be unfairly obtained. The result is that if the creditor does not
take steps to ensure that the would-be guarantor's consent is free and informed, then
any claim which the latter has against the debtor on the ground that her consent was
vitiated may also be pled against the creditor. The security can then be set aside by a
court. To avoid this happening, the creditor should ensure that the would-be guarantor receives independent legal advice.

21.13   *SMITH V BANK OF SCOTLAND*

It was only going to be a matter of time before an attempt was made to extend the
doctrine in *O'Brien* north of the border. The opportunity came in *Smith v Bank of
Scotland* 1997 SC (HL) 111, which reached the House of Lords. Mrs Smith had
executed a standard security, along with her husband, over the house which they
owned in favour of the bank. In return, the bank made a business loan to a firm in
which Mr Smith was a partner. Mrs Smith subsequently raised an action for the
security to be reduced as regards her half share of the property. Her argument was
that her consent was induced by a misrepresentation by Mr Smith. In addition, she
had not been given any independent legal advice, nor a warning as to the consequences of signing, nor even an opportunity to read over the document. Both the
Outer and Inner Houses of the Court of Session found against Mrs Smith on the
basis of the existing law that the creditor had no duty to check that the guarantor
had given free and informed consent. A misrepresentation by the debtor could not
affect the creditor. *O'Brien* was not followed. Lord President Hope stated that
reform of the law here should be a matter for the Scottish Law Commission and
Parliament: see 1996 SLT 392 at 398. The House of Lords, however, allowed the
appeal and, in doing so, openly admitted that it was changing Scots law. Lord
Clyde stated at 1997 SC (HL) 111 at 120–121 :

   'I have not been persuaded that there are sufficiently cogent grounds for refusing the extension to Scotland of the development which has been achieved in
   England by the decision in *Barclay's Bank plc v O'Brien*. On the contrary, I

take the view that it is desirable to recognise a corresponding extension of the law in Scotland'.

This judicial legislation has been criticised by a number of writers and reference is made to the Reading List in this regard. The hook upon which the House of Lords was able to hang its decision was the duty to contract in good faith, at best an uncertain doctrine. See further the contributions of Professors Forte, MacQueen and Thomson to A D M Forte (ed) *Good Faith in Contract and Property Law* (1999). In addition, it must be noted that basing the decision on good faith differentiates it from *O'Brien*, which essentially was based on the doctrine of constructive notice. Consequently, the English and Scottish approaches are not the same. See further S Eden 'Cautionary Tales: the Continued Development of *Smith v Bank of Scotland*' (2003) 7 EdinLR 107.

The exact *ratio* of *Smith* itself is uncertain, although some clarification has been provided by subsequent decisions. Lord Clyde stated that where a creditor should have reasonable suspicion, because of an intimate relationship between the debtor and would-be guarantor, that the consent of the would-be guarantor may not be fully informed or freely given, then he has a duty to act in good faith. This means that he must warn the would-be guarantor of the consequences of agreeing to enter into that role and advise her to take independent legal advice.

21.14   THE NEED FOR A VITIATING FACTOR

One of the immediate uncertainties about *Smith v Bank of Scotland* 1997 SC (HL) 111 was whether there actually had to be a vitiating factor in the first place, before the doctrine established in that case could be invoked. Was it necessary that the debtor had exercised undue influence over the guarantor or made a misrepresentation to her? Thus, if the debtor had done nothing wrongful, but the circumstances were such that the creditor should have insisted that the guarantor received independent legal advice but had not, the issue was whether this failure alone could enable the guarantor to have the security reduced. The view that no proof of a vitiating factor was required could be justified by some of Lord Clyde's judgment (see especially 1997 SC (HL) 111 at 121F). It also commanded some academic support: see S F Dickson 'Good Faith in Contract, Spousal Guarantees and *Smith v Bank of Scotland*' 1998 SLT (News) 39. But, it was established in *Braithwaite v Bank of Scotland* 1999 SLT 25, that wrongful conduct on the part of the debtor must be proven. Lord Hamilton stated at p 33C :

'The concept of good faith is used in the sense that a party may not be entitled to enforce his apparent rights because he is aware of or put on enquiry to discover some prior vitiating factor. The existence in fact of such a factor is a pre-requisite to the applicability of that concept'.

A similar statement is made by Lord Macfadyen in *Wright v Cotias Investments Inc*

2001 SLT 353 at 359. See also *The Royal Bank of Scotland plc v Wilson* 2001 SLT (Sh Ct) 2, affirmed 2003 SLT 910. In establishing a vitiating factor, the guarantor needs to show that this caused her to sign the security which she is seeking to reduce. For example, in *Ahmed v Clydesdale Bank plc* 2001 SLT 423, the pursuer sought to have a standard security set aside because of an alleged wrongful act at a later date. The action unsurprisingly failed. See K G C Reid and G L Gretton *Conveyancing 2000* (2001), pp 89–90.

21.15   WHEN DOES THE DUTY TO ACT IN GOOD FAITH ARISE?

It is important to know precisely what type of relationship between the debtor and guarantor will impose a duty on the creditor to ensure that the guarantee has been entered into on a free and informed basis. Lord Clyde stated in *Smith v Bank of Scotland* 1997 SC (HL) 111 at 121–122 that a duty arises:

'. . . if the circumstances of the case are such to lead a reasonable man to believe that owing to the personal relationship between the debtor and the proposed cautioner the latter's consent may not be fully informed or freely given. Of course if the creditor, acting honestly and in good faith, has no reason to believe that there is any particularly close relationship between the debtor and the proposed cautioner the duty will not arise'.

Obviously, the relationship of husband and wife falls within that definition and the vast majority of the decisions following *Smith* have involved spouses. For an exception, involving a mother and a son, see *Wright v Cotias Investments Inc* 2001 SLT 353 (discussed above). It seems that, spouses aside, the courts will consider this matter on a case to case basis. Creditors, therefore, would be well advised to take a cautious approach and insist that independent legal advice is advised in the case of family members and cohabitants, including same-sex partners.

21.16   WHAT STEPS NEED TO BE TAKEN?

As mentioned in para 21.13, the steps which should be taken by the creditor where there appears to be a close relationship between the debtor and would-be guarantor are to warn of the consequences of entering into guarantee and to advise that independent legal advice be sought. See Lord Clyde in *Smith v Bank of Scotland* 1997 SC (HL) 111 at 122. In the English case of *The Royal Bank of Scotland plc v Etridge (No 2)* [2001] 4 All ER 449, the House of Lords laid down extremely detailed rules as to what the solicitor advising the would-be guarantor needs to do. Specifically, he or she must:

- explain the nature of the guarantee and its legal effect;
- explain the risks involved in signing;

- explain what debts are involved;
- discuss with the would-be guarantor her financial means and those of the debtor;
- explain that she is not obliged to sign and check that she wishes to proceed; and
- ask her permission to write to the creditor confirming that she has received independent legal advice.

See in particular the speech of Lord Nicholls. There is a useful summary in K G C Reid and G L Gretton *Conveyancing 2001* (2002), pp 94–96 and see also D J Cusine and R Rennie *Standard Securities* (2nd edn, 2002), para 2.04. Whilst the court made it clear that the same solicitor could act for both the debtor and the would-be guarantor, provided that he saw the latter on her own, it was noted that a potential conflict of interest could arise here.

However, in *Clydesdale Bank plc v Black* 2002 SLT 764, an Extra Division of the Inner House decided to take a less prescriptive approach than that in *Etridge*. Lord Coulsfield stated at 771: 'To lay down . . . detailed and prescribed requirements would . . . be difficult to reconcile with the normal approach of Scots law to questions of good faith.' The court also made it clear that less onerous requirements are imposed on creditors in respect of guarantees entered into before *Smith*, because that case changed the law. A similar approach was taken by the Second Division in the subsequent case of *The Royal Bank of Scotland plc v Wilson* 2003 SLT 910.

Notwithstanding *Black*, the consequences of *Smith* are awkward for solicitors. Where a guarantor's action to set a security aside fails on the basis that she received independent legal advice, the solicitor who provided that advice may well find himself the subject of a claim against him. The Law Society of Scotland's Conveyancing Committee has recently stated that the same solicitor must not advise both debtor and guarantor. It has also published a *pro forma* letter for use by solicitors advising guarantors: see 'Inter-Spouse Guarantees: An Update' 2003 JLSS Oct/34. Any solicitor advising a would-be guarantor who has a close relationship with the debtor, requires to act, in the words of Professors Reid and Gretton, with 'the utmost circumspection': *Conveyancing 2002* (2003), p 63. Undoubtedly, the safest option in terms of avoiding a later claim against him, will be to recommend not to enter into the guarantee.

21.17 Solicitors' duties to creditors

The past few years have seen a marked increase in the number of actions by creditors against solicitors for breach of contract or professional negligence. When the debtor becames insolvent and, for some reason, it is not possible to recover all the debt by enforcing the security, the creditor's next course of action is often to raise proceedings against the solicitor who advised in relation to the loan. So, for example, in *The Mortgage Corporation v Mitchells Roberton* 1997 SLT 1305, the claim was made on the basis that the solicitors involved had not followed the creditor's instructions. In *Bank of East Asia v Shepherd & Wedderburn WS* 1995 SC 255, the argument that a solicitor can have a duty of care to advise a lender of something which might be a determining factor in whether or not to lend on security was held to be relevant. Accordingly, in such circumstances a solicitor should take a cautious approach. In the case of standard securities, regard has to be had to the Council of Mortgage Lenders' *Lenders' Handbook for Scotland* (see para 22.2) and the instructions contained therein. For a further account of the law in relation to claims against solicitors, reference is made to the writings of Professor Rennie in the Reading List for this Chapter.

Chapter 22

Standard Securities

22.1 Introduction

Normally, the most valuable asset which people own is land. This of course includes buildings. Typically, the purchase price will have been funded by a loan from a lending institution, for otherwise it would be beyond the means of the individual. The words of Lord Diplock, in the English case of *Pettit v Pettit* [1970] AC 777 at 824, that we are 'a real property mortgaged to a building society owning democracy', is a reasonably accurate statement of the position in Scotland three decades on. Strictly speaking, 'mortgage' is a technical term of English law which means the security which the owner grants in favour of the lender, although it is normally used to refer to the loan itself. The mortgage will be repayable over a considerable period of time: 25 years is fairly normal. A large number of mortgage packages are available. These include capital and interest mortgages, where both the loan advanced and the interest are repaid directly by the borrower, and endowment mortgages where the capital is repaid through the mechanism of an insurance policy to which the borrower contributes and which matures either on the borrower's death or at a fixed date in the future. For further detail, see paras 33.15–33.20 and G L Gretton and K G C Reid *Conveyancing* (2nd edn, 1999), Chapter 19.

22.2 Lenders

Loan finance is usually obtained from a lending institution such as a high street bank or building society. The main institutions are part of a body known as the Council of Mortgage Lenders (CML). There is a helpful list of some of these in the June 2003 edition of the *Journal of the Law Society of Scotland* at p 58, together with the contact details of relevant officers. The CML publishes its *Lenders' Handbook for Scotland*, the second edition of which came into effect on 1 January 2003. The *Handbook* is only available online, the web address being www.cml.org.uk/handbook. It is divided into two parts. The first part has general rules which apply to mortgages with all CML members. The second part is lender specific. The rules are designed to have contractual effect between solicitors and lenders, as mortgage instructions will incorporate them. They cover such issues as communication, valuation, title, searches and representation for guarantors. It goes without saying that they need to be adhered to carefully. For an excellent commentary on the second edition of the *Handbook*, see K Swinton 'Council of Mortgage Lenders Handbook (2nd edn)' (2002) 70 SLG 173.

22.3   Heritable security

The essential element of a mortgage is that a security is granted over the land belonging to the borrower or debtor. This is known as heritable security. At common law, four distinct types of heritable security were recognised. These were:

(1) the bond and disposition in security;
(2) the bond of cash credit and disposition in security;
(3) the *ex facie* absolute disposition; and
(4) the pecuniary real burden.

In fact, (3) was a functional rather than a true right in security in that ownership was actually conveyed to the creditor, under an apparently normal (hence the term '*ex facie* absolute') disposition. It was then reconveyed when the debt was discharged. Under the Conveyancing and Feudal Reform (Scotland) Act 1970, Part II (ss 9 to 32 and Schedules 2 to 7), the whole law of heritable securities in Scotland was fundamentally changed from and after 29 November 1970. It is now no longer competent to use the traditional forms of heritable security (including the bond and the *ex facie* absolute disposition), and, in lieu, the 1970 Act provides a new form of heritable security, known as the standard security, which must now be used for all types of security transaction, and which replaces all existing traditional forms. Some doubt remained about whether it was still competent to use the pecuniary real burden, after 1970. Accordingly, this form of security has now been formally abolished by the Title Conditions (Scotland) Act 2003, s 117. The old forms of heritable security are treated in depth in Chapter 21 of the sixth edition of this book, but they are mainly a matter of historical interest, except to the extent that they influenced the development of the standard security. The legislation for pre-1970 heritable securities has now been broadly equated with that for the standard security by the Abolition of Feudal Tenure etc (Scotland) Act 2000, s 69.

The background to the introduction of the standard security is set out in the Halliday Committee Report *Conveyancing Legislation and Practice* (Cmnd 3118, 1968), Chapter 8, paras 102–106. An important recent development has been the passing of the Mortgage Rights (Scotland) Act 2001, which is discussed below. This chapter, however, is not intended to be an exhaustive treatment of standard security law. More detailed accounts are to be found in J M Halliday *Conveyancing and Feudal Reform (Scotland) Act 1970* (2nd edn, 1977), Chapters 6–10; I J S Talman (ed) *Halliday's Conveyancing Law and Practice in Scotland* (2nd edn, 2 volumes 1996–97), Chapters 51–55; D J Cusine and R Rennie *Standard Securities* (2nd edn, 2002); and M Higgins *Scottish Repossessions* (2002).

22.4   **Exclusion of other forms of security**

The use of the standard security to secure a debt over land is made obligatory by the Conveyancing and Feudal Reform (Scotland) Act 1970, s 9(4). If a deed is granted to secure a debt over an interest in land which is not in the form of a standard security but which contains a disposition or assignation, then it is void as a security. (Following feudal abolition the expression 'land or real right in land' will replace 'interest in land'). If such a deed has been recorded, then the grantee is bound to clear the record. But, under s 31 of the 1970 Act, this does not apply to, nor affect, the validity of any heritable security recorded before 29 November 1970.

The word 'debt' in the 1970 Act covers payments of every kind and also obligations *ad factum praestandum*: s 9(8)(b). In this regard, see para 21.4. Negative obligations, such as a prohibition in relation to land use cannot be secured. In practice, standard securities are drafted so that all sums owed by the debtor are secured. See also para 21.5.

22.5   **Style of deed**

There are two forms provided in the Conveyancing and Feudal Reform (Scotland) Act 1970, Schedule 2: Form A and Form B. Both are express security documents and therefore more closely resemble the old bond and disposition in security than the *ex facie* absolute disposition.

Form A contains an undertaking to pay. This may cover not merely fixed advances already made, but also future or fluctuating advances, to a stated limit or advances of indefinite amount without limit. Section 10(1) of the 1970 Act provides an elaborate interpretation for the short form of undertaking incorporated in Form A; it does not apply to Form B.

Form B, in contrast, although *ex facie* a security document, does not contain *in gremio* (within the body of the deed) any personal obligation or undertaking whatsoever. Instead, it simply refers to the debt or obligation constituted in a collateral document which itself constitutes the personal obligation and defines the undertaking to repay. There is no implied personal obligation in Form B.

In terms of s 53(1) of the 1970 Act, standard securities must conform 'as closely as may be' to Form A or B. It is therefore sensible to draft the deed following the statutory form as carefully as possible. In *Royal Bank of Scotland v Marshall,* Glasgow Sheriff Court, 5 June 1996, reported in R R M Paisley and D J Cusine *Unreported Cases from the Sheriff Courts* (2000), pp 445–447, Sheriff Gordon stated that the level of deviation allowed 'comes to one of impression and degree'. He held in this regard that a distinction should not be made between the parts of the forms in italics and those in ordinary print. See also *Spowart v Wylie* 1995 GWD 23-1257.

The 1970 Act formerly required that the security subjects should be described by a particular description, or a statutory description by reference. However, the relevant provision, note 1 to Schedule 2 to the 1970 Act, has now been amended so that the subjects need only be described in a manner 'sufficiently to identify them'. See above, para 8.14. As a standard security requires to be registered in either the Register of Sasines or the Land Register, it must satisfy s 3 of the Requirements of Writing (Scotland) Act 1995. Normally, this is achieved by the deed being witnessed. See Chapter 2.

22.6   Statutory effect of security

Under s 11(1) of the Conveyancing and Feudal Reform (Scotland) Act 1970, a standard security, when registered, operates to give the creditor a real right in security for the performance of the contract to which the security relates. The debtor remains owner and may in principle transfer the subjects, although they will remain subject to the security. However, many lenders expressly prohibit transfer without their consent.

As mentioned in the preceding paragraph, a standard security must be recorded in the Register of Sasines or registered in the Land Register. In the case of a standard security granted by a limited company, the security, being a charge, must also be registered in the Register of Charges within 21 days of the date of recording or registration. A failure so to register means that the charge is void against the liquidator or administrator and any creditor of the company (Companies Act 1985, s 410). It is not competent to re-register the security as of new, if it is otherwise valid: see *Bank of Scotland v T A Neilson & Co* 1990 SC 284. However, the Scottish Law Commission in a recent discussion paper has proposed that the requirement for registration in the Register of Charges be scrapped. There appears to be no serious justification for it, given that publicity is already achieved by registration in the Register of Sasines or Land Register. See *Registration of Rights in Security by Companies* (Scot Law Com Disc Paper No 121, 2002), paras 3.5–3.11. For discussion, see Lord Eassie 'Reforming Registration of Company Charges' 2002 JLSS Dec/26 and D Guild 'The Registration of Rights in Security by Companies' 2002 SLT (News) 289.

22.7   Deduction of title

The Conveyancing (Scotland) Act 1924, s 3, introduced an innovation for the disposition but not for any other form of writ by permitting a person having right to land by a title not recorded in the Register of Sasines to grant that disposition, provided that, in the disposition, a clause of deduction of title was introduced in a statutory form. This facility was not available to the grantor of a bond and disposition in security and is still not available to the grantor of a lease.

Under the Conveyancing and Feudal Reform (Scotland) Act 1970, s 12, however, the deduction of title facility has been extended, on very similar lines to the facility provided for the disposition under the 1924 Act, s 3, which permits a proprietor, without a recorded title, to grant a standard security over his interest in heritable property. A statutory form of deduction of title is provided on very similar lines to the 1924 Act form; and s 12(2) of the 1970 Act further provides that, on the recording of a standard security containing the statutory clause of deduction of title, the title of the grantee shall, for the purpose of the standard security but for no other purpose, be of the same effect as if the grantor thereof had a recorded title. For the purposes of this deduction, mid-couples are as defined in the 1924 Act. See again on this topic under Chapter 31 and also C Waelde (ed) *Professor McDonald's Conveyancing Opinions* (1998), pp 166–169. Deduction of title is not necessary where the subjects have been registered in the Land Register: see the Land Registration (Scotland) Act 1979, s 15.

22.8 Standard conditions

Every standard security embodies, by statutory implication under the Conveyancing and Feudal Reform (Scotland) Act 1970, s 11(2), the standard conditions contained in Schedule 3, with or without such variation as the parties may agree. These conditions operate both in relation to Form A and Form B: see Schedule 2. Note, particularly, that those conditions in Schedule 3 which relate to power of sale or foreclosure, and to the exercise of those powers, cannot be varied. The power of redemption may only be varied to the limited extent prescribed in the Redemption of Standard Securities (Scotland) Act 1971. The effect of the 1971 Act is that, while the parties may validly agree on certain matters, including in particular the duration of the loan and the period of notice, the actual procedure on redemption specified in standard condition 11 may not be altered. This is referred to again below.

22.9 Variation

Except as noted above, the terms of a standard security including a standard condition may be varied by agreement, either at the time when the standard security is granted in which case the variation is embodied in the loan documents or at any subsequent date, under the Conveyancing and Feudal Reform (Scotland) Act 1970, s 16. This applies even where the condition to be varied (for example, the rate of interest in Form A) appears in the security itself, and so on the record; but in that case the deed of variation must itself be recorded.

In practice, it is unusual to find a standard security in which the variable standard conditions have not been altered. The variations which are commonly encountered deal with the insurance of the subjects, prohibitions against parting with possession or transferring the security subjects, alterations in use, improvement grants, power to deal with any moveables left on the premises, the creation of other securities, expanding the circumstances in which the debtor will be in default and permitting the lender to accelerate the requirement to repay the loan in such an event. Many building societies and other lenders produce booklets with the standard conditions in their original form and the standard conditions in the altered form and some of these have been registered in the Books of Council and Session. For a table showing the standard conditions used by the main lenders in 1999, see D J Cusine and R Rennie *Standard Securities* (2nd edn, 2002), Appendix 3.

22.10   Ranking of standard securities *inter se*

Under s 11 of the Conveyancing and Feudal Reform (Scotland) Act 1970, where a standard security is duly recorded, it operates to vest the interest over which it is granted in the grantee as security for performance of the contract to which that security relates. Although the 1970 Act does not specifically so provide, it is generally accepted that, for the purposes of determining preference, the recording of a standard security has exactly the same effect as the recording of a bond and disposition in security had prior to 29 November 1970. In other words, as with the bond so with the standard security, notwithstanding the vesting of the heritable property in the creditor, that vesting is initially for the purpose of security only. The debtor remains the heritable proprietor.

The question of ranking is dealt with in the 1970 Act, s 13, but only to a limited extent. Except in so far as that section provides, therefore, common law rules and statutory provisions operating prior to 1970 continue to apply, to determine the order of preference as between competing rights in land, including the rights secured for the creditor under a recorded standard security.

22.11   PRIORITY OF REGISTRATION DETERMINES PREFERENCE

By the combined effect of the Registration Act 1617 and the Real Rights Act 1693, real rights in land are preferred strictly according to priority of registration. This rule applies to security rights as it applies to proprietary rights. Suppose A, as heritable proprietor grants a standard security to X recorded in 1975; a second standard security to Y recorded in 1980 and a third standard security to Z recorded in 1985. X has the first registration in security, and takes an absolute priority over Y and Z; similarly Y is preferred to Z. If the property is sold on A's default, X is therefore entitled to payment in full of his principal, interest and penalties before Y can take anything; and similarly Y is paid in full before Z can take anything. This order of preference amongst heritable creditors *inter se* is termed 'ranking'; and their ranking *inter se* is prior or postponed, strictly according to the respective dates of registration.

22.12 *PARI PASSU* RANKING

But, in certain cases, two or more creditors fall to be ranked not prior and postponed *inter se*, but equally *pro rata* in proportion to the respective amounts of their several loans. This is termed *pari passu* ranking. Where two or more creditors rank *pari passu*, they share *pro rata* in the proceeds of any sale. *Pari passu* ranking may be constituted in three ways, outlined in the following three paragraphs.

22.13   The Titles to Land Consolidation (Scotland) Act 1868, s 142 and the Land Registration (Scotland) Act 1979, s 7(2).

If two or more standard securities are received by the Keeper of the Registers on the same day they are deemed to be recorded simultaneously and, therefore, rank *pari passu*.

22.14   Two or more lenders

Normally, the personal obligation to pay is in favour of a single creditor; but it is equally competent in a single standard security to incorporate several obligations to pay in favour of several creditors. If this is done, and if the standard security is then recorded on behalf of the several creditors at the same time, they all rank *pari passu*.

Note, however that to achieve *pari passu* ranking by this method, the standard security must be recorded on behalf of all the creditors. This means that, prior to the abolition of need for warrants as of 28 November 2004 (see para 6.27), there must be a warrant of registration on behalf of each creditor, duly signed, before the standard security is presented for recording. If, in such a case, the standard security was presented for registration with a warrant on behalf of one creditor only and not on behalf of the other creditor or creditors thereunder, that one creditor named in the warrant would have a prior ranking unless there was a special ranking clause in the standard security itself. In the Land Register, a Form 2 will need to be completed on behalf of each creditor.

22.15   Subsequent partial assignation

The priority of a standard security is established as at the date of its registration. If the original creditor later assigns the whole security to an assignee, the assignee completes his right by registering the assignation – see below. If the creditor, fraudulently, grants two or more assignations of the same security, in whole, to different assignees, then as between these competing assignees the preference *inter se* would normally be determined strictly according to the order of registration of the respective assignations. But, as between any such assignee and a third party deriving right from the debtor, the assignee has the benefit of the preference established by the original registration of the standard security, and ranks accordingly.

A single standard security may competently be assigned in part, or in several parts to several assignees. If so, such assignees rank *pari passu inter se*; but again, in a question with third parties deriving right from the debtor, each several assignee enjoys the benefit of the preference established by the registration of the original standard security, *quoad* his portion thereof.

22.16 RANKING CLAUSES

The ordinary rules of ranking may be varied by express ranking clauses in one or several (contemporaneous) standard securities. But, if a standard security to A has been registered and contains no express reference to ranking, a clause in a standard security in favour of B, registered later, purportedly ranking B's standard security prior to A's, is ineffective. Because the first registered security contains no contrary express ranking provision, priority of registration determines the order of ranking and the preference.

In many instances, where there is more than one security, it is common for the parties to enter into a ranking agreement rather than have ranking clauses in the security deeds. This device is adopted, particularly where the ranking arrangement is complex. See *Alloa Brewery Company Ltd v Investors in Industry plc* 1992 SLT 121. To be fully effective, such agreements should always be recorded or registered on behalf of all the creditors thereto.

22.17 **Statutory limitation on amount secured**

The Conveyancing and Feudal Reform (Scotland) Act 1970, s 13, is headed 'Ranking of standard securities', but that section is in fact restricted in scope. Contrast the much more detailed statutory provision for the ranking of floating charges, dealt with in the next chapter.

Ranking, therefore, still depends on priority of registration; and is determined by the date of registration of the standard security as explained above. Section 13 merely provides a procedure which limits the priority of an existing all sums (general) standard security. The creditor under a second or subsequent security can send the creditor in the existing security a notice. The effect of this is to restrict that security to advances already made (with interest and expenses) at the date on which the notice is received. But, the existing security will still cover any future advances, not yet made, but which the creditor is bound to make in terms of the security documents. It is of the utmost importance that a solicitor acting for the subsequent security holder validly serves the notice in terms of s 13. For further discussion, see D J Cusine and R Rennie *Standard Securities* (2nd edn, 2002), paras 7.09–7.12.

22.18 Creditor's rights and remedies

The creditor's primary right is to receive payment or repayment of the principal sum in loan; or to insist on implement of the obligation or performance of the contract to which the security relates. He has no other interest, and in particular no true proprietary right, in the security subjects, notwithstanding the registration of the standard security in the Register of Sasines or Land Register except as security for the secured debt or obligation.

Standard conditions 1 to 7 in Schedule 3 to the Conveyancing and Feudal Reform (Scotland) Act 1970 impose a variety of obligations on the debtor which, under the older forms of security, were normally provided for by back letter or collateral agreement, but which are now statutory. All these standard conditions are capable of variation and may be supplemented in any way which the parties agree upon, subject only to the restrictions referred to above which are unlikely to affect a variation of any of the standard conditions 1 to 7.

22.19 IMPORT OF STANDARD CONDITIONS I TO 7

Without going into full detail, standard conditions 1 to 7 impose the following obligations on the debtor:

(1) to maintain the security subjects;
(2) to complete any uncompleted buildings;
(3) to observe all the conditions in the title;
(4) to inform the creditor as soon as the debtor receives any notice or order under the Town and Country Planning Acts;
(5) to insure the security subjects or, if the creditor prefers, to allow the creditor to insure in which case the debtor pays the premium; and, in this case, in contrast to the position under the bond and disposition in security, the amount insurable is the market value of the subjects. The insurable risks are fire and such other risks as the creditor may reasonably require. The debtor must also intimate any claim and give the creditor the opportunity to negotiate a settlement thereof;
(6) The debtor is prohibited from letting the security subjects which, by virtue of his proprietary title, he would otherwise have power to do. See *Trade Development Bank Ltd v Warriner & Mason (Scotland) Ltd* 1980 SC 74;
(7) The creditor is authorised at his own hand to carry out any obligation imposed on the debtor under standard conditions 1 to 6, if the debtor himself fails to implement that obligation and to recover the costs thereof from the debtor. Such

costs, if so incurred, are deemed to be secured by the standard security and therefore have a preference over other creditors.

22.20 Default by the debtor: standard conditions 8 to 10

Standard conditions 8 to 10 deal with default by the debtor, but with this major caveat that the provisions of these three standard conditions, and in particular the rights of the creditor under standard condition 10, are very substantially restricted by the provisions of ss 19 to 28 of the Conveyancing and Feudal Reform (Scotland) Act 1970. In addition, these standard conditions must be read along with these provisions in the 1970 Act, all of which must be strictly observed. Otherwise, any purported action by the creditor in the exercise of the powers conferred on him under the standard conditions may be void and, in addition, the creditor runs the risk of an action for damages for failure to observe his statutory obligations in these sections. There are three alternative default situations, which are outlined in standard condition 9, and amplified in detail in ss 19 to 24 of the 1970 Act.

22.21 CALLING-UP NOTICE: STANDARD CONDITION 9(1)(a)

A calling-up notice can be used where the creditor has the right under the security to demand immediate repayment of the whole debt. Failure to comply with this notice entitles the creditor, on the expiry of the two-month period of notice, to exercise all or any of the powers in standard condition 10 which include sale; entering into possession; carrying out repairs; foreclosure: see the Conveyancing and Feudal Reform (Scotland) Act 1970, s 20.

Section 19 of the 1970 Act contains the statutory provisions as to the form, service and effect of the notice.

22.22 Form of notice

The form of notice calling up the sum in loan secured by a standard security is prescribed in the Conveyancing and Feudal Reform (Scotland) Act 1970, Schedule 6, Form A, which has recently been amended by the Mortgage Rights (Scotland) Act 2001. It is designed primarily for monetary obligations but can be used for obligations *ad factum praestandum* with appropriate adaptation.

Section 19(9) of the 1970 Act deals with the case where the sum in loan is not a definite ascertained amount. The standard security may be used to secure future and fluctuating debt and provision is made for this in the calling-up notice Form A. In such cases, it is competent to include in that notice a proviso to the effect that the amount required to redeem the loan is subject to adjustment. In *Clydesdale Bank plc v Findlay & Co* 1989 SLT (Sh Ct) 77, the debtor sought unsuccessfully to take advantage of this provision to prevent the creditor from entering into possession and proceeding to sell the security subjects, founding on a letter by him to the creditor calling for amendment/adjustment of the sum in loan. Failure by the creditor to comply with the provisions of this section invalidates the calling-up notice; and this underlines the importance of meticulously observing all the statutory requirements on the exercise of these powers.

22.23 Service of the notice

The statutory procedure should invariably be followed to the letter and it is prudent, before serving the notice, to study in detail the provisions of ss 19 and 20 of the Conveyancing and Feudal Reform (Scotland) Act 1970 to ensure that all the statutory requirements have been meticulously complied with. In brief, these statutory requirements are as follows:

- Section 19(2) requires notice to be served on the person holding the last recorded title or his representatives.
- Section 19(3) makes detailed provision for situations where there is difficulty in determining on whom to serve the notice. Thus, where a company has been removed from the Register of Companies, or where the person holding the last recorded title is deceased and has left no representatives, the notice is served on the Lord Advocate.
- Section 19(4) and (5) amplify these provisions.
- Section 19(6), (7) and (8) contain detailed provision for the method of service of the notice, which may be personally made to the debtor or by recorded delivery. Where recorded delivery is used, it has been held effective service for the notice to be signed for by a neighbour at the debtor's house: see *Household Mortgage Corporation plc v Diggory*, Peterhead Sheriff Court, 21 March 1997, reported in R R M Paisley and D J Cusine *Unreported Property Cases from the Sheriff Courts* (2000), pp 455–462. In order to preserve evidence of service either Form C or D of Schedule 6 should be used. Form C is a written acknowledgment by the debtor that he has received the notice. As an alternative, Form D can be signed by the creditor, but must be accompanied by the postal receipt relating to the service. Professor McDonald's opinion is that Form D cannot be used as evidence of personal service, given the specific wording of s 19(6) in this regard. See C Waelde (ed) *Professor McDonald's Conveyancing Opinions* (1998), pp 169–171.

22.24 Period of notice

Section 19(10) of the Conveyancing and Feudal Reform (Scotland) Act 1970 deals with the period of notice which is two months. In terms of the statutory Form A in

Schedule 6, failing payment of the sum in loan with interest and expenses within that two-month period, the security subjects may then be sold. The notice is normally valid for a period of five years from the date thereof.

Formerly, the period of notice could always be dispensed with, given the appropriate consents of the debtor and *pari passu* or postponed creditors. This is no longer possible in relation to subjects to which the Mortgage Rights (Scotland) Act 2001 applies: see para 22.34. In such cases, the notice period cannot be reduced to under one month. The written consent of the debtor, the debtor's spouse (if the property is a matrimonial home), any other person entitled to make an application under the 2001 Act, as well as any *pari passu* creditors is required. The statutory reformulation here is rather awkward in that s 1(8)(a) of the 2001 Act inserts and deletes provisions in s 19 of the 1970 Act, which only apply where the 2001 Act applies.

22.25 ADDITIONAL NOTICE REQUIREMENTS UNDER THE MORTGAGE RIGHTS (SCOTLAND) ACT 2001

Where the Mortgage Rights (Scotland) Act 2001 applies, a copy of the Form A, together with Form BB of Schedule 6 to the Conveyancing and Feudal Reform (Scotland) Act 1970, must be served on 'the occupier' of the subjects: see the 1970 Act, s 19A(1). This gives details of the rights available under the 2001 Act. According to the 1970 Act, s 19A(2), Form BB 'shall be sent by recorded delivery'. If this is not done, then s 19A(3) provides that the calling up notice is ineffective. These provisions are problematic, because if recorded delivery is the only method of service, the debtor can avoid the security being enforced by refusing to accept the notice from the postman.

The matter made the front page of *The Herald* newspaper on 21 December 2001. It is discussed in detail by Mr Higgins in his *Scottish Repossessions* (2002), paras 4.2.26–4.2.28 and also by Sheriff Cusine and Professor Rennie in *Standard Securities* (2nd edn, 2002), para 8.25. These authors focus on the argument that 'send' may have a different meaning to 'serve', so it does not matter if delivery is refused. The suggestion is also made that service by sheriff officers should be carried out too, on a 'belt and braces' approach, although Mr Higgins rightly raises the point that this could be a breach of the debtor's human rights if not justified by the statute. Professors Reid and Gretton in *Conveyancing 2001* (2002), p 84 conclude tentatively that refusal to accept delivery could prevent enforcement. The Scottish Executive, however, are apparently satisfied with the drafting. The view expressed here is that the legislation needs clarified, to make it clear that personal service is effective. Further, it is submitted that if the current wording can allow a debtor to frustrate enforcement by not answering the door, then a court would be forced to strike down the relevant provision in the 2001 Act, in terms of s 29(1)(d) of the Scotland Act 1998. This is because the creditor would be being deprived of his security which would infringe Article 1, Protocol 1 of the European Convention on Human Rights.

22.26 DEFAULT NOTICE: STANDARD CONDITION 9(1)(b)

Where there has been a failure to comply with any other requirement arising out of the security, for example, if the debtor has failed to pay interest on the due date or has failed to maintain the security subjects in good repair, the creditor may alternatively serve a default notice under standard condition 9(1)(b), to which ss 21 to 23 of the Conveyancing and Feudal Reform (Scotland) Act 1970 apply. That the calling-up notice and default notice procedures are direct alternatives and in no way mutually exclusive was confirmed by the Inner House in *Bank of Scotland v Millward* 1999 SLT 901.

Under s 9(1)(a) of the 1970 Act, service of the notice is required to create default. Under s 9(1)(b), the debtor is in default automatically by mere failure to comply. This would normally entitle the creditor to serve a calling-up notice. But he may, as an alternative to calling-up, where appropriate, serve on the debtor a notice of default, calling upon the debtor to remedy his default (such as failure to repair etc) within a period of one month. Failure to comply with an effective notice of default entitles the creditor to exercise the powers of sale, of carrying out repairs and of foreclosure; but it does not entitle him to enter into possession.

There is a different form of notice, Form B of Schedule 6, for a 9(1)(b) default as opposed to a calling-up notice Form A; but otherwise the provisions of s 19 of the 1970 Act apply generally to the service of the notice Form B, for which see above. Again, it is possible for the period of notice to be waived, but not in cases where the Mortgage Rights (Scotland) Act 2001 applies: see s 1(8)(b) of that Act. As with calling-up notices, Form BB will need to be served in a 2001 Act case, there being the same problems with the service provisions as discussed in the previous paragraph.

22.27 Objection by debtor

The notice of default may be objected to under s 22(1) of the Conveyancing and Feudal Reform (Scotland) Act 1970 by application to the sheriff who adjudicates thereon. In contrast, the notice calling up the security under s 9(1)(a) of the 1970 Act is not open to objection in this way. Rather, it may be challenged by an action of reduction: see *Wilson v Target Holdings* 1995 GWD 31-1559. As an alternative, the debtor may petition for suspension of the notice. This is precisely what the debtors did in *Gardiner v Jacques Vert plc* 2001 GWD 38-1433, reversed 2002 SLT 928. In the Outer House, Lady Paton granted the petition because she was not satisfied that the alleged secured debt was due. However, her decision was reversed by the Inner House. It held that, in fact, the petitioners had not made a stateable case that the debt was not owed.

The sixth edition of this book, at para 22.28, suggests that the best advice in many cases may be to serve both a calling-up notice and a notice of default. This follows J M Halliday *Conveyancing Law and Practice* (1st edn, vol 3, 1987), para

39.20. See also I J S Talman (ed) *Halliday's Conveyancing Law and Practice in Scotland* (2nd edn, 2 volumes, 1996–97), para 54.22. The advantage of the shorter period with the notice of the default can be viewed as tempered by there being an express statutory right for the debtor to challenge it. But as the two cases in this paragraph demonstrate, it is possible to challenge a calling-up notice too. Further, as Sheriff Cusine and Professor Rennie point out in *Standard Securities* (2nd edn, 2002), para 8.16 where objection to a notice of default is made the creditor can make a counterclaim under s 22(3) of the 1970 Act to exercise immediately any of the remedies available under standard condition 10. Additionally, Mr Higgins in *Scottish Repossessions* (2002), para 2.7 points out that there are disadvantages in using both procedures simultaneously where the Mortgage Rights (Scotland) Act 2001 applies. Accordingly, the suggestion made in the sixth edition of this book merits reconsideration.

22.28   INSOLVENCY: STANDARD CONDITION 9(1)(c)

Where the proprietor of the security subjects has become insolvent, default is automatic. But the creditor acquires no powers unless and until he applies to the court under s 24 of the Conveyancing and Feudal Reform (Scotland) Act 1970; or, alternatively, serves a calling-up notice or a default notice.

There is a detailed definition of 'insolvency' in standard condition 9(2). Whilst the point has not been definitively settled, the better view is that 'insolvency' includes the situation where the debtor is a company and is apparently insolvent. See Cusine and Rennie *Standard Securities* (2nd edn, 2002), para 8.21.

22.29   APPLICATION TO THE COURT

In terms of s 24 of the Conveyancing and Feudal Reform (Scotland) Act 1970, where the debtor is in default under s 9(1)(b) or s 9(1)(c) of the 1970 Act, the creditor may apply to the court for a warrant to exercise any of the powers available to the creditor under s 9(1)(a). Many agents take decree in every case as a precautionary policy.

Under s 24(2) of the 1970 Act, where an application is made to the court on default under s 9(1)(b), a certificate in terms of Schedule 7 may be lodged in court which is *prima facie* evidence of the facts therein stated.

Where the security relates to land used for residential purposes, ie where the Mortgage Rights (Scotland) Act 2001 applies, once again there are additional requirements involving the problematic issue of service by recorded delivery. In terms of s 24(3) of the 1970 Act, the creditor must send a notice conforming with Form E of Schedule 6 to the 1970 Act to the debtor, as well as to the proprietor if he and the debtor are different individuals. A notice conforming with Form F of the same schedule must be sent to the occupier of the subjects.

22.30 Procedure

Section 29 of the Conveyancing and Feudal Reform (Scotland) Act 1970 deals with procedure. The appropriate court for all actions under Part II of the 1970 Act is the sheriff court in whose jurisdiction any part of the security subjects is situate. Any application to the court, in terms of this section, is by way of summary application. This has given rise to a number of recent cases where a creditor has applied to the court by summary action under s 24 of the 1970 Act and has incorporated, in that summary application, a crave for ejection of the debtor-proprietor and for a warrant to enter into possession of the security subjects. There is no doubt as to the creditor's right to eject the debtor in such circumstances; but that right is conferred by the Heritable Securities (Scotland) Act 1894, s 5. It is not therefore a right arising under Part II of the 1970 Act. The doubts about the correct procedure were resolved by the Act of Sederunt (Amendment of Sheriff Court Ordinary Cause, Summary Cause, and Small Claim, Rules) 1990, SI 1990/661. This provides that if a creditor is seeking only the remedies in standard condition 10, this must be done by summary application. If on the other hand, an additional remedy is sought, for example ejection, an ordinary action must be raised. For a recent example, see *Clydesdale Bank v Hyland* 2002 GWD 37-1229.

22.31 The creditor's powers on default

Standard condition 10 outlines the creditor's remedies on default as defined above in standard condition 9.

22.32 Creditor must act reasonably

At common law, a creditor is under a duty to act reasonably. Reference can be made in this regard to *Rimmer v Thomas Usher & Son Ltd* 1967 SLT 7, a case involving the old *ex facie* absolute disposition.

The standard security legislation imposes strict controls on the creditor, under the Conveyancing and Feudal Reform (Scotland) Act 1970 itself and under the standard conditions. Specifically, it imposes a duty upon the creditor upon sale to obtain the best price reasonably obtainable: see para 22.43. Nonetheless, the view was held by many that, as originally drafted, the 1970 Act as a whole failed to adequately protect debtors. Some comfort was provided by the decision in *Armstrong, Petitioner* 1988 SLT 255, which involved a competition between a heritable creditor and a judicial factor on a partnership estate. A calling-up notice had already been served before the judicial factor was appointed and in the circumstances the court held that the subsequent appointment of the factor did not disable the creditor from exercising rights which he already possessed. But Lord Jauncey commented that the creditor must exercise these rights *civiliter* and with proper regard for the interests of the debtor. The creditor's primary interest is recovery of the debt and on that basis Lord Jauncey did not consider that the creditor has unlimited discretion as to which one or more of the powers he should exercise. Accordingly, if the creditor elects to exercise his powers under condition 10 in a manner which does not produce the best result for the debtor, then he might very well be restrained from so acting; or be liable in damages if he acted in such a way. As Lord Jauncey put it in 1988 SLT 255 at 258

> 'A heritable creditor cannot use his powers for the primary purpose of advancing his own interest at the expense of the debtor when he has the alternative of proceeding in a more equitable manner'.

However, in the important Inner House decision of *Halifax Building Society v Gupta* 1994 SC 13, *Armstrong* was regarded as a decision limited to its peculiar facts. The normal position was held to be that the court has no discretion but to allow the creditor to exercise the powers under the 1970 Act.

22.33   Mortgage Rights (Scotland) Act 2001: introduction

The law in Scotland, as set out in *Halifax Building Society v Gupta* 1994 SC 13, contrasted with that in England, where the Administration of Justice Act 1970 confers a discretion upon the courts to suspend the enforcement rights of creditors in certain circumstances. The disparity between the jurisdictions was regarded as unacceptable by the new Scottish Parliament, which gave its support to a member's Bill introduced by Cathie Craigie MSP, which soon became the Mortgage Rights (Scotland) Act 2001. The legislation came into force on 3 December 2001 in terms of the Mortgage Rights (Scotland) Act 2001 (Commencement and Transitional Provision) Order 2001, SSI 2001/418. The use of the word 'mortgage' is controversial, because other than in respect of aircrafts and ships, this is not a term of art in Scotland. 'Perhaps we should just abandon Scots law now' commented Sheriff Nigel Morrison QC at (2001) 42 Greens Civil Practice Bulletin 2. Another difficulty, which has already been noted in para 22.24, is that the 2001 Act needs to be read along with the Conveyancing and Feudal Reform (Scotland) Act 1970 and indeed also s 5 of the Heritable Securities (Scotland) Act 1894 (ejection of the debtor). Sheriff Cusine and Professor Rennie in *Standard Securities* (2nd edn, 2002), para 8.23, rightly regard this as 'cumbersome'.

22.34   WHICH SECURITIES?

The Mortgage Rights (Scotland) Act 2001, s 1(1), in its post-feudal wording, applies to standard securities over 'land or a real right in land used to any extent for residential purposes'. For a discussion as to whether it applies to pre-1970 heritable securities, see Higgins *Scottish Repossessions* (2002), para 4.2.6. Obviously, the 2001 Act will apply to securities over residential property, in particular flats and houses. But commercial property, which has private accommodation as part of it, such as a public house with a flat for licensee would also be covered. So, too, would a farm with a farmhouse on it. Section 1(1) of the 2001 Act is qualified to an extent by s 1(2) which provides that the property, in whole or in part, must be the applicant's sole or main residence. Sheriff Cusine and Professor Rennie, in *Standard Securities* (2nd edn, 2002), para 8.24, argue that a hotel could not be a debtor's sole or main residence. This, however, is not necessarily true in all cases. See A F Deutsch 'Circumventing the Mortgage Rights (Scotland) Act 2001' (2002) 43 Greens Civil Practice Bulletin 1; the author correctly regards a small hotel as covered by the 2001 Act.

22.35 WHO IS ENTITLED TO USE THE 2001 ACT?

Five parties can apply for a suspension of enforcement procedures. Each of these must satisfy a general pre-requisite, namely that the security subjects are his or her 'sole or main residence'. The first is the debtor: see the Mortgage Rights (Scotland) Act 2001, s 1(2)(a). The second is the proprietor, but only if he is not the debtor, for otherwise he would already be covered: see s 1(2)(a). This would be where there is third-party security: see para 21.8. Mr Higgins, in *Scottish Repossessions* (2002), para 4.2.7, notes correctly that 'proprietor' is not defined in the 2001 Act. He speculates that it could include a trustee in sequestration, although such an individual would probably not wish to delay enforcement. In fact, a trustee in sequestration cannot fall within the meaning of 'proprietor' as the security subjects will not be his sole or main residence.

The third party is the debtor or proprietor's non-entitled spouse, provided that the security subjects are either wholly or partially a matrimonial home within the meaning of the Matrimonial Homes (Family Protection) (Scotland) Act 1981: see the Mortgage Rights (Scotland) Act 2001, s 1(2)(b). This is rather uncontroversial, as it simply makes the 2001 Act achieve the same policy objectives as the legislation of 20 years before.

More novel is the inclusion of the fourth and fifth parties. The fourth is the cohabitant of the debtor or proprietor: see s 1(2)(c) of the 2001 Act. Both heterosexual and same-sex relationships qualify. In the former, the cohabitant must be 'living together with the debtor or proprietor as husband or wife'. In the latter, their relationship must have 'the characteristics of the relationship between husband and wife except that the persons are of the same sex': see s 1(2)(c) of the 2001 Act. It will be of interest to see how the courts interpret these definitions. As regards heterosexual cohabitants, Mr Higgins in *Scottish Repossessions*, at para 4.2.7, comments that reference might be made to the doctrine of marriage by cohabitation with habit and repute. With regard to same sex partners, the drafting, although also found in the Housing (Scotland) Act

2001, Schedule 3, para 2(1)(a)(ii), is suggested by Professors Reid and Gretton to be problematic: see their *Conveyancing 2001* (2002), p 77. Perhaps the intended introduction of civil partnership legislation may lead to a more appropriate substitute provision.

The fifth party is the debtor or proprietor's former heterosexual or same sex cohabitant who continues to live in the subjects, although the debtor or proprietor does not any longer, together with a child of the parties who is under the age of 16: see s 1(2)(d) of the 2001 Act. Such a party must have lived with the debtor/proprietor for at least six months prior to the latter's departure. In addition the subjects must also be the child's sole or main residence. In terms of s 1(3), stepchildren and 'any person brought up or treated' by the parties as their child will also count.

To what extent spouses and cohabitants will take advantage of their new rights is unclear. As will be seen below, one of the factors which the sheriff must take into account when making a suspension order, is the applicant's ability to remedy the default within a reasonable period. Professors Reid and Gretton in *Conveyancing 2001* (2002), p 78, fairly anticipate that applicants who are neither the debtor or proprietor may be loath to take on repayment of the loan.

22.36   WHEN CAN AN APPLICATION FOR SUSPENSION BE MADE?

Under the Mortgage Rights (Scotland) Act 2001, s 1(1), an application for suspension is competent where the creditor has taken steps to enforce the security by:

(1)   serving a calling-up notice;
(2)   serving a notice of default;
(3)   making an application under the Conveyancing and Feudal Reform (Scotland) Act 1970, s 24; or
(4)   raising an action under the Heritable Securities (Scotland) Act 1894.

The application for suspension is a summary application to the sheriff: see the 2001 Act, s 1(6), and the Act of Sederunt (Amendment of Ordinary Cause Rules and Summary Applications, Statutory Applications and Appeals etc Rules) (Applications under the Mortgage Rights (Scotland) Act 2001) 2002, SSI 2002/7.

Where a calling-up notice has been served, the application must be made before the period of notice (two months) has expired: 2001 Act, s 1(4)(a). Where a notice of default has been served, it must be made not later than one month after the expiry of the period of notice, which as noted above is a one month period: 2001 Act, s 1(4)(b). However, the additional month can be shortened if the consent of the parties set out in s 1(5) of the 2001 Act is obtained. These parties are:

(1)   any other person on whom the notice is served;
(2)   where the subjects are a matrimonial home, the spouse; and
(3)   persons who can apply for a suspension under s 1(2)(c) and (d) of the 2001 Act (see the previous paragraph).

Where an application has been made under the 1970 Act, s 24, or an action raised under s 5 of the 1894 Act, the 2001 Act application needs to be made before 'conclusion of the proceedings': 2001 Act, s 1(4)(c). This would seem to mean before decree is granted. See Higgins *Scottish Repossessions* (2002), para 4.2.9. Once an application has been made, the creditor's right to enforce the security is suspended until it has been determined by the sheriff: see the 2001 Act, s 1(7)(b).

22.37 DETERMINATION OF THE APPLICATION

Under s 2(1) of the Mortgage Rights (Scotland) Act 2001, the court is empowered to suspend the enforcement of the security to an extent, period and subject to conditions as it thinks fit. In the case of proceedings under s 24 of the Conveyancing and Feudal Reform (Scotland) Act 1970 or s 5 of the Heritable Securities (Scotland) Act 1894, the court may continue these proceedings until a date of its choosing. But the court may only make an order if it is convinced that it is 'reasonable in all the circumstances': 2001 Act, s 2(2). This obviously gives the court a wide discretion, but that is slightly reined in by a requirement to have regard to four specific factors. These are:

(1) the nature of and reasons for the default;
(2) the applicant's ability to fulfil within a reasonable period the obligations under the standard security which are in default;
(3) any action taken by the creditor to assist the debtor to fulfil these obligations; and
(4) the ability of the applicant and any other person residing at the security subjects to secure reasonable alternative accommodation.

Judicial interpretation is keenly awaited. For the moment, the most detailed commentary is that of Mr Higgins in *Scottish Repossessions* (2002), paras 4.2.11–4.2.19. There would seem to be a difficulty with the framing of factor (2). If a calling-up notice has been served requiring repayment of the entire loan, because the debtor has been defaulting on his monthly repayments, the chance of him being able to discharge the whole debt 'within a reasonable period' is extremely low. Similar wording was used in the equivalent English legislation, but this had to be amended when the problem was highlighted in *Halifax Building Society v Clark* [1973] Ch 307. It may be that the same has to be done in Scotland. See further Cusine and Rennie *Standard Securities*, para 8.30 and Reid and Gretton *Conveyancing 2001*, pp 79–81. With regard to factor (4), in *Abbey National v Briggs,* Glasgow Sheriff Court, 20 June 2002, unreported (see www.govanlc.com/abbeynational_v_briggs), evidence was led from the local manager of the charity Shelter Scotland as to the availability of alternative accommodation in the area.

22.38 REGISTRATION OF ORDERS

If an order is made, s 3(1) of the Mortgage Rights (Scotland) Act 2001 requires that the clerk of court must send a certified copy 'as soon as possible' to the Keeper, so it can be registered in the Register of Inhibitions and Adjudications. A prescribed notice must also be sent: see s 3(2) and the Mortgage Rights (Scotland) Act 2001 (Prescribed Notice) Order 2001, SSI 2001/419. As Sheriff Cusine and Professor Rennie note in *Standard Securities* (2nd edn, 2002), para 8.32, the 2001 Act is sadly silent on the effect if the clerk fails to register the order, the effect of registration itself and on how the order is to be removed from the Register. What is clear, however, is that purchasers from a heritable creditor will need to carry out a search to ensure that no order is made. But, lamentably, the 2001 Act does not even state against whose name the order is to be registered. The Keeper's practice is to register the order against both parties to the application and any other relevant party. See K G C Reid and G L Gretton *Conveyancing 2001* (2002), p 81. Accordingly, a search against the creditor is the correct course of action. See para 32.17.

22.39 Interrelationship between the standard conditions and statutory provisions in the 1970 Act

Standard condition 10 outlines the various remedies which the creditor may resort to on default by the debtor. Note, firstly, that these remedies are without prejudice to the exercise by the creditor of any other remedy arising out of the contract to which the security relates. Accordingly, depending on the nature of the obligations secured by the standard security, there may be other and more appropriate remedies than those listed in standard condition 10. The remedies there listed include:

(1) sale of the security subjects;
(2) entering into possession and, when in possession, granting leases etc;
(3) carrying out repairs;
(4) foreclosure.

As stated above, however, the standard conditions have to be read along with the provisions of the Conveyancing and Feudal Reform (Scotland) Act 1970 itself; and there are now three default situations involving either a calling-up notice, a default notice, or insolvency. Different provisions apply to each of the three alternative default situations.

Under s 20 of the 1970 Act, when the debtor fails to implement a calling-up notice and is therefore in default under s 9(1)(a), the creditor can exercise all or any of the powers in standard condition 10. His power to grant leases, however, which is unqualified in standard condition 10(4), is restricted by the statutory provisions of s 20.

In contrast, where the debtor fails to implement a default notice and has not effectively objected to it under s 22 of the 1970 Act, then, under s 23, the creditor is given power to sell under standard condition 10(2), to carry out repairs under 10(6), and to foreclose under 10(7). But he is not entitled to enter into possession, to grant leases etc. If he wants to have these powers under standard condition 10(3) to 10(5), then he must apply to the court under s 24.

In the third default situation under s 9(1)(c), namely insolvency, the creditor does not acquire any powers. Instead, he must always apply to the court for power to exercise any of these powers under s 24.

22.40   Particular powers

Turning now to the particular powers conferred by standard condition 10, and keeping in mind that the powers there conferred are a summary only and must be read along with the statutory provisions in the Conveyancing and Feudal Reform (Scotland) Act 1970, together with the common law, there are five main powers:

(1)   sale (see paras 22.41 ff);
(2)   entering into possession (see paras 22.49 ff);
(3)   carrying out repairs (see para 22.51);
(4)   foreclosure (see para 22.52); and
(5)   adjudications (see para 22.53).

22.41   SALE

The statutory provisions for sale under a standard security are commendably simple and brief. The Conveyancing and Feudal Reform (Scotland) Act 1970, s 25, provides that the creditor may sell either by private bargain or by public roup. In either event, it is his duty to advertise the sale and to take all reasonable steps to ensure that the price at which the security subjects are ultimately sold is the best price that can be reasonably obtained. Section 25 will be amended by the Land Reform (Scotland) Act 2003, s 40(6), which is not yet in force, to provide that the creditor may only sell subject to ss 37(5)(e) or 40(1) of that Act. These are provisions which prevent sale of land on the open market where a community body is applying for registration of or has a community interest registered over the land. For the background, see A Steven and A Barr 'The Land Reform (Scotland) Act 2003' (2003) 66 Greens PLB 5.

22.42   Advertisement requirements

There are no provisions prescribing the period or number of advertisements, newspapers, place of sale, or upset price. The word 'advertise', as used in s 25 of the Conveyancing and Feudal Reform (Scotland) Act 1970, is not defined. Looking to the elaborate provisions in the Conveyancing (Scotland) Act 1924 which governed the old bond and disposition in security, and the general duty of the creditor, referred to above, to take reasonable steps to protect the debtor's interests, it was originally assumed, without question, that advertisement implied public advertisement in the public press. See J M Halliday *The Conveyancing and Feudal Reform (Scotland) Act 1970* (2nd edn, 1977), para 10.38, and in particular his reference to certificates of advertisement from the publishers.

Three separate instances have been brought to the notice of the Keeper of the Registers in relation to the Keeper's indemnity in registration of the title. In each of these three instances, the property was sold by the creditor in the exercise of the power of sale but not by advertisement in the public press. The Keeper is believed to take the view, however, that s 25 of the 1970 Act does not prescribe the mode of advertisement and indeed, in this context, it is significant that, in the 1970 Act, no provision whatever is made for preservation of evidence of advertisement as in the earlier legislation regulating the power of sale under a bond and disposition in security. If the view is accepted, then anything which lets it be known to the public by whatever medium that the property is for sale could be construed as advertising. In particular, advertisement in the local solicitors' property centre weekly guide should suffice. However, marketing over the internet, may currently at least, be insufficient. See D J Cusine and R Rennie *Standard Securities* (2nd edn, 2002), paras 8.37–8.38. It would certainly be safer to follow the advice of Professor Halliday referred to above. See Professor McDonald 'Advertising Requirements on a Sale by a Heritable Creditor' (1994) 7 Greens PLB 5. The application forms for registration in the Land Register ask the purchaser to confirm that the statutory requirements of the 1970 Act have been complied with, so the onus is placed on his or her solicitor to be satisfied in this regard. See the *Registration of Title Practice Book*, para 6.73.

22.43   Obligation to secure the best price

The duty to advertise is linked to the obligation to achieve the best price that can reasonably be obtained. This obligation protects the debtor and prevents the heritable creditor simply selling the security subjects for a figure matching the debt, when they are actually worth far more so that the excess value, on sale, should be returned to the debtor.

In *Associated Displays (In Liquidation) v Turnbeam Ltd* 1988 SCLR 220 a heritable creditor, acting under his power of sale, concluded missives for the sale of the security subjects. The debtor then sought to prevent the sale going through until such time as the creditor satisfied the court that he had taken all reasonable steps to ensure that he had obtained the best price. The sheriff held that the debtor's application was incompetent on two grounds. First, the creditor was under no duty to satisfy the debtor about anything; and, secondly, it was in any event too late, after missives had been concluded, to seek to prevent the creditor from proceeding with the sale. In the light of the decisions in *Rimmer v Thomas Usher & Son Ltd* 1967 SLT 7 and *Armstrong, Petitioner* 1988 SLT 255 (see para 22.32), this is a somewhat surprising decision. See also, on the same point, *Bank of Credit v Thompson* 1987 GWD 10-341, *Gordaviran Ltd v Clydesdale Bank plc* 1994 SCLR 248 and *Thomson v*

Yorkshire Building Society 1994 SCLR 1014, which have followed the approach in *Associated Displays*. If these decisions are correct, it would follow that even if the debtor sees the property being advertised at a very low figure, he must wait until after the sale before taking any action. In other words, the appropriate remedy is damages and not interdict. See further Higgins *Scottish Repossessions* (2002), para 8.11.

The creditor's obligation to obtain 'the best price' was discussed in the leading case of *Dick v Clydesdale Bank plc* 1991 SC 365. The Clydesdale Bank had a standard security over two areas of ground, one of which was used for commercial purposes and a larger area for agricultural. The bank called up their standard security and instructed professional advisers to market the property. The debtor wrote to the bank asking them to consider a number of matters before they proceeded with the sale and he suggested that the land would become more valuable as soon as the route for a new by-pass had been announced. He clearly wanted the bank to delay until the circumstances were more favourable. The bank, however, advertised the subjects and an offer for both areas of ground was accepted. The debtor then raised an action against the bank for damages for the loss which he claimed he had sustained because the agricultural ground had not been sold having regard to the expected rise in value.

While the Inner House dismissed the debtor's averments of loss as irrelevant, they did go on to discuss the creditor's obligations. In that connection, they made four points:

(1) the creditor has a duty to the debtor as well as to himself;
(2) the creditor is entitled to sell the security subjects at a time of his own choosing, provided he has taken all reasonable steps to ensure that the price at which he sells is the best that can reasonably be obtained at that time (in *Bank of Credit v Thompson* 1987 GWD 10-341, the sheriff thought that, because any further delay in the marketing of the property would have resulted in interest running against the debtor, that factor had to be weighed against the requirement that the creditor must try to get the best available price);
(3) in the ordinary case, the creditor will be regarded as having fulfilled the duties imposed upon him if he takes and acts upon appropriate professional advice. The implication may be that in an unusual case the creditor has to do more than just take professional advice; and
(4) what matters is the reality of the market place in which the property is exposed for sale at the time when the creditor decides to sell. As long as the creditor takes all reasonable steps to attract competition in that market, he will not be criticised for not taking further steps to attract an appropriate purchaser, unless there is evidence to show that a better bargain would have been achieved.

The extent to which the creditor can point to reliance on professional advisers as satisfying his duty to obtain the best price was discussed in *Bissett v Standard Property Investment plc* 1999 GWD 26-1253. Lord Hamilton, under reference to the Australian decision of *Commercial and General Acceptance Ltd v Nixon* [1983] 152 CLR 491, decided that such reliance could not of itself discharge the creditor's duty. It was for the creditor to keep himself appraised of what the agents were doing. The dictum of the court in *Dick v Clydesdale Bank plc* 1991 SC 365 that it is sufficient in the ordinary case to take and act upon appropriate professional advice cannot be safely followed. Another aspect of *Bissett* was an argument that it was inappropriate to sell the subjects by public roup. Lord Hamilton allowed a proof on the matter.

In *Davidson v Clydesdale Bank plc* 2002 SLT 1088, it was argued that the creditors had failed to satisfy their duty because they had not marketed the minerals within the land being sold separately. It was held, however, on the facts that this had made no difference to the price achieved. Of comparative interest is the recent Privy Council decision of *Newport Farm Ltd v Damesh Holdings Ltd* [2003] UKPC 54, an appeal from the New Zealand Court of Appeal. Creditors there are under a similar duty to their Scottish counterparts and one of the grounds on which the appeal failed here was that it was not established that a higher price could have been achieved.

22.44   Missives

The missives for the sale of subjects which are being sold by a heritable creditor may differ in some respects from the norm. For example, because the property may have been vacant for some time and, in any event, the heritable creditor will not have been in occupation, it is unlikely that the heritable creditor will grant some of the warranties which are customarily asked of sellers, particularly in the sale of domestic property. The heritable creditor is unlikely to be willing to warrant the ownership of the moveables, or that the central heating system and electrical appliances are in good order. In addition, the heritable creditor may put the onus on the purchaser to ascertain whether the erection of the building and any alterations complied with local authority requirements and that all other consents have been obtained. The heritable creditor is unlikely to be willing to clear the Personal Registers of any inhibitions which post-date the granting of the standard security and any letter of obligation will be qualified to that extent.

22.45   Clearing the record

Prior creditors are not affected in any way by a sale by a postponed creditor; are entitled to be paid, in full, the principal sum in loan due to them with interest and expenses; and, unless and until so paid, are not obliged to grant the necessary discharge which will clear the record. Accordingly, if a postponed creditor sells under the power of sale and there is a shortfall, he may find himself personally liable to make good the difference in order to clear the record.

As to other securities, the creditor is still bound to account to the debtor for his intromissions but, with the standard security, there is no requirement to produce a formal certificate of surplus or no surplus. Instead, the record is cleared of the selling creditor's own security, all *pari passu* and postponed securities and diligences, merely by the registration of the disposition in favour of the purchaser, which in its terms bears to be in implement of the sale. The old rule which required the consent of *pari passu* creditors was abolished for the standard security by the Conveyancing and Feudal Reform (Scotland) Act 1970, ss 26(1) and 27(1).

In *Newcastle Building Society v White* 1987 SLT (Sh Ct) 81 the building society, on default of the debtor, duly exercised their power of sale and, in the customary form, undertook in the contract of sale and purchase to deliver a clear search. It then emerged that, after the recording of the standard security but before the sale, an inhibition had been registered against the debtor proprietor. The purchaser maintained that, in these circumstances, the search was not clear; but the sheriff principal held that, in view of the provisions of s 26(1) of the 1970 Act referring to diligences postponed to the security of the selling creditor, it was clear *ex facie* of the record that the property had been disencumbered and accordingly no further action was required on the part of the building society.

22.46 Application of proceeds of sale

Under s 27(1) of the Conveyancing and Feudal Reform (Scotland) Act 1970, the proceeds of sale are to be held by the selling creditor in trust and applied thus:

(1) to pay the expenses properly incurred in connection with the sale;
(2) to pay the whole amount due under prior securities;
(3) to pay the whole amount due under his own security and *pari passu* securities, *pro rata* if the proceeds are insufficient;
(4) to pay the amounts due to any heritable creditors with postponed ranking, according to their ranking;
(5) finally, any residue remaining is to be paid to the person entitled to the security subjects at the time of sale.

22.47 Problems of accounting

Clearly, this may cause problems to the selling creditor and so, under s 27(2) of the Conveyancing and Feudal Reform (Scotland) Act 1970, if the creditor cannot obtain a receipt or discharge for any of the foregoing payments, he is obliged to account for his intromissions but may consign the amount due in the sheriff court for the benefit of the persons having best right thereto.

The decision in *Halifax Building Society v Smith* 1985 SLT (Sh Ct) 25 illustrates the difficulties which may confront the selling creditor. In that case, the Halifax Building Society properly exercised its power of sale and there was a resulting surplus. After the standard security had been recorded but before the sale was concluded, a number of inhibitions were registered against the debtor. There was no doubt that, in the circumstances, these inhibitions did not interfere with the sale and that the record was cleared under s 26(1) of the 1970 Act; but the question was whether, for the purposes of s 27(1), inhibiting creditors held securities with a ranking postponed to that of the selling creditor. If so, then they were entitled to share in the distribution of the surplus. The sheriff principal held that, for the purposes of s 27(1)(d), inhibitions were securities. This decision was followed in *Abbey National Building Society v Barclays Bank plc* 1990 SCLR 639, but the opposite position was taken in *Alliance & Leicester Building Society v Hecht* 1991 SCLR 562. That is that an inhibitor must take the further step of either adjudication prior to the sale or arrestment after the sale in order to obtain a preference: see G L Gretton *The Law of Inhibition and Adjudication* (2nd edn, 1996), pp 148–150. The Scottish Law Commission in its *Report on Diligence* (Scot Law Com No 183, 2001), paras 6.60 to 6.64, has recommended amending legislation to the effect that the decision in *Hecht* is correct.

22.48 Protection of the purchaser

This is regulated by the Conveyancing (Scotland) Act 1924, s 41(2), in the form substituted by the Conveyancing and Feudal Reform (Scotland) Act 1970, s 38. The effect of that section is that, where a disposition bearing to be in implement of a power of sale has been duly recorded and where the exercise of the power of sale was *ex facie* regular, the title of a purchaser in good faith for value is not open to challenge either:

(1) on the grounds that the debt had ceased to exist; or
(2) on the grounds of any irregularity in the sale procedure.

The protection afforded to the purchaser, however, does not exclude a claim for damages at the instance of an aggrieved debtor against a selling creditor who has abused his powers.

It is not clear exactly what enquiry the purchaser must make to establish his good faith; but the prudent agent will at least investigate the sale procedure to ensure that the same was *ex facie* regular.

22.49 ENTERING INTO POSSESSION

Standard condition 10(3) empowers the creditor, on default, to enter into possession and receive the rents and feuduties. This power is not available to a creditor under standard condition 9(1)(b) without authority from the court. In any event, even if the creditor is proceeding under a calling-up notice and standard condition 9(1)(a), a decree of maills and duties or its equivalent is required unless the debtor consents. It was held in *UCB Bank Ltd v Hire Foulis Ltd (In Liquidation)* 1999 SC 250 that the creditor is only entitled to the rents from the date upon which he enters into possession. He has no right to any arrears.

Once in possession, whether by decree or of consent, the creditor may let the security subjects. The power to let is, however, restricted by the Conveyancing and Feudal Reform (Scotland) Act 1970, s 20(3) to leases for a term not exceeding seven years, except with the consent of the sheriff. The creditor in possession also has the same rights as the debtor in relation to management and maintenance if the property is already let.

22.50 Implications for creditor in possession

The exact implications of 'entering into possession' are not clear. On the one hand, where a default notice has been served under s 9(1)(b) of the Conveyancing and Feudal Reform (Scotland) Act 1970 and not complied with, the creditor has power of sale but does not automatically have power to enter into possession unless he applies to the court for that power. It is a little difficult to see how a creditor can sell the security subjects without being in possession thereof, but that seems to be the implication of s 23(2) of the 1970 Act.

Whatever the meaning of the term, entering into possession is not something to be undertaken lightly and without some prior investigation. For one thing, a creditor in possession undoubtedly becomes liable for feudal prestations and for the liabilities of the proprietor in a question with the public which, as a mere security holder, he would not incur. In *David Watson Property Management Ltd v Woolwich Equitable Building Society* 1992 SC (HL) 21 the question of what additional liabilities might be imposed upon the heritable creditor was raised. A building society repossessed security subjects with a view to sale. At the time they entered into possession, there were arrears of common charges which had been incurred by the debtor. The House of Lords held that an obligation in the title to maintain was enforceable against singular successors. However, when resulting obligation to pay a specific amount arose, that was a debt which was personal to the owner at the time the work was done and did not transmit against a heritable creditor in possession. The position here has been altered by the Title Conditions (Scotland) Act 2003: see para 17.66.

In this connection it is worth noting that there are various statutes which impose obligations on the 'owner', for example, the Housing (Scotland) Act 1987 which deals with statutory repairs notices. It remains to be decided whether a heritable creditor in possession is the 'owner' for such purposes, but it is arguable that he is. See Cusine and Rennie *Standard Securities* (2nd edn, 2002), para 8.69. As regards obligations on 'owners' under the Building (Scotland) Act 1959, Professor Halliday's view is that the heritable creditor is not liable. See D J Cusine (ed) *The Conveyancing Opinions of Professor J M Halliday* (1992), pp 336–338. The term 'owner' is also used in the replacement legislation, the Building (Scotland) Act 2003, which is not yet in force. It has also been decided that he is not liable for the community charge. See *Northern Rock Building Society v Wood* 1990 SLT (Sh Ct) 109. In the case of council tax, which replaced the community charge, subjects into which the heritable creditor has entered possession are exempt. See the Council Tax (Exempt Dwellings) (Scotland) Order 1997, SI 1997/728, Schedule, para 13.

As a general rule, a postponed creditor can exercise his statutory powers notwithstanding subsisting prior securities. Thus, a postponed creditor can sell the security subjects although he must then pay off the prior security in full in order to obtain a discharge thereof and to clear the record. However, that rule does not apply to entering into possession: see *Skipton Building Society v Wain* 1986 SLT 96, where Lord Stewart held that the creditor holding the earlier of two competing decrees was the creditor entitled to possession.

22.51   CARRYING OUT REPAIRS ETC.

Standard condition 10(6) empowers the creditor, when the debtor is in default, to effect necessary repairs, reconstruction or improvement, and to enter on the subjects for this purpose. There are no statutory limitations on this right; and, in particular, the creditor need not, first, be lawfully in possession.

22.52   FORECLOSURE

The statutory requirements are set out in the Conveyancing and Feudal Reform (Scotland) Act 1970, s 28, and are as follows:

(1) exposure for sale by public roup at a price not exceeding the amount due under the security, and all prior and *pari passu* securities;
(2) the expiry of two months from first exposure;
(3) an application to the sheriff served on the debtor, the proprietor and any other heritable creditor disclosed by a 20-year search. On such application, the sheriff may either:
    (a) allow time to pay not exceeding three months;
    (b) order re-exposure, with power to the creditor to bid; or
    (c) grant decree of foreclosure, declaring the right of redemption extinguished.

If a decree is granted, recording that decree has the following consequences:

(1) the right of redemption is extinguished;
(2) the subjects are disburdened of the foreclosing creditor's security and all post-poned securities. But prior and *pari passu* securities are unaffected. The creditor may redeem these as the debtor might have done;
(3) the creditor's title is unchallengeable on grounds of irregularity in procedure; but
(4) the debtor's personal obligation to the foreclosing creditor is not discharged.

Foreclosure is very rare.

22.53   ADJUDICATION

This is also a common law remedy which is rarely used because the creditor will not acquire ownership of the subjects until the expiry of ten years from the date of the original decree ('the legal'). The Scottish Law Commission has recommended that adjudication should be abolished and replaced with a new statutory diligence to be known as land attachment. See *Report on Diligence* (Scot Law Com No 183, 2001), Parts 2–4. Under the new diligence, the creditor may register a notice of land attachment in the Register of Sasines or Land Register. This will confer a judicial heritable security, which may be enforced by application to the court for permission to sell after six months. In its *Enforcement of Civil Obligations in Scotland: A Consultation Document* (available at www.scotland.gsi.gov.uk/consultations/justice/CivOb-00.asp), published in April 2002, the Scottish Executive confirmed its intention to implement the Commission's proposals. It also made clear that the new diligence can be used against dwellinghouses. This was a matter which the Commission reserved its view upon. However, in such cases there will be special rules protecting the debtor.

22.54 Transmission

Like other securities, there are two elements to a standard security: real security and the personal obligation.

(1) *Real security.* The creditor's preference is established at the date of creation of the real right by the registration of the standard security; but the debtor is not divested. Accordingly, the debtor can still deal with the property by way of sale or second security; and, on his death or on sequestration the security subjects will transmit to his representatives, or trustee. Any such dealing with the debtor's proprietary right is subject to, and cannot affect, the preference created for the creditor by the recording of the standard security. This is a rule which applies to securities in general: see para 21.1.

(2) *The personal obligation.* As discussed in para 22.5, two different forms of standard security are provided in the Conveyancing and Feudal Reform (Scotland) Act 1970, Schedule 2: Form A and Form B. In Form A the personal obligation appears on the face of the deed; whereas, with Form B, the security is granted by the debtor for the purpose of securing a separate obligation contained in a collateral agreement, which is referred to and detailed in Form B. In both cases, the personal obligation subsists until the debtor fully implements his obligations therein; that obligation (unless otherwise expressly so provided which is virtually unknown) is not restricted to the value of the security subjects; and the personal obligation subsists and remains enforceable against the original debtor as a personal debt even although he may have parted with the security subjects.

22.55 CHANGE OF DEBTOR: LIABILITY OF SINGULAR SUCCESSOR

A singular successor acquiring heritable property subject to a standard security does not, at common law, incur any element of personal liability although, notwithstanding his proprietary right, he cannot prevent the creditor from exercising any of his real remedies as against the security subjects which the singular successor has acquired from the original debtor, although he would have the right to make an application under the Mortgage Rights (Scotland) Act 2001. Suppose, then, that A owns land subject to a loan secured by a standard security. He sells the property to B on the footing that B will take over responsibility for the outstanding loan. Some years elapse. B then defaults. The creditor can still sue A on the personal obligation, but cannot sue B by way of personal action; alternatively the creditor can exercise his power of sale and recoup himself out of the proceeds, which does not directly affect A, the original debtor.

This is unsatisfactory, and in practice it is unusual for a purchaser or disponee to take over a loan in this way. Instead, the loan is normally paid off and the disponee borrows of new. But, if taking over the loan is the arrangement between the parties, then the disponer, A, would normally wish to be relieved of personal liability; and the creditor would not normally release him unless he got a personal obligation from B in lieu. The creditor is not, in any event, bound to release A, the original debtor.

22.56   Modes of transferring personal liability

The personal obligation can be made to transmit against B, as singular successor in two ways:

(1) Bond of corroboration. This is a separate deed in terms of which the disponee expressly undertakes personal liability.

(2) The Conveyancing (Scotland) Act 1874, s 47 (as amended by the Conveyancing (Scotland) Act 1924, s 15 and Schedule A2). The object of this provision is to render the bond of corroboration unnecessary. These sections are not excluded by the Conveyancing and Feudal Reform (Scotland) Act 1970 and continue to apply to the standard security. The combined effect of the sections is:

   (a) Where the disponee takes by succession, gift, or bequest, he incurs personal liability up to the value of the subjects taken by him.

   (b) Where the disponee takes by conveyance, other than on succession, gift or bequest, the disposition in his favour may contain an express undertaking by the disponee of personal liability in lieu of obtaining a separate bond of corroboration. A statutory form is provided in the 1924 Act, Schedule A2, which is equally applicable to the taking over of personal liability for a standard security.

The mere fact that a singular successor undertakes the personal obligation in a standard security does not, of itself, release the original debtor from personal liability; and a separate personal discharge is required. Being purely personal, such a discharge is not registrable in the Register of Sasines or Land Register.

22.57   CHANGE OF CREDITOR

The benefit of the personal obligation undertaken by the debtor is an asset in the estate of the creditor. This applies whether the personal obligation is undertaken *in gremio* of the standard security Form A or in a collateral obligation secured by Form B: see Schedule 2 to the Conveyancing and Feudal Reform (Scotland) Act 1970. The right of the creditor under a standard security, accordingly, involves both the benefit of the personal obligation of the debtor and the real security granted by the debtor in support of that personal obligation. If the benefit of the personal obligation is to transmit as it may, by *inter vivos* or *mortis causa* deed, then it is essential that the person succeeding to the debtor's obligation should take over both the benefit of the personal obligation of the debtor and the real security created for the benefit of the original creditor.

22.58　Transmission *inter vivos*

Looking to the special features of this form of asset involving, as it does, both the personal obligation of the debtor and the real security, transmission *inter vivos* involves some specialties. In particular, the transferee or assignee will require an effective transfer of the personal obligation so that the assignee in turn can enforce it directly against the debtor; and he will also require a transfer of the security subjects in a form which will allow him to exercise all the powers enjoyed by the original creditor under the standard security when originally granted in his favour by the debtor. With a Form B security, this means that the assignation must refer expressly to the separate document under which the principal obligation is constituted, otherwise it will not carry that obligation: see *Watson v Bogue (No 1)* 2000 SLT (Sh Ct) 125.

Special provision is duly made for the transfer of both elements in the standard security, the personal obligation and the real security, by way of a statutory form of assignation authorised by the Conveyancing and Feudal Reform (Scotland) Act 1970, s 14(1) and Schedule 4, Form A. In appropriate cases, a partial assignation is competent. On such assignation being duly recorded, the security or the part thereof assigned, vests in the assignee as if the security or that part thereof had originally been granted in his favour.

In addition, under s 14(2) of the 1970 Act, the assignation carries with it to the assignee the benefit of all corroborative obligations; the right to recover from the debtor all expenses properly incurred by the creditor; and the benefit of any notices served by the creditor before the assignation.

There are a number of notes to Schedule 4 dealing with various specialties. In particular:

(1) Note 1. If the assignor does not himself have a recorded title, deduction of title is necessary in the assignation.
(2) Note 2. This deals with securities for uncertain amounts and prescribes the method of defining what is assigned.

22.59　Transmission *mortis causa*

See Chapter 30: Transmission on Death.

22.60 **Extinguishing the debtor's obligation**

As already explained, the standard security is granted to secure performance by the debtor of a pecuniary obligation or an obligation *ad factum praestandum*. If the debtor fails to implement his obligations, then the creditor has remedies, both personal and real, which have already been dealt with. But, in the great majority of cases, the debtor does fulfil his obligations in the fullness of time either by payment or performance; and, when the obligations are thus fully implemented, the debtor is entitled to a discharge.

22.61 DISCHARGE

The purpose of the discharge is two-fold:

(1) to release the debtor from his continuing personal obligation to the creditor; and
(2) to release the security subjects from the burden of the standard security as a real security thereon.

A short statutory form is provided in the Conveyancing and Feudal Reform (Scotland) Act 1970, s 17, which achieves both objectives by the granting of a discharge, following Form F of Schedule 4 to the Act.

Notes 1 and 2 to Schedule 4, referred to above in para 22.58, likewise apply to the discharge Form F. Section 17 further provides that, on the recording of the discharge in the statutory form, the security subjects are disburdened thereof.

22.62 ALTERNATIVE MODES OF DISBURDENMENT

Whilst a discharge is normally used to release the debtor and clear the record, in fact very much less will serve to achieve the same purpose although this is not normally relied on in practice, because of the obligation to provide a clear search. See para 32.35. So, the security subjects may be disburdened of a subsisting security not merely by discharge but also in one or other of the following ways:

(1) redemption;
(2) *confusio*;
(3) prescription; and
(4) payment.

These methods are outlined in the following four paragraphs.

22.63 **Redemption**

Under the debtor's power of redemption and related procedure, without the intervention of the creditor, the record is cleared: see the Conveyancing and Feudal Reform (Scotland) Act 1970, s 18(3).

22.64 *Confusio*

This is a rule of general application to obligations in Scots law and applies where the same person in the same capacity becomes both the debtor and the creditor in an obligation. The effect, as regards heritable securities, is that the security is absolutely extinguished and cannot be revived.

22.65 **Prescription**

In principle, as a real right, a standard security is subject to long negative presciption under the Prescription and Limitation (Scotland) Act 1973, s 8. But in practice no creditor would fail to enforce the security for such a period.

22.66 **Payment**

'An infeftment in security may be extinguished by payment or discharge of the debt': see Lord Kinnear in *Cameron v Williamson* (1895) 22 R 293 at 298, where part of a sum in loan was repaid but no formal discharge was granted. The remaining balance of the loan was later discharged by a formal partial discharge which referred expressly to the earlier partial repayment. It was held that the record was clear of the whole security. Where, however, as is typical in practice the security is for all sums rather than a fixed amount, a formal discharge is required. Otherwise, fresh indebtedness to the creditor will reactivate the security. See G L Gretton and K G C Reid *Conveyancing* (2nd edn, 1999), para 20.18.

22.67 **Restriction**

A standard security creates a real right on the whole of the security subjects and on every individual part thereof. Thus, if the owner of a tenement of flats grants a standard security thereon for £20,000 and one flat is later sold, the sold flat remains liable as real security for payment of the whole debt. The creditor, following on such sale, may then in his option exercise his power of sale over the sold flat alone and satisfy his debt out of the proceeds; or he may proceed against the whole, or other parts, of the tenement.

As a result, no purchaser will take a title to heritable subjects forming part of a larger whole where the larger whole is subject to a subsisting security. In such a case, the debtor may pay off the whole loan and have the standard security discharged, which undoubtedly clears the record and renders the title marketable. But this may be inconvenient to the debtor on a sale of a small portion only of the larger whole. So, as an alternative, a debtor frequently bargains with the creditor in such circumstances for the release by the creditor of the sold portion, on such terms and conditions as the debtor and creditor mutually agree. Where such a release is arranged, it would be inappropriate for the standard security to be discharged; if that were done, the creditor would lose his security for the remaining outstanding loan. Instead, the sold portion can be taken out of the creditor's security by two methods.

22.68   DEED OF RESTRICTION

This is a separate formal deed granted by the creditor. The Conveyancing and Feudal Reform (Scotland) Act 1970, s 15(1), provides that the security constituted by a standard security may be restricted as regards any part of the subjects burdened thereby by a deed of restriction following Form C of Schedule 4 to the 1970 Act and on such deed being registered, the security shall be restricted to those subjects under exception of the land disburdened by the deed; and the part so disburdened is cleared from the security. Again, notes 1 and 2 to Schedule 4 apply.

22.69   CONSENT *IN GREMIO*

Instead of using the separate deed of restriction, it is competent and effective for the creditor to consent to the disposition in favour of the purchaser of the portion sold. A clause is inserted in the narrative of the disposition to the effect that the creditor agrees to release the subjects disponed from his security. The disposition is then executed by the creditor and registration thereof disburdens the part so disponed.

Chapter 23

Floating Charges

23.1 Introduction

This chapter provides an overview of the floating charge. In particular, it considers the rules on creation and ranking. The consequences of this form of security for conveyancing transactions are dealt with in Chapter 34. Reference should also be made to para 4.4 for discussion of the important floating charge case of *Sharp v Thomson* 1997 SC (HL) 66.

It is a general principle of Scots law that every heritable security affects a particular heritable property. It becomes effective only when a writ relating to that particular property enters the Register of Sasines or Land Register; the date of registration is the criterion of preference and of ranking; and the security subsists on the security subjects until it is later actively discharged. The result is that, as with proprietary rights, the Register of Sasines and Land Register are the measure of, and the index to, all security rights affecting heritable property in Scotland.

In the case of companies this fundamental principle was radically altered by the Companies (Floating Charges) (Scotland) Act 1961, later repealed and re-enacted by the Companies (Floating Charges and Receivers) (Scotland) Act 1972, now consolidated in the Companies Act 1985 and the Insolvency Act 1986. Under the 1961 Act (now the 1985 Act), following English precedent, a new type of security known as a 'floating charge' was introduced into Scotland.

The Companies Act 1985, ss 462 to 466 deal with the creation, effect, ranking and alteration of floating charges in Scotland; and ss 410 to 424 deal in detail with the registration of charges, both fixed and floating. The Insolvency Act 1986, ss 50 to 71, superseding the Companies Act 1985, ss 467 to 485, deal in detail with the appointment and powers of receivers in Scotland; and s 72 of the 1986 Act deals with the cross-border operation of receivership provisions in Great Britain as a whole. Receivers enforce the floating charge on behalf of its holder. However, the ability to appoint a receiver has now been curtailed by the Enterprise Act 2002: see para 23.4.

For the sake of completeness, it should be noted that limited liability partnerships, industrial and provident societies and European Economic Interest Groupings may also grant floating charges: see W M Gordon *Scottish Land Law* (2nd edn, 1999), para 20.205. But, undoubtedly, it is floating charges created by companies which are the most important in practice.

23.2   Creation of the charge

The Companies Act 1985 applies only to 'an incorporated company (whether a company within the meaning of this Act or not)'. Guarantee and unlimited companies are included, and also companies registered outside the UK. Any such company may create an effective security for any debt or obligation, including guarantees. The method is to grant a floating charge over all or any part of the property, which may from time to time belong to the company ('be comprised in its property and undertaking'). This includes, *inter alia,* heritable property in Scotland. In the case of Scottish companies, under the Companies (Floating Charges) (Scotland) Act 1961, a floating charge could only competently be created by an instrument of charge in statutory form, as set out in a Schedule to that Act. But the statutory form was dispensed with in the Companies (Floating Charges and Receivers) (Scotland) Act 1972, and there is now no prescribed form of charge.

23.3   Effect of the charge

The benefit to the creditor of the security effected by the floating charge is limited, under the Companies Act 1985, in various ways. We shall consider them under the following headings:

(1) property affected (see para 23.4);
(2) registration (see para 23.5);
(3) ranking (see para 23.6); and
(4) variation (see para 23.7).

23.4   PROPERTY AFFECTED

Under the Companies Act 1985 a charge may be created either:

(1) on the whole property; or
(2) on a specified part of the property (for example, 'all heritable property in Scotland').

In either case (notwithstanding the reference to 'property from time to time comprised in the property and undertaking of the company'), the floating charge in fact only attaches to those assets actually owned by the company at one or other of:

(1) the date of commencement of winding up; or
(2) the date when a receiver is appointed.

At that point, the charge becomes a fixed security and the creditor obtains a real right in respect of the property. In the case of a partial charge, only those assets comprised in the specified part of the property at such date are attached. Thus any asset owned by the company but disposed of before such date escapes from the charge; and any such asset not owned by the company at the date of creation of the charge but subsequently acquired and still owned at such date comes within the charge. In relation to heritable property, it was held in *Sharp v Thomson* 1997 SC (HL) 66 that this ceases to form part of the 'property and undertaking' of a company upon delivery of a disposition to a purchaser who takes entry in return for payment. This decision is treated in paras 4.4, 34.7, 34.12, 34.15 and 34.25 and will not be discussed further here, other than to note that property held in trust by the company will also excluded from the ambit of the charge by virtue of it.

In terms of the Enterprise Act 2002, s 250 (as amended), which came into force on 15 September 2003, it is not possible to appoint a receiver in respect of most floating charges created since that date. However, an adminstrator may be appointed, if the charge is appropriately drafted. But such an appointment will not cause the charge to attach. There are eight types of floating charge which are exempt from the new provisions, namely (1) capital market charges; (2) public–private partnership charges; (3) utilities charges; (4) project finance charges; (5) financial market charges; (6) registered social landlord charges; (7) urban regeneration project charges; and (8) certain water, rail and air traffic company charges.

23.5 REGISTRATION

A floating charge requires to be registered in the Register of Charges. This was a new Register set up in Scotland under the Companies (Floating Charges) (Scotland) Act 1961 and is kept by the Registrar of Companies. Detailed provision is made in the Companies Act 1985, ss 410 to 424, for registration of charges in this Register; and, in particular, time limits are prescribed to meet various circumstances. For discussion, see G L Gretton 'Registration of Company Charges' (2002) 6 Edin LR 146.

In the case of a Scottish company the floating charge must be registered within 21 days of its date. If not so registered, it is void as against the liquidator or administrator and any other creditor; the only remedy is to petition the court to allow late registration, but such petitions will not necessarily be granted. See *Prior, Petitioner.* 1989 SLT 840. The same rule applies to any company incorporated outside Great Britain which creates a charge on property in Scotland.

Provided that the charge is duly registered within 21 days, its date of creation will be regarded as the date on which it was executed: see the Companies Act 1985, s 410(5)(a). It will therefore prevail over a standard security executed on the same day, if it contains a clause giving it priority over such a security, because under the 1985 Act, s 410(5)(b) a standard security is not created until it becomes real. This does not happen until registration in the Register of Sasines or Land Register. See *AIB Finance Ltd v Bank of Scotland* 1995 SLT 2. This rule is inexplicable and unjustifiable. See also paras 34.7 and 34.9.

Until 22 December 1981 companies registered in Scotland, having a place of business in England, were treated exactly as if they were companies registered outside

Great Britain and had to register floating charges over their assets in both the Scottish and English Registers. Since that date, the registration requirement has been altered so that floating charges have to be registered only once in the Register of Charges appropriate to the situation of the registered office of the company concerned (which was the rule for English companies prior to that date). See the Companies Act 1985, ss 396 and 410. See also in this regard C Waelde (ed) *Professor McDonald's Conveyancing Opinions* (1998), pp 172–176.

It is further provided in the 1985 Act, s 462(5), that a floating charge, although registrable in the Register of Charges, does not require to be registered in the Register of Sasines nor in the Land Register, even if heritable property in Scotland is included in the property affected by the charge.

23.6 RANKING

The property is attached by the floating charge subject to certain preferential claims, including the rights of any person who has effectually executed diligence on the property (on which, see *Professor McDonald's Conveyancing Opinions,* pp 176–180) and any person holding a fixed or floating charge ranking prior to the charge in question. Three possibilities are covered in the Companies Act 1985, s 464:

(1) a floating charge in competition with a fixed security arising by operation of law, such as lien. In this case, the fixed security always has priority. It was held in *Cumbernauld Development Corporation v Mustone Ltd* 1983 SLT (Sh Ct) 55 that the landlord's hypothec does not have preference over a floating charge, but this decision is generally accepted to be incorrect. It was rejected in *Grampian Regional Council v Drill Stem (Inspection Services) Ltd* 1994 SCLR 36;

(2) when there are express ranking clauses. Ranking as between a floating charge and a voluntary fixed security not arising by operation of law and between two or more floating charges may be regulated by express ranking clauses. Thus the instrument of charge may, and invariably does, prohibit the creation by the debtor company of (a) any fixed security; or (b) any floating charge having priority over, or ranking *pari passu* with, the floating charge which the instrument creates. See also para 34.9.

The instrument of charge may, by such express provision therein, regulate the order of ranking, *inter se*, of the floating charge and any other specific charge, fixed or floating, present or future. But a pre-existing charge or fixed security is not affected by such a provision, unless it also contains a corresponding clause;

(3) where there is no operative ranking clause, then:

(a) a fixed security which has become real by registering in the Register of Sasines or the Land Register before the floating charge attaches to the property (ie on the commencement of a winding up or the appointment of a receiver) ranks before a floating charge, even although the latter is first registered;

(b) two or more floating charges, if and when they attach to property of the company, rank according to their respective dates of registration.

Note that, under this provision, future fixed securities with prior ranking can validly be prohibited. So, on taking security from a company, the Register of Charges should always be checked. But a subsequent fixed security, so prohibited, is not voided, merely postponed. It is thought that the charge cannot validly prohibit outright disposal by the company to a purchaser. So a search in the Register of Charges is not in theory necessary on sale except for the purpose of disclosing whether or not a receiver has been appointed. But the appointment of a receiver instantly converts a floating charge into a fixed security, the effect of which will transmit against a purchaser of any heritable property of the company. Since sale may trigger off the appointment of a receiver and crystallise the charge, a search is for practical purposes required. This is dealt with again in Chapter 34.

23.7 VARIATION

The Companies Act 1985, s 466 (formerly the Companies (Floating Charges and Receivers) (Scotland) Act 1972, s 7) allows for alteration of the terms of a floating charge, once granted. This was not competent under the Companies (Floating Charges) (Scotland) Act 1961, with unfortunate results on additional lending. For a comparable difficulty in relation to fixed securities and its solution, see para 22.9.

Variation requires a deed executed by the company, the creditor and any other fixed or floating creditors affected by the variation; and the deed must be registered if it makes certain alterations, for example, by ranking clauses, or by releasing property or increasing or decreasing the amount secured.

23.8 Effect of floating charges on property

If, in accordance with the foregoing requirements, a floating charge does effectively attach to property at the date of winding up, or of appointment of a receiver, then it has effect as if the charge had become, at such date, a fixed security over the property to which it has attached in respect of the principal sum in loan and interest due and to become due thereon: see the Companies Act 1985, s 463(1) and the Insolvency Act 1986, s 53(7) and s 54(6).

23.9 Petition for rectification

If a charge is not registered in the Register of Charges within the 21-day time limit, then an application to the Court of Session is competent and necessary for a rectification of the Register. The court may allow the 21-day limit to be extended: Companies Act 1985, s 420. See *Allan Black & McCaskie, Petitioners* 1987 GWD 19-709; *Prior, Petitioner* 1989 SLT 840.

23.10   Miscellaneous

Special provision is also made in the Companies Act 1985 for various miscellaneous matters including:

(1)   time limits for registration of charges created out of the UK: 1985 Act, s 411(1);

(2)   time limits for registration of charges created in the UK but which include property situated outwith the UK: 1985 Act, s 411(2);

(3)   an obligation on every company to make up and maintain its own private register of charges, in which are to be entered copies of instruments creating charges. This is in addition to, and separate from, the requirement to register in the Register of Charges maintained by the Registrar of Companies. The register of charges of each individual company is available for public inspection: 1985 Act, s 422;

(4)   suitable entries will be registered in the Register of Charges when property is released from a charge, by restriction or discharge. The appropriate entry is by memorandum of satisfaction, or partial satisfaction as appropriate: 1985 Act, s 419.

Special forms are provided for these various registration requirements under the Companies (Forms) Regulations 1985, SI 1985/854 (as amended).

23.11   Companies Act 1989

Part IV of the Companies Act 1989 contains provisions to alter the system for registration of charges. These were outlined in paras 23.13–23.21 of the sixth edition of this book. But they have never been brought into force, because they are regarded as unsatisfactory. See G L Gretton 'Registration of Company Charges' (2002) 6 Edin LR 146 at 147. Instead, new proposals have been brought forward by the Scottish Law Commission.

23.12   Reform of registration provisions for floating charges

The Scottish Law Commission has recently published a discussion paper entitled Registration of Rights in Security by Companies (Scot Law Com Disc Paper No 121, 2002). It covers registration of security rights in general, but only the proposals for floating charges will be covered here. See further Lord Eassie 'Reforming Registration of Company Charges' 2002 JLSS Dec/26 and D Guild 'The Registration of Rights in Security by Companies' 2002 SLT (News) 289.

The Commission proposes that floating charges should only be created upon registration in the Charges Register. This departs from the current problematic rule that they are effective upon execution, provided that they are registered within 21 days. In a similar vein, transfers of floating charges would only take effect upon registration of the assignation and variations upon registration of the instrument of alteration. Likewise, a charge would be only extinguished upon registration of a deed of discharge. It is also proposed that floating charges should rank with other securities, both fixed and floating, by date of creation, although this could be altered by a ranking agreement. Under the current law, whilst the default position is that a floating charge will rank below a subsequent fixed security, this is invariably altered in the deed creating the floating charge. It is sensible for the law to recognise the universal practice here and change the default position. The Commission also consults on the question of whether priority notices should be introduced in respect of floating charges. This would allow prospective creditors to achieve a preferential ranking by registering a notice ahead of the actual charge.

Chapter 24

Leases: General

24.1 The creation of a lease

At one time, leases in Scotland were used for residential property and for small commercial and industrial premises, such as shops. However, it has been common for many years for leases to be used in larger properties, such as shopping developments, where the rent paid for any one unit may be fairly considerable. Such leases will usually be for lengthy periods and will almost certainly be registered. The whole topic is therefore of greater practical significance than was the case say 30 years ago. However, it is important to bear in mind that something which may be described as a lease may not be one (see *Millar v McRobbie* 1949 SC 1) and something which is not described as a lease may be one (see *Brador Properties Ltd v British Telecommunications plc* 1992 SC 12). Furthermore, in many leases, the tenant may have security of tenure, for example, in an agricultural holding (see Chapter 26 for more detail). However, there is a great deal of legislation dealing with such matters and although the precise detail is outwith the scope of this Manual it is worth noting, in passing, that strict adherence to the time limits is very often a feature of this legislation.

It is assumed that the reader is already familiar with the general law of landlord and tenant; and no attempt is made in this Manual to rehearse the general principles which apply to that relationship. All we are concerned with here is, briefly, some points to note on the practical aspects of leases in everyday practice. For a more detailed, up-to-date account of the modern law of leases, see A McAllister *Scottish Law of Leases* (3rd edn, 2002). See also C Waelde (ed) *Professor McDonald's Conveyancing Opinions* (1998), pp 181–204.

Under the rules laid down by the Requirements of Writing (Scotland) Act 1995, a lease for more than one year falls under the category of a contract relating to an interest in land. Such a contract is one of the exceptions to the basic principle laid down by the 1995 Act: that writing is not required for the constitution of a contract. However, it is no longer the case that the writing need be probative; a subscribed document is valid (although it may be witnessed to establish self-proving status if desired). The statutory personal bar, which closely resembles its common law counterpart, will apply to a purported lease which falls short of these requirements. If the lease is for less than a year the 1995 Act does not apply. Instead, *rei interventus* and homologation may apply: see *Goldston v Young* (1868) 7 M 188; *Ferryhill Property Investment Ltd v Technical Video Productions* 1992 SCLR 282. There must, of course, be consensus on the subjects to be let, the rent or other consideration, and the term, and without that, there will not be a lease: see *Gray v Edinburgh University* 1962 SC 157.

Until recently there was no general limit on the length of a lease although residential leases are restricted to a maximum of 20 years under the Land Tenure Reform (Scotland) Act 1974, s 8: see para 24.10 below. Leases for very long periods are not uncommon, even up to 999 years. As noted in para 6.28, abolition of the feudal system opened the possibility that a new backdoor feudal system could be introduced by the use of long leases with many of the same defects. To counter this possibility, a restriction on the length of leases was introduced under the Abolition of Feudal Tenure etc (Scotland) Act 2000, s 67. Leases executed on or after 9 June 2000 are restricted to a maximum of 175 years. Leases executed before that date are unaffected. There was no period specified in the Scottish Law Commission *Report on the Abolition of the Feudal System* (Scot Law Com No 168, 1999). The period was set at 125 years when the Bill was introduced into the Scottish Parliament but this period was the subject of debate in the Parliament and it was pointed out that certain commercial developments require a longer period than 125 years. The Scottish Executive accepted this argument and the period was increased to 175 years. For further discussion, see K G C Reid and G L Gretton *Conveyancing 2000* (2001), pp 139–141.

The subject of long leases generally and possible claims for the conversion of tenants' rights into ownership is currently being considered by the Scottish Law Commission. See *Conversion of Long Leases* (Scot Law Com Disc Paper No 112, 2001), discussed in A McAllister 'Long Residential Leases: Some Unfinished Business' (2002) 7 SLPQ 141.

24.2   Lease as a real right

At common law, a lease is essentially a personal contract between the registered proprietor, in this context 'the landlord', and a temporary occupant, in this context 'the tenant'. The tenant is permitted by the landlord, for a limited period of time and for payment of a rent, to enjoy the benefit of the property to the temporary exclusion of the landlord throughout the duration of the lease.

This fundamental characteristic of the lease as a personal contract carries with it two consequences, concerned with:

(1) assignability by the tenant; and
(2) transmission against the landlord's successor.

24.3   ASSIGNABILITY BY TENANT

The selection of the tenant in most cases involves some element of *delectus personae*. In the result, in the great majority of cases, either by implication or by express provision in the lease, the tenant is prohibited from parting with possession of the whole or any part of the subjects of let either by way of assignation of his interest, in whole or in part, or by subletting. This is one feature which distinguishes occupation of property under a lease from occupation as owner where, generally speaking, there is freedom of disposal.

24.4 TRANSMISSION AGAINST LANDLORD'S SUCCESSOR.

Since a lease is essentially a personal contract, the common law rule was (and is) that the lease is not binding in a question with a singular successor of the landlord because the tenant has no real right. That common law rule has been excluded, in the great majority of cases, by the Leases Act 1449.

The principal purpose of this Act was, originally, to give some security of tenure to tenant farmers; but it has since been extended to include leases of almost every kind of property with very limited exceptions.

The main result of the 1449 Act is to create for the tenant a right to maintain himself in possession in terms of his lease, when the landlord dispones the property to a singular successor who becomes owner as proprietor in his place. As a result of the provisions of this Act, the tenant is equally entitled to insist on the terms of the lease in a question with a singular successor as he was with the original landlord on the basis of contract. So the tenant acquires, under the 1449 Act, a real right which transmits against singular successors for the duration of the original lease.

As an extension of this principle, by later statutes, tenants of particular types of property are given much more extensive security of tenure, and certain other rights as well, including, in some cases, the right to continue in occupation at a controlled rent. Two particular cases where statute further controls the relationship of a landlord and tenant in this way are agricultural property under the Agricultural Holdings Acts, and dwelling-houses under the Rent (Scotland) Act 1984 and the Housing (Scotland) Act 1988. These statutory provisions are referred to later in Chapters 26 and 27 respectively.

The 1449 Act, in contrast, protects the tenant strictly according to the terms of the original contract and not beyond. To produce this result, however, the lease must first satisfy certain basic requirements.

(1) It must be in writing in compliance with the Requirements of Writing (Scotland) Act 1995, except for leases of one year's duration or less.
(2) There must be a definite and continuing rent and the rent must not be illusory.
(3) There must be a definite termination date (sometimes referred to as 'the ish'), however far into the future.
(4) The tenant must have entered into possession. The tenant is not protected during any period of possession prior to the date of entry specified in the lease. Without possession, the tenant is merely the personal creditor of the landlord: see *Millar v McRobbie* 1949 SC 1 at 6.

If a lease is entered into which fails to satisfy these requirements, it may be binding, on the basis of contractual agreement, between the original landlord and his universal successors on the one hand and the tenant and his successors on the other; but it will not bind a singular successor of the landlord. The same applies to a lease which complies with the above requirements but where the subjects of let are not within the scope of the 1449 Act, such as fishings. That particular exception has, however, largely been negatived by the Freshwater and Salmon Fisheries (Scotland) Act 1976, s 4 in relation to leases of fishings in inland waters. This provision is to be repealed and replaced by the Salmon and Freshwater Fisheries (Consolidation) (Scotland) Act 2003, s 67, which is not yet in force. The new provision is to similar effect.

24.5   **Rent**

As with feus in earlier days, so with leases the contractual arrangement between landlord and tenant starts off, in the ordinary way, on a strictly commercial basis with the tenant paying to the landlord an annual rent of full commercial value. In other words, the landlord as proprietor receives by way of rent a return on his property equivalent to what he might expect to receive as a return on any other form of investment. But, taking into account improvements to the premises carried out by the tenant, and the steady increase in property values particularly in periods of inflation, rents tend to diminish in real value to the landlord with the passage of years, which has two results.

(1) As time passes, the lease becomes an asset of increasing value to the tenant, particularly in commercial premises with the build up of goodwill; and

(2) in modern leases, this tendency for the rent to get out of line with current rental values is counteracted by the introduction into the lease of a rent review clause. The effect of this clause is that, at regular intervals throughout the period of the lease, the rent is reviewed and may be increased in line with increases in real values.

24.6   **Possession**

So far as the tenant is concerned, the lease has two substantial disadvantages compared with ownership of property.

(1) Sooner or later, the lease comes to an end, whereupon at common law, and in the absence of contrary provision in the lease, the property, with all buildings, fixtures and improvements generally reverts to the landlord without any compensation to the tenant. This is the case even where these have been provided at the expense of the tenant. This, in effect, means that the value of the

tenant's asset is written down to nil at the termination of the lease. To some extent this disadvantage can be counteracted either:

(a) by entering into a lease for a long initial term or by providing in the lease for an option to the tenant to renew his lease for successive terms; or

(b) by providing expressly for compensation for tenant's improvements.

Note, however, the terms of the Tenancy of Shops (Scotland) Acts 1949 and 1964. These provide that a shop tenant can, within 21 days of receipt of the landlord's notice to quit, and in circumstances where a renewal of the tenancy cannot be negotiated on satisfactory terms, make application to the sheriff for renewal of the lease for a period of up to one year on such terms and conditions as the sheriff thinks reasonable. Such an application is made by way of summary cause.

(2) Because of the requirement that, to qualify for the protection of the Leases Act 1449, the tenant must enter into possession, a lease could not be used as security for borrowed money. This is because the essence of any heritable security is that the borrower is left in possession to enjoy the benefits of the property, while the lender has security without actual occupation. Given the requirements of the 1449 Act, a creditor of a tenant could not obtain security over the lease except by taking possession of the subjects of let; and in any event that would probably be prohibited either by implication or by the express terms of the lease itself.

In many cases, the tenant takes land on a long lease with the intention of building. If the lease is for a long enough term, the tenant may find it economically viable to put buildings on the land even although, at the end of the lease, the buildings pass to the landlord without payment. Such leases were and are commonplace in England. Until recently, in Scotland, building leases were much less commonly encountered, but, for technical reasons, did regularly occur. In recent urban re-developments they are now frequently used, particularly in commercial and industrial precincts.

One consequence of this type of lease is that the tenant invests substantial sums of money in building, or in improving and fitting out buildings on land, although he is not the owner thereof. Inevitably, in many such cases, the tenant has to borrow the money required for such development; but, under the 1449 Act, he is not in a position to grant security. Borrowing for development on leasehold land was therefore impracticable, notwithstanding the protection of the 1449 Act. For an example of the dangers facing tenants in such leases, see *Dollar Land (Cumbernauld) Ltd v CIN Properties Ltd* 1992 SLT 211 affirmed 1992 SLT 669; 1997 SLT 260 affirmed 1998 SLT 922.

24.7 **Registration**

These difficulties, which the tenant on a long lease encountered, were removed by the Registration of Leases (Scotland) Act 1857. The main purpose of this Act was to permit publication of the tenant's right by recording of the lease in the Register of Sasines in place of, or as an alternative to, the publication of that right by the taking of possession.

When registration was first introduced for titles under the Registration Act 1617 and the Real Rights Act 1693, the essential feature of the registration legislation was that recording of a deed in the Register of Sasines became an essential element in the obtaining of the real right. In contrast, under the Registration of Leases (Scotland) Act 1857, registration was optional in this sense that the tenant could secure his real right under his lease simply by entering into possession, without recording any deed in the Register of Sasines. However, as the whole of Scotland is now operational for land registration, the tenant no longer has this option; and registration of all new long leases and of writs relating thereto is, in all cases, obligatory: see paras 11.23 and 24.10. We shall consider four aspects of registration:

(1) benefit of registration;
(2) short-term leases;
(3) amendments to the 1857 Act; and
(4) forms.

24.8   BENEFIT OF REGISTRATION

The principal benefit to the tenant of this legislation is that it allows the tenant, while taking possession, at the same time to grant security on his lease and to borrow money on that security so as to allow him to develop his leasehold property.

A further effect of the Registration of Leases (Scotland) Act 1857 is that, if a lease is recorded before the landlord has disposed of the subjects to a singular successor, then no rent is necessary and no definite termination date is required. This contrasts with the position where the Leases Act 1449 alone is relied on. This is because the 1857 Act does not define the term 'lease' and, in particular, does not incorporate the statutory prerequisites laid down in the 1449 Act. For a recent discussion on this aspect of a registration of a lease, see *Palmer's Trustees v Brown* 1989 SLT 128. See also C Waelde (ed) *Professor McDonald's Conveyancing Opinions* (1998), pp 192–197.

24.9   SHORT-TERM LEASES

Leases of short duration are commonplace. To allow every lease to be recorded in the Register of Sasines, regardless of its duration, would have vastly increased the volume of writs entering the Sasines Register and created a major administrative problem there. Therefore, to prevent overloading of the system, the Registration of Leases (Scotland) Act 1857 originally restricted the recording of leases to those leases:

(1) where the term of the lease was not less than 31 years; and
(2) where the subjects of let did not exceed 50 acres in extent.

24.10   AMENDMENTS TO THE 1857 ACT

The Registration of Leases (Scotland) Act 1857 has been amended by two later provisions, as follows:

(1) The Land Tenure Reform (Scotland) Act 1974, Schedule 6, reduced the necessary term for a recordable lease to a term of more than 20 years, and abolished the 50-acre limit. At the same time, the 1974 Act introduced a prohibition against the granting of a long lease of property intended to be used as a dwelling-house.

    The reason behind the prohibition is also to be found in the 1974 Act which prohibited the imposition of new feuduties. It was thought that developers might move to leasing residential property and thus recover, by way of rent, what they previously would have been paid as feuduty.

    There are, however, some long leases of residential property which predate the 1974 Act and they are unaffected by its provisions. Indeed, they may be renewed for a period in excess of 20 years (see Law Reform (Miscellaneous Provisions) (Scotland) Act 1985, s 1). Other long leases (ie for more than 20 years) are not affected by the 1974 Act. However, if there is an obligation on the landlord in these leases to renew the lease at its expiry, the sheriff has power to grant a renewal if the landlord is unknown or his consent is otherwise not forthcoming: see the Land Registration (Scotland) Act 1979, s 22A. Note here the reform proposals of the Scottish Law Commission discussed in para 24.1.

(2) Under s 3 of the 1979 Act, when an area has been declared operational for the purposes of registration of title, which is now the position throughout Scotland, then the tenant under a long lease no longer has the option either to take possession or to register the lease. Registration of the lease in the Land Register is an essential requirement to the obtaining of a real right; and to that extent the Leases Act 1449 is excluded.

24.11   FORMS

No statutory form of lease is provided by the Registration of Leases (Scotland) Act 1857; and any normal conventional form of lease will serve for the purposes of registration. The 1857 Act does, however, provide statutory forms of assignation and of renunciation of a lease; and also provides forms of heritable security over leases with appropriate forms for assignation and discharge of such securities. The forms have been amended and adapted by the following provisions.

24.12   The Conveyancing (Scotland) Act 1924, s 24

The general purpose of this section is to assimilate lease forms with the forms in use for proprietary rights; and, in particular, for the purposes of any assignation or security writ, the subjects of let are to be described in terms of Schedule J to the Conveyancing (Scotland) Act 1924.

Further, by s 24 of the 1924 Act, all the powers, rights and forms applicable to proprietory rights are, with necessary adjustments, made applicable to leases and securities over leases as if the right of the tenant thereunder were a proprietary right.

24.13   The Long Leases (Scotland) Act 1954, s 27

This section removed certain earlier requirements for the description of the subjects of let, and simplified the forms of writ above referred to.

24.14   The Conveyancing and Feudal Reform (Scotland) Act 1970, s 32 and Schedule 8

The statutory modifications introduced by the 1970 Act in relation to heritable securities were applied, by these provisions, to registered leases in the same way as to proprietary rights; and, in consequence, certain provisions in the Registration of Leases (Scotland) Act 1857 dealing with assignations in security etc were abolished.

As a result of the 1970 Act provisions, heritable securities over registered leases can be constituted by standard security in either Form A or Form B, found in Schedule 2 to the 1970 Act, using the Conveyancing (Scotland) Act 1924 provisions for description; and otherwise with the same general results as apply to a standard security over proprietary rights.

24.15   The Land Tenure Reform (Scotland) Act 1974, ss 8–10 and Schedule 6

The principal modifications in this Act are, as above noted:

(1) the reduction in the required period of a registrable lease to 20 years; and
(2) the prohibition on the granting of long leases of dwellinghouses.

The Land Tenure Reform (Scotland) Act 1974 also abolished casualties in leases granted after the passing of that Act; but casualties in pre-existing leases continued to be exigible until abolished under the Leasehold Casualties (Scotland) Act 2001: see para 24.18.

Finally, Schedule 6 to the 1974 Act amends the Registration of Leases (Scotland) Act 1857, s 16, in such a way that a registrable lease should always be registered; and possession alone should not be relied on. See I J S Talman (ed) *Halliday's Conveyancing Law and Practice in Scotland* (2nd edn, 2 volumes, 1996–97), para 41.06.

24.16 **Procedure and effect of registration**

Where the lease itself has not been recorded by the original tenant, it can be registered by any subsequent tenant in right thereof for the time being as assignee, by the registration of the lease together with, in Register of Sasines cases, a notice of title. The new tenant must use the notice of title Form 2 of Schedule B to the Conveyancing (Scotland) Act 1924, and specify the links in title connecting him with the original tenant. As with the use of that form in other situations, the notice of title carries the warrant of registration (although warrants of registration will not be necessary after feudal abolition) and the lease carries a docquet referring to that notice.

Once the lease has been registered, whether by the original tenant or by a successor in the manner above referred to, it can then be transmitted by the tenant in right thereof for the time being, whether or not he himself has a registered title. In this case, the tenant must use the form of assignation provided by the Registration of Leases (Scotland) Act 1857 (as amended by the later enactments referred to at para 24.10).

Similarly, the tenant in right of the lease for the time being can grant a standard security thereon.

24.17 **Real right without possession**

The combined effect of the enactments above referred to is that a lease, on recording or registration, effectively secures a real right for the tenant thereunder as at the date of recording or registration in a competition with all other recorded titles which enter the Register of Sasines or Land Register subsequent to the date of the recording or registration of that lease.

24.18 **Transmission by the tenant**

In the case of unrecorded or unregistered leases, where the right transmits by assignation as it may do, subject possibly to the prior consent of the landlord, the title of the assignee is completed by intimation of the assignation to the landlord.

In the case of recorded or registered leases, consistently with the provisions for the recording or registration thereof, the title of an assignee of a recorded or registered lease is completed by the recording or registration of the assignation in the Register of Sasines or Land Register. The recording or registration of the assignation effectively vests the lease in the assignee to the extent to which the lease is assigned.

In relation to all the foregoing forms, whether of assignation of the lease itself or securities thereon, and of renunciation of leases, the whole lease may be dealt with, using the forms provided by the Registration of Leases (Scotland) Act 1857 (as amended).

In that case, it is unnecessary to describe the subjects of let; and all that is required is to assign the lease itself thus:

'I AB (design) in consideration of the sum of   pounds (£) now paid to me by CD (design) hereby assign to the said CD a lease granted by EF (design) in my favour of the subjects therein described lying in the County of   dated and recorded in the Division of the General Register of Sasines for the County of   on   ; With entry as at   .'

Where part only of the subjects of the lease is to transmit, then a description is required to indicate the part assigned. In that case, the foregoing form is used but with a description of the lease modified on the following lines:

'but in so far only as regards the following portion of the subjects of lease, namely ...'

The portion assigned is then described or referred to as in Schedule D to the Conveyancing (Scotland) Act 1924 for proprietary writs.

Until recently the transmission by assignation of a lease, whether registered or not, created a special problem in relation to leasehold casualties: see the sixth edition of this book at para 24.19. A leasehold casualty was a payment in addition to the rent due by a tenant to a landlord from time to time, which could arise in various circumstances as provided for in a lease. In some cases it was a payment made at regular intervals, commonly every 19 years. Leasehold casualties were similar to feudal casualties which were abolished under the Feudal Casualties (Scotland) Act 1914. Leasehold casualties escaped such abolition and in practice were forgotten about until recently when certain landlords, commonly known as 'title raiders', bought landlords' interest in various properties with a view to exercising the rights to casualty payments for financial gain. Under the Leasehold Casualties (Scotland) Act 2001, leasehold casualties are automatically abolished from 10 May 2000, the date the Bill was introduced into the Scottish Parliament. The 2001 Act provides a limited compensation mechanism. See further R Rennie 'Leasehold Casualties' 2001 SLT (News) 235.

Instead of assigning the lease, the tenant may wish to sub-let the leased subjects in whole or in part. The tenant then becomes the landlord in the sub-lease but, as with an assignation, the original lease may prohibit sub-leases or impose restrictions on the circumstances in which they are permissible.

While there may be restrictions on the tenant's ability to assign or sub-let, there is no such restriction on the landlord who is the proprietor, and the tenant may find himself with a new landlord without being able to object. If the conditions under the Leases Act 1449 or the Registration of Leases (Scotland) Act 1857 or the Land Registration (Scotland) Act 1979 have not been met, the tenant will not have a real right against successors of the original landlord and so the new owner would not be bound to recognise the lease at all.

24.19 Interposed leases

As an alternative to selling his interest outright, the landlord may interpose the lease which creates a sub-tenancy at his instance. The landlord grants the lease of his interest to a new tenant who then becomes the landlord of the existing tenant. The Land Tenure Reform (Scotland) Act 1974 recognises interposed leases and gives effect to those which were created prior to the Act: see s 17. One of the common reasons for interposing a lease is where a developer has leased out various units in the completed development but, rather than sell the interest, wishes to retain it but without having the day-to-day management responsibility. That responsibility can be passed on to the interposed tenant/landlord. For two cases illustrating the potential dangers which may arise as a result of such an arrangement, see *Dollar Land (Cumbernauld) Ltd v CIN Properties Ltd* 1992 SLT 211 affirmed 1992 SLT 669 and *Kildrummy (Jersey) Ltd v Calder (No 2)* 1997 SLT 186.

24.20 Succession to the tenant

On the death of the tenant, the lease vests in his executors (Succession (Scotland) Act 1964, ss 14 and 36(2)) and the executor is given power to assign the lease where the tenant has not made any valid provision in his will or other testamentary document. In such a case, the executor may transfer the lease to one of the persons entitled to succeed on intestacy, or in satisfaction or partial satisfaction of claims with prior or legal rights. This power must be exercised within one year, otherwise the lease will terminate: 1964 Act, s 16(4). See also the Rent (Scotland) Act 1984, s 1(1) and the Housing (Scotland) Act 1987, s 52.

However, the tenant may make a testamentary disposal of the lease in favour of any one of the persons who would be entitled to succeed on intestacy: 1964 Act, s 29(1)).

Special conditions apply to agricultural leases: see Chapter 26.

24.21 Examination of the landlord's title

It is an essential requirement that, for the granting of an effective lease, the landlord must be registered as owner, subject only to the rules of accretion which apply to leases as they apply to the granting of a disposition. The facility for deduction of title which applies to the granting of a disposition and, now, to the granting of a standard security, has not yet been extended to the granting of leases.

Further, not only must the landlord be registered as owner as a preliminary to the granting of an effective lease but he must also have a valid and marketable title.

This is a point which is frequently overlooked by the tenant's agent when revising the lease. But it is just as important to a tenant as it is to a purchaser to ensure that the landlord granting the lease has a valid title so to do.

Therefore, the solicitor for the tenant should insist, in the preliminary contract, that the landlord has a valid and marketable title. In addition, as part of the procedure of revising the lease produced by the landlord's solicitor, the tenant's solicitor should insist on examining the landlord's title to assure himself of its validity. Such an examination should consider such things as the description of the subjects, rights of access, use of services and conditions of title.

The tenant's solicitor must also bear in mind that there may be conditions in the title, for example, restricting the use of the property etc which apply not only to the ownership of the property by the landlord but to the use to be made of the property by the tenant. All writs referred to for burdens, or Section D of the Land Certificate if the subjects are registered in the Land Register, must therefore be carefully examined just as in the case of sale and purchase.

The tenant's solicitor should also insist on production of searches in exactly the same way in which a purchaser's solicitor insists on searches before completing a transaction of sale and purchase.

Further enquiry may be necessary, for example, where there is a heritable security, in which case the consent of the heritable creditor may be necessary (see *Trade Development Bank v Warriner & Mason (Scotland) Ltd* 1980 SC 74).

Finally, exactly the same principles apply to settlement obligations on completion of a lease as apply to settlement obligations on completion of sale and purchase.

24.22 Real and personal conditions

Even though a lease is binding on a singular successor of the landlord, it is still necessary to ascertain which of its conditions are real and bind singular successors and which of its conditions are personal and, as such, are not binding. The general rule is that only those conditions which are *inter naturalia* of a lease run with the land: see *Bisset v Aberdeen Magistrates* (1898) 1 F 87 and *Optical Express (Gyle) Ltd v Marks and Spencer plc* 2000 SLT 644. The class of conditions which have been held to bind singular successors is quite restricted. For example, an obligation to grant renewals has sometimes been held to bind singular successors. Each case must be considered according to its circumstances. As a result, care should be taken when framing conditions which are designed by the contracting parties to be permanent. Of particular importance to a tenant is the question of how best to draft an option to purchase so as to ensure its enforceability against singular successors of the landlord. Unfortunately there are no *voces signatae* – a declaration that such a provision is deemed to be *inter naturalia* of the lease will not suffice. However, in *Davidson v Zani* 1992 SCLR 1001 the element of personal bar and knowledge was deemed to play a significant part in the decision as to whether such a provision was binding.

24.23 Notices to quit: common law

At common law, the rules on removing from urban subjects depended on local custom. For example, the practice of 'chalking' involved the burgh officer chalking the most prominent door of the building in the presence of a witness, 40 days before the appropriate term of removing, either Whitsunday or Martinmas.

24.24 Notices to quit: Sheriff Courts (Scotland) Act 1907

Most current requirements are now derived from the Sheriff Courts (Scotland) Act 1907, ss 34 to 38. However, it has been said that this Act has 'thrown the whole matter, which was by no means devoid of confusion at any rate, into still greater confusion': *Campbell's Trustees v O'Neill* 1911 SC 188 at 192.

24.25 Periods of notice

The Sheriff Courts (Scotland) Act 1907 provides that notices to quit must be in writing. The Schedule to the 1907 Act also lays down the form of notice. The periods of notice required vary according to circumstances. It is of course open to the landlord and the tenant to agree a longer period of notice to be specified in a lease. It is questionable whether or not the parties can agree to a shorter period. When calculating the last date by which notice must be served, it is advisable to disregard both the date of service and the date of receipt. It is essential that 28 or 40 (as the case may be) clear days' notice is given: see *Esson Properties Ltd v Dresser UK Ltd* 1977 SLT 949.

24.26 Service of notice

All notices should be served in terms of the lease. It is also advisable to serve all notices by recorded delivery post. In *Capital Land Holdings Ltd v Secretary of State for the Environment* 1996 SLT 1379 the court held that the notice ought to have been served on the landlord at his registered office, as the parties, having made specific provision for the places to which notices had to be sent, were entitled to hold each other to them. By contrast, in *McGhie v Dunedin Property Investment Company Ltd* 1998 GWD 39-2019 as the lease did not give specific instructions as to where the notice was to be served, it was held competent to serve it on agents of the company.

The importance of serving termination notices by recorded delivery post was confirmed in the case of *Netherfield Visual Productions v Caledonian Land Properties Ltd* 1996 GWD 19-1107, where the landlords claimed never to have received the tenants' notice of termination of the lease which the tenants contended had been posted to the landlords. In that case, however, the court held that the presumption of delivery had not been rebutted by the landlords. A similar decision was reached in *Chaplin v Caledonian Land Properties Ltd* 1997 SLT 384. Notwithstanding these decisions, however, service by recorded delivery post is strongly recommended in order to avoid potential dispute. Care should also be taken when the term of removing is either Whitsunday or Martinmas. See the Term and Quarter Days (Scotland) Act 1990 and the re-definition of the terms of Whitsunday and Martinmas and the inherent conflict with the Removal Terms (Scotland) Act 1886.

A notice to quit, served timeously, may prevent tacit relocation from applying. However, it should be borne in mind that the actual removal of the tenant is regulated by the Sheriff Courts (Scotland) Act 1907 and it may take some time to recover the property from a tenant who refuses to remove from the premises on the expiry date.

The need for clarification or simplification of the law has been recognised and certain recommendations were made by the Scottish Law Commission in its *Report on The Recovery and Possession of Heritable Property* (Scot Law Com No 118, 1989). These recommendations are yet to be implemented, however, and the current statutory requirements continue to be complicated and unsatisfactory.

Chapter 25

Commercial Leases

25.1 Introduction

The approach to leasehold tenure in general in Scots law and English law is fundamentally different. In the law of Scotland reference is often required to the general
law of contract. In England a lease confers an estate in land on the tenant; and the
position is largely governed by a number of Landlord and Tenant Acts. In Scotland,
there is no equivalent legislation to the Law of Property and the Landlord and Tenant
Acts. As mentioned in Chapter 24, the main Scottish statute is the Leases Act 1449.
Naturally, linked to this statutory intervention in England, there is a vast amount of
case law on all aspects of the law from both the viewpoint of the landlord and of the
tenant. These English cases and articles thereon must be read with caution by the
Scottish practitioner who should always remember the different principles applied in
Scots law. However, within the last three decades, investment leases on a full repair-
ing and insuring basis have been introduced into Scotland, closely following the
English pattern.

It can now be fairly said that this is an established area of the law of landlord and
tenant in Scotland. The principal Scottish text on the subject is M J Ross and D J
McKichan *Drafting and Negotiating Commercial Leases in Scotland* (2nd edn,
1993). Reference is also made to A McAllister *The Law of Leases in Scotland* (3rd
edn, 2002) for a good general view of the subject, and to D W Cockburn *Commercial
Leases* (2002) for a practical insight into the modern 'FRI lease'.

It is still common for the agreement between landlord and tenant to enter into a
lease to be documented in an exchange of missives between their solicitors. This contract, whether short or long, ought to cover the foregoing points together with all
other relevant provisions to protect the parties. The contract should also contain the
obligation on the landlord to grant and the tenant to accept a lease of the subjects in
accordance with an agreed draft. In larger developments, however, it is the norm for
all such issues to be dealt with in an Agreement for Lease. No matter which form is
used, it is essential that all salient issues are covered.

As a matter of professional practice in Scotland, the lease is normally drafted by
the landlord who therefore inserts all the clauses in the form which will best protect
his interests. The purpose of this chapter is to discuss briefly some of the clauses
which regularly occur in commercial leases in Scotland and to suggest possible
revisals on behalf of the tenant. Only the major points in a commercial lease will be
dealt with here, but the whole document should always be considered when acting on

behalf of a tenant. It must always be kept in mind that a lease is a contract and, as such, may well be strictly enforced according to its terms.

There are many different types of commercial lease, for example offices, shopping centre developments, industrial units etc. Each lease has its own characteristics and every clause must therefore be considered fully and carefully revised so as to take account of each tenant's individual circumstances. Care should be taken to avoid using a style of lease that is not suitable for the property to be let.

25.2   Duties of a tenant's solicitor

The tenant's solicitor should first carefully read all the documents received from the landlord before commencing to revise the draft lease. Under no circumstances should the bargain be concluded prior to the terms of the draft lease being agreed by the landlord and the tenant. The tenant's solicitor should first take a copy of the draft lease and use this as a working draft. This draft should then be revised and sent to the client with a report outlining the salient terms thereof. After a meeting with the client, alterations can be made to the fresh draft and forwarded to the landlord with a qualified acceptance to his offer to lease. If then the landlord refuses to accept certain revisals made by the tenant's solicitor, the tenant can be advised of the consequences of such rejections.

In revising the draft, it is suggested that the tenant's solicitor should read it through from beginning to end before making any form of detailed revisal. This is important, because many related clauses are often separated by a number of pages in the deed. Use of a checklist highlighting the salient points to look for could be helpful. If there is a definition or interpretation section in the lease document, it should be studied carefully. The lease should then be revised where applicable to safeguard the tenant's interests. At all times, the solicitor should keep the client advised as to the state of negotiations and request instructions on all points of principle.

Once the terms of the lease have been agreed and an engrossment executed and delivered to the landlord's solicitor, it is recommended that a synopsis of the lease be prepared summarising the salient dates and important clauses. Such lease summaries can be of great benefit to the tenant during the lease and especially prior to rent review. The best time to prepare such a summary is when the terms of the revised draft are clearly in one's mind.

The foregoing is a very brief outline of the general steps to be followed by a tenant's solicitor in revising a commercial lease. There are a number of important areas which require specific mention. These are:

(1)   the essentials (see paras 25.3 ff);
(2)   use clauses (see para 25.13);
(3)   keep-open clauses (see paras 25.14 ff);
(4)   monetary obligations of the tenant (see paras 25.19 ff);

(5)   rent review (see paras 25.29 ff);
(6)   the tenant's repairing obligation (see paras 25.61 ff);
(7)   insurance (see paras 25.68 ff);
(8)   alienation (see paras 25.79 ff);
(9)   irritancy (see paras 25.88 ff); and
(10) hypothec (see paras 25.92 ff).

25.3 The essentials

By the essentials, we mean the following:

(1) the landlord's title to the lease;
(2) designations of parties to the lease;
(3) description of the leased subjects; and
(4) the duration of the lease.

25.4 THE LANDLORD'S TITLE TO THE LEASE

The landlord's title to the lease can be considered under three headings:

(1) sub-leases;
(2) heritable creditors; and
(3) planning permission etc.

25.5 Sub-leases

The landlord may himself hold the subjects on lease as principal or sub-tenant. In this case, the head lease should be examined in addition to the head landlord's title. An important consequence of the landlord holding title by virtue of a lease is that, if the landlord's lease is brought to an end, any derivative rights will fall with it. Unlike the situation in England, sub-tenants under commercial leases in Scotland are not protected under statute. The tenant should seek to obtain an undertaking from the head landlord (ie the registered proprietor), that, if the immediate landlord's lease falls, the head landlord will grant a new lease on the same terms for the remaining duration of the original lease. This is dealt with further under 'Irritancy': see para 25.88. Such an undertaking will not be enforceable against singular successors of the registered proprietor as head landlord. The landlord may be taken bound to transmit the obligation under penalty of damages.

25.6 Heritable creditors

The premises may be subject to a standard security. In this event, it is essential that the tenant see a letter of consent to the lease from the heritable creditors in order to satisfy Standard Condition 6 of Schedule 3 to the Conveyancing and Feudal Reform (Scotland) Act 1970. Failure to comply with this procedure could be fatal for the tenant: see *Trade Development Bank v Warriner & Mason (Scotland) Ltd* 1980 SC 74.

25.7   Planning permission etc.

Exhibition of all planning permissions, building warrants, certificates of completion and other necessary permissions and consents should be requested to satisfy the tenant that the landlord has complied with all relevant legislation etc. In addition, the usual enquiries should be made of the local authorities regarding roads, footpaths, and planning, drainage, water supply, and of the statutory undertakers (electricity, gas, British Telecom) as applicable. A valid fire certificate should also be exhibited, if applicable. Environmental issues must also be borne in mind: see the Environmental Protection Act 1990 and related legislation discussed in Chapter 20. More than ever before, careful checks require to be made so as to avoid incurring responsibility for pollution on the site.

25.8   DESIGNATIONS OF PARTIES TO THE LEASE

We shall consider this from the point of view of:

(1)   the tenant; and
(2)   guarantors.

25.9   The tenant

Privity of contract, as known in English law, is not implied in Scots law. Indeed, such a continuing obligation requires to be expressly provided for in the lease before it will be effective. Accordingly, any attempt to provide that the original tenant continues to be bound along with assignees should be resisted. It is still common to find this continuing obligation or privity of contract inserted in leases. Such references should be deleted. The privity of contract rule in English law has been amended by the Landlord and Tenant (Leasehold Covenants) Act 1995.

Where the tenant is an individual or a limited company, the position is relatively straightforward. However, the case of a firm or a partnership deserves separate treatment. Until 28 November 2004, partnerships could not own heritage in Scotland in the partnership name, but a partnership has always been capable of becoming a tenant. Landlords usually insist that the individual partners must act as trustees for the firm. Frequently, however, the obligations are deemed to extend to existing partners at the date of commencement of the lease and to all persons who may subsequently become partners at any time during the period of the lease. Effectively, the landlord is trying to bind future partners of the firm before they even become partners. Such a clause should be strongly resisted. On 28 November 2004, when s 70 of the Abolition of Feudal Tenure etc (Scotland) Act 2000 comes into force, a partnership will be able to take a title to land in its own name and thus be a landlord. See para 6.27.

It is essential that the parties to a lease are distinct from one another: see *Clydesdale Bank plc v Davidson* 1996 SLT 437.

25.10 Guarantors

A landlord may well request that the tenant's obligations be guaranteed by a third party. Such a request should be resisted if possible by the tenant. If it is agreed that a guarantee be given, the landlord will obviously wish to ensure that it is a worthwhile one. Therefore, in the case of a limited company, only a director being a major shareholder with a certain proportion of the issued share capital will be accepted by the landlord, with an obligation that, if he leaves the company, then another similar guarantor, approved by the landlord, should be obtained. If the guarantor is a company, the landlord may request confirmation that it can competently give guarantees in terms of its memorandum and articles. If the guarantee is given, the guarantor's solicitor should read the definition of 'guarantor' carefully so as to ensure that there is no possibility of the guarantee continuing once the original tenant assigns his interest in the lease. This is a common fault. From the landlord's point of view, care should be taken to ensure that the benefit of the guarantee is transferable to singular successors of the landlord: see *Waydale Ltd v DHL Holdings (UK) Ltd* 1996 SCLR 391 and *Waydale Limited v DHL Holdings (UK) Ltd (No 3)* 2000 GWD 38-1434. The landlord may also request that a rent deposit agreement be entered into whereby rental for, say, six months is placed on deposit as a form of security against the tenant failing to meet his obligation to pay rent in terms of the lease.

25.11 DESCRIPTION OF THE LEASED SUBJECTS

It is essential that the tenant obtains the subjects which he thought he was to obtain together with all necessary pertinent rights for their proper use and enjoyment. Careful investigation of plans and the landlord's title is therefore essential. If possible, a site visit should be made. The tenant's solicitor should also obtain a copy of the prospective tenant's survey report and plans.

There is no reason why a description in a lease should be any different from a description in any deed of conveyance. This is often not the case in practice, however. In complex office blocks or shopping centres, great care will have been taken when drawing the description of the subjects, indeed, it is advisable to incorporate an adequate conveyancing description in the lease, whether or not the lease is to be registered. Reference ought also to be made to a plan – Ordnance Survey, if suitable. As well as the subjects themselves, the tenant will require all necessary pertinent rights such as access, use of services etc. This should be revised into the lease if omitted by the landlord. The exceptions and reservations made by the landlord should also be noted carefully by the tenant's solicitors, as their import can often be far reaching.

Such reservations will normally take the form of reservations to the landlord of various rights such as the right to lay and maintain services etc. It is not uncommon for such reservations to be scattered throughout the lease. It is advisable therefore that a summary be given to the tenant of all the rights which he has in the subjects whether exclusive or common; and what exceptions or reservations have been made in favour of the landlord. Ensure that the landlord is obliged to make good any damage caused to the subjects by reason of the exercise of such reserved rights.

In many office block or shopping centre leases, one often finds that the tenant is leasing no more than the airspace within the unit. In such cases, the landlord will retain responsibility for the main walls and roof etc, but will recover the cost of repairing and renewing such items by way of a service charge. It is therefore essential that when investigating the description of the subjects, the tenant's solicitor should consider the whole lease so that he may report to his client on the extent of his holding and the restrictions on it, if any.

Questions may arise as to what constitutes a 'common part' in a multi-occupancy situation: see *Marfield Properties v Secretary of State for the Environment* 1996 SC 362.

25.12 DURATION

The date of entry in the lease should be a definite stated date not earlier than the actual date of entry – howsoever it may be determined. The term of a lease may vary depending on a number of factors such as the individual characteristics of the landlord and the tenant and perhaps the state of the commercial market in the area. The period of lease may be prolonged by the operation of tacit relocation if the contractual term of the lease expires without either party having given notice to the other of his intention to terminate it and there is nothing in the conduct of the parties which might rebut the presumption that renewal of the lease was intended. For a review of the common law principle, see *MacDougall v Guidi* 1992 SCLR 167. Note also the limited protection afforded to shop tenants in Scotland in terms of the Tenancy of Shops (Scotland) Acts 1949 and 1964.

Long leases must be registered in the Land Register in order to have effect against singular successors of the landlord. See para 24.10. The longer the lease, the greater the amount of stamp duty land tax payable. See para 5.6.

25.13 USE CLAUSES

The use to which the premises may be put will be regulated in the lease. This is usually done by specifying a type of use with provision that no other use is permitted without the consent of the landlord – such consent not to be unreasonably withheld. If the permitted use is tightly controlled, this is likely to have a detrimental effect on the rent obtainable at review. It is not uncommon to find use defined by reference to the appropriate class in the Schedule to the Town and Country Planning (Use

Classes) (Scotland) Order 1997, SI 1997/3061. The lease is also likely to prohibit certain types of use that might be a nuisance to adjoining proprietors.

25.14 KEEP-OPEN CLAUSES

We shall consider these under the following headings:

(1) general;
(2) common law;
(3) recent case law; and
(4) summary.

25.15 General

It is not uncommon to find commercial leases of premises in shopping centres that contain an obligation on the tenant to trade from the premises for the duration of the lease. Such obligations are commonly known as 'continuous trading' or 'keep-open' clauses. An example of such a clause is as follows:

> 'The Tenant shall take possession of and use and occupy and trade from the premises for the aforementioned purposes within one calendar month from the date of entry and shall thereafter continue so to do throughout the whole period of this Lease. The Tenant shall not keep the premises nor shall it allow the premises to be kept closed for any period longer than twenty-one consecutive days in any one year'.

Landlords argue that such an obligation is essential for the benefit of the development of which the premises form part. A tenant, on the other hand, will always try to resist such an obligation, arguing that while it is prepared to continue to pay rental until a suitable assignee or sub-tenant is found it is not prepared to trade from the premises at a loss. If such an obligation is accepted by a tenant, it is likely that it will wish there to be concession for closure during works of repair or refurbishment or where the tenant is seeking to assign the lease or sub-let the premises with the consent of the landlord. If such a provision is accepted by the landlord, it is likely that it will be time-limited.

25.16 Common law

In cases where there is no continuous trading obligation in the lease but where a use is prescribed and other uses are prohibited, there is nonetheless an obligation at common law to keep the premises plenished. Accordingly, even without a continuous trading clause or an obligation to trade in whatever fashion, the premises will have to be stocked.

In the case of a shop (in the absence of an express provision to this effect), the tenant cannot be compelled to carry on business from the premises. He must, however, furnish the shop, keep it heated and air it: *Whitelaw v Fulton* (1871) 10 M 27. The landlord enforces his right by a plenishing order in the Sheriff Court.

25.17 Recent case law

There was, for some time, little case law on the subject of 'keep-open' clauses in Scotland. Then came the case of *Grosvenor Developments (Scotland) plc v Argyll Stores Ltd* 1987 SLT 738, which was followed by the decision in *Postel Properties Ltd v Miller and Santhouse plc* 1993 SLT 353. There have been a number of recent cases on this subject, however, both north and south of the border. See *Church Commissioners for England v Abbey National plc* 1994 SLT 959; *Overgate Centre Ltd v Wm Low Supermarkets Ltd* 1995 SLT 1181; *Retail Parks Investments Ltd v Royal Bank of Scotland plc (No 2)* 1996 SLT 669; *Co-operative Insurance Society Ltd v Halfords Ltd (No 2)* 1999 SLT 685; *Highland & Universal Properties Ltd v Safeway Properties Ltd* 2000 SLT 414; and, perhaps most importantly, in England, *Co-operative Insurance Society Ltd v Argyll Stores (Holdings) Ltd* [1997] 1 WLR 898.

25.18 Summary

The above cases demonstrate the problems which can occur with the enforcement of keep-open clauses. In general, there has been a divergence in approach between the English and Scottish courts. In Scotland, the courts are prepared to enforce such clauses by means of an order for specific implement, whereas their English counterparts have viewed damages as the appropriate remedy for breach. See Reid and Gretton *Conveyancing 2000* (2001), pp 67–69. Much, however, will depend on the wording in each lease and the individual circumstances of each case.

Many tenants refuse to accept such obligations in new leases and the logic of their argument can often be difficult to resist. In addition, it is possible that the existence of the clause may lead to there being a discount at review.

25.19 Monetary obligations of the tenant

The monetary obligation of the tenant can be considered under the following headings:

(1) rent;
(2) turnover rent;
(3) interest;
(4) insurance premiums;
(5) rates and other charges;
(6) service charges;

(7) common charges etc;
(8) expenses; and
(9) VAT.

25.20 RENT

The amount of rent to be charged by the landlord may well have already been agreed by the tenant before a solicitor is consulted. The annual rental may be fixed for the initial period of the lease, say five years, or it may be staged over this period. Depending on the state of the market, there may be a rent-free period available to the tenant which should, if possible, cover his initial fitting out works. The period granted will vary depending on the type of unit involved. An alternative to a rent-free period is for the tenant to commence payment of rental at the date of entry but at a reduced rate for a certain period. Frequently, such rent-free periods are documented by way of back letter and are not incorporated in the lease itself, in an effort not to weaken the position of the landlord on rent review. The landlord's agent should exercise care in the granting of such back letters since the court might hold them to be binding in this context: see *Kleinwort Benson Ltd v Barbrak* [1987] AC 597.

Rent is usually payable quarterly in advance. Indeed it is not uncommon to find rent being paid monthly in advance. Payment half-yearly in advance is onerous and should be resisted. The landlord may also provide for rent to be payable by banker's order. Quarterly payments are generally made on the Scottish quarter days of Candlemas, Whitsunday, Lammas and Martinmas. In terms of the Term and Quarter Days (Scotland) Act 1990, these quarter days are, in the absence of provision to the contrary, deemed to be the 28th days of February, May, August and November respectively. Note, however, the 'old' quarter days of 2 February, 15 May, 1 August and 11 November, which are still commonly found in leases: see, for example, *Provincial Insurance plc v Valtos Ltd* 1992 SCLR 203.

At common law, a tenant has the right to retain rent as a compulsitor on the landlord to implement its obligations under the lease. If however there is a head lease and the sub-tenant retains rent, the head lease could well be irritated, thus causing derivative rights (for example the sub-lease) also to fall. Therefore in such circumstances, the tenant's revisal may be refused. In practice, landlords do not wish anything to interfere with the regular payment of rent on the due date and accordingly any attempt to write this into the lease is likely to fail.

25.21 TURNOVER RENT

The concept of turnover rent is common in America and is often found in the UK in shopping centre developments. An additional sum over a flat-rate rent (which itself is subject to review) is usually paid. This additional sum is a percentage of gross sales over a minimum figure of sales. In most cases, a base rent is set between 75% and

80% of the estimated open market rental value, thus guaranteeing the landlord a minimum return. Turnover rent is therefore only payable when the percentage (less agreed deductions) exceeds the base rent. Turnover rent, unlike normal rental payments, is normally paid in arrears. The machinery for calculating this form of rent should be examined carefully.

25.22 INTEREST

There will undoubtedly be an interest provision either in the rent clause or in a separate clause to which reference is made throughout the lease. Generally, the rate provided for by landlords is high and should be reduced if possible. The reason for a high interest rate is to prevent the landlord becoming the 'unofficial and unpaid banker' of the tenant. If at all possible, the tenant should not be committed to paying a penal rate of interest and a period of grace before interest becomes due should be requested. Some older leases have a clause providing for payment of a fifth part more by way of liquidate penalty for failure to pay rent when due. This is certainly penal and should be deleted. There will probably also be other clauses throughout the lease which contain interest provisions. Interest at the rate applicable for non-payment of rent should not be accepted in respect of any payment due by the tenant to the landlord of any balance between the rent previously payable and the new rent payable following on a rent review.

25.23 INSURANCE PREMIUMS

If the landlord insures, the tenant will be required to pay the premiums on demand. The tenant will also have to pay any premiums for risks against which he himself must insure, such as plate glass, public liability etc.

25.24 RATES AND OTHER CHARGES

Rates will be the responsibility of the tenant. The other charges should however be restricted, if possible, to those of an annual or recurring nature. Taxes arising out of the landlord's dealing or deemed dealing with the subjects should be excluded along with any rents payable to a head landlord. If possible, the tenant should also try to avoid paying commission or factorial charges to the managing agents. Such a provision should always be deleted in the lease of a single free-standing building; but deletion is less likely to be acceptable to the landlord in a multi-occupancy complex. It is common to find a provision to the effect that such a charge is to relate to the work done by the landlord or its agents but not to the collection of rent.

25.25 SERVICE CHARGES

Many leases contain a clause obliging the landlord to carry out certain services for which he then charges the tenant(s). Such clauses can be very onerous. There are a number of essential points to be considered in the service charge clause. Briefly, however, the most important items to be excluded from the cost of the services are:

(1) damage caused by the insured risks;
(2) damage caused by latent or inherent defects: see para 25.65; and
(3) the cost of the initial provision of the subjects or any part thereof.

The basis of apportionment should also be investigated, especially if there are unlet units in the development. Provision is sometimes made for a sinking fund to ensure regular payments from the tenants towards the ultimate cost of repair, renewal etc. If there is a sinking fund, however, the tenant must ensure that it is placed outwith the control of the landlord in order to safeguard the tenant's position in the event of insolvency of the landlord. The services to be performed by the landlord for which the service charge is to be levied must be carefully considered so as to ensure that the landlord is not, in essence, given a 'blank cheque' to carry out whatever repairs, refurbishment or other services the landlord may think desirable. The terms of a service charge clause or schedule should be considered carefully and, in the case of a new letting, details of previous years' service expenditure and accounts should be inspected.

25.26 COMMON CHARGES ETC

These will be ascertainable following upon an examination of the title deeds. The tenant's potential liability should thus be calculated prior to conclusion of missives. Note in particular the provisions of the title deeds of a tenement or other multi-occupancy building in respect of the liability for roof and other common repairs especially where liability is shared on a rateable value basis and you are acting for a prospective tenant of the ground-floor shop premises.

25.27 EXPENSES

It is suggested that it is an outdated feature of the practice of landlord and tenant that the tenant must pay the landlord's legal fees in respect of the preparation of a lease. Resist this if at all possible. At the very least, the tenant's solicitor should seek to impose an upper limit on legal costs. If the tenant must pay these fees, the solicitor should ensure that they are reasonable and properly incurred and, if possible, introduce a cap or maximum limit. Most certainly the tenant should refuse to pay the landlord's surveyors' and other professional advisers' costs. There may also be expenses throughout the lease in respect of the service of schedules of repair and applications for consent etc. These are unavoidable. However, the tenant should provide that these charges must be reasonable and properly incurred.

25.28   STAMP DUTY LAND TAX AND VAT

It has always been the tenant's obligation to pay any stamp duty that might arise on the grant of a lease, such duty being charged on an *ad valorem* basis. Changes introduced in the Finance Act 2003 saw stamp duty being replaced with stamp duty land tax: see Chapter 5. These changes have a significant effect on the practice of dealing with leases.

Changes in the UK VAT legislation were made in the Finance Act 1989, in the main taking effect from 1 April 1989. As a result, many leases expressly state whether the rent is inclusive or exclusive of VAT. Since the effective date, landlords have had the choice of obtaining exempt rental income or of charging VAT on rent. Many landlords reserve the option to elect to tax at some time in the future. Note in particular however the position of certain types of tenant who may be unable to recover VAT on rental payments. Such tenants will often attempt to insert a provision in the lease to the effect that the rent is VAT inclusive or that the landlord is prohibited from electing to charge VAT. Such provisions are rarely acceptable. For further comment on VAT, see Chapter 5.

25.29   **Rent review**

Rent review can be considered under the following headings:

(1) object of review;
(2) rent review dates;
(3) timetable for review;
(4) basis for review;
(5) determination of reviewed rental in the event of dispute;
(6) miscellaneous matters.

25.30   OBJECT OF REVIEW

The object of a rent review clause is to minimise the consequence of inflation on the landlord's investment in a particular property. Such a clause allows the landlord to take account of fluctuations in market value so that the tenant is paying throughout the duration of the lease a rent which equates in real terms with the market rental value of the subjects. Therefore, the rent review clause will have been drafted carefully by the landlord's solicitor – possibly in conjunction with the landlord's surveyor. Essentially, a rent review clause provides for the rent to be reviewed after a set period following agreement between the parties. If there is no agreement, the matter will be decided by some independent third party. Clauses are not so straight-forward in practice however and there are a number of elements of a rent review clause which require further comment. In this area of the law, comparisons are often made with English precedents, of which there are many. For a detailed discussion on rent review clauses in general, see the series of articles by E D Buchanan in the 'workshop' section of the Journal of the Law Society of Scotland, commencing April 1983. See also M J Ross and D J McKichan *Drafting and Negotiating Commercial Leases in Scotland* (2nd edn, 1993), Chapter 6, and D W Cockburn *Commercial Leases* (2002), Chapter 8.

The following is a summary of some of the major elements in the rent review clause, which merit careful consideration.

25.31 RENT REVIEW DATES

The frequency of reviews will vary with location, the norm being three or five years. It is essential for a landlord that these dates are clearly and unambiguously expressed in the lease. Phrases such as 'in the fifth year of the lease' are not recommended.

Older leases often provide for longer periods between reviews. In such cases, the landlord may well attempt to obtain a premium rent, ie a higher rent than that which would have been the case had the review interval been less. In other words, the tenant would be paying a premium rent for the advantage of infrequent rent reviews. Even if accepted, such a clause has the disadvantage however that the market rent may rise dramatically, in which event, the premium would not adequately compensate the landlord.

In leases of a longer duration than, say, 25 years, it is common to see procedure for a review of reviews. This will probably take the form of an option exercisable by the landlord entitling him to review the frequency of reviews or redraft the rent review clause so as to produce a new clause which conforms to the prevailing market practice. Such a clause is really another attempt to protect the landlord's investment.

25.32 TIMETABLE FOR REVIEW

The main considerations here are:

(1) notice;
(2) counter-notice; and
(3) postponed reviews.

25.33 Notice

Certain leases provide that the rent will be reviewed without the necessity of any form of notice from the landlord to the tenant. Many leases however provide for some form of notice to trigger the operation of the review machinery. As a result, these leases are drafted to ensure that, even if the landlord fails or omits to serve notice, he may do so at a later date without penalty. There have been a number of decisions on this point in England, where the general rule now is that time is not of the essence in relation to rent review procedure unless the parties expressly so stipulate or it could be inferred from the circumstances that the parties so intended. See, for example, *United Scientific Holdings Ltd v Burnley Borough Council* [1978] AC 904.

The law in Scotland on this matter is now settled following the judgment of the Inner House in *Visionhire Ltd v Britel Fund Trustees Ltd* 1992 SCLR 236. In this case, Lord President Hope undertook a comprehensive review of both English and Scottish cases on the whole subject of whether or not time is of the essence in contracts. To avoid any possible argument, the landlord's clause may well dispense with the requirement of notice altogether and specify that time is not of the essence.

The question, whether time is of the essence in a particular case, is very important to the parties. Every case must be considered on its own merits. This involves a consideration not merely of the rent review clause but also the import of that clause in the context of other clauses in the lease as a whole.

Any notice of the landlord's intention to review the rent should be clear and unequivocal; and should be served in accordance with the provisions of the lease: see *Dunedin Property Investment Co Ltd v Wesleyan & General Assurance Society* 1992 SCLR 159. But see also *Prudential Assurance Co Ltd v Smiths Foods* 1995 SLT 369.

Acceptance of rent at the old rate by the landlord after the stipulated review date may amount to acquiescence in the situation. The result would therefore be that the landlord would be barred from insisting on the missed rent review: see *Banks v Mecca Bookmakers (Scotland) Ltd* 1982 SLT 150 and *Waydale Ltd v MRM Engineering* 1996 SLT (Sh Ct) 6. In light of these decisions therefore, landlords often insert a provision to the effect that demand for and/or acceptance of rent at the old rate after a review date shall not constitute a waiver of the landlord's right to review.

25.34 Counter-notice

Some leases are drafted so that once the landlord serves notice of review the tenant only has a specified period within which he can object or else be deemed to have accepted the reviewed rental. This can be beneficial for a landlord but should be avoided by the tenant who could be faced with an inflated reviewed rental with only a short period within which to object. If the tenant omits to serve such notice due to error or administrative failure he will pay the penalty. The 'time of the essence' cases are of direct significance when considering the effect of such counter-notice provisions.

25.35 Postponed reviews

Failure on the part of a landlord to initiate the rent review procedure will result in back rent being due. If such a late rent review takes place, it is only equitable for the tenant that the level of the market rent should reflect the level that would have applied at the original rent review date. In addition, the tenant should not suffer a penalty when he has not been in a position to pay the increased rent which was unknown. Therefore, the increased rent should be payable only from the postponed date and not backdated to the original rent review date. The tenant must also ensure that he is not required to pay interest on any balancing payment at the rate chargeable in the event of non-payment of rent.

25.36 BASIS FOR REVIEW

By necessity, the world of rent review is a hypothetical one. At each rent review date, the premises must be valued and the rent assessed on the basis of a hypothetical letting involving a hypothetical landlord and a hypothetical tenant. In determining the reviewed rental, the parties will have regard to certain valuation guidelines (assumptions and disregards) as provided for in the lease. For a long time, these valuation guidelines were relatively straightforward. However, now this is often not the case.

One of the valuation guidelines which has been under the judicial microscope has been that relating to rent-free periods. The whole point at issue was whether or not the hypothetical letting should take account of rent-free periods. The landlord's argument was that a rent-free period, if applicable at all, should apply only at the commencement of the lease – not at each review date throughout the term. The tenant, on the other hand, argued that if rent-free periods were being granted to potential new tenants of similar premises at the review date, then a similar concession should be assumed in the hypothetical letting. Alternatively, the tenant would seek a discounted rent to reflect the fact that, unlike a tenant in an open market letting, he will not have the benefit of a rent-free period.

In an effort to avoid such disputes, landlords have commonly inserted additional valuation guidelines into the rent review clause. These take the form of either

(1) an assumption that any rent-free period or concessionary rent or other inducement which may be offered in the open market at the review date in question shall have expired immediately prior to the review date; or

(2) a disregard of the rent-free period or other such inducement.

Indeed, it is common to find a combination of both. Such attempts to minimise the effect of rent-free periods at review are found in many forms and few, if any, provisions can be said to be totally free from possible ambiguity.

Whether or not a rent-free period is given at the commencement of a lease depends on (a) market conditions at the time and (b) the strength of the parties' bargaining power. A rent-free period is essentially a concession to the tenant to encourage him to take a lease at the then open-market rental.

If such inducements have been the norm, however, where does that leave the parties to a review (or in default, the arbiter/expert) in seeking to establish the true open-market rental value of neighbouring premises in the same development? Are the rental levels of the comparable premises truly passing rentals in the open market, or are they headline rents?

For an illustration of the sometimes complex issues debated when seeking to interpret such provisions on the occasion of rent review, see *Co-operative Wholesale Society Ltd v National Westminster Bank plc*; *Broadgate Square plc v Lehmann Brothers Ltd*, *Scottish Amicable Life Assurance Society v Middleton*; and *Prudential Nominees Ltd v Greenham Trading Ltd* [1995] 1 EGLR 97. The matter has also been judicially considered in Scotland: see *Church Commissioners for England and Sears Property Glasgow Ltd v Etam plc* 1997 SLT 38.

It is now often argued that an effective disregard of a rent-free period will itself be viewed as an onerous term in a lease which should have a discounting effect on review. The various assumptions to be made and the facts to be taken into account in establishing the current market rental value of the subjects are an essential part of the review process. Indeed, without such a basis for review being specified, the whole rent review may be void by reason of uncertainty. See *Beard v Beveridge, Herd & Sandilands* 1990 SLT 609; *Crawford v Bruce* 1992 SLT 524; and *Colonial Mutual Group (UK Holdings) Ltd v National Industrial Fuel Efficiency Services Ltd* 1994 GWD 29-1761. It is essential therefore that the lease contains details as to the basis on which the rent is to be reviewed. These details should be clear and unambiguous to avoid dispute. Accordingly, both the landlord and the tenant must ensure that the lease, as agreed, enables their surveyors (and in default of agreement the arbiter or expert) to establish clearly the market rent of the hypothetical letting of the subjects. See *Scottish Mutual Assurance Society v Secretary of State for the Environment* 1992 SLT 617. One lesson which can be learned from case law is that artificial assumptions and disregards in rent-review clauses can produce unexpected and often quite costly results. See also *Unilodge Ltd v University of Dundee* 2001 SCLR 1008. The salient matters are:

(1) upwards-only review (see para 25.37);
(2) valuation (see para 25.38);
(3) assumptions (see para 25.47); and
(4) disregards for valuation (see para 25.52).

25.37   Upwards-only review

Most leases provide for the rent to be reviewed in an upwards-only direction. However, this may not be commercially viable, from the tenant's point of view, especially in poor market conditions. This has been commented on in England in the case of *Stylo Shoes Ltd v Manchester Royal Exchange Ltd* [1967] 204 EG 803. Notwithstanding these comments, it is extremely unlikely that landlords will even countenance the possibility of a 'downwards' review. From time to time there is pressure for reform of upwards-only reviews: see S Brymer 'Upwards-only rent Reviews' (2001) 54 Greens PLB 3.

25.38 Valuation

There are a number of important definitions and assumptions built into a rent review clause – especially as regards the definition of 'the current market rental value' of the subjects. The most important of these are considered in the following paragraphs.

25.39 Best rent

It is suggested that the existence of this phrase in a rent review clause might allow a special rental to be considered for the purposes of comparison. A tenant's solicitor will normally seek alternative wording akin to 'fair' or the omission altogether of a descriptive word.

25.40 Willing landlord and willing tenant

These hypothetical characters are assumed, because they may not be present in the negotiation. This assumption is consistent with the hypothetical open-market assumption. The implication of this assumption was clearly dealt with in the English case of *F R Evans (Leeds) Ltd v English Electric Co Ltd* [1977] 245 EG 657. See also *Dennis & Robinson Ltd v Kiossos Establishment* [1987] 1 EGLR 133. The willing landlord assumption prevents the actual landlord from arguing that he would not in fact let the property to the tenant at the review date, for example because the market was depressed at that date. The term was initially introduced in England by s 34 of the Landlord and Tenant Act 1954, presumably for this reason. It also prevents the landlord arguing that, due to personal difficulties, he could only accept a certain level of rent. The term thus recognises the fact that, with a rent review, a settlement must at some stage and by some means be reached, for example a notional letting must be effected and there is a rent on which a willing landlord and willing tenant would agree.

25.41 User

It is a fact that a restrictive user clause will result in the rent available at a review date being less than what would otherwise have been available. This was demonstrated by the English case of *Plinth Property Investment Ltd v Mott, Hay & Anderson* [1978] 249 EG 1167, CA. To counter this fact, many landlords attempt to introduce an assumption that notwithstanding the actual use, the use at the review date will be any use within a certain use class under the Town and Country Planning Acts. This should be resisted by the tenant who should insist upon the review being in the context of the user clause in the lease. A landlord should not be entitled to unilaterally consent to uses not specifically requested by the tenant solely in order to benefit his case on a rent review. The existence of an enforceable keep-open or continuous trading obligation is also likely to have a restrictive effect on the rent obtainable at review.

25.42 Duration

In the absence of any provision, the unexpired period of the lease at the review date will be the assumed period of the hypothetical letting. It is strongly recommended, however, that this important matter be dealt with by way of express wording in the rent review clause. The assumed duration of the hypothetical letting may either be for a period equal to the original term of the lease or for a period equal to the unexpired term. The former is better for the landlord in most cases and the latter for the tenant. Many leases are drafted with a compromise based on an assumed duration of either the unexpired residue or a set number of years, whichever is the greater. The property market regularly changes however and it is recommended that specific valuation advice be taken at the time of drafting to take account of the nature of the subjects being let. In many cases, it is more straightforward to specify that hypothetical letting will be for a set period of years running from the relevant review date.

25.43 Lease whether as a whole or in parts

Most landlords require such a provision in the rent review clause in order that account may be taken of the possibility of the sub-letting of the whole or part of the premises as individual units. Its omission may not, however, be detrimental; and regard must be had to the terms of the alienation clause in the lease in that the hypothetical letting is usually deemed to be on terms and conditions similar to those in the existing lease.

25.44 Vacant possession / rent-free periods

Where a rent review clause provides for the yearly rental value to be assessed on the basis of a letting with vacant possession, a discount may be applied to the rent to compensate for the fact that no rent-free period will occur at the rent review. Tenants should beware of the vacant possession assumption where there are sub-tenants. Furthermore, the assumption may also negate the effect on rent of a restrictive user clause as the courts may hold that, if vacant possession is to be assumed at a review date, it is illogical also to assume that only the existing tenant can occupy the subjects.

The whole question of whether a rent-free period is to be assumed or disregarded can have significant valuation implications and much depends on the wording in individual leases: see *99 Bishopsgate Ltd v Prudential Assurance Co Ltd* [1985] 1 EGLR 72. It is not uncommon to find preventive drafting on the part of landlords' agents, to such an extent that many of the valuation guidelines commonly found in leases bear little resemblance to the reality of the circumstances of the actual letting or open-market conditions at the review date. One thing is certain, however, and that is that over-complicated drafting may well backfire at the end of the day. See also para 25.36.

25.45   *Terms and conditions*

There is an assumption that the lease is 'on the same terms and conditions as the existing lease – other than the amount of rent and the provisions of the rent review clause.' The latter part of this assumption is often referred to as the 'overage factor'. Taken literally, the landlord is entitled to assume that the hypothetical letting does not contain any provisions as to rent review. As a result, a higher rent would be payable by the 'willing tenant'. There have been several English decisions on this point; and, in particular, the principles laid down in *National Westminster Bank plc v Arthur Young McLelland Moores & Co* [1985] 2 All ER 817 have been debated in a series of subsequent cases. Reference is made in particular to the decisions in *Pugh v Smiths Industries Ltd* [1982] 264 EG 823 and *British Gas Corporation v Universities Superannuation Scheme Ltd* [1986] 1 All ER 978, particularly the opinion of the Vice-Chancellor in the latter case.

The point has not yet been judicially decided in Scotland but it is suggested that, where the lease contains clear words which require the rent review provision (as opposed to all provisions as to rent) to be disregarded, then, as was the case in *Pugh* and as was envisaged by the Vice-Chancellor in *British Gas Corporation*, effect must be given to this direction. Faced with such possible difficulties in interpretation, the tenant should amend the clause so as to specify expressly that the review provisions are to be taken into account.

25.46   *Rent to be without premium*

This condition is designed to ensure that, on each rent review, any premium or inducement offered to the tenant at the commencement of the lease is not to be taken into account on reviewing the rent. This is to avoid the possibility of such a payment or inducement distorting the annual rental to be paid.

25.47   **Assumptions**

In practice, it is now increasingly common for detailed lists of 'assumptions' and 'disregards' to be specified in the rent review clause. In such circumstances, it is essential that these provisions are considered and the rent review clause read as a whole, so as to ascertain the exact intention of the parties. We shall now consider typical 'assumptions'.

25.48   *Compliance with the tenant's obligations*

The rent review clause may provide for the valuation to be on the assumption that the tenant has performed all his obligations under the lease. This is not unreasonable. What is objectionable, however, is an assumption that the landlord has complied with all his obligations under the lease.

25.49 Damage to premises repaired

It is not unreasonable for it to be assumed that for the purposes of rent review, damage by an insured risk has been restored. What may be unreasonable, however, is blanket extension of this assumption to any other form of damage.

25.50 Fully fitted-out unit

Most modern rent review clauses include an express assumption as to the extent to which the premises are to be taken to be available, ready, fitted out and/or equipped for occupation and use by the hypothetical willing tenant. This assumption can be phrased in a number of different ways but the tendency is for the wording to be interpreted in a fairly restrictive manner. See also the cases referred to in paras 25.36 and 25.44.

25.51 VAT

It is sometimes assumed that the tenant (and the hypothetical willing tenant) is able to recover VAT chargeable on the rent and other monies payable under the lease. The view expressed here is that 'artificial' assumptions, such as that the landlord will grant consent to a change of use or assignation, are unreasonable if the terms of the lease in this regard are restrictive.

25.52 Disregards for valuation

The tenant's agent should ensure that the effect (if any) on rent of certain matters is not to be taken into account when the landlord reviews the rent. Express provision of these disregards is essential as, unlike the position in England, on a renewal of a lease (Landlord and Tenant Act 1954, s 34) they will not be implied in a Scottish lease. The 'usual' disregards are as follows:

(1) occupation by the tenant or any predecessor in title or permitted sub-tenant of the tenant;
(2) goodwill attached to the subjects by reason of the trade of the tenant or his foresaids;
(3) initial shop-fitting works – especially in a shop unit; and
(4) alterations or improvements carried out by the tenant otherwise than in pursuance of any obligation to the landlord. This is an important disregard as failure by the tenant to include this in the rent review clause will result in all his improvements being taken into account by the landlord at the review date. This was demonstrated in the case of *Ponsford v H M Aerosols Ltd* [1979] AC 63. See also *Standard Life Assurance Co v Debenhams plc* 1995 GWD 9-514 and *GREA Real Property Investments Ltd v Williams* [1979] 250 EG 651. If the lease is a ground lease where the tenant has paid for and erected buildings on the ground, then the landlord ought to be entitled only to a revised rent based on his interest in the subjects, ie the ground alone. In light of the problems which can be asso-

ciated with improvements on the occasion of rent review, it is recommended that both landlord and tenant should keep a comprehensive record of works undertaken and by whom. The tenant's solicitor should also attempt to revise the clause so as to provide that all work done pursuant to any statutory obligation on the tenant is also to be disregarded.

The landlord may also add that the fact that the subjects have been damaged or destroyed is to be disregarded.

The list of 'disregards' and indeed 'assumptions' appears to grow with each new lease produced on the computer. Is there not a risk that drafting may become unnecessarily over-complicated? For a more detailed consideration of this important topic, see M J Ross and D J McKichan *Drafting and Negotiating Commercial Leases in Scotland* (2nd edn, 1993) pp 71–114 and D W Cockburn *Commercial Leases* (2002) pp 78–95.

25.53 DETERMINATION OF REVIEWED RENTAL IN THE EVENT OF DISPUTE

If there is no agreement between the parties by a given date, the lease usually provides for the matter to be referred to the decision of some independent person to be agreed between the parties or failing agreement, to be appointed by a third party. The usual procedure is by way of a reference to arbitration. However, many landlords prefer that the matter be referred to an expert, ie a surveyor having specialised knowledge of the area. The referral to an expert is designed to accelerate the process of determining the new rent. It is arguable, however, exactly how valid the distinction between the arbiter and the expert is: see *AGE Ltd v Kwik-Save Stores Ltd* 2001 SLT 841. The essential distinction is that the arbiter, unlike the expert, can only decide on the basis of the facts as presented to him in the parties' submissions. Many leases expressly state that the third party is to act as an 'expert and not an arbiter'. Note that an expert, unlike an arbiter, may be sued for negligence.

Some leases provide that s 3 of the Administration of Justice (Scotland) Act 1972 shall be excluded where the determination is by an arbiter (right of appeal to the court on a point of law). This should be deleted by the tenant if possible. It is important to remember, however, that such a right to appeal by way of stated case does not exist if the arbiter or expert's award has been issued in its final form. The tenant should also resist any provision that he pays for the independent determination of rent. Each party should pay their own costs unless the award of the arbiter or expert, as the case may be, declares otherwise.

25.54 MISCELLANEOUS MATTERS

When considering the terms of a rent review clause, the following matters should be taken into consideration.

25.55   Rent pending determination of review

If the reviewed rental has not been ascertained by the review date, the landlord may be entitled to assess a provisional rent. The tenant will therefore pay this new rent, which may be high. Such a clause ought to be resisted by the tenant. If it is to be accepted, there should be an accounting between the parties upon the determination of the reviewed rental with interest at a high rate if possible. However, many leases provide that the existing rental will continue to be chargeable in such circumstances with the increased sum due by the tenant as a debt to the landlords. If interest is to be chargeable on this debt, then the tenant should attempt to reduce the interest rate as much as possible.

25.56   Counter-inflation legislation

Many leases contain clauses dealing with the possibility of rent increases being prohibited or restricted in the future by statutory control. These clauses are a result of controls imposed in the now repealed counter-inflation legislation of the 1970s. The regulations, if re-imposed, would probably only restrict or prohibit collection of increased rentals. Therefore, it will still be competent for the rent to be reviewed on the normal dates in the normal way. Any increase will be payable in whole or in part as soon as the relevant regulations permit. The tenant should avoid clauses providing for interim reviews, but, if such a clause must be accepted, the tenant should ensure that any such review or reviews will contain a valuation based on market values at the original review date and not at any later date.

25.57   Memoranda

Once the review has been agreed, that agreement should be incorporated into a formal addendum to the lease. Try to ensure that the tenant does not have to meet all the expenses of this. In particular, the tenant should not meet the landlord's surveyor's costs. In the past, it has also not been uncommon for 'privacy' or 'confidentiality' agreements to be used whereby a landlord, having made some form of inducement, insists that the tenant enter into an agreement that the information may be suppressed.

25.58   The retail prices index

Review clauses often provide for the rent to be increased in accordance with the appropriate increase in the retail price index between the date of entry and the review date. The use of indexed rents which provide for automatic increases in line with the retail price index may seem an attractive proposition in times of difficult open market rent reviews and falling rental values. However, landlords and tenants generally prefer the revised rent to be fixed by real people rather than by an anonymous index.

A major problem with this procedure is that all the indices measure rises in prices and no official index is related to property. The use of such review provisions can be a gamble for both parties. If the matter is non-negotiable, resist the tendency to panic at the sight of a mathematical formulation.

25.59 Affordability models

The argument that such models be utilised in seeking to assess the market rent of subjects at review is linked to the fact that they are widely used by tenants when seeking to identify the viability of subjects prior to agreeing to enter into a lease. The argument has been successful in a number of rent review third-party determinations.

25.60 English law

As mentioned previously, English law has had a major influence on the development of the law of commercial leases in Scotland. There are numerous English cases on each of the salient points of the review clause and there are a number of excellent English publications such as the Estates Gazette which provide useful up-to-date commentary and case reports. See also the excellent Bernstein and Reynolds *Handbook of Rent Review* (Sweet and Maxwell looseleaf). In recent years in England, however, there has been a tendency to seek to adopt a 'presumption in favour of reality'. It is important to remember that such a presumption is only an aid to the determination of the commercial purpose of the rent review in question. If a lesson is to be learned from these English cases, it is that landlords' solicitors should draft their review clauses with care and attention so as to avoid litigation, if possible. Although the English cases may not always be followed in Scotland, they cannot be ignored.

25.61 Tenant's repairing obligation

The tenant's repairing obligation can be considered under the following headings:

(1) the common law position;
(2) damage by insured risks;
(3) extent of the tenant's repairing obligation;
(4) limiting the tenant's liability for latent defects;
(5) back letters; and
(6) effect of description on the repairing obligation.

25.62 THE COMMON LAW POSITION

The institutional writers state that once a tenant is in possession under an urban lease, the landlord is bound to repair any defect which makes the subjects less than wind and water tight and not in a tenantable condition. Such an obligation is very rarely found in a modern commercial lease. The position at common law in Scotland is that there is an implied warranty by the landlord that the subjects are reasonably fit for the purpose for which they are to be let, and that the landlord has a duty to keep the subjects in tenantable repair and wind and water tight throughout the period of the lease: see *Dickie v Amicable Property Investment Society* 1911 SC 1079; *Blackwell v Farmfoods (Aberdeen) Ltd* 1991 GWD 4-219; and *Lowe v Quayle Munro Ltd* 1997 GWD 10-438. It is now invariably qualified to some extent, if not altogether excluded. However, the wording of such an exclusion from liability at common law must be carefully drafted: see *Turner's Trustees v Steel* (1900) 2 F 363.

Without proper repair, the landlord's investment in the property is put in jeopardy. However, the division of responsibility for maintenance/renewal can give scope for endless disputes. In recent years, the clear trend has been for the landlord to transfer all the responsibilities on to the tenant. The aim is, from the landlord's point of view, to ensure that the landlord incurs no financial liability whatsoever and so receives the rent in full without any deduction. Many landlords have taken the view that an undivided repairing obligation reduces the scope for argument. However, there are always situations where a building is or may be converted into multi-occupation and where significant structural work and even external decoration can only be appropriately done by someone with an interest in the whole property. In such circumstances, the cost of these works will undoubtedly be recovered by the landlord by way of a service charge payable by all the tenants.

Each lease will differ according to circumstances. Therefore, a tenant's agent must read the entire lease carefully, especially the link between the repairs and the insurance clauses. Indeed, a major problem arises where damage is caused to the subjects by a risk for which there is no insurance cover. Accordingly, it is essential to the tenant that his liabilities should be mitigated wherever possible.

The two main areas where such qualification can be made are as follows:

(1)   damage by insured risks; and
(2)   the extent of the tenant's repairing obligation.

25.63   DAMAGE BY INSURED RISKS

Generally, the landlord will insure the subjects and recover the premium from the tenant. Therefore, there will be a specified list of risks against which the landlord is obliged to insure. The tenant should insist on seeing the insurance policy or an extract thereof. To cover the situation where damage is caused by an insured risk, the tenant's agent will require to make an exception to the repairing obligation on the tenant so as to provide that reinstatement of such damage should not be the responsibility of the tenant, because it is the landlord who will recover the cost thereof from the insurance company. Any such qualification will, however, normally be further qualified by the landlord to the effect that the cost of such reinstatement will remain with the tenant if the insurance policy has been vitiated, or payment of the insurance monies has been withheld in whole or in part, by reason of the act or default of the tenant himself.

25.64 EXTENT OF THE TENANT'S REPAIRING OBLIGATION

One of the most common sources of argument, when revising a lease, is the extent of the repairing obligation of the tenant. In England, the word 'repair' has a different interpretation: see *Lurcott v Wakely & Wheeler* [1911] 1 KB 905. There are a number of English precedents on the same point. The position in England appears to be that it is always a question of degree whether that which the tenant is asked to do can properly be described as a repair, or whether it would involve giving back to the landlord a wholly different thing from that initially let. In other words, the approach in England is to look at the particular subjects, consider the state which they are in at the date of the lease, consider the terms of the lease and then come to a decision as to whether the requisite work can be fairly called repairs. However onerous the obligation, it is not to be looked at *in vacuo*.

The whole question of what constitutes a 'repair' was dealt with *inter alia* in the English case of *Ravenseft Properties Ltd v Davstone (Holdings) Ltd* [1980] 1 QB 12. This case established that the tenant's repairing obligation did extend to repairs caused by inherent defects and to the work required to remedy that defect. Furthermore, that result would have ensued, even if the obligation had merely been 'to repair' as opposed to 'repair, renew, rebuild, uphold ... and keep the premises ...'.

The critical test in England seems to be whether or not, if the tenant carries out the reinstatement, he would be giving back to the landlord something totally different from what was originally leased to him.

It has been suggested however that there is no such test in Scots law which would take works of repair, no matter how extensive, out of the tenant's repairing obligation in the lease. In other words, in Scots law, regard should be had to the scope of the rebuilding obligation against the background of the common law doctrine of *rei interitus*: see A I Phillips 'The Scottish Commercial Lease Grows Up' 1985 JLSS 99. See also *House of Fraser plc v Prudential Assurance Co Ltd* 1994 SLT 416. In that case, the tenant contended that works to a retaining wall in the premises amounted to extraordinary repairs for which the landlord had responsibility at common law. Accordingly, reimbursement did not arise. The court held that the landlord was indeed responsible for both ordinary and extraordinary repairs to the building as the common law would have imposed, but that the tenant was liable to reimburse the landlord for the cost of these works, given the terms of the lease.

The important point which distinguishes this case from the type of case which might be encountered in practice, however, is that it was the landlord who was responsible for carrying out all such repairs and charging the tenant therefor by way of a service charge. It would certainly be a different result altogether if it was the tenant who had responsibility for repairs to the leased subjects and there was no reference to renewal or rebuilding in the event of damage to or destruction thereof. It is now common for a lease to impose an obligation on the tenant to repair, renew and rebuild the subjects irrespective of the cause of damage to or destruction thereof and notwithstanding the age or state of repair of the subjects. Such obligations will be interpreted strictly according to their terms. See *Taylor Woodrow Property Co Ltd v Strathclyde Regional Council* 1996 GWD 7-397, however, for an illustration of circumstances where reasonableness will be implied. The onus is, however, on the landlord to transfer the obligations to repair, rebuild, renew and reinstate the subjects to the tenant. A simple obligation to repair does not amount to an undertaking to restore the subjects if they are accidentally destroyed: see *Allan v Robertson's Trustees* (1891) 18 R 932.

In each instance, it is still a matter for construction of the relevant lease. If the lease is silent on the question of extraordinary repairs, it is clear that the matter has to be regulated at common law.

Parties to a lease also require to have careful regard to the terms of the Disability Discrimination Act 1995, which will be fully operational when the provisions relative to educational institutions come into force. This legislation is likely to have a marked effect on the landlord/tenant relationship both with regard to the repairing obligation itself but also at rent review and at the termination of the lease.

25.65   LIMITING THE TENANT'S LIABILITY FOR LATENT DEFECTS

A lease, being a contract, may well be interpreted strictly according to its terms. To avoid argument, landlords always seek to incorporate a clear and unambiguous obligation on the tenant to rebuild, reinstate and renew. The more explicit the provision, the better from the landlord's point of view. The doctrine of *rei interitus*, and the common law obligations and warranties of the landlord, can competently be excluded by express provision. Accordingly, the tenant must always attempt to amend the wording used in the repairing clause. However, landlords generally resist such revisals, taking the view that it is the tenant who is in possession of the subjects on a full repairing lease.

Generally speaking, in every case, the landlord will insist on expressly excluding the implied common law duty on the landlord. Such defects may, however, have been caused by some negligent design or bad workmanship on the part of the landlord or his contractors or architects in the initial design or construction of the subjects. Accordingly, the defect may have been inherent in the structure of the subjects. If the repairing and rebuilding obligation of the tenant is not qualified, the landlord will invariably require the tenant to repair and make good all such defects occurring at any time throughout the lease, provided the terms of the repairing obligation on the tenant so permit. Some landlords may agree to carry out such reinstatement but this should not be regarded as a general rule. The landlord will have his own contractual rights against his contractors etc, whereas the tenant has no such right of recourse. It is not uncommon therefore for a tenant to attempt to revise this clause by excepting liability for reinstatement necessitated by latent or inherent defects. If such a revisal is acceptable by the landlord, care should be taken to ensure that such liability is also excepted from the service charge provisions in the lease if any, so as to avoid the possibility of the landlord still being able to charge the tenant under this provision.

If the landlord accepts this revisal (which it must be said is unlikely), the tenant should also seek to provide for compensation for any loss or damage to the tenant during the execution of such reinstatement by the landlord. Reference should also be made in the insurance clause to the exclusion of the tenant's liability for inherent defects etc. In addition, if the subjects are of recent construction, the tenant should, if possible, require an assignation from the landlord of his rights against contractors, architects and others. If this is not possible, then a back letter should be obtained from the landlord to the effect that the landlord will enforce his rights against the contractors and others at the expense of the tenant if so required. It may also be possible to obtain either a warranty or a 'duty of care' agreement from the professional team responsible for the design and construction of the building. Indeed in most cases, it should be sufficient for a tenant to accept a full repairing and rebuilding obligation in a lease if coupled with a comprehensive warranty package and appropriate insurance indemnity. Such packages require careful assessment. In the case of recently constructed property, enquiries should also be made to see if there is a decennial insurance policy in place in respect of the subjects. Such insurance policies, which are more common in the United States and mainland Europe, are a means of insuring the building against design fault etc and tend to be very costly. All of these possibilities should be explored, so as to minimise as far as possible the tenant's liability to reinstate under the repairing and rebuilding provisions.

Basically, all tenants should be advised before taking a lease of subjects, whether new or old, that they should have the subjects surveyed. The survey should be carried out prior to the bargain being concluded. The surveyor can also be asked to comment on the level of rent being sought and the rent review patterns. On obtaining the survey, the prospective tenant can either refuse to take a lease or negotiate for a reduced rent or reduced liability to reinstate if the subjects are not in good tenantable condition, for example internal repairing only.

The tenant's solicitors should also attempt to reduce the tenant's obligation to repair and reinstate by introducing an exception in respect of 'fair wear and tear'. This could be a useful protection for a tenant of an old building in that it would absolve him of liability to carry out major repairs or reinstatement due to the age or dilapidated state of the building.

If a survey discloses wants of repair, there are a number of possible scenarios:

(1) the prospective tenant chooses not to proceed with the lease;
(2) all wants of repair are remedied by the landlord prior to the date of entry and the tenant's assumption of a full repairing obligation; or
(3) the tenant takes the lease subject to it not being liable for any works of repair or renewal as a result of the premises not being in perfect condition at the date of entry.

In the third case, it is essential for the lease to be carefully revised, otherwise the tenant may find itself still being liable for major works of repair or renewal as a result of the wording in the lease or its acceptance of the premises and the common parts as being in good, tenantable condition and repair.

The only safe way of limiting the tenant's potential liability in such circumstances is for the parties to agree a record of the condition of the premises at the date of entry and for that record to be referred to in the lease. It is unfortunately only too common for the parties to go to the expense of preparing such a record, but then to fail to make any reference to it in the lease document itself. To be fully effective, the record or schedule of condition should be referred to wherever there is any possibility of the tenant directly or indirectly being liable for works of repair or renewal. It is essential that there is no room for ambiguity in this regard.

In addition, it is recommended that such records of condition contain a photographic schedule. The photographs should be numbered by reference to the content of the schedule itself. If a photographic record of condition is to be used, it should be prepared in duplicate so that each party has a copy. Indeed, if the lease is to be registered in the Books of Council and Session, for example, the parties might consider having three copies prepared. This saves problems once the lease is registered and the colour photographs are reproduced in black and white in the extract registered copy of the lease. Note that each page of text and every page of photographs must be signed by the parties in order to comply with the Requirements of Writing (Scotland) Act 1995.

Quite commonly, the parties are uncertain as to the respective repairing liability of landlord and tenant. Most leases nowadays contain a full repairing and rebuilding obligation on the tenant. The tenant should consider the whole lease carefully to establish the extent of his liability, the meaning of the repairing obligations in the lease, and whether or not this obligation is reasonable, given the nature and state of repair of the subjects. From the tenant's point of view, much depends on the age and state of repair of a property at the date of entry. This should be taken into account before a lease is issued to a prospective tenant. Unfortunately, however, this is not often the case. The tenant should therefore be aware of the extent of the obligations which it may be about to assume and the alternatives available to it before the lease is signed. Blind acceptance of the landlord's solicitors' style lease without regard to the state of repair of the premises could have serious consequences.

25.66   BACK LETTERS

It is quite common for back letters to be prepared to the effect that, notwithstanding the terms of the lease, certain items will not require to be repaired by the tenant. Such important matters ought perhaps to be regulated in the lease itself, however, in order to avoid any problem with transmission against singular successors of the landlords.

25.67   EFFECT OF DESCRIPTION ON THE REPAIRING OBLIGATION

The definition of the subjects, perhaps elsewhere in the lease, should also be considered carefully in order to discover whether the tenant is directly liable for repairs to external walls, roof, drains and other services etc. For a case in point, see *Mothercare UK Ltd v City Wall (Holdings) Ltd* 1994 GWD 28-1712. As previously stated, many leases provide the tenant with no more than a right to the air space within the internal walls, with the landlord maintaining the external walls etc and recovering the cost by way of a service charge. In practice, the tenant cannot argue against carrying out day-to-day maintenance or repairs of a decorative nature. However, arguments arise where there are major repairs. In such cases, the definition of the subjects can be critical. If the title to the subjects in question includes a right of common property in the roof, such right of ownership forms part of the subjects so that, if the obligation merely says that the tenant must repair the subjects, the tenant is liable for the repair of the relevant material parts. However, if part of the subjects or the building of which the subjects form part remains in the landlord's control or if the landlord has retained a contractual duty of repair, then he has an implied contractual duty to take reasonable care that his tenant shall not suffer damage. What constitutes 'reasonable care' in this context has, however, to be determined by reference *inter alia* to the landlord's knowledge of the defect or potential defect which gives rise to a risk of damage.

25.68 Insurance

Insurance can be considered under the following headings:

(1) object of insurance provision;
(2) choice of insurance company;
(3) extent of cover;
(4) liability in the event of a shortfall in insurance monies;
(5) damage by insured risks;
(6) insurance in joint names of landlord and tenant;
(7) rent abatement;
(8) reinstatement;
(9) *rei interitus*; and
(10) other insurance.

25.69 OBJECT OF INSURANCE PROVISION

As has been previously stated, the insuring obligation is the complement of the repairing obligation. Basically, the insuring obligation is designed to secure that financial resources will be available to restore insured risk damage and to reinstate the subjects when destroyed by an insured risk. Insurance will either be carried out by the landlord, with the tenant normally repaying the premiums or by the tenant under the supervision of the landlord who will request sight of the policy and premium receipts etc. Most leases contain an obligation of the former type since landlords prefer to keep reinstatement under their control. Therefore, the usual arrangement is that the landlord insures the subjects and the tenant refunds the premium or an allocated portion thereof, often as 'quasi rent'.

There are two supplementary reasons for this common arrangement:

(1) the tenant automatically bears the full cost of increased premiums; and
(2) a refund of premium is not rent, and so attracts no stamp duty land tax.

The main points to be noted in this very broad area are as set out below.

25.70 CHOICE OF INSURANCE COMPANY

Normally, the landlord decides the amount of cover and selects the appropriate insurance company. It is therefore essential for the tenant to have the right at any reasonable time to have sight of the insurance policy, or an extract thereof and the premium receipts. This will enable the tenant to check the sufficiency of cover and that the policy is in force. The landlord is not likely to accept a revisal allowing the tenant to alter the insurance company if he can find a better quotation. The insurance company should be an office of repute. The tenant's agent should investigate this matter fully, and refer a copy of the relevant provision in the lease to the tenant's insurance broker for comment if necessary.

25.71 EXTENT OF COVER

The tenant should consider the definition of 'the insured risks' carefully. The definition may be in a totally separate place in the lease from the insurance clause itself. This definition ought at least to list the minimum risks to be covered. Any discretion in the landlord's favour to insure against other risks should be limited to other 'normal commercial' risks if possible. If the risk of terrorism is to be insured against, this should be expressly stated in the lease. It is suggested that it is not sufficient for such insurance to be imposed on a tenant by implication. The value insured should be no greater and no less than the full reinstatement value with associated fees and loss of rent. This will require constant reappraisal however in order to keep it in line with inflation and building costs generally. Loss of rent insurance is designed to provide cover for the landlord when the subjects are destroyed, in whole or in part, and he is receiving no rent or at the most partial rent. The period of cover is linked to the likely period of reinstatement, this presently being for a minimum of three years. The tenant will pay the premium on such insurance.

25.72 LIABILITY IN THE EVENT OF A SHORTFALL IN INSURANCE MONIES

If the landlord insures, the tenant should always revise the lease so as to provide that the landlord is liable for any such deficiency out of his own resources. It is the landlord after all who is in control. Although it would be better to express this in the lease, the common law may in fact provide a remedy for the tenant where the landlord has not fully insured. It is not uncommon for landlords (for reasons perhaps best known to themselves) to resist this revisal.

25.73 DAMAGE BY INSURED RISKS

If the landlord has sole control of insurance, it is essential that the tenant qualify his repairing obligation with regard to the restoration of insured damage. This emphasises the point made previously when discussing the reinstatement obligation of the tenant. If damage from an insured risk occurs, the insurance company may, except where the tenant is one of the insured (see para 25.74), have the right to enforce the contractual obligation of the tenant to reinstate the subjects, if this is so provided. Therefore, as previously stated, it is essential to exclude from the tenant's repairing obligation the restoration of insured risks damage unless the policy or claim has been invalidated because of some act or default of the tenant.

25.74 INSURANCE IN JOINT NAMES OF LANDLORD AND TENANT

Fire insurance is a contract of indemnity against loss or damage by fire. Therefore, the insurance company will have a right of subrogation entitling them, on indemnifying the insured, to be put into the position of the insured and to exercise all rights competent to the insured against third parties in respect of the fire damage. Accordingly, if the tenant is one of the insured and was responsible for the damage to the subjects, then the insurers would have no such claim. This is because it is generally no answer to a fire policy claim that the damage resulted from the negligence (without fraud) on the part of the insured or one of them: see *Barras v Hamilton* 1994 SLT 949.

Some insurance companies now waive their subrogation rights and such a waiver should always be requested by the tenant. In addition, the tenant's agent should also seek to introduce into the lease a provision for the insurance policy being endorsed with the interest of the tenant. It has been argued that this may be recognition of the tenant's interest in the insurance monies. One result of such an endorsement may be that the insurance company, in the event of damage or destruction, might issue their cheque in settlement in the joint names of the landlord and tenant. Many leases now provide that, in the event of reinstatement being impossible or unacceptably costly, the insurance monies belong exclusively to the landlord who at his option may terminate the lease. For a full discussion, see A I Phillips 'The Scottish Commercial Lease Grows Up' 1985 JLSS 99.

25.75   RENT ABATEMENT

The provision that a lease endures notwithstanding damage will be dealt with below. However, if there is such a provision, the tenant may well be liable to continue paying rent for a period during which he may not be able to obtain access to the subjects. This is unacceptable. In practice, the landlord insures against loss of rent in addition to the usual perils as aforementioned. Accordingly, in the event of damage to or destruction of the subjects, and the landlord's insurance policy not being vitiated in whole or in part or insurance monies being withheld due to the actions of the tenant, the 'loss of rent' insurance monies (designed also to cover any provisions for rent review) will compensate the landlord during the period when the tenant's obligation to pay rent is suspended. It is now common for a lease to provide that the rent is suspended until reinstatement is effected or until the expiry of the period of cover for loss of rent insurance monies, whichever is the earlier. The common law provides that in circumstances where the damage caused does not amount to *rei interitus*, actual or constructive, and is the fault of neither party to the lease, the tenant will be entitled to an abatement of rent according to the nature and extent of the damage and loss suffered: see *Muir v McIntyres* (1887) 14 R 470. This is unlike the position in England, where express provision must be made before there is an abatement of rent.

A rent abatement provision is designed to protect a tenant so that he is not obliged to pay rent in the circumstances previously described. It would also be advisable to ensure that service and other common charges are abated with rent. Abatement may be for a period during which the whole or any part of the subjects are destroyed. Therefore, it may be that only a proportion of the rent etc, payable will be abated. It may also be worth considering whether the tenant ought to attempt to introduce a 'long stop provision' into the lease which would enable the tenant to bring the contract to an end if the subjects are not restored within a specified period. Landlords, however, do not generally accept this revisal: see para 25.77.

25.76   REINSTATEMENT

There is no general rule as to who should reinstate subjects damaged or destroyed by an insured risk. In theory, under a full repairing and insuring lease, the reinstatement obligations should rest with the tenant. However, many landlords prefer to undertake reinstatement works. Indeed, some landlords declare that it shall be in their option whether or not to rebuild the subjects at all. If the landlord reinstates, the lease will normally provide that he shall apply the proceeds of the insurance monies towards reinstatement within a definite period. It is preferable that a set period of say three years is laid down in the lease within which the landlord must complete the reinstatement works.

If the tenant reinstates, the landlord will wish to retain some control, for example over the type of building or plans to be submitted and approved etc. The landlord may also provide for the insurance monies to be consigned in joint names in a bank and only released upon receipt of the tenant's architect's certificate of completion.

While it is quite proper, when dealing with a lease in Scotland, to take into account the implications of the rules at common law, it is suggested that some agents are over-anxious on this question. If the reinstatement period is of sufficiently long duration, taking into account the nature of the subjects and the type of damage sustained, the landlord should not object to a provision in the lease that the lease be terminated if reinstatement is not completed within, say, five years of the damage occurring, or such longer period as may be agreed, assuming both parties to be acting reasonably.

25.77 REI INTERITUS

At common law, if subjects are destroyed or can be regarded as constructively destroyed through the fault of neither the landlord nor the tenant, the lease comes to an end and the loss is divided equally between the landlord, who will lose rent, and the tenant, who will lose possession. Indeed, the circumstances of each individual case must be decided on the respective merits. Destruction of a part of the subjects may be enough if the part in question was essential for the purposes for which the subjects were let: see *Allan v Markland* (1882) 10 R 383 at 389–390, per Lord Shand. An institutional investor in the landlord's interest will not accept this. Accordingly, it has become common for leases to contain a contractual provision to the effect that, the lease will remain in full force and effect notwithstanding damage or destruction of the subjects. Such a provision will often be found in various places in the lease, most notably in the repairing and insurance clauses.

A landlord's solicitor is likely to try to avoid the application of the doctrine of *rei interitus*. Indeed, one often finds that as well as stating that the lease will continue as aforesaid, the landlord is often successful in stating that the tenant will be fully liable for repairing, renewing and, if necessary, rebuilding the subjects if damaged or destroyed by any defect latent or patent.

The common law recognises that, while it is possible for parties to bind themselves to perform some particular act no matter what may happen, it is rarely their intention to do so, and that to enforce performance after a material change in circumstances would often be to bind the parties to a contract which they did not intend to make. In other words, the common law principle rests on the basic 'frustration of contract' rule.

The landlord's solicitor may therefore seek to combat the application of these principles in whatever way possible – especially if there is an investor involved. Therefore, the lease will be drafted so as to transfer all obligations onto the tenant so as to give him little room to plead frustration. However, it becomes increasingly difficult to avoid the operation of *rei interitus* in respect of a lease of premises within a larger building, control of the remaining units of which does not lie with the landlord.

It is suggested that it is now settled that since the case of *Cantors (Properties) (Scotland) Ltd v Swears & Wells Ltd* 1980 SLT 165, in the absence of express or necessarily implied stipulations to the contrary, the effect of total and accidental destruction by fire of the whole leased subjects is that the contract is terminated. It is always, however, open to the contracting parties to provide otherwise. If they do not, then the contract will terminate if the subject matter is totally destroyed so that neither party is bound and neither party can compel performance of any of the stipulations to the contract. Such provisions are not unreasonable.

25.78   OTHER INSURANCE

The tenant may also be liable to insure against a selection of other risks such as public liability, plate glass insurance, loss of licence (if applicable) etc. Exhibition of the policies and/or premium receipts will be required by the landlord. Always check that there is no possibility of double insurance occurring.

25.79   **Alienation**

Alienation may be considered under the following headings:

(1)   common law freedom;
(2)   alienation of part only of the subjects;
(3)   alienation of the whole;
(4)   assignation to related or associated companies;
(5)   franchises / concessions;
(6)   pre-emption; and
(7)   miscellaneous.

25.80   COMMON LAW FREEDOM

At common law, a tenant has freedom to assign and sub-let unfurnished urban subjects (which will, of course, include all normal commercial properties). This right however is severely curtailed in most, if not all, modern commercial leases. Modern clauses are drafted so as to provide the landlord with a degree of control over the tenant. As noted in para 25.9, privity of contract, in the sense that the term is understood in English law, has not really been a feature of the law of landlord and tenant in Scotland. Accordingly, a provision in a Scottish lease that the original tenant guarantees the whole terms of the lease throughout its endurance should be rejected. This is essentially an attempt to import into Scottish leases what was, until removed by legislation, an implied term of similar leases in England: see the Landlord and Tenant (Leasehold Covenants) Act 1995.

A landlord will have investigated the financial standing of his original tenant thoroughly and may well be reluctant to release him for a substitute who may not be as acceptable. A feature of the landlord's control over the identity of his new tenant may be that he will insist upon the new tenant being of 'sound financial standing'. In practice, landlords' agents use a wide variety of phrases to attempt to obtain such control: see para 25.82 below. If there is any doubt as to the financial standing of the proposed assignee, the landlord may request that the original tenant stand as guarantor for his successor throughout the unexpired period of the lease. Such a request should be resisted if possible.

25.81 ALIENATION OF PART ONLY OF THE SUBJECTS

Alienation of part of the subjects, whether by assignation or sub-lease, is generally prohibited. There are sound reasons supporting such a prohibition unless the subjects are of such proportions that a dealing with part only would be beneficial.

25.82 ALIENATION OF THE WHOLE: ASSIGNATION

Assignation of the tenant's interest in the whole of the subjects will almost always, by express provision, require the landlord's consent. If there is an element of *delectus personae* in the lease, consent may well be required notwithstanding the absence of express provision. The matter of consent, and any other restriction on the right of the tenant to assign the lease or indeed to sub-let the subjects, will be read according to its terms. A simple provision for the landlord's consent, for example 'but excluding assignees, legal or conventional, without the previous written consent of the landlord' may give the landlord an absolute discretion as to whether to grant or withhold his consent. Questions may arise, however, as to an implication of reasonableness in such circumstances. The most common revisal to such a clause and in fact elsewhere in the lease is to add the phrase 'which consent shall not be unreasonably withheld'. Without such a revisal being made, the basic Scottish common law position as stated in the case of *Duke of Portland v Baird & Co* (1865) 4 M 10 would prevail, namely that the landlord's power to refuse consent is absolute. It is true that there are the provisions of common law mentioned above and statutory provisions of general application, such as s 31 of the Sex Discrimination Act 1975 and s 24 of the Race Relations Act 1976, which make it unlawful for the landlord to discriminate on grounds of sex or race against a person by withholding consent for disposal of premises to him or her. However, there is little control over the absolute discretion of the landlord to withhold or grant consent, save such as may be contained in the lease itself. The landlord may have good reasons as to why he should have full power to decide whether a prospective substitute tenant is acceptable to him. Basically, however, each case will be decided on its own merits with the onus of proof being firmly on the tenant. Such a revisal may in fact do no more than provide for the possibility of the question being referred to the objective consideration of a neutral arbiter as a control on the subjective view taken by the landlord. For examples of cases involving conditions imposed on a grant of landlord's consent to assignation, see *Lousada & Co Ltd v J E Lesser (Properties) Ltd* 1990 SC 178; *John E Harrison Ltd v Sun Life Assurance Society plc (No 1)* 1991 GWD 29-1761; *John E Harrison Ltd v Sun Life Assurance Society plc* (No 2) 1992 GWD 38-226; and *Scotmore Developments Ltd v Anderton* 1996 SLT 1304.

Many clauses also lay down detailed qualifications as to the financial standing and suitability etc of the prospective tenant. It has been argued, however, that such phrases may possibly weaken the landlord's power to withhold consent if the assignee fulfils these additional qualifications. Such a provision may run, for example, 'not without the written consent of the landlord, which consent shall not be unreasonably withheld in the case of a respectable and responsible assignee'.

From the tenant's point of view, such a clause will fall to be considered in two stages. If the assignee is not a 'respectable and responsible person' as evidenced by bank and trade references, then the landlord will have an unqualified right to withhold consent. It would only be if the proposed assignee complied with this provision that the landlord's power to withhold consent would be fettered and could only be exercised if it was reasonable to do so.

The case of *Renfrew District Council v A B Leisure (Renfrew) Ltd (In Liquidation)* 1988 SLT 635 dealt with the right of the landlord to grant or withhold consent. The same question has also been considered by the English courts: see *International Drilling Fluids Ltd v Louisville International Ltd* [1986] 1 All ER 321. An assessment of the financial strength of the proposed assignee is critical: see *Continvest Ltd v Dean Property Partnership* 1993 GWD 40-2675.

Guidance has been given by recent case law in Scotland as to when consent may be reasonably withheld: see *Legal and General Assurance Society Ltd v Tesco Stores Ltd* 2001 GWD 18-70. However, there are still likely to be a number of instances where landlords may appear to act capriciously in order to take advantage of the position in which the tenant and potential assignee find themselves. An understanding of what in many instances may be the landlord's quite justifiable concerns, however, may go a long way towards ensuring the ultimate grant of consent within the preferred time-scale. As is often the case, negotiation is likely to be more successful than confrontation.

25.83   ALIENATION OF THE WHOLE: SUBLETTING

The landlord may not *per se* object to the tenant subletting the whole subjects, because he will retain his rights against the original tenant. This right is, however, still likely to be regulated in the lease. The landlord will insist upon the rent in the sub-lease not being less than the open market rent. Indeed, he may insist on the rent not being less than the rent in the head lease. This should be resisted, if possible, by the tenant, especially in a recessionary economic climate where rents are actually falling. The landlord may prohibit the sub-tenant from granting further sub-leases so that he does not become too distant from the actual tenant in occupation. However, this is not a valid objection as he does retain his rights against the original tenant, and, if that lease falls, all derivative rights from it also terminate in the absence of express provision to the contrary. As mentioned earlier however, landlords will usually expressly prohibit subletting of parts. See also the case of *Brador Properties Ltd v British Telecommunications plc* 1992 SC 12, where agreements entered into by a tenant with third parties were regarded as being sub-leases. The court held that the definition in Scots law of a lease is different from the definition in English law and is wide enough to include contracts which would not be regarded as leases in England. In *Brador,* it was held that the agreements with third parties amounted to a device to circumvent the express provisions of the lease.

25.84   ASSIGNATION TO RELATED OR ASSOCIATED COMPANIES

If a tenant is a large multiple company, it may be desirable to obtain the landlord's consent to an assignation to another company within the same group. Landlords will generally refuse permission unless the original tenant company or the parent company continues to guarantee the lease. Otherwise, the tenant could assign the lease to an associated company, liquidate that company and thus walk away from its responsibilities under the lease. The landlord may also be approached for his consent to the occupation of the subjects by an associated company of the tenant company as defined in the Companies Act 1985, s 538. Once again, however, this may be permitted only subject to the landlord having prior notification and on the strict understanding that no rights of landlord and tenant are thereby created.

25.85   FRANCHISES AND CONCESSIONS

It is common to find franchises and concessions being offered in large leased subjects such as superstores. Franchisees and concessionaires do not have security of tenure as their exact pitch within the subjects may be uncertain. They thus lack particular subjects of let. Landlords usually allow franchises but often impose an upper limit on their number and the maximum amount of retail floor space which may be so occupied.

25.86   PRE-EMPTION

Beware of a lease containing a right for the landlord to buy back the lease on the occasion of an assignation. This can delay the sale of the tenant's interest quite substantially. In general, this clause should be read carefully in order to advise the tenant of the restriction on his ability to deal with his interest in the lease at some time in the future. The clause may also restrict the tenant from dealing in any manner of way with his interest or the subjects themselves. Such a comprehensive prohibition could also exclude the tenant's right to create a security over the subjects.

25.87   MISCELLANEOUS

If the alienation clause provides for a rent review on the occasion of an assignation or sub-letting, then it should be deleted. It has been suggested that such a provision is contrary to s 16 of the Land Tenure Reform (Scotland) Act 1974, which prohibited the creation of casualties in leases. If a lease contains such a provision, it is suggested that it will have a restrictive effect on the marketability of the tenant's interest in the lease and, as such, would have a detrimental effect on the rent obtainable on rent review.

25.88   **Irritancy**

Irritancy may be considered under the following headings:

(1)   legal or conventional;
(2)   Law Reform (Miscellaneous Provisions) (Scotland) Act 1985, ss 4–7; and
(3)   Scottish Law Commission proposals.

25.89   LEGAL OR CONVENTIONAL

An irritancy may be legal (ie imposed by law) or conventional (ie agreed upon by the parties to a particular contract). The parties to a lease are free to make any lawful stipulation for the conventional irritancy of that lease and consequently irritancy clauses vary in form from lease to lease. Their stipulations, however, must be lawful.

The only legal irritancy in a lease is currently for non-payment of two successive years' rent. Such irritancies are purgeable.

At common law, conventional irritancies, unless they merely expressed what the law implied, were not purgeable once incurred, notwithstanding questions of hardship. A tender of payment after irritancy has been incurred but before declarator came too late. The court could grant relief if the landlord's exercise of his right to terminate the lease amounted to oppression. See the decision of the House of Lords in *CIN Properties Ltd v Dollar Land (Cumbernauld) Ltd* 1992 SLT 669, where the claim of oppression was made but rejected. If, however, rent is accepted by the landlord after notice of irritancy has been served and the tenant remains in occupation of the subjects, the landlord may lose his right to irritate the lease: see *HMV Fields Properties Ltd v Bracken Self-Selection Fabrics Ltd* 1991 SLT 31. This will be a question of fact in each case.

At common law, the tenant was always at risk of losing his lease, possibly by mere oversight or inadvertence, for non-payment of rent on the due date or some other quite minor infringement; and heritable creditors and sub-tenants were similarly affected. See *Dorchester Studios (Glasgow) Ltd v Stone* 1975 SC (HL) 56.

25.90   LAW REFORM (MISCELLANEOUS PROVISIONS) (SCOTLAND) ACT 1985, SS 4–7

This statute implemented the recommendations of the Scottish Law Commission and resulted in a measure of statutory protection for tenants in certain circumstances.

In general, the Law Reform (Miscellaneous Provisions) (Scotland) Act 1985 makes provision for two forms of protection for a tenant against the penal enforcement of irritancies in leases. The first is a notice procedure in s 4 applicable where a landlord seeks to terminate a lease on the basis of the tenant's failure to make any monetary payment due under the lease. The second, which is applicable to all other conventional irritancies in leases, is a development of the equitable power of the court to grant relief from abuse or oppressive use of irritancies. Both forms of protection also cover the possibility of breach of a contractual term which is, or which is deemed to be, material as well as a reliance by the landlord on a conventional irritancy clause. The 1985 Act does not apply to leases of land used wholly or mainly for residential purposes or to crofts, cottars, and other holdings to which the Small Landholders (Scotland) Acts 1886 to 1931 apply.

Section 4(3) of the 1985 Act stipulates a minimum period of 14 days for payment of arrears by a tenant. This must be specified in the notice. Account is taken of the possibility of 'days of grace' being permitted. The notice must be served by recorded delivery at an address in the United Kingdom. For comment on the form of the notice, see *Bellevue Cash and Carry Ltd v Singh* 1996 GWD 4-220.

Section 5 of the 1985 Act is designed to restrict a landlord's powers of termination in circumstances other than those covered in s 4 by reference to the test of the 'fair and reasonable landlord'. This test is based on the proviso to s 26(1) of the Agricultural Holdings (Scotland) Act 1949. All the material facts will be looked at in each particular case. The onus of proof is on the tenant. The test is applicable only to the particular circumstances in which a landlord seeks to rely on the irritancy clause. It is not intended to exclude the possibility that in certain circumstances it may be fair and reasonable for a landlord to resort to irritancy without offering the tenant an opportunity to remedy the relevant breach. Furthermore, in considering the circumstances of a case, regard will be had as to whether a reasonable opportunity has been afforded to the tenant to enable the breach to be remedied. The test is how a 'fair and reasonable landlord' would act: see *Blythswood Investments (Scotland) Ltd v Clydesdale Electrical Stores Ltd (In Receivership)* 1995 SLT 150. See also *Euro Properties Scotland Ltd v Alam and Mitchell* 2000 GWD 23-896.

Section 6 of the Law Reform (Miscellaneous Provisions) (Scotland) Act 1985 provides that the parties to a lease cannot contract out of any provisions of ss 4 or 5.

The 1985 Act undoubtedly provides a degree of protection for tenants, but only to a limited extent. No protection is provided for third parties having an interest in the lease whether as heritable creditors, sub-tenants or otherwise.

In the result, no heritable creditor will lend to the tenant on the security of his lease unless the lease contains an express provision to the effect that the creditor is to receive notification of any impending action of irritancy, including the possibility of purging the irritancy.

Sub-tenants would be advised to insist upon similar protection.

Finally, if the tenant is a company, and a liquidator, administrator or receiver is appointed, the tenant's interest in the subjects may have substantial value, which the liquidator, administrator or receiver may wish to realise for the benefit of the tenant's creditors by finding an assignee acceptable to the landlord. The tenant's agent should therefore ensure that a period of time is given to the liquidator, administrator or receiver so as to enable him so to do, provided always that he undertakes liability for performance of all the obligations of the lease which may include payment of the rent in arrears as well as rent accruing during the period itself.

The general aim in revising the irritancy clause in a lease has been to produce a clause which effectively acts as a *compulsitor* to performance of the relevant contractual obligations rather than as a means by which a landlord can rid himself of an unsatisfactory tenant. While the 1985 Act, ss 4–7 go a long way towards protecting a tenant from the rigours of irritancy clauses, it is suggested that the tenant's solicitor should, whenever possible, carefully revise the irritancy clause, so as to procure the maximum protection for the tenant. It is still quite difficult to prove a claim for unjust enrichment following an action being raised for irritancy: see *Dollar Land (Cumbernauld) Ltd v CIN Properties Ltd* 1998 SC (HL) 90.

25.91   SCOTTISH LAW COMMISSION PROPOSALS

As a result of various judicial comments, the Scottish Law Commission has considered the law of irritancy further in order to assess whether the current law strikes the right balance between providing adequate protection to tenants and retaining an effective remedy for breach of contract. See *Report on Irritancy in Leases of Land* (Scot Law Com No 191, 2003). The Commission found that irritancy is a useful remedy and that it should be retained. However, it is recommended that the exercise of the right to terminated a lease should be controlled and that the Law Reform (Miscellaneous Provisions) (Scotland) Act 1985 be replaced by a new comprehensive scheme of statutory regulation across all leases of land. The key changes proposed are as follows.

(1) A right to terminate a lease will only be exercisable by the service of a termination notice on the tenant.

(2) Before a lease can be terminated by reason of a remedial breach, the tenant should be given a reasonable opportunity to remedy the breach. Landlords will

be required to serve a warning notice requiring the tenant to remedy the breach within a period of not less than 28 days. Failure to remedy the breach within the period will entitle the landlord to terminate the lease.

(3) In the case of an insolvency event affecting the tenant and there is no absolute right to prevent the tenant's interest being assigned, it is recommended that the tenant be given the opportunity to dispose of the tenancy. Accordingly, before a landlord can terminate the lease, he will be required to serve a moratorium notice offering the tenant a six-month period within which to negotiate an assignation of the lease.

(4) In other cases, a landlord should be entitled to terminate a lease unless to do so would be a manifestly excessive response to the circumstance of the case. 28 days' notice would be required and, during that period, the tenant can apply to the court to strike down the notice or delay its effect.

(5) It is recommended that the three existing rights to terminate for non-payment of rent implied by law should be abolished and replaced by a single statutory right to terminate for non-payment of six months' rent. This right would apply to leases which do not contain a contractual right to terminate for non-payment of rent and would be regulated under the statutory scheme.

(6) The Commission proposes that any existing rights of relief from the effects of irritancy be abolished. All of the tenant's protections against termination would be contained in the statutory scheme.

(7) Standard forms of warning notice, moratorium notice and termination notice are contained in the draft Bill annexed to the Commission's Report.

25.92 Hypothec

Hypothec may be considered under the following headings:

(1) general definition;
(2) sequestration for rent;
(3) summary; and
(4) reform.

25.93 GENERAL DEFINITION

In addition to his ordinary remedies as a creditor, a landlord has a special remedy for the recovery of rent due to him, in the form of a right in security without possession of the subjects over which it extends. This right is implied by law and is called a right of hypothec.

Hypothec has been described as being 'a real right in security', implied by law as between landlord and tenant over subjects allowed to remain in the tenant's possession. Essentially, it represents a right to have retained upon the subjects and to recover from those in whose possession they are, if they have been removed in breach of the right, the produce of the subjects or other articles and effects which are upon them. The property covered is known as the *invecta et illata*. Money, bonds, bills, the tenant's clothes and the tenant's tools of trade are not included: *Macpherson v Macpherson's Trustees* (1905) 8 F 191. While hypothec may cover goods brought onto the subjects although they do not belong to the tenant, as in the case of hired furniture, it does not cover goods which are on the subjects for a purpose which is merely temporary, such as goods sent to be repaired or for exhibition. Nor does it cover goods which are the property of a member of the tenant's family. Goods of a sub-tenant, however, may be sequestrated for the rent due by the principal tenant, and also for the rent due by the sub-tenant himself: *Steuart v Stables* (1878) 5 R 1024.

25.94   SEQUESTRATION FOR RENT

Hypothec secures one year's rent but not prior arrears. The process whereby the right of hypothec is converted into a real right is known as sequestration for rent. The right of hypothec falls if not put into force by sequestration within three months of the last term for payment. It is standard practice to sequestrate for the rent actually due and in security for that to become due at the next term. The right of a landlord to sequestrate for rent is not affected by the insolvency of the tenant. Such right is, however, subject to certain preferential claims, insofar as is possible, from the proceeds of the sale of the *invecta et illata*.

Sequestration for rent is exclusively a sheriff court process. The ordinary course of procedure is that a warrant to sequestrate is granted on an *ex parte* statement, the goods are inventoried and valued by a sheriff officer and ultimately sold under a separate warrant from the sheriff by auction. After they have been inventoried, the goods cannot be removed unless the person who removes them, if in good faith, accounts for their value. If in bad faith, he is liable for the rent. Without applying for sequestration, a landlord may interdict the removal of the *invecta et illata* and, if they have been removed, may obtain a warrant to have them brought back. It should be noted however that interdict and recovery of goods, being exceptional remedies, will render the landlord liable in damages, if either the statement on which he obtains authority proves untrue or if there is a genuine dispute as to the rent and the circumstances render extreme measures unnecessary.

After obtaining warrant to sequestrate and having the goods inventoried, the landlord may proceed with their sale. For this, a separate warrant is required from the sheriff and it must be executed by an officer of the court or another person appointed by the sheriff. The sale is by public roup or auction and has to be reported to the court within 14 days. The sheriff may order the gross proceeds of the sale to be consigned whereupon the accounts are taxed and the sale approved; and the landlord is then paid in full or *pro tanto* if not enough is realised. Where the landlord is paid in full, the balance, if any, is paid to the tenant less commissions and expenses. This balance can be attached by ordinary diligence by creditors of the tenant, including the landlord for any arrears of rent.

25.95 SUMMARY

While the landlord's right of hypothec has several advantages over other remedies for collection of rent arrears, it should be remembered that a landlord's claim is postponed to those of certain other creditors. Hypothec is, however, a useful deterrent although, given the preferential claims which it may be subject to, it is a remedy which is often used only as a last resort.

25.96 REFORM

In 2002, the Scottish Executive published a consultation paper on the enforcement of civil obligations: *Enforcement of Civil Obligations in Scotland: A Consultation Document* (April 2002). It proposed the abolition of sequestration of rent, but stated that this would not affect the right of hypothec. This seems ill considered, as the two are directly related. For further discussion, see A McAllister *Scottish Law of Leases* (3rd edn, 2002), paras 5.77–5.79.

Chapter 26

Agricultural Leases

26.1   Introduction

Immediately after World War II approximately 70% of all farms in Scotland were owned by landlords and leased to tenants. Since then, largely a result of legislation, only about 25% of farms remain within the landlord and tenant system. It is anticipated that the advent of the Agricultural Holdings (Scotland) Act 2003 ('the 2003 Act') coupled with a decline in the prosperity of the agricultural industry will see a further decline. For this reason farm lettings are unlikely to be encountered other than by solicitors specialising in agricultural matters. The reader is referred to the specialist texts in the Reading List.

Agricultural leases are amongst the most heavily regulated private contracts and the tenants' security of tenure created by the Agricultural Holdings (Scotland) Act 1948 has resulted in many leases being continued by tacit relocation long after the stipulated ish. Leases granted in the early twentieth century with nominal terms of, for example, 14 years are still current. Subsequent legislation and ever increasing restrictions on the parties' freedom to contract have rendered the text of many older but still extant leases of little value in ascertaining the legal relationship of the parties in many matters. The then existing statute law was consolidated in the Agricultural Holdings (Scotland) Act 1949 which was, itself, along with no fewer than 17 subsequent measures consolidated into the Agricultural Holdings (Scotland) Act 1991 ('the 1991 Act'). This Act has now been extensively varied by the most recent legislation, the Agricultural Holdings (Scotland) Act 2003, which restricts freedom of contract still further and introduces two new types of statutory tenancy. All provisions of the 2003 Act, except those in relation to the tenant's right to buy, came into force on 27 November 2003. See the Agricultural Holdings (Scotland) Act 2003 (Commencement No 3, Transitional and Savings Provisions) Order 2003, SSI 2003/548. Since the early 1970s, very few lettings intended to confer *de facto* security of tenure have been granted. The almost invariable practice has been to lease farms to a vehicle, usually a limited partnership or occasionally a company, over which the landlord could exercise control sufficient to ensure that vacant possession could be recovered at the ish. These mechanisms are discussed below.

The new types of tenancy introduced by the 2003 Act do not enjoy security of tenure beyond the stipulated term, and where land is to be let in future, these are likely to be the types of letting used. The greater likelihood, however, is that other ways of separating ownership from use, such as contract farming, will be further developed.

26.2   Types of leases

A general point is that writing is not necessary to constitute an agricultural lease if it has a duration of one year or less, though unwritten leases are not common. The normal rule under the Requirements of Writing (Scotland) Act 1995 that leases over a year in length must be in writing does apply. Leases can also arise from the parties' actings: see *Morrison-Low v Paterson* 1985 SLT 255.

Disregarding some rarely found instances, agricultural leases can be simply categorised as follows:

(1) 1991 Act leases;
(2) grazing and mowing leases;
(3) 1991 Act, s 2 leases;
(4) short limited duration tenancies; and
(5) limited duration tenancies.

26.3   1991 ACT LEASES

These are leases conferring security of tenure which pre-date the Agricultural Holdings (Scotland) Act 2003 and, in some cases, may have been continued by tacit relocation since the 1930s or 1940s. It is most unlikely that such leases will ever be granted in future due to the extensive and very often retrospective statutory rights of tenants including, under the 2003 Act, a pre-emptive right to buy on sale. In the unlikely event of parties agreeing that a new lease be regulated by the Agricultural Holdings (Scotland) Act 1991, this must be expressly provided. Before the coming in force of Part I of the 2003 Act (due to take place in late 2003), a lease permitting agricultural use expressed to be for less than a year is, by statute, declared to be a lease from year to year. In this way (other than in a few cases) security of tenure is conferred: see the 1991 Act, s 3. Unwritten leases were automatically subject to the 1991 Act.

26.4   GRAZING AND MOWING LEASES

These used to be granted under the Agricultural Holdings (Scotland) Act 1991, s 2, or its precursors. They permit the occupation of agricultural ground only for the purposes of grazing or mowing and only for a period of less than one year. If such a lease extends for a year it becomes a 1991 Act lease and is covered by security of tenure under the 1991 Act. The Agricultural Holdings (Scotland) Act 2003 repeals s 2 of the 1991 Act, but, by s 3, substitutes an alternative arrangement for such leases, which may not exceed 364 days.

26.5 1991 ACT, S 2 LEASES

These are leases granted under the Agricultural Holdings (Scotland) Act 1991, s 2, following the approval of the Scottish Executive Environmental and Rural Affairs Department (SEERAD).

Such leases will soon be phased out as the Agricultural Holdings (Scotland) Act 2003 (which repeals s 2 of the 1991 Act) is brought into force. Where prior written approval has been granted by SEERAD, a lease of up to one year which does not confer security of tenure can be granted to a tenant over the approved area. SEERAD will not normally grant approval for more than one or two years in succession for the same area.

26.6 SHORT LIMITED DURATION TENANCIES (SLDTs)

These are leases for periods not exceeding five years granted under the Agricultural Holdings (Scotland) Act 2003. Any lease of agricultural land granted for a period between 5 and 15 years will take effect as an LDT for 15 years: 2003 Act, s 5(4). If an SLDT is extended for more than five years, it automatically becomes an LDT. The same land cannot be let to the same tenant on successive SLDTs unless there is an interval of not less than one year from the expiry of the first SLDT to the start of the second SLDT, without the two periods being merged. If the addition of the two periods takes the total duration over five years, an LDT is created: 2003 Act, s 4.

26.7 LIMITED DURATION TENANCIES (LDTs)

These are leases of not less than 15 years granted under the Agricultural Holdings (Scotland) Act 2003.

26.8 **Other arrangements for occupying land**

The commonest other arrangements for occupying agricultural land are:

(1) contract and share farming; and
(2) a lease to a limited partnership.

26.9 CONTRACT AND SHARE FARMING

Due to the complexities of the statutory provisions affecting leases, it has become increasingly common for owners of agricultural land to arrange for it to be farmed by a contractor on their behalf. In many instances, the contractor does virtually all the work that would be carried out by a traditional agricultural tenant, although he will not normally have a lease of a farmhouse as was the case in the old-style farming leases granted under the Agricultural Holdings (Scotland) Act 1991. Contract farming agreements and share farming agreements take diverse forms, sometimes including arrangements for the leasing of livestock, and are not considered further in this chapter.

26.10   THE LEASE TO A LIMITED PARTNERSHIP

In response to the statutory provisions granting security of tenure to agricultural tenants, means were sought by which such security of tenure could be avoided. The most common such device used before the passage of the Agricultural Holdings (Scotland) Act 2003 was the lease to a limited partnership. Many of these still exist. The scheme was that the actual occupier of the farm became the general partner in a limited partnership under the Limited Partnerships Act 1907, with a limited partner who was a person acting under the instructions of the landlord. In the agreement constituting the limited partnership, the limited partner had a right to dissolve the limited partnership. An agricultural lease was then granted to the limited partnership which was entitled to the benefit of the security of tenure provisions under the Agricultural Holdings (Scotland) Act 1991 and its precursors. When the agreed duration of the arrangement had been reached the limited partner would serve notice of dissolution of the limited partnership thereby causing the limited partnership, which was the tenant, to cease to exist and thereby bringing the lease to an end. The legal standing of this arrangement was considered and endorsed in *Macfarlane v Falfield Developments Ltd* 1997 SLT 518. The 2003 Act contains detailed provisions in ss 72 and 73 on the parties' rights in such an arrangement after 1 July 2003. These are not further considered.

The 2003 Act, while not actually prohibiting the granting of leases to limited partnerships, makes it impossible in practice to use the above procedure to bring an agricultural tenancy to an end: see 2003 Act, s 70. In the case of leases to limited partnerships following the coming into force of the 2003 Act, the general partner can, in effect, substitute himself as tenant if the limited partnership is dissolved.

26.11   **Terms of a lease**

In earlier editions of this Manual, an example of an agricultural lease was given as an Appendix. Practice following the changes which will be introduced by the Agricultural Holdings (Scotland) Act 2003 has yet to become established but the removal of 'automatic' security of tenure, and the considerable changes to the law may well result in different styles being adopted. There have been a wide variety of forms of agricultural lease used over the past years, some short, some highly detailed, especially when produced on behalf of institutional investors more accustomed to commercial leases. The example at Appendix B is therefore only an illustration of the kind of lease that has been used in the past.

26.12 PARTIES

The parties to the lease must be correctly named and designed. It was generally accepted that a landlord can let property to a group of which he is a member, following *Pinkerton v Pinkerton* 1986 SLT 672. But it is now also accepted that several *pro indiviso* proprietors cannot competently grant a valid lease to one of their number: see *Clydesdale Bank plc v Davidson* 1998 SC (HL) 51. While it may be possible to reconcile these two decisions as consistent, the decision in *Pinkerton* should now be treated with caution. Leases to a company which is merely a nominee of the true proprietors by those same proprietors will be treated as a nullity, on the view that this is equivalent to trying to contract with oneself: see *Kildrummy (Jersey) Ltd v Inland Revenue Commissioners* 1992 SLT 787.

26.13 DESTINATION

Exclusion of assignees and sub-tenants is implied at common law, but express exclusion is common. Some writers draw a distinction between leases of ordinary duration and leases of extraordinary duration of 21 years or more where there is no implied exclusion of assignees and sub-tenants. However, in practice this is of little consequence because of the element of *delectus personae* which is invariably present. It has also been usual to expressly exclude legatees and successors. Notwithstanding the terms of s 16 of the Succession (Scotland) Act 1964, there is warrant for the view that an exclusion of successors effectively brings the tenancy to an end on the death of the tenant: see *Kennedy v Johnstone* 1956 SC 39. However, this point has not been conclusively established. A statutory right to assign a tenancy held under the Agricultural Holdings (Scotland) Act 1991 and an LDT (but *not* an SLDT) is introduced by the Agricultural Holdings (Scotland) Act 2003, ss 7 and 66. Where not expressly excluded in the lease, a bequest of a 1991 Act lease, SLDT or LDT is possible: see 2003 Act, s 21; 1991 Act, s 10A. Where there is no effective bequest, the transfer of the tenant's interest is governed by the Succession (Scotland) Act 1964, s 16 (as amended by the 2003 Act, s 20).

26.14 DESCRIPTION OF SUBJECTS

Measurements should be given in hectares and there should always be a carefully prepared detailed plan showing the Ordnance Survey parcels and their respective areas expressed in hectares. A schedule of measurement detailing the Ordnance Survey number, area and land category (ie arable, permanent pasture, rough grazings) should be annexed and executed as relative to the lease. Such a schedule may prove invaluable during future rent negotiations or arbitration, particularly if, as frequently happens, a record of holding is not prepared.

26.15   DURATION

In the recent past, before the Agricultural Holdings (Scotland) Act 2003, in view of the provisions of ss 21 and 22 of the Agricultural Holdings (Scotland) Act 1991, it was common practice to provide that the lease itself would be for a period of one year or two years only and for the duration of the letting to be effectively regulated by the limited partnership contract or whatever method has been used to permit effective termination of the lease. If, however, the lease was to be granted for a period of years, it was usual to provide breaks to coincide with the statutory rent review period, at present three years in 1991 Act tenancies and LDTs. Notice of intention to invoke the break normally mirrors the statutory provision of giving notice of not less than one and no more than two years prior to an anniversary of the end of the original period of the lease. Following the introduction of SLDTs and LDTs it is essential to provide a clear statement of the duration. Continued occupation and paying of rent for more than five years converts an SLDT into a 15-year LDT.

26.16   RENT

The traditional practice of providing for payments of rent on a forehand or backhand basis is becoming much less frequent and the normal practice is for the rent to be referable to the period of possession and payable either half-yearly, quarterly, or even monthly in arrears. Rent review provisions have been relatively uncommon. The statutory rent review period for 1991 Act leases on tacit relocation is every three years, if either party gives notice. In LDTs, there is also a statutory three-year rent review although the parties can make contractual provision: see the Agricultural Holdings (Scotland) Act 2003, s 9. Any rent review in an SLDT would have to be contractual.

26 17   RESERVATIONS TO THE LANDLORD

Minerals are invariably reserved to the landlord, as are woods, wayleaves, roads, powers to alter marches and very often powers of entry.

26.18   GAME

It is also usual for game to be reserved to the landlord. The tenant has statutory rights under the Ground Game Act 1880 to kill rabbits and hares and, under the Deer (Scotland)

Acts 1959 and 1996, to kill deer on enclosed ground. Express rights to kill deer should be given notwithstanding a general reservation of game if the landlord is to avoid claims for damage caused by them: see *Auckland v Dowie* 1964 SLT (Land Ct) 20. The normal reservation and the substitution of 31 October for the end of the calendar year, as provided under the Agricultural Holdings (Scotland) Act 1991, is now regarded as sensible practice, notwithstanding the tenant's powers under the Deer (Scotland) Acts.

26.19   ACCESS BY THE LANDLORD

It is probably unnecessary to include this as a reservation as it is implied at common law and made the subject of a special power under s 10 of the Agricultural Holdings (Scotland) Act 1991, but if unusual rights are needed by the landlord it is best to be explicit.

26.20   RESUMPTION

Resumption, that is taking back ground from a lease by the landlord, can only be contractual. It is usual to reserve wide powers of resumption, for any purpose other than agriculture, but it is good practice to specify the purposes, especially if unusual. A resumption may not be so major as to amount to a 'fraud on the lease'. It is usual in 1991 Act leases for there to be at least two to three months' notice given of a resumption, to allow the tenant to make his waygoing claims against the landlord.

In an LDT or SLDT, at least one year's notice must be given of a resumption: see the Agricultural Holdings (Scotland) Act 2003, s 17(2).

26.21   REINSTATE AND INSURE

Section 4 of the Agricultural Holdings (Scotland) Act 1991 enables the landlord or tenant to secure a written lease. In the circumstances narrated in s 4 of the 1991 Act, a landlord or tenant may require a revision of an existing lease in order to bring the lease in line with the provisions contained in Schedule 1 to the 1991 Act. The Agricultural Holdings (Scotland) Act 2003, s 13 makes similar provision for SLDTs and LDTs. Paragraph 5 of Schedule 1 to the 2003 Act embodies an undertaking by the landlord to apply insurance monies received in the event of damage by fire towards the replacement of fixed equipment in accordance with the requirement of the paragraph. It is usual for the tenant to be bound to insure his crops and stock.

26.22   LANDLORD'S OBLIGATION FOR FIXED EQUIPMENT

Prior to the provisions of the Agricultural Holdings (Scotland) Act 2003 coming into force, it is the landlord's obligation under the Agricultural Holdings (Scotland) Act

1991, s 5 to provide and maintain fixed equipment – that is buildings, drains, fences etc, to allow the tenant to farm the holding. These statutory provisions are almost invariably made the subject of a contracting-out agreement as contemplated by s 5(3) of the 1991 Act. Such an agreement, or 'post-lease agreement' as it is commonly called, stipulates in detail the contractual as opposed to the statutory obligations of the parties. It was the common, but not universal, practice for tenancies to be placed on a tenant's full repairing and renewing basis, including such repairs and renewals as may be occasioned by fair wear and tear. To be effective, a post-lease agreement had to post-date the lease, and this is usually narrated in the agreement itself. The 2003 Act will make it compulsory in SLDTs and LDTs for the landlord to provide at least basic fixed equipment, which must be specified in the lease. The tenant's oblig-ation is to maintain that fixed equipment in no worse condition than when he took occupation, or when it was provided, fair wear and tear excepted. The landlord in an SLDT or LDT may no longer pass on this responsibility to the tenant by a post-lease agreement: see the 2003 Act, s 16. Existing post-lease agreements continue in force, but the 1991 Act tenant can oblige the landlord to take back his responsibilities: see the 2003 Act, s 60.

26.23   RECORD

Records are made under the Agricultural Holdings (Scotland) Act 1991, s 8. While records were frequently dispensed with in the past, a number of potential claims by either party to a lease are dependent upon a record at the commencement of the ten-ancy having been made. So far as the landlord is concerned, compensation for dilap-idation and deterioration of the holding under s 45 of the 1991 Act will not be enforceable in regard to new leases unless a record of the holding has been made under s 8 of the 1991 Act. The converse applies in regard to a claim by the tenant under s 44 of the 1991 Act for the continuous adoption of a special standard of farming.

The Agricultural Holdings (Scotland) Act 2003, s 61 has amended this to allow records to be made otherwise than by written description.

26.24   ALTERATIONS TO FIXED EQUIPMENT IMPROVEMENTS

In tenancies held under the Agricultural Holdings (Scotland) Act 1991, it was com-mon for parties to agree in their lease, or in a subsequent agreement, that the value of improvements carried out by the tenant referred to in Schedule 5 to the 1991 Act would be written down over a period of years. At least as regards some of those improvements which a landlord would have been obliged to carry out to fulfil his obligations to provide fixed equipment, the tenant's entitlement to compensation at waygo cannot be contractually restricted: see the Agricultural Holdings (Scotland) Act 2003 Act, s 60.

In SLDTs and LDTs the tenant's rights to compensation are protected by the 2003 Act, ss 45–49.

26.25 TENANT'S FIXTURES

Some leases held under the Agricultural Holdings (Scotland) Act 1991 exclude the tenant's right to remove fixtures and buildings under s 18 of that Act. The question as to whether or not it is competent to contract out of this section has not been judicially decided.

26.26 USE OF THE HOLDING

In 1991 Act tenancies it was common to restrict the type of farming for which the farm was let, to exclude the landlord's responsibility for providing, for example, specialised fixed equipment for dairy farming. The restriction on the use of the holding is enforceable as is the prohibition against the breaking up of permanent pasture unless the tenant succeeds in having the provisions varied by invoking s 9 of the 1991 Act. In LDTs and SLDTs, the use of the holding should be carefully specified as the landlord's obligations to provide fixed equipment under the Agricultural Holdings (Scotland) Act 2003, s 16, depend on the kind of produce specified in the lease.

26.27 MUIRBURN

The provisions of any lease in regard to muirburn are overridden by ss 23 to 27 of the Hill Farming Act 1946. These sections set time limits within which muirburn is lawful and to entitle tenants to carry out muirburn in certain circumstances regardless of the terms of the lease. The safeguard for the landlord, so far as overburning is concerned, is contained in s 24(1) of the 1946 Act which enables the landlord to refer any dispute on muirburning to the Scottish Ministers.

26.28 ALTERNATIVE USES

It has been common to prohibit use of farms for purposes other than agriculture, such as camping and caravanning. While this is valid contractually, the position for leases held under the Agricultural Holdings (Scotland) Act 1991 and LDTs has been changed by the provisions permitting diversification into other uses in the Agricultural Holdings (Scotland) Act 2003, Part 3 (ss 39–42). These rights override any prohibition in the lease. Conservation activities are not contrary to good husbandry: 2003 Act, s 69.

26.29 WAYGOING YEAR

Freedom of cropping and disposal of produce does not extend to the year before the expiration of the lease: see the Agricultural Holdings (Scotland) Act 1991, s 7(5)(b).

It is therefore customary, in order to ensure the continuity of husbandry, to stipulate the cropping to which the tenant will be bound to adhere in the year immediately preceding his waygo. Provision is also made for the landlord or incoming tenant to take over certain crops which will still be in the ground at the outgoing tenant's waygo.

26.30   RESIDENCE

It was common before the Agricultural Holdings (Scotland) Act 2003 to oblige the tenant to reside on the holding. This obligation has been overridden by the 2003 Act, s 65, which allows the tenant to permit someone else with relevant skill and experience to reside there in his place.

26.31   IRRITANCY

An irritancy clause gives the landlord the option to terminate the lease on the occurrence of a forbidden event and, being a conventional irritancy, cannot be purged. Great care should be taken when revising an irritancy clause and solicitors acting for tenants should endeavour wherever possible to have the terms watered down. A landlord on the other hand, will seek to make this as wide as possible. In leases held under the Agricultural Holdings (Scotland) Act 1991, an irritancy incurred by the tenant might be one of the few chances of terminating a lease running on tacit relocation. Mutuality of contract applies to irritancies unless excluded. The defences to an action of removal following a conventional irritancy are limited and that the provisions of the Law Reform (Miscellaneous Provisions) (Scotland) Act 1985, ss 4 and 5 do not apply to agricultural leases. There are proposals from the Scottish Law Commission to amend the law of irritancy affecting agricultural leases: *Irritancy in Leases of Land* (Scot Law Com No 191, 2003).

26.32   REMOVING

It was common to insert a clause into leases held under the Agricultural Holdings (Scotland) Act 1991 stating that the tenant would remove at the ish. Such clauses were, after the Agricultural Holdings (Scotland) Act 1949, completely unenforceable due to security of tenure. A tenant of an agricultural holding under a 1991 Act lease cannot be compelled to remove otherwise than by an order of the court following either a notice to quit or a finding that a conventional irritancy has been incurred. Informal undertakings to remove are of less certain effect, following the decision in *Morrison's Executors v Rendall* 1986 SLT 227. The parties can, however, waive strict compliance with the statutory provisions: *Kildrummy (Jersey) Ltd v Calder* 1994 SLT 888. In SLDTs and LDTs, so long as the appropriate statutory notice provisions are operated, a tenant will have to remove at the termination date. If notice is not given, an LDT will continue on a cycle of continuations, as described in the Agricultural Holdings (Scotland) Act 2003, s 8.

26.33 Taking instructions to lease

A landlord contemplating the lease of a farm usually seeks advice from his factor or land agent who will deal with the practical matters involved, advising on the overall terms and conditions upon which the farm should be leased, and referring only matters of law to the owner's solicitor. A prospective tenant will very often depend on his solicitor for the whole spectrum of advice required in connection with the lease. It is for the landlord to decide the type of lease, whether SLDT or LDT. The lease must then follow the statutory requirements for the type of tenancy in question.

26.34 RENT REVIEW

The landlord should be informed of the statutory provisions with regard to the variation of rent and that scarcity value must be discounted by an arbiter when reviewing a rent. Accordingly, it is quite possible that a rent tendered at the commencement of the tenancy may be reduced at the first review.

26.35 CONSENTS

If the property is subject to a heritable security, the consent of the creditor is required in terms of Standard Condition 6 of Schedule 3 to the Conveyancing and Feudal Reform (Scotland) Act 1970, before a lease is entered into. If there is a heritable creditor, his consent to the letting should be sought at an early stage.

26.36 EXPENSES

The landlord should also be informed of the cost of preparing and agreeing a lease and whatever other charges are to be made for managing the property or collecting the rents and so forth.

26.37 QUOTAS AND PREMIUM SCHEMES

Following the reforms in the Common Agricultural Policy of the EU in 1992/93, the number and complexity of subsidy schemes for many types of agricultural 'produce' have increased. These include Milk Quota introduced in 1984; Sheep Premium Scheme; Suckler Cow Premium Scheme; Arable Aid; Beef Special Premium Scheme; and Setaside. At the time of writing, the EU has agreed a significant reform of the Common Agricultural Policy (CAP) which will largely substitute these with a 'single farm payment' less closely tied to agricultural production. The complex rules have altered markedly in the few years during which the schemes have been in operation and are beyond the scope of this Manual. The sums payable under the schemes frequently form a considerable part of the total income which can be derived from farming a holding, and entitlement to them in the case of livestock premiums, or whether or not the whole of the holding qualifies for them, in the case of arable schemes, have been of great practical significance.

Landlords will often seek to ensure that entitlements under the livestock schemes remain with the holding on the waygo of the tenant, sometimes without payment to the tenant. While this may be acceptable in part where the tenant was allocated a Quota at no cost, the opposite applies where the rights were bought in by the tenant. Such provisions must be scrutinised carefully and specialist advice taken where appropriate. This whole area of practice is currently changing due to the recently agreed EU alterations to the CAP.

26.38   RECORDING CONDITION OF HOLDING

The necessity or otherwise to have a record of holding prepared should be discussed. If the fixed equipment on the holding is in good condition and the lease is to be drawn on a traditional basis, the landlord would be well advised to meet the expenses involved in having a record prepared. On the other hand, if the fixed equipment is in poor condition, it is more than likely that the tenant, if he is properly advised, will insist on a record being prepared. The form of the record may now be agreed between the parties: see the Agricultural Holdings (Scotland) Act 2003, s 61.

26.39   Selecting a tenant

Although most new lettings are now conducted by a firm of chartered surveyors or resident factors, there are occasions when solicitors are instructed to carry out this work. The usual procedure is to prepare detailed particulars, to draft the lease, and then to advertise the farm to let, outlining briefly the terms and conditions which the landlord has in mind. The letting particulars should require prospective tenants to provide the landlord with details of their experience, financial standing and probably details of the working capital required, model cashflows and profit and loss accounts. In the event of tenders being sought, it is usual to find a fairly wide variation in the range of rents offered and care requires to be taken to select a tender where the rent is such that the tenant is able to make a reasonable profit.

26.40 PARTICULARS AND ADVERTISEMENT

The particulars of the farm should include matters such as:

(1) description and situation;
(2) type of land, including whether or not it is classed as in the Less Favoured Area (LFA) of the country, whether Disadvantaged or Severely Disadvantaged;
(3) area;
(4) plan;
(5) number of houses and steading accommodation;
(6) services such as water, electricity, telephone, gas and drainage;
(7) details of waygoing valuations and the method by which these will require to be determined;
(8) viewing arrangements;
(9) nature of the tenancy agreement; and
(10) whether any subsidy rights are available with the holding, and how such rights are to be dealt with.

Following advertisement, it is customary to set a closing date for the submission of offers and it is normal for a number of offers to be received. Very often, some of the most suitable candidates will be local farmers or their sons known to the landlord and probably to the solicitor or other letting agent. In such cases, enquiries as to competence and financial standing may be very straightforward. In the case of applicants from another locality, it may be wise to inspect the applicant's existing holding and, if he is a tenant, to make enquiries of his landlord or landlord's factor. The proceedings will usually end in the form of a short list of, say, three applicants and it may almost be immaterial which candidate is eventually chosen. Formal missives should then be entered into and the draft lease and plan of the farm incorporated in these missives.

26.41 Inheritance tax

Agricultural property relief is available on a death or on a lifetime transfer for both owner-occupiers and landlords. It takes the form of a reduction for tax purposes in the value of the property which is liable to tax. Since 10 March 1981, in order to qualify for relief, the deceased or transferor must have either owned the agricultural property for seven years prior to the death or transfer, or occupied it for two years prior to the death or transfer. The rules are relaxed where one agricultural property replaces another or where the property has been inherited from a spouse within these periods.

The relief is a 100% reduction in the value for tax if the deceased or the transferor has the right to or can obtain vacant possession within 12 months, or the property was let by a lease commencing after 1 September 1995. In other cases, relief is 50% except, in some circumstances, in the case of property let before 10 March 1981.

Agricultural property relief may be lost wholly or partly if the property has been the subject of a potentially exempt transfer (PET) for inheritance tax (usually a gift) and is sold or disposed of by the recipient within seven years of the date of transfer, followed by the death of the donor within the seven-year period. This can seriously affect the original transferor's tax liability and may result in inheritance tax being payable by the recipient. The grant of an agricultural tenancy for full consideration is not a transfer of value for inheritance tax purposes. Following the case of *Baird's Executors v Inland Revenue Commissioners* 1991 SLT (Lands Tr) 9, a tenant's interest in an agricultural tenancy can have a value for tax purposes. However, following the Finance (No 2) Act 1992, the value of that interest can obtain 100% relief for inheritance tax purposes, if it can be classed as business property, as will usually be the case.

Chapter 27

Residential Leases

27.1 Public and private sectors

The letting of houses is divided broadly between houses in the public sector where the landlord is now known as a social landlord and houses in the private sector which are leased by private landlords. A new regime for the public sector was introduced under the Housing (Scotland) Act 2001 and applies to tenants of local authorities, housing associations and the former Scottish Homes. Under Part 4 of this Act, Scottish Homes has been converted into a new executive agency known as Communities Scotland.

27.2 Public sector tenancies

The letting of houses in the public sector is now regulated by the Housing (Scotland) Act 2001 which has replaced the previous elaborate code under various statutes, including the Housing (Scotland) Act 1987 and the Housing (Scotland) Act 1988. It introduces a new type of tenancy to cover all public sector tenancies known as a 'Scottish secure tenancy'. A Scottish secure tenant has a right to a written lease and generally to security of tenure. There are provisions for succession to the tenancy on the death of the tenant by a wide category of persons including same sex cohabitants. A new statutory regime for the right to purchase is also introduced in the 2001 Act: see para 28.59. For a general discussion, see A McAllister *Scottish Law of Leases* (3rd edn, 2002), Chapter 16.

27.3 Private sector tenancies

The private sector covers all residential leases not in the public sector. There are two main statutes:

(1) the Rent (Scotland) Act 1984, which consolidates all previous Rent Act legislation; and

(2) the Housing (Scotland) Act 1988, which came into force on 2 January 1989.

In practice, almost all future private sector residential leases will be governed by the 1988 Act; but many of the provisions of the 1984 Act have been left intact and still apply to existing leases. Both Acts contain lengthy and detailed provisions, particularly in relation to security of tenure, recovery of possession and control of rents. What follows is a brief outline only of these provisions and no attempt is made to deal with them exhaustively.

27.4   Rent (Scotland) Act 1984

The principal features of the Rent (Scotland) Act 1984 are security of tenure, statutory transmission of tenancy on the death of the tenant and a system of rent control.

27.5   PROTECTED TENANCIES

Section 1 of the Rent (Scotland) Act 1984 provides that a tenancy is a protected tenancy where a house is let as a dwellinghouse, unless the rateable value exceeded £200 on 23 March 1965. If the house was not completed until after that date, then a lease thereof created a protected tenancy if the rateable value first assigned to the dwellinghouse on completion did not exceed £600; or, from and after 1 April 1985, £1,600. The 1984 Act covered both unfurnished and furnished tenancies; but the provisions relating to furnished tenancy contracts falling under Part VII were repealed by the Housing (Scotland) Act 1988.

In order to establish a protected tenancy under the 1984 Act, there must have been a lease of a house or part of a house as a separate unit with exclusive possession. During the currency of the lease, the tenant of a protected tenancy is known as the contractual tenant. On expiry of the contractual term, the tenant becomes a statutory tenant by virtue of s 3 of the 1984 Act.

A statutory tenant cannot be removed by the landlord except on one of the grounds specified in Schedule 2 to the 1984 Act. There are 21 possible grounds. Part I of Schedule 2 contains those grounds on which a court may grant an order for possession (the discretionary grounds); Part II states those grounds on which the court must grant an order for possession (the mandatory grounds). Additionally, the court may grant an order for possession if it is satisfied that suitable alternative accommodation is available and it is reasonable to grant an order for possession: s 11(1)(a) of the 1984 Act.

27.6   NOTICE TO QUIT

To entitle the landlord to recover possession, a notice to quit must first have been served on the tenant. The style of notice is contained in the Sheriff Courts (Scotland)

Act 1907. Certain prescribed information must also be appended to the notice advising the tenant of his or her right to remain in possession after expiry of the notice, and that possession may only be recovered on the grounds set out in the Rent (Scotland) Act 1984. Failure to include the prescribed information renders the notice invalid.

27.7 PROTECTION OF STATUTORY SUCCESSORS

The Rent (Scotland) Act 1984 provides statutory security of tenure not only for the original contractual tenant, but also for successors. These rights of succession have since been restricted by the Housing (Scotland) Act 1988, s 46, for deaths occurring after that section comes into operation. The resulting position is that, on the death of the original tenant, the spouse or cohabitee is automatically entitled as of right to remain in possession as a statutory tenant. Failing such spouse or cohabitee, any other member of the family of the original tenant, or of his or her spouse, may in certain circumstances be entitled to succeed to the tenancy either on the first or on the second death. However, this is subject to complex residential requirements which are now contained in the 1988 Act, s 46 and Schedule 6, amending the original provisions in the 1984 Act.

27.8 SHORT TENANCIES

The Rent (Scotland) Act 1984, s 9, also introduced the concept of the short tenancy. To qualify, the tenancy must be for a fixed period of between one and five years, at a registered fair rent. The fair rent must have been registered before the commencement of the lease and the tenant must have received notice in the prescribed form before the commencement of the lease that the tenancy was to be a short tenancy in terms of the 1984 Act. Compliance with these conditions entitles the landlord to recover possession at the end of the period of lease; provided he serves the appropriate notices timeously, the tenant has no statutory right to remain in possession as tenant.

27.9 RENT CONTROL

The Rent (Scotland) Act 1984 effectively controls the level of rent payable in the private sector by providing for a system of rent registration. Either or both parties jointly may apply to the rent officer for the registration of a fair rent. Such fair rents are generally substantially below open market value because, in determining the level of rent, the rent officer takes into account the age, character, location and state of repair of a dwellinghouse as well as the quality and quantity of furniture provided. However, he must disregard the element of scarcity value and any circumstances personal to the landlord and tenant in question. Appeal from the decision of the rent officer is to the Rent Assessment Committee. Once a fair rent has been established, it cannot be reviewed or increased for a period of three years unless there is a material change of circumstances. Further, even although the tenant may have agreed to pay a higher rent in terms of the lease, any excess above the fair rent is irrecoverable by the landlord.

27.10   Housing (Scotland) Act 1988

The principal purpose of the Housing (Scotland) Act 1988 was to relax the statutory controls on private sector leases and to widen the scope for open market negotiation on rent between the landlord and tenant. Two new types of tenancy were introduced: the assured tenancy and the short assured tenancy. The 1988 Act repealed Part VII of the Rent (Scotland) Act 1984, which previously governed certain furnished lettings. The provisions relating to the new types of tenancy are contained in Part II of the 1988 Act (ss 12–55).

27.11   ASSURED TENANCIES

An assured tenancy is defined in s 12 of the Housing (Scotland) Act 1988 as a tenancy under which a house is let as a separate dwellinghouse and the tenant, or one of the joint tenants, is an individual who occupies the dwellinghouse as his or her only or principal home. A tenancy which falls within any paragraph in Schedule 4 to the 1988 Act cannot qualify as an assured tenancy. These exclusions embrace, *inter alia*, tenancies rent–free or at very low rents, lettings to students by educational institutions, some tenancies by resident landlords and other special cases.

Section 14(1) of the 1988 Act extends the definition of assured tenancy to those tenants who have exclusive occupation of accommodation forming part of a dwellinghouse, with shared accommodation of other parts of the same dwellinghouse where that accommodation is shared with persons other than the landlord.

27.12   TERMINATION OF ASSURED TENANCIES

A contractual assured tenancy will not come to an end unless and until the landlord has served the appropriate notice to quit in the prescribed form. The purpose of the notice is intended primarily to bring the contractual tenancy to an end. It is not necessarily an indication that the landlord is to take steps to recover possession. If, following on that notice, the tenant remains in possession, a statutory assured tenancy is created which cannot be terminated unless the landlord obtains an order for possession from the sheriff in accordance with the provisions of the Housing (Scotland) Act 1988. The grounds of removal are set out in Schedule 5 to the 1988

Act, 17 in all, of which 1 to 8 are mandatory (Part I of Schedule 5) and 9 to 17 are discretionary (Part II of Schedule 5). In seeking to remove the tenant by court action, the landlord must first have served notice of his intention to raise such court action on the tenant in terms of s 19 of the 1988 Act.

On the death of an assured tenant, the tenancy passes, under s 31 of the 1988 Act, to the spouse or cohabitee living with the tenant at the time of the tenant's death as a statutory assured tenant. There are no further rights of succession to an assured tenancy.

27.13   RENT CONTROL

Under the Housing (Scotland) Act 1988, the landlord and his tenant are free to negotiate the initial rent at the commencement of the tenancy and there is no statutory restriction on the level of rent so agreed for the assured tenancy. Thereafter, however, the landlord cannot increase the rent of an assured tenant except by serving notice on the tenant proposing an increase in the rent. The tenant may then refer the notice to the Rent Assessment Committee who will, in terms of s 25 of the 1988 Act, determine a market rent for the property. The committee may take into account scarcity factors. The rent fixed by the committee will be effective from the date specified by them; but will not apply if the landlord and tenant have in the meantime reached agreement on the variation of the terms of the tenancy.

27.14   THE SHORT ASSURED TENANCY

A short assured tenancy is defined in s 32 of the Housing (Scotland) Act 1988 as an assured tenancy for a term of not less than six months, in respect of which a notice in a prescribed form has been served on the tenant by the landlord before the creation of the tenancy. The short assured tenant has no statutory security of tenure whatsoever when the contractual term comes to an end. Instead, if the landlord so requires, the sheriff must make an order for possession provided he is satisfied that the ish has been reached, that tacit relocation is not operating, that no further contractual tenancy is in existence and that the landlord has given the prescribed notice to the tenant stating that he wishes to obtain possession. Certain of the grounds of removal, for example, grounds 1 and 2 of Schedule 5 to the 1988 Act, require notice in writing to be given to the tenant prior to the commencement of the lease that the landlord may seek to recover possession on these grounds.

27.15   RENT CONTROL

In contrast to the assured tenancy, where the tenant cannot apply for a review of the rent unless the landlord serves notice proposing an increase, the short assured tenant may, subject to certain qualifications in s 34 of the Housing (Scotland) Act 1988,

apply to the Rent Assessment Committee at any time on his own initiative for a determination of the rent which the landlord might reasonably obtain.

27.16   Provisions which apply under both Acts

A number of provisions apply both to tenancies under the Rent (Scotland) Act 1984
and under the Housing (Scotland) Act 1988 with minor differences. The more important of these can be summarised as follows.

27.17   WRITTEN LEASE

In every case, the tenant is entitled to require the landlord to provide him with a written lease setting out the full terms of the tenancy. If the landlord refuses or delays in providing the tenant with a written lease, the tenant can, under s 30(2) of the Housing
(Scotland) Act 1988, by summary application to the sheriff, request that the sheriff draw
up a lease reflecting the agreement between the parties, or adjust the terms of the same.

27.18   RENT BOOKS

Where the rent is collected weekly (but not rent collected at longer periods) the landlord is required by statute to provide the tenant with a rent book or alternatively to
give a rent receipt, which, in either case, must also contain additional information
setting out explicitly the tenant's rights under the relevant Act.

27.19   NOTICES

Notice has always been required in Scotland to terminate a lease, failing which it will
continue by tacit relocation. The same general principle applies to residential leases
controlled under the 1984 and 1988 Acts but with this difference that, in addition to
the normal notice to quit, further notices are or may be required prior to the commencement of the lease, or to convert the lease from a contractual to a statutory
tenancy, or to allow the landlord to take proceedings. In each case, statutory forms
are prescribed and additional information must be provided to the tenant. Otherwise
the notice and subsequent proceedings are invalid.

27.20   MINIMUM PERIODS FOR RENT INCREASES

Under the Housing (Scotland) Act 1988, ss 24(4) and 34(4), no further new rent fixed
by the committee for an assured, or a short assured, tenancy can take effect until after
the first anniversary of the previous determination. Under the Rent (Scotland) Act

1984, the comparable period is three years and there are provisions phasing any increase over that period.

27.21 PREMIUMS

Part VIII of the Rent (Scotland) Act 1984 prohibits the taking of premiums. A premium includes any payment made for the grant or for the assignation of a lease, and the Act contains special deeming provisions to prevent evasion. So, an obligation on a tenant to acquire furniture at an inflated price is to be regarded as a premium. Where a premium has been paid, it is recoverable by the party who paid it. The same prohibition applies to assured and short assured tenancies under the Housing (Scotland) Act 1988, s 27.

With furnished leases, it is common practice to take a deposit as security for damages, often amounting to one or two months' rent. Such a deposit, not exceeding two months' rent, is not to be regarded as a premium: 1984 Act, s 90.

27.22 HARASSMENT AND UNLAWFUL EVICTION

Under s 22 of the Rent (Scotland) Act 1984, it is a criminal offence to remove a tenant without a court order or to harass him. In practice, however, the police are reluctant to interfere in such cases because they consider these to be matters of civil rather than criminal jurisdiction. Additional provisions are also made for unlawful eviction and harassment in the Housing (Scotland) Act 1988, ss 36 to 38. These provisions apply generally to all types of tenancy.

27.23 Phasing out of the Rent (Scotland) Act 1984

The Rent (Scotland) Act 1984 meantime continues to apply to tenancies protected by that Act. But, under the Housing (Scotland) Act 1988, s 42, no tenancy commencing after 2 January 1989 is a protected tenancy under the 1984 Act except in the limited situations specified in s 42 of the 1988 Act. As a result, the 1984 Act provisions are gradually ceasing to apply, as pre-1989 tenancies come to an end and new ones are created.

27.24 Health and safety and multiple occupancy

It is appropriate to make specific reference to two sets of regulations and an order which may affect landlords and/or agents who let out residential property.

27.25   GAS REGULATIONS

The Gas Safety (Installation and Use) Regulations 1994, SI 1994/1886 came into force mainly on 31 October 1994 and also on 1 January 1996 and 1 January 1997. The important regulation is reg 35(2), which states:

> 'It shall be the duty of any person who owns a gas appliance or installation pipe-work installed in premises or any part of premises let by him to ensure that such appliance or installation of pipe work is maintained in a safe condition so as to prevent risk of injury to any person.'

The regulations go on to state that the person should 'ensure that each appliance to which that duty extends is checked for safety at intervals of not more than 12 months by an employee of a member of a class of persons approved for the time being'.

It has been held that this regulation imposes only criminal and not civil liability and cannot be relied upon by a tenant against a landlord in delict: see *Mackenzie v Aberdeen City Council* (2002) Hous LR 88.

27.26   FIRE REGULATIONS

The Furniture and Furnishings (Fire) (Safety) Regulations 1988, SI 1988/1324 (as amended) are aimed at improving safety by requiring all furniture and furnishings to pass certain flammability tests. Since 1 January 1997 any furniture or furnishings provided in let furnished accommodation has had to comply with the regulations. At present, there is some doubt whether the regulations affect the private individual landlord who lets out his property – for example, if he is going abroad – as they apply only to furniture or furnishings which are 'supplied' in terms of the Consumer Protection Act 1987. Section 46(5) of the 1987 Act defines 'supply' as 'supply ... in the course of a business'.

27.27   LICENSING OF HOUSES IN MULTIPLE OCCUPATION

The Civic Government (Scotland) Act 1982 (Licensing of Houses in Multiple Occupation) Order 2000, SSI 2000/177 introduced a scheme of mandatory licensing for houses in multiple occupancy. Owners of such houses with a certain size threshold are required to obtain a licence from their local authority to allow them to let the house or individual rooms to tenants. This allows the local authority to exercise some form of control over the standard of accommodation in granting a licence. The scheme was introduced in October 2000 for houses with an occupancy threshold of six persons which was reduced to five in October 2001, four in October 2002 and three in October 2003.

PART 5

TRANSMISSION

Chapter 28

Contracts of Sale and Purchase

28.1 Constitution and essential content of the contract

'It is remarkable that there has been no attempt to formulate, in an Act of Parliament, the law on the general subject of sale of Scottish heritable property as has been done in the case of land in England and the sale of goods both in Scotland and in England.' *Green's Encyclopaedia*, Volume 13, para 318. More than 70 years later this remains the position.

The Contracts (Applicable Law) Act 1990, implementing the Convention on the Law applicable to Contractual Obligations (1980), allows parties to select the law applicable to a particular contract or part thereof. It is unlikely, however, that this Act will be used, other than in exceptional circumstances, in any contract relating to the sale and purchase of heritage in Scotland. Subject thereto, contracts for the sale and purchase of heritage are, therefore, governed by the ordinary common law rules of contract. Only the special features of such contracts are dealt with here.

There are three basic requirements:

(1) form and authentication;
(2) content; and
(3) *consensus in idem.*

28.2 FORM AND AUTHENTICATION

Since these are contracts relating to land, they must, under the general rule, be in writing; and they must be bilateral. For a recent case confirming that a verbal agreement to convey heritage is not binding, see *Gawthorpe v Stewart* 2000 GWD 39-1461. There are three recognised forms:

(1) a formal, bilateral contract of sale and purchase executed by the parties;
(2) articles of roup, being the appropriate document for sales by auction and constituting a formal offer which is completed by endorsation of a minute of preference and enactment, binding the purchaser to the purchase. See I J S Talman (ed) *Halliday's Conveyancing Law and Practice in Scotland* (2nd edn, 2 volumes, 1996–97), paras 30-170 to 30.179; and

(3) an exchange of missive letters between seller and purchaser or their respective agents.

Exchange of letters between agents is by far the commonest method.

The foregoing references to formal contracts are, of course, to be read in the context of the Requirements of Writing (Scotland) Act 1995, for which see Chapter 2. Very briefly, the implications are that there must be a written document subscribed by a party or agent but without any further formality of execution. See the 1995 Act, s 1(2) and s 2. Under s 2(2), in the case of missives, several such documents taken together may form the contract. The provisions of s 8 on annexations may also apply.

A unilateral undertaking to convey land may bind the grantor, but will normally be construed merely as an offer, requiring acceptance. See *Haldane v Watson* 1972 SLT (Sh Ct) 8: 'I ... undertake to sell to X the flat occupied by me at (address) for £625, when I vacate the flat.' It was held that this was a mere offer; there was no acceptance, and hence no binding obligation.

28.3   Missives

In the ordinary case, the purchaser's agent submits an offer to purchase, in letter form addressed to the seller's agent and which is accepted by the seller's agent, again by letter addressed to the purchaser's agent. But an offer to sell, followed by an acceptance thereof, is equally competent.

Under the Requirements of Writing (Scotland) Act 1995, a formal contractual document must be subscribed but does not require attestation unless it is intended to be self-proving. In the case of missive letters, all that is now required is the subscription of each letter by the party or agent; and, as stated above, two or more such missive letters can together constitute the contract.

In order to signify that a missive letter is a formal letter, many agents have the signature on the missive letter witnessed, although this is not necessary for formal validity but is merely to highlight the formal letter. Others do not, and the profession is roughly equally divided on this practice.

28.4   Agents

Normally, missive letters pass between agents who may bind the principal, whether purchaser or seller, if the agent has special authority. Under the ordinary rule of agency, a contract by an agent duly authorised on behalf of a disclosed principal binds the principal only, and not the agent; otherwise, the agent is personally bound.

At common law, the agent's special authority need not be in writing; it may be verbal. It is presumed that this rule still applies for contracts signed by an agent notwithstanding the provisions of the Requirements of Writing (Scotland) Act 1995, s 1(2)(a)(i). But note that the agent, when making an offer on behalf of a named principal, warrants his authority, although he does not warrant that his principal is solvent nor that his principal will duly carry out the contract. Accordingly, if an agent makes an offer without due authority, he is personally liable in damages to the offeree; and, of course, cannot recover from his alleged principal. Verbal authority, at a meeting or on the telephone, though competent, is often hard to prove; the agent should normally insist on having authority in writing, from his principal, to avoid incurring personal liability. For a recent case involving, *inter alia*, a disagreement as to whether or not the agents purportedly acting had due authority to do so, see *Hopkinson v Williams* 1993 SLT 907: see Digest of Cases 1.3. In an unusual case, *Glasgow City Council v Peart* 1999 GWD 29-1390, a solicitor signed a letter accepting an offer to sell which had been sent to a client who had since died and it was held that the solicitor had no authority to sign.

In relation to faxes, it was held in *McIntosh v Alam* 1997 Hous LR 141 that missives can be concluded by fax. See also *Merrick Homes Ltd v Duff* 1997 SLT 570, and para 2.3. However, it remains good practice to post a letter after it has been faxed.

If the agent is duly authorised to act generally for either party to the contract, he does not require to seek specific authority in relation to every individual clause therein.

28.5 Formal contract

Under the Requirements of Writing (Scotland) Act 1995, missive letters must be signed to constitute a formal contract.

At common law, a contract made by one or both parties furth of Scotland does not require to comply with the strict Scottish formalities provided that it is valid, in point of form, as a contract for sale and purchase of land, according to the law of the place of execution. For a recent illustration, see *Hamilton v Wakefield* 1992 SCLR 740. There is no express provision in the 1995 Act which allows for this relaxation in formalities. The only reference to deeds executed validly under some other jurisdiction is in the context of registration and does not advance matters one way or another. It is presumed, but only presumed, that the courts would apply the old common law privilege accorded to foreign documents but there is as yet no authority for this proposition. *Halliday's Conveyancing Law and Practice*, para 3–169 takes the opposite view.

Any defect in point of form may be cured by the operation of statutory personal bar: see para 28.10 below.

A formal contract, once duly concluded, cannot subsequently be rescinded or discharged by mere verbal agreement. But a formal written offer, whether to sell or to purchase, may be withdrawn if intimation of the withdrawal is made to the other party before the offer is formally accepted, and, unexpectedly, a mere verbal withdrawal suffices if so made. See *McMillan v Caldwell* 1990 SC 389. As a general rule, any informal agreement, verbal or written, which purportedly adds to or modifies the formal contract, whether entered into before or after conclusion thereof, is normally ineffective and unenforceable. But this may introduce elements of error, lack of consensus, personal bar, innocent or fraudulent misrepresentation, for some of which see below.

28.6   CONTENT

In addition to the formal requirements, the contract must contain two essentials, namely, proper identification of the subjects of sale and a statement of the price. Given these two essentials, the law will supply by implication all the remaining conditions and obligations of seller and purchaser; in practice, many of these conditions and obligations are expressed in the contract in a number of standard supplementary clauses, for which see below.

In an attempt to achieve some element of standardisation in the content of such contracts, and to speed up and simplify the process of completion thereof, the Law Society of Scotland in 1991 suggested standard missive clauses which were revised in a second edition issued in 1992. These were not popular with the profession and were not widely used.

In certain areas, for example Dundee and Inverness, local agents have endeavoured to adopt a common approach to adjusting missives, with some degree of success: see C T Graham 'Standard missives: a success story' 1995 JLSS 142. The Law Society of Scotland's Conveyancing Committee is currently investigating the scope for using *pro forma* offers to sell, incorporating standard conditions of contract. This approach has been encouraged by the Housing Improvement Task Force: see para 28.13 below.

28.7   CONSENSUS IN IDEM

The third requirement, as in any contract, is that the parties should be at one, at least on the main essentials of the contract. Thus, an offer (valid in point of form and content) to purchase heritable property can never be binding on either party if not accepted because, until accepted, there is no competent evidence of consensus and hence no contract. In *Grant v Peter Gauld & Co* 1985 SC 251, a provision in missives to the effect that 'the actual boundaries will be agreed ...' between the parties was held not sufficiently precise to establish consensus. Similarly, an offer to purchase identified heritage but without fixing the price, which is accepted, would not be binding, again, because of want of evident consensus. So, in *MacLeod's Executor v Barr's Trustees* 1989 SC 72, no price was stated and there was no agreed basis for determining the same in the contract. Since there was no evident consensus, the contract was invalid.

The principal application of the rule as to consensus in practice involves the qualified acceptance of an offer. An offer to purchase heritage normally lays down conditions; and others are implied (see below). An unqualified acceptance completes the contract on those conditions. If the acceptor does not agree *de plano* with the whole conditions, express and implied in the offer, he may accept, but subject to qualifying conditions. That acceptance, in turn, binds neither party, unless and until those qualifications are in turn accepted, in proper form, by the original offeror. The acceptance may, in its turn, lay down further qualifying conditions. If so, then again neither party is bound unless and until those qualifications are accepted *de plano*. In practice, a contract of sale and purchase often comprises several missive letters from seller and purchaser (or agents) each qualifying to some extent the previous missive letter. It is only when the final qualification has been accepted *de plano* that the contract is complete; and, to indicate that this point has been reached in a series of missive letters, it is commonplace (although unnecessary) to embody in the final letter a statement that the party 'holds the bargain as concluded'. It is now also usual in the final letter holding the bargain as concluded to specify all the letters which taken together constitute the completed contract. This is desirable as it identifies precisely which letters are included and therefore excludes all other letters which might otherwise be regarded as forming part of the contract. This was less necessary prior to the Requirements of Writing (Scotland) Act 1995 because letters forming part of the contract had to be adopted as holograph or otherwise formalised.

Even the old rule as to consensus and formality of documentation seems to have suffered some measure of relaxation in the decision in *McClymont v McCubbin* 1995 SLT 1248, where it was held that, if the missives did not contain all the matters agreed on between the parties and necessary to a sale and purchase of heritage, the additional omitted matters could be proved and the documentation rectified under the Law Reform (Miscellaneous Provisions) (Scotland) Act 1985, s 8. See further para 29.17 on judicial rectification of defectively expressed documents.

28.8 The effect of a qualified acceptance

In the ordinary case, any qualified acceptance of a previous offer or acceptance falls to be treated, in turn, as a fresh offer. It is then in the option of the other party to accept or reject those conditions. See *Dickson v Blair* (1871) 10 M 41, where an acceptance of an offer contained an additional condition that the seller would not give a search, and that additional condition was never explicitly accepted by the purchaser. It was held that there was no consensus.

The effect of a qualified acceptance on the preceding offer is discussed by Lord Caplan in *Rutterford Ltd v Allied Breweries Ltd* 1990 SLT 249. Lord Caplan held, following the decision in *Wolf & Wolf v Forfar Potato Co* 1984 SLT 100, that the effect of a qualified acceptance was to set up a counter-offer. In *Rutterford*, the purchasers' initial offer was met by a qualified acceptance. The qualifications therein were accepted by the purchaser but subject to further qualifications; and these in turn were subsequently qualified in an exchange of successive formal missive letters culminating in a qualified acceptance by the purchasers of the previous qualifications made by the sellers dated 11 October 1988. Thereafter, an interval occurred during which the parties continued to negotiate by informal correspondence but without any formal modification to the contract. This is just one illustration of the risks above referred to created by the relaxation in the required formalities under the Requirements of Writing (Scotland) Act 1995 and underlines the need for distinguishing between formal contractual documentation and informal negotiation. Finally, in January 1989, the purchasers, in an endeavour to conclude the bargain which had not yet been finalised, purportedly withdrew the qualifications in their letter of 11 October 1988, accepted the prior qualifications made by the sellers in their immediately preceding missive letter and purportedly held the bargain as concluded. Lord Caplan held that this purported acceptance was ineffective. He supports the views expressed by Lord Robertson in the earlier case of *Wolf & Wolf* to the effect that, when an offeree replies by qualified acceptance, he is in effect saying that this is his response to the offer. The focus then shifts to the original offeror who has to consider whether or not he will accept the counter proposals. In the result, on Lord Caplan's view of the matter, supported by earlier authority, every qualified acceptance in effect represents a new offer and the party who made that qualified acceptance is not then free to withdraw it in order to accept the bargain on the terms previously proposed.

The same point was again considered by the Second Division in *Findlater v Maan* 1990 SC 150. Although the facts in that case are more complex, the decision in *Findlater* clearly supports the view above expressed that, in the ordinary way, if a party to a contract makes a qualified acceptance, that is a counter-offer, and the original offer is no longer open to de plano acceptance. Because of the unusual circumstances in *Findlater*, the court held that a valid bargain had been concluded. But it would seem that, in the ordinary case, every qualified acceptance represents a new offer; and, as a result, it is no longer competent for the maker of the qualified acceptance subsequently to withdraw it, and to revert to and accept the original offer.

W W McBryde, in *The Law of Contract in Scotland* (2nd edn, 2001), at para 6.96, takes a somewhat different view of the decision in *Wolf & Wolf*. Certainly the decision in *Rutterford* runs counter to the view previously held within the profession that, if an offer is met by a qualified acceptance, the acceptor is free at a later stage to withdraw the qualification and substitute an unqualified acceptance, thus concluding the bargain. But clearly this can no longer be relied on.

Finally, where an offer is accepted apparently subject to qualifications but where the qualifications simply state explicitly what, in any event, the law would imply, that will be treated as an unqualified acceptance and will conclude the bargain. It is assumed that this rule continues to apply notwithstanding the recent decisions as to qualified acceptance.

28.9 'Subject to contract'

This precautionary phrase is commonplace in England but is not much used in Scotland. The object is to prevent the parties being bound unless and until a formal contract is entered into following on a concluded agreement not intended to be irrevocably binding. The effect in Scotland is not settled. As Lord President Cooper said in *Stobo Ltd v Morrison's (Gowns) Ltd* 1949 SC 184 at 192:

'The only rules of Scots law which it appears to me to be possible to extract from past decisions and general principles are that it is perfectly possible for the parties to an apparent contract to provide that there shall be *locus poeni- tentiae* until the terms of their agreement have been reduced to a formal contract; but that the bare fact that the parties to a completed agreement stipu- late that it shall be embodied in a formal contract does not necessarily import that they are still in the stage of negotiation. In each instance, it is a matter of the construction of the correspondence in the light of the facts proved, or averred, on which side of the borderline the case lies'.

For a comparable case, see *Westren v Millar* (1879) 7 R 173 where a purchaser introduced an element of doubt into an otherwise completed contract by writing 'I will finally arrange it on my return'.

For a discussion of the English situation, see Law Commission Memorandum No 65 'Transfer of Land'. This is a report on 'subject to contract' agreements, where the English practice is discussed in detail and commented on. But the Law Commission concluded that, while the existing procedure had drawbacks, it was based on the sound concept that the buyer should not be bound until he has had full opportunity to obtain legal and other advice, to arrange finance, and to make the necessary inspec- tions, searches and enquiries.

In Scotland, this is all incorporated in the initial contract by appropriate suspensive or resolutive conditions; and, therefore, 'subject to contract' agreements are not gen- erally used.

28.10 Statutory personal bar

The Requirements of Writing (Scotland) Act 1995 introduced a statutory form of per- sonal bar to replace the previous rules on *rei interventus* and homologation. Prior to the 1995 Act, missives required to be attested or adopted as holograph to be valid and any defect in formality might be cured by the operation of *rei interventus* or homolo- gation. See para 28.5 of the sixth edition of this book for details. Under the 1995 Act, the only requirement for validity is that the missives must be in writing and sub- scribed. Under s 1(5) of the 1995 Act, the old rules of *rei interventus* and homologation are replaced by a new statutory form of personal bar.

Where a purported contract for the sale and purchase of heritage has not been con- stituted in writing in terms of the 1995 Act and one of the parties has acted or refrained from acting in reliance on the contract with the knowledge and acquies- cence of the other party to the contract the statutory personal bar will apply under s 1(3). The contract will not be regarded as invalid and the acquiescing party will cannot withdraw from the contract on the ground that it has not been formally con- stituted in writing and signed. Under s 1(4) of the 1995 Act, it is essential that the party wishing to uphold the contract has been affected to a material extent and that party would be adversely affected to a material extent if the other party was allowed to withdraw. Professor Rennie notes in his article 'Statutory Personal Bar: *Rei Interventus* Replaced' (2001) 6 SLPQ 197 that the requirements under the 1995 Act are very similar to Bell's definition of *rei interventus* and that the new statutory provisions require five hurdles to be overcome for the statutory personal bar to operate. These are:

(1) there must be a preceding contract;
(2) the actings or omission to act must be in reliance on the contract;
(3) the actings or omission to act must be with the knowledge and acquiescence of the other party;
(4) the actings or omission to act must result in material consequences;
(5) there must be material consequences if the other party withdraws.

It is still uncertain how the rules in the 1995 Act, s 1(3) and (4) will apply compared with the operation of *rei interventus* under the old rules. Generally speaking, however, the position would not seem to be significantly altered and *rei interventus* is thus preserved more or less in its old form. For a discussion of 'old' and 'new' *rei interventus*, see R Rennie and D J Cusine *The Requirements of Writing* (1995), paras 3.03–3.07.

On the other hand, there seems to have been no intention to re-enact provisions comparable to homologation and, according to Professor Reid, in his annotations to the 1995 Act, it thus disappears as a legal doctrine. While he may be right in this, it does seem possible to figure a case, on the wording of s 1, which would, for practical purposes, fall to be treated as equivalent to homologation under the old rules. Compare Rennie and Cusine, para 3.08.

Much of the case law on *rei interventus* will remain relevant to the new statutory personal bar. It must be noted that it is not clear whether the 1995 Act in abolishing *rei interventus* for the purposes of formality of execution has replaced *rei interventus* for all purposes, or only for the purposes with which the 1995 Act is concerned directly, namely solemnities and informalities in the execution of documents. See Rennie and Cusine, para 3.09, and the sixth edition of this book.

There have been few cases on the 1995 Act provisions. In an unreported case, *Bryce v Marwick* (19 March 1999, unreported), Aberdeen Sheriff Court, discussed by Professor Rennie in his above article, the question of what is required to constitute a preceding contract was discussed. This case supports the view that that the term 'contract' in s 1(3) of the 1995 Act should be given a broad interpretation and not a narrow, technical one.

The requirement that the actings should be in reliance on the contract arose in *Super (Tom) Printing and Supplies Ltd v South Lanarkshire Council* 1999 GWD 31-1496 and 1999 GWD 38-1854. In this case a company entered into negotiations with the Council and a preliminary agreement was reached whereby the company would buy a retail unit from the Council and the Council would buy the company's property. Several months later the terms were varied to allow the company some compensation for the delay by the Council in providing the retail unit. There was no formal written contract. In a subsequent dispute it was argued that there were various actings, particularly in relation to the retail unit which amounted to personal bar under s 1(3) and (4) of the 1995 Act. It was held that to enable personal bar to operate the actings must be referable to the informal contract as varied, not to the original informal contract. As the actings were not so referable there was no personal bar.

28.11 Factors which affect the normal content of missives

In addition to the matters which are essential to the constitution of a valid contract, it is commonplace to include a number of conditions, many of which are in more or less standard form, in order to protect the interest either of the purchaser or of the seller, as the case may be. The reason for inclusion of certain clauses is fairly obvious. Thus, although a date of entry is not strictly necessary, it is clearly desirable that a date of entry should be expressly specified. In the 1980s and early 1990s, it was usual to insert a clause that the unimplemented terms of the missives would remain in force notwithstanding delivery of the disposition to the purchaser, to avoid the rule in *Winston v Patrick* 1980 SC 246 that delivery of the disposition supersedes the missives. It was also usual to insert a clause that the *actio quanti minoris*, the right to retain the subject matter of the purchase and claim damages if it was defective, would be available in the event of a breach of contract by the seller, to avoid the rule that the *actio quanti minoris* is not an implied contract term. These two rules, along with the rule that extrinsic evidence is not generally admissible to prove additional terms of a contract, were referred to as 'Three Bad Rules in Contract Law' by the Scottish Law Commission in its Report No 152, 1996 which led to the Contract (Scotland) Act 1997 which abolished these three rules.

Some comments on the more important factors which give rise to additional conditions commonly included in contracts follow.

28.12 THE RULE OF *CAVEAT EMPTOR*

As mentioned below, the law implies, in a contract of sale and purchase of heritage, that the seller will provide a marketable title. To that extent, the purchaser is therefore protected by implication. Beyond that, it is up to the purchaser to satisfy himself on such matters as the fitness of the subjects for his purpose; the structural condition of all buildings on the property; planning and other statutory matters which may affect the property, its use and its amenity; and the possibility of future developments in the area which may have an adverse effect. There are two ways in which this problem can be dealt with, with a view to protecting the purchaser:

(1) by the inclusion of appropriate conditions in the contract relating to such matters which, if not satisfied, will allow the purchaser to escape from the bargain. The seller may be reluctant to accept clauses of this type, and may reject or qualify

the purchaser's offer accordingly. But in practice such clauses are often accepted; and

(2) by obtaining a survey report in advance of submitting the offer, and by making other relevant enquiries so that, before the purchaser makes his offer, he is satisfied on some or all of the foregoing matters and can therefore make his offer without reference to these items in the contract, relying on the survey report and his own preliminary enquiries.

In the majority of cases, the seller will not accept an offer which is subject to a survey report satisfactory to the purchaser, although this condition is occasionally agreed to in missives. That being so, I J S Talman (ed) *Halliday's Conveyancing Law and Practice in Scotland* (2nd edn, 2 volumes, 1996–97), at para 30.68, suggests that a solicitor, if consulted, should always advise that an independent professional survey be obtained in advance of conclusion of the contract. The purchaser, on the other hand, is often reluctant to incur the expense of an independent survey and may prefer to rely on the survey report of his lending institution if he is obtaining a loan to assist in the purchase.

As Halliday points out in para 30.68, an independent survey will found a claim for damages against the surveyor but only in respect of defects which should have been disclosed and in respect of which no disclaimer is included in the surveyor's report. A report provided for the purchaser's lending institution and relied on by the purchaser may not provide the same degree of protection.

28.13 SURVEY REPORTS

For a useful article explaining the three general types of survey report commonly available and the implications of each of these three reports, see C Slater 'House valuations and surveys' 1988 JLSS 89. For a comment on the liability of a surveyor for negligence in the preparation of a report and on the assessment of damages, see J Blaikie 'Surveyors' negligence' 1986 JLSS 484, discussing the decision in *Martin v Bell-Ingram* 1986 SC 208. See also A D M Forte 'Disclaiming liability for negligence in property surveys' 1986 SLT (News) 293, which discusses the same decision. Note, however, that the Law Reform (Miscellaneous Provisions) (Scotland) Act 1990, s 68 has amended the Unfair Contract Terms Act 1977. The right of a surveyor to exclude or limit liability for negligence by way of a non-contractual notice of disclaimer is now as a result severely restricted and the foregoing references must be read with this amendment in mind. See J M Thomson and others, in their commentary on the 1990 Act, for further details of this amendment

Changes in the way surveys are conducted may arise as a result of the proposals of the Housing Improvement Task Force. This Task Force was set up in December 2000 by the Minister for Communities to undertake a comprehensive review of policy relating to private sector housing in Scotland. The Task Force issued its final report in March 2003. One of the proposals is that a 'purchaser's information pack' be introduced. Such a pack would include a detailed survey of the property, paid for by the seller, the cost of which would be reimbursed by the successful purchaser. See further Swinton (2003) 71 SLG 33. It remains to be seen whether such a scheme will come into operation. It has been indicated that a pilot study requiring provision of a seller's survey will commence in April 2004 in Edinburgh, Glasgow, Dundee and Inverness.

Apart from the question of structural defects, other matters which may affect the property under various statutory controls will be disclosed by enquiries to appropriate authorities, in particular, local councils who issue property certificates on such matters as town and country planning and roads. It is not normal for the purchaser to make enquiries on certain of these matters prior to contract. Instead, protective clauses are normally included in the contract which the seller may or may not accept, with or without qualification.

A number of further cases of negligence by surveyors, actual or alleged, are included in the Digest of Cases under this sub-head. As the decision in *Alliance & Leicester Building Society v J & E Shepherd* 1995 GWD 11-608 discloses, liability in such cases is by no means automatic.

28.14 THE PASSING OF THE RISK

Contrary to popular expectation, the risk of damage or destruction to the property passes to the purchaser immediately on conclusion of the bargain unless the contract contains suspensive conditions which are never purified so that, in the result, there is no contract. See Scottish Law Commission Discussion Paper No 81, *Passing of Risk* (March 1989) and *Report on Passing of Risk* (No 127, 1990), commented on at para 28.42 below.

But the seller has a duty to take reasonable care of the property and appropriate precautions to ensure, as far as possible, that damage does not occur. See *Meehan v Silver* 1972 SLT (Sh Ct) 70.

28.15 TIME OF THE ESSENCE

In contracts of sale and purchase of heritage, time is not of the essence by implication, but can be made of the essence by express provision. It is now standard practice for the seller's solicitor to insist on making time of the essence in relation to payment of the price on, or exceptionally within a short period following, the date of entry. There are circumstances, however, where it is also in the interests of the purchaser that time should be of the essence of the contract; and his solicitor should carefully consider whether or not to make such an express provision. For comment on such express provision, see Lord President Hope in *Visionhire Ltd v Britel Fund Trustees Ltd* 1992 SCLR 236.

28.16   THE NEED FOR EXPRESS PROVISION

All the foregoing rules apply by implication to a contract of sale and purchase of heritage, in the absence of an express provision in the contract varying or excluding any one or more of these rules which would otherwise apply. Such a provision is normally competent and, as indicated below, fairly standard clauses have become commonplace to modify or avoid the effect of some or all of the foregoing rules in the great majority of contracts.

28.17   Effect of conditions in contracts whether suspensive or resolutive

This distinction is not normally significant in contracts of sale and purchase of heritage in that, whether a condition in a contract of sale and purchase is suspensive or resolutive, neither party is bound to proceed with the contract, nor to settle the transaction, unless and until all the conditions have either been implemented or, by agreement, departed from.

For a discussion as to whether a particular condition in a contract is suspensive or resolutive, see *McKay v Leigh Estates (Scotland) Ltd* 1987 GWD 16-609. It is clear from this decision and other cases mentioned in the Digest of Cases at para 28.58 that, whatever the nature of the condition, each party is entitled to expect that the other will act reasonably.

For a case reaffirming this proposition, see *Rockcliffe Estates plc v Co-operative Wholesale Society Ltd* 1994 SLT 592. Lord Maclean at p 595L quotes with approval an earlier decision of Lord Clyde, who states: 'Each party must have intended that the other would act reasonably and I do not consider that it could have been the intention that the purchasers would have been enabled to act arbitrarily or unreasonably in the operation of 'a certain condition'. The condition in the contract in *Rockcliffe Estates* provided that payment would only be made after the purchasers were satisfied with the terms of a lease. The terms 'satisfaction' and 'reasonable satisfaction' and other comparable expressions cause difficulties in a variety of contexts including, in particular, sale and purchase and in construing title conditions and are to be avoided. It is, however, often impossible to avoid such subjective tests. On the requirement to act reasonably, see also *McFadden v Wells* (15 November 1994, unreported), referred to in R R M Paisley and D J Cusine *Unreported Property Cases from the Sheriff Courts*, p 139.

For an unusual case of a resolutive condition still operative after settlement, see *Gilchrist v Payton* 1979 SC 380. Here the property was purchased subject to a condition to the effect that the contract was subject to the seller obtaining approval, for dedication of part of the property, from the Forestry Commission. The application for dedication was then rejected. The purchaser then sought to waive the condition in order to proceed with the bargain, tendering the price in full in exchange for a disposition already delivered. That in itself is very unusual. It was held that the condition relating to dedication was resolutive and the bargain accordingly came to an end automatically when the application for dedication was refused. Therefore, the purchaser was not in a position to waive that condition and to proceed.

In *Park v Morrison Developments Ltd* 1993 GWD 8-571 there were in effect two suspensive conditions. One of these made the contract subject to the acquisition of an adjoining property by a stated date; the other contained a condition as to obtaining planning permission, again by a specified date. Neither condition was purified by the respective dates. Despite arguments on the part of the seller that the conditions had been purified or withdrawn, her claim failed. This case illustrates the general rule and underlines the importance of following up such conditions with formal evidence of purification or failure to purify by the date or dates specified.

In *Khazaka v Drysdale* 1995 SLT 1108 the contract was again conditional upon the obtaining of planning permission by the purchaser who was required to lodge his planning application by a stated date. In addition, if permission was not granted by a later stated date, the purchaser was free to resile or to appeal. The purchaser failed to lodge his application within the period specified and the seller purportedly resiled on that account, arguing that time limits specified in a suspensive condition must be strictly adhered to. That argument was, however, rejected on the footing that the date for lodging the application was not suspensive and was not in itself material. What mattered was whether or not permission was obtained within the stated time. The time limit for lodging the application could, of course, have been made a material condition and of the essence by express provision, and this is usually advisable. Failing such provision, the ultimatum procedure must be adopted if the condition is truly material to the interests of either party.

28.18 EFFECT OF CONDITIONS INSERTED FOR THE BENEFIT OF ONE PARTY

The rule above stated, that neither party is bound to proceed until all conditions are satisfied, suffers this qualification, that a condition inserted in a contract exclusively for the protection or benefit of one of the parties may be waived, unilaterally, by that party even if not purified. If so waived, the contract is then immediately binding on both parties. Clearly, it may be very important to determine which, if any, conditions in a contract can be said to be for the exclusive benefit of the seller or of the purchaser, and therefore capable of being unilaterally waived in this way.

For a discussion and analysis of this problem, see *Ellis & Sons Ltd v Pringle* 1975 SLT 10. The facts in that case were, briefly, that an offer to purchase heritage contained, *inter alia*, the following condition:

'This offer is conditional on our clients obtaining planning permission for the use of the subjects as office premises. Our clients undertake to apply for this as soon as possible'.

The seller accepted the offer, but subject to a qualification allowing the seller to resile from the bargain if planning permission had not been obtained by a certain date.

Before that date arrived, the purchaser unilaterally purported to withdraw the condition in his offer as to planning permission and sought settlement of the contract at the stated date of entry, tendering the price in full. Thereafter, planning permission which had been applied for was refused; and the seller then refused to complete the bargain. The purchaser sued for implement, claiming that the condition as to planning permission was inserted solely for the protection of the purchaser and accordingly that the purchaser was entitled unilaterally to waive that condition and had effectively done so. In argument, the purchaser founded on the earlier case of *Dewar & Finlay Ltd v Blackwood* 1968 SLT 196, where, on a similar set of facts, the court had found in favour of the purchasers.

In *Ellis*, however, the court took the opposite view holding that, in this contract, there was no implied right allowing the purchaser unilaterally to waive the planning condition which could, therefore, only be waived with joint consent. Therefore, the seller was entitled to resile. This view is confirmed indirectly in the decision in *Findlater v Maan* 1990 SLT 465 at p 469.

28.19   CATEGORIES OF CONTRACTUAL CONDITIONS

In the course of his opinion in *Ellis & Sons Ltd v Pringle* 1975 SLT 10, Lord Dunpark classifies contractual conditions in three categories:

(1) conditions which can be waived unilaterally. These are principally conditions which cannot in any circumstances be construed as having been inserted for the benefit of both parties. Examples of these are the normal conditions requiring the seller to provide a good title, which can only be for the benefit of the purchaser. Similarly, an offer made 'subject to surveyor's report on structure' can only be for the benefit and protection of the purchaser. Such conditions can clearly be waived unilaterally by the purchaser. In *Zebmoon Ltd v Akinbrook Investment Developments Ltd* 1988 SLT 146, it was held that a condition can be waived unilaterally if (a) it is conceived solely in the interests of one party; and (b) it is severable and not inextricably connected with other parts of the contract;

(2) conditions which cannot be so waived. These include conditions which, although *ex facie* inserted by one party in his own interests, may also operate incidentally for the benefit of the other. Thus, if one party makes an offer 'subject to formal contract' and this is accepted, the condition as to formal contract affects both parties and cannot be unilaterally waived. A condition of this kind is illustrated in *Manheath Ltd v H J Banks & Co Ltd* 1996 SCLR 100. The condition in that case required planning permission to be obtained within five years. Two days before the five-year period expired, the purchaser intimated to the seller that this suspensive condition had been purified although planning per-

mission had not in fact been granted. The seller rejected these arguments and was upheld; and

(3) borderline cases which include conditions of such a kind that only one of the parties normally would have an interest in that condition but in which the other party may exceptionally have an interest. According to Lord Dunpark, on the facts in *Ellis*, the planning condition fell into this third category and in the circumstances could not be waived by one party. Of course, as he later pointed out in his judgment, it is open to the parties to provide expressly in the contract that a condition may be waived unilaterally by one or other of them; and this is often done. It was not done in this case with the result above stated.

In appropriate cases, both parties should therefore carefully consider whether to include or exclude an express provision permitting one or other party unilaterally to withdraw or waive a particular condition.

In *Burnside v James Harrison (Developers) Ltd* 1989 GWD 11-468, it was held that a provision in a contract, which entitled either party to resile if a certain certificate was not obtained by a specified date, was enforceable strictly according to its terms even although the certificate was in fact later obtained; and that the terms of the missives rendered the ordinary common law ultimatum procedure inapplicable.

28.20 Normal content of a contract of sale and purchase of heritage

For examples, see Styles 30A and 30B in Chapter 30 taken from I J S Talman (ed) *Halliday's Conveyancing Law and Practice in Scotland* (2nd edn, 2 volumes, 1996–97), and the relevant style in the Appendix to this Manual. See also several articles on special matters listed in the Reading List for this chapter. Contracts of sale and purchase of heritage can be considered under the following headings:

(1) identification of the subjects sold;
(2) price;
(3) entry;
(4) title;
(5) servitudes and wayleaves serving the property;
(6) feuduty and other liabilities;
(7) planning and other statutory matters;
(8) contaminated land;
(9) structure and passing of the risk;
(10) contract to remain in full force and effect;
(11) occupancy rights under the Matrimonial Homes (Family Protection) (Scotland) Act 1981;
(12) loan clause;

(13) evidence of compliance;
(14) time of the essence; and
(15) time limit.

We shall consider these matters in turn.

28.21 IDENTIFICATION OF THE SUBJECTS SOLD

A formal 'conveyancing' description is unnecessary, and the barest specification or identification is usual. But care is required here, and a full description, possibly with a plan, is often desirable and sometimes essential. In a great number of cases, particularly in the case of the purchase of a dwellinghouse, postal address alone is used to identify the subject matter of the purchase. There is no objection to this common practice subject to the undernoted comments.

28.22 Doubt as to identity

Where a short description of this kind is used, as is usual, and when a dispute then arises as to what was intended to be sold and purchased, it is competent to refer to prior communings in order to determine the extent and nature of the subjects sold. See *Macdonald v Newall* (1898) 1 F 68, where the subjects were simply described in the contract as 'the property known as The Royal Hotel at Portmahomack ... belonging to Peter Macdonald ...'. The parties subsequently disagreed as to the subject matter of the sale; and extrinsic evidence was admitted to prove the facts.

The true question, where a doubt arises as to the nature and extent of the subjects of sale, is not what the contract says, but rather what the parties thought was being sold and purchased. 'In my view, these negotiations are crucial, and all that passed, either orally or in writing, is admissible in evidence to prove what was in fact the subject of the sale; not to alter the contract, but to identify its subject': Lord Chancellor Loreburn in *Houldsworth v Gordon Cumming* 1910 SC (HL) 49. See also *Martone v Zani* 1992 GWD 32-1903.

This rule, however, cannot be invoked to alter or modify the plain terms of the contract. See *Murray v Cherry* 1980 SLT (Sh Ct) 131.

In *N J and J Macfarlane (Developments) Ltd v MacSween's Trustees* 1999 SLT 619 the subjects of the proposed sale were two workshops, a garage unit with adjoining land and also 'approx 8 ? acres of rough undeveloped land lying to the East of the above property'. It was held that the subjects of the proposed sale were insufficiently identified, the price was insufficiently precise and that there was no contract. See para 28.26 below.

Even if the subjects are not described by particular description in the contract, which is commonplace, there must be *consensus in idem* between seller and purchaser as to what is being sold and purchased. So, in *Grant v Peter Gauld & Co* 1985 SC 251, where the missives provided that 'the actual boundaries will be agreed between the parties', this was held not to be sufficiently precise; and so there was no consensus and therefore no valid contract.

Angus v Bryden 1992 SLT 884 is clearly a borderline case. An offer was made for certain salmon fishings which were described in the offer in fairly detailed terms. The seller in a qualified acceptance deleted the description in the offer entire and, instead, introduced into the missives a description by reference to the titles which clearly, in their terms, included not only fishings in a river but fishings in the sea at the river mouth. The disposition in implement followed that description. Some two years later the seller challenged the terms of the disposition and sought to rectify it on the footing that the sea fishings were included by error. The matter was disposed of at procedure roll without hearing evidence as a matter of plain construction gleaned from the terms of the missives themselves. In the course of his judgment, Lord Cameron usefully reviews the authorities and concludes:

(1) that an unintentional essential error known to and taken advantage of by the other party necessarily implies bad faith; and
(2) that, in the result, the missives and the disposition were not capable of rectification since the purchasers appreciated the error made by the seller in the missives and so could not have intended, when concluding those missives, to agree to purchase the subjects as plainly defined in the missives.

In *Aberdeen Rubber Ltd v Knowles & Sons (Fruiterers) Ltd* 1995 SLT 870, there was a dispute between seller and purchaser as to what was actually intended to be sold. The missives referred to four areas of ground. The disposition purportedly in implement thereof actually conveyed a fifth area. The sellers then raised an action of declarator that the fifth area had never been included in the missives and that the disposition accordingly failed to implement the agreement of the parties. It was held in the Inner House that, since the missives were not challenged by the purchasers, they must prevail over prior communings and accordingly the disposition fell to be reduced to the extent of excluding the fifth area. Again, in the decision in this case, there is a useful review of the earlier authorities on error in consensus. The appeal to the House of Lords was dismissed.

28.23 Separate tenements

Subject to the observations in the preceding paragraph, the rules which apply in interpreting a description in a conveyance, and which make it obligatory to incorporate, expressly, all separate tenements, also apply to contracts for sale and purchase. Therefore, if separate tenements are the subject of sale and purchase, each tenement should be separately specified; this applies, typically, to such rights as salmon fishing. See *McKendrick v Wilson* 1970 SLT (Sh Ct) 39 and para 8.3.

28.24 Fixtures and fittings

In the absence of special provision, it is implied in a sale and purchase of heritage, as in a conveyance, that all corporeal heritable property is included in the subjects of sale and all corporeal moveable property is excluded; therefore, the character of a fixture or fitting, whether heritable or moveable, determines whether or not it is included in the price. But of course parties may (and almost always do) make special contractual provision as to fixtures and fittings.

In practice, under this clause, certain items which in any event are heritable fixtures are often included in the contract by express provision (unnecessarily); and, in addition, a large number of other items, principally in the category of fittings, not being heritable by nature and therefore by implication excluded, are by express provision included in the price. For an exhaustive list of items which may or may not be included in the sale by implication under this general head, see *Green's Encyclopaedia*, Volume 7, paras 361–385 concerning fixtures, and *Halliday's Conveyancing Law and Practice*, paras 30-40.

Items which may require special provision in the ordinary case include television aerials, washing machines, refrigerators, electric and gas fires, and other electric fittings, floor coverings, summerhouses, garden sheds and even keys.

Further, in the case of sale and purchase of business premises, such as hotels, public houses, shops etc or agricultural property, an elaborate clause may be necessary, with a long inventory of items. See *Halliday's Conveyancing Law and Practice*, paras 30-42 and 30-43. It is commonplace, in sale and purchase of business premises, to provide, in addition that certain corporeal moveables, typically furniture, stock, machinery etc shall pass from seller to purchaser at date of entry at a price to be agreed or fixed by valuation. If so, then it should be made clear whether or not the provision is binding on both parties, or optional to both or either of them. The date of take-over should be specified, with a proviso that it is only such items as then exist which are to be purchased, but subject to a proviso that the seller should not unduly increase, nor unduly run down, the stock etc prior to that date.

If the items are to pass at valuation, then additional provisions will have to be made appointing the valuer and providing for payment of his fees.

28.25   PRICE

This is the second essential of the contract. It is normally payable in one sum at the date of entry, in cash; but payment of the price by instalments is not uncommon; and sometimes the price is represented in whole or in part by shares or by some other consideration such as an exchange; and occasionally no price is payable.

Some special points to note in regard to price are as follows.

28.26   Precision

If the price is not expressly stated, the contract must contain a precise provision for the fixing of the price. Otherwise, on this ground, there will be no consensus and therefore no valid contract: see *McLeod's Executor v Barr's Trustees* 1989 SLT 392. Compare *Scottish Wholefoods Collective Warehouse Ltd v Raye Investments Ltd*

1994 SCLR 60. In an option to purchase contained in a lease, 'the current open market price pertaining …' on a specified date was held to be an adequate formula to enable the price to be ascertained.

In *Rockcliffe Estates plc v Co-operative Wholesale Society Ltd* 1994 SLT 592 there was a contract of sale and purchase for a whole portfolio of properties at a single global price. The purchasers were to intimate the individual prices allocated on each individual property for inclusion in the relevant disposition. The contract also permitted the purchasers to withdraw any property from the portfolio if they were not satisfied with the lease or leases relative thereto, in which case the purchase price was to be reduced by the amount so allocated by the purchasers. The purchasers exercised this right by intimating a list of properties which they wished to withdraw from the portfolio; but the sellers refused to complete the sale of the remaining properties on the footing that the price allocated by the purchasers on the properties to be withdrawn was too high. In the subsequent action, it was held that there could be no inference in such a contract that the purchasers would allocate individual prices on a reasonable basis, having regard to market values, since this would be contrary to the express terms of the contract, but that it was an implied term of the contract that the purchasers should act reasonably and not capriciously or arbitrarily in exercising their discretion to withdraw properties. While there may no doubt have been special circumstances in this case and good reasons for conferring these options on the purchasers, greater precision in the method of fixing individual prices and a much more strictly drawn option would normally be desirable.

In *N J and J Macfarlane Ltd v MacSween's Trustees* 1999 SLT 619 the price was to be determined by an arbiter but as there was uncertainty as to whether the proposed sale was subject to tenant's rights and as to the date of entry it was held that there was no proper agreement on an adequate mechanism for fixing the price and therefore no contract. In addition there was insufficient identification of the subject matter: see para 28.22 above.

28.27 Deposits

In Scotland it is unusual, but nevertheless competent, to stipulate for a deposit, except in articles of roup. If there is to be a deposit, then the clause should be carefully framed and should make it clear whether or not the deposit is forfeit absolutely if the purchaser fails to complete: *Commercial Bank v Beal* (1890) 18 R 80.

In *Zemhunt (Holdings) Ltd v Control Securities Ltd* 1992 SC 58 it was held that a deposit will normally be construed as a pledge or guarantee of performance by the purchasers, not simply an advance of part of the purchase price, and accordingly the deposit in this case was forfeited, the purchasers being in material breach of contract. In contrast, in *Inverkip Building Co Ltd v Cityploy Ltd* 1992 GWD 8-433 a purchaser was held entitled to recover a deposit where the contract could not be implemented but the fault was not his. See also *Singh v Cross Entertainments Ltd* 1990 SLT 77.

28.28   Interest on the price

Interest is due by law from the date of entry if the purchaser is in possession and if the price is not then paid. This rule applies, even where the delay is mainly or solely due to the fault of the seller.

There is no legal rate of interest; 5% used to be usual, but this depends on interest rates generally, which fluctuate.

This rule as to interest can be avoided if the purchaser, at the date of taking possession, deposits the whole purchase price in joint names of himself and the seller (or their respective agents). Following on such consignation, the seller is entitled to the deposit receipt interest only. See *Prestwick Cinema Co v Gardiner* 1951 SC 98. As a result, missives now almost invariably include express provision for payment of interest by the purchaser if there is delay in settlement not attributable to the fault of the seller. As to whether or not this interest clause can operate where the seller repudiates the contract because of the purchaser's default, see para 28.72.

In *Bowie v Semple's Executors* 1978 SLT (Sh Ct) 9, the sheriff principal held that a purchaser is not obliged to agree to take entry, and to pay the price or interest thereon, unless and until the seller is in a position to fulfil his part of the bargain by delivering a valid disposition. In such circumstances, if the purchaser in his option prefers to wait until the title is ready, no interest runs between the date of entry and the date of actual settlement. If the purchaser fails to pay the price on the due date through no fault of the seller, the seller's ultimate remedy is to rescind the contract and claim damages. See para 28.72 concerning default by purchasers.

If, however, the transaction proceeds and the price is ultimately paid some time after the due date; and if, in the interim, the seller has retained possession, he cannot claim interest on the unpaid price unless there is an express provision in the missives to that effect. Such a provision is now commonplace. The rule is based on equitable grounds; the seller cannot, in equity, claim to have both the benefit of the property and interest as well. See *Tiffney v Bachurzewski* 1985 SLT 165.

While this rule operates logically enough in a landed estate or commercial property which is let and earning rent, it operates harshly in the case of the ordinary sale and purchase of a dwellinghouse; and, as a result, counter-provision is regularly now made in the acceptance of an offer to purchase, for the protection of the seller.

In *Lloyds Bank plc v Bamberger* 1993 SCLR 727 the purchaser defaulted and the seller sought to recover interest under this clause. The claim failed on the footing that the provision for interest was clearly intended to apply only where the contract was actually to be performed and the price would eventually be paid. The decision is therefore dealt with below in the context of default by the purchaser in a subsequent claim for what was in effect damages. Their claim under this head was rejected on the footing that the interest provision was intended to apply only where the contract was being performed and was therefore inapplicable where the contract had been repudiated. The same decision was reached in *Rapide Enterprises v Midgeley* 1998 SLT 504. For a comparable case, see *Field v Dickinson* 1995 SCLR 1146. The full text of a typical interest clause is included in the rubric of this case and is a useful reference.

It differs in its terms from the clause in *Lloyds Bank* and was clearly intended to circumvent the limitations of the *Lloyds Bank* clause. In contrast to the *Lloyds Bank* decision, however, the purchasers in this case did in fact pay the price although several months after the due date; and the sellers were clearly entitled to interest for that period under this provision since the contract here was in fact implemented. The speciality in this case is that, in addition, the sellers claimed further damages resulting from the delay in payment and were held entitled so to do by the sheriff principal on appeal.

In *Zani v Martone* 1997 SLT 1269 a tenant in occupation of subjects under a lease had an option to purchase as at 9 February 1987 which was duly exercised. The validity of the option was unsuccessfully challenged by the landlord who was ordained to execute and deliver a disposition. He refused and the Clerk of Court subscribed the disposition. The date of entry was therefore 9 February 1987 but the price was not paid until 10 April 1996. In a dispute as to the interest payable it was held that the tenant/purchaser was obliged to pay interest from the date of entry to the date of payment as he was in possession of the subjects. The appropriate rate was deposit receipt rate up to the date of granting of the disposition and thereafter the judicial rate until payment. The negative prescription extinguished interest due more than five years preceding.

When a seller has been in breach and then offers performance, it is not possible for the purchaser to deduct interest payable under the contract. In *Keenan v Aberdeen Slating Co* 2000 SC 81, missives were concluded which provided for entry and vacant possession to be given on 28 March 1995 but payment of the price was postponed to 29 February 1996. Interest was to be paid on the price from the date of entry. It was paid, but the sellers defaulted on their obligation to give full vacant possession which limited the intended use by the purchaser. At settlement he sought to pay the price less the interest already paid. It was held that the full price was due and the remedy of the purchaser was to have withheld payment of interest or claim for damages.

28.29 Price by instalments

Contracts involving payment of the price by instalments over a period of years are now almost unknown. For further information on this now obsolete form of transaction, see 'Sale of Heritage: Price Payable by Instalments' 1968 JLSS 46, and *Reid v Campbell* 1958 SLT (Sh Ct) 45.

28.30 ENTRY

A date of entry is not essential to the constitution of a valid contract: *Sloan's Dairies v Glasgow Corporation* 1977 SC 223, followed in *Gordon District Council v Wimpey Homes Holdings Ltd* 1988 SLT 481. But in practice a date of entry is almost invariably specified. Failing express provision, the Conveyancing (Scotland) Act 1874, s 28 applies; or possibly immediate entry would be implied.

Does 'entry' imply 'vacant possession'? Professor Walker states, in *Principles of Scottish Private Law* (4th edn, 1988), that the seller must give actual possession of the subjects, unless this is excluded by the contract, citing *Heys v Kimball & Morton* (1890) 17 R 381. Admittedly, in that case, 'immediate entry' was so construed; but from the outset, actual possession had been a known and accepted requirement of the purchasers. Elsewhere in *Principles*, Walker states that a title tendered is good notwithstanding leases usual in such a property. J Burns *Conveyancing Practice* (4th edn, 1957) at p 343, suggests that leases are unexceptionable failing express provision. Both refer to *Lothian and Border Farmers v McCutcheon* 1952 SLT 450 as authority (lease not a breach of warrandice). Certainly, express provision in the contract for actual occupation is desirable, if not necessary. For a commentary on the terms 'vacant possession' and 'actual occupation' and their implication when used in missives, see *Stuart v Lort-Phillips* 1976 SLT 39. In *Sinclair-MacDonald v Hiatt* 1987 GWD 7-232 warrandice was held not to warrant vacant possession. However, Professor Reid in 'Good and Marketable Title' 1988 JLSS 162 at 164 takes the view that a purchaser is entitled to rescind if he finds that the property is let, even although there may be no express provision in the contract as to vacant possession. He refers to his article in D J Cusine (ed) *A Scots Conveyancing Miscellany: Essays in Honour of Professor J M Halliday* (1987), where the point is further discussed.

If the property is being purchased subject to tenant's rights, it is normal so to stipulate, and to make further provision: see below.

Care should be taken in the missives differentiating the date of entry from the date of settlement. Otherwise, if the transaction fails to settle on the specified date of entry, there will be problems. See *Spence v W & R Murray (Alford) Ltd* 2002 SLT 918, discussed in Reid and Gretton *Conveyancing 2002* (2003), pp 55–57.

28.31   TITLE

All Scotland is now operational for registration of title: see para 11.16. Prior to this, the contractual position, whether by express provision or by implication at common law, depended on three possible situations. The subjects of sale could be in a non-operational area for land registration, in an operational area with the title already registered in the Land Register or in an operational area without the title registered in the Land Register. Different provisions relating to the title were made in an offer for each of these three situations. Now the latter two only are relevant.

It should be noted that recent statutory developments, such as those relating to contaminated land – see para 28.41 below – have meant that specific provisions to protect the purchaser in such matters are generally included in an offer, in addition to the normal clause providing that a good marketable title will be given. Whether or not, in the absence of specific protective provision for that purpose, a title might be treated as unmarketable by implication where any of the requirements under statutory provisions of this kind are not complied with is a point which has not been decided. That being so, the only safe assumption is that express provision is necessary.

28.32 Good and marketable title

It is implied in any contract of sale and purchase of property that the seller will deliver a valid disposition in favour of the purchaser, and will deliver or exhibit a valid marketable title and clear searches. This implied obligation is normally the subject of express provision in the contract of sale and purchase, usually with a further provision specifying the period of search. See generally an article by Professor Reid called 'Good and Marketable Title' 1988 JLSS 162. The question of 'clear' searches is also dealt with in Chapter 32.

By far the most important question arising under this express or implied obligation on the seller is as to marketable title. A marketable title means a title so clear as to protect the purchaser, not only from actual eviction, but also from the risk of any reasonable challenge; a title which is so regular in form and so correct in all particulars that no one, later dealing with the purchaser on sale or for security, will take any exception to it on any ground. The points summarised under this head are dealt with in the article by Professor Reid referred to above.

This obligation may, of course, be varied by express provision in the contract, of a general or a particular nature. See below for examples. In the absence of any such provision, the rule carries the following implications:

(1) *exclusive and absolute right of property*. Ownership satisfies this requirement; but not a leasehold title, even for a term of 999 years. See *McConnell v Chassels* (1903) 10 SLT 790;

(2) *title to whole and identical property*. It will not suffice to tender a title to practically the whole of the property; and the title tendered must cover the identical property referred to in the missives. On this, the purchaser is absolutely entitled to insist, and his motives are irrelevant. The best illustration is in the case of minerals. In the ordinary way, a conveyance of, or contract to purchase, an area of ground, carries by implication subjacent minerals. But, of course, if minerals have already been severed from the surface, before a sale, the seller's title to the surface does not carry them. In that event, in the absence of special provision in the missives, the title is not marketable and the purchaser is not bound to accept it; and this applies even to urban properties where minerals are not being worked. This longstanding rule was reaffirmed in *Campbell v McCutcheon* 1963 SC 505. Lord President Clyde: 'In such circumstances, in my opinion, the purchaser is not obliged to take something less than he purported to buy and is entitled to withdraw his offer, as he did';

(3) *burdens and conditions*. The purchaser is entitled to the property freed from all unusual burdens and incumbrances affecting the subjects. But much will depend on circumstances. Thus, in the purchase of a vacant lot of ground, an absolute prohibition in the title against building would render it unmarketable. See

Louttit's Trustees v Highland Railway Co (1892) 19 R 791 and *Urquhart v Halden* (1835) 13 S 844.

In *Smith v Soeder* (1895) 23 R 60, a foreign purchaser, acting without legal advice, was held entitled to resile from a contract to purchase a two-storeyed cottage, when he discovered that the titles contained the typical restriction limiting the use of the land to the building of one house only, but also requiring the proprietor thereof not to open up windows in the rear of the house and to leave part of the ground unbuilt on. 'But it can hardly be the law that the purchaser of a house is entitled to resile because the title contains a provision that it shall be used as a private dwellinghouse only': J Burns *Conveyancing Practice* (4th edn, 1957), p 211.

Similarly, in the purchase of a shop, a prohibition against sale of liquor may render the title unmarketable – at least so says Burns *Practice*, p 211, referring to *McConnell v Chassels* (1903) 10 SLT 790; but in that case, the purchaser explicitly stated his intention to apply for a licence, and the seller stipulated for a further payment on his obtaining it.

In *Umar v Murtaza* 1983 SLT (Sh Ct) 79, following on the sale of a shop, the purchasers discovered, on examining the title, that there was a prohibition against the sale of alcohol on the premises. They objected to the title on that ground. The sheriff, quoting from *McConnell*, and following Lord Keith in *Armia Ltd v Daejan Developments Ltd* 1979 SLT 147, held that the seller was bound to disclose all restrictions which might materially diminish the value of the property, except where the purchaser knew or must be deemed to have known of the restrictions. This decision has been severely criticised: see Professor Reid in the article referred to above.

Servitudes affecting the subjects of sale are a narrower case; and it may depend, to some extent, on how burdensome the servitude is. See, typically, *Welsh v Russell* (1894) 21 R 769, where the indications are that a purchaser can object to any adverse servitude right, if it detracts from the value of the subjects and if he was not aware of it when making his offer. See also *Armia Ltd*, where a servitude right of access, ten-feet wide, across the property rendered the title unmarketable.

In *Morris v Ritchie* 1991 GWD 12-712 and 1992 GWD 33-1950, following on a contract of sale and purchase in which no reference was made to a proposed right of access across the subjects of sale, the seller tried to introduce such a right into the disposition in favour of the purchaser who objected thereto, and sought to resile. Lord Clyde held that the objection was properly taken, in that the seller was obliged to disclose any burdens, existing or proposed; and that the purchaser was entitled to rely on the missives and his examination of the titles. On a subsequent proof as to the materiality of the proposed servitude, Lord Kirkwood held that the test to be applied was whether it materially diminished the market value of the subjects, and on the facts held that the purchaser was entitled to resile. In assessing value, it was legitimate to take into account the purchaser's intention to develop the subjects.

This point should, of course, have been specifically provided for in the missives, for which see below.

28.33 Variation of the obligation as to marketable title

There are two ways in which this general rule, whether arising by implication or by express provision in a contract, may be varied or qualified, either by the seller or the purchaser.

28.34 *Express modification in the contract*

This is commonplace and may take various forms. For a more detailed discussion on the implied obligation and express modification thereof, see Professor Reid in 'Good and Marketable Title' 1988 JLSS 162. Typical forms are:

(1) express partial qualification on a particular point, for example that minerals are excluded; or are included in the sale, only in so far as the seller has right and title thereto;

(2) a more general qualification, for example that the property is sold subject to the burdens and conditions in the title deeds. This throws the onus on the purchaser to examine the title for himself and to satisfy himself as to the nature, extent and effect of the burdens therein contained. But it does not protect the seller against adverse rights not disclosed on examination of the title, for example a positive servitude constituted by prescription or by an undisclosed and unrecorded agreement;

(3) a general provision that the purchaser must take the title as it stands; commonly called the *tantum et tale* clause. Such a clause is standard in articles of roup, but may be used in missives, although less commonly. It may or may not be coupled with a clause to the effect that the purchaser has satisfied himself as to the identity, extent and particulars generally and to the burdens and conditions affecting the property in the hands of the seller. The language varies. In its ordinary form, it is implied that the beneficial right of property in the subjects of sale (or at least a substantial portion of them) is vested in the seller; but that any curable defect in the title must be put right at the expense of the purchaser, and that the purchaser must suffer any burdens on the property. If, however, the title proves to be incurably bad, or if the seller is unable to show that he has the substantial beneficial right, the purchaser is entitled to resile. 'But, under some present day contracts, the conditions are wide enough and strict enough to compel the purchaser to proceed, even in the second case': J Burns *Handbook of Conveyancing* (5th edn, 1938), p 180. This proposition is, at best, doubtful, on equitable grounds.

For a typical clause, see Burns *Practice*, p 192. Whatever form the clause may take, a purchaser cannot be barred from objecting to defective stamp duty.

28.35 *Personal bar*

The purchaser may have private knowledge, when making the offer, of a subsisting adverse right. If so, and even if there is no reference to this in the contract, the purchaser is not entitled to require of the seller, when the bargain has been closed, something which the purchaser knew, *ab initio*, that the seller could not give him. See *Mossend Theatre Co v Livingstone* 1930 SC 90, where a purchaser, discovering that minerals were not included in the sale, although this was not referred to in the contract, was held entitled to resile. The main ground of argument between the parties was as to whether the purchaser knew, or could be presumed from circumstances to have known, that minerals were excluded from the sale, because in the district all minerals generally were reserved to the superiors in all previous titles. In this case, the facts and circumstances were not sufficient to impute knowledge to the purchaser. But it is implicit in the decision that, had he known in fact of the mineral reservation, he could not later have taken advantage of that fact after completion of the bargain, but would have been personally barred from resiling.

In *Morris v Ritchie* 1991 GWD 12-712, the purchaser's right to object to a proposed burden not provided for in the missives was challenged on the footing that the purchaser already knew that the seller was under obligation to impose a servitude right of access in the purchaser's title; but, in allowing proof before answer, Lord Clyde excluded the seller's averments on this point, presumably being satisfied that the purchaser had no such knowledge and was not therefore personally barred from raising this objection. The point was not further pursued at the proof in 1992.

For a case involving a complex series of successive transmissions, see *MacDougall v MacDougall's Executors* 1994 SLT 1178. The significant point of that decision is that a purchaser was put on his inquiry by the plain terms of the titles and failed to discharge his obligation to inquire, thereby denying himself the protection afforded to a *bona fide* purchaser for value without notice.

28.36   Property where the title is not yet registered

Not only must the purchaser's solicitor be satisfied as to the validity of the seller's title but, in addition, he must satisfy the Keeper thereon when applying for registration of the purchaser's title. He must therefore make appropriate provisions in the missives and in the settlement obligation to ensure that the Keeper will not take exception to the title; and, in particular, that he will not seek to qualify his indemnity.

The title clause in a transaction of this type will require the seller to deliver a valid disposition and a valid marketable title; and, in addition, the seller will be taken bound to produce such documents and evidence, including a plan, as the Keeper may require to enable him to issue a land certificate containing no exclusion of indemnity and disclosing no entry, deed or diligence prejudicial to the interests of the purchaser other than those for which the purchaser himself is responsible, for example a standard security granted by the purchaser to finance the purchase. See the *Registration of Title Practice Book*, Chapter 5.

The provisions on searches are dealt with in Chapters 32 and 33.

28.37   Property already registered

The sale of property held on a registered title is technically referred to as a dealing. The same general rules apply to a contract for sale and purchase of property on a dealing; but there is of course this significant difference that the seller's title is now represented by a land certificate which, within itself, contains all the information on title including in particular the identification of the property, the ownership thereof, securities affecting the same other than floating charges, and burdens; and all of this information is guaranteed. The title is, nonetheless, subject to overriding interests, some of which may materially affect the interest of the purchaser. This includes servitudes.

Bearing these differences in mind, the seller, in the title clause, will be taken bound to deliver a duly executed disposition in favour of the purchaser and to exhibit or deliver to the purchaser the land certificate containing no exclusion of indemnity; any necessary links in title between the registered proprietor and the seller; and such documents and evidence as the Keeper may require to enable the interest of the purchaser to be registered in place of the seller, again without exclusion of indemnity. As on first registration, it should also be provided expressly that the land certificate to be issued to the purchaser will disclose no entry, deed or diligence prejudicial to the purchaser's interest except such adverse interests as may have been created by the purchaser himself. See the *Registration of Title Practice Book*, Chapter 5.

The title clause makes different provisions in relation to searches. Again, these are dealt with in Chapters 32 and 33.

28.38 SERVITUDES AND WAYLEAVES SERVING THE PROPERTY

In urban property, mains services normally enter the subjects of sale directly from the public road, which requires no special provision. But occasionally, as in *More v Boyle* 1967 SLT (Sh Ct) 38, services pass through adjoining property. If so, it is important that any such services are adequately supported by servitude rights, and express provision may be necessary. See *Murray v Medley* 1973 SLT (Sh Ct) 75. A mains water supply to the part of the property retained by the seller, and passing through the part sold, did not justify a servitude of necessity. So the purchaser was free to remove the pipe and the seller lost his mains water. Without appropriate provision in the contract, a purchaser of the remaining property from the seller might have found himself without mains water and without redress against the seller.

In the case of registered titles, servitude rights serving the registered property may appear in the property section of the land certificate; but remember that, while the Keeper guarantees that rights so entered were originally duly constituted, he does not guarantee that they still remain enforceable. Other servitude rights may not be registered but be overriding interests.

In cases where a servitude was constituted by an unrecorded agreement or by mere prescriptive possession, it may by inadvertence have failed to enter the title sheet on first registration. If the registered proprietor can satisfy the Keeper that any such servitude right has been duly constituted, then the Keeper has power to rectify the title sheets both of the benefited and burdened tenements to give effect to the omitted right. In the case of prescription, the Keeper insists on a court declarator. See the *Registration of Title Practice Book*, para 6.58.

For a cautionary case, see *Watson v Gillespie MacAndrew* 1995 GWD 13-750 where a purchaser claimed damages from his solicitor for failing to warn him of the existence over part of the subjects of purchase of servitude rights of access and wayleaves for electricity and pylons which the purchaser maintained had diminished the value and the development potential of the property.

28.39   FEUDUTY AND OTHER LIABILITIES

Feuduty will be abolished on the appointed day of 28 November 2004 under the Abolition of Feudal Tenure etc (Scotland) Act 2000, s 7: see Chapter 6. Provision in missives dealing with feuduty will continue until then. From the appointed day feuduty will no longer be a relevant consideration in missives. It will be abolished and the superior's right to compensation under Part 3 of the 2000 Act will be a personal debt due by the person who is the vassal immediately before abolition. This will not attach to the land and a person purchasing land after the appointed day has no liability. In addition, any arrears of feuduty will also be separated from the land: see para 8.25. The following comments on feuduty apply until the appointed day.

A reasonable feuduty does not render the title unmarketable. Probably, the same would apply to stipend and standard charge. But again, since 1 September 1974, where feuduties, etc, are allocated, they are automatically redeemed and do not affect the purchaser. Unallocated burdens must be disclosed to render the title marketable.

Apart from these, the occupier of heritage (except dwellinghouses after 31 March 1989 when council tax was introduced) is subject to occupier's rates and in appropriate cases there may also be various other liabilities, not of their nature rendering the title unmarketable. These include, in the case of frontagers within a burgh, liability for the cost of making up and maintaining roads and foot pavements under statutory provision; in the case of tenement property, a proportionate share of the cost of maintaining the roof, main walls and other common items in the tenement; and, in certain cases, a service charge for maintaining common access and parking areas and the like.

The making-up of roads and foot pavements presents particular difficulties. In new residential and other developments, completion certificates for buildings are not withheld by the local authority pending completion of roads and certain other works, for example boundary walls. The buildings are usually completed, and completion certificates therefore issued, some time before the roads and foot pavements have been made up. Normally, the developer will have undertaken to make up the roads in terms of the building contract. Having so undertaken, the developer then sells and dispones the houses, receives the price, and then fails to make up the road and/or becomes bankrupt, leaving individual frontagers directly liable for the cost of making-up, when the local authority issues the relevant statutory notice. So, in the result, the purchasers of individual dwellinghouses in effect pay for the road twice. Under the Roads (Scotland) Act 1984, s 17 the local authority have power to require private developers to provide security, usually in the form of a road bond, to ensure that the roads and foot pavements will be duly completed by the developer. It is important, however, to insist on this in the contract of sale and purchase and to check, on examination of title, that a road bond has in fact been lodged with the local authority under that section.

It is usual, but of course not essential, to specify the exact amount of feuduty payable, if not redeemable; to provide that, apart from the stated feuduty, there are no other charges, annual or otherwise; and to make express provision that the road and foot pavement have been made up and are taken over. If this is done, all these matters become, by express provision, conditions in the contract, and any discrepancy between the contractual and the actual liability entitles the purchaser to resile.

28.40 PLANNING AND OTHER STATUTORY MATTERS

Heritable property may be adversely affected, in a variety of ways, under the Town and Country Planning Acts, Housing Acts, Public Health Acts, and various other Acts dealing with or restraining statutory nuisances: see Chapter 20. None of these things affects the title, as such, and the existence of any of them does not, therefore, render a title unmarketable. Further, except in the case of marketability of title, where certain obligations are implied, a contract of sale and purchase of heritage is not a contract *uberrimae fidei*; and there is no obligation on the seller to disclose any such adverse matter to the purchaser, except under express provision in the contract. Thus, if an offer is made without reference to such statutory matter, the purchaser may later find, after the bargain is closed, that the property is adversely affected by some statutory control.

The maxim *caveat emptor* applies; he is bound to proceed, even although he knew nothing of the existence of any of these matters.

Special clauses may be necessary in special circumstances. A general catch-all clause is generally incorporated to protect the purchaser against most known forms of adverse statutory matter.

In *Hawke v W B Mathers* 1995 SCLR 1004 the contract contained a typical catch-all clause relating to building warrants and the like. On conclusion of the bargain, the sellers then found themselves unable to produce a completion certificate which, as was later discovered, had never in fact been obtained. They tendered, instead, a letter of comfort from the local authority. The purchasers were held entitled to resile, on the footing that a letter of comfort was not sufficient compliance with the terms of this clause. See, for illustration, clause 9 of the offer in Appendix A.

In the case of new buildings, dealt with below, and, equally importantly, in the case of existing buildings where there have been additions, improvements or alterations, planning permission will usually be required as well as a building warrant under the Building (Scotland) Acts 1959 and 1970. The Scottish Parliament recently passed the Building (Scotland) Act 2003 but it will not be brought into force for some time. On this new Act, see A D Anderson 'The End of Letters of Comfort' (2002) 70 SLG 172. In addition, where a building warrant has been issued, a completion certificate is required to certify that the work has been carried out in accordance with the warrant. Again, a general catch-all clause is now usually included in an offer to ensure that the purchaser is not adversely affected by some undisclosed matter of this kind. See D A Johnstone 'Planning and Building Control Warranties' 1989 JLSS 206.

For another cautionary case on the terms of missives, see *Hood v Clarkson* 1995 SLT 98, where the offer contained the normal catch-all clause to the effect that the seller had no knowledge of any intended applications or other notices etc and requiring a certificate from the local authority to that effect. The seller modified that clause to the effect that 'the usual local authority letter will be exhibited prior to the date of entry'. If that letter disclosed any matter materially prejudicial to the purchaser's full enjoyment of the subjects as a dwellinghouse, the purchaser would be entitled to resile. A letter from the local authority in normal terms was duly delivered. Subsequently, it emerged that the authority had previously applied for planning permission to construct a road which would directly affect the subjects of purchase of which the seller was aware. The purchaser sought damages from the seller on the grounds of fraudulent or negligent misrepresentation. His claim failed on the footing that, while the clause in the offer, if unqualified, might have sufficed to support a claim for damages, the qualification of that clause limited the liability of the seller to delivery of 'the usual letter' from the local authority and nothing more. That was held to exclude any question of misrepresentation. While this may seem harsh, it underlines the need for extreme caution in framing protective clauses in the purchaser's offer and in accepting qualifications thereof in the seller's acceptance.

Any such development may also have required the prior consent of the superior or neighbouring proprietors; and it is as well to provide for this expressly in the offer although probably this risk is covered by the marketable title provision, whether express or implied.

Where the purchaser proposes to develop, he must include appropriate clauses in his offer, making it conditional upon the obtaining of planning permission and the necessary consents. The case of *Khazaka v Drysdale* 1995 SLT 1108 underlines the risks. Again, extreme care is required in the drafting of these clauses, as that case shows. Depending on circumstances and location, further enquiries may be necessary. The question of contaminated land is dealt with in more detail in para 20.34. For subsidence risks, see para 9.4.

The Construction (Design and Management) Regulations 1994, SI 1994/3140 are relevant here. See the articles thereon in Greens Property Law Bulletin, Issues 20 and 21 referred to in the Reading List. As the authors of these two articles observe, the regulations will require, in some cases, a change of attitude to health and safety issues on the part of those undertaking projects involving construction work; and this in turn may require special provision in the missives.

28.41 CONTAMINATED LAND

A new regime for dealing with contaminated land came into force in 2000: see para 20.34. This is a new potentially problematic area for conveyancers to deal with and the position on conveyancing procedures to be followed is at an early stage of development. The Law Society of Scotland issued a leaflet on contaminated land in April 2003 and there has been a series of articles in the Journal of the Society advising solicitors on the best course of action when dealing with property which may be affected by contaminated land provisions. See L Lewin 'Commonsense Approach to Contaminated Land' (2003) JLSS Apr/30, K Ross 'Issue of Contaminated Land must be Discussed with Clients' (2003) JLSS May/65 and K Ross 'Prepare the Ground to Stop Contaminated Land Disputes' (2003) JLSS Jun/55. See also K Ross 'Contaminated Land: Advice for Conveyancers' (2003) 71 SLG 141. It is important that provision is made in an offer to protect the purchaser's position. A clause should be inserted to the effect that there are no entries relating to the subjects of the offer in the register maintained by the local authority under the scheme set out in the Environmental Protection Act 1990 and the Contaminated Land (Scotland) Regulations 2000, SSI 2000/178. It should also be stated that no notices have been served by the local authority under the 1990 Act. It is also prudent to provide that there are no entries and no notice has been served in respect of adjacent land relating to matters which might affect the subjects of the offer.

28.42 STRUCTURE AND PASSING OF THE RISK

The question of surveys has already been dealt with, in para 28.13. The offer may be made subject to the obtaining of a survey report in terms satisfactory to the purchaser but this is not normally acceptable to the seller.

In addition and separately, the purchaser, in his offer, now commonly makes a number of provisions to protect himself against unexpected or undisclosed matters. Such provisions vary widely, but may include:

(1) a provision that, so far as the seller is aware, the subjects are not affected by any structural defect, including wet or dry rot, rising damp or woodworm;

(2) a provision that, if there has been any specialist treatment to the building, for example for woodworm or dry rot, and if this is supported by guarantees, that the guarantees with all relevant particulars will be delivered, and the rights thereunder assigned, to the purchaser, and that the guarantees are still valid;

(3) a provision that all services, including drainage, plumbing, gas and electric supply, and the central heating system will be in good working order at the date of entry;

(4) a provision that the seller will be responsible for maintaining the property in good condition and repair until the date of entry, with a right to the purchaser to resile if the subjects are seriously damaged in the interval. For an illustration of resulting difficulties, see *Fallis v Brown* 1987 GWD 13-466;

(5) a provision as to passing of the risk. 'The risk passes with the making of the contract, though the seller remains liable for fault till delivery of possession':

Green's Encyclopaedia following the Latin brocard *periculum rei venditae non-dum traditae est emptoris.* See *Sloan's Dairies Ltd v Glasgow Corporation* 1977 SC 223. The purchaser acquires a *jus ad rem specificam* at the date of completion of the contract; his right of action is an action for delivery, or *ad factum praestandum*, and so the risk of damage passes from seller to purchaser at the date of the contract. The purchaser should therefore insure the subjects of sale immediately on the completion of the bargain. Alternatively, the purchaser may require his interest to be endorsed on the seller's insurance policy as 'purchaser, price unpaid', but this is not always satisfactory.

Notwithstanding this common law rule, however, it is also implied at common law that the seller is personally liable for any damage caused by him to the subjects prior to the date of entry; and he must take reasonable precautions against any such damage occurring. Although not directly in point, see *Bosal Scotland Ltd v Anderson* 1988 GWD 30-1275 and *Meehan v Silver* 1972 SLT (Sh Ct) 70. The Scottish Law Commission, in its *Report on Passing of Risk* (No 127, 1990), makes various recommendations for the alteration of the common law rules. First, they recommend that, if property is destroyed or substantially damaged, the contract should be regarded as frustrated. Secondly, if property is damaged but not substantially, the contract should continue in force but the seller should be under obligation to repair the damage and pass the subjects over to the purchaser in the same condition in which they were when the contract was concluded. Failure by the seller would allow the purchaser certain remedies. Finally, the Commission recommends that parties should be free to contract out of the suggested new rules: see the editorial article in the General News at 1990 SLT (News) 308.

The case of *Hall v McWilliam* 1993 GWD 23-1457 underlines the serious risks arising from the foregoing rules. Following on a contract of sale and purchase of a dwellinghouse and before the date of entry, the house was flooded. The missives contained a precautionary clause to the effect that the dwellinghouse would remain in substantially the same condition as it was at the date of conclusion of the contract. Following the flood, the seller undertook remedial work which was completed by the date of entry but the purchaser then maintained that the house was, nonetheless, no longer in the same condition in terms of the missives, and purportedly resiled. Lord Marnoch held that the provision in the missives was ambiguous but that the ambiguity could be resolved by reference to subsequent correspondence between the parties and on that footing found in favour of the seller. Otherwise, on the missives alone, he would have found for the purchaser.

For a recent case illustrating that care must be taken in drafting a clause dealing with passing of risk, see *Homecare Contracts (Scotland) Ltd v Scottish Midland Co-operative Society Ltd* 1999 GWD 23-111.

28.43   CONTRACT TO REMAIN IN FULL FORCE AND EFFECT

Prior to the Contract (Scotland) Act 1997, it was usual to insert a clause that the missives would remain in force for a certain period notwithstanding delivery of the disposition. This was to avoid the rule in the case of *Winston v Patrick* 1980 SC 246, referred to at para 28.11 above, which was abolished by the 1997 Act, s 2. The usual period specified was two years. For details of the position prior to the 1997 Act, see the sixth edition of this book. The 1997 Act does not alter the period for which obligations in missives remain in force. This is a period of 20 years for obligations directly relating to land until the long negative prescription applies under the Prescription and Limitation (Scotland) Act 1973, s 6 and a period of five years for other obligations. After the 1997 Act, it continues to be the usual practice to make provision for the supersession of missives. The reason for doing this before the 1997 Act was to prevent supersession, whereby any unfulfilled obligations were no longer enforceable, taking place immediately on delivery of the disposition. The reason for doing this after the 1997 Act is to prevent unfulfilled obligations continuing for long after settlement .

The usual period specified is two years. This period was first suggested by Professor Cusine on the ground that by that time the search in a Sasines transaction or the land certificate would have been produced: see D J Cusine *'Winston v Patrick* Revisited—Briefly' 1986 JLSS 16. See also Professor Reid 'Five years on: Living with *Winston v Patrick'* 1986 JLSS 316. A period of two years may not be sufficient, however, as a number of recent cases show. In *Hamilton v Rodwell* 1998 SCLR 418 missives were concluded without disclosure of outstanding unimplemented statutory repair notices. At settlement the parties agreed to a retention on deposit receipt of a sum of £10,500 to enable the repairs to be carried out. There was a non-supersession of missives clause with a time limit of two years. The repairs were carried out within the two-year period but the seller did not pay for them. The purchaser was liable to the local authority under the relevant legislation. After the two-year period had expired the purchaser raised an action to receive the money on deposit receipt. The action failed as the time limit had expired and the money on deposit receipt went to the seller as part of the purchase price. See also *Albatown Ltd v Credential Group Ltd* 2001 GWD 19-738 and *Spence v W & R Murray (Alford) Ltd* 2002 SLT 918.

Care should be taken in ensuring that a period of two years is appropriate for the obligations concerned. Similarly, the wording of such clauses should clearly state when the two-year period is to commence. See *Lonergan v W & P Food Service Ltd* 2002 SLT 908 where the wording of such a clause was held void from uncertainty as to when the period of non-supersession started.

28.44　OCCUPANCY RIGHTS UNDER THE MATRIMONIAL HOMES (FAMILY PROTECTION) (SCOTLAND) ACT 1981

Under the Matrimonial Homes (Family Protection) (Scotland) Act 1981, which came into operation on 1 September 1982, occupancy rights have been created for the benefit of the 'non-entitled spouse' on the break-up of a marriage. In the ordinary case, a 'non-entitled spouse' is a wife where the title stands in name of the husband alone.

Without the protection of the 1981 Act, the husband at common law would be in a position to eject her from the matrimonial home. The purpose of the 1981 Act is to create overriding rights for the benefit of the non-entitled spouse to allow her to remain in occupation of the matrimonial home. These 'occupancy rights' transmit against, and are enforceable in a question with, third parties, whether as purchasers or creditors from the entitled spouse who has the title to the property.

Consistent with that general intention, occupancy rights of a non-entitled spouse are overriding interests for the purposes of registration of title.

Whether the title be recorded in the Register of Sasines or the Land Register, nothing will appear in the Register of Sasines, in the Land Register or in the Personal Register to give warning to third parties of the existence of such occupancy rights. But see the Land Registration (Scotland) Rules 1980, SI 1980/1413, r 5 (as amended). Under this rule, the Keeper will endorse a note on the title sheet that there are no subsisting occupancy rights of spouses of persons formerly entitled, if satisfied that this is so. Such endorsements are covered by indemnity. The Keeper, however, gives no assurance as to the current registered proprietor; and anyone dealing with the registered proprietor must make his own enquiries and take the necessary precautions to ensure that there are no subsisting occupancy rights.

In order to protect the *bona fide* purchaser against the possibility of such occupancy rights, any offer to purchase a dwellinghouse or to lend on heritable security thereon should include a clause dealing with potential rights under the Matrimonial Homes (Family Protection) (Scotland) Act 1981.

Minor amendments were made to the provisions of the 1981 Act by the Law Reform (Miscellaneous Provisions) (Scotland) Acts 1985 and 1990: see para 32.67.

For a recent case dealing with the protection of purchasers where an unentitled spouse has occupancy rights, see *Stevenson v Roy* 2002 SLT 445.

28.45 LOAN CLAUSE

In the great majority of cases of house purchase (and in other cases as well), the purchaser requires a loan to allow him to complete his purchase. Normally, the availability of a loan is established prior to making the offer but occasionally this is not possible, in which case it is prudent to make the offer subject to the purchaser obtaining a loan of an amount and on conditions which are acceptable to him. The seller is unlikely to accept this provision; but it will probably suffice to give the purchaser time to secure his loan before the bargain is concluded.

28.46 EVIDENCE OF COMPLIANCE

It is not sufficient simply to include in the contract provisions on the lines above referred to. All these matters must be followed up and investigated prior to settlement. Otherwise, the purchaser may find himself seriously disadvantaged. To avoid any argument with the seller's solicitors, it is prudent to insert a specific provision, either separately or incorporated in the appropriate clauses, to the effect that, where appropriate, evidence will be produced before settlement to satisfy the purchaser's agents that the relevant provisions have in fact been implemented.

28.47 TIME OF THE ESSENCE

It is not normally in the purchaser's interests that time should be of the essence of the contract, although in certain cases it may be; but it certainly is very much in the interests of the seller in most cases to have a provision of this kind in the contract linked to a provision for payment of interest if the price is not paid at date of entry. Recognising this fact, most agents are now incorporating an appropriate clause in the offer to purchase including an appropriate interest clause. If not included, then the seller's agents will normally incorporate a provision to the effect that at least payment of the purchase price on the date of entry is of the essence of the contract. The clause usually includes specific provisions as to the consequences of default and a provision for payment of interest, at a specified penal rate, to exclude the rule in *Tiffney v Bachurzewski* 1985 SLT 165: see para 28.28.

Note that a clause providing that timeous payment of the price is of the essence applies to that clause only. It may be appropriate to make time of the essence in relation to other clauses also, in which case further express provision is required.

28.48 TIME LIMIT

An offer, when made, remains open for acceptance for a reasonable time or until withdrawn. It is standard practice to incorporate in an offer a time limit within which the offer must be accepted, failing which it falls. This would not normally preclude withdrawal of the offer before expiry of the time limit, but it may be prudent to be specific on this point.

28.49 Special clauses

There are any number of specific circumstances for which special clauses are necessary. Only six typical specialties are mentioned here. A number of other special situations are dealt with in Greens Property Law Bulletin, most of which are noted in the Reading List for this chapter. The six typical specialties concern:

(1) let property;
(2) flats;
(3) new houses;

(4) intended development;
(5) purchase of public sector houses and the right to buy; and
(6) the modernised right to buy.

28.50   LET PROPERTY

Nowadays the purchaser usually stipulates for vacant possession; but quite often let property changes hands. If so, then special provision in the contract is desirable, specifying:

(1) the rent or rents receivable, and the basis of apportionment thereof;
(2) whether or not the property is subject to any statutory controls under the Rent Act, the Housing (Scotland) Act 1988 or the Agricultural Holdings Acts;
(3) the terms of the lease or leases, including duration and landlord's obligations, which may in certain circumstances be quite onerous.

28.51   FLATS

There are two main points here.

(1) *What is included in the purchase?* The starting point is the law of the tenement, which may of course be varied in the titles of each flat. The normal common law rule is that the ground floor flat gets the *solum*, front garden, and the back ground. It is prudent to make this a matter of express stipulation when purchasing a ground floor flat; although on the rule in *Campbell v McCutcheon* 1963 SC 505, involving an undisclosed minerals reservation, an offer for a ground floor flat necessarily includes *solum* and ground. In contrast, there is no general inference that each upper flat carries with it a right in common to the *solum* or to the use of the back green. Cellars and other pertinents should also be separately identified.
(2) *Burdens.* The roof is the most onerous; and if purchasing a top flat, it is very important to stipulate expressly that the property is burdened with a proportionate share only and not the whole of the cost of maintenance of the roof, in terms of the titles.

28.52   NEW HOUSES

In order to counteract gerry-building in new houses, with consequent loss to innocent purchasers, the National House-Building Council extended its operations to Scotland on 7 February 1969. Builders registered with NHBC are subject to a set of rules. The rules of the scheme as originally introduced were substantially altered with effect from 1 January 1980, and again with effect from 1 April 1988 when the current scheme, known as 'Buildmark', was introduced. Since the cover on houses completed before 1 January 1980 has now expired, the rules which operated prior to that date are not dealt with here. The current rules were introduced on 1 January 2003.

The following points should be noted with reference to the Council.

(1) It is a voluntary body, which builders or developers may join; but they are not obliged to do so. In practice, a very large percentage of builders do belong, and almost all new houses for sale or letting are built under the NHBC Scheme.

(2) In Scotland, any house which is less than ten years old and which does not have NHBC or equivalent cover may not qualify for a mortgage unless construction was supervised throughout and is certified by an architect.

(3) A builder's registration with NHBC is conditional upon his implementing certain obligatory conditions, which include:
   (a) that all new houses must conform to NHBC standards, which are laid down in considerable detail. To ensure this, the Council make regular inspection of buildings in course of construction;
   (b) that the builder, when selling a new house to a purchaser, must deliver the NHBC Scheme documents as soon as missives have been concluded;
   (c) that the builder must complete the house according to standards and requirements laid down by the Council.

28.53 The risks

It is perhaps worth summarising very briefly the main areas of risk which a purchaser runs when purchasing new property.

(1) *Purchase of an uncompleted dwellinghouse.* There are two possibilities here. Where there is a contract but no title, and deposits or other payments have been made, the purchaser may lose the whole or at least part of these payments because of supervening insolvency of the builder; and will be denied the benefit of the property, which will be disposed of by the liquidator, receiver or trustee in sequestration for the benefit of the creditors. Alternatively, where the purchaser has a title, he will not lose the property; but will be left with an uncompleted building, partly paid for, which, in the nature of things, will cost more to complete (by employing another builder) than on the original contract.

(2) *Condition of dwellinghouse after completion and payment.* The building may turn out to be defective in that:
   (a) minor defects may show up within a short period after completion which were not evident at completion date; and/or
   (b) major structural defects may develop, possibly a considerable time after completion;
   and in either event, for whatever reason (including insolvency) the builder may be unable or unwilling to put matters right.

28.54   Cover under the NHBC Scheme

The principal point which concerns the solicitor in relation to the scheme is whether the purchaser is covered. The essential conditions are:

(1) The cover extends to new dwellinghouses completed less than ten years ago. This includes detached, semi-detached and flatted houses; with garage, boundary and retaining walls, internal footpaths and drains.

   The Scheme did not originally cover converted or sub-divided dwellinghouses or additions or alterations to houses whether already covered under the Scheme or not; and it only covers commercial property in very limited circumstances (generally where the commercial property forms part of the same building as the residential units). It has, however, since been extended to cover conversions and renewals on comparable terms to those for new dwellinghouses.

   The Scheme does not cover roads and footpaths *ex adverso*, and amenity areas, even if the builder is under obligation to complete these as part of the contract. Until comparatively recently, road bonds, in the form of an insurance company guarantee, were commonly used to ensure that the builder did complete the work; or, if not, that money was made available for its completion. Road bonds are now commonly rendered unnecessary by the Roads (Scotland) Act 1984, s 17, and regulations made thereunder, in terms of which security in the form of a road bond or deposit must be given to the road authority; and work should not start on the construction of a private dwellinghouse until such security has been provided. But the position should be checked with the local authority:

(2) Before the introduction of Buildmark, only private purchasers, if acquiring for their own occupation, were covered; but the benefit of the protection transmitted to singular successors of the first purchaser without any special assignation or otherwise. Under the new Buildmark scheme as from 1 April 1988, every purchaser is protected without any exclusions, and 'purchaser' means the first purchaser, each subsequent purchaser and any heritable creditor in possession of the house. In either case, however, the second (and any subsequent) purchaser can only claim for defects which first emerge after the second purchaser acquired the house. The second (or subsequent) purchaser has no rights in respect of patent or known defects which either should have been reported to the NHBC or should have shown up on a survey.

(3) The purchaser must have entered into a binding contract with the builder or developer. So, deposits before missives are completed are not covered.

(4) Under the old rules, the purchaser must also have entered into the House Purchaser's Agreement. The 1988 changes in the rules removed this requirement by dispensing with the House Purchaser's Agreement.

(5) For structural defect claims, the notice of insurance cover/ten year notice must have been issued to the purchaser.

28.55   Documentation

Under the Buildmark scheme, introduced as from 1 April 1988, the documents comprise:

(1) *the offer of cover*. This is the offer by the builder and the NHBC to the purchaser of the house of the protection set out in the Buildmark booklet;

(2) *the acceptance*. The purchaser accepts the offer of cover by completing the acceptance and returning it to the NHBC;

(3) *the NHBC Guide*. This document is issued to the purchaser for information. It is not part of the Buildmark insurance cover, but it does include useful information and advice to the purchaser;

(4) *the ten-year notice of insurance cover* (known as the insurance certificate since 1 April 1999). This is issued by the NHBC in duplicate to the purchaser's solicitor once the acceptance of cover has been received by it and the house has been completed. One copy is intended for the purchaser and one for his lender.

The new documentation is intended to simplify and improve the procedures for obtaining the cover afforded under the scheme. The documents (with the exception of the lender's copy of the certificate) must be passed to the purchaser.

28.56   The cover provided

The main cover provided by the policy, against the risks above referred to, includes the following:

(1) loss *before* the issue of the notice of insurance cover. This normally means loss to the purchaser before the building is actually completed.
The purchaser is indemnified against the consequences of the insolvency of the builder, to a maximum limit of £10,000 or 10% of the original purchase price, whichever is the greater;

(2) loss *after* the issue of the notice of insurance cover. There are two separate provisions.

   (a) The initial guarantee period, which is two years from the date of the issue of the notice of insurance cover. During this period, the purchaser deals directly with the builder and requires the builder to remedy defects. But if the builder fails to satisfy the purchaser and the dispute goes to court or arbitration, the NHBC undertake to implement any arbitration award.

   (b) The structural guarantee period, which is after two years but within ten years of completion of the dwellinghouse. During this period, the NHBC undertake to pay to the purchaser the cost, for dwellinghouses registered for cover prior to 31 March 1999, of remedying any major structural defect or subsidence and resulting damage. For dwellinghouses registered from 1 April 1999, the insurance covers a list of defined defects subject to a minimum claim value of £500. The minimum claim value is index linked and increases over the life of the cover.

The Scheme is subject to certain limits on liability but these are now inflation-proofed automatically and increase as average building costs increase.

No special provisions are required in a contract of sale and purchase either to ensure the issue of the Council's ten-year notice or insurance certificate or to ensure its transmission. The only point of enquiry is, prior to the contract, to ascertain whether or not the builder is registered with the Council. If he is, then all the foregoing automatically follows. If he is not, then comparable provisions must be introduced into the contract in lieu. The terms of the NHBC documents can be used as a style for suitable clauses in a contract with an unregistered builder.

28.57   Earlier arrangements

As mentioned above, there are certain limits on the liability incurred by the NHBC. This has always been so. Due to inflation, the cover provided under earlier NHBC certificates got out of line with the cost of repairs. As from 31 March 1979, however, inflation proof cover has been provided as part of the Scheme.

The extent of the cover against defects under the NHBC scheme is discussed in *Cormack v NHBC* 1997 GWD 24-1218.

28.58   INTENDED DEVELOPMENT

Very often, the purchaser has in mind, at the time of his purchase, some immediate or early development. He may be frustrated in two ways.

28.59   Restrictions in the title

It is normal to stipulate in the offer that the property is free of any title conditions; or at least any which would effectively prevent the proposed use. Normally, the seller will place the onus on the purchaser by stipulating that, at least quoad burdens, the purchaser must take the title as it stands. But at least the purchaser then gets the chance to see what the restrictions are. He may then have to stipulate that the offer is subject to the requisite waivers.

The wording in these clauses requires some care: see the Inner House decision in *Armia Ltd v Daejan Developments Ltd* 1979 SLT 147, referred to at para 28.32. In that case there was a condition in an offer in these terms: 'There is nothing in the titles of the said subjects which will prevent demolition and redevelopment'. On subsequent examination of the title, it turned out that the property was burdened by a servitude of access for adjoining subjects, a building restriction, and a right to build an external stair for the benefit of the adjoining property. In the Outer House in *Armia Ltd* reported at 1977 SLT (Notes) 9, Lord Wylie held that the existence of these restrictions on title did not constitute a breach of this condition, because demolition and some redevelopment was possible. Redevelopment of the whole site was excluded by the servitude and conditions; but the clause in the contract did not specify redevelopment of the whole. But, on appeal, the House of Lords held the title to be unmarketable, and the purchaser was free to resile.

28.60 Planning permission and building committee approval

Almost all development (including change of use) is subject to planning permission; and any structural work is subject to building regulations. Special restrictions are imposed on listed buildings. There may also be, in special cases, additional special requirements, for example the fire authorities for various types of property, and special needs under the licensing laws, for public houses. See generally Chapter 20. If planning and other permissions cannot be obtained prior to the making of the offer, then the contract must be subject to the obtaining of these consents. Otherwise, the purchaser runs the risk of finding himself committed to a purchase of property which he cannot use for the proposed development.

The special problem of making up roads and foot pavements is dealt with in para 28.39 and must not be overlooked.

Any development involving access on to, or an alteration to, a public road or footpath will normally require special permission.

Often the clause includes a provision that the permission is to be to the purchaser's entire satisfaction. A phrase on these lines is frequently used in such clauses and is often intended by the purchaser as an escape clause which will allow him to resile from the bargain for reasons unconnected with the planning permission but ostensibly on the footing that he is dissatisfied therewith. For a typical illustration of such a situation see *Gordon District Council v Wimpey Homes Holdings Ltd* 1988 SLT 481, and at 1989 SLT 141, although, in that case, the clause did not include the word 'entire'. The seller sought to hold the purchaser to his bargain on the footing that, although dissatisfied, he was acting unreasonably. Lord Clyde held that, as a matter of construction, each party must have intended that the other would act reasonably; and a decision not to develop for reasons unconnected with the planning permission would not suffice to allow the purchaser to escape from his bargain. But, on the facts in this case, he came to the view that a developer could reasonably declare that he was dissatisfied with the conditions imposed in the planning permission and, on that ground, was not obliged to proceed.

See also *McKay v Leigh Estates (Scotland) Ltd* 1987 GWD 16-609. The missives contained a condition that the purchaser should receive a satisfactory report on the suitability of the ground for development. The purchaser subsequently resiled on the basis that the engineer's report of ground conditions was unsatisfactory; but, in fact, no trial pit investigation had been carried out. Held that the purchaser was under a duty first to obtain a report which justified terminating the contract before he could competently do so.

The question of acting reasonably is again discussed in *John H Wyllie v Ryan Industrial Fuels Ltd* 1989 SLT 302. Lord Milligan, in that case, took the view that each party intended that the other would act reasonably.

28.61   PURCHASE OF PUBLIC SECTOR HOUSES AND THE RIGHT TO BUY

The Housing (Scotland) Act 1987, principally ss 61 to 84, gives almost all secure tenants of public landlords the right to buy their homes at varying discounts on their market value, with the power to enforce that right by application to the Lands Tribunal. The 1987 Act consolidated the previous legislation which commenced with the Tenants' Rights etc (Scotland) Act 1980. Significant changes to this right to buy scheme under the 1987 Act, as amended, were introduced under Part 2 of the Housing (Scotland) Act 2001.

The right to buy is set out in s 61 of the 1987 Act, as amended by s 43 of the 2001 Act. It now extends to virtually all public sector secure tenants including those who are tenants of local authorities, housing associations and registered social landlords. It excludes co-operative housing associations, registered social landlords which are charities and housing designed for people with special needs. There is a limitation on the right to buy from a registered social landlord, as s 44 of the 2001 Act adds a new s 61A to the 1987 Act which provides that for new Scottish secure tenancies the right to buy does not apply for ten years unless waived by the landlord and enables the landlord to apply to the Scottish Ministers to extend the period.

The 2001 Act introduced new provisions imposing limitations on the right to buy in ss 45 to 47. These sections add new sections 61B, 61C and 61D to the 1987 Act. Under s 61B a local authority can request an area be designated a pressured area by Scottish Ministers for a period up to five years. The intention is that this will apply to areas where there is pressure on housing resources and where so designated the right to buy will not operate. Under s 61C an application to buy can be refused where the tenant is in arrears of rent, council tax or water or sewerage charges and under s 61D the right to buy can be suspended where the landlord raises proceedings for recovery of possession due to the tenant's adverse conduct.

The new provisions in the 2001 Act are known as 'The Modernised Right to Buy.' However, as these are less generous than the previous provisions, the Scottish Executive has introduced a statutory instrument, the Housing (Scotland) Act 2001 (Scottish Secure Tenancy etc) Order 2002, SSI 2002/318. This preserves the right to buy provisions in respect of the calculation of discount under the old system for tenants who became tenants prior to 30 September 2002. The effect of this is that there are now two parallel systems operated by local authorities: the old system where the right to buy legislation was significantly more generous, allowing discounts up to 70%, and The Modernised Right to Buy. The following paragraphs relate to The Modernised Right to Buy only. Where a tenancy was created prior to 30 September 2002, reference should be made to the Housing (Scotland) Act 1987 as amended by the Housing (Scotland) Act 2001.

In order to have the right to buy, tenants must have a secure tenancy, the house being let as a separate dwelling and the tenant being an individual and having the house as his only and principal home (s 44 of the 1987 Act). The term 'house' (s 338 of the 1987 Act) includes any part of a building occupied or intended to be occupied as a separate dwelling and any land, outhouses and pertinents let therewith.

28.62 THE MODERNISED RIGHT TO BUY

We shall consider this under the following five headings.

28.63 Application to purchase

In order to exercise his right to buy, a tenant must complete and serve on his landlord an application to purchase in the prescribed form: see the Housing (Scotland) Act 1987, s 63. When the application is served, this becomes 'the relevant date' both for a strict statutory timetable and for valuation of the house.

A secure tenant must have been in continuous occupation of a house or a succession of houses provided by certain public landlords for at least five years prior to the date of service of his application to purchase: see the 1987 Act, s 61(2), (10) and (11) (as amended by the Housing (Scotland) Act 2001, s 44). He may exercise the right to purchase with one or more members of his family acting as joint purchasers if they are at least 18 years of age and have had their only and principal home with the tenant for six months prior to the date of application to purchase.

28.64 Notice of refusal

Where a landlord disputes a tenant's right to purchase a house, he must serve a notice of refusal within one month of the relevant date. If the landlord is of the opinion the information in the application is incorrect the tenant must be given reasonable opportunity to amend it, within two months.

28.65 Valuation

The house is valued either by a qualified valuer nominated by the landlord, if accepted by the tenant, or the district valuer as the landlord thinks fit, on the basis that the house is available for sale on the open market with vacant possession at the relevant date. In order to ascertain the price, however, a discount is deducted from the valuation. The discount normally represents a minimum of 20% of the valuation rising by 1% per year for each year beyond five of continuous relevant occupation to a maximum of 35% or £15,000, whichever is less.

28.66 Offer to sell

The landlord must serve on the tenant a notice ('offer to sell') within two months of the relevant date, assuming no notice of refusal has been served. The conditions of sale of the house must ensure that the tenant has as full enjoyment and use of the house as owner as he has had as tenant and must include such additional rights as are necessary for the tenant's reasonable enjoyment and use of the house as owner, for example common rights. See the Housing (Scotland) Act 1987, s 64(1).

If the tenant is unhappy about the terms of the offer he must make a request to the landlord in writing to strike out or vary the conditions or include a new condition within one month of the service of the offer to sell; and, if the landlord agrees, he must serve an amended offer to sell within one month of the service of the request. If the landlord refuses to accede to the request or is dilatory in serving such an amended offer or has not served an offer, the tenant may refer the matter to the Lands Tribunal within one month of the refusal or failure (or two months with the landlord's consent) for determination. The Lands Tribunal has power to order the service of the offer or an amended offer on the tenant if it thinks fit.

If the tenant does not dispute the terms of the offer or such dispute has been resolved, he must serve a notice of acceptance on the landlord within two months of service of the offer to sell or the amended offer as the case may be. See s 66 of the 1987 Act.

28.67   Repayment of discount

There is a liability to repay the discount in whole or part to the landlord if the house or part thereof is sold before the expiry of three years from the date of service of the notice of acceptance by the tenant under s 72 of the Housing (Scotland) Act 1987. The exceptions to this are:

(1) a disposal from one of the original purchasers to another;
(2) where the remainder of the house continues to be the only or principal home of the seller;
(3) a disposal by the deceased owner's executor acting in that capacity: see *Clydebank District Council v Keeper of the Registers of Scotland* 1994 SLT (Lands Tr) 2. But problems still remain in Sasines titles: see D J Cusine 'The Right-to-Buy Legislation: Sales by Executors' 1991 JLSS 186;
(4) a disposal as a result of a compulsory purchase order; and
(5) a disposal to a member of the owner's family who has lived with him for 12 months before the disposal and is for no consideration, provided that if the disponee disposes of the house before the end of the three-year period it is treated as a first disposal and he as the original purchaser. The discount repayable in the event of a sale not falling within the exceptions is 100% in the first year, 66% in the second and 33% in the third and nothing thereafter. The landlord can secure the liability to make repayment by a standard security but it is ranked postponed to any security granted for the purchase or improvement of the house, but not a security for any other loan unless the landlord consents.

If the house is sold within the three-year period a discharge will be required but, if it is sold outwith the same, the Law Society of Scotland recommends that provision is made in the re-sale missives to cover the point concerning the discount standard security appearing in the search undischarged. Under the former legislation, the period during which discount was repayable was five years. Therefore if the house was bought before 7 January 1987 the record will show a five-year discount standard security. The Housing (Scotland) Act 1986, s 23 (not repealed or consolidated) provides that the reduced three-year period will apply retrospectively and therefore no repayment or discharge would be required though it may be a matter of convenience to obtain a suitable discharge from the landlord to clear the record in the circumstances.

28.68 Resulting obligations of seller and purchaser

In the absence of special provision in the contract, or to the extent to which special provision is not made, both parties come under certain obligations.

28.69 SELLER'S OBLIGATIONS

The seller's obligations are:

(1) to deliver or exhibit a good and marketable title which complies with the provisions of the missives. In transactions which induce first registration, the seller is normally under an obligation to provide a good marketable title which implies a valid prescriptive progress of titles to the whole and identical property included in the missives. It also means that the seller must satisfy the purchaser on all matters expressly, or by implication, dealt with in the contract in relation to title. If, on examination of the title, the purchaser finds some fault with it, then he is entitled at the seller's expense, to have any such doubt in the title cleared to the extent of an Outer House judgment; but the normal rule as to expenses would apply on appeal. See Professor K G C Reid 'Good and Marketable Title' 1988 JLSS 162.

In transactions where the title has already been registered, ie in the case of a dealing, the seller will normally be under obligation in the missives to produce a land certificate which discloses no exclusion of indemnity. Here, examination of title is substantially simplified in that the land certificate is complete and self-contained and guaranteed; but of course it must still be examined to ensure, in particular, that there are no outstanding securities and that the burdens as set out in the burdens section are all acceptable to the purchaser in terms of the missives. In addition, it has to be borne in mind that every registered title is subject to overriding interests and these, particularly servitudes and public rights of way, may be objectionable as being contrary to provisions in the missives;

(2) to give possession. Further, the seller must tender title and possession timeously.

This does not mean that, if title or possession is not available on the actual date of entry, the seller is automatically in default. In *Heys v Kimball & Morton* (1890) 17 R 381 the term 'immediate entry' in a contract was held to mean such early possession as is practicable; and possession tendered four days after the contract date did not put the seller in breach. In the ordinary case, the seller must be given reasonable time to implement his obligation, which of course depends on circumstances. But time may be made the essence of the contract, either expressly or by implication, in which case the purchaser is then entitled to insist on title and possession on the due date, failing which the seller is immediately in breach.

In *Stuart v Lort-Phillips* 1976 SLT 39, following on an offer to purchase with actual occupation, failure to give vacant possession timeously to seven acres out of a total of 21 acres purchased under the missives was held to be a material breach of contract, entitling the purchaser to resile, even although the occupant apparently had no legal right or title to be there. The date of entry in the contract was 16 January 1974; and the purchaser intimated his intention to resile on 26 March 1974. There is no suggestion in the report that the seller should have been given time to secure the eviction of the occupant, notwithstanding Lord Stott's comment, on the strength of English authority, that it was for the seller to eject the third party 'before completion';

(3) to deliver a valid disposition in favour of the purchaser or his nominees, containing absolute warrandice. Note, however, that absolute warrandice is not, in any circumstances, an alternative or substitute for marketable title;

(4) to deliver or exhibit clear searches (see paras 32.17 ff); and

(5) to implement any other special obligations in the contract, for example to exhibit planning permission.

In *Davidson v Tilburg Ltd* 1991 GWD 2-115 and 1991 GWD 18-1109 the court held that a purchaser could not be compelled to settle except in exchange for delivery of a valid disposition; and his refusal to settle on this ground did not entitle the sellers to resile, notwithstanding express provisions in the missives which, arguably, gave them the right. This follows *Bowie v Semple's Executors* 1978 SLT (Sh Ct) 9. If the title is defective, the seller cannot compel the purchaser to settle on the footing that the seller will grant absolute warrandice. Likewise, the seller cannot insist on settlement in such circumstances by providing a property title indemnity unless the purchaser agrees. The defect in title must first be cured unless the purchaser otherwise agrees.

28.70   PURCHASER'S OBLIGATIONS

The purchaser's obligations are:

(1) to pay the purchase price on the due date; but see *Bowie v Semple's Executors* 1978 SLT (Sh Ct) 9 and *Davidson v Tilburg Ltd* 1991 GWD 2-115 and 1991 GWD 18-1109; and

(2) to implement any other special obligations in the contract, for example to obtain planning permission within a time limit.

28.71 Breach of contract

Where the transaction has not yet settled and where, as a result, *restitutio in integrum* is almost always possible, both seller and purchaser have the alternative remedies of an action for implement, or rescission and damages. But the court will not order implement in circumstances where implement is clearly impossible; and, in such cases, the only effective remedy is to rescind and claim damages.

Where *restitutio in integrum* is no longer possible, neither party can rescind because *restitutio* is an essential pre-requisite for rescission. Accordingly, if *restitutio in integrum* has become impossible (for which see below) then the remedy is specific implement, if that is practicable; or damages. The entitlement to damages depends on various factors discussed elsewhere in this chapter. It has also been possible since 21 June 1997, when the provisions of the Contract (Scotland) Act 1997 came into force, for a purchaser to retain the subjects and sue for damages under the *actio quanti minoris.*

28.72 DEFAULT BY THE PURCHASER

This normally only arises before settlement of the transaction, while *restitutio in integrum* is normally still possible. In almost all such cases, it takes the form of failure or refusal by the purchaser to pay the price. The seller may either:

(1) sue for implement, by an action for payment of the purchase price in exchange for which the seller tenders a disposition; or
(2) rescind the contract, following on which the seller is free to resell the property at the best price obtainable and thereafter may sue for damages, which will include the difference between the original and the resale price, plus expenses etc.

If the seller decides to rescind the contract and claim damages, he must proceed with caution for two reasons.

28.73 The ultimatum rule

Unless the contract otherwise expressly provides, time is not of the essence; and, therefore, failure by the purchaser to pay the purchase price on the due date does not entitle the seller immediately to rescind. Instead, the seller must give notice that, if the price is not paid within the period of notice, then he will hold the purchaser in breach: see *Rodger (Builders) Ltd v Fawdry* 1950 SC 483. Under missives, the price was payable on 11 November but the purchaser was not ready to settle on that date.

On 25 November, the seller's agents gave an ultimatum, requiring payment of the price by 28 November, which was not forthcoming. On 28 November, purporting to rescind, the seller entered into a second contract of sale. (In fact, the purchase price was available on 29 November.) Held that the seller had acted too precipitately, and was not entitled to rescind on such short notice.

The 'ultimatum rule' applies to any obligation in a contract of sale and purchase, whether that obligation falls to be implemented by the purchaser or by the seller, if the party has it in his own power to implement that condition or not as he chooses, but has unnecessarily, or unjustifiably, delayed or refused to implement it. In such cases, time is not of the essence of the contract unless the contract otherwise expressly provides. So, an ultimatum must be given by the aggrieved party and must expire before he is in a position to rescind. For a discussion on provisions making time expressly of the essence, see Lord President Hope in *Visionhire Ltd v Britel Fund Trustees Ltd* 1992 SCLR 236.

Not surprisingly, there is no definitive ruling as to the length of notice required under the ultimatum rule. In *Rodger (Builders) Ltd v Fawdry* 1950 SC 483, three days' notice was held to be too short, but Lord Sorn observed that, provided the time limit is a reasonable one in the circumstances, failure to pay within that time will be treated as entitling the seller to rescind.

In *Johnstone v Harris* 1977 SC 365, after a period of several months during which the parties litigated, the sheriff finally fixed a period of six weeks within which the price should be payable. This is at least a guide as to what might be thought by the court to be a reasonable period of notice.

In *Inveresk Paper Co Ltd v Pembury Machinery Co Ltd* 1972 SLT (Notes) 63, the purchaser failed to pay the price for a long period after the stipulated date. The seller did not, however, give any formal intimation that failure to pay within a reasonable time would be treated as breach. In the absence of that ultimatum, the seller was held not entitled to rescind the contract.

In *Toynar Ltd v R & A Properties (Fife) Ltd* 1989 GWD 2-82, the missives stipulated that, failing payment on the due date, the seller would have the option 'immediately thereafter' to resile. Six weeks elapsed after the due date without payment; and, after sundry communings, the seller was held entitled to resile. 'Immediately thereafter' qualified the option; it did not require the seller to resile at once. In *Atlas Assurance Co Ltd v Dollar Land Holdings plc* 1993 SLT 892 the purchaser claimed that, by delay in enforcing the contract, the seller had waived or abandoned his right to resile on account of non-payment; but the claim was rejected in the circumstances.

In contrast, in *Packman & Sons v Dunbar's Trustees* 1977 SLT 140, where a long period had elapsed since the date of entry, Lord Stott expressed the view that the seller was entitled to resile without notice; and was not bound first to impose on the purchasers a time limit for performance.

If, however, neither party is at fault, and if the fulfilment of a condition in the contract depends not on the seller or purchaser but on a third party or on extraneous circumstances, the ultimatum rule is not appropriate. Instead, the rule seems to be that such conditions must be implemented either: (1) before the date specified in the contract by which the condition is to be fulfilled. In that case, the date must be strictly adhered to and time is in effect of the essence of such a condition; or (2) where no special date is fixed for fulfilment of a condition, it must be fulfilled before the date for completion of the contract; or (3) in the absence of either date, which is very rare indeed, any such condition must be fulfilled within a reasonable time. See *Boland & Co Ltd v Dundas Trustees* 1975 SLT (Notes) 80. That decision was followed in two later cases.

In *Ford Sellar Morris Properties plc v E W Hutchison Ltd* 1990 SC 34, a leasehold case, it was provided expressly that the contract was conditional upon certain consents being obtained. It was declared a material condition that, if the consents were not obtained by a stated date, either party could resile. Consent was obtained but after the stipulated date; and was intimated to the other side who thereupon resiled. They were held entitled so to do on the footing that, where a date has been set and is of the essence of the contract, it must be adhered to. The party resiling is obliged to exercise his right to do so within a reasonable time but in this case, where eight days had elapsed beyond the stipulated date, that period was held not to be excessive.

The decision in *Ford Sellar Morris Properties plc* was apparently not followed in *Cumming v Brown* 1993 SCLR 707 and indeed is not referred to in the report of that case. The purchaser in *Cumming* failed to meet a time limit where time was of the essence and so, as a result, the seller became entitled to resile. The purchaser thereafter tendered the price and was held entitled so to do, thus holding the seller to the bargain notwithstanding that the time limit had expired. The reasoning of the sheriff principal was that, while the seller was no doubt entitled to resile, he had not actually done so and so could not refuse an offer of performance. But that decision, in turn, seems inconsistent with the later case of *Charisma Properties Ltd v Grayling* 1996 SLT 791, where the Inner House rejected a comparable finding by Lord Penrose, based on somewhat special wording in the missives in question, and held that the seller had effectively repudiated the contract and was not bound to proceed with it.

In *Burnside v James Harrison (Developers) Ltd* 1989 GWD 11-468 missives of sale and purchase provided that either party might resile if a completion certificate was not obtained by a specified date, by giving written notice within three days thereof. A completion certificate was in fact obtained but six days after the stipulated date. Within the three-day time limit provided for, the sellers resiled from the bargain by a written letter to that effect and were held entitled so to do.

The importance of adhering strictly to the procedure detailed in the contract is well illustrated by *Grovebury Management Ltd v McLaren* 1997 SLT 1083. In this case the missives provided that if the price was unpaid 28 days after the date of entry the seller was entitled to treat the non-payment as repudiation of the contract on giving written notice to the purchaser to that effect. The price was not paid at the expiry of the 28-day period. Two weeks later the purchasers intimated by fax that they were ready to settle the transaction. On receipt of this the sellers sent a fax purporting to rescind the contract. It was held that as the purchaser was prepared to tender performance before the seller rescinded in accordance with the procedure set out in the contract the seller was not entitled to rescind.

28.74   Measure of damages

The seller must make every endeavour to minimise his loss by reselling the property at the best possible price obtainable – see *Johnstone v Harris* 1977 SC 365 – but he need not anticipate breach by the purchaser before completion date. On the question of quantum of damages and the various elements making up the seller's claim, see *Grant v Ullah* 1987 SLT 639 and *Tainsh v McLaughlin* 1990 SLT (Sh Ct) 102.

In *Mills v Findlay* 1994 SCLR 397 the sheriff awarded solatium over and above the ordinary elements of damages and was upheld by the sheriff principal who, however, reduced the award to £500. In *Palmer v Beck* 1993 SLT 485 solatium was held to be an element in a claim for damages if the claim involved fraudulent misrepresentation.

In *Lloyds Bank plc v Bamberger* 1993 SCLR 727, 1994 SLT 424, the missives contained the usual clause providing for payment of interest on the purchase price if not duly paid on the date of entry. The purchasers then defaulted and the sellers repudiated the bargain. In the subsequent action of damages, the sellers claimed that the purchasers were liable for interest at the rate specified in this clause. The court, however, held that the interest clause, on its wording, restricted the rights of the sellers to interest on the price if duly paid but beyond the due date; but that the clause had no application whatsoever to a case where the purchase price was never paid at all. This did not, of course, exclude a claim for damages but this particular item was disallowed. Following on that decision, Professor Rennie and Sheriff Cusine put forward some comments on such claims for damages and suggested styles of clause for insertion in the missives to ensure that this particular aspect of a claim was properly covered, along with other elements which go to make up the claim. All this is conveniently summarised in their article 'Penalty Interest Clauses after the *Lloyds Bank* Decision' 1993 JLSS 450.

Whether or not the courts will give effect to such clauses is, however, a different matter. See the comments by the Lord Justice-Clerk in particular in *Lloyds Bank plc v Bamberger* 1994 SLT 424 at 427L:

'It thus appears to me to be contrary to principle for the pursuers now to be seeking payment of interest on the price when, by rescinding the contract, they for their part are declaring themselves to be unwilling to perform their part of the bargain'.

In *Colgan v Mooney* 1994 GWD 1-43, in negotiations for a sale of a guest house, it was alleged that the seller advised the purchaser that the guest house could not accommodate a sufficient number of guests to require a fire certificate, which was not correct. In the subsequent missives, the purchaser introduced a condition to the effect that the premises complied with the Fire Precautions Act 1971 and had a fire certificate. The seller qualified this provision to the effect that it applied only to the extent that the subjects were too small to require a fire certificate, and disclosed the fire officer's letter which confirmed that the safety standards were met. His letter was based on the seller's assurance that no more than six guests were ever accommodated. The purchaser claimed damages but, perhaps somewhat surprisingly, the claim failed on a strict application of the terms of the missives on the basis that the seller in fact never took in more than six persons per night, even although more guests could have been accommodated. The missives contained an *actio quanti minoris* clause but Lord Clyde doubted whether or not a claim in this case came within the terms of such a clause.

28.75 DEFAULT BY THE SELLER

This can arise, from various causes, both before and after settlement of the transaction.

28.76 Before settlement

Restitutio in integrum is still normally possible. The purchaser's remedies are as follows.

(1) An *action of implement*, to have the seller ordained to deliver a valid disposition, or, failing that, to acquire a title by adjudication. This remedy is, of course, only appropriate where the seller can implement the contract (ie he has a title and the beneficial right) but refuses or lacks capacity to implement.

An action of implement is competent either in the Court of Session or in the sheriff court; an action of adjudication can only be raised in the Court of Session. Decree in an action of adjudication operates as an active title to the successful pursuer, for which see para 30.2. A decree in an action of implement does not have the same affect and simply obliges the seller to grant a disposition to obtemper the decree. In an action of implement in the Court of Session, under the *nobile officium*, the court has always had power to authorise the clerk of court to sign a disposition where the seller refuses so to do. See *Boag, Petitioner* 1967 SC 322. The same power is now conferred on the sheriff by the Law Reform (Miscellaneous Provisions) (Scotland) Act 1985, s 17. In such cases, however, it would seem to be a prerequisite that there should be a disposition in existence ready for signature which, for whatever reason, the seller will not sign; and that it is only in these circumstances that the clerk of court could be authorised to sign in the seller's place. But apparently in *Martone v Zani* 1992 GWD 32-1903 the court granted decree, *inter alia* ordaining the defender to execute and deliver a disposition, failing which the clerk of court was authorised to subscribe. The result is not altogether clear; but at least in some cases it would seem that notwithstanding these powers, an action of adjudication may be necessary. Compare the much wider and more explicit powers conferred on the sheriff under the Housing (Scotland) Act 1988, s 30 to adjust the terms of a lease where the parties cannot agree, and to declare that the resulting document reflects the terms of the tenancy whereupon it is deemed to be duly executed by both parties.

(2) *Rescission and damages.* Normally, in an action of implement, there is an alternative conclusion for damages. Where the seller cannot implement the contract, because he lacks title, this is the only competent remedy. Again if time is not expressly of the essence of the contract, notice is appropriate. If the seller fails to implement because of some technical defect in the title which is curable, then the court would normally give him time to put matters right; but not where the defect is complete want of title, even although he may be able and willing to remedy the defect. See *Campbell v McCutcheon* 1963 SC 505, where Lord President Clyde, at p 510, distinguishes between defects in the title and want of title for this purpose. In that case, property had been sold without reference to a reservation of minerals. The seller offered to acquire the minerals and convey them to the purchaser, but the purchaser insisted on rescinding. The court declined to allow the seller time to acquire the minerals, and held the purchaser entitled to immediate rescission on the grounds of want of title.

In a comparable situation in *McLennan v Warner & Co* 1996 SLT 1349, the sellers were unable to produce a marketable title following on conclusion of missives. The purchaser then issued an ultimatum requiring the title to be corrected within a 28-day time limit. The seller, for technical reasons, was unable to produce a marketable title within the stipulated time limit and appeared unlikely to be able to produce such a title within a reasonable time. In these circumstances, the purchaser was held entitled to resile on the authority of *Rodger (Builders) Ltd v Fawdry* 1950 SC 483.

(3) *Retention and damages* under the *actio quanti minoris*. Prior to the passing of the Contract (Scotland) Act 1997, this was only available if a clause to this effect was inserted in the missives. After 21 June 1997, this is available automatically to the purchaser. He can insist on proceeding with the bargain but claim damages (in effect a reduction in the price) in respect of any contractual obligation which the seller is unable to implement.

(4) *Interdict.* In the unlikely, but possible, situation of a seller attempting to sell to another party, it will be possible for the purchaser to obtain an interdict against the seller.

28.77   After settlement

The remedy of rescission and damages remains available to the purchaser, on breach by the seller of any material obligation in the contract, so long as matters remain entire or, to put it another way, so long as *restitutio in integrum* is still possible. See *Louttit's Trustees v Highland Railway Co* (1892) 19 R 791. In that case, a purchaser, in exchange for the price, took delivery of a disposition of an area of land on which he intended to build and then later discovered a restriction in the titles against building. No work had been carried out when the discovery was made.

Notwithstanding this restriction, the purchaser sought to retain the subjects but to claim damages from the seller for breach of contract. The court was clearly not disposed to grant a remedy on these lines since the purchaser would be retaining the subjects and claiming damages, which is a clear case of the *actio quanti minoris*. But the seller, for special reasons, agreed to settle the claim on this footing; and matters were therefore dealt with on that basis. Surprisingly, there is no subsequent reported Scottish case where a purchaser, having taken delivery of a disposition and paid the price, thereafter exercised his apparent right to rescind and claim damages on the grounds of a subsequently emerging breach of the seller's obligations in the contract. In *Mowbray v Mathieson* 1989 GWD 6-267 a purchaser had taken possession, and the transaction had settled, two years previously. The purchaser then sued for implement. Finally, he sought to rescind but, in the circumstances, was held not entitled so to do.

In contrast, in *Caledonian Property Group Ltd v Queensferry Property Group Ltd* 1992 SLT 738 purchasers settled a transaction while the seller's obligation to produce a completion certificate was still outstanding. In anticipation of receiving the certificate within the stipulated time limit, the purchasers then carried out extensive work on the subjects. The certificate was not duly produced and, as a consequence, the purchasers had to abandon plans to sell on the property; and the property market then deteriorated. In the result the purchasers calculated that they would incur a loss on ultimate resale, including loss of interest on the price, and sued for damages accordingly. The report includes a discussion on the claim for interest and the appropriate rate of interest. Given that the transaction was between two property companies, it was held that the seller should have anticipated that the purchaser would borrow at least part of the price and that the interest rate should be fixed with that in mind; and accordingly a proof before answer was allowed on that footing.

There are, of course, other instances where a disposition has been reduced after delivery but not on the grounds of breach of contract by the seller. Such cases involve other elements, for example error common to both parties as in *Anderson v Lambie* 1954 SC (HL) 43; or the rule penalising private knowledge of a prior right, referred to as the 'offside goals' rule, as in *Rodger (Builders) Ltd v Fawdry* 1950 SC 483.

Contrary to clear indications in the decision in *Louttit's Trustees v Highland Railway Co* (1892) 19 R 791, it seems to have been generally accepted in the profession that, after settlement of the transaction, *restitutio in integrum* is no longer possible. To some extent that view may be justified by reference to the nature of the transaction. In *Louttit's Trustees*, the purchaser had acquired a vacant piece of ground with a view to building and, before going further, the restriction on building was discovered. Clearly, in such a case, neither party would be significantly prejudiced if the transaction were reversed, the disposition reduced, and the purchase price repaid to the purchaser.

In ordinary domestic conveyancing, however, it is rather a different matter in that, if the purchaser of a dwellinghouse takes delivery of a disposition in exchange for the price, he will almost certainly, in the process, have sold his own house; will have taken possession, moved in his furniture and taken up residence in the new dwelling-house. Can it be said in that situation that matters are still entire?

In any event, whatever the correct view of the decision in *Louttit's Trustees* may be, it seems necessarily to follow that, even after settlement of the transaction, the purchaser will have the right to retain the subjects and to claim damages *quanti minoris* by virtue of the Contract (Scotland) Act 1997, whether *restitutio* remains possible or not.

28.78   COLLATERAL OBLIGATIONS

Under the Contract (Scotland) Act 1997 collateral obligations are enforceable for a period of 20 or 5 years, depending on the nature of the obligation, unless there is a clause in the missives imposing a time limit on their enforceability. See para 28.43.

28.79   BOTH PARTIES IN BREACH

For a complex case where both parties were in breach and where, in addition, the pursuers as purchasers under concluded missives maintained that their solicitors had acted negligently, see *Mason v A & R Robertson & Black* 1993 SLT 773.

Following conclusion of missives for the purchase of a farm, the purchasers paid a substantial sum, over £100,000, towards the purchase price and took possession. The sellers' agents granted a letter of obligation undertaking to deliver a valid disposition in exchange for the remaining balance of the price. Some time later they intimated that they were in a position to deliver that disposition but the purchasers refused to settle on the footing that the acreage of the farm had been misrepresented. This in turn led to an action of implement by the sellers against the purchasers which was defended on these grounds. The purchasers further averred in the course of that action that the sellers' alleged breach of contract amounted to repudiation; that the contract fell to be rescinded; and, on that account, counterclaimed for repayment of the part of the purchase price already paid over. The sellers refused to accept rescission of the contract at which point, apparently, the sellers' solicitors withdrew from the action. The purchasers obtained a decree of dismissal and a decree by default in their counterclaim. They were, however, unsuccessful in enforcing that decree, and so petitioned for the sellers' liquidation. Creditors in a standard security over the farm then entered into possession and resold it.

The basis of the claim for negligence against the purchasers' solicitors was failure on the part of the solicitors to advise the purchasers that obtaining decree in the principal action would probably be worthless and that, in addition, by obtaining that decree, they would render the letter of obligation worthless as well. Lord Cameron of Lochbroom did not accept that the taking of decree amounted to an irrevocable election to terminate the contract and accordingly that the pursuers' averments, that the letter of obligation had become ineffective, were irrelevant.

The case serves as a warning but does not produce any significant matter of principle. Lord Cameron declined to reach a firm conclusion on the averments of the parties beyond what is stated above but put the case out by order and, in the subsequent procedure, decree of dismissal was pronounced.

Chapter 29

Statutory Titles

29.1 Statutory limitation of the real right

The real right is the foundation of ownership; and it is of the essence of the real right that it is secure against challenge from all comers. In heritage, the real right depends upon registration in either the Register of Sasines or the Land Register.

At common law, if the real right is to transmit *inter vivos*, it can only do so by means of an ordinary disposition granted by the registered proprietor or, at least, a general disposition by him which satisfies the minimum requirements of the Conveyancing (Scotland) Act 1874, s 27 in that it contains a word or words importing a conveyance or transference or a present intention to convey. Nothing less will do.

But this general rule is subject to certain qualifications. In the first place, in certain circumstances, the court will intervene to give effect to personal or equitable claims affecting the real right vested in a registered proprietor. In the second place, by statute, certain bodies, especially local authorities and certain ministers, are given powers of compulsory expropriation in the national interest, in the exercise of which, failing co-operation by the registered proprietor, the acquiring authority can obtain a valid title under statutory procedure.

29.2 Adjudication in implement

The registered proprietor may, in various ways, voluntarily undertake obligations which affect his real right in heritage, and may create valid and enforceable personal claims at the instance of some other party. Normally, he implements such obligations by granting an appropriate title in favour of the grantee; but, if he declines to grant the appropriate title, then the grantee may invoke the assistance of the court.

The appropriate process is adjudication in implement, a form of diligence under which a person in right of land, or for whose benefit a debtor has agreed to grant a heritable security, may obtain a title to land or security over land. An action of adjudication is competent only in the Court of Session and cannot be raised in the sheriff court.

29.3   AN EXAMPLE

Suppose that A, the registered proprietor, enters into a contract, valid in point of form and content, to sell his heritage to B. In terms of such a contract, A undertakes to convey the heritage to B, but the contract does not contain 'any other word or words importing conveyance or transference, or present intention to convey or transfer' to satisfy the requirements of the Conveyancing (Scotland) Act 1874, s 27. Accordingly, while it confers on B a valid and enforceable right to the heritable property, it does not *per se* operate as a title. In the ordinary way, following on such a contract, A will convey the property to B. But suppose he declines to do so. B may then raise an action of adjudication in implement against A for implement of the contract of sale and purchase.

The decree supplies the want of the conveyance by A to B. The extract operates as a title, and may be recorded direct in the Register of Sasines or given effect to by the Keeper in the Land Register to complete the adjudger's right; or it may be used, unregistered, as a link in title. In a competition, the date of preference is the date of registration of the extract decree, not the date of the decree itself: see the Titles to Land Consolidation (Scotland) Act 1868, ss 62 and 129 (as amended by the 1874 Act, ss 62 and 65). The same applies to titles registered in the Land Register.

29.4   **Adjudication *ad factum praestandum***

Although an action of adjudication in implement is the recognised formal method of obtaining a title where a title cannot be obtained by voluntary means, it is also competent, both in the Court of Session and in the sheriff court, in appropriate circumstances to raise an action of implement *ad factum praestandum*. This is done to ordain the defender to grant the appropriate title in favour of the pursuer which, for whatever reason, the defender fails or refuses to grant. The difficulty here is that, while a decree may be obtained in appropriate terms, it cannot of itself operate as a title in contrast to a decree in an action of adjudication which is itself a title and can be recorded in the Register of Sasines or registered in the Land Register to procure ownership for the pursuer in that form of process.

Admittedly, in the Court of Session in such an action the court has power under the *nobile officium* to authorise the Principal Clerk of Session or his deputy to sign a disposition in place of the defender who refuses or is unable to sign. But this would normally presuppose that there is in existence a writ in appropriate and agreed form available for signature; and all that is required is the signature of the defender.

In similar circumstances, now, under the Law Reform (Miscellaneous Provisions) (Scotland) Act 1985, s 17, in a sheriff court action, the sheriff has the like power to authorise the sheriff clerk to sign a disposition but again this presupposes that there is a disposition in existence available and ready to sign which may not always be the case. Certainly, s 17 reads as if there were such a deed available for signature and all that the sheriff can do is authorise the execution thereof. If so, he would seem to have no power to authorise the preparation of an appropriate disposition in implement; and the power of the Court of Session under the nobile officium may be subject to the same limitation. This can be contrasted with the position under the Housing (Scotland) Act 1988, s 30(2), which empowers the sheriff in prescribed circumstances to draft a lease or adjust the terms thereof. See para 27.17.

29.5 Adjudication for debt

The whole of a man's estate, both heritable and moveable, is liable for payment of his whole debts. As we have seen, a secured debt creates a preference for the creditor at the date of the security; and such creditors obtain, *ab initio*, a nexus on the security subjects and powers of enforcement, such as sale. The unsecured creditor has no equivalent, *ab initio*; but can later acquire rights to some extent equivalent to those enjoyed by the secured creditor through the process of adjudication for debt. This takes two forms, adjudication for payment and adjudication in security. This type of adjudication differs from adjudication in implement in that the intention here is not to confer an absolute title on the creditor, but rather to secure payment for the creditor out of the heritable property adjudged to him.

29.6 ADJUDICATION FOR PAYMENT

This process is competent to a creditor holding a liquid document of debt, for example a personal bond or a decree for payment.

Decree, when obtained, is registrable in the Register of Sasines or in the Land Register. It operates as a judicial security to the creditor over the heritable property adjudged, for payment of the debt, but subject to a power of redemption at the instance of the debtor at any time within ten years of decree. This ten-year period is the legal period of redemption, otherwise known as the 'legal'. In the result, the creditor's title under an adjudication for payment is initially a right in security, whereas under adjudication in implement the pursuer's title is immediately indefeasible. At any time within the legal, the creditor can be forced to denude in favour of the debtor if he receives payment of his claim in full. In the result, the creditor has a mere security only, which he cannot convert into cash to liquidate his debt for at least ten years. This is because, under a decree of adjudication for payment, recording of the decree provides security, but it does not confer any power of sale in contrast to the powers of a creditor under a standard security.

The Scottish Law Commission has proposed that adjudication be abolished and replaced with a new statutory diligence known as land attachment: see para 22.53.

29.7   ADJUDICATION IN SECURITY

Adjudication in security is competent, but now virtually unknown, where there is no liquid document of debt, in special circumstances only. It differs from adjudication for payment in that there is no 'legal' and the right of redemption persists indefinitely.

29.8   **Bankruptcy and sequestration**

Adjudication for debt, although still competent, is rare in modern practice. Instead, it is usual for the estate of the debtor to be sequestrated for the general benefit of the whole body of creditors. The procedure is regulated by the Bankruptcy (Scotland) Act 1985 (as amended by the Bankruptcy (Scotland) Act 1993).

We are concerned here with the effect of sequestration on heritable titles; and the procedure introduced by the 1985 Act is touched on by way of introduction to that aspect of the Act only.

Sequestration follows on a petition to the court, by the debtor or by a creditor, for the appointment of a trustee to whom the whole of the debtor's estate is transferred. The trustee holds and administers the estate in trust for the general body of creditors. Under the 1985 Act, the appointment of the trustee proceeds in two stages. Firstly, an interim trustee is appointed under the 1985 Act, s 13 to take immediate control of the debtor's estate. Thereafter, following on a meeting of creditors, a permanent trustee is appointed in his place. The same person may, and normally will, act as both interim and permanent trustee.

Note the proposal regarding the timing for a trustee in sequestration to complete title in the Scottish Law Commission Discussion Paper on *Sharp v Thomson*. See para 4.6.

29.9   THE ACT AND WARRANT

For the purposes of title, the act and warrant of the court, confirming the appointment of the permanent trustee, transfers the whole property of the debtor, heritable and moveable, to the permanent trustee absolutely and irredeemably as at the date of sequestration; but only so far as belonging to the debtor. The effect of the act and warrant on heritable estate of the debtor in Scotland is as if a decree of adjudication in implement and a decree of adjudication for payment but subject to no legal reversion had been pronounced in favour of the permanent trustee.

In contrast to a decree of adjudication in implement in ordinary form (see above), the act and warrant in a sequestration operates as a general disposition in favour of the trustee on which he may, if he wishes, complete title; but he cannot record the act and warrant *de plano*. He will normally complete title immediately in order to exclude the possibility of some other party acquiring a valid adverse real right. Thus, if the debtor, prior to sequestration, has granted a standard security which has not been recorded at the date of sequestration; and if, thereafter, the creditor records it before the permanent trustee completes title, the creditor will be secured. Completion of title by the permanent trustee before the competing deed excludes that possibility, although this was challenged in *Burnett's Trustee v Grainger* 2002 SLT 699, which is under appeal to the House of Lords at the time of writing: see para 4.5.

29.10   COMPLETION OF TITLE BY TRUSTEE

Special provision is made in the Bankruptcy (Scotland) Act 1985, s 31(3) to allow the permanent trustee to complete title to heritage to which the debtor's title was not completed at the date of sequestration.

Under s 32 of the 1985 Act, assets subsequently acquired by the debtor after sequestration, for example as beneficiary under the will of a person who dies after that date, automatically vest in the permanent trustee; and production by the trustee of the act and warrant is sufficient to compel the custodier of any such asset to make it over to the permanent trustee. This is subject to two provisions:

(1)   where someone in good faith and without knowledge of the sequestration has made over after-acquired assets to the debtor, he is not liable to account to the permanent trustee; and

(2)   where a third party had acquired an interest in some such after-acquired asset in good faith and for value his title to that asset is beyond challenge: see s 32(6) of the 1985 Act. In a heritable transaction involving third parties, good faith will be difficult if not impossible to establish, given the customary entries in the Personal Register relating to the sequestration. In contrast to the position prior to the 1985 Act, such vesting of after-acquired assets is automatic and does not now require the intervention of the court nor any further procedure by way of recording of a notice in the Register of Sasines or applying to the Keeper for registration in the Land Register as was previously necessary.

For a discussion of the position where the bankrupt has granted a security, see para 3.21 and K G C Reid and G L Gretton *Conveyancing 2000* (2001), pp 88–101. Under s 33 of the 1985 Act, any asset genuinely vested in the debtor as trustee for some other person is excluded from the sequestration and does not vest in the permanent trustee.

Further, under s 33(3), the vesting provisions in ss 31 and 32 are without prejudice to the right of any secured creditor which is preferable to the rights of the permanent trustee. A short provision in s 39(4), which regulates the relationship of the trustee in sequestration and heritable creditors.

Under s 31(2) of the 1985 Act, however, the powers conferred on the permanent trustee under the act and warrant are immune from challenge by an inhibiting creditor and an inhibition is of no effect in a question with the permanent trustee, except in a question of ranking.

29.11   REGISTRATION IN THE PERSONAL REGISTER

Under the Bankruptcy (Scotland) Act 1985, s 14(1), the clerk of court is required, forthwith after the date of sequestration, to send a certified copy of the relevant court order to the Keeper of the Register, for recording in the Personal Register. Recording of the certified copy has the effect, as from the date of sequestration, of an inhibition and of a citation in an adjudication of the debtor's estate, thereby effectively preventing the bankrupt from disposing or otherwise dealing with his heritable estate.

29.12   GRATUITOUS ALIENATION AND UNFAIR PREFERENCES

Any gratuitous alienation by the sequestrated debtor can be reduced at common law. In addition, gratuitous alienation is struck at, but with certain qualifications and within certain time limits, under the Bankruptcy (Scotland) Act 1985, s 34. Under s 34(4), however, any third party who has acquired right from the gratuitous transferee in good faith and for value is protected. In practice, however, it would probably be impossible to establish good faith in any heritable transaction under this proviso.

A gratuitous transfer includes not only a transfer for no consideration but also a transfer for inadequate consideration, which is always exceedingly difficult to establish. This can cause serious problems for the seller. If the transferee is an associate of the debtor, which includes husband and wife, relatives, and partners, the effect of this provision lasts for five years. For other transferees, the period is two years. During that period, the gratuitous alienation can be challenged by any creditor or trustee in sequestration or under a trust deed. Admittedly, the effect of this section can be excluded if it can be shown that, at any time after the alienation, the debtor's assets were greater than his liabilities or that the alienation was made for adequate consideration; but these are difficult facts to establish.

Accordingly, if there is any suggestion on the face of the title that there has been a transaction for less than full consideration, the purchaser should proceed only with extreme caution. For illustrations of reductions following on gratuitous alienations, see the Digest of Cases at para 29.13.

Similarly, under s 36 of the 1985 Act, any transaction entered into by a debtor which creates a preference for a creditor to the prejudice of the general body of creditors (termed an unfair preference), can be challenged under this section if the unfair preference was created within six months prior to the sequestration. Transactions in the ordinary course of trade, and payments in cash are exempted unless the cash payment was collusively made.

For a discussion on the effect of a gratuitous alienation at common law, which still also applies, see *Boyle's Trustee v Boyle* 1988 SLT 581.

Under the fraudulent preference provisions in the Bankruptcy Act 1696 (now repealed) it was held that, in calculating the six-month period to determine whether or not a disposition was struck at by the fraudulent preference rules, the date of recording of the disposition, not the date of delivery, was the critical date: see *Grant's*

Trustee v Grant 1986 SLT 220. The same rule may be expected to apply under the 1985 Act.

29.13 **Reduction**

A real right in land in principle is secure from challenge against all comers. But the real right only has this characteristic of invulnerability if it has proceeded on, and been constituted in virtue of, a valid antecedent title, or series of titles. The title or series of titles on which the real right is based must be probative writing(s). This does not mean, however, that a probative writing is automatically exempt from challenge. It may be challenged on a variety of grounds including, for example, want of capacity, error, fraud, force, or defect in the solemnity of execution; but the onus of establishing any such latent defect in a probative writ lies on the challenger and not on the person acquiring right thereunder, whose interest is to sustain the writ.

Suppose, then, that A is registered in a heritable property as owner but is insane. He executes a disposition thereof to B. Any deed by a person, insane, is invalid from want of capacity; but the deed may be ex facie valid. Suppose this deed is. B records it in the Register of Sasines or the Land Register, apparently perfects his real right thereby, and takes possession. A guardian is then appointed to A. How does the guardian recover the property from B as ostensible owner? He must raise an action of reduction against B, the disponee, seeking to have the disposition to B reduced.

The onus lies on A's guardian to establish and prove that A, at the date when the disposition was executed, was insane; but if he satisfies the court on this point, then, notwithstanding the apparent probative quality of the disposition by A, the court will then grant decree of reduction, the effect of which is to avoid and invalidate the disposition. This has the further consequence that all titles following on, and deriving their validity through that disposition are also reduced and rendered wholly invalid. In other words, the title to the heritable property in question is restored, by reduction, to the state it was in immediately prior to the granting of the invalid disposition by A.

This is the position in the case of titles in the Register of Sasines. Where a title had been registered in the Land Register, however, the House of Lords in *Short's Trustee v Keeper of the Registers of Scotland* 1996 SLT 166 upheld the decision of the Court of Session that a decree of reduction was not registrable in the Land Register, but the trustee was required to apply for rectification. The decision, which is problematic, particularly in light of its sequel case, *Short's Trustee v Chung (No 2)* 1999 SLT 751, is discussed in greater depth at para 11.35.

This underlines the fundamental difference between registration in the Land Register and recording of a deed in the Register of Sasines which is an essential step in the creation of the real right but carries no guarantee of validity or invulnerability. In contrast, an interest registered in the Land Register under the Land Registration (Scotland) Act 1979 is guaranteed by the Keeper except to the extent to which he has qualified his indemnity. Rectification of the Register to give effect to any inaccuracy therein can be exercised by the Keeper, or ordered by the court, only in very limited circumstances, if such rectification would prejudice the proprietor in possession. See further paras 11.31 to 11.35.

For an illustration of reduction of a power of attorney and a discussion on the standard of proof required, see *Sereshky v Sereshky* 1988 SLT 426.

29.14   REDUCTION AND ADJUDICATION COMPARED

Note the difference in effect between a decree of reduction and a decree of adjudication; the latter operates as an active title, equivalent to a disposition, in favour of the pursuer. A decree of reduction has a purely negative effect, invalidating existing writs. In the ordinary way, a decree of reduction invalidates the deed entire, but partial reduction seems to be competent in appropriate circumstances: see *McLeod v Cedar Holdings Ltd* 1989 SLT 620 and *Broadley v Wilson* 1991 SLT 69.

It follows from what has been said that every heritable title in Scotland is, theoretically, open to challenge at any time on the grounds that one of the deeds relating thereto is invalidated by a latent defect of the kind described above. In practice, actions of reduction affecting heritable title are rare; and this risk is one which a person dealing with a heritable proprietor on an *ex facie* valid title must simply accept.

29.15   PROTECTION OF PURCHASERS

As a further protection to a purchaser dealing with a heritable proprietor on the faith of the record, the Conveyancing (Scotland) Act 1924, s 46 provides that where a deed, decree or other writing recorded in the Register of Sasines (or forming an unrecorded mid-couple in a recorded title) has been reduced by action of reduction, the extract decree must be recorded in the Register of Sasines. Further, the decree is not pleadable against a third party who has *bona fide* onerously acquired a right to the heritage in question prior to the registration of the decree in the Register of Sasines or the Land Register. In the Land Register, however, the decree can only enter the Register by means of an application for rectification. It cannot be directly registered. See paras 11.35 and 29.13.

The intention of this section may have been to extend and enhance the security of a recorded title in a question with *bona fide* purchasers for value. But in *Mulhearn v Dunlop* 1929 SLT 59, the court held that the section, in its terms, protected a *bona fide* purchaser acquiring the disputed subjects, but only during the short period between the granting of the decree and the recording of that decree; the section did not protect a purchaser who had acquired the heritage in question prior to the date of granting of the decree.

So, in the A–B case above, B (the disponee of the insane A) sells and dispones the property to X, a *bona fide* purchaser, who believes the disposition A–B is valid. X records the disposition B–X before A's guardian is appointed. The guardian is thereafter appointed and raises an action of reduction to invalidate the two dispositions and obtains decree. X loses the property; but could claim against B under warrandice.

For a detailed discussion of the 1924 Act, s 46, and the implications of *Mulhearn v Dunlop*, see G L Gretton 'Reduction of Heritable Titles' 1986 SLT (News) 125.

The Family Law (Scotland) Act 1985, s 18, empowers the court, in a matrimonial dispute, to set aside or vary any transfer of, or transaction involving, property by a party to a marriage made within the preceding five years; but no order can be made under this section which would prejudice the rights of a *bona fide* purchaser for value. This replaces the Divorce (Scotland) Act 1976, s 6.

29.16 DISCHARGE OF HERITABLE SECURITY

The Conveyancing and Feudal Reform (Scotland) Act 1970, s 41, introduced a novel provision in regard to discharges of heritable securities. Prior to this Act, if a security had been discharged at any time within the last 20 years, it was still necessary to examine the security, its transmissions and discharge(s) for intrinsic and extrinsic validity. When the security was discharged, say, 18 years ago, this was patently rather a waste of time. Section 41 provides that, where a discharge has been duly recorded more than five years previously, the subsequent reduction of that discharge (because, presumably, it was improperly granted) is not to affect the title of a bona fide purchaser for value; and s 46 of the Conveyancing (Scotland) Act 1924 ceases to apply to that decree of reduction.

29.17 Judicial rectification of defectively expressed documents

At common law, unless and until a probative writ had been set aside by an action of reduction, it was bound to receive effect. This was altered by the Law Reform (Miscellaneous Provisions) (Scotland) Act 1985, ss 8 and 9, in terms of which, as an alternative to an action of reduction, it is now competent to apply to the court for the rectification of a document if either party can satisfy the court that it fails to express accurately the intention of the grantor or, in the case of a contract, the intention of the parties. Under s 8(4), if a document is so rectified, then it takes effect as if it had always been so rectified; and, under s 8(5), if the deed was registered in the Register of Sasines or the Land Register, the order rectifying the document should also be registered whereupon the deed as originally registered falls to be treated as having been registered in its rectified form *ab initio*.

When such an action has been raised, it is competent, under s 8(7) of the 1985 Act, to record a notice of litigiosity in the Personal Register.

There have been a large number of cases on the subject of rectification under s 8, and the courts are interpreting the provision widely. Thus in *Bank of Scotland v Graham's Trustee* 1992 SC 79, a standard security was rectified when it had been signed only once, and not twice as was provided for in the deed. In *Bank of Scotland v Brunswick Developments (1987) Ltd* 1995 SLT 689 the name of the wrong grantor was inserted in the deed. Proof before answer was allowed. The court stressed that the deed must be executed by the right person, and if that person was then misdescribed in the deed, that could be rectified. In *Sheltered Housing Management Ltd v Cairns* 2003 SLT 578 builders executed a deed of conditions relating to a sheltered housing complex built by them. The deed mistakenly omitted a clause which related to a management scheme for the complex with the result that there was no provision for payment of a service charge. A petition for rectification was granted.

Whereas it would appear that many different types of error can now be rectified, if what is required is rectification of a deed that is so extensive that it almost amounts to a rewriting, that will not be permitted: see *Huewind Ltd v Clydesdale Bank Plc.* 1996 SLT 369. In addition, for rectification under s 8(1)(a) of the 1985 Act, some 'common intention' of the parties that has not been expressed in the document must be demonstrated. In *Rehman v Ahmad* 1993 SLT 741 Lord Penrose held that to justify rectification the applicant had to prove that there had been an agreement, made independently of and prior to the date of the document. This could be difficult to show in the case of missives not expressing a common intention of the parties, but easier to prove where a disposition does not implement the terms of the missives. In *Bank of Ireland v Bass Brewers Ltd* 2000 GWD 20-786 a bank sought rectification of a letter of consent by a company to a standard security granted by another company in favour of the bank which created a doubt as to the order of ranking. In allowing proof before answer, it was accepted that rectification was possible when the language of the document repeated exactly the language that the grantor intended to use but which failed to achieve the intended result.

For further discussion of judicial rectification, see Gretton and Reid *Conveyancing* (2nd edn, 1999), Chapter 17. See also C Waelde (ed) *Professor McDonald's Conveyancing Opinions* (1998), pp 251–256.

29.18 Appointment of trustees, judicial factors, guardians etc

This is another case where, on the application of an interested party, the court will intervene to appoint a new trustee on a pre-existing trust, where for some reason or other the existing trust machinery has broken down; or to appoint a guardian, judicial factor to take over and/or administer an estate on behalf of an incapax, missing, or unknown, proprietor. In such cases, the decree of the court either operates as a conveyance in favour of the trustee or factor so appointed, in virtue of which he can make up title to the trust heritage; or it operates as a judicial power of attorney, entitling the factor to deal with heritable estate in name of an incapax. See Chapter 3.

29.19 Compulsory purchase

In any developing industrial society, the individual's right of property in land must yield to the overriding needs and interests of society as a whole. Otherwise, if the individual right of property in land is to be paramount, then any individual owner, by declining to co-operate, can frustrate all manner of developments, typically, railways, canals, trunk roads, water and sewage. Of course, many landowners appreciate this need and are willing to co-operate, when required, in disposing of land to the appropriate authority by agreement. But inevitably there will be cases where, for one reason or another, the landed proprietor cannot or will not co-operate; and to meet these cases it is necessary for the State or certain public bodies to have powers of expropriation, subject always to payment of the appropriate compensation. What we are concerned with here is the effect, in outline, *quoad* title, of the exercise by an appropriate authority of powers of compulsory acquisition of land.

In the exercise of such powers, there are two elements to consider, namely, the conferment, by statute, of the actual power to acquire; and, secondly, the procedure regulating the exercise of the power, to prevent oppression and injustice, including regulations for payment of compensation.

Prior to 1845, both elements were normally conferred together on the acquiring authority by a single Act of Parliament especially passed for the purpose. But in all cases the procedure became more or less standard; and accordingly, to avoid the necessity of repeating at length, in each separate Act of Parliament conferring power to acquire, provisions as to procedure, an Act was passed in 1845 known as the Lands Clauses Consolidation (Scotland) Act 1845. This contained a detailed and elaborate procedural code to be adopted in any future Act of Parliament conferring power of compulsory acquisition on an acquiring authority, where that was considered appropriate. The 1845 Act has been subsequently modified, and the statutory procedure expanded by later Acts, principally the Acquisition of Land (Authorisation Procedure) (Scotland) Act 1947, the Land Compensation (Scotland) Acts 1963 and 1973, the Planning and Compensation Act 1991, and the Town and Country Planning (Scotland) Act 1997. In England the comparable older legislation has been repealed and new statutory provision made. So far, there is no Scottish equivalent; subject to these modifications, the Lands Clauses Consolidation (Scotland) Act 1845 still applies.

From the point of view of heritable title only, compulsory acquisition of land implies, in the final analysis, the divesting of an individual heritable proprietor and the investing of the acquiring authority as owner. This, of course, can always be achieved by conventional means where the proprietor is willing and able to co-operate and where, by agreement, he conveys his heritage to the acquiring authority. In practice, this very commonly happens. But in the majority of cases, the acquiring authority urgently requires land for its development and, in practice, it will initiate the compulsory purchase procedure, even although it later acquires land by conventional titles, with a view to the ultimate acquisition, if necessary, of land by compulsory purchase.

The commonest cases of compulsory purchase in modern practice are by a local authority for roads, planning and housing purposes.

There are two different procedures under which the acquiring authority can obtain a statutory title to heritage in Scotland. Initially the procedures are similar and are regulated by the Acquisition of Land (Authorisation Procedure) (Scotland) Act 1947.

In outline (and ignoring altogether specialities of which there are any number), both procedures commence in the following form. For further detail, see J J Rowan Robinson *Compulsory Purchase and Compensation* (2nd edn, 2003), especially Chapter 3.

29.20   COMPULSORY PURCHASE ORDER

The acquiring authority makes an order, known as a compulsory purchase order, specifying the land to be acquired, which is published by advertisement and served on owners and lessees. Individual owners are given an opportunity to object, and objections may be followed by a public inquiry. None of this has any effect *quoad* title.

29.21   CONFIRMATION

The compulsory purchase order must be confirmed by the Scottish Ministers (or other confirming authority). Confirmation must be advertised and affected persons notified, and only then does the order become final. This has still no effect *quoad* title.

Thereafter the procedures differ and are dealt with separately.

29.22   Ordinary procedure under the Lands Clauses Consolidation (Scotland) Act 1845 (as amended)

(1) *Notice to treat.* This is a notice, served by the acquiring authority on the individual heritable proprietor, intimating the intention to acquire compulsorily and, when served in accordance with the statutory procedure, has the effect of creating a notional binding contract of sale and purchase of heritage between the owner and the acquiring authority under which the owner has agreed to sell his land to the acquiring authority, and is bound thereafter to convey it in implement of that agreement, as under any normal contract of sale and purchase. The purchase price is represented by compensation, computed in accordance with statutory formulae. After serving the notice to treat, the acquiring authority may

take possession of the subjects, on 14 days' written notice, under the Acquisition of Land (Authorisation Procedure) (Scotland) Act 1947, Schedule 2, para 3(1).

In *Rush v Fife Regional Council* 1994 SCLR 231 the council served notices to treat under the Lands Clauses Consolidation (Scotland) Act 1845 in respect of various subjects which they wished to acquire. The validity of the notices were challenged by Rush on the grounds that the descriptions therein did not conform to his title. His challenge was dismissed and he appealed. It was held that the notices to treat were valid in that they adequately showed the location and extent of the lands to be acquired. There was no requirement in the 1845 Act that the notice to treat should refer to the title.

(2) Following on this notice to treat, the proprietor may convey the land to the acquiring authority, in which case the conveyance may take one of two forms, namely, a statutory form, as prescribed in schedules to the Lands Clauses Consolidation (Scotland) Act 1845, which is known as a schedule conveyance; or a common law (or conventional) conveyance such as any heritable proprietor grants in favour of any ordinary purchaser.

(3) If the proprietor, having been served with notice to treat, declines to convey, whether by conventional or schedule conveyance, the acquiring authority is statutorily empowered to record a notarial instrument at its own hand, which, by statute, has the same effect as the recording of a schedule conveyance.

(4) In the case of other compulsory acquisition procedures, the effect on servitudes and burdens is unclear but will be clarified by the Title Conditions (Scotland) Act 2003. See para 18.65.

(5) *Disposal.* Provision is made in the 1845 Act (as amended) for the disposal of surplus lands compulsorily acquired but no longer needed for their original purpose. Following on a well-known case in England, the statutory provisions were supplemented by a Government Circular, now Circular 38/1992 issued by the Scottish Office: The Disposal of Surplus Government Land – The Crichel Down Rules. The purpose of these rules, which are non-statutory, is to require a local authority when disposing of surplus land first to make an offer thereof to the original owner. In a recent case, *JDP Investments Ltd v Strathclyde Regional Council* 1996 SCLR 243, the pursuers entered into missives of sale to the regional council of some six hectares of land through which it was proposed to construct a new road. The road proposal was later abandoned and the regional council decided to dispose of part of the site on the open market. The pursuers applied for a declarator that the Crichel Down Rules were applicable to the disposal but their claim was rejected because the land was originally acquired not by compulsory acquisition or under threat thereof but by a purely voluntary arrangement to which the rules had no application. There is a useful discussion in Lord Hamilton's judgment as to how the rules operate in practice.

It has recently been proposed that the Rules be placed on a statutory footing in England because they are not being followed. See J J Rowan Robinson *Compulsory Purchase and Compensation* (2nd edn, 2003), pp 80–81.

29.23 **General vesting declarations**

General vesting declarations are regulated by the Town and Country Planning (Scotland) Act 1997, s 195 and Schedule 15.

When a compulsory purchase order has come into operation, ie after the statutory procedure for compulsory purchase has run its course, the acquiring authority may execute a general vesting declaration. It must contain a particular description or a statutory description by reference of the land to be acquired. The intention to make a general vesting declaration must be published in the press not less than two months before the vesting declaration is actually made and this is usually done in conjunction with the advertisement of the confirmation of the order. Immediately on executing the declaration the acquiring authority must intimate its terms to every owner and occupier (except short-term tenants) having an interest in the affected land.

On the expiry of a period to be specified in the declaration (at least 28 days):

(1) the Lands Clauses Consolidation (Scotland) Act 1845 (those parts adopted by Schedule 24 to the Town and Country Planning (Scotland) Act 1972, now Schedule 15 to the 1997 Act) and the Land Compensation (Scotland) Acts 1963 and 1973 apply as if notice to treat had been served on each owner and occupier; and

(2) the land described in the declaration, and the right to take possession thereof, vests in the acquiring authority subject only to short tenancies. Notice to short-term tenants is required.

The declaration is to be registered in the Land Register, because a general vesting declaration will induce first registration where the title is not already registered in the Land Register; and thereupon has the same effect as a schedule conveyance duly recorded under s 80 of the 1845 Act.

Chapter 30

Transmission on Death

30.1 Scope of the chapter

We are not here concerned with the substantive rules which determine the beneficial entitlement to property, heritable or moveable, on the death, testate or intestate, of the proprietor thereof, but with the technical machinery by which the person beneficially entitled, on testacy or intestacy, acquires a title and perfects his real right to heritable property passing to him from his deceased ancestor and to which he has succeeded as a beneficiary on the death.

30.2 Position before the Succession (Scotland) Act 1964

For details of transmission of heritable property in testate and intestate succession before the Succession (Scotland) Act 1964, see the sixth edition of this book, at para 31.2.

30.3 Succession (Scotland) Act 1964

The Succession (Scotland) Act 1964 made fundamental changes to the way title to heritage is administered and transferred. Under s 14 of the 1964 Act, heritable property vests in the executor, provided that he is duly confirmed thereto and the duly confirmed executor is the only person who can make up title to heritable property, with limited qualifications as noted below.

30.4 Confirmation as a title to heritage

In relation to heritage, the Succession (Scotland) Act 1964, ss 14(2) and 15(1) provide that an executor is not to be taken as having duly confirmed to heritable property unless a description of that heritable property is included in the confirmation in accordance with, now, the provisions of the Act of Sederunt (Confirmation of Executors Amendment) 1966, SI 1966/593. The requisite description is such a description 'as will be sufficient to identify the property or interest therein as a separate item in the deceased person's estate', ie (normally) the postal address. A formal 'conveyancing' description is clearly not required; and, not uncommonly, the postal address alone may suffice. In the case of tenement property, however, the location of the flat within the tenement should also be included properly to identify it as a separate item in the deceased's estate. See I J S Talman (ed) *Halliday's Conveyancing Law and Practice in Scotland* (2nd edn, 2 volumes, 1996–97), para 21–04.

Assuming the executor has duly confirmed to heritage belonging to the deceased, the nature and quality of the title conferred on the executor by confirmation is defined in s 15 of the 1964 Act. This section proceeds by applying to heritage generally the limited provisions of the Conveyancing (Scotland) Act 1924, s 5 which applied only to heritable securities and only if they were moveable in the succession as they usually were in practice. The necessary amendments to the 1924 Act, s 5 are contained in the 1964 Act, s 15 and Sch 2. The result is that, under the 1924 Act, s 5(2)(a) (as amended), where the proprietor of any estate in land, which vests in an executor under the 1964 Act, s 14, has died, with or without a recorded title, whether testate or intestate, confirmation in favour of the executor which includes the appropriate description shall of itself be a valid title to such estate in land. Such confirmation is also a valid mid-couple for any deduction of title, but is not recordable in the General Register of Sasines.

It is not clear from these provisions whether confirmation is intended to be the only effective title to heritage. Provided it includes the appropriate description, confirmation is in itself a valid title, equivalent to a general disposition in favour of the executors; and it is certainly arguable that no other title can competently be used. But the professors of conveyancing, in an opinion delivered in April 1965, took the view that testamentary trustees and executors could use the will as an alternative link in title; and two of them took the view that a legatee could also so use the will where it contained a direct bequest of heritage in his favour. See the memorial at 1965 JLSS 153, and the comments thereon at 1965 JLSS 189 and the opinion at 1966 JLSS 84.

30.5 Probates

The amendment to the s 5(2)(a) of the Conveyancing (Scotland) Act 1924 also affects probates and letters of administration issued in England. But with this difference, that under the 1924 Act, s 5(2)(b), probates or letters of administration were deemed to include heritable securities, without actually containing these items; in fact, a probate cannot 'contain' any items since it carries no inventory.

The intention, obviously, is to make probate and letters of administration valid links in title to Scottish heritage vested in a deceased of English domicile; but some doubt arose as to whether the Succession (Scotland) Act 1964, s 15 in fact accomplished this.

This difficulty is now resolved by the Law Reform (Miscellaneous Provisions) (Scotland) Act 1968, s 19 which provides that s 15(1) of the 1964 Act shall have effect, 'and be deemed always to have had effect', as if it had read:

'provided that a confirmation (other than an implied confirmation within the meaning of the said section 5(2)) shall not be deemed, for the purposes of the said section 5(2) to include any such interest unless a description of the property ... is included or referred to in the confirmation'.

This made it perfectly clear that a resealed probate etc being an 'implied confirmation' under the 1924 Act, s 5(2)(b), operated as a valid link without containing any description or identification of the subjects.

Further, under the Administration of Estates Act 1971, English and Northern Ireland probates etc no longer require to be resealed, but operate automatically as titles to Scottish land without resealing.

30.6 Special destinations generally

Any conveyance of land, such as a disposition or heritable security, may contain a special, as opposed to a general, destination directing the devolution of the property on the death of the initial disponee along a particular line of devolution, for example 'to A, and on his death to B, and on B's death to C'; or 'to A and B and the survivor of them'. The special destination raises problems, particularly:

(1) as to whether or not it can be revoked (or 'evacuated');
(2) if revocable, as to whether or not it has been revoked by some other testamentary writing, for example a will; and
(3) as to completion of title thereunder.

Normally, such destinations are revocable, except for:

(1) contractual destinations; and
(2) survivorship destinations in gifts.

Failing revocation, the destination still determines the beneficial succession; but, since the Succession (Scotland) Act 1964, apart from special cases, it has ceased to have any effect *quoad* title.

In fact, since 1868, the use of such destinations is increasingly less common because of the facilities provided by the Titles to Land Consolidation (Scotland) Act 1868, s 20, with reference to wills; and, with the exception of destinations to husband and wife and survivor, they are rarely met with in practice.

30.7   TERMS USED IN DESTINATIONS

A special destination may take the form of a conveyance to a series of named persons, one succeeding to the other, which was rare; or it may restrict the line of devolution by reference to derivative terms, which was common; or it may take the form of a survivorship destination. In the second case, quite a number of terms were used in practice and acquired technical legal meanings, such as 'heir male of the body' etc. But, whatever form the destination takes, all destinations have this in common, that they are embodied in a *de praesenti* conveyance of heritage to a series of persons who take in succession. The person first called in this conveyance was known as the institute; any person called to take in succession to the institute was known as a substitute.

30.8   THE EFFECT OF DESTINATIONS ON THE RIGHTS OF THE PARTIES

In the ordinary case, where the destination in a disposition takes a simple and typical form, for example 'to A and on his death to B', both parties being named and being strangers *inter se*, A is the institute, being the disponee first called. When the disposition is delivered to A, he becomes the immediate and absolute proprietor, in fee, of the subjects thereby conveyed. The disposition is registered in the Register of Sasines or the Land Register making A owner. The presence, in his title, of the destination-over to B does not in any way detract from, or affect, his unfettered and unqualified right, as absolute proprietor, to dispose of the property by *inter vivos* or *mortis causa* deed, onerously or gratuitously. Any such *inter vivos* disposal by the institute evacuates the destination and wholly defeats the rights of the substitute B; and B has no subsequent claim either on the property itself, nor on the proceeds of sale if A has disposed of it for a consideration.

A also has unfettered power of *mortis causa* disposal which, again, evacuates the destination and defeats the rights of B, provided that:

(1)   the destination is revocable; and
(2)   A observes certain rules as to revocation of the destination.

But if A dies without effectively evacuating the destination, then B, the substitute, takes in preference to A's representatives or heirs whomsoever.

30.9   Revocability

Where the proprietor of heritage dispones it gratuitously to a disponee or several disponees, the disponer as donor is entitled to dictate the terms of any special destination. Alternatively, in an onerous conveyance, it is the disponee as purchaser who dictates the terms of the destination.

Obviously, where there are two (or more) disponees who are jointly putting up the price, they can, together, dictate the terms of the destination in the conveyance; and where they agree to a special destination (for example to A and B and the survivor) then, because they are jointly contributing, the element of survivorship introduced into the destination would be held to be a matter of contract between A and B.

Any provision as to devolution of property, taking effect on death, is normally revocable; but a party may competently contract to make a testamentary disposition in certain terms, and such a contract is enforceable. The net result is that, where a special destination is contractual, the parties to the destination are deprived of their right of *mortis causa* disposal; and cannot, by *mortis causa* deed, evacuate the destination. Their power of *inter vivos* disposal, onerously or gratuitously, is not affected. See Lord Mackay in *Brown's Trustee v Brown* 1943 SC 488. In *Smith v Mackintosh* 1988 SC 453, M conveyed her house to herself and her daughter equally between them and the survivor of them. Later, by a second *inter vivos* disposition, she conveyed her own one-half *pro indiviso* share to her son. The disposition was challenged by the daughter, following on her mother's death, on an averment that her mother had agreed that the daughter should have the whole house on the mother's death for services rendered. Her claim was dismissed on the footing that there was no evidence of this contractual arrangement on the face of the first disposition; and in any event, the second disposition in favour of the son, being an *inter vivos* deed, was not in any way invalidated by the presence of the special destination in the earlier title.

In fact, in modern practice, by far the commonest destination is the 'A and B and the survivor' case; and very often, these are in fact contractual, because the parties have jointly contributed, or have borrowed part or the whole of the price and jointly and severally granted a mortgage on the subjects. In the result, the only question which in the ordinary way now arises in regard to the interpretation of destinations is whether or not, by being contractual, they are revocable at the instance of one or other of the parties to the destination.

Thus, where there is a disposition of heritable property to 'A and B and the survivor of them' registered in the Register of Sasines or the Land Register on behalf of A and B, the effect is to vest each of A and B with an immediate and indefeasible right to a one-half *pro indiviso* share of the subjects; and each of A and B is thereupon immediately entitled to dispose of that share *inter vivos*, gratuitously or for onerous consideration.

The following points should be noted with regard to *mortis causa* disposal.

(1) Where the price was jointly contributed by A and B, or where A and B have jointly granted security, then neither A nor B can by testamentary writing alter the survivorship destination or prevent the survivor from taking the predeceaser's one-half *pro indiviso* of the property. But this does not in any way interfere with the right to dispose *inter vivos* of the one-half *pro indiviso* share of each party. See *Shand's Trustees v Shand's Trustees* 1966 SC 178.

(2) Where the price was contributed solely by A, then A can alter the survivorship destination *quoad* his own one-half *pro indiviso* share of the property. B cannot,

by *mortis causa* deed, alter the survivorship destination *quoad* his one-half *pro indiviso* share of the property. But either A or B may dispose *inter vivos* of his one-half *pro indiviso* share, thus, in effect, evacuating the destination: *Brown's Trustees v Brown* 1943 SC 488.

For a full discussion of the effect of such a destination in various circumstances, see *Hay's Trustee v Hay's Trustees* 1951 SC 329. In this case subjects were conveyed to a husband and wife and the survivor of them on the narrative that the price had been contributed equally. It was agreed, in subsequent litigation, that the narrative was incorrect and that in fact the wife had provided the whole price. Lord President Cooper, with some hesitation, admitted extrinsic evidence to prove this fact which was not disputed by the other side. This particular point caused some difficulty in *Gordon-Rogers v Thomson's Trustees* 1988 SLT 618, where the circumstances were very similar but the parties failed to agree on the facts. Lord Morison distinguished this case from *Hay's Trustee* on the footing that, in the instant case, the facts were not agreed and so extrinsic evidence was not admissible.

(3) Where the subjects were donated by X to A and B and the survivor, then neither A nor B can alter the survivorship destination by *mortis causa* deed. But again, either can dispose *inter vivos* of his one-half *pro indiviso* share. See *Brown's Trustees v Brown*.

30.10   Express additional provisions

The express terms of the destination or express provisions in the deed containing it may modify these rules and further restrict the rights of co-disponees. See J Burns *Conveyancing Practice* (4th edn, 1957), pp 371 and 372 for some illustrative styles which set out the rights of co-disponees explicitly, and it is thought would receive effect. Burns, however, makes no attempt in these styles to modify or take away the right of the co-owner to dispose of his *pro indiviso* share *inter vivos*. He deals with *mortis causa* disposal only. It is arguable that, on principle, the *pro indiviso* owner must have this *inter vivos* right.

For an unusual case, see *Munro v Munro* 1972 SLT (Sh Ct) 6. In this case, heritage had been disponed by a father to his three children, under an arrangement between all parties, the full nature of which is not disclosed in the report. The disposition was in favour of the father in liferent, and the three children equally between them and to the survivors and the last survivor of them, and the heirs of the last survivor in fee. This was followed by an express declaration that none of them might revoke, alter or affect the destination to the last survivor. The sheriff held that, in the circumstances, the destination created a right of joint ownership, and not of common property. Hence, apparently, no one of the three children had any ascertainable share which he could deal with *inter vivos* or *mortis causa*. He quotes, with approval, Lord President Cooper in *Magistrates of Banff v Ruthin Castle* 1944 SC 36 to the effect that joint property can only exist where the plural disponees are inter-related by virtue of some trust, or contractual or quasi-contractual bond (such as partnership), so as to create an independent relationship. The sheriff doubts if this independent relationship is created in this case by the disposition alone; but he finds sufficient in the surrounding circumstances to justify his view:

'It is a reasonable inference that the common thought was that each child ... should, throughout his life, have the opportunity to live in or return to the family home ... There was, on my understanding, a pre-existing agreement to keep the family home open for each of them during their respective lives, and the destination was conceived with this in mind'.

If so, why not so provide in the deed; or confer a conjunct fee and liferent? As a result of the terms of the very special arrangement in this case, express and implied, it would seem as if the three children were in effect trustees under a self-imposed trust for themselves and the survivors in conjunct liferent and the last survivor in fee, and this quasi-trust provided joint, not common, ownership.

For a criticism of this decision, see K G C Reid 'Common Property: Clarification and Confusion' 1985 SLT (News) 57.

30.11 EVACUATION

As to evacuation of a destination, the old rule was that, where the destination was not created by the deceased himself, any will, earlier or later in date, revoked the destination. Where the deceased himself had been responsible for creating the destination, a will later in date than the destination might revoke it; but only if the two were patently incompatible *inter se*. Otherwise, destination and will both receive effect as the joint testamentary instruction of the deceased.

Now, by the Succession (Scotland) Act 1964, s 30, any will executed after 10 September 1964 revokes a revocable special destination only if it refers to it and expressly revokes it. Otherwise, the destination stands. See *Stirling's Trustees v Stirling* 1977 SLT 229, where there was no express clause and therefore no revocation; and likewise *Marshall v Marshall's Executor* 1987 SLT 49.

30.12 COMPLETION OF TITLE UNDER DESTINATIONS

Where the deceased's title contained a special destination, not revoked at the death, the property passed, not to the heir-at-law, but to the 'heir of provision' under the special destination. He in turn acquired a title by serving as heir of provision, in special or in general, to the deceased institute or substitute.

The decree of service, special or general, had exactly the same effect for the heir of provision as a decree of service in favour of the heir-at-law, ie it operated as his title. If the decree was special, he could record it *de plano*; if general, he could complete title by notice of title.

In either case, the benefit thereof transmitted to his successors if he failed to complete title.

30.13   SURVIVORSHIP DESTINATIONS

These represent a technical specialty. A disposition to A and B and to the survivor operates as an immediate conveyance of one-half *pro indiviso* of the property to each of A and B as institutes, coupled with a substitution of the survivor of them to succeed, as substitute, to the one-half *pro indiviso* vested originally in the predeceaser. Therefore, on the recording of a disposition to A and B and the survivor, with the warrant of registration on behalf of A and B, each becomes registered as owner in one-half of the property *pro indiviso*.

If B predeceases survived by A, then A takes B's original one-half of the property as substitute unless B, the predeceaser, could competently have evacuated the special destination as being non-contractual and effectively did so, bearing in mind the special provision of the Succession (Scotland) Act 1964, s 30, referred to above at para 30.11. Logically in that situation A, the survivor and as such substitute in the destination to A and B, should, in feudal theory, make up title to B's one-half share as heir of provision, and obtain a decree of service in that capacity. But, in the case of survivorship destinations, the strict rule was not applied and, in the illustration, A, as survivor, did not require to serve or to carry through any other procedure in order to make up title to B's one-half share. By mere survivance, following on a survivorship destination, A as survivor became owner automatically in the share of the predeceaser. For the origin of this unexpected rule, see G L Gretton 'Trust and Executry Conveyancing' 1987 JLSS 111 at 116.

This rule also creates an unexpected problem on separation or divorce where the title to the matrimonial home has been taken in joint names of A and B and the survivor, which is commonplace in practice. If, as part of the financial settlement, A agrees that B should have the matrimonial home, it is not sufficient simply for A to convey his or her one-half *pro indiviso* share to B. That does effectively vest the whole property in B. But the survivorship destination in the title is almost certainly a contractual one and as such is irrevocable by *mortis causa* deed. So, if B then dies first, B's original one-half *pro indiviso* share would pass back to A under the special destination in the original title, notwithstanding the subsequent conveyance by A to B and irrespective of the terms of B's will. See *Gardner's Executors v Raeburn* 1996 SLT 745. Accordingly, in such situations, A and B should jointly convey the whole subjects to B in order to evacuate the special destination in the original conveyance by an *inter vivos* deed, which is always competent. See G L Gretton 'Destinations' 1989 JLSS 302.

The cases mentioned in the Digest of Cases at para 7.14 'Common Property – Division and Sale' indicate a number of situations where the presence of a special destination in the title has created problems, particularly on divorce or separation or on the break-up of a relationship where property was owned in common.

In *Redfern's Executors v Redfern* 1996 SLT 900, a similar situation to that in *Gardner's Executors v Raeburn* arose. The title to a matrimonial home was taken in joint names of husband and wife and survivor. Both contributed to the price. Subsequently, the parties separated and raised actions of divorce. They then entered into a minute of agreement providing for the dismissal of both actions and further providing for the disposal of the matrimonial home. It was agreed that the house should be sold and the proceeds divided in certain proportions. Except as otherwise provided, 'neither party shall have any claim of any nature against the other either now or at any time in the future and the parties hereby relinquish all rights of succession to the estate of the other party in the event of the death of either of them'. The house was put on the market but, before it was sold, the husband died. Thereafter, his widow withdrew the instructions to sell the house. As a result, the husband's executors raised an action of declarator against her, craving the court to hold that the minute of agreement still subsisted and bound the parties notwithstanding the husband's death. The widow argued that the agreement was at an end, and so, as she maintained, the disclaimer provisions ceased to apply, thus allowing her to succeed to her husband's one-half share of the house. Her argument was rejected on the footing that, under the disclaimer clause, each party had voluntarily waived the normal bar to evacuation of the special destination. As a result, the husband's executors were entitled to his half share of the house.

A recent case has clarified that a person takes a share of heritable property under a special destination subject to any debts. In *Fleming's Trustee v Fleming* 2000 SLT 406, a husband and wife owned a house, the title to which was in their joint names with a survivorship destination. The husband was sequestrated and subsequently died. The trustee in sequestration had not completed title at the date of death. The widow argued that she should receive her husband's share of the house under the destination free from his debts, as was decided in a previous case, *Barclays Bank Ltd v McGreish* 1983 SLT 344 which has been subject to criticism. It was held that she took her husband's share under the destination, but subject to his debts up to the value of that share.

30.14 Special destinations under the 1964 Act

Special administrative provisions are made by the Succession (Scotland) Act 1964, ss 18, 30 and 36(2). The effect of s 30 has been noticed already. By the combined effect of the 1964 Act, ss 18 and 36, the administrative position post-1964 is as follows.

(1) If a special destination in the title has been effectively revoked by the deceased, the property is part of his estate and vests in his executor as if it had been held on a general destination.

(2) If the special destination has not been effectively revoked, then the heritable property does not form part of the deceased's estate. The property passes to the substitute next called in the destination.

As to title:

(1) if the substitute requires a title (as he does in all cases except in the case of survivorship destinations) the heritable property vests in the executor by virtue of confirmation thereto, but only for the limited purpose of enabling the executor to convey the property to the substitute next called in the destination;

(2) if the substitute does not require a title, as in the case of survivorship destinations, then the property does not vest in the executor at all, and he cannot competently confirm thereto. Even if he does confirm, the confirmation in this case is not an effective title.

30.15 Entails

Similarly, under s 18(1) of the Succession (Scotland) Act 1964, all entailed property vests in the executor by confirmation but only for the purpose of conveying it to the next heir of entail. New entails have been incompetent since 1914. All remaining entails will be abolished on 28 November 2004, when the Abolition of Feudal Tenure etc (Scotland) Act 2000, s 50 comes into effect.

30.16 Subsequent transactions by the executor with heritable property

There are three possible situations following on a death.

(1) The executor is to retain the heritage to which he has confirmed, typically, in a continuing trust. In this case, the confirmation is his title. He can use the confirmation to expede a notice of title and thereby take ownership as executor. But he is not obliged to take ownership; and, instead, can hold the property on the confirmation as proprietor in trust.

   He cannot register the confirmation *de plano* in the Register of Sasines with a view to completing his title, but in the Land Register he can send it to the Keeper, who, if satisfied, will enter him as proprietor.

(2) The property is to be transferred to a beneficiary. A specific procedure is provided here by the Succession (Scotland) Act 1964, s 15(2). Under the old rule prior to 1964, where the whole estate was conveyed to trustees with a direction to make over heritage to a particular beneficiary, the will was the trustees' link in title but they then had to grant a formal disposition in favour of the beneficiary. Now, under the 1964 Act, any such transfer can be effected to a testamentary beneficiary, to a statutory successor, or to a surviving spouse or child claiming prior or legal rights by endorsing a short docquet on the confirmation (or on a certificate of confirmation). A short statutory form of docquet is given in Schedule 1 to the 1964 Act. Any such docquet, so endorsed, may be specified as

a mid-couple or link in title in any deduction of title, but is not registrable in the Register of Sasines or the Land Register with a view to completing the beneficiary's title. In the Land Register, the Keeper may change the proprietor details, if he is satisfied with the application.

This procedure is optional, in that it still remains competent to transfer heritage to a beneficiary by disposition etc, as before.

(3) The property is to be sold by the executor. Confirmation is his title. He may complete title using it as a link or he may dispone as unregistered proprietor, using the Conveyancing (Scotland) Act 1924, s 3. He cannot use a docquet on the confirmation to give a title to a purchaser.

30.17 **Protection of purchasers**

Prior to the Succession (Scotland) Act 1964, where a man died testate leaving a will dealing with heritage, a purchaser from the trustee under that will, or from a legatee, had to satisfy himself that the will was intrinsically and extrinsically valid and that the seller had a valid title thereunder to sell the property to him. Further, prior to the Trusts (Scotland) Act 1961 in the case of trustees, it was necessary to consider whether trustees had power to sell. If it later turned out that the will, as a title, was defective in any respect, or if the trustees (prior to 1961) did not have the requisite power, then in any of these events the purchaser's title might later be reduced on the grounds of any such defect. As a result, a purchaser only took a title from the deceased's representatives, whether testate or intestate, after careful enquiry into the title; but he was bound to accept the risk of reduction on these grounds. See *Sibbald's Heirs v Harris* 1947 SC 601.

Under the 1964 Act, confirmation is a title to heritable property. But, as with any other form of title, confirmation is open to reduction on a variety of grounds, for example that the will was invalid because of latent defect, or otherwise void because of want of capacity, fraud, revocation etc; or, in the case of a confirmation-dative, on the grounds that the wrong person had been confirmed.

Were it not for the provisions of the 1964 Act, s 17, a purchaser or other person dealing with the title would require to consider the terms of the will, or the terms of the petition on which confirmation proceeded, and the validity and propriety of endorsed docquets etc, or dispositions to beneficiaries etc (s 17 is not confined to docquets). All such enquiry is rendered redundant. Section 17 provides that, where any person has, in good faith and for value, acquired title to an estate in land which has vested in an executor by confirmation thereto, whether such person takes his title directly from the executor or from a person deriving title directly from the executor, the title so acquired is not open to challenge on the grounds that the confirmation was reducible or has in fact been reduced; nor can the title be challenged on the grounds that the property has been conveyed, by the executor, to the wrong beneficiary (by docquet or disposition).

The decision in *MacDougall v MacDougall's Executors* 1994 SLT 1178 illustrates a number of points referred to in the foregoing paragraphs. The facts, however, are complex and are not here narrated. The principal point in the context of succession and completion of title also involves the effect of such completion in a question with a *bona fide* purchaser for value. In this context, there are two statutory protections to a purchaser:

(1) Under the Trusts (Scotland) Act 1961, s 2, where the trustees enter into a transaction with another party which falls within the statutory of powers conferred on them under the 1921 Act, s 4, including sale, any title acquired by that other party is exempt from challenge on the grounds that the trustees acted at variance with the terms or purposes of the trust. Accordingly, when purchasing from Scottish trustees, a purchaser is protected to that extent, whether he is acting in good faith or not. See *Brodie v Secretary of State for Scotland* 2002 GWD 20-698.

(2) The Succession (Scotland) Act 1964, s 17 provides comparable protection as noted above, provided in this case that the purchaser acts in *bona fide* and for value.

(3) Alternatively, at common law, where one of the writs within the prescriptive progress of titles is voidable as opposed to void *ab initio*, a *bona fide* purchaser for value without notice is likewise protected against a subsequent challenge of the antecedent title. See Gretton and Reid *Conveyancing* (2nd edn, 1999), para 7.15. As the professors point out in that passage, however, the common law protection to the purchaser in the circumstances narrated has no application in any case where an antecedent title in the prescription progress is void. Further, even in the case of voidable titles, the purchaser is not exempt from challenge if he had notice or was put on his enquiry by something in the antecedent titles which might raise a suspicion that an earlier title was in some way or other defective.

For a detailed account of *MacDougall v MacDougall's Executors*, see the sixth edition of this book, para 31.26.

30.18 Proposed reforms

In 1990 the Scottish Law Commission carried out a general review of the whole law of succession in Scotland following on three consultative memoranda published in 1986: see the *Report on Succession* (Scot Law Com No 124, 1990). The Commission recommended a complete recasting of the law of intestate succession and legal rights and certain specific changes in relation to testate succession, executries and other matters.

So far as this chapter is concerned, the relevant recommendations of the Commission are contained in Part VI, Special Destinations, and Part VIII, Executry Questions, in the Report.

30.19 SPECIAL DESTINATIONS

After making extensive investigations and consultations, the Commission made the following recommendations:

'25 In future proprietory titles, destinations should cease to be competent but excluding from that sweeping recommendation, survivorship destinations; destinations in liferent and fee; destinations to a person as a trustee or holder of an office or position and his successors as such; and destinations giving effect to the terms of a will executed prior to the passing of the relevant Act.

26 This recommendation relates only to testamentary writings, not to titles.

27 A special destination should be defined as a destination by which the property in question is to devolve on a named or identified person or persons or on a class of persons, other than "heirs".

28 These recommendations deal with administrative machinery only, for which see chapter 31.

29 A successor under a destination should be personally liable for the debts of the predeceaser up to the limit of the value of the property to which the survivor succeeds.

30 (a) The owner of property subject to a destination in the title should have power to dispose of that property, for value or gratuitously, *inter vivos* or *mortis causa*, whether or not the destination is contractual and regardless of who paid for the property, but

(b) this should apply only to destinations created after the commencement of the relevant legislation'.

There are also further recommendations in regard to leases.

30.20 EXECUTRY QUESTIONS

A number of recommendations are made by the Commission on executry matters in Part VIII of the Report. The only one which is significant in the context of this chapter is:

'44 It should be competent for an executor or trustee to use the deceased's will as a link in a clause of deduction of title; and the same facility should be extended to legatees or general disponees under the will'.

Whether or not this would improve the present position is open to question, but at least it has the merit of clarifying the position and removing the doubts expressed in para 30.4 above.

The Commission's proposals have not been implemented and are unlikely to be implemented in the foreseeable future.

Chapter 31

Completion of Title

31.1 The desirability of registration

As between two parties acting at arms' length, such as a seller and a purchaser of heritage, the purchaser at settlement obtains from the seller a title in the form of a disposition which contains all the essential elements to allow of its recording *de plano* in the Register of Sasines or registration in the Land Register. In all such cases, it is desirable to record the disposition in the Register of Sasines or register it in the Land Register on behalf of the disponee with the minimum of delay to avoid the possibility of some supervening impediment to the title, such as the sequestration of the grantor. Failure to record the disposition immediately may mean that the purchaser's title is defeated by a writ which enters the Record before it. The classic case is the *Ceres School Board v McFarlane* (1895) 23 R 279, where a feuar under a feu charter, which had been delivered but not registered, occupied the land for many years undisturbed on that unrecorded title. However, several years later, the estate of which the land formed a small part transmitted as a whole to a *bona fide* purchaser for value who had no warning of the existence of the feuar's rights and himself recorded the disposition of that landed estate. In a subsequent competition between the feuar under the prior but unrecorded feu charter and the purchaser of the landed estate with a recorded title, priority of registration determined priority of right and the purchaser of the landed estate, having the real right in the whole property, was preferred to the feuar in occupation thereof on an unrecorded title.

On the other hand, where a registered owner of a particular heritable property dies leaving the property to trustees under his will for the liferent of his wife and to his issue in fee, the position is undoubtedly different, in that the possibility of the trustees' title being defeated by some valid intervening and adverse right is exceedingly remote. Moreover, in any event, the form which the title of the trustees takes, whether it be the will of the deceased or confirmation in their favour as executors, is not of itself recordable in the Register of Sasines or registrable in the Land Register, although in the Land Register a confirmation can be sent to the Keeper who, if satisfied, will enter the executors as proprietors. As a result, in the great majority of cases where property is to be retained in trust or by a beneficiary as absolute proprietor, no title enters the record and the trustees or the beneficiary as the case may be remain as unregistered proprietors. The risk of any adverse interest defeating their title is so remote that for practical purposes it can be ignored.

There are, however, intermediate cases where the risk may be more significant;

and, in any event, even in the case of trustees holding heritable property for the liferent of the beneficiary, it may be desirable to convert their valid personal title into an effective real right by the recording of an appropriate writ in the Register of Sasines or registration thereof in the Land Register.

Under the feudal system, a person who has not completed title is known as an 'uninfeft proprietor'. This terminology is removed by the Abolition of Feudal Tenure etc (Scotland) Act 2000 and replaced with the expression 'unregistered proprietor'. The new term is used in this chapter.

31.2   THE GENERAL DISPOSITION

The commonest situation where a general disposition is used is following on a death because, in every such case, the title takes a form which is not suitable for recording itself. But there are a variety of other such cases. In all such situations, the title will take the form of a general disposition or its equivalent, such as confirmation, a deed of assumption of new trustees, or the like.

Before considering the methods of completion of title, it is convenient here to deal with various cases where a general disposition may operate as a link in title, otherwise than on death. The following list is illustrative but not by any means exhaustive.

31.3   **Trusts**

We have noticed already the situation where a will or trust disposition and settlement operates as a direct conveyance of heritage by the deceased to his trustees. Since 1964, confirmation is recommended as the appropriate title in all cases rather than using the will as a link; but, nonetheless, in the opinion of the professors of conveyancing, the will itself can still be used as a valid link, at least by trustees, as being a general disposition. See para 30.4.

In exactly the same way, although less commonly, a heritable proprietor can grant a general disposition of his whole estate to operate *inter vivos*, such as a trust deed for creditors, or, possibly, a general disposition of his whole estate for *inter vivos* trust purposes. But, normally, when setting up an *inter vivos* trust, specific assets are conveyed by special conveyance rather than by way of a general disposition of the whole estate.

31.4   ORIGINAL DEED AS A LINK IN TITLE TO TRUSTEES

In all these cases, where there is a general disposition conveying heritage, the constituent deed operates as the link in title to the trustees.

31.5 ORIGINAL DEED AS A LINK IN TITLE TO BENEFICIARY

Alternatively, in the case of wills, it was and is possible for the deceased to convey his estate directly to the beneficiary and the view of two of the professors was that, in that situation, the will operates as a valid link. But because of the doubts expressed in the professors' opinion, it is undesirable in any circumstances to use the will as a link for a beneficiary post-1964. Under the Succession (Scotland) Act 1964, notwithstanding the direct conveyance to a beneficiary of heritage in a will, the executors or trustees have power to confirm to that heritage and, if they so confirm, it vests in them and the confirmation is their title.

31.6 DEED OF ASSUMPTION AND CONVEYANCE

The trustees acting under any trust, *inter vivos* or *mortis causa*, normally have power to assume new trustees by virtue of the Trusts (Scotland) Act 1921, s 3; and, under the 1921 Act, executors nominate have the like power. But, in addition to their appointment, the new trustees will require a title to the trust assets. The appropriate deed is, therefore, a combined deed of assumption, operating as an appointment of the new trustees, and conveyance, operating as a general disposition of the trust assets in favour of the new trustees.

It is technically competent, in a deed of assumption and conveyance, to incorporate a special conveyance of heritage, but this is now never done. As a result, the deed of assumption and conveyance operates as a general disposition in favour of the new trustees and can be used as a link in their title.

In *inter vivos* deeds, the truster may reserve, or may have by implication, a power to appoint new trustees. Having divested himself of his assets which are invested in the original trustees, the truster has no power to give a title to new trustees appointed by him. Thus, by *inter vivos* deed of trust, A appoints B and C to act as trustees and conveys certain heritable estate to them. B and C both then die. A, the truster, then appoints X as trustee but cannot give X a title. In that situation, X could obtain a title to the trust assets from the executors of C, the last surviving trustee, if they confirm to the trust estate, under the Executors (Scotland) Act 1900, s 6: see below.

The same applies in unusual cases where some third party has the power to nominate new trustees. This does not give him power to confer a title on the new trustees.

31.7 RESIGNATION OR REMOVAL OF A TRUSTEE

A trustee or executor nominate normally has power to resign office, by a minute of resignation. This effectively divests the trustee of his interest in the trust assets, including heritage, which devolve on the continuing trustees without the necessity of any conveyance or other transfer by the resigning trustee: see the Trusts (Scotland)

Act 1921, s 20. Nonetheless, it is the custom to include a minute of resignation in any narration of links in title in a clause of deduction of title etc: see below.

Alternatively, in certain situations, the court may remove a trustee: see the 1921 Act, s 23. Removal has exactly the same effect as resignation, and the decree of removal would normally be included in the links in title.

31.8 LAPSED TRUSTS

If all trustees on an existing trust have died, new trustees must be appointed to continue the administration; and in all such cases the new trustees will also require a title. The new trustees appointed in a lapsed trust, or the beneficiaries, may derive their title in the following ways, whether the deceased died before or after the Succession (Scotland) Act 1964.

31.9 Trusts (Scotland) Act 1921, s 22

Where no one has power to appoint new trustees, for example typically, in a testamentary case, where all the trustees have died without assuming any new ones, then the court may appoint trustees under the Trusts (Scotland) Act 1921, s 22. In terms of that section, the decree appointing the new trustees had to include a warrant authorising them to complete title; but this requirement as to warrant in the decree has been removed by the Conveyancing Amendment (Scotland) Act 1938, s 1. In the result, a decree of appointment, standing alone, operates as a general disposition in favour of the new trustees appointed thereunder.

31.10 Trusts (Scotland) Act 1921, s 24

As an alternative, in the case of certain lapsed trusts, to avoid the necessity of appointing new trustees, it is competent for beneficiaries, where the administration in the trust is complete, to petition the court for authority to allow the beneficiaries to make up title to the trust estate. The situation here envisaged is that A has died leaving a will in favour of a trustee B and directing B to make over the residue of his estate to X, Y and Z. B administers the estate but dies before the assets are actually made over; but, at B's death, nothing remains to be done except to make over the assets. X, Y and Z could then petition the court for authority to complete title thereto. In such cases, under s 24 of the Trusts (Scotland) Act 1921, the decree in favour of the beneficiaries operates as a general disposition in their favour.

31.11 Confirmation of executors

If the deceased died after 10 September 1964, then new trustees may be appointed by the court; or title can be made up through the medium of the executors of the last surviving trustee under the Executors (Scotland) Act 1900, ss 6 or 7.

To illustrate the working of the rules as to confirmation in a practical situation, assume that A died as registered owner of a heritable property, testate or intestate. B confirms as A's executor and includes A's heritage in the confirmation, which therefore vests in B as executor by virtue of confirmation thereto. Normally, B will deal with A's heritage either by selling it or passing it on to A's successors, by disposition or by a docquet given under the Succession (Scotland) Act 1964, s 15. But suppose he fails to do so and then dies. The title to A's heritage lapses on B's death and has to be revived.

31.12   Executors (Scotland) Act 1900, s 6

B's executor, nominate or dative, if he is willing so to do, may include A's heritable estate in the inventory of B's estate, and so in B's confirmation, under a special heading of estate held in trust. See *Currie on Confirmation* (8th edn), Chapter 16, for full details. Such confirmation allows B's executor to transfer A's unadministered heritage either (1) to new trustees appointed in A's estate or (2) to A's successors, but does not confer any further power of administration on B's executor.

31.13   Executors (Scotland) Act 1900, s 7

If procedure under s 6 of the Executors (Scotland) Act 1900 is not practicable, anyone interested in A's estate may petition the sheriff for appointment of an executor dative *ad non executa* who, when appointed, may confirm to A's unadministered heritage. The confirmation *ad non executa* is a valid title; and the executor *ad non executa* has full power to administer.

31.14   JURISDICTION IN TRUST PETITIONS

In all the foregoing situations, the sheriff court now has jurisdiction to appoint or remove trustees and to give authority to beneficiaries to make up title under the Trusts (Scotland) Act 1921, ss 22–24, by virtue of the Law Reform (Miscellaneous Provisions) (Scotland) Act 1980, s 13, which substantially reduces the costs of these procedures.

31.15   Judicial factors

The decree appointing a judicial factor, prior to the Conveyancing Amendment (Scotland) Act 1938, had to contain a warrant authorising the judicial factor to complete title to the estate coming under his charge as factor. However, this is no longer necessary by virtue of the 1938 Act, s 1, in terms of which any decree appointing a factor operates as a general disposition in his favour of all heritable estate coming under his charge. It can, therefore, be used as a link in title for the purpose of dealing with that estate.

31.16   Sequestration

The decree confirming the appointment of the permanent trustee, termed 'the act and warrant', vests the whole estate of the bankrupt in the permanent trustee under the Bankruptcy (Scotland) Act 1985, s 31. Accordingly, the act and warrant is equivalent to a general disposition in his favour, and can be used as such when dealing with the bankrupt's heritage. There is no obligation on him to complete his title by recording a notice of title; but normally he will do so in order to exclude possible competing titles or securities. In that case, he will use the notice of title – see below. For a recent example of a trustee using a notice of title, see *Burnett's Trustee v Grainger* 2002 SLT 699.

31.17   *ACQUIRENDA* IN SEQUESTRATION

Where, after the date of sequestration, the bankrupt acquires right to other estate, for example as a beneficiary under the will of a deceased testator, this estate also vests in the permanent trustee automatically under the Bankruptcy (Scotland) Act 1985, s 32(6). Any such after-acquired estate will, no doubt, be held by a third party, for example a trustee under the will of the deceased in which the bankrupt is the beneficiary. In terms of the 1985 Act, s 32(6), the trustee under that will, on production to him of the act and warrant of the permanent trustee, is obliged to make over to the permanent trustee any assets falling to the bankrupt as beneficiary. In that event, if assets are made over *in specie*, the conveyance by the executor under the will of the deceased in favour of the permanent trustee will operate as the trustee's title and will probably be in the form of a special disposition, in the case of heritage, which can be recorded *de plano*. Accordingly, in the case of such assets, the question of completion of title presents no problem.

31.18   Completion of title and ownership following thereon

No real right of ownership in land can be created without:

(1)   written title; and
(2)   registration in the Register of Sasines under the Registration Act 1617, or, where appropriate, registration of the title under the Land Registration (Scotland) Act 1979. The same principles apply to both registers, although the procedure differs. See para 31.23 below.

31.19   The general disponee

After the Titles to Land Consolidation (Scotland) Act 1868 and the Conveyancing (Scotland) Act 1874, it became very much more common in practice for a person to have a right to land under a general, as opposed to a special, disposition. Such a general disposition was, undoubtedly, a valid title, but was not of itself recordable for the procuring of proprietorship. Such cases arose in the following, typical, situations.

31.20 WILLS

The Titles to Land Consolidation (Scotland) Act 1868, s 20, validated wills generally as links in title. Such wills were normally in the form of a general disposition either to trustees or to a beneficiary direct.

31.21 TRUSTS

The increasing use of trusts produced a consequent increase in deeds of assumption and conveyance and minutes of resignation, not containing any description of the trust heritage.

31.22 HERITABLE SECURITIES AND CONFIRMATION

Heritable securities became moveable estate under the Titles to Land Consolidation (Scotland) Act 1868 (in the great majority of cases), with a consequent increase in the number of cases where confirmation, as a general disposition, operated as a link in title, not of itself recordable.

31.23 **Procedure for completing title**

Under the system of recording title in the Register of Sasines, machinery existed to enable a person in right of land under a general disposition or its equivalent to put his title on record and so become heritable proprietor. This was by means of a new writ, a notarial instrument, which was introduced in the Titles to Land (Scotland) Act 1858. The elaborate provisions in the 1858 Act were re-enacted and extended in the Titles to Land Consolidation (Scotland) Act 1868. These were largely superseded with the introduction of the notice of title in the Conveyancing (Scotland) Act 1924. The position under land registration is different. If the title has already been registered, a notice of title is no longer required. The unregistered proprietor simply applies to the Keeper to be registered as proprietor under the Land Registration (Scotland) Act 1979, s 3(6). Under the 1979 Act, s 3(1), registration has the effect of vesting in the registered proprietor a real right in the registered property and the date at which the real right is so created is the date of registration under s 3(4). Until all land throughout Scotland is held on a registered title, the need for notices of title will remain, although their use will diminish.

The provisions on the notice of title are set out in ss 4–6 of the 1924 Act. But the effect of the notice of title is equated, under the 1924 Act, to the effect of a notarial instrument; and it is therefore necessary in the first place, to look briefly at the 1868 provisions.

The main provisions, in the 1868 Act, relating to completion of title to land, are ss 17, 19, 23 and 25. Sections 125 to 128 deal with heritable securities.

31.24   Notarial instrument

Speaking generally, the notarial instrument is a semi-official narrative under the hand of a notary public but is a narrative only, simply setting out certain facts, or purported facts, which have been brought to the attention of the notary. It is not an operative deed and does not of itself create or confer rights. It merely serves as a necessary and convenient vehicle for transporting a personal title to land onto the Record, so as to convert that personal title into a real right, and procure ownership. On this aspect of the effect of the notarial instrument, see *Kerr's Trustee v Yeaman's Trustee* (1888) 15 R 520 (the opinion of Lord Rutherfurd Clark; ignore the other judgments) and *Sutherland v Garrity* 1941 SC 196.

31.25   Notice of title

In practice, the notarial instrument was superseded, although not abolished, by the notice of title, introduced under the Conveyancing (Scotland) Act 1924. The main purpose of the 1924 Act was simplification. In place of the numerous sections in the Titles to Land Consolidation (Scotland) Act 1868 dealing, separately, with completion of title to land and to heritable securities, the use of the notice of title for completing title to land and securities in all circumstances is dealt with in one relatively simple section: see s 4 of the 1924 Act. In addition, various forms of notice of title are introduced, replacing all the various forms of notarial instrument under the earlier Acts.

Further, the notice of title may be signed by any law agent, not merely a notary public. Hence the change of name.

31.26   THE RIGHT TO LAND

Section 4 of the Conveyancing (Scotland) Act 1924 provides:

'Any person having right either to land or to a heritable security by a title which has not been completed by being recorded in the appropriate Register of Sasines, may complete his title in manner following'.

Four separate situations are then dealt with under subsections (1), (2), (3) and (4); and the section then concludes:

'And on such notice of title being recorded, as in this section provided, the title of the person on whose behalf it is recorded shall be, in all respects, in the same position as if his title were completed as at the date of such recording by notarial instrument in the appropriate form duly expede and recorded according to the present law and practice'.

31.27 NATURE OF THE TITLE

Generally speaking, there are three distinct categories of person who may be said to have a right to land:

(1) the heritable proprietor, having a registered title. Clearly, the section has no application in his case, because his title is already completed;
(2) the unregistered proprietor whose right is constituted by an active but unregistered title, such as a special but unrecorded disposition or, much more commonly, a general disposition or its equivalent. The notice of title is available for any such disponee;
(3) a purchaser under missives or a beneficiary in a trust, although undoubtedly having right to land, does not have right to land by title. A contract is not a title, since it contains no words of conveyance. The trust deed is a title to the trustees. It is not (normally) a title to the beneficiary, whose right is a *jus crediti* only, a mere *jus ad rem*, which entitles him to call on the trustees to denude.

31.28 LAST REGISTERED PROPRIETOR

The Conveyancing (Scotland) Act 1924, s 4 makes no distinction between the case where the immediate predecessor in title of the person expeding the notice was registered, and the case where he was not. The procedure under this section applies equally to either case. Thus A died, leaving a will containing a general conveyance to B. B is a person in category (2) above, and might complete title to A's heritable property by notice of title. He is not bound to complete title. Suppose in fact, that he failed to do so. He died without a registered title, leaving a will in favour of C. Again, C is a person in category (2), even although B was unregistered; and C might complete title to the heritable estate originally belonging to A, again by notice of title under s 4.

31.29   ALTERNATIVE FORMS OF NOTICE

The Conveyancing (Scotland) Act 1924, s 4(1) and (2) contain two alternative procedures for completing title to land. 'Land' is defined in the 1924 Act, s 2(1) to exclude securities, but otherwise has the definition assigned to it in the Titles to Land Consolidation (Scotland) Act 1868, s 3, and the Conveyancing (Scotland) Act 1874, s 3, which is very wide. Section 4(1) of the 1924 Act deals with the normal case; s 4(2) provides an alternative for very special circumstances, and is rarely used. Section 4(3) and (4) make comparable alternative procedures for completing title to heritable securities.

31.30   FORM B1

Section 4(1) of the Conveyancing (Scotland) Act 1924 (as amended by the Abolition of Feudal Tenure etc (Scotland) Act 2000, with effect from 28 November 2004) provides:

'A person having such right to land may complete a title thereto by recording in the appropriate Register of Sasines a notice of title in or as nearly as may be in the terms of form No 1 of Schedule B to this Act, in which notice of title such person shall deduce his title from the person having last recorded title'.

'Deduction of title' is defined in s 2(3) of the 1924 Act as implying the specification of the writ or series of writs, without narration of the contents thereof, by which the person expeding the notice has acquired right from the person last with the last recorded title. In other words, however many unrecorded mid-couples may intervene between the person last registered and the person now completing the title, the deduction of title starts with the last registration and then narrates all the intervening unrecorded links.

31.31   Links in title

Broadly speaking, anything which operates as a title to land, *inter vivos* or *mortis causa*, may be used as a link in title in a deduction of title for this purpose. Even were this not implied, it is express in terms of the Conveyancing (Scotland) Act 1924, s 5(1), which defines the writs which can be used as links in this context as including any statute, conveyance, decree, or other writing whereby a right to land is vested in, or transmitted to, any person. The definition of 'conveyance' in the 1924 Act, s 2(1)(c) is extremely wide; and the definitions of the same term in the Titles to Land Consolidation (Scotland) Act 1868, s 3, and the Conveyancing (Scotland) Act 1874, s 3 are expressly adopted for the purpose of the 1924 Act by s 2(1). The definition is extended to include, not only the principal writs themselves, but also extracts and office copies, as defined in the 1924 Act, s 2(2). For an equivalent provision in the case of probates and letters of administration, see the 1874 Act, s 51 and the Conveyancing (Scotland) Acts (1874 and 1879) Amendment Act 1887, s 5.

31.32 Statutory vesting provisions

For an illustration of a statute operating as a vesting writ for this purpose see the Scotland Act 1998, s 60, and the Transfer of Property etc (Scottish Ministers) Order 1999, SI 1999/1104. Under that Act and Order all rights and interests in property in Scotland belonging to a Minister of the Crown or government department which is used wholly or mainly for functions which are devolved are transferred to and vest in the Scottish Ministers. The combined effect of the 1998 Act and the 1999 Order is simply to give the Scottish Ministers a title under a general disposition. It does not create any registered title for them. Therefore, when disponing land, the Scottish Ministers must deduce title through the Act and Order.

Compare the Church of Scotland (General Trustees) Order Confirmation Act 1921, in terms of which property is transferred to the transferees thereunder to the same effect as if dispositions had been granted and recorded in the appropriate division of the General Register of Sasines. Obviously, in the latter case, the transferees are deemed to be heritable proprietors although having no recorded title.

The first form of statutory provision is common; the second is rare.

31.33 'Conveyance'

'Conveyance' includes any general disposition (eg, before the Succession (Scotland) Act 1964, a will, or after it, a confirmation) or special disposition (which means the ordinary type of disposition). Suppose A, with a recorded title, grants a disposition to B. Normally, B completes title by recording it. He may equally well, if he wishes, record a notice of title using the disposition as a link, though there is normally no point in so doing.

31.34 Content of Form B i

The normal form of notice for completing title to land in the Conveyancing (Scotland) Act 1924, Schedule B1, is straightforward. In outline, its content is:

(1) *narrative*. This defines the person expeding the notice and having the right to the land;
(2) *description*. The subjects to which title is being made up are described in conventional form;
(3) *burdens*. It is appropriate to refer to burdens in the usual way. In addition, however, it may be necessary (although this is extremely rare) to set out at length in the notice of title the terms of any real burden or condition running with the land and contained in one of the unrecorded mid-couples or links in title on which the notice proceeds. Special provision is made for this in Schedule B1, in terms of

which, in addition to setting out the burden at full length, it is necessary to specify the writ in which the burden appears. See *Cowie v Muirden* (1893) 20 R (HL) 81;

(4) *deduction of title*. This is the clause which complies with the instruction in the 1924 Act, s 4(1) to deduce title. It contains three essential elements:

  (a) identification of the person with the last recorded title, by name and designation. Note particularly that he must be designed;

  (b) a specification of his recorded title. Only the minimum detail is required, normally the division of the Register and the date. It may be that the date of the last recorded title has been incorrectly specified or omitted, but, if so, provided that the writ can be identified, the error may not be fatal, by analogy with the provision for statutory descriptions by reference. See para 8.22;

  (c) deduction of title proper, being the specification of the writ, or writs, by which the person expeding the notice acquired right from the person with the last recorded title. There may be one, or several. Each writ must be separately specified, giving sufficient information to identify the writ, for example the type of writ, the party or parties without designations, its date, and date of registration; but narration of the content of each writ is unnecessary;

(5) *presentment of writs to the official*. As already mentioned, under the 1924 Act, the notice of title may now be signed by any law agent, not merely a notary public. It is generally stated that the agent executing the notice should have no direct interest therein; but it is quite unobjectionable for a solicitor to expede a notice on behalf of a client and this is regular practice. The clause simply states 'Which last recorded title and subsequent writ(s) have been presented to me YZ (designed), law agent'.

The notice is executed by the law agent and the testing clause is added in the usual way. Attestation, by one witness, is still necessary since the notice is to be recorded: see the Requirements of Writing (Scotland) Act 1995, s 6 and Schedule 4.

The writ is then sent to Register House for recording. The title of the person expeding the notice is thus completed in accordance with the statutory formula.

31.35   FORM B2

Form B2 was used for certain special situations which are now rare. See the sixth edition of this book at para 32.28.

31.36   HERITABLE SECURITIES

The Conveyancing (Scotland) Act 1924, s 4(3) and (4) make equivalent provision for the ordinary, and the special circumstances, procedure for completing title to a heritable security (or part thereof) which for all practical purposes nowadays means the standard security.

Section 4(3) applies to any heritable security already recorded; for that case, Form B3 is the appropriate form (equivalent to Form B1).

Section 4(4) applies to unrecorded securities. It provides for the recording thereof, along with the special form of notice set out in Form B5.

31.37 Effect of recorded notice

Finally, the Conveyancing (Scotland) Act 1924, s 6, provides that a notice of title expede in terms of the Act is equivalent to a notarial instrument expede according to the pre-1924 law and practice. As a result, for practical purposes, the notarial instrument is superseded, although it can still competently be used.

31.38 Deeds by unregistered proprietors

As a general property law principle, a real right can originate only from a proprietor who is himself registered. It follows that, where the proprietor of heritage is unregistered and wishes to grant a lease or a standard security, he must still first complete title by the recording of an appropriate notice. The old rule has now been altered, but with limitations, under three different provisions:

(1) continuity of trust ownership;
(2) disposition etc by person with unregistered title; and
(3) standard securities.

31.39 CONTINUITY OF TRUST OWNERSHIP

The Titles to Land Consolidation (Scotland) Act 1868, s 26, and the Conveyancing (Scotland) Act 1874, s 45, relate to trusts; and the object is to render unnecessary completion of title of new, in the case of a trust, on the occasion of the assumption of a new trustee. The 1868 provision applies only to religious and educational trusts, where the title to trust heritage has been taken in the name of office bearers or trustees for behoof of the association, and their successors in office. The 1874 provision applies to any trust, but only where the office of trustee is conferred upon the holder of that office *ex officio* and his successors in office, or on the proprietor of a landed estate and his successors as such proprietor.

In these limited circumstances, when the trustees have taken an original registration, then, notwithstanding subsequent changes in the body of trustees, there is notionally a deemed continuity of registration; and the present trustees for the time being (as successors in the office under the 1868 provision, or as the holder of the office or owner of the estate for the time being under the 1874 provision), are deemed to be registered, even although there is no title on the Record in their name. This is a useful, but very limited, provision. It is particularly appropriate in the case of churches and other similar associations.

31.40 DISPOSITION ETC BY PERSON WITH UNRECORDED TITLE

See the Conveyancing (Scotland) Act 1924, s 3. This is a statutory short-cut available in all cases (not merely in the case of trusts) to any person having right to land or to a heritable security whose title thereto has not been completed by being recorded in the Register of Sasines or registered in the Land Register. Compare s 4 of the 1924 Act and note the similarity in wording. In other words, the short-cut is available to a person in category (2) of the three categories referred to in para 31.27 above, who holds an active title in his favour which is of itself an entitlement to registration by expeding a notice of title.

31.41 Deduction of title

In the case of a person in category (2) (see para 31.27), s 3 of the Conveyancing (Scotland) Act 1924 provides:

(1) In the case of land, that the person entitled may grant a disposition. If, in such disposition, he deduces his title from the person with the last recorded title, by incorporating, in the disposition, a clause of deduction of title in terms of Schedule A1 to the 1924 Act then, on such disposition being recorded, the title of the disponee is in all respects in the same position as if, at the date of recording of the disposition, the disponee had completed title by recording a notarial instrument. Put shortly, an unregistered proprietor can now dispone provided he deduces title.

The only significant difference between a disposition by an unregistered proprietor and a disposition by an registered proprietor is the incorporation of the clause of deduction of title in terms of Schedule A1 to the 1924 Act; and this clause is identical in form to the clause of deduction of title in a notice of title. Deduction of title is not required where the subjects are already registered in the Land Register.

(2) In the case of a heritable security duly constituted by having been recorded in the Register of Sasines, the creditor for the time being in right thereof may deal with that security by way of assignation, restriction or discharge, without first completing title, provided, again, that in such assignation, deed of restriction or discharge, the unregistered creditor deduces title in terms of note 2 to Schedule

K to the 1924 Act, and two alternative methods of deduction of title were provided for dealings with heritable securities. This provision is further amended by the Conveyancing and Feudal Reform (Scotland) Act 1970, s 47 and Schedules 10 and 11. The effect of this amendment is that, where the grantor of the assignation etc, has a recorded title, no further specification or deduction is necessary. Where the grantor has no recorded title in his own name, he deduces title from the last recorded title to the security.

Again, under the 1924 Act, s 3, when the assignee etc, records the assignation containing this deduction of title, his title is in all respects in the same position as if he had completed it by notarial instrument under the pre-1924 rules.

The same rules apply to dealings with standard securities under the 1970 Act.

31.42 STANDARD SECURITIES

See the Conveyancing and Feudal Reform (Scotland) Act 1970, s 12. In the past, heritable securities (not being dispositions under the Conveyancing (Scotland) Act 1924, s 3) could not be granted by the unregistered proprietor. However, s 12(1) of the 1970 Act allows unregistered proprietors to grant a standard security: 'a standard security may be granted over land or a real right in land by a person having right to that land or real right in land but whose title thereto has not been completed by being duly recorded'. But such a person must deduce title. Notes 2 and 3 of Schedule 2 to the 1970 Act provide the style of deduction.

Note 2 deals with the normal case where A, as unregistered proprietor, is granting a standard security. He inserts a clause of deduction of title identical in form to the 1924 Act, Schedule A, except that, here, the person with the last recorded title need not be designed. Deduction of title is not required where the standard security is registered in the Land Register.

In cases where deduction of title is appropriate, the 1924 Act, s 5 (deduction of title) is applied by s 12(3) of the 1970 Act to define mid-couples or links in title.

See I J S Talman (ed) *Halliday's Conveyancing Law and Practice in Scotland* (2nd edn, 2 volumes, 1996–97), para 36–21 ff.

31.43 CONTINUING NEED FOR COMPLETION OF TITLE

As a result of these provisions, the notice of title is far less common than its predecessor, the notarial instrument. But completion of title by way of notice of title is still commonplace. For one thing, it is generally accepted that, as stated in para 31.38, a lease cannot competently be granted by an unregistered proprietor, notwithstanding the provisions in the Conveyancing (Scotland) Act 1924 for a disposition by the proprietor without a recorded title. The same applied to granting heritable security before the Conveyancing and Feudal Reform (Scotland) Act 1970, s 12, which first introduced deduction of title for the standard security. For another thing, if property is to be retained indefinitely, it may be prudent to complete title in order to establish the real right and to exclude any possibility of challenge to the title as having been extinguished by the long negative prescription under the rule in *Pettigrew v Harton* 1956 SC 67. For a recent illustration, see *Porteous's Executors v Ferguson* 1995 SLT 649.

In the case of registered titles, see para 31.23 above. But completion of title for this purpose would now seem no longer to be necessary. See para 32.77.

Chapter 32

Examination of Title

32.1 First registration

Since 1 April 2003, the whole of Scotland has been operational for land registration: see para 11.16. Accordingly, almost all transactions will lead to a first registration. The main exception is where a property is not sold or leased on a long lease but is transferred for no consideration. In such cases the transfer of a property which is not already registered in the Land Register will not lead to a first registration and the disposition transferring the title will be recorded in the Register of Sasines. This chapter deals with examination of title in transactions leading to a first registration and where the title is already registered. For those few transactions where the disposition will be recorded in the Register of Sasines, many of the details relating to a first registration apply but reference should also be made to the sixth edition of this book at paras 33.2 to 33.79. For further details on the matters covered in this chapter, see the *Registration of Title Practice Book*.

The selling solicitor will normally know whether the title has already been registered. If there is any doubt, an application to the Keeper for a Form 14 report will clarify the position.

32.2 CONDITIONS IN THE CONTRACT

As already explained at some length in Chapter 28, certain general obligations in the contract of sale and purchase are implied; and several special conditions are now almost invariably expressed. The first step in examining a title is to read the contract through from beginning to end; and to note all the special conditions and points to look for when examining the title, such as: what is the liability for roof repairs?

In this context, it is particularly important when examining the title to check in addition that any previous alteration to the property, including installation of the double glazing, and any change of use was duly authorised and completion certificates duly obtained under the relevant statutory provisions referred to in Chapter 20. Particular care must be taken in the case of listed buildings.

In the case of new developments, it is also important to check not only that planning permission and a completion certificate have been obtained, but also that the road and foot pavement have been made up *ex adverso* of the subjects of purchase. If they have not, one should check to see if a road bond or its equivalent has been lodged with the local authority under the Roads (Scotland) Act 1984, s 17. On these points, see para 28.39.

Changes lie ahead due to the enactment of the Building (Scotland) Act 2003. The current practice of obtaining a letter of comfort from a local authority or a private report from an architect where the appropriate local authority building warrant or completion certificate cannot be produced will cease when the relevant provisions of the 2003 Act come into force, currently expected to be in 2005. This Act will replace the Building (Scotland) Act 1959, in compliance with the relevant EC Directive, and includes changes in procedures relating to building warrants and completion certificates. Where an owner requests a local authority to confirm that a building conforms to building regulations, a Building Standards Assessment will be issued instead of a letter of comfort. The Scottish Executive initiated a consultation process on the detailed regulations, which ended on 31 October 2003. See www.scotland.gov.uk/library5/development/dbsr05-00.asp. For a brief outline of the implications of the Building (Scotland) Act 2003 in relation to letters of comfort, see A D Anderson 'The End of Letters of Comfort' (2002) 70 SLG 172.

Another change relates to the new regime for dealing with contaminated land which came into force in 2000. It is necessary to ensure that there are no entries relating to the property in the register maintained by the local authority. See paras 20.34 and 28.41.

32.3 PROPRIETARY TITLE

The main point to establish is the validity and sufficiency of the seller's proprietary title, ie that he has the legal title. On a first registration, the purchaser's solicitor first examines the title and satisfies himself thereon. Having taken a disposition in favour of the purchaser, he must then in turn satisfy the Keeper that the title as presented to the Keeper, including the disposition in favour of the purchaser, is a title which the Keeper can accept without any exclusion or qualification of indemnity. For this purpose, the whole prescriptive progress of title must be carefully examined, starting with the foundation writ. But, for this purpose, nothing earlier than that deed need be considered. The points to look for are set out below.

32.4 Foundation writ

The quality of the foundation writ has been dealt with in Chapter 12. Under the Prescription and Limitation (Scotland) Act 1973, possession must be founded on and follow the recording of a deed sufficient in its terms to constitute a title to the interest in land (here, the proprietary interest). By such possession the validity of the title is put beyond challenge, except for forgery, or *ex facie* invalidity. Therefore, we are only concerned with the intrinsic validity of the foundation writ; extrinsic matters can be ignored. Assuming that the foundation writ is a disposition, then the points to look for are as follows.

(1) *Stamp duty.* Where stamp duty was payable, the writ must be properly stamped, although insufficiency of stamp duty is not a bar to prescription. For details of the new stamp duty land tax, see Chapter 5.

(2) *Narrative.* In a foundation writ, nothing in the narrative can affect the intrinsic validity. See *Cooper Scott v Gill Scott* 1924 SC 309.

(3) *Dispositive clause.* The points to check are:

   (a) the disponee and the destination. Check this information against the next writ in the progress;

   (b) description. Does this correspond exactly with the contract; and does it correspond exactly with what the purchaser imagines he has purchased? Ideally, this requires a physical check on the ground by the client, or possibly by a surveyor. Where the foundation writ contains a description by reference, check the description for intrinsic validity and also check the description referred to in the prior writ;

   (c) reservations and burdens. Note, for reference, all writs referred to for burdens, and note the content of any new reservations or burdens in this writ; and

   (d) remaining clauses. Note any specialities but, in the ordinary case, nothing in the subordinate clauses could affect the intrinsic validity of the foundation writ. When a conveyance is granted on or after 4 April 1979, several of the old traditional subordinate clauses are now implied and will not be repeated expressly in the great majority of cases unless there are specialities requiring special treatment. See Chapter 10.

(4) *Authentication.* The writ must be probative. The Requirements of Writing (Scotland) Act 1995, s 6, requires deeds to be self-proving as a precondition of registration.

(5) *Warrant of registration.* This must coincide with the dispositive clause.

(6) *Certificate of registration.* This should also be checked.

32.5 Subsequent titles

Each writ following the foundation writ must then be meticulously checked, whether recorded or not. In the case of each subsequent title, the concern is with extrinsic as well as intrinsic validity. If the next writ in the progress is, for example, a disposition granted by the disponee under the foundation writ, the points to check are as follows.

(1) *Stamp duty.* As above.

(2) *Grantor.* Does he connect up with the grantee under the prior title?

(3) *Narrative.* This must be scrutinised in detail and any material facts must be checked by reference to extrinsic sources, for example the date of confirmation in the case of a sale by an executor.

(4) *Dispositive clause.* Check the disponee and destination. Check the description, make sure that it coincides with the foundation writ or, if it differs, whether the differences are in order. Check the burdens clause and note the content of any

new burdens. Check all the subordinate clauses, noting any specialties. In particular, check carefully any clause of deduction of title, and vouch it by reference to the links narrated therein.

(5) *Authentication, warrant of registration and certificate of registration.* These must be checked as in the case of the foundation writ.

In addition, there may well be other points which are material in a writ within the progress, although not material in the case of the foundation writ. Typically, questions of capacity are significant, although they cannot affect the validity of a foundation writ. The same applies to, for example, powers of sale of trustees.

This meticulous check is then repeated for each subsequent writ in the progress down to and including the seller's own title.

If this examination discloses no defect in the title, then the seller has a valid proprietary legal title.

32.6   PLANS AND BOUNDARIES

In the Register of Sasines, in many cases, the purchaser satisfies himself as to title and marketability without reference to any plan. This is because, if the title is not bounding, possession of the property within the physical boundaries on the ground for more than ten years establishes the title to the property within those boundaries by prescriptive possession. But, in registration of title, a plan is essential to the making-up of the title sheet and land certificate. So, the purchaser must ensure that there is sufficient accurate information with the title to allow the property to be identified accurately on the Ordnance Survey map. If not, the seller must produce this information; and is taken bound to do so in the suggested missives clause.

A seller, except in the case of tenement flats where there is no exclusive ground held as a pertinent, such as a garden, must apply to the Keeper for a Form P16 report in a transaction leading to first registration for examination by the purchaser. The main function of the application Form P16 is to request the Keeper to compare the boundaries as they appear in the title with the occupied extent as depicted on Ordnance Survey map, to see whether or not there are any discrepancies. Although an on-site comparison can be made, the comparison is more conveniently made through the medium of a P16 report obtained from the Keeper. The form must give the Keeper sufficient information to allow him to compare the description in the titles with the physical boundaries of the property as they appear on the Ordnance Survey sheet. A deed plan or a detailed particular description with measurements taken from the titles will normally be sufficient. For other methods of providing the required information, see the *Registration of Title Practice Book*, para 4.9.

It should be emphasised that the P16 report issued by the Keeper is intended simply to deal with the question of boundaries and nothing more. Accordingly, where such a report confirms that the boundary features on the ground coincide with the titles is not an assurance that the title itself will be registered without exclusion of indemnity. It merely clears one area of enquiry at the preliminary stage, which is always desirable.

32.7 Dealing with discrepancies

If the P16 report does not indicate any discrepancy, the report need merely be enclosed with the application for registration (listing it on inventory Form 4) and an affirmative answer given to the first part of question 2 on the Form 1. If the P16 report discloses any discrepancies between the boundaries in the title and the physical boundaries on the ground ('the occupational boundaries'), then the implications of these discrepancies must be explored at the examination of title stage because, as a result, the title may not be marketable; and the Keeper may exclude indemnity as to part of the subjects.

The seller's obligation to produce a marketable title in the suggested missives clause covers any such material discrepancy; and the purchaser should insist that the seller puts matters right before settlement. Action of some form will require to be taken before the application is submitted for registration, the nature and extent of such action depending upon circumstances and the nature of the discrepancy. As a first step, an on-site comparison between the legal boundaries and the Ordnance Survey map may be advisable in order to check that features on the ground have not altered since the map was last updated. If the comparison shows that the physical and theoretical boundaries cohere, the presumption arises that the map is erroneous. In this situation the only further action needed is to answer the second part of Question 2 of Form 1 in the affirmative.

If the comparison confirms the accuracy of the P16 report, and the area occupied by the seller includes land outwith the legal boundaries, the Keeper will not include that land in the registered title since there is no legal basis upon which he could do so. If therefore the purchaser wishes to include land outwith the legal boundaries in his registered title, remedial conveyancing will be necessary.

In the reverse situation, where the occupied extent is less than the legal extent, the purchaser can choose to limit his title to the occupied extent, relinquishing such land as lies within the title deed boundaries but outwith the occupied extent. This may be a sensible course of action where the occupied extent corresponds to the purchaser's expectation, based on a visual inspection, of what he is buying. Question 2(b) of Form 1 gives the applicant a convenient opportunity to advise the Keeper accordingly. Conversely, the purchaser may wish to assert title to the full legal extent (where it is larger than the occupied extent), in which case the opposite answer should be given to Question 2(b). The latter course carries the risk that the Keeper will exclude indemnity as regards the ground outwith the occupied extent because of the possibility that a third party has a competing title fortified by possession.

In cases of discrepancies in boundaries, the Land Registration (Scotland) Act 1979, s 19 – agreement as to common boundary – provides a convenient method of resolving such difficulties as between adjoining proprietors. In terms of that section, where there is a boundary discrepancy and where the adjoining proprietors, both having registered titles, have agreed to and have executed a plan of the correct boundary as represented by the physical feature on the ground, the plan is then registrable; and, on being so registered, it is binding on singular successors of both parties, even although there is no formal excambion and no formal conveyance by each party to the other of the discrepant areas. If one of the titles is a title still recorded in the Register of Sasines, the s 19 agreement, with plan annexed, is both recorded and registered to produce the same result. It appears that no consents, discharges or restrictions are required from heritable creditors who have securities over the properties concerned. Section 19 agreements can be used only where the discrepancy is relatively minor. If a larger area is effectively being transferred from one property to another a disposition or, where appropriate, an excambion should be used.

32.8   ENCUMBRANCES

Establishing proprietary title in this way does not, however, mean that the title is unencumbered. There are two main types of encumbrance which may materially affect the property in the hands of the purchaser: real burdens and heritable securities.

32.9   Real burdens

Real burdens are a type of title condition. See para 14.1. The provisions of the Abolition of Feudal Tenure etc (Scotland) Act 2000 and the Title Conditions (Scotland) Act 2003 mean that what is required in examining the title in relation to real burdens differs for real burdens created before and after 28 November 2004. The existence of the burdens will be established by an examination of the progress of titles and any writs referred to for burdens. However, the question arises as to whether the burdens created in a feu disposition are enforceable after the appointed day. Real burdens which are validly created after the appointed day are straightforward and will affect the title. See Chapter 15 for the constitution of real burdens under the 2003 Act. Real burdens created before 28 November 2004 need careful consideration.

Those which are not feudal real burdens will continue to be enforceable after 28 November 2004 if the benefited proprietor has a title and interest to enforce: Title Conditions (Scotland) Act, s 8(2). One of the problems, however, is in identifying who has a title. Implied rights for third parties to enforce real burdens continue but in a different form. Reference must be made to the detailed treatment of enforcement of real burdens in Chapter 17 which is essential to examination of title.

Feudal real burdens are no longer enforceable by a superior after 28 November 2004: Abolition of Feudal Tenure etc (Scotland) Act 2000, s 17. However, some may be converted or preserved under Part 4 of the 2000 Act in conjunction with the 2003 Act. Some burdens are automatically converted. This applies to facility and service burdens and maritime burdens: see paras 19.27 to 19.29. Others can be preserved by a superior realloting the burdens: see paras 19.30 to 19.73. The procedure involves registration of a notice on or after 1 November 2003: see para 19.25. In examination of title it will be necessary to check whether such a notice has been registered to real-lot the feudal real burden.

Certain feudal real burdens may be preserved as conservation burdens by registration of a notice against the burdened property: see para 19.75. Other feudal real burdens may be preserved as economic development burdens, health care burdens or development value burdens: see paras 19.79 to 19.97.

Under s 53 of the 2003 Act, burdens imposed by a superior on a community of properties may still be enforceable by neighbours in related properties: see paras 17.31 to 17.35.

Various types of real burden are considered briefly in the following paragraphs. They can be divided into three main categories:

(1) building conditions;
(2) other real burdens; and
(3) reservation of minerals.

32.10 *Building conditions*

All building conditions and restrictions must be read carefully and it must be considered whether any of the burdens, being of an unusual or unexpected nature, is objectionable in terms of the contract or is contrary to express contractual provision. For a cautionary case see *Spurway, Petitioner* 1987 GWD 2-65.

Normally, building conditions fall into three categories:

(1) *conditions* ad factum praestandum. These include, typically, an obligation to build a house, to enclose the site and to make up roads, all within a time limit;
(2) *money payments*. These include, typically, payments to the developer for roads; and payments to neighbouring proprietors for one-half of the cost of erecting mutual walls, or fences; and
(3) *restrictions on use etc*. These conditions are, of course, continuing. The question is whether they are still being duly complied with. If not, consider: (1) whether the consent of the benefited proprietor to some deviation has been obtained or whether the benefited proprietor has acquiesced; and (2) whether the neighbouring proprietors have a right to object and if so whether they have consented.

32.11 *Other real burdens*

These include clauses of pre-emption and redemption again normally (but not necessarily) contained in the original break-off deed. See *Spurway, Petitioner* 1987 GWD 2-65. Under the Abolition of Feudal Tenure etc (Scotland) Act 2000, s 18, a superior can preserve these which would otherwise cease to be enforceable. See para 32.14 and para 19.78.

(1) *Personal pre-emption and personal redemption burdens*. A superior can preserve a right of pre-emption or redemption by nominating a benefited property

and registering a notice against the burdened property. If this is done before the appointed day, the right is preserved as a personal burden provided that the right was enforceable on the day immediately preceding the appointed day. See para 19.78.

(2) *Community right to buy.* Under Part 2 of the Land Reform (Scotland) Act 2003, there is provision in certain areas of the country, in terms of s 33 and to be confirmed by statutory instrument, for local community bodies to buy land in their area when the current proprietor decides to sell. This is expected to be brought into force in early 2004. Such bodies can register a notice of their interest under the 2003 Act, which effectively gives the community body a right of pre-emption. The Keeper of the Registers of Scotland will establish a new Register of Community Interests in Land for this purpose, which has not been done at the time of writing. It will be necessary to search this Register, if the property is in an area where this right may exist, to see whether such a notice has been registered.

32.12   Reservation of minerals

Normally, the original reservation occurs in the original break-off deed; but this is not necessarily so. As a result, a reservation of minerals can easily be missed.

32.13   Heritable securities

It is, of course, necessary to ensure that the title is disencumbered of all subsisting heritable securities. Positive prescription does not assist in this case, although negative prescription is of some help. The general working rule is:

(1) Examine the Form 10 report which will list any deed creating or affecting securities in the last 40 years to the date of the report and any discharges in the last five years.

(2) Any security discharged more than five years ago can be ignored, because under the Conveyancing and Feudal Reform (Scotland) Act 1970, s 41, a discharge by the ostensible creditor cannot be challenged, in a question with a *bona fide* purchaser, more than five years after recording.

(3) If any security was finally discharged within the five-year period, then check the original security deed, all transmissions thereof, and the final discharge, all in detail, to ensure a proper and valid discharge.

(4) Any remaining securities in the 40-year period are presumably still subsisting, unless they have been effectively restricted. Check the titles for deeds of restriction or clauses *in gremio* in dispositions disburdening the subjects thereby disponed, and, if there are any such, make sure that the property has been effectively disburdened of these securities. If the subsisting securities have not been so restricted, then the purchaser's agents should see and revise draft discharges of the remaining outstanding securities. These discharges should be delivered at settlement, along with the selling solicitor's cheque for the appropriate registra-

tion dues. However, most agents are prepared to take an obligation from the seller's agents to deliver valid discharges, in terms of the revised drafts, within a few weeks after settlement of the transaction. See para 32.28.

32.14 POSSESSION

There are two points to consider here: prescription and vacant possession.

32.15 Prescription

In any examination of title, one relies on the positive prescription. This requires both title and possession. The quality and duration of possession have been dealt with in Chapter 12. Strictly speaking, it is not enough simply to examine the title in isolation; one should also enquire into the extent and quality of possession over the ten-year period since the date of the foundation writ. This can be of particular importance with regard to evidence as to whether or not the property is a matrimonial home. But, in practice, evidence of possession is rarely called for by the purchaser, although the seller would require to satisfy the purchaser on this point, if called upon to do so. There is an interesting discussion of the extent of possession required in an article by Professor Rennie in 1994 SLT (News) 261.

32.16 Vacant possession or subject to tenant's rights

This is a point which should be dealt with in the contract. If the property is purchased with vacant possession, then an inspection of the property will normally show whether or not vacant possession can be given.

If the property is purchased subject to tenant's rights, the purchaser's agent should always call for and examine in detail the lease or leases. He does this not only to establish the benefits flowing to the landlord under these leases, but also to satisfy himself as to the obligations incumbent on the landlord, since these benefits and these obligations (unless personal to the original landlord, which they would rarely be) will transmit and be enforceable by and against the purchaser.

32.17 FORM 10 AND FORM 11 REPORTS

A search for encumbrances may or may not be produced with the titles. The search for encumbrances was used in Sasines transactions to check the title position. This comprised details of entries in the appropriate property register, the Register of Sasines, and in the Register of Inhibitions and Adjudications, usually referred to as the Personal Register. On first registration the seller must produce a Form 10 report and, usually, a Form 11 report updating it, or the equivalent forms from a private searching organisation. This replaces the search for encumbrances. However, there may be circumstances when that search needs to be examined, in particular if the Form 10 report does not cover the personal register for all parties who held title during the prescriptive period.

With these points in view, the *Registration of Title Practice Book*, para 8.9 suggests a clause in the following form in an offer where the transaction will lead to first registration:

> 'In exchange for the price, the seller will deliver a duly executed disposition in favour of the purchaser and will deliver or exhibit a valid marketable title together with a Form 10 report, brought down to a date as near as practicable to the date of settlement and showing no entries adverse to the seller's interest, the cost of the said report being the responsibility of the seller. In addition, the seller will furnish to the purchaser such documents and evidence including a plan as the Keeper may require to enable the Keeper to issue a land certificate in name of the purchaser as registered proprietor of the whole subjects of offer and containing no exclusion of indemnity in terms of s 12(2) of the Land Registration (Scotland) Act 1979. Such documents shall include (unless the whole subjects of offer comprise only part of a tenement or flatted building and do not include an area of ground specifically included in the title to that part) a plan or bounding description sufficient to enable the whole subjects of offer to be identified on the ordnance map, and evidence (such as a Form P16 report) that the description of the whole subjects of offer as contained in the title deeds is habile to include the whole of the occupied extent. The land certificate to be issued to the purchaser will disclose no entry, deed or diligence prejudicial to the purchaser's interest other than such as are created by or against the purchaser, or have been disclosed to, and accepted by, the purchaser prior to the date of settlement. Notwithstanding any provision of the missives to the contrary, this clause shall remain in full force and effect until implemented and may be founded upon.'

The seller should exhibit the Form 10 and the Form 11 reports.

32.18   The Form 10 report

If not produced with the titles, then the purchaser should ask for this at once. The report is in three parts. The first part discloses the following:

(1) the whole prescriptive progress of titles from the foundation writ to date (not merely from the last date of search), but only back to date of recording of the foundation writ;

(2) all undischarged heritable securities created within the past 40 years, and any deed or deeds relating thereto;

(3) all discharges of heritable securities granted within the preceding five years but already fully discharged: see the Conveyancing and Feudal Reform (Scotland) Act 1970, s 41, for the significance of this disclosure; and

(4) any other deed within the past 40 years which affects the title, such as a deed of servitude, a minute of waiver, a notice of improvement grant etc.

The second part is a report from the Land Register which discloses whether the subjects or any part of them has been registered and, if so, the title number.

The third part is a report from the Register of Inhibitions and Adjudications against the parties listed by the applicant. The significance of this is discussed at paras 32.20 to 32.33 below.

The search for encumbrances is therefore not normally relevant to the examination of the title and would not normally be examined; but it may be helpful in particular cases. For example, a tenement search will show the sale of individual flats; and it may be relevant to examine each break-off disposition to establish the position regarding common rights and mutual repairing obligations. Similarly, if the presence of a deed outwith the 40-year period is suspected, and if that is material to the title, then a reference to a search going back more than 40 years and/or to the prior titles may be appropriate, for example to establish the position of minerals if that is material. Unless the Keeper expressly states in the title sheet and land certificate that minerals are included in the title, that fact is not guaranteed. Even when minerals are included the Keeper may not grant indemnity.

32.19   The Form 11 report

As already explained, the Form 10 report should be obtained by the seller before missives are concluded. So, there is bound to be a gap, probably of at least some weeks, between the date when the Form 10 report was prepared and the date of settlement. It is prudent to cover that gap by updating the Form 10 report to a date within a day or two prior to the date of settlement. The application Form 11 and the resulting report by the Keeper are used for this purpose. The seller's solicitors will normally produce, with the titles, a draft application Form 11, to be revised by the purchaser in the course of his examination of the title. One revisal which the purchaser's solicitor will normally make is to include the purchaser(s) in the application Form 11, to be searched against in the personal register. Obviously, this will not have been done when the Form 10 report was obtained, pre-sale. Form 11 is lodged with the Keeper in duplicate.

32.20   THE REGISTER OF INHIBITIONS AND ADJUDICATIONS

This is a purely diligence register. The Register of Inhibitions and Adjudications (commonly known as 'the Personal Register'), is not concerned with land, or with titles to land as such. It is only concerned with persons and the personal capacity of persons to grant deeds affecting land. Originally, there were several such registers; but all these have now been amalgamated together into a single register under this name: Conveyancing (Scotland) Act 1924, s 44.

The Personal Register is now the only register for the publication of personal diligence. Further, interdict apart, a third party cannot create any effective bar on the capacity of a heritable proprietor or prevent him from dealing with heritage unless an entry appears against that heritable proprietor in the Personal Register. This has no application to natural incapacity. If a heritable proprietor lacks capacity, he is automatically barred from effectively dealing with his heritable estate, but no entry to that effect appears in the Personal Register.

32.21   NATURE OF ENTRIES

The law provides equitable remedies for the benefit of persons having valid claims on heritable property where there is a registered proprietor: see Adjudication, Reduction and Sequestration in Chapter 29. But these equitable remedies involve delay. Meanwhile, in the period between the raising of the action and the granting of the decree, the registered proprietor remains ostensibly owner and may confer an active title on a *bona fide* purchaser for value who is unaware of the pending action, to the prejudice of the person claiming an interest in the heritable property in question. To prevent such prejudice, immediate interim procedures are available to the pursuer in an action (or a creditor) whereby he can effectively prevent the debtor in the obligation from dealing with heritage. These procedures do not, in themselves, provide an active title for the claimant (or creditor). To be effective, an entry must be made against the registered proprietor in the Personal Register, and it is only by making the appropriate entry in this register that this result can be achieved. There are four common types of entry, each producing a similar effect:

(1) notice of litigiosity;
(2) inhibition;
(3) sequestration; and
(4) trust deed for creditors.

These are dealt with below. For a full list of various possible entries in this register, see G L Gretton *Guide to Searches* (1991), p 27.

32.22   Notice of litigiosity

Heritable property becomes litigious when it is the subject matter of a depending real action (for example adjudication or reduction). When heritage is litigious, this implies a prohibition against alienation of the heritage to the prejudice of the pursuer in the action (or to the prejudice of a creditor who has done real diligence), where the object of that action (or real diligence) is to acquire a title to the heritage, absolutely (or in security). Note that the registered proprietor is not absolutely barred from dealing with the property, simply because his property has become litigious. He may deal with it, but anyone taking a title from the registered proprietor has notice of the potential claims upon it; and a title so taken may later be reduced at the instance of the person who has rendered the property litigious.

Originally, the mere calling in court of a real action affecting heritable title was sufficient publication, and of itself rendered the property litigious. But by the Conveyancing (Scotland) Act 1924, s 44(2)(a), no action relating to land shall, *per se*, make property litigious. In addition, in order to produce a state of litigiosity, a notice in the form of Schedule RR to the Titles to Land Consolidation (Scotland) Act 1868 must be recorded in the Personal Register. Property only becomes litigious at the date of the recording of such notice.

Since 30 December 1985 every notice of summons of reduction, adjudication etc must incorporate a description of the lands to which the summons relates; and Schedule RR is amended accordingly. See the Law Reform (Miscellaneous Provisions) (Scotland) Act 1985, s 59 and Schedule 2, paras 4 and 5. Likewise, every notice of application to rectify a deed relating to land must contain a description of land to which the application relates: see s 8(8) of the 1985 Act.

Further, by s 44(2)(b) of the 1924 Act, decree in an action of adjudication does not, of itself, make property litigious.

The notice of litigiosity has no effect on the proprietor's capacity to deal with other heritage; it affects only the heritable property to which the action relates. It was previously impossible to tell what property was affected by litigiosity because the lands were not described; but this defect in the system has been cured under the amending provision referred to above.

Further, litigiosity strikes only at future, voluntary deeds; and so cannot bar the subsequent granting of a disposition of heritage which has been made litigious if it is in implement of a contract dated prior to registration of the notice.

The Scottish Law Commission has proposed that adjudication be abolished and replaced with a new statutory diligence known as land attachment: see para 22.50.

32.23 Inhibition

In any real action, the *status quo* may be preserved, and prejudice to the pursuer may be avoided, by rendering the property litigious, through the recording in the Personal Register of the appropriate notice. A personal action, for example for payment of a debt, as opposed to a real action, is not directed at, nor does it directly affect, heritable property belonging to the defender. But the whole estate of the debtor is liable for payment of his whole debts. The pursuer in a personal action for payment is therefore indirectly interested in heritage belonging to the debtor in that, if he succeeds in his action, he may then have recourse, by diligence, against heritage of the debtor.

In order to protect his potential interest in heritable property belonging to the debtor, a creditor may, by the appropriate procedure followed by the appropriate entry in the Personal Register, inhibit the debtor. The effect of an inhibition is similar to litigiosity, in that, by inhibition, the inhibited proprietor is effectively prevented from granting any future voluntary deed affecting any heritable estate or interest belonging to him at the date when the inhibition becomes effective. Again, deeds granted by an inhibited party are not, of themselves, void; but they remain voidable at the instance of the prejudiced creditor. The inhibition now differs from the notice of litigiosity in that the inhibition strikes at all heritable property generally, not merely the property described in the notice.

An inhibition is purely negative. It never operates to confer an active title on the inhibitor; and it only affects heritable estate. But an inhibition may confer a certain preference on the inhibitor in a sequestration. For articles on ranking, and recent cases, see the Reading List. Care should be taken by those instructing inhibitions that they have accurate information about the person who it is proposed to inhibit. For an example of this, see *Atlas Appointments Ltd v Tinsley* 1998 SLT 395.

32.24   Procedures

There are two alternative procedures: letters of inhibition and inhibition on the dependence.

(1) *Letters of inhibition*. This procedure is competent only in execution, where the creditor holds a liquid document of debt; or in security, where the creditor holds an illiquid document of debt and the debtor is approaching insolvency or con- templating flight.

   No formal action is necessary; instead, all that is required is to present the document of debt with a bill in the Petition Department of the Court of Session, which is granted by the clerk of court. The form of letters of inhibition is statu- tory under the Titles to Land Consolidation (Scotland) Act 1868, s 156 and Schedule QQ.

   The letters are signeted, and served on the debtor and, thereafter, entered in the Register of Inhibitions and Adjudications. They are effective only from the date of such registration.

(2) *Inhibition on the dependence*. Where a debt is illiquid, it requires formal constitu- tion by action in court. But it is competent to include, in the summons of any Court of Session action concluding for payment, a warrant to inhibit; and where so included, the summons (after service on the debtor) may be registered in the Personal Register. The effect is to inhibit the defender as from the date of such reg- istration, which is in practice a very useful device. However, see *Karl Construction Ltd v Palisade Properties plc* 2002 SC 270, in which it was held that inhibition on the dependence without judicial involvement contravened Article 1, Protocol 1 of the European Convention on Human Rights. An actual hearing is not required: see *Advocate General for Scotland v Taylor* 2003 SLT 1340.

   Inhibition on the dependence may also be effected in a sheriff court action. The procedure is to apply to the Petition Department of the Court of Session, producing the initial writ or a certified copy thereof, and other appropriate doc- uments. See Macphail *Sheriff Court Practice* (2nd edn, 1998), paras 11.37 to 11.38 for details.

32.25   Notice of inhibition

Where the creditor intends to inhibit the debtor by either method, he may register in the Personal Register a notice of inhibition under the Titles to Land Consolidation

(Scotland) Act 1868, s 155 and Schedule PP. This is a form of advance warning that an inhibition is on the way; but it has no effect whatever unless letters of inhibition, or a summons containing the warrant to inhibit, are subsequently registered within 21 days following on the registration of the notice. In that event only, the letters, or summons, date back to the date of registration of the notice.

32.26 Sequestration

The effect of an act and warrant appointing a trustee in sequestration, as a title to the debtor's heritage, has been noticed already. Under the Bankruptcy (Scotland) Act 1985, s 14, the clerk of court is now obliged forthwith to send a certified copy of the relevant court order to the Keeper of the Registers for recording in the Personal Register. Such registration has the force of an inhibition. It, therefore, prevents the bankrupt from disposing of his heritable estate to the prejudice of other creditors, pending completion of title, subsequently, by the trustee in sequestration. Similarly, property acquired by a bankrupt after the date of sequestration *may* vest in the trustee in sequestration. See *Halifax plc v Gorman's Trustee* 2000 SLT 1409 and other cases referred to at para 3.21.

32.27 Trust deed for creditors

Under the Bankruptcy (Scotland) Act 1985, s 59 and Schedule 5, para 2, the trustee may register a notice in a prescribed form which has the effect of an inhibition. This provision is quite new. Note that it is permissive, not obligatory. But the trustee should be advised to record such a notice at once, if the debtor owns heritage.

32.28 DURATION OF ENTRIES IN THE PERSONAL REGISTER

(1) *Notice of litigiosity*. The effect of such notice expires five years from the date of registration; or on the expiry of six months from the date of final decree in the action, whichever shall first happen: Conveyancing (Scotland) Act 1924 s, 44(3)(a).

(2) *Inhibition*. An inhibition is of no effect after the expiry of five years from the date on which it first became effective: see the 1924 Act, s 44(3)(a).

(3) *Abbreviate of sequestration*. Under the Bankruptcy (Scotland) Act 1985, s 14(4), if the permanent trustee was not discharged within three years of the date of sequestration, he was required to send a memorandum in a prescribed form to the Keeper for registration in the Personal Register before the expiry of the original three-year period. Although this requirement was mandatory it was not always observed, and s 14(4) of the 1985 Act was amended by para 3 of Schedule 1 to the Bankruptcy (Scotland) Act 1993, to the effect that registration of a memorandum in a continuing sequestration is now at the trustee's discretion. The trustee's registration of the memorandum in the Personal Register renews the effect of the original registration of the relevant order, but only for a

further period of three years. If still not discharged after six years, the permanent trustee can register further memoranda to keep renewing the order for further periods of three years until finally discharged.

(4) *Trust deed for creditors.* Such a trust deed subsists until discharged.

Apart from the statutory prescriptions, the effect of any of these entries in the Personal Register can be removed by discharge at the instance of the creditor or trustee who made the original entry; or may be recalled or restricted by the court. Appropriate entries are then made in the Personal Register.

32.29   EFFECT OF STATUTORY PRESCRIPTIONS

It is generally accepted that the effect of the statutory prescription under the Conveyancing (Scotland) Act 1924 is two-fold:

(1) when five years have expired from the date of registration of a notice of litigiosity or an inhibition, the debtor/proprietor is released from the effect thereof, and he is then absolutely free from any prohibition against alienation; and

(2) even if the debtor/proprietor has alienated his heritage during the five-year period, the party in right of the inhibition or notice absolutely forfeits his right to reduce the alienation by the debtor/proprietor immediately on the expiry of the full five-year period.

It is not altogether clear whether the 1924 Act, s 44, achieves this second effect. Most solicitors are of the view that the second result is effectively achieved by the legislation, and act on that view in the instructing of searches. But, as Professor Gretton points out in *The Law of Inhibition and Adjudication* (2nd edn, 1996), p 69, the practice of the profession is by no means necessarily conclusive.

32.30   PURPOSE OF PERSONAL SEARCH

A search in the Register of Inhibitions and Adjudications is intended to disclose any legal bar which may still be effective against the present proprietor or any predecessor in title within the prescriptive period. This is in case such a legal bar (for example, an inhibition) might have rendered a title granted by such a person reducible at the instance of a third party (for example, the inhibitor). A search in the Personal Register is normally combined with a search in the Property Register by means of the Form 10, for convenience; but it serves an entirely separate purpose and may be separately instructed.

32.31   Period of search

The practical rules governing period of search and persons searched against in the Personal Register take into account three main factors:

(1) inhibitions and notices of litigiosity prescribe in five years: Conveyancing (Scotland) Act 1924, s 44; but

(2) under the Bankruptcy (Scotland) Act 1985, the effect of the registered court order expires in three years, although that effect can be renewed for successive three-year periods; and

(3) extrinsic invalidity (ie granting deeds under disability) is cured after ten years by positive prescription.

The practical rule is that all persons having the legal title, or any beneficial right, to the property within the past ten years should be searched against in the Personal Register, but for a period of five years only prior to the date of completion of the purchaser's title. The Form 10 and Form 11 applications, as printed, imply that a search will be made only against owners in the five-year period prior to the report, not owners in the ten-year period prior to the report. However, all owners in the ten-year period should be searched against for a five-year period. This search information may appear in a search for encumbrances if this is made available.

32.32 PRACTICAL ASPECTS

The working practice is:

(1) Make a list of all the parties having the legal title or a beneficial right to the property at any time within the past ten years.

(2) Check to see if any of these parties have already been searched against for a full five-year period prior to divestiture; and, if they have, delete them from the list.

(3) The remaining parties now fall to be searched against on this occasion. For this purpose the full name and addresses of individuals should be given.

There are some specialities to take into account.

(1) *Trustees or executors.* The practice is to search against them as a body, naming and designing the truster, but not naming individual trustees. The truster or the deceased, as the case may be, may also fall to be searched against under paragraph (3) above.

(2) *Firms.* The practice is to search against all individual partners as individuals and as trustees for their firm; and against the firm in the firm name. If, as often happens, the trustees for the firm are not the current individual partners, the trustees as a body should be searched against in their trust capacity.

(3) *Purchaser(s).* As a courtesy, the seller will normally agree to the inclusion of the purchaser(s) in the Form 11 application if they are granting a standard security. This usually causes no problem.

In all cases, the period in the personal search is for five years prior to divestiture or completion of the current transaction.

32.33   IS THE PERSONAL SEARCH CLEAR?

The point is that an inhibition strikes only at future voluntary deeds granted by the inhibited party. Thus, if a contract of sale and purchase is duly concluded and if, thereafter, the seller is inhibited before delivery of the disposition in favour of the purchaser, that disposition is not struck at by the inhibition and cannot be challenged by the inhibiting creditor. However, this does not appear *ex facie* of the Record because, of course, the missives are not recorded. On the strength of the decision in *Dryburgh v Gordon* (1896) 24 R 1, it is generally accepted in the profession that, in such circumstances, the search is not clear because, *ex facie* of the Record, when the disposition was recorded, the grantor was under inhibition. See I J S Talman (ed) *Halliday's Conveyancing Law and Practice in Scotland* (2nd edn, 2 Volumes, 1996–97) Volume 2, para 38.15.

A similar question can arise in relation to heritable securities. In *Newcastle Building Society v White* 1987 SLT (Sh Ct) 81, the debtor, in a standard security granted to and recorded by the building society, was subsequently inhibited. Thereafter, the building society exercised its power of sale and the purchaser challenged the title on the footing that the search was not clear. The sheriff principal took the view in that case that, looking to the provisions of the Conveyancing and Feudal Reform (Scotland) Act 1970, s 26(1), it was clear *ex facie* of the Record that the property had been disencumbered and accordingly the search was clear. For a more detailed discussion, see G L Gretton *The Law of Inhibition and Adjudication* (2nd edn, 1996), p 190.

32.34   COMPANIES

A search in the Register of Charges is only appropriate in the case of a limited company dealing with heritage. It discloses floating charges. It also discloses all fixed securities, although these would, in any event, be disclosed by a search in the Property Register. Accordingly, when a company is granting a standard security, or a floating charge, a search in the Register of Charges is always required because a floating charge may competently prohibit the company from granting any subsequent fixed security ranking prior to the floating charge. In the absence of such a prohibition, which absence is very unusual in practice, a subsequent fixed charge automatically takes priority. Floating charges rank *inter se* according to their dates of registration, subject to the terms of the earlier charge.

When heritable property is being sold by a limited company, as a going concern, the property is automatically released from a floating charge on sale, and, strictly speaking, no search is required. But, when the company goes into liquidation, or when a receiver is appointed, the floating charge becomes a fixed security. A search in the Register of Charges would not reveal the liquidation of the company but would reveal the appointment of a receiver which is noted in that register.

In the case of liquidation, there is a time-lag of anything up to 15 days during which, under statute, the resolution putting the company into liquidation may be lodged; for the appointment of a receiver the statutory time limit is seven days. Therefore, a search in the company register is never right up to date.

When purchasing from, or lending to, a company, one should accordingly search the company's file in the Register of Companies, not merely the Register of Charges, and take other appropriate action, if necessary, as discussed in detail in Chapter 34.

If a search is required in the Register of Charges, it will normally be from 27 October 1961, which was the date of commencement of this register; or from the date of incorporation of the company, if later.

For a full discussion on the content and effect of searches, with illustrative styles, see G L Gretton *A Guide to Searches* (1991). See also the Scottish Law Commission Discussion Paper on *Sharp v Thomson* (No 114, 2001).

32.35 SETTLEMENT OBLIGATIONS

At the settlement of a transaction, one of the seller's contractual obligations is to clear the records of any adverse entry, evidenced by the subsequent receipt of a land certificate without exclusion of indemnity and by exhibition of a Form 10 or Form 11 report with clear entries in the Personal Register. The seller can never implement this at the date of settlement, and some delay is inevitable.

It is therefore usual, at settlement, to require the seller's agents to grant a letter of obligation undertaking to implement this contractual obligation. It is customary to include in such letters of obligation an undertaking implement to any other conditions of the contract which are not fully implemented at settlement, for example delivery of a discharge of a standard security repaid by the seller out of the purchase price. But a purchaser is not obliged to agree to this.

Note that such obligations are always personally binding on the sellers' solicitors, unless expressly worded otherwise: see *Johnston v Little* 1960 SLT 129 and the article by Professor Henry 'Settlement Obligations' 1959 JLSS 135. So the purchaser's agent is relying on the personal integrity and standing of the other agent; and the agent granting the obligation guarantees his client to that extent. Again, he should grant such obligations only with circumspection. The obligation is also binding on the seller himself; and the purchaser, or his agents, can sue both the selling solicitor and the seller jointly for implement of the obligation: see *McGillivray v Davidson* 1993 SLT 693. The purchaser himself also has a title to sue, notwithstanding that the obligation is granted by one solicitor to another: see D J Cusine 'Letters of Obligation: A Few More Thoughts' 1991 JLSS 349.

32.36 IMPLICATIONS OF THE OBLIGATION SYSTEM

The conveyancing system in Scotland very largely depends for its efficient working on the use of the letter of obligation granted by the seller's solicitor at settlement. Indeed, letters of obligation have been described as 'the lubricant of the daily settlement of transactions involving the sale and purchase of heritable property': Professor Henry 'Settlement Obligations' 1959 JLSS 135. See also *Cheval Property Finance plc v Hill* 2003 GWD 36-999.

After the Presentment Book at Register House was computerised on 1 April 1992 it is, in effect, up to date to within 24 hours prior to the preparation of a Form 10 or 11 report. As a result, the risk of any adverse entry is, or will be, remote and, unless the circumstances are very special indeed, there should be no valid reason why the seller's solicitors should not grant a letter of obligation in traditional or 'classic' form as described below. There is, however, no legal obligation on a solicitor acting for a seller to grant a letter of obligation. If a solicitor acting for a seller does not propose to grant a personal letter of obligation in usual terms, then he or she has a professional duty in practical terms to advise the purchaser's solicitor that no obligation will be available at settlement. This must be done at the earliest opportunity and preferably before the conclusion of missives so that an alternative method of settlement can be agreed upon.

From the point of view of the purchaser, notwithstanding that the risk is now very slight, his solicitor should never settle a transaction without such an obligation because, otherwise, the purchaser is virtually unprotected. In such a situation, where the selling solicitor declines to grant a letter of obligation and where there is no special contrary provision in the missives, the seller is not in a position at settlement fully to implement all his obligations in the contract. In the absence of express provision in the missives, no purchaser is obliged to proceed with a contract unless and until the seller has implemented all his obligations; and no purchaser should ordinarily agree, in the missives, to any such express contrary provision.

The Law Society of Scotland's view has consistently been that in a domestic property transaction the purchaser's solicitor is entitled to expect a personal obligation from the seller's solicitor unless otherwise stated. See the note from the Society's conveyancing committee at 1991 JLSS 171 and 'Clarifying the Classic Letter of Obligation' 2003 JLSS Apr/26. If the seller's solicitor will not grant a letter of obligation, then settlement at Register House is the only safe alternative, which is impracticable.

In the case of sales by individuals, firms, trustees etc, the problem has not become serious and is largely resolved by computerisation of the Presentment Book, as explained above. In the case of companies, however, for reasons explained in Chapter 34, solicitors acting for a selling company will not normally grant a letter of obligation to produce a clear search in the company file or Charges Register. This in turn produces serious problems which are dealt with in detail in that chapter.

32.37 MATTERS DEALT WITH IN THE LETTER OF OBLIGATION

The recommended form of letter of obligation in the *Registration of Title Practice Book*, para 8.14 is in the following terms:

'Dear Sirs,

[Seller's name]

[Purchaser's name]

[Address of subjects]

With reference to the settlement of the above transaction today we hereby (1) undertake to clear the records of any deed, decree or diligence (other than such as may be created by or against your client) which may be recorded in the Property or Personal Registers or to which effect may be given in the Land Register in the period from * to ** inclusive (or to the earlier date of registration of your client's interest in the above subjects) and which would cause the Keeper to make an entry on or qualify his indemnity in the Land Certificate to be issued in respect of that interest and (2) confirm that to the best of our knowledge and belief as at this date the answers to the questions numbered 1 to 14 in the draft Form 1 adjusted with you (in so far as these answers relate to our client or to our client's interest in the above subjects) are still correct.

Yours faithfully.'

* Insert date of certification of Form 11 report or, if only a Form 10 report has been instructed, the date of certification of that report.

** Insert date 14 (now 21) days (or such other period as may be agreed) after settlement. (Note the change in period from 14 to 21 days referred to in para 32.39.)

The importance of the undertaking (2) in this suggested letter of obligation, regarding the accuracy of the answers to the questions in the application form, is dealt with below.

32.38 Appropriate additions

Under the Sasine system, where an outstanding heritable security was being discharged, an undertaking was included to deliver the recorded discharge within an agreed period. Such an undertaking is no longer appropriate where the purchaser's interest is being registered. In the majority of cases the discharge will no longer be recorded in the Sasine Register at all. Even in those cases where recording is appropriate, the purchaser's concern is not that the discharge has been recorded but that effect is given to the discharge in the Land Register when his interest is registered. There are occasions when a purchase has to be settled before a signed discharge is in the seller's hands. If settlement has to take place on this basis, an appropriate addition to the letter of obligation may be made in some such terms as:

'We further undertake to deliver to you within [   ] days (i) a duly executed Discharge of the Standard Security granted by [   ] in favour of [   ] in terms of the draft Discharge approved by you; (ii) a completed Application (Form 2) for Registration of the said Discharge duly signed; and (iii) an Inventory (Form 4) completed in duplicate with reference to that Application and cheque in respect of registration dues.'

32.39   Time-limits

One of the difficulties which arose from time to time in relation to Sasine letters of obligation was the question of time-limits for recording the disposition: see *Warners v Beveridge & Kellas* 1994 SLT (Sh Ct) 29. As a result of these difficulties, the Law Society of Scotland's Conveyancing Committee, in conjunction with the Insurance Committee, introduced what has come to be known as the 'classic' letter of obligation. This style of obligation made it clear that the obligation to deliver a clear search as such is a separate obligation from the obligation to deliver a search which actually discloses the disposition. In the classic obligation, the undertaking to exhibit or deliver the search was qualified to the effect that it would cover a clear search only up to a date 14 days (now 21) after the date of the letter of obligation. This was to protect the seller's solicitor from his obligation being extended indefinitely. In so far as the obligation to deliver a search disclosing the disposition was concerned, again this only applies provided the disposition was recorded within 14 days (now 21) of the date of the letter of obligation.

In land registration letters of obligation, this principle is continued, as the wording above shows. The obligation to clear the record is only for a period until 14 days (now 21) after settlement to ensure that the application for registration is dealt with timeously. This original 14-day period in the classic letter of obligation has been extended to 21 days with effect from 1 November 2002 to take account of delays at the Stamp Office in 'turning round' deeds duly stamped and possible delays due to holiday periods at Register House which can mean 14 days is insufficient time. See 'Classic Letters of Obligation' 2002 JLSS Oct/12 and 'Clarifying the Classic Letter of Obligation' 2003 JLSS Apr/26.

32.40   RISKS INHERENT IN THE OBLIGATION SYSTEM

From the purchaser's point of view, his agents should not settle a transaction if the subscribed disposition is not ready for delivery. The only protection in such circumstances is for the price to be consigned in joint names, pending delivery of a disposition; but the seller will normally not agree to that because, once the price is consigned, the pressure by the purchaser ceases, and the purchaser's agent tends then to drag his feet. In the result, there is a delay in the seller obtaining the price. Therefore, the seller's agent will normally only agree to early settlement if the price is paid in full, even although he is not in a position to deliver a disposition to the purchaser in exchange. As a result, the purchaser's agent may agree to hand over the price without title but, as a measure of protection, will then insist on an undertaking by the seller that a disposition will be delivered to the purchaser in due course. Solicitors acting on behalf of a seller are strongly advised against granting a personal obligation in such circumstances. Any personal obligation so granted would be regarded as 'non-classic'. Such a practice can be quite unsatisfactory and does involve serious risks for both agents and parties.

The risks can be summarised as follows:

(1) the risk to the purchaser;
(2) the risk to the parties' agents; and
(3) the risk to the seller.

32.41   The risk to the purchaser

The risk here is that, in the end of the day, the seller may prove unwilling or unable to implement the obligation, although contractually bound to do so. If he is merely unwilling to do so, then the purchaser has a remedy through the action of implement; but this may involve him in considerable delay and expense.

However, the seller may be totally disabled from completing the transaction by supervening circumstances, for example insolvency. In that case, the property, although subject to a contract, will pass to the trustee in sequestration who can repudiate the contract. The purchaser has no real right but merely a contractual claim against the seller; and the trustee in sequestration is not bound to implement that claim. In the result, even though the purchaser has paid over the price and is in possession, and even though he has a binding contract with the seller and a binding obligation by the seller's agent to deliver a disposition, he cannot maintain his position in a question with the trustee in sequestration who can eject him and resell the property to some other purchaser. The purchaser's only remedy against the seller in such a situation is to rank in the sequestration and claim damages for a breach of contract; but if, as often happens, there is nothing for the ordinary creditors, then in the result the purchaser has lost his money.

Alternatively, the property could be subject to a heritable security, or several heritable securities, and the seller may have sold at a price less than sufficient to pay off all the creditors in full. In the ensuing delay, one of the heritable creditors gets tired of waiting and exercises his power of sale which, of course, he is perfectly entitled to do, notwithstanding the binding contract of sale and purchase. Again, as a result, the purchaser may lose his money.

32.42   The risk to the parties' agents

If the purchaser's solicitor has explained the position in detail to the purchaser, made the purchaser aware of the risks and has then settled without title on the purchaser's express instructions, the agent will not be liable. But in some cases, the purchaser's agent settles without title against the seller's obligation without putting the purchaser in the picture. In that case, he is almost certainly guilty of professional negligence and would be liable in restitution to the disappointed purchaser.

Every practising solicitor is obliged to carry professional indemnity insurance under a master policy negotiated by the Law Society of Scotland. The liabilities of agents, both for seller and purchaser, are understood to be covered by the master policy, but only within certain limits and subject to possible exceptions.

Clearly, if a 'non-classic' obligation is granted, the seller's solicitor may well not be insured. Non-classic letters of obligation are all types of undertaking, other than an obligation to deliver a search and a discharge, where the solicitor personally undertakes to do something more – typically, for example, to deliver some other deed not available at settlement, or to produce a completion certificate. For an indicative (and sadly non-exhaustive) list of such obligations, see 'Classic Letters of Obligation' 2002 JLSS Oct/12 and 'Clarifying the Classic Letter of Obligation' 2003 JLSS Apr/26.

Any solicitor who grants an obligation of this type and cannot implement it will suffer a double excess or double deductible on any claim made under the Master Policy. If a firm's normal excess is £12,000, the excess on a claim of this type will be £24,000. In many cases, this will mean that the firm will have to pay the whole cost of the claim.

32.43   The risk to the seller

Where the transaction settles in this way, the seller gets the purchase price in full, and his risk is minimal. Nonetheless, there are certain risks. For example, it is possible that, notwithstanding payment of the price, the transaction may not settle in the end of the day; for example, the purchaser may claim that the title is unmarketable.

If the unmarketability in title is of a minor nature, it may be that, by paying over the price and taking possession, the purchaser has barred himself from rescinding the contract on grounds which otherwise would have entitled him to do so. See *Macdonald v Newall* (1898) 1 F 68.

But, clearly, there could be certain situations where, because of a major defect in the title, the purchaser is entitled to rescind and claim repayment. Meantime the seller may have paid off heritable securities out of the money paid to him by the purchaser; or he may have purchased another house. In either case, the seller might have difficulty then in finding the money to repay.

32.44   ILLUSTRATIONS OF THE RISKS

For a cautionary case, which illustrates the dangers of settling without a validly executed title, see *Gibson v Hunter Home Designs Ltd* 1976 SLT 94. Mr Gibson bought a house from Hunter Homes Ltd, which he paid for on 31 October 1974, and took possession, without getting delivery of his feu disposition. Shortly thereafter, Hunter

Homes Ltd went into liquidation before the feu disposition had been delivered. Mr Gibson then sued for implement but the court held, without difficulty, that the house remained the property of the company, and that Mr Gibson had a mere personal right but no real right therein. As a result, the liquidator was entitled to repudiate the contract of sale to Mr Gibson, as he did, and to resell the property, defeating Mr Gibson's claim in the process. This left Mr Gibson with a claim for damages as an ordinary creditor in the liquidation.

It appears from the report that the solicitors for Hunter Homes Ltd had granted a letter of obligation undertaking to deliver a validly executed disposition, which of course they could not do. Mr Gibson was encouraged by the judges in that case to institute proceedings against the solicitors who granted that obligation, presumably for damages for failure to implement the same. Obviously, this put the solicitors granting the obligation in a position of some difficulty, and they may well have had to pay Mr Gibson in full, and then claim as ordinary creditors in the liquidation.

This case underlines the risks both to the purchaser, and to the seller's solicitors who granted the obligation.

A letter of obligation prescribes after five years under the Prescription and Limitation (Scotland) Act 1973, s 6: see, for example, *Lieberman v G W Tait & Sons* 1987 SLT 585. However, arguably, a letter of obligation contains obligations relating to land under Schedule 1, para 2(e). If so, the relevant period is 20 years, not five years: see *Barratt (Scotland) Ltd v Keith* 1993 SC 142 and *Wright v Frame* 1992 GWD 8-447. This point was not raised in *Lieberman*.

For some further comments, see an article 'Script for Two Nightmares: Letters of Obligation' by R A Edwards in 1975 JLSS 260. See also the commentaries on the more recent cases of *Sharp v Thomson* 1997 SLT 636 and *Burnett's Trustee v Grainger* 2002 SLT 699, as listed in the Reading List for Chapter 4.

32.45 SUMMARY OF INSURANCE PROVISIONS

It is perhaps useful to summarise the current position under the Law Society of Scotland's Master Policy in relation to letters of obligation.

(1) If a solicitor grants a classic letter of obligation undertaking only to clear the record and to deliver a discharge and:
   (a) has made due enquiry (which means having obtained a search in the computerised Presentment Book, which should be no more than three days old);
   (b) has asked the client to disclose any secured loans;
   (c) is unaware of any other security; and
   (d) has sufficient funds to pay off the existing security,
   the solicitor will be fully covered by the Master Policy with no excess or deductible whatsoever in the event of a claim arising.
(2) If a solicitor grants a classic letter of obligation without having made due enquiry (as aforesaid), the solicitor will suffer the normal excess or deductible in the event of the claim arising.

(3) In the event of a solicitor granting a non-classic letter of obligation (to deliver a disposition or some other such matter), the solicitor will suffer a double excess or deductible in the event of a claim arising.

(4) In the event of a solicitor recklessly granting a non-classic letter of obligation, knowing that the obligation is unlikely to be implemented, so as to raise an inference of bad faith on the part of the solicitor, there may be no cover at all.

See further 'Clarifying the Classic Letter of Obligation' 2003 JLSS Apr/26.

32.46   MISCELLANEOUS ITEMS

According to circumstances, there may be quite a number of other things which affect the validity of the title to a greater or lesser degree, or which impose some restraint on the proprietor, and which may not emerge from mere scrutiny of the titles and the search. In practice, however, an examination of the title will normally disclose the risk. Some of the more important of these undisclosed items are as follows.

32.47   Lack of capacity

There is no way of telling from the titles if a deed has been granted by persons under age or otherwise lacks capacity. Normally the purchaser's agents accept this risk without enquiry; but it does sometimes happen.

32.48   Forgery

Again, there is no way of telling, by a scrutiny of the title, whether one of the writs is forged. But again, the purchaser's agents normally accept the risk.

32.49   Latent defects.

Any writ, or decree, although *ex facie* valid, may be void or voidable and open to reduction on various grounds, as we have seen. In *Sibbald's Heirs v Harris* 1947 SC 601 at 604 Lord President Cooper states:

'The obligation on a seller is to produce an *ex facie* valid prescriptive progress of titles, not to guarantee the purchaser, by policies of insurance or otherwise, against every risk of subsequently emerging latent defect. In so far as these risks are taken into account in our system of conveyancing, they have been left to rest on the classical obligation of warrandice, and warrandice is offered here.'

32.50   Statutory protection

The Conveyancing (Scotland) Act 1924, s 46, provides that a decree of reduction is not to have any effect in a question with a *bona fide* purchaser for value who has acquired right prior to the extract of the decree being recorded in the Register of Sasines. Whatever the underlying purpose of this section may have been, it is arguably of very limited application following on the decision in *Mulhearn v Dunlop* 1929 SLT 59, as discussed in Chapter 29, para 12. Recent commentators, however, seem to discount the effect of this decision.

More positive protection is afforded under other statutory provisions, but only with limited effect.

(1) *The Succession (Scotland) Act 1964, s 17.* Where a person has, in good faith and for value, acquired a title to heritage which has vested in an executor, either directly or indirectly, from the executor or from someone deriving title from the executor, then his title is not challengeable on the ground that the confirmation was reducible. Nor is it challengeable on the ground that the executor should not have transferred the property to a particular beneficiary.

(2) *The Trusts (Scotland) Act 1961, s 2.* A sale of heritable property by trustees may be contrary to the terms or the purposes of the trust, in which case the trustees have no implied power of sale under the Trusts (Scotland) Act 1921, s 4. Until 1961, this meant that, in a question with a *bona fide* purchaser for value, the beneficiary could challenge the title of a disponee who purchased heritage from the trustees without the necessary powers. Under this section, notwithstanding the lack of power, a disposition by trustees to a purchaser is put beyond challenge, and good faith is not required. See *Brodie v Secretary of State for Scotland* 2002 GWD 20-698.

The section protects only persons transacting with the trustees in a Scottish trust. It does not apply in English or other trusts. Further it protects only the purchaser from trustees. If the trustees, mistakenly, convey heritable property to the wrong beneficiary and the beneficiary then sells the property, that sale is not covered by the 1961 Act, s 2.

In contrast, if the executor dispones or transfers the heritage to the wrong beneficiary, who then sells the property to a *bona fide* purchaser for value, the purchaser is still protected against that defect in title by the 1964 Act, s 17.

(3) *The Companies Act 1985, ss 35, and 35A (as amended by the Companies Act 1989, s 108).* This affords a measure of protection to persons dealing with a company, with particular reference to the *ultra vires* rule which applied at common law. This is dealt with more fully in Chapter 34.

32.51 Unregistered interests

Generally, real rights are more powerful than personal rights. Real rights are enforceable against the world, whereas personal rights are enforceable only against an individual (or identifiable category of individuals). This can be illustrated in various contexts, but is particularly marked in considering rights and obligations encumbering land. An example can be seen in the case of *Ceres School Board v McFarlane* (1895) 23 R 279, where A granted a feu disposition to B who entered into possession of the land, but did not complete title by registration. Years later, D, in ignorance of the feu disposition by A to B, took a conveyance from A of the whole estate. This conveyance was registered. It was held that D's right to land was unaffected by the prior unregistered feu disposition in favour of B. See also *Young v Leith* (1848) 2 Ross LC 81, affirming (1847) 9 D 932 and *Burnett's Trustee v Grainger* 2002 SLT 699.

Or consider the following case where A and B own neighbouring plots of ground. They enter an agreement whereby A undertakes that he will not build on certain parts of his property and that he will impose a similar obligation on any purchaser. However, when A sells on the plot to C no obligation is imposed. If C then proposes to build, B can do nothing to prevent it. The agreement between A and B created a personal right enforceable only against A. It cannot be enforced against C. See *Morier v Brownlie and Watson* (1893) 23 R 67.

The general principle is well established. However, in some exceptional cases a personal right enforceable against an owner of property (or other holder of a real right in the property) may also be enforceable against a successor of that owner (or holder). In such cases the successor is bound by the prior personal obligation in certain cases where the successor is in bad faith through his or her knowledge of the existence of the prior personal obligation. In *Morison's Dictionary* this is referred to as the rule penalising 'Private Knowledge of a Prior Right'. Modern textbooks refer to 'the offside goals rule'.

32.52   *The rule penalising private knowledge of a prior right*

The doctrine whereby a prior personal right can bind a singular successor of property has been known to Scots law for over 400 years. The earliest decision is *Stirling v White and Drummond* (1582) Mor 1689 and there has developed a small body of case law over the centuries. In recent years the leading illustration of the doctrine is *Rodger (Builders) Ltd v Fawdry* 1950 SC 483. Here, Fawdry owned a farm and contracted to sell it to Rodger (Builders) Ltd. At settlement Rodger (Builders) did not pay the purchase price. Fawdry then resold the farm to Bell. Bell knew about the prior contract but relied on an assurance from Fawdry that the prior contract had fallen. The second sale proceeded and a conveyance was delivered to Bell, who registered. Bell's registration went ahead in full knowledge that Rodger (Builders) were preparing to assert their rights. The company duly went to court, arguing successfully that the disposition in favour of Bell should be reduced on account of Bell's bad faith in proceeding with the transaction while aware that there was an earlier transaction. Bell was not entitled to rely on the assurance of Fawdry, and was under a duty to inquire as to the true position. The effect of the decision is that as a result of Bell's bad faith the prior personal right of Rodger (Builders) exercisable against Fawdry, could found an action against Bell. The personal right trumped Bell's real right.

32.53   Parameters of the doctrine

Although the doctrine has been well established over the years, its parameters have been subject to little sustained analysis. The leading modern treatment is that of

Professor Reid in *The Law of Property in Scotland* (1996), paras 695 to 700. He suggests that the doctrine is based on civil law fraud (when interpreted as meaning 'bad faith') and that the case law originally suggested that the second purchaser is penalised because he or she is a participant in the seller's attempt to defraud the first purchaser. This approach may be criticised as its suggests the application of the doctrine is based on the conduct of the seller – which was rejected by a line of cases beginning with *Petrie v Forsyth* (1874) 2 R 214, where the seller genuinely believed that he was entitled to enter the second transaction.

Previous editions of this book (including the sixth edition at paras 33.58 to 33.61) have rightly suggested that the parameters of the doctrine are unclear. In attempting to identify these parameters it was argued that the origins of the doctrine lie in the law of personal bar, ie that the second purchaser is personally barred from founding on his real right in a competition with the first purchaser. This approach seems based on comments of Lord Gifford in *Petrie v Forsyth* (1874) 2 R 214 at 223. It is noteworthy, though, that in Lord Gifford's classic statement of the doctrine in *Stodart v Dalzell* (1876) 4 R 236, he does not use the language of personal bar. It has recently been persuasively argued by Professor John Blackie that personal bar cannot form the juristic basis of the doctrine: see 'Good faith and the doctrine of personal bar' in ADM Forte (ed) *Good Faith in Contract and Property Law* (1999) p 129, at pp 147 to 150. The present writers would therefore depart from the analysis of the previous editions of this book.

Other writers have suggested alternative approaches to the juristic parameters of the doctrine, but these fall outwith the scope of this Manual. For a detailed analysis of the approaches, see S Wortley 'Double sales and the offside trap: Some thoughts on the rule penalising private knowledge of a prior right' 2002 JR 291, who suggests that the doctrine is based on the publicity principle applicable in property law.

32.54 When does the doctrine apply?

The case law can be analysed as follows.

(1) A is an owner of land or of a real right in land who is under an obligation to B.
(2) This obligation relates to the land and gives B a correlative personal right that is capable of being made a real right (subject to one exception, detailed in para 32.62).
(3) A then enters a subsequent transaction with C whereby C will acquire a real right in the same piece of land.
(4) The transaction between A and C breaches the obligation owed by A to B.
(5) In entering the transaction with A, C was in bad faith in that C knew (or wilfully closed his or her eyes to the existence) of the prior obligation owed by A to B. The appropriate remedy available to B is discussed in paras 32.58 to 32.62.

This analysis is illustrated by consideration of examples where the doctrine applies – as discussed in paras 32.58 to 32.61 (where instances of double grants in the same property are considered) and para 32.62 (where other cases are examined).

However, some elements require further preliminary explanation. There are three particular areas of difficulty: the requirement that B's personal right be a personal right capable of being made real; the meaning of bad faith; and when C is to be in bad faith.

32.55 A personal right capable of being made real

This qualification stems from *Wallace v Simmers* 1960 SC 255. There, a farm owner had granted a licence to occupy the land to a party – the licence being only a personal right. When the owner sold the property on to a third party with knowledge of the licence, the third party was not encumbered by the licence-holder's personal right and could remove him from the property. The justification for this is that the licence was not a real right, and could not become a real right. Where the transaction with B is a contract of sale or a contract for the grant of servitude or other subordinate real right, while the contract creates a personal right, the personal right is a *jus ad rem acquirenda* (a personal right to acquire a real right). However, the qualification extends beyond instances where B has a contract with A to acquire a real right. It also applies where B has a right to enter a contract to acquire a real right, such as an option to purchase – *Davidson v Zani* 1992 SCLR 1001 – or a right of pre-emption – *Matheson v Tinney* 1989 SLT 535 and *Roebuck v Edmunds* 1992 SLT 1055.

While this qualification was criticised in para 33.61 of the sixth edition of this book, it is now well established (and if – as is generally argued – the roots of the doctrine lie in property law would be an understandable qualification). Indeed in *Optical Express (Gyle) Ltd v Marks & Spencer plc* 2000 SLT 644 – one of the recent cases on the doctrine – the approach in *Wallace v Simmers* seems to be endorsed.

Although Professor Reid endorses this qualification, in *The Law of Property in Scotland* (1996), para 697, he suggests that the basis of the decision in *Wallace* 'appears to be that, unlike a *jus ad rem*, an ordinary personal right contains no grant of warrandice, either express or implied. Consequently when a subsequent real right comes to be granted there is no breach of the antecedent personal right and hence no scope for the rule against offside goals'.

Professor Reid's analysis attempts to reconcile the decision in *Trade Development Bank v Warriner & Mason* 1980 SC 74 with the general thrust of decisions on the doctrine. In that case the Lyon Group were tenants of an industrial estate. They had created a security over the estate in favour of the bank. The security contained the usual prohibition on the debtor granting leases. However, contrary to this prohibition Lyon Group granted a sub-lease in favour of Warriner and Mason. It was held that this sub-lease could be reduced at the instance of the bank. The reasoning for this is difficult to discern in the judgment but appears to be based on Warriner and Mason's bad faith. Here, the personal right of the bank is a prohibition, not a right capable of being made real. Instead, it is a personal right inherent in the bank's real right in security. The decision had no precursors, and has not been directly followed as an example of the doctrine. It is suggested that, since the authority stands alone, it may not truly be an illustration of the doctrine. Despite contrary analysis within the decision, it may (as Professor Reid originally suggested in his article 'Real Conditions in Standard Securities' 1983 SLT (News) 173 and 189 at 191), be rationalised as an example of the general principle in the law of securities that the debtor shall not act in a way to prejudice the creditor's security. See *Reid v McGill* 1912 2 SLT 246 and *Edinburgh Entertainments Ltd v Stevenson* 1926 SLT 286.

32.56 What is the meaning of bad faith?

It is not the action of A – the party that makes the double grant – that triggers the doctrine. Instead, the actions of C are examined. C will be in bad faith if C knows that the transaction with A contravenes an earlier obligation between A and B. This is clear from *Petrie v Forsyth* (1874) 2 R 214. The knowledge of the earlier obligation is enough to put C on notice, requiring C to make enquiries to determine whether or not the obligation between A and B subsists. Such enquiries cannot rely on assurances of A that the prior obligation no longer applies. This proposition has been asserted regularly in the cases: see for example, *Lang v Dixon* 29 June 1813 FC, *Marshall v Hynd* (1828) 6 S 384, and *Rodger (Builders) Ltd v Fawdry* 1950 SC 483.

Bad faith may also arise as a result of the constructive knowledge of C. Thus, if the obligation A owes to B appears on the register (as would be the case with a right of pre-emption), C is deemed to know of the existence of the obligation.

Bad faith additionally arises where C's transaction with A is gratuitous. This proposition is stated by academic commentators: see Reid *The Law of Property in Scotland* (1996), para 699, and *Baron Hume's Lectures, 1786–1822*, Volume IV, p 317 (as edited by G C H Paton and published as Volume 17 of The Stair Society (1955)). However, only one case appears to confirm this: *Andersons v Lows* (1863) 2 M 100.

32.57 When is C to be in bad faith?

In *Alex Brewster & Sons v Caughey* 2002 GWD 10-318 it was suggested in *obiter* comments of Lord Eassie that C is in bad faith if C knew of the prior obligation owed by A to B at any time prior to completion of the real right. Despite observations to the contrary within the judgment, this represents an extension of the law. These comments have been criticised by S Wortley in 'Double sales and the offside trap: Some thoughts on the rule penalising private knowledge of a prior right' 2002 JR 291. He suggests that C should not be punished for knowledge acquired after conclusion of the contract with A, but prior to completion of the real right. This difficult question remains open for consideration.

32.58 Double grant cases

The usual situation where the rule penalising private knowledge of a prior right applies is where A enters two transactions, each of which would create a real right affecting the land (or real right in land). There are three broad categories of case:

(1) successive transfers by A;

(2) competition between transfer of the property and the grant of a subordinate real right; and

(3) competition between subordinate real rights.

32.59 Successive transfers

This is the principal example where A agrees to transfer to B, and then to transfer to C and C completes title first. Typically, both transactions will be sales. In these cases if the requirements set out in paras 32.54 to 32.57 apply, then B will be able to reduce the conveyance by A in favour of C: see, for example, *Rodger (Builders) Ltd v Fawdry* 1950 SC 483, discussed above. Alternatively, if B raises an action prior to C completing title, B can interdict C from completing title: see, for example, *Spurway v Oversudden Ltd* (10 December 1986, unreported), OH; the transcript is available on LEXIS. As shown in paras 11.31 to 11.35, once C has registered title to the property in the Land Register reduction cannot enter the register unless the Land Register is rectified under s 9 of the Land Registration (Scotland) Act 1979. It is suggested that the bad faith of C may be sufficient to permit rectification, even against a proprietor in possession, on the grounds of the 'fraud or carelessness' of C. For further discussion, see para 11.34. However, if this is not possible it seems arguable that the nature of the doctrine should allow B to exercise his or her personal right to acquire a real right against C (adopting the approach in *Greig v Brown & Nicolson* (1829) 7 S 274).

32.60 Transfer competing with a subordinate real right

There are two possible scenarios: (1) A agrees to transfer to B, and then creates a subordinate real right (such as a security or servitude) in favour of C who completes the real right first in knowledge of B's right; or (2) A agrees to create a subordinate real right in favour of B, but then transfers the property to C (who has knowledge of B's right). In the former case the real rights can co-exist. In the latter the transfer to C will prevent the real right in favour of B being created (as the grant would now be from a non-owner).

(1) *Transfer followed by subordinate real right.* The case law indicates that although the rights are compatible B can reduce the grant of the subordinate real right in favour of C, meaning B's acquisition of ownership is unencumbered. This approach is long-established: *Bouack (or Bowack) v Croll* (1748) Mor 1695 and 15280 (competition between an assignation of lease and the grant of a sub-lease) and *Trade Development Bank v David W Haig (Bellshill) Ltd; Trade Development Bank v Crittall Windows Ltd* 1983 SLT 510 (competition between an assignation of a lease and the grant of a standard security over the lease).

(2) *Grant of subordinate real right followed by transfer.* Case law here is mixed. It has been held that where B had a right to obtain a servitude and C acquired ownership with knowledge of B's right, then B was entitled to assert the personal right to acquire the servitude against C: *Greig v Brown & Nicolson* (1829) 7 S

274. However, where B had a right to obtain a lease and C acquired ownership with knowledge of B's right, B could not reduce the conveyance in favour of C nor assert the personal right against C: *Jacobs v Anderson* (1898) 6 SLT 234, and *Millar v McRobbie* 1949 SC 1. Given the development of the doctrine in the latter half of the twentieth century, the latter cases appear wrongly decided. It would seem that, following *Greig*, in such cases B should be able to exercise the personal right against C. Reduction of the conveyance in favour of C, however, would not seem possible.

32.61 Competing subordinate real rights

The situation here is where A agrees to grant a subordinate real right (such as a lease or security) in favour of B, then grants a subsequent subordinate real right in favour of C. C acquires the real right first. Sometimes the subordinate real rights will be incompatible, such as where A grants a lease to B, and a proper liferent to C. Both B and C will expect exclusive possession of the property. Although there is no case law it is suggested that the principles outlined above would mean that the doctrine should apply if C is in bad faith as to B's right.

Where the rights are compatible there is no case law other than in relation to competing heritable securities: *Blackwood v The Other Creditors of George Hamilton* (1749) Mor 4898; *Henderson v Campbell* (1821) 1 S 103 (NE 104); and *Leslie v McIndoe's Trustees* (1824) 3 S 48 (NE 31). The doctrine was not applied in these cases (the argument attracted the court in *Blackwood*, but the matter did not need to be decided). In each case, the primacy of the order of creation of real rights was asserted for ranking purposes (where there is no agreement between the creditors). It is not clear how the developments in the doctrine in other competitions affect these cases, but the competing security decisions (despite a suggestion in the headnote of *Trade Development Bank v David W Haig (Bellshill) Ltd; Trade Development Bank v Crittall Windows* 1983 SLT 510) have never been overturned. One reason may be the risk of creating circles of priority where there are three or more competing securities.

32.62 Other cases

There are two other situations where the doctrine has applied beyond the instance of double grants: (1) where B's right is as a beneficiary in a trust; and (2) where B's right is an option to purchase or right of pre-emption.

(1) *Beneficiary in a trust.* This is one example where B's personal right is not capable of being made real being merely a beneficiary's interest in a trust. However, it was held in *Redfearn v Somervail* (1813) 1 Dow 50, 5 Pat 707 that where C acquired a real right with knowledge of B, the beneficiary's interest, then B could assert his or her right against C. The common law position has been amended by s 2 of the Trusts (Scotland) Act 1961. This provides that a third party (C) will be protected in a sale, or grant of security, even if C was in bad faith.

(2) *Option to purchase and rights to pre-emption*. In these cases, where B has a right
to enter an agreement to acquire the property, and C has acquired the property in
knowledge of B's right, it has been held that B can reduce the conveyance in
favour of C: see *Matheson v Tinney* 1989 SLT 535 and *Roebuck v Edmunds* 1992
SCLR 74. Alternatively, B can enforce his or her personal right against C:
Davidson v Zani 1992 SCLR 1001.

32.63   Servitudes

Prior to 28 November 2004, both positive and negative servitudes may have been
duly constituted by a writ which need not have entered the Record. Admittedly, in the
case of positive servitudes, there must have been publication by possession, but this
was a very uncertain protection; and for negative servitudes publication was unnecessary and possession impossible. Further, a servitude right may have been registered
in the benefited, not in the burdened, title. See *Balfour v Kinsey* 1987 SLT 144.
However, under the Title Conditions (Scotland) Act 2003, s 80, no new negative
servitudes can be created and existing negative servitudes are converted into real burdens from the appointed day which subsist for a period of ten years and are then extinguished unless preserved through registration of a notice of converted servitude. See
para 16.11 and paras 17.16 to 17.21. Under the 2003 Act, s 75(1), a new positive servitude must be registered in both the benefited (formerly the dominant) and the burdened (formerly the servient) title. Accordingly, the only servitude rights which may
be difficult to identify are a positive servitude created prior to 28 November 2004
which has not been registered, for example a servitude by prescription, and a converted servitude in the ten-year period until it is extinguished or a notice is registered.

32.64   Heritable securities

Securities recorded more than 40 years ago may not be disclosed in a Form 10 report,
although the risk is small.

32.65   Gratuitous alienations

Under the Bankruptcy (Scotland) Act 1985, s 34(4), any gratuitous alienation within
a maximum period of five years prior to sequestration may be reduced, subject to certain safeguards. The provisions of this subsection are without prejudice to any right
or interest acquired in good faith and for value from or through the transferee in the
gratuitous alienation. So a *bona fide* purchaser for value from a donee of the bankrupt
is absolutely protected.

Under the 1985 Act, s 36, any unfair preference is similarly open to reduction if created within the six months prior to sequestration or the granting of a trust deed. In the
majority of cases, the title will show the risk. Further, if the transaction is the purchase
of a property from the creditor in a challengeable security exercising his power of sale,
a *bona fide* purchaser for value would normally be protected. There were also rules at

common law which differed in certain respects from the statutory rule introduced under the Bankruptcy Act 1621 by virtue of which gratuitous alienations could be attacked. These common law rules still apply and may still be used; and in *Bank of Scotland v T A Neilson & Co* 1990 SC 284, the court further held that these common law rules applied to companies as they applied to individuals.

In *Short's Trustee v Keeper of the Registers of Scotland* 1996 SLT 166, referred to above at para 11.35, the original dispositions by the bankrupt had been reduced as gratuitous alienations and the subsequent dispositions by the original disponee were in themselves gratuitous. However, perhaps surprisingly, counsel does not appear to have seriously pressed the argument that, in these circumstances, rectification of the Register was appropriate under the Land Registration (Scotland) Act 1979, s 9(3)(a)(iii). This would have been on the footing that the Register was inaccurate, in that it no longer truly represented the position according to the titles on which registration had proceeded; that the inaccuracy was caused initially by the fraud or carelessness of the original disponee who took the titles at under-value; and that the registered proprietor, being a gratuitous alienee from him, was not protected by the 1985 Act, s 34(4). Protection is afforded under s 34(4) of the 1985 Act only to a person who has acquired an interest in the subjects in good faith and for value through the original gratuitous alienee. The wife of the original disponee in *Short's Trustee*, having herself received the properties gratuitously, did not qualify for protection under that proviso. In these circumstances, could the registered proprietor properly claim that the inaccuracy had not been caused by her fraud or carelessness? It was held that she was entitled so to do and was protected by the provisions of the 1979 Act, s 9. Certainly to hold otherwise would produce formidable difficulties and serious defects in the system of registration of title. However, this decision has been thrown into doubt by *Short's Trustee v Chung (No 2)* 1998 SC 105, 1998 SLT 200, affirmed 1999 SLT 751, discussed in para 11.35.

32.66 Unrecorded leases and tenants' rights

In practically all cases, leases transmit against singular successors under the Leases Act 1449.

Except in the case of registered leases, for which see Chapter 24, nothing appears on the Record, and therefore nothing appears in the search to indicate the existence of such rights. But an examination of the property should disclose the position.

32.67 Occupancy rights of non-entitled spouses

The Matrimonial Homes (Family Protection) (Scotland) Act 1981 (as amended by the Law Reform (Miscellaneous Provisions) (Scotland) Act 1985) which came into operation on 1 September 1982, creates occupancy rights for the benefit of the non-entitled spouse as described in para 28.44. The 1981 Act was further amended by the Law Reform (Miscellaneous Provisions) (Scotland) Act 1990, Schedule 8, para 31.

When acting for a purchaser or creditor, it is important to ensure that the property is not affected by any occupancy rights; and to bear in mind that the existence of any such rights will not be disclosed either in the Register of Sasines or in the Personal Register or as regards rights of the former owner's spouse in the Land Register. For a recent case, see *Stevenson v Roy* 2002 SLT 445. Once the title is registered, occupancy rights are overriding interests and the Keeper will state on the title sheet that there are no subsisting occupancy rights of spouses of persons formerly entitled, if satisfied that this is so. The statement is backed by indemnity. It does not cover the current proprietor, so that enquiry is still necessary as to his/her position.

Under s 6 of the 1981 Act, the 'non-entitled spouse' may consent to the dealing (by sale or by security) with the matrimonial home; and such consent excludes any subsequent claim for occupancy rights in that matrimonial home. The Secretary of State, by statutory instrument (the Matrimonial Homes (Forms of Consent) (Scotland) Regulations 1982, SI 1982/971), prescribed two separate forms of consent:

(1) a clause of consent to be inserted in the deed effecting the dealing, for example the disposition in favour of the purchaser from the entitled spouse; and
(2) a deed of consent as a separate document.

In appropriate cases, either of these prescribed forms should be used, and should comply strictly with the statutory requirements.

Alternatively, the non-entitled spouse may renounce his or her occupancy rights by renunciation under s 6 of the 1981 Act. This is uncommon in practice.

If there is no 'non-entitled spouse', the 1981 Act provides for an affidavit which, under ss 6 and 8, protects a third party dealing with the entitled spouse against the possibility of any subsisting occupancy rights adversely affecting the property. The forms of affidavit and renunciation are not prescribed by statutory instrument. The Law Society provided suitable forms in circulars to members dated 28 July and 5 November 1982, updated in 1986 JLSS 214. These forms should be followed in practice. They are reproduced in I J S Talman (ed) *Halliday's Conveyancing Law and Practice in Scotland* (2nd edn, 2 Volumes, 1996–97) Volume 2, paras 36.31 to 36.33.

32.68   *Documentation*

On first registration, the purchaser's solicitors will have to satisfy the Keeper that, in the case of every person having a relevant interest in the property during the preceding five years, no occupancy rights are subsisting. The applicant will have to produce the appropriate documents in relation to each previous proprietor, other than the applicant himself, such as a consent or a renunciation by a non-entitled spouse or an affidavit. Assuming the Keeper is satisfied, on the evidence produced, that there are no subsisting occupancy rights at the time of first registration, then he will endorse the proprietorship section of the land certificate accordingly.

Note particularly, in relation to subsequent dealings with that registered interest, that the certificate applies only to previous proprietors, not to the present registered proprietor. Accordingly, on each subsequent transaction with a registered title, the purchaser or lender must still obtain from the registered proprietor the appropriate consent, renunciation or affidavit etc relating to that sale or loan. See the *Registration of Title Practice Book*, paras 6.28 to 6.48 for a detailed discussion of these and other related points on the Matrimonial Homes (Family Protection) (Scotland) Act 1981. See also 1985 JLSS 486 for a note by the Registers of Scotland on the effect of the Law Reform (Miscellaneous Provisions) (Scotland) Act 1985 on the evidence to be produced to the Keeper for those purposes. This has, of course, been modified by the Law Reform (Miscellaneous Provisions) (Scotland) Act 1990, as noted above.

Some practical points on the effect of the 1981 Act on normal transactions are set out below.

32.69   Title in joint names

Where the title to a dwellinghouse is in joint names, no special action is required, on sale, on purchase, or on granting security because both parties grant the deed(s); but note the following:

(1) Title in joint names, and security granted by one of the spouses only, on his or her one-half *pro indiviso* share. This is a very unusual situation and will only rarely occur; but if it does, consent of the other spouse would not seem to be required because it is impossible to occupy a *pro indiviso* share.

(2) Title in joint names, followed by a divorce. If, after divorce, one of the parties to the marriage remains in occupation of the original matrimonial home (as may easily happen), and then remarries, the title may remain in the original joint names; but on remarriage the new spouse may acquire a right under the Act and become a 'non-entitled spouse'.

There is a strong argument that, in situation (2), the new spouse may not qualify as a 'non-entitled spouse' because of the provisions of the Matrimonial Homes (Family Protection) (Scotland) Act 1981, s 6(2)(b).

However, the ultra cautious course would seem to be, when selling property on behalf of husband and wife, where the title is in joint names, to confirm with them that they are still the same husband and wife, and that there has been no intervening divorce. When purchasing property from a husband and wife, confirmation should be obtained from the selling agent that there has been no intervening divorce and no second marriage.

An appropriate case in point is *Murphy v Murphy* 1992 SCLR 62, where a house was purchased in joint names of A and B. B subsequently married C and moved into the house which became their matrimonial home. The marriage broke up and B moved out leaving C in occupation. The court held that since A had never occupied the house and had allowed B to occupy it with his wife C, A had waived her rights of occupation in favour of B under s 1(2) of the 1981 Act.

32.70   Title in one name

There are two main situations where title in one name is important.

(1) *Sale*. When selling a dwellinghouse, and when the title is in the name of one spouse only, or in name of one or more unmarried owners then either:
   (a) if there is no non-entitled spouse, the seller's solicitor should obtain an affidavit to that effect (one from each owner if more than one); or
   (b) if there is a non-entitled spouse, the solicitor should get a renunciation or consent (*in gremio* or separate) from the non-entitled spouse.
   These will be delivered to the purchaser at settlement.
(2) *Security*. When arranging heritable security, either at the time of purchase or as an additional advance, if the title is not in joint names of the spouses, the procedure is the same as in a sale.

If the security is granted simultaneously with the purchase, the same affidavit or renunciation will serve. But, if the non-entitled spouse is consenting, and has not granted a renunciation, consent (*in gremio* or separate) is required to the granting by the entitled spouse of a standard security.

In the case of a subsequent advance, a new affidavit must be obtained (from each borrower if more than one); or the non-entitled spouse must either renounce, or consent to the additional security.

32.71 Protecting the purchaser

When purchasing a dwellinghouse, in all cases where there is no non-entitled spouse, insist on an affidavit by the seller to be delivered at settlement and then registered in the Books of Council and Session. This was essential before the amendments in the Law Reform (Miscellaneous Provisions) (Scotland) Act 1990 and is still desirable to ensure that the affidavit is delivered; but, under the 1990 amendments, affidavits are effective even if produced after a dealing or after the granting of security.

In all cases where there is a non-entitled spouse, take a renunciation or the consent (*in gremio* or separate) of the non-entitled spouse. The renunciation should be delivered to the purchaser at settlement, and then registered in the Books of Council and Session.

32.72 Death

Occupancy rights automatically terminate on the death of an entitled spouse, and so the surviving non-entitled spouse has no protection. Most agents take an affidavit or renunciation from a sole beneficiary to whom the deceased's heritable property has been bequeathed; and that may be a prudent safeguard in appropriate cases.

32.73 EXAMINATION OF OTHER TITLES

Normally, only the title of the property being purchased needs examination. But in certain limited cases an examination of titles to adjoining properties may be appropriate or necessary. There are three common illustrations:

(1) boundary features;
(2) tenements; and
(3) part disposals, with restrictions on the part retained.

32.74 Boundary features

Although a proprietor can normally establish possession of the land within the boundaries, he can rarely establish exclusive possession of the boundary feature itself. Suppose, then, that there was a disposition by A in favour of B in 1970 which disponed the lands of X and described them as bounded 'on the north by the north face of a boundary wall separating the said subjects hereinbefore disponed from other subjects belonging to C, which said wall is erected wholly on the subjects hereinbefore disponed'. On delivery of the disposition, B enters into possession. It would seem from his title that he is the exclusive proprietor of the boundary wall on the north boundary; and therefore can use it as he pleases, for example for a garage, etc. But suppose that, in a disposition by A in favour of the said C of the adjoining subjects on the north recorded prior to the 1970 disposition, the same boundary in C's disposition is referred to as 'the centre line of the mutual wall separating the said subjects hereinbefore disponed from other subjects belonging to me'. Normally, neither B nor C can establish exclusive possession of the boundary feature itself. Therefore, the titles would be conclusive as to the ownership of the boundary feature; and as C's title was recorded before B's, B could not prevail in a competition with C and, accordingly, the wall would be mutual and not B's property. This might frustrate B in some development.

The same sort of problem can occur in other, less usual circumstances, for example with fishings, lochs, common property etc.

See further paras 8.15 and 8.28 and the Scottish Law Commission *Report on Boundary Walls* (Scot Law Com No 163, 1998).

32.75 Tenements

In the absence of express provision in the titles, the law of the tenement supplies, by implication, certain rights and imposes certain obligations on tenement proprietors *inter se*. This can, and often does, cause difficulties. Suppose that A in 1970 dispones the top flat in a tenement to B and imposes on B the burden of payment of a one-eighth share of the cost of maintaining the roof, chimneyheads, main walls, and other common items in the tenement. *Prima facie*, this supersedes the law of the tenement, (at least as regards the roof) and limits B's liability for roof repairs to a one-eighth share only.

But suppose that A, when selling off the remaining flats in the tenement, fails to insert any comparable obligation in the dispositions of the other flats. Since the other titles are silent, the law of the tenement will apply in their case; and, as regards the roof, the law of the tenement provides that the top flat proprietor pays the whole cost of maintaining the roof above his flat. Therefore, contrary to what appears in the title, (which is also the earliest separate title) B is in fact burdened with the payment of the whole, not merely a one-eighth share, of the cost of roof repairs. This may be a very serious liability.

Accordingly, it is necessary to examine the titles of other flats in a tenement. For further details and proposals for reform, see paras 8.6 to 8.11 on the law of the tenement and the Tenements (Scotland) Bill.

32.76   Part disposals, with restrictions on the part retained

Suppose A owns a house and garden, with a half-hectare of spare amenity ground. He sells the half-hectare to B, to build a house on. In the contract, and in B's disposition, A undertakes not to use his own house for any purpose other than as a residence. A then sells his own house to C but without inserting any restriction on use. C converts the house to a licensed hotel. B cannot prevent C from so doing. See *McLean v Kennaway* (1904) 11 SLT 719, where a right of pre-emption was conferred on a disponee A of part of a tenement, entitling him to acquire the remainder, ie it entered the disponee's title in the General Register of Sasines. The disponer then sold the remainder, without first offering it to A under the pre-emption. A then sought to reduce the disposition of the remainder to the disponee thereof but was held not entitled, in that the pre-emption had not effectually created a real burden on the remainder.

Note incidentally that, in this case, the fact that the pre-emption appeared on the Record, in the title to another property, was held not to be public notice thereof, and not equivalent to intimation to the disponee of the remainder, warning him of the right and putting him on his enquiry. Otherwise, the principle in *Rodger (Builders) Ltd v Fawdry* 1950 SC 483, discussed above, would have applied. But, if C could be shown to have known the whole position, an argument on the *Rodger (Builders) Ltd* principle might succeed.

Note also that, had the right conferred on A been in the nature of a servitude, he could have enforced it against the successor in the remainder. Indeed, the case was argued on the basis of dominant and servient tenement, but Lord Low rightly rejected that argument.

This type of problem does not arise with burdens created under the Title Conditions (Scotland) Act 2003, because of the requirement for dual registration. See para 15.45.

Despite what may be serious risks in some cases, titles of adjoining property, flats in tenements etc are rarely examined in practice by purchaser's agents, except as regards roof liability. According to Professor K G C Reid in 'Good and Marketable Title' 1988 JLSS at p 164, the purchaser is not entitled, as of right, to require the seller to produce the title deeds of other properties unless the contract so provides. This should therefore be covered by the 'evidence of compliance' clause in the missives: see para 28.46.

32.77 NEGATIVE PRESCRIPTION

The long negative prescription reintroduced in its new form by the Prescription and Limitation (Scotland) Act 1973, ss 7 to 11, may indirectly affect heritable titles. In summary, ss 7 and 8 provide that:

(1) if any obligation has subsisted unpursued for 20 years and not acknowledged by the obligee, or

(2) a right has become exercisable and has remained unenforced for 20 years,

then the right or obligation is altogether extinguished.

Certain rights and obligations are, however, declared to be 'imprescriptible' and are excluded from the operation of these sections by Schedule 3. The rights which cannot be extinguished by the negative prescription are set out below.

(1) Real rights of ownership apply only to real rights and do not prevent the extinction of mere personal rights or personal titles: see *Macdonald v Scott* 1981 SC 75. The obligation to deliver a disposition under a contract of sale and purchase is personal and will prescribe. In the light of the decision in *Barratt (Scotland) Ltd v Keith* 1993 SC 142, that obligation falls to be treated as an obligation relating to land for the purposes of the Prescription and Limitation (Scotland) Act 1973 and Schedule 1, para (2)(e); and so the 20-year period would apply. The same would seem to apply to a personal but unrecorded title as being imprescriptible under the 1973 Act, Schedule 3, para (h). A right duly made real by registration, however, can never be lost by the negative prescription alone. Of course, such a right so constituted may be lost if the registered proprietor neglects his rights by permitting adverse possession by a third party who has a title habile to create a right for him by positive prescription. In the case of personal titles, it is now generally thought that these are now imprescriptible under the 1973 Act, Schedule 3, para (h).

Three cases in 1992, *Barratt (Scotland) Ltd v Keith*; *Wright v Frame* 1992 GWD 8-447; and *Stewart's Executors v Stewart* 1993 SLT 440 appear to confirm the decision in *Macdonald* in two respects:

(a) that the long negative prescription, not the short prescription, applies in the case of mere personal rights, for example the right of a purchaser under missives; but

(b) once a conveyance has been delivered, although it creates only a personal title, the right thereunder is imprescriptible under the 1973 Act, Schedule 3, para (h), which applies to completion of title to the land.

(2) Similarly, the rights of a tenant under a recorded lease cannot be lost, under the negative prescription, by failure on the part of the tenant to exercise his rights for however long a period.

(3) *Res merae facultatis* cannot prescribe and are not extinguished by non-use. The right of a proprietor of landlocked land is an important example: see *Bowers v Kennedy* 2000 SLT 1006.

32.78   The effect on heritable title

Bearing these exceptions in mind, the main cases where the negative prescription affects heritable title are:

(1) *Heritable securities.* If no action is taken by the creditor to enforce a heritable security, and no interest has been paid throughout the 20-year period, the obligation and the security is then automatically extinguished and cannot in any circumstances revive. Therefore, by implication, the title is disburdened thereof, although this does not disclose itself on the Record.

(2) *Servitudes.* In contrast to *res merae facultatis*, servitudes are extinguished by the long negative prescription. Further, under the 1973 Act, the period is now 20 years in all cases, in contrast to the earlier period of 40 years plus non-age etc.

In the case of positive servitudes, the period starts to run from the date when the servitude was last exercised. In the case of negative servitudes, the period starts to run from the date when the negative servitude was infringed without objection. In order to exclude the long negative prescription under the 1973 Act, a relevant claim must have been made, which means either by appropriate proceedings in court, by diligence or by arbitration.

Alternatively, in the case of obligations, the long negative prescription is interrupted by 'relevant acknowledgment' which means such performance by the debtor as clearly indicates that the obligation subsists or unequivocal written acknowledgment by the debtor or on his behalf: see ss 9 and 10 of the 1973 Act. Deeds *ex facie* invalid or forged are not exempted from challenge by the negative prescription; this mirrors the equivalent provision for positive prescription in ss 1 to 3 of the 1973 Act.

32.79   DOCUMENTS USED IN FIRST REGISTRATION

There are three main documents used in first registration:

(1) the disposition;
(2) standard securities; and
(3) inventory of writs.

32.80   The disposition

The disposition is the deed most commonly used to implement a contract of sale and purchase; but the comments here apply with equal force to a lease.

The form of disposition used for first registration does not differ materially from the form of disposition used in a Sasine transaction. Remember, at this stage, notwithstanding the impending registration of the title, that there is, so far, no title number. In particular, applications for Form 10 and Form P16 reports will not produce a title number for that property. A title number is never allotted until an actual application for registration of the title is received. It is therefore not possible to incorporate in the description in the disposition any reference to the title number of the property; and so the Land Registration (Scotland) Act 1979, s 4(2)(d), does not yet apply.

(1) *Description and plan*. As already explained, a plan will be essential in most cases to allow the Keeper to identify and map the property on the Ordnance Survey sheet, which is then to be incorporated in the title sheet and land certificate. But this does not mean that the disposition in favour of the purchaser must itself incorporate a plan on the appropriate scale. The plan can be separately provided with the application form and need not be formally executed by the seller. Not infrequently, a plan or a sufficiently detailed particular description will be contained in one of the earlier titles submitted with the application; and if so, a new plan may not be required at all.

It is not necessary for the existing description in the Sasine title to be redrafted in the disposition in favour of the purchaser in different or in bounding terms. The repetition of the existing Sasine description in the disposition in favour of the purchaser will suffice in almost all cases, even although that disposition is then to be the subject of a first registration.

If a new, separate, plan is required, it must accompany the application and must be certified by the applicant as defining the subjects in respect of which registration is sought. With effect from 1 October 1995, primary measurements used in new descriptions or on new plans should be metric in order to comply with the relevant EC Directive on Units of Measurements. Existing (pre-1 October 1995) plans and conveyancing descriptions are unaffected, and the effect of the directive is also mitigated to allow the acre to be used for land registration purposes and imperial measurements to be used as supplementary indicators to metric measurements. See the *Registration of Title Practice Book*, paras 4.44 to 4.51.

(2) *Burdens*. The reference to burdens is in exactly the same terms as in a Sasines title. The requirements for valid constitution of real burdens under the Title Conditions (Scotland) Act 2003 are set out in detail in paras 15.25 to 15.45.

(3) *Warrandice*. A warrandice clause is included, as in a Sasines transaction.

32.81 Standard securities

In the great majority of cases in practice, the purchaser will be obtaining a loan to finance the purchase; and will grant a standard security to the lender in security thereof. The standard security will fall to be registered contemporaneously with the disposition in favour of the purchaser.

The purchaser cannot grant an effective security until he himself has title; and, in this case, his title is to be registered. Therefore, strictly speaking, the standard security is a dealing, registrable under s 2(4) of the Land Registration (Scotland) Act 1979; and a separate application Form 2 will in fact be required – see below. Nonetheless, if the standard security is to be lodged for registration along with the disposition (which is standard practice), the description in the standard security, although strictly speaking a dealing, will take the same form as in a Sasines transaction; and so will normally repeat the description in the disposition in favour of the purchaser.

If that is a new description of a new unit of property on a first split, containing a particular description and incorporating a plan, it is probably most convenient, in the majority of cases, to repeat that particular description in the standard security and incorporate a copy of the disposition plan therein.

Since a title number will not yet have been allotted, it cannot be referred to in the standard security description, which must therefore be in compliance with note 1 of Schedule 2 to the Conveyancing and Feudal Reform (Scotland) Act 1970.

32.82   Inventory of writs

Form 4 provides an inventory of writs. Note that no warrant of registration is necessary on any deed presented for registration, as this is replaced by the relevant application form.

32.83   THE LETTER OF OBLIGATION

See para 32.35 above.

32.84   APPLICATIONS FOR REGISTRATION

See the *Registration of Title Practice Book*, Chapter 5. The procedure to be followed by the purchaser's solicitor is:

(1) Obtain/encash the loan cheque and intimate completion to the building society.
(2) Complete the disposition and standard security with appropriate testing clauses.
(3) Arrange for payment of stamp duty land tax, if appropriate.
(4) For the purpose of registering the disposition, complete the application Form 1 already agreed in draft with the seller's solicitors and revised by them. In registration of title, application forms are essential for every writ presented for registration; and an inventory of writs Form 4 must also accompany every application form, along with a cheque/remittance for the appropriate registration dues. The application form, submitted in duplicate, supersedes and renders unnecessary the warrant of registration.

There are three application forms for registration:

●   Form 1 for first registration (pink).
●   Form 2 for a dealing, where the whole property is transferred (blue).

- Form 3 for a dealing involving a transfer of part of a registered interest only (yellow).

With each application form, notes for guidance are also issued and these should be consulted when the application form is being completed. Copies of all the forms, including Forms 1, 2, 3 and 4, are reproduced at the end of the *Registration of Title Practice Book* together with the notes for guidance for the four forms, to which reference is made.

32.85 Forms: general

The general procedure for dealing with application forms for registration is set out below.

(1) Each of the three application Forms 1, 2 and 3 must always be accompanied by an inventory Form 4; but if, for example, Form 1 and Form 2 are lodged together, only one Form 4 (in duplicate) is required.

(2) A separate application Form 1, 2 or 3, as appropriate, is required for each separate deed presented for registration. There is only one exception to this rule, namely where, on sale and purchase, an existing heritable security is being discharged or restricted and the discharge or deed of restriction of that security is presented for registration along with the application for registration of the purchaser's interest. This applies both on first registration and on a subsequent dealing.

(3) When an application Form 2 is submitted along with application Form 1 on first registration (which is commonplace on a purchase with a standard security), the title number is not yet known. So the box for the title number at the bottom right hand corner of Form 2 may be left blank.

(4) Application Forms 1, 2 and 3 are coloured pink, blue and yellow respectively; and are deliberately colour-coded for administrative convenience in the Land Register. The Keeper will therefore not accept a photostat copy of Forms 1, 2 or 3 reproduced on white paper. It is now possible to generate the forms from computer disc. Obviously, such forms are not coloured. They are identified with the appropriate form number and are acceptable to the Keeper.

(5) Every application form, to be acceptable, must be signed and dated otherwise the Keeper will reject it.

32.86 Form 1 (pink)

See the *Registration of Title Practice Book*, paras 4.14 to 4.16 and 5.2. Form 1 replaces the warrant of registration, but goes much further. In contrast to the application for recording in the Register of Sasines, the applicant is required to provide basic information which the Keeper requires to enable him to complete the registration. Great care must be taken in answering these questions and in formulating the supplementary information, where appropriate. The reason is that, on the basis of the answers to the questions in these forms, the Keeper then decides whether or not he is to exclude or qualify his indemnity. The application form is, in part, an application for a guarantee by the Keeper and all information given in the application form is *uberrimae fidei*. In the result, if there is any inaccuracy in answering the questions this may invalidate the Keeper's indemnity in the land certificate which he then issues.

32.87 Form 2 (blue)

See the *Registration of Title Practice Book*, paras 5.4 and 8.46. If a standard security is to be recorded contemporaneously with the purchaser's disposition, which is commonplace, Form 2 must be completed as well. A separate application form is always required for each separate writ, with very limited exceptions.

32.88 Form 4 (the inventory of writs)

See the *Registration of Title Practice Book*, para 5.5. Form 4 must be lodged with every application form; but one Form 4 will normally suffice if two associated writs, for example disposition and standard security are presented together by the same agent at the same time. In every case Form 4 must be lodged in duplicate. The Keeper returns one copy of Form 4 to the applicant as his acknowledgement of receipt and, when so doing, enters on the front of Form 4 the following information:

(1) the title number allocated to the particular title;
(2) the date of receipt, which is the date of registration; and
(3) an application number.

In all subsequent correspondence or communications with the Keeper, the title number and the application number must be quoted.

In the case of an application for first registration (Form 1), the relevant deeds and documents to be listed on Form 4 are:

(1) a sufficient progress of titles including the deed inducing registration and unrecorded links in the title;
(2) all prior writs containing rights or burdens affecting the subjects;
(3) any redemption receipt for feuduty or other annual payments;
(4) any existing heritable securities and deeds relating thereto;
(5) where appropriate, consents to leases and sub-leases and assignations of recorded or registered leases;
(6) Form P16, if obtained;
(7) matrimonial homes evidence;
(8) any other relevant documents.

32.89 DRAFTING AND REVISING

The purchaser's solicitor will draft and the seller's solicitor will revise the disposition in favour of the purchaser(s). The seller will produce a Form 10 report obtained pre-sale; and should also produce, for revisal by the purchaser, the draft application Form 11.

The purchaser's solicitor will also draft and submit to the seller's solicitor for revisal the application Form 1 for the registration of the disposition along with the draft Form 4, which is referred to in Form 1. The point of this is that, in terms of the recommended missives clause, the seller undertakes that the purchaser is to obtain a land certificate without exclusion of indemnity, and the seller's solicitors confirm, in their letter of obligation, that the answers to the questions in application Form 1, so far as relating to the seller's interests, are still correct at settlement. The seller therefore has an interest in the information provided in the application Form 1 to this extent.

As in Sasines practice, the seller's solicitor will draft and the purchaser's solicitor will revise any discharge or deed of restriction of subsisting standard securities and the draft letter of obligation.

The seller's solicitor is not concerned with, and need not revise, the draft application Form 2 for the registration of the standard security. But, where separate agents are acting for borrower and lender, the Form must be adjusted between them.

32.90 SETTLEMENT

See the *Registration of Title Practice Book*, paras 8.20 to 8.21. In particular, the purchaser's solicitor, in exchange for the price, will take delivery of the disposition in favour of the purchaser, together with the supporting titles, the seller's solicitor's letter of obligation, the Form 10 and Form 11 reports, the Form P16 report, and the keys. In practice, the seller's solicitor often retains the Form 10 report (or a copy) for future reference in later related transactions, for example when selling flats in a tenement. But it is probably good practice in multiple sale transactions on a Sasines title, each of which induces first registration, to order a separate Form 10 report for each separate sale. See the Conveyancing Guidance Note 1991 JLSS 203 for detailed comment.

The only special point to note is that, for first registration, the purchaser's solicitor will usually have to produce to the Keeper, with his application for registration, any earlier writs referred to for description or burdens which may be common to his own and other titles. In tenement or estate titles, however, where the Keeper has already seen, and noted the content of, these earlier writs, production may be unnecessary. In a Sasines transaction, these writs are not delivered at settlement; but are retained by the seller's solicitor or returned by the seller's solicitor to the custodian thereof. In a registration of title transaction, however, the purchaser's solicitor should borrow these at settlement for production to the Keeper. They will later be returned by the Keeper to the purchaser's solicitor; by him to the seller's solicitor; and, by him, to the custodian, if different.

32.91   ACCEPTANCE OF APPLICATION BY KEEPER

See the *Registration of Title Practice Book*, paras 8.22 to 8.27. In the ordinary way, provided the forms are correctly completed and lodged, the Keeper will normally accept an application even although all the information has not yet been provided when the application is lodged. It is therefore possible to maintain the priority of registration, which is the date of receipt of the application, even although certain documents have still to be produced before the Keeper can complete registration. If, however, there is undue delay in producing required additional information, then, under the Land Registration (Scotland) Rules 1980, SI 1980/1413, r 12, the Keeper may exclude indemnity or reject the application altogether.

Where a security is being discharged at the same time as the purchaser's title is being registered, a separate application form is not required, provided the discharge is submitted with the application Form 1 and is included in the Form 4 relative thereto. The Keeper will then give effect to the discharge without further procedure. In that case, a fixed fee is charged.

If, however, the discharge is submitted separately, a separate application form is required for its registration and the appropriate scale fee is chargeable.

It is not only unnecessary but inappropriate to record the discharge in Sasines unless, exceptionally, the discharge also affects other security subjects which are to remain unregistered. Such a discharge will require to be recorded in Sasines – but only in respect of the unregistered subjects – with an appropriate warrant of registration. The Sasine recording can take place contemporaneously with registration in the Land Register provided the Keeper is specifically instructed that dual recording/registration is required. Alternatively, since the Sasine recording is irrelevant to the interest being registered in the Land Register, it can be effected separately either before or after first registration.

The Keeper will examine the writs during the registration process to ensure that the title is valid and indemnity should not be excluded. The Keeper may issue requisitions during this process requesting deeds or plans or other information. If these requisitions are ignored by the purchaser's solicitor, or not responded to within the appropriate time-limit, the Keeper may reject the application and priority of registration will be lost.

32.92   PROCEDURE AFTER REGISTRATION

See the *Registration of Title Practice Book*, paras 8.28 to 8.33. In due course, following on completion of first registration, the Keeper will issue to the applicant a land certificate and a charge certificate.

On receiving the land and charge certificates, the purchaser's solicitors should then:

(1) check the land certificate to make sure that the details are correct;

(2) check the charge certificate. Note that, where the standard security was granted by a limited company, the certificate of registration thereof in the Register of Charges must be produced to the Keeper in due course before he issues the charge certificate. Otherwise, he will exclude indemnity;

(3) mark the selling solicitor's letter of obligation as implemented and return it, if fully discharged;

(4) return common titles to the seller's solicitor;

(5) send the land certificate and charge certificate to the lender for retention, along with additional relevant documents not covered by these certificates, such as NHBC documentation, building completion certificates etc.

(6) dispose of the title deeds.

32.93   DISPOSAL OF PRIOR TITLE DEEDS

See the *Registration of Title Practice Book*, para 8.31. In the ordinary way, following on first registration, the title deeds cease to have any relevance. In practice, except for some older titles prior to 1858, the whole progress of titles will have been recorded in the Register of Sasines or in the Books of Council and Session and extracts can always be obtained if required. The only cases where a reference to the actual prior title deeds may be required would normally be:

(1) where a deed, with a plan, was recorded prior to 1934. No copy of the plan will normally be held in the GRS and it may be relevant to determine boundaries. But see *Marshall v Duffy* 2002 GWD 10-318;

(2) where a deed with a plan was recorded after 1934 but the plan exceeds the maximum size 28″ × 22″, the plan will not have been photocopied;

(3) in the case of plans which have been copied in the record volume, colouring on the plan may be material to the rights conferred on the disponee and may not show up effectively on the photocopy.

In any of these cases, however, a duplicate plan may have been lodged under the facility provided by the Conveyancing (Scotland) Act 1924, s 48; but it is probably desirable in such cases to retain the principal deed.

In cases where the Keeper has qualified or excluded his indemnity, it may be prudent to retain the whole title deeds, until prescription has run.

Otherwise, with the exception of common writs which are returned to the seller or custodian following on registration, the title deeds, subject to the foregoing considerations, could be consigned to the wastepaper basket without any adverse results for the purchaser. Nonetheless, there is a natural reluctance on the part of many solicitors to destroy original title deeds for historical or archival reasons. Certainly, no title deeds should be destroyed except with the express authority of the client to whom they belong. Many clients like to keep the title deeds for historical interest but lenders are not keen to store bundles of old Sasine titles.

To some extent, the position is covered by the Land Registration (Scotland) Act

1979, s 3(5). Once a title has been registered, any existing obligation (whether express or implied by s 16) to assign or produce titles, other than a land or charge certificate, ceases to have any effect unless the Keeper has excluded indemnity.

It must also be kept in mind that the land certificate will not disclose a warrandice obligation; and, if the purchaser requires to found on this clause in any subsequent claim, he will have to rely on and produce the principal disposition containing this clause.

The invulnerability in principle of the registered title as compared to a Sasines title has already been commented on in Chapter 11.

32.94 Dealings

For the remainder of this chapter we shall look at dealings, which can involve transfers of land either in total or in part.

32.95 DEALINGS WITH WHOLE OR PART

Once the title has been registered, it remains permanently on the Land Register and only in very exceptional and rare circumstances can it be taken off the Land Register and transferred back into the Sasines Register. Accordingly, for practical purposes, once registered, every subsequent transaction with that title, whether by way of a transfer of the whole (which is the commonest case) or a transfer of part, or the granting of security or lease thereon is in every case a dealing with that registered interest.

32.96 DISPOSITION OR LEASE

A sale and disposition of the whole property implies a transfer of the whole. In contrast, a lease of the whole property is treated as a transfer of part, because of the grantor's continuing interest as landlord. Likewise, any conveyance or lease of the whole but under exception of a part retained by the grantor is a transfer of part. On the other hand, a standard security granted by the registered proprietor over part of the registered subjects is classed as a dealing with whole, because heritable title remains with the grantor.

32.97 TRANSFER OF WHOLE

The title having been registered, identification of the property and the subsisting burdens are determined conclusively by the terms of the title sheet. It is of course possible either to transfer the whole or only a part thereof. The procedure in either case is substantially the same but, for convenience, transfers of whole are dealt with first; and thereafter the differences, such as there are, are noted in paras 32.110 ff.

32.98 Pre-sale procedures

See the *Registration of Title Practice Book*, paras 8.34 to 8.37. In contrast to first registration, the position here is more straightforward. The seller's solicitor proceeds as follows:

(1) He examines the seller's land certificate, in particular, the title plan, and the title conditions in the burdens section D therein, in order to prepare for completion of missives. Only the land certificate need be consulted. Regardless of what earlier titles may have provided, there cannot be any subsisting title conditions other than the conditions set out in the burdens section and any overriding interests not disclosed in the title sheet.

(2) He instructs a pre-sale report, using application Form 12. The seller's land certificate will show the position of the title as at the date to which it was made up; and that date will be shown, as the last date to which the land certificate was made to coincide with the title sheet, in the boxes on page 2 of the land certificate. But of course there may be later entries on the title sheet which are not reflected on the land certificate prepared down to the last date shown therein.

In the ordinary way, this will not occur because, for normal transactions, the land certificate has to be submitted along with any dealing and would be amended and updated at that time. But there are exceptions to this rule. For example, where the registered proprietor grants a second security or where an adverse title to part of the registered interest is also registered in name of an adjoining proprietor, the Keeper does not call in the land certificate: see the Land Registration (Scotland) Rules 1980, SI 1980/1413, r 18. It is also possible to obtain a substitute land certificate if the original has been lost. If it is subsequently found it may not be up to date.

32.99 *Application Form 12*

See the *Registration of Title Practice Book*, paras 3.7 and 8.40. Form 12 is equivalent to Form 10, and is submitted in duplicate. It differs from the application Form 10 in that:

(1) the property is already defined exactly on the title sheet; and all that is required is to identify it by reference to the title number. It is unlikely that there will be any doubt as to the boundaries because the boundaries are exactly defined in the existing title sheet. If, however, there is a doubt as to boundaries, which can occur in unusual situations, then an application Form P17 is available, equivalent to the application Form P16 and serving that same purpose, requesting the Keeper to confirm that the occupational boundaries coincide with the title boundaries; and

(2) in the Form 12 report, the registered proprietors are searched against automatically in the Personal Register. Normally, no other party would have to be
searched against at this stage.

As with the Form 10 report, so with Form 12, it can be updated shortly prior to settlement by a supplementary Form 13 report.

Form 12 and Form 13 reports or their equivalent can be obtained either from the
Keeper or certain private searchers. See the Registers of Scotland article 'When to
get Form 10 Reports' 1992 JLSS 500 and the letter by T Brown published at 1993
JLSS 9.

32.100   *Missives*

See the *Registration of Title Practice Book*, para 8.37. Again, as on first registration,
the only clause in the missives which requires adaptation is the marketable title
clause; but further adaptation of that clause is recommended in the case of a dealing,
taking account of the fact that the seller's title has already been registered. The suggested clause in the Practice Book reads:

> 'There are no outstanding charges, no unduly onerous burdens and no overrid-
> ing interests adversely affecting the subjects of sale. In exchange for the
> purchase price there will be delivered a duly executed disposition in favour of
> the purchaser and there will be delivered or exhibited to the purchaser (i) either
> (a) a land certificate (containing no exclusion of indemnity under s 12(2) of the
> Land Registration (Scotland) Act 1979 or (b) if the land certificate has not been
> released by the Keeper pending a previous application, then certified copies of
> all documents sent to the Keeper in support of the outstanding application(s) or
> required by the Keeper to process the outstanding application(s), together with
> the Form 10 of Form 12 report(s) (and any updated reports) and (if appropri-
> ate) the Form P16 report or Form 17 report, and the receipted Form(s) 4 in
> respect of the outstanding application(s); (ii) all necessary links in title evi-
> dencing the seller's exclusive ownership of the subjects of offer; and (iii) a
> Form 12 report, brought down as near as practicable to the date of settlement,
> and showing no entries adverse to the seller's interest, the cost of said report
> being the responsibility of the seller. In addition, the seller will furnish to the
> purchaser such documents and evidence (including a plan if necessary) as the
> Keeper may require to enable the interest of the purchaser to be registered in
> the Land Register as registered proprietor of the whole subjects of offer with-
> out exclusion of indemnity under s 12(2). The land certificate to be issued to
> the purchaser will disclose no entry, deed or diligence prejudicial to the pur-
> chaser's interest, other than such as are created by, or against, the purchaser, or
> have been disclosed to and accepted by the purchaser prior to the date of set-
> tlement. Notwithstanding any provision of the missives to the contrary this
> clause shall remain in full force and effect and may be founded upon.'

32.101 Examination of title: the land certificate

See the *Registration of Title Practice Book*, para 8.39. It is on a sale or other dealing with a registered interest that the full practical changes under registration of title come into play. Assuming the land certificate contains no exclusion of indemnity (and exclusions of indemnity are relatively rare), the purchaser's solicitor will examine several documents, the most important of which is the land certificate. Here he will have to pay particular attention to:

(1) the identification of the subjects, to make sure that the land certificate covers the whole subjects of purchase in terms of the missives. But, since the missives usually refer to the land certificate, or at least a copy of its plan, no problem normally arises.
(2) the proprietorship section and the destination therein, if any. This may also involve the checking of subsequent unregistered links in title.
(3) the charges section, to make sure that all existing heritable securities are to be duly discharged by the seller.
(4) the burdens section and the details of the burdens therein contained. Remember that no other burdens or conditions can affect the title except:
    (a) the burdens and conditions set out in the land certificate; and
    (b) any overriding interest.

In particular, there is never any need to examine prior titles unless the title contains an exclusion of indemnity. In that case, examination of the prior writs will normally be necessary to assess the risk of accepting the exclusion. Otherwise, examination of prior titles is not necessary because everything which affects the registered interest must appear in the land certificate unless it is an overriding interest. If the overriding interest was disclosed in the prior titles, the Keeper will have noted it on the title sheet, except for short leases and occupancy rights under the Matrimonial Homes (Family Protection) (Scotland) Act 1981. The land certificate will normally contain a statement (which is guaranteed) that there are no subsisting occupancy rights for the spouse of any previous proprietor.

The common law rights of common interest and common property, however, are overriding interests. Accordingly, when dealing with a flat in a tenement, examination of the titles of other flats in the same tenement is normally necessary in order to establish the common rights and mutual repairing obligations. In an increasing number of cases, the titles to the other flats in the tenement will have been registered and examination of the whole of the tenement titles is to that extent made easier.

It is just possible that there may have been other dealings, relating to the interest, but not yet registered. If so, it would normally be necessary to examine these.

32.102 Examination of title: other documents

Having examined the land certificate, the purchaser's solicitor must then look at:

(1) the Form 12 report and any Form P17 report;

(2) the draft application Form 13 which he will revise. The application Form 13 is lodged with the Keeper in duplicate; and

(3) any charge certificate and draft discharge of an outstanding heritable security.

Note particularly that the purchaser's solicitor need not concern himself with the validity of the title, because that is guaranteed by the Keeper unless there is an exclusion of indemnity. Likewise, the Keeper guarantees that any heritable security not appearing in the charges section has been discharged; and that any burden not entered in the burdens section is no longer enforceable. The Keeper does not, however, guarantee that the title is marketable. The purchaser's solicitor must examine the burdens section, in particular, to ensure that no reservation or burden or condition is so onerous as to render the title unmarketable.

32.103   Deeds

See the *Registration of Title Practice Book*, para 8.47. In contrast to the registration system in England, no special forms of deed are provided in the Scottish system. Accordingly, traditional forms of deed are used to deal with registered interests in exactly the same style as for Sasines titles, but with certain differences in detail, summarised below. In particular, it is still competent to grant a disposition, a lease, a standard security, or any other document which, in the Sasines system, is capable of being recorded in the Register of Sasines; and any such document, when so used in relation to a registered interest, has the same result as its counterpart in the Sasines system.

The registered interest is exactly defined in the title sheet and title plan, and an exhaustive statement of the rights pertaining to, and of the burdens affecting, that interest is contained therein. This, taken together with the statutory provisions for the vesting of the interest in the Land Registration (Scotland) Act 1979, s 3, allow for substantial simplification in the content of deeds. Further, under s 15(1) of the 1979 Act and the Land Registration (Scotland) Rules 1980, SI 1980/1413, r 25 and Schedule B, a shorthand style of description is provided which should be followed in all cases.

Under s 3 of the 1979 Act, registration has the effect of vesting in the registered proprietor a real right in and to the registered interest itself, and in and to any right, pertinent or servitude, express or implied, forming part of that registered interest; but subject to any adverse interests, including burdens, set out in the title sheet and to overriding interests. It follows, therefore, that there is no need, in describing a registered interest, to incorporate in the description any narration of, or reference to, parts, privileges or pertinents, servitudes and the like; and there is no need to refer to burdens. All these are inherent in the registration of the title. Accordingly, any dealing necessarily carries with it the benefit thereof and is necessarily subject thereto: see s 15(1) and (2).

In the result, the *Registration of Title Practice Book*, at para 8.47, illustrates a disposition representing the transfer of the whole of a registered interest in the following simple terms:

'I, AB (design) in consideration of (state price or other consideration) hereby dispone to CD (design) All and Whole the subjects (here insert postal address of subjects where appropriate) registered under title number(s) ( ); with entry on; and I grant warrandice.'

Note that no warrant of registration is required.

32.104 Deeds by unregistered proprietors

In the Sasines system, the unregistered proprietor, being a person having right to land by a title not recorded in the Register of Sasines, may complete his title by the recording of a notice of title under the Conveyancing (Scotland) Act 1924, s 4. Alternatively, such a proprietor may:

(1) grant a disposition (but not a lease), so long as he deduces his title in that disposition in terms of the 1924 Act, s 3; or

(2) grant a standard security, so long as he deduces his title therein under the Conveyancing and Feudal Reform (Scotland) Act 1970, s 12.

That rule continues to apply up to the point where a title is registered. So, it applies to a disposition which will induce first registration. However, once an interest has been registered, the rule as to registration is modified by the Land Registration (Scotland) Act 1979, s 15(3), the general effect of which may be summarised as follows.

(1) Once a title has been registered, any subsequent unregistered proprietor no longer has to use a notice of title to complete title. Instead, he merely produces his link(s) in title to the Keeper with the appropriate application Form 2, and the Keeper will register him as proprietor.

(2) Where the person in right of a registered interest is not himself registered as proprietor, he can still validly grant a disposition or standard security. A clause of deduction of title is no longer necessary. Instead, the grantee simply produces the relevant deed (disposition or standard security) granted by the unregistered proprietor in his favour, along with the unregistered links (for example confirmation) connecting the grantor to the last registered proprietor and the application form for registration of the disposition or standard security. This replaces the formal deduction of title clause, which is now redundant.

32.105 Letters of obligation

A similar letter of obligation is used for a dealing to that used on first registration. The style is set out in the *Registration of Title Practice Book*, para 8.43, with minor adaptations to take account of the different number of questions in application Form 2 and the fact that the relevant reports are Forms 12 and 13, not 10 and 11.

32.106   Settlement

The procedure on settlement is substantially the same on a dealing as on first registration, but with differences in detail. At settlement, the purchaser's solicitors will
take delivery of:

(1) the executed disposition in favour of the purchaser;
(2) the discharge or deed of restriction of any outstanding standard security, duly
     executed;
(3) the land certificate and charge certificate;
(4) the links in title, if any, between the seller and the registered proprietor;
(5) the letter of obligation;
(6) the Form 12 report, updated, if appropriate, by the Form 13 report;
(7) the Form P17 report, if any; and
(8) the keys.

32.107   Application for registration

The procedure for registering the title of the purchaser is basically the same on a
dealing as on first registration, but with differences in detail:

(1) For a dealing involving a transfer of the whole, the blue application Form 2
     should be used.
(2) An inventory Form 4 is required, listing the documents submitted to the Keeper
     with the application. The inventory is completed and lodged in duplicate; and
     the Keeper will acknowledge receipt by returning one copy of the inventory. As
     with first registration, so on a dealing, documents can be listed but marked 'To
     follow' if not available at the date of application. In contrast to first registration,
     however, the applicant must lodge the land certificate; but will not normally be
     asked to produce any other title deeds. If there are outstanding securities, then
     the charge certificate should be lodged along with the discharge thereof. If the
     two are lodged together, a separate application form for the registration of the
     discharge is not required; but the discharge should be listed in the inventory
     Form 4.
(3) In terms of the notes for guidance for completing Form 4, to accompany an
     application Form 2, the relevant deeds and documents to be listed are:
     (a) the land certificate;
     (b) any relevant charge certificate;
     (c) all writs which affect the registration, including all writs containing burdens
          not already specified in the land certificate or varying or discharging bur-
          dens since the certificate was last issued – it is not likely that there will be
          any;
     (d) where appropriate, consents to leases, sub-leases and to assignations of
          recorded or registered leases;
     (e) Form P17, if obtained;

(f) matrimonial homes evidence under the Matrimonial Homes (Family Protection) (Scotland) Act 1981 (as amended);

(g) all unregistered links in title.

The Keeper may raise requisitions during the registration process and these should be responded to by the purchaser's solicitor within the appropriate time-limit.

32.108 Concurrent standard security

If the purchaser is obtaining a loan and has granted a standard security, then, as on first registration, so on a dealing, a separate application Form 2 should be lodged with the standard security itself for registration, which reduces the fees. Again, however, a separate Form 4 for the standard security is not required if the standard security is listed in the Form 4 lodged with the application Form 2 relating to the transfer of the interest.

32.109 Procedure after registration

In due course, following a transfer of the whole, the Keeper will issue to the applicant a land certificate and, if appropriate, a charge certificate for any standard security. The purchaser's solicitor should check the amendments made to the previous land certificate to ensure that it is correct. The land certificate is not a historic document; and alterations are not made simply by scoring out spent information and inserting new data. For example, on the sale of a registered interest, the proprietorship section and the charges section are freshly prepared, so that no trace appears in the new land certificate of previous proprietors nor of discharged securities. The new land certificate must be checked carefully to ensure that all entries therein are correct.

32.110 TRANSFERS OF PART

A transfer of part occurs where only a part of the registered interest (as distinct from the whole or a *pro indiviso* share of the whole) is conveyed to a new proprietor. The most common example is the purchase of a new plot from a builder where the whole development is registered. The procedure for transfer of part follows almost exactly the procedure applicable to the transfer of the whole of the registered interest dealt with under para 32.97. Accordingly, in the case of dealing with transfer of part only, paras 32.95 to 32.109 above apply with minimal variations. The principal point of difference is that, on a transfer of part of the registered interest, it is necessary for the relevant deed to contain a description in identifying terms of the part dealt with in the particular transaction. This makes no difference whatsoever to the applicability of and procedure on pre-sale procedures (see para 32.98) and application Form 12 (see para 32.99).

32.111   Missives

Missives, however, for transfers of part differ from those for transfers of whole (see para 32.100). In a transfer of part, there are almost certain to be special provisions as between the part dealt with and the part retained, for example division boundary walls, servitude rights both serving and imposed on the respective parts, and a number of other possible special features. The fact that the title is registered, however, does not in itself produce any further speciality as compared with a transfer of part of a property held on a Sasines title.

Apart from the foregoing difference, para 32.100 on missives applies without variation. Paras 32.101 and 32.102, on examination of title, involve exactly the same procedures. In para 32.103, however, which deals with deeds, while the same general principles apply, the speciality above referred to must here be dealt with by the incorporation of the appropriate description of the part transferred. So, in contrast to the style of disposition illustrating a transfer of whole and incorporated in para 32.103, the style of disposition on a transfer of part is illustrated in the *Registration of Title Practice Book*, para 8.47. A skeleton disposition, following that form, might read:

'I, AB [   ] in consideration of [*state price or other consideration*] hereby dispone to CD [   ] All and Whole [*describe the part conveyed in sufficient detail, preferably by reference to a plan, to enable the Keeper to identify it on the Ordnance Map*   ] being part of the subjects registered under Title Number(s); but always with and under the following reservations, burdens and conditions, namely: [*insert additional burdens or conditions where appropriate*   ]; with entry on [*date of entry*   ]; and I grant warrandice.'

Note that no warrant of registration will be required.

The *Registration of Title Practice Book*, para 8.47 then continues to discuss in some detail some of the specialities which may be encountered in a transfer of part including. In particular, there is a need to consider and, if need be, define parts, privileges and pertinents; conditions already imposed by prior disposals of parts; and new burdens now required to give effect to the rights of the disponee of part, and the rights of the disponer as registered proprietor of the remainder. All of this is, of course, familiar and the same general principles apply as in Sasines titles. But great care must be taken to deal with these in detail and exhaustively, as in a Sasine title. Since the transfer of part is to be registered, the applicant for registration will have to satisfy the Keeper on all the points in the transfer itself including the points above referred to. Otherwise, there is a risk that the Keeper may feel it necessary, at least to some extent, to qualify or limit his indemnity.

32.112   Subsequent procedure on transfer of part

There are only very minor variations in the subsequent procedure as compared with the transfer of the whole of the registered interest. These can be summarised thus:

(1) letters of obligation: see para 32.105. The same considerations apply;
(2) settlement: see para 32.106. The same conditions apply;
(3) application for registration: para 32.107. The same general principles apply here, but there is a special form of application for the registration of a transfer of part: Form 3 (yellow).

Form 3 follows the same pattern as Forms 1 and 2 but there are 13 questions to be answered compared with 8 questions in Form 2 and 14 questions in Form 1.

For practical purposes, however, the substance of the questions in all three Forms is identical, save only that, in Form 3, question 11 relates to boundaries, taking account of the fact that part only is being dealt with, whereas Form 1 contains detailed question 1 relating to identification.

32.113   Inventory Form 4

As with Forms 1 and 2, so with Form 3 on a transfer of part, the application form must be accompanied by a duly completed inventory Form 4 in duplicate but the content is identical with Form 4 supporting an application Form 2 on transfer of the whole and there are no specialities.

32.114   Concurrent standard security

Exactly the same considerations apply here as apply on a dealing with whole.

32.115   Effect of transfer of part

Following on a transfer of part, there are significant variations on the post-registration effects as compared with first registration. The point is, of course, that the existing registered interest, previously held on a single title sheet for which a single land certificate will have been issued, has now been sub-divided, part disposed of and part retained, with two separate proprietors. It logically follows that not only must the title sheet for the existing registered interest be amended or endorsed to show the part-disposal; but, in addition, a new title sheet must be created and a new title number allotted to the part disposed.

32.116   *Points of difference*

As a subordinate point, it is frequently the case that the original single registered interest, now sub-divided, was previously subject to one or more securities; and, in the ordinary way, the part disposed of will fall to be released from the heritable security over the original whole. Taking account of the special factors, the following points of difference apply.

(1) The land certificate in respect of the whole registered interest now sub-divided, will, of course, fall to be surrendered to the Keeper along with the application

Form 3. That land certificate will be amended to show the part disposal and returned, so amended, on completion of the registration procedure. It will, however, retain its original title number. Depending on the nature of the part-disposal and the associated provisions, the original title sheet may either fall to be amended or a new title sheet may be made up, still retaining the old title number, probably to give effect to the provisions in the part-disposal. In addition, a fresh land certificate with a new title number will be issued to the applicant in respect of the part disposed of. Both certificates, the amended original, and the new certificate for the part disposed of, will be returned to the solicitor who applied for the registration of the title to the disposed part; and he in turn must, of course, return the original amended land certificate to the seller's solicitor.

(2) Where the registered interest was subject to a real security, it would also be necessary for the applicant, when presenting Forms 3 and 4 to lodge with the documents the charge certificate(s) in respect of the secured interests. Unexpectedly, although the charge certificate(s) must be so lodged, the Keeper will not amend them to show the part-disposal, even although the part disposed of is released from the security. The reason is that, since we are dealing here with registered titles, a heritable security will not continue to operate as a security on any part of the subjects originally embraced therein unless, following on a part-disposal, the new title sheet of the part disposed of shows that security as a continuing charge thereon; and this will not happen if, as is usual, the part disposed of has been released from the security. But of course the Keeper must be satisfied on this point if he is to register the title of the part disposed of without showing the security in the charges section.

(3) For this purpose, the charge certificate is required by the Keeper together with appropriate evidence of restriction in whatever form showing the part disposed of as released therefrom. This produces the somewhat unexpected consequence that a charge certificate which originally covered, say, 100 hectares in a registered title, where the registered proprietor has subsequently disposed of substantial parts thereof, will still apparently operate as a security on the original 100 hectares. Anyone therefore examining that charge certificate may be misled into thinking that the charge certificate still covers the original whole area. There will be nothing on the charge certificate to indicate any amendment to the extent of the security. The reason for this has already been explained but it can cause confusion.

(4) The unamended charge certificate will also be returned to the solicitor for the applicant lodging the application to register the part-disposal and he in turn will, of course, return it to the seller's agents for transmission to the creditor.

32.117   Builder's development

See the *Registration of Title Practice Book*, paras 4.35 to 4.43. Builder's development is a further facility provided for the benefit of builders and developers who are to give off a number of separate titles to individual purchasers of houses on a developing estate. In such cases the builder may, if he wishes, proceed as follows.

Firstly, the builder himself must have a registered title. The facility cannot be used where the builder's title is recorded in Sasines. But of course he may apply for a voluntary registration of his title to comply with this requirement, and this is the type of voluntary registration which the Keeper is most disposed to accept.

The builder submits a layout plan of the proposed development for approval by the Keeper before any transfer of part is made. This allows any initial questions on the development boundaries to be ironed out before sales proceed.

In the subsequent sales of individual houses, the Form 12 report with an office copy of the title plan can be issued simply by reference to the plot number. Each disposition will contain a description appropriate for a transfer of part; but the description in the disposition is very much simplified by using an excerpt from the approved plan as the deed plan in each individual case. The solicitors for each purchaser can accept the approved layout plan as conclusive that the individual plot forms part of the registered title.

The requirement in the Land Registration (Scotland) Rules 1980, SI 1980/1413, r 18, that an application for registration, whether on a transfer of the whole or on a transfer of part, must be accompanied by the appropriate land certificate is avoided. Instead, the builder's land certificate is deposited with the Keeper who, in turn, issues the builder with a deposit number. Each subsequent application for registration on a transfer of part (ie on the sale of each house) simply quotes the deposit number in the application Form 3 for registration of a dealing; and the applicant is not then required to produce the land certificate with that application. In association with this facility, the use of office copies conveniently surmounts the problem of several purchasers each seeking to examine the same title at the same time.

In the letter of obligation granted by the builder's solicitors, it would be appropriate to include a specific undertaking that the builder has not, and will not, deviate from the approved plan; but the seller's solicitor may not be prepared to grant such an obligation.

Otherwise, subsequent procedure following on application for registration of a transfer of part creates no other specialities.

Chapter 33

A Typical Conveyancing Transaction

33.1 Sale and purchase of a dwellinghouse

This description of a typical conveyancing transaction tries to set in context the various deeds and documents which are drafted and completed. It does not deal with any technical conveyancing points in regard to either the examination of title or the drafting of deeds. On these matters, see Appendix A and the preceding chapters in this Manual, especially Chapter 32. If a property is already registered in the Land Register the title will be guaranteed and will be checked by means of the land certificate. Accordingly, certain of the stages described in this chapter will not be necessary and this is indicated where appropriate. The procedures to be followed, in cases where a first registration will take place or where a title is already registered in the Land Register, are set out in detail in the *Registration of Title Practice Book*.

In describing a 'typical' conveyancing transaction, a number of assumptions have to be made since there is really nothing of the sort. The majority of transactions involve, so far as each solicitor acting for one client is concerned, the sale of one house and the discharge of a loan secured over it, coupled with the purchase of another house and the securing of a fresh loan over the new house. In this transaction, however, in the interest of clarity, the seller and the purchaser are treated as being involved only with the one property. In other words, the seller is selling his house and discharging the loan over it, but is not involved in buying a new house; while the purchaser is buying the seller's house and is securing his loan over that house, but is not involved in selling his own present house. Separate solicitors act for the seller and the purchaser respectively. If the seller were to buy a new house and if the purchaser were to sell his present house, the steps required would be the same as described here.

The outline of the transaction is therefore as follows. The seller is selling his house over which a building society holds a standard security in respect of the loan advanced when the house was bought. The purchaser is buying the house with the assistance of a loan from a building society and additional security is afforded by the purchaser/borrower taking out a life assurance policy.

When moving house, the main difficulty is faced by the individuals and not the solicitors involved. There is no guarantee that, if someone buys a house before selling his present one, he will in fact sell his present house either at a satisfactory price or at all; or that, if he sells his present house before buying a new one, he will find a suitable new house at a price he can afford. When houses are selling well, as has been the position in the early years of the twenty-first century, there is usually no problem, although there may be a difference between settlement dates. When the housing market is not buoyant, however, the problem becomes acute. It is up to the solicitor involved to try to ensure that houses are sold and bought with the minimum of worry and trouble to clients. Therein lies the way to a satisfied client. This is not always possible to achieve, however, and it should always be clearly explained to clients what the potential problems and liabilities are; for example, overdraft interest, hotel bills etc. The key element is communication – in terms which the client can understand. With transactions running concurrently, the solicitor should ensure that the respective settlement dates are as closely matched as possible. Many clients prefer not to have to move out of their existing house and into the new one on the same day.

How long a particular sale/purchase transaction takes to complete will depend on the property and other factors such as price. The normal period considered as realistic between the conclusion of missives and settlement (when the price is paid, and entry to the house is given to the purchaser) is approximately six weeks. However, there is an increasing trend for conclusion of missives to be deliberately delayed for longer, especially when the client seller is purchasing or client purchaser is selling another house.

It is normal practice for the solicitor who acts for a purchaser or seller also to act for the building society or other lender. This is not, however, an invariable practice and, since the interests of the purchaser and the lender providing the money to make the purchase will be different, it is always open for the lender to instruct separate solicitors. If this does happen, it may cause delay in the transaction as well as increase the fees the purchaser has to pay. On the other hand, it does point out clearly that the interests of the purchaser (who is borrowing the money) and the lender (which is lending the money) are distinct. A solicitor instructed to act on behalf of both purchaser and society must remember that he is representing these separate interests and that he is not simply acting on behalf of the purchaser. Of particular interest to solicitors is Rule 22 of the Solicitors (Scotland) Accounts Rules 2001, which prohibits a solicitor who is a partner in a law firm from acting for his or her lender in a house purchase. The prohibition extends to acting for his or her spouse, partner or other connected person. This prohibition was deemed necessary in an attempt to reduce the risk of fraudulent schemes being perpetrated.

Conflict of interest is obviously of paramount importance and there must be awareness of this potential problem, especially in light of the Solicitors (Scotland) Practice Rules 1986. For convenience, the Rules are printed in para 33.71 below.

In the following sections, references to 'building society' should be taken to include also other lending institutions.

33.2 Preparation for the sale

There is nothing to stop an owner advertising his own property for sale himself, either by press advertisement or by erecting a noticeboard in the front garden. He may go to an estate agent and the first a solicitor may hear of the sale is when offers have been received by the estate agent and they are passed to him for attention.

So far as is possible, however, a solicitor should ensure that every client consults him before selling a house. The solicitor should try to have a meeting with his client. He should make clear that the assistance he can give does not relate simply to the actual transfer of the property. The solicitor should be aware of the state of the housing market both in general and in particular. If the market is buoyant and the house is in reasonable condition, is reasonably sited and is reasonably priced, then the sale should (hopefully) be accomplished relatively quickly, say in four weeks or so. The solicitor should q ualify any statement as to when a sale may be expected; there may be a house advertised one day and sold the following day, but a similar house in an apparently similar location may not be sold for several months.

Fixing the correct level of price at which to advertise the house is of the utmost importance and, unless the solicitor is sure on the area, he should consult a valuer – always advising the client of this and getting his confirmation that he approves and will meet the fee. A solicitor's office may employ its own valuer or estate agent, whose services the solicitor may use. Nowadays, local solicitors' property centres keep a computerised database of sale prices and it may be helpful to consult this. A price is generally better fixed at slightly under rather than slightly over the figure hoped for. The client may have ideas about the enhanced value of his house, based on what he has spent on it. This need not always be the case. Improvements such as central heating generally increase the value, however, but initially not by the same amount as that expended. The solicitor should not encourage the client to expect a top-of-the-market price but be realistic in his approach. The indication of price should be as accurate as possible since this is a matter on which the solicitor will be holding himself out as a professional adviser. Remember, however, that a successful sale involves there being a willing seller and a willing purchaser.

The solicitor will need to elicit information on various matters from his client, in addition to the date on which he hopes to move, to allow him to carry out his part in the sale. He will also have to obtain the following documents and information.

If the recommendations of the Housing Improvement Task Force are introduced, the preparation for a sale will include the compilation of a purchaser's information pack by the seller, which will be made available to potential purchasers. See further para 28.13.

From 1 December 2003, a solicitor undertaking residential conveyancing for a private client must provide the client with a terms of business letter detailing the work to be carried out, an estimate of the total fee and outlays and who will principally carry out the work. See the Solicitors (Scotland) (Client Communication) (Residential Conveyancing) Practice Rules 2003.

33.3   THE TITLE DEEDS OF THE HOUSE

A solicitor should not advertise property for sale without having examined the title deeds or land certificate, as the case may be. If the title is already registered in the Land Register there should be no need to check the title deeds prior to the land certificate. The solicitor must check not only the validity of the title itself, but the description given in the title against the property itself and any conditions which regulate the use of the property. This normally implies inspection of the property either by himself or by someone in his office; or by a surveyor.

In the case of a sale where the property is not already registered in the Land Register and which will lead to a first registration, an application should be made to the Keeper for a Form 10 report: a report prior to registration. This has three parts. The first part lists a prescriptive progress of titles, undischarged securities in the 40-year period prior to the report, discharges recorded in the 5-year period prior to the report and other types of deed, such as minutes of waiver or servitudes recorded in the 40-year period prior to the report. The second part discloses whether the property or any part of it has been registered with the title number. The third part is a report from the Register of Inhibitions and Adjudications against the persons requested in the application for the report. This Form 10 report will enable the solicitor to satisfy himself as to the state of the title and take any appropriate action prior to the sale.

It is also necessary, except in the case of tenement flats, to apply to the Keeper for a Form P16 report to have the boundaries on any plan in the title deeds and/or the bounding description in the title deeds checked with the Ordinance Survey map, which will be used for the plan annexed to the land certificate. This will identify any discrepancies in advance which can then be investigated. See the *Registration of Title Practice Book*, paras 4.8 to 4.10.

Firms of private searchers also provide equivalent reports.

The solicitor should ask his client where the title deeds are held and if there is a loan secured over the property. If the client is an established one or if the solicitor bought the house for him, the solicitor should of course know this.

If there is a loan secured over the property, the title deeds will be held by the lender. If there is more than one loan secured over the property (for example, a building society loan with a second top-up loan from another lender), the title deeds will be held by the building society as first lender and the second lender will normally hold only the standard security granted in its favour. This, of course, should have been intimated to the first lender. The solicitor should obtain from the client the name of the building society, the branch at which the account is held and the account number. If there is a second loan, the solicitor should obtain the same information about this loan. The solicitor should then write to the building society and request the title deeds. The solicitor will be sent the title deeds on loan subject to the condition that they are held by the solicitor to the order of the society and that they will not be allowed out of his control except in connection (temporarily) with the proposed sale and (permanently) on repayment of the balance of the loan outstanding. If the sale takes longer than anticipated, the solicitor will receive requests for information from the building society and the solicitor should keep them in the picture as to how the sale is progressing and as to why the solicitor still requires the titles.

If there is no loan over the property, there will have been no requirement for the title deeds to have been lodged in any particular place. They may be in the solicitor's own strong room if the client is an established one. If they are held for safe keeping on his behalf by a bank it is normally sufficient for the solicitor to write and request them, either enclosing a letter from his client or having previously asked him to contact the bank manager to arrange for their release. If they are held by another solicitor (whose client the solicitor has now gained), then the solicitor should obtain a mandate from his client and send this to the other solicitor, requesting that the title deeds be sent to him. It is possible that a fee may be charged for forwarding the documents in such circumstances.

In a few cases the title deeds may have vanished and the solicitor will have to obtain extracts from the Scottish Record Office. The difficulty here is that if the title deeds have been lost, the solicitor will have to establish what they consist of, either by inspecting the search sheets himself or, more likely, by instructing a search. In the case of a property already registered in the Land Register, a replacement land certificate or charge certificate as the case may be can be ordered.

When the solicitor does receive the title deeds, he should always acknowledge receipt, after checking them to ensure that all the titles and other documents listed as delivered are in fact present. He should check whether there is a prescriptive progress of titles with a foundation writ, and that all the deeds referred to for description or burdens are there. If not, he should try to obtain them or get extracts or quick copies from the Scottish Record Office or direct from the searchers, as doing so at this stage will save time later. The solicitor should see all the titles, especially burden writs, before concluding a bargain; and it is more efficient if the solicitor can, after conclusion of missives, send the purchaser's solicitor all the deeds which he will require to examine. If there are titles which appear to be required but are not there, they may relate to larger property (of which the solicitor's client's house forms only a part) and will be held by the solicitors who act for the owners of the remainder of that larger property or the superiors. The solicitor should write to them and ask them for the prior writs. If they cannot be traced, or if the missing deed has obviously been mislaid, the solicitor should write to the Scottish Record Office in Edinburgh and request either a quick copy, which is simply a xerox copy of the deed and is not certified as a true copy, or an extract. An extract is certified by the Keeper, takes slightly longer to obtain, and is more expensive but has the same quality as the principal deed in terms of the Conveyancing and Feudal Reform (Scotland) Act 1970, s 45.

The solicitor will be under obligation to exhibit or deliver a marketable title and the purchaser's solicitor is entitled to demand from the solicitor all that he (reasonably) needs to satisfy himself as to this. Solicitors holding titles on behalf of an estate, builder or superior or former superior will charge a lending fee to the solicitor if he wishes to borrow these titles, and the client will have to meet this. Many solicitors, however, try to pass on the whole or at least half of the cost of Scottish Record Office copies or extracts to the purchaser's solicitor. If the deed is required to confirm the seller's title, the purchaser's solicitor should not be asked to pay. It may be, however, that it is not absolutely necessary to support the title, in which case there may be something (though not a lot) to be said for sharing the cost. There is no justification for the seller's solicitor requiring the return of a quick copy or extract which relates purely to the property being sold simply because he has had to pay for it. In the context of the average fee, the cost of the average quick copy is hardly of major importance.

33.4   LOCAL AUTHORITY CERTIFICATES

Property is or may be affected by numerous statutory controls: see Chapter 20. The solicitor should therefore request from the appropriate local authority, and the appropriate water authority, certificates confirming the position with regard to these various matters. It is now necessary to ask whether there are any entries in the local authority contaminated land register. At the time of writing, local authorities have set up these registers but there are no entries in them yet. To provide maximum protection, certificates should be obtained within the shortest practicable period prior to settlement. It is normal for a comprehensive enquiry letter to be sent to the appropriate authority. In some cases specific additional information may be required and appropriate alterations should be made to the standard letter. The appropriate fee must accompany the request and charges vary. Obtaining the replies is much quicker than previously and usually takes only five or six days. There are now several private firms of searchers who will provide the appropriate information even more quickly and sometimes at a lower price than the local authorities. Their certificates are backed by indemnity insurance, unlike the local authorities' own certificates.

Difficulties can be caused if the written reply is at variance with the verbal report. The difficulty with property enquiries comes when the enquiry produces information which may be unexpected, such as when the roads department proposes to route a major new road through the foot of the solicitor's client's garden. In cases such as this, obviously, further enquiry has to be made and the client advised. Furthermore, it is often not enough simply to search against the client's property, since a proposal relating to a neighbouring property may adversely affect the subjects. The purchaser's agent may make provision for this in the contract of sale by introducing a warranty in respect of such matters. It is unusual for additional certificates to be requested. If possible, a plan of the subjects together with a note of adjoining roadways etc might be annexed to the local authority enquiry letter.

33.5   CONSENTS ETC REQUIRED UNDER THE MATRIMONIAL HOMES (FAMILY PROTECTION) (SCOTLAND) ACT 1981

Unless the title to the property is held in common by a husband and wife, the seller's solicitor should consider at this stage the necessary affidavit, consent or renunciation which will be required and arrange, in due course, for the appropriate party to sign or swear it. Offers for the house will contain a condition relating to the position under the Matrimonial Homes (Family Protection) (Scotland) Act 1981 (as amended).

Even where property is in joint names, it is prudent for the solicitor to establish, by discreet enquiry, if he is dealing with the same husband and wife as those named in the title, unless this fact is personally known to him. See Chapter 32.

33.6 RECEIPTS FOR OUTGOINGS

These may be required to confirm the amount or the position relative to feuduty until feudal abolition takes place on 28 November 2004 and common charges, and will be needed in due course to vouch the state for settlement. The client should be asked to produce them at an early stage. The outgoings include:

(1) *Feuduty* until feudal abolition on 28 November 2004. If the feuduty has been redeemed, the certificate should be with the title deeds. If the feuduty has not been redeemed, the solicitor should obtain the last receipt, or the current notice, or at least information about the superiors, from his client.
(2) *Common charges.* These will normally arise in tenement property or in housing estates where there are common areas maintained by the various house owners. The solicitor should obtain the last receipt for charges or the current notice together with details of the factoring or other arrangements.

33.7 OTHER TITLE ISSUES

Having obtained the title deeds and examined them, the solicitor should deal with any matters in the title which may later give rise to problems. So, if there is a subsisting right of pre-emption, write formally to the person having right thereto. It is also common to find a provision stating that if any alterations have been made to the property, which require the consent of the superior or neighbouring proprietor, such consent will be produced. After 28 November 2004, former superiors will not be able to enforce such burdens unless they have them preserved: see Chapter 19.

33.8 PLANNING PERMISSION AND BUILDING WARRANT

Every house erected in recent years required planning permission and building warrant. Alterations to the structure of the house (for example, dormer windows, kitchen extension, a garage) may require planning permission, and will normally need a building warrant followed by a completion certificate when the works are completed. Particular attention must be paid regarding the installation of double glazed units as practices differ among local authorities as to whether or not a building warrant is required. In all cases, however, such windows must comply with the relevant regulations. Alteration to the use of the house or part of the house may require planning permission but will not, unless structural alterations are also required, need a building warrant.

So far as planning permission is required, the solicitor should check the position with his client and the planning authority, if necessary, as to whether any changes have taken place. In the case of a new house or a house where alterations have obviously taken place, the question of planning permission will almost certainly be raised by the purchaser's solicitor. A copy of the permission or a letter confirming that the development in question was permitted without formal planning permission being necessary will be required. In the case of building warrant approval, the warrant and the certificate of completion (or certificate of habitation) will be required. In each case the relevant documents should be placed with the titles: see Chapter 32.

33.9   OTHER GUARANTEES, CERTIFICATES ETC

Depending on the type and age of property, the solicitor should, for example, confirm that if the house was built within the last ten years there is an NHBC Buildmark ten-year notice and guarantee with the titles, or, if the house has had remedial treatment for rot or woodworm, that his client has the appropriate guarantee and the original survey reports and quotations for the work involved. If not immediately available, these should be obtained. It is also essential to ascertain whether the company which granted the guarantee is still trading. If it is not, the guarantee could be worthless.

33.10   **Advertisement**

The solicitor cannot sell property efficiently without having seen it for himself. Once he has checked the title and the public land use position, he or his firm's property valuer or estate agent should visit the house. He should check the boundaries against the titles and, if necessary, the planning permission. Discrepancies do occur where, for example, fences are replaced or extended or even erected on the wrong line. It is better to discover potential problems before missives are concluded rather than after, when rectification may be difficult and expensive. The solicitor should confirm which fittings are to be left in the house and are included in the price (for example, the stair carpet, kitchen fittings etc) and which may be available to a purchaser but at a separate – and additional – price. The solicitor should explain to his client in what state he should leave the house – for example, if he wants to take the chandelier in the hall with him, he must replace it with a light socket and not just leave the wire hanging from the ceiling.

The solicitor should discuss with the client the advertising of the property, when and in what papers or via the internet. He should confirm the viewing arrangements. This will depend on the owner's wishes, but too restrictive arrangements do not make for an easy sale, except in the case of a very desirable property. 'Come at any time' will lead to a total disruption of the client's social life. It is better to stick to set hours (for example, 2–4 pm and 7–8 pm) or viewing by individual arrangement with the client (arranged by telephone) on production of a card. The solicitor should take care with unaccompanied viewing for security reasons. Similarly, he should try to avoid placing his client's telephone number in the advertisement. He should make sure he knows how and when he can contact the client.

33.11   SCHEDULE OF PARTICULARS

The solicitor will now prepare a schedule of particulars of the house, with a photograph and plan, if possible, and a press advertisement. He should confirm the details of these with the client, remembering the terms of the Property Misdescriptions Act 1991 which prohibits the making of false or misleading statements about property matters in the course of estate agency and property development business. The solicitor should instruct the advertisements in the press, if appropriate, remembering that he is advertising his client's house and not his firm. The solicitor registers the schedule in the local solicitors' property centre along with the appropriate fee. At the same time he makes the necessary arrangements in his office so that incoming calls in response to the advertisement will not be met by mystification on the part of the telephonist. He notes down details of enquirers, has available a supply of schedules to send to them or capable of being downloaded from the firm's website if there is one and, before the advertisements appear, advises his client of the dates on which they will appear.

The final matter which the solicitor should at this stage impress on the client is never to commit himself to any approach from a potential purchaser without consulting his solicitor first. He should explain in outline how the sale of property in Scotland is carried through so that the client is aware of the binding nature of an offer once it has been accepted, especially in light of the terms of the Requirements of Writing (Scotland) Act 1995: see Chapter 3. The solicitor should discourage the client from grasping at a tempting verbal offer when in fact it is possible that a higher offer may be negotiated or may be received later. The seller should be instructed simply to pass on any approaches to his solicitor and in the meantime to indicate that 'considerable interest has been expressed'. There can be an element of bluff at the selling stage; after all, the seller wants the highest price he can get.

The period of waiting now begins.

33.12   **The issues for the purchaser**

The purchaser has in the meantime been looking for a house, and should have consulted his solicitor at an early stage. However, all that his solicitor can do at this point is offer general advice, note that his client is actively looking for a new house, and discuss the price bracket in which the purchaser can operate. Unless the latter has won a large sum of money on the Lottery or has inherited a fortune, it is likely that the price he can pay will depend on (1) his income and the loan which that will support and (2) the price which his present house will fetch, less the existing loan and outlays and expenses. This is particularly significant if the housing market is depressed and prices are falling, with the result that the existing loan might exceed the price obtained after exposure on the open market. At settlement, the outstanding loan over a seller's house has to be repaid out of the proceeds of sale. Once the date of settlement is known, the solicitor writes to the building society for a note of the sum required to redeem the loan as at that date.

A potential purchaser should have some idea of his price range as well as the likely cost of outgoings and repayments on a house of this value and a loan of this size before he starts looking. While not wishing to over-extend a client financially, it is as well for the solicitor to point out that there are certain costs involved in making offers (for example, survey fees) which recur with each unsuccessful offer, and it may be more sensible (in the long run) for a purchaser to offer just a little more than he may comfortably be able to afford to secure a house.

33.13 CONFIRMATION THAT FUNDS ARE AVAILABLE

The purchaser or his solicitor as an independent financial adviser should confirm at this stage that he will be able to obtain a loan of the likely amount he will need and on the date when he is aiming to buy his new house. In many instances a loan may be arranged by the purchaser direct with a building society, bank or insurance company. Care should be taken so as to ensure that the type of loan selected is best for the client. It is for his solicitor, however, to advise him on the best type of loan for his particular needs and if necessary to arrange this loan for him. It should be possible for a loan to be arranged without the involvement of a mortgage broker. The financial services industry is very competitive and the purchaser should beware the salesmanship of certain companies. In particular, if he does wish to take an endowment loan, he should wait until the loan has been confirmed before signing up for any new life policy.

What a purchaser needs at this stage is the promise of a loan to be available at the time when he is hoping to move into his new house.

33.14 FINDING THE PROPERTY

The purchaser, particularly if he is new to a district, should then be advised where to look for property; ie the local solicitors' property centre or its website and the property pages of the local press. His solicitor can also circulate other solicitors in the area or suggest that the client looks at their websites. Thereafter, the choice of a house is a matter for the client.

33.15 Finance for house purchase

The financial services industry has changed dramatically in recent years. Today, the provision of finance for house purchase is very competitive. Building societies, banks, insurance companies and other institutions provide mortgage finance. There is no shortage of availability of funds for prospective borrowers who have sufficient income and are creditworthy. Such borrowers can normally obtain finance for a mortgage on suitable terms. In previous years, mortgage funds were not so freely available and different types of lending institution had different approaches to lending. See the sixth edition of this book, paras 34.15 to 34.20.

33.16 Methods of repaying a mortgage

There are three main methods of repaying a loan on a mortgage:

(1) capital and interest repayments;
(2) endowment method;
(3) personal pension plans.

33.17 CAPITAL AND INTEREST REPAYMENTS

For some time, this was the most popular method of repaying a mortgage. The applicant is charged interest on the capital sum being borrowed and repays instalments of the sum, plus interest, on a month-to-month basis. Obviously, the composition of that monthly payment will consist of capital and interest, with the interest being charged on the outstanding amount of the mortgage at the end of the financial year. This method is known as the annuity method of payment. With a mortgage of this type it is generally advisable that the borrower should make arrangements for some form of mortgage protection assurance. Such insurance is generally tailored to fit the capital outstanding at the outset of the mortgage and decreases over the period of the agreed term. Whilst at the outset future changes of interest rates cannot be forecast, the cover generally provided is enough in this relatively inexpensive type of insurance policy to discharge all or a very substantial proportion of the mortgage, on death occurring during the term of the mortgage. Alternatively, the borrower may take out a level-term assurance policy. This has the advantage, in later years, of providing more than enough cover on death to discharge the mortgage. In the earlier years, however, interest represents almost the whole of the month's payment; and so sufficient cover may not be available in the event of early death.

33.18 ENDOWMENT METHOD

With an endowment loan, the borrower pays only interest every month to the lender. The capital element of the mortgage is repaid at the end of the agreed term from the proceeds of an endowment policy taken out with an insurance company, or on earlier death. An endowment policy is an investment type of life assurance. The most popular type of policy being used as collateral security for a building society mortgage is known as a low-cost endowment plan. This type of policy comprises two parts:

(1) a with-profits endowment policy which is designed in such a way that, if the company continues to achieve profits of only 80% of its current level, there will be sufficient capital at the end of the term to repay the mortgage; and

(2) decreasing term insurance such that the policy carries a minimum guaranteed death benefit which is never less than the original amount of the loan.

In a recessionary climate, however, even this type of loan can come under pressure in circumstances where the sum insured is insufficient to repay the loan. Serious problems with the sale of such policies have occurred in recent years. Many borrowers have found themselves in this position of having insufficient funds from the policy to repay the loan and many of these have been awarded compensation for the 'mis-selling' of such policies.

33.19   PERSONAL PENSION PLANS

This method of repayment of mortgage loans has risen in popularity in recent years. The main points of relevance to the lender are that they are utilised mainly by people who are self-employed or in non-pensionable employment and the benefits can be taken by the policyholder between the ages of 50 and 75 whether or not they have retired. The policy cannot be assigned as collateral security for a loan.

An eligible person is entitled to invest a certain percentage of his relevant income in a personal pension plan policy. The policyholder is then entitled to tax relief at his highest rate on the premiums payable, which are then invested in a tax-free fund and consequently that fund grows at a much faster rate than a normal life fund. Unit-linked pension plans will also be acceptable to the lender. At maturity, the policyholder is given the option of using all of the fund to purchase a pension or to take part as a tax-free lump sum with a reduced pension. It is the tax-free lump sum that the society looks to in order to repay the advance and which makes the scheme possible. As the pension plan policy cannot be assigned to the building society, the society requires a level-term assurance, which may be in the form of a separate policy or part of the pension plan, to be assigned to it.

It is also possible that another suitable life policy be used for this purpose. The borrower is then asked to sign an undertaking that he will, amongst other things, repay the outstanding debt from the proceeds of the personal pension policy. Generally, a building society's normal lending terms will not be altered because of this particular method of repayment. Note that certain aspects of executive/directors' pension plan policies differ from personal pension plan policies.

33.20 **Individual's borrowing capacity**

This is normally calculated by taking the individual's gross annual salary and multiplying it by an appropriate factor. This factor has increased in recent years as mortgage finance has become freely available and the norm is now three and a half times salary or two and a half times the combined salary in a joint purchase, although higher factors are possible. In addition to the basic salary, a proportion of any commission or overtime worked on a regular basis can be taken into consideration. Prudent lenders will appreciate that the amount of the advance is not simply an automatic paper exercise. It is necessary to try to ascertain the applicant's existing or future financial commitments and, on receipt of all information, make the necessary decision. All lenders now carry out a credit check against each borrower.

33.21 **Survey and valuation of the property**

A building society is required by law to obtain a valuation of a property on which an advance may be required and the regulations regarding that valuation are now contained in s 13 of the Building Societies Act 1986. The different types of survey are detailed below at para 33.27.

33.22 **General percentage lending terms/insurance guarantees**

As mortgage finance is widely available, it is possible to obtain a maximum 100% mortgage (or an even higher percentage with certain lenders), although this has not always been the position. The Building Societies Act 1986 came into effect on 1 January 1987 and the regulations relating to insurance companies under the Building Societies Act 1962 are still current. Under the relevant sections, a building society normally cannot make an advance exceeding 75% of the purchase price without additional security. This, however, does not mean that it is restricted to a maximum of 75%; but may lend the balance by way of an excess which must not exceed 25% of the purchase price. The excess advance under terms of s 28 of the 1962 Act must be covered by some form of additional security which can take several forms. It can include a security over another heritable property, over funds deposited in the building society account, or assignation of a portfolio of shares, but typically the guarantee is given by an insurance company nominated by the building society. This indemnity guarantee policy provides that, in the event of a repossession by the building society and the sale of the property should a shortfall occur, this will be covered by the insurance company up to the amount of the excess advance. It should be remembered that in the event that the insurance company is required to indemnify the building society under the policy, the borrower remains personally liable for the capital sum. The insurance company receives a single premium for this facility: see para 33.57.

33.23   **Taking final instructions**

It is recommended that the method of purchasing property in Scotland (the system of offers, surveys and so on) should be explained to the purchaser at this stage so that he is generally aware of the various steps which require to be taken. In particular, the purchaser should be advised not to write to the seller himself offering to purchase the property as, if accepted in writing, a binding contract may be created. See the Requirements of Writing (Scotland) Act 1995, discussed in Chapter 2.

The purchaser visits the seller's house, likes it and expresses interest to the seller. The seller, however, having been well briefed by his solicitor, indicates that offers should be made to his solicitor but may go on to add – without committing himself – that in principle the price, date of entry and so on indicated by the purchaser are acceptable. The purchaser should not push in these circumstances for a decision, however keen he may be on the house. The purchaser's solicitor will have advised him of the need for a survey to be made at least on behalf of the building society which will be providing the loan and the purchaser should find out when a surveyor will be able to obtain access. Throughout the sale period the seller and his solicitor should keep in touch and when there are any firm expressions of interest, the seller should notify his solicitor.

The purchaser now discusses the proposed purchase with his solicitor. The solicitor should obtain full details of the house. He should, if possible, obtain a copy of the schedule of particulars and any arrangements made as to other matters such as fittings and fixtures. At this stage, he is generally aware of his client's financial position and confirms that the price of the house is within his client's financial reach and that there appears to be no difficulty about a suitable loan. He will also discuss the date of entry with his client since this will have to take into account – so far as possible – completion of the sale of his client's present house to allow the financing of the sale and purchase to be simplified. If there is to be a period between the date of settlement of the new house and the date of settlement of the present house, some form of bridging loan for the purchase must be available on the date stipulated. It is as well to discuss this possibility with a client at this stage and to suggest he arranges the necessary bridging loan with his bank in the event of this being required. Banks will normally lend where a customer's house has already been sold and it is simply a question of waiting till a particular date for the sale proceeds (a 'closed bridge') but are most unlikely to agree to provide bridging finance on an open-ended basis where the present house has not been sold and there appears to be no other source from which funds to repay the bridging loan are likely to come.

33.24 Action by purchaser's solicitor

He contacts the seller's solicitor to confirm that the house is still on the market; if this is so, he 'notes his client's interest' in the property. Noting interest ensures (or should ensure) that the seller will not conclude the sale of the house without allowing all those who have noted interest to be given the opportunity of making an offer. He should also find out whether a 'closing date' has been fixed. This is the date by which offers have to be in the hands of the seller's solicitor. It is useful also at this stage to try to elicit information from the selling solicitor about the price level likely to be acceptable, the most suitable date of entry, the fittings to be included and so on. It is also becoming common for properties to be offered for sale at fixed prices whereby the first offer received at the advertised price will be accepted so long as there are no other unusual conditions.

33.25 OFFER PRICE

The price which the purchaser should offer is of the greatest importance since, if there are other interested potential purchasers, it will normally have to be higher than any other competing offer. In arriving at the final price to be offered various factors have to be borne in mind such as the amount of loan which may be obtained. This will depend on both the property and the purchaser's income, and the funds which the purchaser can himself raise, for example, from the sale of his present house. Two factors finally are present: the purchaser must be advised (if he has not already been) as to the likely cost of the move, both practical, such as removal costs, new carpets, curtains etc, and legal, such as stamp duty land tax, registration dues, legal fees, cost of survey etc. He must weigh the total cost of the move against the fact that he may have to move again and that if he does not manage to buy this house he will incur further costs in trying to buy another house. The purchaser and his solicitor must therefore consider very carefully the price which the purchaser can and should offer, and whether, when the amount is settled on, this is likely to be successful. This is one area where the solicitor's experience and expertise are of great importance to the client who wants to buy the house but not to pay over the odds for it. The difficulties of fixing a price should not be under-estimated. One of the reasons for odd prices (for example, £140,253) being offered is not because it includes some fitment valued at £253 but so that, in theory, the client will have a slight edge (of £253) over another offerer.

33.26 Confirming loan arrangements

The purchaser has already asked about access arrangements and with this information he, or his solicitor, will now instruct a survey of the house. Alternatively, his building society will instruct a survey for loan purposes. The building society will normally instruct a valuation survey (carried out on its behalf, not the purchaser's) unless instructions are given for a more detailed form of survey: see para 33.21. The purchaser's solicitor should advise the purchaser of the possible need for a more detailed survey. If a structural survey, for example, is necessary, it is possible for this to be done by the same surveyors and a reduced fee to be charged. A valuation survey can usually be carried out fairly quickly and if necessary the building society will advise the purchaser's solicitor by telephone of the result of the survey, the amount of the loan it is prepared to make and when the loan funds will be available. Ask the building society to confirm the actual amount of the loan which will be available on the date of settlement, and to indicate any deductions or retentions.

33.27   Surveys and valuation inspections

The importance of a survey has already been mentioned. There are basically three types of inspections that can be instructed: mortgage valuation (normally for loan purposes); house buyer's report and valuation/private report (known as a 'Scheme 2 report'); and full structural survey. A full structural survey can only be undertaken now by a building surveyor and not by a chartered surveyor, as was previously possible. In addition there are various types of specialist survey.

33.28   MORTGAGE VALUATION

This type of inspection is the most usual one and will be carried out by a chartered surveyor on instructions from a lending institution (for example, a bank or building society) before the latter makes an offer of loan on a property.

The valuation inspection is instructed by the institution although the prospective purchaser/borrower will pay for it and will also receive a copy of the report.

Its purpose is simply to assure the institution that the property provides adequate security for the loan. The intention of the inspection is to arrive at a value which reflects the value for mortgage purposes of the property. The surveyor will normally point out any immediate defects which are visible and apparent but will not inspect the underfloor area, roof spaces or any other area where special access is required. For the purposes of arriving at a valuation, these will be assumed to have no significant defects. Floor coverings (for example fitted carpets or vinyl) and furnishings will not be moved to gain access. The roof coverings will be inspected from ground level only and none of the services, ie water system, heating system or electrical circuits, will be checked or tested. Comment may be made on systems which are obviously outdated or clearly defective. The surveyor will not normally note items which do not seriously affect the possible security value of the property such as rotten windowsills, frames, leaking gutters or broken windows. However, these items may be mentioned for the guidance of a prospective purchaser.

Particular problems arise with regard to tenement property. The surveyor will normally not attempt (or be able) to gain access to communal roof spaces or other common parts and for valuation purposes the condition of these areas will be assumed to be satisfactory, no regard being had to any mutual repair obligations.

If a retention is suggested, this may or may not reflect accurately the likely cost of repair; this is a matter for the purchaser/borrower to resolve himself. It is suggested that in this event an accurate estimate should be obtained from an appropriate contractor or other specialist and it would be advisable for a detailed inspection to be instructed.

33.29 HOUSE BUYER'S REPORT AND VALUATION/PRIVATE REPORT

The purpose of this inspection is to establish the general condition and value of the house/flat. While it is less detailed than a full structural survey, it is more detailed than the inspection carried out for mortgage valuation. It will take the form of either the house buyer's report pre-printed form under a scheme introduced by the Royal Institution of Chartered Surveyors which is completed by the surveyor, or a surveyors' firm's own private report. Again, a surveyor will not be able to examine those parts of the property to which he cannot gain access, but he will inspect under the floors where access is available and roof coverings when visible from the attic windows or skylights or readily opened hatches.

He will also comment on drains, heating and electric, gas and water services. These services will not, however, be tested. The surveyor may also report on double glazing and any potential unauthorised alterations.

33.30 FULL STRUCTURAL SURVEY

The purpose of this is to establish the full physical condition of the property and this can only be carried out by a building surveyor.

A full structural survey is much more detailed and in the majority of cases requires to be specially instructed by the purchaser. Despite the term, however, the surveyor is unlikely to be able to look at parts of the property to which he cannot get access (for example if there are fitted carpets he is unlikely to lift these, and it may be impossible to obtain access to the foundations or the attic space). It is nonetheless the most comprehensive type of survey which is available and is normally essential when considering large or old property where an accurate idea of any defects and the necessary repairs to rectify these will be of importance. The surveyor will almost certainly comment on the services in addition to the state of the property, and he may be authorised to engage the services of such electricians or other specialist contractors as he may consider necessary in order to carry out his instructions properly. If damp or rot is suspected or obvious, he may recommend further inspection by a specialist.

The cost of a full structural survey will depend on the property and the time spent by the surveyor (and any other specialists which he requires to instruct) but is unlikely to be less than £500 and will range upwards from that figure.

If the purchaser can arrange for the same surveyor to carry out the structural survey and any required valuation survey, the total cost to him is likely to be modified.

33.31   SPECIALIST SURVEYS

Particularly when damp, woodworm or wet or dry rot is either obvious or suspected, the surveyor may well recommend obtaining a report from a specialist firm, and indeed it may be in the interest of the prospective purchaser to do this in any event. These surveys are normally free since they are carried out by firms who hope to carry out the work which they recommend, and it is sensible therefore to obtain a number of estimates since the quality and the thoroughness of the inspection do vary as in some cases do specialist opinions on the seriousness or complexity of the problem. A specialist surveyor should be instructed to examine all parts of a building, and not confine his inspection only to the areas where a surveyor has first noticed the likely defect.

A guarantee will be given on completion of the work, usually for 30 years, and again it is worth considering the length of time a firm has been in business when valuing the worth of a guarantee. Some guarantees are backed by an insurance company to reassure the customer. Such a guarantee is normally transmitted to successors in title without any formal assignation.

Other forms of specialist survey may relate to the wiring, drains or, if there is a potential problem with the structure, a structural engineer may be called in to investigate. These surveys are fee based and can be expensive, depending on the extent of the work required.

33.32   SURVEYORS

Surveyors, other than specialists, are normally chartered surveyors, and members of the Royal Institution of Chartered Surveyors which operates a code of practice for members. Specialist surveyors may either be members of their own professional associations or, in certain cases, may not have a professional association, in which case reputation is what counts.

33.33   **The offers**

With confirmation from the building society about a loan and a satisfactory survey available, the purchaser is now in a position to go ahead. If a closing date is suddenly fixed and no time is available to obtain a survey or offer of loan, an offer can still be made provided it is made subject to suitable conditions.

The purchaser then instructs his solicitor to make an offer for the seller's house and should be asked to confirm in writing the property, the price, the date of entry, the fittings to be included in the price and those (if any) being bought separately. The name(s) of the purchaser(s) should also be confirmed. The purchaser's solicitor then prepares an offer for the house (which will no doubt follow his firm's standard form) which is subscribed by the purchaser, or more usually his solicitor, and sends it to the seller's solicitor. The purchaser's solicitor should send a copy of the offer to the purchaser on the same day.

The offer will include (in addition to the price, a brief description of the subjects offered for, and the date of entry) such other – hopefully relevant – conditions as appear to the purchaser's solicitor and the purchaser as being necessary or appropriate. These will vary, depending on the property and the circumstances. If a style offer is used, it should be altered to suit the property being offered for although many standard forms of missives are framed to be appropriate for all types of residential properties, it should be borne in mind also that the more stringent the conditions which are attached, the more chance there is (unless there is only one offer) that a similar offer subject to fewer or less stringent conditions will be accepted. The aim of the solicitor making the offer is both to protect the purchaser's interests and to buy the property for him; and the various factors involved should be balanced. The offer will usually conclude by stating the time limit within which an acceptance has to be received: this should be realistic. It is usual, unless a closing date has been fixed, for the formal offer to be sent with a simple covering letter. If a closing date has been fixed, the offer may well be enclosed in a further sealed envelope marked 'Offer for [property] to be opened at [time] on [date])'.

33.34 The bargain concluded

In the meantime, the seller's solicitor and the seller will have been gauging interest in the property. The noting of interest and a survey being carried out are indicative of serious interest in the property, and at this stage the seller's solicitor should consider with the seller whether to fix a closing date. If there are a number of interested parties, a closing date will probably be set, though it is difficult to be categoric about this; and every party who has noted interest or otherwise expressed interest should be notified. It is obviously sensible to list those firms who have noted interest on behalf of clients in some way. If a closing date has been fixed, the solicitor should adhere to it. Whether to set a closing date or to accept the first reasonable offer is a matter for agreement with the seller.

33.35 NO CLOSING DATE

If no closing date has been fixed, the solicitor will contact the seller when he receives any offer and will 'take instructions', though in most cases the seller will seek advice from the solicitor. The difficulties centre round the proverb 'a bird in the hand is worth two in the bush'. If a reasonable offer is received, even though it is possible that a higher one might come in, the seller may well consider accepting the present offer to avoid further disruption. The trauma which is often associated with buying and selling a house should not be lost sight of. In any event, a higher offer may not in fact materialise. The seller should, however, see the offer or have its terms summarised and he should be aware of all the relevant conditions, not just the price offered. It is then for the seller to instruct his solicitor whether to accept it or not.

33.36   CLOSING DATE

If a closing date has been fixed, the practice is for the offers to be opened at that time and not before. The seller may wish to be present when the offers are opened at the 'appointed hour' on the closing date. The seller will, after all, be very interested in the proceedings. His solicitor should try to accommodate such a request if possible, although it may not be possible due to the pressures of business today. There is no need to have offerors present. The seller will then be advised of all the offers and terms. Price, date of entry, other conditions (particularly suspensive conditions) are all relevant in deciding which offer to accept. Even though a closing date has been fixed, the seller is not obliged in law to accept any offer; nor need he accept the highest. So, for example, an earlier date of entry may be preferable to a slightly higher price, while an offer subject to a survey condition is not as immediately acceptable as one without such a condition. The seller has to decide which offer he is to accept and he should formally advise his solicitor of this. The solicitor should therefore ensure that he can contact his client. On the other hand, there is no reason normally why the seller should be forced into taking an immediate decision, though it is unfair to keep offerors unnecessarily in suspense and most offers will have time limits. On the closing date, the seller should be advised that, although not bound to accept the highest or indeed any offer, if he or she instructs the solicitor to enter negotiations with a view to concluding a bargain with a party who has submitted an offer at the closing date, the solicitor will not be able to enter into any subsequent negotiations with or accept an offer from another party unless and until the negotiations with the original offeror have fallen through. In the event that the solicitor is instructed to negotiate with a third party in such circumstances, he should decline to act further in the sale.

The Law Society of Scotland has issued Guidelines on Closing Dates and Noting Interest, the latest version of which are available on the Society's website at www.lawscot.org.uk/members/common_rules/law_scot_guide/conflict.

33.37   CHECKING THE SUCCESSFUL OFFER

Once the seller has confirmed which offer is to be accepted, his solicitor will, if he has not done so already, check the conditions in the offer against the title deeds, the local authority and, if appropriate, water authority, certificates and any other relevant information. He will advise the solicitor who made the successful offer that it is to be accepted and will detail any qualifications which are to be made, probably by telephone initially. He will then accept the offer either (1) unconditionally, if there are no qualifications (which is unlikely) or (2) subject to any necessary qualifications. This letter of acceptance is a formal letter, and is usually sent subject to final acceptance being forthcoming within a brief time limit. If the seller's solicitor has received an assurance from the purchaser's solicitor that the qualifications are acceptable, he may also advise the other offerors that their offers were unacceptable: this should, however, be deferred if there is any doubt about the successful offer concluding the bargain.

The purchaser's solicitor confirms with the purchaser that the qualifications are acceptable, and then sends a further formal letter to the purchaser's solicitor to this effect 'holding the bargain as concluded'. It may be that a further exchange of formal letters will be required before this stage is reached; whether or not this is so, 'missives' – the comprehensive term for the various letters which comprise the bargain for the sale/purchase of heritage – must, before they can be considered to be concluded, deal with every point in the offer and the ensuing letters: both parties must be in agreement on all the points dealt with. At this stage the bargain for the sale/purchase of the property is complete.

It is unfortunately becoming increasingly common for the seller's solicitor to send the title deeds for the property to the purchaser's solicitor so that 'he can satisfy himself as to conditions A, B and C' of his offer. This practice, while sometimes necessary, ought to be avoided, where possible, as it leads to an inevitable delay in conclusion of missives and there is an increased possibility that either party may decide not to proceed. It is suggested that this is not in either party's best interests. The seller's solicitor ought to be able to stand by his client's title, having examined the same pre-sale; and he should have obtained in advance all the documents and information referred to above.

33.38 ADVISING THE CLIENTS

The seller's solicitor then advises the seller that the sale is concluded; cancels the advertising, withdraws the schedule of particulars from the local solicitors' property centre and removes any advertising signs from the house itself.

The purchaser's solicitor formally advises the purchaser that the purchase is concluded. He may require to arrange temporary insurance cover for the property because the risk is deemed to have passed to the purchaser on conclusion of the bargain, unless the seller accepts responsibility in terms of the missives which is the usual practice.

33.39 **Titles and drafts**

Once missives have been concluded, and indeed quite often before such conclusion, the next stage of a transaction proceeds. It includes the conveyancing and the examination of the title offered and commences with the seller's solicitor sending the purchaser's solicitor the following documents.

33.40   THE TITLE DEEDS

These should include all the deeds which the Keeper will require to see if the sale leads to a first registration. If the title is already registered in the Land Register, the title deeds will simply comprise the land certificate, the seller's charge certificate, if any, and any ancillary documents.

33.41   SEARCHES

The seller's solicitor is under obligation to deliver or exhibit a marketable title, which is why he forwards the title deeds to the purchaser's solicitor to allow the latter to examine them, and a clear search which will have to be continued to show the conveyance to be granted by the seller to the purchaser. Under land registration, the search is contained in a Form 10 report for a first registration. The seller's solicitor should have obtained this when instructed in the sale: see para 33.3. To continue this search, a Form 11 report is required and the seller includes a draft application for this report which the purchaser's solicitor must complete. If the title is already registered, instead of the Form 10 report and draft application for a form 11 report, a draft application for a Form 12 report – a report on a registered title is sent to the purchaser's solicitor. The Form 12 report is similar to the Form 10 report. A Form 12 report can be updated by means of a Form 13 report.

The draft which the seller's solicitor sends to the purchaser's solicitor will not be complete (he will not know the purchaser's full name and address, for instance). If the purchaser's solicitor also acts for the building society which will require a search to be made in the Personal Registers against the purchaser, he will extend the application to provide for a personal search against the purchaser/borrower. In these respects the revisals to the draft application are made by the purchaser's solicitor who in the latter instance is acting on behalf of the building society. The seller is not bound to pay for the search being extended to disclose the purchaser's financial arrangements, but in practice no objection is normally taken. In the property search, only recorded writs will be disclosed; deeds which are not recorded such as the assignation of a life policy or a deed of assumption and conveyance will not be disclosed, but may be referred to in other entries.

33.42   THE DRAFT LETTER OF OBLIGATION

It is normal practice for a letter of obligation to be granted at settlement, covering, principally, an undertaking to clear the records of any entry in the Property or

Personal Registers which would prevent the Keeper issuing a land certificate without exclusion of indemnity and, if the seller has a loan over the property, delivery of a recorded discharge of that loan. Other matters which have not been delivered or completed will also be included.

The seller's solicitor drafts the letter of obligation, again perhaps using an office style or a pre-printed form, so long as it is in 'classic' terms. The importance (from the purchaser's point of view) of ensuring that the obligation is granted personally by the seller's solicitor and not 'on behalf of' the seller has already been stressed: see para 32.35 ff.

It will reflect the position as the seller's solicitor sees it and amendments may have to be made to it by the purchaser's solicitor now or at a later stage in the transaction. The scope of a letter of obligation should not be extended to extraneous matters or matters outwith the control of the seller's solicitor. See the articles by Lionel Most and the Law Society of Scotland's Conveyancing Committee 'Classic Letters of Obligation' and 'Clarifying the Classic Letter of Obligation' in 2002 JLSS Oct/12 and 2003 JLSS Apr/26.

33.43   A DRAFT DISCHARGE OF ANY SECURITY

The seller's solicitor will, if there is an outstanding loan secured over the property, draft a discharge of this security. In the case of a building society loan, a form of discharge will probably be printed on the principal standard security. If this form is to be adopted, one should photocopy the blank discharge, complete it with the necessary details and use this as the draft. If no printed or draft form of discharge is available, a style form is given in the Conveyancing and Feudal Reform (Scotland) Act 1970. If there is more than one loan over the property, a separate draft discharge will be prepared for each loan.

33.44   A FORM P16 REPORT

If this report has been obtained to check the description of the property in the title with the Ordnance Survey map which will be used in the land certificate, this should be included: see para 33.3.

33.45   ANCILLARY DOCUMENTS

Any other documents which are relevant and which have not already been sent to the purchaser's solicitor in support of any conditions in or qualifications to the missives (such as local authority certificates, affidavits etc under the Matrimonial Homes (Family Protection) (Scotland) Act 1981, as amended) should be included.

Once a letter has been sent to the purchaser's solicitor, with the title deeds and usual drafts, the seller's solicitor can sit back (if only briefly) since the ball is now firmly in the court of the purchaser who must proceed to examine the title and prepare a draft disposition.

33.46   Examination of title

This subject has already been dealt with in greater detail in Chapter 32. The purchaser's solicitor has to ensure that the title is, in accordance with the missives, and 'a good and marketable title' and that the search is 'clear'. The purpose of examining the title is to ensure that this is so and that it will allow the purchaser freely to enjoy the use and ownership of the property and to be able in due course to sell it without difficulty. Until a title has been registered in the Land Register, the practice is that in each transaction, whether on purchase or on obtaining a loan, the solicitor acting for the purchaser or the lender requires to make a full examination of title to ensure that his client's position is fully protected. Although his client should in due course receive a land certificate guaranteeing the title, the Keeper requires to be satisfied that the title is good before issuing a land certificate. If the title is already registered, then the title only needs to be checked from the date of the land certificate and the following comments on title relate mainly to a first registration.

When the purchaser's solicitor receives a letter enclosing the title deeds and 'the usual drafts', he should check the enclosures. If there are omissions from the enclosures, he should advise the seller's solicitor at once. Letters enclosing title deeds or other important documents should always be acknowledged without delay. If the solicitor can deal with the examination of title in the course of a day or so, he may feel that a separate acknowledgement is not necessary, but it is good practice to do so – there may be other causes of delay in an office.

Before examining a title, particularly if the solicitor did not himself conclude the missives, he should check the file to see what has happened, and the missives to see that a proper contract has been completed and what special conditions it contains. He should separate the title deeds into the property title (which will include the writs referred to for burdens) and the security title; in other words extract from the main body of titles all standard securities, discharges etc.

33.47   PROCEDURE ON EXAMINATION OF TITLES

In first registration cases, the solicitor checks through the property title for the foundation writ. The foundation writ is the first recorded writ outwith the prescriptive period of ten years. This may be a disposition, a feu disposition, a notice of title etc. Assuming in the case of a particular transaction that the date of entry is to be 28 June

2004, the solicitor will require to find a deed recorded on or before 27 June 2004. In the case of a title where the property has not changed hands frequently, the foundation writ may be 20 or more years old; in other cases, it may be only a matter of days or weeks beyond the ten-year date. A review of the search or Form 10 report may be helpful in ascertaining the foundation writ.

If the foundation writ is valid, there is no need to check any other prior writ. Where, however, the foundation writ, or indeed any other writ in the progress of titles, refers for description to a writ outwith the progress of titles and earlier than the foundation writ, then this writ should also be examined to confirm the accuracy of the description.

Having found the foundation writ, the solicitor will want to check that there is a continuous series of transfers of the property from that date down to the seller. The grantee in one writ should be the grantor of the next writ in the progress of titles; and if there is a gap or if the name of the grantee is not the same as the grantor of the next writ, further investigation should be made. For example, if the grantee was a company, it may have changed its name or alternatively a liquidator may have been appointed before the next deed was granted; or an individual grantee in one writ may have died and the grantor of the next writ may be his executor or trustee. In these cases the appropriate linking writs, such as a confirmation or special resolution, should form part of the progress of titles offered to allow the purchaser's solicitor to check the validity of the various links. All writs referred to for burdens should be examined, whether or not they are within the prescriptive progress of titles.

It is a matter of judgment as to whether the older titles, even if they are referred to for burdens, are required. Some resistance may sometimes be found on the part of sellers' solicitors to the production of these writs since it may be difficult to trace who holds them and the costs of obtaining the necessary extracts may be considerable. It is, however, for the seller's solicitor to produce such writs as are reasonably required by the purchaser's solicitor and there is no reason why the purchaser should meet the cost of obtaining extracts or quick copies of writs from the Scottish Record Office or the searchers. If a deed is referred to for burdens, it should be examined.

The purchaser's solicitor should compare the written description in the title and the plan (if any) against the missive description and against the actual property. If a Form P16 report has been obtained this is also checked to ensure there are no discrepancies with the Ordnance Survey map.

Where the title is already registered, only the titles subsequent to the date of the land certificate are checked.

33.48 INSPECTION OF PROPERTY

A solicitor acting for a purchaser should, ideally, always inspect the property which he is buying, preferably before missives are concluded, so that he has some idea of the property and so that he can foresee potential problems (for example a private roadway). But, this is seldom possible due to the pressures of modern business. What he should certainly do is to write to the purchaser (and possibly the surveyor if one was instructed) once he has the titles, sending him (or them) a copy of the description and the plan (if any) asking him (or them) to confirm that the description and the plan accurately define the property which is being purchased. The written description should also be checked against the survey report.

33.49   BURDENS

The purchaser's solicitor will also inform the purchaser of the burdens which affect the property and whether they are in conformity with the provisions of the missives. He will check the local authority and water authority certificates (when he receives them) against the missives and he will check any superior's certificates against the title. If necessary he will require the seller's solicitor to obtain any other certificates.

If he requires to examine other writs, he will request these from the seller's solicitor. If he wishes further information about particular points he will raise these points also with the seller's solicitor. Before he reaches the point of raising these 'observations on title' he will have examined the title in detail.

33.50   POINTS TO CHECK

The following list is not exclusive but indicates the main points which the solicitor should consider. It is helpful to have available some form of checklist which can be completed as the examination proceeds. This avoids any relevant points being omitted from consideration: see Chapter 32.

(1) Check that there is a prescriptive progress of titles, and that each writ is correctly framed, executed and recorded.
(2) Check the description of the property.
(3) Check the burdens in the title.
(4) If there are burdens in the title, were these referred to in the missives? If there is a right of pre-emption, does it affect the sale to the client? Have all the title conditions been complied with?
(5) If the property is less than ten years old, is there an NHBC certificate? Is there a copy of the planning permission and building warrant?
(6) If the property is in a tenement, are there rights to *inter alia* the *solum* and are the obligations for maintenance apportioned on an equitable basis and conform to the missives?
(7) Check the local authority and, if necessary, water authority, certificates as to the planning position and as to whether the roads, pavements, water supply and main drains are publicly maintained. (In rural areas, this may well not be the case.)

(8) Check whether there have been any additions or alterations to the property and if so:
  (a) check the planning position;
  (b) check the building warrant and completion certificate;
  (c) check that any superior/neighbouring proprietor(s) have consented, if such consent is required.
(9) Check any securities over the property. Have they been discharged?
(10) Check the search and, if necessary, the prior search for undischarged securities, etc.
(11) Check the position regarding evidence under the Matrimonial Homes (Family Protection) (Scotland) Act 1981.

33.51 NOTING TITLE

It is normal and good practice to prepare notes on title (a summary of the salient points of each relevant deed in the titles).

The property title should be dealt with first; thereafter, in order, the writs referred to for burdens, the security title, and the search. There is no need to repeat every word in every deed. It is always useful, particularly in the case of a deed of conditions in an estate title which is referred to for burdens, to photocopy the burdens section and, where there is a plan, it is helpful to attach a copy of this.

As well as providing confirmation of the sufficiency of the title, notes on title are a valuable record of the title which will be retained in the office once the transaction file is closed and once the title deeds are lodged elsewhere. Particularly if the titles have to be lodged with a building society, it is important that the notes on title are sufficiently full to answer any queries which may be subsequently raised on the title by the client. They provide an initial reference to the title, though, if the query is important, the solicitor may need to obtain the actual titles. They may be useful also if the client is buying or selling another house on the same estate. The notes on title may not be completed until other information is obtained from the seller's solicitor but they should be prepared as the purchaser's solicitor is going through the title.

33.52 OBSERVATIONS ON TITLE

At the same time as the purchaser's solicitor is examining the title he will also note down any queries he may have and any points on which he wishes further clarification. These should be raised with the seller's solicitor at the same time as the purchaser's solicitor sends the draft disposition for revisal and returns the title deeds. If these observations relate to what may be serious defects in the title or if other information or other writs are necessarily required, then the observations will be raised before the purchaser's solicitor drafts (or can draft) the disposition. There is clearly no point in preparing a conveyance in favour of the purchaser if the validity of the title is in doubt, since, unless this can be rectified, the purchaser will resile from the bargain.

The purchaser requires to complete a Form 1 when applying for a first registration. This form asks detailed questions regarding the title, the answers to which must satisfy the Keeper before the title will be registered and guaranteed. Any queries regarding the answers to the questions in this application form should be raised with the seller's solicitor.

Examining and raising observations on the title efficiently and selectively require experience; having identified the points in the title on which further information is required, the purchaser's solicitor should list them in order of importance, and, if certain that they are of minor if not minimal significance, may consider that they can safely be ignored. However, points of any significance should never be ignored and the solicitor should not feel embarrassed by raising them. In the letter to the seller's solicitor, however, rather than listing the points deed by deed, the solicitor should detail them in order of importance. In some cases, the seller's solicitor may consider some of the purchaser's solicitor's requests for information or confirmation less than reasonable; or some of the information sought may be unobtainable or not able to be confirmed (for example, a request to obtain an unrecorded feu charter of 1805 which is referred to for burdens, or a planning permission of 1972). Some degree of practical expediency is necessary when raising observations on title – but without ever compromising the duty of the solicitor acting for a purchaser as to the title being offered. If he overlooks or accepts something in the title which is incorrect, rest assured that when he is selling the property, a more meticulous conveyancer will raise the point and he will have to resolve it.

A letter raising observations on title should always be courteously phrased, whatever the solicitor may think about the quality of the conveyancing offered. There are innumerable ways of requesting information and each letter will be different depending on the circumstances of the transaction.

The seller's solicitor is responsible for the title he is offering. It is up to him to satisfy the purchaser's reasonable doubts and to rectify any curable defects therein. On the other hand, the purchaser's solicitor may wish to suggest a solution rather than leaving it to the seller's solicitor along the following lines: 'We note that' [the flaw] 'and await your comments. We would suggest that this might be rectified by ...'.

The seller's solicitor should obtain the information, writs, etc requested and deal with any queries raised: he must satisfy the purchaser's solicitor as to the validity and marketability of the title. If the latter is, however, satisfied, he then prepares the conveyance in the purchaser's favour.

33.53   DRAFTING THE DISPOSITION

The conveyance to the purchaser is by way of disposition.

Prior to concluding the missives, the purchaser's solicitor should have confirmed with his client the disponee(s) and the destination to be inserted in the disposition.

Over the years every solicitor will acquire his or her own personal set of styles (copies or drafts of deeds required to carry into effect out-of-the-ordinary transactions should always be retained). There are also published style books. In most ordinary cases, however, involving the straightforward conveyance of a whole property, the conveyancer will use the last disposition (in favour of the seller) in the title as a draft and by amending that disposition as necessary will produce the draft disposition in favour of the purchaser. While this is standard and convenient practice, it is also a frequent source of error. For example, if the last disposition describes the property by reference to an earlier deed, say 'by A B Limited in my favour ...', 'my' is no longer appropriate in the new draft.

If the title is already registered in the Land Register, a short form of disposition is appropriate. See the *Registration of Title Practice Book*, para 8.47.

33.54 REVISAL/APPROVAL OF SELLER'S DRAFTS

The purchaser's solicitor will approve or revise the draft letter of obligation; will revise the draft application for a Form 11 report by checking it against the search part of the Form 10 report. He will amend it, if necessary, to take account of the purchaser's personal details and building society, and will approve (almost certainly) the draft discharge by comparing it with the standard security. So far as the search in the Form 11 report is concerned, he will also ask for this to be obtained as close as possible to settlement. If the seller is a limited company, a search in the Register of Charges and the company's file will usually be required to be prepared or continued to a date 22 days after the date of recording of the disposition in favour of the purchaser. Certain other safeguards may also be insisted upon by the purchaser's solicitor such as a certificate of solvency by the directors or by a director and the company secretary, or a certificate of non-crystallisation of a floating charge (incorporating a deed of release) if appropriate. See Chapter 34.

The purchaser's solicitor then returns the title deeds to the seller's solicitor along with his draft disposition and the draft letter of obligation, draft Form 11 report application and any draft discharge, all of which have been approved or revised. He will also enclose his draft Form 1 application for first registration and draft Form 4 which is simply an inventory of the writs to be sent to the Keeper with the application for first registration.

If the title is already registered, the seller will have sent the land certificate instead of the title deeds and a draft application for a Form 12 report instead of a Form 10 report plus an application for a Form 11 report. This will be revised by the purchaser's solicitors and returned with the land certificate, the draft short form of disposition and the revised drafts of the letter of obligation and any discharge. In addition, the purchaser's solicitor will enclose his draft Form 2 application to register, which is used instead of Form 1, and draft Form 4. If there is any delay in settlement, an up-to-date Form 13 report, equivalent to Form 11 on first registration, can be applied for. This is drafted by the seller's solicitor and approved by the purchaser's solicitor.

33.55   The purchaser's loan

The purchaser's loan can be considered under the following headings:

(1) first stage;
(2) guarantees;
(3) repairs; and
(4) acceptance of loan.

33.56   FIRST STAGE

The purchaser's solicitor has in this case (as is usual where building societies are involved) been instructed to act also – in a separate capacity – for the building society. Prior to the offer being made for the house, the purchaser's building society will have confirmed that a loan would be available if the particular property was suitable. The fact that a society is asked to survey a property does not necessarily mean that the purchaser proceeds with the purchase or, if he does so, that he is successful. When missives have been concluded, however, the purchaser or his solicitor will inform the building society that the offer for a particular property (which has been surveyed) has been successful and ask the society to start processing the loan.

The building society will then make an offer of loan to the purchaser/borrower, usually via his solicitor, and, either at the same time, or once the offer has been accepted, will instruct the solicitor to act on its behalf in connection with the loan. An important innovation in relation to the conveyancing procedures to be followed where a solicitor is acting for both borrower and lender was the introduction of the Council of Mortgage Lenders' Handbook. Now in its second edition, which is only available online at www.cml.org.uk, this sets out the conveyancing procedures to be followed in all transactions involving its members, which includes almost all lenders of mortgage finance. Part 1 of the Handbook sets out the instructions that apply to all transactions and Part 2 sets out the individual instructions of its members, as most lenders have slightly different procedures. It is important that the solicitor explains clearly the type of loan and the terms and conditions of the offer of loan to the borrowing client.

When a building society makes a loan, it will base the loan on the value placed on the property by its surveyor, not the price which the purchaser is prepared to pay for it. If, for example, the price offered is £120,000 but the property is valued at only £118,000 by the surveyor, and the loan offered is 90%, then the sum which will be advanced is 90% of £118,000. In other words, the purchaser will receive by way of loan £106,200 and not the £108,000 which he might have expected had the value and the price been the same. This is the first point which should be explained to a potential borrower at the stage when the solicitor is discussing his general financial position with him.

33.57 GUARANTEES

As noted at para 33.22, if a building society is lending more than 75% of valuation, any excess percentage will normally be covered by a single premium guarantee policy taken out by the society with an insurance company. At the present time most building societies will absorb the payment themselves if the loan is between 75% and 90%. If it is over that amount it will normally be charged to the borrower with the payment spread over the repayment period.

33.58 REPAIRS

In some cases, if the property requires a substantial amount of repairs, the society may retain a proportion of the loan until the repairs have been carried out. This can obviously cause the purchaser financial problems and must be taken into account in working out the financing of a purchase. Such retentions, however, are less common than previously, unless the repairs are fairly substantial.

33.59 ACCEPTANCE OF LOAN

Assuming that the purchaser/borrower is satisfied with the offer of loan, he should sign any acceptance required and return it to the society as soon as possible. Some societies do not require a formal acceptance. The solicitors' instructions will then be issued if not already issued and the loan processed.

The loan instructions to the solicitor will include details of the society's procedures and blank copies (usually in duplicate to allow for a draft and a principal copy) of the various forms and other documents required. The loan instructions should be acknowledged and it should be confirmed that the solicitor is prepared to act on behalf of the society.

If there is a second loan, the procedures adopted by the lending institution, the borrower and the solicitor are similar; and details of what documents are required will also be given.

Before completing the security documents, the purchaser's solicitor should, however, wait until the seller's solicitor has approved and returned the draft disposition in case the latter has made any revisals which would affect the security documents.

33.60 **The disposition approved**

When the seller's solicitor receives the letter from the purchaser's solicitor returning the titles and the drafts, and enclosing the draft disposition, he will deal with any queries and obtain any other information, documents or deeds required and send this/these on. He will approve or revise the draft disposition and, in the case of a first registration, the drafts of Form 1 and Form 4 or, in the case where the title is already registered, the drafts of Form 2 and Form 4, and return these to the purchaser's solicitor. In a first registration he will also send off the application for a Form 11 report to the Keeper to have the search brought down to a date as close as possible to settlement or where the title is already registered the application for a Form 13 report, if necessary. The titles and approved/revised draft letter of obligation will be filed away pending settlement, and the approved draft discharge will be engrossed.

The purchaser's solicitor now engrosses the disposition. It will be compared to ensure its accuracy, and a schedule of signing attached. The engrossment, the schedule of signing and the draft 'for comparison and return' will then be sent to the seller's solicitor. The purchaser's solicitor should, however, ensure, before posting the draft and the engrossment, that he has either completed the standard security or has kept a copy of the draft to allow this to be done.

33.61   LOAN: SECOND STAGE

Complete the standard security in draft and have it engrossed; prepare, if this is required, in draft, the personal bond or other agreement regulating the terms of the loan and have this engrossed. These documents require to be signed by the purchaser and, while they can certainly be sent to him for this purpose, it may be sensible to ask him to call at the office. There is no shortage of witnesses there – the signatures will all require to be witnessed – and there may be points about the purchase on which he wishes further information. In any event, it is easier to explain verbally the purpose of the various deeds he is signing and where the signatures should appear than attempt to put this in writing in a letter. If the solicitor does have to send deeds out to a client to sign, he should explain clearly and concisely where the signature has to go and where the witness's signature (if required) has to go; and mark clearly in pencil exactly where each party has to sign. Always enclose a schedule of signing to be completed, even if details are to be given on the deed. Not infrequently, they are omitted there. Always send a stamped addressed envelope for the return of the signed deeds. At this point, if there is a shortfall between the price for the new house and the funds which will be received from the sale of the purchaser's present house and the new loan, it is wise to indicate what funds will be needed to settle and say when the cheque will be required. It is probably easier therefore to invite the client to the office both to sign the security deeds and to deal with settlement arrangements.

33.62   SIGNING THE DEEDS

When the purchaser arrives for this meeting, the various deeds which he requires to sign should be ready; and his solicitor should be prepared for any explanation which is necessary. He should also have prepared (if this has not already been done) an estimated statement showing the various parts of the transaction from a financial point of view so that the client knows exactly what is required of him. The solicitor will require at settlement the full purchase price, plus or minus any outlays and if these funds are not to be available (if the sale of his present house only settles after the purchase, for example) then bridging finance should be arranged, preferably by the client. If bridging finance is requested, an irrevocable mandate will be signed, in duplicate, by the purchaser; and the solicitor will require to confirm to the bank that he will implement the terms thereof when the loan cheque is encashed. If additional funds are to be found by the client, he should be made aware of this and he should be told that his cheque should be in his solicitor's hands a few days before settlement to allow it to clear, though there is no personal reflection here on his credit rating. His solicitor should explain to him that stamp duty land tax (if charged) and the registration dues need to be paid immediately following settlement in order that the conveyance in his favour can be recorded and again the solicitor should be in funds to settle this. If a cheque in settlement of the amount of stamp duty land tax and the registration dues is not available, the solicitor should not delay paying the tax and then registering the disposition – especially if a standard security is being granted in favour of a lender. The solicitor also owes a duty of care to the lender if he or she is acting on behalf of the lender.

At the same time, once the security writs have been signed, the purchaser's solicitor will, if he is satisfied with the title, confirm to the building society that the title is in order and will request the loan cheque to be made available shortly before the settlement date. Building society loan cheques, if not cashed within a brief period of issue (usually 7 or 14 days), may require to be returned for redating to the society. They should not therefore be requested for issue too soon before settlement.

33.63 Settlement

Settlement can be considered under the following headings:

(1) the seller's part;
(2) the purchaser's part; and
(3) procedure on settlement.

33.64   THE SELLER'S PART

When the seller's solicitor receives the engrossment of the disposition and the draft, he compares the one with the other and returns the draft to the purchaser's solicitor. The seller's solicitor will then arrange for the seller to sign the disposition and any forms under the Matrimonial Homes (Family Protection) (Scotland) Act 1981, if applicable. He may send the engrossment of the disposition to the seller for signature along with the schedule of signing; if so, he will explain clearly what signatures are required (including that of a witness), and enclose a stamped addressed envelope for the return of the signed disposition. Alternatively, he may suggest that the seller comes into his office to sign the deed. The solicitor should remember to establish that the seller is going to be available to sign – there is nothing worse than a seller disappearing close to settlement, without having signed the necessary deeds. If the seller will be away at the relevant time, it is sensible to have him sign a power of attorney.

The seller's solicitor will also engross the discharge (the draft of which was approved by the purchaser's solicitor since it is required to clear the title of the security writ encumbering it) and send this document to the seller's building society to execute, again accompanied by a schedule of signing. He will also request a note of the amount required to repay the outstanding balance of the loan on the settlement date and will undertake not to release the executed discharge until payment of this balance has been made and the loan repaid.

The seller's solicitor will also forward the Form 11 report or any Form 13 report when he receives it and at any rate prior to settlement. Until recently it was usual to send a state for settlement detailing the purchase price payable and any adjustment to this for example, extra moveables agreed to be purchased by the seller. This is not usual now except in purchasers of new homes from builders.

When the seller has signed the disposition and the relative schedule of signing has been completed and the seller's building society returns the executed discharge (again with a completed schedule of signing), the solicitor's seller will complete as necessary the details of execution on the discharge (this is a deed affecting the seller) but will not put a testing clause on the disposition (this is a deed prepared on behalf of the purchaser). He will simply retain the signed disposition and schedule of signing with the titles. He will file the redemption figure for the loan. When any draft state for settlement is returned approved by the purchaser's solicitor, the seller's solicitor will retype this if necessary and retain it on the file; he will also have typed the letter of obligation, dated for settlement, and will retain this and the draft on the file. He will have arranged with the seller how the purchaser is to get access and where the keys will be. It is sensible for one key to be held by the seller's solicitor; but, provided keys are not handed over until the price has been paid, any other suitable arrangements can be made. He may have to advise the seller on how to deal with services, such as gas and electricity. He is, however, at this stage now in a position to await the date of settlement.

33.65   THE PURCHASER'S PART

The purchaser has signed the security writs and these have been attested. The purchaser's solicitor has:

(1) requisitioned the building society loan cheque;
(2) instructed his client to let him have a cheque for any balance of price necessary

(including outlays such as stamp duty land tax) or has arranged for bridging finance to be available;

(3) approved the Form 11 or Form 13 report sent to him by the seller's solicitor (he should examine the report carefully with particular reference to any entries in the Personal Register against the seller, and, if the purchaser is obtaining a loan, against the purchaser); and

(4) approved/revised and returned any draft state for settlement and supporting vouchers, if any.

He also is (or will be) in a position to settle. It is courteous, however, to confirm to the seller's solicitor that he is in funds and is in a position to settle.

Some days before settlement, he will confirm that the client's cheque has been received and banked. He will make the necessary arrangements with the seller's solicitor as to when settlement will take place. He will ensure that the loan cheque when it arrives is also banked on the day of settlement.

33.66 PROCEDURE ON SETTLEMENT

Settlements can be carried out by post or personally. The only difference is that, in the case of a postal settlement, arrangements have to be made to ensure that a signed cheque is on the desk of the seller's solicitor or the funds have been electronically transferred to his client account and the various documents etc (and keys) are on the desk of the purchaser's solicitor. So far as personal settlement is concerned, the arrangements will have been made by telephone, probably the same day, or some days before; the normal rule is that the purchaser's solicitor goes to the seller's solicitor. The purchaser often wishes settlement to take place early so that the removal can be got underway – especially if the purchaser is to be selling his existing house on the same day.

All the purchaser's solicitor requires is a signed cheque drawn on his client account and made out in favour of the seller's solicitor for the amount brought out in the state for settlement (the price plus or minus any outlays or apportionments). The seller's solicitor should remember to check the amount and to ensure that the cheque is signed. Before drawing this cheque, the purchaser's solicitor will have encashed (possibly some days before) any cheque from the purchaser to ensure that it is met; and, on the morning of settlement, but not before, any bank cheque in respect of a bridging loan and the building society loan cheque. He will check (again), before he encashes the loan cheque, that the borrower/purchaser has signed the security writs. He should satisfy himself that he is in funds to settle before he draws the cheque in favour of the seller's solicitor. Particular care should be taken if a cheque in settlement of the purchase price is to be held as undelivered. It is not normally necessary for a solicitor to have specific consent to release a cheque since by the drawing and issuing of the general client cheque, a solicitor has given control of the transaction to the selling solicitor. If a cheque is to be held as undelivered, this should be clearly referred to either in the missives or in a subsequent exchange of correspondence.

33.67 Documents etc

In exchange for the cheque or the alternative of electronic transfer of funds, the seller's solicitor will hand over:

(1) the disposition, signed by the seller, and the schedule of signing; the signatures and the schedule should be checked;
(2) the title deeds falling to be delivered;
(3) the executed discharge of the seller's loan; this will have been attested and completed by the seller's solicitor. It will usually have attached to it a standard form of letter to the Keeper signed by the seller's solicitor and the selling solicitor's cheque for the appropriate recording dues payable to the Registers of Scotland;
(4) the principal letter of obligation duly subscribed, together with the draft previously approved; the purchaser's solicitor should check the one against the other there and then just in case the seller's solicitor has omitted any of his revisals;
(5) documentation under the Matrimonial Homes (Family Protection) (Scotland) Act 1981 (if applicable);
(6) any receipted copy of the state for settlement; and
(7) the keys (unless other arrangements have been made), which is all that the purchaser is in fact really interested in.

33.68 After settlement: the purchaser

Immediately following settlement, both the purchaser's solicitor and the seller's solicitor have a number of matters which should be attended to without delay.

The purchaser's solicitor will advise his client that settlement has now taken place; he will hand him the keys (if he received them at settlement) and will tell him that the removal vans can now roll, that he can start redecoration or digging up the garden if he wishes.

He will then prepare the testing clause for the disposition and type it on to the draft; after checking he will insert it on to the disposition. He will (if he has not done so already) complete the testing clause on the standard security in favour of the purchaser's building society. He will stamp or type (if this has not been done before) the name and address of his firm together with his firm's FAS Number for registration purposes on the bottom segment of the backing of both deeds so that they will be returned to the correct address. He will then sign the completed Form 1 or Form 2, as appropriate and send this to the Keeper with the disposition and the standard security along with a cheque for the appropriate registration dues payable to the Registers of Scotland. These should be sent in the special envelopes prepared by the Keeper for this purpose to facilitate the administrative procedures at Register House. A receipt is returned to the presenting agent as evidence of the provisional date of recording.

He will, if necessary, first arrange for stamp duty land tax to be paid. See Chapter 5.

He will, if requested, advise the building society that the loan cheque has been encashed and the advance made, by returning the completion form duly completed.

He will cancel any temporary insurance cover taken out at the time missives were concluded. If a building society is involved, permanent property insurance will often be arranged by the society. If not, or if the purchaser is buying from his own resources, a permanent property insurance should be arranged immediately.

He will pass any receipted state for settlement to the cash room.

He will file the letter of obligation, in accordance with office practice. It is not normally a good idea to file letters of obligation on a correspondence file since they may be overlooked there, but to file them on a separate 'Obligations' file where they can be reviewed at regular intervals.

He will then prepare a statement of the outlays incurred in connection with the purchase and loan, which will include his fee, and will either write to the purchaser for payment or, if he has requested payment in advance of settlement, will simply account to the purchaser. It is good practice for the seller's solicitor to keep his client informed at all times, to advise him of the cost of whatever transaction he is involved in and to recover from him any outlays, such as stamp duty land tax, before they are incurred. Otherwise the firm will effectively be lending the client the money. It is also good practice for the seller's solicitor to render a statement of account before the date of entry or as soon as possible after the purchase has been settled. In any event, such a statement of account or a fee note must be rendered to the client either before or at the same time as the fees are debited.

He will, if the building society requires this, make an inventory and send to the society the title deeds which have been delivered to him. Most building societies, however, prefer that this be done only when the borrower's title – the land certificate – and the charge certificate are returned from the Register House.

Finally, he will check through his file to confirm that everything which should have been done has been done. The golden rule, for both the purchaser's solicitor and the seller's solicitor, at this stage in any transaction, is to leave no loose ends in a file.

33.69 **After settlement: the seller**

Immediately following settlement, the seller's solicitor will cash the purchase cheque and will repay the outstanding balance of the seller's building society loan on the basis of the statement which was requested earlier. In due course the society will send the seller direct a statement of the mortgage account down to its close. The society will cancel any property insurance charged to the seller and will refund any balance of the premium due.

The seller's solicitor will return any titles he has borrowed from other solicitors, and will, if he has not already done so, settle their lending fee.

He will ensure that he or the seller cancels any banker's orders or other debits in respect of monthly mortgage payments etc.

He will then prepare a statement of outlays and his fee. If he has money in hand, it is necessary for him under the accounts rules to seek his client's approval before deducting the fee and outlays from the balance, leaving a net balance to be forwarded to the client, or as he may direct, or in response to a mandate, for example, to a bank. If the client (for some reason) wants the full proceeds to be sent to him without first deducting the fee, the solicitor should retain sufficient to cover the outlays, and should ensure that the note of fee is submitted at the earliest possible moment.

The solicitor will pay any outlays which remain outstanding, for example, advertising accounts. Finally, he will check through the file once again to ensure that everything has been dealt with and that there are no loose ends.

33.70   Final stages

The final stages of a transaction may take some time to complete in a first registration. This is due to the fact that the Keeper will be issuing a land certificate which guarantees the title. The Keeper requires to be satisfied with the title before issuing the land certificate which may take time, especially as there will be a plan included, which must correspond to the Ordnance Survey map. Where the title is already registered, however, the title only needs checking from the date of the existing land certificate and the process is much quicker. Accordingly, the current average time to receive a land certificate is approximately one hundred days for a first registration and less than a month where the title is already registered.

Once the purchaser's solicitor receives the land certificate, this should be checked carefully against the prior deeds and if it is order the letter of obligation should be returned duly discharged to the seller's solicitor. The land certificate and charge certificate, if a loan is involved, are then sent to the lender.

Solicitors are advised to keep a diary of dates when matters such as delivery of a land certificate or discharge should take place, or placing letters of obligation (both incoming from other solicitors and those granted by the firm) on a separate file where they can be easily and regularly reviewed. This is so as to avoid problems which may be caused by dilatoriness or forgetfulness in completing the final stages of a transaction. The case of *Burnett's Trustee v Grainger* 2002 SLT 699 is a salutary lesson in this regard. Indeed, with most missives now specifying varying periods during which they are to remain in full force and effect, it is essential that important dates are noted. If not, the purchaser can find himself without any recourse against the seller – although he probably may still have a justifiable complaint against his own solicitor.

Once the letter of obligation has been implemented and returned to the seller's solicitor the transaction is finally closed. Both solicitors can now close their files, always assuming, of course, that the fees have been paid.

33.71 Solicitors (Scotland) Practice Rules 1986

In the light of the comments at para 33.1 on conflict of interest, these Rules are repro-duced here for ease of reference. The Law Society of Scotland's website at www.lawscot.org.uk/members/conveyancing/index should be consulted for any updates to these.

'1. (1) These rules may be cited as the Solicitors (Scotland) Practice Rules 1986.

(2) These Rules shall come into operation with respect to transactions commenced on or after 1 January 1987.

2. (1) In these Rules, unless the context otherwise requires:

"the Act" means the Solicitors (Scotland) Act 1980;

"client" includes the prospective client;

"Council" means the Council of the Society;

"established client" means a person for whom a solicitor or his firm has acted on at least one previous occasion;

"employed solicitor" means a solicitor employed by his employer for the purpose, wholly or partly, of offering legal services to the public whether or not for a fee;

"firm" includes any office at which that firm carries on practice and any firm in which that firm has a direct interest through one or more of its partners, or members;

"the Society" means the Law Society of Scotland established under the Act;

"solicitor" means a solicitor holding a practising certificate under the Act, or an incorporated practice;

"transaction" includes a contract and any negotiations leading thereto.

(2) The Interpretation Act 1978 applies to the interpretation of these Rules as it applies to the interpretation of an Act of Parliament.

3. A solicitor shall not act for two or more parties whose interests conflict.

4. Without prejudice to the generality of Rule 3 hereof an employed solicitor whose only or principal employer is one of the parties to a transaction shall not act for any other party to that transaction; provided always that such solicitor may, where no dispute arises or appears likely to arise between the parties to that trans-action, act for more than one party thereto, if and only if:

(a) the parties are associated companies, public authorities, public bodies, or government departments or agencies;

(b) the parties are connected one with the other within the meaning of section 533 of the Income and Corporation Taxes Act 1970.

5. (1) Without prejudice to the generality of Rule 3 hereof, a solicitor, or two or more solicitors practising either as principal or employee in the same firm or in the employment of the same employer, shall not at any stage, act for both seller and purchaser in the sale or purchase or conveyance of heritable property, or for both landlord and tenant, or assignor and assignee in a lease of heritable property for value or for lender and borrower in a loan to be secured over heritable property; provided, however, that where no dispute arises or might reasonably be expected to arise between the parties and that, other than in the case of exception (a) hereto, the seller or landlord of residential property is not a builder or developer, this rule shall not apply if:

(a) the parties are associated companies, public authorities, public bodies, or Government Departments or Agencies;

(b) the parties are connected one with the other within the meaning of section 533 of the Income and Corporation Taxes Act 1970;

(c) the parties are related by blood, adoption or marriage, one to the other, or the purchaser, tenant, assignee or borrower is so related to an established client; or

(d) both parties are established clients or the prospective purchaser, tenant, assignee or borrower is an established client; or

(e) there is no other solicitor in the vicinity whom the client could reasonably be expected to consult; or

(f) in the case of a loan to be secured over heritable property, the terms of the loan have been agreed between the parties before the solicitor has been instructed to act for the lender, and the granting of the security is only to give effect to such agreement.

(2) In all cases falling within exceptions (c), (d) and (e) both parties shall be advised by the solicitor at the earliest practicable opportunity that the solicitor, or his firm, has been requested to act for both parties, and that if a dispute arises, they or one of them will require to consult an independent solicitor or solicitors, which advice shall be confirmed by the solicitor in writing as soon as may be practicable thereafter.

6. A solicitor shall unless the contrary be proved be presumed for the purposes of Rules 4 and 5 hereof to be acting for a party for whom he prepares an offer whether complete or not, in connection with a transaction of any kind specified in these Rules, for execution by that party.

7. A solicitor acting on behalf of a party or prospective party to a transaction of any kind specified in Rule 5 hereof shall not issue any deed, writ, missive or other document requiring the signature of another party or prospective party to him without informing that party in writing that:

(a) such signature may have certain legal consequences, and

(b) he should seek independent legal advice before signature.

8. Where a solicitor, or two or more solicitors practising as principal or employee in the same firm or in the employment of the same employer, knowingly intends or intend to act on behalf of two or more prospective purchasers or tenants (other than prospective joint purchasers or tenants) of heritable property (in this Rule referred to as "the clients"), the clients shall be informed of such intention, and a single solicitor shall not, where he has given any advice to one of the clients with respect to the price or rent to be offered, or with respect to any other material condition of the prospective bargain, give advice to another of the clients in respect of such matters.

9. The Council shall have power to waive any of the provisions of these Rules in any particular circumstances or case.

10. Breach of any of these Rules may be treated as professional misconduct for the purposes of Part IV of the Act (Complaints and Disciplinary Proceedings).'

Chapter 34

Transactions with Companies

34.1 General

Transactions with incorporated companies, including most commonly companies incorporated under the Companies Act 1985 and earlier Companies Acts, raise particular issues and produce special problems. Some of these have been mentioned in earlier chapters; and, to some extent, the material in this chapter repeats what has gone before. The purpose of this chapter is to collect together and deal with, in one chapter, the main problems which the practitioner should be aware of when dealing with a company (or sales by companies in liquidation, receivership or administration), on the sale or purchase of heritable property in particular and in certain other situations.

34.2 Foreign companies

The material in this chapter predominantly deals with companies incorporated under the Companies Acts and having their registered office either in Scotland or in England and Wales. Increasingly, in practice, practitioners find themselves dealing with companies registered abroad, particularly in tax havens. To a limited extent, some provision is made for such companies in UK statutes referred to later in this chapter. But, generally speaking, when dealing with a company registered outwith Scotland, England and Wales, advice and/or a legal opinion should be sought from a lawyer in the country in which the company is registered, because the rules which apply to that company may well be different from the rules which would otherwise apply if the company were registered in Great Britain.

34.3 Company name

It is peculiarly important that deeds granted by or in favour of an incorporated company should state the name of the company precisely as rendered in its certificate of incorporation or certificate of incorporation on change of name. See I J S Talman (ed) *Halliday's Conveyancing Law and Practice* (2nd edn, 2 Volumes, 1996–97), para

4.04. The registered number and registered office of the company should also be narrated in the deed. The separate legal *persona* created on the incorporation of a company exists only in the company whose name is so registered. Accordingly, a deed granted by or in favour of a company whose name is not correctly and exactly reproduced is, in effect, a nullity. For example, see the case of *Modern Housing Ltd v Love* 1998 SLT 1191 where the court stated that an error as to the company name must plainly be regarded as of first importance. See also D J Cusine (ed) *The Conveyancing Opinions of J M Halliday* (1992), pp 265–266 and C Waelde (ed) *Professor McDonald's Conveyancing Opinions* (1998), pp 14–15, where the opinion was expressed that the omission of an apostrophe in a company's name is fatal. See also G L Gretton and K G C Reid *Conveyancing* (2nd edn, 1999), para 28.04.

To this strict rule there are very limited exceptions, such exceptions being predicated on the general question as to whether the inaccuracy is one of form or substance. The abbreviation of the word 'Michael' to 'M' will invalidate a document, whereas an abbreviation of the word 'Limited' to 'Ltd' or 'and' to '&' will not: see *Durham Fancy Goods Ltd v Michael Jackson (Fancy Goods) Ltd* [1968] 2 All ER 987. Furthermore, the abbreviation of 'Company' to 'Co' has been held in England not to invalidate the document at common law: see *Banque de L'Indochine et de Suez SA v Euroseas Group Finance Co Ltd* [1981] 3 All ER 198. But, in the case of a company called 'L & R Agencies Ltd', an English court held that a document in which the '&' was omitted did not reproduce the company name correctly, which underlines the need for exactitude: see *Hendon v Adelman* (1973) 117 SJ 631. However, this case can be compared with the Scottish case of *Orkney Islands Council v S J D Robertson & Company Ltd* 2003 SLT 775. Here, Temporary Judge T G Coutts, QC granted a motion to amend a court summons which narrated the name of the company as 'S & J D Robertson & Company Ltd' instead of its true name 'S & J D Robertson Oils Ltd'. Compare *Modern Housing Ltd v Love* 1998 SLT 1191.

In reviewing such cases, it is suggested that the following general principles may be applied in deciding whether a deed of conveyance will be invalidated. However, such guidance must be regarded as tentative, as the decisions relied upon are not Scottish conveyancing cases, there being a dearth of these.

(1) The misspelling of a word will generally be insufficient to render a deed void: see *Jenice Ltd* [1994] BCC 43 at 48F–G.
(2) The omission of a word will usually be fatal, for example the omission of the word 'Limited' in *Penrose v Martyr* (1858) 120 ER 595.
(3) An abbreviation of a word featured in a company name will not render a deed void if:
   (a) the abbreviation is treated as the equivalent of the word abbreviated;
   (b) there is no other word which is abbreviated to that particular abbreviation; and
   (c) there is no possibility that the Registrar of Companies would accept for registration two companies if it was presented with both companies' names (ie one with the full name and the other with the abbreviation): see the said case

of *Banque de L'Indochine et de Suez SA v Euroseas Group Finance Co Ltd* [1981] 3 All ER 198.

In addition, in the case of a charitable company limited by guarantee whose name does not include the words 'charity' or 'charitable', it is a legal requirement that any deed of conveyance, *inter alia*, clearly states in English in legible characters that the company is a charity: see s 112(6) of the Companies Act 1989. Failure to do so may lead to criminal penalties, but will not invalidate the deed.

If, in terms of the Companies Act 1985, s 36B, a company chooses to have a common seal, the name of the company must be engraved on it. It is thought that the name of the company must be rendered exactly correctly on the seal to comply with this direction; but the same special exceptions to the rule may apply also to the seal. Of course, since 30 July 1990, a company incorporated under the Companies Acts no longer requires to have a common seal. Accordingly, from a purely practical viewpoint, save in the context of an examination of the prescriptive progress of writs on an examination of title in a first registration transaction (where the foundation or other writs were signed and sealed by an incorporated company possessing a company seal) and in the rare event that a company chooses to have a seal, the practitioner will rarely encounter company seals in the context of property disposals.

In the case of heritable titles, these rules may suffer some qualification in the case of foundation and earlier writs in the progress which may not be invalidated by the use of the wrong name because, in order to check whether or not the correct name has been used, extrinsic enquiry beyond the four corners of the deed is necessary, and that is excluded by positive prescription. However, this will only be relevant in the rare event of a Sasines transaction or a property transaction which induces a first registration in the Land Register. In other cases the Land Register Title Sheet will be conclusive and an examination of the prior heritable titles will no longer be required.

34.4 Capacity

This has already been fairly fully dealt with in Chapter 3, to which reference is made. See also *Halliday's Conveyancing Law and Practice,* para 2.116 ff. In the ordinary case of sale and purchase under the Companies Act 1985, capacity did not normally present any problem because the company, in the objects clause in its memorandum of association, would almost invariably have the power to sell or purchase heritable property or borrow on the security thereof. Under s 35 of the 1985 Act (as amended by s 108 of the Companies Act 1989) the capacity of the company is not to be permitted to be called into question by reason of any limitation imposed in the memorandum. Non-observance of any limitations imposed in the memorandum can now only result in liability on the directors, although such liability may be negated by ratification of the director's actions at board level, save in the case of *mala fides* or fraud. As far as the power of the directors to bind the company was concerned, at least in a question with a person dealing with the company in good faith, prior to the 1989 Act, any transaction decided on by the directors was deemed to be one within the capacity of the company. Furthermore, there was no duty on the other party to make enquiry as to whether or not this was so. See the 1985 Act, s 35. Under s 35A and s 35B of the Companies Act 1985 (added by the Companies Act 1989), the difficulties encountered with the *ultra vires* rule and the authority of a director to bind the company under the 1985 Act have been further ameliorated, at least as far as the duty of the third party to investigate the authority of directors is concerned. The third party is now presumed to be dealing in good faith, unless the contrary can be shown: s 35A(2)(c) of the 1985 Act. A person will not be taken to be acting in bad faith for the sole reason that he is aware of the fact that an act is beyond the powers of the directors. This presumption of 'good faith' is not negated by a failure to investigate the powers of the directors, or by actual knowledge of limitation on their powers: see s 35B of the 1985 Act. For reasons later explained, the same applies in the case of an administrator.

In circumstances where the holder of a floating charge has appointed a receiver, he has statutory powers which cover sale, trading and borrowing on security. In addition, the floating charge will usually add to the receiver's statutory powers of sale, trade and borrowing. The liquidator, in a winding-up, has statutory powers of sale and borrowing on security; but his power to continue trading is restricted.

Care must, however, be taken when dealing, not with companies, but with other bodies corporate not incorporated under the Companies Acts, to whom the *ultra vires* rule continues to apply. Such bodies include universities and other corporate bodies (such as The Standard Life Assurance Company) incorporated by Royal Charter or Act of Parliament, and housing associations registered under the Industrial and Provident Societies Acts or the Friendly Societies Acts. In *Piggins & Rix Ltd v Montrose Port Authority* 1995 SLT 418, the question arose as to whether the Montrose Port Authority had power to sell land which was surplus to requirements. In a special case presented to the court, the answer was negative, although it was mentioned, *obiter*, that the Port Authority may have the power to grant long leases.

34.5   Execution of deeds

The execution of deeds by companies has already been dealt with fairly fully in Chapter 2 and as was mentioned there, the Requirements of Writing (Scotland) Act 1995 governs the matter. See also *Halliday's Conveyancing Law and Practice*, para 3-117. The situation can be summarised thus:

(1) If executed on or before 30 July 1990 while the company is still a going concern, the execution of a deed intended to be probative should follow the provisions of the Companies Act 1985, s 36(3). This required the affixing of the common seal of the company and the signatures of two directors or a director and the secretary on the last page of the deed and on the last page of each schedule or other addendum.

On 31 July 1989, the 1985 Act, s 36 was replaced by a new s 36B, by the Companies Act 1989. That section was not satisfactory and was in turn replaced on 1 December 1990, but with retrospective effect as from 31 July 1990, by the Law Reform (Miscellaneous Provisions) (Scotland) Act 1990, s 72. The new s 36B of the 1985 Act was replaced by the Requirements of Writing (Scotland) Act 1995. The requirement now is execution by two directors, or one director and the secretary, or by two persons authorised by the company to subscribe. In each case, witnesses are unnecessary and the deed need not be sealed. A deed so executed is probative. See para 2.13.

For the execution of deeds by a foreign company on or after 16 May 1994, see the Foreign Companies (Execution of Documents) Regulations 1994, SI 1994/950. These provide that a foreign company may execute a deed by the subscription of two directors; by the subscription of a director and the secretary; or by the subscription of one person authorised to subscribe the document on behalf of the company.

(2) When a company is in liquidation, or a receiver or administrator has been appointed, the best view is that the deed runs in name of the company and of the liquidator, receiver or administrator. There should be a statement in the narrative giving details of the liquidation or appointment of a receiver or administrator, as the case may be, following the style approved in *Liquidator of Style & Mantle Ltd v Prices Tailors Ltd* 1934 SC 548. Given that the title remains vested in the company, it is not clear whether the liquidator, receiver or administrator need be conjoined in the deed as co-grantor, but this is standard practice. It rests on the argument that he or she is the person entitled to administer the estate by virtue of the statutory or contractual power vested in him or her.

The deed is signed by the liquidator, receiver or administrator as the case may be on the last page; and, in each case, the signature requires attestation by one witness. For the same reason as stated above, some agents require the liquidator, receiver or administrator, as the case may be, to sign the deed twice, representing his dual capacity; although, again, it is doubtful if this is necessary. Any deed so executed before 31 July 1990 also required the common seal of the company; but, under s 36B(1) of the Companies Act 1985, as well as under the Requirements of Writing (Scotland) Act 1995, a company no longer requires a common seal and accordingly sealing of the deed on or after 31 July 1990 is unnecessary in all cases.

34.6 Purchase of heritable property from a company as a going concern

This transaction is dealt with first because it is the transaction which causes most problems to practitioners.

It is well known that certain types of company, especially building and property development companies, are particularly vulnerable, and frequently go into liquidation or have an administrator or receiver appointed, in many cases with little or no warning.

The same fate may, of course, overtake an individual or a firm or partnership. Any of these may become insolvent; and may be sequestrated or have a judicial factor appointed.

34.7 FLOATING CHARGES

The particular risk involved in dealing with a company arises out of the facility available to a company to grant a floating charge over the whole or certain specified assets, a facility which is not, of course, available to individuals or firms. The danger which the floating charge presents is that it can immediately become a fixed security on all the assets covered by the charge without prior notification and, in particular, without any entry appearing either in the Companies Register, the Register of Charges, or the Personal Register. The Scottish Law Commission has, however, consulted on whether the law should be changed here: see *Sharp v Thomson* (Scot Law Com Discussion Paper No 114, 2001), paras 4.41 to 4.44. The current automatic conversion into a fixed security occurs immediately upon the liquidation of a company or on the appointment of a receiver in respect of the assets included in the charge. Note, however, the new curb on appointing a receiver introduced by the Enterprise Act 2002. See para 23.4. In practice, a floating charge normally extends to the whole assets of the company; but it may be restricted. The appointment of an administrator does not have the same effect. Admittedly, there are statutory provisions requiring notification of the liquidation or the appointment of a receiver or administrator in the Register of Charges and elsewhere. But the validity of the fixed security created immediately upon liquidation or on the appointment of a receiver is not dependent on such notification. Moreover, it is not affected by failure to register the appropriate information with the Registrar of Companies or to publish it in the *Gazette* or public press. A floating charge may also automatically crystallise on the happening of particular events as specified in the instrument of charge by virtue of a 'conversion clause'; and in that case notice of crystallisation must be lodged with the Registrar. For an illustration of an automatic crystallisation, by special extra provision in the deed itself, subsequently followed by the appointment of a receiver, see *Norfolk House plc v Repsol Petroleum Ltd* 1992 SLT 235. It was held in the special circumstances of this case that the Insolvency Act 1986, s 72, which deals with the cross-border operation of receiverships, was intended to bridge the transaction from the creation of the charge to the appointment of the receiver, to ensure that he could exercise his powers under the Act. However, see at p 237 Lord Penrose's reservations about conversion clauses and the automatic attachment of floating charges where the charge instrument provides that the secured indebtedness becomes immediately repayable.

It is also possible for a company to grant more than one security, for example a floating charge and a standard security. In these circumstances an agreement determining the order of ranking will be required. A recent example is *Bank of Ireland v Bass Brewers Ltd* 2000 GWD 28-1077. Here, an order for rectification under s 8(1)(b) of the Law Reform (Miscellaneous Provisions) Act 1985 was sought when the question of ranking arose between the holder of a fixed security and the holder of a floating charge.

A floating charge, when created, must be registered in the Register of Charges within 21 days after the date of its creation, with limited exceptions for charges created outwith the UK. *AIB Finance Ltd v Bank of Scotland* 1995 SLT 2, which is also discussed in para 23.5, states that the word 'create' in ss 410(5) and 464 of the Companies Act 1985 means:

(1) in relation to a fixed security, the date of the real right coming into existence and accordingly, the date of recording of the fixed security in the Register of Sasines or registration in the Land Register; and
(2) in relation to a floating charge, the date of execution of the floating charge instrument.

But the Scottish Law Commission has proposed that floating charges are not created until registration: see para 23.12.

Failure to register within the 21-day time limit invalidates the charge. Therefore, a failure to register within such 21 days is a serious concern as this will leave the floating charge void as against the liquidator and other competing creditors in terms of s 410(1) of the Companies Act 1985. See also D J Cusine (ed) *The Conveyancing Opinions of J M Halliday* (1992), pp 41–43. However, there is a statutory provision in the guise of Companies Act 1985, s 420 (s 404 of the Companies Act 1985 in England) which enables a creditor to apply to the court to extend the period for registration. But it is very unlikely that the court would permit an extension of time to the prejudice of a third party purchaser: see *Prior, Petitioner* 1989 SLT 840 and para 35.15 below.

The Companies Act 1985, s 462(5), expressly provides that the charge is fully effective, both as a floating charge and as a fixed security, notwithstanding that the deed creating it is not registered in the Register of Sasines or Land Register. As a result, at the date of settlement of a transaction with a company, there may be in existence an effective charge which has already become a fixed security on the heritable property in question without any official notification of these facts in any public register. Further, a charge which is still floating at settlement may, immediately thereafter, become a fixed security on the property, even after delivery of the disposition thereof to the purchaser against payment of the price. Prior to the decision of the House of Lords in *Sharp v Thomson* 1997 SC (HL) 66, it was considered that this would apply even after delivery of the disposition to the purchaser against payment of the price. In *Sharp*, in the unusual circumstances of more than a year after settlement of the transaction, a company signed and delivered a disposition to a purchaser. The disposition was recorded in the General Register of Sasines 12 days later. The day after the delivery of the disposition to the purchaser, a receiver was appointed to the company. The Court of Session held that the property remained vested in the company as the delivery of the disposition did not transfer property in land. Transfer of property occurred only when the disposition was recorded. However, the House of Lords reversed the decision. It held that in receivership, on delivery of the disposition and entry being taken in return for payment, the property no longer forms part of the 'property and undertaking' of the company within the meaning of the Insolvency Act 1986, s 53(7) and thus will not be attached on crystallisation of the charge. For a discussion of the implications of the case, see the Reading List for this chapter. See also paras 4.4 to 4.6. The Scottish Law Commission has recommended that *Sharp* be overturned by statute and replaced by a new set of priority rules, protecting disponees who register timeously. See *Sharp v Thomson* (Scot Law Com Discussion Paper No 114, 2001).

34.8 METHODS OF PROTECTING THE PURCHASER

In the ordinary case, when purchasing heritage from a company as a going concern, the problems outlined above may be dealt with as suggested below. Reference may also be made to A J McDonald and S Brymer 'Transactions with companies – *caveat emptor*' (1994) 13 Greens PLB 2.

34.9 Power of sale

There are two possible limitations on the power of sale:

(1) Improbably, but just conceivably, the company does not have power of sale in the objects clause of its memorandum of association. Some agents prefer to establish that the company has this power by examining the memorandum; but in practice, except in very unusual circumstances, a *bona fide* purchaser for value is fully protected by the Companies Act 1985, s 35.

   From 16 November 1989 under the Companies Act 1985, s 35 (as substituted by the Companies Act 1989, s 108), the validity of an act done by a company cannot be called into question on the ground of lack of capacity by reason of anything in the company's memorandum. This is discussed in more depth above.

(2) If the company has granted a floating charge, it is perfectly competent and commonplace expressly to provide in the instrument of charge that the company will grant no other floating charge and no fixed security ranking prior to or *pari passu* with the floating charge itself. Occasionally, this provision goes further and prohibits the granting of any security, whether prior or postponed. Finally, some lending institutions include in their standard form of floating charge an absolute prohibition against disposal of any asset without the consent of the creditor. Such provisions are commonly known as a 'negative pledge'. The cumulative effect of *AIB Finance Ltd v Bank of Scotland* 1995 SLT 2, *Griffith and Powdrill, Petitioner* 1998 GWD 40-2037 and *Bank of Ireland v Bass Brewers Ltd* 2000 GWD 28-1077 is that:

(a) the existence of a negative pledge (albeit in a negative rather than a positive manner) is sufficient to displace the order of ranking set out in subs (2) and (4) of s 464 Companies Act 1985 (this is now expressly reflected in s 464(1A) of the Companies Act 1985); and

(b) there is no universal rule to the effect that the existence of a negative pledge in a floating charge will, as a matter of course, elevate such floating charge to a prior ranking security, notwithstanding the terms of the Companies Act 1985, s 464(1A). Each negative pledge will be interpreted and applied strictly according to its terms.

Accordingly, in the context of a property acquisition by a limited liability company, where such corporate purchaser (1) has previously granted a floating charge containing a negative pledge to a lender and (2) is obtaining borrowing from a different lender to acquire the property, the practitioner would be best advised to contact the original floating charge holder and the lender for their views as to ranking, prior to effecting the floating charge and/or standard security over the property in favour of the lender. Otherwise, the lender advancing funds to enable the company to purchase the property will automatically end up with a postponed ranking standard security, contrary to their legitimate expectations of priority ranking.

34.10 The 'floating' characteristics of a floating charge

The whole essence of a floating charge is that property owned by a company 'floats out' of the charge on disposal and so, in the ordinary way, when purchasing from a company, the purchaser has no concern with the terms of a floating charge because, once disposed of, the charge no longer affects that property. So *Halliday's Conveyancing Law and Practice,* para 36-92 states that, in strict theory, it is unnecessary to search the Register of Charges in the case of an outright sale, on the footing that a floating charge of its nature does not prevent the company from selling its heritable property. But the author then points out that the sale of a property may be an event which would precipitate the appointment of a receiver, and so convert the floating charge into a fixed security with possible adverse consequences.

Whether or not an absolute bar on disposal without the creditor's consent could in any circumstances affect a purchaser is doubtful; but conceivably an argument might be developed along the lines of the 'duty of enquiry' rule, as laid down in *Rodger (Builders) Ltd v Fawdry* 1950 SC 483. It could be argued that, since the charge is registered, a purchaser by implication is deemed to have notice of its terms – despite the fact that the public information available to a prospective purchaser from a review of any Form 395 or 410 registered with Companies House is of limited value. (Indeed, it is often the case that the Registrar of Companies does not keep a copy of the floating charge.) The purchaser should therefore have enquired as to whether or not the creditor had consented to the sale. Against that, such an absolute prohibition in a floating charge can only be, in its nature, a personal contract between the creditor and the debtor therein, and on general principle should not be capable of affecting singular successors.

Clearly, however, to avoid future challenge, the best advice is to obtain the consent of the creditor. This is standard practice: see para 34.18 below.

34.11   Title

Apart from the situation outlined above where the floating charge totally excludes any disposal without consent, the existence of a floating charge does not of itself affect the title of the company to dispone. Accordingly, in the ordinary way, the selling company will grant a disposition in favour of the purchaser, without requiring any consent *in gremio* (within the body of the disposition). On registration, the disposition will perfect the real right of the purchaser and give him a valid and marketable title free and disencumbered of the charge.

To ensure a marketable title as in other situations, all fixed securities, such as standard securities, outstanding at the date of sale must either be discharged or restricted in order to release the part sold. This presents no particular difficulty and no specialties, as compared with taking a title from an individual. Of course, Forms 419(a) or (b) (memoranda of satisfaction) must be registered with Companies House once any standard security over the property sold has been discharged or restricted, but there is no time limit for this.

34.12   Risks inherent in floating charges

In the case of floating charges, however, there are serious risks involved, against which precautions must be taken. The risks are that the company may go into liquidation before the transaction has settled, without the purchaser knowing anything about it; a receiver may be appointed; or similarly, one of the events as specified in the instrument of charge may have occurred. See *Norfolk House plc (In Receivership) v Repsol Petroleum Ltd* 1992 SLT 235, referred to at para 34.7. This means that when the disposition is delivered to the purchaser, the charge will already have become a fixed security and therefore the purchaser's title is burdened therewith. Further, until the disposition in favour of the purchaser is recorded, the company is arguably not finally divested. When, however, the disposition is delivered to the purchaser who takes entry in return for payment, the property will no longer form part of the property and undertaking of the company, and so on receivership a floating charge will not attach to the property. See *Sharp v Thomson* 1997 SC (HL) 66, referred to at para 34.7. However, in the case of liquidation, there could still be a race to the register: see *Burnett's Trustees v Grainger* 2002 SLT 699. But liquidators rarely take steps to complete title.

Under the Companies Act 1985, s 403 (introduced by the Companies Act 1989, s 98) (in the case of a floating charge granted by a company registered in England and Wales) and s 419 (in the case of a floating charge granted by a company registered in Scotland), a memorandum of satisfaction duly delivered to the Registrar of Companies renders the charge void as against a *bona fide* purchaser for value even if, in fact, the charge continues to be effective after the date of such registration. An informal release may also suffice to release the property from the floating charge. In *Scottish and Newcastle Breweries plc v Ascot Inns Ltd* 1994 SLT 1140 an informal letter from the creditor in a floating charge to the solicitors for the company amounted to a release of the properties specified in the letter. The letter did not require to be registered to be valid.

34.13 NECESSARY SEARCHES

Searches will therefore be required in:

(1) the Property Register, to disclose the existence of any standard security or other fixed security affecting the property;
(2) the Personal Register to disclose any diligence registered against the company, such as an inhibition relative to the property; and
(3) the Companies Register, to disclose whether or not there are floating charges (and standard securities or other fixed securities) and, if so, whether or not a receiver has been appointed; whether the company has gone into liquidation; and whether the company has been struck off the Register and so ceased to exist.

34.14 Searches in the Companies Register

In relation to searching in the Companies Register, the traditional method was to obtain and search a microfiche relative to the particular selling company which contained copies of all of the documents registered on the Company's File. However, since December 2002 company fiches are no longer available, save in exceptional circumstances. Companies House now provides an on-line internet search service. See www.direct.companieshouse.gov.uk. Basic information relative to a company can be accessed free of charge, for example registered number, registered office, history of name changes, SIC code and filing history (which shows all documents registered with Companies House for an approximate period of ten years). More detailed information can be retrieved subject to payment of a fee, for example annual returns, statutory accounts, copies of registered Companies House Forms, copy shareholder resolutions, notices of appointment of a receiver, liquidator etc. All information is compiled in chronological order online.

Where the title is registered, when a company is selling property, the Keeper relies on the answers given on the application forms. He does not take it on himself to search the Companies Register in order to ascertain the position as to floating charges; as to whether or not a receiver or administrator has been appointed; or whether or not the company has gone into liquidation; or whether or not the company has been struck off the Register. See the *Registration of Title Practice Book*, para 5.46. It is therefore entirely up to the agent to make these enquiries for himself by appropriate searches on-line of the Companies Register in terms of the previous paragraph or the obtaining of a charges search from a firm of professional searchers. For professional indemnity insurance reasons, the latter route is preferred and by far the most prudent. Professional searchers provide protection for the solicitor in the event that inaccurate information is supplied. A search of the position from the Companies House on-line service, while worthwhile, will expose the solicitor to liability in the event that the information retrieved and relied on by the solicitor in concluding the transaction ultimately transpires to be erroneous. In this situation, Companies House accepts no liability for any such inaccuracies: see www.companieshouse.gov.uk/.

34.15　Period of search

In order to ensure that all the necessary information is disclosed, the search in the Companies Register runs from 27 October 1961 (being the date from which floating charges first became competent in Scotland), or from the date of incorporation of the company, if later, up to a date 22 days after the date of registration of the disposition. The reason for the 22-day period is that the holder of a floating charge has 21 days within which to register the charge if it is to be fully valid. If a receiver is then appointed under that charge before the purchaser's disposition is delivered, the protection offered by *Sharp v Thomson* 1997 SC (HL) 66 (discussed in para 34.7) is not applicable, and the floating charge becomes a fixed security on the property in the hands of the purchaser. The 21-day period might be extended by application to the court under the Companies Act 1985, s 420 (or s 404 in the case of an English company). However, it is very unlikely that the court would permit an extension of time to the prejudice of a third-party purchaser: see *Prior, Petitioner* 1989 SLT 840 and *Barclays Bank plc v Stuart Landon Ltd* [2001] BCLC 316 (CA) (in the context of the English provisions in s 404 of the Companies Act 1985). So, for practical purposes, a period of 22 days after the date of registration suffices.

34.16　Searches in the Property and Personal Registers

When dealing with an individual and searching in the Property and Personal Registers, there is always a short gap between the closing date of the search and the settlement date during which, possibly, some adverse deed might be delivered or recorded. The purchaser or lender is protected by the seller's letter of obligation. When dealing with a company, a purchaser or lender will also be concerned to ensure that there have been no floating charges registered or receivers appointed prior to the delivery of the disposition. The registration of a floating charge may not show up until 21 days after the delivery of the disposition. Notice of appointment of a receiver should be delivered to the Registrar of Companies for registration within seven days of execution: Insolvency Act 1986, s 53. Until computerisation of the Presentment Book for Register of Sasines titles was introduced by the Keeper in 1992, there was a very real risk that the seller might record a standard security or other adverse deed during the gap of some months (as it then was) between the date of the close of the search on an interim report in the Property Register and the date of settlement. That risk in the Property Register is now virtually eliminated by computerisation. The

Personal Register has always been up to date within 24 hours of close of search. See Chapter 32 for further comment on computerisation. Accordingly, the seller's solicitor can normally safely give an obligation to produce a clear search on behalf of an individual and in so doing does not incur any significant risk.

In the case of a selling company, however, the risks are thought to be greater. As a result, most solicitors, particularly when acting for the vulnerable building or development company, specifically provide in their missives that they themselves do not undertake to give a clear search in the Companies Register, and possibly in the other Registers as well. As regards the Companies Register, this is best practice, as such an undertaking is not covered by the classic letter of obligation. See the article by the Law Society of Scotland Conveyancing Committee 'Clarifying the Classic Letter of Obligation' 2003 JLSS Apr/26.

34.17 LETTER OF OBLIGATION

The letter of obligation traditionally granted at settlement undertaking to deliver clear searches in the Property and Personal Registers is personally binding on the solicitor who grants it, thereby effectively putting him in the position of a guarantor for the seller. Given computerisation of the Presentment Book and the comment above, the risk to the solicitor acting for a selling company in relation to the Property and Personal Registers is now generally thought to be acceptable. However, because of the special provisions for companies, already dealt with in Chapter 32, the agent acting for the selling company should not commit himself to produce a clear search in the Companies Register or Register of Charges. Moreover, such an obligation would not be covered by the classic letter of obligation. See the article by the Law Society of Scotland Conveyancing Committee 'Clarifying the Classic Letter of Obligation' 2003 JLSS Apr/26. To ensure that he does not come under such an obligation and that settlement is not delayed on that account, a provision to this effect should be inserted in the missives. It is, however, now standard practice to undertake to provide a clear Companies Search *on behalf of the client* in letters of obligation, where a company is the seller.

34.18 ALTERNATIVE METHODS OF PROTECTING THE PURCHASER

To protect the purchaser against unforeseen emerging fixed securities resulting from liquidation or the appointment of a receiver following on the granting of a floating charge, two devices are commonly adopted.

(1) *Grants by the creditor*. The creditor in the floating charge(s) may agree to grant either:
   (a) a deed of release in terms of which, possibly subject to certain conditions, he formally releases the property from the charge. This is similar to a deed of restriction of a standard security and is the most satisfactory solution because it avoids the risk referred to in (1) in para 34.9. Alternatively, an

informal letter of release may suffice: see *Scottish & Newcastle Breweries plc v Ascot Inns Ltd* 1994 SLT 1140; or

(b) a certificate of non-crystallisation, in terms of which, again subject to certain conditions and usually within a fairly short time limit, the creditor undertakes that he will not take any steps to appoint a receiver or to put the company into liquidation. That is binding on the creditor; but it does not protect the purchaser against the possibility of liquidation at the instance of some other party, on which event the floating charge would automatically become a fixed security, notwithstanding the granting of the letter of non-crystallisation. The letter of non-crystallisation remains necessary even after the decision in *Sharp v Thomson* 1997 SC (HL) 66 to protect the purchaser for the period prior to the delivery of the disposition.

Furthermore, the above methods only protect the purchaser against floating charges of which the purchaser is aware at settlement. They do nothing to protect the purchaser from (i) floating charges granted by the selling company immediately prior to settlement or (ii) the appointment of a receiver, administrator or liquidator immediately prior to settlement, where notice of such floating charge(s) and appointment(s) has not made their way on to the Companies Register. For these reasons it is not uncommon for the purchaser to attempt to protect their position by introducing provisions into commercial missives to retain part of the purchase price until clarification of the position to the purchaser's satisfaction has been secured, ie 22 days or more after settlement.

(2) *A certificate of solvency.* This takes the form of a certificate, granted personally by one or more directors, or by a principal shareholder of the company concerned, warranting that, so far as they are aware, the company is solvent, that no steps have been or are about to be taken to put it into liquidation or to appoint a receiver, and that no floating charge has been granted which does not appear in the search of the Companies Register. The qualification 'so far as aware', though usual, seriously weakens the protection. At first sight, it might be thought that this is a satisfactory solution to the problem; but such a certificate may well be worthless. In any event, it cannot amount to a release from the security and is at best a personal guarantee by the grantors thereof which, in turn, for its efficacy, depends on the honesty and financial standing of the grantors. Purchasers will, however, be given extra protection where the selling company goes into receivership or liquidation, if the proposals of the Scottish Law Commission in its Discussion Paper on *Sharp v Thomson* (Scot Law Com Disc Paper No 114, 2001) are implemented.

34.19 Purchase of heritage from an administrator

On the appointment of an administrator, the company remains a going concern and retains its corporate powers and title to its assets but the powers of directors are taken over by the administrator. The office of administrator is dealt with in Part II (ss 8–27) of the Insolvency Act 1986. It involves an application to the court for an administration order. The general effect is that, on the making of an order, the administrator takes over the management of the company in place of its directors. The directors are not, however, removed from office although their powers are suspended during the period of administration. The main purpose of the administration order is to provide machinery to rescue an ailing company; but the order will not be granted unless there is a genuine prospect of success.

The administrator is required to intimate his appointment to the Registrar of Companies within 14 days of the making of the order under the Insolvency Act 1986, s 21, and to the Keeper for insertion in the Personal Register.

34.20 DISCLAIMER OF CONTRACTS

An administrator has no power to disclaim contracts entered into by the company before his appointment and so, even if the administrator is appointed after the property has been sold by the company, the contract is valid and binding. The following comments are therefore equally applicable whether the property was sold by the company before the administrator was appointed or was sold by the administrator himself under his administrative powers.

34.21 POWERS

Under the Insolvency Act 1986, Schedule 1, an administrator has power to sell by private bargain and, thereafter, to grant the necessary deeds. Under the Insolvency Act 1986, s 14(6), there is a general provision to the effect that a person dealing with an administrator in good faith and for value is not concerned to enquire as to whether the administrator is acting within his powers. Accordingly, a purchaser can safely purchase property from an administrator, relying on these statutory provisions.

34.22 TITLE

The appointment of an administrator has no effect on title; and all the company's assets remain vested in the company.

The question of searches and outstanding securities is less significant than when purchasing from a company as a going concern. This is because, under the Insolvency Act 1986, s 15, the administrator has a further power to dispose of property of the company which is subject to a security as if the property were disencumbered. In the case of fixed securities, the consent of the court is required. Secured creditors are protected as against the administrator; but, under s 14(6) of the 1986 Act, that cannot affect a *bona fide* purchaser. In particular, under s 16(1) of the

1986 Act, a disposition by an administrator, when registered, has the effect of disencumbering the property conveyed of all outstanding fixed securities, which of course would include standard securities and floating charges which have become fixed.

34.23 MORATORIUM ON ADVERSE ACTIONS

Under the Insolvency Act 1986, s 11, during the period of administration, no effective resolution can be passed to put the company into liquidation; no steps can be taken to enforce any existing security; and no other proceedings and no diligence may be commenced or continued without consent of the court. The position of a preexisting inhibition against the company, registered prior to the appointment of the administrator, is not entirely free from doubt. It was argued in the sixth edition of this book, at para 35.23 that, notwithstanding such an inhibition, the administrator has power to sell and to grant an unchallengeable title by virtue of the provisions of the 1986 Act, s 11(3)(d). This provides that no diligence may be 'continued' against the company or its property without leave of the court. We depart from that view here, on the basis that an inhibition is complete upon registration and that there is nothing to be 'continued': see G L Gretton *The Law of Inhibition and Adjudication* (2nd edn, 1996), p 180. Further, the existence of the inhibition would preclude the exhibition of a clear search.

34.24 **Purchase of heritage from a receiver**

If the company has granted a floating charge and if, thereafter, the creditor has appointed a receiver, the resulting position is dealt with in the Insolvency Act 1986, ss 50–71. In outline, the position is as follows.

34.25 APPOINTMENT

Firstly, under the Insolvency Act 1986, s 51, the holder of the floating charge over all or any property of the company has power to appoint a receiver; or he may apply to the court for such an appointment. But note para 34.32 in relation to floating charges created on or after 15 September 2003.

The circumstances justifying appointment are prescribed in s 52 of the 1986 Act; and the mode of appointment in s 53. In particular, under s 53(7), on the appointment of a receiver, the floating charge attaches to the property included therein and has effect as if the charge was a fixed security over that property. In line with *Sharp v Thomson* 1997 SC (HL) 66, the charge will not attach to property after delivery of the disposition where the purchaser has taken entry in return for payment. The receiver, when subsequently dealing with the property attached by the charge, does not rely on his security as such as conferring any powers, but on express statutory provisions as undernoted.

If the receiver is appointed by the creditor himself as is competent by instrument of appointment, a certified copy of that instrument must be notified to the Registrar of Companies within seven days after its execution under the 1986 Act, s 53(1). Alternatively, if the receiver is appointed by the court under s 54 of the 1986 Act, the petitioner applying for the appointment is required to make intimation to the Registrar within the same period (ie seven days) under s 54(3).

Notwithstanding the risks created by *Sharp v Thomson* in a purchaser taking title from a receiver, the Keeper has, so far, taken the approach of accepting titles from receivers without exclusion of indemnity. See the following terms in the *Registration of Title Practice Book*, para 5.37:

'The Keeper considers that the risk of a latent unregistered disposition surfacing once registration has been completed is too small to justify a policy of blanket indemnity exclusion for all sales by receivers. Accordingly, an application for registration of a conveyance by a receiver will not result in an exclusion of indemnity solely because of the risk that an unregistered disposition may come to light. Nevertheless, the Keeper expects that a purchaser acting in good faith will make appropriate enquiries of the receiver. If the receiver's response to those enquiries is less than satisfactory, or points to some difficulty or anomaly, the purchaser should seek the advice of the Keeper's Pre-Registration Enquiries Section before proceeding to settle the transaction. Pre-Registration Enquiries will take a measured view of the circumstances and consider the risk to the Keeper's position.'

34.26 DISCLAIMER OF CONTRACTS

As in the case of the administrator, the receiver has no power to disclaim contracts entered into by the company prior to his appointment. See the Insolvency Act 1986, s 57(4). So, if the company has sold the property prior to the appointment of a receiver he is bound to implement it according to its terms.

34.27 POWERS

The statutory powers relied on by the receiver are:

(1) the powers given to him by the instrument creating the charge; and
(2) the powers specified in Schedule 2 to the Insolvency Act 1986.

Under s 55(4) of the 1986 Act, a person dealing with a receiver in good faith and for value is not concerned to enquire whether the receiver is acting within his powers. But the powers do in fact include, under Schedule 2 to the 1986 Act, power to sell or lease the property, power to use the company's seal which is no longer relevant as noted above, and power to grant deeds in the name and on behalf of the company to implement the power of sale etc.

34.28   TITLE

The position as to title is somewhat anomalous. On the appointment of the receiver, the whole assets of the company, whether included in the charge or not, remain vested in the company which retains the title thereto.

The effect of the appointment is to convert the floating charge into a fixed security in terms of s 53(7) of the Insolvency Act 1986; but that section is not apparently intended to confer any titular powers; its purpose is simply to establish a preference. The receiver therefore relies on the powers referred to above which allow him, amongst other things, to deal with and dispose of property belonging to the company and attached by the charge.

The exercise of these powers is subject to the rights of any creditor holding a fixed security or floating charge having priority over the charge in question; and to the rights of any person who has effectually executed diligence on any of the property concerned.

34.29   PRECEDENCE AMONG RECEIVERS

Under the Insolvency Act 1986, s 56, if there are two or more floating charges sub-sisting, a receiver appointed under the prior charge takes priority over a receiver appointed under a postponed charge. In practice, if a receiver is appointed by the holder of a postponed charge, this simply triggers off the appointment of a receiver by the prior creditor so that, for practical purposes, in almost every case, one is deal-ing with the receiver under the first-ranking floating charge.

As a result, on examining a title, the agent is concerned with any fixed security ranking in priority to the first ranking floating charge and effectually executed dili-gence. In this context, however, an inhibition registered after the creation of the charge and before the appointment of a receiver but not followed by a decree of adju-dication, is not effectually executed diligence and so for practical purposes falls to be ignored. So far as clearing the record is concerned, these statutory provisions pro-duce a similar result to sale by a heritable creditor under a standard security in terms of the Conveyancing and Feudal Reform (Scotland) Act 1970: see para 22.45.

34.30   CONSENT OF CREDITOR OR APPLICATION TO THE COURT

Under s 61 of the Insolvency Act 1986, if property under the control of the receiver is already subject to an effective fixed security or effectually executed diligence (for example, an adjudication decree), and if the relevant creditor will not give consent, the receiver may apply to the court for authority to sell and to disburden the property of the security or diligence in question. Where the court has approved of a sale under s 61(2), the receiver grants to the purchaser or disponee a disposition of the property. On being recorded, this has the effect of disencumbering the property of the security and freeing it from any pre-existing effectual diligence or fixed security under s 61(8).

34.31 SEARCHES

As a result of these provisions, the position as to searches against the company is, again, of less significance than when a company is a going concern because of the disencumbering effect of the disposition in favour of the purchaser. But searches are, of course, still required, looking to the terms of the Insolvency Act 1986, s 61.

34.32 ENTERPRISE ACT 2002

In terms of the Insolvency Act 1986, ss 72A–72H (added by the Enterprise Act 2002, s 250), which were brought into force on 15 September 2003, it is normally incompetent to appoint a receiver, where the floating charge was created on or after that date. Certain categories of floating charge are excepted from this rule: see para 23.4. In other cases, it will be possible to appoint an administrator, but only if the charge is drafted in accordance with requirements laid down by the 2002 Act.

34.33 **Liquidation**

The winding-up of a company incorporated under the Companies Acts is dealt with in ss 73–219 of the Insolvency Act 1986, with some supplementary provisions in ss 230–251. No attempt is made here to deal with the detail of the liquidator's appointment but, broadly speaking, there are two general liquidation situations.

(1) Where the company is solvent and the members decide nonetheless to terminate its activities. This is known as a members' voluntary liquidation.

(2) Where the company is insolvent, the company itself or any of its creditors may put the company into liquidation on the footing that it can no longer meet its obligations, pay its debts etc: see the criteria listed in s 123 of the Insolvency Act 1986. In this situation, there are two alternatives:

    (a) a creditors' voluntary winding-up where the company takes the initiative, passes a special resolution to wind up the company, and appoints a liquidator subject to confirmation by the creditors; or

    (b) a winding-up by the court. This involves a petition to the Court of Session or the sheriff court in Scotland (High Court or County Court in England) applying for the winding-up of the company.

There are technical differences in detail between these various methods of winding-up but, in all cases:

(i)   a liquidator is appointed;

(ii) the directors are no longer entitled to exercise any of their powers;

(iii) the assets of the company remain vested in the company; and

(iv) the liquidator alone can competently deal with assets on behalf of the company.

To the rule that the assets of the company remain vested in the company there is one exception. In the case of a winding-up by the court, under the Insolvency Act 1986, s 145, in special circumstances, the court, may, on the application of the liquidator, direct that all or any part of the assets of the company shall vest in the liquidator by his official name. However, this facility is rarely used.

34.34   APPOINTMENT AND POWERS

When the property in question belonged to the company at the date of liquidation and is to be sold by the liquidator, the position is relatively straightforward. Statutory powers are conferred on the liquidator by Schedule 4 to the Insolvency Act 1986. Certain of these powers require prior sanction. However, others, including power to sell and power to execute in name of the company all deeds necessary for that purpose, require no prior sanction. In addition, in Scotland, under the 1986 Act, s 169(2), the liquidator has the same powers as a trustee in sequestration, subject to the rules prescribed in the 1986 Act. This relates principally to the relationship between the liquidator and secured creditors.

In contrast to what is thought to be the position of the administrator and is, by statute, the position of the receiver, a liquidator has at common law and by statute the right either to adopt and implement any contract entered into by the company prior to liquidation or to refuse to implement it. Of course, if he refuses to implement a contract, the other contracting party has a claim for damages against the company, but ranks only as an ordinary creditor in the liquidation of the company. This means that, where the company has contracted to sell property prior to the liquidation but the sale has not yet been implemented by delivery of a disposition, the purchaser may or may not lose the benefit of his contract, depending on the decision of the liquidator.

34.35   TITLE

In a sequestration, the appointment of the trustee (and issue of the act and warrant by the court) operates as a general disposition in his favour of all estate, heritable and moveable, so that he takes over all the assets of the bankrupt in his own name. In a liquidation, in contrast, the assets remain vested in the company but the powers of the directors are suspended. Under the Insolvency Act 1986, s 145, the liquidator may apply for a vesting order; and that would operate as a general disposition in his favour as an individual. As of 28 November 2004, a liquidator may complete title to land or dispose land by deducing title under ss 3 and 4 of the Conveyancing (Scotland) Act 1924. See the Abolition of Feudal Tenure etc (Scotland) Act 2000, Schedule 12, para 8(9).

34.36 FIXED SECURITIES

Liquidation has no direct effect on pre-existing fixed securities such as a standard security validly granted by the company and duly recorded and registered unless the same is challenged by the liquidator and subsequently cut down as an unfair preference. Further, on liquidation, any floating charge validly granted by the company and duly registered automatically becomes a fixed security, thereby securing a preference for the benefit of the holder of the charge.

Under the Insolvency Act 1986, s 185, which applies generally to all forms of winding up in Scotland, the Bankruptcy (Scotland) Act 1985, s 37(1) to (6) and s 39(3), (4), (7) and (8) are applied, *mutatis mutandis*, as they apply to a sequestration. The position generally speaking is as follows.

(1) If the liquidator is able to sell the property at a price more than sufficient to cover all securities on the property, then he is empowered to proceed with a sale without the consent of the secured creditors although they, of course, have a preference on the proceeds.
(2) If the liquidator intimates to a secured creditor that he intends to sell, that prevents the creditor from taking steps to enforce his security.
(3) Conversely, if a secured creditor has intimated to the liquidator that the creditor intends to embark on sale procedure under his power of sale, the liquidator is precluded from selling that asset.

Accordingly, in such cases, if the liquidator sells, existing securities will be discharged in the ordinary way; or, if a secured creditor sells, the sale will proceed under his statutory powers.

There is no provision in the Insolvency Act 1986 for a liquidator equivalent to that for a receiver (see para 30.30) which would disencumber property of pre-existing securities if sold by a liquidator. This can cause problems.

In so far as diligence is concerned, there still seems to be some doubt as to whether or not an inhibition registered against the company prior to liquidation is effective to prevent disposal of heritable property in Scotland or not. See G L Gretton *The Law of Inhibition and Adjudication* (2nd edn, 1996), p 174.

34.37 Second securities by companies

In the case of an individual, the granting of a second security is relatively straightforward. All that is required is a search in the Property Register and in the Personal

Register to see what securities have already been registered and whether or not the debtor is under effective diligence, such as an inhibition. Because an individual cannot have granted a floating charge, there are no complicating factors. The position therefore is very similar to the position on purchase of heritage from a selling proprietor.

In the case of companies, however, again because of the floating charge facility, the position is more complex, whether a company is granting a first fixed security or a second or subsequent fixed security. The relevant provision is the Companies Act 1985, s 464. It provides:

(1) under s 464(1)(a), it is expressly provided that the instrument creating the charge may contain provisions prohibiting or restricting the creation of any fixed security having priority over or ranking *pari passu* with the floating charge in question. Such a provision is commonly referred to as a 'negative pledge' which will be effective as to ranking (see para 34.9). Accordingly, any such 'negative pledge' provision is undoubtedly effective in a question with a second creditor; and

(2) a fixed security, if not so excluded under s 464(1)(a), takes priority over a floating charge provided the right of the creditor thereunder is made real before the floating charge itself becomes fixed. For a discussion on ranking of charges see *Alloa Brewery Co Ltd v Investors in Industry plc* 1992 SLT 121. But note the reform proposals of the Scottish Law Commission, discussed at para 23.12.

Where a creditor is lending to a company as a going concern and securing the loan either by a floating charge or by a standard security, many of the issues relevant to a purchase from a company as a going concern, dealt with above in paras 34.6 onwards are pertinent here too.

Appendix A

Styles

Notes

(1) The styles which follow, as listed in this Inventory, are skeleton styles only, intended merely to illustrate the form and content of each writ or document. They are not meant to be used as styles in practice and indeed, in many cases, important clauses are either truncated or omitted altogether, rendering them quite unsuitable for use as practical styles. This is particularly applicable to the missives of sale and purchase.

(2) For full styles of the relevant writs, with variants to meet a number of special cases, see I J S Talman (ed) *Halliday's Conveyancing Law and Practice in Scotland* (2nd edn, 2 volumes, 1996–97).

(3) Registers of Scotland Forms 1, 4, 10 and 10A are Crown copyright. They are reproduced here with the kind permission of the Controller of Her Majesty's Stationery Office and the Queen's Printer for Scotland.

Inventory of Style Writs

1. Feu Charter by Andrew Brown in favour of County Developments Limited, recorded GRS Lanark 13 November 1980
2. Floating Charge by County Developments Limited in favour of the Lanarkshire Bank Limited, dated 15 and registered in the Register of Charges 23 March 1981
3. Deed of Conditions by County Developments Limited, recorded said GRS 20 June 1981
4. Feu Disposition by County Developments Limited in favour of Mr and Mrs Edward Fox and the survivor, recorded said GRS 28 December 1983
5. Standard Security by the said Mr and Mrs Edward Fox in favour of The Larklanark Building Society, recorded said GRS 20 January 1984
6. Searches: Property, Personal and Company Registers
7. Death Certificate of Edward Fox (not reproduced here)
8. Certificate of Confirmation in favour of the Executors of the late Mrs Grace Fox, issued from the Commissariot of South Strathclyde, Dumfries and Galloway on 20 April 2002
9. Discharge by The Larklanark Building Society in favour of the Executors of the late Mrs Grace Fox of Standard Security number 5 hereof, recorded said GRS 3 June 2002

10. Missives of Sale and Purchase of dwellinghouse number 3 Larklanark Road, Lanark, dated 12, 17 and 18 September 2002
11. Disposition by the Executors of the late Mrs Grace Fox in favour of Peter Quinn, registered in the Land Register on 5 November 2002
12. Application Form 10 and Form 10A Report thereon
13. Application Form 1 for registration of the Disposition number 11 hereof and Inventory of Writs Form 4 accompanying same
14. Land Certificate for 3 Larklanark Road, Lanark
15. Charge Certificate for 3 Larklanark Road, Lanark
16. Disposition by Peter Quinn in favour of Clinton Blair

I. Feu Charter by Andrew Brown in favour of County Developments Limited

STAMP DUTY: £2,000

I, ANDREW BROWN, Accountant, residing at Larklanark House, Glasgow Road, Lanark (who and my successors as superiors of the subjects and others hereinafter disponed are hereinafter referred to as 'the Superiors') in consideration of the sum of One Hundred Thousand Pounds (£100,000) Sterling paid to me by COUNTY DEVELOPMENTS LIMITED incorporated under the Companies Acts and having their Registered Office at One Glasgow Square, Lanark of which sum I hereby acknowledge the receipt and of the feudal prestations hereinafter contained, HAVE SOLD and do hereby IN FEU FARM DISPONE to and in favour of the said County Developments Limited and their successors and assignees whomsoever but excluding assignees before infeftment on these presents and under declaration that these presents shall not be a valid warrant for infeftment after the expiry of six months from the date hereof (the said County Developments Limited and their foresaids as proprietors for the time being of the *dominium utile* of the Feu being hereinafter referred to as 'the Feuars') heritably and irredeemably ALL and WHOLE that plot or area of ground (hereinafter referred to as 'the Feu') situated on the south side of Glasgow Road, Lanark in the Parish of Larklanark and County of Lanark extending to Ten hectares or thereby and bounded as follows *videlicet*: on or towards the north by the north face of a stone wall separating the Feu from Glasgow Road aforesaid along which it extends two hundred metres or thereby; on or towards the east and south by the centre line of a post and wire fence separating the Feu from other subjects belonging to me along which it extends five hundred metres and two hundred metres respectively; and on or towards the west by the east face of a stone wall separating the Feu from other subjects belonging to me along which it extends five hundred metres or thereby, the Feu being delineated and outlined in red on the plan thereof annexed and signed by me as relative hereto (which plan is demonstrative only and not taxative) and forming part and portion of ALL and WHOLE the lands and estate of Larklanark in the said Parish and County more particularly described in and disponed by Disposition by the Testamentary Trustees of the late Bernard Brown in my favour dated Tenth and recorded in the Division of the General Register of Sasines for the County of Lanark on Fifteenth, both days of May, Nineteen Hundred and Sixty Six; and the Feu is hereby disponed TOGETHER WITH the whole fittings and fixtures therein and thereon, the whole parts, and privileges and pertinents of and effeiring thereto and my whole right, title and interest present and future in and to the *dominium utile* thereof; with free ish and entry to and from the Feu by Glasgow Road aforesaid; RESERVING to the National Coal Board constituted by the Coal Industry Nationalisation Act 1946 the whole coal and other minerals vested in them under that

Act so far as situated in or under the Feu; but the Feu is disponed with and under the real burdens and conditions following videlicet: (First) the Feuars shall be bound in all time coming to maintain in good order and repair, and whenever necessary to re-erect or reconstruct with the like materials, the whole of the stone wall extending along the north boundary of the Feu except for that part thereof to be demolished in order to give access to the Feu from Glasgow Road aforesaid as hereinafter provided; (Second) . . .

Note
A number of further burdens would be included in this Feu Charter in practice
in order to ensure a good standard of development and of future maintenance
in order to preserve the amenity of the Superior's adjoining property.

All which real burdens and conditions hereinbefore specified are hereby declared to be real burdens and conditions on and affecting the Feu and shall be inserted in any infeftment hereon and inserted or validly referred to in any future conveyance or transmission of the Feu or any part thereof; Declaring further that, if the Feuars contravene or fail to implement any of the foregoing feuing conditions, then this Feu Charter and all that may have followed thereon shall, in the option of the Superiors, become null and void and the Feuars shall forfeit their whole right, title and interest in and to the Feu which, with all buildings thereon, shall revert to and belong to the Superiors free and disencumbered of all burdens thereon as if these presents had never been granted; With entry and vacant possession on Eleventh November, Nineteen Hundred and Eighty: TO BE HOLDEN the Feu of and under the Superiors as immediate lawful superiors thereof in feu farm, fee and heritage forever; and I grant warrandice: IN WITNESS WHEREOF I have subscribed these presents, consisting of this and the preceding page together with the plan annexed hereto, at Lanark on the Tenth day of November, Nineteen Hundred and Eighty before these witnesses John Smith and Allan Robertson, both Solicitors of Three Glasgow Square, Lanark.

John Smith, Witness

                                          Andrew Brown
Allan Robertson, Witness

REGISTER on behalf of the within named COUNTY DEVELOPMENTS LIMITED in the REGISTER of the COUNTY of LANARK

                Holdsworth & Hepburn, Solicitors, Lanark, Agents

Registers of Scotland
General Register of Sasines
County of Lanark Book 14132 Folio 5
Presented and recorded on 13 November 1980.

This is the plan referred to in the foregoing Feu Charter by Andrew Brown in favour of County Developments Limited.

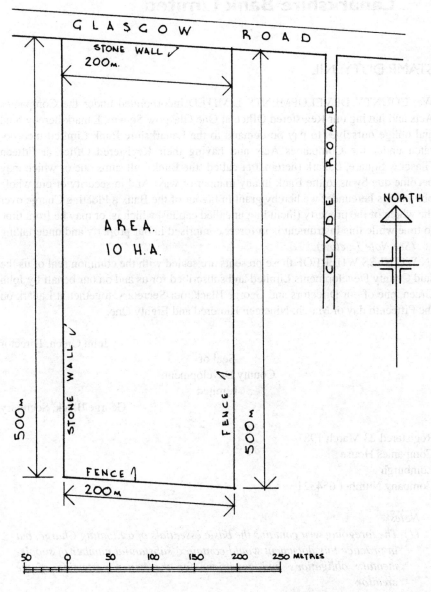

Andrew Brown

2. Floating Charge by County Developments Limited in favour of the Lanarkshire Bank Limited

STAMP DUTY: NIL

We, COUNTY DEVELOPMENTS LIMITED incorporated under the Companies Acts and having our Registered Office at One Glasgow Square, Lanark hereby bind and oblige ourselves to pay on demand to the Lanarkshire Bank Limited incorporated under the Companies Acts and having their Registered Office at Fifteen Glasgow Square, Lanark (hereinafter called 'the Bank') all sums due or which may become due by us to the Bank in any manner or way; And in security of our whole obligations hereunder we hereby grant in favour of the Bank a Floating Charge over the whole of the property (including uncalled capital) which is, or may be from time to time while this Instrument is in force, comprised in our property and undertaking . . . *(See Note 1 below)*

IN WITNESS WHEREOF these presents are sealed with the common seal of us the said County Developments Limited and subscribed for us and on our behalf by John Green, one of our Directors and George Black, our Secretary, together at Lanark on the Fifteenth day of March, Nineteen Hundred and Eighty One.

John Green, Director

Seal of
County Developments
Limited

George Black, Secretary

Registered 23 March 1981
Companies House
Edinburgh
Company Number 654321

Notes
(1) The foregoing writ contains the basic essentials of a Floating Charge, but in practice this document would contain a substantial number of supplementary obligations and conditions for the better protection of the creditor.
(2) The Floating Charge would not have been recorded in the GRS but, to be valid, would have to have been registered with the Registar of Companies in the Register of Charges within 21 days of its date of execution.

3. Deed of Conditions by County Developments Limited

STAMP DUTY: 50P

We, COUNTY DEVELOPMENTS LIMITED incorporated under the Companies Acts and having our Registered Office at One Glasgow Square, Lanark, heritable proprietors of ALL and WHOLE that plot or area of ground situated on the south side of Glasgow Road, Lanark in the County of Lanark, extending to Ten hectares or thereby, more particularly described in and disponed by and delineated and outlined in red on the plan annexed and signed as relative to the Feu Charter by Andrew Brown in our favour dated Tenth and recorded in the Division of the General Register of Sasines for the County of Lanark on Thirteenth, both days of November, Nineteen Hundred and Eighty; CONSIDERING that we intend to develop the said subjects by the erection of villa dwellinghouses thereon and to dispone the same to individual purchasers and that it is desirable to execute these presents in order to define the rights, interests, obligations and liabilities of the proprietor of each individual dwellinghouse to be erected on the said subjects; THEREFORE we do hereby declare and provide as follows:

First   Definitions

In this deed, unless the context otherwise requires, the following expressions shall have the following meanings respectively, viz:

'the Development' means the said area of ground extending to ten hectares or thereby.
'the Superiors' means us and our successors as proprietors for the time being of the *plenum dominium* of the development or so much thereof as has not been feued and of the *dominium directum* of those parts of the whole of the development which, at the relevant date, have been feued.

Notes
(1) Depending on the type of development proposed, a number of further definitions will follow.
(2) If the Land Registration (Scotland) Act 1979, s 17 has not been disapplied in this Deed of Conditions, all the burdens and conditions therein will become real burdens affecting the whole development and every part thereof immediately on recording the Deed. Accordingly, a reference to this Deed in subsequent conveyances of parts of the development would be strictly unnecessary, although in practice the Deed of Conditions is always so referred to.
(3) If s 17 of the 1979 Act is disapplied, which is competent, the burdens and conditions will become real, as regards each portion of the development subsequently feued or disponed if, but only if, the Feu Disposition (or

Disposition) of such portion expressly refers to the Deed of Conditions for burdens.

(4) The Deed of Conditions may contain a clause permitting the Superiors to vary the terms thereof which can cause problems and must be carefully drafted. Since such a clause is often desirable, s 17 of the 1979 Act is commonly disapplied; but that does not solve all drafting problems.

(5) For convenience, the definition clause in the Deed of Conditions may contain provisions as to ownership in common of those parts of the development which are to remain common to the whole proprietors thereof, including internal roads and footpaths; lighting; parking and amenity areas; and possibly other special features. This is usually a necessary provision for the purpose of defining common repairing obligations. Whether or not s 17 of the 1979 Act is disapplied, a Deed of Conditions may conveniently be used to define and identify common parts, but it cannot of itself create any right of common ownership in those common parts. Such rights of common ownership must therefore be separately and explicitly conferred on each individual disponee in each subsequent Feu Disposition (or Disposition) of each Feu, normally by reference to the definition in the Deed of Conditions.

(6) Note that s 17 of the 1979 Act will not apply to deeds granted on or after 28 November 2004, when the provisions of the Title Conditions (Scotland) Act 2003 come into force.

Second   The dwellinghouse erected on the Feu shall be used in all time coming as a private residence for use by one family only and for no other purpose whatsoever.

Note
The foregoing clause is purely illustrative. A much fuller clause would normally be used and a substantial number of further clauses would normally then follow to provide for the maintenance and amenity of the development as a whole; the maintenance of common parts; insurance and reinstatement; the constitution, formation and powers of a feuars' association; the conferring of an express jus quaesitum tertio on each individual proprietor to enforce the conditions as against his neighbours; and a declaration of real burdens and irritancy clauses on the lines of these clauses as they appear in the Feu Charter No. 1 above.

IN WITNESS WHEREOF these presents consisting of this and the (   ) preceding pages are sealed with the common seal of us the said County Developments Limited and subscribed for us and on our behalf by John Green, one of our Directors and George Black, our Secretary, together at Lanark on the Fifteenth day of June, Nineteen Hundred and Eighty One.

John Green, Director

Seal of
County Developments
Limited

George Black, Secretary

REGISTER on behalf of the within named COUNTY DEVELOPMENTS LIMITED
in the REGISTER of the COUNTY of LANARK

Holdsworth & Hepburn, Solicitors, Lanark, Agents

Registers of Scotland
General Register of Sasines
County of Lanark Book 14134 Folio 20
Presented and recorded 20 June 1981

4. Feu Disposition by County Developments Limited in favour of Mr and Mrs Edward Fox and the survivor

STAMP DUTY: £1,200

We, COUNTY DEVELOPMENTS LIMITED incorporated under the Companies Acts and having our Registered Office at One Glasgow Square, Lanark, heritable proprietors of the subjects and others hereinafter disponed In Consideration of the sum of Sixty Thousand Pounds (£60,000) Sterling paid to us in equal shares by Edward Fox and Mrs Grace Hunter or Fox, Spouses, presently residing at Sixteen Glasgow Road, Lanark, HAVE SOLD and do hereby IN FEU FARM DISPONE to the said Edward Fox and Mrs Grace Hunter or Fox equally between them and to the survivor of them and to the executors and assignees whomsoever of the survivor (the said Edward Fox and Mrs Grace Hunter or Fox and their foresaids as proprietors for the time being of the *dominium utile* of the Feu being hereinafter referred to as 'the Feuars') heritably and irredeemably ALL and WHOLE that plot of ground extending to twenty decimal or one hundredth parts of a hectare or thereby forming Plot 20 of the Development hereinafter referred to with the dwellinghouse and ancillary buildings erected thereon known as Three Larklanark Road, Lanark, in the County of Lanark all as the said Plot is delineated and outlined in red on the plan thereof annexed and signed as relative hereto, which said plot of ground hereinbefore in feu farm disponed is hereinafter referred to as 'the Feu' and forms part and portion of our Glasgow Road Development comprising ALL and WHOLE that plot or area of ground situated on the south side of Glasgow Road, Lanark in the said County extending to ten hectares or thereby, more particularly described in, in feu farm disponed by and delineated and outlined in red on the plan annexed and signed as relative to the Feu Charter by Andrew Brown in our favour dated Tenth and recorded in the Division of the General Register of Sasines for the County of Lanark on Thirteenth, both days of November, Nineteen Hundred and Eighty; and the Feu is so disponed together with (One) a right in common with all other proprietors of every part of the said Glasgow Road Development, including ourselves so long as we still remain heritable proprietors of any part of the *dominium utile* thereof, to the common parts of the said Glasgow Road Development all as the said common parts are more particularly described in a Deed of Conditions relative to the said Development, which said Deed of Conditions was granted by us dated Fifteenth and recorded in the said Division of the General Register of Sasines on Twentieth, both days of June, Nineteen Hundred and Eighty One; (Two) the whole parts, privileges and pertinents of the Feu; (Three) our whole right, title and interest, present and future in and to the *dominium utile* of the Feu; With free ish and entry to the Feu from Larklanark Road aforesaid fronting the Feu on the west side thereof: But always with and under the

reservations, real burdens and conditions specified and contained in *(here refer to (i)*
the Feu Charter Number 1 hereof; and (ii) the Deed of Conditions Number 3 hereof.
Note that, since the Deed of Conditions contains the whole conditions relative to the
Development, including a declaration of real burdens and an irritant and resolutive
clause, these clauses do not need to be repeated in this Feu Disposition); With entry
and actual occupation to the Feu on Twenty First December, Nineteen Hundred and
Eighty Three; To be holden of and under the Superiors, as defined in the said Deed of
Conditions, as immediate lawful superiors thereof in feu farm, fee and heritage forever; And we grant warrandice: IN WITNESS WHEREOF these presents consisting
of this and the ( ) preceding page(s) together with the plan annexed hereto are sealed
with the common seal of us the said County Developments Limited and subscribed
for us and on our behalf by John Green, one of our Directors and George Black, our
Secretary, together at Lanark on the Fifteenth day of December, Nineteen Hundred
and Eighty Three.

John Green, Director

Seal of
County Developments
Limited

George Black, Secretary

REGISTER on behalf of the within named EDWARD FOX and MRS GRACE
HUNTER or FOX in the REGISTER of the COUNTY of LANARK

White & White, Solicitors, Lanark, Agents

Registers of Scotland
General Register of Sasines
County of Lanark Book 14139 Folio 215
Presented and recorded 28 December 1983

This is the plan referred to in the foregoing Feu Disposition by County Developments Limited in favour of Edward Fox and Mrs Grace Hunter or Fox.

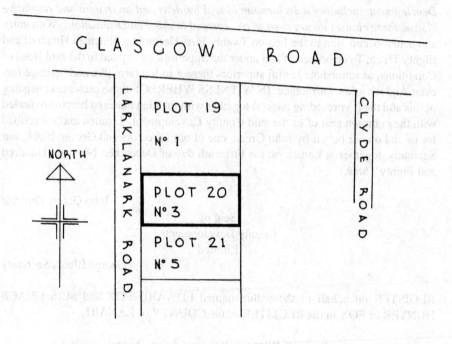

Seal of
County Developments
Limited

John Green, Director
George Black, Secretary

5. Standard Security by Edward Fox and Mrs Grace Hunter or Fox in favour of the Larklanark Building Society

Note
Building Societies normally use a boxed style of Standard Security, as in this illustration. For alternative styles, see the Conveyancing and Feudal Reform (Scotland) Act 1970, Schedule 2, Forms A and B; styles in I J S Talman (ed) Halliday's Conveyancing Law and Practice in Scotland (2nd edn, 2 volumes, 1996–97); and the Diploma Styles.

Stamp Duty: Nil

The expressions set out below shall have the meanings and effects respectively set opposite them:

The Borrower	EDWARD FOX and MRS GRACE HUNTER or FOX, both sometime residing at Sixteen Glasgow Road, Lanark and now at Three Larklanark Road there
The Guarantor	None
	Where the Borrower or the Guarantor is more than one person, the singular includes the plural and all obligations of the Borrower and the Guarantor are undertaken jointly and severally
The Society	The Larklanark Building Society having its Chief Office at Four Glasgow Square, Lanark
The Advance	Fifty Thousand Pounds (£50,000) Sterling
The Advance Date	Fifteenth January, Nineteen Hundred and Eighty Four
The Interest Rate	10 per cent per annum or such other rate as may be fixed by the Society from time to time in terms of its Rules
The Property	Dwellinghouse No. 3 Larklanark Road, Lanark, being the subjects herinafter described

The Borrower hereby undertakes to pay to The Society The Advance made on The Advance Date and all other sums due and which may become due by The Borrower to The Society in respect of any further advances to be made by The Society to The Borrower with interest computed in accordance with the practice of The Society at The Interest Rate . . .

Note
Special provisions will normally follow the foregoing undertaking to provide for, inter alia, repayment of capital by instalments, payment of interest and establishing the balance of capital outstanding and due to The Society under the security, together with arrears of interest, at any future date.

For which The Borrower grants a Standard Security in favour of The Society over The Property, being ALL and WHOLE the plot or area of ground with the dwelling-house and others erected thereon known as Three Larklanark Road, Lanark, in the County of Lanark, being the subjects more particularly described in, in feu farm disponed by, and delineated and outlined in red on the plan annexed and executed as relative to, the Feu Disposition by County Developments Limited in favour of The Borrower dated Fifteenth and recorded in the Division of the General Register of Sasines for the County of Lanark on Twenty eighth both days of December, Nineteen hundred and Eighty Three.

The Standard Conditions specified in Schedule 3 to the Conveyancing and Feudal Reform (Scotland) Act 1970 as varied by the Rules of The Society and a Deed of Variation made by The Society dated Sixth and Registered in the Books of Council and Session on Sixteenth June Nineteen Hundred and Seventy One (a copy of which The Borrower hereby acknowledges to have received) and any lawful variation thereof operative for the time being shall apply;

And The Borrower grants warrandice; And The Borrower consents to the registration hereof and of any certificate granted in terms hereof as aforesaid for execution: IN WITNESS WHEREOF these presents, consisting of this and the preceding page, are subscribed by the said Edward Fox and Mrs Grace Hunter or Fox both together at Lanark and on the Fifteenth day of January, Nineteen Hundred and Eighty Four before these witnesses Alan Brown and James Jones, both Solicitors, of Nine Glasgow Square, Lanark.

| Alan Brown | Witness | Edward Fox |
| James Jones | Witness | Grace Fox |

REGISTER on behalf of the within named THE LARKLANARK BUILDING SOCIETY in the REGISTER of the COUNTY of LANARK.

Brown & Jones, Solicitors, Lanark, Agents.

Registers of Scotland
General Register of Sasines
County of Lanark Book 14140 Folio 162
Presented and recorded 20 January 1984

Note
The County of Lanark became an operational area for registration of title on 3 January 1984. The foregoing writ, although granted after the date on which Lanarkshire became operational, is not a writ which would induce first registration and therefore falls to be recorded in the Register of Sasines.

6.   Searches: Property, Personal and Company Registers

𝔖𝔈𝔄𝔯𝔠𝔥 in 𝔕egister
of 𝔠harges
against

COUNTY DEVELOPMENTS LIMITED No. 654321 a

Company incorporated under the Companies Act

and having their Registered Office situated

in Scotland.

From 30 Sept. 1980 Date of Incorpor-
                    ation of Company
To 19 Jany. 1984

_____

Date of Registration

23 March 1981

BOND AND FLOATING CHARGE dated 15 March 1981 by County

Developments Limited,- To Lanarkshire Bank,- of the

whole of the property and undertaking - for securing

all sums due or to become due. Under declaration as to

ranking.

SEARCHED THE REGISTER OF

CHARGES AND FOUND AS ABOVE

N.B. There were no adverse notices on the Company's

File relating to Liquidation, Receivership,

Administration Order, Winding Up or Striking off as at

19 January 1984

Authorised Signatory

Search for Incumbrances Affecting

All and Whole that plot of ground extending to 0.20 hectare, Plot 20 on Plan, together with the dwellinghouse etc. erected thereon known as 3 Larklanark Road, Lanark, being the subjects more particularly described in Feu Disposition by County Developments Limited in favour of Edward Fox and his wife Grace Hunter or Fox dated Fifteenth and recorded in the Division of the General Register of Sasines applicable to the County of Lanark on Twenty eighth both days of December Nineteen hundred and eighty three, which subjects are part of All and Whole 10 hectares of ground, bounded on the north by Glasgow Road, Lanark, described in Feu Charter by Andrew Brown in favour of County Developments Limited dated Tenth and recorded in the said Division of the General Register of sasines on Thirteenth both days of November Nineteen hundred and eighty.

GEN: REG: OF SAS:

From 13 Novr. 1980

To 20 Jany. 1984

FEU CHARTER by Andrew Brown,- To County Developments Limited,- of 10 hectares of ground, bounded on the north by Glasgow Road, Lanark, in Parish of Larklanark, part of the lands and Estate of Larklanark /

2.

Millar & Bryce Limited

Larklanark, reserving Minerals. Dated 10 November 1980.

NOTE:- Superiors interest and burdens, if any, by him or his Authors not traced.

20 June 1981 14134 - 20	DEED OF CONDITIONS by County Developments Limited - Declaring real burdens etc. affecting said 10 hectares of ground. Dated 15 June 1981.
28 Decr. 1983 14139 - 215	FEU DISPOSITION by County Developments Limited,- To Edward Fox and Grace Hunter or Fox, equally and survivor,- of the Subjects of Search. Dated 15 December 1983. NOTE:- Superiors interest not further traced.
20 Jany. 1984 14140 - 162	STANDARD SECURITY for £50,000 and further sums by Edward Fox and Grace Hunter or Fox,- To Larklanark Building Society,- over the Subjects of Search. Dated 15 January 1984.

SEARCHED the General Register of Sasines for the County of Lanark from the Thirteenth day of November Nineteen hundred and eighty to the Twentieth day of January Nineteen hundred and eighty four, both dates inclusive,

Inhibs: over
Page 1

and found as on this and the preceding page.

Authorised Signatory.

SEARCH 239283746   MILLAR & BRYCE LTD   Page 1

SEARCH

IN THE REGISTER OF

INHIBITIONS AND ADJUDICATIONS

AGAINST

COUNTY DEVELOPMENTS LIMITED

EDWARD FOX

GRACE HUNTER OR FOX

From 21 Jany. 1979

To 20 Jany. 1984   2400 HOURS

8302345   5 April 1983
Notice of Letters of Inhibition, Michelangelo
and Partners, Chartered Architects, St. Peter's
Buildings, Rome Square, Glasgow,- against
COUNTY DEVELOPMENTS LIMITED, 1 Glasgow Square,
Lanark. Signetted 5 April 1983. Per L. Sharpe,
Writer, Edinburgh.

8303456   11 April 1983
Letters of Inhibition, Michelangelo and Partners,
Chartered Architects, St. Peter's Buildings,
Rome Square, Glasgow:- against COUNTY
DEVELOPMENTS LIMITED, 1 Glasgow Square,
Lanark. Per L. Sharpe, Writer, Edinburgh.

8306578   25 Octr. 1983
Discharge by Michelangelo and Partners,
Chartered Architects, St. Peter's Buildings,
Rome Square, Glasgow - of Inhibition (recorded
11 April 1983) against COUNTY DEVELOPMENTS
LIMITED, 1 Glasgow Square, Lanark. Per J. Bloggs,
Registers of Scotland.

SEARCHED THE REGISTER OF INHIBITIONS
AND ADJUDICATIONS AND FOUND AS ABOVE

AUTHORISED SIGNATORY.

7.   Death Certificate of Edward Fox (not reproduced here)

8.   Certificate of Confirmation in the estate of the late Mrs Grace Hunter or Fox

Certificate of Confirmation (see the Act of Sederunt (Confirmation of Executors) 1964, SI 1964/1143, Schedule D (as amended by the Act of Sederunt (Confirmation of Executors Amendment) 1971, SI 1971/1164))

<u>Confirmation was issued</u> from the Commissariot of South Strathclyde, Dumfries and Galloway on Twentieth April, Two Thousand and Two in favour of Alan Brown and James Jones, both Solicitors of Nine Glasgow Square, Lanark as executors nominate of Mrs Grace Hunter or Fox sometime of Sixteen Glasgow Road, Lanark and late of Three Larklanark Road, there who died on Tenth March, Two Thousand and Two.

<u>DOMICILED IN SCOTLAND</u>

It is hereby certified that the said Confirmation contained *inter alia* the following item of estate situated in Scotland.

<u>HERITABLE ESTATE IN SCOTLAND</u>

1.   ALL and WHOLE the dwellinghouse and pertinents
      known as Three Larklanark Drive, Lanark.   £145,000

      Given under the seal of office of the Commissariot of South Strathclyde, Dumfries and Galloway and signed by the Clerk of Court at Lanark the Twentieth day of April, Two Thousand and Two.

John Gibson
Sheriff Clerk Depute   Seal

9. Discharge by The Larklanark Building Society in favour of the Executors of the late Mrs Grace Hunter or Fox

(endorsed on the Standard Security: see Writ 5 above)

We, The Larklanark Building Society having our Chief Office at Four Glasgow Square, Lanark IN CONSIDERATION of the sum of FIFTY THOUSAND POUNDS STERLING, being the whole amount secured by the Standard Security aftermentioned, paid to us by Alan Brown and James Jones both Solicitors of Nine Glasgow Square, Lanark, Executors Nominate of the late Mrs Grace Hunter or Fox sometime of Sixteen Glasgow Road, Lanark and late of Three Larklanark Road, Lanark conform to Confirmation in their favour granted by the Sheriff of South Strathclyde, Dumfries and Galloway at Lanark on Twentieth April, Two Thousand and Two Do Hereby Discharge the foregoing Standard Security granted by Edward Fox sometime of Sixteen Glasgow Road aforesaid and late of Three Larklanark Road, aforesaid, and the said Mrs Grace Hunter or Fox in our favour recorded in the Register for the County of Lanark on Twentieth January, Nineteen Hundred and Eighty Four: IN WITNESS WHEREOF these presents partly printed and partly type-written on this page are subscribed for us and on our behalf by David McDonald our Principal Deeds Officer at Lanark on the Thirtieth day of May Two Thousand and Two before the witness, Evelyn Anderson, clerk at our Chief Office at Lanark.

Evelyn Anderson witness

David McDonald
Principal Deeds Officer

REGISTER on behalf of the within named Alan Brown and James Jones as Executors within mentioned in the REGISTER of the COUNTY of LANARK

Brown & Jones, Solicitors, Lanark, Agents

Registers of Scotland
General Register of Sasines
County of Lanark Book 14203 Folio 21
Presented and recorded 3 June 2002

Notes
(1) See Note on the Standard Security (Writ 5 above).
(2) Although this Discharge is endorsed on the Standard Security, the forego-ing information relating to the Standard Security must be inserted in the endorsed Discharge to give the Keeper the required information for pur-poses of recording the Discharge in Sasines.
(3) See Note on Writ 5 as to recording/registration.

10. Missives of Sale and Purchase for Number 3 Larklanark Road, Lanark

Brown & Jones	Our Ref: JK/SR/JDM	King & Co
Solicitors	Your Ref:	Solicitors
9 Glasgow Square		10 Glasgow Square
Lanark		Lanark

12 September 2002

Dear Sirs

Peter Quinn
3 Larklanark Road, Lanark

On behalf of our client Peter Quinn of 20 Clyde Street, Lanark, we hereby offer to purchase from your clients the dwellinghouse known as Three Larklanark Road, Lanark and garden ground pertaining thereto, together with the garage and garden shed at present erected thereon, and that on the following terms and conditions:

1. Price

    The price will be One Hundred and Forty-Five Thousand Pounds (£145,000) Sterling payable on the date of entry hereinafter specified.

2. Fittings and Fixtures

    The purchase price includes all fittings and fixtures in and upon the subjects of sale and any items, the removal of which would cause damage to the fabric of the property, including all growing trees, flowers, plants and shrubs in the garden ground pertaining to the subjects of sale.

3. Entry

    Entry with vacant possession to the whole subjects will be given on Thirty First October 2002 or on such other date as may be mutually agreed.

4. Interest on Price

    It is a material condition of the bargain to follow hereon that (a) the purchase price will be paid on the date of entry and (b) the sellers will give entry with vacant possession to the whole subjects of sale on the date prescribed in Clause 2. Without prejudice to the foregoing, if (but only if) at the date of entry the sellers have (a) implemented all obligations incumbent on them in terms of the bargain to follow hereon and (b) are in a position to give possession of the whole subjects of sale to the purchaser, the purchaser will pay to the sellers interest on any part of the purchase price outstanding at said date at a rate of 4% per annum above the lowest base rate for lending charged by any of the Scottish clearing banks during the period of non-payment (together with any arrangement fee or other charges incurred by the sellers on any borrowing by them necessitated by the purchaser's failure to pay the purchase price timeously); and that notwithstanding consignation and whether or not the purchaser shall have taken occupation of the subjects of sale; and in the event of any part of the purchase price remaining unpaid on the expiry of a period of two weeks form the date of entry, the sellers will be entitled but not obliged, forthwith to resile from said bargain to follow hereon and to resell the subjects of sale on giving written notice to that effect, under reservation of all claims which may be competent to the sellers to recover from the purchaser all loss and damage sustained by the sellers on any such resale and interest as aforesaid.

5. Maintenance, condition and existence of subjects of sale

(i) The sellers will maintain the subjects of sale in their present condition (fair wear and tear excepted) until the purchase price is paid or the purchaser takes possession, whichever date is the earlier. In the event of the subjects being destroyed or materially damaged prior to that date, either party shall be entitled, but not obliged, to resile from the contract to follow hereon with penalty and without prejudice to any entitlement to claim damages from the other party.

(ii) The risk of damage to or destruction of the subjects of sale will remain with the sellers until the purchase price is paid or the purchaser takes possession, whichever date is the earlier.

(iii) The sellers will be responsible for the cost of any repairs to the subjects of sale instructed prior to the date of entry. In addition, and without prejudice to the foregoing, the sellers will be responsible for the cost of any repairs required under Notices issued by the Local Authority or any other competent body prior to the date of entry.

(iv) The central heating system (if any is included in the price) shall be in full working order as at the date of entry. Any material defect in the system as at the date of entry, which is notified to the sellers or their agent within 7 days of the date of entry, will be remedied at the sellers' expense.

(v) The sellers are not aware of the existence in the subjects of sale of woodworm, dry rot, wet rot or rising damp and, in the event that a Guarantee has been issued in respect of any of these, said Guarantee is valid in all respects and the benefit thereof shall be transferred to the purchaser. Further, the said Guarantee, with the specification and estimate to which it refers, shall be delivered at settlement.

6. Roads, sewerage and water supply etc

The sellers will provide at their expense a certificate prior to the date of entry from the appropriate local authority confirming (i) that the roadways, footways, waterchannels and sewers *ex adverso* and serving the subjects of sale have been taken over and are maintained by the local authority (ii) that there are no road proposals which will affect the subjects of sale and (iii) that the subjects of sale are connected to the public water supply and sewer. Furthermore, the sellers warrant that they are not aware of any proposals by or rights in favour of a public or local authority, statutory undertaker or other party which would affect the subjects of sale.

7. Planning etc

The sellers will provide at their expense prior to the date of entry a certificate (dated not earlier than twenty eight days prior to the conclusion of the bargain to follow hereon) from the appropriate local authority confirming that the subjects of sale are (i) in an area designated in the Development Plan primarily for residential purposes; (ii) not adversely affected by any planning schemes, orders, notices or proposals under the Town and Country Planning (Scotland) Acts, Building (Scotland) Acts, the Civic Government (Scotland) Act 1982 or other Statutes; (iii) not included in any proposals or orders under the Housing (Scotland) Acts or other Statutes; (iv) not subject to any such matters which are outstanding in the knowledge of the said local authority; and (v) not designated for compulsory acquisition for any planning purposes of the said local authority. The subjects of sale are not included in a list of buildings of special architectural or historic interest nor located within a conservation area.

8. Amenity and Neighbourhood

The Sellers warrant:

(i) that they are unaware of any proposals by any public or local authority, statutory undertaker or other party which would, in any way, materially and adversely affect the subjects of sale.

(ii) that there are no pecuniary burdens affecting the subjects of sale.

(iii) that the titles do not contain any provisions of an unusual or unduly onerous nature, which materially and adversely affect the said subjects, as to which the purchaser, acting reasonably, shall be the sole judge.

9. Structural alterations etc

If the subjects of sale have been converted or altered in the 20-year period prior to the date of conclusion of the bargain to follow hereon, the sellers will provide at their expense such evidence as may reasonably be required by the purchaser that (i) the relevant works were carried out and completed in conformity with all necessary local authority permissions and warrants, and (ii) all other necessary consents and permissions were obtained and any conditions attaching thereto were fully implemented.

10. NHBC

If the subjects of sale were constructed within ten years prior to the date of conclusion of the bargain to follow hereon a Buildmark 10-year Protection Notice will be delivered at settlement.

11. Title

The sellers will at or prior to settlement deliver or exhibit a good marketable title together with a Form 10 Report brought down to a date as near as practicable to the date of settlement and showing no entries adverse to the sellers' interest, the cost of the said report being the responsibility of the sellers. In addition, the sellers, at or before the Date of Entry and at their expense shall deliver to the purchaser such documents and evidence as the Keeper may require to enable the Keeper to issue a Land Certificate in name of the purchaser as the registered proprietor of the whole subjects of Offer and containing no exclusion of indemnity in terms of Section 12(2) of the Land Registration (Scotland) Act 1979; such documents shall include (unless the whole subjects of Offer only comprise part of a tenement of flatted building) a plan or bounding description sufficient to enable the whole subjects of Offer to be identified on the Ordnance map and evidence (such as a Form P16 Report) that the description of the whole subjects of Offer as contained in the title deed is habile to include the whole of the occupied extent. The Land Certificate to be issued to the purchaser will disclose no entry, deed or diligence prejudicial to the purchaser's interest other than such as are created by or against the purchaser, or have been disclosed to, and accepted by, the purchaser prior to settlement. Notwithstanding the delivery of the Disposition above referred to, this Clause shall remain in full force and effect and may be founded upon until implemented.

12. Mineral reservations

The minerals are included in the purchase price in so far as the sellers have right thereto. In the event of the minerals being reserved to the sellers, the superior or some other third party, the titles of the subjects of sale contain a provision affording full rights of compensation to the proprietor in respect of any surface damage, damage to buildings or other damage occasioned by working of the minerals. In the case of coal and associated minerals, the statutory protection afforded by the Coal Mining Subsidence Act 1991 shall be deemed sufficient protection to the purchaser for the purposes of this clause.

13. Occupancy and other rights

At the date of entry there will be no subsisting occupancy rights of a non-entitled spouse in terms of the Matrimonial Homes (Family Protection) (Scotland) Act 1981, as amended, and the sellers will deliver appropriate evidence to that effect on or before the date of entry.

14. Missives to remain in force

This offer and the missives following hereon will form a continuing and enforceable contract notwithstanding the delivery of the disposition in favour of the purchaser except insofar as fully implemented thereby. Without prejudice to the special provisions in Clause 11 hereof, the missives will cease to be enforceable after a period of two years from the date of delivery of said disposition, except insofar as they are founded upon in any court proceedings which have been commenced within the said period. A clause to his effect will, at the option of the purchaser, be included in the disposition in his favour.

15. Time Limit for Acceptance

This offer is open for acceptance by letter reaching us not later than 5.00 pm on 19 September 2002.

Yours faithfully

(King & Co)

Our Ref: AB/TM
Your Ref: JK/SR/JDM

Brown & Jones
Solicitors
9 Glasgow Square
Lanark

17 September 2002

King & Co
Solicitors
10 Glasgow Square
Lanark

Dear Sirs

Mrs Grace Fox's Executry

Peter Quinn

<u>3 Larklanark Road, Lanark</u>

On behalf of and as instructed by our clients, the executors of Mrs Grace Fox, late of 3 Larklanark Road, Lanark we hereby accept your offer of 12 September 2002 to purchase the above Subjects at the price and on the terms and conditions therein contained but that subject to the following qualification viz:

In Clause 9 of your said offer the period of 10 years shall be substituted for the period of 20 years therein specified.

This qualification is open for immediate acceptance only.

Yours faithfully

(Brown & Jones)

Brown & Jones   Our Ref: JK/SR/JDM   King & Co
Solicitors   Your Ref: AB/TM   Solicitors
9 Glasgow Square   10 Glasgow Square
Lanark   Lanark

18 September 2002

Dear Sirs

Peter Quinn
3 Larklanark Road, Lanark

On behalf of and as instructed by our client, Peter Quinn, we hereby accept the qualification in your letter of 17 September to our offer of 12 September and hold the
bargain as concluded in terms of those two letters and this letter.

Yours faithfully

(King & Co)

11. Disposition by the Executors of Mrs Grace Hunter or Fox in favour of Peter Quinn

STAMP DUTY: £1,450

We, Alan Brown and James Jones both Solicitors and both of Nine Glasgow Square, Lanark Executors Nominate of the deceased Mrs Grace Hunter or Fox sometime of Sixteen Glasgow Road, Lanark and late of Three Larklanark Road, Lanark conform to Confirmation in our favour as Executors aforesaid issued from the Commissariot of South Strathclyde, Dumfries and Galloway at Lanark on Twentieth April, Two Thousand and Two and as such Executors, uninfeft proprietors of the subjects and others hereinafter disponed; IN CONSIDERATION of the sum of One Hundred and Forty Five Thousand pounds (£145,000) Sterling now paid to us as Executors aforesaid by Peter Quinn of Twenty Clyde Street, Lanark of which sum we hereby acknowledge receipt, HAVE SOLD and do hereby DISPONE to and in favour of the said Peter Quinn and his Executors and Assignees whomsoever heritably and irredeemably ALL and WHOLE the dwellinghouse and pertinents known as and forming Three Larklanark Road, Lanark in the County of Lanark being the subjects more particularly described in, in feu farm disponed by, and delineated and outlined in red on the plan annexed and executed as relative to, the Feu Disposition by County Developments Limited in favour of Edward Fox and another dated Fifteenth and recorded in the Division of the General Register of Sasines for the County of Lanark on Twenty eighth both days of December Nineteen Hundred and Eighty Three TOGETHER WITH (One) the whole fittings and fixtures therein and thereon (Two) the whole parts, privileges and pertinents of the said subjects hereinbefore disponed and (Three) our whole right title and interest present and future as Executors aforesaid in and to the said subjects; BUT ALWAYS WITH and UNDER *(here refer to prior writs for burdens as in the Feu Disposition No. 4 hereof. Since there are no additional burdens in that Feu Disposition, it need not be referred to)*; WITH ENTRY and vacant possession on the Thirty First October Two Thousand and Two; which said subjects hereinbefore disponed were last vested in the said Mrs Grace Hunter or Fox; and from whom we acquired right as Executors aforesaid by the said Confirmation in our favour; and we, as Executors aforesaid, grant warrandice from our own facts and deeds only and, in so far as we can competently do so, we bind the beneficiaries entitled to the estate of said Mrs Grace Hunter or Fox in absolute warrandice: IN WITNESS WHEREOF these presents are subscribed by us the said Alan Brown and James Jones as Executors aforesaid both together at Lanark on the Twenty Seventh day of October, Two

Thousand and Two before the witness hereto subscribing whose designation is appended below his signature.

Witness	A Smith	Alan Brown
Address	9 Glasgow Square, Lanark	
Designation	Secretary	James Jones

Note

No Warrant of Registration is required on this Writ because it induces first registration. The relevant application forms 1 and 4 follow.

12. Application Form 10 and Form 10A Report thereon

REGISTERS OF SCOTLAND EXECUTIVE AGENCY **FORM 10**
(Land Registration (Scotland) Rules 1980 Rule 24(1))

APPLICATION FOR A REPORT PRIOR TO REGISTRATION OF THE SUBJECTS DESCRIBED BELOW
Note: No covering letter is required and an existing Search should not be submitted.

Please complete in DUPLICATE

VAT Reg No. GD 410
GB 888 8410 64

FOR OFFICIAL USE
REPORT NUMBER
DATE OF RECEIPT
SEARCH SHEET NOS.
FEE

FROM King & Co.
Solicitors
10 Glasgow Square
LANARK

DX 570829
LANARK

TO
Keeper of the Registers of Scotland

Meadowbank House
153 London Road
EDINBURGH EH8 7AU

Telephone: 0131 659 6111

County LANARK

Applicant's Reference JK/SR/JDM

FAS No. 1234

Telephone No. 01555 875436

FAX No. 01555 875346

FAX response required [ ] X here

Postal Address of Subjects

| Street No. | 3 | House Name | | Street Name | Larklanark Road |
| Town | Lanark | | | Post code | ML11 0TX |

Other: Description of Subjects

The above subjects being edged red on the accompanying plan [1,2]
being (part of) the subjects described in [1,3]

Feu Disposition by County Developments Limited in favour
of Mr and Mrs Edward Fox and the survivor recorded GRS
Lanark 28 December 1983.

I/We apply for a report

(1) on the subjects described above, for which an application for registration in the Land Register is to be made, from

(a) the **REGISTER OF SASINES** and

(b) the **LAND REGISTER** stating whether or not registration of the said subjects has been effected [4]

1. Delete if inapplicable
2. A plan need not be attached if a verbal description will sufficiently identify the subjects
3. Describe by reference to a writ recorded in the Register of Sasines
4. If the subjects have been registered, the Keeper will supply an Office Copy of the Title Sheet only on specific request.
Faxed applications should not be followed up by a written request and may not be accepted if a plan is included.

and (2) from the Registers of Inhibitions and Adjudications for 5 years prior to the date of Certificate against

1. Surname(s)

Fox

Forename(s)

Grace

Address(es)

Latterly of 3 Larklanark Road, Lanark

2. Surname(s)

Fox

Forename(s)

Grace, Exors of

Address(es)

3. Surname(s)

Forename(s)

Address(es)

4. Surname(s)

Forename(s)

Address(es)

5. Company/ Firm/ Corporate body

Address(es)

6. Company/ Firm/ Corporate body

Address(es)

Note: Insert full names and addresses of the persons on whom a Report is required.

Signature: _____

Date: _____

Form 10A

REGISTERS OF SCOTLAND
(Land Registration (Scotland) Rules 1980 Rule 24(1))
REPORT PRIOR TO REGISTRATION

Report No.

4415/LAN/02

REGISTER OF SASINES

1. Prescriptive progress of titles

Deed	Recording date

Feu Charter — County Developments Ltd. — 13 Nov. 1980

Feu Disposition — Edward Fox and another — 28 Dec. 1983

2. Statement of Securities recorded within 40 years prior to the date of certificate and for which no final Discharge has been recorded.

No deed.

3. Statement of Discharges (of Securities) recorded within the 5 years prior to the date of the certificate.

Discharge — Fox/Larklanark Building Society — 3 Jun. 2002

4. Deeds, other than transfers or deeds creating or affecting securities, recorded within the 40 years prior to the date of the certificate.

Deed of Conditions — County Developments Ltd. — 20 Jun. 1981

Certified correct to   10 September 2002   Initials XY

LAND REGISTER

The subjects have not been registered

~~The subjects have been registered under Title Number~~ ....

~~An Office Copy is enclosed as requested~~

~~The subjects are in course of being registered under Title Number~~ ....

~~An Office Copy will be sent in due course~~

Certified correct to   10 September 2002   Initials XY

REGISTER OF INHIBITIONS AND ADJUDICATIONS

FOR OFFICIAL USE

Nat. Grid ref.

See Report annexed

No deed to 10 Sep. 2002

13. Application Form 1 for registration of the Disposition and Inventory of Writs Form 4

REGISTERS OF SCOTLAND EXECUTIVE AGENCY   **FORM 1**   *Please complete in BLACK TYPE*   Typewriter Alignment Box
(Land Registration (Scotland) Rules 1980 Rule 9(1)(a))   No covering letter is required   Type XXX in centre

APPLICATION FOR FIRST REGISTRATION

1 Presenting Agent. Name and Address (see Note 1)

King & Co
Solicitors
10 Glasgow Square
LANARK   DX 570829   Lanark   **Part A**

Keeper of the Registers of Scotland
Meadowbank House
153 London Road
EDINBURGH EH8 7AU
Telephone: 0131 659 6111

2 FAS No. (see Note 2)	**3 Agent's Tel No.** (include STD Code)	**4 Agent's Reference**
1234	01555 875436	JK/SR/JDM

5 Name of Deed in respect of which registration is required

Disposition

6 County (see Note 3)   Mark X in box if more than one county

LANARK

7 Subjects (see Note 4)

Street No.	3	Street Name	Larklanark Road
Town	Lanark		
Other		Post code	ML11 0TX

8 Name and Address of Applicant (see Note 5)

1. Surname   Quinn   Forename(s)   Peter

Address   20 Clyde Street, Lanark

2. Surname   Forename(s)

Address

and/ or company/ firm or council, etc.   Mark X in box if more than 2 applicants

Address

9 Granter/Party Last Infeft (see Note 6)

1. Surname   Fox   Forename(s)   Grace (Party Last Infeft)

2. Surname   Forename(s)

and/ or company/ firm or council, etc.   Mark X in box if more than 2 granters

10 Consideration (see Note 7)	**Value** (see Note 8)	**Fee** (see Note 9)	**Date of Entry**
£145,000.00		A £319.00	

11 If a Form 10 Report has been issued in connection with this Application, please quote Report No.   4415/LAN/02

12 I/ We apply for registration in respect of Deed(s) No 8 in the Inventory of Writs (Form 4). I/ We certify that the information supplied in this application is correct to the best of my/our knowledge and belief.

FOR OFFICIAL USE

Signature   Date

Notes 1-9 referred to are contained in Notes and Directions for completion of Applications for First Registration

PART B

Delete **YES** or **NO** as appropriate
N.B. If more space is required for any section of this form, a separate sheet, or separate sheets, may be added.

---

1. Do the deeds submitted in support of this application include a plan illustrating the extent of the subjects to be registered?
    If **YES**, please specify the deed and its Form 4 Inventory number:
    Feu Disposition by County Developments Limited in favour of Mr & Mrs Edward Fox – Item No. 3 on Form 4

    If **NO**, have you submitted a deed containing a full bounding description with measurements?

    If **YES**, please specify the deed and its Form 4 Inventory number:

    N.B. If the answer to both the above questions is NO then, unless the property is part of a tenement or flatted building you must submit a plan of the subjects properly drawn to a stated scale and showing sufficient surrounding features to enable it to be located on the Ordnance Map. The plan should bear a docquet, signed by the person signing the Application Form, to the effect that it is a plan of the subjects sought to be registered under the attached application.

    YES/~~NO~~

    ~~YES~~/NO

---

2. Is a Form P16 Report issued by the Keeper confirming that the boundaries of the subjects coincide with the Ordnance Map being submitted in support of this Application?

    If **NO**, does the legal extent depicted in the plans or descriptions in the deeds submitted in support of the Application cohere with the occupational extent?

    If **NO**, please advise:-

    (a) the approximate age and nature of the occupational boundaries, or

    (b) whether, if the extent of the subjects as defined in the deeds is larger than the occupational extent, the applicant is prepared to accept the occupational extent as viewed, or

    (c) whether, if the extent of the subjects as defined in the deeds is smaller than the occupational extent, any remedial action has been taken.

    YES/~~NO~~

    YES/NO

    YES/NO

    YES/NO

---

3. Is there any person in possession or occupation of the subjects or any part of them adversely to the interest of the applicant?
    If **YES**, please give details:

    ~~YES~~/NO

---

4. If the subjects were acquired by the applicant under any statutory provision, does the statutory provision restrict the applicant's power of disposal of the subjects?
    If **YES**, please indicate the statute:

    YES/NO
    N/A

---

5. (a) Are there any charges affecting the subjects or any part of them, except as stated in the Schedule of Heritable Securities etc. on page 4 of this application?
    If **YES**, please give details:

    ~~YES~~/NO

    (b) Apart from overriding interests are there any burdens affecting the subjects or any part of them, except as stated in the Schedule of Burdens on page 4 of this application?
    If **YES**, please give details:

    ~~YES~~/NO

(c) Are there any overriding interests affecting the subjects or any part of them which you wish noted on the Title Sheet?
If **YES**, please give details:

~~YES~~/NO

(d) Are there any recurrent monetary payments (e.g. feuduty, leasehold casualties) exigible from the subjects or any part of them?
If **YES**, please give details:
Variable annual service charge to Superiors/Feuars Association under Deed of Conditions Item Number 2 on Form 4

YES/~~NO~~

6. Where any party to the deed inducing registration is a Company registered under the Companies Acts
    Has a receiver or liquidator been appointed?
    If **YES**, please give details:

N/A
YES/NO

    If **NO**, has any resolution been passed or court order made for the winding up of the Company or petition presented forits liquidafion?
    If **YES**, please give details:

YES/NO

7. Where any party to the deed inducing registration is a Company registered under the Companies Acts can you confirm

N/A

(a) that it is not a charity as defined in section 112 of the Companies Act 1989 and

YES/NO

(b) that the transaction to which the deed gives effect is not one to which section 322A of the Companies Act 1985 (as inserted by section-109 of the Companies Act 1989) applies?

YES/NO

Where the answer to either branch of the question is **NO**, please give details:

8. Where any party to the deed inducing registration is a corporate body other than a Company registered under the Companies Acts

N/A

(a) Is it acting *intra vires?*
If **NO**, please give details:

YES/NO

(b) Has any arrangement been put in hand for the dissolution of any such corporate body?
If **YES**, please give details:

YES/NO

9. Are *all* the necessary consents, renunciations or affidavits in terms of section 6 of the Matrimonial Homes (Family Protection)(Scotland) Act 1981 being submitted in connection with this application?

YES/~~NO~~

N.B. If sufficient evidence to satisfy the keeper that there are no subsisting occupancy rights in the subjects of this application is not submitted with the application then the statement by the keeper in terms of rule 5(j) of the Land Registration (Scotland) Rules 1980 will not be inserted in the Title Sheet or will be qualified as appropriate without further enquiry by the Keeper.

10. Where the deed inducing registration is in implement of the exercise of a power of sale under a heritable security

N/A

Have the statutory procedures necessary for the proper exercise of such power been complied with?

YES/NO

---

11. Where the deed inducing registration is a General Vesting Declaration or a Notice of Title pursuant on a Compulsory Purchase Order

N/A

Have the necessary statutory procedures been complied with?

YES/NO

---

12. Is any party to the deed inducing registration subject to any legal incapacity or disability?
If **YES**, please give details:

~~YES~~/NO

---

13. Are the deeds and documents detailed in the Inventory (Form 4) all the deeds and documents relevant to the title?
If **NO**, please give details:

YES/~~NO~~

---

14. Are there any facts and circumstances material to the right or title of the applicant which have not already been disclosed in this application or its accompanying documents?
If **YES**, please give details:

~~YES~~/NO

SCHEDULE OF HERITABLE SECURITIES ETC.
N.B. New Charges granted by the applicant should not be included

As per Item Number 4 on Form 4.

SCHEDULE OF BURDENS

As per Item Numbers 1, 2 and 3 on Form 4.

REGISTERS OF SCOTLAND EXECUTIVE AGENCY
(Land Registration (Scotland) Rules 1980 Rule 9(2))

FORM 4

Typewriter Alignment Box
Type XXX in centre

INVENTORY OF WRITS RELEVANT TO APPLICATION FOR REGISTRATION *(see Note 1)*
(to be completed in duplicate)

King & Co
Solicitors
10 Glasgow Square
LANARK

DX 570829 Lanark

FAS 1234

(see Note 2)

Title Number(s)
(to be completed for a dealing with
registered interests in land.)

Subjects *(see Note 3)*   3 Larklanark Road, Lanark

Registration County   LANARK

Applicant's Reference   JK/SR/JDM

Please complete Inventory overleaf as in this specimen

Item No.	Please mark "S" against writs submitted	Particulars of Writs *(see Note 4)*		
		Writ	Grantee	Date of Recording
		Land Certificate*		
		Charge Certificate*		
1	-	Feu Charter	Upright Builders Ltd	2 May 1938
2	S	Feu Disposition	Smith	4 Feb 1939

* Delete if inapplicable

Notes 1-4 referred to are contained in Notes and Directions for Completion of Inventory of Writs Relevant to Application for Registration.

FOR OFFICIAL USE ONLY

APPLICATION NUMBER	**DATE OF RECEIPT**	**TITLE NUMBER**

The writs marked "S" on this inventory were received on the Date of Receipt stamped on this page.

INVENTORY

Particulars of Writs *(see Note 4)*

Typewriter Alignment Box
Type XXX in centre

Please mark "S" against writs submitted

Item No.		Writ		Grantee	Date of Recording
		~~XXXXXXXXXX~~*			
		~~Charge Certificate~~*			
1.	S	Feu Charter		County Developments Limited	13 NOV 1980
2.	S	Deed of Conditions			20 JUN 1981
3.	S	Feu Disposition		Mr and Mrs Edward Fox	28 DEC 1983
4.	S	Standard Security		Larklanark Building Society	20 JAN 1984
5.	S	Death Certificate of Edward Fox			
6.	S	Certificate of Confirmation		Fox's Executry	
7.	S	Discharge of No. 4 hereof		Executors of the late Mrs Grace Fox	03 JUN 2002
8.	S	Disposition		Peter Quinn	
Note:		Of the foregoing 10 Writs in this progress of Titles No: 2 - The Floating Charge and No: 9 - the Missives are not included in the foregoing Inventory Form 4 not being registrable or relevant to the Keeper's examination of the title.			

* delete if inapplicable

14. Land Certificate for 3 Larklanark Road, Lanark

(Land Registration (Scotland) Rules 1980, Rule 14)

LAND REGISTER OF SCOTLAND

LAND
CERTIFICATE

Title Number: LAN91460

Subjects: 3 LARKLANARK ROAD. LANARK

This Land Certificate, issued pursuant to section 5(2) of the Land Registration (Scotland) Act 1979, is a copy of the Title Sheet relating to the above subjects.

STATEMENT OF INDEMNITY

Subject to any specific qualifications entered in the Title Sheet of which this Land Certificate is a copy, a person who suffers loss as a result of the events specified in section 12(1) of the above Act shall be entitled to be indemnified in respect of that loss by the Keeper of the Registers of Scotland in terms of that Act.

ATTENTION IS DRAWN TO THE NOTICE AND GENERAL INFORMATION OVERLEAF.

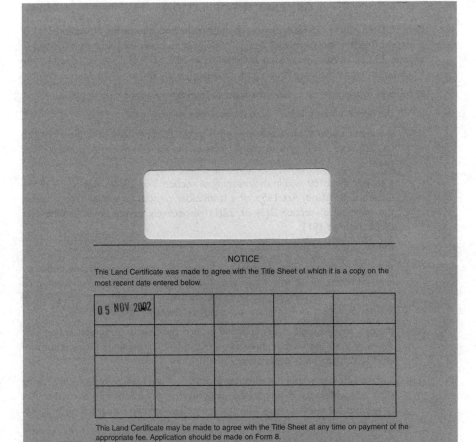

NOTICE

This Land Certificate was made to agree with the Title Sheet of which it is a copy on the most recent date entered below.

0 5 NOV 2002				

This Land Certificate may be made to agree with the Title Sheet at any time on payment of the appropriate fee. Application should be made on Form 8.

GENERAL INFORMATION

1.   OVERRIDING INTERESTS. A registered interest in land is in terms of section 3(1) of the Land Registration (Scotland) Act 1979 subject to overriding interests defined in section 28 of that Act (hereinafter referred to as "the 1979 Act") as amended by the Matrimonial Homes (Family Protection) (Scotland) Act 1981 as:

in relation to any interest in land, the right or interest over it of

(a)   the lessee under a lease which is not a long lease;

(b)   the lessee under a long lease who, prior to the commencement of the 1979 Act, has acquired a real right to the subjects of the lease by virtue of possession of them;

(c)   a crofter or cottar within the meaning of section 3 or 28(4) respectively of the Crofters (Scotland) Act 1955, or a landholder or statutory small tenant within the meaning of section 2(2) or 32(1) respectively of the Small Landholders (Scotland) Act 1911;

(d)   the proprietor of the dominant tenement in a servitude;

(e)   the Crown or any Government or other public department, or any public or local authority, under any enactment or rule of law, other than an enactment or rule of law authorising or requiring the recording of a deed in the Register of Sasines or registration in order to complete the right of interest;

(ee)   the operator having a right conferred in accordance with paragraph 2, 3 or 5 or schedule 2 to the Telecommunications Act 1984 (agreements for execution of works, obstruction of access, etc);

(ef)   a licence-holder within the meaning of Part I of the Electricity Act 1989 having such a wayleave as is mentioned in paragraph 6 of Schedule 4 to that Act (wayleaves for electric lines), whether granted under that paragraph or by agreement between the parties;

(eg)   a licence-holder within the meaning of Part I of the Electricity Act 1989 who is authorised by virtue of paragraph 1 of Schedule 5 to that Act to abstract, divert and use water for a generating station wholly or mainly driven by water;

(eh)   insofar as it is an interest vesting by virtue of section 7(3) of the Coal Industry Act 1994, the Coal Authority;

(f)   the holder of a floating charge whether or not the charge has attached to the interest;

(g)   a member of the public in respect of any public right of way or in respect of any right held inalienably by the Crown in trust for the public;

(gg)   the non-entitled spouse within the meaning of section 6 of the Matrimonial Homes (Family Protection) (Scotland) Act 1981;

(h)   any person, being a right which has been made real, otherwise than by the recording of a deed in the Registrer of Sasines or by registration; or

(i)   any other person under any rule of law relating to common interest or joint or common property, not being a right or interest constituting a real right, burden or condition entered in the title sheet of the interest in land under section

6(1)(e) of the 1979 Act or having effect by virtue of a deed recorded in the Register of Sasines,

but does not include any subsisting burden or condition enforceable against the interest in land and entered in its title sheet under section 6(1) of the 1979 Act.

2.   THE USE OF ARROWS ON TITLE PLANS

(a)   Where a deed states the line of a boundary in relation to a physical object, e.g. the centre line, that line is indicated on the Title Plan, either by means of a black arrow or verbally.

(b)   An arrow across the object indicates that the boundary is stated to be the centre line.

(c)   An arrow pointing to the object indicates that the boundary is stated to be the face of the object to which the arrow points.

(d)   The physical object presently shown on the Plan may not be the one referred to in the deed. Indemnity is therefore excluded in respect of information as to the line of the boundary.

3.   Lineal measurement shown in figures on title plans are subject to the qualification "or thereby". Indemnity is excluded in respect of such measurements.

4.   SUBMISSION OF LAND CERTIFICATE WITH SUBSEQUENT APPLICATIONS FOR REGISTRATION

In terms of Rule 9(3), this Land Certificate should be submitted to the Keeper of the Registers of Scotland with any application for registration.

5.   CAUTION. No unauthorised alteration to this Land Certificate should be made.

	Officer's ID / Date	TITLE NUMBER
LAND REGISTER OF SCOTLAND	3174 7/7/2003	**LAN91460**
ORDNANCE SURVEY NATIONAL GRID REFERENCE		Scale
		1/1250
		Survey Scale
NS8942 NS8943		1/2500

CROWN COPYRIGHT © – This copy has been produced from the ROS Digital Mapping System on 07/07/2003 and was made with the authority of Ordnance Survey pursuant to Section 47 of the Copyright, Designs and Patents Act 1988. Unless that act provides a relevant exception to copyright, the copy must not be copied without the prior permission of the copyright owner.

LAND REGISTER OF SCOTLAND

TITLE NUMBER LAN91460   **A 1**

A. PROPERTY SECTION

DATE OF FIRST REGISTRATION
05 NOV 2002

DATE TITLE SHEET UPDATED TO
05 NOV 2002

DATE LAND CERTIFICATE UPDATED TO
05 NOV 2002

INTEREST
PROPRIETOR

MAP REFERENCE
NS9239

DESCRIPTION

Subjects 3 LARKLANARK ROAD, LANARK ML11 9XN edged red on the Title
Plan; Together with a right in common with all other proprietors of
every part of the Glasgow Road Development, to the common parts of the
said Development as described in the Deed of Conditions in Entry 2 of
the Burdens Section.

LAND REGISTER OF SCOTLAND

TITLE NUMBER LAN91460

B 1

B. PROPRIETORSHIP SECTION

ENTRY NO	PROPRIETOR		
1	PETER QUINN 20 Clyde Street, Lanark.	**DATE OF REGISTRATION** 05 NOV 2002	**CONSIDERATION** £145,000
			DATE OF ENTRY 31 OCT 2002

Note: There are in respect of the subjects in
this title no subsisting occupancy
rights, in terms of the Matrimonial Homes
(Family Protection) (Scotland) Act 1981,
of spouses of persons who were formerly
entitled to the said subjects.

LAND REGISTER OF SCOTLAND

TITLE NUMBER LAN91460   C 1

C. CHARGES SECTION

ENTRY NO	SPECIFICATION	DATE OF REGISTRATION
1	Standard Security for £120,000 and further sums by PETER QUINN to ALLIANCE & LEICESTER PLC incorporated under the Companies Act and having its Customer Service Centre at Narborough, Leicester.	5 Nov 2002

LAND REGISTER OF SCOTLAND

TITLE NUMBER LAN91460　　　　　　　　　　**D 1**

D. BURDENS SECTION

ENTRY NO	SPECIFICATION
1	Feu Charter by Andrew Brown (who and whose successors are hereinafter referred to as "the Superiors") to County Developments Limited and their successors and assignees (hereinafter referred to as "the Feuars"), recorded G.R.S. (Lanark) 13 Nov. 1980, of 10 hectares of ground ("the Feu") of which the subjects in this Title form part, contains the following burdens:

(First) the Feuars shall be bound in all time coming to maintain in good order and repair, and whenever necessary to re-erect or reconstruct with the like materials, the whole of the stone wall extending along the north boundary of the Feu except for that part thereof to be demolished in order to give access to the Feu from Glasgow Road, Lanark as hereinafter provided: (Second) .... Note: The burdens which are set out in the said Feu Charter No.1 above will be repeated here.

2　Deed of Conditions, recorded G.R.S. (Lanark) 20 Jun. 1981, by County Developments Limited, proprietors of 10 hectares of ground, of which the subjects in this Title form part, contains burdens &c. in the following terms:

CONSIDERING that we intend to develop the said subjects by the erection of villa dwellinghouses thereon and to dispone the same to individual purchasers and that it is desirable to execute these presents in order to define the rights, interests, obligations and liabilities of the proprietor of each individual dwellinghouse to be erected on the said subjects; THEREFORE we do hereby declare and provide as follows; FIRST: Definitions: In this deed, unless the context otherwise requires, the following expressions shall have the following meanings respectively, viz: "the Development" means the said area of ground extending to ten hectares or thereby; "the Superiors" means us and our successors as proprietors for the time being of the plenum dominium of the development or so much thereof as has not been feued and of the dominium directum of those parts or the whole of the development which, at the relevant date, have been feued; SECOND: Each of the dwellinghouses erected on the Development shall be used in all time coming as a private residence for use by one family only and for no other purpose whatsoever. Note: The burdens which are referred to in the said Deed of Conditions No.2

LAND REGISTER OF SCOTLAND

TITLE NUMBER LAN91460   **D 2**

D. BURDENS SECTION

ENTRY NO	SPECIFICATION

above will be set out in full here.

3   Feu Disposition by County Developments Limited to Edward Fox and Grace Hunter or Fox, recorded G.R.S. (Lanark) 28 Dec. 1983, of the subjects in this Title, contains no further burdens.

15. Charge Certificate for 3 Larklanark Road, Lanark

(Land Registration (Scotland) Rules 1980, Rule 15)

LAND REGISTER OF SCOTLAND

CHARGE CERTIFICATE

Title Number: LAN91460

Subjects: 3 LARKLANARK ROAD, LANARK

The within-mentioned Charge has been registered against the subjects in the above title

STATEMENT OF INDEMNITY

Subject to any specific qualifications entered in the Title Sheet of which the Charge Certificate relates a person who suffers loss as a result of the events specified in section 12(1) of the Land Registration (Scotland) Act 1979 shall be entitled to be indemnified in respect of that loss by the Keeper of the Registers of Scotland in terms of that Act.

NOTICE

1.   This Certificate must be presented to the Keeper on every transaction affecting the interest of the within-mentioned Register Creditor.

2.   The relative Title Sheet contains a specification of the reservations and burdens affecting the subjects in the above title. An Office Copy of the Title Sheet may be obtained on application to the Keeper.

3.   No unauthorised alterations to this Charge Certificate should be made.

NOTICE

This Charge Certificate was made to agree with the Title Sheet to which it relates on the most recent date entered below.

0 5 NOV 2002				

This Charge Certificate may be made to agree with the Title Sheet at any time on payment of the appropriate fee. Application should be made on Form 8.

LAND REGISTER OF SCOTLAND

CHARGE CERTIFICATE

TITLE NO: LAN91460

SUBJECTS: 3 LARKLANARK ROAD, LANARK

REGISTERED PROPRIETOR OF SUBJECTS
          Peter Quinn, 20 Clyde Street, Lanark.

THIS IS TO CERTIFY THAT ALLIANCE & LEICESTER PLC incorporated under the Companies Act, having its Customer Services Centre at Narborough, Leicester is the Registered Creditor in the heritable security attached.

Registered on 5 Nov 2002

Note: There are no heritable securities ranking prior to or pari passu with the above mentioned heritable security appearing on the register affecting the subjects

CC 1

Alliance & Leicester plc
SCOTLAND

Standard Security

Account No	1234567890123

I, the Borrower described below, whereas the expressions set out below shall have the meaning respectively set opposite them:

The Borrower:
PETER QUINN residing at 20 Clyde Street, Lanark

The Owner: the said —
Peter Quinn

The Guarantor (if any): Not applicable

Where any Borrower or Owner or Guarantor is more than one person the singular includes the plural and all obligations of the Borrower or the Owner or the Guarantor are undertaken jointly and severally which means that if there is more than one person named the obligations apply to all the persons together and to each of the persons on their own

The Lender:	Alliance & Leicester plc, incorporated under the Companies Acts and having its Customer Services Centre at Narborough, Leicester, LE9 5XX
The Offer of Loan:	The offer from the Lender to the Borrower to make the Loan
The Loan:	£120,000 The Loan Date: 31 October 2002
The Property: (Postal Address)	3 Larklanark Road, Lanark Being the subjects hereinafter described
The Mortgage Conditions:	Alliance & Leicester Mortgage Conditions 1997 (Scotland) dated Thirteenth and registered in the Books of Council and Session on Fourteenth both days of March Nineteen Hundred and Ninety Seven, receipt of a copy of which is acknowledged by the granters hereof

Hereby undertake to pay to the Lender the Loan and other sums due, in accordance with the Offer of Loan and the Mortgage Conditions, made or about to be made by the Lender to me and all other sums due and that may become due by me to the Lender in terms of this Standard Security or in respect of any further loan or other obligations for which I am or may become liable or responsible to the Lender in any way with interest computed in accordance with the Offer of Loan or the practice of the Lender and I agree that a Certificate signed by an Official of the Lender duly authorised for that purpose shall be sufficient to ascertain and constitute conclusively the amount due by me to the Lender at the date of the Certificate; for which the Owner grants a Standard Security in favour of the Lender over the Property being ALL and WHOLE the subjects known as and forming 3 Larklanark Road, Lanark and being the whole subjects registered in the Land Register under Title Number LAN91460.

And the Guarantor undertakes for himself and his executors the obligations to the Lender specified in this Standard Security and in the Mortgage Conditions specified in Schedule 3 to the Conveyancing and Feudal Reform (Scotland) Act 1970 as varied by the Offer of Loan and Mortgage Conditions and any lawful variation thereof operative for the time being shall apply to this Standard Security; and the owner grants warrandice; and the whole granters hereof consent to the registration hereof and of any such Certificate as aforesaid for execution: IN WITNESS WHEREOF these presents partly printed and partly typewritten on this and the two preceding pages are subscribed by me the said Peter Quinn at Glasgow on the thirty first day of October, Two thousand and two in the presence of Alan Tyre, Solicitor, 2002 Park Circus, Glasgow.

Alan Tyre (witness)   P Quinn

REGISTER on behalf of the within named ALLIANCE & LEICESTER plc in the REGISTER of the COUNTY of

Agents

NOTE TO GUARANTORS(S) – By signing this Standard Security, you may become liable instead of or as well as the Borrower for all the money owing under this Standard Security. You are advised to take independent legal advice before signing.

16. Disposition by Peter Quinn in favour of Clinton Blair

I, Peter Quinn, formerly of Twenty Clyde Street, Lanark and now of Three Larklanark Road, Lanark, in consideration of the price of One Hundred and Seventy Thousand pounds, hereby dispone to Clinton Blair of Sixteen Bush Drive, Lanark All and Whole the subjects Three Larklanark Road, Lanark registered under title number LAN91460; with entry as at First September Two Thousand and Three; and I grant warrandice: IN WITNESS WHEREOF subscribed by me at Lanark on Thirtieth August Two Thousand and Three before the witness, Campbell Brown of Fourteen Clyde Street, Lanark.

C Brown (Witness)   Peter Quinn

This illustrates the form of Disposition for transfer of a registered interest. No warrant of registration is necessary. Note that a stamp clause would be inserted if required, as here. The stamp duty payable on this Disposition was £1,700.

Appendix B

Agricultural lease

Note
This style, which is reproduced with kind permission of the Law Society of Scotland from 'Workshop' July 1980, is for illustrative purposes only. It will require adaptation for use in practice. It pre-dates the Agricultural Holdings (Scotland) Act 2003.

LEASE

between

[insert name]

(who and whose successors as Landlord under this Lease are hereinafter referred to as 'the Landlord')

and

[insert name]

(hereinafter referred to as 'the Tenant')

IT IS AGREED between the parties hereto as follows:

The Landlord in consideration of the rent and other benefits and with and under the reservations, conditions and others hereinafter specified, hereby LETS to the Tenant, excluding successors, assignees and sub-tenants whether legal or conventional without the written consent of the Landlord ALL and WHOLE the Farm of

extending to   all as
delineated on the plan thereof annexed and signed as relative hereto together with the farmhouse and all other buildings thereon (which subjects are hereinafter referred to as 'the Farm').

The Farm is let from   for a period
of
The yearly rent payable by the Tenant will initially be   payable in

equal instalments at Fifteenth May and Eleventh[1] November in each year, beginning the first payment at
for the term preceding
and the next payment at
and so forth half-yearly thereafter with interest on any sum outstanding (whether in respect of rent or otherwise) at a rate three percentage points above the Base Rate of the   Bank of
in force from time to time. The Landlord will not at any time be barred from claiming damages from the Tenant for failure to implement any obligation under this Lease by reason of the fact that the rent may have been accepted by the Landlord.

The rent will be subject to review every three years, the first review date being   and the subsequent review dates occurring at intervals of three[2] years thereafter. The new rent (which will take effect from the relevant review date) will be fixed by agreement between the Landlord and the Tenant, failing which by arbitration.

RESERVATIONS
There are reserved to the Landlord:

(A) the whole ores, minerals and mineral substances, whether metalliferous or not, including precious and other metals, and sand, gravel and building stone on or under the Farm with full power to do everything necessary to prospect for, work, win and carry away, let or dispose of the same, including power to erect buildings and plant in connection therewith, but subject to payment for surface damage (which in the case of crops shall include temporary grass) or for damage to fixed equipment or other property of the Tenant and to an adjustment of rent which, failing agreement, will be fixed by arbitration;

(B) power to alter marches and excamb land with any neighbouring proprietor, an adjustment of rent being made on the basis of annual value of any additions to or deductions from the Farm, which adjustment will, failing agreement, be fixed by arbitration;

(C) power at any time to resume any part or parts of the Farm for any purpose other than agricultural purposes on giving at least   months' written notice;

(D) all water in rivers, streams, burns, springs, lochs, ponds, wells, reservoirs, dams, drains, conduits, canals, or underground channels with all necessary rights of access thereto subject to the use thereof by the Tenant for the proper purposes of the Farm only;

(E) the whole shootings and fishings on the Farm with the exclusive right of sporting, shooting, fishing, trapping and snaring, subject to the Tenant's common law

---

1 Now Twenty Eighth May and Twenty Eighth November: see the Term and Quarter Days (Scotland) Act 1990.
2 See now the Agricultural Holdings (Scotland) Act 1991, s 13.

and statutory rights; declaring that the Tenant is hereby granted permission to kill deer if found on arable land or enclosed pasture; and the period of twelve months ending Thirty-First October in each year will be substituted for the calendar year for the purposes of Section 52(1) of the Agricultural Holdings (Scotland) Act 1991; and the Tenant, so far as in his power and subject as aforesaid, will protect the game on the Farm and will prevent all poachers and others from trespassing thereon and will immediately give notice to the Landlord of poaching, suspected poaching or trespassing;

(F) all woods, trees, brushwood and plantations (with grass therein) and the ground occupied thereby on the Farm, with power on payment for surface damage (a) to cut, prune and remove the same and to plant others in their place; (b) to fence the same and also the stools of trees and shrubs when cut; (c) to enclose any unenclosed woods and plantations, all without compensation to the Tenant, it being understood that all such plantations or woodlands occupied by the Tenant will be so occupied by mere tolerance and such permission may be withdrawn by the Landlord at any time; and (d) to cart wood through the Farm from the woods and plantations thereon or from neighbouring woods or plantations; declaring that if any trees, woods or plantations and the fences round the same are destroyed or injured by the Tenant or his employees or by the Tenant's machinery or by the Tenant's livestock, the Tenant will be liable to the Landlord for the damage so done;

(G) all existing rights of way, wayleaves and servitudes, with power to grant further wayleaves and servitudes, subject to payment for surface damage (which in the case of crops shall include temporary grass);

(H) a right to use all roads and means of access over the Farm to other lands and subjects;

(I) the right to enter and to authorise others to enter all parts of the Farm for the purpose of satisfying the Landlord that the conditions of this Lease are being properly carried out, or fulfilling the Landlord's obligations or exercising his rights hereunder;

declaring that if any ground damaged or resumed under any of the foregoing powers is restored to an arable state and if possession thereof is given to the Tenant at any time during the currency of this Lease, the abatement of rent in respect of such ground will cease and the Tenant will thereafter be bound to cultivate such land along with the rest of the Farm in accordance with the terms of this Lease.

FURTHER CONDITIONS

(1) The Tenant will pay all rates, taxes and other charges, including water rates, usually payable by tenants or occupiers.

(2) The Landlord will reinstate or replace any building on the Farm which is damaged or destroyed by fire if its reinstatement or replacement is required to enable him to fulfil his obligation to manage the Farm in accordance with the rules of

good estate management; and the Landlord will also effect in his own name a policy or policies of insurance against damage by fire for all buildings on the Farm to their full reinstatement value.

(3) The Tenant will in the event of the destruction by fire of harvested crops grown on the Farm for consumption thereon return to the Farm for full equivalent manurial value of the crops so destroyed insofar as the return thereof is required for the fulfilment of his obligation to farm in accordance with the rules of good husbandry; and the Tenant will insure to their full value against damage by fire, all live and dead stock on the Farm and all such harvested crops as aforesaid with an insurance office to be reasonably approved of by the Landlord and will exhibit the receipts for the premiums paid therefor to the Landlord and, if required, will assign the policy or policies of assurance to the Landlord who will be entitled to recover any sum due under the same and to apply such sum in payment of all or part of the rent due or current at the time and any other sums due by the Tenant to the Landlord, and if the Tenant fails to pay the premiums on the said policy or policies as they become due, the Landlord will be entitled to do so and recover payment thereof from the Tenant; [the Tenant will also insure the stock against anthrax and foot and mouth disease and brucellosis].

(4) The Landlord undertakes to put the fixed equipment on the Farm into a thorough state of repair, and to provide such buildings and other fixed equipment as will enable the Tenant, provided he is reasonably skilled in husbandry, to maintain efficient production as respects both the kind of produce specified in the Lease and the quality and quantity thereof; and will, during the tenancy, effect such replacement or renewal of the fixed equipment as may be rendered necessary by natural decay or by fair wear and tear.

(5) The Tenant agrees that the undertaking of the Landlord to put the fixed equipment on the Farm in a thorough state of repair has been duly implemented; and the Tenant binds himself during this Lease to maintain the fixed equipment on the Farm in as good a state of repair (natural decay and fair wear and tear excepted) as it was in immediately after it was put in repair as aforesaid, or, in the case of equipment provided, improved, replaced or renewed during the tenancy, as it was immediately after it was so provided, improved, replaced or renewed, the dykes and fences having the cope and wire on (as the case may be); and all being left 'slap free', natural decay and ordinary fair wear and tear alone being excepted.

Notwithstanding the foregoing, the cost of maintaining or replacing those fences which form the boundaries of the Farm will, where the Farm adjoins other subjects belonging to the Landlord, be shared equally between the Tenant and the Landlord.

(6) Without prejudice to the generality of the foregoing obligation to uphold the fixed equipment, the Tenant undertakes:

(a) to employ skilled tradesmen as necessary to replace loose or broken slates and glass, overhaul roofs, chimneys, rhones, gutters, pipes, roads and

bridges, walls, dykes and fences, gates and gate pillars and to scour the
ditches, drains and water courses;

(b) to keep all tile and surface drains and sewage disposal systems clear and
efficient, and to repair all burst and choked drains;

(c) to dig and clean the roots of and switch all the hedges, and not to remove or
destroy any hedges on the Farm;

(d) to cut down and spray all thistles, dockens and weeds on the Farm once
before they come into flower and again in August in each year, and to take
all practicable steps to prevent the growth of wild oats;

(e) to keep down all rabbits, moles, rats and other vermin and pests on the
Farm;

(f) to paint, once in every _____ years, the whole outside woodwork and
ironwork of the buildings on the Farm in such manner as shall be approved
by the Landlord;

(g) to paint, once in every _____ years, the internal walls and woodwork of
the farmhouse which have previously been painted in such manner as shall
be approved by the Landlord;

(h) to whitewash or limewash, once in every _____ years, all those parts of
the farmhouse and other buildings which have previously been white-
washed or limewashed.

If any of the foresaid operations is neglected or not duly performed, the
Landlord shall have power to employ workmen to execute the necessary operation and the Tenant will be bound to meet the expenditure thereby incurred; and
the Tenant will perform free of charge all cartage of materials required for any
improvements or repairs, which may be executed or made on the Farm during
the currency of this Lease. No capital improvements will be carried out by the
Tenant except with the prior written consent of the Landlord.

(7) The Landlord and the Tenant agree that a record of the condition of the fixed
equipment on, and the cultivation of, the Farm will be made at the commencement of this Lease. At the termination of this Lease the Tenant will have a right
to compensation for improvements and the Landlord to compensation for dilapidations.

(8) The Tenant will not alter or add to any or erect new fixed equipment unless with
the prior written consent of the Landlord.

(9) The Tenant's fixtures are specified in Schedule I annexed hereto. At the termination of this Lease the Landlord or the incoming tenant will take over at valuation
all the Tenant's fixtures. These fixtures will be kept in proper repair by the
Tenant at all times.

(10) The Tenant will always keep the Farm fully stocked and equipped with his own
stock and crop and the Tenant accepts the Farm at entry in the then state of cultivation without claim or objection; and the Tenant will manage, manure, labour
and crop the Farm as an arable and/or livestock rearing farm only, according to
the rules of good husbandry in all respects and shall not use the Farm or any part
or parts of it for any other business whatsoever; declaring that no permanent

pasture land (or any part of the hill) will be broken up without the prior written permission of the Landlord, and in the last year of this Lease the Tenant will be bound to have the Farm under a rotation according to the rules of good husbandry as recognised and practised in the district; and the Tenant binds himself not to sell or remove from the Farm, but to consume thereon, the whole straw, turnips, and fodder (except potatoes and grain) growing yearly thereon and to apply to the Farm yearly the whole dung thereon and to manure the same and to leave the whole dung made thereon and not used at the expiry of this Lease to the Landlord or incoming tenant who will take over the dung at a valuation to be fixed, failing agreement, by arbitration.

(11) The Tenant may burn one-tenth of the heather, muir, whins or bracken on the Farm in each year, but only on written intimation to the Landlord before the Twentieth day of March in each year. The Tenant will, when appropriate, give notice to neighbouring occupiers of his intention to burn and will take every precaution to avoid injuring any wood or trees and generally to control the burning.

(12) The Tenant will ensure that no part of the Farm is used for camping or caravanning.

(13) If the Tenant uses any part of the Farm as a market garden or for commercial flower or vegetable cultivation, or as a dairy farm, or for pig or poultry production, he will have no claim against the Landlord for alterations or improvements or for compensation at the termination of this Lease.

(14) The Tenant will at the proper season in the last year of this Lease, sow, if required so to do by the Landlord or incoming tenant, with such kinds and quantities of clover and grass seed as either of them may specify, such part of the Farm in grain crop in that year as may be fixed by the Landlord or incoming tenant; the Tenant will be bound to harrow and roll in said seed and protect the grass therefrom against injury by cattle or sheep or otherwise, all free of charge, the Landlord or incoming tenant paying for the grass seed; and further, in the last year of this Lease, the Tenant will allow the Landlord or incoming tenant to enter into such part of the Farm as may be intended to fallow at the separation of the penultimate crop from the ground and to labour, manure and dress the same accordingly; and generally in the last year the Tenant will allow the Landlord or incoming tenant access to the whole land under crop as soon as the crops are carried off the ground; and the Landlord or incoming tenant will take the whole of the waygoing fodder and grain crop and outgoing turnip crop of the last year of this Lease at a valuation to be fixed, failing agreement, by arbitration; and the Tenant further binds himself at the termination of this Lease to leave the Landlord or incoming tenant the one year old grass and all straw on the Farm, and to plough and harrow the fallow ground.

(15) The Tenant will reside in the farmhouse, and the habitable buildings will be occupied only by employees of the Tenant unless the Landlord agrees otherwise in writing.

(16) The Tenant will be bound at his own expense to reclaim any areas of waste ground on the Farm which are capable of being reclaimed as soon as it is practical to do so.

(17) If, during this Lease, the Tenant becomes apparent insolvent or grants a Trust Deed for behoof of his creditors or, without the prior written consent of the Landlord, assigns this Lease or sub-lets the Farm or any part or parts of it, or allows one half-year's rent to remain unpaid for one month after it has become due or for fourteen days after receipt of a written demand from the Landlord, whichever is the later, or fails to cultivate the Farm according to the rules of good husbandry, or if the farmhouse or buildings is or are not occupied in accordance with Condition 15 hereof, or if the Tenant fails within a reasonable time to remedy any breach, capable of being remedied, of any condition of this Lease, not inconsistent with his responsibilities as Tenant, or commits a breach of a condition of this Lease which materially prejudices the Landlord and is not capable of being remedied, then and in any of these events, it will be in the power of the Landlord by written intimation addressed to the Tenant at the Farm and sent by Recorded Delivery post or Registered Letter forthwith to put an end to this Lease and to resume possession of the Farm in whatever state it may then be without any declarator or process of law and without prejudice to the Landlord's claim for past, due and current rents and all other claims competent to him, and neither the Tenant nor any of his creditors will in such an event have any right or claim for improvements or otherwise against the Landlord[1].

(18) The Tenant binds and obliges himself to flit and leave the Farm vacant for the Landlord or incoming tenant at the termination of this Lease without the necessity of any warning or process of removing.

(19) And the parties consent to registration for preservation and execution:

IN WITNESS WHEREOF

---

1 See the Law Reform (Miscellaneous Provisions) (Scotland) Act 1985.

SCHEDULE I

(Tenant's fixtures)

Note

An agricultural lease is frequently followed up by the conclusion of an Agreement between the parties to vary certain provisions of the lease, to an extent not inconsistent with statute, in the following terms.

AGREEMENT
between

[insert name]
(hereinafter called 'the Landlord')
and

[insert name]
(hereinafter called 'the Tenant')

The parties have agreed that their obligations under the lease of the Farm of dated   be varied in manner underwritten:

(1) Notwithstanding the terms of the said Lease the Tenant hereby accepts the fixed equipment on the Farm as being in a thorough state of repair and sufficient in all respects to enable him to maintain efficient production, and further the Tenant undertakes that he will during the tenancy effect at his own expense on behalf of the Landlord such replacement or renewal of the buildings or other fixed equipment on the Farm as may be rendered necessary by natural decay or by fair wear and tear.

(2) Except in so far as varied hereby, the parties confirm the terms of the said Lease:
IN WITNESS WHEREOF

Index

Manager burdens
  characteristics, 15.2
  duration, 15.21, 15.49
  generally, 15.19
  mixed tenure estates, 15.21
  related properties, 15.20
  sheltered housing, 15.20, 15.21
Mansfield, Earl of, 6.3
Maritime burdens
  automatic preservation, 19.27, 19.29, 32.9
  generally, 15.2, 15.16
  title to enforce, 17.49
  waiver, 18.8
Marketing properties, 33.2, 33.10–11
Matrimonial homes
  consent to dispositions, 7.4, 32.67, 33.5, 33.50
  death of entitled spouses, 32.72
  division and sale, 7.11
  examination of title, 32.67–72
  land certificates, 11.28, 32.101
  missives, 28.44
  Mortgage Rights Act, 22.35
  occupancy rights, 28.44
  protection of purchasers, 32.71
  reduction of transactions, 29.15
  registration of title, 28.44
    dealings, 32.107
    documentation, 32.68
  renunciation of rights, 32.67
  security for business debts, 21.8, 21.12
  special destinations, 7.13
  titles in joint names, 32.69
  titles in one name, 32.70
Measurements
  descriptions in dispositions, 8.16, 32.80
  land certificates, 11.28
  metric measures, 8.16, 32.80
Mental capacity. *See* CAPACITY
Microcopies, title deeds, 11.8
Midlothian, 11.16
Military services, 6.3, 6.18
Milk quotas, 26.37
Minerals
  good and marketable titles, 28.32
  reservations. *See* RESERVATION OF MINERALS
  separate tenements, 8.3, 9.1
Minors. *See* CHILDREN
Minutes of waiver
  community burdens
    by neighbours, 18.23
    complexity, 18.25
    examples, 18.22, 18.24
    generally, 18.19–25
    majority rule, 18.20
    notifications, 18.23
  considerations, 18.4
  feudal real burdens, 19.10, 19.15
  generally, 18.3–26

Minutes of waiver – *contd*
  granters, 18.6
  grassums, 18.4, 18.16, 19.15
  personal real burdens, 18.8
  practice, 18.4
  praedial real burdens, 18.7, 18.13, 18.18
  registration, 11.28, 18.12–15
    certificates, 18.21
    praedial real burdens, 18.13
    servitudes, 18.14
  requirements of writing, 18.11
  rules, 18.5
  servitudes, 18.4, 18.14, 18.26
  unilateral deeds, 18.16
Missives. *See* CONTRACTS FOR SALE OF LAND
Misspelling, 34.3
Monopolies, and real burdens, 15.31–32
Moray, 11.16
Mortgage lenders
  CML Handbook, 21.17, 22.2, 33.56
  generally, 22.2
  instructions to solicitors, 33.59
  lending terms, 33.22
  solicitors acting for, 33.1, 33.56
    duty of care, 33.62
Mortgages
  acceptance, 33.59
  borrowing capacity, 33.20
  completion forms, 33.68
  confirming arrangements, 33.26
  conveyancing practice, 33.55–59, 33.61, 33.66
  financial services, 33.15
  guarantees, 33.22, 33.57
  mortgage valuation surveys, 33.28
  professional advice, 33.13
  and repairs, 33.58
  repayment methods, 33.16–19
    capital and interest repayments, 33.17
    endowment, 22.1, 33.18
    personal pension plans, 33.19
  securities. *See* STANDARD SECURITIES
  and valuation, 33.28, 33.56
Moveable property, 1.4
Mowing leases, 26.4
Muirburn, 26.27
Multiple occupancy housing, 27.25–27

Nairn, 11.16
Names, companies, 34.3
Narrative clauses
  dispositions, 7.2–5
  examination of title, 32.4, 32.5
  style, 7.16
National bodies, SDLT, 5.7
National House-Building Council, scheme,
    28.52, 28.54–57, 33.9, 33.50
Natural gas, 9.2